BRIGADES OF

Gettysburg

The Union and Confederate Brigades
at the Battle of Gettysburg

BRADLEY M. GOTTFRIED

Skyhorse Publishing

Skyhorse Publishing books may be purchased in bulk at special discounts for sales promotion, corporate gifts, fund-raising, or educational purposes. Special editions can also be created to specifications. For details, contact the Special Sales Department, Skyhorse Publishing, 307 West 36th Street, 11th Floor, New York, NY 10018 or info@skyhorsepublishing.com.

Skyhorse® and Skyhorse Publishing® are registered trademarks of Skyhorse Publishing, Inc.®, a Delaware corporation.

Visit our website at www.skyhorsepublishing.com.

10 9 8 7 6

Library of Congress Cataloging-in-Publication Data is available on file.

ISBN: 978-1-61608-401-1

Printed in the United States of America

For my wonderful wife, Linda,
who has supported me at all times

CONTENTS

III Corps (Sickles)   185

V Corps (Meade, Sykes)   233

VI Corps (Sedgwick)   283

XI Corps (Howard, Schurz)   301

CONFEDERATE BRIGADES

First Corps (Longstreet)   399

Second Corps (Ewell)   487

PREFACE

More has been written about the battle of Gettysburg than any other battle of the Civil War. So why yet another book on the topic? Because no brigade-level accounts of the battle have been written. While most students of the battle know that the Iron Brigade fought heroically on McPherson and Seminary Ridges during July 1, few can explain what the unit did during the remainder of the battle. Yet, it played an important role in preventing Culp's Hill from capture.

This book is a companion to Larry Tagg's *The Generals of Gettysburg*. Although I arrived at my idea before Tagg's book was published, it is a natural partner because each exams a unit or its commander.

This book would not have been possible without the help of a number of people. From the publishing side, Ted Savas (Savas Publishing Company) and Robert Pigeon and Fred Francis (both of Da Capo) were a constant source of support and information. The staff of the Gettysburg National Military Park library, especially John Heiser and Scott Hartwig, were very helpful, as was the staff at the United States Army Military History Institute at Carlisle.

Finally, thanks to my past secretary, Carol Hampson, who respected the privacy of my lunch breaks, allowing me to expedite the completion of the book. Most important, I want to thank my wife, Adele, and daughters, Mara and Emily, for their love and support as I plowed through this time-consuming project.

Bradley M. Gottfried
April 2002

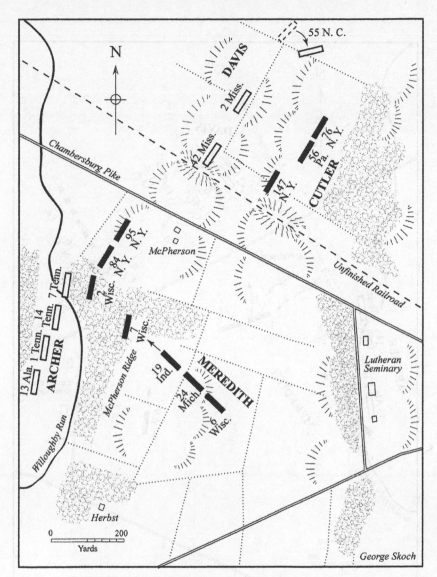

N

55 N. C.

DAVIS

2 Miss.

42 Miss.

36 Pa. 76 N.Y.

147 N.Y.

CUTLER

95 N.Y.

84 N.Y.

2 Wisc.

McPherson

Chambersburg Pike

Unfinished Railroad

7 Wisc.

19 Ind.

MEREDITH

24 Mich.

6 Wisc.

McPherson Ridge

Lutheran Seminary

7 Tenn.

14 Tenn.

1 Tenn.

13 Ala.

ARCHER

Willoughby Run

Herbst

0   200
Yards

George Skoch

Day 1: The Initial Infantry Encounter

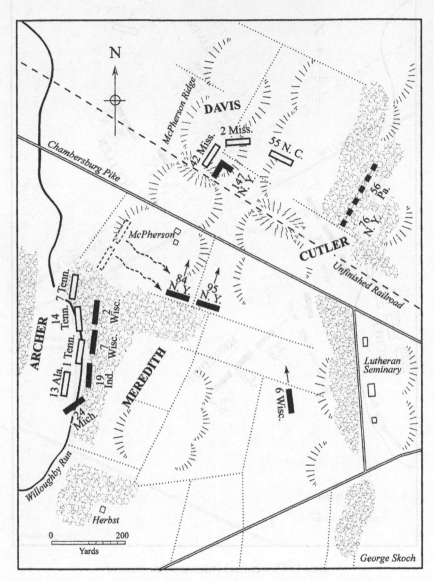

Day 1: Archer's Brigade Defeated by the Iron Brigade;
Cutler's Brigade Defeated by Davis's

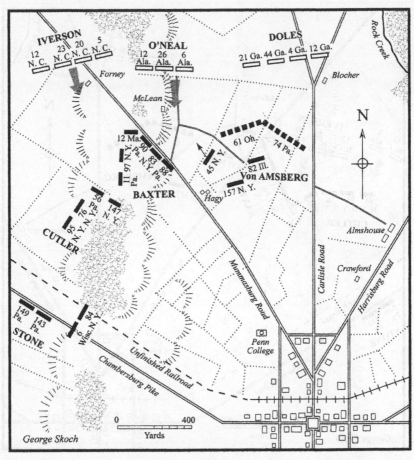

Day 1: Rodes' Division's Initial Attacks against the Federal Right Flank

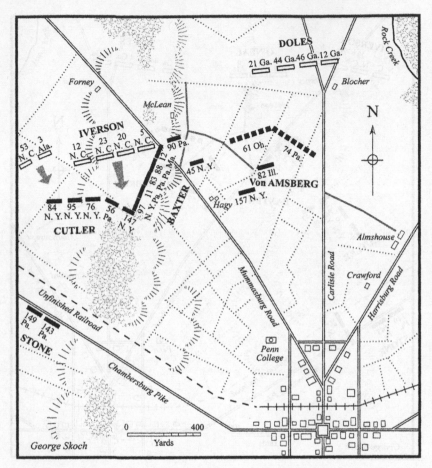

DOLES
21 Ga. 44 Ga. 46 Ga. 12 Ga.

Blocher

Forney

McLean

IVERSON
53 3
N. C. Ala.

12 23 20 5
N. C. N. C. N. C. N. C.

90 Pa.

61 Oh.

74 Pa.

N

45 N. Y.

82 Ill.

Von AMSBERG

Hagy 157 N. Y.

84 95 76 56
N. Y. N. Y. N. Y. Pa.

11 83 88 12
N. Y. Pa. Pa. Pa. Ma.

97
N. Y.

147
N. Y.

BAXTER

CUTLER

Almshouse

Crawford

Unfinished Railroad

149 143
Pa. Pa.

STONE

Chambersburg Pike

Mummasburg Road

Carlisle Road

Harrisburg Road

Penn
College

0   400

Yards

George Skoch

Rock Creek

Day 1: Iverson Attacks Baxter's and Cutler's Brigades

16

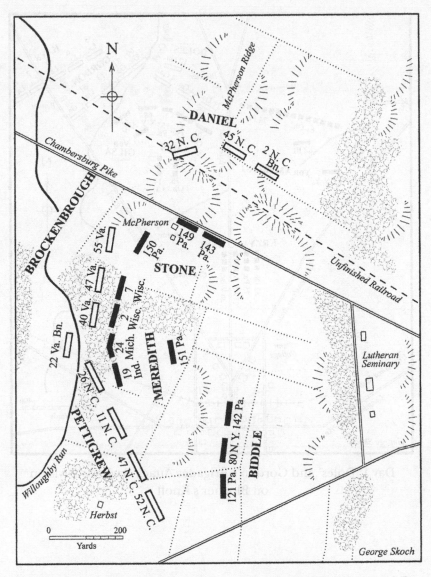

Day 1: Renewal of Confederate Attacks against the Federal Left and Center

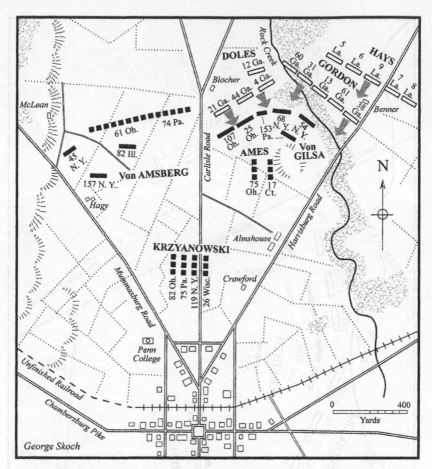

Day 1: Doles' and Gordon's Brigades Attack Barlow's Division
on Blocher's Knoll

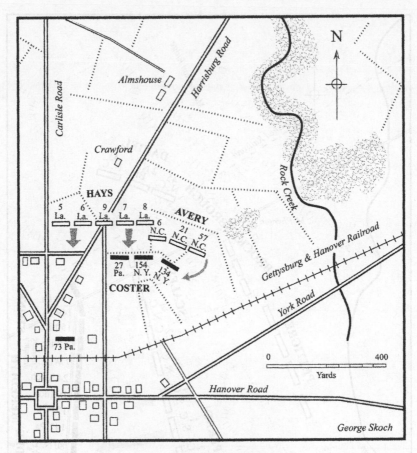

Day 1: The Brickyard Fight

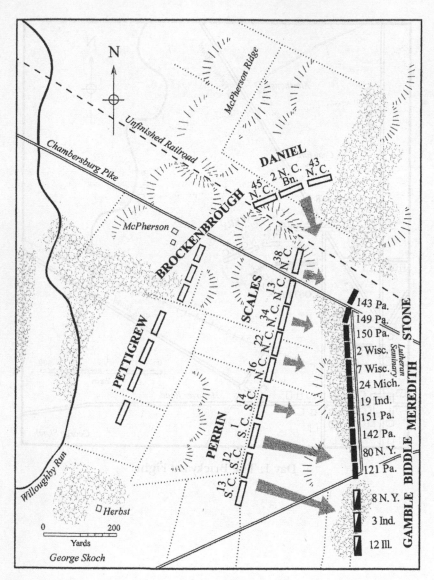

N

McPherson Ridge

Unfinished Railroad

Chambersburg Pike

DANIEL

BROCKENBROUGH

McPherson

45 N.C.   2 N.C. Bn.   43 N.C.

38 N.C.

SCALES

13 N.C.

34 N.C.

22 N.C.

16 N.C.

143 Pa.
149 Pa.
150 Pa.
2 Wisc.
7 Wisc.
24 Mich.
19 Ind.
151 Pa.
142 Pa.
80 N.Y.
121 Pa.

Lutheran Seminary

STONE

PETTIGREW

14 S.C.

1 S.C.

PERRIN

12 S.C.

13 S.C.

Willoughby Run

□ *Herbst*

0   200
Yards

George Skoch

GAMBLE BIDDLE MEREDITH

8 N.Y.
3 Ind.
12 Ill.

Day 1: The Confederate Attack on Seminary Ridge

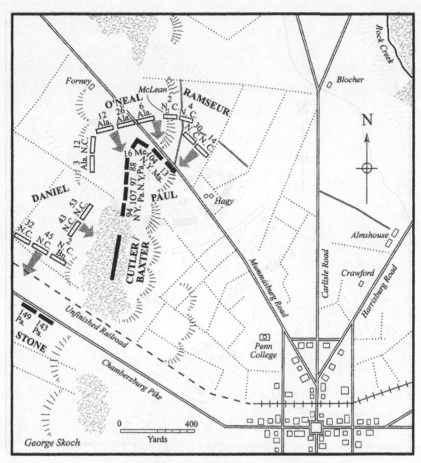

Day 1: Final Attacks on Oak Ridge

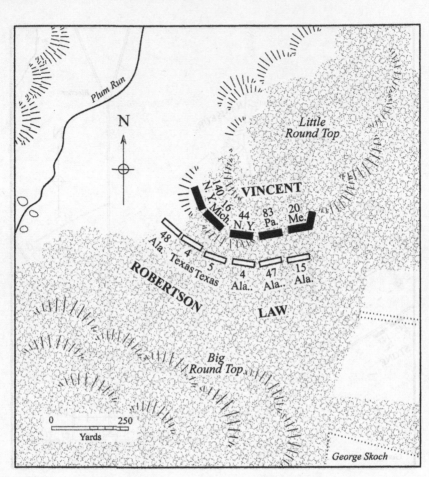

Day 2: The Attacks on Little Round Top

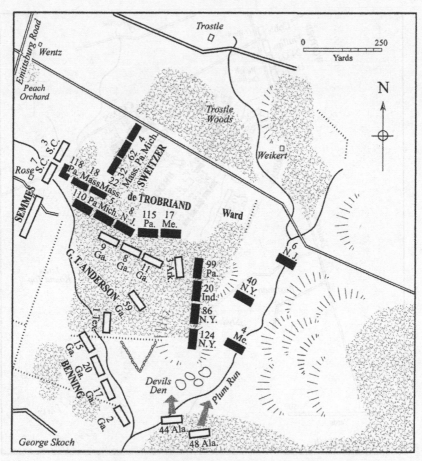

Day 2: Hood Attacks the Wheatfield and Devil's Den

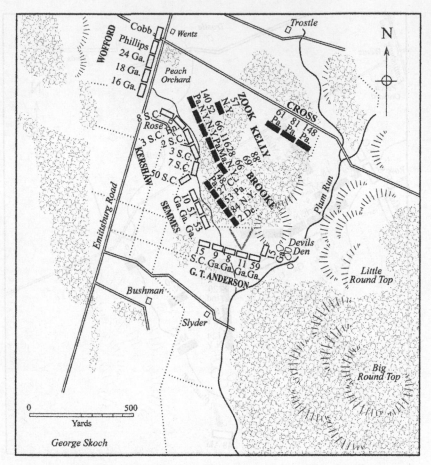

Day 2: McLaws' Division Attacks the Wheatfield and Stony Hill

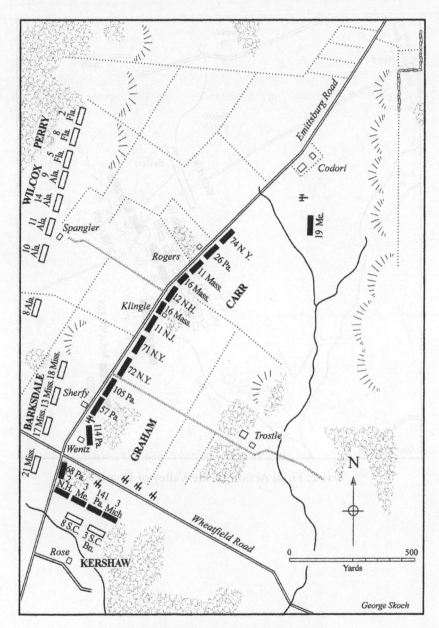

WILCOX
PERRY

2 Fla.
8 Fla.
5 Fla.
9 Ala.
14 Ala.
11 Ala.
10 Ala.
8 Ala.

Spangler

Emmitsburg Road

Codori

19 Me.

74 N.Y.
26 Pa.
11 Mass.
16 Mass.
CARR
12 N.H.
16 Mass.
11 N.J.
71 N.Y.
72 N.Y.
105 Pa.
57 Pa.
114 Pa.
GRAHAM

Rogers

Klingle

BARKSDALE
17 Miss. 13 Miss. 18 Miss.

Sherfy

21 Miss.

Wentz

Trostle

68 Pa.
2 N.H.
3 Me.
141 Pa.
3 Mich.

8 S.C.
3 S.C. Bn.

Rose

KERSHAW

Wheatfield Road

N

0   500
Yards

George Skoch

Day 2: The Emmitsburg Road Line

25

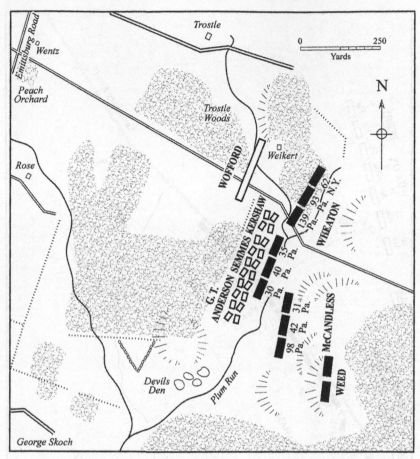

Day 2: Final Action in the Valley of Death

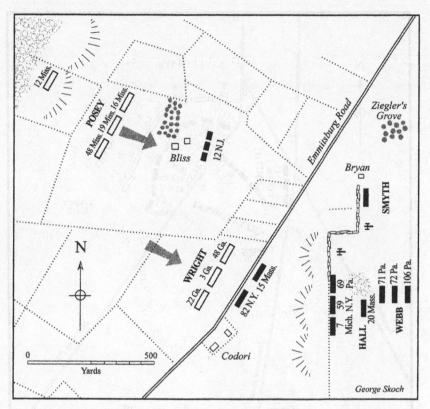

12 Miss.

POSEY

48 Miss. 19 Miss. 16 Miss.

Bliss

12 N.J.

Emmitsburg Road

Ziegler's Grove

Bryan

SMYTH

N

WRIGHT

48 Ga.

3 Ga.

22 Ga.

82 N.Y.

15 Mass.

71 Pa.

72 Pa.

106 Pa.

WEBB

69 Pa.

59 N.Y.

7 Mich.

20 Mass.

HALL

0   500

Yards

Codori

George Skoch

Day 2: Anderson's Division Attacks the Federal Center

27

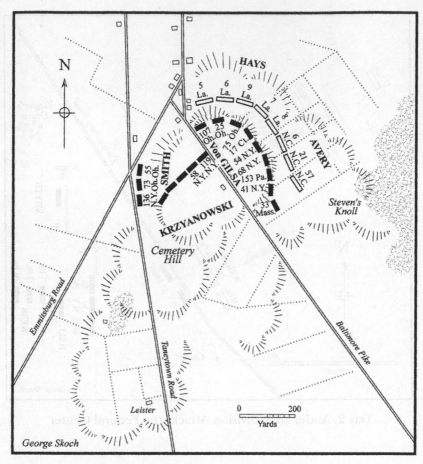

N

HAYS

5 La. 6 La. 9 La. 7 La. 8 La.

107 Oh. 25 Oh. Von GILSA 15 Oh. 17 Ct.

6 N.C. 21 N.C. 57 N.C. AVERY

SMITH

136 N.Y. 73 Oh. 55 Oh.

58 N.Y. 119 N.Y.

54 N.Y. 68 N.Y. 153 Pa. 41 N.Y.

33 Mass.

KRZYANOWSKI

Steven's Knoll

Cemetery Hill

Emmitsburg Road

Taneytown Road

Baltimore Pike

Leister

0   200
Yards

George Skoch

Day 2: Early Attacks Cemetery Hill

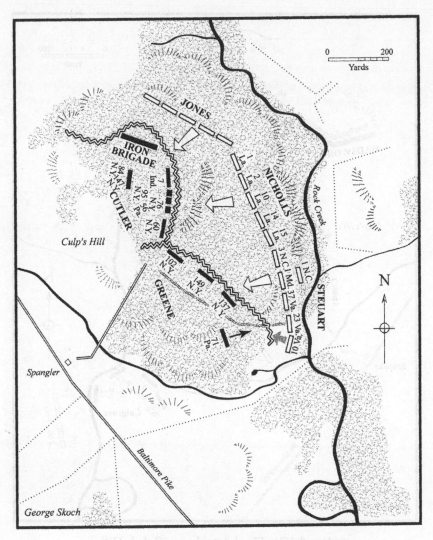

Day 2: Johnson's Division Attacks Culp's Hill

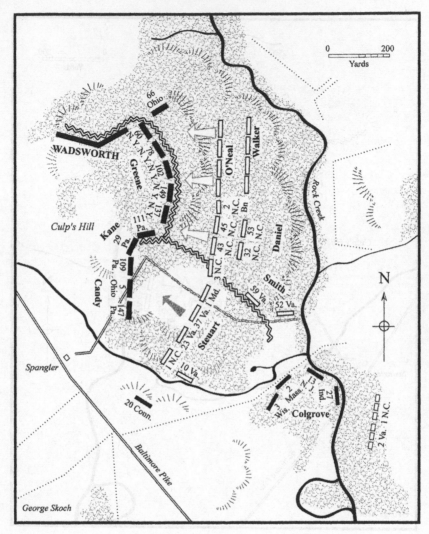

WADSWORTH

66
Ohio

60
N.Y.
78
N.Y.
102
N.Y.
149
N.Y.
137
N.Y.

Greene

O'Neal

Walker

Culp's Hill

111
Pa.

Kane

29
Pa.

2
N.C.

Bn

45
N.C.

43
N.C.

3 N.C.

32
N.C.

53
N.C.

Daniel

Smith

109
Pa.

5
Ohio
Pa.

147
Pa.

Candy

1 Md.

37 Va.

59 Va.

52 Va.

Stewart

23 Va.

10 Va.

1 N.C.

Spangler

20 Conn.

3
Wis.

2
Mass.

13
N.J.

1
Md.

27
Ind.

Colgrove

2 Va. 1 N.C.

N

Rock Creek

Baltimore Pike

George Skoch

Day 3: The Final Attacks on Culp's Hill

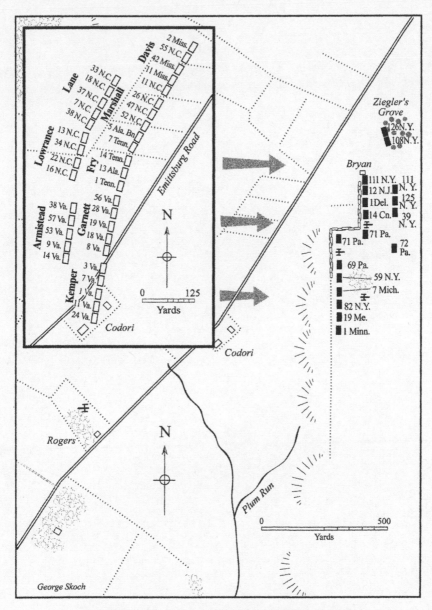

Day 3: The Pickett-Pettigrew-Trimble Charge

Inset map labels:
2 Miss.
55 N.C.
42 Miss.
11 Miss.
Davis
11 N.C.
33 N.C.
18 N.C.
26 N.C.
Lane
37 N.C.
47 N.C.
7 N.C.
52 N.C.
Marshall
38 N.C.
5 Ala. Bn
13 N.C.
7 Tenn.
34 N.C.
Lowrance
14 Tenn.
22 N.C.
Fry
13 Ala.
16 N.C.
1 Tenn.
56 Va.
38 Va.
28 Va.
57 Va.
Garnett
19 Va.
Armistead
53 Va.
18 Va.
9 Va.
8 Va.
14 Va.
3 Va.
7 Va.
Kemper
1 Va.
11 Va.
24 Va.
Codori

Emmitsburg Road

N
0   125
Yards

Main map labels:
Ziegler's Grove
126 N.Y.
108 N.Y.
Bryan
111 N.Y.   111 N.Y.
12 N.J.
1 Del.   125 N.Y.
14 Cn.   39 N.Y.
71 Pa.
71 Pa.   72 Pa.
69 Pa.
59 N.Y.
7 Mich.
82 N.Y.
19 Me.
1 Minn.

Codori
Codori
Rogers
Plum Run

N
0   500
Yards

George Skoch

Day 3: The Bliss Farm–Pettigrew–Trimble Charge

UNION BRIGADES

I CORPS—

Major General John Reynolds/
Major General Abner Doubleday/
Major General John Newton

Not to be confused with the I Corps of the ill-fated Army of Virginia, Major General John Reynolds's I Corps of the Army of the Potomac was formed on September 12, 1862. The corps had the distinction of opening the battle of Antietam under General Joseph Hooker. It ran into several gritty Confederate divisions in the East Woods and Miller's cornfield and suffered horrendous losses before being withdrawn. The heavy losses continued at the battle of Fredericksburg. Chancellorsville was a reprieve for the corps, but by this point it had become a crack unit.[1]

Reynolds had commanded the corps since September 29, 1862. A West Point graduate, he had had an illustrious military career up to the Gettysburg campaign. Reynolds and his brigade fought in the Seven Days battles, and he was captured at Gaines's Mill. Exchanged soon after, Reynolds returned to lead the Pennsylvania Reserve Division with distinction at Second Bull Run. He did not see action at Antietam, because Pennsylvania Governor Andrew Curtin had Reynolds detached from the army to assist in the recruitment and organization of the militia during Lee's first invasion of the North. Returning to the army after the battle, Reynolds assumed command of the I Corps and led it at Fredericksburg and Chancellorsville. Prior to appointing General George Meade to take over the Army of the Potomac during the Gettysburg campaign, Lincoln offered the command to Reynolds. The latter would not accept the position as long as Washington tied his hands. Lincoln was unwilling to turn over so much responsibility to a field officer, so Reynolds rejoined his corps.[2]

The corps' long march to Gettysburg continued on June 28, when the men broke camp at Middletown, Maryland, and reached Frederick that night. The corps reached Emmitsburg on June 29 and camped just north of town. Reynolds thought a fight was imminent, so he selected high ground for the bivouac. The march on June 30 was much shorter—only about four miles to the banks of Marsh Creek, another strong defensive position. According to General Abner Doubleday, "it was General Reynolds's intention to dispute the enemy's advance at this point." During this period Reynolds commanded the army's right wing, composed of the I, III, and XI Corps.[3]

Through a series of telegrams, Reynolds learned that the enemy was concentrating ahead of him. Galloping ahead of his men, Reynolds reached the battlefield at about 10:00 A.M., and sent a number of messages to General Meade and XI Corps commander General Oliver Howard. Reynolds brought up Wadsworth's 1st Division and Hall's battery, and his remaining two divisions hit the road around 90 to 120 minutes later. According to Doubleday, this action caused Wadsworth's two brigades to face the brunt of the initial Confederate onslaught alone and without support. Doubleday did not believe that Reynolds had any grand plan in mind, except to "simply to defend the two roads entering the town from the northwest and southwest, and to occupy and hold the woods between them." Wadsworth's two brigades were attacked by units of General Harry Heth's Division almost as soon as they deployed west of town on McPherson Ridge. After initial setbacks, Reynolds's men defeated two Confederate brigades, causing severe losses. Casualties on the Union side were also heavy—and included John Reynolds. Leading the 2nd Wisconsin of the Iron Brigade to its position, he yelled, "Forward men, forward for God's sake and drive those fellows out of those woods." He was struck by a minié ball and died almost instantly. Doubleday assumed command of the 1st Corps.[4]

General Thomas Rowley, now in command of Doubleday's 3rd Division, formed his two brigades on either side of the Iron Brigade on McPherson Ridge, while Robinson's 2nd Division remained in reserve on Seminary Ridge at midday. The latter did not remain there long, as Rodes's Confederate Division (Second Corps) made its appearance on Oak Hill, forcing Doubleday to send first Baxter's Brigade, and then Paul's, to the right to extend the Federal line.[5] The Confederate attacks were again piecemeal, allowing the outnumbered Federal troops to maintain their positions on McPherson Ridge and Oak Ridge. By 3:00 P.M. the Confederates had finally brought their immense manpower to bear on Doubleday's beleaguered I Corps. The coordinated attacks forced the I Corps to withdraw to Seminary Ridge and then to retreat into Gettysburg.[6]

Unlike the XI Corps, which also battled the Confederates on July 1, Reynolds's men fought like tigers. Rather than make excuses or comparisons, the XI Corps veterans bestowed respect upon their comrades. For example, Private Andrew Sweetland of the 55th Ohio wrote, "I have believed since that day that the First Corps did the hardest and most persistent fighting of any organization in that army up to and including that day."[7]

Reaching Cemetery Hill, Doubleday met General Winfield Hancock of the II Corps, who informed him that he had assumed command of the I and XI Corps. Doubleday was told to deploy his men, but confusion arose almost immediately when General Howard sent contradictory orders. "This occasioned at the time some little delay and confusion," wrote Doubleday. Fortunately, the enemy did not attack during this chaotic period. During the early morning hours of July 2, General John Newton of the VI Corps was ordered to take over the I Corps, forcing a bitterly disappointed Doubleday to return to his 3rd Division. The remainder of the battle found the I Corps on Cemetery and Culp's Hills. Several units were moved south to support the rest of the army on July 2 and 3, and Stannard's Brigade and two regiments of Rowley's (Biddle's) Brigade helped repulse Wright's Brigade (Anderson's Division, Third Corps) on July 2 and Pickett's Division (First Corps) on July 3. The corps left the battlefield on July 6. Although decimated, the men knew that their spirited defense had contributed to the defeat of Lee's army.[8]

1ST DIVISION—

Brigadier General James Wadsworth

The 1st Division had four commanders from the time it was formed on September 12, 1862, until Brigadier General James Wadsworth assumed command on December 27, 1862. Wadsworth's life up to the Gettysburg campaign was unusual. Reared in a wealthy family and without formal military training or experience, Wadsworth climbed the command chart. Initially a volunteer on the staff of General Irvin McDowell, he was soon in command of a brigade and in the late winter of 1862 was placed in charge of the Washington defenses as military governor of the District of Columbia. While in the army, he was on the ballot to be governor of New York, but lost the election, probably because he did not campaign. His meteoric rise continued when in late December 1862 he became the commander of the 1st Division of the I Corps. The men loved him because he took care of them. Gettysburg would be his first real test as division commander.[9]

The evening of June 28 found Wadsworth's Division camped in a meadow. Driving rain drenched the men, so the rail fences looked very tempting. A roaring fire could provide a welcome cup of coffee and dry clothing. Unfortunately, orders prohibited using fences for firewood. Realizing the plight of his men and being independently wealthy, Wadsworth sought out the farmer to purchase his fence. The farmer did not wish to sell, but Wadsworth finally convinced him that it was the right thing to do. The astronomically high amount of $250 also helped. "In less than three minutes every rail had left the fence . . . and prolonged cheers for General Wadsworth fairly rent the heavens," noted one of the men. They had seen Wadsworth's first rule of command: "First protect your men."[10]

The division broke camp on Marsh Creek at 8:00 A.M. on July 1. Cutler's Brigade led the column, followed by Meredith's Iron Brigade. When less than a mile from Gettysburg, at about 10:00 A.M., Reynolds ordered the men to the sound of the fighting. This meant crossing the fields to the left of Emmitsburg Road. Wadsworth immediately deployed three of Cutler's Regiments on the north side of Chambersburg Pike; the two others were on the south side of the road, near McPherson's farm buildings. The three regiments on the north side of Chambersburg Pike were almost immediately attacked by Davis's Brigade, approaching from the west. After less than half an hour, Cutler's Regiments were flanked and forced to retreat. On the opposite side of the road, the two remaining regiments battled skirmishers from Archer's Brigade. The Iron Brigade appeared and formed on their left in Herbst Woods. The left regiments of the Iron Brigade flanked Archer's Brigade, causing it to flee. A number of prisoners from Archer's Brigade fell into the Iron Brigade's hands, including its commander, General James Archer. The decisive victory permitted Cutler's two regiments on the south side of Chambersburg Pike, and the 6th Wisconsin of the Iron Brigade, to turn and take on Davis's Brigade, which was approaching from the north. Although taking heavy losses, the three regiments charged across Chambersburg Pike and captured over two hundred men in the unfinished railroad cut. By 11:00 A.M. Wadworth's two brigades had bested two Confederate brigades from Heth's Division.[11]

The next attack on the Wadsworth's Division came around 3:00 P.M., when the Iron Brigade was again attacked by portions of Heth's Division, and Cutler's Brigade battled units from Rodes's Division. After initially holding their ground, both brigades were ultimately forced back to Seminary Ridge. A sharp encounter occurred there, but the division was again flanked, forcing it to withdraw to Cemetery Hill. The division was sent over to Culp's Hill the next day, where it helped battle Johnson's Division during the evening of July 2 and the morning of July 3. The division remained on the battlefield until July 6.[12]

Without question, the stout defense of Wadsworth's Division helped buy time for the Union army to assemble at Gettysburg and ultimately defeat the Army of Northern Virginia.

1st Brigade—Brigadier General Solomon Meredith

Units: 19th Indiana, 24th Michigan, 2nd Wisconsin, 6th Wisconsin, 7th Wisconsin
Strength: 1829
Losses: 1153 (171-720-262)—63%[13]

Arguably the finest fighting unit in the Army of the Potomac, the Iron Brigade deserved both its name and its designation as the 1st Brigade, 1st Division, I Corps. The five western regiments had been forged into a formidable fighting force that was both feared and respected by the enemy. The men could be easily distinguished by their tall black Hardee hats, pinned back on one side and sporting a feather. "There was something of the

'Western' frontier mentality in all this, a quiet determination to see the job through with the same resolve it took to clear a field of stones, build a rail fence or wait out a Wisconsin winter," wrote two modern historians.[14]

The brigade also had another distinction. At 6'7", its commander, Brigadier General Solomon Meredith, towered above any other officer in the army. Born in North Carolina, Meredith made his way north to Indiana as a young man and became a prosperous farmer and politician. Unfortunately, his leadership did not match his height, and many of his men and senior officers openly questioned his abilities.[15]

The division began its final march to Gettysburg at 8:00 A.M. on July 1. Cutler's Brigade led the column, but the Iron Brigade was about a mile behind. As a result, the veterans of the two units fought over which of them actually led the column to Gettysburg, long after the battle ended. Detached to perform picket duty about two and a half miles up the road toward Gettysburg the night before, the 19th Indiana was ordered to "fall into its proper place in the column as it came marching by," reported its commander, Colonel Samuel Williams. This occurred between 8:30 and 9:00 A.M. The brigade marched toward Gettysburg in the following order: 2nd Wisconsin–7th Wisconsin–19th Indiana–24th Michigan–6th Wisconsin.[16]

Although the men knew that Lee's army was somewhere in front of them, they did not expect an immediate battle. The men were in good spirits, and songs broke out as they marched along. This quickly changed when up ahead "the sullen booming of the artillery and the white smoke of the exploding shells" told them that the enemy was nearby. The pace quickened, and the men knew that it was just a matter of time before they entered the fray. As the column approached Gettysburg, Lieu-tenant Colonel Rufus Dawes of the 6th Wisconsin ordered his drum corps to the front of his regiment and had the flags unsheathed. Within moments, the men were marching to the tune "The Campbells are Coming."[17]

Upon reaching the Codori house at about 10:00 A.M., the brigade followed Cutler's Brigade to the left (west), across fields, toward the Lutheran seminary. The brigade band, which had been playing the tune "Red, White, and Blue," now changed to "Yankee Doodle." The men double-quicked across the open fields. The march was relatively easy because Cutler's men had already flattened the fences.[18]

Passing the seminary, the column went by a two-gun section of Calef's battery tossing shells at the unseen enemy. Led by the 2nd Wisconsin, the Iron Brigade hurried toward McPherson Ridge. They could see Buford's cavalry division hotly engaged with the enemy. Except for the 19th Indiana, which had been on picket duty the night before, the men rushed toward the enemy with unloaded muskets. Some of the officers realized this fact almost too late. Colonel William Robinson of the 7th Wisconsin recalled that "we had not halted to load, and no orders had been received to do so, for the reason, I suppose that no one expected we were to be engaged so suddenly." Colonel Henry Morrow of the 24th Michigan ordered his men to halt to load, but the order was revoked by one of General Wadsworth's staff, who waved them toward Herbst Woods. Some of the officers ordered their men to load while sprinting to the front. Although a difficult task for green troops, the Iron Brigade accomplished this order without missing a step. As the last regiment in the column, the 6th Wisconsin, passed the seminary, a boyish-looking staff officer galloped up to its commanding officer, Lt. Colonel Dawes, with information that General Reynolds was dead and

General Doubleday was now in command of the field.[19]

Reynolds was still alive when the 2nd Wisconsin reached the crest of McPherson Ridge. He saw the line shudder when met by a volley from the 7th Tennessee and 14th Tennessee (Archer's Brigade, Heth's Division, Third Corps) that killed and wounded a number of men. Reynolds yelled, "Forward men, forward, for God's sake and drive those fellows out of the woods." He died soon after. Not waiting for the remainder of the brigade, the men plunged down the slope toward Archer's troops in the woods below, obliquing slightly to the right because of the intensing of the gunfire. The next regiment in line, the 7th Wisconsin, waited momentarily, while the 19th Indiana and then the 24th Michigan formed on its left. Through the dense smoke, Colonel Robinson of the 7th Wisconsin could not discern whether the shots being fired at his men were from the enemy, or from the 2nd Wisconsin, which was somewhere up ahead and to the right. While he was pondering what to do, a staff officer rode up. Robinson asked if he knew the identity of the troops in front of him. The staff officer merely pointed to the left; following his arm, Robinson saw a Confederate battle flag in the ravine below. The staff officer ordered Robinson to charge the enemy. Robinson first ordered a volley, then, drawing his sword, ordered his men to charge. They responded by rushing down the hill, yelling at the top of their lungs. Because there was no time to waste, the three regiments went into action *en echelon*.[20]

While the 7th Wisconsin and part of the 19th Indiana smashed into Archer's front, the left of the 19th Indiana and the 24th Michigan overlapped the right of the Confederate line and circled around it. The battle flared on the banks of Willoughby Run. Realizing their peril, members of the 13th Alabama on the

right of the Conferedate line either fell back or were captured. Within a matter of minutes, the entire right side of Archer's Brigade was rolled up and forced backward. Some hand-to-hand combat broke out, but most of the Confederates realized the futility of resisting an attack on their front, flank, and rear. Colonel Robinson recalled that "the enemy—what was left of them able to walk—threw down their arms, ducked through between our files, and passed to the rear." One of the Confederates purportedly yelled to his comrades, "That ain't no milishy! There's them damn black hats again—that's the Army of the Potomac."[21]

Just prior to these events, the 2nd Wisconsin on the right of the brigade had obliqued farther right, entered Herbst Woods, and slowly pushed back the Tennessee troops in front of it. One veteran from the 2nd Wisconsin observed that "it was . . . the unadorned, long-drawn-out line of ragged, dirty blue against the long-drawn-out line of dirty, ragged butternut." Seeing the Confederates reforming their lines, Major John Mansfield ordered a charge. This put an end to the Confederate resistance, as the Tennesseans ran for the rear. Over seventy-five men were captured, including General James Archer, Lee's first general to be so humiliated. Archer was captured by Private Patrick Maloney, who delivered the general to Major Mansfield. Private Maloney would be killed before the sun set that day.[22]

Continuing their attack, the brigade climbed the incline on the western side of Willoughby Run and fired at Archer's retreating men. Realizing the brigade's vulnerable position, the officers ordered the men back across the run and into position in Herbst Woods. The men lay down and prepared for another attack. By 11:30 A.M., the brigade was realigned. The 7th Wisconsin formed on the right of the 2nd Wisconsin, and the 19th Indiana formed on the brigade's left flank, with the 24th Michigan on its right. The brigade's deposition was, from left to right, 19th Indiana–24th Michigan–2nd Wisconsin–7th Wisconsin. The 2nd Wisconsin initially faced north, but after the realignment, faced west. Because of the disposition of the remainder of the brigade, the right wing of the 24th Michigan was forced to bend backward toward the right to connect with the 7th Wisconsin. This formed an obtuse angle at the center of the regiment. The regiment's left flank extended down the hillside, and was not visible to its right wing.

The 24th Michigan's commander, Colonel Henry Morrow, was unhappy with his regiment's deployment, and sent several aides to report that the position was untenable. Each time the aides returned with the same response: "the position was ordered to be held, and must be held at all hazards." The 19th Indiana was also unhappy with its position, because its left flank hung in the air, dangerously exposed to a Confederate attack. The latter two regiments wanted to occupy the higher ground to the west, closer to Willoughby Run, but Doubleday insisted that the woods be held. It seemed to some of the men that the Union high command had gone into a state of shock after General Reynolds's death. As with the 24th Michigan, aides were sent to find General Meredith to protest their position. Meredith could only say that he was following orders, and when General Wadsworth was approached, he refused to make changes. The Hoosiers felt some relief when Doubleday's Division arrived and took position on either side of the brigade. Stone's Brigade was placed on the right of the Iron Brigade and Biddle's Brigade to the left. Unfortunately, a quarter-mile gap loomed between the latter two brigades. Colonel Williams of the 19th Indiana

wrote in his report that "two regiments afterwards formed *en echelon,* to my left and rear, which however did not prevent a heavy fire on my flank in the action of the afternoon."[23]

Earlier in the day, the brigade's last regiment, the 6th Wisconsin, was also preparing to face the enemy. One of General Meredith's aides galloped up as the unit reached Seminary Ridge and told Lieutenant Colonel Rufus Dawes, "Colonel, form your line, and prepare for action." With a sweep of his arm, the aide indicated that the regiment should form on the 24th Michigan's left flank. The men loaded as they ran toward their assigned position. Before reaching it, another of Doubleday's aides halted the regiment and told Dawes that his unit was designated the division's reserve. Because the men were tired from their run across the fields, Dawes permitted them to lie down. Attached to the regiment at this point was the hundred-man Iron Brigade Guard. Dawes placed half of them on each flank of this regiment.[24]

The 6th Regiment's reprieve was a short one, for yet another aide arrived with orders to move to the right. While the Iron Brigade was defeating Archer's Brigade, Cutler's Brigade on its right, across Chambersburg Pike, was having a more difficult time with Davis's Confederate Brigade. Two Federal regiments had already been forced to retreat, and a third was in danger of being annihilated. Flushed with victory, Davis's men swept toward the Iron Brigade's vulnerable right flank. Dawes was ordered to meet this new threat from the north, and he did so by yelling, "By company into line on the right company."[25]

"The guns of Hall's battery could be seen driving to the rear, and Cutler's men were manifestly in full retreat," Dawes noted after the war. In his official report he wrote, "my men kept up a steady double-quick, never faltering or breaking under the fire, which had become very galling." As the regiment approached Chambersburg Pike, Dawes's horse was shot and the colonel was thrown to the ground. As Dawes scrambled to his feet, the men heartily cheered. Stout fences lined the pike, and beyond them, the men could see the Confederates firing as they advanced. Dawes's men began to fall, so he ordered them to halt and lie down behind the fence. Resting their guns on the lowest rail, the men fired several volleys into Davis's troops. Many of the enemy soldiers simply disappeared. It was not until later that Dawes and his men realized that many of the enemy had sought refuge in an unfinished railroad cut that paralleled Chambersburg Pike.[26]

Seeing the Confederate line waver, Dawes drew his sword and ordered his men over the fences lining the road. The maneuver was a deadly one, as many were hit during their climb. The heavy fire made Dawes realize that the enemy had not retreated, but were firing from a depression in front of them. After crossing the second fence on the opposite side of Chambersburg Pike, Dawes saw the 95th New York of Cutler's Brigade forming on his left. He may not have known it at the time, but another of Cutler's Regiments, the 84th New York, was on the 95th New York's left flank. "I did not know or care where they came from, but was rejoiced to see them," wrote Dawes. These regiments had been on the Iron Brigade's right, south of Chamberburg Pike, and when Davis's movement threatened the Union line, they were also rushed north to halt the Confederate advance.[27]

Rushing up to Major Edward Pye of the 95th New York, Dawes yelled, "We must charge." Pye readily agreed, and the Federal units swept forward. As the three regiments closed on the railroad cut, Davis's men poured destructive volleys into them. Scores of men were hit, but there was no turning back—they had to reach the Confederate position to silence the deadly gunfire. Captain John Kellogg recalled that the three regiments did not attack together—the 6th Wisconsin reached the railroad cut about three minutes before the New York regiments. Dawes recalled giving no orders during this charge, except "Align on the colors! Close up on the colors! Close up on the colors!" As the Federal troops reached the edge of the railroad cut, some of the enemy threw down their arms to surrender.[28]

Some of the men saw the 2nd Mississippi's flag and rushed toward it. The flag bearer, Private William Murphy, recalled that "they still kept rushing for my flag and there were over a dozen shot down like sheep in their madly [sic] rush for the colors. The first soldier was shot down just as he made for the flag . . . and at the same time a lieutenant made a desperate struggle for the flag, and was shot through his right shoulder. Over a dozen men fell killed or wounded, and then a large man made a rush for me and the flag. As I tore the flag from the staff he took hold of me and the color." The large man was Corporal Francis Waller, who later earned the Congressional Medal of Honor for his feat.[29]

Looking down upon the Confederates in the railroad cut, a general cry, "Throw down your muskets! Down with your muskets!" rang through the line. Seeing a potential escape route to his right, Adjutant Edward Brooks took a detachment of twenty men to this part of the railroad cut, and ordered his men to fire into the flank of the rebels. Knowing that he needed to act quickly before the Confederates fled, Dawes yelled, "Where is the colonel of this regiment?" An officer with stars on his collar, Major John Blair of the 2nd Mississippi, approached and asked Dawes who he was. To this question Dawes replied, "I command this regiment. Surrender, or I will fire." Blair did not say a word, but merely handed over his sword. Seeing this act, Blair's men threw down their muskets. Over 225 men, primarily from the 2nd Mississippi, were captured. Six other officers also approached, and as they moved away, Dawes tried to hold seven swords. Adjutant Brooks relieved Dawes of the burden, permitting him to order the captured Confederates to the rear.[30]

The behavior of some of the Confederates angered the men. Private James Sullivan wrote that "some of them would throw down their guns and cry 'I surrender,' and immediately pick them up and shoot some of our unsuspecting men." After the war, Dawes marveled at his men's actions. "The coolness, self-possession, and discipline which held back our men from pouring in a general volley saved a hundred lives of the enemy." The 6th Wisconsin was attached to Cutler's Brigade on the north side of Chambersburg Pike for the next few hours.[31]

While the 6th Wisconsin was fighting at the unfinished railroad cut to the north, the rest of the Iron Brigade remained in their positions in Herbst Woods, under constant shelling by Confederate artillery. They rested and watched their skirmishers engage the enemy. General Doubleday rode up to the men and told them to hold their position at all cost. "If we can't hold it, where will you find men who can?" was the grim reply, according to Doubleday. Six Confederate brigades of General A. P. Hill's Third Corps were moving into position to attack the Federal units on the south side of Chambersburg Pike. Three brigades from Heth's Division led the attack column, supported by three more from Pender's Division. Sometime between 2:30 and 3:00 P.M., the men could see the Confeder-

ates advancing in two lines. What worried the 19th Indiana most was that the Confederate line extended far beyond its vulnerable left flank. The men grimly watched as the long Confederate line approached, with battle flags flapping in the wind. Observing the advance of the 11th North Carolina, and part of the 26th North Carolina of Pettigrew's Brigade (Heth's Division), Williams told his men, "Boys, we must hold our colors on this line, or lie here under them." Although Williams had earlier wanted to pull his men back to a less exposed position, he was ready to defend his assigned position to the death. When the Tar Heels were within range, Williams ordered his men to open fire. Confederates dropped all along the line. The attackers returned the fire, and Hoosiers fell by twos and threes. Because Biddle's Brigade was so far to the left and rear, it did not provide adequate support to the 19th Indiana's left flank. After a valiant fight, the 19th Indiana could hold no longer and the men began to drift backward about 100 yards to assume a new defensive position. They left twenty dead and another hundred wounded behind, about 40% of the regiment's strength. If it was any consolation, the 11th North Carolina was also sustaining heavy casualties. One company entered the fray with thirty-eight men, but only four remained when the sun set.[32]

The 24th Michigan, to the Hoosiers' right, had been ordered to hold its fire until the enemy approached to within fifty yards. When the order was given, the line erupted with sheets of flame. The men of the 24th Michigan were incredulous when the smoke cleared, for the 26th North Carolina still advanced. Colonel Morrow wrote in his report that the "nature of the ground" protected the enemy. "Their advance was not checked, and they came on with rapid strides, yelling like demons," he wrote. Not a Michigander ran. All continued loading and firing into the enemy's ranks. Every shot found its mark and gaps formed in the Confederate ranks. One veteran recalled that "no Rebel crossed that stream [Willoughby Run] and lived." The men spied a Confederate officer on a mule, cheering his men on by yelling, "Give 'em hell boys." A bullet knocked off his hat, which he grabbed in mid-air and returned to his head, continuing to lead his men.[33]

The withdrawal of the 19th Indiana exposed the left flank of the 24th Michigan, which resulted in "the men falling like grass before the scythe." The hail of bullets was so great that even wounded men on the ground were hit additional times. The two left-most companies refused to face the threat on the flank, and held for a short period before the regiment was also forced to retreat.[34]

Taking a new position in the rear, the men opened fire again, exacting a terrible toll. The two lines stood less than twenty paces apart, firing volleys into each other. After holding this position for a few minutes, the 24th Michigan was overwhelmed and again forced to retreat. The line had been bent, but was not broken. If the Confederates wanted the hills west of Gettysburg, they would have to pay an outrageous price for them. Thirteen flag bearers from the 26th North Carolina went down. The flag of the 24th Michigan was carried by a succession of ten soldiers, all but one killed or wounded in the process. As Colonel Morrow of the regiment bent down to pick up the fallen standard, he was approached by Private William Kelly, who shouted above the din, "The colonel of the Twenty-fourth shall never carry the flag while I am alive," and grabbed the standard. Kelly died almost immediately in a hail of bullets. Realizing that he needed to rally his men, Morrow grabbed the flag and was wounded. The 19th Indiana's flag bearers had suffered so severely that an officer ordered the flag to be wrapped and slid back into its shuck, so no more men

would be slaughtered while carrying it. It was unsheathed again later. As the men were pushed backward by the growing horde, they continually stopped and returned the fire, then inched backward again. According to the regiment's historian, the unit stopped four times to turn and face the Confederates, but each time was again forced to continue to fall back to Seminary Ridge. Only one man in five that marched down to McPherson Woods that morning was still standing, and only three officers remained with the unit.[35]

While the enemy's initial advance was directed against the 19th Indiana and 24th Michigan, the men of the 2nd Wisconsin and 7th Wisconsin on the right of the line watched Brockenbrough's Brigade (Heth's Division) making preparations to attack. At first it appeared that the Confederate attack would hit Stone's Brigade on their right, but a second line detached and obliqued toward them. Colonel William Robinson, whose 7th Wisconsin occupied the brigade's right flank, watched the Confederates advance into Herbst Woods, then lie down to open a galling fire on his position. Seventy-year-old Gettysburg resident John Burns fought with the regiment during this part of the battle; he was wounded several times.[36]

General Meredith was struck by an artillery shell. Since Wadsworth was off to the right, no replacement was appointed. Therefore, each regiment subsequently fought independently. As the left side of the line was rolled up under the intense pressure from Pettigrew's Brigade, a staff officer galloped up to Colonel Robinson with orders to pull his 7th Wisconsin and the 2nd Wisconsin back to the safety of Seminary Ridge. Robinson left the 2nd Wisconsin and three companies of the 7th Wisconsin in their positions; the seven remaining companies Wisconsin fell back. Attempting to hold their positions was folly, and after a short time, they joined the seven companies of the 7th Wisconsin on Seminary Ridge. Colonel Robinson wrote that "I retired by right of companies to the rear some 150 or 200 yards, halted, and wheeled into line again to support the other regiments in retiring. Then again retired about the same distance, and again wheeled into line, and so on until I reached the foot of Seminary Ridge."[37]

It appears that the 19th Indiana reached Seminary Ridge first; the 2nd Wisconsin last. As the men approached the seminary, they witnessed both harrowing and uplifting sights. The latter was in the form of a soldier from the 24th Michigan, lying on the ground and holding aloft the unit's flag, even in death. When the 7th Wisconsin approached a nearby orchard, canister and shells that had been passing over their heads from the Federal batteries on Seminary Ridge began to fall among their ranks, killing and wounding several men.[38]

The men received a measure of relief when they saw eighteen cannon arranged on Seminary Ridge. About forty yards in front of the batteries was a two-foot-high barricade "of loose rails, which . . . had been thrown together by some of our troops in the earlier part of the day, behind which I threw the regiment," noted Colonel Robinson of the 7th Wisconsin. Lying down behind it, the men grimly watched Scales's and Perrin's Brigades (Pender's Division) approach. "Here was made out our last and hopeless stand," wrote the commander of the 19th Indiana. Major Mark Finnicum of the 7th Wisconsin watched as the Rebels "came moving on in gallant and splendid style, not withstanding the shot and shell that ploughed through their ranks from our artillery. The waiting infantry screamed, 'Come on, Johnny! Come on!' When within a hundred paces of us, a sheet of flame burst from our line hurling its leaded hail with

such deadly certainty that their confident ranks were checked . . . literally annihilating the Rebel line. In our front not a man was left standing, what few if any were unhurt, sought safety behind the dead bodies of their fallen comrades."[39]

The position was a strong one, particularly with the line of artillery 40 yards to their rear, and could have been held somewhat longer had the 1st South Carolina not broken through the line to the left of the Iron Brigade. Seeing their flank about to be rolled up again, some of the men directed an oblique fire at the Confederates charging from their left. It was futile, for the South Carolinians swept around the Iron Brigade's flank. With the collapse of the XI Corps, enemy soldiers were approaching their right flank as well. In danger of being surrounded, General Doubleday finally ordered the brigade to abandon its position. Colonel Williams of the 19th Indiana wrote that "we could have held out against the line in front but their maneuvers on the left made the position untenable and I gave the order to retreat." Williams wrote to the governor of Indiana soon after the battle that the "men were loath to obey the order . . . [and] returned again to the barricade to pay the enemy one more complement."[40]

The 2nd and 7th Wisconsin were apparently the last units to leave the barricades. Captain Nat Rollins of the 2nd Wisconsin claimed that he did not receive orders to withdraw. Instead, he could see the Confederates drawing around his position and, looking to his right, could see Chambersburg Pike clogged with retreating Union soldiers. "There was no time to waste; so we stood not on order of our going, but went at once." Farther to the right, Lieutenant Colonel Dawes of the 6th Wisconsin saw a staff officer approach, who leaned over his horse and quietly said to Dawes, "The orders, colonel, are to retreat beyond the town. Hold your men together."[41]

The survivors found no solace in Gettysburg. The streets were clogged with soldiers from the XI Corps, and Confederates entered the town, scooping up scores of prisoners. "The streets were jammed with crowds of retreating soldiers, and with ambulances, artillery, and wagons. The cellars were crowded with men, sound in body but craven in spirit, who had gone there to surrender. I saw no men wearing the badge of the First Army Corps in this disgraceful company," wrote Dawes. The Iron Brigade's units had disintegrated to the point that many men made their way to safety without much direction from their officers. Colonel Williams wrote that it was "impossible to form [the units] and we retired, each to care for himself, through the town." There was constant firing, and the men stopped periodically to fire a volley before moving on.[42]

The 6th Wisconsin was one of the few units that moved through the town as an organized unit. When the remnant of the regiment came to an intersection swept by small arms fire, Dawes ordered his men across single file, through a small opening in a fence. Dawes positioned himself by the opening, and any man who dallied was "jerked away without ceremony or apology, the object being to keep the track clear for those yet to come." The regiment lost only two men crossing the street. The weather was extremely hot, and Dawes recalled the sweat streaming down his men's faces. A local citizen received three cheers when he appeared with two buckets of cool water.[43]

Upon reaching Cemetery Hill, the men threw themselves down on the ground in utter exhaustion. After taking stock of their losses, the men's worst fears were confirmed. The brigade had almost been destroyed. Only twenty-six men assembled

under the flag of the 24th Michigan propped up against the wheel of a cannon, while its single remaining captain slumped against a nearby tombstone. Stragglers later swelled the number to ninety-nine men and three officers—out of almost five hundred who had entered the fight, a loss of 73%. Few Federal regiment lost a larger proportion of men during the battle. The 19th Indiana initially mustered seventy-five men on Cemetery Hill, and the 2nd Wisconsin, only sixty-nine. Wadsworth finally ordered Colonel Robinson of the 7th Wisconsin to take command of the brigade during this period.[44]

The men did not have time to rest, for they were ordered to fall in and march to Culp's Hill. The 6th Wisconsin joined them later and formed on the right of the line. This was a special reunion, because the 6th Wisconsin brought its regimental wagon containing entrenching tools. Although Dawes received no orders, he told his men to begin digging after they arrived. "The men worked with great energy. A man would dig with all his strength till out of breath, when another would seize the spade and push on the work," recalled Dawes. The activity was probably therapeutic, for it took their minds off their terrible experiences. Coffee and hardtack were distributed to the exhausted men. Some of the units were also temporarily reorganized during this period. For example, the decimated 24th Michigan was divided into two parts, each under the command of a lieutenant. As additional men returned, the regiment was again reorganized, this time into four battalions.[45]

July 2 was a quiet time for the men. This changed at dusk, when Johnson's Division (Second Corps) attacked Culp's Hill. According to Dawes, "a sound came from the woods to our right, that made us jump for our breastworks. It was the rebel yell, sounded by thousands of voices. . . . I ran to my post, and ordered: 'Down, men, watch sharp, keep your eyes peeled! Shoot low, shoot low, the hill is steep; quiet, now; steady!'" Because the attacks were made farther to their right, the men did not open fire that night.[46]

The night was not over for the 6th Wisconsin. A staff officer ordered Colonel Dawes to report with his regiment to General Greene, who was holding out against extraordinary odds. All but Greene's Brigade had been removed from the breastworks on Culp's Hill just before Johnson's attack. Dawes issued a string of orders to his men: "Attention, battalion, right face, forward by the file right—march." It was an unsettling combination—the night was dark, and the men did not know where they were going or where the enemy was. Stumbling again and again, the men moved toward Greene's vulnerable right flank, which had been bent back by Johnson's charge. Somewhere near them was the 84th New York of Cutler's Brigade, also moving to Greene's aid.[47]

As Dawes's men approached the breastworks, they made an unsettling discovery: they were occupied by the enemy. The enemy soldiers, "who were completely surprised at our sudden arrival, rose up and fired a volley at us, and immediately retreated down the hill," recalled Dawes.

The encounter with the 10th Virginia of Steuart's Brigade lasted but a few moments, but was instrumental in blunting its further advance toward the Federal rear. The 6th Wisconsin remained there until midnight, when it was ordered back to its brigade.[48]

The renewed attacks on Culp's Hill during the morning of July 3 were again directed to the right of the brigade, so it played no role in repulsing the enemy. Later that afternoon, the brigade was rushed over toward Cemetery Ridge, where the Pickett–Pettigrew–Trimble charge was ebbing. Not needed here, the men were again ordered back to their positions on Culp's Hill. This ended the brigade's actions at the battle of Gettysburg.[49]

Three days after the battle, General Wadsworth paid the 24th Michigan's commander, and essentially the entire Iron Brigade, a special tribute, when he remarked, "Colonel Morrow, the only fault I have with you is that you fought too long, but God only knows what would have become of the Army of the Potomac if you had not held the ground as long as you did." Few units could have sustained the punishment meted out to the Iron Brigade on July 1. Its stubborn resistance of the two ridges west of Gettysburg bought valuable time for the Federal army to concentrate.[50]

2nd Brigade—Brigadier General Lysander Cutler

Units: 7th Indiana, 76th New York, 84th New York, 95th New York, 147th New York, 56th Pennsylvania
Strength: 2017
Losses: 1002 (128-509-365)—50%[51]

Like his division commander, Brigadier General Lysander Cutler had no military experience; prior to the war, accumulated

wealth, and hailed from New England. That is where the similarities ended. Two successive business ventures eventually failed, throwing Cutler from the ranks of the affluent into poverty. Starting over again in Milwaukee, Cutler struggled. When the Civil War broke out, Cutler raised the 6th Wisconsin. Hated by his subordinates, but respected for his fighting abilities, Cutler was badly wounded during the Second Bull Run campaign. He received command of the 2nd Brigade on March 26, 1863, and led it at Chancellorsville. Since the corps saw limited action there, Cutler rode toward Gettysburg without battlefield experience at this level. His brigade was a mixed bag of regiments from three states. Four had been together since the brigade was formed, and a fifth, the 147th New York, was added in March 1863. The brigade certainly did not have the same reputation as its sister brigade.[52]

Cutler's Brigade had the distinction of leading the I Corps toward Gettysburg, and therefore it was the first infantry unit to reach the battlefield. Despite the arduous march, the men's spirits were revived by the civilians who lined the road during their march. "Frequently loaves of fresh bread, kneaded by loyal hands and tendered with pleasant smiles of welcome, and aprons full of ripe cherries" were much in evidence, noted one of the men. As the 56th Pennsylvania crossed its state border, the men "sent up cheer upon cheer, showing their appreciation of 'Home sweet, sweet home,'" recalled Lieutenant Abram Smith of the 76th New York.[53]

Up at dawn on July 1, the men ate whatever was available. For Captain J. V. Pierce of the 147th New York, it was two pieces of hardtack and a cup of black coffee. Prior to breaking camp, the men each received sixty rounds of ammunition and one day's rations. The brigade began its march toward Gettysburg at 8:00 A.M. on July 1 without the 7th Indiana, which was left behind on special duty. The 76th New York led the column, followed by the 56th Pennsylvania, 147th New York, 95th New York, and 84th New York (bringing up the rear). The column halted about two miles from Gettysburg during the early morning, where the men watched as General Reynolds studied a large map while standing by the side of the road.[54]

As the column pushed on, the men heard sounds of battle up ahead. Before long, "circular wreaths of smoke" could be seen over trees in the distance, marking where artillery shells had exploded. Staff officers brought word that Buford's cavalry were attempting to hold off a growing horde of Confederate infantry. "The Rebs were thicker than blackberries beyond the hill," they were told. According to Colonel John Bachelder, "the ranks closed up, the head became more firm, and the whole column swept grandly on, and every one seemed anxious to meet the invader."[55]

Realizing that he needed to get his men to the scene of the action as quickly as possible, Reynolds decided to order them to double-quick across the fields. As the head of the column reached the vicinity of the Codori house on Emmitsburg Road, the men heard the orders, "Head of column to the left!" quickly followed by "Forward, double-quick! Load at will!" A "wild rattle of jingling ramrods" filled the morning air. Although the pioneers cleared the path of obstructions, the 76th New York was also required to push down fences, which impeded its movement across the fields. As the men ran forward in the narrow valley between McPherson and Seminary Ridges, shell fragments rained down on them from Confederate batteries on Herr Ridge.[56]

Upon reaching the Lutheran seminary, the head of the column turned left and marched westward. Seeing the infantry arriving, General Buford pulled his cavalrymen back to safety. This was a critical time, as Cutler's Brigade was the only infantry unit on the scene and two Confederate brigades from Heth's Division (III Corps) were approaching. After marching about 150 yards, Cutler divided his brigade. The first three regiments, the 76th New York, 56th Pennsylvania, and 147th New York, marched northward and crossed Chambersburg Pike and took position north of the unfinished railroad. The 84th and 95th New York bringing up the rear were ordered toward the McPherson house. For some reason, Lieutenant Colonel Francis Miller of the 147th New York did not receive the orders to cross the road, and instead remained behind the 95th and 84th New York. Halting his regiment at a garden with a picket fence at the McPherson house, Miller either rode off to seek orders or received them from an orderly while deploying his men. Either way, he issued orders to "By the flank to the right at a double quick" and the men hastily crossed the road, and therefore were over a hundred yards closer to the enemy than the 76th New York and 56th Pennsylvania, which were on its right and rear. This was not an enviable position, given the fact that Davis's Brigade was bearing down on it.[57]

The two other regiments to the north of the road, the 76th New York and 56th Pennsylvania, had already crossed the unfinished railroad cut and formed line of battle about two hundred yards north of it. This accomplished, the line moved about fifty yards west. Reaching the crest of the ridge, the two regiments halted and came under intense small arms fire. The Pennsylvanians could see the 55th North Carolina (Davis's Brigade) approaching from the right. Colonel J. William Hofmann of the 56th Pennsylvania was apparently confused by this sudden turn of events, for he turned to Cutler, who was riding behind the regiment, and asked, "Is that the enemy?" When Cutler replied in the affirmative, Hofmann screamed to his men, "Ready, right oblique, aim, fire!"[58]

As Hofmann gave the order, "aim," Cutler asked whether the enemy was close enough for a volley. Hofmann apparently did not hear him, and the volley exploded from the Pennsylvanians's gun barrels. The first Federal infantry volley of the bat-

tle of Gettysburg had been fired. Cutler received his answer within seconds, when a Confederate volley brought down a number of Pennsylvanians and unhorsed Cutler and two of his aides. The 76th New York encountered a similar situation, but its commander handled it quite differently. Upon reaching their position on the right of the 56th Pennsylvania, the New Yorkers were immediately raked with several volleys. Because the 2nd Mississippi was lying down in a Wheatfield, Major Andrew Grover assumed that the fire was coming from Federal troops. "We were exposed to their fire several minutes without replying. The men were cautioned to hold their fire until the enemy appeared," wrote a grim Captain John Cook in his official report. At least three volleys were fired into the 76th New York before it responded. The long, straight lines of the 55th North Carolina pushing down on its right flank left no doubt in Grover's mind, and he hastily ordered his men to open fire. The regiment soon received fire from its front and flank. To counter this threat, Grover ordered his right flank to "Change front to the rear." No sooner had these orders been issued, than Grover went down with a mortal wound. The men obeyed the order as though the unit was on the parade ground. With its right flank refused, the New Yorkers tried to stem the Rebel advance from the north and west.[59]

Seeing the two regiments' untenable situation, General Wadsworth ordered Cutler to withdraw them to the safety of Seminary Ridge. The regiments lost heavily during the twenty minutes they were engaged. The 76th New York suffered the most, losing 234 men out of the 375 it carried into battle (62%). The 56th Pennsylvania lost about half of its men.[60]

The 147th New York had crossed the road later than her sister regiments, and moved westward—into the path of the 42nd Mississippi. It arrived at a fortuitous time, as the Mississippi skirmishers were bearing down on Hall's battery along Chambersburg Pike. Private Francis Pease recalled seeing the enemy was "not more than 30 or 40 rods off and their colors flying." Adjutant Henry Lyman of the 147th noted that the fighting was "at very short range and very destructive." Captain J. V. Pierce reported that the "bullets from the enemy were flying thick and fast as we marched rapidly towards our opponents." Many of the men dropped down into the wheat to avoid the killing fire of the Mississippians. Captain James Coey recalled that the men would "take deliberate aim, fire and then slide back under their canopy or covering of straw; reload and continue their firing. Those of the regiment wounded here were in the head or upper part of the body, consequently more fatal." While the New Yorkers and Mississippians fought it out, Hall's battery limbered up and galloped to safety.[61]

With its two sister regiments pulling back, the 147th New York was facing the 42nd Mississippi on its front and the 2nd Mississippi and 55th North Carolina on its flank and rear. The regiment's commander, Lieutenant Colonel Miller, had received orders to pull back at about the same time as the two other regiments, but was wounded before he could give the order. Not knowing this, Major George Harney, the new commander, ordered the right companies refused at right angles to face the threat from the north. "The fight was again fierce and hot; the boys on the right [the refused part of the regiment] were falling like autumn leaves; the air was full of lead. Men fell all along the line," wrote Captain J. V. Pierce.[62]

Seeing the regiment's perilous position, Captain Timothy Ellsworth recalled Wadsworth turning to him and saying

"what that regiment was doing up there; said he had given orders some time ago for those troops to be withdrawn, and directed me to go and withdraw them unless there was some special occasion, which was not apparent to him for their remaining." Pressing his head against his horse's neck, Ellsworth galloped through the maelstrom to give orders to Harney. "Major Harney then gave orders, to be communicated along the line, for the men to divest themselves of everything but the rifle and cartridge box. Thus went our rations, and until July 4, only two crackers from a passing regiment sustained us," complained Captain James Coey. With three enemy regiments pushing down on its front, flank, and rear, extracting the 147th New York from its precarious position was not easy. Coey recalled the orders as "the men were to fire, rise up and immediately fall down, thus letting the enemy's fire pass over them, Then bending low, march in quick step to the rear, trailing their guns, loading and firing at will." The regiment fired its volley, then crouched down. When it received orders to rise up and run to the rear, "it seemed to melt away, as it received the retained fire of the enemy's line," recalled Coey. It was now a race for the rear, and in their excitement, many of the inexperienced Southerners neglected to remove their ramrods before firing their rifles. This caused even more terror among the retreating Northern troops. In all, the regiment probably remained in combat for at least ten additional minutes after its comrades withdrew. The seventy-nine survivors (of the original 380) eventually joined the 76th New York and 56th Pennsylvania behind Oak Ridge on the north side of Chambersburg Pike, where they refilled their canteens and rested. The fight of the 147th New York, an untested regiment in its first battle, was said to be a "highlight of the first day's battle." Its gallant stand had helped save Hall's battery from certain capture.[63]

While three of Cutler's regiments were battling Davis's Brigade on the north side of Chambersburg Pike, the two remaining regiments, the 84th and 95th New York, were taking position just to the south of the McPherson farm buildings. Cutler decided to remain with the three regiments across the road, so he ordered Colonel Edward Fowler to take command of the two regiments to the south of it. The demi-brigade almost immediately engaged the skirmishers from Archer's Brigade, whose main body was still beyond Willoughby Creek. It must have been a welcome relief for the New Yorkers to see the black-hatted Westerners from the Iron Brigade arrive and take position on their left.[64]

Looking across Chambersburg Pike to his right, Colonel Fowler was surprised to see the remnants of his three sister regiments streaming to safety to the rear, pursued by a thick mass of Confederates. Knowing that the whole Federal defensive line would collapse if the enemy rolled up its right flank, Fowler about-faced his two regiments and pulled them back a short distance. When about even with the Confederate line across the road, he ordered his men to "change front forward on the right" so that the right-most company pivoted to the right until it faced the enemy. The next company completed this maneuver, then the third, until both regiments faced Davis's Brigade's right flank. Upon reaching Chambersburg Pike, Fowler ordered his men to lie down. Around this time, General Doubleday ordered the 6th Wisconsin forward, which ultimately formed on the 95th New York's right. Although the Badgers claimed otherwise after the war, the New Yorkers insisted that the three regiments had attacked Davis's Brigade together.[65]

Davis's men were disordered at this time and their higher-ranking officers seem to have lost control. The men, however, knew a threat when they saw one, and three Federal regiments lying along the road on their flank stopped them in their tracks. Wheeling to their right, they confronted the new threat. Fowler's troops were not about to make it easy for the Confederates, and, with their muskets barrels resting on the fence rails along Chambersburg Pike, poured volleys into Davis's men. The fire from the thousand muskets was just too hot for the enemy, so they approached the unfinished railroad cut. Only now did Davis realize that the situation had gone from sweet victory to the possibility of defeat, as the three regiments he had driven backward loomed on his flank and three other regiments were in front. The time had come for a retreat.[66]

Colonel Fowler could sense the tide shifting, and ordered his 84th New York to charge. "At the Colonel's command they rushed forward with a cheer . . . as the troops, charging with dash and spirit, reached this little eminence, they were met with a murderous hail of musket bullets. The balls came so thick and fast that the whirring noise they made sounded like the steady rhythm of machinery. For just an instant, as the full force of this terrible fire broke along their front, the line wavered," recalled C. V. Tervis of the regiment. Composing themselves, the units rushed on. Men dropped with each step. The 95th New York and 6th Wisconsin also charged across Chambersburg Pike. Many of the Confederates had jumped into the unfinished railroad cut for safety. It was a trap, as the sides were too steep for an escape.[67]

The 6th Wisconsin sent a detachment to flank the enemy in the railroad cut, thus cutting off their retreat. As the three Federal regiments lined the bank, hundreds of Confederates threw down their rifles to surrender. This action claimed a lasting page in the history of the battle for Cutler's Brigade. After sending the prisoners to the rear, the three regiments joined the remainder of Cutler's Brigade in the woods just to the east on Seminary Ridge. Here the men rested and helped the wounded.

At about 1:00 P.M. that afternoon, Cutler ordered his men forward to reoccupy their former positions. According to a recent analysis by James McLean, the troops were arranged, from south to north (left to right), as 6th Wisconsin–84th New York–95th New York–76th New York–56th Pennsylvania–147th New York. Wadsworth detached the two left regiments, the 6th Wisconsin and the 84th New York, to support Calef's battery, which occupied Hall's battery's old position.[68]

After about forty-five minutes, General Cutler made another disturbing observation: "I discovered the enemy putting a battery in position on my right flank and moving forward large bodies of infantry in the same direction." Rodes's Division had arrived on Oak Hill, squarely on Cutler's flank. Requesting orders, Wadsworth told Cutler to "take such a position as I judged proper." He decided to wheel his four regiments to the right, via a right oblique movement, to face this new threat from the north. His men were not in this position very long when Cutler apparently had second thoughts, so he changed the position of two of his regiments to create a letter L. The 147th New York and the 56th Pennsylvania faced Rodes's Division to the north behind a zigzag fence, while the 95th and 76th New York faced west along the margin of the wood. Again unsupported, Cutler probably wondered whether this would be the attack that would destroy his brigade. He received welcome reinforcements in the form of

Baxter's Brigade (Robinson's Division, I Corps), which formed at right angles to his right wing. The 84th New York and the 6th Wisconsin, which had been supporting Calef's battery, also rejoined the brigade around this time.[69]

Before long, Cutler's men could see the long, well-dressed lines of Iverson's North Carolina Brigade advancing against them from Oak Hill to the north. The 56th Pennsylvania and 147th New York already facing this direction opened fire while Cutler quickly wheeled his other regiments to face Iverson's doomed brigade. They all poured a destructive fire into the approaching enemy. Baxter's men had already risen up from their concealed positions behind a stone wall, and decimated Iverson's men. At least part of the 76th New York along with some units from Robinson's Division counterattacked to capture a number of prisoners. A new threat materialized almost immediately, when Daniel's North Carolina Brigade (Rodes's Division) approached Cutler's left flank. This forced Cutler to swing his left flank backward again toward the woods, so his men had a clear field of fire. Realizing that his ammunition was almost expended, Cutler pulled his brigade back to safety. During the half-hour wait to be resupplied, the men were exposed to shelling from Confederate artillery on Oak Hill and Herr Ridge.[70]

The entire I Corps's position was rapidly crumbling from the immense Confederate pressure, so General Doubleday ordered his troops assembled on Seminary Ridge. In response, the 76th, 84th, and 147th New York were quickly rushed to the left to support Stewart's battery, which was deployed near Chambersburg Pike. Here they helped repel Scales's Brigade's (Pender's Division) valiant but suicidal efforts to capture the battery. "With the rebel yell they rushed up the slope again and again in a splendid series of charges, advancing in line of battle, as if on parade. They were checked again and again with the murderous fire . . . but as one line was wiped out and broken up by grape and canister and musketry another would be reformed at the bottom of the hill," recalled Tervis (84th New York).[71]

Doubleday realized that he had run out of options, so he ordered the I Corps back to Gettysburg. Cutler's orders were to retreat along the railroad tracks and through the town. As Cutler's men complied, they helped drag one of Stewart's guns to safety. Lieutenant Abram Smith of the 76th New York proudly recalled that as the men entered the railroad cut and began their retreat toward Gettysburg, they "marched with perfect steadiness and no excitement . . . [This] had the effect to bring the enemy to a halt, when he threw out skirmishers." Cutler had another horse killed from under him during this retreat.[72]

The men found complete chaos in Gettysburg. Not only were the streets packed with Federal soldiers, Confederate artillery pounded the town, adding to the confusion. At least one shell hit a building, showering the troops with masonry. Colonel John Cook of the 76th New York estimated that he lost eight to ten men while marching through the town. The brigade finally reformed on East Cemetery Hill, where it spent the night. Here it reunited with the newly arrived 7th Indiana. The brigade had fought from 10:00 A.M. to 4:00 P.M. and engaged five Confederate brigades. The brigade had, however, paid a heavy price, losing about a thousand men. It now numbered (without the 7th Indiana) about six hundred.[73]

Although the 7th Indiana did not play a role in the bloody contests, it was destined to have a major impact on the bat-

tle's outcome. Detached from the brigade on June 29 to guard the corps' cattle and ammunition train, the regiment marched slowly toward Gettysburg. Hearing the sounds of battle up ahead, and learning that General Reynolds had been killed, was too much for the regiment's commander, Colonel Ira Grover, to bear. Disobeying orders, he marched his men toward the sounds of battle. He was later court-martialed for abandoning the cattle and trains, but was exonerated.[74]

Arriving at Cemetery Hill at about 5:00 P.M. on July 1, the Hoosiers passed a dejected General Wadsworth sitting on a stone fence by the roadside, his head bowed in grief. Brightening when he saw these familiar fresh troops, Wadsworth exclaimed, "I am glad you were not with us this afternoon . . . all would now be dead or prisoners." The regiment was immediately sent to Culp's Hill, and the remnants of the Iron Brigade formed on its left. Because there were not enough troops to man the entire hill, several companies were sent to its base to form a picket line. In the growing darkness, the men from Company B ran into a reconnaissance party from the 42nd Virginia of Edward Johnson's Division. Most of the Virginians were captured; the others ran back to report that the hill was occupied. This information convinced Second Corps commander, General Richard Ewell, to wait until daylight to attack the hill. This event is commonly cited as one of the reasons why the Confederates lost the battle of Gettysburg.[75]

Early the next morning, the rest of Cutler's Brigade moved eastward to Culp's Hill, where it deployed to the right of the 7th Indiana. The front line, from left (west) to right (east), was 7th Indiana (facing northeast)–76th New York–56th Pennsylvania–95th New York (facing east). The two remaining regiments, 84th and the 147th New York, formed a second line behind their comrades. The brigade spent the remainder of the day strengthening their breastworks, cleaning their guns, and resting.[76]

That evening, the men realized that they were again in a very vulnerable position, as Meade had pulled all of the XII Corps, except Greene's Brigade, off Culp's Hill and sent them to aid the Federal left flank. Johnson's Division attacked Culp's Hill after they departed. Although heavily outnumbered, Wadsworth's depleted division and Greene's Brigade occupied an exceptionally strong position. Jones's Brigade attacked Cutler's front. Colonel Hofmann of the 56th Pennsylvania recalled how the "crest of the works was lighted up as it were, by a long flash of tongued lightning, as the regiments took their place in the woods." The terrain was steep and darkness had all but fallen, and this together with the destructive fire of Cutler's men, halted Jones's attack. Although some of Jones's men came within twenty feet of the breastworks, most were dissuaded long before they came that close.[77]

Greene was having a more difficult time just to the south, as Steuart's Brigade had found his right flank. In response to urgent pleas for assistance, Wadsworth sent the 84th and 147th New York and the 6th Wisconsin. As the relief column made its way slowly toward Greene's right flank, Colonel Fowler was met by Lieutenant John Cantine of Greene's staff, who helped guide his subsequent movements. Colonel Fowler explained what happened next:

> On arriving on the right, we received a fire from the inside of our lines, and, it then being quite dark I was placed in a trying position to determine if we were being fired on by our friends, or if the enemy had penetrated inside of our line.

I formed the Regiment facing the fire, and sent out a scout to reconnoiter, who returned and reported it to be the 10th Virginia and as their fire was continued, I directed a volley to be fired into them, which at once silenced them.[78]

According to a modern historian, James McLean, the actions of the three regiments that evening were instrumental in saving the Union army. If the 10th Virginia had not been stopped, it could have continued southward, reaching Baltimore Pike and the rear of the army. The collision with the Federal troops in the dark effectively eliminated the Virginians' taste for further exploration that evening.[79]

Continuing forward, Fowler found the regiment that he was to relieve, but soon learned that it was already being supported by two lines of battle. Believing that he was not needed, Fowler ordered his men back up the hill to their original positions. Almost as soon as they arrived, Fowler was confronted by one of General Greene's staff officers, who ordered the men to move down the hill once again to relieve a regiment in the trenches. This time, they were successful in finding the correct regiment, the 137th New York, and took its place in the breastworks for the reminder of the night. Early the next morning, the 137th New York returned, so the I Corps troops took a position in the rear. A short time later, they received orders to rejoin the brigade farther up the hill. Upon reaching the summit, the men were permitted to grab a quick breakfast before being ordered back down the hill to again support the XII Corps.[80]

During the early morning hours of July 3, Johnson's Division renewed its attacks on the Federal position on Culp's Hill. While Cutler's four regiments on the front line continued to fire into the flank of the attacking Confederates, the 84th and 147th New York were again ordered down the hill. These two regiments spent the morning hours relieving the troops in the trenches along the front line. Fowler recalled that "the Regiment advanced to the trenches at double-quick, cheering and shouting, and remained there fighting until our ammunition was exhausted. I ordered each man to retain a load in his rifle to be used while being relieved. The men fought in the trenches with great coolness, many of them standing up and looking around for a good range before firing." When it was time for his troops to be relieved, Fowler "ordered our men to fire rapidly to cover their entrance to the trenches, and the relief to fire rapidly to cover our exit." As a result, Fowler lost not a man when undertaking the hazardous task of leaving the breastworks and making for the rear. The 147th New York had similar experiences—at least four times it was ordered to relieve the troops in the breastworks. Every man fired over two hundred rounds at the enemy that morning.[81]

At about 1:00 P.M., the men were exposed to the intense artillery fire that preceded the Pickett–Pettigrew–Trimble charge. Colonel Fowler recalled that the "noise of cannon and explosion of projectiles was almost deafening." The regiment was ordered to return to the brigade at about 4:30 P.M. Although the charge was repelled, Meade was still concerned about further attacks, so he ordered reinforcements to Cemetery Ridge. This included the four regiments from Cutler's Brigade that remained high up on the hill during the battle for Culp's Hill—the 7th Indiana, 56th Pennsylvania, and 76th and 95th New York. The two remaining regiments, the 84th and 147th New York, took their places behind the breastworks. Probably concerned about a renewed attack on Culp's Hill, General Cutler remained behind, while Colonel Hofmann led the

four regiments to Cemetery Ridge. The four regiments were not needed and returned a few hours later. Hofmann led another expedition, this time involving the 7th Indiana and 56th Pennsylvania, into Gettysburg on the morning of July 4. One of Cutler's men was wounded while passing through it—the brigade's last casualty of the battle. The brigade left Culp's Hill again on the morning of July 5, when it was ordered to occupy the western slope of Cemetery Hill. It remained there until the next morning, when it began its pursuit of Lee's army.[82]

Cutler's Brigade earned an important place in the history of the battle. The first infantry unit on the field, it also had the distinction of being the first unit driven back. This was not due to the fighting quality of the men, but to their unfortunate position, which was flanked by Davis's Brigade. Two of its regiments subsequently redeemed the brigade's honor by helping to defeat Davis's Brigade, capturing hundreds in the process. Later in the day, the brigade helped halt Iverson's charge. That night, the 7th Indiana played its important role in discouraging a night attack on Culp's Hill, and through the night of July 2 and the morning of July 3, the brigade was instrumental in repelling repeated Confederate attacks on the hill. As a result of these actions, the brigade lost half of its numbers.

NOTES

1. Frederick H. Dyer, *A Compendium of the War of the Rebellion* (New York, 1959), 284; Stewart Sifakis, *Who Was Who in the Civil War* (New York, 1988), 539–540.

2. Sifakis, *Who Was Who in the Civil War,* 539–540; Larry Tagg, *Generals of Gettysburg* (Campbell, CA, 1998), 10–11.

3. *War of the Rebellion: A Compilation of the Official Records of the Union and Confederate*

Armies, 128 vols. (Washington, DC, 1880–1901), series 1, vol. 27, pt. 1, 243–244. Hereafter cited as OR. All references are to series 1 unless otherwise noted.

4. OR 27, 1, 244; Tagg, *Generals of Gettysburg,* 11–12.

5. OR 27, 1, 247–248.

6. OR 27, 1, 248–251.

7. A. F. Sweetland, "First Day at Gettysburg," *National Tribune,* November 2, 1916.

8. OR, 27, 1, 252, 258, 261–263.

9. Dyer, *Compendium of the War of the Rebellion,* 284; Ezra J. Warner, *Generals in Blue* (Baton Rouge, LA, 1964), 532–533; Tagg, *Generals of Gettysburg,* 15.

10. *New York Monuments Commission for the Battlefields of Gettysburg and Chattanooga—Final Report on the Battlefield of Gettysburg,* 3 vols. (Albany, NY, 1900), vol. 3, 1001. Hereafter cited as *NYG.*

11. OR 27, 1, 265–266, 281–282.

12. OR 27, 1, 266–267.

13. John W. Busey and David G. Martin, *Regimental Strengths and Losses at Gettysburg* (Hightstown, NJ, 1994), 23, 239.

14. Lance J. Herdegen and William J. K. Beaudot, *In the Bloody Railroad Cut* (Dayton, OH, 1990), 160; Richard A. Sauers, *Fighting Them Over—How the Veterans Remembered Gettysburg in the Pages of the National Tribune* (Baltimore, MD, 1998), 74–91.

15. Tagg, *Generals of Gettysburg,* 16–17; Warner, *Generals in Blue,* 319.

16. OR 27, 1, 278–279; "Report of Lt. Col. William W. Dudley," in Bachelder Papers, New Hampshire Historical Society; O. B. Curtis, *History of the Twenty-Fourth Michigan of the Iron Brigade* (Detroit, MI, 1891), 124; David G. Martin, *Gettysburg, July 1* (Conshohocken, PA, 1996), 94.

17. William J. Beaudot and Lance J. Herdegen, *An Irishman in the Iron Brigade* (New York, 1993), 93; Rufus R. Dawes, *Service with the Sixth Wisconsin Volunteers* (Marietta, OH), 164.

18. James P. Sullivan, "The Old Iron Brigade at Gettysburg," *Milwaukee Sunday Telegraph,* December 20, 1864.

19. OR 27, 1, 267, 273, 279; Beaudot and Herdegen, *An Irishman in the Iron Brigade,* 94; "Report of Lt. Col. William W. Dudley."

20. OR 27, 1, 279; Martin, *Gettysburg—July 1,* 152.

Lieutenant Colonel John Callis recalled these moments somewhat differently. While waiting for orders, but under a heavy fire, Callis gave the order to "fix bayonets," as his men had not been given orders to load. As they were rushing forward, one of General Wadsworth's aides arrived to stop the advance, but it was too late. The attack drove Archer's men across Willoughby Run. ("'The Iron Brigade'—7th Wis. Infantry at Gettysburg, Pa.—Report of Lt. Col. John Callis," in Bachelder Papers, New Hampshire Historical Society.

21. OR 27, 1, 279; Donald L. Smith, *The Twenty-Fourth Michigan of the Iron Brigade* (Harrisburg, PA, 1962), 126; Abner Doubleday, *Chancellorsville and Gettysburg* (New York, 1882), 132.

22. OR 27, 1, 274; Cornelius Wheeler, "Reminiscences of the Battle of Gettysburg," in *Wisconsin MOLLUS,* vol. 2, 210; Allen T. Nolan, *The Iron Brigade* (New York, 1961), 236.

23. OR 27, 1, 268, 274, 279; Curtis, *History of the Twenty-Fourth Michigan,* 157–159; William H. Harries, "The Iron Brigade in the First Day's Battle of Gettysburg," in *Minnesota MOLLUS,* vol. 4, 210; William T. Venner, *Hoosiers Honor* (Shippensburg, PA), 170–171; Alan D. Gaff, "Here Was Made Out Our Last and Hopeless Stand," *Gettysburg Magazine* (January 1990), issue 2, 29; Harry Pfanz, *Gettysburg—The First Day* (Chapel Hill, NC, 2001) 271–272.

24. OR 27, 1, 275; Dawes, *Service with the Sixth Wisconsin Volunteers,* 164–165; Rufus R. Dawes to John Bachelder, March 18, 1868, in Bachelder Papers, New Hampshire Historical Society.

25. James P. Sullivan, "Gettysburg: A Member of the 6th Wis. Takes Issue With Carleton," *National Tribune,* May 14, 1885.

26. Dawes, *Service with the Sixth Wisconsin Volunteers,* 166–167; OR 27, 1, 276; James P. Sullivan, "The Sixth Wis. At Gettysburg," *Milwaukee Sunday Telegraph,* June, 21, 1885.

27. OR 27, 1, 276; Dawes, *Service with the Sixth Wisconsin Volunteers*, 167.

According to Sergeant George Fairfield, the men pulled down the fence along the south side of Chambersburg Pike and climbed over the northern one (George Fairfield, "The Capture of the Railroad Cut," *National Tribune*, September 1, 1910).

28. OR 27, 1, 276; Dawes, *Service with the Sixth Wisconsin Volunteers*, 167–168; John Kellogg to John Bachelder, November 1, 1865, in Bachelder Papers, New Hampshire Historical Society; Rufus R. Dawes to John Bachelder, March 18, 1868.

29. W. B. Murphy letter (copy in 2nd Mississippi folder, Gettysburg National Military Park). Hereafter cited as GNMP.

30. Sullivan, *An Irishman in the Iron Brigade*, 95; Dawes, *Service with the Sixth Wisconsin Volunteers*, 169.

31. Sullivan, "Gettysburg"; Dawes, *Service with the Sixth Wisconsin Volunteers*, 169; Rufus R. Dawes to John Bachelder, March 18, 1868.

32. Gaff, "Here Was Made Out Our Last and Hopeless Stand," 31; OR 27, 1, 244; Martin, *Gettysburg—July 1*, 354; John M. Vanderslice, *Gettysburg Then and Now* (New York, 1899), 120.

According to Martin (*Gettysburg—July 1*, 363), Colonel Williams of the 19th Indiana may have mistaken the movement of the 151st Pennsylvania of Biddle's Brigade as a relief for his men, and therefore pulled his men backward.

33. Smith, *History of the Twenty-Fourth Michigan*, 129–130; OR 27, 1, 268, 279.

It appears that there were three attacking lines in front of the 19th Indiana and two in front of the 2nd and 7th Wisconsin.

34. Curtis, *History of the Twenty-Fourth Michigan*, 160, 182; Marc Storch and Beth Storch, "Unpublished Gettysburg Reports by the 2nd and 7th Wisconsin Infantry Regimental Officers," *Gettysburg Magazine* (July 1997), issue 17, 22.

35. OR 27, 1, 268–269; Curtis, *History of the Twenty-First Michigan*, 160–162, 166; Smith, *History of the Twenty-Fourth Michigan*, 130–136; Venner, *Hoosier's Honor*, 179; Craig

L. Dunn, *Iron Men, Iron Will* (Indianapolis, IN, 1995), 192–193.

36. OR 27, 1, 274, 279; John W. Johnston, *The True Story of John Burns* (Philadelphia, 1916), 11; "'The Iron Brigade'—7th Wis. Infantry at Gettysburg, Pa.-Report of Lt. Col. John Callis."

37. Storch and Storch, "Unpublished Gettysburg Reports," 22; OR 27, 1, 280.

Although his wound was not serious, Meredith never returned to the Army of the Potomac. Instead, he was assigned to command posts in Illinois and Kentucky (Warner, *Generals in Blue*, 320).

38. Curtis, *History of the Twenty-Fourth Michigan*, 165; "'The Iron Brigade'—7th Wis. Infantry at Gettysburg, Pa.-Report of Lt. Col. John Callis."

39. Martin, *Gettysburg—July 1*, 398–399; OR 27, 1, 269, 280; Gaff, "Here Was Made Out Our Last and Hopeless Stand," 30; Storch and Storch, "Unpublished Gettysburg Reports," 22; Dawes, *Service with the Sixth Wisconsin Volunteers*, 175.

40. OR 27, 1, 280; Storch and Storch, "Unpublished Gettysburg Reports," 22; Gaff, "Here Was Made Out Our Last and Hopeless Stand," 30, 31.

41. Varina D. Brown, *A Colonel at Gettysburg and Spotsylvania* (Columbia, SC, 1931), 212; Dawes, *Service with the Sixth Wisconsin Volunteers*. 176.

42. Dawes, *Service with the Sixth Wisconsin Volunteers*, 178; Venner, *Hoosier's Honor*, 183; Gaff, "Here Was Made Out Our Last and Hopeless Stand," 31; Smith, *History of the Twenty-Fourth Michigan*, 138.

43. Dawes, *Service with the Sixth, Wisconsin Volunteers*, 176–178.

44. OR 27, 1, 280; Curtis, *History of the Twenty-Fourth Michigan*, 165; Smith, *History of the Twenty-Fourth Michigan*, 139; Venner, *Hoosier's Honor*, 184.

45. Smith, *History of the Twenty-Fourth Michigan*,139–143; Dawes, *Service with the Sixth Wisconsin Volunteers*, 79.

46. Dawes, *Service with the Sixth Wisconsin Volunteers*,181.

47. Dawes, *Service with the Sixth Wisconsin Volunteers*,182.

48. Dawes, *Service with the Sixth Wisconsin Volunteers*, 172.

49. Smith, *History of the Twenty-Fourth Michigan*, 144.

50. Curtis, *History of the Twenty-Fourth Michigan*, 168.

51. Busey and Martin, *Regimental Strengths and Losses*, 24, 239.

52. Dyer, *Compendium of the War of the Rebellion*, 284; Tagg, *Generals of Gettysburg*, 18–19.

53. Smith, *The Seventy-Sixth Regiment, New York Volunteers* (New York, 1867), 232–233.

54. J. V. Pierce, "Gettysburg—Last Words as to What Regiment Opened the Battle," *National Tribune*, April 3, 1884; *NYG*, 3, 990, 2, 736; *Pennsylvania at Gettysburg—Ceremonies at the Dedication of Monuments Erected by the Commonwealth of Pennsylvania*, 2 vols. (Harrisburg, PA, 1904), vol. 1, 340. Hereafter cited as *PAG*; William J. Hofmann, *Remarks on the Battle of Gettysburg* (Philadelphia, 1880), 3.

55. *NYG*, 3, 990; *NYG*, 2, 615; Pierce, "Gettysburg."

56. *NYG*, 2, 615; *NYG*, 3, 990–991; Smith, *The Seventy-Sixth Regiment*, 237.

57. *NYG*, 3, 1001, 991; James McLean, *Cutler's Brigade at Gettysburg* (Baltimore, MD, 1994), 62, 64; J. William Hofmann, "Gettysburg Again," *National Tribune*, June 5, 1884.

58. Hofmann, *Remarks on the Battle of Gettysburg*, 4; Samuel P. Bates, *History of Pennsylvania Volunteers*, 10 vols. (Wilmington, NC, 1993), vol. 3, 220; OR 27, 1, 285; B. E. Parkhurst, "At Gettysburg—Heroism of the 147th New York," *National Tribune*, January 1, 1888.

59. Bates, *Pennsylvania Volunteers*, 3, 220; John Kellogg to John Bachelder, November 1, 1866; OR 27, 1, 285; *NYG*, 2, 616; McLean, *Cutler's Brigade*, 70, 72.

60. *NYG*, 2, 616; Busey and Martin, *Regimental Strengths and Losses*, 239.

61. Coey, "Sketches and Echoes—Cutler's Brigade"; *National Tribune*, July 15, 1915; *NYG*, 3, 991–992, 1001; McLean, *Cutler's Brigade*, 79, 81.

62. *NYG*, 3, 991–992, 1001; J. Volnay Pierce to John Bachelder, November 1, 1882, in Bachelder Papers, New Hampshire Historical Society.

63. *NYG*, 3, 992–3, 99–1002, 1005; Coey, "Sketches and Echoes—Cutler's Brigade"; McLean, *Cutler's Brigade*, 90–92, 95, 96; Parkhurst, "At Gettysburg."

64. OR 27, 1, 286, 287.

65. C. V. Tervis, *History of the Fighting Fourteenth* (Brooklyn, 1911), 83; OR 27, 1, 286, 287; McLean, *Cutler's Brigade*, 106–108. The veterans also disagreed on the role the three Federal regiments played in saving the 147th New York. Lieutenant Pierce of the regiment recalled that men on the left side of the line had jumped into the unfinished railroad cut and were trapped, only to be saved by the charge of the 6th Wisconsin (see J. Volnay Pierce to John Bachelder, November 1, 1882). Other veterans, such as Adjutant Lyman, vehemently denied that the regiment needed assistance (see *NYG*, 3, 1004). The difference of opinion probably relates to where the units were at the time of the retreat.

66. McLean, *Cutler's Brigade*, 109, 111.

67. Tervis, *Fighting Fourteenth*, 83–84; Rufus R. Dawes, "Align on the Colors," *Milwaukee Sunday Telegraph*, April 27, 1890; "With Reference to the 95th." According to Dawes's account to John Bachelder (March 18, 1868), the 6th Wisconsin advanced slightly ahead of the New Yorkers.

68. McLean, *Cutler's Brigade*, 128; Smith, *Seventy-Sixth Regiment*, 239; OR 27, 1, 282.

69. OR 27, 1, 282; J. William Hofmann, "56th Pennsylvania Volunteers in the Gettysburg Campaign," *Philadelphia Weekly Times*, January 13, 1886; McLean, *Cutler's Brigade*, 132.

70. OR 27, 1, 282, 286; McLean, *Cutler's Brigade*, 138.

71. Tervis, *History of the Fighting Fourteenth*, 85.

72. *NYG*, 3, 993; Tervis, *History of the Fighting Fourteenth*, 86; Smith, *The Seventy-Sixth Regiment*, 240; OR 27, 1, 287.

73. OR 27, 1, 285; Tervis, *History of the Fighting Fourteenth*, 87; *NYG*, 3, 1002; McLean, *Cutler's Brigade*, 144. The Confederate brigades were Archer's, Davis's, Iverson's, Daniel's, and Scales's.

74. James Hart diary (copy in the Brake Collection, USAMHI); Paul Truitt, "The 7th Indiana Fighters," *National Tribune*, November 11, 1925.

75. Orville Thomson, *Narrative of the Service Of The Seventh Indiana Infantry* (Baltimore, MD, 1993), 162–163; "At Gettysburg. How A Proposed Night Attack by the Enemy was Foiled," *National Tribune*, February 11, 1886.

76. D. J. Dickson, "At Culp's Hill—Gallant Fighting by the First Corps," *National Tribune*, March 15, 1915.

77. Bates, *Pennsylvania Volunteers*, 3, 221; Hofmann, "56th Pennsylvania Volunteers."

78. Tervis, *History of the Fighting Fourteenth*, 138; Edward Fowler to John Bachelder, October 2, 1889, in Bachelder Papers, New Hampshire Historical Society.

79. McLean, *Cutler's Brigade*, 161.

80. OR 27, 1, 867; Tervis, *History of the Fighting Fourteenth*, 138.

81. Tervis, *History of the Fighting Fourteenth*, 138–139; McLean, *Cutler's Brigade*, 162; *NYG*, 3, 1002.

82. Tervis, *History of the Fighting Fourteenth*, 139; OR 27, 1,288; James Hart, diary; *PAG*, 1, 343.

2ND DIVISION—

Brigadier General John C. Robinson

The 2nd Division began its fighting career by being soundly defeated at the battle of Antietam. Its brigades were sent into the fray piecemeal and were defeated that way, with heavy losses. The division had more success at the battle of Fredericksburg, where it, with Meade's 3rd Division, punched a hole in the Confederate line, which was quickly sealed. Brigadier General John C. Robinson took command of the division five days after Christmas in 1863. It was an action that surprised some of the men. Dismissed from West Point for disciplinary reasons, Robinson had enlisted in the army and spent most of his life in it. He won accolades during the Baltimore riots and later, during the Seven Days battles, where he commanded a brigade. Less conspicuous were his actions at Fredericksburg. Gettysburg would be his real first test as division commander, as the division had played only a supporting role at Chancellorsville.[1]

The 2nd Division brought up the rear of the I Corps during the final leg of the march on July 1. General Robinson heard the sounds of battle up ahead when about three miles from Gettysburg, and ordered the pace quickened. Upon arriving on the battlefield, the division was ordered to form the reserve near the seminary buildings. Confederate troops could be seen approaching Oak Hill on the I Corps's right flank, and almost as soon as the weary troops settled down to rest, General Henry Baxter's Brigade was ordered to extend the Union line in that direction while General Gabriel Paul's Brigade remained behind. Before leaving to oversee the actions of Baxter's Brigade, Robinson ordered Paul's men to begin building breastworks.[2]

Soon after Baxter's men reached their assigned position on Oak Ridge, O'Neal's Brigade (Rodes's Division, Second Corps) attacked. The halfhearted assault was repulsed, but seeing additional Confederate troops massing in preparation for an attack, Robinson rushed Paul's Brigade to Baxter's aid. Baxter next repulsed Iverson's Brigade (Rodes's Division), almost annihilating it in the process. The division continued to exchange fire with the enemy, while Rodes regrouped his division. Having expended its ammunition, Baxter's Brigade was ordered to the left (south), and Paul's fresh brigade took its position. Even with these fresh regiments, Robinson's Division was unable to hold its position in the face of determined charges made on two fronts. Prior to this point, the rest of the I Corps and the XI Corps had begun their retreat toward the town of Gettysburg and Cemetery Hill. Orders to withdraw were tardy in arriving, leaving Robinson and his division in desperate straits. Robinson pulled his men back too late, losing almost a thousand of his men to the Confederates.[3]

With half of his division killed, wounded, or captured, Robinson regrouped his men on Cemetery Hill and sent them to support batteries near Ziegler's Grove, close to Emmitsburg Road. The division's right was at the Bryan farm and its left was just beyond the Copse of Trees on Cemetery Ridge. The division remained there until relieved by units of the II Corps on the morning of July 2. It was now pulled back to Cemetery Hill, where it formed on the right of Doubleday's Division. The men remained there until early evening, when they were rushed south to help thwart Longstreet's attack on the Union left flank. The division halted behind the position originally occupied by Humphreys's Division (III Corps), and although the men were shelled during their journey, they did not engage the enemy, as the attacks had been repulsed prior to their arrival.[4]

Marching back to the rear of Cemetery Hill on July 3, the division was told that it would move to the aid of the XII Corps on Culp's Hill if its help was needed. These orders never arrived; instead, the division was ordered back to Ziegler's Grove, where it formed on the right of the II Corps, which was reeling under the attack of the Pickett–Pettigrew–Trimble charge. Again, it arrived too late to participate in the action. The division held this position until July 6, when it was ordered to march toward Emmitsburg.[5]

Robinson's defense of the Union right flank against overwhelming odds was a high point of July 1. Although the division was decimated, and ultimately defeated, it fought tenaciously.

1st Brigade—Brigadier General Gabriel Paul

Units: 16th Maine, 13th Massachusetts, 94th New York, 104th New York, 107th Pennsylvania, 153rd Pennsylvania
Strength: 1537
Losses: 1026 (50-343-633)—67%[6]

The 1st Brigade had the distinction of being the first unit to attack through bloody Miller's cornfield during the battle of Antietam. On the opposite side was a Confederate brigade behind a fence, just waiting. Unsupported, it lost about a third of its men in a matter of minutes. The brigade did not retreat, instead standing its ground and firing round upon round into the enemy, who was only about 250 yards away.[7]

General Brigadier Gabriel Paul commanded the brigade during the Gettysburg campaign. Although he had shuffled between command of several brigades since the previous autumn, he had had no real combat experience. Appointed to command the 1st Brigade on June 17, 1863, Paul was a stranger to his veterans.[8]

The marches during the waning days of June were a nightmare for the brigade, and June 29 was probably the worst. The 16th Maine arrived outside Frederick, Maryland, at 3:00 A.M., and after only a two-hour rest, the exhausted men were again on the march. By 6:00 P.M., the worn-out troops finally came to a halt outside Emmitsburg, Maryland, after a march of twenty-six miles. In all, the troops marched forty miles between 4:00 P.M. on June 28 and 6:00 P.M. the next day.[9]

The local citizens helped ease the fatigue. Private Austin Stearns of the 13th Massachusetts recalled that "the citizens came out to welcome us and added to our comfort by placing barrels of water within easy reach; the young ladies with baskets of goodies . . . with waveing [sic] flags cheering us on." Newspapers were in short supply, so the men got their information from "citizens, by observation, and instinct."[10]

The brigade left Emmitsburg at about 8:00 A.M. on June 30. A short four-mile march brought them into Pennsylvania, where the men were relieved to learn that they could rest for the remainder of the day and night. The brigade resumed its march toward Gettysburg at about 6:00 A.M. on July 1. The pace was, as one soldier put it, "under no pressure of haste." A gentle shower fell shortly after the march began. This pleased the men,

because it "washed the dust from every blade of grass and from the leaves of every tree; the sun shone brightly and the air was fragrant with woodland odors." If only the Rebels were not somewhere up ahead. The troops choked on the thick clouds of dust as the day grew warmer.[11]

The leisurely pace continued, even after the men began hearing irregular gunfire coming from the northwest. They were told that Buford's cavalry division was engaging the Confederate infantry, and that the two other divisions of the I Corps were making their way toward the firing. With each passing mile, the sounds of battle increased in intensity. Soon the men could make out the bark of artillery and the rattle of Springfield rifles. One of General Robinson's staff officers galloped up and ordered the men to "hurry up" and break into a double-quick pace. When the column reached the Codori house, the brigade cut across the fields toward the seminary on the ridge that bore its name. Shortly after leaving the road, the men passed General Reynold's horse being led to the rear, and learned that their beloved corps commander was dead.[12]

Upon reaching the seminary at about 11:00 A.M., General Abner Doubleday ordered the brigade to "throw up some slight entrenchments, to aid me in holding that point in case I should be driven back." Colonel Abner Small of the 16th Maine recalled that these breastworks were built in a semicircular fashion in front of the seminary. Baxter's Brigade had already been ordered north to help fend off the growing number of Confederates assembling on Oak Hill, leaving Paul's Brigade as the I Corps reserve. This status ended at about 1:00 P.M., when General Paul was ordered to move his brigade northward. Colonel T. F. McCoy of the 107th Pennsylvania recalled that the men were ordered to "move promptly by a flank further to the right." The men advanced at the double-quick over the fields and through small stands of timber toward Chambersburg Pike. The 13th Massachusetts was in the lead, followed by the 104th New York. When they crossed into a field through a gap in a fence, they saw their first casualty of the battle—a wounded officer from the 12th Massachusetts of Baxter's Brigade. Some of the men were ordered to load their muskets while crossing the unfinished railroad north of Chambersburg Pike. The brigade halted and formed line of battle. Stearns (13th Massachusetts) could see a long line of troops in the distance, but could not ascertain their identity. As the Confederates approached, "all doubts were soon set at rest, and that long line began to move directly towards us; we could see their colors, and their dirty uniforms." The brigade's skirmishers were soon engaged, and the remainder of the men were ordered to advance toward the woods on Oak Ridge that harbored Baxter's men.[13]

The brigade arrived just as Iverson's Brigade's ill-fated charge was blunted, and some of Paul's units apparently participated in the counterattack. During the confusion, Sergeant Wilmer Whiston of the 13th Massachusetts carried away four Confederate officers' swords, two in each hand. Confederates from other units opened fire on the victorious Federal troops returning to their lines. Colonel Charles Tilden of the 16th Maine, the only mounted officer on the left side of the brigade, fell to the ground when his horse was hit. He was unhurt, and therefore luckier than several, including the regiment's flag bearer, Corporal William Yeaton, who was killed. Captain William Waldron, in trying to steady his men, yelled for them to keep cool and aim low. Standing while they crouched behind the low stone wall facing Forney's field, he took a bullet in his neck. Unwilling to let surgeons look at his

wound, he steadied himself by holding on to a tree with one hand, trying to staunch the flow of blood with the other.[14]

The brigade was split in two when it arrived. The first regiments in the column, the 13th Massachusetts and the 104th New York, marched north to Mummasburg Road and Baxter's right flank. The remaining regiments joined the left of Baxter's main line, facing west. As a result the 2nd Division's two brigades were intermingled. Facing Forney's field to the west, the regiments were arranged, from left to right, as 94th New York–16th Maine–107th Pennsylvania–11th Pennsylvania–97th New York–83rd Pennsylvania–88th Pennsylvania–12th Massachusetts–90th Pennsylvania. To their right, along Mummasburg Road, were the 104th New York and the 13th Massachusetts. The latter regiment moved into position first, followed a few minutes later by the 104th New York. Colonel Gilbert Prey of the latter regiment thought that General Robinson ordered him to form on the 13th Massachusetts's right. Moving his men obliquely, Prey heard Robinson's stentorian voice screaming, "Colonel Prey, _____ _____ you, where are you going? Form on the left." Realizing his error, Prey ordered his men to flank to the left. Not wanting to stop his men, he ordered them to "load at will." As the 13th Massachusetts and the 104th New York approached Mummasburg Road, they were hit by heavy small arms fire from enemy troops behind a stone wall in front of them. Firing rapidly as they advanced, the men drove the enemy from the wall. A number of prisoners were captured during the charge across Mummasburg Road. The men were ordered back to their defensive positions, "before our weakness was shown," according to the 13th Massachusetts's historian. Taking position along the south side of Mummasburg Road, they exchanged small arms fire with the enemy. The men had not seen General Paul until this time. When he rode up behind the 104th New York, he promptly took a bullet to his face that left him permanently blinded. Colonel Prey's horse was also wounded at the time. Robinson, who was still with this vulnerable part of the line, regretted that Prey was on foot, as he wanted all of his regimental commanders mounted. Yet Prey later did not recall seeing any of the others on horseback.[15]

At the opposite end of Robinson's line, the 16th Maine fixed bayonets and charged into the remnants of Iverson's Brigade. Colonel Small wrote that "Color Sergeant Mower was the first to jump the fence, and the regiment followed with a ringing cheer, and in the face of a galling fire, went double-quick, scattering the rebel line, they going pell-mell to the rear in the woods. Our boys would have followed them, but were recalled." The 94th New York also charged the enemy, but was met by the 3rd Alabama (O'Neal's Brigade, Rodes's Division, II Corps) and the 53rd North Carolina (Daniel's Brigade, Rodes's Division, II Corps) and forced to fall back. The 107th Pennsylvania's behavior was apparently not so gallant. Captain Isaac Hall of the 97th New York noted that "as our regiments [Baxter's] came over the wall with the prisoners . . . this regiment [107th Pennsylvania] became unsteady, though, as yet only under fire of a skirmish line, some began to go to the rear, when Colonel Wheelock immediately ordered his regiment [97th New York] to their rear to rally them."[16]

Out of ammunition, most of Baxter's men (with the 97th New York) were withdrawn at this time (about 3:00 P.M.), leaving only Paul's Brigade to stem the growing Confederate horde. After several disastrous piecemeal attacks, General Robert Rodes finally organized a coordinated attack. Ramseur's fresh brigade, along with O'Neal's and the remnants of Iverson's, engaged Paul's Brigade from the west and the north. Robinson realigned the brigade, ordering the 16th Maine to the right, where its left faced Forney's field and its right refused to face Mummasburg Road. The 94th New York, 107th Pennsylvania, and left flank of the 16th Maine faced Forney's field, while the right flank of the 16th Maine, the 104th New York, and the 13th Massachusetts faced north along Mummasburg Road.[17]

After General Paul was wounded, Colonel Samuel Leonard of the 13th Massachusetts took command of the brigade. Leonard was wounded soon after and Colonel Adrian Root of the 94th New York assumed command, but he too was wounded. Colonel Prey of the 104th New York stopped General Robinson as he rode by and asked him who was in command of the brigade. No one seemed to be in command, and the men were becoming demoralized. Robinson replied, "Where is Colonel Root?" Prey responded, "Don't know, not here." Then he asked, "Where is Colonel Leonard?" and was told he was not with his regiment. Finally, Robinson exclaimed, "You are next in rank, take command of the brigade!"[18]

The situation was becoming increasingly desperate. Baxter's and Cutler's Brigades had already withdrawn (although Baxter's was still somewhat to the south). With no artillery support and men falling by the second, it was doubtful that Paul's Brigade could hold on much longer. Over on the right, the Rebels firing from behind a stone wall were taking a deadly toll. Already seven color bearers from the 104th New York had been shot down, and Colonel Prey realized that he was in danger of losing all of his men to this fire. Ordering a charge, Prey was flabbergasted when the men hesitated. Finally, unsheathing his sword, he yelled,

"I'll lead you, boys." The subsequent charge forced the Confederates from behind the wall. Farther to the right, the 13th Massachusetts moved a bit to the left to help repel the pending Confederate attack. When the Confederates attempted to cross the Mummasburg Road, "we let them have it in good shape as they ascended the bank nearest us. They tried to get back to the other side of the road, and we had them at our mercy." A bayonet charge was ordered, and the Bay Staters scooped up almost 140 prisoners in this ill-fated attack. The men were shocked to see a strong Confederate line of battle advancing on their left, which let loose a volley, killing, wounding, and capturing a number of men and forcing the remainder to quickly make their way back to their original position behind Mummasburg Road.[19]

It was about 3:30 P.M., and the Confederates had broken the XI Corps, exposing Paul's right flank. On the left, the remainder of the I Corps was pulling back as well. Realizing that his men were about to be cut off, General Robinson finally ordered Paul's men to retreat. Actually, all left but the 16th Maine. Knowing that he needed a unit to hold back Rodes's Division while the remainder of the brigade made its escape, Robinson rode up to Colonel Tilden and said, "Take that position and hold it as long as there is a single man left." Tilden replied, "All right, General, we'll do the best we can." Tilden gave the command: "About face, fix bayonets, charge."[20]

"We heard distinctly the commands of a rebel officer directing his men to fire; and a volley crashed, and we saw some of our men fall," wrote Small. The Maine men fired a volley in return and saw the Rebel officer and a flag go down. Beyond these Confederate troops, they could see several other lines. Small bitterly wrote after the war that "we were sacrificed to steady the retreat." Almost surrounded, scores of men fell by the minute, and the survivors began falling back. "They came on, firing from behind the wall, from fences, from the road; they forced us, fighting, back along the ridge," wrote Small. The small unit periodically reformed and turned to face the enemy, only to be driven back again. Lieutenant Lewis Bisbee wrote that "every man commenced to look after himself without further orders." Upon reaching the unfinished railroad cut, they could see a sea of Confederates from Daniel's Brigade approaching from their right as well. It looked as though all was lost, so the flag bearers, "by [the] advice and consent of the colonel and other officers," ripped their beloved flag into pieces and distributed them to the men. The staff was broken as well. When ordered to surrender by Daniel's men, Colonel Tilden thrust his sword into the ground and broke it. All but four officers and thirty-eight men were killed, wounded, or captured. By 4:00 P.M., there were no more defenders—all were lying on the field, being hustled to the Confederate rear as prisoners, or fleeing toward Gettysburg. The regiment lost almost 80% of its men, including 164 wounded.[21]

While the 16th Maine was being sacrificed on Oak Ridge, the remainder of Paul's Brigade was seeking safety. Pender's Division approached from the southwest, and Rodes's troops from the west and north. Even Doles's Brigade, north of the town, changed direction, hoping to cut off Paul's men. Hundreds were captured. Private Charles Davis of the 13th Massachusetts recalled that it was "each man for himself, it being impracticable to do otherwise without losing still more men." Private George Jepson of the same regiment agreed. "It was not as an army corps, nor as brigades, hardly even as regiments, that they got there [Cemetery Hill], but for the most part singly or in twos and threes."

Some men moved along the railroad cut, while others headed directly for the town. Those who chose the latter route found a maze of streets and alleys choked with Union troops, and all too often, Confederates only too willing to relieve them of their firearms and send them to the rear. "The great trouble was to know where to run, for every street seemed to be occupied by the 'rebs,' and we were in imminent danger of running into their arms before we knew it," wrote Davis.[22]

The fortunate men began reaching Cemetery Hill at about 5:00 P.M. While resting there, the men learned that they had a new commander, Colonel Richard Coulter of Baxter's Brigade, accompanied by his 11th Pennsylvania. The brigade was sent to Cemetery Ridge, where it threw up breastworks near the Copse of Trees. Food was scarce, and the little hardtack available was quickly eaten. As night fell, the men remained under arms, expecting a renewal of the attacks at any time. Sleep came easily. It was such a hard sleep that most did not hear the "tramp and clatter of an approaching army." Help was arriving.[23]

The landscape was transformed when the men arose on July 2. "Thousands of troops had gathered during the night, presenting a formidable appearance in the gray morning light," wrote Davis (13th Massachusetts). Wanting to gain a better view, some of the men climbed atop their breastworks, but were quickly shooed down by General Hancock, who told them that they had, "too much d__d curiosity."[24]

Hays's Division (II Corps) arrived before noon, so the brigade was marched back toward Cemetery Hill, where it supported some of the batteries. The men of the XI Corps were busily preparing their defenses all around them. It was quiet, and many spent the time resting and talking with their comrades. All this changed in the afternoon when the Confederate artillery

opened fire, signaling a renewal of hostilities. Orders arrived at around 6:30 P.M. to move south to support Sickles's men. As the small column dashed past Meade's headquarters on Taneytown Road, it came under Confederate artillery fire. Ill-fate again hit the 16th Maine. According to Sergeant William Warner of the 13th Massachusetts, "marching brigade front, a shell struck in line of adjoining Regt [16th Maine] where the men has swayed closely together. Knocking over I should think nearly a dozen men." Eight men of the approximately thirty survivors of the regiment were killed or wounded.[25]

The march south continued. "Before we had reached there it had grown so dark that the smoke & flame of the rebel artillery lighted up like sheets of flame," recorded Warner in his diary. Arriving at their designated position, the men received orders to "By the right flank—march!" This brought the brigade into line of battle just north of the George Weikert farm, on the left of Baxter's Brigade. In the growing darkness, the men did not encounter any Confederate infantry, who had begun their withdrawal before reinforcements had arrived. As Warner put it, "the tide had turned and the Rebel Infantry had gone back."[26]

Later that evening, the men were reformed and moved back toward Cemetery Hill, which was under attack by Early's Division (II Corps). The brigade arrived after the attack was repulsed, and at about 9:00 P.M., were moved toward the north end of the hill, facing the town. They took refuge behind a stone wall while supporting the batteries. The men were ordered to fall in again at sunrise, and marched back to Ziegler's Grove on Cemetery Ridge. Colonel Coulter established his headquarters on the edge of the grove, making sure that the enemy had a clear view of the brigade's flag.[27]

The peace was broken with the Confederate artillery barrage preceding the Pickett–Pettigrew–Trimble charge. Small (16th Maine) recalled,

The earth groaned and trembled. The air, thick with smoke and sulphurous vapor, almost suffocated the troops in support of the batteries. Through the murk we heard hoarse commands, the bursting of shells, cries of agony. We saw caissons hit and blown up, splinters flying, men flung to the ground, horses torn and shrieking . . . solid shot . . . plunging into the ranks, crushing flesh and bone.[28]

The brigade moved back to Cemetery Hill at about 2:00 P.M., where it supported the artillery. "How that short march was made, I don't know," recalled Small. "The air was all murderous iron; it seemed as if there couldn't be room for any soldier upright in motion." The historian of the 13th Massachusetts agreed. "It seemed like jumping out of the frying pan into the fire, so far as danger was concerned." Here they faced both Confederate artillery fire and snipers. After arriving, the men could see a distressed Colonel Coulter tearing up and down the line. "Where in hell is my flag?" he yelled. "Where do you suppose that cowardly son of a bitch has skedaddled to?" Coulter immediately began hunting for the aide charged with holding the flag, and found him and the flag hiding flat behind a stone wall. Grabbing the soldier with one hand and the flag with the other, Coulter carefully shook out the folds in the flag, thrust the staff into the hands of the panic-stricken aide, and double-quicked him toward the front of the brigade. Finally, Coulter stopped and yelled, "There, Orderly; hold it! If I can't get you killed in ten minutes by God, I'll post you right up among the batteries!"[29]

His fighting blood up, Coulter dashed down his line, only to catch a shell fragment in his arm, forcing him temporarily to relinquish command of the brigade to Colonel Peter Lyle of the 90th Pennsylvania. Lyle became the sixth officer to command the brigade during the battle. Coulter returned soon after and resumed command.[30]

As the charge approached Cemetery Ridge, Coulter received orders to rush his brigade back toward Ziegler's Grove again to support Hays's Division. The brigade arrived just in time to see the last of Pettigrew's and Trimble's men turning back or being captured. The brigade was ordered to throw up breastworks, and skirmished with the enemy for the remainder of the day. The skirmishing continued throughout July 4. When the sun rose on July 5, the men were relieved to learn that the enemy had abandoned its positions and was in full retreat. At noon the brigade was moved about a mile south, and at 7:00 A.M. on July 6, it began the movement in pursuit of Lee.[31]

The battle was over for Paul's Brigade, but the sadness would last much longer. The brigade had lost 67% of its men. No other brigade in the army sustained losses of this magnitude. Virtually all of the losses occurred on July 1, when the brigade was probably retained in position longer than necessary. By the time it received orders to retire, Confederate troops were all around them, causing 62% of the brigade's losses to result from its men being captured. While the brigade was not actually engaged during the two remaining days of the battle, it was still a difficult period for the troops. The 13th Massachusetts's historian wrote that "it often happens that this kind of duty turns out to be much more arduous than being stationed in line of battle, inasmuch as you may be called upon to march to any point that needs strengthening."[32]

✂

2nd Brigade—Brigadier General Henry Baxter

Units: 12th Massachusetts, 83rd New York, 97th New York, 11th Pennsylvania, 88th Pennsylvania, 90th Pennsylvania
Strength: 1585
Losses: 649 (41-258-350)—45%[33]

Riding at the head of the 2nd Brigade was hard-luck Henry Baxter, who had been wounded in every engagement he had fought in. The string of injuries began with the Seven Days battles, when he received a severe abdominal wound while leading a company of the 7th Michigan. He returned in time to be wounded again at the battle of Fredericksburg, but not before having the distinction of rowing across the Rappahannock with his men to establish the beachhead on the opposite side of the river. When he returned to the army a third time on February 2, 1863, he was given command of the 2nd Brigade and promoted to brigadier general. He was therefore untested in battle as a brigade commander, but his prior exploits were well known by his new command. The 2nd Brigade had chased Stonewall Jackson around the Shenandoah Valley in the spring of 1862, then fought at Second Bull Run.[34]

The march northward through the rain and mud was exceedingly tiring. Stories of marauding Rebels helped to relieve some of the suffering, as the men became even more anxious to meet the enemy. Private William Clare of the 83rd New York wrote home that "the enemy have passed through all this section of the country plundering as they went along." June 29 was especially hard on the men. Private Robert Coburn of the 83rd New York complained in his diary that the officers had "marched us too fast, men played

out . . . half dead. Heaviest march yet, made 26 miles." The column finally halted at Emmitsburg for the night. Coburn called it a "fine town and bully people." The next day the column crossed the state line into Pennsylvania, which especially moved the men from the Keystone State. Lieutenant Samuel Boone of the 88th Pennsylvania recalled the moment. "Amidst the wildest demonstration of joy, all singing 'home again,' 'home sweet home,' and other appropriate songs."[35]

Although the troops were up before daylight, the column did not move out until sometime between 8:00 and 9:00 A.M. Private John Vautier of the 88th Pennsylvania recalled that "some delay occurred before the division was assembled and ready to march." The day promised to be another hot one. Vautier remembered that the "morning was blistering hot, and the stifling clouds of yellow dust, settling on the ranks like a blanket, filled the eyes, mouth, nostrils, and entire person of the soldier with an impalpable powder, while perspiration, running down the skin, ploughed furrows through the dirt." The brigade marched behind Paul's Brigade, and was therefore the last I Corps unit to reach the battlefield. As the men approached Gettysburg, they could see and hear a battle raging. Lieutenant Boone of the 88th Pennsylvania "heard the distant booming of canon [sic] and a little later the rattle of small arms and could see the little puffs of white smoke from exploding shells from Rebel guns over the tree-tops in the neighborhood of the Seminary." Major Benjamin Look of the 12th Massachusetts recalled that he began hearing the sounds of battle at

10:00 A.M. A wave of excitement passed through the column. The officers constantly shouted, "Close up men, close up." Perhaps to relieve the tension, the 88th Pennsylvania broke out in "Glory Hallelujah," "keeping time with their feet to the words and notes of that inspiring song." The men turned somber when they heard their officers saying, "Step out lively . . . General Reynolds has been wounded, and every man is needed at the front."[36]

Captain George Hussey of the 83rd New York recalled that the column was moving forward "without special orders" until it reached the Codori house on Emmitsburg Road. The column left the road there and crossed the fields on their left. As the men double-quicked toward Seminary Ridge, they tried to reassure each other. "Boys, do your duty today for the old Keystone"; "Home and fireside now"; "The man who runs should be shot in his tracks" were among some of the comments the men could hear as they hurried along.[37]

Baxter's Brigade reached the seminary sometime between 11:30 and noon, where the men were permitted to rest and load their guns. Major Look (12th Massachusetts) recalled hearing that "the whole rebel army was advancing." The 88th Pennsylvania made good use of the reprieve by making coffee, while the 83rd New York constructed a barricade of fence rails. The hiatus did not last long, for masses of Confederates could be seen on Oak Hill, threatening the I Corps's right flank. Baxter was ordered to send two of his regiments, the 11th Pennsylvania and 97th New York, across Chambersburg Pike toward the threatened area. Deploying a skirmish line of two companies from the 97th New York, Colonel Richard Coulter of the 11th Pennsylvania directed both regiments northward. As the skirmishers took position, a cavalryman passed them,

shouting, "There are not troops behind you! You stand alone between the Rebel army and your homes. Fight like hell!" The skirmishers clashed with their Confederate counterparts, who were aligned behind a stone wall on the opposite side of Mummasburg Road. Surveying the terrain, Coulter took position on Cutler's Brigade's right flank.[38]

Concerned about the safety of Coulter's two regiments, Baxter ordered the rest of his brigade northward. The 12th Massachusetts was the first regiment to move off Seminary Ridge, and when it reached Coulter's men, it marched beyond them to take position farther north, along Mummasburg Road. Seeing this movement and the resulting gap, the 97th New York, and presumably the 11th Pennsylvania, were ordered to "flank to the right" and connect with the left flank of the 12th Massachusetts. As the three other regiments arrived, they were placed on the 12th Massachusetts's right flank, facing northeast along Mummasburg Pike. Baxter's line now resembled an arrow, with the 11th Pennsylvania and 97th New York facing northwest toward Forney's field, and, positioned along Mummasburg Road facing northeast from left to right, 90th Pennsylvania–83rd New York–88th Pennsylvania. The 12th Massachusetts formed the tip of the arrow, with its left flank connecting with the 97th New York, and its right, refused to form a right angle, connecting with the 90th Pennsylvania, facing north. These dispositions were completed at about 1:00 P.M.[39]

Confederate General Robert Rodes planned to send three brigades down from Oak Hill to crush the I Corps's right flank. The plan unraveled from the start, when O'Neal's Brigade attacked prematurely with only three of its five regiments. Few of Baxter's men commented on O'Neal's attack on the brigade's right flank. One exception was Vautier (88th Pennsylvania): "Baxter quickly dressed his line and received the Confederate fire as their line of battle, covered by a cloud of busy skirmishers, came driving through the woods from the right of the Mummasburg Road. Waiting until they were in easy range, the order was given, 'Commence firing.' With the sharp crack of the muskets a fleecy cloud of smoke rolled down the front of the brigade and the Minie balls zipped and buzzed with a happy chorus toward the Southern line, which halted, and after a brief contest, retired to the shelter of the woods." O'Neal's men did not get within two hundred yards of the Federal position before falling back.[40]

Baxter's men did not have time to savor this victory, for yells from their comrades on the left flank told them that another force was advancing from the northwest. When General Robinson rode up to survey Baxter's line, he was concerned about the gap between Baxter's and Cutler's Brigades, and ordered the brigade to "change front forward on his left battalion," to close it. The 11th Pennsylvania and 97th New York filed southward. This created a gap between the 97th New York and the 12th Massachusetts. The 83rd New York and the 88th Pennsylvania on the right of the line received orders to "About face, right half wheel, halt; right dress; front," which brought them into position to seal the gap. The 12th Massachusetts and 90th Pennsylvania also filed to the left at this time. The latter regiment extended beyond Mummasburg Road, then was refused to face north to watch for any renewed threat from that sector. Its flag was located in the angle between the two wings of the regiment. The brigade was now deployed, from left to right, as 11th Pennsylvania–97th New York–83rd New York–88th Pennsylvania–12th Massachusetts–90th Pennsylva-

nia. Concerned about Baxter's growing vulnerability, Robinson ordered Paul's Brigade off its reserve perch on Seminary Ridge.[41]

Within moments of completing these complex movements, Iverson's Brigade entered Forney's field in front of the brigade. Baxter's men were amazed by the spectacle before them. Vautier noted that "the field in our front was swarming with Confederates who come sweeping on in magnificent order with perfect alignment, guns at right shoulder and colors to the front." They were most surprised by the absence of skirmishers preceding Iverson's line of battle. Closer and closer the North Carolinians came, seemingly oblivious to the deadly threat directly in front of them and on their left flank. Baxter's men took advantage of a low stone wall, by crouching behind it and taking careful aim against the advancing Confederates. Baxter's men, "with rifles cocked and fingers on the triggers, waited and bided their time." The men were told to "await command and aim low." The wait seemed endless.[42]

When Iverson's men were about fifty yards from Baxter's line, the officers screamed, "Open fire!" Vautier recalled that "Baxter's men arose and poured a withering fire into their faces with terrible effect. Hundreds of the Confederates fell at the first volley, plainly marking their line with a ghastly row of dead and wounded men, whose blood trailed the course of their line with a crimson stain clearly discernible for several days after the battle." Private George Hussey of the 83rd New York added, "rarely has such a destructive volley been fired on any field of battle." Iverson's line halted and attempted to return the fire, but it was a mismatch between troops in a good defensive position and an exposed line of troops. Iverson's men were now falling "like leaves in a storm." The survivors found refuge in a small gully about 150 yards from Baxter's position. Many returned the fire, and several of Baxter's men fell.[43]

Iverson's men were in a desperate situation. No support was in sight, and going forward or retreating across the open fields meant certain death and injury. Lieutenant George Grant of the 88th Pennsylvania recalled that "a steady death-dealing fire was kept up, our men loading in comparative safety, and then resting rifle on boulders before them, would fire coolly with unerring aim." Baxter's men could now see hats and handkerchiefs being waved in a token of surrender. At first, the officers thought it might be a ploy, but Baxter, riding behind the 88th Pennsylvania, yelled, "Up boys, and give them steel." There was considerable confusion in the Union ranks at the time. Adjutant Charles Wehrum of the 12th Massachusetts recalled that "there was a great deal of hollering, some to cease firing, others to charge bayonets no doubt . . . I asked someone . . . 'what is the order?' The answer returned was 'forward,' then I cried, 'forward boys.'" Wehrum believed that "our advance was brought about by the action of the enemy, and not by any general order, and no special credit is due anyone in particular. It was a spontaneous movement which every one that did advance thought was proper." Given the confusion, Wehrum is probably correct. Baxter never claimed credit for ordering the attack. Captain Edmund Patterson of the 88th Pennsylvania claimed that the men attacked because they were all but out of ammunition. Corporal George Kimball of the 12th Massachusetts denied that it was ever a "charge" as much as "only a run forward to drive in Iverson's men, who were willing enough to surrender."[44]

It appears that most of Baxter's regiments took part in this countercharge against Iverson's prone men. The 88th Pennsylvania captured most of the 23rd North Carolina, including its battle flag. The 97th New York did the same to the 20th North Carolina. This was a new experience for Baxter's men. Private George Cramer of the 11th Pennsylvania wrote home that "we fixed Bayonets and made a charge, at which time a whole Regiment of Rebels surrendered. This scene rather affected me when I seen them using white Henkerchif [sic] & Towels for Flags on theyre [sic] Guns for the Signal of surrender." Some of the men were surprised that Iverson's troops had surrendered. Adjutant Wehrum wrote that "it was a surprising spectacle for me for I could easily see they were much stronger in force than we were." So stunned were the North Carolinians that they were "simply ordered to the rear, and I can tell you they needed no second order, but got up and got," claimed Corporal William Miller of the 83rd New York.[45]

While wildly successful, this countercharge led to additional casualties, as Ramseur's and O'Neal's Brigades opened fire on the exposed troops, hitting not only the Union soldiers but Iverson's as well. Colonel Charles James Bates of the 12th Massachusetts was wounded in the neck. Lieutenant Boone recalled that the "course of the bullets could be seen cutting the high grass as if dine [sic] by electricity."[46]

The men now hurried back to their original positions behind the stone wall, and were overjoyed to see that Paul's Brigade had arrived. While some of Paul's regiments moved to Mummasburg Road, the 94th New York and 107th Pennsylvania took position behind the stone wall in what had been the 88th Pennsylvania and 97th New York's position. The returning men of the latter regiment could see that the 107th Pennsylvania was unsteady and some of its men had already broken for the rear. Colonel Charles Wheelock (97th New York) ordered his men to pursue and ultimately rally them. Both brigades now settled down and awaited another attack. Ammunition was dangerously low, so the men scavenged the dead and wounded's cartridge boxes. Wheelock grabbed the captured flag of the 20th North Carolina and waved it defiantly at the Rebels. Seeing this, General Baxter rode over and ordered the flag to the rear for safe keeping. Wheelock was not to be denied. "My regiment captured these colors and will keep them," he yelled in defiance. Outraged, Baxter ordered his subordinate under arrest, but before these orders could be carried out, Wheelock called one of his captains to his side. Placing the flagstaff in the captain's hands, Wheelock ran his saber through the flag, tearing it from the staff. Wheelock twirled the flag around his sword, while the captain waved the staff. A shot rang out, and the captain fell dead with a bullet in his forehead—killed by an infuriated Confederate sniper. The flag was later recaptured by the Confederates. The brigade captured a total of four flags that afternoon.[47]

About 3:00 P.M., Rodes finally attacked the Union right in a coordinated fashion, using Ramseur's fresh brigade, O'Neal's, and the remnants of Iverson's. Baxter ordered Colonel Alfred Sellers of the 90th Pennsylvania to shift its front to the right to meet this new threat. Although not engaged, the men could hear the increasing intensity of gunfire emanating from their right. The two Union brigades initially repulsed these charges. However, there were just too many enemy soldiers moving against Robinson's men. It was disconcerting for the men of the 88th Pennsylvania to hear the sounds of battle gradually getting closer and louder, sug-

gesting the Confederates were having success against Paul's north-facing brigade. Almost out of ammunition, the brigade was finally ordered to pull back. Lieutenant George Grant of the 88th Pennsylvania recalled that the orders were not hastily obeyed. "We halted, fired, and checked the enemy, again and again, loading while retreating to make a stand and deliver another volley." General Robinson halted the brigade near Stewart's battery, which was deployed along Chambersburg Pike. The men were ordered to fix bayonets, as their ammunition was depleted. The troops remained long enough for the gunners to limber up their pieces and gallop to safety. 48

The brigade left two "unmustered" members behind when it retreated. One was Sallie, the 11th Pennsylvania's canine mascot, who remained behind to "guard" the dead and wounded. A second was a fifteen-year-old boy named J. W. Wheatley, who begged Colonel James Bates of the 12th Massachusetts for an opportunity to fight the invaders. He was wounded during the long afternoon fight.[49]

A glance to the west revealed that Pender's Division had broken through the remainder of the I Corps, threatening to get in the brigade's rear and cut off its retreat. Behind them, the men could see Paul's men approaching, and it was just a matter of time before they expected to see the enemy approaching from that direction as well. The situation was so desperate that there was no time to form into any semblance of order—it was every man for himself. Those who ran toward the seminary were gobbled up by Pender's men. Most used the unfinished railroad cut as their route to safety. Confederate troops closely following the brigade poured volleys into the retreating men. Many men avoided being struck by cannon fire by "hitting the ground and then jumping up and running immediately after the Rebel artillery pieces discharged," noted a survivor of the 97th New York. The men who bypassed the town by cutting across fields to make their way to Cemetery Hill generally arrived safely. Most who took the direct route through the town were scooped up by the enemy. The town was a wild melee of activity. Ambulances and wagons blocked many roads, and the complex alley system led many into the arms of Confederate soldiers. Among the prisoners was Colonel Wheelock of the 97th New York, who subsequently escaped and returned to his regiment.[50]

The weary survivors made their way up Cemetery Hill, where they were resupplied with ammunition and finally permitted to rest. The men could now see the extent of the decimation. The 97th New York could muster but seventy-five men at this time; the 83rd New York, only eighty-two; and the 88th Pennsylvania, a hundred. The size of the brigade shrank farther when the 11th Pennsylvania was transferred to Paul's Brigade.[51]

After the short reprieve, the men were marched south to Ziegler's Grove, where they formed a line parallel to Emmitsburg Pike, with their right flank near the Bryan house and the left extending toward the Copse of Trees. Understanding the important role the stone wall had played when they defeated Iverson's Brigade, the men threw up breastworks almost immediately. Few slept that night. Although they were exhausted, "sleep tho [sic] precious, was not permitted lest the enemy should come upon us unawares, which frequent interviews between the pickets seemed to indicate," wrote Clare (83rd New York) to his brother. The brigade remained there until about 10:00 A.M. on July 2, when it was relieved by units of Hays's Division (II

Corps). None of the men were saddened to relinquish the front line. Their new position, a "short distance in the rear," was just fine. The men remained there until 4:00 P.M., when they were ordered to the right to support a XI Corps battery on Cemetery Hill. After two hours, they received orders to collect their muskets and fall into line. This time they moved south to support the Union left flank, which was under attack. The brigade came under artillery fire during this march, losing several men.[52]

Upon arriving at their assigned positions, about two thousand feet east of the Rogers house. Baxter was ordered to throw out a line of skirmishers. He did so, but they encountered no enemy soldiers during their slow forward movement. It was now dark and the battle on the Union left had ended. However, the attack on the Union right was just getting under way. Baxter received orders to rush his brigade to the aid of the XI Corps on Cemetery Hill before his men became acclimated to their new position. Arriving near the area they had occupied late that afternoon, the men waited for the orders to advance and engage the two brigades of Early's Division that had briefly captured the hill. The orders never arrived, and the men rested on their arms all night. Coburn (83rd New York) perfectly captured the brigade's activities that day in his diary: "Hard work. Laying not 5 minutes in one place. On reserve. Drawn up on the left and then double quick to center." That night, the men were not permitted to make fires and, according to Clare (83rd New York), "constant alarms caused us to be watchful."[53]

The morning of July 3 found Baxter's men supporting Osborn's Artillery battalion (XI Corps) on Cemetery Hill. Still another movement was ordered at 9:00

2ND DIVISION �֍ 75

A.M., when Baxter's men were sent toward Culp's Hill to provide support, should the XII Corps need it. The brigade again changed its position at 1:00 P.M., returning to Cemetery Hill, where it again supported the XI Corps's batteries, which were now under a heavy artillery barrage that preceded the Pickett–Pettigrew–Trimble charge. Vautier (88th Pennsylvania) would never forget this period of the battle. "The concussion of the cannon shook the ground, while the air was cut by every form of missile, whistling, hissing and screaming in their terrible course, striking the earth and sending up immense clouds of dust, smashing the rocks into splinters, ripping through the trees, demolishing the tombstones, bounding and ricocheting among the men . . . carrying terror and death in every nook and corner of the ground in range." Coburn (83rd New York) was more succinct, writing in his diary, "horses, men, knocked in every shape." The brigade changed its position at least once as a result of this heavy cannon fire. As the Pickett–Pettigrew–Trimble charge reached its climax, Baxter's men were rushed back toward Ziegler's Woods to help support Hays's Division. The men were ordered to build breastworks while in line of battle.[54]

After the attack was repulsed, the Union line was annoyed by sniper fire, and General Robinson ordered Baxter to send out a strong skirmish line to drive them away. The 12th Massachusetts and a detachment from the 90th Pennsylvania rushed forward with a shout, and successfully drove back the Confederate skirmish line. The detachment remained between Cemetery Ridge and Seminary Ridge to prevent the enemy's return and was relieved by the 97th New York at 1:00 A.M. on July 4. The unit's commander, Major Charles Northrup, was censored in Baxter's report for pulling his line back almost a hundred yards without permission. The remainder of the brigade spent the day lying behind its breastworks. Coburn (83rd New York) recorded in his diary, "expected to be attacked this morning. Have a bully position, think we can hold it." Coburn also called the groans of the wounded on the field "horrid." He explained that no one could help these men because "they are betwixt the pickets." Some of the men did, however, venture out to provide water. After the Confederates had left the battlefield, the men were ordered out to begin burying the dead. Clare (83rd New York) wrote home that the "stench was beyond description, and yet we had to endure it for 24 hours." The brigade occupied the same position through July 6, when it moved about half a mile to the left. It left the field later that day, bound for Emmitsburg.[55]

The actions of Baxter's Brigade on July 1 will always be remembered. During three fateful hours on the battlefield, the unit repulsed two separate Confederate charges and captured over three hundred men from Iverson's Brigade. The latter figure is contested, however. General Robinson and his men believed the figure to be about a thousand men. However, if that were the case, Iverson's Brigade would have had to have been double its actual size. During the two remaining days of the battle, the brigade's actions were minor, as it was moved from place to place "where its services were supposed to be most needed," and thus became a spectator to some of the grand moments in the battle. For example, Major Look of the 12th Massachusetts reported that the brigade reached Ziegler's Woods "just in time to witness the repulse of the enemy." His regiment lost 111 on July 1, but only three the two following days.[56]

NOTES

1. Stephen W. Sears, *Landscape Turned Red* (New York, 1983), 187; Edward J. Stackpole, *Drama on the Rappahannock* (Mechanicsville, PA, 1967), 190; Tagg, *Generals of Gettysburg*, 20–21.

2. OR 27, 1, 289.

3. OR 27, 1, 289; Busey and Martin, *Regimental Strengths and Losses*, 240.

4. OR 27, 1, 290.

5. OR 27, 1, 290.

6. Busey and Martin, *Regimental Strengths and Losses*, 25, 240.

7. Sears, *Landscape Turned Red*, 186–187.

8. Tagg, *Generals of Gettysburg*, 22–23; Dyer, *Compendium*, 285.

9. OR 27, 1, 295; A. R. Small, *The Sixteenth Maine in the War of the Rebellion* (Portland, ME, 1886), 114.

10. Austin Stearns, *Three Years with Company K* (Cranbury, NJ, 1976), 178.

11. OR 27, 1, 295, 297; Charles E. Davis, *Three Years in the Army: The Story of the Thirteenth Massachusetts Volunteers* (Boston, 1864), 225; Harold Small, *The Road to Richmond—The Civil War Memoirs of Major Abner R. Small of the 16th Maine* (Berkley, CA, 1959), 98.

12. Cyndi Dalton, *Sixteenth Maine Regiment: The Blanket Brigade* (Union, ME, 1995), 129; Small, *The Sixteenth Maine in the War of the Rebellion*, 116; Small, *The Road to Richmond—The Civil War Memoirs of Major Abner R. Small of the 16th Maine*, 98; NYG, 2, 752; George Jepson, "Memoirs," in Brake Collection, USAMHI, 17.

13. Davis, *Three Years in the Army: The Story of the Thirteenth Massachusetts*, 226; Small, *The Sixteenth Maine in the War of the Rebellion*, 116; OR 27, 1, 247, 295; Sauers, "The Sixteenth Maine Volunteer Infantry at Gettysburg," *Gettysburg Magazine* (July 1995), issue 13, 36; PAG, 1, 560; NYG, 2, 756; Stearns, *Three Years with Company K*, 179.

14. George Jepson, "Memoirs," 17; Small, *The Sixteenth Maine in the War of the Rebellion*, 117; Small, *The Road to Richmond—The Civil War Memoirs of Major Abner R. Small of the 16th Maine*, 99.

15. Sauers, "The 16th Maine Volunteer Infantry at Gettysburg," 35; Davis, *Three Years in the Army: The Story of the Thirteenth Massachusetts*, 227; NYG, 2, 753, 756.

16. Small, *The Sixteenth Maine in the War of the Rebellion*, 117–118; Dalton, *Sixteenth Maine Regiment: The Blanket Brigade*, 132; OR 27, 1, 290, 299; Isaac Hall, *History of the Ninety-Seventh New York* Volunteers (Utica, NY, 1890), 138–139.

17. Sauers, "The Sixteenth Maine Volunteer Infantry at Gettysburg," 38.

18. NYG, 2, 756.

In his report of the battle (OR 27, 1, 298), Colonel N. Walter Batchelder of the 13th Massachusetts claimed to have commanded the brigade after Colonel Leonard was wounded. This is difficult to believe, given the statements of many of the men and the fact that Colonel Coulter of a different brigade was later placed in command.

19. NYG, 2, 757; OR 27, 1, 298; W. S. Kimball, "The 13th Massachusetts at Gettysburg"; *National Tribune*, May 14, 1885; Davis, *Three Years in the Army: The Story of the Thirteenth Massachusetts*, 227; Stearns, *Three Years in Company K*, 179–180.

Colonel Prey was chagrined when Colonel Batchelder of the 13th Massachusetts relieved these prisoners from the detail of the 104th New York, and claimed them as being captured by his regiment.

20. Octavus H. Tubbs, letter, 16th Maine folder, GNMP; Dalton, *Sixteenth Maine Regiment: The Blanket Brigade*, 134; Small, *The Road to Richmond—The Civil War Memoirs of Major Abner R. Small of the 16th Maine*, 101; OR 27, 1, 295.

21. Small, *The Road to Richmond—The Civil War Memoirs of Major Abner R. Small of the 16th Maine*, 102; Small, *The Sixteenth Maine in the War of the Rebellion*, 118; Lewis C. Bisbee, "War Reminiscences," 9, 16th Maine Folder, GNMP; *Maine at Gettysburg*, 43–44, 47, 51; Busey and Martin, *Regimental Strengths and Losses*, 240.

The 104th New York also destroyed its flag to prevent it from falling into the hands of the enemy (NYG, 2, 751).

22. Martin, *Gettysburg—July 1*, 390–391; Davis, *Three Years in the Army: The Story of the*

Thirteenth Massachusetts, 228; Jepson, "Memoirs," 17–18.

23. *NYG,* 2, 754; Bates, *Pennsylvania Volunteers,* VI, 861; OR 27, 1, 293–294; Davis, *Three Years in the Army: The Story of the Thirteenth Massachusetts,* 229.

24. Davis, *Three Years in the Army: The Story of the Thirteenth Massachusetts,* 233.

25. OR 27, 1, 305; Small, *The Road to Richmond—The Civil War Memoirs of Major Abner R. Small of the 16th Maine,* 103–104; Bates, *Pennsylvania Volunteers,* VI, 861; William Warner, diary, 13th Massachusetts folder, GNMP.

26. Small, *The Road to Richmond—The Civil War Memoirs of Major Abner R. Small of the 16th Maine,* 104; Warner, diary.

27. Davis, *Three Years in the Army: The Story of the Thirteenth Massachusetts,* 233; OR, 27, 1, 296; Small, *The Sixteenth Maine in the War of the Rebellion,* 121; Small, *The Road to Richmond—The Civil War Memoirs of Major Abner R. Small of the 16th Maine,* 104.

Small gives conflicting information in his two books as to when Coulter posted his tent in full view of the Confederates. It was most likely on July 3, not July 2.

28. Small, *The Road to Richmond—The Civil War Memoirs of Major Abner R. Small of the 16th Maine,* 105.

29. Small, *The Road to Richmond—The Civil War Memoirs of Major Abner R. Small of the 16th Maine,* 105–106; Davis, *Three Years in the Army: The Story of the Thirteenth Massachusetts,* 236; Small, *The Sixteenth Maine in the War of the Rebellion,*123–124.

30. Small, *The Road to Richmond—The Civil War Memoirs of Major Abner R. Small of the 16th Maine,* 106; Martin, *Gettysburg—July 1,*

31. Small, *The Road to Richmond—The Civil War Memoirs of Major Abner R. Small of the 16th Maine,* 107–109; OR 27, 1, 294.

32. Small, *The Sixteenth Maine in the War of the Rebellion,* 127; Busey and Martin, *Regimental Strengths and Losses,* 240; Davis, *Three Years in the Army: The Story of the Thirteenth Massachusetts,* 233.

33. Busey and Martin, *Regimental Strengths and Losses,* 26, 240.

34. Warner, *Generals in Blue,* 25; Dyer, *Compendium,* 285; Gary G. Lash, "Brig. Gen.

Henry Baxter's Brigade at Gettysburg, July 1," *Gettysburg Magazine* (January 1994), issue 10, 7–9.

35. Lash, "Brig. Gen. Henry Baxter's Brigade at Gettysburg," 9; William Clare, letter, Duke University; Robert Coburn, diary, CWTI Collection, USAMHI; *PAG,* 1, 486; Samuel Boone, "Memoirs," Michael Winey Collection, USAMHI.

36. Cook, *History of the Twelfth Massachusetts Volunteers (Webster's Regiment),* 100; Bates, *Pennsylvania Volunteers,* V, 154; *NYG,* 2, 677; John D. Vautier, "At Gettysburg," *Philadelphia Weekly Press,* November 10, 1886; Vautier, *History of the Eighty-Eighth Pennsylvania for the War for the Union* (Philadelphia, 1894), 105; OR 27, 1, 311; Samuel Boone, "Memoirs"; Benjamin Look to John Bachelder, February 17, 1884, in Bachelder Papers, New Hampshire Historical Society; William H. Locke, *Story of the Regiment* (New York, 1872), 228.

37. *NYG,* 2, 677; George W. Grant, "The First Army Corps on the First Day at Gettysburg," in *Minnesota MOLLUS,* vol. 5, 48.

38. Bates, *Pennsylvania Volunteers,* I, 257; George A. Hussey, *History of the Ninth Regiment N.Y.S.M.* (New York, 1889), 267; Henry Clare, letter, 83rd New York folder, GNMP Library; Hall, *History of the Ninety-Seventh New York Volunteers,* 135; Benjamin Look to John Bachelder, February 17, 1884; Howard Thomas, *Boys in Blue From the Adirndack Foothills* (Prospect, NY, 1960), 148; OR, 27, 1, 289, 292, 309.

While the Bachelder maps of the first day show the 97th New York on the left of the line, the location of the monuments clearly indicates that the 11th Pennsylvania occupied this position.

39. Charles Wehrum, "The Adjutant of the 12th Massachusetts Replies to the Captain of the 97th N.Y.," *National Tribune,* December 10, 1885; Lash, "Gen. Henry Baxter's Brigade at Gettysburg," 15.

40. Locke, *Story of the Regiment,* 229; Vautier, "At Gettysburg"; Martin, *Gettysburg—July 1,* 222.

41. Vautier, *History of the Eighty-Eighth Pennsylvania for the War for the Union,* 135; Vautier, "At Gettysburg"; Alfred Sellers,

letter (90th Pennsylvania folder, GNMP); *PAG*, 1, 487; Martin, *Gettysburg—July 1*, 226, 227–228.

42. Vautier, "At Gettysburg"; Grant, "The First Army Corps on the First Day at Gettysburg," 49.

43. Vautier, *History of the Eighty-Eighth Pennsylvania for the War for the Union*, 135; Hussey, *History of the Ninth Regiment, N.Y.S.M.* 270; *NYG*, 2, 678.

44. Grant, "The First Army Corps on the First Day at Gettysburg," 50; Charles Wehrum Account, *Bachelder Papers*, vol. 2, 989–990; OR, 27, 1, 307, 311; George Kimball, "Iverson's Brigade," *National Tribune*, October 1, 1885.

In his *Philadelphia Weekly Press* account (but not in his book), John Vautier described a conference of the officers prior to the charge. Some believed that the tokens of surrender were a ploy to get Baxter's men to cease firing and draw them into the open.

45. Vautier, "At Gettysburg"; Vautier, *History of the Eighty-Eighth Pennsylvania for the War for the Union*, 135; "88th Pennsylvania Report," National Archives, RG 94, War Records, vol. 27, boxes 48–52; George Cramer, letter, 11th Pennsylvania folder, GNMP; Charles Wehrum to John Bachelder, January 21, 1884, in Bachelder Papers, New Hampshire Historical Society; Miller, "They All Helped to Do It."

46. Wehrum, "The Adjutant of the 12th Massachusetts Replies"; Boone, "Memoir."

47. Hall, *History of the Ninety-Seventh Regiment*, 138–139; Grant, "The First Army Corps on the First Day at Gettysburg," 51.

A controversy developed after the war when Isaac Hall of the 97th New York claimed that the 12th Massachusetts did not participate in the counterattack against Iverson's men. Adjutant Charles Wehrum rebutted this claim, which covered several issues of the *National Tribune*. Finally, William Miller of the 83rd New York seemed to end the discussion when he wrote that

they were not ordered to charge—the men from all of the regiments participated.

The flags were from the 5th, 20th, and 23rd North Carolina. Captain Edmund Patterson of the 88th Pennsylvania also claimed that his regiment captured the 16th Alabama's. Since this unit was not at Gettysburg, he may have meant the 26th Alabama (OR 27, 1, 311; Martin, *Gettysburg—Day 1*, 233).

48. OR 27, 1, 292; Vautier, "At Gettysburg"; Grant, "The First Army Corps on the First Day at Gettysburg," 52; Cook, *History of the Twelfth Massachusetts Volunteers (Webster's Regiment)*, 101.

According to Pfanz (*Gettysburg—The First Day*, 185), the 97th New York may have been with Paul's men.

49. Elsie Slingmaster, "Sallie," 11th Pennsylvania folder, GNMP; Alan D. Gaff, "The Kid," *Civil War Times Illustrated* (1998), vol. 37, no. 4, 38–41.

50. Bates, *Pennsylvania Volunteers*, V, 72; Vautier, "At Gettysburg"; Hall, *History of the Ninety-Seventh New York*, 141; Grant, "The First Army Corps on the First Day at Gettysburg," 50–51; 88th Pennsylvania Official Report; OR 27, 1, 292, 308;

51. *NYG*, 2, 678; Vautier, *History of the Eighty-Eighth Pennsylvania for the War for the Union*, 135; Lash, "Brig. Gen. Henry Baxter's Brigade at Gettysburg," 27; OR, 27, 1, 292.

52. OR, 27, 1, 308; Clare, letter; *PAG*, 1, 481.

Baxter states in his report that he was relieved by Webb's Brigade of the II Corps, but this unit occupied the area near the Copse of Trees to the south.

53. OR, 27, 1, 308; Coburn, diary; Clare, letter.

54. OR 27, 1, 308, 311; 88th Pennsylvania Official Report; Vautier, "At Gettysburg"; Coburn, diary.

55. OR 27, 1, 309, 311; Coburn, diary; Clare, letter.

56. Busey and Martin, *Regimental Strengths and Losses*, 240; Benjamin Look to John Bachelder, February 17, 1884.

3RD DIVISION—

Major General Abner Doubleday/
Brigadier General Thomas Rowley

The 3rd Division had a distinguished reputation that its troops had not earned. Formerly commanded by General George Meade during the autumn and winter of 1862, the 3rd Division had been the Pennsylvania Reserve Division. It fought with distinction through the war, including Antietam and Fredericksburg, where it was part of the I Corps. Its losses were so horrendous after the latter battle that it was pulled from the Army of the Potomac and sent to the Washington defenses to recuperate. A new 3rd Division was formed in mid-February 1863, when two green brigades from the Washington defenses joined the army. A third brigade, composed of Vermont troops, was added in June 1863.[1]

Although the troops were green, their divisional commander was not. Major General Abner Doubleday was a West Point graduate who had devoted his life to the army. After distinguished service at Second Bull Run as a brigade commander, Doubleday took over the I Corps's 1st Division and led it at Antietam and Fredericksburg. Because the newly formed 3rd Division needed a seasoned commander, Doubleday was transferred to its command during the early part of 1863.[2]

With the assignment of General Reynolds to oversee the activities of the army's left wing and General Doubleday now commanding the I Corps, General Thomas Rowley, who had commanded the 1st Brigade, now led the division, and Colonel Chapman Biddle of the 121st Pennsylvania assumed command of the 1st Brigade.[3]

Breaking camp at about 8:00 A.M. on July 1, Rowley sent Stone's and Biddle's Brigades toward Gettysburg using different routes, which were only 150 to 200 yards apart when they reached the Codori house on Emmitsburg Road. Stannard's 3rd Brigade was left behind to guard the corps' wagons. The two brigades arrived on the battlefield sometime between 11:00 and 11:30 P.M. and therefore missed the initial fight between Wadsworth's Division and Archer's and Davis's Brigades of

Heth's Division. Upon reaching Seminary Ridge, the two brigades again split up and formed on either side of the Iron Brigade. Biddle's brigade formed on the left of the Iron Brigade; Stone's formed on the right.[4]

Both brigades became engaged within a short time. For some reason, both brigades' flanks hung in the air, ultimately causing their defeat. On the right, Stone's Brigade was attacked by Daniel's Brigade (Rodes's Division) early in the afternoon. Colonel Stone skillfully maneuvered his regiments to face the enemy and successfully thwarted the Confederate attacks. Later in the afternoon, Daniel's attack on the brigade's center and right flank was renewed, this time in concert with Brockenbrough's Brigade's attack against its left. On the left, Biddle's Brigade battled the right flank of Pettigrew's Brigade (Heth's Division), but was quickly flanked and forced to withdraw to Seminary Ridge. These attacks, combined with the withdrawal of the Iron Brigade on their right, forced the brigade to seek refuge on Seminary Ridge.[5]

On Seminary Ridge, Stone's and Biddle's Brigades joined the I Corps's artillery and the Iron Brigade in beating back repeated charges by Pender's Division. Biddle's Brigade's left flank, however, again hung in the air, and within a short time, units from Perrin's Brigade overpowered this sector, causing the entire defensive line to fall back through the town. The movement through the town was fairly disorganized, and the survivors finally reformed on Cemetery Hill.[6]

The division's odd dispositions and Biddle's Brigade's erratic movements have caused some to hypothesize that General Rowley was drunk. Lieutenant George Benedict of the 12th Vermont recalled passing Rowley during the afternoon of July 1. "He was asleep, overcome by fatigue, or something, and his aids [sic] would not wake him." Later, a member of the Iron Brigade saw Rowley "giving General Wadsworth's troops contradictory orders, calling them cowards, and whose conduct was so unbecoming a division commander and unfortunately stimulated with poor commissary [whiskey]." A lieutenant became so angry by Rowley's behavior that he placed his commander under arrest. Rowley was later court-martialed and assigned command of the District of the Monongahela.[7]

On July 2, General John Newton of the VI Corps took command of the I Corps, and Doubleday returned to his division. Some believed that Meade held Doubleday in low esteem, and was therefore quick to make the change. Most of the men were not privy to this change and probably did not care. However, Lieutenant Jacob Slagle of the 149th Pennsylvania wrote that "his [Doubleday's] being superceded at that time was a gross outrage." The division was strengthened by the arrival of Stannard's Brigade at about 5:00 P.M. on July 1.[8]

The division spent most of July 2 resting on Cemetery Hill. At about 6:00 P.M., the division was rushed southward to help support Sickles's

Corps. Only the 13th Vermont of Stannard's Brigade was engaged during the early evening, when its bayonet attack helped drive Wright's Brigade (Anderson's Division, III Corps) from its temporary perch on Cemetery Ridge. That evening, two regiments from Biddle's Brigade, the 80th New York and 151st Pennsylvania, became separated from the rest of the division and took a first-line position along Cemetery Ridge. The division came under the heavy artillery fire that proceeded the Pickett–Pettigrew–Trimble charge, but casualties were not heavy. Only Stannard's Brigade and Biddle's two regiments were actually involved in repelling the charge. The former brigade's flank attack played a major role in Pickett's, and subsequently Lang's, defeat. The division finally marched away from the battlefield on July 6.[9]

1st Brigade—Brigadier General Thomas Rowley/ Colonel Chapman Biddle

Units: 80th New York (20th Militia), 121st Pennsylvania, 142nd Pennsylvania, 151st Pennsylvania
Strength: 1361
Losses: 898 (111-557-230)—66%[10]

A cabinetmaker by trade, Brigadier General Thomas Rowley began the war as colonel of a three-month regiment before taking command of the 102nd Pennsylvania. He gained experience during the Peninsula campaign and was promoted to brigadier general just before the Fredericksburg campaign. On March 28, 1863, Rowley was assigned to command the new 1st Brigade of the 3rd Division, which was composed of three Pennsylvania regiments that had never been in combat.[11]

During the long trek toward Gettysburg, the exhausted men of the 1st Brigade learned that the 80th New York was to join their all-Pennsylvania unit. They probably met this news with mixed emotions. Pennsylvanians and New Yorkers never mixed well, but the 80th New York was a veteran fighting unit that would add stability to the inexperienced brigade. Two of the regiments, the 121st Pennsylvania and 142nd Pennsylvania, had been at Fredericksburg and Chancellorsville, but had never been under fire. The 151st Pennsylvania, a nine-month regiment, had not yet been on a battlefield. It was dubbed the "School Teacher's Regiment" because of the large number of faculty in its ranks.[12]

The brigade broke camp at about 8:00 A.M. on July 1 and headed toward Gettysburg. Farm wives stood along the route, distributing pieces of bread to the grateful men. Captain John Cook of the 80th New York bitterly noted that many of his soldiers were denied this delicacy, as they were from New York, not Pennsylvania. Resentment grew because they were defending the Keystone State, but were being treated ungraciously. The New Yorkers finally realized that a little lie was in order. "It was easy enough to say that they were Pennsylvanians, and a little thing like that hardly troubled the conscience of an old campaigner, however much he might resent the necessity for the subterfuge," noted Cook. "Our boys got their portion all right."[13]

After traveling about three miles along Millerstown Road, the column turned sharply to the right, and after a short march, reached Marsh Creek. The sounds of battle could be heard not too far in the distance. Marching on Black Horse Tavern Road for about a mile, the column left the road and made its way toward the battlefield, marching along the west bank of Willoughby Run. Colonel George McFarland of the 151st Pennsylvania recalled that his men were halted as they crossed Hagerstown Road, formed into line of battle, and ordered to fix their bayonets. They apparently attracted the attention of the Confederate gunners on Herr Ridge, for, according to McFarland, "our arrival at this point was greeted by the booming of cannon."[14]

The men were now ordered "by the right flank" and marched about half a mile to the northeast, where they reformed their line of battle, this time facing west. Ordered to unsling their knapsacks, the men threw them into a pile. They knew that serious work was ahead, and all wisecracking ceased. Perhaps detecting a change in the men, the officers reminded the troops that they were on native soil and it was their solemn duty to defend it. They were almost immediately ordered forward toward Willoughby Run. Crossing open fields, the men reached the edge of Herbst Woods, where they were exposed to heavy artillery and small arms fire. Colonel Theodore Gates of the 80th New York recalled that they were "unable to see the enemy from whom the fire came, and did not attempt to reply to it." Captain Cook of the same regiment added that a "swarming flight of artillery missiles showed that we were seen by the enemy." What happened next became the subject of dispute between officers of the various regiments. According to Colonel Theodore Gates (80th New York), "here we first received the enemy's infantry fire, but did not reply to it, and were shortly moved back on to the ridge, all the regiments of the brigade passing over." Over on the right of the line, Colonel McFarland (151st Pennsylvania) recalled it differently. "All firing now ceased for perhaps an hour, when, about noon, the enemy opened on our right. As this was a flank fire, we were soon ordered back into the hollow." Taking the middle ground, Captain Cook (80th New York) recalled that when the men reached their advanced position, they immediately came under fire. "As usual, some of the men began to grumble about what seemed needless exposure," he wrote, suggesting that they remained here for more than a few moments. Whether the brigade remained near Herbst Woods for an hour or for only a few minutes, the officers agreed that the brigade's next position was closer to Seminary Ridge.[15]

The officers and men were unhappy with both their initial exposed position and their subsequent movements to other positions. Some attributed these erratic movements to the inebriated state of General Rowley. A measure of protection was realized when the brigade reached the east side of McPherson's Ridge. Here the brigade was aligned, from left to right, as 121st Pennsylvania–80th New York–142nd Pennsylvania–151st Pennsylvania. Cooper's battery was between the 80th New York and the 142nd Pennsylvania. The men could see the seminary buildings about a third of a mile behind them. In front of them and to their right was Meredith's Iron Brigade. The men were told to lie down to reduce the number of casualties.[16]

Colonel Gates of the 80th New York was ordered to take possession of the Harmon farmhouse during the morning hours. Confederate sharpshooters occupied the house, taking their toll on both the brigade and Cooper's gunners. Company K, and later Company G, finally extracted the Confederates from their lodgings. The two companies held the house all through the afternoon, firing periodically into the Confederate lines. This continued until the enemy surrounded the detachment on three sides. The men barely made good their escape, not joining the rest of the regiment until later that evening.[17]

About 2:00 P.M., Rowley detached the 151st Pennsylvania from its position on the right of the line, and ordered it back to the seminary, where it became the I Corps's last reserve. It replaced Paul's Brigade (Robinson's Division), which rushed to the right to support Baxter's Brigade. The green 151st Pennsylvania climbed behind the rail breastworks constructed by Paul's veterans, and warily awaited further orders.[18]

At about the same time, the Confederate artillery opened fire again, this time throwing an enfilading fire against the brigade's right flank. The brigade was now ordered to move by the left flank and form on the opposite (south) side of Hagerstown Road. After about ten minutes, the enemy gunners again found the brigade's position, and several men fell amid the resulting firestorm. The brigade received some relief when it moved into the road, facing north, where the men were partially protected by a fence and the roadway's bank. Thirty minutes later, the men were ordered back to the position they had vacated on McPherson Ridge, while the enemy artillery fire continued to play on their ranks.[19]

Lieutenant Colonel Alexander Biddle's report on the actions of the 121st Pennsylvania showed how confused the movements were at the time. While moving back toward its position between McPherson and Seminary Ridges, Reynolds's bat-tery had formed on the left of the 142nd Pennsylvania, and interfered with its taking position. "We were therefore ordered to the left or south of the battery and, finding there the Twentieth New York, moved to the left of that regiment," Biddle wrote. It seemed that temporary brigade commander Colonel Chapman Biddle or temporary division commander General Rowley was having problems commanding his units.[20]

As the 121st Pennsylvania finally swung into position behind a fence on the left of the brigade at about 2:30 P.M., the men saw two lines of Confederate infantry slowly approaching. What concerned them most was that the enemy line considerably overlapped theirs on the left. "As the enemy's faces appeared over the crest of the hill [McPherson Ridge], we fired effectually into them, and soon after, received a crushing fire from their [Confederate] right, under which our ranks were broken and became massed together as we endeavored to change front to the left to meet them," noted Biddle. Captain Frank Sterling of Company C watched with wonder, and later wrote to his father, "what an impressive sight was the well-dressed rebel lines approaching with flags waving." The regiment's historian recalled that the men held their fire until the Confederates "had reached within a few yards of the top of the ridge, [when] the men arose and delivered their fire directly in their faces, staggering them and bringing them to a stand." The Confederates returned the fire—some thought they fired first. To Captain Sterling, it felt that whole regiments were mowed down, as the opposing lines were less than 150 yards apart. Attacked from both the left and front, the men tried to hold their position against the 52nd North Carolina regiment of Pettigrew's Brigade (Heth's Division, Third Corps). From Sterling's vantage point, the majority of the 121st Pennsylvania was on the ground, and he felt that if the regiment remained another minute, it would have been annihilated. Biddle finally gave orders for the broken unit to fall back to Seminary Ridge. The regiment's historian recalled that the speed with which the men crossed the quarter-mile stretch to the Seminary "was remarkable, probably the best on record."[21]

Just to the right, the 80th New York was holding its own against the attack of the 47th North Carolina and 52nd North Carolina. Captain John Cook took issue with the perception that the Confederate uniform was gray in color. "In actual service it was butternut brown . . . owing to their long campaign, as dirty, disreputable, and unromantic as can well be imagined . . . but they could shoot all right, and as they stood out there in line . . . and poured in a rapid fire of musketry that gave us no time to criticize their appearance." With the 121st Pennsylvania now gone, the right flank of the 52nd North Carolina wrapped around the 80th New York's flank. Reynolds's battery quickly limbered up and galloped to safety. Seeing the Tar Heels gaining his rear, Colonel Gates took up his regiment's flag and immediately ordered a withdrawal to the seminary.[22]

With the 151st Pennsylvania detached, the 142nd was the right-most regiment. Gearhart of the latter regiment watched intently as the Confederate troops advanced. "They kept steadily advancing until we could see their officers stepping in front swinging their swords." Suddenly, the Confederate line erupted in smoke as they fired a well-aimed volley against the Union position. Gaps formed in the line as many men fell. The Union officers screamed for their men to open fire, which halted the 47th North Carolina in its tracks. The men were firing so quickly that their muskets became red-hot. Many

discarded them, and picked up others that had been dropped by their killed or wounded comrades. As one veteran recalled, "there was no scarcity of muskets, as the dead and wounded were largely in the majority of the regiment." Turning his head, Gearhart had a terrible feeling, for "the enemy [were] getting around on our left, [and] my heart sank within me." The men began inching backward, but "the enemy giving us a heavy volley at pretty close range we broke."[23]

Seeing that all was about to be lost, Colonel Chapman Biddle rode forward, grabbed the regiment's colors, and yelled, "Rally round the flag." The subsequent counterattack against the 47th North Carolina was foolhardy, as the men were mowed down, including the regiment's beloved commander, Colonel Robert Cummins. A few of the men tried to carry him to safety, but they too were hit. Lying on the ground, with blood streaming from his mouth, Cummins uttered his last words, "For God's sake men rally, we can whip them yet." A Confederate soldier from the 47th North Carolina recalled that "the scattered Federals swarmed around him [Cummins] as bees cover their queen." Some of the survivors did try to rally, making another stand at a broken fence, but they too were swept away. Gearhart (142nd Pennsylvania) honestly admitted, "the men were running in retreat without order." The regiment lost its colors during the confused retreat.[24]

The flawed deployment of the brigade, which caused its left flank to hang in the air, spelled doom, as each unit in turn was attacked in front and left flank and forced to retreat. According to Captain Frank Sterling, "if we had remained for minutes longer in our position I don't believe there would have been a single man in our regiment unwounded." Upon reaching Seminary Ridge at about 4:00 P.M., the men took position on the left of the battered Iron Brigade, which occupied the breastworks thrown up by Paul's Brigade during the forenoon. The decimated regiments, which were probably aligned in the same arrangement as before, tried to find fence posts or any other materials that could be used as a barricade.[25]

While the three regiments of the brigade were being thoroughly defeated on McPherson Ridge, the 151st Pennsylvania was having its own problems. Detached earlier in the afternoon to serve as the I Corps's reserve on Seminary Ridge, the men occupied the grounds around the seminary. As Pettigrew's Brigade pressed forward, Rowley rode up to the regiment and ordered it to McPherson Ridge to fill the gap between Biddle's Brigade on the left and the Iron Brigade on the right. As the large 467-man unit approached Herbst Woods, it was greeted by a volley from the 11th North Carolina, which Colonel McFarland said "brought several of my men down, ere I had halted in position." Before this, their first battle, McFarland had ordered additional target practice for his men, so they were fairly good marksmen. Because the North Carolinians were downslope and among the trees, McFarland cautioned his men to fire individually "as he saw an enemy on which to take a steady aim." The unit was in a no-win situation. The 19th Indiana of the Iron Brigade had fallen back, possibly thinking that the Pennsylvanians were their relief, and this allowed the full force of the Confederate attack to fall on these green troops. Still, they held their ground. McFarland proudly wrote in his report, "I know not how men could have fought more desperately, exhibited more coolness, or contested the field with more determined courage." After losing scores of men, McFarland realized that Biddle's Brigade on his left and the Iron

Brigade on his right had pulled back, leaving him in danger of being surrounded, and he quickly ordered a withdrawal. McFarland's survivors eventually took position behind the barricade on Seminary Ridge. An officer arrived with some colors and asked Colonel McFarland, "Colonel, is this your flag?" Recalling his startled reaction, McFarland wrote about "the sensation that quickly passed through me at the thought of having lost my flag. Just then a breeze wafting the flag revealed the inscription, 142d P.V. on its folds and relieved me." McFarland ordered the colors planted on his left, and soon the remnants of that regiment took position there.[26]

After about fifteen minutes behind the barricades, the Confederate lines of attack again appeared, as three fresh brigades from Pender's Division approached. The Union soldiers opened fire, but when the approaching line did not return the fire, the officers told the men to "stop firing on our own men." Suddenly, the approaching line stopped and opened fire, confirming what the enlisted men knew all along. The Union line held for about half an hour, sending Perrin's South Carolina Brigade reeling in defeat. A private in the 14th South Carolina recalled that as they approached Biddle's men, the enemy "rose to their feet and took as deliberate aim as if they were on dress parade, and to show you how accurate their aim was, 34 out of 39 men fell at the first fire." General Perrin later commented that it was "the most destructive fire I have ever been exposed to." Several attempts were made to breach the line, but all met with the same fate. At one point, Perrin was sure that his 14th South Carolina was annihilated, as it was "staggered for a moment by the severity and destructiveness" of the Federal fire. While conferring with Colonel Gates, brigade commander Biddle was struck in the head with a spent minié ball. Several soldiers later recalled the distinct sound it made. After turning command of the brigade over to Gates, Biddle retired from the field. However, Biddle would not be kept out of the fight, and returned a short time later with his head heavily bandaged. The fire was so severe that trees along the Federal line were splintered and limbs fell everywhere.[27]

Looking over to his left, Lieutenant Colonel Alexander Biddle of the 121st Pennsylvania was horrified to see the earlier events of the day being replayed. "Finding the enemy were moving out on our left flank, with the intention of closing in on the only opening in the barricade, I reported the fact to the division commander, and by his directions returned to the fence barricade." It did not take long for Perrin's 1st South Carolina to break through. After a quick discussion with Colonel Gates, Colonel Biddle ordered the men to fall back to Gettysburg.[28]

The retreat to Gettysburg was not an easy one, as the men were exposed to small arms fire from three sides. The majority of the men probably fled to safety along the unfinished railroad with the 80th New York bringing up the rear. When only about twenty paces from the seminary, Colonel McFarland of the 151st Pennsylvania made the mistake of stopping to look back and was almost immediately hit in the leg, which was subsequently amputated.[29]

Finally reaching the safety of Cemetery Hill at about 5:30 P.M., the men were posted behind a stone wall overlooking Taneytown Road. They were resupplied with ammunition and ordered to await the expected attack on the heights. The men were shocked to see how few of them remained. Lieutenant Colonel Biddle reported that he mustered only 48 men

and 2 officers in his 121st Pennsylvania. However, returning stragglers helped swell the depleted ranks to 75 men out of the 256 who had entered the fray in the morning. Of the 466 men of the 151st Pennsylvania, 353 fell or were captured— a 76% loss. The entire brigade could muster only 390 of the 1361 men it had taken into battle. The men were relieved when reinforcements arrived, and, according to Captain Cook of the 80th New York, "no nightfall was ever more welcome than that which came to us, wearied, dispirited, mourning our lost comrades, and filled with apprehension lest the enemy, so far successful, should attack and overwhelm us before our army could be got together to resist."[30]

During the morning of July 2, the brigade was moved into a field south of the cemetery and placed behind a stone wall lining Taneytown Road. The men were later joined by Stannard's Brigade of nine-month recruits. Most of the day was quiet, except for periods of intense cannon fire. To avoid the effects of this fire, the men were moved across the road. About sunset Colonel Gates of the 80th New York received orders to take his regiment and the 151st Pennsylvania south to help support the army's left flank. The fighting had ended by the time the two regiments reached the vicinity of Little Round Top. Without further orders from Rowley, Colonel Gates decided to march his men to the northwest, where the fighting had occurred. Reaching the west side of Cemetery Ridge, he deployed his men on the left of Harrow's Brigade (Gibbon's Division, II Corps). Captain Cook of the 80th New York remembered the isolation, stating that "the night before we were in the very front of the line and seemed to have been misplaced and forgotten." The men cared for the wounded in their front until about midnight.[31]

On the morning of July 3, the 121st Pennsylvania and 142nd Pennsylvania marched about three hundred yards to a position near General Doubleday's headquarters. Here they threw up breastworks, which were partially destroyed by the cannonade preceding the Pickett–Pettigrew–Trimble charge. Three men from the 121st Pennsylvania were wounded. As the charge got under way, the two regiments were rushed forward to the right of Stone's Brigade, behind Hays's Division (II Corps). Because of Hays's firepower, the regiments did little but observe the destruction of the Southern attack. They did, however, fire on sharpshooters who were harassing the Federal cannoneers. The two regiments remained until 9:00 P.M., when they were relieved by other troops and withdrawn to the rear.[32]

About half a mile to the south, the two regiments under Gates's command awoke on July 3 to a view of death and destruction between Seminary and Cemetery Ridges. The men were hungry, for they had not eaten for twenty-four hours. Cook would never forget the cannonade that began about 1:00 P.M.

> The shriek of shot, the scream of shell, and the sounds of exploding missiles seemed incessant. We hugged the ground behind the low pile of rails which partly concealed us, and awaited our destiny with such composure as we could muster. Again and again a shot struck one of these rails and knocked it around to kill or cripple a man lying behind it. Again and again pieces of exploding shells would hit someone in the line with disabling or fatal effect. There was no getting away.[33]

Lieutenant Colonel Jacob Hardenburgh of the 80th New York recalled how his regiment's veterans handled the artillery fire, compared with Stannard's inexperienced troops nearby. "Ours during the cannonade were smoking and joking while they lay there hugging the ground and big drops of perspiration stood out on their foreheads and faces." This form of bravado was not uncommon years after the battle, and it is probable that Captain Cook's recollection of dread was closer to the mark than Hardenburgh's.[34]

The men suddenly saw Kemper's Brigade (Pickett's Division) approach from the direction of Seminary Ridge, and march toward them. The Federal troops "rose up and formed in line . . . the color guard mounted some stones and waved the colors towards the enemy and shouted to them to come on. Some of the men in the excitement of the moment commenced firing," recalled Lieutenant Colonel Hardenburgh. Captain Cook of the same regiment found the Southerners' attack most impressive. "No one who saw them could help admiring the steadiness with which they came on, like the shadow of a cloud seen from a distance as it sweeps across a sunny field." About halfway between the two ridges, Kemper's long line made an oblique movement toward the right of Biddle's two regiments, toward the Copse of Trees. Colonel Gates's fighting blood was up, and he ordered his men to move by the right flank to intercept the Confederate movement, which he characterized as being made with "unusual determination." Hardenburgh incorrectly mentioned that there were no troops between the Copse of Trees and his position before the movement. In actuality, Harrow's Brigade occupied this position. More accurate was Captain Walter Owens's (151st Pennsylvania) recollection that the II Corps units on their right moved toward the Copse of Trees, and Gates's men followed them.[35]

As the men filed to the right, they kept up a constant fire on Kemper's oncoming troops. Reloading while walking was probably easier for the veterans of the 80th New York than for the green troops of the 151st Pennsylvania. Facing the enemy, the Confederates opened "a severe fire upon our exposed ranks causing us to waver and at times it seemed that our line would be compelled to give way," noted Captain Owens. After about ten minutes of exchanging small arms fire, Gates could see that the Confederates were beginning to waiver, and some were returning the Seminary Ridge, so he ordered a charge. "The order was promptly obeyed and with a deafening shout and a gallant dash" the men approached the enemy. Here the story gets murky. Captain Cook recalled that "a curious thing about this fighting was, that although all the men were armed with bayonets, no one seemed to be using them. Those nearest clubbed their muskets and beat each other over the head, while those not so close kept loading and firing as fast as they could." In his report written on July 4, Colonel Gates remarked about "this almost hand-to-hand contest." Given Gates's pension for seeking glory, and the freshness of the event in his mind, he is probably correct that no hand-to-hand fighting occurred. Gates did say that his men "poured a volley into the enemy at very short range, who now completely broke." Many of Kemper's men had taken refuge behind some slashings in front of the Union position. "Our men shouted to them to come in and promised not to hurt them, and at the word hundreds rose us [sic] and came into our lines, dropping their arms and crouching to avoid the fire of their own artillery, which was pouring upon our position."[36]

Justifiably proud of these two regiments, General Doubleday singled them out in his report. The two small regiments, which probably did not number more than 240 men on the morning of July 3, lost about 15% during this short, but sharp encounter with Kemper's men. After the last of Kemper's men had been driven away or captured, the men walked around the contested fields, where they were shocked by the level of devastation wrecked upon Pickett's Division. At 6:00 P.M., the two regiments were pulled back, probably along with the rest of the brigade, to Taneytown Road, where they remained for the night. Hunger, their old enemy, soon returned. Finally, on July 4, a young heifer was driven into camp and eaten with newly arrived hardtack and coffee. The brigade left the Gettysburg area at 6:00 A.M. on July 6.[37]

Biddle's Brigade has come under fire for somehow not fighting as hard or as well as the other I Corps units on July 1. This is unfortunate, because the unit did fight as well as can be expected, given its untenable position on McPherson Ridge with its left flank in the air. In fact, the Iron Brigade was forced to leave its position on the ridge for the same reason. Why Biddle's Brigade did not link up with the Iron Brigade remains a mystery, but may have been because of the intense Confederate artillery fire. Biddle's losses were among the highest in the army—two-thirds were either killed, wounded, or captured. In addition, two of its regiments, the 80th New York and the 151st Pennsylvania, had the distinction of being the only I Corps units, besides Stannard's Brigade, to help repulse Pickett's Division on July 3. The most horrendous total losses were sustained by the 151st Pennsylvania, which lost about 75% of its men. This nine-month regiment was just a shell of its former self when it was mustered out of service on July 27, 1863.[38]

✄

2nd Brigade—Colonel Roy Stone

Units: 143rd Pennsylvania, 149th Pennsylvania, 150th Pennsylvania
Strength: 1317
Losses: 853 (109-465-279)—65%[39]

Although they had never been under fire, Stone's men could sense that a fight with the Confederate invaders was imminent. This was important for some of the men of the second Bucktail Brigade, as they were anxious to gain the kind of reputation that the first Buckail Brigade had earned. They were also buoyed by the knowledge that they were approaching their native soil. "It was a veritable 'triumphal progress,'" recalled Major Thomas Chamberlin of the 150th Pennsylvania. However, this emotion was tempered by the realization that many might not survive the coming battle. "The expressions in [their] faces have changed . . . [they have become] grave and quiet and very reticent and apparently more thoughtful," wrote Private Avery Harris of the 143rd Pennsylvania.[40]

What the brigade lacked in experience, its commanding officer, Colonel Roy Stone, supplied. A grisly veteran of the "real" bucktails, he fought in many of the early battles of the eastern theater. So impressed was the War Department with the bucktails that Stone was dispatched to Pennsylvania to raise another brigade of them. Returning with the 149th Pennsylvania, he was disgusted when it and the two other new regiments were assigned to the Washington defenses. Therefore, they were excited to be transferred to the Army of the Potomac prior to the Gettysburg campaign.[41]

As with the other units, the men were not averse to trying to make a positive impression on the townspeople along the route to Gettysburg. Private William Perry of the 150th Pennsylvania recorded in his diary that as the men passed through the small villages they "found a good deal of cheering to do." As they entered Emmitsburg on June 29, the flags were unsheathed, and as the drums beat, the men tried to take on a military air, despite the long, thirty-mile march they had just completed. Their energy levels were doubtless bolstered by the enthusiastic welcome they received from the citizens. Perry probably understated this feeling when he recorded that "the people seem to be glad to see the Union troops." Townspeople lined the roads, and "fresh bread, cakes and pies easily found the way into their capacious haversacks," recalled Major Chamberlin.[42]

The men welcomed the easy six-mile march to the banks of Marsh Creek on June 30. Reveille was sounded at 7:00 A.M. on July 1, and the men of the 149th Pennsylvania quickly cooked the three-day ration of meat they had received the day before and carefully packed it in their haversacks. The 150th Pennsylvania was apparently not supplied the day before, and the men spent the early morning scrounging about for a suitable breakfast. Although orders to resume the march arrived at 9:00 A.M., the brigade did not take to the road for another thirty to forty-five minutes. The column marched on a different road than Biddle's Brigade. Heading north on Red Rock Road, they probably made contact with Biddle's Brigade at the intersection with Millerstown Road. Here they parted again, moving to Emmitsburg Road. About two or three miles from Gettysburg, the sounds of battle could be heard and the pace increased. Along the way, the men's resolves were hardened as many townspeople passed them in their flight to safety. Among them were two children, "on one horse, crying as if their little hearts would break," wrote Major Chamberlin (150th Pennsylvania). Near the Codori house, one of Reynolds's aides diverted the brigade to the left, double-quicking it across fields and meadows, until it reached Seminary Ridge. By this time, the men's uniforms were black with sweat and their equipment and woolen clothes felt much heavier.[43]

Continuing their march in a northwesterly direction, the men reached Hagerstown Road, where they could see the Confederate lines in the distance. Upon reaching the seminary, the men halted, and were addressed by Generals Doubleday and Rowley, "reminding them that they were upon their own soil, that there was every reason to believe they would do their duty in the uttermost in defence of their State." All the while, shells flew overhead, rattling the green troops. The order to advance was given, and the men moved down the slope in front of the seminary. Upon reaching the bottom of the ridge, the men were ordered to unsling their knapsacks and blankets and throw them in a pile. The time was between 11:00 and 11:30 A.M.[44]

As the men advanced toward McPherson Ridge, some of the soldiers in the 150th Pennsylvania yelled out to their commander, Colonel Langhorne Wistar, that their guns were not yet loaded. The order was immediately given, which was carried out in some merriment, as the men continued their forward movement. The 150th Pennsylvania was in the lead, followed by the 143rd Pennsylvania; the 149th Pennsylvania brought up the rear. Upon reaching the McPherson farm, the

brigade was deployed and faced west. The 150th Pennsylvania was on the left of the farmhouse, separated from the Iron Brigade in Herbst Woods by a three hundred-yard gap. To the right of the 150th Pennsylvania was the 143rd Pennsylvania, which occupied the ground between the McPherson house and barn. To its right was the 149th Pennsylvania, whose right extended to Chambersburg Pike.[45]

In position at about noon, Stone ordered a company from each regiment thrown out as skirmishers. The inexperienced captain of Company B of the 150th Pennsylvania, George Jones, who drew this "honor" asked Colonel Langhorne Wistar how far his men should move to the west. Wistar replied, "to advance until he met the enemy, and engage him." The two army's skirmishers soon collided, with Stone's men gaining the upper hand.[46]

Around this time, a solitary man approached the 150th Pennsylvania. Seventy-year-old John Burns of Gettysburg had come to fight the Rebels. He was closely queried about his shooting abilities and ammunition. Assured that he was prepared, Colonel Wistar suggested that he fight nearer to Herbst Woods, where he would be more protected. Although clearly reluctant, Burns made his way toward the Iron Brigade and immortality.[47]

During the next hour, between noon and 1:00 P.M., the men were ordered to lie down to avoid the shells being occasionally thrown at them. Major David McIntosh, commanding A. P. Hill's artillery reserve, had his guns fire "slowly upon the enemy wherever they brought into view considerable bodies of troops." Lieutenant Francis Jones of the 149th Pennsylvania, like virtually all of the men, had never been under fire before. He observed a "continuous shower of six inch solid shot come over . . . and go on until they struck the ground in our rear and continued their onward rolling and bounding, cutting down men, horses and fences until they passed out of sight, while shells were also bursting all around and over us." [48]

Stone made the first of many changes in troop dispositions during this period. The right wing of the 149th Pennsylvania shifted to the right, so it faced Chambersburg Pike. The regiment's left, now at right angles with its right, still faced west along the farm lane in front of McPherson's house. A new threat soon materialized north of the brigade, as Rodes's Division (II Corps) arrived on Oak Hill. After deploying his artillery, Rodes ordered them to open fire on the Union line. The Confederate artillery on Herr Ridge also opened fire. Many of the shells found their way to Stone's position. Most unsettling were the "whistling shrieks" of the English-made, breech-loading Whitworth guns. This, together with the retreat of Cutler's Brigade to the north, forced Stone to shift the 150th Pennsylvania to the right, to take refuge near the McPherson house, and to move the remainder of the 149th Pennsylvania to face Chambersburg Pike. The ground next to the roadway was lower, providing a measure of cover for Colonel Walton Dwight's men. Unfortunately, this movement was seen by the Confederate gunners, who sent a storm of shells flying toward Stone's brigade. As Captain John Bassler of the 149th Pennsylvania wrote, "the change of position was like jumping out of the frying pan into the fire for the commander of a rebel battery on the pike, westward, and nearer than the other [on Oak Hill] caught a glimpse of the Regiment over the swell of ground before the men lay down, and at once opened a crossfire upon us." [49]

One of the shells exploded among Company B, killing three and wounding five more. One of the wounded came hop-ping up to hard-nosed Colonel Dwight, yelling, "I am killed, I am killed." Dwight growled, "The hell you are killed, go back to your place." A short time later, the soldier stretched out on the ground and died. Other men were killed and wounded as the Confederate gunners found their range. It was a very trying time for the inexperienced men of the 149th Pennsylvania, and probably more than a few eyed the land behind them. Seeing the fear, Colonel Dwight was everywhere, reassuring the troops. More than a few believed that Dwight's courage was the result of the large quantities of army whiskey he had consumed that morning. Whatever its source, he helped hold the regiment together. [50]

The severe shelling continued. In desperation, Colonel Stone came up with a ploy, ordering the 149th Pennsylvania's color guard to move twenty-five yards west and forty-five yards north of the regiment's left flank, where it took refuge behind a pile of fence rails. Stone held his breath, but soon the trajectory of the shells changed, as the enemy gunners assumed that the regiment had moved with the colors. Behind the rails, the color guard hugged the ground, some undoubtedly wishing they could get into it. [51]

The appearance of Confederate infantry on Oak Hill at about 1:30 P.M. caused Colonel Stone to shift the 143rd Pennsylvania to the right of the 149th Pennsylvania, both now facing north. This forced the 150th Pennsylvania, still facing west, to stretch to fill the space that had been vacated by the 143rd Pennsylvania. This was a desperate time for the Union forces, as they were now facing Confederate troops on both flanks. Even after Baxter's Brigade of Robinson's Division arrived to face Rodes's threat, General Doubleday knew the importance of the position. He later wrote, "I relied greatly upon Stone's brigade to hold the post assigned them . . . in truth the key-point of the first day's battle."[52]

Soon the men could see Iverson's Brigade march smartly off Oak Hill, aiming for Baxter's men to the northeast. Stone probably knew that the North Carolinians were out of musket range, but he felt that his men needed to release their pent-up aggression, so he ordered the two regiments along the road to open fire. Colonel Dwight of the 149th Pennsylvania ordered his men to "fire over the heads of my skirmishers at the enemy." Stone wrote in his official report, "we poured a most destructive fire upon their flanks," which perhaps contained more exaggeration than truth. One of his soldiers wrote, "it was here that we gained our baptism of fire." It also attracted the attention of several Confederate officers.[53]

Another Confederate force suddenly materialized from the direction of Oak Hill, but this one was heading directly for Stone's position along Chambersburg Pike. This was the 2nd North Carolina Battalion and the 45th North Carolina of Daniel's Brigade (Rodes's Division), who were advancing seemingly oblivious to the threat of Stone's two prone regiments in front of them. Reaching a fence about seventy-five yards from the unfinished railroad cut, the North Carolinians were scaling it when the Union line erupted in smoke. The orders to the two Federal regiments had been straightforward—fire "as long as a man was seen moving in that field in front of us. In a short time, no living soul was to be seen on that field, but it was covered with the dead of both armies," noted Jones (149th Pennsylvania). Over seven hundred bullets thumped into the Confederate line, sending it reeling. Lieutenant Colonel Wharton Green of the 2nd North Carolina Battalion recalled that "the enemy were some

five or six hundred yards in front, and results showed that they had set a most deadly trap for us." Daniel's two battered units were ordered to retreat to a position halfway back to Oak Hill, where they lay down and awaited further orders.[54]

Seeing the effects of these initial volleys, Stone ordered Dwight's regiment to charge to the railroad cut, about a hundred yards in front of it. Reaching the southern edge of the cut, Dwight ordered his men down into it to take position on the opposite side. This was easier said than done, as the descending bank was steep and lined with loose dirt and stones. Many slid down the slope; others tumbled head over feet until they unceremoniously reached bottom. A few lay at the bottom of the cut with cuts, bruises, and sprained ankles. Then it was up the ascending bank, which proved no easier. Finally reaching the top, Dwight told his men to rest their arms on the bank and told them "to take deliberate aim at the knees of the front rank of the enemy as he came up." The movement was watched with some disdain by the 143rd Pennsylvania, which did not receive orders to join in the movement. "There go the men of the 149th with their tails just a bobbing. What does that mean? Have they got this job by contract? Stone is after a big chunk of glory for his tails and does not intend that the 143rd shall have any of it," wrote Harris (143rd Pennsylvania).[55]

Daniel now reorganized his two units, and brought them, and a third regiment, the 32nd North Carolina, forward again. Dwight noted, "my position [in the railroad cut] was undiscovered by the enemy until he reached a rail fence, 22 paces in my front, when he saw my colors flying." Daniel ordered his men to open fire, but the railroad cut protected most of the Federal troops there. Dwight now ordered his men to "fire by battalion." "The effect on the enemy was terrible, he being at the time brigade en masse, at 9-pace interval. He now broke to the rear in great confusion." While Dwight's men reloaded, Daniel's men prepared for another charge. Waiting until the Tar Heels were almost upon them, Dwight ordered his men to open fire, sweeping away many in Daniel's front ranks. Casualties in Dwight's regiment were surprisingly few during this period, for "our bodies were so well protected below the edge of the railroad cut," recalled Francis Bacon. That is, until "the enemy sent a battery into the south end of the cut and commenced pouring canister shot into our ranks, on our left flank." This forced Lieutenant Colonel Dwight to order a withdrawal back to Chambersburg Pike.[56]

This proved difficult for many of the men. While the railroad cut was fairly shallow on the right, it was deep on the left. Captain John Bassler recalled that "some were shot while climbing up the steep side; others losing their hold slid back, and some ran to the right to get out; and numbers on the left never got out except as prisoners, for the foe was upon them before they could clear it." The survivors quickly made for Chambersburg Pike. The 143rd Pennsylvania, which had retained its position along Chambersburg Pike, now poured a terrific oblique fire into Daniel's triumphant men. Lieutenant Colonel John Musser of the regiment believed that the 149th Pennsylvania "would all have been killed or captured, had we not given the enemy a flank fire compelling them to return behind their brest [sic] works." Colonel Wistar also moved his regiment to the right, and reformed it along Chambersburg Pike, facing north. Here the men fired volleys at Daniel's men.[57]

Daniel now sent the 32nd North Carolina on a flank attack from the left

(west), while the 2nd North Carolina Battalion and the 45th North Carolina drove straight ahead. Around this time, Colonel Stone went down with wounds to his hip and arm, and command of the brigade devolved upon Colonel Wistar of the 150th Pennsylvania. Under a severe fire, Wistar now ordered the 149th Pennsylvania, which had just returned from the railroad cut, to turn and again counterattack toward the cut. Captain Bassler recalled that "the next instant Col. Dwight, without taking time to form the regt. properly into line, headed a charge and carried the regt. back to the cut. This charge cost us dearer than the enemy, but after the previous blunder it was the best thing the Col. could do, and was necessary to preserve the prestige of the regt." Clearly, Bassler did not know that Dwight's actions were ordered by Wistar. Prior to this charge, Harris (143rd Pennsylvania) saw Dwight, "berating them [149th Pennsylvania] in deserved terms in which he loudly proclaims their cowardice." This counterattack was reasonably successful in driving the 2nd North Carolina Battalion and 45th North Carolina from the cut, but did nothing to the 32nd North Carolina firing into their left flank. Dwight had no choice but to pull his men back to the shelter afforded by Chambersburg Pike.[58]

Wistar ordered the three right companies of his 150th Pennsylvania to cross Chambersburg Pike and form at an oblique angle to the rest of the regiment, soon after assuming command of the brigade. "This it did in good order, though under a very severe musketry fire," noted Wistar. After driving back the 149th Pennsylvania, the 32nd North Carolina began making its way toward the McPherson barn. The Tar Heels did not see the 150th Pennsylvania crouching behind a fence. Lieutenant Colonel Henry Huidekoper, who was in command of the right wing, ordered his men to hold their fire as the North Carolinians approached. "At a distance of 50 yards, a volley was poured into the rebels, which staggered them so completely that a second one was fired before an attempt was made to advance or retreat," he recalled. Wistar now ordered the three companies to attack, routing the Tar Heels in front of them. Both sides lost heavily in this short engagement. Wistar was wounded in the mouth at the end of the charge, forcing him to relinquish command of the brigade to Colonel Edmund Dana of the 143rd Pennsylvania. Confederate artillery opened fire soon after, forcing Lieutenant Colonel Huidekoper to withdraw the right wing back to the relative safety of Chambersburg Pike.[59]

Danger loomed to the west as Heth's Division's long-delayed attack was about to begin at about 3:00 P.M. "With no undue excitement, and in thoroughly good order, the regiment swung back to its original position, facing the west, leaving, however, a large gap between our left and the woods [Herbst], which was impossible to fill," recalled Major Thomas Chamberlin of the 150th Pennsylvania. Thus a gap existed between the right of the Iron Brigade and the left of the 150th Pennsylvania. Brockenbrough's small Virginia brigade approached from the west. Because of the continued pressure being brought to bear by Daniel's men to the north, Dana was unable to shift the rest of his brigade to meet this new threat. For some reason, Brockenbrough's advance was slow and deliberate, giving the Pennsylvanians time to take position behind a fence. Once in position, the 150th Pennsylvania opened a "scathing fire which at once checked the enemy's progress, but failed to scatter or confuse him," recalled Chamberlin. The Virginians returned the fire. Chamberlin likened it to a hailstorm, but the Pennsylvanians held firm. The

enemy suddenly began falling back beyond the woods lining Willoughby Run. The Virginians returned and, at the same time, Daniel's men continued their pressure on the brigade's right.[60]

Many officers fell during the fighting and this, coupled with the constant movement of the units, caused some confusion in the ranks. Many men seemed to have lost connection with their units and joined others. Such was the case of Corporal Sandford Boyden of the 149th Pennsylvania, whose movement may have been intentional. "My brother Alfred and self [sic] here held a council of war and decided to go and help the 150th rather than go into a coop and along with a few of the boys we tendered our services to the Major," wrote Boyden after the war.[61]

Meredith's Iron Brigade on the 150th Pennsylvania's left slowly withdrew, as did Robinson's Division, on the brigade's right. This left Stone's Brigade in a dangerous position, with Confederates converging from all directions. The brigade was finally ordered to withdraw toward the town. Although wounded and unable to talk, Wistar remained with the brigade, and recalled that it stopped periodically to fire into the advancing Confederate soldiers.[62]

For some reason, Lieutenant Colonel Dwight never ordered his color guard to safety after the danger from the shelling had passed. Concerned about their wellbeing, one member of the color guard was sent back to the regiment for orders, but he never returned. The survivors of Davis's Brigade who were not captured at the railroad cut earlier in the day spied the colors as they rested. "The flags in front of us became an interesting topic of conversation," reported Sergeant Frank Price of the 42nd Mississippi. Not able to restrain their desire to make up for the embarrassment to their regiment, a handful of men from the 2nd and 42nd Mississippi cautiously approached the barricade. After a lively hand-to-hand fight, the state flag was captured by one of the Mississippians. Three members of the color guard ran off with the national flag, but eventually lost it to a member of the 55th Virginia of Brockenbrough's Brigade. Dwight merely wrote in his report, "to have saved my colors would have been to advance between two forces of the enemy, both my superiors in numbers, also to have put my command under an enfilade battery fire. It would have been certain surrender or destruction. I saved the regiment and lost the colors." In the excitement and turmoil around him, Dwight probably forgot about colors, and his report was simply a way of rationalizing the loss.[63]

One of the retreating soldiers left an impact on Confederate corps commander, A. P. Hill, that was described by an English visitor. "A Yankee color bearer floated his standard in the field and the regiment fought around it, and when at last it was obliged to retreat, the color bearer retreated last of all, turning around now and then to shake his fist in the face of the advancing Confederates." The color bearer, Sergeant Ben Crippen, was shot, much to the sorrow of Hill, and his heroic deeds are now commemorated on the regiment's monument along Chambersburg Pike.[64]

The brigade finally reached Seminary Ridge at about 3:30 P.M., where it halted and attempted to stem the Confederate tide. To the brigade's left were the remnants of the Iron Brigade and Biddle's Brigade. Baxter's Brigade was to their right, on the other side of a number of I Corps's cannon. The men's ammunition was replenished as they nervously awaited the onslaught of Pender's Division. The 150th Pennsylvania was on the left of the line, the 149th Pennsylvania in the center, and the 143rd Pennsylvania extended across Chambersburg Pike to the north. Lieutenant Colonel Dwight recorded that "we made a desperate stand with the fragments of the brigade, and succeeded in holding the ground against vastly superior numbers." They watched the destruction of Scales's North Carolina Brigade by the batteries on the ridge and by their own small arms fire. With the breakthrough of Perrin's South Carolina Brigade to the left, the Federal batteries limbered up, and Dana gave orders for the men to retreat toward Gettysburg. Because the Confederates were closing in from several sides, the brigade sustained heavy losses.[65]

Many of the men found their way to the town by following the railroad cut; others took an overland route. Many were captured. Once in Gettysburg, the men found the streets clogged with soldiers, wagons, and artillery. Confederates making their way into the town also posed significant problems, and not a few of Stone's men were captured there as well. Those who eluded capture usually escaped by "leaping fences, crossing gardens, or passing through shops and dwellings in order to reach streets to which the pursuing forces had not yet penetrated," wrote the 150th Pennsylvania's historian.[66]

The brigade finally reached Cemetery Hill between 5:00 and 6:00 P.M. Captain James Glenn of the 149th Pennsylvania recalled that the men crossed a cornfield and then climbed Cemetery Hill, where they encountered units of the XI Corps. "We passed through their line over the hill, and completely worn out, dropped down on the grass and rested as best we could." The brigade was positioned near a low stone wall on the southern slope of the cemetery, facing the town. It was here that the men fully realized the magnitude of their losses. The survivors of the 150th

Pennsylvania were horrified when they saw that but a handful of the regiment remained. However, they were later overjoyed to find that another group of soldiers from the regiment was resting nearby. After stragglers arrived, the size of the regiment "swelled" to 109. Private William Wright of the 149th Pennsylvania arrived on the hill with a handful of men from his company and began searching for his unit. Finding Captain Glenn and perhaps a hundred men, "we asked for the regiment and to our surprise the captain said that was what left out of 490." A few days later, the regiment could muster but 113 men, a loss of over 70% in its first taste of battle. The 150th Pennsylvania also mourned another loss—their flag had been captured in the streets of Gettysburg. Despite the clamor around them, most of the men stretched out on the hard ground and fell sound asleep.[67]

July 2 dawned bright and warm, and during the morning the brigade moved a short distance to take position between the cemetery and Taneytown Road. The men of the 149th Pennyvania were issued beef rations, as they had lost their haversacks the day before. The men relaxed while supporting batteries on the hill for most of the day. This changed sometime after 6:00 P.M., when the brigade was formed into line and double-quicked down Taneytown Road to the army's left flank to help support the III and V Corps, which were being savagely attacked by Longstreet's Corps. Arriving near the position of Humphreys's Division, the men were ordered to fix bayonets and prepare to charge. Night fell without orders to charge. Not all of the troops remained there, for the 149th and 150th Pennsylvania were ordered toward Emmitsburg Pike to ascertain the position of the enemy and to recover two abandoned cannons. John Badler of the 149th Pennsylvania wrote

home that "the Rebels have our flag, but we took one cannon from them in return the next day." As they struck the road, gunfire rang out in the darkness, and the men were pulled back to a position between Emmitsburg Road and Taneytown Road, where they remained all night. Private John Nesbit of the 149th Pennsylvania vividly recalled that the men "spent the night, when not on duty, carrying water from the well at the Codori house to the wounded of both armies. It was a long and sleepless night. The cries and moans of the wounded and dying, the close proximity of the rebel pickets . . . kept the boys awake and nervous."[68]

Two Confederate cannon opened on the 150th Pennsylvania at dawn on July 3, killing and wounding several men. The brigade moved north soon after, to a position several hundred yards southeast of the clump of trees that would be the target of Pickett's Division later that day. Despite having the protection of the reverse slope of Cemetery Ridge, the men immediately threw up rudimentary breastworks. Not having tools, they created a barricade of rails and stones. This completed, many of the men finally caught up on their sleep after their long night of picket duty or caring for the wounded. The initial artillery rounds preceding the Pickett–Pettigrew–Trimble charge caught some members of the 149th Pennsylvania out of the breastworks, killing and wounding several of them. The men quickly rushed to the breastworks, but casualties mounted, including minor ones from flying splinters from the breastworks. Captain John Musser of the 149th Pennsylvania described the cannonade as "such a storm of shell and solid shot was never heard before. No place was safe. They passed through the regt. killing and wounding, bursting over us, ploughing through the earth under us. It was our duty to remain where we were."

According to Musser, his regiment lost four killed and twenty-one wounded in the cannonade. Later, some of the men apparently fired at Pickett's men during the charge, but it is doubtful that they had much of an impact.[69]

The brigade moved to Taneytown Road on the morning of July 4, where many received their first rations in several days. Captain John Musser's 143rd Pennsylvania did not receive its rations along with the others, so he ordered some of his men to beg for food from other units. Details were sent out on July 5 to bring in the wounded and collect arms and equipment. As Lee pulled his army back to defensive positions along Seminary Ridge, some of the wounded men who had been hiding began returning to the brigade. Sergeant Charles Frey of the 150th Pennsylvania, who had been on detached duty, returned to the regiment and remarked that "they were a sad set of men." The brigade finally left the battlefield on the morning of July 6.[70]

So ended the baptism of fire for the three Pennsylvania regiments. The men were consumed by a mixture of conflicting emotions. One wrote to a local newspaper after the battle that "our brigade covered itself with glory in this, its first battle; but it is torn to pieces!" Like Biddle's Brigade, Stone's Brigade was ordered to occupy an impossible position. The I Corps was not large enough to cover the area assigned to it, and as a result, both of Stone's flanks hung in the air. Attacked on two sides by units from two Confederate divisions, the men fought well, but were ultimately forced to flee for safety. The 336 casualties/prisoners lost by the 149th Pennsylvania ranks third of all regiments in the entire army, and its loss of 75% ranks seventh.[71]

3rd Brigade—Brigadier General George Stannard

Units: 12th Vermont (detached), 13th Vermont, 14th Vermont, 15th Vermont (detached), 16th Vermont
Strength: 3387 (1950 engaged)
Losses: 351 (45-274-32)—18%[72]

One of the newest units in the Army of the Potomac, Brigadier General George Stannard's inexperienced Vermont brigade slipped away from the defenses of Washington on June 25 and headed north to join Doubleday's Division. These troops were the subject of derision for two reasons. Unlike the typical three-year regiments being recruited at the time, these were only nine-month regiments. When they joined the Army of the Potomac, their blue uniforms looked so new that they were quickly dubbed the "Paper Collar Brigade." Their commander had had considerably more combat experience, serving at First Bull Run and the Peninsula campaign. Captured at Harper's Ferry in September 1862, he was exchanged and returned home to take charge of the newly formed Vermont regiments.[73]

The troops averaged eighteen miles a day during the seven-day march, causing Stannard to proudly state, "considering the condition of the roads, the distance traveled could not have been accomplished in less time." Because it was a nine-month brigade whose term of enlistment had almost expired, the quartermasters were reluctant to issue shoes to the men. As a result, more than a few men developed foot problems during the hard march. Yet the men kept their humor, despite these hardships. For example, Lieutenant Edwin Palmer of the 13th Vermont noted that the men were able to buy cakes "at a fair price." He recalled that the men were fond of saying, "Hardtack has played out, whilst green backs last." Toward the end of the march "not a man [could] hardly drag one blistered, bleeding foot after the other," recollected Palmer.[74]

The brigade received orders on June 30 to guard the I Corps's wagon train. As a result, it avoided the blood bath that all of the other I Corps brigades sustained on July 1. At about 9:00 A.M. on that day, Stannard received orders to leave two regiments to guard the train and to march with the rest of his men toward Gettysburg. The men could hear the sounds of battle at about 3:00 P.M. that afternoon, and later, as the men approached the battlefield, they passed fleeing civilians. This caused a change in the demeanor of the inexperienced troops. Palmer observed "little talking, no straggling, each man with a sober, determined look," as the men marched along Emmitsburg Road. Finally arriving at the battlefield at 5:00 P.M. on Emmitsburg Road, there was considerable confusion as to where the brigade was to take position. As a result, several changes of position were made and "General Stannard swore like a piper . . . because so much moving about when their boys were all tired out from the long day's hard march and wanted to rest," recalled Private Ralph Sturtevant of the 13th Vermont. Stannard was in no mood for this incompetence, especially because his inexperienced troops had just completed a 150-mile march in seven days. The brigade finally took position on the south end of Cemetery Hill, in a Wheatfield on its west slope, behind the I and XI Corps. Because the 12th Vermont and 15th Vermont had been detached to guard the wagon trains, the brigade was only at three-fifths strength, but this was still larger than most of the veteran brigades. The 15th Vermont returned the following day, but its stay on the battlefield was short, as it was ordered back to guard duty at noon. The men settled in by 8:00 P.M. that night. All around them they could see the broken condition of their comrades who had fought that day. No one doubted that they would receive their baptism of fire the following day.[75]

The morning and early afternoon of July 2 were fairly quiet. Most of the men received rations, except for the 13th Vermont, which had to scrounge for food and wound up making coffee with muddy water. During the morning hours, Captain John Tidball, who had been attached to General Hunt's staff, rode by Stannard's men and thought that "they were a fine body of men, and were drawn up in close column by division, ready to go to any part of the field at a moment's notice." After inquiring about their identity, Tidball rode away. Soon after this exchange, half of the 13th Vermont was detached and sent to support a battery on the crest of the hill; the other half was moved south and formed behind the II Corps. Regimental commander, Colonel Francis Randall, insisted that "I received no further orders from our brigade headquarters during the remainder of that day." Stannard's men were exposed to their first shelling when the Confederate artillery opened fire on the batteries on Cemetery Hill. Within fifteen minutes, some of the men of the XI Corps broke for the rear, and Randall yelled after them, "See these boys, they don't run and they were never in a battle; you ought to be ashamed to run." Although they didn't run, the Green Mountain boys were clearly unnerved by the cannon fire, causing General Doubleday to ride up to them and say, "Boys, you will fight—won't you? The honor of your State is in your hands."[76]

Disaster loomed for the Union army as Lee's attack rolled toward the II Corps's position on Cemetery Ridge. Earlier, Caldwell's Division had been pulled from its position on the ridge, leaving a yawning gap. At about 6:30 P.M., several Confederate brigades aimed for this vulnerable position. Casting about for reinforcements, General Meade asked about the whereabouts of the VI Corps. Captain Tidball instantly replied, "I do not know, but if you need troops, I saw a fine body of Vermonters a short distance from here, belonging to the First Corps, who are available." About 6:30 P.M., Colonel Randall spied an officer galloping toward him, who proved to be General Doubleday. "After having found what regiment we were, and making a few inspiriting remarks to my men, he directed me to take my regiment in the direction from which he had come, and report to General Hancock," recalled Randall. Doubleday further remarked that Hancock's II Corps was being hard pressed and was in danger of losing most of its artillery. Rushing his men forward under a storm of shot and shell, Randall led the five companies of his regiment not supporting the battery on Cemetery Hill to their prescribed position. As they hurried along, they were carefully watched by Meade and his staff, who were probably relieved to see the 350 men in close formation double-quicking toward the breach in the line. Finding Hancock, Randall was told that the "rebels had captured a battery he had had there, and pointed out to me the way they had gone with it, and asked me if I could retake it." Randall recalled saying to the general, "I thought I could, and that I was willing to try." Hancock cautioned that "it would be a hazardous job, and he would not order it." Hancock would not, how-

ever, stop him "if I thought I could do it, I might try."[77]

Randall's five companies arrived during this exchange, and some of the men strained to hear the conversation. While Hancock anxiously watched, Randall deployed his men from "column by division" to "deployment in line." Randall next gathered his companies' commanders together and hastily told them what to expect. Then, taking his position in front of the five companies, he gave the order to advance. Randall's horse was hit almost immediately and both fell, with the horse landing atop its rider. While lying there, Randall could see the 22nd Georgia of Wright's Confederate Brigade (Anderson's Division, III Corps) moving toward the crest of the Cemetery Ridge, not more than 250 yards in front of him. Randall was more than annoyed that most of the men were more interested in helping him than they were in facing the enemy. He yelled at them, "Go on boys, go on. I'll be at your head as soon as I get out of this damn saddle." The men complied while Randall tried to free himself. Yelling, "On, boys, on," the now-extricated Randall ran down the slope after his men. Palmer summarized the charge by writing that "they now charge down the sloping hill, over the dead and dying, shouting, firing into the foe . . . it seemed but a moment till the rebel lines were breaking all along and flying back in dismay."[78]

The Georgians were surprised to see this line of blue materialize out of nowhere, and immediately fired a volley at it. They were so unnerved that they did not take time to aim. The volley was therefore ineffectual. Suddenly, Randall's men charged, and many of Wright's men either surrendered or made their way back toward Seminary Ridge. The inexperienced Vermonters did not know what to do next: round up the enemy, or counterattack and retake Weir's battery, which had been captured by the enemy. Hancock rode up at about this time, and yelled out to Randall to press on for the guns, and he would take care of the prisoners. Driving forward, they retook Weir's four captured cannon. Looking behind them, the victorious battalion could see the remaining units of the brigade rapidly approaching to provide support. Upon returning to Cemetery Ridge, Colonel Randall was met by General Hancock, who exclaimed, "That was well done! Give me Vermonters for a charge." Most of the men did not know it, but their officers had disobeyed a directive of General John Newton, now commander of their corps, to break off the charge as they ran toward Emmitsburg Road. Stannard had been in the dark about the whereabouts of Randall's Battalion. He recorded in his journal that he was "much annoyed at not knowing where [Randall] was, and sent every way to find him." However, given the exuberance of the moment, the officers were absolved of any wrongdoing.[79]

The men settled down to rest that night in the gap created when Caldwell's Division's moved south to the Wheatfield. Some commotion was caused that evening when mortally wounded General William Barksdale, commander of a Mississippi brigade, was carried by the unit on his way to a field hospital. The night was not an easy one for the pickets of the 16th Vermont, which occupied the no-man's-land between the two armies. According to Colonel Wheeler Veazey, "the mingled impre[c]ations & prayers & groans of the wounded and supplications for help, were literally heart rending . . . I saw scores of wounded men die in the gloom and darkness."[80]

On July 3, the men took refuge from the energetic enemy sharpshooters by lying behind a low stone wall. According

to Benedict, the 13th Vermont was on the left and to the rear of the 14th Vermont. Later in the day, the 14th Vermont received permission to move forward to a more protected area in Plum Run Valley. Seeing his sister regiment change its position, Colonel Randall asked that his 13th Vermont also be permitted to make the same movement, and was granted permission to do so. The men immediately began strengthening their positions with fence rails and loose stones. The 16th Vermont was even farther forward, where some of the men were on the skirmish line.[81]

Hancock was a dominant presence during this period. Whether he was concerned about the men's inexperience or just believed that this was an important part of the line is not known. However, Colonel Randall remembered Hancock "repeatedly coming to me and giving us the benefit of his advice and encouragement, and offered us supports."[82]

The cannonade that proceeded the Pickett–Pettigrew–Trimble charge began shortly after 1:00 P.M. "Shells whizzed and popped and fluttered on every side; spherical case shot exploded over our heads, and rained iron bullets upon us; solid shot tore the ground around us, and grape hurtled in an iron storm against the low breastworks," recalled Benedict (12th Vermont). What amazed their officers even more was the number of men who actually fell asleep as a result of their toils and sleepless nights on the battlefield. Losses were fairly high during the cannonade—the 14th Vermont lost about sixty men. The brigade occupied an advanced frontline position at the start of the charge. No troops were positioned on the left; Harrow's Brigade was on its right. The 13th Vermont's right connected with the Biddle's men, and the 14th Vermont was to its left, and somewhat advanced. The 16th Vermont, except for its skirmishers, was stationed behind the 14th Vermont.[83]

Stannard's men could see that they would be a target of the attack as Kemper's Brigade (Pickett's Division, I Corps) emerged from the direction of Seminary Ridge. Benedict recalled that the sight brought "every man's arms into his hands, and many a man's heart to his mouth." The officers took pains to reassure the men. "Steady, boys! Hold your positions; don't fire till the word is given; keep cool lie low until the order is given to fire" could be heard along the line. The men were ordered to hold their fire until Kemper's men got closer. Finally, orders rang out for the men to "Fire, Fire!" and both forward regiments responded with a volley. Colonel Randall boasted that this volley "seemed to level their front rank and all mounted officers." When the Confederates had reached the midway point, they began to oblique to their left, probably to the relief of many a Vermonter. Stannard proudly stated that the enemy made this change because of the "firm front shown them." In actuality, the maneuver was made to close the gap between the left of Pickett's Division and the right of Pettigrew's.[84]

Seeing Kemper's right flank hanging in the air, Stannard decided upon a bold move. He ordered the 13th Vermont forward into the meadow, marched a few rods to the right, and then "changed front forward on the first company," causing his men to form perpendicularly, one after the other, on the enemy's flank. Orderly Sergeant James Scully had the distinction of being the "pivot of the pivotal movement of the pivotal battle of the war." The Confederates could easily see this maneuver. Captain Henry Owen of Garnett's Brigade (Pickett's Division) recalled seeing a mass of men rushing toward them wearing uniforms that almost looked

black in color and carrying gleaming bayonets. He instinctively knew that it was a race as to whether the Confederate troops would reach the stone wall on Cemetery Ridge first, or Stannard's men would destroy their flank first. The Confederates were taking no chances, and they poured a deadly fire into the 13th Vermont as it rushed forward. This unnerved the inexperienced men who were charging in an open plain. The line wavered, but the officers were able to calm the men, and they continued on.[85]

The 16th Vermont was ordered to form on the 13th Vermont's left flank. This maneuver was more difficult because the 16th Vermont had to first move around the flank of the 14th Vermont before it could begin its movement into the meadow. Colonel Veazey recalled that Kemper's men at this point were "in great masses, without much order, and were rushing rapidly upon the lines to our right [on Cemetery Ridge], and regardless of the exposure of their right flank." The two Vermont regiments opened fire, and because Kemper's men were so close, the results were devastating. Colonel Randall called this fire "the most withering fires I had ever beheld." Veazey recalled that "those great masses of men seemed to disappear in a moment . . . the ground over which we passed after striking their flank was literally covered with dead and wounded men." Seeing the flank attack, many of Kemper's men immediately threw down their arms in surrender. A Confederate officer saw the danger and was in the process of ordering his men to change position to face it when he was struck down by the Vermont marksmen. One Confederate veteran distinctly recalled seeing Stannard's men on the flank and immediately informed his captain. The reply was, "We had nothing to do with that . . . those in the rear would attend to them." Yelling "forward," the captain bolted ahead, but almost immediately, the soldier who observed the flank movement felt a gun against his head and a voice with a New England accent saying, "Wall naouw, I guess you won't go any farther in that direction." The Confederate officer immediately complied. While the 13th and 16th Vermont were in the meadow, the 14th Vermont held its position along the main Federal defensive line on Cemetery Ridge and poured an enfilading fire into the Confederate ranks. One of its victims may have been General Kemper. According to Colonel Veazey, the 13th Vermont was at a 45 degree angle to the 14th Vermont during the charge.[86]

As Kemper's men broke for the rear, the officers of the 13th Vermont told their men not to fire at the retreating foe. Lieutenant Stephen Brown of the 13th Vermont was especially happy when he happened upon an enemy officer trudging to the rear as a prisoner. Arrested earlier in the march for trying to procure water for his men, Brown was released in time for the battle, but was not able to regain his sword. Instead, he used a camp hatchet, which he swung over his head like a sword. The captured officer was only too happy to relinquish his sword when Brown raised the hatchet over his head.[87]

The men were absolutely incredulous when they realized that yet another, but smaller force was bearing down on their rear. These were Wilcox's and Lang's Brigades (Anderson's Division, III Corps), who had been ordered to protect Pickett's right flank and prevent the movement successfully undertaken by Stannard's men. Too late to provide this protection, they marched rapidly forward anyway. Colonel Veazey of the 16th Vermont ordered his disorganized men to "fall in" and marched them in the direction of this new threat. Orders soon arrived from

General Stannard to "double-quick back to our original position and get in front of this new line," recalled Colonel Veazey. The men were ordered to "face obliquely towards the left flank" of the enemy, and, rushing forward without firing a shot, approach the enemy, who had taken temporary shelter behind some low bushes and rocks along Plum Run south of the Codori house. The 13th Vermont again changed direction to follow its sister regiment, but General Stannard ordered it back to Cemetery Ridge, and instead ordered four companies of the 14th Vermont to provide support. Attacking the Confederate flank, Veazey's men "followed it until the whole line had disappeared." Again, the 14th Vermont opened fire from its protected position on Cemetery Ridge, while the 16th Vermont hit the Confederates' flank. The attack was so sudden that the Confederate line could not be shifted to meet it. The result was the same as with Kemper's Brigade—the Confederate attack was quickly broken with heavy losses inflicted. The heaviest losses were sustained by the 2nd Florida on the left of Lang's Brigade's line, which also lost its battle flag. So stunned were the Confederates that they willingly wandered to the Union rear without guards. Stannard's men simply told them "where to go and they went." Colonel David Lang merely wrote in his report, "the enemy paid his undivided attention to us, and our safety from utter annihilation was in retreat." Colonel Veazey was rewarded with a Congressional Medal of Honor for his actions.[88]

Watching the Vermonters' heroics, General Doubleday waved his hat and shouted, "Glory to God, Glory to God! See the Vermonters go it!" After the repulse, the three regiments were moved somewhat to the right, where the 16th Vermont was positioned to the left of the 13th Vermont. The men were almost immediately hit by a hail of Confederate artillery fire, causing them to seek shelter. After the barrage ended, the men lay down on their rubber blankets for a rest, as they did not expect to be relieved any time soon. However, they were relieved at about 9:00 P.M. and ordered to the rear, halting near Taneytown Road. The men were saddened to hear that their source of continual encouragement during the battle, General Hancock, had been wounded near the 14th Vermont during the charge. Stannard also was wounded during the latter part of the repulse. July 4 and 5 were spent resting and burying the dead, and on July 6, the men received the welcome orders to prepare to leave the battlefield for the march after Lee's army.[89]

Although green troops, Stannard's men performed magnificently during the battle. The 13th Vermont arrived at a critical time on July 2 to help seal the breach on Cemetery Ridge and deny Wright's Brigade a victory. Stannard's Brigade's movement on Kemper's Brigade's flank helped destroy the Virginia unit, and was instrumental in blunting the overall attack. With the men's terms of enlistment expired, the brigade was disbanded soon after the battle.

NOTES

1. Dyer, *Compendium*, 286–287.
2. Tagg, *Generals of Gettysburg*, 26.
3. OR 27, 1, 12, 316.
4. OR 27, 1, 312.
5. D. Scott Hartwig, "The Defense of McPherson's Ridge," *Gettysburg Magazine* (July 1989), issue 1, 17–24.
6. OR 27, 1, 313.
7. George G. Benedict, *Army Life In Virginia* (Burlington, VT, 1882), 165; Lance J. Herdegen, "The Lieutenant Who Arrested a General," *Gettysburg Magazine* (January 1991), issue 4, 29–30.
8. OR 27, 1, 258, 316; Jacob Slagle, letter, 149th Pennsylvania file, GNMP.
9. OR 27, 1, 258–260; Bradley M. Gottfried, "Wright's Charge on July 2, 1863: Piercing the Union Line or Inflated Glory?" *Gettysburg Magazine* (July 1997), issue 17, 77, 79.
10. Busey and Martin, *Regimental Strengths and Losses at Gettysburg*, 27, 240.
11. Dyer, *Compendium*, 286; Tagg, *Generals of Gettysburg*, 27–28.
12. Hartwig, "The Defense of McPherson's Ridge," 17; OR 27, 1, 317.
13. John Cook, "Personal Reminisces of Gettysburg," in *Kansas MOLLUS*, 324–325.
14. Seward R. Osborne, *Holding the Left at Gettysburg: The 20th New York Militia on July 1, 1863* (Hightstown, NJ, 1990), 5–6; OR 27, 1, 326–327.
15. OR 27, 1, 320; Theodore B. Gates, *"Ulster Guard" and the War of the Rebellion* (New York, 1879), 433; James W. Downy, *Lethal Tour of Duty: A History of the 142nd Pennsylvania Volunteer Infantry* (M.A. thesis, Indiana University of Pennsylvania, 1995), 26; *History of the 121st Pennsylvania* (Philadelphia, 1893), 44; Cook, "Personal Reminisces of Gettysburg," 325.
16. OR 27, 1, 317, 327; *Supplement to the Official Records of the Union and Confederate Armies* (Wilmington, NC, 1994), vol. 5, 150; Osborne, *Holding the Left at Gettysburg*, 7; Theodore B. Gates to John Bachelder, January 30, 1864, in Bachelder Papers, New Hampshire Historical Society; *History of the 121st Pennsylvania*, 45.
17. Theodore B. Gates to John Bachelder, January 30, 1864; OR 27, 1, 315.
18. OR 27, 1, 327.
19. OR, 27, 1, 318, 320.

According to a report later filed by Colonel Gates of the 80th New York (OR 27, 1, 320), the brigade was formed into two lines in the roadway. Gates commanded the second line and Colonel Biddle commanded the first. There is, however, no other account that confirms this odd disposition, as three regiments were involved.
20. OR suppl., 5, 151.
21. *PAG*, 2, 661; Kevin E. O'Brien, "'Give Them Another Volley, Boys': Biddle's

Brigade Defends the Union Left on July 1, 1863," *Gettysburg Magazine* (July 1998), issue 19, 43; OR 27, 1, 323; Frank Sterling, letter, State University of New Jersey, Rutgers Special Collections and Archives; *History of the 121st Pennsylvania,* 45–46, 48.

22. Jacob Hardenburgh, letter, New York Historical Society; Gates, *The "Ulster Guard,"* 442; Cook, "Personal Reminisces of Gettysburg," 326.

23. Edwin R. Gearheart, "Account," *Daily Times,* March 19, 1900—August 6, 1990, copy in the GNMP Library; Horatio N. Warren, *Two Reunions of the 142nd Regiment, Pennsylvania Volunteers* (Buffalo, 1890), 22.

24. Downey, *Lethal Tour,* 28, 31; Horatio N. Warren, *The Declaration of Independence and War History, Bull Run to Appomattox* (Buffalo, 1894), 30; Gearhart, "Account"; Walter Clark, *Histories of the Several Regiments and Battalions from North Carolina in the Great War 1861–65* (Wilmington, NC, 1996), vol. 3, 90; Hartwig, "The Defense of McPherson's Ridge," 25; Bates, *Pennsylvania Volunteers,* VII, 466.

Colonel Robert Cummins died the following day, July 2, 1863.

25. OR suppl., 5, 151; 121st *Pennsylvania,* 48; J. Frank Sterling, letter.

Although Sterling sustained what he thought was a minor leg wound, he was dead in three months (Pfanz, *Gettysburg— The First Day,* 291).

26. OR 27, 1, 327–328; "Movements of the 151st Penn. Vols. Of Biddle's Brigade," in Bachelder Papers, New Hampshire Historical Society; "Report of Movements of 151st Pennsylvania," in Bachelder Papers, New Hampshire Historical Society.

27. O'Brien, "Give Them Another Volley, Boys," 49; *History of the 121th Pennsylvania,* 49; Gates, *Ulster Guard,* 443; Osborne, *Holding the Left at Gettysburg,* 15; Daniel A. Tompkins, *Company K, Fourtheenth South Carolina Volunteers* (Charlotte, NC, 1897), 19–20; Abner Perrin, letter, copy in GNMP Library; "Report of Movements of 151st Pennsylvania."

Colonel Chapman Biddle never fully recovered from the effects of this wound, and resigned from the army on December 10, 1863.

28. OR 27, 1, 321, 323.

29. OR 27, 1, 318, 328.

30. Gates, *Ulster Guard,* 444; OR suppl., 5, 152; OR 27, 1, 315; "Report of Movements of 151st Pennsylvania"; Cook, "Personal Reminisces of Gettysburg," 330; Bates, *Pennsylvania Volunteers,* vol. 7, 32.

31. OR 27, 1, 316, 321, 325; Cook, "Personal Reminisces of Gettysburg," 331; Walter L. Owens to John Bachelder, August 6, 1866, in Bachelder Papers, New Hampshire Historical Society.

Confusion exists over whether the entire brigade was ordered south. None of the official reports of the 121st Pennsylvania or 142nd Pennsylvania mention this movement, and Captain Cook of the 80th New York indicated that only the 80th New York and 151st Pennsylvania were ordered south. However, Captain Walter Owens, commanding the latter regiment, and Colonel Gates suggest that the entire brigade moved south. They indicated that the two regiments operated independently of the brigade, when, according to Owens, "a portion of the troops engaged in the fight returned, and passed through our brigade separating the 20th New York and 151st Penn. Regts. from the bal [sic] of the brigade. Instead of following Gen. Rowley, we marched by a right file to the top of a hill" (Walter L. Owens to John Bachelder, August 6, 1866).

32. Downey, *Lethal Tour,* 33–35; Bates, *Pennsylvania Volunteers,* VII, 33; OR 27, 1, 316, 325–326.

33. Cook, "Personal Reminisces of Gettysburg," 332–333.

34. Hardenburgh, letter.

35. Hardenburgh, letter; Cook, "Personal Reminisces of Gettysburg," 334; OR 27, 1, 319; Walter L. Owens to John Bachelder, August 6, 1866.

36. Bates, *Pennsylvania Volunteers,* VII, 680; Cook, "Personal Reminisces of Gettysburg," 334–335; Walter L. Owens to John Bachelder, August 6, 1866; OR 27, 1, 319, 322.

37. OR 27, 1, 260, 322; George R. Stewart, *Pickett's Charge* (Boston, 1959), 173, 262; Cook, "Personal Reminisces of Gettysburg," 338–339; Bates, *Pennsylvania Volunteers,* VIII, 681.

38. Bates, *Pennsylvania Volunteers,* VIII, 681.

39. Busey and Martin, *Regimental Strengths and Losses,* 28, 241.

40. Thomas Chamberlin, *History of the One Hundred and Fiftieth Regiment Pennsylvania Volunteers* (Philadelphia, 1895), 115; Avery Harris, journal, USAMHI.

41. Tagg, *Generals of Gettysburg,* 28–29.

42. William Perry, diary, USAMHI; *PAG,* vol. 2, 745; Chamberlin, *History of the One Hundred and Fiftieth Regiment Pennsylvania Volunteers,* 115.

43. Chamberlain, *History of the One Hundred and Fiftieth Regiment Pennsylvania Volunteers,* 117–118; *PAG,* vol. 2, 745; OR 27, 1, 331, 332; Richard E. Matthews, *The 149th Pennsylvania Volunteer Infantry in the Civil War* (Jefferson, NC, 1994), 78–79.

While several soldiers recalled the children on the horse, their stories were usually at odds with each other. For example, Captain John Bassler recalled that the children were not crying, but were "anxious and bewildered."

44. Chamberlin, *History of the One Hundred and Fiftieth Regiment Pennsylvania Volunteers,* 118; Matthews, *The 149th Pennsylvania Volunteer Infantry in the Civil War,* 78; OR 27, 1, 334–335; *PAG,* vol. 2, 745.

45. Chamberlin, *History of the One Hundred and Fiftieth Regiment Pennsylvania Volunteers,* 119; OR 27, 1, 332.

46. Chamberlin, *History of the One Hundred and Fiftieth Regiment Pennsylvania Volunteers,* 119; OR 27, 1, 329.

47. Chamberlin, *History of the One Hundred and Fiftieth Regiment Pennsylvania Volunteers,* 120–122.

48. "Chronicles of Francis Bacon Jones," USAMHI.

49. Chamberlin, *History of the One Hundred and Fiftieth Regiment Pennsylvania Volunteers,* 122; Matthews, *The 149th Pennsylvania Volunteer Infantry in the Civil War,* 80; OR 27, 1, 329; William Ramsey to John Bachelder, April 16, 1883, in Bachelder Papers, New Hampshire Historical Society.

50. Matthews, *The 149th Pennsylvania Volunteer Infantry in the Civil War,* 82–83.

51. Matthews, *The 149th Pennsylvania Volunteer Infantry in the Civil War,* 84.

52. Hartwig, "The Defense of McPherson's Ridge," 20; OR 27, 1, 247, 335; Doubleday, *Chancellorsville and Gettysburg,* 139–140.

53. OR 27, 1, 330, 341; Matthews, *The 149th Pennsylvania Volunteer Infantry in the Civil War,* 86.

54. Hartwig, "The Defense of McPherson's Ridge," 20; Chronicles of Francis Jones; Clark, *N.C. Regiments.,* vol. 4, 255.

55. OR 27, 1, 342; Matthews, *The 149th Pennsylvania Volunteer Infantry in the Civil War,* 87; Harris, journal.

56. OR 27, 1, 342; Frances Bacon, "Chronicles."

57. John H. Bassler to John Bachelder, February 1882, in Bachelder Papers, New Hampshire Historical Society; John Musser, letter, USAMHI; William Ramsey to John Bachelder, April 16, 1883; "Memoranda of Lt. Col. Huidekoper Concerning the 150th Regt. PA," in Bachelder Papers, New Hampshire Historical Society.

58. John H. Bassler to John Bachelder, February 1882; Harris, journal; OR 27, 1, 343.

59. OR 27, 1, 332, 346; *PAG,* vol. 2, 748–749; John Kensill to John Bachelder, February 14, 1882, in Bachelder Papers, New Hampshire Historical Society; Chamberlin, *History of the One Hundred and Fiftieth Regiment Pennsylvania Volunteers,*125–126; John F. Krumwiede, "A July Afternoon on McPherson's Ridge," *Gettysburg Magazine* (July 1999), issue 21, 34–37.

60. *PAG,* vol. 2, 749–750; Krumwiede, "A July Afternoon on McPherson's Ridge," 37; "Memoranda of Lt. Col. Huidekoper Concerning the 150th Regt. PA."

61. Sanford Boyden, letter, copy in the 149th Pennsylvania file, GNMP.

62. OR 27, 1, 333.

63. Frank Price to John Bachelder, January 27, 1878, in Bachelder Papers, New Hampshire Historical Society; J. H. Bassler, "The Color Episode of the One Hundred and Forty-ninth Regiment, Pennsylvania Volunteers," in *Southern Historical Society Papers* (1909), vol. 37, 272–300; Franklin Lehman to John Bachelder, September 29, 1881, in Bachelder Papers, New Hampshire Historical Society Account; OR 27, 1, 342.

Curiously, several members of the 150th Pennsylvania recalled, and Lieutenant Colonel Henry Huidekoper stated in his official report (OR 27, 1, 346), that their regiment recaptured the lost standards and returned them to the regiment. This was not the case, and may have been the 150th Pennsylvania's way of deflecting attention from the loss of its own flag.

64. *PAG*, vol. 1, 696; Bates, *Pennsylvania Volunteers*, VII, 488–489.

It is interesting to note that the historian of the 150th Pennsylvania, believed that Hill was referring to his regiment's standard bearer, who was also acting heroically (*PAG*, vol. 2, 751).

65. OR 27, 1, 333, 336, 343; Chamberlin, *History of the One Hundred and Fiftieth Regiment Pennsylvania Volunteers*,132, 134; Matthews, *The 149th Pennsylvania Volunteer Infantry in the Civil War,* 95.

Several veterans recalled that the artillery officers begged the brigade to halt on Seminary Ridge to buy time for the guns to be removed. However, Wistar's report clearly states that the brigade was ordered to halt on Seminary Ridge and engage the approaching enemy.

66. *PAG*, vol. 2, 753.

67. OR 27, 1, 336; *PAG*, vol. 2, 740–741, 754; Matthews, *The 149th Pennsylvania Volunteer Infantry in the Civil War,* 97–98; Chamberlin, *History of the One Hundred and Fiftieth Regiment Pennsylvania Volunteers,* 137.

This stand of colors was purportedly sent south to Governor Vance of North Carolina, who presented it to President Jefferson Davis (Chamberlin, *History of the One Hundred and Fiftieth Regiment Pennsylvania Volunteers,* 139).

68. OR 27, 1, 333, 348; *PAG*, vol. 2, 741, 754–755; John Badler, letter, copy in 149th Pennsylvania file, GNMP; Matthews, *The 149th Volunteer Infantry in the Civil War,* 98; Slagle, letter; William Ramsey to John Bachelder, April 16, 1883.

69. Matthews, *The 149th Pennsylvania Volunteer Infantry in the Civil War,* 98–99; OR 27, 1, 333, 340; John Musser, letter, copy in 143rd Pennsylvania file, GNMP; Chamber-

lin, *History of the One Hundred and Fiftieth Regiment Pennsylvania Volunteers,*150–151.

70. Matthews, *The 149th Pennsylvania Volunteer Infantry in the Civil War,* 99; Chamberlin, *History of the One Hundred and Fiftieth Regiment Pennsylvania Volunteers,* 153, 154; Musser, letter; OR 27, 1, 337.

71. Matthews, *The 149th Pennsylvania Volunteer Infantry in the Civil War,* 101; Busey and Martin, *Regimental Strengths and Losses,* 262, 263.

72. Busey and Martin, *Regimental Strengths and Losses,* 29, 241.

Only three regiments of the brigade, or 1950 men actually fought; the two other brigades were detached to guard wagon trains.

73. Christopher C. Dickson, "The Flying Brigade: Brig. Gen. George Stannard and the Road to Gettysburg," *Gettysburg Magazine* (January 1997), issue 16, 5–8.

74. OR 27, 1, 348; Edwin F. Palmer, *The Second Brigade or Camp Life* (Montpelier, VT, 1864), 174–175; Christopher C. Dickson, "Col. Francis Voltaire Randall and the 13thVermont Infantry," *Gettysburg Magazine* (July 1997), issue 17, 83.

75. OR 27, 1, 349, 351; "Second Vermont Brigade—Brig. Ben. Geo. J. Stannard, commanding—Extra from General Stannard's diary," in Bachelder Papers, New Hampshire Historical Society; Palmer, *The Second Brigade or Camp Life,* 176; "An Account of the Reunion of the 14th Regiment Vermont Volunteers," copy in 14th Vermont file, GNMP; Ralph O. Sturtevant, *Pictorial History of the Thirteenth Vermont Volunteers* (n.p., 1910), 243–244, 253; Henry Stevens Willey, "The Story of My Experiences During the Civil War," Library of Congress; John C. Williams, *Life In Camp: A History of the Nine Months' Service of the Fourteenth Vermont Regiment* (Claremont, NH, 1864), 138.

The 12th Vermont was detached at Emmitsburg to guard the I Corps's train. According to Quartermaster A. P. Blunt, Sickles ordered him to take the trains south to Westminster with all dispatch as Stuart's cavalry was in the area. It was later ordered to march 2765 prisoners to Ft. McHenry

(National Archives, RG 94, War Records, vol. 27, boxes 48–52).

General Stannard wrote in his official report (OR 27, 1, 349) that his brigade did not join the I Corps on Cemetery Hill until the morning of July 2. This disagrees with Colonel Francis Randall's report (13th Vermont; OR 27, 1, 351) and all of the subsequent first-person accounts.

76. Sturtevant, *Pictorial History of the 13th Vermont Volunteers*, 245; Doubleday, *Chancellorsville and Gettysburg*, 177; OR 27, 1, 351; Palmer, *The Second Brigade or Camp Life*, 186–187.

77. OR 27, 1, 351–352; Doubleday, *Chancellorsville and Gettysburg*, 177; Williams, *Life In Camp: A History of the Nine Months' Service of the Fourteenth Vermont Regiment*, 141–142.

78. OR 27, 1, 352; Palmer, *The Second Brigade or Camp Life*, 196; Sturtevant, *Pictorial History of the 13th Vermont*, 488, 499, 559–560.

79. OR 27, 1, 352; Sturtevant, *Pictorial History of the 13th Vermont*, 488; Dickson, "Col. Francis Voltaire Randall and the 13th Vermont Infantry," 96; "Second Vermont Brigade—Brig. Ben. Geo. J. Stannard, commanding—Extra from General Stannard's diary."

80. Sturtevant, *Pictorial History of the 13th Vermont*, 283, 289; Wheelock Veazey, letter, copy in the 16th Vermont file, GNMP.

81. Benedict, *Army Life In Virginia: Letters from the Twelfth Vermont Regiment*, 173; *An Account of the Reunion*, 11; OR 27, 1, 352.

82. OR 27, 1, 352–353.

83. Benedict, *Vermont at Gettysburg* (Burlington, VT, 1886–88), 12–13; Veazey, letter; George Benedict to John Bachelder, December 24, 1863, in Bachelder Papers, New Hampshire Historical Society; Wheelock Veazey to John Bachelder, December, 1863, in Bachelder Papers, New Hampshire Historical Society; Hess, *Pickett's Charge* (Chapel Hill, 2001), 90.

84. Benedict, *Army Life In Virginia*, 177; Stewart, *Pickett's Charge*, 200; Palmer, *The Second Brigade or Camp Life*, 195; OR 27, 1, 349, 353.

85. OR 27, 1, 350; Stewart, *Pickett's Charge*, 232; Richard Rollins, *Pickett's Charge—Eyewitness Accounts* (Redondo Beach, CA, 1994), 175.

86. Veazey, letter; George G. Benedict, *A Short History of the Fourteenth Regiment, Vermont Volunteers* (Bennington, VT, 1887), 11, 37; Wheelock Veazey to John Bachelder, December 1863.

Colonel Francis Randall gives a different account, suggesting that he ordered his men forward—a move that was encouraged by General Doubleday, who "assured me that my movement would be a success" (OR 27, 1, 353).

According to Colonel Veazey, both regiments were, "facing obliquely to the right and facing the flank of the enemy" (Wheelock Veazey letter). Veazey also took issue with the 13th Vermont's assertion that they charged before the 16th Vermont joined them. "The 13th did not move a step forward before the 16th joined on the left of the 13th," he wrote (Wheelock Veazey to John Bachelder, December 1863).

87. Benedict, *Vermont in the Civil War*, vol. 2, 476; Sturtevant, *Pictorial History of the 13th Vermont*, 309.

88. OR 27, 1, 350; Clement A. Evans, *Confederate Military History—Texas and Florida* (n.p., n.d.), vol. 11, 152; Hess, *Pickett's Charge*, 300–301.

89. Stewart, *Pickett's Charge*, 233; George Benedict George Benedict to John Bachelder, December 24, 1863; Veazey, letter; Palmer, *The Second Brigade or Camp Life*, 198–199, 201–205; Sturtevant, *Pictorial History of the 13th Vermont*, 321; Winfield Hancock to John Bachelder, November 20, 1883, in Bachelder Papers, New Hampshire Historical Society; Tony L. Trimble, "Paper Collars: Stannard's Brigade at Gettysburg," *Gettysburg Magazine* (January 1989), issue 2, 77.

II CORPS—
Major General Winfield Hancock

The II Corps had a long and distinguished career in the Army of the Potomac. Created on March 3, 1862, the corps had performed admirably during the Peninsula campaign, the Seven Days campaign, Antietam campaign, and Fredericksburg, and had become one of the army's most dependable fighting units. Its commanding officer, Major General Darius Couch, resigned on May 22, 1863, because he could no longer stomach the army's commander, Joe Hooker. This opened the door for 1st Division commander General Winfield Hancock to assume command of the corps the same day.[1]

Every inch a soldier, General Hancock had a distinguished career that matched his new command's. His actions at Williamsburg during the Peninsula campaign brought him initial fame. He led a division at Antietam and Fredericksburg and helped save the beleaguered VI Corps at Chancellorsville. One of the most respected men in the army, he was a natural to lead the II Corps.[2]

The II Corps began breaking camp near Falmouth, Virginia, on June 14 and marched to the Stafford courthouse. During this leg of the journey, the II Corps formed the rear guard of the army. The march on June 15 ended at Aquia Creek. It began again at 6:00 A.M. the following day, and continued until about 2:00 P.M., when the column halted a short distance beyond the Occoquan River. The hot weather caused severe straggling. Arriving at Sangster's Station on June 17, the men were permitted to rest until the afternoon of June 19. Some units were detached to guard Thoroughfare Gap for a few days, where they skirmished with Jeb Stuart's cavalry.[3]

The corps crossed the Potomac River on the evening of June 26. Heavy rains fell, making the men miserable. They remained on the Maryland side of the river until 3:00 P.M. on June 27, when the march continued. The column reached Frederick, Maryland, the following day. It left at 8:00 A.M. on June 29 and undertook a forced march of over thirty miles. The ordeal finally ended at about 10:00 P.M. that night. Camped outside Uniontown, the men were excited when they were permitted to rest the next day. The march continued during the early morning hours of July 1. While his men went into bivouac at about 11:00 A.M., Hancock rode over to confer with General Meade.[4]

Hancock received orders at 1:00 P.M. to ride to Gettysburg to assume command of the army's left wing, composed of the I, III, and XI Corps, as General Reynolds had been killed. Turning the corps over to General John Gibbon of the 2nd Division, Hancock spent the first few miles carefully studying maps of the area in the back of an ambulance. Satisfied, Hancock mounted his horse and rode to Gettysburg, where he met General Howard at about 3:00 P.M. and assumed command. This did not go smoothly, as Howard outranked Hancock. The new commander of the left wing liked the defensive position on Cemetery Hill that Howard had selected, and immediately set about positioning the broken I and XI units, while bolstering his men's spirits. Turning command over to newly arrived General Henry Slocum of the XII Corps, Hancock returned to Taneytown, where he conferred with General Meade.[5]

While Hancock was riding to Gettysburg, his corps was trudging there as well. The march began at about 1:30 P.M., and by 4:00 P.M., the exhausted men crossed into Pennsylvania. The column halted that night, about three miles from the battlefield. The corps finally reached the battlefield at about 7:00 A.M. on July 2. After several changes in position, the corps was placed in the center of the Federal line along Cemetery Ridge. Hays's 3rd Division formed on the right, with his right connecting with the XI Corps. Caldwell's 1st Division was placed on the left, with its left connecting to the III Corps, and Gibbon's 2nd Division was placed in the middle. After resting for most of the day, the corps was called into action later that afternoon. Caldwell's Division was rushed south to the Wheatfield, where it was repulsed with heavy losses. Gibbon's Division was more successful in repelling the Confederate attacks against the Union center. One of Hays's Brigades (Willard's) was rushed south, where it was instrumental in blunting a determined Confederate attack made by Barksdale's Brigade. Carroll's Brigade, also from Hays's Division, helped repel the attack on Cemetery Hill that night.[6]

The corps's lasting fame was conferred on it on the afternoon when Gibbon's and Hays's Divisions almost single-handedly beat off the Pickett–Pettigrew–Trimble charge, but not before General Hancock was wounded. General Caldwell took command of the corps, which remained on the battlefield until the evening of July 5.[7]

1ST DIVISION—

Brigadier General John Caldwell

Although Brigadier General John Caldwell's Division boasted four brigades—more than any other in the army—its losses had been so great that it was now an average-size division. General Hancock commanded the division at Antietam, after General Israel Richardson was fatally wounded. Now with Hancock elevated to corps command, Caldwell was given the division. Despite having no military experience prior to the war, Caldwell rose quickly through the ranks. He began the war as a colonel of the 11th Maine, then assumed command of the 1st Brigade of the 1st Division during the battle of Fair Oaks. He led it during the Seven Days battles and at Antietam, where there were persistent rumors about his personal cowardice. Wounded at Fredericksburg, he returned to lead his brigade at Chancellorsville. Now, on May 22, 1863, he was elevated to command the 1st Division.[8]

Arriving on the battlefield during the early hours of July 2, the division rested while stretched across Taneytown Road with its left flank near Big Round Top. The men were roused at 3:30 A.M. and ordered to have breakfast. The division remained there until 6:00 A.M., when it was moved to a patch of woods east of Taneytown Road. Remaining there for an hour, the men were moved once again, this time to the west, where they relieved Robinson's Division (I Corps) on Cemetery Ridge. Gibbon's Division of their corps formed on their right and Humphreys's Division (III Corps) was on their left.[9]

The division took its place on Cemetery Ridge along a narrow 500-yard front "in columns of regiments by brigade," with Cross's Brigade on the left, Kelly's Brigade in the center, and Brooke's Brigade on the right. Zook's Brigade was in the second line, directly behind Kelly's. Rorty's Battery B, 1st New York battery, was stationed between Cross's and Kelly's Brigades. The men spent a quiet morning and afternoon in this position.[10]

The situation changed later in the afternoon, when Hood's Division smashed into the III Corps to their left. Caldwell received orders a short time later to move his command south to reinforce the Union left. Marching by the left flank, the men moved south along Cemetery Ridge. After marching only about half a mile, the men were ordered to halt and retrace their steps back to their original position. This order both frustrated and confused the men. Around 5:00 P.M., the men could see orderlies rushing along the line, so they were not surprised when orders arrived to "fall in." They did not know that General Hancock had received a plea for reinforcements to bolster the Federal left flank. Riding over to his left-most division, Hancock merely said, "Caldwell, get your division ready." This time there was no turning back, as the division passed the John Weikert farm. Cross's Brigade led the column, followed by Kelly's Irish Brigade, and Brooke's Brigade; Zook's Brigade brought up the rear. Because of the desperateness of the situation, the men did not file off by regiments, but simply faced left; the division "marched as it stood, in brigade of columns of regiments, closed en mass." During this march, Zook's Brigade was detached from the column because of a desperate plea from one of Sickles's staff officers. The brigade detached from the rear of the column apparently without Caldwell's knowledge. Caldwell's own orders were to find General Sykes of the V Corps, who would provide additional directives. Since Sykes was nowhere to be found, Caldwell marched his division toward the sound of the fighting. Suddenly, two horsemen galloped up as the head of the column approached Trostle Woods, and Caldwell was told to attack the Wheatfield.[11]

The three remaining brigades turned west, splashed across Plum Run, passed through the Trostle Woods, and halted along Wheatfield Road. In front of them was the wide expanse of the Wheatfield, with its breast-high wheat. De Trobriand's Brigade (Birney's Division, III Corps) had been forced from the field by overwhelming enemy numbers, and Caldwell's Division was ordered to fill the breach. A soldier from Cross's Brigade recalled that "it was the most exhausting run of three-fourths of a mile." The division halted as it reached the vicinity of Wheatfield Road, and deployed with Cross's Brigade on the left, the Irish Brigade on its right, and Brooke's Brigade in reserve.[12]

Because of the desperateness of the situation, the brigades were fed into battle as soon as they arrived and, therefore, in an uncoordinated fashion. The initial orders to deploy into line of battle caused considerable confusion, as the formation was backward as a result of the hasty march south. After correcting their alignment, Cross entered the Wheatfield first on the left, followed by Kelly's Brigade on his right. Brooke's Brigade remained in reserve along Wheatfield Road. Approaching the Wheatfield from further north, after being detached, Zook's Brigade advanced on Kelly's right, toward Stony Hill. Modern historian Eric Campbell hypothesized that the division entered the

Wheatfield by 5:30 P.M. The enemy, composed of Anderson's Brigade (Hood's Division) and Kershaw's Brigade (McLaws's Division), watched as Cross's men approached, and "the moment the heads of Cross's line appear[ed] above the crest of the hill edge of the wood along his entire front and right flank [was] fringed with a blaze of musketry," recalled Lieutenant William Wilson, of Caldwell's staff. While Cross's Brigade pushed Anderson's men out of the Wheatfield, Kelly's Irish Brigade stood almost toe to toe with several regiments from Kershaw's Brigade. Exchanging fire for a few moments, Kelly's men charged, and together with Zook's Brigade, drove Kershaw's men off Stony Hill.[13]

Only at one point did the division act as a unit, and that was when Brooke was driving through the Wheatfield on the left, while Kelly's and Zook's Brigades were throwing Kershaw's men off Stony Hill. However, Kelly's and Zook's men becoming intermixed, Brooke's men advanced too far, and a counterattack by Wofford's Brigade (McLaws's Division) doomed the division's efforts in this part of the field.[14]

The dejected division moved back to Cemetery Ridge. July 3 brought new hope to the men. They were kept busy by building breast-works. "Before noon we had a work which served to protect the men during the artillery fire which followed," Caldwell wrote in his report. The division was essentially a spectator to the grand charge made by Pickett's Division later that day. The division remained there until the evening of July 5, when it began the march to Frederick.[15]

1st Brigade—Colonel Edward Cross

Units: 5th New Hampshire, 61st New York, 81st Pennsylvania, 148th Pennsylvania
Strength: 853
Losses: 330 (57-260-13)—38.7%[16]

As the 1st Brigade marched toward Gettys-burg, turmoil swirled around its comman-der, Colonel Edward Cross. While no one doubted his fighting prowess, some believed that he remained a colonel because he was a gadfly to those of higher rank. He had already alienated the 148th Pennsylvania, which was newly assigned to the brigade. Major R. Forster of the regi-ment felt that "for some cause . . . [Cross], from his first association with us, seemed to have conceived a dislike of the regi-

ment." Because its colonel was on sick leave, Cross assigned veteran commander Colonel H. Boyd McKeen of the 81st Pennsylvania to take command of the unit, instead of its lieutenant colonel. "This act of Colonel Cross was wholly unjustifiable, the culmination of a series of insults and indignities . . . inflicted on the Regiment," recalled Adjutant Joseph Muffly. "As I passed through the camp late at night I found men gathered in groups discussing the act and expressing their indignation in very strong language." The men did not realize that Cross was concerned about their safety under a clearly unprepared officer and apparently decided to weather their wrath rather than see the unit destroyed. Less understandable was Cross's other actions, like striking one of the regiment's noncommissioned officers across the neck with the flat of his sword.[17]

Colonel Cross was dealing with internal turmoil at the time. During a June 28 conversation his aide, Lieutenant Charles Hale, Cross stated that "it will be my last battle." Hale noted that "he used the words in a grave decided way, and it gave me a shock . . . then I recalled . . . that in the last day or so he had at times seemed in a sort of abstracted mood that was not usual with him." Cross asked Hale to attend to his private papers and other belongings after his death.[18]

The march on June 29 was particularly hard on the men, as they traveled over thirty miles that day. Making the journey somewhat easier were the citizens who lined the roads and provided food and warm wishes. Private Henry Meyer of the 148th Pennsylvania recalled how, "at every farm house, and in every village, along our route, the people, old and young, stood in front of their homes with buckets of water, baskets of bread, cakes and other eatables, which they distributed among the boys as they passed, until their provisions were all gone, meantime speaking words of welcome, sympathy and encouragement."[19]

When the long march of June 29 was finally completed, the men, "utterly worn out by the toilsome march, their clothes wet from perspiration, . . . simply dropped down on the bare ground, as they reached the place of bivouac, pulled a rubber blanket or a piece of shelter tent over them, and fell asleep in a moment, without making coffee or partaking of a mouthful of food," noted Private Henry Meyer. The night was cold, and this, coupled with the exhausted condition of the men, caused many to catch colds. Straggling was heavy, and some estimated that over half the men fell out of the ranks. However, a wel-

come rest on June 30 allowed the stragglers to catch up to their units.[20]

The men were again on the march early on July 1. As the day wore on, the men began to pass frightened civilians fleeing to the rear. Meyer recalled passing a group of "young ladies" who "told us that the rebels were not far off, and they 'hoped to God' we would defeat them." The brigade finally halted about three miles from Gettysburg at about 9:00 P.M. that night. Lieutenant Charles Fuller of the 61st New York recalled that the men "stacked arms; ate supper; removed a fence rail and worked it into a line of rifle pits; went to bed, or rather rolled up in blankets and slept the sleep of the just."[21]

The men were awakened at 3:30 A.M. on July 2 and ordered to prepare a quick breakfast. After a "thorough" inspection, the brigade marched about a mile toward Gettysburg at the rear of the division. The column passed their doctors along the way, and many of the officers shook hands with the medical personnel. "We'll see you again later," they told each other, but Lieutenant Fuller recalled, "I tried to say this with a jaunty air, but down in my shoes I did not feel a bit jaunty." As the brigade approached the battlefield, Colonel Cross turned to Lieutenant Charles Hale and said firmly and gravely, "Mr. Hale—attend to that box of mine at the first opportunity." The statement was the last of many that Cross made during the march. It finally convinced Hale that Cross "was in dead earnest and had firm conviction of impending fate." Upon arriving on Cemetery Ridge, the brigade was closed in mass in the same order in which they had marched: the 61st New York in the first line; the 81st Pennsylvania in the second; the 148th Pennsylvania in the next two lines; the 5th New Hampshire in the rear.[22]

Cross's entire demeanor became transformed. Hale recalled that he was "full of fire, showing the sharp impulsive manner . . . on former battlefields; his eyes flashed as he said to us, 'Gentlemen:—it looks as though the whole of Lee's rebel army is right here in Pennsylvania: there will be a great battle fought to-day.'" Cross was also animated with his foot soldiers. While the men waited nervously for orders to advance, Colonel Cross rode up and reassured them with such phrases as, "Men, you know what's before you; give 'em hell!" Some of the men responded, "We will, Colonel!"[23]

The men spent most of the day resting, talking, playing cards, and writing in their diaries or to a loved one back home. They ate their midday meal as though no enemy lurked nearby. The officers' horses were unbridled, and nosebags filled with oats were attached. By 2:00 P.M. firing on the skirmish line increased in intensity. Looking over to the left, the men could see aides and orderlies galloping along the III Corps's lines. The men knew that something was brewing, and they grew tense. By 3:00 P.M. the artillery fire was heating up, and by 3:30 P.M. Lieutenant Charles Hale considered it to be "furious." Private Meyer (148th Pennsylvania) recalled how "some of the boys slept though shells and solid shot came crashing into our midst." The 5th New Hampshire was dispatched to Taneytown Road near the Round Tops on picket duty at about this time. The men were actually happy to be detached, for "it was preferable to advance into action, rather than to wait in expectation of the order to move," wrote Lieutenant Charles Fuller.[24]

As the enemy's activities increased, so too did Cross's. Pacing back and forth with his hands behind his back, he finally stopped and pulled a handkerchief out of his pocket and tied it around his head as though it were a turban. This was a common pre-battle ritual for Cross. What concerned the men most, however, was that the bandana was not the customary red one, but was black.[25]

The III Corps had moved forward by this time to occupy an exposed position near Emmitsburg Road. Shortly after 4:00 P.M., the sounds of small arms fire erupted from the left, as Hood's Division had taken on Birney's. At about 5:00 P.M., General Hancock rode up from the left and stopped near Colonel Cross, who was standing near his horse. "Colonel Cross," he said, "this day will bring you a star." Cross gravely shook his head, and calmly replied, "No General, this is my last battle." A short time later the men watched as Wilson of Hancock's staff galloped up to General Caldwell. Colonel Cross was experienced enough to knew what was in the offing, and said to his staff, "Mount, Gentlemen." The enlisted men were veterans and knew what was about to happen. Watching the intense artillery barrage, Private Meyer (148th Pennsylvania) could see orderlies, "dashing along our lines, and we said, 'Now, look out, we'll get into that too.'"[26]

Cross received orders to move by the left flank. About a half an hour before these orders arrived, the 5th New Hampshire hurried back to the brigade, as the regiment's commanding officer was told that it was "going in." Because Cross's Brigade was on the left, it led the division's column southward. As it approached Wheatfield Road, two aides galloped up to Cross. One was apparently from General Sykes of the V Corps, who screamed, "The enemy is breaking in directly on your right:—Strike him quick!" Cross wheeled his horse and, according to his aide, Lieutenant Charles Hale, gave an unusual order, "By the right flank: March!" Then the men were ordered to "Left face." Hale later related, "of course there was instant confusion, for it brought the line of battle facing by the rear rank, with the file-closers pushing and crowding through." This was a manifestation of Caldwell's Division's rapid movement toward the Wheatfield.[27]

The brigade moved forward obliquely into the Wheatfield in a southwesterly direction, deployed, from left to right, as 5th New Hampshire–148th Pennsylvania–81st Pennsylvania–61st New York. Because of the topography, the right side of the line was more advanced than the left, and all but the 5th New Hampshire and the left of the 148th were in the open field. The latter entered the southeast corner of Rose Woods. So rapid was the movement that Cross did not have time to throw out skirmishers. "As we emerged from the woods into the open ground, the bullets from the enemy's skirmishers came buzzing around like bees and we could see the puffs of smoke from the rifles in every direction," recalled Lieutenant Hale. Cross and his aides dismounted around this time. Kelly's Brigade was on Cross's right, and entered the Wheatfield soon after.[28]

The line of battle advanced about two hundred yards and halted when it reached a knoll. So rapid was this movement that several of the Confederate skirmishers threw up their arms to surrender. Cross yelled to Lieutenant Hale, "Get a file of men for a guard and hold them Mr. Hale." At first, the 5th New Hampshire and seven companies of the 148th Pennsylvania that were in the woods could not see any enemy soldiers. "In a few seconds I saw first one or two men come toward us on a run . . . a brief time passed when a solid line of men in gray appeared," recalled Lieutenant Charles Fuller of the 61st New York. These enemy soldiers were from Tige Anderson's Georgia Brigade (Hood's Division). Lieutenant William Wilson of Caldwell's staff noted that the enemy had taken position behind a stone wall, where they quietly awaited the attack. "Every rock, tree and bush concealed a sharpshooter and the moment the heads of Cross's line appear[ed] above the crest of the hill the edge of the wood along his entire front and right flank [was] fringed with a blaze of musketry," noted Wilson. Orders to open fire rang through the line. The enemy returned the fire. The breast-high ripening wheat was still on the stalks at the time, and Private Meyer (148th Pennsylvania) noticed "how the ears of wheat flew in the air all over the field as they were cut off by the enemy's bullets." The enemy's fire was particularly heavy on the right of the line, where the 61st New York lost almost two-thirds of its men. Lieutenant Colonel K. Oscar Broady commented in his official report that the "wounds received by my men seemed to be of an unusually severe character, and it is to be feared that the greater portion of the wounded will never be fit for active service again."[29]

Realizing that his losses were mounting, particularly on the exposed center and right of his line, Cross decided to order a charge. He told his aides, "Boys, instruct the commanders to be ready to charge when the order is given; wait here for the command, or if you hear the bugles of the Fifth New Hampshire on the left, move forward on the run." He then quickly walked toward the 5th New Hampshire on left side of his line. Upon reaching it, his head was grazed by a bullet. Binding the wound with his bandana, he remained with his old unit until he was wounded by a minié ball that entered his abdomen near his navel and exited near his spine. The mortal wounding occurred at about 6:00 P.M. near the present location of the 5th New Hampshire's monument in the Wheatfield. Carried to the rear, he died around midnight in considerable pain.[30]

Because the stone wall that protected Anderson's men was almost perpendicular to Cross's advance, it was fairly easy for the left of the line, composed of the 5th New Hampshire and part of the 148th Pennsylvania, to flank the right of Anderson's Brigade. The 1st Texas with the 15th Georgia were pushed from their perch behind the wall in short order. Private Meyer (148th Pennsylvania) recalled how "the rebels continued to fire into the right of our line until we leaped on the wall and took them in flank." Now in command of the brigade, Colonel H. Boyd McKeen reported that "the brigade steadily drove the enemy back to the far end of the Wheatfield, a distance of over 400 yards." The brigade finally halted when its right flank had reached the crest of the knoll, about midpoint in the Wheatfield. Major R. Forster (148th Pennsylvania) wrote after the war that "here the battle was desperate and sanguinary, the enemy endeavoring with might and persistency to drive us back, while the brigade held fast with marvelous valor and unyielding tenacity."[31]

The brigade held its position in the center of the Wheatfield for about half an hour, when the right side of the line, having expended its ammunition, was relieved by Brooke's 4th Brigade. The 5th New Hampshire and 148th Pennsylvania retained their positions, and continued to blaze away at the enemy. The large 148th Pennsylvania was deployed in two lines. Private Meyer in the first line was chagrined when the men in the rear rank "fired so close to our heads that the powder burned our faces." Theirs was a tenuous position because they were receiving fire from Anderson's Brigade in their front and from Benning's Brigade from Devil's Den to their left. The two regiments held their position until about 7:15 P.M., when they were relieved by Sweitzer's Brigade (Barnes's Division, V Corps).[32]

All accounts indicate that the brigade, particularly the left side, conducted an orderly withdrawal. Colonel H. Boyd McKeen said the left of the line "retired in splendid order" and finally reached the remainder of the brigade in the rear, resting behind a stone wall near Wheafield Road. Major Richard Cross of the 5th New Hampshire wrote that his regiment "fell back, firing, in good order."[33]

That evening the brigade, along with the rest of the division, made its way back to its original position on Cemetery Ridge. The men were sore and dejected. According to Lieutenant Charles Hale, "it was disheartening; we had held our own, but the losses had been frightful, and we had gained no ground." The men were especially concerned about the next day, "after such a grinding as we had gone through," wrote Hale. Darkness did not bring the needed quiet for sleep. "All night long were heard the monotonous tramp of moving troops, the low rumble of the wheels of ambulances, the ammunition and supply trains, and the artillery over stony roads. The sharp command of the officers, the curses of teamsters heard above the murmur of many voices, the groans of the wounded and dying made a medley of weird and discordant sounds," noted Private Meyer.[34]

At about 8:00 A.M. on July 3, wagons with entrenching tools arrived and the men set to work erecting breastworks. The works were completed by 11:00 A.M. and the men were permitted to rest. As a result of these efforts, the brigade sustained virtually no casualties during the great cannonade, which began shortly after 1:00 P.M. During the Pickett–Pettigrew–Trimble charge, Wilcox's and Perry's Brigades of Anderson's Division attacked in the brigade's front, but "were broken by the artillery just as they were getting within musket-range," reported Colonel McKeen.

The men did help to round up a number of prisoners, however. The brigade remained in its position, resting, on picket duty, and burying the dead through 4:00 P.M. on July 5, when it was ordered to begin the march after Lee's army.[35]

Cross's Brigade, like the other brigades in Caldwell's Division, was placed in the difficult position of trying to seal the breach in the Federal line in the Wheatfield. Although the division ultimately failed, as it was overwhelmed by McLaw's and Hood's units, at least parts of Cross's Brigade (the 5th New Hampshire and 148th Pennsylvania) held their ground on the left and rendered good service long after the rest of the brigade had been withdrawn.

Irish Brigade—Colonel Patrick Kelly

Units: 28th Massachusetts, 63rd New York, 69th New York, 88th New York, 116th Pennsylvania
Strength: 532
Losses: 198 (27-109-62)—37.2%[36]

After fighting in every campaign since First Bull Run and taking exceptionally heavy losses at Antietam and Fredericksburg, the famous Irish Brigade was but a skeleton of its former self. Two of the regiments, the 63rd and 69th New York, each numbered about seventy-five men and the 88th New York could boast only ninety. Private John Noonan of the 69th New York called it "a miserable remnant of the splendid regiment." As a result, the three regiments were combined during the Gettysburg campaign and fought under one green flag and one national standard. Even smaller was the 116th Pennsylvania, which mustered but sixty-six men and had been consolidated into four companies. Only the 28th Massachusetts resembled a regiment, as it carried 224 on its rolls.[37]

June 29 was a particularly hard day for the men, as they struggled along the thirty-four-mile march, carrying sixty pounds of equipment. Stragglers were many, but because the division rested the following day, most of them caught up with their units before the final march to Gettysburg.[38]

July 1 found the brigade, along with the rest of the division, again on the march toward Gettysburg. That night they passed an ambulance carrying the body of I Corps commander General John Reynolds. The brigade halted for the evening at 10:00 P.M., about three miles south of Gettysburg. The march continued sometime between 4:00 and 4:30 A.M. on July 2, when the brigade finally halted by the east side of Taneytown Road. The brigade, along with the rest of the division, was again on the move at 6:00 A.M., this time crossing Taneytown Road. By 7:00 A.M. the men were in position on Cemetery Ridge, facing west. To their left was Cross's Brigade; to their right was Brooke's Brigade. The men were permitted to rest there after completing the task of pulling down fences to make crude breastworks. At this point the brigade was formed in two lines, with the 28th Massachusetts and 116th Pennsylvania in the front line and the consolidated 63rd New York–69th New York–88th New York in the second.[39]

As 4:00 P.M. arrived the men could hear the sounds of battle beginning to erupt to the south and knew that it would probably be just a matter of time before they would be called upon to enter the fray. Perhaps considering the vicious fighting that had occurred the day before, Father William Corby, the brigade's chaplain, asked permission to hold a religious service. Given the hard marching the men had sustained over the past few weeks, this would be the first service in quite a while. Kelly gave his permission, and soon Corby could be seen standing upon a large rock with the members of the brigade deployed in front of him. Noonan (69th New York) described what occurred:

The Chaplain . . . addressed the men in a few simple words, their duties, what he was about to do, also the procedure necessary to gain absolution. When he had concluded his address, every man, Catholic and non-catholic [sic] alike fell on his knee with his head bowed down, and repeated an act of contrition. Extending his right hand towards the brigade, Father Corby pronounced the words of absolution. The scene was more than impressive, it was awe inspiring.[40]

Major St. Clair Mulholland of the 116th Pennsylvania recalled that the men had been standing at "order arms" during the ceremony, and as Corby completed his address, "every man fell on his knees with head bowed down." A hatless General Winfield Hancock silently watched the ceremony, surrounded by his aides.[41]

The men reformed as the service ended and marched by the left flank. They halted near Wheatfield Road, then backtracked along it, and finally entered the Wheatfield to the right of Cross's Brigade. At this point, no units were on Kelly's right, but this soon changed, as its oblique movement brought it close to Zook's Brigade. As the brigade moved forward, it was deployed from left to right as 88th New York–69th New York–63rd New York–28th Massachusetts–116th Pennsyl-

vania. Because the brigade was obliquing through the field in a southwesterly direction, only the New York regiments on the left marched a considerable distance through the Wheatfield. Most of the 28th Massachusetts and 116th Pennsylvania soon left the open field and tramped through the woods leading to Stony Hill. The latter was so named because of its numerous large boulders. No shots had been fired up to this time.[42]

While the brigade was entering the Wheatfield, the 3rd and 7th South Carolina of Kershaw's Brigade (McLaws's Division) were ascending Stony Hill from the opposite side. Although they reached the top first, the South Carolinians were distracted by Zook's Brigade, which was advancing on their left (the Irish Brigade's right). Suddenly realizing the danger in their front, the South Carolinians threw a volley at the right side of Kelly's Brigade, but because they were marching up the incline, most of the bullets flew harmlessly over the men's heads. Now it was the Irish Brigade's turn to fire a volley; theirs found the mark and many South Carolinians fell. Lieutenant James Smith of the 69th New York recounted that "after our line delivered one or two volleys, the enemy were noticed to waver, and upon the advance of our line (firing) the enemy fell back, contesting the ground doggedly. One charge to the front brought us in a lot of prisoners."[43]

Owing to the oblique nature of the brigade's movement, the 116th Pennsylvania on the right of the line made contact with the 7th and 3rd South Carolina before the brigade's other units. A soldier from the 116th Pennsylvania cried out, "There they are," when the enemy was only forty feet away. Major Mulholland recalled that "no orders were given but in an instant every musket on the line was at its deadly work." The Pennsylvanians carried "buck and ball" ammunition in their smoothbore muskets that was deadly at these close ranges. Mulholland noted that "a blind man could not have missed the mark." For ten minutes the two sides blazed away until Colonel Kelly ordered a charge. The South Carolinians held their ground and, in the words of Major Mulholland, "in charging we had literally ran right in among them. Firing instantly ceased, and we found there were as many of the enemy as there were of ourselves . . . [we] looked for a time at each other utterly bewildered; the fighting had stopped, yet the Confederate soldiers stood there facing us, still retaining their arms and showed no disposition to surrender." Realizing that a bold act was needed to halt the standoff, Mulholland yelled, "Confederate troops lay down your arms and go to the rear." To his immense relief, a large number responded. The rest beat a hasty retreat, leaving the Irish Brigade in possession of Stony Hill.[44]

All was quiet for about fifteen minutes, when Mulholland's men spied a movement to their right and rear. Mulholland conducted a quick reconnaissance, which was brought to a speedy conclusion when a breeze unfurled the Confederate flag. These troops proved to be from Wofford's Georgia Brigade (McLaws's Division). Running back to his unit, Mulholland told his men to each "look to his own safety, pointing out the direction they were to take towards Little Round Top." He later honestly admitted that while the official reports, "speak of 'retiring in good order,' 'slowly falling back,' and other such terms, more flattering than truthful."[45]

With Wofford's Brigade approaching their right flank and Kershaw's and Semmes's Brigades threatening their left and front, the Irish Brigade was in a desperate situation. To continue to hold this position was folly. A staff officer arrived

with an obvious order—"You are surrounded; retreat and save as many men as possible." It was each man for himself as the units disintegrated. Lieutenant James Smith of the 69th New York admitted that "it was impossible after falling back to rally the men . . . great confusion . . . prevailed at the time we crossed the [Wheatfield]."[46]

The brigade's colors were planted near the II Corps hospital on Taneytown Road. As the stragglers arrived they were sorted by regiment and put back in formation. What remained of the brigade returned with the rest of the division to its former position on Cemetery Ridge at about 10:00 P.M. that night. The men rested on their arms, but few slept that night.[47]

The men were ordered to throw up breastworks the next morning. There were no entrenching tools, so the men improvised, using plates, utensils, and other equipment. Most of the works consisted of stones. Major Mulholland lamented that "the works that we did attempt were very light, scarcely sufficient to stop a musket ball." When finally completed, the men remained behind them all day. Given the flimsiness of the works, it is surprising that only one man was wounded during the massive artillery barrage unleashed shortly after 1:00 P.M. So exhausted were the men that many actually fell asleep, despite the mayhem around them. After the war, Mulholland found it impossible to describe the bombardment accurately, as "no tongue or pen can find language strong enough to convey any idea of its awfulness." He did try though:

> Streams of screaming projectiles poured through the hot air falling and bursting everywhere. Men and horses were torn limb from limb; caissons exploded one after another in rapid succession, blowing the gunners to pieces. No spot

within our lines was free from this frightful iron rain. The infantry hugged close the earth and sought every shelter that our light earthworks afforded. . . . That awful rushing sound of the flying missiles which causes the firmest hearts to quail was everywhere.[48]

When the barrage ended, the men looked up to see long lines of Confederate infantry approaching their position. Major Mulholland recalled that "our artillery . . . open[ed] with terrible effect upon the advancing lines, tearing great gaps in their ranks and strewing the field with dead and wounded. Notwithstanding the destructive fire under which they were placed, the enemy continued to advance with a degree of ardor, coolness, and bravery worthy of a better cause." Mulholland and the other officers had to go to extremes to keep their men from firing. The Confederate line disappeared in a ravine and soon "the welcome order [was] sounded down the line 'ready' . . . was heard and hundreds of hammers were cocked and guns primed . . . the air [became] filled as though by a great flock of white pigeons," as hundreds of white handkerchiefs fluttering in the breeze,

Wilcox's and Perry's men, "thinking discretion the better part of valor . . . laid down their arms and surrendered."[49]

That night the men were ordered to repair their damaged breastworks in preparation for another attack in the morning. This fear pervaded the Union army and prevented it from celebrating the birth of their nation on July 4. That day, and most of July 5, was spent helping to bury the dead, attending to the wounded, and collecting arms and equipment that lay in abundance around the battlefield. The brigade finally began the march after Lee's army at 4:30 P.M. on July 5. The men were happy to leave because, in the words of Major Mulholland, "the stench from the dead became intolerable, and we tried to escape it by digging up the ground and burying our faces in the fresh earth."[50]

The small but proud Irish Brigade would fight on many more battlefields before the end of the war. Its veterans could hold their heads up high when considering their conduct at Gettysburg. Thrown into the Wheatfield at a critical moment, the brigade held Stony Hill until flanked on both sides and almost destroyed.

3rd Brigade—Brigadier General Samuel Zook

Units: 52nd New York, 57th New York, 66th New York, 140th Pennsylvania
Strength: 975
Losses: 358 (49-227-82)—36.7%[51]

The three New York regiments had been brigaded together since early in the war and had fought on many battlefields. General Samuel Zook assumed command of the brigade in October 1862 and led it on a heroic but futile attack at the battle of Fredericksburg. Charging up Marye's Hill,

the brigade encountered infantry behind a stone wall and massed enemy artillery. Not to be denied, Zook drove his men almost to the wall, but his unit was blown apart, losing over five hundred men in a matter of minutes. Zook was promoted after the battle, but neither he, nor the brigade, saw action for almost six months prior to Gettysburg. Unlike the three New York regiments that had been mustered into Federal service in the fall of 1861, the 140th Pennsylvania did not come into existence until a year later. As a result, the four regiments had never fought together as a brigade prior to the Gettysburg campaign.[52]

As the New Yorkers of Zook's Brigade marched through Maryland in June 1863, they recalled the prior autumn, when they had once before trudged along these dusty roads after Lee's army. Captain Josiah Favill, one of Zook's staff officers, stated that "everybody was, of course, on the streets and showed us the greatest attention, looking in amazement at the interminable lines of infantry, moving day and night without interruption." The army helped stimulate the heavy turnout, because, as Favill related, "in passing through these towns, we usually resume the regular step, and with bands playing and colors flying make a stunning appearance." As the men marched smartly past, the crowd yelled out, "God bless you, boys." Private Robert Stewart of the 140th Pennsylvania recalled that these words "rang in our ears and cheered our hearts."[53]

June 29 was a fearsome day, as the brigade marched over thirty miles with few stops. Captain Gilbert Frederick of the 57th New York noted that "straggling began early and rapidly increased toward evening and was fearful by midnight . . . the day began with route-march and ended with go-as-you-please." The men were most unhappy, and according to Private Jacob Cole of the same regiment, "there was complaining, grumbling, growling, and worse." The regiment's commander, Colonel Alford Chapman, heard the men's complaints and patiently replied that it was "a soldier's privilege to grumble." The men's feet swelled and blisters rose, until by the end of the march, "the man who did not have a limp in his gait . . . was a rare exception among his fellows," recalled Robert Stewart. Riding

at the head of the brigade, General Zook suggested that each of his staff "contribute something for the amusement of the party" to while away the monotony of the long march.[54]

The men certainly welcomed the day of rest on June 30. However, it did not prove to be restful for those who had fallen out of the ranks and were trudging along the dusty roads to catch up with their units. "All day long the stragglers were coming up and one by one joined their regiments. A motley, dirty crowd they were, for, having fallen in their tracks and slept, an early start was made to find their camps, mostly without washing or cleaning," noted Captain Gilbert Frederick of the 57th New York.[55]

Reveille sounded early on July 1. The men grabbed a quick breakfast and then were ordered to fall in to continue the march to Gettysburg. During the early morning hours the brigade was detached from the column and ordered to guard the wagon train. However, these orders were countermanded during the early afternoon, and the brigade set out for Gettysburg.[56]

Like the march on June 29, there were few halts. A short supper-stop, consisting of coffee and hardtack, occurred at 8:00 P.M., then it was on again. When the brigade finally halted about six miles from Gettysburg at 1:30 A.M. on July 2, "the men dropped down on the road and most of them fell asleep immediately," recalled Captain Favill. The young staff officer especially remembered this night because he was unable to wake up enough of the exhausted men to form a guard detail. General Zook finally told Favill to go to General Caldwell with the suggestion that "the troops be allowed to remain in the road for the night, which was obviously the only thing to be done." Favill must have wondered how these thoroughly exhausted troops could be expected to take on Lee's army the next day.[57]

The men were up again two hours later as the march to Gettysburg continued. The reunion finally occurred at about 8:00 A.M. on July 2, when the brigade massed behind the Irish Brigade. At about 10:00 A.M. that morning, the brigade, with the rest of the division, moved to Cemetery Ridge, where it formed between Gibbon's Division (II Corps) on its right and Humphreys's Division (III Corps) on its left. The brigade was massed in column by regiments, with the large 140th Pennsylvania forming the first two lines. The 52nd New York formed the third line, followed by the 57th New York; the 66th New York made up the last line.[58]

The men spent most of the day resting. There was little talking, as the men seemed preoccupied with their own thoughts, or with writing letters home or recording in their diaries. At about 3:00 P.M., they could see the magnificent sight of Sickles's III Corps advancing toward Emmitsburg Road. "It was a grand sight as the regiments deployed into line, with flags flying and rifles glittering in the sun," recalled Major Thomas Rogers of the 140th Pennsylvania. Later that afternoon the division moved south to support the III Corps, which was under a savage attack. Some of the officers gave quick speeches before the men moved. For example, Colonel Richard Roberts of the 140th Pennsylvania stepped in front of his men and said, "Men of the 140th! Recollect that you are now defending your own soil, and are fighting to drive the invader from your own homes and firesides. I shall therefore expect you to conduct yourselves as if in the presence of your wives, your sisters, and your sweethearts, and not disgrace the flag you bear or the name of Pennsylvanians." The men responded with cheers, just as orders to double-quick arrived.[59]

Captain Tremain of Sickles's staff galloped up to the column after it was well on its way, to direct it to its position to help repel the Confederate onslaught. Unfortunately, he came across the tail end of the column, which was composed of Zook's Brigade. Realizing that he didn't have time to waste trying to find Caldwell, Tremain conferred with General Zook and ultimately asked him to detach his brigade from the division and hasten to the Wheatfield. The brigade commander protested, but finally told Tremain, "Sir, if you will give me the order of General Sickles, I will obey it." Tremain answered, "Then, General Sickles's order is that you file your brigade to the right and move into action here." Zook shouted, "File, right!" and his men immediately changed direction to the southwest, where the firing was the greatest.[60]

Crossing Plum Run, the brigade entered Trostle Woods, heading in a southwest direction. Halting prior reaching Wheatfield Road, Zook arranged his command into two lines of battle. The first line consisted, from left to right, 66th New York–52nd New York–140th Pennsylvania; the 57th formed the supporting second line. The men were now ordered to load their guns. As they crossed Wheatfield Road, they gingerly stepped over and around the men of Sweitzer's Brigade (V Corps). Sweitzer's men had already been roughly handled on Stony Hill, so they were happy to have Zook's men between them and the enemy. Many yelled out, "Don't mind us; step anywhere; step on us." The two left regiments, the 66th and 52nd New York, marched through the northeast corner of the Wheatfield, while the 140th Pennsylvania moved primarily through the woods leading to Stony Hill. Stewart of the latter regiment recalled the "scores of huge uprising boulders, so thickly set that we had great difficulty to preserve our alignment." Although Zook's Brigade had brought up the rear of the column, it entered the fray only shortly after Cross's, which headed the column. As the men moved forward, they could see "through a dense pall of smoke and stifling heat . . . a blaze of light in front, revealing the dark forms of a double line of men who were actively engaging the enemy." This proved to be the Irish Brigade. Zook's Brigade had veered too far to the left, so its left flank now overlapped the 116th Pennsylvania of the Irish Brigade. This forced a "right flank" movement to rectify the situation.[61]

During its approach to Stony Hill the brigade encountered many obstructions and continual small arms fire. Up ahead was the right flank of Kershaw's Brigade, composed of the 3rd and 7th South Carolina. The South Caroliniaians's initial volleys were aimed too high, and, according to Stewart (140th Pennsylvania), "the balls rattled and crashed among the limbs of the trees behind and above us." The enemy calmed themselves and their fire now became more deadly. "Men reeled and fell on every side, but with daunting courage those who survived stood their ground until the order came to fall back," recalled Stewart. Colonel Roberts continued to reassure his regiment, yelling, "Steady men! Fire low. Remember, you are Pennsylvanians!" The enemy fire was equally deadly over on the left. Captain Gilbert Frederick recalled that "man after man fell in his tracks, some instantly killed, others wounded. We soon returned the fire still pushing forward over rocks, through underbrush and dense woods." According to Major Peter Nelson of the 66th New York, "we pressed steadily forward through wheat-fields, woods, over rail fences 10 feet high, stone walls, ditches, deep ravines, rocks, and all sorts of obstructions, every one of which had served as cover for the

enemy, and from which a murderous fire was poured upon us as we advanced, but without avail, as nothing could stop the impetuosity of our men."[62]

A majority of the officers had been killed or wounded by this time, making coordinated movement that much more difficult. General Zook had received a mortal wound in his abdomen earlier in the contest, probably as he approached Stony Hill. After Zook had been helped to the rear by his aides, the command devolved on Colonel Charles Freudenberg of the 52nd New York.[63]

Given the heavy fire in their front and Zook's mortal wounding, the brigade's advance ground to a halt. This permitted the Irish Brigade to come up on its left and engage the enemy on Stony Hill. Soon the men could see in their front "an almost continuous blaze of light, behind which we could dimly discern the forms of the men who confronted us." Colonel Freudenberg yelled, "Cease fire!" Moving to the front of the brigade, he shouted "Forward march!" Freudenberg fell wounded by three bullets, but not before he got the brigade moving forward again. Command of the brigade now devolved upon Colonel Richard Roberts of the 140th Pennsylvania. Climbing Stony Hill, the brigade encountered the right flank of Kershaw's South Carolinians. While the Irish Brigade engaged the right flank of the 7th South Carolina, the 66th and 52nd New York also found its front, the 140th Pennsylvania shifted to the right to hit the 3rd South Carolina in front and flank. The right side of the 140 Pennsylvania was hit with bullets from the 2nd and 3rd South Carolina. Orders were issued to "Load and fire at will."[64]

Together with the Irish Brigade on their left, Zook's men pushed Kershaw's men back toward the Rose farmhouse. The men were ordered to halt near the edge of the woods. After about fifteen minutes, Kershaw rallied his troops and returned them to face Caldwell's Division. Of growing concern to the Federal officers was the gap on the right of the 140th Pennsylvania. Masses of troops could be seen moving eastward, and Zook's men fervently hoped that they were from the III Corps pulling back from the Peach Orchard. "On this supposition orders were given to cease firing," noted Stewart. The men realized their mistake when "a volley of musketry which enfiladed our line and revealed the enemy to envelop our flank in such a way as to make escape impossible." This was Wofford's Georgia Brigade of McLaws's Division. Realizing that their position was untenable, Lieutenant Colonel John Fraser, now in command of the brigade after Colonel Roberts was wounded, gave orders to pull back. It was too late to help those on the right of the line. One soldier from the 140th Pennsylvania wrote home after the battle that "it [the regiment] would never have come out if the officers had let us alone. But we would not surrender. We were completely flanked and cut our way out." It became a footrace, as the men ran the deadly gantlet of missiles and "invitations" to surrender. Lieutenant J. Jackson Purman believed that the regiment lost more men during this period than during its advance.[65]

With the 140th Pennsylvania making for the rear, pressure was now applied to the right flank of the 66th New York, while the 52nd New York received pressure on its left from Kershaw. "We fell back to the stone wall then turned and gave the enemy such a volley of lead as, for a time, disordered his advance," recalled Captain Gilbert Frederick of the 57th New York, which was in the second line. To his right, Frederick could see Wofford's Brigade "marching steadily with colors flying as though on dress parade, and guns at right-shoulder-shift." Lieutenant Colonel Alford Chapman of the 57th New York recorded what happened next.

A staff officer rode up to me and stated that the right of the line had broken, and that the enemy [Wofford's Brigade] were coming in rapidly on that flank, advising me to move my regiment to the rear to avoid being taken. I determined and was about to change front forward to the right and endeavor to protect the right flank of the Brigade, when the whole line in front of me [52nd and 66th New York] suddenly gave way, breaking through the ranks of my regiment in considerable disorder . . . [I] moved to the rear in line . . . the enemy following closely. During this retrograde movement I halted my regiment several times, and endeavored to rally men enough on its flanks to check the advance of the enemy, but without success.[66]

The troops finally rallied in the rear and were later marched back to their original position on Cemetery Ridge. Here the men lay down to rest, but, according to Captain Gilbert Frederick, "sleep did not readily kiss the eyelids of these dusty, blood-stained warriors. A gentle breeze came across the battlefield, bearing on its bosom the moans of the suffering wounded, a sound indescribably desolate, which could not be shut out even by covering the head."[67]

The men were up at daylight on July 3. Breakfast was eaten, ammunition replenished, and equipment checked. Crude breastworks were next constructed, and when completed, the men lay down behind them. These served to provide some relief during the great bombardment, which began shortly after 1:00 P.M. Captain Frederick noted that during the artillery duel "both Seminary and Cemetery Ridges seemed on fire with blaze and smoke; the air was full of hissing demons;

the thunder benumbed the ears and shattered the nerves." Like the other brigades of Caldwell's Division, Zook's Brigade did not fire a shot during the Pickett–Pettigrew–Trimble charge. July 4 and early July 5 were spent burying the dead and resting. The brigade left the battlefield during the afternoon of July 5.[68]

Zook's Brigade fought well on July 2 when it helped to clear temporarily the Wheatfield and Stony Hill of Confederates. However, like its sister brigades, it was ultimately placed in an untenable situation when it was attacked on its front and both flanks, forcing it to withdraw with heavy losses.

4th Brigade—Colonel John Brooke

Units: 27th Connecticut, 2nd Delaware, 64th New York, 53rd Pennsylvania, 145th Pennsylvania
Strength: 851
Losses: 389 (54-284-51)—45.7%[69]

Unlike the other brigades comprising the 1st Division, which were formed on March 13, 1862, and participated in all of the major campaigns of the Army of the Potomac, the 4th Brigade did not come into existence until exactly thirteen months later. Although the brigade was new, its units were all veteran, being pulled from the 1st and 3rd Brigades of the division. The brigade's first battle at Chancellorsville left a lasting impression, for while the brigade was not heavily engaged, the 27th Connecticut was almost entirely captured. Colonel John Brooke commanded the brigade from its inception. While he performed commendably in every engagement prior to Gettysburg, the losses had a put stain on his record that he aimed to remove as his men marched toward Gettysburg.[70]

Like so many other Federal units, Brooke's Brigade was warmly received by the local citizens as it marched north. Cattaraugus Freeman of the 64th New York fondly recalled the women who "stood on the sides of the road with fresh water and good large slices of bread and butter—

real soft bread and yankee butter. They could not give all a piece but showed their good will."[71]

The men rested on June 30, after marching over thirty miles the day before. The reprieve did not continue, however, as the men were roused early on July 1 and put back on the road again. A high point of the march occurred when the column crossed the Pennsylvania state line. So excited were the men in the Pennsylvania regiments that, "ringing cheers went up . . . when we found ourselves, after so long an absence, once more treading the soil of our native State." Lieutenant Charles Hatch of the 53rd Pennsylvania noted that the men's "step became more springly [sic], the gait quickened as our forward movement went on." While the march ended at about 9:30 P.M. when the brigade was about three miles from Gettysburg, the exertion did not, as the men were now ordered to build breastworks near Taneytown Road. According to Colonel Daniel Bingham of the 64th New York, the work was completed slowly because "for a regiment with one axe and two shovels, [the job] was rather tedious." Private Martin Sigman of the same regiment recalled that the men were moved to another position just as the breastworks were almost completed. By midnight, the men were asleep. All of them, that is, except the 145th Pennsylvania, which had been detached earlier in the day to guard the division's wagon train. These men did not rejoin the brigade until the early hours of July 2.[72]

If it seemed to the men that reveille sounded soon after they went to sleep, they were right. According to Major Leman Bradley and Sigman of the 64th New York, the men were roused at about 2:30 A.M. on July 2, and ordered to have breakfast, consisting of hardtack and coffee. The column moved out about 4:00 A.M., and finally reached the battlefield around 6:00 A.M. The brigade was initially posted east of Taneytown Road, facing east, but a short time later, it marched across the road and formed the right of the division on Cemetery Ridge, facing west. The men reached this position about 7:00 A.M. and remained there for the rest of the day. Except for occasional skirmishing and artillery fire, the day was fairly peaceful. This changed later in the afternoon, when the artillery fire intensified. The brigade was massed by regiments, in the following order, from front to rear: 2nd Delaware–64th New York–53rd Pennsylvania–27th Connecticut–145th Pennsylvania.[73]

The men's weariness disappeared when the attack on the Union left opened and it appeared that they would be engaged shortly. Most of the officers and men recalled that the orders to fall in and prepare to march to the left arrived at 5:00 P.M. Prior to moving south, many of the officers gave encouraging speeches to their men. Private Benson Wordon of the 53rd Pennsylvania recalled that Brooke told his comrades, "Boys—remember the enemy has invaded our own soil! The eyes of the whole world is [sic] upon us and we are expected to stand up bravely to do our duty!" The men heard their officers yell, "Attention, left face, forward, quick

time, march" and the brigade followed Kelly's Irish Brigade south. When the brigade finally halted along Wheatfield Road, it was in reverse order, like the rest of the division. According to Sigman, "by a change of front our rear rank came in front, and to any but well drilled troops would have been disastrous." The brigade was deployed from left to right as 2nd Delaware–64th New York–53rd Pennsylvania–27th Connecticut–145th Pennsylvania.[74]

While lying along the road, the men watched Cross's Brigade advance through the Wheatfield to engage the enemy. Kelly's Irish Brigade also moved forward, and it too became engaged. After waiting about ten minutes, the brigade was ordered forward through the breast-high wheat to relieve Cross's Brigade. Brooke later recalled that his brigade spanned almost the entire width of the Wheatfield. After reaching Cross's position about halfway through the Wheatfield, the men were ordered to "Halt, fire at will," which continued for about five minutes. The men were dreadfully exposed here, so they were ordered to fix bayonets and continue to advance once again. "It was a deafening roar, and it was very dificult [sic] to hear the commands given, and took some efort [sic] to start the line forward into another charge," stated Sigman (64th New York). Because of the ear-splitting din, some of the men could not hear the orders to advance, so Brooke grabbed hold of the colors of the 53rd Pennsylvania and carried them forward, which got the entire brigade moving. Rapidly advancing, they forced General Tige Anderson's Georgians out of the Wheatfield. Corporal Stephen Osborn of the 145th Pennsylvania recounted after the war that "I think there is nothing that will cause a man to shoot so unsteady and wildly as to have the enemy charging down on him yelling like mad."

This worked during the evening hours of July 2, as Brooke's men scooped up dozens of prisoners.[75]

As Brooke's men rushed through the Rose Woods, their formations were broken by the large rocks and ledges that abounded in this part of the battlefield. Unfazed, the men continued on until they reached the edge of the woods, adjacent to the open pasture north of the Rose Woods. They were now far in advance of the rest of the division. In the open field in front of them was Semmes's fresh Georgia Brigade, "drawn up in readiness just beyond, within pistol range." The two lines immediately exchanged volleys, but Semmes's men got the worst of it, as they were in the open. General Semmes was mortally wounded, and his brigade fell back to safety.[76]

Brooke's line resembled a crescent, with the center most advanced. While Brooke had been successful in clearing his front of Confederates, his rapid advance had outpaced the troops on either side, and as a result, both flanks hung in the air. Equally disturbing was the news that the ammunition was down to an average of five rounds per man. An aide was dispatched to General Caldwell to request immediate support, or at least additional ammunition. Brooke received word that a mass of enemy troops, probably from Anderson's Brigade, were descending upon his left flank. A volley erupted almost immediately into this vulnerable part of Brooke's line. Before Brooke could rearrange his troops to deal with this threat, an aide brought news that Confederate troops (from Kershaw's Brigade) were also bearing down on his right. Sigman confided in his diary that the ridge was "the hottest place we came across that day." So hot was the fire, that the men "loaded their pieces under shelter of the brow of the hill, then rising up,

delivered their fire," related Sergeant Winthrop Sheldon of the 27th Connecticut. The 2nd Delaware's left was refused to deal with the threat on the left. Brooke directed his men while standing on a large boulder near the left center of his line.[77]

Colonel Brooke bitterly wrote in his report, "finding no troops coming to my support, and finding that unless I retired all would be killed or captured, I reluctantly gave the order to retire, and in good order the whole command came off the field slowly, and firing as they retired, succeeded in bringing off nearly all their wounded." Lieutenant Colonel Richard McMichael of the 53rd Pennsylvania estimated that the men held this ridge for about fifteen minutes. The historian of the 2nd Delaware proudly wrote that Brooke's Brigade "reached the farthest point gained by any of the Union troops during the day." Unfortunately for Brooke's men, the enveloping Confederate forces caused them to run a gauntlet of fire, resulting in scores being killed, wounded, or captured.[78]

A wounded John Brooke formed his command along the stone wall near Wheatfield Road. After being relieved by units of the V Corps, the brigade moved off toward Little Round Top. Orders arrived from Caldwell for Brooke to return his brigade to its original position on Cemetery Ridge, which was accomplished that evening.[79]

July 3 brought continued hot, sultry weather, and, like the day before, relative quiet on the Union center and left. Sometime during the morning the men were ordered to form on Zook's Brigade's left. Seeing this movement, the Confederate gunners immediately opened fire, killing and wounding a number of men. The soldiers were ordered to build breastworks, and when completed, they spent the quiet hours writing letters, making entries in their diaries, and, of course, eating. During his morning rounds, General Hancock was hailed by one of the officers of the brigade as he passed the 27th Connecticut, and was told of the gallantry of the regiment on July 2. The regiment went into battle with seventy-five men because all but three companies had been captured at Chancellorsville. Looking gravely at the regiment that now numbered less than fifty, Hancock said, "Boys, stand well by your duty and you will carry with you to your homes the honor of helping to win the greatest battle ever fought on this continent."[80]

The peacefulness ended shortly after 1:00 P.M., when well over a hundred Confederate artillery pieces opened fire. "The shells flew all around us, and killed and wounded quite a number of men and horses [sic] there was a fearful noise and roaring of the cannon, if it had only been one day later, we might have called it a Fourth of July Celebration," described Sigman (64th New York).[81]

The artillery barrage stopped almost as abruptly as it had started. In the distance, the men could see Pickett's Division forming on Seminary Ridge. "First we saw the flags move out and halt, then the line formed on the colors, dress and move to the front, then another line form [sic] and move [sic] front and then still a third line. Finally they [were] all ready, waiting for the word to go," related Osborn (145th Pennsylvania) after the war. The men prepared for the charge by arranging their cartridges on the breastworks and laying their ramrods before them. The men cried out, "Here they come," and all watched in awe as the magnificent line of battle approached. The Confederate lines veered to Brooke's right, taking them out of range. However, the brigade later took a number of prisoners from Wilcox's

Brigade (Anderson's Division, III Corps) when the Alabama soldiers realized that to continue the charge was folly.[82]

The brigade spent July 4 and most of July 5 resting and burying the dead, finally leaving their breastworks at about 4:00 P.M. on July 5.[83]

Modern historian Harry Pfanz wrote that Brooke's charge was "gallant," and one of the few made by the Army of the Potomac during the battle. He was especially complimentary to Colonel John Brooke, for his leadership and heroism. While the brigade was successful in clearing the Wheatfield, it was but a short-lived victory, as it too was finally swept away by mounting pressure from three directions.[84]

NOTES

1. Dyer, *Compendium*, 287.

2. Tagg, *Generals of Gettysburg*, 33–34.

3. Richard A. Sauers, "The 53rd Pennsylvania Volunteer Infantry in the Gettysburg Campaign," *Gettysburg Magazine* (July 1994), issue 11, 80–81.

4. A. M. Gambone, *Hancock at Gettysburg . . . and Beyond* (Baltimore, 1997), 7; OR 27, 1, 367.

5. Almira R. Hancock, *Reminiscences of Winfield Scott Hancock* (New York, 1887), 188–189; OR 27, 1, 367–368.

6. OR 27, 1, 369–372.

7. OR 27, 1, 372–374; Gambone, *Hancock at Gettysburg*, 148.

8. Tagg, *Generals of Gettysburg*, 35–36.

9. Bingham, "From the 64th New York," *The Cattaraugus Freeman*, July 30, 1863; Eric Campbell, "Caldwell Clears the Wheatfield," *Gettysburg Magazine* (July 1990), 28–29.

10. Harry W. Pfanz, *Gettysburg—The Second Day* (Chapel Hill, NC, 1993), 73; Campbell, "Caldwell Clears the Wheatfield," 29.

11. OR 27, 1, 379; Joseph G. Bilby, *Remember Fontenoy! The 69th New York in the Civil War* (Hightstown, NJ, 1995), 87; St. Clair A. Mulholland, *The Story of the 116th*

Pennsylvania Infantry (Philadelphia, 1899), 135; Campbell, "Caldwell Clears the Wheatfield," 31, 32, 34; William P. Wilson, "Statement," in Bachelder Papers, New Hampshire Historical Society.

12. Campbell, "Caldwell Clears the Wheatfield," 34; Wilson "Statement"; Joseph W. Muffly, ed., *The Story of Our Regiment: A History of the 148th Pennsylvania Volunteers* (Des Moines, IA, 1904), 459.

13. Campbell, "Caldwell Clears the Wheatfield," 34, 35; Wilson "Statement."

14. Campbell, "Caldwell Clears the Wheatfield," 43.

15. OR 27, 1, 380, 391, 392.

16. Busey and Martin, *Regimental Strengths and Losses,* 35, 242.

17. *PAG,* vol. 2, 733; Muffly, *The Story of our Regiment,* 244, 716; Pfanz, *Gettysburg— The Second Day,* 74.

There is considerable confusion over when McKeen was assigned command of the 148th Pennsylvania. In addition to Muffly's account, which had McKeen taking over on June 28, Major R. Forster of the 148th Pennsylvania recalled that it was on June 30 and Lieutenant Charles Hale of Cross's staff thought that it occurred on the evening of July 1. When McKeen took over the 148th Pennsylvania, Lieutenant Colonel Amos Stroh assumed command of the 81st Pennsylvania (*PAG,* vol. 2, 733; Hale, "With Cross in the Gettysburg Campaign," USAMHI; OR 27, 1, 385).

18. Hale, "With Cross in the Gettysburg Campaign."

19. Muffly, *The Story of our Regiment,* 534.

20. Muffly, *The Story of our Regiment,* 534; "A Private's Diary, 1863": Pvt. Jacob Lincoln Carter's 148th Reg. Of Pennsylvania Volunteers, Army of the Potomac, copy in 148th Pennsylvania file, GNMP, 24.

21. "A Private's Diary, 1863," 24; Muffly, *The Story of our Regiment,* 171, 534, 590; *NYG,* vol. 2, 459–460.

Differences of opinion exist about when the march commenced. Jacob Lincoln of the 148th Pennsylvania recorded in his diary that it began at 8:00 A.M., while William Child of the 5th New Hampshire recalled that it was at 6:30 A.M. ("A Private's Diary, 1863," 24; William A. Child, *A History of the Fifth New Hampshire* (Bristol, NH, 1893), 206).

Thomas Meyer of the 148th Pennsylvania recalled that the pioneer corps actually chopped down trees to make a strong breastwork. If true, this may have been done because adequate fences were not available nearby (Muffly, *The Story of our Regiment,* 459).

22. *NYG,* vol. 2, 460; OR 27, 1, 381; Charles A. Fuller, *Personal Recollections of the War . . . in the 61st New York Volunteer Infantry* (Sherburne, NY, 1906), 92–93; Hale, "With Cross in the Gettysburg Campaign."

23. Hale, "With Cross in the Gettysburg Campaign"; *NYG,* vol. 2, 460; Fuller, *Personal Recollections of the War,* 93.

24. Muffly, *The Story of our Regiment,* 535; Child, *A History of the Fifth New Hampshire,* 206; Fuller, *Personal Recollections,* 93.

25. Hale, "With Cross in the Gettysburg Campaign."

According to Private Henry Meyer of the 148th Pennsylvania, the men spent the day in line of battle (Muffly, *The Story of our Regiment,* 535).

26. Hale, "With Cross in the Gettysburg Campaign"; Muffly, *The Story of our Regiment,* 536.

27. Child, *A History of the Fifth New Hampshire,* 206; Hale, "With Cross in the Gettysburg Campaign."

Lieutenant Colonel K. Oscar Broady of the 61st New York described this unusual movement as "formed in line of battle by inversion and faced by the rear rank" (OR 27, 1, 384).

28. OR 27, 1, 381; Hale, "With Cross in the Gettysburg Campaign."

29. OR 27, 1, 381, 384; Hale, "With Cross in the Gettysburg Campaign"; Fuller, *Personal Recollections,* 94; *PAG,* vol. 2, 729; Wilson, "Statement"; Muffly, *The Story of our Regiment,* 536, 537.

While some of the men wrote that the wheat was breast-high, Lieutenant Charles Hale of Cross's staff recalled that it had been trampled down by this point by other troops (Hale, "With Cross in the Gettysburg Campaign").

30. Hale, "With Cross in the Gettysburg Campaign"; Carter, "A Private's Diary, 1863"; Child, *A History of the Fifth New Hampshire,* 205, 206, 207.

Cross was apparently killed by a sniper's bullet, fired from a large boulder with a "cleft or fissure along the top on the far side" (Hale, "With Cross in the Gettysburg Campaign"). According to historian Eric Campbell, the rock stands at the northwest corner of the intersection of Cross and Sickles Roads (Campbell, "Caldwell Clears the Wheatfield," 37).

31. OR 27, 1, 381; Campbell, "Caldwell Clears the Wheatfield," 37; *PAG,* vol. 2, 729; Pfanz, *Gettysburg—The Second Day,* 273–274.

32. OR 27, 1, 383, 385; Muffly, *The Story of our Regiment,* 537; Child, *A History of the Fifth New Hampshire,* 206; John Brooke to John Bachelder, November 14, 1885, in Bachelder Papers, New Hampshire Historical Society; Pfanz, *Gettysburg—The Second Day,* 300.

According to a postwar account by Lieutenant William Wilson of Caldwell's staff, the two regiments advanced with Brooke's brigade through the Wheatfield (Wilson, "Statement").

33. OR 27, 1, 382, 383.

34. Hale, "With Cross in the Gettysburg Campaign"; Muffly, *The Story of our Regiment,* 539.

35. OR 27, 1, 382; Muffly, *The Story of our Regiment,* 463, 591.

According to Major R. Forster of the 148th Pennsylvania, General Hancock suggested that the men go toward the town to find fence rails (*PAG,* vol. 2, 731).

36. Busey and Martin, *Regimental Strengths and Losses,* 36, 242.

37. T. L. Murphy, *Kelly's Heroes: The Irish Brigade at Gettysburg* (Gettysburg, PA, 1997), 29–32; Noonan, "The 69th New York History," Kenneth H. Powers Collection, USAMHI; *PAG,* vol. 2, 624–625; OR, 27, 1, 387–388.

38. *PAG,* vol. 2, 619.

39. OR 27, 1, 386, 389, 391; Noonan, "The 69th New York History."

J. Noonan of the 69th New York recalled that the march began from Uniontown at 8:00 A.M. on July 1.

40. J. Noonan, "The 69th New York History"; William Corby to John Bachelder, January 4, 1879, in Bachelder Papers, New Hampshire Historical Society.

41. *PAG,* vol. 2, 623.

There is some disagreement concerning when and where this ceremony occurred. While J. Noonan of the 69th New York and Major Mulholland of the 116th Pennsylvania clearly put the time as just prior to 5:00 P.M., others not associated with the brigade believed that it occurred much earlier—perhaps around noon. Siding with the latter group, the author of a recent short history of the Irish Brigade at Gettysburg concluded that Hancock would never have permitted such a ceremony, as the battle was raging and the units were needed to the south. He also believed that the site of the absolution was as much as five hundred yards to the north of the current monument. It is difficult to believe that the veterans would have allowed the monument to have been placed in the wrong position, and that they were all incorrect in their recollections of when the service took place. Another recent history of one of the brigade's regiments suggested that Corby overheard Hancock say to his division commander, "Caldwell, get your division ready," and immediately asked permission to conduct the service (Murphy, *Kelly's Heroes: The Irish Brigade at Gettysburg,*, 20–26; Patrick O'Flaherty, *History of the 69th Regiment in the Irish Brigade* (New York, 1986), 255.

42. OR 27, 1, 386; Bilby, *Remember Fortenoy!* 89; *PAG,* vol. 2, 625.

43. Bilby, *Remember Fortenoy!* 88–89; OR 27, 1, 389.

44. *PAG,* vol. 2, 625.

45. *PAG,* vol. 2, 626–627.

46. O'Flaherty, *History of the 69th Regiment,* 258–259; Paul Jones, *The Irish Brigade* (Washington, 1969), 196; OR 27, 1, 389.

47. OR 27, 1, 386, 389, 392; Jones, *The Irish Brigade,* 197; *PAG,* vol. 2, 628; James Gardner to John Bachelder, September 20,

1889, in Bachelder Papers, New Hampshire Historical Society.

48. OR 27, 1, 386; *PAG*, vol. 2, 628, 629; O' Flaherty, *History of the 69th Reg.*, 259–260.

49. OR 27, 1, 391, 392–393; *PAG*, vol. 2, 628, 630; O' Flaherty, *History of the 69th Reg.*, 259–260.

50. OR 27, 1, 386, 391; *PAG*, vol. 2, 631.

51. Busey and Martin, *Regimental Strengths and Losses*, 37, 242.

52. Edmund J. Raus, Jr., *A Generation on the March* (Gettysburg, PA, 1996), 65, 66, 69–70, 130–131; Warner, *Generals in Blue*, 577; OR 21, 229.

53. J. Favill, *Diary of a Young Officer* (Chicago, 1909), 240, 241; Robert L. Stewart, *History of the One Hundred and Fortieth Regiment, Pennsylvania Volunteers* (n.p., 1912), 88.

54. Gilbert Frederick, *The Story of a Regiment—The Fifty-Seventh New York Infantry in the War of the Rebellion* (Chicago, 1895), 164; Jacob H. Cole, *Under Five Commanders* (Paterson, NJ, 1906), 188; Wilson Paxton, diary, Civil War Miscellaneous Collection, USAMHI; *NYG*, vol. 2, 419; Stewart, *History of the One Hundred and Fortieth Regiment, Pennsylvania Volunteers*, 88; Favill, *Diary of a Young Officer*, 241.

55. Frederick, *The Story of a Regiment*, 164.

56. Frederick, *The Story of a Regiment*, 165; OR 27, 1, 396; *NYG*, vol. 2, 419.

57. Favill, *Diary of a Young Staff Officer*, 242; Stewart, *History of the One Hundred and Fortieth Regiment, Pennsylvania Volunteers*, 420.

Lieutenant W. S. Shallenberger of the 140th Pennsylvania recalled that so little time was given during this halt for supper that few men were able to make coffee (*PAG*, vol. 2, 683).

58. Stewart, *History of the One Hundred and Fortieth Regiment, Pennsylvania Volunteers*, 420; *PAG*, vol. 2, 683; Cole, *Under Five Commanders*, 193; OR 27, 1, 397; Campbell, "Caldwell Clears the Wheatfield," 29.

59. "St. Louisans Among Gettysburg Heroes," *St. Louis Globe-Democrat*, April 2, 1891; J. Jackson Purman to John Bachelder, November 3, 1871, in Bachelder Papers, New Hampshire Historical Society.

60. Henry E. Tremain, *Two Days of War: A Gettysburg Narrative and Other Experiences* (New York, 1905), 81–84; Campbell, "Caldwell Clears the Wheatfield," 33.

According to Harry Pfanz, Sickles "impressed" several units to help his beleaguered III Corps. There are different variations of this story. One of Zook's aides recalled that Tremain rode up to Zook before the division moved south, with a request that he move to the left to provide assistance. According to Captain Josiah Favill, Zook immediately rode over to see Sickles "who, surrounded by a large staff, was in a state of great excitement; the enemy's shot were dropping about him, and he seemed to be very much confused and uncertain in his movements," recalled Favill. Zook "declared his willingness to act," and galloped back to his command. By the time he returned, Cross's and Kelly's Brigades had already departed, so he quickly ordered his men into line (Favill, *Diary of a Young Officer*, 245). Lieutenant James Purman of the 140th Pennsylvania admitted that "few men would have acted as Zook did" (J. J. Purman, "General Zook at Gettysburg," *National Tribune*, March 25, 1909). That Sickles requested help from Zook is confirmed by Lieutenant William Wilson, an aide to General Caldwell (Wilson, "Statement"). General Caldwell's report suggests that he did not know that the brigade was detached (OR 27, 1, 379).

61. OR 27, 1, 394; Charles Freudenberg to John Bachelder, June 16, 1880, in Bachelder Papers, New Hampshire Historical Society; Philippe de Trobriand to John Bachelder, May 2, 1882, in Bachelder Papers, New Hampshire Historical Society; Stewart, *History of the One Hundred and Fortieth Regiment, Pennsylvania Volunteers*, 104; "St. Louisans Among Gettysburg Heroes"; *PAG*, vol. 2, 684.

The troop deposition used here follows Pfanz's, not Colonel Fraser's (Pfanz, *Gettysburg—The Second Day*, 274; OR 27, 1, 394).

Although all of the official reports from Zook's Brigade state that the movement south occurred at 4:00 P.M., Lieutenant

William Shallenberger recalled looking down at his watch and seeing that it was 6:00 P.M. His perception is probably correct, as Hood's attack was launched until about 4:00 P.M. (OR 27, 1, 394, 396, 397; Stewart, *History of the One Hundred and Fortieth Regiment, Pennsylvania Volunteers*, 422).

There was some controversy about the movement through Sweitzer's Brigade, when after the battle, "Historicus" wrote, "Barnes' disordered troops impeded the advance of the brigade [Zook's]. 'If you can't get out of the way' cried Zook, 'lie down, and I will march over you.' Barnes ordered his men to lie down" (*New York Herald*, March 12, 1864).

62. Stewart, *History of the One Hundred and Fortieth Regiment, Pennsylvania Volunteers*, 105; Frederick, *Story of a Regiment*, 169; OR 27, 1, 396, 398.

63. Benjamin F. Powelson, *History of Company K of the 140th Regiment Pennsylvania Volunteers* (Ann Arbor, MI, 1970), 28; Favill, *Diary of a Young Officer*, 247–248.

Zook died at about 5:00 P.M. on July 3. Captain Gilbert Frederick observed that Zook fell while jumping his horse over a stone wall (*NYG*, vol. 2, 420).

64. Charles Freudenberg to John Bachelder, June 16, 1880; Sara G. Walters, *Inscription at Gettysburg: In Memorium to Captain David Acheson, Company C, 140th Pennsyvlania Volunteers* (Gettysburg, PA, 1990), 107; Stewart, *History of the One Hundred and Fortieth Regiment, Pennsylvania Volunteers*, 105.

Colonel Brooke, commanding the 4th Brigade, later recalled taking command of Zook's Brigade sometime during its charge up Stony Hill, after Colonel Charles Freudenberg "came to me and told me Zook was dead." While Brooke may indeed have exercised some control over Zook's left units, it is doubtful that Freudenberg spoke directly to him (John Brooke to John Bachelder, November 14, 1885 and March 18, 1886).

65. Stewart, *History of the One Hundred and Fortieth Regiment, Pennsylvania Volunteers*, 107–108; unknown writer's letter, Timothy

Brooks Collection, USAMHI; J. Jackson Purman to John Bachelder, November 3,1871.

66. OR 27, 1, 395, 396–397; Frederick, *Story of a Regiment*, 170–171.

67. *NYG*, vol. 2, 420; Frederick, *Story of a Regiment*, 173.

68. Frederick, *Story of a Regiment*, 173, 174; OR 27, 1, 395, 397; Powelson, *History of Company K*, 29; Joseph Woodward, letter, copy in 140th Pennsylvania folder, GNMP.

69. Busey and Martin, *Regimental Strengths and Losses*, 38, 242.

70. Dyer, *Compendium*, 287–289; Tagg, *Generals of Gettysburg*, 42–43.

71. Cattaraugus Freeman, "Recollections," copy in the 64th New York file, GNMP.

72. OR 27, 1, 400, 403, 413; *PAG*, vol. 1, 330; Franklin Ellis, ed., *History of Cattaraugus County, New York* (Philadelphia, 1879), 105; Martin Sigman diary, copy in 64th New York file, GNMP.

73. OR 27, 1, 400, 403, 407, 410; Sigman, diary; Campbell, "Caldwell Clears the Wheatfield," 29.

74. *PAG*, vol. 1, 330–331; OR 27, 1, 400, 407, 409, 412, 414; Benson J. Wordon, "Battle of July 1st, 2nd, and 3rd, 1864 [sic], Indiana State Library (copy in Brake Collection, USAMHI); S. A. Osborn, "The Battle of Gettysburg as I Remember It," *Shenango Valley News*, April 2, 1915; Sigman, diary.

There is some disagreement over the positions of the 53rd Pennsylvania and 64th New York. Pfanz's conventions are not followed here (*Gettysburg—The Second Day*, 272) as they contradict the arrangement of the regiments' memorials on the battlefield.

75. OR suppl., 5, 155; OR 27, 1, 400, 409; John Brooke to John Bachelder, November 14, 1885; Osborn, "The Battle of Gettysburg as I Remember It"; Sigman, diary.

76. OR 27, 1, 400–401; Campbell, "Caldwell Clears the Wheatfield," 45.

77. OR 27, 1, 400–401; A. E. Clark, "The 27th Conn. At Gettysburg," Connecticut Historical Society, copy in 27th Connecticut folder, GNMP; John Brooke to John Bachelder, November 14, 1885; Sigman, diary; Winthrop D. Sheldon, *The "Twenty-Seventh," A Regimental History,* (New Haven

CT, 1866), 75; Pfanz, *Gettysburg—The Second Day*, 286–287.

78. OR 27, 1, 401, 410; Robert G. Smith, *A Brief Account of the Services Rendered by the Second Regiment Delaware Volunteers* (Wilmington, DE, 1909), 24–25.

79. OR 27, 1, 401.

While General Brooke and Martin Sigman recalled that the brigade rejoined the division on Cemetery Ridge that night, the reports of the 2nd Delware and 53rd Pennsylvania indicated that these regiments did not return until the next morning.

Brooke's recollection was probably more accurate (OR 27, 1, 401, 403, 410; Sigman, diary).

80. OR 27, 1, 401; Almond E. Clark, "A Yankee at Gettysburg—The Stand Made by the Remnant of the 27th Connecticut," *National Tribune*, October 10, 1918.

81. Sigman, diary.

82. S. A. Osborn, "The Battle of Gettysburg as I Remember It."

83. *PAG*, vol. 1, 332; OR 27, 1, 401, 404, 408.

84. Pfanz, *Gettysburg—The Second Day*, 286.

2ND DIVISION—

Brigadier General John Gibbon

Formed during the reorganization of the Army of the Potomac, the 2nd Division had fought in most of the battles, from the Peninsula campaign to Chancellorsville. Its darkest day was on September 17, 1862, at the battle of Antietam, when it was unexpectedly attacked in front and flank, losing thousands of men in a matter of minutes. It was the 2nd Division that established the beachhead across the Rappahannock River during the subsequent Fredericksburg campaign. The division had been led consecutively by two officers who rose to command corps at Gettysburg (John Sedgwick and Oliver Howard). Brigadier General John Gibbon took over the division on April 11, 1863, but did not see much action at Chancellorsville. A West Point graduate, Gibbon was best known for forging the Iron Brigade into a tough fighting unit.[1]

The division spent June 29 on a bone-crushing march of thirty-three miles that finally ended at Uniontown, Maryland. The men were given a reprieve from marching on June 30 and remained in camp. The march to Gettysburg resumed at about 7:00 A.M. on July 1, and the column reached the Pennsylvania state line at about 5:00 P.M. The march finally ended at 9:00 P.M., when the division halted near Little Round Top. Awakened at 3:00 A.M., the men marched to the base of Cemetery Hill. The division moved one last time, at 10:00 A.M., to its final position on Cemetery Ridge.[2]

The division faced west on Cemetery Ridge. Caldwell's Division was to their left and Hays's was to their right. The brigades were deployed in column of regiments, to facilitate rapid movements to other parts of the battlefield. Webb's Philadelphia Brigade was positioned near the Copse of Trees, and to its left was Hall's Brigade. Harrow's Brigade formed the divisional reserve in the rear. All was quiet until 4:00 P.M., when Gibbon sent two regiments from Harrow's Brigade, 15th Massachusetts and 82nd New York, forward to Emmitsburg Road to protect Humphreys's Division's right flank. These two regiments bore the initial brunt of

Wright's Brigade's (Anderson's Division, III Corps) attack on Cemetery Ridge. The units were overwhelmed and lost heavily. To help bolster the III Corps's line, Gibbon sent at least four other regiments: the 19th Maine and 1st Minnesota of Harrow's Brigade and the 19th Massachusetts and 42nd New York of Hall's Brigade to the left to provide support. All were engaged and helped stabilize the sector. While the gallant 1st Minnesota charged Wilcox's Brigade (Anderson's Division) on the slopes of Cemetery Ridge, the three other regiments also played a major role in maintaining the Federal position. The Philadelphia Brigade played a major role in repulsing Wright's Brigade's charge against Cemetery Ridge that evening.[3]

That evening it was the Philadelphia Brigade's turn to be broken up. The 106th Pennsylvania was sent to bolster the Cemetery Hill defenses, which were under attack by two brigades of Early's Division (II Corps). It arrived too late to participate in the repulse of this charge. The 71st Pennsylvania was also detached and sent to Culp's Hill. Assigned to form on the right of Greene's Brigade, it came under Confederate small arms fire in the dark. Alarmed by these actions, the regiment's commander marched the men back to the brigade's position on Cemetery Ridge without orders.[4]

July 3 brought lasting fame to the division. Because of its position in the middle of the Federal line on Cemetery Ridge, the division bore the brunt of Pickett's Division's attack. After some difficult moments, where the 71st Pennsylvania of the Philadelphia Brigade was overwhelmed and the 72nd Pennsylvania of the same brigade refused to charge the enemy, the division descended upon Pickett's men near the grove of trees. Gibbon's men ultimately sealed the breach and captured hundreds of enemy soldiers. The losses among the division were high, and included General Gibbon, who took a bullet to his left arm. The division ultimately left the battlefield on July 5.[5]

1st Brigade—Brigadier General William Harrow

Units: 19th Maine, 15th Massachusetts, 1st Minnesota, 82nd New York
Strength: 1366
Losses: 768 (147-573-48)—56.2%[6]

The men of the 1st Brigade harbored some animosities toward their officers as they marched toward Gettysburg. Upon hearing the news that Meade had replaced Hooker, Private Patrick Taylor of the 1st Minnesota recorded that it "[fell] on us like a wet blanket." The brigade also had a new commander, General William Harrow, who was ill during the campaign. He was already highly disliked by his men. Major Henry Abbott of the 20th Massachusetts wrote home that Harrow was "an administration tool . . . a western col. promoted for a bloodless skirmish out west ostensibly, but really for cursing rebels, is here in command . . . he toadies the men & calls them boys." Discontent also arose when Colonel William Colvill of the 1st was placed under arrest. The men were to cross a tributary of the Monocacy Creek without wasting time by taking off their shoes and socks. However, some of Colvill's men ignored Hancock's order, and skipped across on two fallen logs. Watching these actions, and hearing the taunts of men that he thought were from the 1st, but were really from the 15th Massachusetts, incensed II Corps Inspector General Colonel Charles Morgan. He immediately rode up to Colvill and placed him under arrest.[7]

Brigadier General William Harrow was constantly ill during his war-years. An attorney by training, he commanded the 14th Indiana in the Shenandoah Valley campaign, and after a bout with illness, was back with his regiment at Antietam, where he battled the Confederates at the Sunken Road, losing half of his men in the process. Sick again for several months, he finally returned to the army, and was given the 1st Brigade on June 8, 1863. He replaced General Alfred Sully, who was removed by General Gibbon for not shooting members of a mutinous regiment.[8]

The thirty-three-mile march on June 29 left the men numb and thoroughly exhausted. Halting near Uniontown, they were initially disheartened to learn that no campfires could be kindled. This order was countermanded, and campfires with brewing coffee could be seen throughout the camps. Most of the men were content to merely go to sleep. If they were not so tired, the men might have recalled the reception of the citizens earlier that day. "The old men shouted for joy. The women brought out pies, bread & chees [sic] and water, and the girls waved their handkerchiefs and snapped kisses from the second story windows," wrote Private Roland Bowen of the 15th Massachusetts. Sergeant John Plummer of the 1st Minnesota recalled that the citizens yelled, "God bless you! and "Good for you!" "[It] seemed to put new life into all of us," he recalled. Russ Allen told his comrades, "Boys, who wouldn't fight for such as these?"[9]

After resting near Uniontown on June 30, the men were back on the road early on July 1. During the march they passed troops from the XI Corps who told them of the catastrophe that had befallen the Union army that day. According to Sergeant Plummer (1st Minnesota), the men stopped to prepare their dinners when they were about thirteen miles from Gettysburg. They were given the impression that they would remain there, at least through the day. However, after finishing their meal the men were back on their feet, and the march continued. It finally ended that night near Little Round Top, where the men were ordered to build breastworks. According to Sergeant Plummer, "we were pretty tired and couldn't really see the necessity of work that far from the field, [so] we boys did not build any, but laid down to sleep." Roused early on July 2, the men were told to fix breakfast, consisting of hardtack and coffee. Orders to fall in soon followed. "Everything was bustle and excitement," and Private Bowen and his comrades knew that it was just a matter of time before they would be engaged. The men halted near Cemetery Hill. They moved again at 10:00 A.M., this time to Cemetery Ridge, where the men stacked arms and rested. The brigade was massed in column, from west to east, as 82nd New York–19th Maine–15th Massachusetts–1st Minnesota. The latter regiment's position was, according to Colonel Colvill, "a few rods to the left, and in front of a small white building [Leister house] near the Baltimore Pike." The ammunition wagons arrived, and although the men already had sixty rounds of ammunition, they were told to take twenty more, which some put in their haversacks.[10]

General Harrow assembled the men and gave them a speech that afternoon. Drawing his pistol, he yelled to his men, "The first God Damned man I see running or sneaking, I blow him to hell in an instant. This God Damned runing [sic] is played out, just stand to it and give them Hell." About 3:00 P.M., the men yelled out, "The 3rd corps is advancing," and the men "wa[t]ched them at every step with the greatest anxiety," recalled Private Bowen of the 15th. The brigade was subsequently "pulled to pieces" and destined to fight in three separate engagements on July 2.[11]

As the III Corps moved forward off the southern end of Cemetery Ridge, Gibbon decided to help support its right flank by advancing the 15th Massachusetts and the 82nd New York to an exposed position along Emmitsburg Pike. The 82nd New York's left flank was at the Codori house and the 15th Massachusetts took position on its right. While two batteries were in the vicinity, it was a highly vulnerable position, as both flanks hung in the air. The veterans of the two regiments realized their predicament and began throwing up flimsy breastworks of fence rails. These were quickly destroyed when the Southern artillery opened fire on the two regiments shortly after. The men could not see it because they were lying prone in the tall grass along Emmitsburg Road, but sometime between 6:15 and 6:30 P.M. a powerful Georgia brigade under General Ambrose Wright launched its attack on Cemetery

Ridge. The 15th Massachusetts and 82nd New York lay directly in its path.[12]

Realizing that an attack on their position was imminent, the men nervously placed their cartridges and ramrods within easy reach in front of them. Within half an hour of taking their positions, the skirmishers ran back to the main position. Soon after, the Confederates charged with their "demoniac yell," peppering the Union position with a volley at the same time, recalled Private Bowen. "With a shout we sprang up on our knees and resting our muskets over the rails, we gave them one of the most destructive volleys I ever witnessed . . . they hesitated, then reeled, they staggered and wavered slightly, yet there was no panic." These volleys momentarily stunned Wright's men, but did not stop them. To make matters worse, artillery fire from Union batteries in their rear fell among the men of the 15th Massachusetts and 82nd New York, killing and wounding a number of them.[13]

The 82nd New York crumbled first, as its men could not withstand the pressure on their front and left flank. The 15th Massachusetts tried to hold its position, as its men fired away at Wright's oncoming troops. Seeing that his position was being assailed in the front, right, and rear, Colonel J. H. Ward of the of the 15th Massachusetts realized that further resistance was hopeless and ordered a retreat. He went down with a fatal wound as the retreat began. The 82nd New York also lost its commander during this engagement. Private Bowen of the 15th Massachusetts thought it unusual that he did not see any officers at this time. What began as an organized retreat soon degenerated into a rout, as Wright's men gained on the retreating Union troops. One soldier recalled that we "retired in some disorder, being pressed so closely that we lost quite a number of prisoners, captured by the enemy." Another called the retreat a "stampede." The two shattered regiments subsequently reformed on the right of the 1st Minnesota behind the batteries on Cemetery Ridge.[14]

Released from arrest upon his request, Colonel William Colvill of the 1st Minnesota waited on Cemetery Ridge with his men. Soon after the 15th Massachusetts and 82nd New York were detached, Colvill received orders to move his regiment by the left flank along the crest of the ridge, toward a dry ravine (Plum Run) to plug part of the gap left when Caldwell's Division moved south to the Wheatfield. Here the regiment supported Thomas's battery. The men remained there until about 6:00 P.M., when the tide of battle approached them. They could see General Hancock trying unsuccessfully to rally the broken ranks of Humphreys's Division as it streamed to the rear. The Confederates were close behind. "They came at double-quick, and the first line had no sooner reached the foot of the ridge and halted, as I judged to reform its lines, which was . . . broken by the rapid advance," recalled Colvill. Watching the broken units retreat, Sergeant Plummer recalled that he "never felt so bad in my life. I thought sure the day was gone for us." Plummer resolved that he would rather die than suffer the "disgrace and humiliation" of defeat.[15]

Sitting on his horse, Hancock spied Colvill's unit and rode over to it. Yelling through the din, "What regiment is this?" and he was informed that it was the 1st Minnesota. His response was immediate: "Charge those lines!" Wilcox's Alabama Brigade (Anderson's Division), which had helped crush Humphreys's Division, loomed in front of the regiment. Colvill yelled, "Attention, First Minnesota; right shoulder shift; arms. Forward, double quick march," and his regiment was off.

Running down the bank of the ravine, they received the fire of Wilcox's massed regiments. However, most of the rounds were aimed too high and the Minnesotans raced onward. "Bullets whistled past us; shells screeched over us . . . no one took a second look at his fallen companion," wrote Private Alfred Carpenter. The enemy's aim improved. Saregeant Plummer noted that "the bullets were coming like hailstones, and whittling our boys like grain before the sickle." Colvill now ordered his men to charge, and Wilcox's first line melted away. Lieutenant William Lochren understood their reaction, as "the men were never made who will stand against levelled [sic] bayonets coming with such momentum and evident desperation." While Colvill asserted that there was some "bayonet pricking," he admitted that he did not know if anyone was killed in this manner.[16]

The charge halted Wilcox's advance momentarily, and losses to the 1st Minnesota were minimal. Before the Alabamians commenced their attack, Colvill ordered his men to open fire while they took whatever cover they could find in the dry creek bed. For several minutes the two sides fired at each other. The 1st Minnesota was hit in front and both flanks, and the number of casualties grew. Wilcox's men also refused to budge. Lieutenant Lochren recalled that the "ferocity of our onset seemed to paralyze them for a time, and though they poured in a terrible and continuous fire from the front and enveloping flanks, they kept at a respectful distance from our bayonets." Reinforcements arrived in the form of Willard's Brigade, which formed on the left of the 1st Minnesota. Realizing that the number of defenders was increasing and that he was unsupported, General Wilcox ordered his men to fall back to Seminary Ridge. While the 1st Minnesota had heroically sealed the gap in the Union line, it paid a dear price. Of the 262 men that made the charge, 178, or two-thirds of the regiment were killed or wounded in an engagement that lasted only five to ten minutes in Colvill's estimation. Two detached companies returned that evening, and the noncombatants were given muskets, swelling the ranks to 140 men.[17]

After the 15th Massachusetts and 82nd New York departed for Emmitsburg Road, General Hancock also ordered the 19th Maine to the left. Its orders were to support Weir's battery, which occupied an exposed position between Seminary and Cemetery Ridges. Hancock was clearly stressed at this point, for he "gave way to a curious outbreak of temper" as he positioned the battery, noted Colonel Heath of the 19th Maine. To hasten the movement, Heath ordered his men to break ranks to allow the battery to pass, to which Hancock snapped, "If he commanded the regt. he'd be God Damned if he would not charge bayonets on him." Finally in position, Heath ordered his men to lie down.[18]

As the Confederate attack rolled toward them, the men could see Humphreys's Division rapidly approaching, with the victorious Confederates close behind. Colonel Heath "walked in front of the line, cautioning the men to lie still and permit the retreating troops to pass over us," recalled Private John Smith. Humphreys's men were clearly anxious to reach safety, so they disregarded the 19th Maine lying in the path of their retreat. Silas Adams noted that Humphreys's men "swept over us, they stepped over us, they stepped on or between the men and even tumbled over us, having no regard to dignity or military order, or to pick out reasonable paths to walk in, as their only object seemed to be to get to the rear, out of reach of their relentless pursuers." A

general officer, thought to be Humphreys, approached Heath and "ordered me to get my men (who were all lying down) on their feet and stop his men; this I refused to do, fearing that the Regt.would be carried away with the disordered troops." Heath told the general to "get his men out of the way & that we would stop the pursuers." The general was clearly unhappy and rode down Heath's line, ordering his men up. Heath rode behind him, countermanding the order. As Humphreys's men passed, some yelled out, "Run boys, we're whipped, the day is lost." Others tried to encourage the men by shouting, "Hang on, boys! We will form in your rear." Some men from the Excelsior Brigade apparently tried to do so, but they too disappeared after a short time.[19]

The 19th Maine was now alone, except for the 1st Minnesota, which was about 350 yards to their left (south), and other scattered regiments somewhere in the vicinity. This handful of regiments was asked to face a Confederate attack that Humphreys's Division could not stem. Although the 19th Maine had been in the army for almost a year, it had never been in battle. Closely following Humphreys's men was Lang's small Florida brigade. Seeing a tall Confederate color bearer moving ahead of the line of battle, Heath ordered one of his men to shoot him, and within moments the soldier and his flag fell to the ground. John Smith recalled that "the 'rebs' were about thirty-five yards from our lines, when Colonel Heath gave the order to fire. The regiment arose and delivered a deadly fire into the ranks of the enemy that surprised and staggered them." Despite the firepower of four hundred muskets, the Floridians continued on, causing some of the men from Maine to question whether their bullets were reaching their mark. The captain of the left company approached Heath with bad

2ND DIVISION ❧ 141

news—a large enemy force was on his flank. Running over, Heath saw a Confederate regiment in the act of deploying. Heath immediately ordered his left companies to shift position and fire into this new threat, and "the column disappeared at once," he noted.[20]

Heath's second in command now rushed over with news that the enemy had gained the right flank and rear of the regiment, placing it in danger of being cut off and captured. Not waiting to see this threat for himself, Heath ordered the entire regiment withdrawn. After the regiment had retreated about twenty yards, the smoke cleared and Heath could see that it was a false alarm. He immediately ordered his men back to their original positions. Moving forward again, they drove into Lang's Brigade, whose advance one Union soldier called "snail-like," capturing several prisoners in the process. In actuality, Lang pulled back to Emmitsburg Road after receiving the first volleys and realized that he was no longer supported on his right. Therefore, when Heath's men returned, the Confederates were in the process of pulling back anyway. Seeing the Confederates retreat, Heath yelled out, "Come on, boys," and the regiment sprang forward after them.[21]

That evening, the men helped tend to the wounded, who were fairly easy to find because of the bright full moon. One soldier from the 19th Maine recalled that "the cries of the enemy's wounded, whom no friends had cared for, drove sleep from the eyelids of many a soldier." Many thought of home and their loved ones left behind.[22]

On the morning of July 3, Harrow's Brigade occupied a position on the front line of Cemetery Ridge to the left of Hall's Brigade. It was deployed, from left to right, as 15th Massachusetts–1st Minnesota–19th Maine–82nd New York. To its

left were the 80th New York and 151st Pennsylvania from Biddle's Brigade (Doubleday's Division, I Corps). To its right was Hall's Brigade. Because the men did not have entrenching tools, they used whatever they could find to build crude barricades. Some of the men emptied out their knapsacks, filled them with sand, and added them to the breastworks for added protection. Lieutenant William Lochren of the 1st Minnesota described these barricades as being "knee high." This task completed, many of the men went to sleep. However, soon after 1:00 P.M., the great cannonade began. One soldier from the 19th Maine suggested that, "had a knitting-needle stood on end it would have been shot off a dozen times." While the infantry lay prone, the men could see the artillerymen servicing their guns, who in many cases, were swept away by the maelstrom. According to Colonel Heath, all the men had to do was "chew tobacco, watch caissons explode and wonder if the next shot would hit you. On the whole it was not a happy time."[23]

It was almost with relief that the cannonade ended and the Confederate infantry advanced. At first, the right of Pickett's Division marched in close formation straight for their position. However, an oblique movement by the Confederates to the left (to right of the Federals) brought Harrow's men out of harm's way. As Kemper's Brigade forced the Union line to Harrow's right to pull back, Heath quickly ordered his men to the scene of the heaviest fighting. So intent were the men to get there that all order was lost. One veteran from the 19th Maine wrote, "Company, regimental and brigade organizations were lost, and we were a great crowd." Colonel Heath of the regiment agreed: "we went up more like a mob than a disciplined force." Another soldier from the 19th Maine related that "it was a wild charge, with little regard for ranks or files. Volleys were given and received at close quarters." After the men fired, others jumped in front of them to discharge their guns, while the men in the original position reloaded their guns. This maneuver generated a steady stream of small arms fire into Pickett's flank. Amos Plaisted of the 15th Massachusetts recalled that many of the enemy soldiers were lying down behind the stone wall when they approached, which made the process of extracting them more difficult.[24]

The men knew what was at stake and, according to Alfred Carpenter of the 1st Minnesota, "seemed inspired and fought with a determination . . . men fell about us unheeded, unnoticed; we scarcely knew they were falling, so great was the intensity of attention to the fallen foe. Our muskets became so heated we could no longer handle them. We dropped them and picked up those of the wounded . . . many men became deaf . . . it was a grand and terrible scene."[25]

Plaisted estimated that the standoff continued for about five minutes, and Harrow's men took heavy losses. Not able to take it anymore, one soldier from the 15th Massachusetts yelled out, "For Gods sake let us charge . . . theyl [sic] kill us all if we stand here." Continuing his narrative, Plaisted wrote that "we did charge tords [sic] the wall all in a mass, and the enimy [sic] jumped up to run and several atempted [sic] to take their flag off the Wall, but as soon as they started we stoped [sic] and gave them a volley and nearly all lay down again and cried out to us to stop firing and let them come in." Desperate hand-to-hand combat now erupted. While those in the front ranks used their rifle butts against the closest Southerners, John Smith of the 19th Maine observed that "those in the rear of the crowd of Union soldiers fired over the heads of those in front, and some of them hurled stones at the heads of the Confederates." Lieutenant William Harmon of the 1st Minnesota recalled that "if men ever became devils that was one of the times. We were crazy with the excitement of the fight. We just rushed in like beasts. Men swore and cussed and struggled and fought, grappled in hand-to-hand fight, threw stones, clubbed their muskets, kicked, yelled, and hurrahed." Wilbur Clifford of the 19th Maine noted that "we were directly in front of their left flank and not more than 75 yards from them when they turned and ran and we kept sending the lead after them till they got out of reach." The 82nd New York avenged its beating of July 2 by capturing the battleflags of the 1st and 7th Virginia of Kemper's Brigade. Colonel Heath also claimed that his men captured two flags, but they were "torn from the lances by men of other regiments." The 1st Minnesota claimed the flag of the 28th Virginia of Garnett's Brigade, but they lost an additional fifty men, bringing their total losses to over 70% for the battle.[26]

Those who were sent out on the skirmish line after the charge was repulsed encountered dead and wounded enemy soldiers dotting the fields. Clifford found them "groaning, crying for water, praying, swearing, all at once in every direction." The men were famished after the fight. Because their haversacks were empty, the men resorted to rifling through those of the dead and wounded Confederates, who lay about in great numbers. July 4 was spent resting and burying the dead. The brigade finally left the battlefield on July 5.[27]

The brigade acquitted itself well during the battle. The charge of the 1st Minnesota has become one of the legends of the battle, overshadowing a similar one made by the 19th Maine. These two regiments were instrumental in halting the attack of two Confederate brigades that came close to capturing Cemetery Ridge. The 82nd New York and 15th Massachusetts were poorly positioned on July 2 and paid the price by being flanked, causing heavy losses. All of the regiments apparently did well in the repulse of Kemper's Brigade on July 3.

2nd Brigade—Brigadier General Alexander Webb

Units: 69th Pennsylvania, 71st Pennsylvania, 72nd Pennsylvania, 106th Pennsylvania
Strength: 1224
Losses: 491 (114-338-39)—39.5%[28]

Although the Philadelphia Brigade had fought in virtually every engagement in the eastern theater, historian George Stewart believed that "in studying the records, one comes up with a feeling that perhaps all was not well, that beneath the surface it was suffering from some lapse of morale." Almost as soon as Meade assumed command of the army, he removed the brigade's popular, but lax commander, General Joshua Owen, and replaced him with a young "spit and polish" West Pointer with little combat experience. The men knew that General Alexander Webb was a protégé of Meade and realized that nepotism was alive and well in the army. Webb called his officers together and criticized them for no longer wearing their shoulder boards or other accoutrements of rank. The men had discarded the trappings to avoid being conspicuous, but Webb would have none of it. He also told them that all straggling must stop immediately, and that any offenders were to be brought to him and he would "shoot [them] . . . like dogs."[29]

The men's resentment rose during the remainder of the march as their new commander imposed strict discipline. For example, prior to fording the Monocacy Creek, Webb refused to allow the men to remove their shoes and socks. To act as a model, he dismounted in the middle of the creek. One Irishman was not impressed, muttering to Webb as he passed, "Sure its no wonder ye can stand there when ye are [in] leather up to your waist." An officer attempting to scamper across the stream on a fallen log was quickly placed under arrest by Webb. On June 29, Webb pushed his men unmercifully. The brigade marched nineteen miles without a rest, and the men were in a foul mood when they reached Liberty. However, the townspeople were out with cool water, milk, pies, bread, and butter, and these delicacies helped boost the men's spirits. The respite was all too short, for Webb again pushed his men to Uniontown, which they reached at 9:00 P.M. that night after the thirty-five-mile march in fourteen hours. The men were permitted to rest on June 30, and best of all, the paymaster visited the camp.[30]

The march continued at 7:00 A.M. on July 1, and the men crossed the Pennsylvania state line at about 5:00 P.M. that day. Their presence was needed up ahead, so no ceremonies accompanied this special moment. As the men approached the battlefield, they could hear the dull booming of cannon in the distance. They also passed a long line of wounded soldiers, and knew that it was just a matter of time before they would be engaged. The men finally bivouacked for the night between Little Round Top and Taneytown Road at 9:00 P.M.[31]

The men were awakened at 3:00 A.M. on July 2 and told to prepare to march. After about two miles, the brigade halted and Webb addressed the men. He told them that "they would now be called upon to defend their own state by hard fighting, that it would require each man to do his full duty . . . any one found shirking it in the slightest degree would be severely dealt with . . . he would shoot any one leaving the line, and . . . any man [could] do the same to him if he failed in his duty." The men were permitted to rest, make coffee, and eat their hardtack.[32]

The final leg of the march began at 6:00 A.M. on July 2. Almost immediately, the men wheeled to the left to take position along Cemetery Ridge. To their left was Hall's Brigade (Gibbon's Division) and to their right was Willard's Brigade (Hays's Division). Only one regiment, the 69th Pennsylvania, was ordered to take position behind a low stone wall in front of the Copse of Trees, facing the Confederate position on Seminary Ridge. The three other regiments rested on the other side of the ridge, and were hidden from the view of even the most powerful Confederate field glasses.[33]

Before the men had time to get comfortable, each regiment was ordered to send out skirmishers. After the 1st Delaware of Smyth's Brigade was pushed back from the Bliss farm buildings by the 16th Mississippi, a company from the 106th Pennsylvania was foolishly sent forward to try to drive the enemy from the farmyard. The unit's commander quickly realized the impossibility of his task and withdrew, but not before losing eleven men and an officer. The company returned soon after to help the 12th New Jersey drive the enemy from the farm.[34]

That afternoon the men watched the III Corps advance to an exposed position and not much later saw and heard the savage attack launched against it by General James Longstreet's two divisions. That was to the south, but gradually the men could discern that the battle was creeping toward them. The veterans of the 69th Pennsylvania knew what was about to happen. They were not happy that there were no troops to their right, as Willard's regiments had been ordered south. Sharing the low stone wall to the left of them were the 59th New York and 7th Michigan of Hall's Brigade. The three other units of the Philadelphia Brigade were within supporting distance in column of regiments on the reverse slope of the ridge, arranged in the following order from top of the slope to the base: 71st Pennsylvania–72nd Pennsylvania–106th Pennsylvania.[35]

The Confederate artillery opened on the Federal lines late in the afternoon, forcing the men to dive for cover. Even the troops on the opposite side of the ridge were not immune to this cannonade—one officer and several men from the 106th Pennsylvania were wounded. About 6:30 P.M. the men could see long, well-dressed lines of infantry of Brigadier General Ambrose Wright's Georgia Brigade moving in their direction. Fourteen hundred men strong, it was a veteran unit that had won its share of laurels. Corporal John Buckley of the 69th Pennsylvania recalled after the war that these men were "the best clothed soldiers that we had ever come across on their side."[36]

Sweeping aside the six hundred men of the 15th Massachusetts and 82nd New York of Harrow's Brigade that had been deployed along Emmitsburg Road, Wright's men made for the six-rifled cannon of Lieutenant Fred Brown's battery. Realizing the hopelessness of the situation, Brown ordered his guns to the rear, but two cannon had to be abandoned.[37]

The Irishmen of the 69th Pennsylvania watched impatiently as Brown's guns thundered past them. Their front now cleared, the 69th Pennsylvania color bearer calmly shook the folds out of the green flag as his comrades opened fire. Some cannoneers that had dropped to the ground in front of the wall looked up to see a "vivid flame sending messengers of death to the foe."[38]

Captain Michael Duffy of the 69th Pennsylvania became so enraged when a Confederate officer mounted one of the abandoned cannon to encourage his men that he screamed to his own men to "Knock that d____d officer off the gun." A short time later, the enemy officer lay crumpled at the base of the cannon and Captain Duffy was also wounded. Despite the pounding that Wright's men had taken from Brown's guns and the intense small arms fire from the 69th Pennsylvania, the 48th Georgia on the left of Wright's line continued to rush forward. Not a Pennsylvanian ran for the rear. The historian of the 69th Pennsylvania recalled,

Still came on the mad Georgians until they reach point-blank range of our rifles. We met their charge with such a destroying fire that they were forced back in confusion. They rall[ied] again and ma[d]e a second effort and again their lines [were] broken and thinned as we pour[ed] volley upon volley into their disordered rank, until they finally retire[d] a dispirited mob.[39]

Realizing that the 69th Pennsylvania was about to be overwhelmed, Generals Hancock and Webb ordered the three remaining regiments of the brigade forward. The 71st Pennsylvania took position behind a low stone fence to the right of the Copse of Trees, with its right connecting with Arnold's battery. In front of it was Cushing's battery. The 72nd Pennsylvania rushed to the left of the Copse of Trees and the 106th Pennsylvania was brought

up to the crest of the ridge, just to the right of the Copse of Trees. Colonel Curry of the latter regiment recalled what happened that fateful evening:

By order of Brigadier-General Webb, I advanced the regiment by the left flank, and formed in rear of the second line. Shortly after, orders were received to move forward. I advanced the regiment to the crest of the hill, and opened fire upon the enemy. After several volleys, perceiving that we checked his advance, and seeing his lines waver, I ordered bayonets fixed and a charge to be made, which movement resulted in a complete success, the enemy retiring in confusion to his original position in the woods.[40]

The 48th Georgia had already taken horrific losses during its advance and now could see a fresh Federal regiment eagerly jumping over the low stone fence and rushing toward their flank, cheering at the top of its lungs. This was the final straw for the 48th Georgia. Its relatively few remaining men turned around and began to make their way back to the safety of Seminary Ridge. Left behind were 57% of the regiment and its beloved flag.[41]

While the Philadelphia Brigade firmly held the sector on its front, the same was not true on the left of the line, where several of Wright's regiments saw the gap in the Federal line that had been occupied by Caldwell's Division and drove for it, briefly reaching the crest of Cemetery Ridge. Just then they were hit by a savage counterattack by part of the 13th Vermont (Stannard's Brigade, Doubleday's Division) and forced to retreat.[42]

On the opposite side of Gibbon's line, the 106th Pennsylvania was not content to see the backs of the 48th Georgia, and with the 71st Pennsylvania swept forward and recaptured Brown's lost guns. The 72nd also advanced. While the 71st Pennsylvania remained with the cannon, the

106th Pennsylvania and 72nd Pennsylvania crossed Emmitsburg Road after the enemy. What happened next has been debated. According to the historian of the 106th Pennsylvania, the men spied a Confederate officer waving a white handkerchief as they approached the Codori house. Colonel Curry ordered one of his companies forward to investigate and it soon encountered an officer from the 48th Georgia. He informed the Federal troops that his regimental commander, Colonel William Gibson, was seriously wounded and needed immediate medical attention. The story goes that Colonel Gibson was not the only other Confederate soldier in the farmyard—the entire remnant of the 48th Georgia was also present with their beloved commander. The Federal company commander surveyed the situation and told his counterpart that he would honor the request, but only if all of the men surrendered. This demand was immediately rejected, but when the Federal officer persisted, all of the Georgians laid down their arms to surrender. Besides Colonel Gibson, the 106th Pennsylvania supposedly bagged five captains, fifteen lieutenants, and about 250 enlisted men. The story was corroborated by General Webb's after-battle report. While an interesting story, it is probably just that. There are too many holes and improbabilities for it to be taken seriously. The regiment's historian spun other tales about this part of the battle. For example, he wrote that the men captured Colonel Birkett Fry and many men of the 13th Alabama in the basement of the Codori house. These troops were, however, out of harm's way on Seminary Ridge at the time. The regiment also purportedly captured four "Parrot guns" that had been abandoned by the enemy. Yet these guns probably did not exist.[43]

General Webb pulled his men back to the safety of Cemetery Ridge shortly after, and the men took stock of their losses. Although Wright's Brigade had lost almost half of its men in the charge, the Philadelphia Brigade's losses were much more modest—127, or just over 10%.[44]

If the men had visions of a peaceful rest, those dreams were dashed when an officer ordered Colonel Curry to move his 106th Pennsylvania to Cemetery Hill. In the gathering darkness, two brigades from General Jubal Early's Division had made a desperate attack on the hill and troops were needed to drive them off the heights. The regiment apparently arrived too late to participate in this short, but sharp engagement.[45]

At about the same time, Hancock also ordered the 71st Pennsylvania to the right to reinforce the extreme flank of the army on Culp's Hill. This part of the line had been seriously weakened when Meade pulled all but one brigade of General Howard Slocum's XII Corps out of line to assist in blunting Longstreet's attack on the Federal left. General Edward Johnson's Division made several attacks on Culp's Hill, and General "Pap" Greene's thinly stretched brigade needed help, so the 71st Pennsylvania was rushed forward to extend the line. The men had difficulty navigating over the rough terrain in the darkness and, to make matters worse, did not know where to go. Fortunately, the regiment's commander, Colonel R. Penn Smith, met a XII Corps staff officer, who led the men in the right direction. Captain Charles Horton, Greene's adjutant, took the regiment to its assigned position on the right of the 137th New York. As they approached, the men gave three loud cheers to reassure Greene's beleaguered men. The nearby Confederates also heard this noise and opened fire on the Pennsylvanians. Just as the 71st Pennsylvania settled in on the right of the Federal line, Steuart's Confederate Brigade attacked its front and flank. The men of the 137th New York were amazed when the Pennsylvanians suddenly filed out of the breastworks. No panic or disorder was evident. Sergent William Burns of the 71st Pennsylvania recorded in his diary that "it was a blunder on the part of our officers and came near costing us dear. It was the heaviest and wickedest musketry fire for about half an hour that ever I lay under. We lost 15 men and four officers."[46]

Colonel Penn described the incident in his after-battle report:

An adjutant-general directed me to proceed to the front, assuring me that all was safe on either flank. Arriving at the front, I became engaged with the enemy on the front. At the same time he attacked me on my right and rear. I immediately ordered my command to retire to the road in my rear, when I returned to camp against orders. During the engagement, I lost 3 commissioned officers and 11 enlisted men.[47]

As Colonel Smith marched his command back in the direction from which they had come, Captain Horton rushed up and demanded an explanation. Smith angrily told him that he would not have his men murdered, and that he had orders to return to his former position. General Webb's official report tersely read that the regiment "returned at about 12 o'clock without orders." In recalling this incident after the war, Horton wrote that the men of the 71st Pennsylvania appeared mortified by the actions of their commanding officer. With the 71st gone, the Confederates attacked the 137th New York in its front, flank, and rear, forcing it backward with heavy losses. Some of the breastworks were captured. The men of the 71st Pennsylvania subsequently returned to their original positions on Cemetery Ridge, where they stacked arms and went to sleep.[48]

The morning of July 3 was quiet, giving the men time to rest and find something to eat, as none had done so in twenty-four hours. The men became more apprehensive as noon approached, as it was too quiet on their front. Private Joseph McDermott of the 69th Pennsylvania observed that "anxious looks could clearly be seen on the faces of the men, and feelings of mingled dread and determination pervaded the minds." In anticipation of an attack, Webb reviewed the alignment of his brigade. The 69th Pennsylvania remained in its position behind the low stone wall in front of the Copse of Trees, with Cushing's cannons on its right and Hall's regiments on its left. The 71st Pennsylvania and 72nd Pennsylvania were again in reserve on the opposite side of the ridge, and all but two companies of the 106th Pennsylvania remained with Howard's XI Corps on Cemetery Hill.[49]

A single cannon fired shortly after 1:00 P.M. and then most of the Confederate artillery opened fire on the Union line. McDermott recalled that "the air [was] filling with the whirling, shrieking, hissing sound of the solid shot and bursting shell; all threw themselves flat upon the ground, behind the little stone wall; nearly 150 guns belched forth messengers of destruction, sometimes in volleys, again in irregular, but continual sounds, traveling through the air, high above us, or striking the ground in front and ricocheting over us, to be imbedded in some object to the rear." Joseph McKeever, of the same regiment, noted that "after the cannonading began, we were all hugging the earth and we would have liked to get into it if we could."[50]

The firing stopped as suddenly as it had started and during the subsequent lull the officers prepared their men for an attack they knew would surely come. Some felt the need to address their men.

Colonel Dennis O'Kane of the 69th Pennsylvania told his men to conserve their ammunition and not fire until they could see the "whites of their eyes" and reminded them that they were defending their beloved state. He concluded his remarks by saying, "Let your work this day be for victory to the death." Webb also told the men not to fire until the enemy had crossed Emmitsburg Road and "gave them all the encouragement in his power," recalled one of the men. The brigade commander also made last-minute adjustments to his line. With Cushing's battery all but destroyed, he moved the 71st Pennsylvania to the low stone wall that extended to the right of the 69th Pennsylvania. Since Webb elected to leave a few of Cushing's cannon in place, the entire 71st Pennsylvania could not fit behind the wall, so two companies were positioned behind a continuation of the wall about two hundred feet in the rear and right. Noted modern historian George Stewart speculated that "by this shift at a critical moment, most of the regiment was sent into a position with which it was unfamiliar. In such a situation, troops are likely to be nervous."[51]

Webb's line now consisted of the 69th Pennsylvania in front of the Copse of Trees and to its right, eight companies of the 71st Pennsylvania, with the two remaining companies just behind it and to the right. All were positioned behind low two-foot-high stone walls. Some volunteers from the 71st Pennsylvania helped man Cushing's depleted gun crews, which occupied the gap between the 69th and 71st Pennsylvania. The 72nd Pennsylvania continued occupying its reserve position behind the Copse of Trees. Concerned about his men's ability to withstand a determined charge, Webb sent a small detail of forty-five men under the command of a captain to stand behind the

brigade with orders to shoot any man who tried to get past them.[52]

The men could soon see the long line of Pickett's Division breaking from the protection of Seminary Ridge. As the Confederates steadily approached, the men could see that most were heading directly for their position. General Webb panicked and began searching for ways to handle this deadly situation. He requested the services of Captain Andrew Cowan's battery near Cemetery Hill, and despite the fact that it belonged to the VI Corps, its commander redeployed his guns near the Copse of Trees. Webb was everywhere during this time, encouraging and eyeing his new command. The brigade's skirmishers stubbornly held their ground against General Richard Garnett's Brigade (Pickett's Division), but were finally forced to scamper for the protection of the Union line.[53]

When Garnett's Brigade was within 250 yards, the prone men of the Philadelphia Brigade sprang up on their knees and opened fire. The smoke from the initial volley enveloped the Virginians, and when it cleared there were many fewer men standing. Half the battle flags went down, but were quickly picked up by other soldiers. All the Confederate troops could see was the glitter of the sun on the Philadelphia Brigade's rifle barrels, red flashes as they fired, and their flags. These initial volleys were unusually intense and rapid because the Federal soldiers had scoured the area for guns prior to the attack, and each had two to five loaded guns behind him.[54]

If the men had had time, they could have counted about ten Confederate regimental battle flags in front of them. Defending this five hundred-foot sector were less than four hundred infantry and a few cannon that had all but expended their ammunition. Inviting gaps in the line existed in two places to allow the two batteries to fire through the Federal line. The 28th, 56th, and part of the 19th Virginia of Garnett's Brigade aimed for the 71st Pennsylvania and the gap to its left. Realizing the seriousness of the situation, Webb quickly ordered the unbloodied 72nd Pennsylvania and the two companies of the 106th Pennsylvania to advance from their reserve position to plug the hole on the right side of his line. Before he could bring them up, Garnett's men surged forward and overpowered the 71st Pennsylvania. Sergeant William Burns of the 71st Pennsylvania recorded in his diary that "the fight soon became awful. We mowed the rebs right and left but still they came on. We had to retreat." Garnett's men rushed for the stone wall and captured it, along with those Pennsylvanians who tenaciously held their ground.[55]

Suddenly materializing farther up the ridge was a mass of blue—the 72nd Pennsylvania had arrived. No sooner had they reached this position than they were ordered to fire a volley into Garnett's troops. Lieutenant George Finley of the 56th Virginia vividly remembered the scene: "A terrific fire burst upon us from our front, and looking around I saw close to us, just on the crest of the ridge, a fresh line of Federals attempting to drive us from the stone fence, but after exchanging a few rounds with us they fell back behind the crest, leaving us still in possession of the stone wall. Under this fire . . . General Garnett had fallen dead."

Most of Garnett's men elected to remain at the stone wall and wait for Armistead's Brigade. They exchanged fire with the 72nd Pennsylvania near the crest of the ridge. Webb realized that the Southern position was vulnerable at this point and ordered a charge by the 72nd Pennsylvania. To his horror, the men would not obey his orders. Some veterans

recalled after the war that if these were his orders, they did not hear them because of the din of battle. Not to be deterred, Webb decided to take action, as he recalled after the war. "The color bearer and myself stood together, I holding onto the staff and he did not move forward with me. I ordered him forward; this was the color bearer of the 72nd regiment. I know of no words said when I ordered him forward, he moved in his place but did not carry the colors out of the regimental line." The color bearer would soon be dead, riddled with thirteen bullet wounds. Webb's spirits sank. He had witnessed the 71st Pennsylvania flee and now he could not get the 72nd Pennsylvania to charge. Webb admitted in a letter to his wife, "when they [Garnett's Brigade] came over the fences, the Army of the Potomac was near being whipped than it was at any time of the battle. When my men fell back I almost wished to get killed." Perhaps to do so, Webb walked down to the 69th Pennsylvania's position, which was under heavy attack.[56]

The furious attack on the 69th Pennsylvania was made by several of Kemper's and Garnett's regiments. Cowan's battery belched canister at the oncoming Confederates, but some of the balls bowled over the 69th Pennsylvania's men as well. The Virginians were undeterred and continued their advance. The men of the 69th Pennsylvania refused to budge. It became a standoff. Some of the enemy actually jumped over the crouched men of the 69th Pennsylvania at the wall and ran for Cowen's guns, only to be blown away by canister at short range. The pressure was just too great, and parts of the regiment were forced back toward the Copse of Trees. McKeever (69th Pennsylvania) recalled that "we all fell back just as they were coming in to the inside of the trees and they made a rally, and then they were coming in all around, but how they fired without killing all our men I do not know." All order was lost and the unit could only be called a "mob." Still the men desperately fought on.[57]

Back on the right of the Philadelphia Brigade's line, General Armistead, twirling his hat on his sword, arrived at the head of his brigade. Sizing up the situation, he yelled to his men, "Come on, boys, give them the cold steel! Who will follow me?" Climbing over the stone wall, they overwhelmed the right of the 69th Pennsylvania and drove for the 72nd Pennsylvania. To counter this new threat, the right companies of the 69th Pennsylvania were ordered to refuse the line, to face Armistead's men on their right and rear. The three right-most companies promptly obeyed the order, but the captain of the next company (F) was shot just as he was about to give the order. The company therefore held its position and was overwhelmed by Armistead's men. Most were killed, wounded, or captured. A rapid counterattack helped secure the right of the 69th Pennsylvania's line. At this point, both the 69th Pennsylvania's right and left companies were refused backward, and the center ones tenaciously held the area in front of the Copse of Trees.[58]

Webb walked into this maelstrom. Pointed out by Confederate officers, Webb was fired on by the enemy infantry, but surprisingly was only grazed in the thigh. He provided encouragement upon reaching the right flank of the 69th Pennsylvania. One of the soldiers admitted that "we thought we were all gone." Just as Armistead touched one of Cushing's now abandoned cannons, he fell mortally wounded. The 72nd Pennsylvania had brought down a second Confederate brigade commander. Realizing that their numbers were too few to defeat the 72nd Pennsylvania, many of Armistead's men

dropped to the ground and opened fire. Others ran to their right to fire into the backs of the 69th Pennsylvania.[59]

Help was on the way, as other regiments converged on the scene of this desperate fighting. Two of Hall's regiments, the 19th Massachusetts and 42nd New York, charged toward the Copse of Trees, smashing into the disordered mass of Confederates and closing the gap on the right of the 69th Pennsylvania. Captain William Hill of the 19th Massachusetts later complimented the men of the 69th Pennsylvania. "They were doing some pretty good fighting. They did not yield one inch, and the enemy swarmed right over them, but whenever they got a chance to get in a shot here and there they let the enemy have it." All was now pandemonium. Captain Cowan later wrote that "the 69th Pa. Regt. was before our guns, but I do not think . . .there was such a thing as *regiments*. The men were fighting pretty much at will." All order was lost, as individual fights broke out between the men on both sides. Finally realizing that to continue was foolhardy, the Southerners either surrendered or tried to escape.[60]

Attempts were still being made to get the right side of Webb's Brigade to charge the enemy at the stone wall. An aide to General Gibbon, Lieutenant Frank Haskell, tried without success to get the 71st Pennsylvania to charge and then turned his attention to the 72nd Pennsylvania. Whether it was his actions, the approach of other Federal regiments, or just a decision that it was time, the 72nd Pennsylvania finally charged Pickett's men. Major Samuel Roberts recalled that "the color bearer, seizing the stump of the staff of the colors, whirling his hat around his head, moved with the regiment down to the wall; many of our men being wounded or killed in the advance and the men behind that wall, besides men out in the field surrendered; the men out in the field throwing up their hands and shouting 'Don't shoot.'" A total of seven men carried the 72nd Pennsylvania's flag that day. Six others lay dead or wounded on the field. According to Sergeant Burns, the 71st Pennsylvania also participated in the charge, which he said, was led by Webb. "He went right in front of us and led us when we gave a yell and charged on them and drove them back with great slaughter," he noted.[61]

The 69th Pennsylvania, the "Rock of Erin," had magnificently held its position despite overwhelming odds. The men were so stunned after the engagement that they neglected to pick up the Confederate regimental flags lying in abundance all around them. As a result, other units, "captured" flags (the 71st Pennsylvania picked up five) and received recognition. At the other end of the spectrum was the behavior of the 72nd Pennsylvania. In his report, General Webb wrote that "the Seventy-second Pennsylvania Volunteers were ordered up to hold the crest, and advanced to within 40 paces of the enemy's line . . . [it] fought steadily and persistently." Yet Colonel Devereux of the 19th Massachusetts recalled Webb saying immediately after the repulse that the

72nd would receive a "severe scolding" for its behavior. Interestingly, Webb tried to amend his official report long after the war by adding the statement, "the portion of the 72nd PA volunteers near me remained steadily in their position, a little retired from the crest, and fired at the advancing enemy."[62]

The brigade's two-day losses were almost 50%, and it now numbered less than seven hundred men. That night the men were issued three days' rations, but a drenching rain saturated the men and reduced their hardtack to a pulpy mush that even the hungriest would not eat. Each man slept that night with several loaded guns by his side. The brigade continued burying the dead the next day. Sergeant Burns, who had recorded little of the havoc or misery of past battles, now showed how thoroughly he was moved when he wrote, "Shocking sights." The men heard the welcome news that Lee was retreating back toward Virginia on July 5, and they followed soon after.[63]

While the 69th Pennsylvania and 106th Pennsylvania had performed superbly during the battle, the behavior of the brigade's two other regiments was suspect. The cloud of doubt about the brigade's effectiveness would follow it through the remainder of the war.[64]

3rd Brigade—Colonel Norman Hall

Units: 19th Massachusetts, 20th Massachusetts, 7th Michigan, 42nd New York, 59th New York
Strength: 922
Losses: 377 (71-282-14)—40.1%[65]

Although the 3rd Brigade had been in most of the campaigns of the Army of the Potomac, it claimed lasting fame when its

men paddled across the Rappahannock River to establish a beachhead there during the Fredericksburg campaign. Colonel Norman Hall commanded the brigade. A West Point graduate, Hall served at Ft. Sumter when it fell in 1861. During the early years of the war he commanded artillery, became a staff officer, and led the 7th Michigan. He probably rode toward Gettysburg questioning why he had not been promoted.[66]

The march to the battlefield was a difficult one for the 3rd Brigade, but the men made the best of it. Sergeant McGinnis usually could be found at the front of the 19th Massachusetts leading his "glee club" in song. "March along, we are marching along," they sang. Private Cornelius Linehan would never forget June 29, when the men marched a total of thirty-two miles in thirteen hours "with knapsack, haversack, canteen, gun, cartridge box, equipments, shelter tent, rubber blanket, sixty rounds of cartridges . . . not boys' every day play." The men received a day's rest at Uniontown, Maryland, where they were well cared for by the small town's citizens. Colonel Arthur Devereux of the 19th Massachusetts wrote that they "manifested a spirit unexpected and worthy of the name of the town, something we had been unaccustomed to in our considerable previous experience with the population of Maryland." The men were on the march again early on July 1, and before long began passing streams of wounded men heading for the rear. The men finally approached the battlefield at about 9:00 P.M. and were permitted to rest. The brigade, and the remainder of the II Corps, had just completed a very tiring 190-mile march. So intent was Hancock on reaching the battlefield that he ordered each regiment to post a guard in its rear to arrest any man who fell out of the ranks to get a drink of water. Perhaps equally vexing was the pervasive dust, which "enveloped us [so that] nothing was anywhere visible. For all that we knew we might have been passing through a treeless desert," recalled George Bruce of the 20th Massachusetts.[67]

The men were up at daybreak on July 2, refreshed and ready to go. After a quick breakfast, the men were back in column at about 5:00 A.M. and heading north in the following order: 42nd New York–20th Massachusetts–19th Massachusetts–7th Michigan–59th New York. After a short march, the brigade was ordered to the right of the Taneytown Road, where it formed in column of regiments. The men rested for about an hour before being ordered across the road to Cemetery Ridge, near the Copse of Trees. Hall sent the 7th Michigan and the 59th New York to the left of the 69th Pennsylvania of Webb's Brigade, taking position behind a low stone wall. The rest of the brigade remained behind the ridge. The day was a quiet one, except for the skirmishing between the two opposing armies.[68]

The Confederate army's attack began at about 4:00 P.M. and soon the sounds of battle erupted to the south. Colonel Hall was not happy when he learned that Caldwell's Division, which had been on his left, was ordered south to help defend the Wheatfield. This left a yawning quarter-mile gap between Humphreys's Division's right flank and Hall's left. The men could see and hear the battle rolling toward them, and soon Humphreys's exposed division of the III Corps came under attack. A staff officer, Lieutenant Henry Christiancy, ordered Hall to detach two regiments to help plug the gap and support Humphreys's Division. Hall immediately dispatched the 19th Massachusetts and 42nd New York. The 19th Massachusetts leading the column had gone less than a mile when it saw Humphreys's Division "completely broken, and running to the rear in great confusion." Observing these events, Colonel Arthur Devereux asked the staff officer about the object of the two regiments' mission and was told that they were to support Humphreys's Division. Devereux immediately "pointed out to him how useless to attempt to form a support for a division in the open field with two small regiments, numbering but 290 men together." He further protested that it was too late to provide support, as the division "was much broken and fleeing in such confusion." The staff officer could give no additional information or orders and, to Devereux's dismay, galloped off.[69]

A veteran of many battles, Devereux knew an impossible situation when he saw one, so he suggested to Colonel James Mallon of the 42nd New York that the two small regiments form behind a small knoll. "Lie down, wait until our retreating line . . . [has] passed, deliver a volley by the rear and front ranks, to check the pursuing enemy, and then make good our retreat," he suggested. Wasting no time, the men sprinted forward to their assigned positions and lay down; the New Yorkers formed on the right of the Bay Staters. They did not have long to wait before they could see the right flank of General Richard Anderson's Confederate Division composed of Wilcox's and Lang's Brigades rapidly approaching. Both regiments fired two volleys, then jumped up and ran to the rear to avoid capture, as both their flanks were overlapped by the enemy. Devereux recalled that the enemy was so close that when his men sprang up they captured several prisoners. The retreat was orderly, according to Devereux. Soon they passed several lines of Union troops, probably from Harrow's Brigade, which ultimately stemmed the Confederate advance. Reaching the crest of Cemetery Ridge, the men passed over it and rested on the opposite side. The losses were modest. The 42nd New York lost three killed and twelve wounded; the 19th Massachusetts's losses were probably similar. Darkness had descended on the battlefield by this time, and Hall sent orders to return to the brigade.[70]

While the two regiments were moving to the left to support Humphreys,

Wright's Brigade from Anderson's Division prepared to attack Cemetery Ridge. While the enemy marched in close formation across the wide plain between Seminary and Cemetery Ridges, the men of the 7th Michigan and 59th New York nervously waited. Earlier, the men had improvised a barricade by stripping a nearby fence of its rails. To their right was the 69th Pennsylvania of the Philadelphia Brigade; to their left was the gap left by Caldwell's move south. The 3rd and 22nd Georgia advanced to within thirty to forty yards of the Union line, when they came to a protective swale. Here they halted and opened fire. Seeing Weir's battery to their right, Wright's men lunged at it and captured several pieces of artillery. The Georgians infuriated the Union troops when they posted one of their flags on the guns. The two Federal regiments poured volleys into the Confederates near the gun at a distance of less than thirty yards. Sergeant Cyris Tyler of the 7th Michigan wrote home after the battle that "we killed most every reb we shot their colors down more than twenty times. I never saw such plucky men before for they stood not more than five rods from us after they took the batteries and kept whaling [sic] away at us tho [sic] hit most of the boys in the head. They would stand and wave their colors and as fast as one color bearer was shot another would take it and they kept on till we killed and wounded most of them and took the rest prisoners." Major Sylvanus Curtis of the 7th Michigan noticed that the volleys were so effective that "several of the enemy, were seen to throw down their guns, and, creeping along the ground to our lines, surrendered as prisoners." The rest "retreated in considerable disorder."[71]

With a yell, those Georgians not near the cannons rushed toward the Union line, but, according to Curtis, "the enemy's line was fast melting away under the scathing fire of our men, who remained unflinchingly at their posts, and they [the enemy] soon retreated in utter confusion, leaving a large number of killed and wounded." Private Ralph Rea of the 7th Michigan concurred, writing home that "the 2nd [July] they charged on us but we shot them down as fast as they came up to us. What we did not kill and wound we took prisoners." [72]

While its four sister regiments were engaged with the enemy, the 20th Massachusetts remained in its reserve position on Cemetery Ridge. Its only losses resulted from the cannonade that had preceded the attack on the Union center. That night the regiment was joined by the 19th Massachusetts and 42nd New York, which formed on its right, toward the Copse of Trees, about a hundred yards behind the front line. The three regiments supported Rorty's battery. Although only a single shovel was available, the men of the 20th Massachusetts shared it throughout the night to throw up a crude breastwork that was about a foot deep and a foot high. [73]

As the morning progressed, the heat and humidity sapped the men's energy. Many improvised shelters by fixing their bayonets to their rifles, thrusting them down into the ground and tying blankets and pieces of shelter tents between them affixed to the triggers. After only two days of heavy fighting, most of the men knew that Lee was not yet done. The men spent time cleaning their guns and inspecting their ammunition. Private Frederick Oesterle of the 7th Michigan noted that "there was no hilarity, no joking no laughing, and in many cases you could see good Christian boys praying, and in this manner we waited calmly, either death or victory." Officers passed frequently, offering reassurance. [74]

The men had never experienced the fiasco that occurred during the massive bombardment that preceded the Pickett–Pettigrew–Trimble charge. Ernest Waitt of the 19th Massachusetts described it as "fragments of bursting shell . . . flying everywhere. There seemed to be no place where they did not strike and no spot from whence they did not come." While trying to maintain their alignment, the men sought whatever protection they could find. Hiding behind his flimsy barricade of fence rails, Oesterle wrote, "oh how we hugged the ground and how we stuck our heads and as much as possible of our body out of the way of these merciless, approaching and bounding shells." A relieved Oesterle related that few shells found their mark, as most either overshot their positions or struck the ground and bounced over them. The same could not be said for nearby batteries, which suffered heavy losses during the bombardment. Lieutenant Fred Brown's battery, which had been decimated during Wright's charge the previous day, was again hard hit. Few men remained to man the guns, causing an exasperated Brown to yell to Devereux, "For God's sake Colonel, let me have twelve men to work my gun." [75]

Suddenly shouts of "Here they come! Here they come! Here comes the infantry!" filled the air. Before long the men could see the long lines of Pickett's Division advancing toward them. Only the 7th Michigan and 59th New York occupied the front line at the time—the three other regiments were in reserve to the left of the Copse of Trees. Tyler (7th Michigan) silently watched the enemy advance with a sense of dread. Suddenly, the Federal artillery opened fire on the well-dressed Confederate lines. "I never saw men slaughtered by artillery before—it did not seem as though a man could get out alive," he wrote. Colonel Hall called their advance "fearfully irresistible." Hall decided to bring the 20th Massachusetts up to the front line about this time, placing it to the right of the 7th Michigan. The 19th Massachusetts and 42nd New York also moved closer to provide support. When the enemy line was within two hundred yards of Hall's three regiments, some of the men opened fire. The remainder waited until the enemy got nearer. "We let the regiment in front of us get within 100 feet of us, & then bowled them over like nine pins, picking out the colors first," noted Major Henry Abbott of the 20th Massachusetts. Oesterle recalled that "when their columns were within 100 yards, we got orders to fire and the whole of that blue line, raising up as seemingly out of the earth, and poured a withering volley . . . almost into their faces. This for a moment, checked their foremost line, but on they pressed in quick time, only to be mowed down like grass." Still the enemy advanced. The fire became so intense that some of Kemper's Brigade (Pickett's Division) began crowding to the left. This forced Hall's men to fire obliquely at the enemy. As they approached, the Federal batteries changed to canister, mowing down hundreds. Tyler marveled: "I never saw men march up in as good style as they did under such a terrible fire—they was [sic] the best troops they had."[76]

Bruce (20th Massachusetts) recalled that the thick smoke did not affect the men's deadly marksmanship, as the enemy's ranks were still full. Some of the men ran forward to engage the enemy while others stood their ground. Any semblance of order was lost, as the men fought singly or in small groups, all the while pouring a deadly fire into the enemy ranks. The musketry finally broke the charge and all that remained were "groups of two or three men running round wildly, like chickens with their heads off," wrote Abbott. In their joy, the men yelled, "Fredericksburg" at the defeated Rebels.[77]

The volleys from Harrow's and Hall's Brigades, coupled with the flank attack by Stannard's Brigade, destroyed the enemy's attack. Looking to his right, Hall could see the enemy breaking through the gap in the line between his brigade and Webb's on the right that had been created for Cowan's cannon to fire through and saw part of the 59th New York give way, Hall ordered his three frontline regiments to turn and face this new threat. Colonel Steele of the 7th Michigan was to form his regiment at right angles to its former position and attack the enemy's right flank. Because of the intense noise, only those men closest to Steele on the regiment's right flank heard the order and obeyed it. The rest thought that their comrades were retreating, but held their position and continued pouring an oblique fire onto the enemy. The 20th Massachusetts, on the 7th Michigan's right, received orders to "face to the right and to file to the right," according to Captain Henry Abbott. They, too, could not hear the precise nature of the orders, but thinking they were to retreat and reform their lines, the regiment retired about "two rods." Realizing their error, the officers ordered the men to charge toward the Copse of Trees. Finding the enemy behind a fence, the men were exposed to a heavy fire and many fell. Here they joined a wild melee where several of Hall's and Harrow's regiments were intermixed, "each man fighting on his own hook," according to Abbott.[78]

Somewhat earlier, the 19th Massachusetts and 42nd New York, just to the left of the Copse of Trees, nervously watched as Pickett's men breached the Federal line to their right. Realizing that no time could be lost, Colonel Devereux called out to Colonel Mallon of the 42nd New York, "Mallon, we must move." Just then General Hancock rode by and Devereux called out to him, "See, General, they have broken through! The colors are coming over the stone wall! Let me go in there!" Hancock quickly replied, "Go in there pretty God-damned quick!" and the two regiments raced through Cowan's battery toward the scene of the heaviest fighting. Colonel Hall rode up to encourage the men as they moved forward. The 42nd New York reached the scene first, quickly followed by the 19th Massachusetts. Colonel Devereux explained that "there was considerable confusion here, from the men running to the rear from the first line." The two regiments were joined by the 20th Massachusetts, which had just shifted position from along the line facing Seminary Ridge.[79]

The fighting was bloody and intense. Colonel Devereux reported that the two sides stood at the Copse of Trees less than fifteen paces apart and "for an instant it seemed to hang in the balance whether we should drive the enemy out of the works, which they had entered, or they succeed in carrying the position." Other regiments finally converged on the area, and in places the men stood five and six lines deep. Waitt (19th Massachusetts) recalled that "every time a man [stooped] to load, others crowd[ed] in ahead of him so that he [would] have to elbow his way through in order to get another chance to fire." So anxious were the men to fire at the enemy that many tried to shoot through openings in the ranks that formed in front of them. "Muskets [were] exploding all around, flashing their fire almost in one's face and so close to the head as to make the ears ring," related Waitt. Unfortunately, the bullets were as likely to hit one of their comrades. Continuing his narrative, Waitt wrote that "foot to foot, body to body and man to man they struggled, pushed, and strived and killed. Each had rather die than yield. The mass of wounded and heaps of dead entangled the feet of the contestants . . . [the men] hatless, coatless, drowned in sweat, black with powder, red with blood, stifling in the horrid heat, parched with smoke and blind with dust, with fiendish yells and strange oaths they blindly plied their work of slaughter." The sheer weight of numbers overwhelmed Pickett's depleted ranks as, Waitt noted, "the men sprang forward like a thunderbolt and followed their colors. A strange resistless impulse seemed to seize the whole Union line." The enemy survivors either threw down their arms in surrender or tried to make their way to safety. During this intense fighting, the 19th Massachusetts apparently captured four flags. Three are known: from the 14th, 19th, and 57th Virginia.[80]

By the end of the fighting regiments no longer existed, as the men were so badly intermingled. The officers spent the next half-hour or so reforming their units and determining the extent of the losses. The stunned men could see the effects of the melee all around them. Dead and wounded soldiers of both sides lying all around, prisoners being hustled to the rear, and massive amounts of equipment littered over every foot of the ground. The brigade remained in position until July 5, when it left the battlefield.[81]

Hall's Brigade acquitted itself quite well during the battle. Like Harrow's, the brigade was broken up and fought in two or three units. Two of its regiments, the 59th New York and 7th Michigan, occupied the front line and helped repulse both Wright's charge on July 2 and Pickett's charge on July 3. The 19th Massachusetts and the 42nd New York also fought gallantly in helping to blunt the charge of Perry's and Wilcox's Brigades on July 2 and Pickett's Division on July 3. The members of the brigade basked in the glory of their achievements for the rest of their lives.

NOTES

1. Dyer, *Compendium*, 289; Tagg, *Generals of Gettysburg*, 45; Stackpole, *Drama on the Rappahannock*,136.

2. OR 27, 1, 416; Joseph Ward, *History of the One Hundred and Sixth Pennsylvania Volunteers* (Philadelphia, 1883), 179–180.

3. OR 27, 1, 416–417; Gottfried, "Wright's Charge on July 2, 1862," 74.

4. OR 27, 1, 417; Bradley M. Gottfried, *Stopping Pickett—The History of the Philadelphia Brigade* (Shippensburg, PA, 1999),164.

5. OR 27, 1, 417–418; Gottfried, *Stopping Pickett*, 172–173, 175; Tagg, *Generals of Gettysburg*, 46.

6. Busey and Martin, *Regimental Strengths and Losses*, 39, 243.

7. Patrick Taylor, diary, in Bachelder Papers, New Hampshire Historical Society; Henry Abbott, *Fallen Leaves—The Civil War Letters of Major Henry Abbott* (Kent, OH, 1991), 191; R. I. Holcombe, *History of the First Regiment Minnesota Volunteer Infantry* (Gaithersburg, MD, 1987), 349–350; William Lochren, "The First Minnesota at Gettysburg," in *Minnesota MOLLUS*, 45; William Colvill, "Statement," copy in Brake Collection, USAMHI.

8. Tagg, *Generals of Gettysburg*, 47.

9. Charles Muller, "Narrative," Brake Collection, USAMHI; Gregory Coco, *From Ball's Bluff to Gettysburg . . . and Beyond* (Gettysburg, PA, 1994), 192; John W. Plummer, letter, *The State Atlas* (Minnesota), August 26, 1863.

10. John Q. Imholte, *The First Volunteers: History of the First Minnesota Volunteer Regiment* (Minneapolis, 1963), 115; Colvill, "Statement"; Coco, *Ball's Bluff to Gettysburg . . . and Beyond*, 193, 195–196; William Colvill, Jr. to John Bachelder, June 9, 1866, in Bachelder Papers, New Hampshire Historical Society.

According to Imhof, (*Gettysburg—Day Two*, 22–23) the regiments were deployed from left to right: 15 Massachusetts–82nd New York–1st Minnesota–19th Maine. None of his citations show this deposition; I used Private Bowen's letter, written within a year of the battle.

11. Coco, *Ball's Bluff to Gettysburg . . . and Beyond*, 196–197; Holcombe, *The First Minnesota*, 339.

12. OR 27, 1, 436; Coddington, *The Gettysburg Campaign*, 416, 420; *NYG*, vol. 2, 663–664.

13. Andrew Ford, *Story of the Fifteenth Massachusetts Volunteer Infantry . . .* (Clinton, MA, 1898), 267; Coco, *Ball's Bluff to Gettysburg . . . and Beyond*, 196–201.

14. OR 27, 1, 419–420, 423, 425–426; OR 27, 2, 628; Ford, *Story of the Fifteenth Massachusetts Volunteer Infantry*, 268–269; Coco, *From Ball's Bluff to Gettysburg . . . and Beyond*, 201–202; Wiley Sword, "Defending the Codori House and Cemetery Ridge: Two Swords with Harrow's Brigade in the Gettysburg Campaign," *Gettysburg Magazine* (July 1995), issue 13, 46–47. *NYG*, vol. 2, 664; William Paul, "Severe Experiences at Gettysburg," in *Confederate Veteran*, (1912), vol. 19, 85.

15. William Colvill, Jr. to John Bachelder, June 9, 1866; Lochren, "The First Minnesota at Gettysburg," 48–49; J. N. Searles, "The First Minnesota Volunteer Infantry," in *Minnesota MOLLUS*, vol. 2, 106; Plumber, letter, August 26, 1863.

16. William Colvill, Jr. to John Bachelder, June 9, 1866; Plumber, letter; Lochren, "The First Minnesota at Gettysburg," 48–49; Searles, "The First Minnesota Volunteer Infantry," 106; Alfred Carpenter, letter, Minnesota Historical Society, copy in Brake Collection, USAMHI.

17. Lochren, "The First Minnesota at Gettysburg," 50–51; Colville, "Account"; Meinhard, "The First Minnesota at Gettysburg," 82; Holcombe, *First Minnesota Volunteers*, 345, 364; William Colvill, Jr. to John Bachelder, June 9, 1866.

18. Francis Heath, letter, copy in 19th Maine file, GNMP; Francis Heath Account, *Bachelder Papers*, vol. 3, 1651.

19. Heath, letter; John D. Smith, *History of the Nineteenth Regiment of Maine Volunteer Infantry* (Minneapolis, 1909), 68–69; Silas Adams, "The Nineteenth Maine at Gettysburg," in *Maine MOLLUS,*, vol. 4; John Lancaster, letter, copy in 19th Maine file, GNMP; Maine Gettysburg Commission, *Maine at Gettysburg: Report of the Maine Commissioners Prepared by the Executive Committee* (Portland, ME, 1898), 292–293.

20. *Second Reunion of the Nineteenth Maine,* 10–11; Smith, *History of the Nineteenth Maine Volunteer Infantry,* 254–255; *Maine at Gettysburg,* 292.

21. Heath, letter; *Second Reunion of the Nineteenth Maine,* copy in the 19th Maine folder, GNMP, 11; *Maine at Gettysburg,* 293–294; OR 27, 2, 631–632; Lancaster, letter.

22. *Maine at Gettysburg,* 295; Holcombe, *History of the First Regiment Minnesota Volunteer Infantry,* 346; *Second Reunion of the Nineteenth Maine,* 12.

23. Holcombe, *History of the First Regiment Minnesota Volunteer Infantry,* 364; OR 27, 1, 422; Stewart, *Pickett's Charge,* 50; *NYG,* vol. 2, 665; Searles, "The First Minnesota Volunteer Infantry," 110; Lochren, "The First Minnesota at Gettysburg," 51; Heath, letter.

24. OR 27, 1, 420, 423, 425; Holcombe, *History of the First Regiment Minnesota Volunteer Infantry,* 345; *Second Reunion of the Nineteenth Maine,* 13; Heath, letter; *Maine at Gettysburg,* 297.

25. Carpenter, letter.

26. Coco, *Ball's Bluff to Gettysburg . . . and Beyond,* 163; Smith, *History of the Nineteenth Maine Volunteer Infantry,* 83; Meinard, "The First Minnesota at Gettysburg," 87; Wilbur Clifford, letter, copy in Brake Collection, USAMHI; *NYG,* vol. 2, 666.

This figure, and other losses to the regiment cited above, have been determined by modern historian Robert Meinhard ("The First Minnesota at Gettysburg," 87).

27. Clifford, letter; *Second Reunion of the Nineteenth Maine,* 13; Imholte, *The First Volunteers: History of the First Minnesota Volunteer Regiment,* 125.

28. Busey and Martin, *Regimental Strengths and Losses,* 40, 243

29. Stewart, *Pickett's Charge,* 59; Gottfried, *Stopping Pickett,* 152.

30. Ward, *History of the One Hundred and Sixth Pennsylvania Volunteers,* 179–180; William Burns, diary, Save the Flag Collection, USAMHI; John Wheaton Lynch, letter, Pennsylvania Historical Society.

31. OR 27, 1, 429; Ward, *History of the One Hundred and Sixth Pennsylvania Volunteers,* 181–187.

32. Charles H. Banes, *History of the Philadelphia Brigade* (Philadelphia, 1876), 178–179; Ward, *History of the One Hundred and Sixth Pennsylvania Volunteers,* 187–188.

33. OR 27, 1, 430–431

34. Ward, *History of the One Hundred and Sixth Pennsylvania Volunteers,* 188–189; Banes, *The Philadelphia Brigade,*180–181.

35. Gottfried, "Wright's Charge on July 2, 1863," 71–72.

36. OR 27, 1, 427, 434; John Buckley to John Bachelder, n.d., in Bachelder Papers, New Hampshire Historical Society.

37. John H. Rhodes, *The History of Battery B, First Regiment, Rhode Island Artillery* (Providence, RI, 1914), 200–202.

38. *PAG,* vol. 1, 415, 550–551; Rhodes, *History of Battery B, First Regiment, Rhode Island Artillery,* 202–203.

39. Anthony McDermott, *A Short History of the 69th Regiment Pennsylvania Veteran Volunteers . . .* (Ann Arbor, MI, 1968), 28.

40. OR 27, 1, 427, 434, 436, 447–448.

41. Ward, *History of the One Hundred and Sixth Pennsylvania Volunteers,* 191–192, *PAG,* vol. 1, 550–551; Busey and Martin, *Regimental Strengths and Losses,* 294.

42. Sturtevant, *Pictorial History of the Thirteenth Vermont Volunteers,* 267–269.

43. Ward, *History of the One Hundred and Sixth Pennsylvania Volunteers,* 193; OR 27, 1, 427; Gottfried, "Wright's Charge, July 2, 1863," 81–82.

44. Gottfried, "Wright's Charge, July 2, 1863," 81–82; OR 27, 1, 424, 432, 433.

45. Harry W. Pfanz, *Gettysburg—Culp's Hill and Cemetery Hill* (Chapel Hill, NC, 1993), 220; Ward, *History of the One Hundred and Sixth Pennsylvania Volunteers,* 196; OR 27, 1, 434.

46. Charles Horton to John Bachelder, January 23, 1867, in Bachelder Papers, New Hampshire Historical Society; Burns, diary.

47. OR 27, 1, 432.

48. Charles Horton to John Bachelder, January 23, 1867; Pfanz, *Gettysburg—Culp's Hill and Cemetery Hill*, 221, 443; Banes, *Philadelphia Brigade*, 186; Ward, *History of the One Hundred and Sixth Pennsylvania Volunteers*, 196.

49. *Gettysburg Compiler*, June 7, 1887; McDermott, *A Short History of the 69th Regiment Pennsylvania Veteran Volunteers . . .* , 29; Stewart, *Pickett's Charge*, 67–68.

50. McDermott, *A Short History of the 69th Regiment Pennsylvania Veteran Volunteers . . .* , 30; Joseph McKeever testimony, in *Survivors of the Seventy-second Regiment of Pennsylvania Volunteers, Planintiffs vs. Gettysburg Battlefield Memorial Association . . .* (1891), 266. Hereafter cited as *Trial.*

51. McDermott, *A Short History of the 69th Regiment Pennsylvania Veteran Volunteers . . .* , 31; Anthony McDermott to John Bachelder, June 2, 1886, in Bachelder Papers, New Hampshire Historical Society; Joseph McKeever testimony, *Trial*, 259.

52. Gottfried, *Stopping Pickett*, 169; OR 27, 1, 428, 432; Stewart, *Pickett's Charge*, 166; Andrew Cowan, "When Cowan's Battery Withstood Pickett's Splendid Charge," *New York Herald*, July 2, 1911.

The number of companies next to the 69th Pennsylvania has been disputed. Some have argued there were eight; others, two. The former figure is supported by both the regimental and brigade commanders.

53. Gottfried, *Stopping Pickett*, 169–170.

54. John Buckley to John Bachelder, n.d.; Smith, "The Battle of Gettysburg—The Part Taken by the Philadelphia Brigade in the Battle," *Gettysburg Compiler*, June 7, 1887.

55. Stewart, *Pickett's Charge*, 206–208; Kathy G. Harrison and John W. Busey, *Nothing But Glory—Pickett's Division at Gettysburg* (Gettysburg, PA, 1993), 64; George W. Finley, "The Bloody Angle," *Buffalo Evening News*, May 29, 1894," Burns, diary; Smith, "The Battle of Gettysburg."

56. Samuel Roberts, testimony, *Trial*, 35; Finley, "The Bloody Angle"; Stewart, *Pickett's Charge*, 212–213; James Clay, "About the Death of General Garnett," in *Confederate Veteran* (1905), vol. 14, 81; Alexander Webb, letter, *Trial*, 317; Alexander Webb, testimony, *Trial*, 160–161; Henry Russell, testimony, *Trial*, 99.

57. Report of Lieutenant Col. Charles Morgan, *Bachelder Papers*, vol. 3, 1362; Anthony McDermott account, Bachelder Papers, vol. 3, pp. 1648, 1656–1657; Stewart, *Pickett's Charge*, 222–223. Joseph McKeever, testimony, *Trial*, 260, 267, John Buckley, testimony, *Trial*, 135.

The grove of trees during the battle included brush, which restricted movement through parts of it; hence, it formed a barrier to the 69th's Pennsylvania's retreat.

58. Martin and Smith, "The Battle of Gettysburg," 186–187; John B. Bachelder, "The Third Day's Battle," *Philadelphia Weekly Times*, December 15, 1877; OR 27, 1, 431, Alexander Webb, testimony, *Trial*, 160.

59. Anthony McDermott to John Bachelder, June 2, 1886; Harrison and Busey, *Nothing But Glory*, 104, 111.

60. Andrew Cowan to John Bachelder, December 2, 1885, in Bachelder Papers, New Hampshire Historical Society.

61. Frank A. Haskell, *The Battle of Gettysburg* (Boston, 1969), 112; Thomas Read testimony, *Trial*, 56; Samuel Roberts, testimony, *Trial*, 150; Gary G. Lash, "The Philadelphia Brigade at Gettysburg," *Gettysburg Magazine* (July, 1992), issue 7, 110; Burns, diary.

62. Anthony McDermott to John Bachelder, June 2, 1886; OR 27, 1, 428; Stewart, *Pickett's Charge*, 213–214; Lash, "The Philadelphia Brigade at Gettysburg," 112; "Testimony of Captain Charles H. Banes," in Bachelder Papers, New Hampshire Historical Society; William Porter, testimony, *Trial*, 63, James Wilson, testimony, *Trial*, 139, Alexander Webb, testimony, *Trial*, 165, 179; Arthur Devereux, testimony, *Trial*, 187.

63. OR 27, 1, 430–431; Burns, diary; Ward, *History of the One Hundred and Sixth Pennsylvania Volunteers*, 213–214; Rollins, *Damned Red Flags of the Rebellion*, 228.

64. Gottfried, *Stopping Pickett*, 229–230.

65. Busey and Martin, *Regimental Strengths and Losses*, 41, 243

66. Tagg, *Generals of Gettysburg*, 51–52.

67. Ernest L. Waitt, *History of the Nineteenth Massachusetts Volunteer Infantry* (Salem, MA, 1906), 221; Cornelius Linehan, letter, copy in the Brake Collection, USAMHI; OR, suppl., 5, 161; George A. Bruce, *The Twentieth Regiment of Massachusetts Volunteer Infantry* (Cambridge, MA, 1906), 268–269; OR 27, 1, 435.

68. Bruce, *The Twentieth Regiment of Massachusetts Volunteer Infantry*, 273; OR 27, 1, 442, 447, 452.

69. OR 27, 1, 442; Pfanz, *Gettysburg—Second Day*, 376.

70. OR 27, 1, 443, 451; OR suppl., 5, 163; Waitt, *History of the Nineteenth Massachusetts Volunteer Infantry*, 230–231.

Devereux reported that the issue of seniority between the two officers was not resolved, but Mallon "cheerfully waived all claim on his part and obeyed my orders." He also suggested in this report written in 1878, that Mallon's men fired first and retreated; then the 19th followed suit (OR suppl., 5, 162–163).

71. OR 27, 1, 447–448; Cyris Tyler, letter, Duke University Library; Gottfried, "Wright's Charge on July 2, 1863," 79.

72. OR 27, 1, 448–449; Ralph Rea, letter, copy in 7th Michigan file, GNMP.

73. OR 27, 1, 445, 451.

In his regimental history of the 19th Massachusetts, Waitt recalled that the 20th Massachusetts was in front of the two regiments (*History of the Nineteenth Massachusetts Volunteer Infantry*, 234).

74. Waitt, *History of the Nineteenth Massachusetts Volunteer Infantry*, 237; Hugh D. Purcell, "The Nineteenth Massachusetts Regiment at Gettysburg," in *Essex Institute Historical Collections* (October 1963), 281; John Reynolds, "The Nineteenth Massachusetts at Gettysburg," copy in the 19th Massachusetts file, GNMP; Frederick Oesterle, "Memoirs, "CWTI Collection, USAHMI.

75. Purcell, "The Nineteenth Massachusetts Regiment at Gettysburg," 283.

76. Edmund Rice, "Repelling Lee's Last Blow at Gettysburg," in *Battles and Leaders of the Civil War*, Vol. 3, 387; OR 27, 1, 439, 448; Oseterle, "Memoirs"; Tyler, letter; Abbott, *Fallen Leaves*, 188.

While Hall reported in his official report (OR 27, 1, 439) that he ordered his men to open fire when the enemy was about two hundred yards away, virtually all of the other primary accounts from soldiers in his regiments indicates that they waited until the enemy came much closer.

77. Bruce, *The Twentieth Regiment of Massachusetts Volunteer Infantry*, 294; Abbott, *Fallen Leaves*, 188; OR, 27, 1, 445.

78. OR 27, 1, 445–446, 450.

79. OR 27, 1, 443–444, 451; Purcell, "The Nineteenth Massachusetts Regiment at Gettysburg," 285; OR suppl., 5, 165.

80. OR 27, 1, 444; OR suppl., 5, 165; Waitt, *History of the Nineteenth Massachusetts Volunteer Infantry*, 240–243.

81. OR suppl., 5, 165; Waitt, *History of the Nineteenth Massachusetts Volunteer Infantry*, 244.

3RD DIVISION—
Brigadier General Alexander Hays

Like many other officers, General Alexander Hays joined his new division immediately before the battle of Gettysburg. Prior to June 28, 1863, he had been fairly inactive since receiving a wound at Second Bull Run. Hays was a fairly flamboyant character and his men quickly got to know him. Hays was proud to be a Pennsylvanian, and his zeal at Gettysburg was particularly high. His division was a mixed bag, composed of two veteran brigades and a brigade that had been ignominiously captured at Harper's Ferry during the Antietam campaign. All three brigades were led by colonels, which may have erroneously suggested their level of competence.[1]

The division reached Frederick, Maryland, with the rest of the corps on June 28. A grueling march began at 3:00 A.M. on June 29 and continued through the day and night. It finally ended at 3:00 A.M. on June 30 after the men had marched thirty miles. The division remained near Uniontown, Maryland, until the morning of July 1, when the march to Gettysburg continued at about 6:30 A.M. Marching on Taneytown Road, the column crossed the Pennsylvania state line at about 5:00 P.M. The division finally rested for the night near the Round Tops between 8:00 and 9:00 P.M.[2]

The command was up early on July 2 and marched north to the base of Cemetery Hill. After resting for about an hour, the division moved west to occupy Cemetery Ridge, from the Copse of Trees on the left to Ziegler's Grove on the right. The division was initially deployed in column of regiments. Willard's Brigade formed the left, Smyth's in the center, and Carroll's on the right. Except for some skirmishers, the men were not called upon to battle the enemy during the morning. This changed in the afternoon, when Smyth's Brigade sent a succession of individual units to capture and hold the Bliss farm buildings. This seesaw battle continued through the morning of July 3, until Hays ordered the buildings burned.[3]

As the attacks on the Federal left flank gained momentum, Willard's Brigade was sent south to provide support. Arriving just as Barksdale's (McLaws's Division) victorious brigade approached Cemetery Ridge, Willard's men barreled into it, halting the attack and forcing the Confederates to return to Seminary Ridge. Later that evening, Early's Division's successful attack on Cemetery Hill caused Carroll's Brigade to be rushed to the scene of the action. Driving through the Evergreen Cemetery gatehouse, they saw Avery's Brigade engaged in hand-to-hand combat with the Federal gunners at the top of the hill. The resulting fight was sharp but short, resulting in the enemy's retreat from the summit of the hill.[4]

In addition to the battle for the Bliss farm, Smyth's, Willard's, and the 8th Ohio of Carroll's Brigade were instrumental in defeating the six brigades from Pettigrew's and Trimble's Divisions that charged Cemetery Ridge in conjunction with Pickett's Division to the south. So exuberant was General Hays after the Confederates's defeat that he grabbed an enemy flag emblazoned with the name "Harper's Ferry." He dragged it in the dirt while riding back and forth behind Willard's Brigade, exclaiming, "So we wipe out Harper's Ferry." This was in reference to the capture of almost the entire brigade at Harper's Ferry during the Antietam campaign.[5]

The division performed magnificently at Gettysburg and played three major roles in defeating Lee's army: the repulse of the two attacks on either end of the Federal line on July 2, and the defeat of Pettigrew's and Trimble's Divisions on July 3. The division left the battlefield on July 5.[6]

1st Brigade—Colonel Samuel Carroll

Units: 14th Indiana, 4th Ohio, 8th Ohio, 7th West Virginia
Strength: 977
Losses: 211 (38-166-7)—21.6%[7]

Samuel Carroll's Brigade had the distinction of being one of the few in the army with a special name (Gibraltar Brigade), in addition to its numeric designation. Like the tough Iron Brigade of the I Corps, it was composed of western regiments with natural fighting abilities. According to historian George Stewart, the men of the Gibraltar Brigade had gained a reputation throughout the army as "fighting fools" for their tenacity.[8]

The brigade had been commanded by Colonel Samuel Carroll since April 1863. A West Point graduate, Carroll had originally commanded the 8th Ohio. Well-liked by his men and his commanders, Carroll had already commanded two other brigades, one during the Shenandoah Valley campaign in the spring of 1862 and one at Fredericksburg. He probably rode toward Gettysburg wondering what he would need to do to get his star.[9]

During the hellish marches in pursuit of Lee's army many men had difficulty remaining in the ranks. Private Charles Merrick of the 8th claimed that only eighteen men were present at the conclusion of the thirty-mile march from Frederick that began on June 29. The remainder eventually caught up. Despite these hardships, the men were in fairly good spirits.[10]

The brigade led the II Corps during the march toward Gettysburg on July 1. After traveling about four miles, the unit halted and an order was read to the men announcing that Meade had replaced Hooker in command of the army. The men met this information with indifference. "There was an apparent distrust on the part of the men, who had always seemed more anxious for 'real business' than their general officers," recalled William Keppler of the 4th Ohio. The order also stated the "duty of defending our homes and driving back the invader." Keppler and others took issue with this order, thinking it too tame. They believed that "we ought to *destroy* the invader instead of driving him back." Colonel Carroll tried to placate the men by simply saying, "Do as you always have done."[11]

Despite the abundance of fruit along the way, not a man fell from the ranks to collect it. As the brigade marched north, it could hear the faint sounds of battle up ahead. During the afternoon the column passed an ambulance carrying the body of General John Reynolds, who had been killed that morning. Keppler noted that "there was profounder silence than ever; no more jokes, and as usual before a battle, hundreds of playing cards were strewn along the road." At sunset, the men saw Carroll conferring with General Hancock. After Hancock explained the situation to his subordinate, Carroll asked, "General, have we a good position?" Hancock firmly responded, "If Lee does not attack before all our forces are up, we can hold the position I have selected against the whole Confederacy."[12]

The march continued for several hours and ended when the brigade arrived near Powers Hill, where it bivouacked for the night. The men did not have much sleep that night, for they were roused sometime between 3:00 and 4:00 A.M., and after a quick breakfast, moved to Cemetery Ridge. Here they took up a position between Woodruff's battery on their left and Taneytown Road on their right. The men were securely in place by 8:00 A.M. All were surprised when the morning did not bring a continuation of the hostilities.[13]

At about 9:00 A.M. on July 2, Carroll was ordered to throw out four companies of skirmishers to support the hard-pressed ones already in position. He sent out four companies from the 4th Ohio, who marched out to Emmitsburg Road. The remainder of the brigade spent the morning and afternoon preparing for battle and resting. The brigade shifted its position at least once when it moved to support Woodruff's battery. The skirmishing increased in intensity after 3:00 P.M. when the enemy's line became much more aggressive. Carroll responded by sending out the entire 8th Ohio to bolster the skirmish line. Sergeant Thomas Galway recalled that "we moved down the hill in line of battle in fine style, our colors flying and the artillery as well as the rest of our brigade cheering us." The artillerymen enthusiastically applauded this movement because the enemy skirmishers were picking them off. Also watching the movement were Generals Hancock and Hays. Lieutenant Colonel Franklin Sawyer proudly wrote in his report that his men performed this action "moving forward gallantly under a smart fire of the enemy's pickets and sharpshooters." Before Sawyer left his original position, he recalled Colonel Carroll telling him to "hold my line to the last man."[14]

As the 8th Ohio advanced, "the balls came thick and spitefully among us, the men began to fall . . . but on we swept until we came to the fence along Emmitsburg Road," noted Sawyer. They quickly dispersed a group of Confederates positioned there. As Sawyer's men scrambled over the fences, they were hit by artillery fire from Seminary Ridge. Undeterred, they continued forward until they encountered a group of Confederates who were unwilling to depart. After a short fight, the enemy soldiers were forced to either retreat or surrender. Sawyer threw out two of his companies as skirmishers and arranged the remainder of the regiment in a natural depression on the east side of the road. The men immediately began pulling down the fence rails to make a crude breastwork and then lay down along the side of the road.[15]

The Confederates moved forward again at 4:00 P.M., this time in greater force. Sawyer responded by ordering the remainder of his regiment to its feet to join the skirmish line "on a run, cheering, and firing." The Confederates must have believed the force around the road to be larger than it really was, for they quickly retreated back toward Seminary Ridge. Nightfall ended the action for the 8th Ohio. Later that evening, Sawyer sent Carroll information about the situation in his front. To his surprise, he received a message from General Hays, informing him that Carroll had moved the rest of the brigade to defend Cemetery Hill.[16]

While Sawyer's men were skirmishing with the enemy, the remainder of Carroll's Brigade had been resting on Cemetery Ridge. At 6:00 P.M., the brigade shifted to the left to occupy Willard's Brigade's position, which had been rushed to the left to help thwart the enemy's drive toward the southern part of Cemetery Ridge. Almost immediately upon taking this position, Carroll received orders to leave the 4th Ohio and return to his original position with his two remaining regiments. Carroll received new orders after dark to march his men quickly to the right to help thwart the Confederate attack on Cemetery Hill. With the 14th Indiana in the lead and the 4th Ohio bringing up the rear, Carroll rushed his men through the cemetery to the edge of the hill. In front of him, Confederate units from Hays's and Avery's Brigades (Early's Division) had successfully gained a foothold on Cemetery Hill, and were now battling the artillerymen, who refused to relinquish their cannon. Keppler observed that the "maddened gunners of captured batteries raved and swore, or cried in very madness, vowing death to meet rather than give up their guns, striking the rebels with fist, rammer, ammunition and stones."[17]

Carroll would never forget that night, when, "owing to the artillery fire from our own guns, it was impossible to advance by a longer front than that of a regiment, and it being perfectly dark, and with no guide, I had to find the enemy's line entirely by their fire." As the men approached the right of the cemetery's gatehouse, Colonel Carroll yelled, "Halt! Front face! Charge bayonets! Forward, double-quick! March! Give them_____," recalled Sergeant J. Dickelman of the 4th Ohio. Captain David Beem of the 14th Indiana wrote home soon after the battle that "we arrived just in the nick of time. They had already surrounded one gun . . . when we approached, the officers of the battery threw their fists in the air and shouted for joy." The men were hit by a savage cross fire, so Carroll immediately dispatched the 7th West Virginia to clear out the opposition along a stone wall, which they successfully accomplished.

The men of the 14th Indiana could see the 21st North Carolina milling around a captured cannon. According to Captain Beem, his men "pushed right on to the rebel horde and got right among them, but they did not long stand our rapid volleys. They ran pell mell." Not content to drive the enemy from the cannon, Colonel John Coons ordered his men to dash down the hill after them. Lieutenant Colonel Elijah Cavins of the 14th Indiana recalled that the fight was brief, writing, "it was a headlong dash in the dark—a yell—and a few rounds aimed at the flash of the enemy's guns, and all was over for the night." The remainder of the brigade, which followed the 14th Indiana, took position on either side of the Hoosiers. The 7th West Virginia formed on their left; the 4th Ohio on their right.[18]

Other than a few shots, the battlefield grew quiet by 10:00 P.M. One of General Ames's aides approached Carroll and asked that the brigade remain in its position because he did not trust the men of his XI Corps. Carroll told the aide to return to Ames with the message, "Damn a man who had no confidence in his troops." Carroll received the same request from General Howard, and Ames's men formed on both sides of the brigade.[19]

Several of Carroll's men took pains to single out the cowardice of the XI Corps. Although his regiment was not present during the attack on Cemetery Hill, Galway (8th Ohio) wrote that as Carroll's men charged the heights "an immense mob of Union fugitives came sweeping back over the Baltimore Pike." Captain Beem (14th Indiana) wrote home that "we had no confidence in the Dutch of the 11th . . . the Dutch ran like cowards." Captain R. Bruce Ricketts, whose battery was saved by Carroll's men, stated that "all the credit due to the infantry in that affair is due to Carroll's Brigade alone."[20]

After the battle, another war was waged by the survivors of Carroll's Brigade and the XI Corps, each discounting the other's role. Historian Harry Pfanz seemed to support both sides, believing that while Carroll's Brigade had performed well, some of its veterans claimed too much glory. Part of the problem stemmed from the fact that parts of two Confederate brigades reached the heights of Cemetery Hill. While Carroll's men were instrumental in extracting Avery's Brigade, Pfanz believed that Hays's men were driven back primarily by troops from the XI Corps.[21]

July 3 found Carroll's three regiments at the base of Cemetery Hill. Except for skirmishing in their front and sharpshooter fire coming from the town, the battle was essentially over for these men. The same was not true for Carroll's 4th regiment, the 8th Ohio, which still occupied its position between the two armies along Emmitsburg Road. The regiment spent a miserable night in its vulnerable position. "A gloomier night . . . can scarcely be imagined. We were a good way in advance of our division, without any direct support, with no knowledge whatever as to the event of the great battles of the day; ignorant of the hopes, probabilities or prospects of the morrow; threatened by a stealthy and skulking enemy, amid our dead and wounded," recalled Sawyer.[22]

The skirmishing reopened at first light on July 3. It became so intense at one point that Sawyer ordered his entire regiment up to the skirmish line and ordered volley after volley fired into the pesky Confederate troops from Thomas's Brigade. "We went without any well-defined lines or well-defined companies, but we dashed in among the skirmishers," Sawyer recalled. The audacious move was successful, for the Confederate skirmish line and its supports quickly fell back. Sawyer sent a messenger to Carroll with a request that the regiment be withdrawn. Events were unfolding too rapidly for this to occur, however. [23]

Noon arrived and the temperature continued to soar. The water in the canteens became so hot that the men could not drink it. Soon after 1:00 P.M. the massive Confederate bombardment commenced, and Colonel Sawyer would never forget it.

Nothing more terrific than this storm of artillery can be imagined. The missiles of both armies passed over our heads. The roar of guns was deafening, the air was soon clouded with smoke, and the shriek and startling crack of exploding shells above, around, and in our midst; the blowing up of our caissons in our rear; the driving through the air of fence-rails, posts, and limbs of trees; the groans of dying men, the neighing of frantic and wounded horses, created a scene of absolute horror.[24]

The fire suddenly stopped, and the men could see two long lines of Confederate troops emerge from Seminary Ridge to their left-front. Sawyer recalled looking back at his main lines and seeing a flurry of activity. "An order just then recalling the Eighth would have been to us very pleasant. None came," wrote Sawyer after the battle.[25]

Forming his 150 men in a single line, Sawyer did the unthinkable: he ordered a charge gainst Brockenbrough's Brigade, which formed the left flank of the great Pickett–Pettigrew–Trimble charge. Brockenbrough's men were a weak link in the attack because the men were demoralized and poorly led. After his regiment poured several volleys into the Virginians, at a distance of 100 yards, Sawyer noted that "some fell, some run back, most of them, however, threw down their arms and were

made prisoners." These men "stuck up handkerchiefs and coats to ask us to quit firing." Galway felt that "had they [Brockenbrough's men] continued their advance with the same spirit shown by their comrades in Pickett's column . . . many days might have been added to this war!" Sawyer ordered his men to change front and prepare to charge into Brockenbrough's flank. Just then, the Federal artillery opened on the Confederate line.

Arms, heads, blankets, guns, and knapsacks were thrown and tossed into the clear air. Their track, as they advanced, was strewn with dead and wounded. A moan went up from the field, distinctly to be heard amid the storm of battle, but on they went, too much enveloped in smoke and dust now to permit us to distinguish their lines or movements, for the mass appeared more like a cloud of moving smoke and dust than a column of troops. Still it advanced amid the now deafening roar of artillery and storm of battle.[26]

Sawyer's men showed no sympathy for the enemy, pouring volleys into their vulnerable left flank. First Brockenbrough's Brigade broke, then the fire was applied to Davis's Brigade's left flank, and it too began to falter. The Ohioans's ammunition was now depleted, as hundreds of Confederates approached their position. Fortunately for Sawyer's men, these men were merely attempting to surrender, not to continue the hostilities. After the war Sawyer felt that many of these men were confused and ran into the 8th Ohio by mistake. Other enemy soldiers tried to make their way back to Seminary Ridge. "We dashed in amongst them, taking prisoners by the droves," recalled Galway. In addition to the hundreds of prisoners, at least three battle flags were secured. The latter was of special interest to

Sawyer, who recalled that while most of the enemy surrendered willingly, the color guards tried to save their flags, but were thwarted by "counter squads," who chased them down and forced them to relinquish their prizes. Sawyer saw hundreds of men lying on the ground and ordered some of his men to capture them. These men were all dead, however, and beyond capture.[27]

Sawyer finally received Carroll's orders to "come in as soon as I pleased," and it was immediately obeyed by the 8th Ohio. With fixed bayonets, the regiment approached in a "sandwich" formation— half marched in front of the hundreds of prisoners, and the other half brought up the rear. Upon approaching the main line, Colonel John Coons of the 14th Indiana, which had just returned from Cemetery Hill, ordered his men to "present arms" and the remainder of the brigade erupted in cheers for their gallant comrades who had helped to break the great charge. Carroll was so excited by the sight that he yelled out, "Look you fellows!— there comes my old Eighth with the balance of Lee's army!"[28]

So audacious were Sawyer's actions that distinguished historian John Bachelder at first did not believe the exploits to be true. He even went so far as to suggest that Sawyer had a drinking problem that led to illusions of grandeur. This was not the first time that someone suggested this trait— those who observed the regiment's exploits at Gettysburg also thought that Sawyer must be either drunk or mad.[29]

When the men awoke on July 4, they found the ground around them teeming with dead and wounded. Galway called it "a great hospital." The day was mostly quiet, except for sniper fire. Burying the dead commenced and continued into the next day as well. Those men who could be recognized by their comrades were buried with headboards marking their identities; the unrecognizable were buried in long trenches. The Confederate dead were buried in separate trenches.[30]

Although the brigade's casualties were light, its exploits were not. Its counterattack against Avery's Brigade on Cemetery Hill during the evening of July 2 has been highlighted as an important aspect of the battle. Yet its significance can be questioned, given the relatively small number of unsupported Confederates who occupied the summit at this point. The same is not true of the exploits of the 8th Ohio, which truly played a major role in blunting the Pickett–Pettigrew–Trimble charge.

2nd Brigade—Colonel Thomas Smyth

Units: 14th Connecticut, 1st Delaware, 12th New Jersey, 108th New York, 10th New York Battalion
Strength: 1069
Losses: 360 (59-275-26)—33.8%[31]

One of the younger brigades in the army, the 2nd Brigade was formed on September 12, 1862, with regiments that had not seen prior action. The brigade was quickly baptized at Antietam, where it was repulsed at the bloody sunken lane. The brigade was again defeated during its attack up Marye's Heights at the battle of Fredericksburg. It therefore marched to Gettysburg without having tasted the fruits of victory. Colonel Thomas Smyth of the 1st Delaware assumed command of the brigade on May 16, 1863. While an experienced regimental commander, he had never commanded a brigade in battle.[32]

The brigade's march through Maryland was a pleasant experience for most of the men of Smyth's Brigade. Even the 12th New Jersey, which had pulled the undesirable assignment of guarding the division's trains, found some diversions. Captain Az Stratton summed it up when he wrote "what a picnic we had; cherries everywhere; the trees were soon blue with the boys; the wagon train forgotten; the boys scattered all over the fields, in groups and in squads; some to the houses, and they especially fared well." Passing through the town of Liberty, the brigade encountered the townspeople lining the streets, distributing bread smeared with butter, buttermilk, and ice water. The merriment ended sometime during June 29, when the men were well into their thirty-three-mile march. By the time the march ended, the brigade was but a skeleton of its former self, as many had fallen from the ranks.[33]

The brigade spent June 30 in the vicinity of Uniontown, Maryland, where those men who fell out of the ranks during the strenuous march rejoined their comrades. The brigade set off sometime between 6:30 and 7:00 A.M. on July 1 and crossed into Pennsylvania at about 5:00 P.M. Cannon fire could be heard up ahead and soon another army was encountered—an army of "stragglers and Coffee Coolers, niggers, servants, and all the non-combatants that follow an army, coming toward us getting away from the point of danger," recalled Sergeant George Bowen of the 12th New Jersey. After participating in several campaigns in enemy territory, Bowen felt "strange to be in a country where we are welcome and to feel we are among friends and well wishers." This reaction was not uniformly felt, however. Charles Cowtan of the 10th New York Bat-

talion sadly contrasted how the troops had been "generously met with open hands and generous hearts by the hospitable and loyal farmers" of Maryland compared with the "numberless rebuffs at the thresholds of farm houses, and the prices of bread and other little luxuries" by the farmers in southern Pennsylvania. Cowtan even recalled that some farmers went so far as preventing the troops from drawing water from their wells. Private Albert Emmel of the 12th New Jersey concurred, writing home that "the Marylanders treat us well, much better than the Pennsylvania Dutch."[34]

The column halted at about 11:00 A.M. that day, and the men rested until 1:00 P.M., when the march to Gettysburg continued. The brigade halted for the night between 8:00 and 9:00 P.M. near the Round Tops, about three miles south of the town. Some of the men groused about "massing the brigade in column." One soldier from the 1st Delaware cried out, "Give us dress parade." The men were roused at 4:00 A.M. and double-quicked north toward Cemetery Hill. Many were "swearing at their luck, as they hoped their march was over," noted Bowen (12th New Jersey). Filing to the left, the brigade halted between Emmitsburg Road and Taneytown Road, where it took position in column by regiments behind, and in support of, Woodruff's battery. As the mist lifted, the men could begin to see the cemetery to their front-right and the spires of Gettysburg. They could also make out the positions of Carroll's Brigade to their left and the XI Corps in their front. Units from Robinson's Division (I Corps) were also in the sector.[35]

The brigade moved west to Cemetery Ridge later that morning, where it relieved units from the I Corps. The men could look across the wide plain and see the Confederate position on Seminary

Ridge, about three-quarters of a mile away. To their left was Willard's Brigade, and to their right was Carroll's. The brigade was arranged from left to right as 12th New Jersey–14th Connecticut–108th New York. The 1st Delaware was behind the 12th New Jersey. The 108th New York was in Ziegler's Grove, with its left flank resting at the Bryan house. General Hays actually formed the New Yorkers behind Woodruff's battery, between its guns and limbers. No one was happy with this arrangement, but Hays was adamant. The 12th New Jersey's left was next to Arnold's battery. After Willard's Brigade rushed south to help blunt Longstreet's attacks that afternoon, the 14th Connecticut was shifted two hundred yards to its left to help fill the resulting gap. The regiment was posted behind a stone wall near Hays's headquarters. It remained there for the remainder of the battle. The brigade was now deployed from left to right as 14th Connecticut–1st Delaware–12th New Jersey –108th New York.[36]

At about 8:00 A.M., the 1st Delaware and a company of the 12th New Jersey were thrown out on the skirmish line, about five hundred yards in front of Cemetery Ridge. Hays and Smyth accompanied the head of the column for at least part of the way. A lively encounter erupted with the skirmishers from Scales's and Lane's North Carolina Brigades as the command approached the Bliss farm. The Federal troops got the upper hand because, as Bowen noted, "the 1st Del. being a very superior skirmishing Regt . . . soon had them [the enemy] comparatively silenced."[37]

All was quiet until about 2:30 P.M., when Confederate artillery opened fire on Smyth's main line on Cemetery Ridge. Longstreet's attack was unleashed at about 4:00 P.M., and around this time, the Confederate skirmishers returned in

greater force. This time, the 19th Mississippi, and most of the 16th Mississippi (Posey's Brigade, Anderson's Division), approached the Bliss buildings. Sergeant Bowen (12th New Jersey) realized the desperateness of the situation when "looking around [I] saw the men of the 1st Del. running to the rear." Part of the reason for the retreat was the overwhelming numbers of enemy troops suddenly materializing in the area. The other was the cowardice of the regiment's commander, Lieutenant Colonel E. P. Harris. As the situation became more desperate, Lieutenant John Brady sought out his commanding officer, but could not find him. He finally found him in the basement of the Bliss barn. According to Brady, "whereupon, he [Harris] after carefully venturing from his safe retreat and taking a very hasty glance over the situation, turned and *fled* precipitously towards our main line, leaving that portion of the field in the immediate charge of Lieutenant Tanner and myself." Brady was not the only officer to have a negative encounter with Harris. As Sergeant Bowen of the 12th New Jersey was making to the rear, he also encountered Colonel Harris, "who was getting to the rear as fast as he could, he swung his sword around, called me a hard name, telling me to go back." After dodging a swarm of enemy bullets, Bowen finally approached the Federal line. He quickly realized that he was directly in front of Woodruff's battery, which was about to open fire on the enemy. "I threw myself on the ground and lay as flat as I could, they fired over me," recorded Bowen in his diary.[38]

Lieutenant Colonel Harris had escaped from the enemy, but was still not safe. Watching Harris's shameful conduct, General Hancock rode over, and "standing in his stirrups interviewing him in the most choice and forcible language deemed suitable for the occasion which resulted in Harris being then and there, 'ordered under arrest for cowardice in the face of the enemy,'" recalled Lieutenant Brady.[39]

Although a number of other units from Carroll's and Webb's Brigades were on the skirmish line, they were not able to drive Posey's Confederates from the Bliss farm. According to Captain Richard Thompson, the enemy sharpshooters "made themselves particularly disagreeable when any mounted officers came" into view. Frustrated, General Hays approached Smyth and asked, "Have you a regiment that will drive them out?" Smyth responded, "Yes sir, the 12th [New Jersey] will do it!" Then, turning to Major John Hill, Smyth said, "But I don't want all of you, Major." For some reason, Smyth opted to send only four companies from the veteran 12th New Jersey. Returning to his command, Major Hill immediately assembled his company commanders and asked for volunteers. All readily did so, and Hill selected the four companies. With the order, "Fall in, Companies B, H, E and G! Right dress! Front! Right face! Forward march," the detachment was off. Smyth again accompanied this two hundred-man detachment as it made its way to the front. His aides were apparently not pleased to be needlessly exposed to the enemy fire and were relieved to be permitted to return to Cemetery Ridge, with "bullets flying around us like drops of water in an April shower," Captain Parsons recalled.[40]

As the detachment approached the Bliss buildings, Captain Samuel Jobes ordered the men to "Forward, double-quick, march!" Giving three loud yells, the men closed on the enemy positions. Many fell, but still the line advanced. Jobes's men finally opened fire with their "buck and ball" ammunition, which acted like a shotgun blast. Some of the men ran to the barn windows and opened fire. Enemy sol-diers could soon be seen fleeing and the barn was captured. Those who didn't escape were captured. The Confederates were "terror stricken and many of them with their faces covered with blood, the Johnies rush out from their hiding places behind walls and from hay mows and cry for mercy," Private Emmel noted. A total of seven officers and eighty-five enlisted men were captured and sent to the rear. Writing home after the battle, Corporal Christopher Mead felt that the Confederates "perceiving our determination to take the place at the point of the bayonet, the most of them escaped by running away when, at the same time, if they had displayed the courage that we did, they might have killed us all or taken us prisoners."[41]

Jobes's men were content with the barn's capture. However, Mississippians still occupied the Bliss house and continued firing at Woodruff's cannoneers. Again frustrated by the situation, Hays sought out a courier who could "have the men in the barn take that damned white house and hold it at all hazards." No one responded to Smyth's call for volunteers. Finally, a sick Captain A. Parke Postles of the 1st Delaware volunteered. Mounting his horse, he made a mad dash through a hail of bullets to deliver the message. Barely stopping to convey the information to Jobes, Postles was off again. When he reached a safe distance, he stopped and shook his cap at his Confederate tormentors. "They immediately set up the 'rebel yell' and ceased firing at me," recalled Postles. For his bravery, Postles was awarded the Congressional Medal of Honor.[42]

Although Jobes's men captured the house, they realized that they could not hold their positions much longer, as Confederate shells rained down on the structures, killing and wounding a number of men. In addition, Confederate infantry were applying pressure from three directions. After about an hour, Jobes pulled his men back to the safety of Cemetery Ridge. The detachment's return to Cemetery Ridge was met with cheers from their comrades.[43]

While skirmishing continued, the remainder of the brigade rested behind a two-foot-high stone wall. Some men piled fence rails atop the fence to strengthen it further. The 10th New York Battalion was detached from the brigade to occupy the reverse slope of Cemetery Ridge along Taneytown Road. Its hundred or so men spent the remainder of the battle there acting as a provost guard, or as their commander, Major George Hopper put it, "for the purpose of arresting stragglers."[44]

Smyth's exhausted men settled down to sleep after dark. Sergeant E. B. Tyler of the 14th Connecticut recalled that they put their "knapsacks plumb up to the base of the stone wall and pillowed our heads thereon, not being allowed to divest ourselves of any other arms or equipment, we sought for the rest and sleep we so much needed."[45]

As the sun rose on July 3, the brigade was arranged from left to right as 14th Connecticut (with its left touching the 71st Pennsylvania of the Philadelphia Brigade)–1st Delaware–12th New Jersey–108th New York. Willard's Brigade was behind them. During the night, Posey's Confederates had again taken possession of the Bliss buildings, forcing Hays's hand. This time he sent out five companies of the 12th New Jersey and most of the 1st Delaware. With the arrest of Colonel Harris and the wounding of several officers, a lieutenant now commanded the 1st Delaware. Smyth therefore put Captain Richard Thompson of the 12th New Jersey in charge of the detachment. Forming in column of companies, the men moved grimly forward. As with the prior

advances, the men initially marched toward the buildings until they were within musket range, at which time they double-quicked the remaining distance. The Confederates fled from the buildings after firing a few harmless volleys at them, perhaps not wanting to repeat the defeat that they had sustained when the 12th New Jersey had last ventured forward. Some of the men raced after the fleeing Mississippians, capturing a handful of prisoners. Although successful in securing the buildings, the men could see large numbers of Confederate infantry stealthily approaching. The Union soldiers did not know that the Confederates had formed a wide arc around them, and when they opened fire, the men at first believed that they were surrounded. A panic set in and the men fled back toward Cemetery Ridge, thus leaving the Bliss buildings again in the hands of the enemy.[46]

Utterly frustrated by his men's inability to hold the Bliss buildings, and angry at the toll taken on Arnold's battery's cannoneers by the enemy snipers, Hays decided to throw out the 14th Connecticut to do what his other units could not. Except for two companies out on the skirmish line along Emmitsburg Road, the regiment had not faced the enemy and was fresh. The unit had its work cut out for it, as "Confederate sharp-shooters were not long in seeing the advantage of this improvised fort [Bliss barn] and soon every window, door, and crevice showed the protruding muzzles of long range rifles ready to do their dirty work." This time, Smyth ordered the men to stay put after they captured the buildings. If they couldn't, he gave them a new option—"burn the buildings and return to the line," he told Lieutenant Frederick Seymour.[47]

At first, only four companies made the trek in a "go as you please" type of approach. This meant the detachment was to scatter and run without formation toward the barn to avoid taking serious losses. After sustaining some casualties, the small detachment reached the barn and saw the Confederates "skeedaddling" to the rear. Taking possession of the barn, the men were met by heavy gunfire when they tried to take the house as well. Closely watching these events, Smyth ordered the remainder of the 14th Connecticut forward to reinforce their comrades. As these troops passed Long Lane on their right, they were exposed to volleys fired by Thomas's Brigade and sustained a number of losses. Still double-quicking, they reached the Bliss house and captured it. Those who entered the house found it to be a very dangerous place. Bullets constantly pierced the thin siding or flew through the windows. Several soldiers abandoned the house and ran to the barn or to a woodpile. These men were exposed to heavy fire from the Confederates occupying the orchard and other locations around the farm buildings. To make matters worse, a Confederate battery began shelling the buildings. At least one case shot entered the barn and exploded, killing and wounding a number of the men. The men later learned that the cannoneers were ordered to "place ten shells beside each of the four guns of the battery and to continue firing them leisurely at the buildings until they were vacated." It was actually worse than this, for all sixty-three guns of A. P. Hill's III Corps opened fire on the structures.[48]

This was a difficult time for the Nutmeggers, as it was becoming obvious that the buildings could not be held. The time was right to torch the buildings, but there was one problem: Lieutenant Seymour had been wounded and no one else knew of Smyth's orders. At about noon, Hays sent Sergeant Charles Hitchcock of the 111th New York (Willard's Brigade) with orders for the 14th Connecticut to burn the buildings. Receiving this order and the matches that Hitchcock brought with him, Major Theodore Ellis of the 14th Connecticut immediately complied. Flames were soon racing through the buildings. As Hitchcock left the dangerous area, he quickly picked a bunch of flowers growing in the Bliss garden. Returning to his lines, he handed them to Hays, who promoted Hitchcock to the rank of lieutenant on the spot.[49]

Upon returning to their lines, the exhausted men of the 14th Connecticut found that the 1st Delaware had taken their places, forcing them to form behind their comrades. They searched their haversacks for whatever meager rations they could find. The other regiments had spent a quiet morning behind the stone wall, "seeing little and doing less." The veterans of the 12th New Jersey were uneasy about the overall quiet, and had a feeling that an attack was imminent. They cleaned and checked their guns and some decided to gain an advantage by manipulating their ammunition. Equipped with buck and ball ammunition, which included one leaden ball and three small buckshot, the men carefully opened the paper casing, poured out the ball, and replaced it with ten, fifteen, and in some cases, even twenty-five buckshot. These rounds would act like a shotgun blast—deadly at close range.[50]

The great bombardment began shortly after 1:00 P.M. Captain Az Stratton recalled that "I almost tremble when I think what an awful din it made, the shrieking shells bursting . . . . how we hugged the ground . . . thinking it might stop shot or shell." Emmel wrote to his aunt that "if I ever hugged the ground in my life, I did then. We fairly rooted and felt most grateful and thankful that we were alive to root." Emmel knew that any shell would go through the rails atop the stone wall as if they were "rotten cheese." Still, he was happy for the added protection. The men of the 108th New York, who were supporting Woodruff's battery, suffered terribly during the cannonade. "Our regiment came in for its full share of shot and shell aimed at Woodruff's guns," recalled Surgeon Francis Wafer. The men were called upon at times to help move the guns. Arnold's battery was so decimated by the Confederate shells that many of the guns were pulled away from the wall.[51]

After the firing suddenly stopped, "we rose from the ground and stretched our cramped limbs and, in our inexperience, thought the battle was over, but Major Ellis was better posted than we. 'No' said he. 'They mean to charge with all their infantry,'" recalled the historian of the 14th Connecticut. The men did not have long to wait to see that their commander was correct, for the Confederate infantry broke from the woods on Seminary Ridge. The regiment numbered but a hundred men at this point, and was stretched thinly in a single line. The regiment, which had been behind the 1st Delaware, now occupied the gap to the right that had been occupied by Arnold's battery.[52]

The men looked up to see General Hays riding in front of their line, shouting, "They are coming, boys; we must whip them, and you men with buck and ball, don't fire until they get to that fence [along Emmitsburg Road]." Hays's behavior helped to steel the men, and their feelings of fear began to dissipate. "I think every man thought we would whip them," wrote Captain Stratton.[53]

Stratton would also never forget the sight of the Confederate infantry marching toward him. "I think the grandest sight I ever witnessed unfolded itself to our view, as the different lines came marching toward us, their bayonets glistening in the sun, from right to left, as far as the eye could reach; but on they come, their officers mounted, riding up and down their lines, apparently keeping them in proper formation. The lines looked to be as straight as a line could be, and at an equal distance apart." Major Theodore Ellis of the 14th Connecticut agreed, writing in his official report that "the spectacle was magnificent. They advanced in perfect order, the line of skirmishers firing." Charles Page of the same regiment noted that "gay war flags fluttering in the gentle summer breeze, while their sabers and bayonets flashed . . . the advance seems as resistless as the incoming tide."[54]

When the Confederate line was about halfway to the Federal position, all hell broke loose. Stratton related that "pandemonium seemed to be let loose among our artillery; the ground fairly shook under us. From the Round Tops to Cemetery Hill, the cannon hurled forth death and destruction in the advancing lines; we could see our shells burst in their lines, and it looked as though they had all been cut down in that place, but they would close up the gap and come on again." Coming in contact with the Federal skirmishers, the Confederate line drove them "like so many frightened sheep, although they fought well until they saw there was no chance," wrote Corporal Christopher Mead of the 12th New Jersey. Emmel of the same regiment wrote that Pettigrew's men approached, "trying to strike terror into Yankee hearts by unnatural shrieks and yells. But it was no go."[55]

Some of the men opened fire as the Confederate line came within rifle range, but most waited until the line reached Emmitsburg Road. The men of the 1st Delaware saw General Hays riding behind them, waving his divisional flag and yelling, "Show them your colors and give them hell boys!" Smyth related that the men were ordered to hold their fire until the enemy was within fifty yards. Over on the left, the men of the 14th Connecticut watched as the Confederates slowly but steadily advanced. "The men [Pettigrew's] mounted to cross [the fence] when the word 'fire! fire!' ran along the Union line, 'crack! crack!' spoke out the musketry, and the men dropped from the fence as if swept by a gigantic sickle . . . great gaps were formed in the line, the number of slain and wounded could not be estimated by numbers, but must be measured by yards," wrote the historian of the 14th Connecticut. William Seville observed that the Confederate "ranks melted away like wax" under the concentrated fire from the Union position. Smyth was equally impressed, noting that "so effective and incessant was the fire from my line that the advancing enemy was staggered, thrown into confusion." These were troops from Marshall's (Pettigrew's) and Fry's (Archer's) Brigades. Behind them marched Lowrence's (Scales's) and Lane's Brigades.[56]

While the muskets of the 12th New Jersey loaded with buckshot blew giant holes in the Confederate formation, two companies from the 14th Connecticut were also creating havoc, as its men were armed with Sharps repeating rifles. The men worked in pairs—one loaded while the other fired a second rifle. The Confederate color guards approached, but when the fire proved too hot, many lay down for protection. Several came within a few rods of the Federal position. The firing was so rapid that the men's gun barrels became too hot to touch. Some of the men attempted to cool them off by dousing them with water. A shell fragment hit Colonel Smyth during the charge and Colonel F. Pierce of the 108th New York

took his place while the wound was being dressed. When some members of the 12th New Jersey ran out of ammunition, they resorted to throwing rocks at the enemy.[57]

Seeing that the charge was broken, Major Ellis of the 14th Connecticut asked for volunteers to dash over the wall to capture the prized battle flags and their color guards. They subsequently captured the flag of the 14th Tennessee (Fry's/Archer's Brigade). Five other flags, including those from the 16th North Carolina and 52nd North Carolina, were captured later. No other regiment on either side captured more flags, and three Nutmeggers received the Congressional Medal of Honor for their actions in capturing these banners.[58]

With the defeat of Pettigrew's Division, the men could look over to their left and see that Webb's Philadelphia Brigade was in danger of being overrun by Pickett's Division. The commanders of both the 14th Connecticut and 1st Delaware ordered their men to "Left oblique, fire!" Caught between two fires, Pickett's men either surrendered or began their retreat. With the charge destroyed, the 1st Delaware jumped over the wall with bayonets fixed and gathered up scores of prisoners.[59]

The sights stunned the men. Reverend Stevens of the 14th Connecticut called them "indescribable." "Poor wounded wretches, scattered or lying in heaps, over the field . . . were writhing in agonies or straightening out in the last death shiver . . . those upon the ground, now thoroughly bereft of hope and filled with fear, raised handkerchiefs, that looked like leaflets fluttering in the breeze, and waved them above their heads crying out mightily for quarter." Another soldier later wrote, "I never saw dead and wounded men lay so thick. From a space about seventy-feet back to the opposite side of the pike you could walk over the dead bodies of men."[60]

In his excitement, General Hays took one of the Confederate flags and dragged it on the ground after his horse as they trotted along the lines. The men responded with cheers. Their hunger now returned. Some, like Private Loring Goodrich of the 14th Connecticut, had nothing in their haversacks and in desperation, leaped over the wall to search the dead and dying Confederates' haversacks for food. "I am ashamed to own it but then the pangs of hunger will do most anything," he wrote after the war. The brigade spent July 4 resting, tending the wounded, and burying the dead.[61]

Much of Smyth's activities on July 2 centered on attempting to capture and hold the Bliss farm. The brigade made several efforts to achieve this goal, but each met with only limited success. Part of the problem was that Smyth sent out only portions of his command in every case, and never once sent more than a regiment and a half. His tactics have been questioned, and one can only assume that General Hays prevented him from sending out a larger force to prevent bringing on a general engagement around the barn for which the Federal sector was unprepared. Smyth's men are much better known for their heroic defense of Cemetery Ridge on July 3, when the brigade almost single-handedly took on two of Pettigrew's Brigades and two of Trimble's and defeated all of them.[62]

3rd Brigade—Colonel George Willard

Units: 39th New York, 111th New York, 125th New York, 126th New York
Strength: 1508
Losses: 714 (139-542-33)—47.3%[63]

A dark cloud followed Willard's Brigade as it marched toward Gettysburg. Within a month of taking the field in August 1862, the regiments surrendered to Lee's forces at Harper's Ferry during the Antietam campaign. Finally exchanged, the regiments were assigned to the 3rd Division, II Corps, on June 25, 1863. The men had the twin stigma of never being in battle and the reputation of being cowards. Their II Corps comrades called them the "Harper's Ferry brigade" and "band-box soldiers."[64]

Unlike the soldiers of many other units, Willard's men generally obeyed orders to respect private property during the march. The men were especially excited about marching through the small villages along the way. As they approached, the flags were unfurled and the bands played. "Instantly new life would pervade the exhausted troops. Guns which had been carried 'any way' were brought to position, limping steps became firm and cadenced to the music; the line straightened itself and the men were *soldiers all over*," recalled A. Willson of the 126th New York. These feelings did not last long, for once they left the village "the flags were furled, the men drooped and limped again, and crawled along through the rough field or stony highway, faint, but still obedient."[65]

The worst day of the march was June 29, when the brigade marched about thirty-three miles. Beginning at 5:00 A.M., the men marched along the dusty roads with few breaks until the early morning hours of June 30, when the brigade halted at Uniontown, Maryland. Men fell out of the ranks by the hundreds along the way. Colonel Benjamin Thompson of the 111th New York complained that the men "waded every stream on the way" despite the fact that there were ways that could have been employed to keep the men's feet dry. As a result, sand often got into their shoes, and with the chafing of the wet socks and shoes, blisters erupted. The hard march also caused many a pair of shoes to give out, forcing the soldier to march along barefoot. In an effort to keep up, the men began throwing away equipment and clothes, but for many it was but a stopgap measure. "Men would fall out every few rods, declaring they could not go another step, but coaxing and carrying their muskets for them, and more by keeping up a constant stream of funny stories, and songs, were able to hold them on for miles," recalled Thompson. Some of the officers also freely distributed whiskey as a stimulant. By the time the brigade halted at Uniontown, it was but a skeleton of its former self. For example, Company H of the 126th New York arrived with only 8 of its 54 men, and Company C mustered only 12 men of the 60 that began the march earlier that day. The survivors collapsed where they halted. The men of the 126th New York were incredulous when they were almost immediately ordered to perform picket duty. Realizing that the men were in desperate shape, their commanding officer, Colonel Eliakim Sherrill, ordered them back to their slumbers, and personally performed picket duty with his lieutenant colonel in their stead.[66]

The morning of June 30 came all too soon, and the men were again ordered into line. However, after marching about a mile, the column halted and the men were ordered to fall out. They rested for the remainder of the day. The quartermaster visited them with new shoes, and the paymaster brought another needed

commodity. The march continued at about 11:00 A.M. on July 1. Entering Pennsylvania, the men continued to suffer more than their comrades, who were in better marching shape because they had been in the field for many months. Since the brigade had led the division on June 29, it rotated to the rear of the column on July 1, where it was detached to guard the corps' wagon train. The men watched the commotion, as staff members dashing madly about. They did not know it, but the battle of Gettysburg had begun and they were soon ordered to rejoin the division. The brigade finally halted by Taneytown Road near the Round Tops at 9:00 P.M. that evening.[67]

The men were roused sometime between 3:00 and 4:00 A.M. on July 2, and ate what little they had in their haversacks. It was the last meal that many would eat until the following afternoon. The brigade marched with the remainder of the division toward Cemetery Ridge, finally halting near the Bryan farm. Here General Hays ordered the brigade assembled in "columns of battalions." According to Captain Aaron Seeley of the 111th New York, the regiments were deployed in the following manner: the 126th New York in front (west), followed by the 125th New York and the 111th New York; the 39th New York formed in the rear (east). The 39th New York was almost immediately thrown out on the skirmish line. The rest of the men inspected and cleaned their muskets, received additional ammunition, and waited for the fight to begin. Regimental bands serenaded the men during part of the day.[68]

About 3:00 P.M., the enemy batteries opened fire on the Federal line. Orders of "Boys, lie down!" rippled down the line as the officers tried to steady the men. According to Major Charles Richardson, the 126th New York was ordered forward to take advantage of the cover provided by a low stone wall. The cannonade produced a deafening noise but few casualties.[69]

The men heard small arms fire emanating to the south, which appeared to be moving in their direction. Events were taking a turn for the worst for Meade's army. As Hood's, and now McLaw's Confederate Divisions were launched against the Federal left flank, they achieved some successes. Among the most successful was Barksdale's Brigade of Mississippians, which had crushed Graham's Brigade (Birney's Division, III Corps) in the Peach Orchard, and had turned, and rolled up Humphreys's Division's (III Corps). Flushed with victory, it was now driving toward Cemetery Ridge. Hancock desperately cast about for fresh Federal troops to help blunt the attack. A courier arrived a short while later while General Hays and Colonel Willard were conferring. The request was for a brigade, and Hays looked at Willard and said, "Take your brigade over there and knock the H_____ out of the rebs." Orders to "Fall in!" were followed by "fix bayonets; shoulder arms; left face; forward march." These orders were probably issued sometime after 5:00 P.M.[70]

Because Sickles was wounded, Meade placed Hancock in charge of the III Corps. Since he was moving south on Taneytown Road anyway, Hancock decided to lead Willard's men to their position. Marching by the left flank, the brigade moved about a half a mile to the south before halting north of Weikert's Woods. It formed line of battle facing to the right (west). The brigade halted when it reached its appointed position. The 126th New York formed on the right of the 125th New York. About two hundred yards behind the 126th New York, and slightly to its right was the 111th New York, and over to the left, behind the 125th New York, was the 39th New York, which faced

southwest. McGilvery's artillery reserve was deployed in front of the brigade. The noise was deafening and devastation laid all around them.[71]

Willard's men realized that it was just a matter of time before the enemy appeared as streams of III Corps units moved to the rear. The men did not know that they were up against the brigade that had flanked their position at Harper's Ferry, therefore guaranteeing their capture. As the Mississippians approached a swale containing an almost dried up Plum Run and trees and bushes, General Barksdale halted them to redress their disordered lines of battle. They had already smashed through two Federal positions and had their eye on a third. The sun was sinking low on the horizon as Willard moved his men toward the swale, and soon they could see men on the other side. Chaplain Ezra Simons of the 125th New York reported what occurred next. "Our men commenced to fire, but the word was shouted: 'firing on your own men!' Upon which the command was given by Colonel Willard: 'Cease firing!'" Many of the men were not so sure about the accuracy of their officers' assessment, but reluctantly obeyed orders. This reprieve gave Barksdale's men time to reload and the knowledge that a potentially large Federal force was in front of them.[72]

The volley that the 125th and 126th New York subsequently received was both well aimed and deadly. Men fell by the score. Lieutenant Colonel James Bull, who prepared the brigade's after-battle report, wrote with some bitterness that "contrary, as is evident, to the expectations of the brigade commander [Willard] the rebels in considerable force were found in the underbrush." Perhaps with some hyperbole, Thompson (111th New York) wrote that the "constant rain of missiles at this point was terrific. A large number of cannon at close range were pouring shell and shrapnel upon us without intermission, and in our whole front was a line of riflemen giving us minie balls with such rapidity that it seemed as if nothing could live an instant exposed to their fire." Realizing his mistake, Willard ordered the two regiments forward. As the men advanced through the swale, firing as they went, a soldier yelled out, "Remember Harper's Ferry." The cry was taken up by hundreds of others. After the men crashed through the swale and reached the other side, they were ordered to "charge bayonets." They almost immediately came upon Barksdale's men. So rapid was this charge that many Mississippians threw down their weapons and surrendered. Others ran for the rear.[73]

Seeing that total victory was within their grasp, the men charged after the fleeing Confederate soldiers. After going about 175 yards, they were hit by heavy Confederate artillery fire. "The commander, finding his brigade unable to stand so severe a fire, ordered the regiments to retire, which was done in good order down the hill and through the underbrush," noted Lieutenant Colonel Lewis Crandell of the 125th New York in his diary. He explained that only "reluctantly the boys fell back." An artillery round took away most of Willard's face at this time, and command of the brigade passed to Colonel Eliakim Sherrill.[74]

While the 125th and 126th New York were dealing with Barksdale's Brigade, Wilcox's Alabama Brigade was attacking on Barksdale's left, threatening Willard's right flank. General Hancock galloped up to Colonel Clinton MacDougall of the 111th New York and ordered him to move his regiment to the right to hit Wilcox's right flank. MacDougall immediately put his men into motion, and formed them on the right of the 126th New York. Advanc-

ing, they crashed into Wilcox's line, driving its right wing backward. This pressure was an important reason for General Wilcox's subsequent decision to break off his attack on Cemetery Ridge. Captain Aaron Seeley graphically described how his men "hurled themselves upon the advancing foe. The rebel ranks were broken through, and, as they hurriedly retreated, volley after volley was poured into them by our still advancing regiment." The 111th New York paid dearly for its victory, however. Approximately 185 of its 390 men were casualties.[75]

The 39th New York on the second line on the left of the brigade also played a role in defeating Barksdale's men. The 21st Mississippi parted from the rest of the brigade and advanced rapidly in a southeasterly direction, capturing Watson's battery in the process. While the Confederates were in the process of turning the cannon to fire into the retreating Federal troops, Captain John Fassett, an aide to General Birney, realized the devastation it could wreck. Seeing the 39th New York nearby, he rode over and ordered Major Hugo Hildebrandt to recapture the guns. "By whose orders?" asked the major. "By order of General Birney," replied a fast-thinking Fassett. "I am in General Hancock's Corps," was Hildebrandt's response. Not missing a beat, Fassett said, "Then I order you to take those guns, by order of General Hancock." Probably seeing the precarious situation, Hildebrandt ordered his regiment to double-time and it crashed into the 21st Mississippi, causing it to retreat toward Seminary Ridge. Captain Fassett won a Congressional Medal of Honor for his heroics.[76]

High praise was heaped upon the brigade. Hancock wrote that the brigade's actions were "equal to any regular brigade I ever saw." Not only had it blunted Barksdale's and Wilcox's attacks, it recaptured several cannon. The action was not without some controversy, however. As darkness fell, Colonel Sherrill ordered his men back to their original positions on Cemetery Ridge. Spying this movement, General Hancock rode up and "with a stream of profanity which one might have expected from a drunken sailor, but not from a gentleman, demanded where we were going and who was in command," recalled Thompson (111th New York). Placing Sherrill under arrest, Hancock turned the column around, and according to Thompson, "ordered us to stay there until told to move." A short time later, the brigade was ordered to return to its original position on Cemetery Ridge.[77]

As the brigade reached Ziegler's Grove, it was unable to take its original position because some units of Smyth's Brigade occupied it. The brigade therefore formed two lines. The 126th New York moved to the front line, to the right of the 108th New York (Smyth's Brigade), while the other regiments took position behind Smyth's Brigade, from left to right, as 39th New York–125th New York–111th New York. Given the exertions of the march and the battle with Barksdale's and Wilcox's Brigades, it is not surprising that the men "slept like logs until day dawn," according to Thompson (111th New York).[78]

The following day Colonel MacDougall and General Hays went to see Hancock and eventually won Sherrill's release. Some would say it was too bad that Sherrill did not remain under arrest, for a few hours later he would be mortally wounded. While Hays was visiting a recuperating Hancock in Norristown, Pennsylvania, after the battle, the latter remarked, "What has become of that Col. of your Division I put in arrest at Gettysburgh. I guess I ought to apologize to him." Hays sadly responded, "That's just like all your

d_____d apologies, Hancock. They come too late. He's dead."[79]

Upon arising on July 3, the men were issued not food and coffee, but sixty rounds of ammunition. This provided a strong hint of what was to be expected of them. Details were sent out from each regiment for the skirmish line during the morning hours. As the sun rose, the heat became insufferable. Rations were short, especially among the officers, and many had to make do by rubbing ripened wheat between their hands and eating it. Many of the enlisted men grumbled that Meade was unreasonable in expecting them to fight without food or coffee. The noon hour was deathly silent, and one did not need to be a veteran to know that something was brewing. The suspense ended shortly after 1:00 P.M., when the Confederate artillery began their massive bombardment. "From the southwest, west, north, and northeast poured the missiles of death . . . the air all over the wide field was fierce and heavy with the iron hail. The greater portion of the field was swept by the fiery shot. Horses and men dropped, crushed and dead," wrote Simons (125th New York). The artillery projectiles were not the only problem. "Limbs of trees, splinters of rails, gravel and dirt, pieces of stone from the stone walls filled the air and wounded many," recalled Colonel Clinton MacDougall of the 111th New York.[80]

Chaplain Simons graphically described the charge:

See! From the woods covering Seminary Ridge that magnificent line of men—a mile long, three lines, deep, and each line at a double line . . . as they come nearer, the shell burst among them; nearer still and the canister rains upon them. They are at the Emmitsburg Road. They mount the fence. Now at them, men! Commanded "to hold the fire until the enemy come near enough," the moment to strike has come. And the infantry, along the crest of the assaulted hill, arise and pour full into the faces of the foe the death-winged bullet.[81]

During the height of the cannonading, the 111th New York moved to the right, where it formed behind the 12th New Jersey (Smyth's Brigade). Not having access to the stone wall that sheltered the New Jerseyans, the men had to make do by lying close to the ground. Lieutenant S. B. McIntyre recalled that the right of the 111th New York actually occupied the first line behind the stone wall, and only the left was behind the 12th New Jersey.[82]

As the Confederate line advanced, Captain Samuel Armstrong of the 126th New York ordered the seventy-five-man picket reserve to fall in and double-quick about three hundred yards to get at the Confederate flank. Finding a rail fence, Armstrong ordered his men to take position behind it, and with the 8th Ohio, they poured a withering fire into the Confederate left flank.[83]

The rest of the line waited until the Confederate line approached Emmitsburg Road. As it approached, "General Hays ordered us all to our weapons and we were quickly formed in line of battle and moved to the left about forty rods and ordered to lie down behind the broken fragments of an old stone wall," recorded Sargeant Charles Belknap of the 125th New York. This stone wall was actually behind the first line occupied by Smyth's men. Almost immediately, the men were ordered up again and moved forward another hundred yards to the front line. Ezra Simons of the same regiment noted that "other troops were mingled with our regiment at the crucial point." Belknap wrote that "here we waited in almost breathless suspense for the enemy who was moving on toward us like a vast avalanche." The sus-

pense soon ended when the officers yelled, "Open fire," and thousands of muskets responded. The Rebels fell by the hundreds. Over on the extreme right of Willard's line, the 126th New York was ordered to wheel to the left to pour a deadly fire into the Confederate flank.[84]

The 111th New York was also pouring a destructive fire into the enemy. "The volley you gave them on the fence [along Emmitsburg Road] threw them into confusion; but they reformed, even rectifying their lines and advanced with redoubled fury. The fire now became general. As the effect of each volley could be seen, the cheers and the confusion were wild. Many of them came within a few feet of this low stone wall; but the fire was too severe, the resistance too great," wrote Colonel Mac-Dougall after the war.[85]

Seeing the Confederate charge losing steam, Willard's men jumped over the low stone wall and charged into the enemy, capturing hundreds of prisoners. Chaplain Simon recalled the reaction of one Confederate officer when he was escorted into the Federal position. "Where are your men?" he asked. When told that the relatively few he saw were all that had repelled the charge, he exclaimed, "If I had known that this was all you have, I would not have surrendered!" General Hays, who happened to be within earshot, told the Confederate officer to "Go back and try it over," as the prisoner was escorted to the rear.[86]

The dead Confederate soldiers lay in heaps in front of the wall. Private Norman Eldred of the 111th New York recalled that the dead were so thick he could "almost jump from one body to another." The loss of life in the Union ranks was also severe, particularly among the officers, who made good targets as they provided encouragement to their men. Colonel Sherrill was mortally wounded near the left of the line and Colonel

MacDougall of the 111th New York and Major Hildebrandt of the 39th New York were also wounded.[87]

The men had performed exceptionally well. On July 2, they were instrumental in halting both Barksdale's and Wilcox's Brigades as they drove toward Cemetery Ridge, and they played an important role in blunting Pettigrew's Division on July 3. The men did well enough for General Hays, their former brigade commander, to tell them that "the Harper's Ferry boys wiped out Harper's Ferry."[88]

NOTES

1. Faust, *Historical Times Illustrated Encyclopedia of the Civil War,* 354; Tagg, *Generals of Gettysburg,* 54.

2. OR 27, 1, 455; Francis Wafer, diary, copy in 108th New York file, GNMP.

3. OR 27, 1, 465

4. OR 27, 1, 454, 457, 472.

5. OR 27, 1, 465; Benjamin W. Thompson, "Personal Narrative of Experiences in the Civil War, 1861–1865," Civil War Times Illustrated Collection, USAMHI.

6. OR 27, 1, 455.

7. Busey and Martin, *Regimental Strengths and Losses,* 42, 244.

8. Stewart, *Pickett's Charge,* 56.

9. Dyer, *Compendium,* 292; Tagg, *Generals of Gettysburg,* 55–56.

10. Charles Merrick, letter, copy in 8th Ohio folder, GNMP.

11. Thomas Keppler, *History of the Three Months and Three Years' Service . . . of the Fourth Regiment Ohio Volunteer Infantry in the War for the Union* (Cleveland, OH, 1886), 123–124.

12. Keppler, *History of the Three Months and Three Years' Service . . . of the Fourth Regiment Ohio Volunteer Infantry in the War for the Union,* 124–125; Franklin Sawyer, *A Military History of the 8th Regiment, Ohio Volunteer Infantry . . .* (Cleveland, OH, 1881), 123.

Colonel Franklin Sawyer recounted a slightly different version of the story, recall-ing that Hancock stated that "I have selected a position from which Lee cannot drive us, and there the battle will be fought" (Sawyer, *A Military History of the 8th Regiment, Ohio Volunteer Infantry . . . ,* 123).

13. Thomas F. Galway, *The Valiant Hours: Narrative of "Captain Brevet," An Irish-American in the Army of the Potomac* (Harrisburg, PA, 1961), 100–101; OR, 27, 1, 456; Sawyer, "The 8th Ohio at Gettysburg," address, copy in 8th Ohio folder, GNMP, 3

According to Captain David Beem of the 14th Indiana, his men did not have breakfast (David Beem, letter, Indiana Historical Society).

14. Keppler, *History of the Three Months and Three Years' Service . . . of the Fourth Regiment Ohio Volunteer Infantry in the War for the Union,* 126–127; Sawyer, "The 8th Ohio at Gettysburg," 3–4; Galway, *The Valiant Hours: Narrative of "Captain Brevet," An Irish-American in the Army of the Potomac,* 103; OR 27, 1, 461.

There is some confusion about when these four companies were relieved by two other companies of the regiment. Carroll said it was at noon; Colonel Leonard Carpenter of the 4th Ohio thought it occurred at 3:00 P.M. (OR 27, 1, 457, 460).

15. Sawyer, *8th Ohio,* 126–127; Thomas Galway to John Bachelder, May 19, 1882, in Bachelder Papers, New Hampshire Historical Society.

16. Franklin Sawyer, "The 8th Ohio at Gettysburg," 5; Sawyer, *A Military History of the 8th Regiment, Ohio Volunteer Infantry . . . ,* 128.

According to Thomas Galway, units from the XI Corps (specifically the 55th Ohio) attempted to advance in support of the 8th Ohio, but were unsuccessful (Thomas Galway to John Bachelder, May 19, 1882).

17. OR 27, 1, 457; Keppler, *History of the Three Months and Three Years' Service . . . of the Fourth Regiment Ohio Volunteer Infantry in thw War for the Union,* 128–129.

18. OR 27, 1, 457, 459; Elijah Cavins to John Bachelder, May 9, 1878 and "Statement of Lt. Col. Elijah H.C Cavins," in Bachelder Papers, New Hampshire Historical Society;

Dickelman, "Gen. Carroll's Gibraulter Brigade at Gettysburg"; David Beem, letter.

19. Pfanz, *Gettysburg—Culp's Hill and Cemetery Hill*, 274; Keppler, *History of the Three Months and Three Years' Service . . . of the Fourth Regiment Ohio Volunteer Infantry in thw War for the Union*, 129.

20. Galway, *The Valiant Hours: Narrative of "Captain Brevet," An Irish-American in the Army of the Potomac*, 106; Captain R. Bruce Ricketts to John Bachelder, March 2, 1866, in Bachelder Papers, New Hampshire Historical Society.

21. A. F. Sweetland, "Repulsing the 'Tigers' at the Cemetery," *National Tribune*, November 2, 1916; H. H. Caines, "A Gettysburg Diary," *National Tribune*, December 23, 1909; Jonah Bayles, "On Cemetery Hill," *National Tribune*, September 1, 1910; Pfanz, *Gettysburg—Culp's Hill and Cemetery Hill*, 274–275.

22. OR 27, 1, 457, 458, 460; Sawyer, *8th Ohio at Gettysburg*, 5.

23. Sawyer, *8th Ohio at Gettysburg*, 5–6; Franklin Sawyer to John Bachelder, October, 20, 1885, in Bachelder Papers, New Hampshire Historical Society.

24. T. S. Potter, "The Battle of Gettysburg," *National Tribune*, August 5, 1882; Sawyer, *A Military History of the 8th Regiment, Ohio Volunteer Infantry . . . ,*130.

25. Sawyer, *8th Ohio at Gettysburg*, 7.

26. Sawyer, *A Military History of the 8th Regiment, Ohio Volunteer Infantry . . . ,*132; Galway, *The Valiant Hours: Narrative of "Captain Brevet," An Irish-American in the Army of the Potomac*, 116; Horace Judson to John Bachelder, October, 17, 1887, in Bachelder Papers, New Hampshire Historical Society.

Two of the flags were from the 38th Virginia and 34th North Carolina.

27. Sawyer, *8th Ohio at Gettysburg*, 7–8; Franklin Sawyer to John Bachelder, October 20, 1885; Galway, *The Valiant Hours: Narrative of "Captain Brevet," An Irish-American in the Army of the Potomac*, 118; The Ohio Boys at Gettysburg, Ohio Historical Society.

28. Sawyer, *A Military History of the 8th Regiment, Ohio Volunteer Infantry . . . ,*132; Sawyer, *8th Ohio at Gettysburg*, 8.

29. Franklin Sawyer to John Bachelder, October 20, 1885; Stewart, *Pickett's Charge*, 270.

30. Galway, *The Valiant Hours: Narrative of "Captain Brevet," An Irish-American in the Army of the Potomac* 120–122; Keppler, *History of the Three Months and Three Years' Service . . . of the Fourth Regiment Ohio Volunteer Infantry in the War for the Union*, 132.

31. Busey and Martin, *Regimental Strengths and Losses*, 43, 244.

32. Dyer, *Compendium*, 292; Tagg, *Generals of Gettysburg*, 57.

33. William P. Haines, *History of the Men of Co. F* (Woodbury, NJ, 1983), 36; Edward Longacre, *To Gettysburg and Beyond: The Twelfth New Jersey Volunteer Infantry* (Hightstown, NJ, 1988), 115; diary of Francis Wafer (copy in 108th New York file, GNMP).

34. Poriss and Poriss, *While My Country is in Danger,* 68; Seville, *History of the First Regiment,* 80; Bowen, "The Diary of Captain George A. Bowen," 128; Cowtan, *Services of the Tenth New York Volunteers,* 205; Albert Emmel, letter (copy in the 12th New Jersey file, GNMP).

35. Francis Wafer, diary; OR 27, 1, 464, 469; Report of the Joint Committee, 6; Page, *History of the 14th Connecticut*, 138–139; Bowen, "Diary of Captain George A. Bowen," 128.

36. Haines, *History of the Men of Company F,* 38; Christ, *The Struggle for the Bliss Farm,* 19–20; Page, *History of the 14th Connecticut,* 140–141; Stevens, *Souvenir of the Excursion to the Battlefield,* 14; Poriss and Poriss, *While My Country is in Danger,* 69; Major Theodore Ellis, account, *Bachelder Papers*, vol. 1, 79; Hess, *Pickett's Charge*, 105.

37. OR 27, 1, 465; *Report of Joint Committee*, 7; Bowen, "Diary of Captain George A. Bowen," 128.

38. Christ, *Hot Crimson Plain*, 27–28; John Brady, account, *Bachelder Papers*, vol. 3, 1388; Bowen diary, "Diary of Captain George A. Bowen," 129.

Lieutenant John Dent, who filed the 1st Delaware's report, put a different spin on the matter, saying that Harris had ordered the regiment back to the main line because its ammunition was almost exhausted. (OR 27, 1, 469).

39. Brady, account, *Bachelder Papers*, vol. 3, 1389.

40. OR 27, 1, 465; Haines, *History of the Men of Company F*, 38; Christ, *Hot Crimson Plain*, 36; Longacre, *To Gettysburg and Beyond: The Twelfth New Jersey Volunteer Infantry*, 125–126.

41. Gerry H. Poriss and Ralph G. Poriss, *While My Country is in Danger: The Life and Letters of Lieutenant Colonel Richard S. Thompson*, 70; Albert Emmel, letter, copy in Brake Collection, USAMHI; Christopher Mead, letter, copy in Brake Collection, USAMHI.

42. W. F. Beyer and O. F. Keydel, *Deeds of Valor* (Stamford, CT, 1994), 228–230.

43. Poriss and Poriss, *While My Country is in Danger: The Life and Letters of Lieutenant Colonel Richard S. Thompson*, 79; Longacre, *To Gettysburg and Beyond: The Twelfth New Jersey Volunteer Infantry*, 127.

44. OR 27, 1, 471.

45. Charles D. Page, *History of the Fourteenth Regiment, Connecticut Volunteer Infantry* (Gaithersburg, MD, 1987), 142.

46. Stevens, *Souvenir of the Excursion*, 15; Haines, *History of the Men of Company F*, 39; Longacre, *To Gettysburg and Beyond: The Twelfth New Jersey Volunteer Infantry*, 129–130.

There is some confusion over the number of companies participating from the 12th New Jersey. Some believe it was four, others five.

47. Page, *History of the Fourteenth Regiment, Connecticut Volunteer Infantry*, 144.

48. Stevens, *Souvenir of Excursion*, 17–21; Hamblen, *Connecticut Yankees at Gettysburg*, 96; Wilbur Fiske, account, *Bachelder Papers*, vol. 3, 2007.

49. Poriss and Poriss, *While My Country is in Danger: The Life and Letters of Lieutenant Colonel Richard S. Thompson*, 71.

All the 14th Connecticut veterans (and even some recent writers) mistakenly thought that Lieutenant Postles brought the order. However, his heroics were clearly performed on July 2.

50. Longacre, *To Gettysburg and Beyond: The Twelfth New Jersey Volunteer Infantry*, 131;

Page, *History of the Fourteenth Regiment, Connecticut Volunteer Infantry*, 148.

51. Haines, *History of the Men of Company F*, 41; Washburn, *History and Record of the 108th Regiment N.Y.*, 50; Francis Wafer, diary.

52. Page, *History of the Fourteenth Regiment, Connecticut Volunteer Infantry*, 150–151; Stevens, *Souvenir of Excursions*, 26; OR 27, 1, 467.

53. Haines, *History of the Men of Company F*, 41

54. Haines, *History of the the the Men of Company F*, 42; OR 27, 1, 467; Page, *History of the Fourteenth Regiment, Connecticut Volunteer Infantry*, 151.

55. Haines, *History of the Men of Company F*, 42; Christopher Mead, letter, copy in Brake Collection, USAMHI; Emmel, letter.

56. *Report of Joint Committee to Mark the Positions Occupied by the 1st and 2nd Delaware at the Battle of Gettysburg* (Dover, DE, 1887), 14; OR 27, 1, 465; Haines, *History of the Men of Company F*, 42; Page, *History of the Fourteenth Regiment, Connecticut Volunteer Infantry*, 152; William P. Seville, *History of the First Regiment, Delaware Volunteers . . .* (Baltimore, MD, 1986), 81.

57. Charles P. Hamblen, *Connecticut Yankees at Gettysburg* (Kent, OH, 1993), 105; Page, *History of the Fourteenth Regiment, Connecticut Volunteer Infantry*, 152; Seville, *History of the First Regiment, Delaware Volunteers . . .*, 82.

58. Page, *History of the Fourteenth Regiment, Connecticut Volunteer Infantry*, 154; H. S. Stevens, *Souvenir of the Excursion to the Battlefield by the Society of the 14th Connecticut Regiment* (Washington, 1893), 32; Rollins, *The Damned Red Flag of the Rebellion*, 228.

59. Stevens, *Souvenir of the Excursion to the Battlefield by the Society of the 14th Connecticut Regiment*, 31; Seville, *History of the First Regiment, Delaware Volunteers . . .*, 83; OR 27, 1, 469.

60. Stevens, *Souvenir of the Excursion to the Battlefield by the Society of the 14th Connecticut Regiment*, 31; *Report of Joint Committee Committee to Mark the Positions Occupied by the 1st and 2nd Delaware at the Battle of Gettysburg*, 15.

61. Loren Goodrich, "Memoir," Connecticut Historical Society; Stevens, *Souvenir*

of the Excursion to the Battlefield by the Society of the 14th Connecticut Regiment, 36.

62. Elwood W. Christ, *The Struggle for the Bliss Farm at Gettysburg* (Baltimore, MD, 1993), 69.

63. Busey and Martin, *Regimental Strengths and Losses,* 44, 244.

The 322 men of the 39th New York had been consolidated into four companies just prior to Gettysburg (*NYG,* vol. 1, 284).

64. *NYG,* vol. 2, 882, 905; Tagg, *Generals of Gettysburg,* 59.

65. Arabella M. Willson, *Disaster, Struggle, Triumph* (Albany, NY, 1870), 154–155.

66. Benjamin W. Thompson, "Personal Narrative of Experiences in the Civil War, 1861–65," copy in Brake Collection, USAMHI; Wayne Mahood, *Written in Blood* (Shippensburg, PA, 1997), 113; Willson, *Disaster, Struggle, Triumph,* 155.

67. Mahood, *Written in Blood,* 114; Thompson, "Personal Narrative"; Lewis Crandell, diary, copy in 125th folder, GNMP; Charles Belknap, diary, copy in 125th New York folder, GNMP.

68. N. Eldred, "Only a Boy," copy in the Brake Collection, USAMHI; OR 27, 1, 472, 475; Thompson, "Personal Narrative"; Ezra D. Simons, *A Regimental History: The One Hundred and Twenty-fifth New York State Volunteers* (New York, 1886), 102.

69. Simons, *A Regimental History: The One Hundred and Twenty-fifth New York State Volunteers* 103; *NYG,* vol. 2, 905.

70. OR 27, 1, 475; Eric Campbell, "'Remember Harper's Ferry:' The Degradation, Humiliation and Redemption of Colonel George L. Willards's Brigade," *Gettysburg Magazine* (July 1992), issue 7, 64; Willson, *Disaster, Struggle and Triumph,* 168.

71. *NYG,* vol. 2, 905; R. L. Murray, *Redemption of the Harper's Ferry Cowards: The Story of the 111th and 126th New York State Volunteer Regiments at Gettysburg* (Wolcott, NY, 1994), 96–97; OR 27, 1, 474.

72. *NYG,* vol. 2, 886.

73. *NYG,* vol. 2, 906; OR 27, 1, 472; Thompson, "Personal Narrative"; Willson, *Disaster, Struggle and Triumph,* 169.

74. *NYG,* vol. 2, 906; Crandell, diary.

75. OR 27, 1, 475, 476; Mahood, *Written in Blood,* 131; Pfanz, *Gettysburg—The Second Day,* 406.

76. OR 27, 1, 474; *NYG,* vol. 2, 906; Beyer and Keydel, *Deeds of Honor,* 240–241.

77. Mahood, *Written in Blood,* 132–133; Thompson, "Personal Narrative."

According to Colonel Charles Mac-Dougall, Sherrill was only following Willard's instructions before he was struck down. When told to move to the rear and right, MacDougall demurred, saying that it would weaken the Federal center, but obeyed at Sherrill's insistence. MacDougall believed that Sherrill "misunderstood Willard's order, for you know W.(illard) was a good tactician" (C. D. MacDougall, letter, copy in GNMP).

78. Mahood, *Written in Blood,* 140; *NYG,* vol. 2, 907; Thompson, "Personal Narrative."

79. MacDougall, letter.

80. Thompson, "Personal Narrative"; OR 27, 1, 473; George Yost, letter, copy in 126th folder, GNMP; *NYG,* vol. 2, 800, 801, 889.

81. Simons, *A Regimental History: The One Hundred and Twenty-fifth New York State Volunteers,* 135–136.

82. OR 27, 1, 476; S. B. McIntyre, letter, copy in 111th folder, GNMP.

83. Simons, *A Regimental History: The One Hundred and Twenty-fifth New York State Volunteers,* 137–138.

84. Belknap, diary; *NYG,* vol. 2, 890, 907.

85. *NYG,* vol. 2, 802.

86. *NYG,* vol. 2, 891, 908.

87. Eldred, "Only a Boy"; Michael Bararella, *Lincoln's Foreign Legion* (Shippensburg, PA, 1996) 139.

88. Bararella, *Lincoln's Foreign Legion,* 140.

III CORPS—
MAJOR GENERAL DANIEL SICKLES

Created on March 3, 1862, the III Corps was originally commanded by Major General Samuel Heintzelman through the fall of 1862. It was a veteran unit, having seen action at Yorktown, Williamsburg, Fair Oaks, Glendale, and Fredericksburg. It was not engaged at Second Bull Run or Antietam. A colorful politician, Major General Daniel Sickles took over the corps on February 5, 1863, making it the only one not commanded by a West Pointer. Sickles got to show his mettle at the battle of Chancellorsville, when he took on Stonewall Jackson's corps. He fought well, but General Hooker ordered him to pull back and he lost many men because of it.[1]

Sickles took a leave from the army after the battle and did not resume command of his corps until it reached Frederick on June 28. His defeat at Chancellorsville still weighed heavily on him when he returned. The corps began its march the following day at about 6:00 A.M. and it ended between Taneytown and Emmitsburg. The men remained in camp until between 2:00 and 3:00 P.M. on June 30, and then proceeded to Emmitsburg. The morning of July 1 found the corps covering Fairfield Road north of the town. Being in the left wing of the army, Sickles sent an aide to seek out General Reynolds for orders on July 1. Reynolds responded that Sickles should march toward Gettysburg. This put Sickles in a quandary, as Meade had told him to remain at Emmitsburg. A hurried order from General Howard, telling Sickles that Reynolds was dead and that he should rush his men to the battlefield finally settled the matter. Leaving a brigade from each division behind at Emmitsburg, Sickles ordered his men to Gettysburg at 2:00 P.M. The corps marched along Emmitsburg Road, with Birney's 1st Division in the lead. Because the two divisions took different roads as they approached the battlefield, Birney's 1st Division arrived several hours before Humphreys's 2nd Division. The corps was assigned the sector from Little Round Top to the southern portion of Cemetery Ridge. Birney's Division became the left-most unit of the army. Humphreys's 2nd Division formed on its right, with its right connecting with Caldwell's Division's (II Corps) left flank.[2]

Fretting about the high ground in front of his assigned position, Sickles petitioned Meade for permission to move his corps forward about two thousand feet to occupy it. Meade was more concerned about other sectors, so he sent his artillery chief, General Henry Hunt, to examine Sickles's position. After Sickles sent out a reconnaissance-in-force that found a large enemy force in Pitzer's Woods on Seminary Ridge, Sickles became even more insistent about moving forward. As the afternoon wore on, Sickles became increasingly agitated, and finally moved his corps forward to the high ground without orders to do so.[3]

All hell broke loose at about 4:00 P.M., when the Confederate attack against Sickles's position was launched. General Sickles was grievously wounded in the leg by a cannon ball as he sat on his horse near the Trostle house at about 6:30 P.M. Hoping to harden his men, Sickles nonchalantly puffed on a cigar as he was carried away on a stretcher. It didn't work, for his wounding had a great impact on the men. Not only was he extremely popular with his men, it could not have come at a worse time, as the III Corps was in danger of being destroyed. "Our division and corps feel disheartened at this [Sickles's wounding], and we feel a little panic stricken," recalled Daniel Crotty of the 3rd Michigan (de Trobriand's Brigade).[4]

General Birney took over the corps and was thrust into the position of holding an increasingly vulnerable spot. Hood's and McLaws's Confederate Divisions smashed into Devil's Den/Houck's Ridge, the Wheatfield, and the Peach Orchard, and after a tenacious defense, Birney's Division, now commanded by General J. Hobart Ward, was forced to fall back. The same was true of Humphreys's Division on the right, which was pulled back before it was overwhelmed by units from McLaws's and Anderson's Divisions. The corps was devastated by its gallant defense and spent the remainder of the battle in the rear.

1ST DIVISION—

Major General David Birney

Cold and colorless Major General David Birney had led the 1st Division since October 30, 1862. Although not a West Pointer, he threw himself into the study of strategy and tactics as the war approached. A politically well-connected attorney, Birney rose from commanding the 23rd Pennsylvania in the summer of 1861 to brigade command and a brigadier general's commission in February 1862. The division, with Birney's Brigade, fought at Fair Oaks, Glendale, and the Second Bull Run campaign. Birney assumed command of the division prior to the Antietam campaign, but the division did not participate in it. Charged with dereliction of duty for not supporting Meade's Division at Fredericksburg, he was later exonerated. The division participated in the defeat at Chancellorsville and was now ready for redemption.[5]

The division's march to Gettysburg mirrored that of the III Corps, except that de Trobriand's 3rd Brigade was left behind at Emmitsburg on July 1 to watch the army's flank. The unit was recalled, however, during the early morning hours of July 2 and arrived in time to participate in the battle. The remainder of the division reached the battlefield at 5:30 P.M. on July 1 and relieved Geary's Division (XII Corps) near Little Round Top the following morning. According to Birney, his left flank connected with Little Round Top and his right with Humphreys's Division. Except for some minor shifts in position, the division remained there through the day. One exception was Berdan's Sharpshooters and the 3rd Maine (Ward's Brigade), who ventured forward to Seminary Ridge to ascertain the enemy's position. They found them in strength, and after a heated action in Pitzer's Woods, returned with the information.[6]

Upon receiving his orders to advance to occupy the high ground in front of his position, Birney took possession of the Devil's Den–Wheatfield–Peach Orchard axis. Ward's Brigade was on the left, de Trobriand's in the middle, and Graham's on the right. Because of the terrain, the two left brigades faced southwest, while Graham's faced northwest. This created a vulnerable salient at the Peach Orchard. Hood's Division's attack hit Ward's and de Trobriand's Brigades at about 4:00 P.M., and after several hours of hard fighting, the two units were forced back from Devil's Den/Houck's Ridge and the Wheatfield toward their original positions. On the right, Graham's Brigade in the Peach Orchard was overwhelmed by McLaw's Division, and it too was forced to withdraw, but not before sustaining heavy losses, including the capture of its commander. Sickles's wounding during the early evening forced Birney to assume command of the corps and General Ward to take over the division. The division reassembled near Taneytown Road in the rear, where it spent the remainder of the battle.[7]

1st Brigade—Brigadier General Charles Graham

Units: 57th Pennsylvania, 63rd Pennsylvania, 68th Pennsylvania, 105th Pennsylvania, 114th Pennsylvania, 141st Pennsylvania
Strength: 1516
Losses: 740 (67-508-165)—48.8%[8]

As General Charles Graham's Pennsylvania Brigade marched slowly but steadily toward Gettysburg, many of the men still harbored thoughts of Chancellorsville, where several of its regiments had been roughly handled. For example, the 141st Pennsylvania lost 234 men out of the 419 that had entered that bloody battle. In command of the 1st Brigade since March 1863, Charles Graham had been a political ally of Sickles in New York. When the war broke out he encouraged four hundred of his dockworkers to join his 74th New York of the Excelsior Brigade. Sickly from the start of the war, Graham had seen little action. He was actually promoted to the rank of brigadier general in November 1862, but was unable to take the field until four months later. Thus, he rode toward Gettysburg with virtually no

experience commanding any men in battle, let alone a full brigade. The brigade that Graham inherited was battle-tested, having been at Yorktown, Seven Oaks, Malvern Hill, Second Bull Run, Fredericksburg, and Chancellorsville.[9]

Now, during the march toward Gettysburg, the men's spirits rose as they marched through Jefferson and Middletown, Maryland. The men witnessed "the first expression of Union sentiment that had gladdened our eyes and hearts for several months," wrote Gilbert Hays of the 63rd Pennsylvania. "Old Glory was displayed from most of the houses and fair ladies greeted the soldiers with approving smiles and words of welcome. A thousand handkerchiefs waved from windows and house tops," he noted. Flowers and food were freely provided, and when the men camped, the citizens visited the camps to see how soldiers really lived.[10]

The news that Meade had replaced Hooker as commander of the army was received with indifference by most of the men. "Most of us were not greatly concerned in the change, for changes had occurred so often that we hardly had time to become very much attached to any one of them," wrote Sergeant John Bloodgood of the 141st Pennsylvania.[11]

The men continued their march from their bivouac between Taneytown and Emmitsburg sometime between 1:30 and 2:00 P.M. on July 1. A heavy thundershower had earlier drenched the troops, and as is so common in Pennsylvania summers, was followed by the sun's appearance. Although the rain disappeared, the high humidity remained, and many soldiers were forced to drop from the ranks from the energy-zapping combination of high temperature and humidity. The column halted beyond Emmitsburg at about 6:00 P.M. that night, and the men began preparing supper. Before long, bugles sounded, and the weary men continued their march toward Gettysburg. The march was not made any easier by the fact that two infantry corps, artillery, and wagons had already traversed this road, making it exceedingly muddy.[12]

As the men crossed into Pennsylvania they encountered a new group of people—the Pennsylvania Dutch. Bloodgood recalled that these citizens "love money about as well as they do beer and whisky . . . and though they were glad to see us it was more on account of what they wanted us to do than for any great affection for us." In fairness to these people, it is probable that many of the other citizens felt the same way.[13]

The last leg of the trip was especially hard on the men, for they had to witness the heart-wrenching passage of civilians fleeing their homes. Sergeant William Loring of the 141st Pennsylvania recalled that "every conceivable vehicle had been pressed into service and filled with women, children and baggage, and was jolting along by the side of the road—the troops taking the center . . . the women,

some in tears, wringing their hands, lamenting that we were too late, telling us the Union army was already whipped; while others, waving their handkerchiefs, cheered us on with 'God bless you all.'" Private Frank Rauscher of the 114th Pennsylvania noted that the wagons contained "an indiscriminate gathering of household furniture and utensils."[14]

The brigade finally reached the vicinity of Gettysburg around 10:00 P.M. on July 1. General Graham led his troops to the right of Emmitsburg Road, where they were finally permitted to rest in a field just south of George Weikert's farm. The brigade was bivouacked in column of regiments—the 63rd Pennsylvania in front (west), followed by the 105th Pennsylvania, 57th Pennsylvania, 114th Pennsylvania, and 141st Pennsylvania (east) in that order. Colonel Calvin Craig of the 105th Pennsylvania proudly noted in his report that only three of his men fell out of the column during this leg of the march. Many soldiers grumbled when told that no fires could be lit, and, according to the historian of the 141st Pennsylvania, had to "forego their much coveted hot coffee, after their long and fatiguing march."[15]

At daylight the next morning, the brigade moved to the right of Wheatfield Road. The 63rd Pennsylvania and four companies of the 105th Pennsylvania were thrown out on the skirmish line at 9:00 A.M., taking position behind a fence, just behind the Joseph Sherfy house. The rest of the men were permitted to prepare breakfast, which included hot coffee. Loring (141st Pennsylvania) noticed that like before other battles "old feuds and strifes [sic] were dropped and a feeling of fraternity pervaded every breast."[16]

The brigade received orders at midmorning to march to the vicinity of the Trostle house (northwest), where it eventually deployed "in columns doubled on the center." Graham arranged his brigade from left to right as 68th Pennsylvania–141st Pennsylvania–57th Pennsylvania. Behind them were the 105th Pennsylvania and the 114th Pennsylvania. Clark's battery was deployed in front of the brigade. Captain Edward Bowen of the 114th Pennsylvania (Collis's Zouaves) considered this to be a "naturally strong and defensible position, and where, if the enemy had had the temerity to attack us, we could and would have made a successful resistance."[17]

The next several hours were fairly uneventful, as the men rested and speculated. At 3:00 P.M., Graham received orders to move his command forward to its new position along Emmitsburg Road. The brigade was deployed, facing west, from left to right, as 68th Pennsylvania–114th Pennsylvania–57th Pennsylvania–105th Pennsylvania. The 68th Pennsylvania on the left of the line was positioned at the intersection of Wheatfield and Emmitsburg Roads with its right resting on the former road. To the right was the Zouave-attired 114th Pennsylvania, which supported four guns of Bucklyn's battery in front of it. Next came the 57th Pennsylvania, directly across the road from the Sherfy house, and in position to support the other two cannon of Bucklyn's battery and two more from Thompsons's. The last regiment in line was the 105th Pennsylvania, whose right rested on the Trostle farm lane. The brigade's fifth regiment, the 141st Pennsylvania, formed at right angles to the remainder of the brigade, facing south along the Wheatfield Road. Other infantry units and batteries would form along Wheatfield Road, causing a salient to form at the 68th Pennsylvania's position. Two regiments from Brewster's Brigade were aligned along Emmitsburg Road to the right of the 105th Pennsylvania.[18]

The enemy's batteries on Seminary Ridge opened fire on Graham's men shortly after 4:00 P.M. Losses mounted, as the men occupied exposed positions. Bloodgood (141st Pennsylvania) recalled the order, "cover" and "we all got, flat on our faces, so as to give the rebel shells plenty of room to operate over our heads." Colonel Edward Bowen of the 114th Pennsylvania noted that the hostile artillery fire was concentrated on their front. "We were in the midst of a terrific shower of shot and shell and every conceivable kind of missile, which made terrible havoc among us." A soldier from the 68th Pennsylvania recalled that "the artillery fire bearing upon it [the regiment], was terrific, carrying away men at every discharge." The soldiers' only option was to press themselves against the ground and hope that their time was not up. Some of the units, particularly the 141st Pennsylvania, were protected by the sunken nature of Wheatfield Road. Bucklyn's battery, and others in the vicinity of the Peach Orchard, engaged the enemy's, but the return fire was so heavy that the losses among the cannoneers mounted. Responding to pleas from the battery commanders, a call for volunteers was issued, and some of the men from the 141st Pennsylvania helped carry ammunition while others from the 68th Pennsylvania helped serve the guns of the Rhode Island battery.[19]

At 5:30 P.M., while the fighting was still restricted to the left, the 63rd Pennsylvania was pulled back from the skirmish line. During the seven hours of performing this duty, the regiment had expended most of its ammunition. Instead of replenishing its ammunition and returning to the brigade, it remained in the rear, and did not participate in the defense of the Peach Orchard.[20]

The artillery fire stopped as quickly as it had started, and the men who lay prostrate on the ground knew that it was only a matter of time before the enemy infantry appeared. As Barksdale's Mississippi Brigade (McLaws's Division), approached from the west, Captain George Randolph, the III Corps's chief of artillery, rode up to Captain Bowen of the 114th Pennsylvania, and yelled, "If you want to save my battery, [Bucklyn's] move forward." Not able to find his commanding officers, and knowing it was "now or never," Bowen gave the order to advance. "The regiment sprang forward with alacrity and passed through and to the front of the battery, which hastily limbered up and go to the rear," Bowen proudly wrote after the war. Passing the Sherfy buildings, the men moved forward "loading and firing as rapidly as possible." Barksdale's men gave as good as they got, and Bowen's men fell by the second.[21]

The two regiments to the right of the 114th Pennsylvania, the 57th and 105th Pennsylvania, also crossed the road as Barksdale's men approached. The three regiments were now alone in battling Barksdale's men. "Standing on elevated ground, with open fields on all sides, the steady fire of the men, as the enemy's infantry pushed forward, was delivered with excellent effect," wrote a soldier from the 114th Pennsylvania.[22]

To the south side of the Peach Orchard, the left wing of Kershaw's Brigade attempted to capture the Federal cannon concentrated there. Loring (141st Pennsylvania) heard his officers yell, "Attention! Forward," as the men moved through the trees to support the guns. The regiment was now flanked on either side by other regiments in Birney's Division that had been on the skirmish line—the 3rd Maine on the right and the 3rd Michigan on the left, which let loose a "murderous volley" that staggered the South Carolinians and halted their advance. Bloodgood recounted that the 141st Pennsylvania "poured out a tempest of leaden hail upon them." As a result of this volley, the Confederates "reeled, and staggered like drunken men, then scattered and ran in every direction like a flock of frightened sheep." General Graham now ordered the three regiments to advance against the enemy, along with the 2nd New Hampshire to the right. A Federal soldier wrote that "the regiment, which had lain concealed from view, leaped the wall and dashed forward upon the foe. Bewildered by its sudden appearance, and firm front, his forces gave ground, and the regiment held its advanced position until the guns could be dragged by hand to a place of safety."[23]

While the four Federal regiments met with initial success in battling Kershaw's Brigade, the enemy was determined to succeed. Colonel Henry Madill of the 141st Pennsylvania was dismayed to see the regiment on either side of him (3rd Maine and 3rd Michigan) halt, turn, and march to the rear. Madill tried to hold his ground, but the odds were just too great, and he ordered his men to take position behind the 68th Pennsylvania along Emmitsburg Road, which was already engaged with Barksdale's right flank, composed of the 21st Mississippi. Colonel Andrew Tippin of the 68th Pennsylvania ordered his men to "reserve their fire until [the enemy] reaching a certain point, when a destructive fire was opened, the enemy halting and dropping behind a fence." The 17th Mississippi soon arrived on the Pennsylvanians' right flank, and now the two Mississippi regiments again advanced on the 68th Pennsylvania's position while Kershaw's regiments approached from the south. With its right flank in danger of being turned, Colonel Tippin pulled his men back behind the batteries on the east side of the Peach Orchard.[24]

Here Tippin was met by General Graham, who ordered him to "engage the enemy coming down on our right flank." Charging into the 17th Mississippi across Emmitsburg Road toward the Sherfy farm, the Pennsylvanians were ultimately repulsed. General Graham was wounded about this time and Tippin assumed command of the brigade.[25]

Back around the 68th Pennsylvania's original position, the 141st Pennsylvania was trying to hold its ground despite the enemy approaching on two sides. According to Colonel Madill, "I was thus left alone on the hill occupied by the brigade in the afternoon." As the Mississippians advanced they unleashed a volley that staggered the 141st Pennsylvania. Bloodgood recalled that the men of the regiment "continued to pour into their solid ranks the death-dealing missiles, while the rebel bullets cut the air around us like hail." Captain John Clark rushed up to Madill and asked him if it was time to retreat. "I have no order to get out," replied Madill. Gazing at his small numbers, he exclaimed, "If I had my old regiment back again, I could whip all of them." Finally realizing that to remain was suicide, Madill ordered his men to the rear. He estimated that his men had held up the Rebel advance for about twenty minutes. Barksdale's men paid dearly during the 141st Pennsylvania's retreat, for it frequently halted and threw deadly volleys into the 21st Mississippi before continuing toward Cemetery Ridge. General Sickles watched them trudge past, and remarked, "Colonel! For God's sake can't you hold on?" With tears in his eyes, Madill replied, "Where are my men?"[26]

Colonel Madill was incorrect in his assumption that the entire brigade had withdrawn. Just to the north, at the Sherfy house, the 114th, 57th, and 105th Pennsylvania continued to hold their ground

against Barksdale's men. The 57th Pennsylvania had immediately opened fire on the enemy when the Mississippians approached the Sherfy farm. The 13th and 17th Mississippi did not respond until they reached a rail fence about a hundred yards from the Pennsylvanians. Their initial volleys were so tremendous that the 114th Pennsylvania's left flank collapsed on its right. The men realized that they could no longer hold their positions and began withdrawing up Emmitsburg Road. In position behind them was the 73rd New York (Brewster's Brigade), which temporarily held the enemy in check. The remnants of the 114th Pennsylvania halted periodically to pour volleys into the victorious Confederates. With the 114th Pennsylvania in full flight, the 57th Pennsylvania now felt the full fury of the Confederate attack on its front and flank. According to Sergeant Ellis Strouss, the men had been confident that they could have held their position, but "we learned that the enemy had broken through the angle at the Peach Orchard, and were swarming in our rear . . . so we were obliged to fall back."[27]

Prior to Barksdale's attack, a number of men from the 57th Pennsylvania had taken position in the Sherfy farm buildings, from where they effectively sniped at the approaching enemy. Most did not know that the enemy had flanked them, making their position precarious. Back on the 57th Pennsylvania's main line, Captain Alanson Nelson watched the 114th Pennsylvania and other regiments run past, and said to his commanding officer, Colonel Peter Sides, "It looks as though we will soon have to move out of here, or be captured." Turning his head, Sides quickly said, "Yes, I think we will go now." As Sides was issuing orders to withdraw, Nelson remonstrated that many of the men had taken shelter in the buildings and should be withdrawn before the regiment left. Sides was more concerned about saving the majority of his men, so shrugged off Nelson's suggestion and told him that he could stay behind with a detail, if he so desired. The noise was deafening and Nelson and his men had to yell in the ears of the troops in the building to make themselves understood. Nelson barely escaped capture, but was able to get several men safely out of the house. Others were not so fortunate, and were captured by the 18th Mississippi.[28]

This left the 105th Pennsylvania on the right of the line as Graham's only regiment along Emmitsburg Road. When they saw the three Mississipi regiments advancing along Emmitsburg Road, the men were ordered to swing around and face them. Some of the 57th Pennsylvania formed on their flank and together they opened fire on the enemy. Before long the men could see the enemy enveloping their left flank. Colonel Craig admitted that "the regiment being so small and both flanks being entirely unprotected, I ordered the regiment to retire slowly, and formed line again a short distance to the rear." A veteran of the unit wrote after the war that the retreat was "in good order, re-forming at short intervals and at every favorable point, keeping up all the while a deliberate fire." The writer estimated that the regiment rallied "eight or ten times after the rest of the brigade had left us." At one point the defense was so spirited that the enemy was pushed back toward the Sherfy house. During this period of adversity, the men's battle cry was "Pennsylvania."[29]

So chaotic was the situation, that some units did not return to the brigade for some time. For example, Captain Bowen's 114th Pennsylvania did not find the brigade until early the next morning.[30]

The brigade finally occupied a small grove of trees near the Weikert house,

about three-quarters of a mile in the rear on the morning of July 3. Here the men rested, ate, and cleaned their guns. Most were appreciative of the whiskey ration served to the survivors. Private Lewis Schaeffer wrote in his diary that it is "dreadful to look at our brigade this morning. So many gay and happy fellows who were anxious for the fight yesterday are now bushed in death or lay frightfully wounded." At the beginning of the tremendous artillery barrage that preceded Pickett's charge, many of the men were sleeping with their heads on their knapsacks. None were happy when they were ordered into line at the height of the cannonade, faced right, and marched double-step to an open field about half a mile to the north.[31]

The move placed the brigade squarely in the teeth of the cannonade. A somewhat bitter Captain Edward Bowen wrote after the war that "Colonel Tippen was ordered to move the brigade still further to the right, and whether it was that the brave Colonel didn't know the right from the left, or just which way it was he was ordered to go, or whether it was that his soldierly instinct led him to lead the brigade towards the enemy, doubtless glad of an opportunity to repay them in the same coin for the way they had served us on the previous afternoon the writer does not know, but this much he does know, that in less time than it has taken to tell this we were in the midst of a most severe shower of flying missiles of all sorts and kinds." Colonel Tippin was wounded, and command of the brigade devolved upon Colonel Henry Madill of the 141st Pennsylvania, who, according to Captain Bowen, "quickly withdrew it from the exposed position Colonel Tippen's indiscretion had placed it in."[32]

The brigade marched quickly to the right and toward the front, where it formed the second line of defense behind the Philadelphia brigade. While most of the brigade were bystanders during the charge, the 114th Pennsylvania and 141st Pennsylvania were detached, and sent to General Webb, who ordered them to support Cowan's battery near the Copse of Trees.[33]

That night, the men were detailed to pick up rifles that were strewn around the fields in front of them. The 114th Pennsylvania picked up over three hundred rifles. Later, the 57th and 114th Pennsylvania were sent out on picket duty in the fields between Cemetery and Seminary Ridges,

where they spent a peaceful night. July 4 was spent burying the dead and looking after the wounded. The brigade pulled back on July 5, and remained there until 4:00 A.M. on July 6, when it started after the retreating enemy.[34]

The battle was a tough one for Graham's Brigade. Placed in an untenable position with a salient in the middle of the line, the Pennsylvania troops fought as well as could be expected. It did not help that they were up against a fired-up Mississippi brigade on one side that sought victory at any cost, and a determined South Carolina Brigade on the other.

2nd Brigade—Brigadier General J. Hobart Ward

Units: 20th Indiana, 3rd Maine, 4th Maine, 86th New York, 124th New York, 99th Pennsylvania, 1st U.S. Sharpshooters, 2nd U.S. Sharpshooters
Strength: 2188
Losses: 781 (129-484-170)—35.7%[35]

Brigadier General J. Hobart Ward's civil war experience matched that of his brigade's. Ward had joined the regular army at the age of eighteen and fought in the Mexican War. He later returned to New York, where he became assistant commissary general and then commissary general. Forging political connections, he became the colonel of the 38th New York when the war broke out. Ward's unit saw action at First Bull Run, and he assumed command of Willcox's Brigade when its commander was wounded. Ward also performed solidly at Williamsburg and Seven Pines. With the elevation of David Birney to divisional command, Ward was given his brigade. The brigade lost heavily at both Fredericksburg and Chancellorsville. During the latter battle the brigade made

a rare night attack, which went awry, causing it to flee to safety in the darkness. The brigade was one of the rare units in the army that could boast stability—it had the same commander for ten months.[36]

The men of Ward's Brigade were not happy at 3:00 P.M. on July 1. Having reached Emmitsburg, they were in the process of preparing to go into bivouac when orders arrived to stop, repack their gear, and prepare to continue the march to Gettysburg. According to Sergeant Wyman White of the 2nd U.S. Sharpshooters, "we had hardly put our tents up and had our noon ration when the long roll sounded and that meant for us to pull down our tents . . . and fall into line for further tramping." The march was made at "quick-time," which was difficult because of the road conditions, which General Ward categorized as "horrible." So angry was one soldier that he yelled out, "G-D your Pennsylvania. The rebels ought to destroy the whole state if you can't afford better roads. This road is worse than Virginia roads." Private Peter Ayars of the

99th Pennsylvania later noted that there was only "one stop, a breathing spell of about 15 minutes" during this rapid march. In an effort to keep up, many of the men threw away their personal belongings to lighten their loads. Some officers dismounted so that their horses could carry the heavy muskets of the men who were struggling to keep up. As the men approached Gettysburg, they passed streams of women and children fleeing for safety.[37]

The march up to this point had not been much more pleasant. Captain Charles Weygant of the 124th New York recorded in his diary that the men "lost considerable flesh during the last week, and complain bitterly whenever we start the march, of their swollen, blistered feet." The march was made easier by the townspeople, who gathered by the side of the roads and cheered the men as they passed. Many of the citizens had hung lanterns over their doorways to help light the way during the night march of June 30. Old Glory was also very much in evidence along the route. Sometimes the men were embarrassed by all the attention. When schoolchildren gave three cheers for the men, a sergeant from the 2nd U.S. Sharpshooters yelled out to them, "You better wait until we lick them rebels before you give us so much cheering." The brigade finally reached the battlefield between 8:00 and 8:30 P.M., and filed east from the Emmitsburg Road to Wheatfield Road, where it camped near the George Weikert farm. The men were permitted to make small fires for coffee before turning in for the night. Not all of the men enjoyed this pleasure, however, as the 4th Maine was detached for picket duty west of Emmitsburg Road. Those who turned in for the night were told not to "take off an article of clothing or any accouterments," for an attack was expected at any time.[38]

About 7:30 A.M., Colonel Hiram Berdan received orders to detach a hundred men from his 1st U.S. Sharpshooters to "discover, if possible, what the enemy was doing." General Ward sent the 3rd Maine to provide support. The 99th Pennsylvania was also sent out on picket duty near the Sherfy house. Thus, in addition to the hundred sharpshooters from the 1st U.S., Ward had three of his other regiments (e.g., 3rd Maine, 4th Maine, and 99th Pennsylvania) aligned near Emmitsburg Road. The remaining men were up early on July 2 and moved to the left sometime between 7:30 and 8:00 A.M. They eventually halted near Little Round Top. The brigade now had the distinction of being on the extreme left flank of the army. Prior to this movement the remainder of the 1st and 2nd U.S. Sharpshooters were detached and sent beyond Emmitsburg Road to form a skirmish line. The 2nd U.S. Sharpshooters was later ordered back to form a skirmish line near Little Round Top.[39]

The hundred sharpshooters of the 1st U.S. moved cautiously forward in a northwesterly direction with its left flank eventually resting near the Peach Orchard. According to Colonel Berdan, the detachment came under small arms fire, which stopped its advance. He sent word to General Birney that he could not get the desired information, and was subsequently ordered to send another hundred men from the 1st U.S. Sharpshooters to join the detachment. Lieutenant Colonel Casper Trepp, who commanded the 1st U.S. Sharpshooters because Berdan was placed in command of both sharpshooter units, was angry with his commanding officer. There had been bad blood between the two men, but now it was reaching the boiling point. Trepp angrily wrote in his official report that "I conducted this second detachment directly to and followed the road in plain view of the enemy. This detachment might have been marched . . . perfectly concealed from view of the enemy and without loss of time. As we marched, the enemy must have seen every man from the time we reached the road until we entered the woods on Fairfield road, giving the enemy time enough to counter-maneuver." Trepp was also annoyed that the 3rd Maine, which had been ordered to support the two hundred sharpshooters, halted on Emmitsburg Road in accordance with Berdan's orders, in full view of the enemy. "For this violation of rules of secret expeditions we paid dearly," he wrote.[40]

Continuing forward in a northwesterly direction, the men approached Pitzer's Woods. As they approached, a boy ran up to them and yelled, "Look out! There are lots of rebels in there in rows." The men discounted the boy's story and continued their march. They soon ran into the 11th Alabama of Wilcox's Brigade (Anderson's Division), which was moving south along Seminary Ridge, and a sharp fight broke out. "We attacked them vigorously on the flank, and from our having come upon them very unexpectedly, and getting close to them, we were enabled to do great execution, and threw them for a time into confusion," reported Berdan. The sharpshooters' Sharps breechloaders also assisted in routing the enemy.[41]

The confusion caused by Berdan's men was only temporary, for as the sharpshooters entered Pitzer's Woods they ran into the 10th Alabama, which opened fire. Realizing that he was up against large numbers of enemy troops, Berdan quickly brought up Colonel Moses Lakeman's 3rd Maine at the double-quick. Lakeman groused in his report that his men "labored under a decided disadvantage . . . the skirmishers [Berdan's Sharpshooters] were well secured behind trees, while my battalion filled the intervals."

The two sides blazed away at each other for about twenty minutes. Having ascertained that enemy troops occupied the woods in heavy numbers, Berdan considered his mission accomplished and ordered his troops withdrawn. The men halted occasionally to fire volleys at the enemy, which served to lessen their ardor in following them.[42]

Reaching Emmitsburg Road, Lakeman reformed his broken ranks and began the march back to the brigade. The column had progressed only a short distance when a messenger from General Birney arrived with orders to move to the Peach Orchard. The regiment was deployed as skirmishers, facing south, with its right flank touching Emmitsburg Road and its left in contact with the skirmishers of the 3rd Michigan (de Trobriand's Brigade). General Ward later rued this order, as he would desperately need their services later that day. The 1st U.S. Sharpshooters also reformed on Emmitsburg Road before being redeployed as skirmishers in front of Carr's Brigade (Humphreys's Division).[43]

While the 1st U.S. Sharpshooters and the 3rd Maine were off to the northwest, the remainder of Ward's brigade was spending a quiet morning near Little Round Top. At about 10:00 A.M., the 86th New York was sent to the front to demolish the stone walls and fences in front of the brigade. This was an odd order, given that these low fences proved to be strategic defensive positions in other parts of the field. The men did not think to throw up protective breastworks during this period. "We had not yet learned by bitter experience the inestimable value of breastworks, and instead of spending our leisure time in rolling together the loose stones . . . we lounged about on the grass and rocks, quietly awaiting the coming shock," recalled Weygant (124th New York). There was some excitement at about noon, when the 124th New York found some cows, which were quickly slaughtered; the meat was distributed to the hungry men.[44]

After receiving the report that Confederate troops were on Seminary Ridge in force, Sickles ordered Birney to change front to meet this potential threat. Ward's Brigade advanced about five hundred yards to the Wheatfield. After resting there for about half an hour, the brigade was ordered to move by the left flank to its final position on Houck's Ridge.[45]

At about 2:00 P.M., General Ward sent the 2nd U.S. Sharpshooters back to the skirmish line, toward Emmitsburg Pike, where they encountered their counterparts to their right. This forced Major Homer Stoughton to pull back his men, lest they be flanked. Around 3:00 P.M., the Confederate batteries opened fire on the Federal positions. "Presently a shell came shrieking, and bursting near us," wrote Sergeant J. Harvey Hanford of the 124th New York. "We needed no order or invitation to get behind the rocks." The fire was especially hot because of the regiment's position near Smith's battery. Colonel A. Van Horne Ellis moved his 124th New York to the woods on his right flank, but when he found that this position was just as dangerous, he returned the regiment to its original position.[46]

While waiting between Little Round Top and Emmitsburg Road, Stoughton's Sharpshooters could see a long line of battle approaching. The sharpshooters calmly took aim at Law's Alabama Brigade (Hood's Division, I Corps), killing and wounding many enemy soldiers. Stoughton claimed that as a result of his sharpshooters' accurate fire, one Confederate regiment "broke three times, and rallied before it would advance." When the Confederate line of battle came within a hundred yards, Major Stoughton finally ordered his men to fall back, firing as they went. It appears that the regiment split in two as it retreated. One took up new defensive positions in front of Big Round Top, while the other mingled with Ward's Brigade around Devil's Den. The former group of regiments engaged the 15th and 44th Alabama on the right of the Confederate line, and were again forced to withdraw after inflicting heavy losses on the enemy. This detachment split again, with a portion scrambling up Big Round Top and a second taking position with Company B of the 20th Maine in the saddle between Big and Little Round Tops.[47]

Over to the right, or north, of the 2nd U.S. Sharpshooters, the rest of the brigade nervously fingered their rifles and waited for the Confederate attack to bear down upon them. The brigade was arranged, from left to right, as 4th Maine–124th New York–86th New York–20th Indiana–99th Pennsylvania on Houck's Ridge. The three right regiments occupied the eastern fringes of Rose's Woods; the two left regiments occupied open ground and could more easily see the Rebel advance. Plum Run Gorge was to their left. Because of the considerable space the brigade had been ordered to defend, it occupied only a single line; there were several gaps between the regiments. For example, there was a large gap between the right of the 124th New York and the left of the 86th New York. Two batteries galloped up and took position nearby—Smith's battery unlimbered behind the brigade and Winslow's battery deployed in the Wheatfield to their right.[48]

An argument developed when Captain James Smith deployed four of his guns to the left of the line near Devil's Den. Striding over to Colonel Elijah Walker of the 4th Maine, Captain Smith asked if the regiment could move to his left. Walker recalled that "he [Smith] contended he could take care of his front, but the enemy would come up the woods on our left and I could better protect his guns from that place." Walker vigorously disagreed for a variety of reasons. Most important, he did not like the looks of the wooded Plum Run Gorge. Smith was undeterred and sought out General Ward to plead his case. He convinced the brigade commander, who ordered Walker to move his regiment to the left to form across Plum Run Valley. Walker "remonstrated with all the power of speech I could command" but knowing that the enemy was approaching, he reluctantly obeyed the order. While this placated Smith, it left a gaping hole in the line, which Smith claimed he could defend, but in the end, couldn't.[49]

An ominous quiet settled over the field after the heavy cannonade suddenly stopped. "The firing suddenly ceased and as the smoke blew away we could see the enemy coming toward us in four distinct lines of battle," noted Lieutenant Henry Ramsdell of the 124th New York. Ward did not like the looks of the situation. "The supports of the first two lines of the enemy were now coming up in columns en masse," he wrote, "while we had but a single line of battle to receive the shock." The men of the 124th New York did not like it either, primarily because they were still cooking the beef they had killed earlier. As they quickly assembled, Lieutenant Ramsdell looked over his regiment's thin line, which resembled more of a skirmish line than a line of battle. The brigade's skirmish line slowly fell back under the relentless Confederate pressure. As it did, Ward ordered the men not to fire until they could plainly see the enemy, probably at a distance of no more than two hundred yards. As the 1st Texas and 3rd Arkansas of Robertson's Brigade (Hood's Division, I Corps) approached to within two hundred yards, the men deliv-

ered a devastating volley, which halted the Confederates in their tracks. The reprieve gave the men time to reload and send a second volley into the enemy ranks.[50]

Private A. W. Tucker of the 124th New York recalled the defense somewhat differently. "When the enemy got within 100 yards of us Col. Ellis ordered us to fix bayonets, at the same time directing not a man to fire a shot until he gave the command . . . it was a trying position, the bullets pattering around . . . we lay still until the enemy . . . were not 50 feet away, when Col. Ellis gave the order to up and fire. There was never a more destructive volley fired. It seemed to paralyze their whole line."[51]

Although Ward didn't mention it in his report, the 17th Maine had taken position behind a stone wall to the right of his brigade and was firing volleys into the 3rd Arkansas's flank. Seeing disorder in the enemy's ranks, Ward advanced his right regiments to a stone wall about 160 yards in his front. It was a mistake, for the enemy reformed and fired several volleys that stopped the Federal advance in its tracks and then pushed it backward. The 124th New York in the center of the line also charged forward. According to Private Tucker, "Colonel Ellis gave the command to 'Charge bayonets! Forward; double-quick—March!'" The 1st Texas gave way and scampered to the rear. Tucker recalled that "the rebel line withered. They ran like frightened sheep." The 124th New York now occupied an advanced position with both of its flanks hanging unsupported in the air. Unlike the upper echelon of the other regiments, Colonel Ellis and his officers remained mounted during the attack. When it was suggested that they would become targets, Major Cromwell explained that "the men must see us to-day." They did just that, and all three officers were either killed or wounded within minutes. The 1st Texas reformed, and with Benning's Brigade (Hood's Division) coming up behind them, the pressure was so great that the 124th New York fell back in some disorder to its original line. Lieutenant Charles Weygant described the sound of the battle as "roaring cannon, crashing rifery [sic], screeching shots, bursting shells, hissing bullets, cheers, shouts, shrieks and groans." As the men moved up the ridge in disarray, Colonel Ellis rallied them by yelling, "My God! Men! Your major's down; Save him! Save him!" This halted their retreat, and they wheeled around and fired a volley into the victorious Confederates, momentarily halting their advance. Too few men remained for the regiment to mount a serious defense, so the New Yorkers were eventually forced to continue their trek to the top of the ridge.[52]

The 4th Maine on the left of the line did not participate in these actions. However, it soon had its hands full as the two left regiments of Law's Alabama Brigade approached. Seeing the 44th Alabama approach in his front, Walker ordered his men to open fire, which slowed and ultimately halted the Confederate advance. Lieutenant Charles Sawyer described his regiment's predicament. "Our men then engaging the enemy in our front. Scouts were then sent on our left, the movements of the enemy . . . reported the enemy advancing a column on the hill to flank us. A column of the enemy was then seen moving rapidly to our left, not over 50 yards distant, in the woods." Colonel Walker immediately refused his left flank to face this new threat from the 48th Alabama which was in an area now called, the "Slaughter Pen." Thinking all was well with his left, Walker quickly walked to the right of his line and found that the enemy was about to capture several of Smith's guns

and were getting into his rear. "Our principal loss was in this place," wrote Sawyer, as his men fell by the score. After firing about twenty-five rounds at the advancing Confederates, the regiment pulled back twenty to thirty rods, where Walker halted his men and ordered them to fix bayonets. "I shall never forget the 'click' that was made by the fixing of bayonets, it was as one," Walker wrote after the war.[53]

Prior to this point, Ward realized that he had to plug the large gap in his line that formed when the 4th Maine moved to the left. He had no reserve, so in desperation he ordered the 99th Pennsylvania on the right to move "by the left flank, left in front, in rear of the brigade, double-quick." The move destabilized the right of the line, where the 20th Indiana now faced Anderson's Brigade and the 3rd Arkansas along its front and right. Two companies were moved to the right to face that threat, but the regiment's position was becoming increasingly precarious.[54]

As the 99th Pennsylvania double-quicked to the left, the 4th Maine was also moving in that direction by the right oblique to escape from the relentless pressure from the 44th Alabama. The Pennsylvania formed on the left of the 4th Maine and the remnants of the 124th New York formed on its right flank. Therefore, almost by accident, the three regiments attacked the 1st Texas, left wing of the 44th Alabama and elements of Benning's Brigade for possession of Houck's Ridge. Walker admitted that "it was close quarters for a few minutes." Private Peter Ayars recalled that the 99th Pennsylvania fired "one volley, and with a dash . . . were into the thick of the fight. Above the crack of the rifle, the scream of shell and the cries of the wounded could be heard the shout for 'Pennsylvania and our homes.'" The fight was desperate and sharp, and ultimately the Confederates were driven off.[55]

Ward reformed his line farther east along Houck's Ridge and continued to put up stiff resistance against the Confederates. Eventually the enemy withdrew to what Colonel Walker of the 4th Maine called "a respectful distance . . . the enemy taking cover behind the rocks and boulders and in the Devil's Den."[56]

Desperate for help, Ward sent a plea for assistance to General Birney, who ordered the 40th New York (de Trobriand's Brigade) and the 6th New Jersey (Burling's Brigade) quickly to the area. There is little evidence that these two regiments received any supervision from Ward; they probably fought it out alone.[57]

The unceasing attacks of Benning's Brigade, coupled with pressure by parts of three other Confederate brigades (Anderson's, Robertson's, and Law's), meant that it was just a matter of time before Ward's men were overwhelmed. It appears that the right regiments retired before the left ones. Lieutenant Erastus Gilbreath of the 20th Indiana on the far right of the line recalled that the men were ordered to pull back because of their heavy losses and low supply of ammunition. "The Rebels laughed at us as we marched back, and their fire was concentrated on our color," he recalled. A number of men from the 4th Maine on the left side of the line were captured during the withdrawal. A wounded Colonel Walker almost fell into this category, but was helped away just in time. More would have been lost had it not been for the 6th New Jersey and 40th New York, which remained behind to cover the retreat.[58]

While Ward's line was engaged on the left of the Federal line, the 3rd Maine was on the skirmish line in front of the Peach Orchard. It missed the attack of Barksdale's Brigade on its right and rear, but its time came shortly after, when the 8th South Carolina and 3rd South Carolina

Battalion (Kershaw's Brigade, McLaws's Division) approached. The men put up a stiff resistance, but were forced back to the main line. The men rested after passing through the line of south-facing cannon. They were next ordered back to the front line, taking position to the left of the 2nd New Hampshire. To their left were the 141st Pennsylvania and the 3rd Michigan. These four regiments now braced for Kershaw's attack from the southwest. They should have held their own, except for the fact that Barksdale's Brigade's attack on their right was enfilading their line.[59]

For some unexplained reason, the 3rd Maine and the 3rd Michigan pulled back, destabilizing the line. This caused the two other regiments to change their positions as well. A new line formed, facing west, with the 3rd Maine to the left and rear of the 2nd New Hampshire. The Confederates attacked almost immediately, but the regiment continued to put up a stiff resistance.[60]

Colonel Moses Lakeman of the 3rd Maine reported that "I engaged them and held them for some fifteen minutes, when I received a severe flank fire on my left. I then saw a large force marching round to cut me off, and ordered my regiment to retire, and while doing so we received a most distressing fire, which threw my command in much confusion." The flanking force bearing down on them along Wheatfield Road was Wofford's Brigade (McLaws's Division). A chagrined Lakeman reported the loss of his regiment's flag. Because of the confusion, no one realized it was missing until the following morning. After reforming his regiment in the rear, Lakeman marched it southward, where he joined the rest of the brigade.[61]

The brigade spent the night just north of Little Round Top. At about 11:00 A.M. the next morning, the brigade was moved to the right, where it supported several batteries on Cemetery Ridge. Although the brigade was in the general vicinity of the Pickett–Pettigrew–Trimble charge, it did not assist in repelling it. The brigade remained there through the following day. The 20th Indiana, 3rd Maine, 4th Maine, and 99th Pennsylvania were deployed as skirmishers during July 3 and 4. Although skirmishing was brisk, few casualties resulted. The remainder of the brigade collected arms, tended to the wounded, and helped bury the dead. The brigade returned to the position it had occupied near the George Weikert farm on the morning of July 5 and remained there during the day.[62]

About a hundred men from the 1st U.S. Sharpshooters were deployed as skirmishers to cover the VI Corps's front on July 3 and skirmished with the enemy for most of the day. The sharpshooters made a charge toward evening and captured eighteen enemy soldiers. The rest of the regiment, and the 2nd U.S. Sharpshooters, remained with the brigade. All of the sharpshooters were thrown out as skirmishers on July 4 and 5.[63]

On the left of the Federal line, the brigade was attacked by parts of three Confederate brigades. Although the brigade was eventually overwhelmed, it did as well as could be expected, wisely using the excellent defensive positions afforded by Devil's Den and Houck's Ridge. The fighting in this sector was especially intense. Captain Edwin Libby counted thirty-one bullet holes in the 4th Maine's new flag. In the end, Ward's Brigade earned lasting distinction for its spirited defense of its position.[64]

3rd Brigade—Colonel Philippe Regis de Trobriand

Units: 17th Maine, 3rd Michigan, 5th Michigan, 40th New York, 110th Pennsylvania (six companies)
Strength: 1387
Losses: 490 (75-394-21)—35.2%[65]

Colonel Philippe Regis de Trobriand was very different from any other brigade commander in either army. Born and raised in an aristocratic family in France, he emigrated to New York in 1841, where he married an heiress. When the war broke out, de Trobriand was given command of the predominately French 55th New York, and led it at Williamsburg. He did not see further action until Chancellorsville, where his regiment (now combined with the 38th New York) was held primarily in reserve. Despite his limited combat experience, de Trobriand was given command of the new 3rd Brigade when it was reformed after Chancellorsville. As a result, the brigade marched toward Gettysburg with an inexperienced brigade commander and veteran units that had not fought together.[66]

June 29 was a special day for de Trobriand's Brigade for the men drew two months' pay (like the rest of the army) and many were issued vitally needed shoes. More than a few had been marching with bare feet, and hundreds more wore shoes about to fall apart. Their new shoes and pockets full of money probably helped the men weather some of the negative reactions of the civilians. One soldier from the 17th Maine recalled that the people in one part of Maryland had "more of the spirit of secession than we had found in coming the entire length of Maryland. The people were more sulky than the Virginians even and bestowed nothing but scowls on us as we passed and muttered curses which they had not the courage to come out openly and declare." The officers, nevertheless, tried to enforce rules respecting private property. Colonel de Trobriand wrote home that "we take particular care to respect the property, and the army in its passage, only burns a small number of 'fences' to cook the rations of the soldier."[67]

The citizens' reception changed when the column reached the vicinity of Frederick Maryland. According to de Trobriand, "the population is loyal [and] gave us a real ovation. The flags floated from almost every house; the ladies were everywhere at the windows waving their handkerchiefs." De Trobriand was especially pleased when a "pretty young girl" presented him with a huge bouquet of flowers, which he gratefully carried as he rode through the streets of the city. Years after the war, Captain Charles Hamilton of the 110th Pennsylvania still recalled the generosity of some of the civilians. For example, the column passed a farmer and his two daughters standing next to a table piled high with bread and pies, which they liberally distributed to the men, along with milk, without any thought of compensation.[68]

After marching about two miles with the rest of the division on July 1, de Trobriand was ordered to take his brigade and Burling's (Humphrey's Division, III Corps) to Emmitsburg, where they were to prevent a Confederate turning movement through the South Mountain passes. After deploying his men, de Trobriand established his headquarters at the Convent of the Sisters of Charity. No Confederate movements were detected, and de Trobriand was awakened at 2:00 A.M. on July 2, with orders to rejoin the division. The men grabbed a quick breakfast before breaking camp. Private John Haley of the 17th Maine complained that "we hadn't a

solitary thing to lay our jaws to except coffee." However, orders to move out immediately precluded the men from even getting coffee. There was plenty of grousing as the column marched through the quiet streets of Emmitsburg at daybreak. When the column halted a short time later, the men quickly boiled water for the coffee. This effort was also aborted when one of General Birney's aides galloped up to de Trobriand with orders to march with all dispatch to the battlefield. The entry into Pennsylvania was hailed with "cheers and much enthusiasm," recalled Lieutenant Edwin Houghton of the 17th Maine. As the men approached the battlefield, they began passing streams of fleeing civilians who were loaded down with bedding and clothes. The brigade finally rejoined the division by 10:00 A.M. that morning, halting in column of regiments just to the west of Taneytown Road.[69]

The exhausted men were pleased to fall out and begin preparing their long-awaited coffee. The men were almost immediately ordered back into line, however, and backtracked along Taneytown Road toward the Peach Orchard. The men were permitted to catch up on their lost sleep during most of the late morning and early afternoon. This was not true of the 5th Michigan, which was detached at about 1:00 P.M. to support a battery. The regiment remained there about an hour, when General Birney ordered it back to the brigade. Sickles moved his corps forward toward Emmitsburg Road about 3:00 P.M. De Trobriand's Brigade was positioned west of the Wheatfield, on wooded Stony Hill, between Ward on the left and Graham on the right. The attack on Birney's Division began with an intense artillery barrage, which sent the men scrambling for cover. De Trobriand sent the 3rd Michigan out on the skirmish line west of Birney's Division. The 110th Pennsylvania was advanced to the base of Stony Hill, near Rose Run, facing southwest. On its left was the 5th Michigan. The two other regiments formed in the rear, and at right angles to these regiments, facing northwest. The 40th New York was on the left, and the 17th Maine was on its right.[70]

As Hood's Division launched its attack, Ward's Brigade to the left came under increasing pressure. The 17th Maine was ordered to move by the left flank to help fill the gap between Ward's and de Trobriand's Brigades. The men took position behind a low stone wall along the south side of the Wheatfield. They arrived just as Robertson's Brigade was about to smash into Ward's beleaguered men. The men of the 17th Maine were cautioned not to fire until the skirmishers returned. "We heard again that furious [Rebel] yell and saw our men coming in. We lay quiet until our men got by and the rebs got within close range," described Franklin Whitmore. Another soldier noted that the enemy "continued to advance, coming on with rapid strides so that it seemed as if nothing under heaven could, or would stop them short of annihilation."[71]

The stone wall that the 17th Maine took shelter behind was at an oblique angle to the left of Robertson's Brigade, so when the men opened fire they caught the 3rd Arkansas in a deadly flank fire. Ward's men sent volleys into the 3rd Arkansas's front at the same time. Captain George Verrill of the 17th Maine recollected that because of the woods, the Arkansas troops were in an open formation rather than in a compact line of battle. That probably saved many Confederate lives, as the 17th Maine opened fire when the enemy was only seventy-five yards away. The fire was deadly, but "it did not annihilate him or apparently discourage him, but it checked his rush and presently his advance," Verrill recalled.

Whitmore added, "we opened upon them so furiously that they began to skedaddle." As could be predicted, the greatest disorder occurred along the 3rd Arkansas's left flank, which took the full brunt of the initial volleys. The infantry were greatly aided by Winslow's battery, which threw canister into the approaching Rebels.[72]

The 3rd Arkansas was forced to abort its attack. However, Captain Verrill was upset to see the enemy moving toward the 17th Maine's vulnerable right flank, "concealing themselves as much as possible, and using the shelter of the bank of the main branch of Plum Run." Robertson's Brigade, now joined by Anderson's Brigade, soon launched another attack. "The enemy speedily advancing as far as he had previously come, and then working up as a strong body of skirmishers, using every rock and tree for his protection," observed Verrill. The "Down Easters" were now up against the 11th and 59th Georgia (Anderson's Brigade). "Nearer and nearer they came; never was loading and firing of muzzle-loaders done more rapidly than by the 17th at that time, but it did not check them as before," recalled Verrill. "They brought their colors close up to the wall, just a handful of men with them . . . [they] received such a scorching fire at short range" that the Confederates aborted their second attack.[73]

While the right regiments of Anderson's Brigade (11th and 59th Georgia) were attacking the 17th Maine and Ward's Brigade, the 8th and 9th Georgia headed for the gap to the right of the 17th Maine and the left of the 5th Michigan. Help was on the way. The 115th Pennsylvania and 8th New Jersey of Burling's Brigade (Humphreys's Division) plugged the gap. The Georgians found other gaps in the defensive line, causing the two regiments to fall back. To compensate, the 17th Maine refused its right three companies.

De Trobriand's last reserve regiment, the large 40th New York, was no longer available, as Birney was forced to send it to the left to bolster Ward's sector. This apparently occurred soon after the 17th Maine took its position behind the stone wall. Following Plum Run, the 40th New York passed in front of Winslow's battery, continued beyond Ward's Brigade, and halted in the Plum Run Valley.[74]

The men of the 5th Michigan and 110th Pennsylvania on the right of de Trobriand's line could also see signs that an attack on their position was imminent. They heard the familiar Rebel yell and then a flock of cattle and hogs ran hurriedly in their direction. Before long the men could see the legs of soldiers of Anderson's Brigade's 8th and 9th Georgia. De Trobriand noted in his report that he only had two regiments to hold this line, but "fortunately, my position was a strong one, in a wood commanding a narrow ravine, which the enemy attempted in vain to cross under our fire." Captain Charles Hamilton of the 110th Pennsylvania observed that the Federal fire was so severe as the enemy approached Rose Run that the enemy took "position behind the trees under the bank of which they hid and delivered us [sic] a deadly fire." He estimated that some enemy soldiers came to within twenty yards of the Federal line. But the line held and the 8th Georgia and part of the 9th Georgia of Anderson's Brigade were forced to retreat. Anderson's men attacked again, and again were repulsed. Captain Hamilton believed that the "nature of the ground broke their lines and enabled us to hold them at a distance by the rapidity and precision of our fire." The 17th Maine poured an enfilading fire into Anderson's right flank, while the 110th Pennsylvania and 5th Michigan faced the enemy directly.[75]

Kershaw's Brigade (McLaw's Division) formed on Anderson's left and, a short time later, the two brigades renewed the attacks. Seeing Tilton's Brigade on the right of the 110th Pennsylvania about to be flanked, General Barnes ordered its withdrawal. De Trobriand watched in horror and yelled out to them, "Where are you going?" They responded, "We are ordered to fall back." An incredulous de Trobraind screamed, "Fall back? There is no necessity for it." De Trobriand tried to explain that he had already repelled two attacks, and given their strong position, could repel more of them. He bitterly noted that Barnes's men retired without firing a shot. In his official report, de Trobriand claimed that "two regiments from the Fifth Corps, sent there to my support, having fallen back without engaging the enemy (by what orders I could never ascertain). . . . I found myself in danger of being surrounded." This left de Trobriand's three regiments vulnerable to being flanked on either side. Private A. S. Shattuck of the 3rd Michigan watched de Trobriand gallop toward his skirmish line, yelling, "Third Michigan, change front to the right. I give ze order tree or four times. Change quick, or you all be gobbled up; don't you see you are flanked? Ze whole rebel army is in your rear." Shattuck admitted, "Never did a regiment change it front in quicker time." The regiment tried to hold the line, but was ultimately driven to the rear.[76]

This exposed the flank of the 110th Pennsylvania on the 3rd Michigan's former left flank. At this point, Captain Hamilton noted that his regiment was "holding on only in fragments." Realizing that he was in danger of being surrounded, de Trobriand ordered the 110th Pennsylvania and 5th Michigan withdrawn. In his report, de Trobriand had only the highest praise for the 5th Michigan, which had done so much to hold the line. "The unflinching bravery of the Fifth Michigan, which sustained the loss of more than one-half of its number without yielding a foot of ground, deserves to be especially mentioned here with due commendation." The two regiments probably held their position for about two hours.[77]

With the regiments forming his right flank in full retreat, Colonel de Trobriand rode over to the left, where a regiment was holding its ground behind a stone wall. He inquired about its identity and when he was told that it was his own 17th Maine, he ordered it to "Fall back, right away!" Haley recalled that the men did not hear the order because of the din of battle, so they maintained their steady fire. Some may have heard the order, but knew that they would become dreadfully vulnerable if they left the protective cover of the stone wall. This sentiment was conveyed by a soldier in the 17th Maine. "We knew that the very minute we abandoned that position the Rebels would occupy it and we should then be in the same fix as they were then." De Trobriand knew that all of the Federal troops to the right had been swept away, making his position untenable.[78]

After falling back to Wheatfield Road, the officers sent desperate messages for ammunition. It was shortly after 6:00 P.M., and the men had rested but ten minutes when General Birney appeared, apparently in an agitated condition. The enemy was advancing toward the flank and rear of the army, and while Caldwell's Division (II Corps) was rushing south to blunt this thrust, it had not yet arrived. After learning that he had encountered the 17th Maine, Birney ordered it to return to the Wheatfield and halt the enemy's advance. When told that the men were almost out of ammunition, he ordered bayonets fixed. Riding to the front of the regiment, Birney

told the men to follow him, which they did with a cheer. When about halfway to their original position, Birney ordered the men to halt, kneel, and prepare to hold the position. The 5th Michigan returned and formed on the 17th Maine's left flank. Some of the 110th Pennsylvania may have formed on the right of the 5th Michigan. The Confederates of Anderson's Brigade did not renew the attack, except in small groups. Most were content to claim the stone wall, which provided a measure of protection. De Trobriand's troops were relieved when Caldwell's troops finally arrived, and they were permanently withdrawn from the Wheatfield.[79]

While most of de Trobriand's regiments were attempting to hold the area around the Wheatfield, the 40th New York had been rushed to support Ward's Brigade. As the regiment neared Devil's Den, the men could see Smith's battery deployed on Houck's Ridge. Colonel Thomas Egan of the 40th New York noted that "he [Smith] called upon me in beseeching terms to save his battery." Egan ordered his men to charge, which he described as being done "with great alacrity [as] they pushed forward at a double-quick, crossing a marsh up to their knees in mud and water." Not to be deterred, the men smashed into the 2nd and 17th Georgia near the Slaughter Pen. (Benning's Brigade), forcing it back. Knowing that he must continue to press his advantage, Egan ordered his men after the slowly retreating Confederates. The latter took refuge in the rocks of Devil's Den. "All attempts to dislodge them from the second line proving unsuccessful, and discovering that they had gained ground upon my right, which threatened a flank movement . . . I was compelled to fall back, rallying my men upon the ridge over which I passed," wrote a frustrated Egan in his report. Colonel Wesley

Hodges of the 17th Georgia counted seven attacks by the 40th New York before it gave up.[80]

Unfortunately for Egan, the enemy, which included the 2nd and 17th Georgia, (Benning's Brigade) and the 48th Alabama (Law's Brigades), were not content to hold their ground and surged forward, forcing the 40th New York to continue its withdrawal. Fire from the 6th New Jersey (Burling's Brigade) helped the New Yorkers pull back. Egan finally halted his men near Winslow's battery, where he received orders to rejoin the brigade. That was easier said than done, as Egan could not find it, so his men bivouacked near the position they had occupied earlier that afternoon. Although Egan's men had failed to stop the Confederate tide, Captain Smith emphatically stated that the actions of the regiment had slowed the Confederate attack and were instrumental in saving Little Round Top.[81]

Minus the 40th New York, the brigade spent the night along Taneytown Road, where most of the men went to sleep supperless. More concerning was the lack of water. The limited supply was, according to Crotty (3rd Michigan), "reserved for the wounded, and of course the officers."[82]

The morning of July 3 was a happy one, as rations arrived at about 9:00 A.M. "It is safe to say that we indulged in a general fill up," noted a private in the 17th Maine. Later that morning the brigade moved to the position it had occupied during the prior forenoon, now behind the V Corps, where it reunited with the 40th New York. The brigade spent a quiet morning in this position, but this changed shortly after 1:00 P.M. Captain Charles Hamilton never forgot the destructiveness of the cannonade that preceded Pickett's charge, when the brigade lost seventy-six men. "There were thus more than two hundred shells in the air at once. The air was thick with the

bursting shells and the flying fragments full of thick clouds of white smoke hanging in the hot air that beat down in scorching rays." Lieutenant Charles Mattocks of the 17th Maine noted that the men "did nothing but stick our noses in the ground." The brigade double-quicked by the right flank toward the Copse of Trees, where it supported a battery during the latter part of the cannonade. It watched as the three Confederate divisions attacked, but was not an active participant in blunting the charge. Probably feeling somewhat slighted, Private Haley (17th Maine) wrote after the war, "true we didn't do any shooting there, but we were there if needed, and did as much as many regiments which have claimed great credit." The night was a sleepless one for most of the men, as the brigade was sent out on picket duty. Returning once again to its original position on July 4, the brigade was ordered to throw up breastworks.[83]

The men tended the wounded during the latter part of July 3 and most of July 4. They were excited by the news that Lee's army had retreated sometime during the early morning hours of July 5. The brigade remained on the increasingly foul-smelling battlefield through July 6. It did not leave the battlefield until July 7 at 5:00 A.M.[84]

De Trobriand's brigade had the distinction of being involved in three actions on July 2. While the 5th Michigan, 110th Pennsylvania, and 17th Maine fought in the vicinity of the Wheatfield, the 3rd Michigan fought near the Peach Orchard (at least its right flank), and the 40th New York fought near Devil's Den. All of the regiments seemed to acquit themselves well. Probably most deserving of praise was the 17th Maine, which stubbornly held its position behind a stone wall and helped repulse several Confederate attacks. The actions of the 40th New York, whose men charged a superior number of enemy troops in a futile effort to halt their advance toward Little Round Top, were also noteworthy. Although General Birney freely commended his three brigade commanders in his report, he saved his most glowing praise for de Trobriand, writing, "Colonel de Trobriand deserves my heartiest thanks for his skillful disposition of his command by gallantly holding his advanced position until relieved by other troops."[85]

NOTES

1. Dyer, *Compendium*, 295; Tagg, *Generals of Gettysburg*, 61–63.

2. Tremain, *Two Days of War*, 18–19; Edward J. Hagerty, *Collis' Zouaves: The 114th Pennsylvania in the Civil War* (Baton Rouge, LA, 1997), 231; W. A. Swanberg, *Sickles The Incredible* (New York, 1956), 196, 202; OR 27, 1, 482; Pfanz, *Gettysburg—The Second Day*, 43–44.

3. OR 27, 1, 482; Swanberg, *Sickles the Incredible*, 209–211.

4. OR 27, 1, 483; Swanberg, *Sickles the Incredible*, 217; Daniel Crotty, *Four Years Campaigning with the Army of the Potomac* (Grand Rapids, MI, 1874), 91.

5. Dyer, *Compendium*, 295; Warner, *Generals in Blue*, 34.

6. OR 27, 1, 482.

7. OR 27, 1, 482–483.

8. Busey and Martin, *Regimental Strengths and Losses*, 49, 245.

9. William E. Loring, "Gettysburg," *National Tribune*, July 9, 1885; Dyer, *Compendium*, 295; Tagg, *Generals of Gettysburg*, 67–68; Richard A. Sauers, *Advance the Colors* (Harrisburg, PA, 1987), vol. 1, 159.

10. Gilbert A. Hays, *Under the Red Patch—The Story of the Sixty-Third Regiment, Pennsylvania Volunteers* (Pittsburgh, PA, 1908), 190–191; *History of the Fifty-seventh Regiment, Pennsylvania Veteran Volunteer Infantry, First Brigade, First Division, Third Corps, and Second*

Brigade, Third Division, Second Corps, Army of the Potomac (Kearny, NJ, 1995), 85–86.

11. John D. Bloodgood, *Personal Reminiscences of the War* (New York, 1893), 127–128.

12. Loring, "Gettysburg"; David Craft, *One Hundred and Forty-First Regiment Pennsylvania Volunteers* (Towanda, PA, 1885), 116–117; OR 27, 1, 500, 502; Bloodgood, *Personal Reminiscences of the War*, 130–131.

13. Bloodgood, *Personal Reminiscences of the War*, 124.

14. Loring, "Gettysburg"; Frank Rauscher, *Music on the March: 1861-'65 with the Army of the Potomac* (Philadelphia, 1892), 85.

15. Lash, "'A Pathetic Story—The 141st Pennsylvania at Gettysburg" (January 1966) issue 14, 85; OR 27, 1, 497, 500; Bates, *Pennsylvania Volunteers*, vol. VII, 441.

That the men could not light fires was contradicted by John Bloodgood of the 114th Pennsylvania. He wrote, "we ate a few crackers and pork sandwiches, drank a cup of coffee, and lay down to sleep" (Bloodgood, *Personal Reminiscences of the War*, 131).

16. Bates, *Pennsylvania Volunteers*, vol. III, 495; Loring, "Gettysburg."

17. Bates, *Pennsylvania Volunteers*, vol. IV, 785; OR 27, 1, 504; John P. Dunn, "Report," Pennsylvania State Archives; Edward R. Bowen, "Collis' Zouaves—The 114th Pennsylvania at Gettysburg," *Philadelphia Weekly Times*, June 22, 1887.

18. *PAG*, vol. 356; Pfanz, *Gettysburg—The Second Day*, 314.

19. Bloodgood, *Personal Reminiscences*, 134–135; Bowen, "Collis' Zouaves—The 114th Pennsylvania at Gettysburg"; Bates, *Pennsylvania Volunteers*, vol. IV, 676; vol. III, 251; vol. VII, 441; A. J. Adams, "The Fight at the Peach Orchard," *National Tribune*, April 23, 1885; Loring, "Gettysburg."

According to an account written by a member of the 68th Pennsylvania soon after the war, General Graham was wounded during his cannonade and carried to the rear. Command of the brigade devolved upon Colonel Tippin. Graham purportedly returned to the field a little later in the engagement and was subsequently captured (Bates, *Pennsylvania Volunteers*, vol. VI, 676).

20. OR 27, 1, 497, 498; Bates, *Pennsylvania Volunteers,* vol. III, 495; Pfanz, *Gettysburg—The Second Day,* 322.

21. OR 27, 1, 502.

A slightly different version was given by Bowen after the war: "You boys saved this battery once before at Fredericksburg, and if you will do it again move forward" (Bowen, "Collis' Zouaves—The 114th Pennsylvania at Gettysburg").

22. Bates, *Pennsylvania Volunteers,* vol. VI, 1183.

23. Loring, "Collis' Zouaves"; OR 27, 1, 504–505; Bloodgood, *Personal Reminiscences of the War,* 138; Bates, *Pennsylvania Volunteers,* vol. VII, 442.

24. OR 27, 1, 505, 499; Lash, "A Pathetic Story—The 141st Pennsylvania at Gettysburg," 91.

25. OR 27, 1, 499; Lash, "A Pathetic Story—The 141st Pennsylvania at Gettysburg," 95.

According to William Loring, "The General, in his impetuous bravery, rode through and so far in advance of the line as to be surrounded by the enemy and capture" (Loring, "Gettysburg").

26. OR 27, 1, 505; Bloodgood, *Personal Reminiscences of the War,* 140–141; Craft, *One Hundred and Forty-First Regiment,* 122, 123.

27. *PAG,* vol. 1, 356; Bates, *Pennsylvania Volunteers,* vol. VI, 1183; Bowen, "Collis' Zouaves—The 114th Pennsylvania at Gettysburg"; OR 27, 1, 497; Frank E. Moran, "A Fire Zouave—Memoirs of a Member of the Excelsior Brigade," *National Tribune,* November 6, 1890; Given diary, Philadelphia Civil War Library and Museum.

Colonel Michael Burns of the 73rd New York reported to General Humphreys that the Pennsylvanians gave way before he arrived in position, and he subsequently faced the enemy alone (Andrew Humphreys to John Bachelder, November 14, 1865, Bachelder Papers, New Hampshire Historical Society).

28. Robert Fuhrman, "The 57th Pennsylvania Volunteer Infantry at Gettysburg" (July 1997), issue 17, 64; *PAG,* vol. 1, 356; Alanson

H. Nelson, *The Battles of Chancellorsville and Gettysburg* (Minneapolis, 1899), 149–152.

29. Bates, *Pennsylvania Volunteers,* vol. VI, 785; OR 27, 1, 501; Pfanz, *Gettysburg—The Second Day,* 331–332.

30. OR 27, 1, 503.

31. *PAG,* vol. 1, 357; James M. Martin, *History of the Fifty-Seventh Regiment, Pennsylvania Veteran Volunteer Infantry* (Meadville, PA, 1904), 91; Nelson, *The Battles of Chancellorsville and Gettysburg,* 157; Lewis Schaeffer, diary, West Virginia University; Bates, *Pennsylvania Volunteers,* vol. III, 252; Hays, *Under the Red Patch,* 195–196.

32. Bowen, "Collis' Zouaves—The 114th Pennsylvania at Gettysburg."

According to Colonel Henry Madill's diary (Greg Coco Collection, USAMHI), Tippin relinquished command, not because he was wounded, but because he was arrested. Lewis Schaeffer helped resolve the issue when he wrote in his diary on July 4, "Our colonel was put under arrest yesterday for being drunk. He left for Washington this morning where he was ordered to report himself." Tippin himself wrote in his report, "we remained here until evening, when I was relieved of the command" (OR 27, 1, 499).

33. OR 27, 1, 503, 506; Robert Kenderdine, "A California Tramp," copy in the 114th Pennsylvania folder, GNMP; Bowen, "Collis' Zouaves—The 114th Pennsylvania at Gettysburg."

34. OR 27, 1, 503; Bowen, "Collis' Zouaves—The 114th Pennsylvania at Gettysburg."

35. Busey and Martin, *Regimental Strengths and Losses,* 50, 245.

36. Tagg, *Generals of Gettysburg,* 69–70.

37. OR 27, 1, 493; *NYG,* vol. 2, 697; "The 124th at Gettysburg," *Middletown Whig Press,* July 22, 1863; Wyman S. White, "The Civil War Diary of Wyman S. White," copy in the Brake Collection, USAMHI, 85; Charles H. Weygant, *History of the One Hundred and Twenty-Fourth Regiment* (Newburgh, NY, 1877), 172; Peter B. Ayers, "The 99th Pennsylvania," *National Tribune,* February 4, 1886; N. S. Baker; diary, Rochester Public Library.

38. Weygant, *History of the One Hundred and Twenty-Fourth Regiment,* 169; Francis A. Osbourn, "The Twentieth Indiana Infantry," Indiana State Library; Wyman White, diary, 85–86; Elijah Walker to John Bachelder, January 5, 1885, Bachelder Papers, New Hampshire Historical Society Account; Gary G. Lash, "The March of the 124th New York to Gettysburg," *Gettysburg Magazine* (July, 1993), 13.

39. OR 27, 1, 493, 515, 518; Pfanz, *Gettysburg—The Second Day,* 87.

40. *Dedication of the Monument to the Fourth New York Company, First Regiment, U.S. Sharpshooters* (n.p., n.d.), 18; OR 27, 1, 515, 516–517; Wiley Sword, *Sharpshooter: Hiram Berdan, His Famous Sharpshooters and their Sharps Rifle* (Lincoln, RI, 1988), 25.

41. *Dedication of 4th New York Company Monument,* 19–20; Charles A. Stevens, *Berndan's Sharpshooters in the Army of the Potomac* (St. Paul, MN, 1892), 303, 309; OR 27, 1, 514.

42. OR 27, 1, 507, 515, 517; *Maine at Gettysburg,* 128.

43. OR 27, 1, 508, 517; John D. Imhof, *Gettysburg, Day Two, A Study in Maps* (Baltimore, MD, 1999), 71.

44. Weygant, *History of the One Hundred and Twenty-Fourth Regiment,* 173; Henry P. Ramsdell, "Account," Brake Collection, USAMHI, 7–8.

45. Lash, "The March of the 124th New York to Gettysburg," 15.

46. OR 27, 1, 518–519; J. Harvey Hanford, "The Experiences of a Private of the 124th N.Y. in the Battle," *National Tribune,* September 24, 1885; A. W. Tucker, "Orange Blossoms—Services of the 124th New York at Gettysburg," *National Tribune,* January 21, 1886.

47. OR 27, 1, 518–519; John J. Pullen "Effects of Marksmanship," *Gettysburg Magazine* (January 1990), issue 2, 57–58; *Maine at Gettysburg,* 348, 351.

According to Pullen (56), the sharpshooters first engaged the enemy in a position 500 yards west of Emmitsburg Road.

48. OR 27, 1, 506, 509, 511.

49. Elijah Walker to John Bachelder, January 5, 1885.

50. OR 27, 1, 493; Ramsdell, "Account," 7–8.

51. Tucker, "Orange Blossoms—Services of the 124th New York at Gettysburg."

52. OR 27, 1, 493; Weygant, *History of the One Hundred and Twenty-Fourth Regiment,* 175, 176.

53. OR 27, 1, 509–510; Elijah Walker to John Bachelder, January 5, 1885; *Maine at Gettysburg,* 163.

54. OR 27, 1, 506, 513; *Maine at Gettysburg,* 166.

55. Elijah Walker to John Bachelder, January 5, 1885; Ayars, "The 99th Pennsylvania."

56. Garry E. Adelman and Timothy H. Smith, *Devil's Den—A History and Guide* (Gettysburg, PA, 1997), 42–43; Elijah Walker to John Bachelder, January 5, 1885.

57. OR 27, 1, 494, 519, 526–527.

To emphasize their feelings of isolation, some of the men exaggerated the activities of the units around them. For example, Charles Weygant of the 124th New York wrote, "A brigade with Maltese crosses, the regulars, I think, lie just over the hill there, boiling coffee" (Weygant, *History of the One Hundred and Twenty-Fourth Regiment,* 177–178).

58. Adelman and Smith, *Devil's Den—A History and Guide,* 50, 52; Erasmus Gibreath, "Recollections," copy in the Brake Collection, USAMHI.

59. OR 27, 1, 499; Pfanz, *Gettysburg—The Second Day,* 332.

60. Pfanz, *Gettysburg—The Second Day,* 332.

61. OR 27, 1, 508.

62. Gilbreath, "Recollections"; OR 27, 1, 506, 509, 512, 514; Captain N. S. Baker, diary, Rochester Public Library.

63. OR 27, 1, 515, 518, 519.

64. OR 27, 1, 511.

65. Busey and Martin, *Regimental Strengths and Losses,* 51, 246.

66. Dyer, *Compendium,* 295–296; Tagg, *Generals of Gettysburg,* 71.

67. Unknown, "Private's Recollections," copy in 17th Maine folder, GNMP; William

B. Styple, *Our Noble Blood* (Kearny, NJ, 1997), 111.

68. Regis de Trobriand, *Four Years With the Army of the Potomac* (Boston, 1889), 479, 480; Styple, *Our Noble Blood*, 112–113; Charles C. Hamilton, "Memoirs," Philadelphia Civil War Museum and Library.

69. OR 27, 1, 519, 524; Styple, *Our Noble Blood*, 116; Charles Mattocks, *Unspoiled Heart, The Journal of Charles Mattocks of the 17th Maine* (Knoxville, TN, 1994), 48; Hamilton, "Memoirs"; Franklin Whitmore, letter, copy in the 17th Maine folder, GNMP; John W. Haley, *The Rebel Yell & the Yankee Hurrah: The Civil War Journal of a Maine Volunteer* (Camden, ME, 1985), 100–101; Edwin B. Houghton, *Campaigns of the Seventeenth Maine* (Portland, ME, 1866), 90–91.

Modern historian Harry Pfanz questioned why these two brigades, both commanded by colonels, were left behind, as opposed to at least one brigade with a commander with general's rank (Pfanz, *Gettysburg—The Second Day*, 474, n. 43).

70. *Michigan at Gettysburg, July 1st, 2nd and 3rd, 1863 . . .* (Detroit, MI, 1889), 76; George W. Verrill, "The Seventeenth Maine at Gettysburg and in the Wilderness," in *Maine MOLLLUS*, vol. 1, 262; John Pulford to John Bachelder, December 20, 1864, Bachelder Papers, New Hampshire Historical Society; Frederick C. Floyd, *History of the Fortieth (Mozart) Regiment, New York Volunteers* (Boston, 1909), 201; Verrill, "The Seventeenth Maine at Gettysburg and in the Wilderness," 263–264; Philippe Regis de Trobriand to John Bachelder, August 24, 1869, Bachelder Papers, New Hampshire Historical Society.

71. Whitmore, letter; unknown, "Private's Recollections."

72. Verrill, "The Seventeenth Maine at Gettysburg and in the Wilderness," 263–264; *Maine at Gettysburg*, 193–194.

Private John Haley told a different story—that the Confederates were engaged at a greater distance, so that the initial volleys had little impact on them, and that their initial formation was denser than normal (Haley, *The Rebel Yell & the Yankee Hurrah:*

The Civil War Journal of a Maine Volunteer, 101). Verrill's version is probably more accurate.

73. Verrill, "The Seventeenth Maine at Gettysburg and in the Wilderness," 264–265; George W. Verrill to John Bachelder, February 11, 1884, Bachelder Papers, New Hampshire Historical Society; *Maine at Gettysburg*, 195, 212; Kevin E. O'Brien, "Hold Them with the Bayonet: de Trobriand's Brigade Defends the Wheatfield," *Gettysburg Magazine* (July 1999), issue 21, 84.

74. OR 27, 1, 526–527; Pfanz, *Gettysburg—The Second Day*, 242, 245; De Trobriand, *Four Years in the Army of the Potomac*, 498.

75. Hamilton, "Memoirs"; OR 27, 1, 520.

76. OR 27, 1, 520; *New York Herald*, March 23, 1864; *Michigan at Gettysburg*, 76.

77. Hamilton, "Memoirs"; OR 27, 1, 520; O'Brien, "Hold Them with the Bayonet," 82.

78. Haley, *The Rebel Yell & the Yankee Hurrah: The Civil War Journal of a Maine Volunteer*, 101; unknown, "Private's Recollections."

There is some confusion over who finally got the 17th Maine to withdraw. According to an anonymous private, Colonel de Trobriand brought the order the third time, while Private John Haley recalled that it was General Birney (Haley, *The Rebel Yell & the Yankee Hurrah: The Civil War Journal of a Maine Volunteer*, 102; John Haley to John Bachelder, February 6, 1884, Bachelder Papers, New Hampshire Historical Society). Both sources agreed that the two leaders tried to get them to pull back during this phase of the battle.

79. Verrill, "The Seventeenth Maine at Gettysburg and in the Wilderness," 267–268; OR 27, 1, 522; Houghton, *Campaigns of the Seventeenth Maine*, 93; John Pulford to John Bachelder, December 20, 1864.

Lieutenant Verrill told a slightly different story. The men's ammunition was replenished along Wheatfield Road before the order was given to move back into the Wheatfield. While the order was given by Birney, the regiment was actually led by one of his aides (George W. Verrill to John Bachelder, February 11, 1884).

80. OR 27, 1, 526–527.

81. OR 27, 1, 527; Floyd, *History of the Mozart Regiment*, 202.

82. Unknown, "Private's Recollections"; Crotty, *Four Years Campaigning with the Army of the Potomac*, 91.

The 40th New York received food and ammunition that night (Floyd, *History of the Mozart Regiment*, 203).

83. Unknown, "Private's Recollections"; OR 27, 1, 522–523, 524, 529; John Haley to John Bachelder, February 6, 1884; John Pulford to John Bachelder, December 20, 1864; Hamilton, "Memoirs"; Mattocks, *Unspoiled Heart: The Journal of Charles Mattocks of the 17th Maine*, 52; Daniel Gookin, letter, Lewis Leigh Collection, USAMHI.

84. Haley, *The Rebel Yell & the Yankee Hurrah: The Civil War Journal of a Maine Volunteer*, 107; Mattocks, *Unspoiled Heart: The Journal of Charles Mattocks of the 17th Maine*, 53.

85. OR 27, 1, 484.

2ND DIVISION—

Brigadier General Andrew Humphreys

Many of the men in the ranks were ambivalent about their new division commander. The men called General Andrew Humphreys "Old Goggle-eyes," and, according to Fifer Charles Bardeen of the 26th Pennsylvania, he was "another man we did not like before the battle, but whom after the battle we were ready to swear by, for he showed himself to be a hero and a leader." Tough and unyielding, he was called "one of the loudest swearers" the men had ever seen. Yet, when a battle raged, Humphreys was usually at the head of his command. A West Point graduate, Humphreys entered the war as chief engineer on General George McClellan's staff. He jumped from staff position to command of a V Corps division of nine-month troops, which he commanded at Antietam. Fredericksburg was a high point for Humphreys, as he drove his men up Marye's Hill in gallant fashion. With the expiration of his division's term of enlistment after Chancellorsville, Humphreys was given the III Corps's 2nd Division. Unlike his former command, it was a veteran division that had been commanded by Hooker, Sickles, and Hiram Berry. Humphreys was probably disturbed by the fact that two of his three brigade commanders had limited combat experience.[1]

The division's march toward Gettysburg was fairly uneventful. It crossed the Potomac River at 5:00 P.M. on June 25 and reached Frederick three days later. The evening of June 30 found the division midway between Taneytown and Emmitsburg. Reaching the latter community the following day, Humphreys rested his division. He received orders at 3:00 P.M. to march to Gettysburg, a distance of about twelve miles. Burling's 3rd Brigade was left behind to guard the South Mountain approaches.[2]

As the division approached Marsh Run that evening, Humphreys was ordered to take position "on the left of Gettysburg." Humphreys was set to take Emmitsburg Road, but one of Sickles's aides, Lieutenant Colonel Julius Hayden, told him to march by way of Black

Horse Tavern. Lieutenant Colonel Clark Baldwin wrote later that Hayden "was more noted for frouth [sic] and foam than for common sence [sic]." Along the route the head of Humphreys's column approached a Confederate picket post. Fortunately for Humphreys, he realized his mistake before the enemy, and ordered his men to "about face" and quickly and quietly march to the rear. Humphreys reported that he might have attacked the enemy at daylight, but decided against it because he was so far from the rest of the army. As a result of this misstep, the division did not arrive in the vicinity of Gettysburg until 1:00 A.M. on July 2.[3]

Burling's Brigade rejoined the division at about 9:00 A.M. on July 2. Shortly after noon, Humphreys received orders to form line of battle, with his left connecting with Birney's 1st Division and his right making contact with Caldwell's Division (II Corps). Humphreys placed Carr's Brigade in the first line, with one regiment from Brewster's Brigade. The rest of Brewster's Brigade occupied the second line, two hundred yards behind the first, and Burling's Brigade was in the third line, two hundred yards behind the second. No sooner had these depositions been completed than Humphreys received orders to move Burling's Brigade to the left, where it was to report to General Birney for further orders. Shortly after 4:00 P.M., Humphreys moved the division forward to its new line on Emmitsburg Road, in accordance with General Sickles's orders.[4]

Lieutenant Jesse Young of the 84th Pennsylvania (Carr's Brigade) watched as the division moved forward. "Battle flags waved above the heads of the gallant soldiers; the bright gleam of their muskets flashed along their extended line; aides were to be seen galloping in every direction to execute the orders for the advance; bugles sounded out their stirring blasts, indicating the will of the corps commander." The division came under enemy artillery fire almost immediately.[5]

Humphreys did not have long to wait before the Confederate attack fell on his vulnerable division. Attacked on the left by Barksdale's Brigade (McLaws's Division, I Corps) and on his front by Wilcox's and Perry's Brigades (Anderson's Division, III Corps), the line began to crumble. He received orders from General Birney, now in command of the III Corps, to pull back to Cemetery Ridge. Humphreys was furious with the order. "I would have sustained myself, weakened as I was," he wrote later. According to Captain Asa Bartlett of the 12th New Hampshire, the enemy "now poured its almost unobstructed torrent of destruction through the widening breach; sweeping regiments and batteries and finally the whole division in confusion from the field." Humphreys remained in the thick of it, providing much-needed encouragement to his men. He went to his death lamenting the way his division had been misused. "Had my division been left intact, I would have driven the enemy back, but this ruinous habit (it doesn't deserve the name of system) of putting troops in position & then drawing off its reserves & second line to help others, who if similarly disposed would need no such help, is disgusting," he wrote.[6]

July 3 opened with the enemy batteries again finding the range of Humphreys's men. When the pounding ended, Birney ordered the division to the left, where its ammunition was replenished. It was rejoined here by Burling's Brigade, which had been split up and its regiments used where needed. Now behind the V Corps, the division was rushed to the right at 4:30 P.M. and formed behind the II Corps batteries. It did not participate in the repulse of the Pickett–Pettigrew–Trimble charge. This ended the battle for Humphreys's beleaguered division. It remained on the battlefield until 3:00 A.M. on July 7, when it began its march back toward Emmitsburg.[7]

1st Brigade—Brigadier General Joseph Carr

Units: 1st Massachusetts, 11th Massachusetts, 16th Massachusetts, 12th New Hampshire, 11th New Jersey, 26th Pennsylvania, 84th Pennsylvania (absent, guarding wagons)
Strength: 1718 (without 84th Pennsylvania)
Losses: 790 (121-604-65)—46.0%[8]

Appointed to lead the 1st Brigade the day before the battle of Antietam, Brigadier General Joseph Carr was familiar with his men and they with him. Many did not like their commander, as they considered him to be a "dandy" and some openly questioned his abilities. He fought the brigade well at Fredericksburg and Chancellorsville. During the latter battle, the brigade lost over five hundred men, and Carr briefly assumed command of the division when General Berry was killed. As he rode toward Gettysburg, Carr suffered from malaria-like symptoms and was heavily medicated.[9]

The march to Gettysburg was grueling for the brigade. Carr reported that the march was "one of the most severe in my experience, the air being almost suffocating, the dust blinding, and the heat intolerable. Many men suffered from *coup de soleil* [sunstroke], and a large number sank by the wayside, utterly helpless and exhausted." While the march had been difficult on the men, it was especially hard on their clothes, particularly their shoes. Most were worn fairly thin, and it was not uncommon to see a barefoot soldier. The situation improved somewhat on June 30, when the brigade's supply train caught up and distributed shoes and socks.[10]

The halt allowed citizens to come from all directions to see the troops. The soldiers were quite a curiosity, as the civilians had never seen such a large aggregation of troops. The men were especially impressed by the people's hospitality. William Cudworth of the 1st Massachusetts remembered that the townspeople "waved handkerchiefs and flags as the troops went by, and supplied the hungry with bread, pies, milk, and poultry, for a reasonable compensation." Bardeen (26th Pennsylvania) never forgot the Maryland hospitality that the men received. "We got well acquainted with Maryland bread, huge loaves baked in ovens outside the house, and tasting to us like manna in the wilderness." As the column left Maryland and entered Pennsylvania, the citizens became more generous. One soldier from the 1st Massachusetts recorded in his diary that "folks quite generous in this town—gave away whole loaves of bread . . . some wouldn't take any money." The civilians were apologetic when their supplies became depleted, remarking that they would have been better prepared had they known there were so many soldiers.[11]

The grueling marches took their toll on the men and many fell from the ranks. Lieutenant Henry Blake of the 11th Massachusetts recalled the soldiers "walking with an irregular step and carrying their guns 'at will,' retaining their strength by rarely talking, but staying with their companies to prevent 'straggling.'" If the men were weary from their exertions, there were times when they didn't feel it. Marching along a road lined with cheering civilians always added spring in the soldiers' steps. They were not, however, above yelling catcalls at able-bodied men lining the road. Corporal William Wheeler of the 16th Massachusetts felt grateful to the women who "done [sic] all in their power to help the boys along not only by cheering them on but by giving good substantial food to them." Crossing the Pennsylvania state line also brought a wave of enthusiasm, particularly from the men who lived there. Their regimental bands played "Home, Sweet Home," as cheers erupted from the ranks. Many of

the officers also tried to inspire their men with speeches. For example, Colonel Robert McAllister of the 11th New Jersey formed his regiment in a square, and standing in the middle, told his men that they must stand shoulder to shoulder with their Pennsylvania brethren to drive the enemy from the state's borders.[12]

Many of the men were less than pleased to learn that Meade had replaced Hooker as their commander. Gustavus Hutchinson of the 11th Massachusetts bitterly wrote that "our old and tried commander was thus displaced by a general regarding whose ability we had no knowledge, at the onset of a struggle with the flower of the Confederate army." Most, however, were more concerned about the commanders of their companies and regiments.[13]

The men could hear cannon fire at around 10:00 A.M. on July 1, and they reached Emmitsburg several hours later. After halting there for about two hours, the brigade hastened toward Gettysburg. Veterans hated to get their shoes and socks wet while fording a stream, especially when they had hard marching to do, for it raised blisters. Therefore, the men were not happy when they were ordered to splash across Marsh Creek in the darkness of July 1. About midnight, the men were told to "keep silent and not smoke or light matches, articles making a tinkling sound were tied closely," as the enemy was just ahead. Lieutenant Henry Blake of the 11th Massachusetts recalled that the "generals and their staffs, who were riding at the head, looked and rode backward" as the column retraced its steps after almost running into Wilcox's Brigade (Anderson's Division, III Corps) in the darkness. The men were especially furious when they had to reford Marsh Creek. Blake knew that "if an inexcusable blunder like this had been committed in Virginia, where every house furnished a spy . . . the consequences would have been disastrous for the national cause." Many of the men blamed Humphreys for this mistake. Fifer Bardeen (26th Pennsylvania) recalled his lieutenant colonel's profanity, which included calling Humphreys "Goggle-eyes."[14]

When the brigade finally reached its bivouac site "under the shadow of Round Top Hill," about two miles from Gettysburg at 2:00 A.M. on July 2, it deployed in column of regiments. The men were so exhausted from their long march that most simply fell to the ground and went to sleep without supper. The men were roused the following morning, but they did not feel much better. One soldier from the 1st Massachusetts complained in his diary that the "blankets [a] little wet—still tired this morn—head aches."[15]

At about 11:00 A.M., the 1st Massachusetts relieved the 3rd Maine (Ward's Brigade, Birney's Division, III Corps) on picket duty. The 26th Pennsylvania was also dispatched to the front to pull down fences that might impair the troops' movements. The remainder of the brigade formed in column of regiments and rested, ate, and prepared for battle, during the morning. These activities ended at 12:30 P.M., when the brigade moved west to take its position on the front line. Carr's Brigade was now on the extreme right of the III Corps line, with its regiments deployed from left to right as 11th New Jersey–12th New Hampshire–16th Massachusetts–11th Massachusetts–26th Pennsylvania. Caldwell's Division (II Corps) was to its right, and units of Brewster's Excelsior Brigade were on its left and rear.[16]

All was quiet until 4:00 P.M., when General Humphreys ordered the brigade to advance about three hundred yards. Colonel Robert McAllister of the 11th New Jersey described this movement as being "executed handsomely." At the same time, Carr ordered a hundred men from the 16th Massachusetts to occupy the Klingle log cabin on the left of the line. The men immediately began poking holes through the mortar between the logs of the house so they could fire at the enemy.[17]

The rest of the brigade was ordered to lie down when they reached their positions between Emmitsburg Road and Cemetery Ridge. A short time later, a Confederate battery opened fire on the brigade and soon found its location. Seeley's battery arrived, and an artillery duel ensued. "Tons of metal hurtled over and fell around us, and it was only by hugging the ground closely that we escaped serious loss," recollected Thomas Marbaker of the 11th New Jersey. He admitted that lying unprotected under artillery fire truly tested the men's nerves. Perhaps most unnerving was the solid shot, which "struck the earth, bounded into the air, and leaped like a rock skipped upon the surface of the ocean by the powerful arm of a giant," related Henry Lieutenant Blake of the 11th Massachusetts.[18]

By about 6:00 P.M., the fight to the south (left) was hot and heavy, and seemed to be moving progressively toward the brigade. Bartlett (12th New Hampshire) recalled that the sound of battle "increased into such a roar and crash of arms as to make even the veteran's heart to tremble, who, with quickening pulse and thrilling nerves, awaits the coming tide of awful carnage." The men could see the 114th Pennsylvania (Graham's Brigade) give way on their left, and before long Barksdale's Mississippi Brigade (McLaws's Division) materialized on their left flank. According to General Carr, this "compelled me to change my front."[19]

To face Barksdale's threat, Carr ordered the 11th New Jersey shifted to face south, rather than west (with the rest of the brigade). Also orientated south at this time were several regiments from Brewster's Brigade. According to historian John Imhof, Humphreys formed a new defensive line, from left to right: 73rd New York–70th New York–72nd New York–11th New Jersey–5th New Jersey (Burling's Brigade), with the 73rd New York's left on Trostle Lane and the right of the 5th New Jersey on Emmitsburg Road. As the Mississippians approached, Colonel McAllister of the 11th New Jersey calmly gave orders for his men to "fire by rank, rear rank first, so as to be enabled to hold in check the enemy after the first fire." Unfortunately for McAllister and his men, the move exposed the regiment's right flank to Wilcox's Brigade (Anderson's Division), which was bearing down on the brigade from the west. This posed future problems for the regiment. More pressing was the need for McAllister's men to realize that Federal skirmishers were in front of them, so they were not to open fire. Over on the right of the line, Blake (11th Massachusetts) insisted that Carr told his regiment not to fire because some of their own troops were in front of them. Blake believed that Humphreys's orders were misunderstood—that the men were to exercise care not to fire on their own skirmish line. Instead, Carr believed that this was a blanket order not to fire.[20]

A steady stream of orders was given by the line officers to calm and instruct the men. "Keep cool"; "Steady boys"; "Aim low"; "Wait for orders"; "Don't be in a hurry"; "Don't fire yet," were among the expressions that the men heard as they nervously handled their weapons. They knew that they were dangerously exposed, particularly because they had not prepared breastworks or any protective barriers.[21]

As the enemy approached, the 1st Massachusetts scampered back toward the brigade from the skirmish line. When he asked where to position his troops, Lieutenant Colonel Clark Baldwin was told "in front" of the 26th Pennsylvania. Baldwin thought the order must be a mistake, as his troops would mask the Pennsylvanians's fire. When he asked about the originator of the order, Baldwin was told "General Carr." Baldwin admitted after the war that he "could not understand it, but [I] formed my regiment in obedience to the order." It appears, however, that the regiment shifted somewhat to the right to unmask the 26th Pennsylvania. A later conversation with General Carr convinced Baldwin that an aide had miscommunicated the order.[22]

The situation was becoming desperate for Carr's Brigade. In his report, Carr related that almost as soon as he shifted some units to face south (left), "the enemy made his appearance on my right flank, pouring in a most destructive crossfire." Despite the fact that Barksdale's Brigade was advancing on his left and Wilcox's and Lang's Brigades (Anderson's Division) were moving toward his front and right, Carr felt that he could have maintained his position. "I have no doubt that I could have charged on the rebels and driven them in confusion, for my line was still perfect and unbroken, and my troops in the proper spirit for the performance of such a task," he wrote in his report. The brigade, and Seeley's and Turnbull's batteries, opened fire on the advancing enemy troops. The initial volleys must have been fairly powerful, for gaps appeared in Wilcox's and Lang's ranks, and they halted momentarily to redress before continuing. The men of the 11th Massachusetts on the right side of the line, who had been told not to fire, nervously watched as the enemy bore down on them. Finally realizing that they could wait no longer, they too opened fire on the enemy, disregarding the "absurd command."[23]

Colonel McAllister of the 11th New Jersey on the opposite end of the line was immediately wounded when Barksdale's regiments returned the fire. Both friends and enemies fell in droves, and the New York regiments to the left fell back. Although the Confederates were taking serious losses, they continued to advance. The men could not have been cheered when they saw Seeley's battery limber up and gallop to safety. Lieutenant John Schoonover, who now commanded the 11th New Jersey because of heavy losses to the officers, recalled that the regiment continued firing at the approaching enemy. He characterized it as being "effective." However, he admitted that "the fire of the enemy was at this time perfectly terrific; men were falling on every side. It seemed as if but a few minutes could elapse before the entire line would be shot down, yet the galling fire was returned with equal vigor." Over on the right of the line, Lieutenant Henry Blake of the 11th Massachusetts recalled that "the companies about-faced in pursuance of the orders of some stupid general, and executed a right half-wheel under a severe fire, with as much regularity as if they had been upon parade." He apparently did not realize that Perry's small Confederate brigade was bearing down on his right regiment's flank.[24]

Carr was never given the opportunity to make good on his boast that he could have withstood the Confederate assault, because he received orders from General Birney, now commanding the III Corps, to fall back to Cemetery Ridge. Bartlett (12th New Hampshire) recalled receiving the order to "change fronts to the rear," which was immediately obeyed. He complained that "it was hardly possible that any regiment, much less a whole brigade,

could remain intact while endeavoring to obey the command, and it seemed but the folly of madness to attempt it."[25]

Captain Matthew Donovan of the 16th Massachusetts did not indicate, however, that he received orders to retreat. "We were attacked in front and on the flank," he wrote. "Our men stood it bravely until overpowered by numbers; were forced to fall back a distance of 300 yards." While admitting that his regiment was forced to retire, Schoonover also said nothing about receiving such orders from Carr. Lieutenant Colonel Baldwin of the 1st Massachusetts agreed, stating that "the enemy's three lines of battle proving too much for our one, we were obliged to give way before such superior odds."[26]

Although the enemy was bearing down on two sides, the retreat was fairly orderly. Units stopped periodically and fired at the oncoming foe before continuing their retreat. The brigade continued to sustain heavy casualties during the retreat. Blake (11th Massachusetts) recalled that "in the execution of these orders, hundreds [were] pierced by balls or struck by shells, fell in blood." Blake proudly stated that his regiment gave as good as it got, as it was using buck and ball in their smoothbore muskets. Captain John Langley of the 12th New Hampshire recalled that a number of his men were captured as the Confederates pressed their victory.[27]

After retreating several hundred yards, the men rallied around their colors. Probably seeing several regiments from Willard's (Hays's Division) as well as Harrow's and Hall's (both of Gibbon's Division) stubbornly holding their ground, Carr ordered his brigade to turn and face the enemy. Some of the officers apparently needed no such orders. Lieutenant William Fernal of the 12th New Hampshire "shook his sword defiantly toward the enemy, and then waving it over his head as a beckoning sign to his men and with a trumpet shout, 'come on,' he led his troops against the victorious enemy." The Confederate attack was essentially spent by this time, and as the masses of blue-coated Federal troops appeared, the Confederates knew it was time to retreat to the protection of Seminary Ridge. The brigade finally stopped at its former position along Emmitsburg Road. The position was still exposed, and the men were ordered to fall back to a more secure location. "The men were very indignant, because they wished to enjoy that rest which is so precious to every soldier,— a sleep upon the field which they had won by their bravery," wrote Blake (11th Massachusetts). The brigade pulled back to the vicinity of the Hummelbach house, west of Taneytown Road, where the men tended to the wounded of both armies for most of the night.[28]

The Confederate artillery opened fire again early on July 3, but losses were minimal among Carr's men. The brigade was ordered farther to the rear at 6:00 A.M., where it joined the remainder of the III Corps. Three days' rations were issued.

For some of the men, it was the first food they had received in thirty-six hours. The weakened men greedily consumed the food, and then fresh ammunition was distributed. Fed and restocked, the brigade returned to the front, where it supported Barnes's Division (V Corps). The brigade rushed to the right at about 3:20 P.M. to help support some of the II Corps's artillery, which were under attack by Pickett's Division. Here the brigade was massed "in columns of battalions" and was vulnerable to the enemy batteries on Seminary Ridge.[29]

At dusk, Carr was again ordered to the left to retake his former position. The brigade remained there until 3:30 A.M. on July 7, when it began its march toward Emmitsburg.[30]

Carr's Brigade and the rest of Humphreys's Division were placed in the untenable position of trying to hold Emmitsburg Road. Attacked on two sides, it was forced to retreat, sustaining heavy losses in the process. It was another example of a good fighting unit being placed in an untenable position.

2nd Brigade—Colonel William Brewster

Units: 70th New York, 71st New York, 72nd New York, 73rd New York, 74th New York, 120th New York
Strength: 1837
Losses: 778 (132-573-73)—42.4%[31]

Formed by Daniel Sickles in the fall of 1861, the Excelsior Brigade had fought in most of the campaigns of the Army of the Potomac. The same could not be said of its commanding officer, Colonel William Brewster. Originally the colonel of the 73rd New York, he was with the regiment at Williamsburg and Fredericksburg, but

was curiously absent during most of its other engagements. When Brewster returned to his unit after the battle of Chancellorsville, he learned that he was the senior brigade officer and would lead it during the Gettysburg campaign. How the men felt about this is unknown, but as they marched northward they probably wondered whether their new commanding officer would be present when the fighting started.[32]

During the march toward Gettysburg, the Excelsior Brigade encountered cheering citizens who supplied the men with food and water. One negative incident occurred north of Emmitsburg, when a farmer objected to the men of the 73rd New York pulling down his fence. Instead of receiving the $0.22 he demanded, Major Michael Burns ordered him into the ranks, and he was marched at least six miles. Whether it helped fan his patriotic ardor is not known.[33]

The men were so exhausted when they arrived at the battlefield at 2:00 A.M. on July 2 that they stacked arms, immediately dropped to the ground, and fell sound asleep. The commander of the 120th New York bragged in his report that despite their over-exertion "there was scarcely any straggling, and the regiment was marched to the battle-field almost to a man."[34]

At about noon on July 2, Colonel Brewster received orders from General Humphreys to move his brigade to the front and form into line of battle. Brewster deployed behind Carr's Brigade, and sent two regiments, the 71st and 72nd New York, to the front to form on Carr's left and connect the division with Birney's 1st Division. At the same time, the 74th New York advanced to form on Carr's right flank. The 73rd New York, Brewster's old regiment, advanced to an exposed position at the crest of a hill near the Klingle house on Emmitsburg Road with orders to "hold it at all hazards." The men spent some of their idle time pulling down fences that could impede the division's movement. The two remaining regiments, the 70th New York and 120th New York, remained behind Carr's Brigade.[35]

The regiments retained their relative positions when they advanced with the rest of the III Corps after 3:00 P.M. Shortly after assuming their new positions along Emmitsburg Road, the men were exposed to a severe artillery barrage. Brewster recalled that the shelling came

from batteries on his left, and called it "most destructive, killing and wounding many men." Private Henri Brown of the 72nd New York called this shelling "the heaviest artillery fire the corps had ever experienced."[36]

The men remained under this shelling for about ninety minutes. At 5:30 P.M., the 73rd New York, which occupied the advanced position along Emmitsburg Road prior to the movement of the division, was rushed south to help support Graham's Brigade, which was under attack by Barksdale's Mississippi Brigade (McLaw's Division). Facing his regiment to the left, Major Michael Burns led the men across Trostle's Lane toward Wheatfield Road. He was assisted by Major Henry Tremain of Sickles's staff.[37]

The 73rd New York arrived in time to see the 114th Pennsylvania under heavy attack along Emmitsburg Road. Reaching a rise in the ground near the Sherfy house, they received a volley from the Mississippians in their front, which they couldn't return because the Pennsylvanians masked their front. The Excelsiors could see Barksdale's men for the first time, "swarming up from the woods, yelling like demons," according to Captain Frank Moran. As the out-of-breath New Yorkers formed into line of battle, the clicking of the musket hammers as the men prepared to fire comforted Moran. The Pennsylvanians finally were forced to fall back, clearing the way for the New Yorkers. The regiment "poured a quick and well-directed volley at the enemy who fell in scores . . . they staggered under our fresh fire, but seeing their supports close at hand, rallied and returned it," he recalled. Moran also noted that his men were falling by the score from both musket and artillery fire. Barksdale's men briefly halted at the Sherfy barn, and to

Moran, "the smoke grew thicker each minute and the sound of exploding shells was deafening." The men heard that they were going to charge and let out a cheer. The officers reconsidered this action when they realized how depleted their ranks had become. Seeing that their left was being flanked, the regiment received orders to fall back. The men retired grudgingly. According to Colonel Rafferty, his men would "fire at the enemy, walk to the rear, loading as they went, take deliberate aim and fire again, and so on . . . so deliberately that the enemy kept at a respectful distance." The New Yorker's actions along Emmitsburg Road bought time for Graham's Brigade to retreat.[38]

Realizing that it was just a matter of time before the Confederate onslaught hit his left flank, Humphreys ordered the 11th New Jersey (Carr's Brigade) to face to the south (left). Although none of the New Yorkers reported it, eminent Gettysburg historian Harry Pfanz believed that the 71st and 72nd New York, which had been on the left of the 11th New Jersey, were also swung around to face Trostle Lane at this time to maintain their connection with the Garden Staters. Pfanz also believed that the 120th New York, which was in reserve, also shifted its orientation to form a supporting line. John Imhof believed that the new defensive line also included the 70th and 73rd New York. Humphreys's two brigades thus formed at a right angle to each other. Most of Carr's Brigade faced west to take on Wilcox and Perry's Brigade, while Brewster's Brigade faced south to halt Barksdale's victorious Mississippians.[39]

The veterans wrote little about their participation in the fight. Pfanz believed that the men did not describe this maneuver because they performed so poorly in this position. It appears that when Barksdale's men charged, most of the New Yorkers, particularly the 71st and 72nd New York, broke without putting up much of a fight. The 72nd New York's historian merely wrote that "the division changed front and rallied three times, but was compelled to fall back to the second line."[40]

Members of the 19th Maine (Harrow's Brigade, Gibbon's Division) recalled seeing soldiers from the Excelsior Brigade running past them on their way to the rear. They recalled some New Yorkers calling out, "Run boys, we're whipped, the day is lost." Others tried to encourage the men by shouting, "Hang on, boys! We will form in your rear." Some apparently tried to do so, but they too apparently disappeared.[41]

Not all of the New Yorkers fled from the south-facing line. It appears that the 120th New York held its ground. Colonel Charles Westbrook related how the regiment watched hopelessly as one after another Excelsior regiment was fed into the battle, until it was the only reserve. The regiment was finally ordered to move fifty yards and take position behind a low stone wall. The men knew that they were in for the fight of their lives, and many prayed. "I offered a silent prayr [sic] to the preserver of all as I rose to take my musket: for myself and the loved ones at home," wrote Eseck Wilber after the battle. The regiment was apparently isolated, for it could not see its sister regiments nearby. Westbrook recalled that Barksdale's attack was launched against Brewster's line at 6:30 P.M. Charles Santvoord noted that the "order came and the whole line rose as a man and poured into their ranks such a terrible fire of musketry, as to bring them to a standstill when within a few rods of us." The 120th New York held its position until 7:00 P.M., when it was about to be overwhelmed by Barksdale in the front and Wilcox on the right. An unknown regiment suddenly materialized and poured a concentrated fire into the enemy, allowing the New Yorkers to retire safely. The regiment fell back, stubbornly contesting every foot of ground. Colonel Brewster appeared at this time and acted as a file closer for the regiment.[42]

The brigade ultimately reformed in the rear. As Barksdale's men continued their attack, they could see a brushy area in front of them, and not knowing what it was, momentarily halted. To Private Felix Brannigan of the 74th New York, this was a fatal error, for it gave the Federals a chance to regroup, survey the situation, and launch a counterattack, which ultimately drove the Confederates back with heavy losses. Because there were so few officers, Brannigan recalled that, "everyone was his own General." An artillery officer rode up to them and pointed to some cannon captured by the enemy. He yelled to the disorganized men, "Boys! You said you'd stick to us, is this the way the brigade is going to leave the field? There's the guns! If you're men, come on!" Spurring his horse, he rode forward, followed by a number of men from the brigade. "It was irresistible—and glorious—oh we went through their shattered columns like a thunderbolt, and in the thrilling excitement of the desperate rush, we seemed to be borne on wings," recalled Brannigan. Wilber likened it to driving the Southerners "like Chalf [sic] before the wind." A number of Confederate battle flags were left standing by the cannon, only to be captured by the onrushing New Yorkers. Realizing that they had to withdraw the guns before the Confederates could launch a counterattack, the Confederate prisoners were given ropes to pull the cannon to safety. Few admitted that it was actually Willard's Brigade (Hays's

Division II Corps) that spearheaded this drive.[43]

The brigade was pulled back several hundred yards to regroup, where it spent the rest of the night. The moon that night was full and rose early, so many of the men decided to return to the scene of the early evening fighting. "Strewn all over the field, and lying side by side, were the blue and gray," recalled Santvoord. The men could see doctors and stretcher bearers plying their trade, as they desperately tried to address the needs of the wounded. Few men were able to sleep that night because of the scenes they had witnessed, and because of the continual sound of artillery and small arms fire that pierced the night.[44]

The brigade was pulled back farther during the early morning hours of July 3, where it was fed and resupplied. Between 2:00 and 3:00 P.M. the brigade marched to the northwest (toward the front lines) to support the II Corps batteries. While the brigade was exposed to the heavy artillery fire at this time, and lost several men, it did not directly participate in repulsing Pickett's charge. At 7:00 P.M., the brigade moved back to the position it had occupied that morning and went into bivouac. The brigade remained there until July 6, when the men were ordered into line and marched half a mile. The column suddenly halted, and the men "about-faced" and returned to their original positions. The brigade finally left the battleground during the early morning hours of July 7, when it began its march after Lee's army.[45]

Placed in a difficult situation, Brewster's Brigade probably did as well as it could. The 73rd and 120th New York fought well and received accolades. The same is probably not true of some of the brigade's other regiments, such as the 71st and 72nd New York, which apparently fled without much provocation.

✂

3rd Brigade—Colonel George Burling

Units: 2nd New Hampshire, 5th New Jersey, 6th New Jersey, 7th New Jersey, 8th New Jersey, 115th Pennsylvania
Strength: 1365
Losses: 513 (59-376-78)—37.6%[46]

As the 3rd Brigade marched toward Gettysburg, the men probably wondered how their new commander, Colonel George Burling, would perform. They knew him from the beginning of the war, as he was a captain in the 6th New Jersey. He took over the regiment in August 1862, after having fought with it (and the rest of the brigade) at Seven Pines. The brigade did not see much action during the Seven Days battles. About to be overwhelmed at the battle of Second Bull Run, the brigade pulled back. Burling did not notice the withdrawal, and as a result, his regiment sustained heavy losses. Burling was wounded, but returned for the battle of Fredericksburg, but the brigade did not see action. The brigade was engaged at Chancellorsville, where Burling was again wounded. When he returned in June 1863, he was put in command of the brigade because its permanent commander, General Gershom Mott, had also been wounded at Chancellorsville.[47]

The march through central and northern Maryland was a special time for many of the men. Private John Burrill of the 2nd New Hampshire wrote home that he had "fallen in love with 'My Maryland.'" It was "as fine a country as I have ever seen—so handsome, and what fields of grain . . . the people as loyal as any I ever seen. They are willing to do for us and give us everything they have." Burrill even went so far as to state that "they are more loyal than those of N.H." Private Martin Haynes of the same regiment agreed, recording in his diary that "we are getting into God's country, now, where there are loyal people, and where American flags and cheers for the Union are the rule, and not the exception." These experiences not withstanding, the men were exhausted. Captain William Evans of the 7th New Jersey wrote home that "we have marched 200 miles . . . our march has been the severest I've ever had, and we have suffered dreadfully, but it is all for the flag."[48]

The brigade, along with the remainder of the division, reached Emmitsburg at noon on July 1. The brigade was detached at 2:00 P.M. and with de Trobriand's Brigade (Birney's Division, III Corps) ordered to watch the mountain passes. The men were happy to have this reprieve, and were even more excited when they found an abundance of hay to soften their beds. The men were told that they would spend the night there. As a result of the prospects for a long rest, many of the men slipped away to buy food from the farmers in the area. Some prepaid for bread that was to be baked that night and delivered to them in the morning. Unfortunately, the men never received their goods, for at about 1:30 A.M. on July 2, Colonel Burling received orders to march his men toward Gettysburg, where the army was assembling. Colonel Burling wrote that the march did not actually begin the march until 4:00 A.M. because "my command covering so much ground, and the night being so very dark," it took him two and a half hours to get under way. The brigade was considerably dispersed because of the number of roads it was expected to picket.[49]

The men made good time on the deserted road and were permitted to halt for ten-minute breaks at the end of each hour. The brigade finally rejoined the division at 9:00 A.M. on July 2, where it was massed in column of regiments in the Trostle Woods. It moved twice that morning, each time closer to Emmitsburg Road. At about noon, General Humphreys ordered the brigade to move behind the division's two other brigades in the woods on the west side of Wheatfield Road, where it formed the reserve. Because an attack was expected momentarily, Burling received orders to move his brigade to the left and report to General Birney at about 4:00 P.M.[50]

Skirmishing soon erupted in Birney's front, and Burling's Brigade was ordered out of the woods and into the Wheatfield. Enemy batteries opened fire almost immediately from a distance of less than a thousand yards. After remaining there for about half an hour, Burling was approached by several of his regimental commanders with a request that he pull back the brigade about a hundred yards, where it would be protected by a rise of ground. Considering the officers to be "equally competent with myself" and feeling the uneasiness of his first brigade command, Burling decided to take their advice, and ordered the men to "about face" and move back. The men had not moved very far when Captain John Poland of General Sickles's staff tore up to Burling and demanded to know by whose authority the move was made. "By my own," was his reply. Poland was in no mood to accept the disregard of a direct order and told Burling to move the brigade back to its exposed position. Burling complied, but before his men had reached this position, one of Birney's aides rode up with orders to move to Trostle Woods on the left and take up a position perpendicular to the original one.[51]

Shortly after reaching this position, another of Birney's aides arrived with orders to "detail two of my largest regiments to report to General Graham." Burling dutifully detached the 2nd New Hampshire and 7th New Jersey and rushed them toward the Peach Orchard. Still another aide arrived with orders to send the next largest regiment to General Humphreys for picket duty. Burling selected the 5th New Jersey, and sent it west to form in front of the division. This left Burling with three small regiments, which were ordered into the Wheatfield to form on the left of de Trobriand's Brigade. Another messenger soon arrived to take another regiment, which was sent to Ward's Brigade's aid on the left. Burling rode over to the 6th New Jersey to give it orders, when "the Eighth New Jersey Volunteers was taken from me without my knowledge, leaving me with the One hundred and fifteenth Pennsylvania Volunteers, numbering 140 muskets." A frustrated Burling wrote in his official report that "my command being now all taken from me and separated, no two regiments being together, and being under the command of the different brigade commanders to whom they reported, I with my staff, reported to General Humphreys for instructions, remaining with him for some time."[52]

While Colonel Burling was cooling his heels with his division commander, his units were having the fights of their lives. The 6th New Jersey was moving south to support Ward's Brigade, the 115th Pennsylvania and 8th New Jersey were in the Wheatfield, the 2nd New Hampshire and 7th New Jersey were in the Peach Orchard, and the 5th New Jersey had relieved the 63rd Pennsylvania on the skirmish line.

The 6th New Jersey had the farthest distance to march, and it didn't help matters much that no guide was provided. Instead, the regiment advanced to a fence in the vicinity of Devil's Den. The men could see the enemy in the distance, so they formed into line of battle just west of Plum Run and opened fire on the 44th and 48th Alabama (Law's Brigade, Hood's Division). The initial fire was ineffective because the regiment was at least four hundred yards from the Alabamians. The return fire brought down of number of men, however. Moving forward another two hundred yards into an open field, Lieutenant Colonel Stephen Gilkyson deployed his men directly in front of the two guns of Smith's battery posted in the rear. In its new position, the 6th New Jersey was to the right of the 40th New York (de Trobriand's Brigade), and behind the 4th Maine (Ward's Brigade), where it took on the right wing of Benning's Brigade, composed of the 2nd and 17th Georgia. It appears that Gilkyson was operating independently, barely noting the actions of the regiments around him, much less trying to coordinate with them. Seeing the 40th New York and Ward's Regiments withdrawing to his right, Gilkyson held his ground, permitting them to escape. Realizing that his position was untenable, Gilkyson ordered his men to fall back also. Halting in close proximity to Ward's Brigade, Gilkyson approached its brigade commander for orders. Ward told him that "he had been relieved, ordering me to join my brigade, which we did about 7 P.M."[53]

The 115th Pennsylvania and the 8th New Jersey had their hands full in the Wheatfield to the north. Deployed to fill the gap between the 17th Maine on their left, and the 5th Michigan and 110th Pennsylvania (all of de Trobriand's Brigade), the two regiments took position in the Rose Woods. The 115th Pennsylvania formed on the left; the 8th New Jersey on its right. Here, the men held their position against increasingly heavy pressure from the 8th and 9th Georgia of Anderson's Brigade (Hood's Division). However, the gaps on their left and right placed the two regiments in an untenable position. After about half an hour, the enemy found the gap to the right of the 8th New Jersey, forcing it to fall back. This opened another gap to the right of the 115th Pennsylvania, forcing its officers to order a withdrawal. Despite the loss of these two units, de Trobriand's regiments held their ground. Falling back about fifty yards, Major John Dunn of the 115th Pennsylvania was approached by Captain George Winslow with a plea that the regiment defend his battery in the Wheatfield until its guns could be limbered up and moved to safety. Dunn complied, ordering his men to the right of the battery, where they lay down. The 115th Pennsylvania later rose and made two charges to keep the enemy at bay. When their ammunition was almost exhausted, the Pennsylvanians fell back toward Taneytown Road, about half a mile from the front. Here they rejoined the brigade, stacked arms, and rested for the night. Despite its vulnerable positions, the 115th Pennsylvania sustained the lightest casualties in the brigade—16%.[54]

The most gallant fight was being waged by the 2nd New Hampshire in the Peach Orchard, where it supported Ames's battery. Rushing forward, the regiment formed into a double-row line of battle, facing southwest, with its right flank perpendicular to, and touching, Emmitsburg Road. Behind its right flank, facing the road, was the 68th Pennsylvania; to its left was the 3rd Maine of Ward's Brigade. As a result, the 2nd New Hampshire had the dubious honor of being positioned at the

Peach Orchard angle. Realizing that his right flank hung in the air, Colonel Bailey ordered it refused so it faced Emmitsburg Road. The two wings of the regiment were therefore at right angles to each other at this time. One company (B), armed with Sharps repeating rifles, was sent to the right, where it deployed as sharpshooters around the Wentz farm buildings.[55]

Colonel Bailey again changed the regiment's position at about 3:15 P.M. This time all of its companies faced south, with its right in the garden behind the Wentz house. Ames's battery initially had the upper hand in its battle with its Confederate counterparts, until another enemy battery emerged from the woods on Seminary Ridge and opened an enfilading fire. "Never, in all its history, was the regiment exposed to such a terrific artillery fire as it received while lying upon the ground to the rear of this battery [Ames's]," wrote Haynes. "The air was fairly alive with bursting shell and whistling canister; the leaves fell in showers from the peach trees, and the dirt was thrown up in little jets where the missiles were continually striking." John Burrill wrote home that the heavy artillery fire "made the earth tremble and the air shook and was so full of smoke you could not see." The men lay on the ground for over two hours, praying that the shells would continue flying harmlessly overhead.[56]

The men's concerns grew when the Confederate artillery fire escalated and enemy troops could be seen massing on Seminary Ridge during the late afternoon. The skirmishers came lopping back soon after. Colonel Bailey accurately described the enemy forces in his front. "A brigade of the enemy [Barksdale's] was advancing on our right, in column of battalions massed, while two regiments [from Kershaw's Brigade] were moving directly parallel with my front to the left, evidently

with the design to turn that flank." Bailey immediately sought out General Graham, commanding this sector, and requested permission to charge. Haynes claimed that Graham's reply was, "Yes, for God's sake, go forward!" So hopeless was the defense that at least one battery commanders ordered his guns spiked. Haynes recalled that Bailey's order was, "Forward, guide center!" "With a roar of defiance from three hundred throats the Second went tearing down the slope. They did not have to hunt for the enemy—there he was right before them," noted Bailey. The men of the 8th South Carolina (Kershaw's Brigade, McLaws's Division) did not expect this response and momentarily halted before taking to the rear.[57]

Bailey's report graphically describes this gallant charge. "My regiment started immediately, and advanced 150 yards at a run with a yell and such impetuosity as to cause the enemy to retire to a ravine 250 yards in our front, where they were covered from our fire, when I directed the fire of my battalion of the left . . . my fire was so galling . . . as to cause them [the enemy] to break and seek shelter." Although most did not mention it, the 3rd Maine, 3rd Michigan, 2nd 141st Pennsylvania also advanced to the left[58]

Although the 2nd New Hampshire had charged beyond the Peach Orchard, driving Kershaw's men before it, the situation did not look good. Bailey ordered his men to take cover behind a fence. All was quiet for about twenty minutes as the Confederates massed for another charge. Bailey knew that his men could not hold this line, so he sent his adjutant back to tell the batteries to withdraw. As the enemy renewed their attack, the pressure forced the 68th Pennsylvania and the 3rd Maine to retire. The enemy line pivoted, taking the 2nd New Hampshire on its front and flank, and forced Colonel Bailey to give the order to fall back. He halted the regiment in the Peach Orchard to fire into the 21st Mississippi (Barksdale's Brigade) approaching from the right. Bailey estimated that the two sides were no more than twenty yards apart at this point. Haynes claimed that "so near were the rebels upon us that the worst shot in the army could not well have missed his mark." Reforming his ranks behind a rise in the Peach Orchard, Bailey was pleased to see the 68th Pennsylvania about forty feet to its right and rear and the 3rd Maine on its left and rear. The pressure became too great for these regiments to withstand, and soon they were streaming to the rear. Bailey ordered his men to join their comrades in the withdrawal. He proudly reported that the movement was accomplished "quite rapidly, yet coolly, and without excitement as they went." Burrill wrote that "we [had] to fall back. They pour[ed] an awful fire into us. Men dropped fast." The regiment was smaller, but still full of fight when it rejoined the rest of the brigade at about 6:30 P.M. that evening.[59]

The 2nd New Hampshire was not the only regiment from Burling's Brigade occupying the Peach Orchard—the 7th New Jersey was also sent there. Its story is quite different, however. Assigned to support the batteries, the regiment faced southwest, to the left and behind the 141st Pennsylvania (Graham's Brigade). Because of its proximity to the Federal artillery, the regiment was pounded by Confederate batteries, causing Colonel Louis Francine to order his men to lie down. All was chaos around them, and casualties mounted until Colonel Francine decided to pull his regiment back to a more protected position. Just then an aide from General Graham galloped up and told Francine to hold his position. Francine replied, "I will support the battery. I was only trying to get

a better position for my men, who I am losing very fast."[60]

The 7th New Jersey held its position until the 8th South Carolina from Kershaw's Brigade attacked the batteries. Clark's battery quickly limbered up; in the words of Major Frederick Cooper, "the battery broke through our ranks, creating considerable confusion for a time, but through the exertions of the officers the line was reformed." With the threat on his left, Colonel Francine threw his right wing forward, and ordered the entire regiment to open fire. "After firing a few rounds, a charge was ordered," wrote Major Cooper, "which was attempted, but the enemy's fire was so severe that we were compelled to fall back a short distance." Francine went down, followed by Lieutenant Colonel Francis Price, leaving Major Cooper in command of the regiment. He tried to hold his position, but with Kershaw on his left and Barksdale's Brigade bearing down on his right, Cooper decided it was time to withdraw. The regiment eventually rejoined the brigade that evening. Despite the fact that it occupied only a supporting position in the Peach Orchard, the regiment lost over 40% of its men.[61]

At about 4:00 P.M., the 5th New Jersey was detached from the brigade to relieve the 63rd Pennsylvania on the skirmish line in front of Humphreys's Division. Moving by the right flank at a double-quick pace, the men deployed in front of Seely's battery. They dodged spherical case shells being fired by a Confederate battery in their front as they took position. Before long, other enemy batteries took position in preparation for the assault on the Union line. Particularly nasty was the enfilading fire coming from the left. This heavy fire continued for over an hour, as losses mounted. Colonel William Sewell intently watched Seminary Ridge for signs of enemy infantry, and when they broke from cover, he immediately sent word to General Humphreys. The left of Sewell's line became engaged first, but the men stubbornly held their ground. They could see Birney's regiments being driven from the Peach Orchard on their left, but still they held on, hoping that the fresh troops in their rear would advance. The pressure soon became too great on their front (from Wilcox's Brigade) and left flank (from Barksdale's Brigade), so Sewell ordered the men to mass near Seely's battery along Emmitsburg Road to buy time for its withdrawal. Colonel Sewell fell wounded as the regiment withdrew. The regiment, which lost almost half of its men on the skirmish line, rejoined the brigade later that night.[62]

The brigade reassembled in the Trostle Woods, but did not rejoin the division until the next day, when it took the position it had occupied the day before. It remained there until after noon, when it was moved to the right to support some of the batteries. Here the men lay in position for about two hours under the full force of the artillery barrage that preceded the Pickett–Pettigrew–Trimble charge. When night finally fell, the brigade marched back to its earlier position, where it remained until Lee's army retreated. With time on their hands, the men walked around the battlefield. Although veterans of many fights, the men were incredulous at the amount of death and destruction wrought by the two armies. One unidentified soldier from the 2nd New Hampshire probably exaggerated when he wrote home, "you may as well believe I had rather go into a fight than to see the effects of it." The brigade finally left the battlefield at 3:00 A.M. on July 7.[63]

The brigade had the dubious distinction of being one of the few in either army that was entirely broken apart with its regiments being sent to different sectors. The

effectiveness of its units was mixed, depending almost solely on the commanding officers. For example, the 2nd New Hampshire performed well under the effective leadership of Colonel Edward Bailey. The same cannot be said of the 6th New Jersey, which never really assisted Ward's Brigade, or the 7th New Jersey, which merely supported the batteries in the Peach Orchard until it belatedly charged the enemy. General Birney summarized his feelings about the brigade when he wrote in his report, "I cannot estimate too highly the services of the regiments from Burling's Brigade . . . most gallantly did they sustain the glorious reputation won by them in former battles."[64]

NOTES

1. Charles W. Bardeen, *A Little Fifer's War Diary* (Syracuse, NY, 1910), 216; Tagg, *Generals of Gettysburg*, 73–74; Dyer, *Compendium*, 298.

2. OR 27, 1, 530–531.

3. OR 27, 1, 531; Clark Baldwin to John Bachelder, May 20, 1865, Bachelder Papers, New Hampshire Historical Society.

4. OR 27, 1, 531–532.

5. Jesse B. Young, *What a Boy Saw in the Army: A Story of Sight-Seeing and Adventure in the War for the Union* (New York, 1894), 300.

Young was serving as an assistant provost marshal at Humphreys's headquarters and was therefore away from his regiment.

6. OR 27, 1, 532–533; A. A. Humphreys, letter, copy in Brake Collection, USAMHI; Asa W. Bartlett, *History of the Twelfth Regiment, New Hampshire Volunteers in the War of the Rebellion* (Concord, NH, 1897), 124, 127; Tagg, *Generals of Gettysburg*, 74–75.

7. OR 27, 1, 536.

8. Busey and Martin, *Regimental Strengths and Losses*, 52, 246.

9. Dyer, *Compendium*, 298; Tagg, *Generals of Gettysburg*, 75–76.

10. OR 27, 1, 542; Thomas D. Marbaker, *History of the Eleventh New Jersey Volunteers* (Trenton, NJ, 1876), 90.

11. Marbaker, *History of the Eleventh New Jersey Volunteers*, 90; William H. Cudsworth, *History of the First Regiment Massachusetts Infantry* (Boston, 1866), 390; Bardeen, *A Little Fifer's War Diary*, 212; anonymous, diary, Civil War Times Collection, USAMHI.

12. Henry Blake, "Personal Reminiscences of Gettysburg," copy in the USAHMI; Cudsworth, *History of the First Regiment Massachusetts Infantry*, 392–393; W. H. Wheeler, "War Record and Reminiscences," Duke University; Marbaker, *History of the Eleventh New Jersey Volunteers*, 92.

13. Hutchinson, *A Narrative of the Formation and Services of the Eleventh Massachusetts Volunteers*, 48.

14. Blake, *Three Years in the Army of the Potomac*, 203; O'Brien, "To Unflinchingly Face Danger and Death," 8–9; Blake, "Pernsonal Reminiscences of Gettysburg; Bardeen, *Little Fifer's Diary*, 216.

15. Cudsworth, *History of the First Regiment Massachusetts Infantry*, 392–393; OR suppl., 5, 176; anonymous diary.

16. OR 27, 1, 543, 553, 555; Marbaker, *History of the Eleventh New Jersey Volunteers*, 97; Bartlett, *History of the Twelfth Regiment, New Hampshire Volunteers in the War of the Rebellion*, 121; Pfanz, *Gettysburg—The Second Day*, 146.

In a letter written soon after the war, Lieutenant Colonel Clark Baldwin reported that he advanced at 7:30 A.M. However, his after-battle report, written on July 28, 1863, said it was at 11:00 A.M., and this was supported by Carr's official report (OR suppl., 5, 176; OR 27, 1, 543, 547).

17. OR 27, 1, 543, 553.

18. OR 27, 1, 553; Marbaker, *History of the Eleventh New Jersey Volunteers*, 97; Blake, *Three Years in the Army of the Potomac*, 206–207.

19. Bartlett, *History of the Twelfth Regiment, New Hampshire Volunteers in the War of the Rebellion;* 122; OR 27, 1, 543.

20. OR 27, 1, 553; Marbaker, *History of the Eleventh New Jersey Volunteers*, 97–98; Pfanz, *Gettysburg—The Second Day*, 365; Blake, "Personal Reminiscences of Gettysburg"; Imhof, *Gettysburg: Day Two*, 161.

21. Blake, "Personal Reminiscences of Gettysburg."

22. OR suppl., 5, 178; Pfanz, *Gettysburg—The Second Day*, 366.

23. OR 27, 1, 543, 553, Blake, "Personal Reminiscences of Gettysburg"; Kevin E. O'Brien, "To Unflinchingly Face Danger and Death: Carr's Brigade Defends Emmitsburg Road," *Gettysburg Magazine* (July 1999), issue 19, 17.

Henry Blake was still fuming over how Carr handled his troops at Gettysburg, when his memoirs were published in 1865. One quote is particularly memorable: "orders were duly transmitted from a blockhead, terms upon the muster-roll a brigadier-general, not to discharge a musket, because they 'would fire on their own men' . . . " He also called Carr a coward for his behavior during the battle (Blake, *Three Years in the Army of the Potomac*, 209; Blake, "Reminiscences of Gettysburg").

24. OR 27, 1, 553–554; Blake, *Three Years in the Army of the Potomac*, 208; Pfanz, *Gettysburg—The Second Day*, 369.

25. OR 27, 1, 543; Bartlett, *History of the Twelfth Regiment, New Hampshire Volunteers in the War of the Rebellion*, 124.

26. OR 27, 1, 553–554; Cudworth, *History of the First Regiment Massachusetts Infantry*, 394; OR suppl, 5, 179; Blake, "Personal Reminiscences of Gettysburg."

27. OR 27, 1, 543; Blake, "Personal Reminiscences of Gettysburg"; John F. Langley to John Bachelder, March 24, 1864, Bachelder Papers, New Hampshire Historical Society.

28. OR 27, 1, 543, 554.

29. OR 27, 1, 544, 550, 551.

Thomas Marbaker recalled that the 11th New Jersey assisted the II Corps before it had a chance to eat (Marbaker, *History of the Eleventh New Jersey Volunteers*, 101).

30. OR 27, 1, 544.

31. Busey and Martin, *Regimental Strengths and Losses*, 53, 246.

32. Tagg, *Generals of Gettysburg*, 77–78.

33. "Fourth Excelsior N.Y. Vols," Bachelder Papers, New Hampshire Historical Society.

34. OR 27, 1, 565, 568.

35. OR 27, 1, 558–559; *NYG*, vol. 2, 605.

According to Pfanz, the 74th New York formed behind the 26th Pennsylvania of Carr's Brigade (Pfanz, *Gettysburg—The Second Day*, 147).

36. OR 27, 1, 559; Henri L. Brown, *History of the 3d Regiment, Excelsior Brigade* (Jamestown, NY, 1902), 104.

37. OR 27, 1, 559.

38. Frank E. Moran, "A New View of Gettysburg," *Philadelphia Weekly Times*, April 22, 1882; *NYG*, vol. 2, 606.

39. Pfanz, *Gettysburg—The Second Day*, 347–348; Imhof *Gettysburg: Day Two*, 161.

40. Pfanz, *Gettysburg—The Second Day*, 347–349; Brown, *History of the 3rd Regiment, Excelsior Brigade*, 104.

41. Adams, "The Nineteenth Maine at Gettysburg," 253; John Lancaster, letter, copy in 19th Maine file, GNMP; *Maine at Gettysburg*, 292–293.

42. C. D. Westbrook, "The 120th N.Y.'s Firm Stand on the Second Day at Gettysburg," *National Tribune*, September 20, 1900; Esick Wilber, letter, Murray Smith Collection, USAMHI; Cornelius VanSantvood, *The One Hundred and Twentieth N.Y.S.* (Rondout, NY, 1894), 74.

Westbrook believed that the unknown regiment may have been from Willard's Brigade.

43. Felix Brannigan, letter, copy in Brake Collection, USAMHI; Wilber, letter.

This counterattack was probably made in conjunction with Willard's Brigade.

44. VanSantvoord, *The One Hundred and Twentieth N.Y.S.*, 75

45. OR 27, 1, 559, 562, 566.

46. Busey and Martin, *Regimental Strengths and Losses*, 54, 247.

47. Tagg, *Generals of Gettysburg*, 79–80; Dyer, *Compendium*, 298.

48. John Burrell, letter, Civil War Times Illustrated Collection, USAMHI; Martin A. Haynes, *History of the Second New Hampshire: Its Camps, Marches, and Battles* (Manchester, NH, 1865), 165; William Evans, letter, New Jersey Historical Society, Newark.

49. OR 27, 1, 570; Haynes, *History of the Second Regiment, New Hampshire Volunteers*, 136; Martin A. Haynes, *A History of the Second Regi-*

ment, New Hampshire Volunteer Infantry in the War of the Rebellion (Lakeport, NH, 1896), 166.

50. Haynes, *A History of the Second Regiment, New Hampshire Volunteer Infantry in the War of the Rebellion*, 167; George Burling to John Bachelder, February 8, 1884, Bachelder Papers, New Hampshire Historical Society

51. OR 27, 1, 570.

52. OR 27, 1, 570–571.

Although modern historian Harry Pfanz wrote that Burling stated in his official report that with all of his other regiments gone, he ordered the 115th Pennsylvania to report to General Birney, there is no reference to this action in the report (OR 27, 1, 571).

53. OR 27, 1, 577–578; Pfanz, *Gettysburg—The Second Day*, 199; Kathleen G. Harrison, "Our Principal Loss was in the Place, Action at the Slaughter Pen and at South end of Houck's Ridge, Gettysburg, Pennsylvania, 2 July, 1863," *Gettysburg Magazine* (July 1989), issue 1, 64–65.

54. OR suppl., 5, 185–186; Pfanz, *Gettysburg—The Second Day*, 246; John Dunne to John Bachelder, June 30, 1884, 1865, Bachelder Papers, New Hampshire Historical Society; Busey and Martin, *Regimental Strengths and Losses*, 247.

55. OR 27, 1, 573; Haynes, *A History of the Second Regiment, New Hampshire Volunteer Infantry in the War of the Rebellion* 169–170; Haynes, *History of the Second Regiment, New Hampshire Volunteers: Its Camps, Marches and Battles*, 138–139; John Dearborn to John Bachelder, April 4, 1889, Bachelder Papers, New Hampshire Historical Society

In his report, Colonel Edward Bailey mistakenly wrote that his regiment took position on the right of the 63rd Pennsylvania, and that the 3rd Maine was on the skirmish line. In reality, the 63rd Pennsylvania was on skirmish line, and the 3rd Maine was to its right. The relative positions are confusing, as witnessed by the contradictory maps in recent publications. I have used Imhof's convention (*Gettysburg—Day Two*, 113) rather than Pfanz's (*Gettysburg—The Second Day*, 314) as the layout of the monuments suggests that the former interpretation may be more accurate.

56. Haynes, *A History of the Second Regiment, New Hampshire Volunteer Infantry in the War of the Rebellion* 171; Haynes, *A History of the Second Regiment, New Hampshire Volunteers: Its Camps, Marches and Battles,* 139; John Burrill, letter, Civil War Times Illustrated Collection, USAMHI.

57. OR 27, 1, 574; Haynes, *A History of the Second Regiment, New Hampshire Volunteer Infantry in the War of the Rebellion,* 171, 176.

58. OR 27, 1, 574.

59. Edward Bailey to John Bachelder, March 29, 1882, Bachelder Papers, New Hampshire Historical Society; Haynes, *History of the Second Regiment, New Hampshire Volunteers: Its Camps, Marches and Battles,* 142; Burill, letter.

60. OR 27, 1, 578–579; Samuel Toombes, *New Jersey in the Gettysburg Campaign* (Orange, NJ, 1888), 222; Paul J. Lader, "The 7th New Jersey in the Gettysburg Campaign," *Gettysburg Magazine* (January 1997), issue 16, 58–59.

61. OR 27, 1, 578–579; Lader, "The 7th New Jersey in the Gettysburg Campaign," 61–70; Busey and Martin, *Regimental Strengths and Losses,* 247.

62. OR 27, 1, 575–577.

63. George Burling to John Bachelder, February 8, 1884; OR 27, 1, 571; unidentified letter, Brake Collection, USAMHI.

64. OR 27, 1, 483.

V CORPS—

Major General George Meade/
Major General George Sykes

Formed on May 18, 1862, the V Corps had been commanded by Fitz John Porter, Joseph Hooker, Daniel Butterfield, and, since Christmas 1862, George Meade. The corps found glory on the battlefields near Richmond in the spring and summer of 1862, fighting in the battles of Hanover Courthouse, Mechanicsville, and Gaines's Mill. The latter battle was particularly noteworthy, for Porter's Corps held the high ground for many hours against heavy Confederate attacks. The corps ultimately vacated the heights, but not before inflicting tremendous casualties on the enemy. One division held the center of the line at the battle of Glendale, but was overwhelmed by the concentrated Confederate infantry. It more than made up for it during the bloody repulse of the enemy at Malvern Hill. A dark stain was placed on the corps' record during the Second Bull Run campaign, when army commander John Pope accused Porter of not moving his troops into battle soon enough. It was a frivolous charge, but led to Porter's removal. The corps was not engaged at Antietam. Under Butterfield at Fredericksburg, the corps suffered heavy losses as it assailed Marye's Hill. Meade assumed command of the corps prior to the battle of Chancellorsville, but it was not heavily engaged there. Never a fan of Hooker, Meade rode toward Gettysburg with the hope that his corps would see action.[1]

After long, hard marches from Virginia, the V Corps camped within two miles of Frederick, Maryland, on the evening of June 28. That night, Meade assumed command of the Army of the Potomac, and he turned the V Corps over to General George Sykes, who had commanded the 1st Division. The march continued on the morning of June 29 through Frederick, which was decked out in flags and other buntings to welcome the Federal troops. The column continued for another eighteen miles and halted between Liberty and Johnsville. The hard rain that night soaked most of the men. Reveille sounded before daylight on June 30, and the men were on the road shortly after 4:00 A.M. for a twenty-three-mile march. The men remained in camp until 8:00 A.M. on July 1, when they were ordered to fall in and continue the march toward Pennsylvania. Like the troops of many of the other commanders, General Sykes's men formally celebrated when they crossed the Pennsylvania state line that day. The column reached Hanover, Pennsylvania, at about 4:00 P.M., where the men could see signs of a recent cavalry battle. After a short rest, the march continued into the night. It ended at about 1:00 A.M., when the corps was approximately four miles from the battlefield. The rest was a short one, for reveille sounded at 3:30 A.M., and the corps finally reached the battlefield shortly after 7:00 A.M. on July 2.[2]

Private John Smith of the 118th Pennsylvania (Tilton's Brigade) recalled the approach of the V Corps toward Wolf Hill on the early morning of July 2. "The alignment perfected, with colors unfurled and pieces at a right shoulder, the masses advanced, preserving their alignments and distances with all the force, effect and impressiveness attending a display occasion. The fences were removed and grass, grain, bush and weed were crushed by the heavy tramp of the solid advance." The corps made several subsequent changes in position before it finally halted between Powers Hill to the west and where Rock Creek intersects Baltimore Pike. According to the Bachelder maps, Barnes's Division was on the right, astride Baltimore Pike, Ayes's Division was to his left, and Crawford's formed behind them.[3]

The corps received orders to move south to help support the left wing were between 4:00 P.M. and 5:00 P.M., and Generals Sykes and Barnes led the column southward. The destination was the southern end of Cemetery Ridge and Little Round Top. Several III Corps aides rode up, pleading with Sykes for assistance, but he refused all requests, as he would not divide his forces. General Warren was, however, able to divert Vincent's Brigade, and later Weed's Brigade, to Little Round Top, where they helped to beat off determined Confederate attacks. The rest of the corps made its way to their assigned position. Four brigades from Barnes's and Ayres's Divisions were sent to the Wheatfield, where all were ultimately forced to withdraw. Crawford's Division counterattacked from Little Round Top, helping to dissipate the last vestige of the Confederate attack.[4]

The corps was distributed along the south end of the field on July 3. It was not engaged except for McCandless's Brigade (Crawford's Division), which advanced and captured a portion of the 15th Georgia (Benning's Brigade, Hood's Division). July 4 was spent resting, skirmishing, and burying the dead. The corps finally left the battlefield during the late afternoon of July 5.[5]

1ST DIVISION—

Brigadier General James Barnes

Falling ill in early May, Brigadier General Charles Griffin left the army for treatment, leaving the 1st Division temporarily in the hands of Brigadier General James Barnes of the 1st Brigade. One of the oldest generals in the army at age sixty-one, Barnes was a West Pointer who rose through the ranks beginning as colonel of the 18th Massachusetts. Although never having been under fire, Barnes received command of the 1st Brigade on July 10, 1862. It was not until the Fredericksburg campaign that Barnes actively engaged the enemy, and that was in a losing cause. Barnes did not see much action at Chancellorsville. Thus, as the Gettysburg campaign began, Barnes found himself temporarily leading a division, despite having limited combat experience.[6]

June 28 brought ambivalence to the men of Barnes's Division when they learned that their corps commander, General George Meade, now commanded the army. According to Captain Francis Donaldson of the 118th Pennsylvania (Tilton's Brigade), the move was "one not likely to inspire the greatest amount of confidence." Prior to his appointment, Donaldson wrote that Meade "appears to be a man universally despised in the Corps."[7]

The division marched through Frederick at 11:00 A.M. on June 29 amid the celebrations of its citizens. The march continued at 4:00 A.M. on June 30, and after another long day, the division finally camped at Union Mills at 6:00 P.M. The men broke camp at 10:00 A.M. on July 1 to orders that any straggler would be shot. Colonel Strong Vincent's 3rd Brigade led the division during this leg of the march, followed by Colonel Jacob Sweitzer's 2nd Brigade; Colonel William Tilton's 1st Brigade brought up the rear. The division crossed the Pennsylvania state line at 11:00 A.M. among hurrahs and drumbeats. The men halted at 4:00 P.M. near Hanover. With the battle raging up ahead at Gettysburg, the officers received orders at about 5:00 P.M. to continue the march. Colonel Sweitzer recalled that since his brigade was closest to the road, he assumed that his unit would lead the column. Colonel Vincent, however, ordered his brigade to take a short cut to reach the head of the column. Seeing this attempt to usurp his position, Sweitzer ordered his men to double-quick. So did Vincent. "Then commenced the most exciting little run I ever saw," wrote Sweitzer, whose brigade won the race and remained at the head of the column.[8]

The march continued until 3:30 A.M., when the men were permitted to rest. The column moved out again at 5:00 A.M. The division reached the vicinity of Wolf Hill on July 2, where it halted and deployed "in line of masses, the battalions doubled in the center." The division was deployed, from left to right, as Vincent's Brigade–Sweitzer's Brigade–Tilton's Brigade. Lieutenant Edward Bennett of the 44th New York explained that "the length of time we staid in this position is uncertain, as the 36 hours' march just completed rendered nearly every officer and man indifferent as to time and place." The men did not know that they had actually reached the battlefield at this point. After a short time, Bennett saw a horseman galloping up to General Barnes, and knew what was to come next. Bugles soon sounded the call to "fall in." During its march to support the III Corps that afternoon, the column moved west, then south toward Little Round Top, with Vincent's Brigade in the lead.[9]

General Warren's observations caused Vincent's Brigade to peel off from the column and rush toward Little Round Top while the rest of the division continued toward the Wheatfield. Sweitzer's Brigade arrived first, followed by Tilton's, and both passed through the broken ranks of the III Corps to reach their positions. Barnes was especially concerned about his vulnerable right flank, and when it looked as though it was about to be turned, he pulled both brigades back to safety. According to modern historian Harry Pfanz, Barnes withdrew the two brigades without permission, leading to "insinuations and accusations" even before the battle ended.[10]

Barnes's troubles had not yet ended. A frantic General Caldwell found Barnes and practically begged him to support his beleaguered division, which had entered the Wheatfield. Sweitzer's Brigade was sent back into the maelstrom, where it was hit in front, both flanks, and the rear by a growing host of enemy troops. The brigade miraculously extricated itself, but not before sustaining devastating losses. The division received a measure of redemption when Vincent's Brigade successfully defended Little Round Top.[11]

Despite the fact that Barnes was wounded in the thigh on July 2, the division's permanent commander, General Charles Griffith, refused to assume command when he arrived on the field on July 3. He apparently said, "To you, General Barnes, belongs the honor of the field; you began the battle with the division, and shall fight it to the end." Some of the veterans questioned Barnes's behavior during the battle. One member of Vincent's Brigade wrote: "if he gave an order during the battle to any brigade commander I fail to find a record of it in any account I have read." Others had difficulty finding him during the battle. Some soldiers insinuated that Barnes was drunk during the battle. Except for minor movements, the division held its ground on July 3 and was not engaged. It departed the field on July 5.[12]

1st Brigade—Colonel William Tilton

Units: 18th Massachusetts, 22nd Massachusetts, 1st Michigan, 118th Pennsylvania
Strength: 655
Losses: 125 (12-102-11)—19.1%[13]

With the ascent of General Barnes to temporary division command, the 1st Brigade went to its senior colonel, William Tilton of the 22nd Massachusetts. Tilton served with the 1st Brigade for most of the war up to the Gettysburg campaign, and both saw action at Yorktown and Gaines's Mill. They did not see action at Second Bull Run or Antietam, but were called upon to charge the heights at Fredericksburg. The brigade was in reserve at Chancellorsville. Therefore, Tilton, like his divisional commander, had little experience directing large numbers of men as the Gettysburg campaign began.[14]

When the brigade crossed the Potomac River, there were "ejaculations of Joy at getting off the sacred soil of old Virginia," reported Corporal William Read of the 118th Pennsylvania. Many of the southern Maryland citizens were Confederate sympathizers. This changed as the column reached Frederick, Maryland, on June 28, where "the citizens lined the sidewalks and crowded the windows. The reception was generous and the people demonstrative," an appreciative Private John Smith

wrote after the war. The men's spirits soared as "each Regiment marching, Company front. The colors unfurled & music playing," recalled Chilion Lukens of the 118th Pennsylvania. After the long years in Virginia, the men were impressed by the countryside. "What a delightful Country this is!" Corporal William Read recorded in his diary. "The farms are in a high state of cultivation, the soil good and the houses neat and comfortable and many of them beautiful."[15]

This awe did not stop the men from vandalizing private property. A soldier from the 1st Michigan disgustedly wrote in his diary about the large cherry trees. "The boys break off the limbs instead of picking the cherries. Spoilt all the trees. Not allowed to burn rails but they do it for all that is there is no other wood round here. Must cook and eat."[16]

June 28 also brought word that the soldiers' own corps commander, George Meade, was now commander of the Army of the Potomac. Many were less than enthusiastic. Upon hearing the news, Surgeon Joshua Wilbur wrote his wife, "Meade has commanded our corps and is a perfect old granny. The men all have a supra-comtempts [sic] for him . . . there is only one consolation to draw from it and that is that we have got rid of him as a corps commander." They had earlier heard rumors that beloved General George McClellan had taken command. "The announcement was received with shout and yell and cheer," recalled Smith (118th Pennsylvania). Surgeon Wilbur added that "they gave three cheers, the band played and everyone seemed to feel new life."[17]

The morning of July 1 found the brigade, along with the rest of the division, trudging toward Hanover, Pennsylvania. The church bells rang wildly and civilians joyfully distributed food and water to the men. The column reached the Pennsylvania line at about 1:00 P.M. that afternoon, but the men did not know it at the time. Passing a small house, Lukens asked a "little dutch woman" what state they were in and she sang out, "Adams Co., Pennsylvania." The regiment's colonel rode down the line, ordering the flags to be unfurled and three cheers. The Pennsylvanians responded heartily and were soon joined by the men from the other states. The Corn Exchange Regiment's historian claimed that there "was a firmer step, better closed ranks, more determined countenances."[18]

The men finally reached Hanover at 4:00 P.M. on July 1. They were cheered by the news that they would bivouac there after their long march. Local citizens descended upon the camps, wanting to get a peek at camp life and the ways of the soldier. This abruptly ended at about 6:00 P.M., when the bugle sounded "that almost hated call, 'strike tents,'" and soon after the men were back on the road to Gettysburg. The Federal I and XI Corps had been roughly handled at Gettysburg and the V Corps's presence was sorely needed. Lukens (118th Pennsylvania) wrote home that the moon shone brightly, and at least for a while, the drum corps struck up the tune, "The Girl I Left

Behind Me." The column halted at about 1:30 A.M., and the men quickly fell asleep by the side of the road.[19]

The men were roused a few hours later, between 5:00 and 5:30 A.M. and, after a hasty breakfast, continued their movement west toward Gettysburg. The men expected a resumption of hostilities in the early morning hours, but this was not the case, causing an anonymous soldier from the 1st Michigan to write in his diary, "very quiet and still, don't like that much." The division finally halted when it reached the vicinity of Wolf Hill at about 11:00 A.M. Tilton's Brigade was on the right of the line and was deployed, from left to right, as 22nd Massachusetts–1st Michigan–118th Pennsylvania. The 18th Massachusetts was detached for picket duty and therefore was not with the brigade for most of the day. After a few changes in position, the brigade massed near an orchard where Rock Creek flowed under Baltimore Pike. The men were now able to catch up on their sleep, write letters home, and talk with their comrades. Rock Creek proved to be too tempting for some of the men, and many bathed in its cool waters.[20]

Artillery fire increased after 3:00 P.M., and about ninety minutes later, the men heard the orders to "Fall in, attention, load at will!" They marched by the left flank in an southwesterly direction toward the sound of heavy firing. Because of the arrangement of the brigades during this march, Vincent's Brigade was in the lead, and had the "honor" of being detached to Little Round Top and everlasting glory. Several of Tilton's veterans later bemoaned this turn of fate, which sent their brigade to the Wheatfield and relative future obscurity.[21]

The sounds of battle intensified as the men approached the Wheatfield on Granite Schoolhouse Lane. Along the way they passed horribly mangled wounded men making their way to the rear. It was not a sight for the weak of heart. Turning to the left, the men made their way toward the wooded Stony Hill. On their right and rear was Sweitzer's Brigade, and to their left was de Trobriand's embattled III Corps brigade. Tilton deployed the brigade in the same manner as before, except that the 18th Massachusetts was directly behind the 1st Michigan. Because there were no Federal troops between Stony Hill and the Peach Orchard, the right companies of the 118th Pennsylvania were refused to face the orchard. Sergeant Henry Peck of this regiment thought that the position was "a tolerably good one—a splendid one if approached only on the front."[22]

While the men couldn't see any enemy in front of them, their officers knew that it was just a matter of time before they came under attack. Therefore, strong warnings were issued "to restrain themselves long enough, in case of attack, to permit the skirmishers to retire," recalled Smith (118th Pennsylvania). The left side of the brigade came under attack first by units of Kershaw's Brigade (McLaws's Division), as the skirmishers on this part of the line scampered back to the main line. The enemy closely followed them through the smoke, "moving with a shout, shriek, curse and yell," noted Smith. Some could see that the enemy "were moving obliquely, loading and firing with deliberation as they advanced, begrimed and dirty-looking fellows, in all sorts of garb, some without hats, others without coats, none apparently in the real dress or uniform of a soldier." The men responded with spirited volleys, which halted the Rebel advance. One Michigan soldier simply recorded in his diary, "got a good view of the Rebels and drove them back right quick."[23]

Tilton's men stood erect as they fired at the oncoming enemy troops, rather than seeking cover among the numerous rocks or behind trees. Each stepped back a pace or two to reload, then stepped forward to the firing line again to discharge his weapon. Although the men were achieving success in repelling the attacks by the right wing of Kershaw's Brigade on their front, they were distressed about the South Carolinians's slow, but perceptible movement around their right flank. The men of the 118th Pennsylvania at this end of the line realized that they must either change front or be annihilated. Captain Donaldson noted that "our line wavered, trembled and commenced to give ground." Making matters worse were the sheer numbers of the enemy. "They were so thick that you could shut your eyes and fire and could hit them, and they jumped behind every tree and stump for cover, according to Private Smith of the same regiment.[24]

New to brigade command, Colonel Tilton was also suffering from considerable anxiety. His troops were attacked almost as soon as they took position. Walking along his line, he could see the losses mounting and, according to his report, was "somewhat doubtful if our line could withstand it [the enemy charge]." He quickly sent an aide to communicate these feelings to General Barnes. The aide returned with orders allowing Tilton to "fall back in good order if unable to hold the position." The men had already repelled two enemy charges, and some of his colonels, particularly those on the left, insisted that they be permitted to counterattack. However, Tilton was worried about a flank attack against his right, and when he felt that it was about to be launched, he realized that he could wait no longer. The 118th Pennsylvania was ordered to "Change front to the rear on 10th company, battalion about face, by company right half wheel, march!" A surgeon later commented that most of the wounded he saw were either shot in the side (from the flank attacks) or in the back (during their retreat).[25]

The brigade fell back firing, finally taking position about three hundred yards to the right and rear, near the Trostle house, where it supported Bigelow's battery. As the 1st Michigan approached a low stone wall, the men saw that the 118th Pennsylvania had reformed behind it, waiting for its front to clear before firing into the approaching Confederates of Barksdale's Brigade (McLaws's Division). The enemy was also on Tilton's flanks, and an anonymous soldier from the 1st Michigan wrote, "shot, shell and bullets flying pretty thick here. Men are dropping pretty fast. We are outflanked both right and left and fall back." What really upset the Michigan soldiers was when the 118th Pennsylvania broke "thru' [sic] our ranks and confus[ed] our line." Tilton reported that he ordered his men to fall back to a new position in the Trostle Woods to the right of the Ayres's Division to avoid being flanked again. Seeing General Sykes, he rode up to him for orders. During this latter retreat, Tilton tried to maintain order and reported that he was "greatly embarrassed by squads of men and parts of regiments, who, hurrying from the front, broke into and through my line." While Smith (118th Pennsylvania) generally agreed that the brigade fell back in a fairly organized manner, he admitted that during the retreat from the Trostle house "there were moments when regularity of formation was lost, and loud tones of command and defiant waving of colors indicated vantage grounds and gave assurance of strength and confidence to the hesitating ranks." He was quick to point out, however, that "at no time, though, was there panic or demoralization." Despite the heavy fighting all around

them, Tilton's Brigade remained in Trostle Woods. That night, the men were issued ammunition and went to sleep on their arms, although many helped the wounded, whose cries made resting impossible.[26]

At daylight on July 3 the brigade was shifted to the southern portion of Little Round Top, where it relieved Vincent's Brigade. While the men appreciated the large boulders that provided protection, they were unnerved by the continual sniper fire that took its toll.[27]

The historian of the 118th Pennsylvania recalled the great cannonade that preceded the Pickett–Pettigrew–Trimble charge: "screech, whistle, roar, crash, thug, explosion, so filled the air with inharmonious conflicting noise as to drown the human voice." Many of the men had a good vantage point from which to watch the charge. Smith noted that the enemy's "standards fluttered defiantly, the muskets, at a right-shoulder, glistened brightly . . . there was no crescendo yell, no wild, weird shriek, and the tramp was steady, solemn, silent . . . the Union guns reserved their fire. Then deep, sonorous, rapid, they plied their terrible punishment, and yet, with unflinching nerve and steady grandeur, the formidable charging column pressed right along in the full seep of a resistless energy." When the guns opened, "everything disappeared in the gloom of the impenetrable smoke," he wrote.[28]

July 4 brought no celebrating, as Lee's army was still dangerously poised on Seminary Ridge. About 10:00 A.M. the brigade was ordered forward to "feel and develop the enemy." As they advanced, the men could see the devastation wrought by the two armies. A volley rang out when the unit reached the Wheatfield, indicating that a considerable enemy force was still in front of them. Having fulfilled his mission, Tilton pulled his men back to safety. The brigade began its march after Lee's army at 10:00 A.M. on July 6.[29]

Tilton's Brigade's actions on July 2 were questioned after the war. Some believed that the brigade had pulled back too quickly, thus spelling doom to de Trobriand's defensive line. In explaining his actions on July 2, Colonel Tilton wrote in his report, "I think . . . I saved my brigade from great disaster after it could no longer do any good in front, and succeeded in forming a new line, which was retained through the night." Obviously, only those who were on Stony Hill that afternoon know the real truth.[30]

2nd Brigade—Colonel Jacob Sweitzer

Units: 9th Massachusetts, 32nd Massachusetts, 4th Michigan, 62nd Pennsylvania
Strength: 1423
Losses: 427 (67-239-121)—30.0%[31]

Unlike Colonel Tilton, Colonel Jacob Sweitzer had commanded a brigade prior to Gettysburg. Sweitzer's first fighting experience was as lieutenant colonel of the 62nd Pennsylvania. He was present at Yorktown and Gaines's Mill. Badly wounded at the later battle, he missed the rest of the Seven Days campaign and Second Bull Run, but was back by the Antietam campaign. He was in command of the 62nd Pennsylvania during the campaign, but the brigade did not see any action. He led the brigade during its ill-fated charge up Marye's Hill at Fredericksburg, losing 222 men in the process. He relinquished command of the brigade when the senior colonel returned, but assumed command again at Chancellorsville, although the unit was not engaged.[32]

Sweitzer's men were welcomed with open arms by the citizens as they marched through northern Maryland and southern Pennsylvania. Sergeant James Houghton of the 4th Michigan recalled that as the men trudged through Unionville, Maryland, "we kept step by the beat of the drums. The ladies and children were on the porches waving the Stars and Stripes and singing the Star Spangled Banner . . . this made us forget our tired limbs and sore feet for a while." Upon reaching Pennsylvania, the brigade halted and the commanders gave short speeches. For example, Colonel Harrison Jeffords of the 4th Michigan told his men that "you are now standing on free soil once more and now give three cheers for the free states." The men gladly responded at the tops of their lungs.[33]

Sometimes the citizens' welcome was silent. "The farmers and countrymen hanging on fences along our line of march gazed at our ranks in open-mouthed silence. Here and there we received a word of welcome, and grins of satisfaction were visible as they viewed our seemingly interminable columns of infantry," noted Sergeant Daniel MacNamara of the 9th Massachusetts. The citizens frequently distributed water and food as the men passed.[34]

Rumors abounded. One of the more pervasive was that Hooker had been replaced by beloved General George McClellan. "Instantly the space was filled with the hats and caps of the gratified soldiers. They shouted and hollered, and kicked up their heels, and were frisky with the supposed good news," recalled Sergeant Oruey Barrett of the 4th Michigan.[35]

The brigade, with the rest of the division, reached Hanover at about 5:00 P.M. on July 1, where the men were permitted to rest and eat. They could see the aftermath of the recent cavalry fight all around them. Most of the men realized they would be pushed on, as the sounds of battle could be clearly heard up ahead. Sure enough, at 8:00 P.M. the men were on the road again. The column finally halted at midnight near Bonaughtown, about four or five miles from the battlefield. Campfires soon blazed, for while the men were exhausted, they were not about to forego their coffee. They had trouble sleeping that night, not only because of the anticipation of battle, but because of "the arival [sic] of other troops coming in and taking their positions. The heavy tred [sic] of infantry the ratling [sic] of canteens and the command of officers was herd [sic] all night," reported Houghton (4th Michigan).[36]

The men were up again between 3:00 and 3:30 A.M. on July 2. After preparing breakfast, they cleaned their muskets and drew additional ammunition. The column moved out at about 6:00 A.M. and arrived on the battlefield three hours later. After resting along the right of Hanover Road, south of Wolf Hill and the XII Corps, the division marched to the left (south). It massed in a field near a stone bridge where Baltimore Pike intersected Rock Creek. While the men rested here, John Patton of the 62nd Pennsylvania noted that he "saw signs of something going on. Orderlies & aids [sic] began running in every direction, every one was up watching with deep interest every rider that came along & the movements of every General." A bugle call sounded, and within five minutes the men were hurrying southward toward Little Round Top. General Barnes rode up to the 4th Michigan and told the men, "Boys, I want you to put in a few licks for Pennsylvania; the

Bucktails [62nd Pennsylvania] will go in on your left. Forward."[37]

The brigade was already weakened, as the 9th Massachusetts had been detached to perform picket duty on Brinkerhoff Ridge near Hanover Road. The 32nd Massachusetts had originally been assigned this duty, but its commanding officer, Colonel George Prescott, complained to Sweitzer that his regiment was inexperienced and suggested that a more experienced regiment be assigned in its place. Sweitzer agreed, and the 9th Massachusetts was soon in motion.[38]

The remainder of Sweitzer's Brigade formed on the west side of Stony Hill, facing the Peach Orchard to the northwest. In front of it was an open field. The brigade was at right angles to Wheatfield Road on their right and de Trobriand's Brigade (Birney's Division, III Corps) and Tilton's Brigade on their left. The brigade was initially arranged, from left to right, as 32nd Massachusetts–62nd Pennsylvania–4th Michigan. However, Sweitzer did not like the low, open position of the 32nd Massachusetts and its exposed left flank, so he refused it at right angles to the rest of the brigade. It now faced southwest, bringing it in line with the left of Tilton's Brigade.[39]

The men were not in position long before Kershaw's Brigade attacked Tilton's and de Trobriand's Brigades. The 32nd Massachusetts was already facing this direction and, according to Francis Parker, "we were hardly established in our position, such as it was, before the attack came, the enemy piling down in great numbers from the opposite slope and covering themselves partially under the hither bank of the little stream." Seeing no enemy troops in front of the rest of the brigade, Sweitzer gave orders for them to change direction, and soon the 62nd Pennsylvania and 4th Michigan were in a supporting position behind the 32nd Massachusetts. General Barnes was apparently not optimistic about his men's ability to hold their ground, so he sent Sweitzer a message explaining the retreat route, should it be needed. This information was communicated to Colonel George Prescott of the 32nd Massachusetts, who thought he was to immediately withdraw. "I don't want to retire; I am not ready to retire; I can hold this place," he exclaimed. Prescott was relieved when the order was subsequently clarified, and his men continued to fire at the enemy.[40]

The initial volleys effectively halted Kershaw's Brigade's (Hood's Division) in its tracks. Sweitzer later termed his position "elegant," and he felt that "the old Second could have held it against considerable odds 'till the cows came home."' He believed that the only way that the Confederates could get him off Stony Hill was to flank his position, and that's just what happened. When the pressure on Tilton's Brigade on the right became too strong to resist, it was pulled back toward Wheatfield Road. This exposed Sweitzer's Brigade's right flank. Barnes gave Sweitzer orders to pull back, which he did by marching his men out by the left flank. Sweitzer probably exaggerated when he recalled after the war that his men "came back in as good order and with no more confusion than if on drill." The brigade ultimately took position along Wheatfield Road. Stray shots were still finding their mark, so the officers ordered the men to lie down along the road. Caldwell's Division (II Corps) soon arrived and passed over them to engage the victorious Confederates. While there is some evidence that Sweitzer's men threw Zook's Brigade's ranks into some disorder, some of the veterans recalled that Sweitzer's men yelled encouragement as they moved into the Wheatfield.[41]

The men could hear the small arms fire flare up in front of them, as Caldwell's men engaged the victorious Confederates and drove them out of the Wheatfield. After what seemed to be about fifteen minutes, Caldwell apparently rode up to Sweitzer in great haste with news that his brigades were "driving the enemy like hell over yonder in the woods . . . and asked if I [Sweitzer] would give him . . . support." Sweitzer directed Caldwell to General Barnes. According to Sweitzer, Barnes soon approached him and "asked me if I would take the brigade in." Sweitzer told him that he would, "if he wished me to do so." Barnes indicated that he did, and soon the men were called to attention. Barnes moved to the front of the brigade and made a few patriotic remarks, and the men responded with cheers.[42]

The tide of battle was turning as Confederate reinforcements forced Caldwell's men from the Wheatfield. Sweitzer's Brigade stepped smartly into the Wheatfield, hoping for better fortune than when it had last ventured forward. Captain W. J. Patterson of the 62nd Pennsylvania recalled that as the men advanced, a "straggling line came back through our ranks" as Caldwell's men retreated to safety. The brigade continued into the Wheatfield in the same arrangement as before: the 32nd Massachusetts was on the left, the 4th Michigan was on the right, and the 62nd Pennsylvania was in the center. The thousand-man man brigade probably extended for three hundred yards from flank to flank, stretching across most of the Wheatfield.[43]

After Zook's troops fled past them, the 4th Michigan was exposed to a deadly flank fire. Sweitzer believed this fire was from "our troops aimed over us at the enemy in the woods beyond and falling short." The unit's flag bearer suddenly shouted, "Colonel, I'll be _____ if I don't think we are faced the wrong way; the rebs are up there in the woods behind us, on the right." Through the din of battle Houghton heard the "rattling of canteens and a heavy tread of infantry . . . in our rear, observing a little closer, we saw that they wore the gray uniform and were not over 10 rods distant. They were on double quick passing through the woods out into the wheat field east of us." These were Georgians from Wofford's Brigade, who had already crushed Zook's Brigade's right flank and now were about to do the same to Sweitzer's.[44]

Sweitzer immediately ordered the 4th Michigan to face right to take on this new threat, and within moments he ordered the 62nd Pennsylvania to do the same where they took on Kershaw's Brigade. At about the same time, Sweitzer dispatched an aide to find Barnes for immediate help. The aide, Lieutenant John Seitz, went to the place he had last seen Barnes, but found enemy infantry instead. His horse was killed and Seitz barely avoided capture. He raced back to Sweitzer on foot with the news that the Confederates were in his rear. Realizing that there was little more he could do, Sweitzer immediately ordered his men to fall back, which he said "was done in order, the command halting and firing as it retired." Sweitzer did not know it at the time, but his three small regiments were up against four Confederate brigades (Anderson's, Kershaw's, Semmes's, and Wofford's). It was not uncommon to now see hand-to-hand combat between Confederate soldiers and members of the 62nd Pennsylvania and 4th Michigan. Seeing his flag captured, Colonel Harrison Jeffords of the latter regiment ran back to retrieve it. During the resulting melee, he was bayoneted and later died.[45]

Realizing that he could not fall back the way he had come, Sweitzer ordered his men to retire diagonally across the Wheatfield, toward its eastern corner. Corporal Oscar West of the 32nd Massachusetts recalled the order as, "Left face, and every man get out of this the best way he can." Because the enemy had almost completely surrounded the brigade, losses to the 4nd Michigan and 62nd Pennsylvania were high, over 40%, and many men were captured. Houghton related that as the men of the 4th Michigan ran the gauntlet, "the crash came—a storm of lead swep [sic] through our ranks like hail. Many of our noble boys fell to the ground."[46]

The remnant of the brigade formed on the right of Tilton's Brigade, just north of the J. Weikert farm, where it spent the remainder of the battle. The 9th Massachusetts, which had been skirmishing with the 2nd Virginia (Walker's Brigade, Johnson's Division), rejoined the brigade shortly after it had reached this position. The brigade was not involved in repelling the grand charge on July 3, but was exposed to the heavy cannonade that preceded it. "The whole line was ablaze. Firing was incessant. Salvos after salvos, of artillery belched forth. The air was full of flying missiles—death everywhere," recalled Barrett (4th Michigan).[47]

According to Sweitzer, General Barnes could not be found during the evening of July 2, so he took command of the division. He remained in command until the early hours of July 3, when Barnes suddenly reappeared. The men rested and buried the dead on July 4 and most of July 5. The brigade left the battlefield that evening.[48]

The brigade fought valiantly in the Wheatfield on July 2. While its first foray into the Wheatfield was understandable from a command point of view, the second was less so. Why General Barnes thought that three regiments could stem the Confederate tide when Caldwell's full division was unable to do so is unclear. Sweitzer heard after the battle that when Barnes saw the enemy on the brigade's flank and rear, he commented to his aides that he might as well say "good-bye to the Second Brigade." No troops could have survived that maelstrom, and it is a wonder that the brigade was not annihilated. Indeed, Colonel Patrick Guiney of the 9th Massa-chusetts wrote after the war that "when we arrived at Colonel Sweitzer's Head Quarters, we could scarcely be said to *join* the Brigade; it seemed to me that it would be more appropriate to say that we *constituted* the Brigade. There were the flags of regiments, a remnant of a splendid regiment around each."[49]

3rd Brigade—Colonel Strong Vincent

Units: 20th Maine, 16th Michigan, 44th New York, 83rd Pennsylvania
Strength: 1336
Losses: 352 (88-253-11)—26.3%[50]

Organized in May 1862, and initially commanded by General Daniel Butterfield, the 3rd Brigade originally contained six regiments. However, considerable changes occurred a year later. The terms of enlistment of two of the regiments expired and they went home, leaving the brigade with only four. Equally disturbing to the men was the fact that they had received yet another commander. This time it was Colonel Strong Vincent of the 83rd Pennsylvania. True to his name, he had a strong physique and personality and was well respected by his men. He had, however, no experience commanding a brigade.[51]

The march on July 1 was one that the men would never forget. Beginning at about 9:00 A.M., the brigade reached the Pennsylvania state line at about 2:00 P.M. Colonel Vincent told his officers that a suitable display would be appropriate to buoy the men's spirits. Colonel Amos Judson of the 83rd Pennsylvania caught the scene:

> The drum corps struck up our thrilling old national air of Yankee Doodle, and as the glorious old banner, shattered and rent by the shocks of a dozen battle fields, floated once more proudly upon

the inspiring breezes of the old Keystone State, long and loud shouts of joy from ten thousand iron throats broke upon the morning air. The enthusiasm was contagious. In a few moments it had spread from regiment to regiment, and from brigade to brigade, until every banner was flying, every fife screaming, and every drum beating.[52]

Private Alfred Apted of the 16th Michigan was less dramatic, recording in his diary, "drums beating and flags flying." Vincent's idea was a success, as evidenced by Private John Berry's diary entry for the day: "we march in better spirits. Although footsore and wornout with the late long marches & want of natural rest—we hurry along singing . . . as if we were in a pleasure excursion. At the head of the regiment marches the . . . drum corps . . . the musicians do all they can to impart cheerfulness among themselves and the soldiers by singing patriotic songs, as we pass through each village & farm." Civilians along the route freely gave of their food and good cheer. Berry noted that "as we pass through this country the people welcome us with the greatest enthusiasm, all turning out & many is the 'hurrah for the Union and God bless the Army of the Potomac.'"[53]

The brigade reached Hanover at about 3:00 P.M. on July 1, and Vincent again ordered the fife and drum corps of the 83rd Pennsylvania to play and had the flags unsheathed. Keenly watching his men march by, Vincent exclaimed, "What death more glorious can any man desire than to die on the soil of old Pennsylvania fighting for that flag?" The men were permitted to break ranks and rest, and soon the aroma of coffee filled the area. Many thought they would spend the night there, so they prepared their bedrolls. Hardly had they received their rations when they heard orders to return to the ranks and continue the march. Colonel Joshua Chamberlain of the 20th Maine recalled that his men moved out with "promptitude and spirit extraordinary, the cheers and welcome they received on the road added to their enthusiasm." Private Seth Ward of the 83rd Pennsylvania recorded in his diary how "the people bringing water to us on the march and evry [sic] where showing signs of patriotism . . . we passed many towns last night and were evry [sic] where greeted with cheers and demonstrations of joy." As the march continued well into the night, some of the men's positive feelings were replaced by negative ones. Lieutenant Ziba Graham of the 16th Michigan noted that the "animation of our march of the forenoon . . . in the darkness of the night seemed to have been lost, in our tired condition. Confidence seemed to be lacking, and hope seemed to have almost forsaken us . . . we were fearful." The twenty-two-mile march finally ended at 1:00 A.M. on July 2.[54]

The men were awakened at 5:00 A.M. and told to prepare their guns for inspection. One soldier in the 44th New York noted that "the captain told us he did not care for the outside but wanted the inside of the gun to be all right." The men knew that they were in for a fight and the typical gloom fell over them. The march contin-

ued and the brigade reached Powers Hill at 7:00 A.M., where the men were permitted to prepare breakfast. The brigade initially remained massed with the rest of the division along the west side of Taneytown Road, but was later moved several times to the left (south). Private John Berry of the 16th Michigan complained that he "spent the whole forenoon manuvering [sic] & marching around." Because a battle was imminent, the men were kept in some semblance of line of battle. Many men stripped off their clothes to deal with "greybacks" (body lice) during the wait. Others made coffee and wrote letters home. Colonel Vincent was heard to announce that "Today will either bring me my stars or finish my career as a soldier."[55]

When the left of the Federal line came under attack at 4:00 P.M., Barnes was ordered to move his division to the front. Theodore Gerrish of the 20th Maine recalled that the orders were to "Fall in! Fall in! By the right flank! Double quick! March!" Vincent's brigade led the column toward the Wheatfield. Unbeknownst to the men, General Gouverneur Warren was watching the approaching Confederate troops from his undefended perch on Little Round Top. Realizing that this vital hill was the key to the Union line, Warren cast about for immediate help. Finding General George Sykes of the V Corps nearby, Warren quickly explain the situation and requested immediate assistance. Sykes readily understood the situation, and sent an aide to find General Barnes with orders to move a brigade to the hill.[56]

The brigade halted near the George Weikert house and awaited orders. Vincent saw an orderly galloping in his direction, and hailed him. "Captain, what are your orders" he asked. The aide had his own question: "Where is General Barnes?" According to Private Oliver Norton, an aide to Vincent, Barnes should have been at the head of the column, but was nowhere to be found. Knowing this, and sensing that the aide brought critical orders, Vincent again asked, "What are your orders? Give me your orders!" The aide finally relented, blurting out, "Genl. Sykes directs Genl. Barnes to send a brigade of his division to occupy that hill, yonder," pointing behind him, toward Little Round Top. Norton recalled that Vincent immediately said, "I will take responsibility myself for taking my brigade there."[57]

Upon making the decision to move his brigade to Little Round Top, Colonel Vincent turned to Colonel James Rice of the 44th New York, which was leading the column, and said, "Colonel, bring the brigade as quickly as possible on to that hill. Double quick where the ground will permit." With that, he sent two of his aides down the line to repeat this command to the other regiments, and he galloped off to Little Round Top.[58]

Norton followed Vincent up the side of Little Round Top, carrying the brigade flag. Upon reaching the top, Vincent met General Warren, who pointed at the approaching enemy troops and said, "Hold this point at all hazards, if you sacrifice every man of the 3rd Brigade. I will bring you re-inforcements." Shells suddenly began bursting around them in quick succession. Vincent turned to Norton and yelled, "They are firing at the flag. Go behind the rocks with it." The brigade soon arrived in column of fours. Initially approaching from the north of Little Round Top, the brigade circled around to its less imposing east face before climbing it. Vincent eagerly awaited his brigade's arrival and positioned the regiments as they arrived. Upon being shown his position on the right of the line, Colonel Rice told Vincent, "Colonel, in every battle the 44th

has always fought by the side of the 83d [Pennsylvania]. I wish it might be so today." Nodding, Vincent said, "It shall be. Let the 16th [Michigan] pass you." Therefore, the brigade was arranged, from left to right, as 20th Maine–83rd Pennsylvania–44th New York–16th Michigan. Knowing the desperateness of the situation, the noncombatants of the 83rd Pennsylvania grabbed muskets and joined their comrades.[59]

The men took position behind whatever cover they could find, which was usually behind the abundant large rocks. Lieutenant Charles Salter of the 16th Michigan noted that "as we arrived on top, [we] saw a long line of rebels coming over and down a range of hills opposite us. If we had been 5 minutes later, the enemy would have gained the ridge we were on." Colonel Joshua Chamberlain added that "the enemy's artillery got range of our column as we were climbing the spur, and the crashing of the shells among the rocks and the tree tops made us move lively along the crest. One or two shells burst in our ranks." A few men also fell from the small arms fire being directed at the hill. Scarcely had the men had time to settle into their new position, when the 4th and 5th Texas of Robertson's Brigade (Hood's Division) and 4th Alabama of Law's Brigade launched their first attack from the west. Lieutenant Colonel Freeman Conner of the 44th New York noted that the enemy came within forty yards of his line. "A sheet of smoke and flame burst from our whole line, which made the enemy reel and stagger, and fall back in confusion," wrote Judson (83rd Pennsylvania). The attacks were folly, and the three regiments were easily repulsed. The Confederates made another attack, and it too was repulsed. It appears that the first attack hit the 44th New York and 83rd Pennsylvania and the second one spread to the right, including the 16th Michigan in the maelstrom. Medal of Honor recipient Edward Hill characterized the desperate fighting as "teeth-a-set and hand to throat."[60]

Joined by the 48th Alabama from Law's Brigade, the Confederates attacked a third time. This time it was different. After the men of the 44th New York repelled the 5th Texas in its front, they turned to their right and poured an oblique fire into the 4th Texas and 48th Alabama that were assaulting the 16th Michigan. Private W. W. Colestock recalled that there was no semblance of a line of battle because of the terrain, so the men took refuge between rocks and trees. The men could see the right side of the 16th Michigan's line giving way. Some historians believed it was the Confederate pressure on that part of the line. Others, like Lieutenant Colonel Norval Welch, believed it was because of a mistaken order. "Some one (supposed to be General Weed or Major-General Sykes) called from the extreme crest of the hill to fall back nearer the top, where a much less exposed line could be taken up." Welch observed that most of the men ignored this order. However, Lieutenant William Kydd obeyed the order and sent the colors to the rear. "None left with them, however, but three of the color-guard." Welch was wrong, as over a third of the regiment followed the colors.[61]

Vincent dashed over when he saw his line about to crumble. He carried his wife's riding crop, as his sword was still hitched to his horse. Mounting a large rock, Vincent yelled, "Don't give an inch, boys, don't give an inch!" He probably used more direct words along with his whip to restore the line. A shot rang out, and Vincent fell with a mortal wound to the groin. Vincent purportedly muttered as he was being carried away, "This is the

fourth or fifth time they have shot at me and they have hit me at last." As the Alabama and Texas troops surged toward the summit of Little Round Top, it looked as though the hill would be lost. However, the 140th New York of Weed's Brigade (Ayres's Division, V Corps) arrived just in time to staunch the tide. The 44th New York also poured an oblique fire from the left, which helped dissipate the Confederate charge.[62]

In noting the intensity of the fighting, Lieutenant Charles Salter of the 16th Michigan wrote, "although we had been engaged in other battles . . . we never had such a terrible, close bayonet fight before. It seemed as if every man, on both sides, was activated by the intensest [sic] hate, and determined to kill as many of the enemy as possible."[63]

The men were cheered by the arrival of Lieutenant Charles Hazlett's battery on the hill. Captain Eugene Nash of the 44th New York recalled that, when the cannon opened fire on the surging Confederate troops, "no military music ever sounded sweeter and no aid was ever better appreciated." When the din of battle subsided somewhat, the New Yorkers lustily cheered the cannoneers.[64]

The time was about 6:00 P.M. After their frequent repulses, the Texans and Alabamians were content to fall back and snipe at Vincent's troops on Little Round Top. Colonel James Rice was now in command of the brigade. To its right stood Weed's Brigade. The threat to this sector had now ended.[65]

However, the battle for Little Round Top was far from over. Over to the left, Colonel Joshua Chamberlain was still attempting to cope with the attacks being made on his front. In positioning the regiment on a "spur" facing south, at almost right angles to the rest of the brigade, Vincent made it very clear to Chamberlain that his unit was the left-most regiment on the Army of the Potomac's line, and could expect an attack. Chamberlain recalled that Vincent told him that "I was to 'hold that ground at all hazards,'" Chamberlain recalled. These were the last words ever exchanged between them.[66]

Chamberlain did not like what he saw around him. In front of him was the "saddle" between Little Round Top and Big Round Top. The ground, in Chamberlain's words, was "rough, rocky, and stragglingly [sic] wooded." The men also despaired over the heavy cannon fire that raked their position. "Shells were crashing through the air above our heads, making so much noise that we could hardly hear the commands of our officers. The air was filled with fragments of exploding shells and splinters torn from mangled trees," recalled Private Gerrish. After forming on the spur of Little Round Top, Chamberlain detached Captain Walter Morrill's Company B and sent it to the left. He was given the latitude to "act as occasion might dictate, to prevent a surprise on my exposed flank and rear."[67]

The 47th Alabama (Law's Brigade) broke out of the woods in the "saddle" almost as soon as Chamberlain completed his depositions, and assaulted the center and right flank of the 20th Maine. Eventually, the entire regiment opened fire on the approaching Alabamians. The fighting was occasionally hand-to-hand, when many Confederates reached the Union position.[68]

While the fight with the 47th Alabama was raging, an officer from the 20th Maine's center company ran up to Chamberlain with news that a considerable enemy force had arrived and threatened his left flank and rear. Captain Ellis Spear first saw the new arrivals' legs through the underbrush. With no reinforcements available, Chamberlain had no choice but to extend his left flank so the regiment occupied a position approximately double its original length. Where there was natural cover the companies were arranged in a single line. Chamberlain also refused his left flank, so that it lay at right angles to the rest of the regiment. Five of his companies now faced southeast, four faced southwest, and one, Company B, was to the left.[69]

This new force, the 15th Alabama, continued forward, apparently not realizing that Chamberlain had extended his line to the left. When the Alabamians were at close range, the Federal line suddenly erupted in a blaze of fire. This staggered the Confederate line and then stopped it, and enemy soldiers could be seen withdrawing. The Maine men did not have long to celebrate for, in the words of Chamberlain, the enemy "burst forth again with a shout, and rapidly advanced, firing as they came. They pushed up to within a dozen yards of us before the terrible effectiveness of our fire compelled them to break and take shelter." So desperate was the situation that the regiment's flag bearer, Sergeant Andrew Tozier, picked up a musket and continually fired it while holding the colors in the crook of his arm.[70]

The two sides continued to battle for over an hour. "Squads of the enemy broke through our line in several places, and the engagement was literally hand to hand," recalled Chamberlain. He characterized the fight as being like ocean waves, rolling back and forth. Several times his men were forced back, only to surge forward again to reclaim their original positions. As ammunition began to give out, the men rummaged through the cartridge boxes of their fallen comrades. Some of Chamberlain's men also discarded their Enfield muskets in favor of the Springfields laying nearby.[71]

Chamberlain reformed his line as the enemy retreated yet again. He was growing increasingly concerned about his depleted numbers and questioned whether his regiment could sustain another determined attack. The enemy suddenly emerged from the woods again. Chamberlain's men immediately opened fire, but the Confederate charge seemed to be irresistible. Many of his men were down to their last cartridge, and others had none. Many of the latter changed the grip on their muskets so they could use them as clubs.[72]

It was now or never, and Chamberlain yelled for his men to fix bayonets. In the words of Chamberlain,

> The word was enough. It ran like fire along the line, from man to man, and rose into a shout, with which they sprang forward upon the enemy, now not 30 yards away. The effect was surprising; many of the enemy's first line threw down their arms and surrendered . . . Holding fast by our right, and swinging forward our left, we made an extended 'right wheel,' before which the enemy's second line broke and fell back, fighting from tree to tree, many being captured, until we had swept the valley and cleared the front of nearly our entire brigade.[73]

As the enemy broke in confusion, Captain Morrill and his Company B, along with some men from the 2nd U.S. Sharpshooters, opened fire, creating even more havoc. They also captured scores of Alabamians.[74]

Realizing the vulnerability of his exposed position, Chamberlain quickly ordered his men back to the spur. It was at this point that Colonel Rice arrived on the left to confer with Chamberlain. Rice brought news of Vincent's fall and expressed concerns about Big Round Top, which seemed to be teeming with Confederates, who were sniping at the Union soldiers on Little Round Top. Rice indicated that Colonel James Fisher's Brigade (Crawford's Division) had been ordered to clear Big Round Top, much to the relief of Chamberlain. As 9:00 P.M. approached, and Fisher's men had still not claimed the hill, Rice became more apprehensive. Feeling that he could wait no longer, he approached Chamberlain, whose depleted regiment was closest to the large hill. "Col. will you do it?" Rice asked. Despite the fact that his men's ammunition had not been replenished, Chamberlain decided to take the hill.[75]

Walking over to his color guard, Chamberlain called for volunteers. "I am going, the colors will follow me. As many of my men as feel able to do so can follow us." To Chamberlain's relief, every man sprang to his feet, subjugating the exhaustion they felt after the long day. The regiment began its ascent at about 9:00 P.M. with bayonets fixed. The ground was rugged, with large rocks often barring their paths. Many tripped on unseen rocks and tangled vegetation. To make matters worse, the men could hear squads of the enemy falling back before them. All expected a shattering volley to break the evening calm. When it did come, several of Chamberlain's men fell. The weakened unit doggedly moved up the hill, scooping up about twenty enemy soldiers in the process.[76]

Deploying his men behind rocks at the summit of Big Round Top, Chamberlain prepared his men for the night. Not knowing what was on the opposite side of the hill, Chamberlain sent a picket line down to explore. The squad saw Confederate campfires up ahead, and worse, a group of the enemy from the 4th Texas, which they captured and sent up the hill. Not seeing Fisher's Brigade, Chamberlain sent a messenger to Colonel Rice for aid, and received the 83rd Pennsylvania.[77]

As dawn approached, Vincent's Brigade continued its lonely vigil on the summits of Little and Big Round Tops. Snipers at Devil's Den continued to make the men's lives miserable on Little Round Top. At about 9:00 A.M., Tilton's Brigade arrived to relieve Vincent's weary men. The men now received orders to move to the right to occupy their old positions, about a third of a mile to the north. The 20th Maine and 83rd Pennsylvania on Big Round Top did not leave their positions until about noon. When the brigade was reunited to the east of Cemetery Ridge, the line was arranged, from left to right, as 16th Michigan–44th New York–83rd Pennsylvania–20th Maine. Within a short time, the men found themselves in the teeth of the Confederate cannonade that preceded the Pickett–Pettigrew–Trimble charge. Judson (83rd Pennsylvania) recorded that "hundreds of the enemy's shells which failed to explode, flew shrieking through the skies . . . those striking nearer would plow a huge furrow in the ground, and then ricochetting and leaping upward to the height of a hundred feet, could be seen whirling away." Losses were exceptionally small because the brigade took refuge behind the abundant stone walls. Some of the men strengthened the walls with added materials.[78]

The brigade remained there until about noon on July 4, when it was thrown forward on a reconnaissance to ascertain the enemy's position. Not finding any, the brigade returned to Little Round Top, where it helped bury the dead. Their own dead were laid in individual graves, each marked with a headboard fashioned from cartridge boxes, which bore the unfortunate soldier's name. The enemy dead were buried in long trenches. The men also constructed breastworks. Many threw away their Enfield muskets and replaced them with Springfields that were laying around in abundance throughout the battlefield. The march after Lee's army began at about 5:00 P.M. on July 5.[79]

Vincent's Brigade made a lasting name for itself on Little Round Top. However, Lieutenant Charles Salter of the 16th Michigan could not know this when he wrote to a friend on July 12, 1863. "All the papers that I have seen yet seem to lay the blame of our former defeats to our former generals, and give the credit of the victory to General Meade. But our army knows this to be not the true state of affairs for we will fight better in Pennsylvania and Maryland than we will in Virginia . . . the rebels they fight better in Virginia than they do here . . . we are not fighting for generals, but for our country."[80]

NOTES

1. Dyer, *Compendium*, 301; John J. Hennessy, *Return to Bull Run* (New York, 1993), 464–465.

2. OR 27, 1, 592, 599–600; Eugene A. Nash, *A History of the 44th New York Infantry* (Chicago, 1911), 140–141; W. H. Sanderson, "Sykes's Regulars," *National Tribune*, April 2, 1891.

3. John L. Smith, *History of the 118th Pennsylvania Volunteers, Corn Exchange Regiment* (Philadelphia, 1909), 238.

4. OR 27, 1, 593, 600.

5. OR 27, 1, 593.

6. Warner, *Generals in Blue*, 20; Tagg, *Generals of Gettysburg*, 83–84.

7. Gregory Acken, *Inside the Army of the Potomac* (Mechanicsburg, PA, 1998), 289, 293.

8. OR suppl., 5, 189; Acken, *Inside the Army of the Potomac*, 294–295.

9. Acken, *Inside the Army of the Potomac*, 297–298; Edward Bennett, "The Battle as Seen by a Member of the 44th N.Y.," *National Tribune*, May 6, 1886; Smith, *History of the 118th Pennsylvania Volunteers, Corn Exchange Regiment*, 238; Edward J. Merrill, scrapbook, copy in 44th New York folder, GNMP; OR 27, 1, 610.

10. Pfanz, *Gettysburg—The Second Day*, 260–262.

11. OR 27, 1, 601–602.

12. OR 27, 1, 494; Tagg, *Generals of Gettysburg*, 84; James H. Nevins and William B. Styple, *What Death More Glorious* (Kearney, NJ, 1997), 72.

13. Busey and Martin, *Regimental Strengths and Losses*, 59, 247.

14. Tagg, *Generals of Gettysburg*, 86.

15. William Read, diary, copy in the 118th Pennsylvania folder, GNMP; Smith, *History of the 118th Pennsylvania Volunteers, Corn Exchange Regiment*, 232; Chilion Lukens, letter, Duke University.

16. Unidentified, diary, copy in the 1st Michigan folder, GNMP.

17. Joshua Wilbur, letter, Civil War Misc. Collection, USAMHI; Smith, *History of the 118th Pennsylvania Volunteers, Corn Exchange Regiment*, 237.

18. Lukens, letter; Smith, *History of the 118th Pennsylvania Volunteers, Corn Exchange Regiment*, 235.

19. Henry T. Peck, letter, copy in the Brake Collection, USAMHI; Lukens, letter; unidentified, diary; Wilfred McDonald, diary, University of Texas Library.

When the brigade halted for the night is disputed. Some veterans recalled that it was around midnight (John L. Parker, *Henry Wilson's Regiment: History of the Twenty-second Regiment, Massachusetts Infantry* [Boston, 1887], 277); others believed it was 1:00 or 1:30 A.M. (see above); and still others recalled it to be around 3:30 A.M. (Henry T. Peck, *Historical Sketch of the 118th Regiment Pennsylvania Volunteers* [n.p., 1884], 203; Smith, *History of the 118th Pennsylvania Volunteers, Corn Exchange Regiment*, 237).

20. Lukens, letter; Parker, *Henry Wilson's Regiment: History of the Twenty-second Regiment, Massachusetts Infantry*, 277; Tagg, *The Generals of Gettysburg*, 86; unidentified, diary; Smith, *History of the 118th Pennsylvania Volunteers, Corn Exchange Regiment*, 238–239.

21. Smith, *History of the 118th Pennsylvania Volunteers, Corn Exchange Regiment*, 240.

22. Smith, *History of the 118th Pennsylvania Volunteers, Corn Exchange Regiment*, 242;

23. Smith, *History of the 118th Pennsylvania Volunteers, Corn Exchange Regiment*, 244; unidentified, diary.

According to Imhof's maps (*Gettysburg—Day Two*, 82, 85–86), these attacks appear to have been made by the right flank of Kershaw's Brigade (McLaw's Division) and the left of Anderson's (Hood's Division).

24. Smith, *History of the 118th Pennsylvania Volunteers, Corn Exchange Regiment*, 244–245; Peck, letter; Acken, *Inside the Army of the Potomac*, 304; John L. Smith, letter, Historical Society of Pennsylvania.

25. OR 27, 1, 607; Smith, *History of the 118th Pennsylvania Volunteers, Corn Exchange Regiment*, 245; Wilbur, letter.

26. Smith, *History of the 118th Pennsylvania Volunteers, Corn Exchange Regiment*, 245, 251; OR 27, 1, 607–608; unidentified, diary; McDonald, diary.

27. Unidentified, diary; Smith, *History of the 118th Pennsylvania Volunteers, Corn Exchange Regiment*, 254, 263.

28. Smith, *History of the 118th Pennsylvania Volunteers, Corn Exchange Regiment*, 258, 260.

29. Smith, *History of the 118th Pennsylvania Volunteers, Corn Exchange Regiment*, 262; Parker, *Henry Wilson's Regiment: History of the Twenty-second Regiment, Massachusetts Infantry*, 277; Peck, letter; unidentified, diary.

30. Styple, *Our Noble Blood*, 125; OR 27, 1, 608.

31. Busey and Martin, *Regimental Strengths and Losses*, 60, 248.

32. Dyer, *Compendium*, 30; Tagg, *Generals of Gettysburg*, 87–88.

33. James Houghton, journal, Bentley Library, University of Michigan.

34. Daniel G. Macnamara, *The History of the Ninth Regiment, Massachusetts Volunteer Infantry . . .* (Boston, 1899), 314; O. S. Barrett, *Reminiscences, Incidents, and Battles of the Old Fourth Michigan Infantry in the War of the Rebellion* (Detroit, MI, 1888), 21.

35. Barrett, *Reminiscences, Incidents, and Battles of the Old Fourth Michigan Infantry in the War of the Rebellion*, 21–22.

36. *PAG*, vol. 1, 382; Macnamara, *The History of the Ninth Regiment, Massachusetts Volunteer Infantry . . .*, 314–315; Lieutenant Robert Campbell, "Account," copy in Brake Collection, USAMHI; Houghton, journal.

37. John Milton Bancroft, diary, copy in Brake Collection, USAMHI; Oscar W. West, "On Little Round Top—The Fifth Corps' Fight at Gettysburg—Particularly the 32nd Mass's Part," *National Tribune*, November 22, 1906; "The Sixty-Second Pennsylvania Volunteers Dedicatory Exercises at Gettysburg, September 11, 1889," copy in the 62nd Pennsylvania folder, GNMP; John S. Patton, "Papers," Historical Society of Western Pennsylvania, copy in 62nd Pennsylvania folder, GNMP; OR 27, 1, 610; Barrett, *Reminiscences, Incidents, and Battles of the Old Fourth Michigan Infantry in the War of the Rebellion*, 22.

38. Frank Flynn, *The Fighting Ninth for Fifty Years and the Semi-centennial Celebration* (Ann Arbor, MI, 1972), 34; Francis J. Parker, *The Story of the 32nd Massachusetts Infantry* (Boston, 1880), 165–166.

39. Pfanz, *Gettysburg—The Second Day*, 244, 246; OR 27, 1, 610–611.

40. Parker, *The Story of the 32nd Massachusetts Infantry*, 168; OR 27, 1, 611.

While Sweitzer explained that the 32nd Massachusetts formed in the front line to the left of Tilton's Brigade, Pfanz's map shows the regiment to have formed behind the First Brigade (OR suppl., 5, 191; Pfanz, *Gettysburg—The Second Day*, 246).

41. OR suppl., 5, 191–192; *PAG*, vol. 1, 363; "The Sixty-Second Pennsylvania Volunteers Dedicatory Exercises at Gettysburg, September 11, 1889," 12–13.

42. OR 27, 1, 602, 611.

43. *PAG*, vol. 1, 363; Pfanz, *Gettysburg—The Second Day*, 290.

44. *PAG*, vol. 1, 383; OR 27, 1, 611–612; Houghton, journal.

According to Francis Parker and Oscar West of the 32nd Massachusetts, Sweitzer was a no-show during this phase of the battle and the regimental commanders made their decisions independently. When Sweitzer finally appeared, "he demanded with an oath" that the brigade turn around and continue engaging the Confederates, who had almost surrounded the brigade. It seems reasonable that the Bay Staters did not see Sweitzer because he was with the men on the right flank (Parker, *The Story of the 32nd Massachusetts Infantry*; West, "On Little Round Top").

45. OR 27, 1, 612; Pfanz, *Gettysburg—The Second Day*, 292.

The 4th Michigan's monument purportedly stands where Jeffords fell (Campbell, "Account").

46. OR 27, 1, 612; West, "On Little Round Top"; Houghton, journal; Bates, *Pennsylvania Volunteers*, vol. III, 458; Bancroft, diary.

47. OR 27, 1, 613; Pfanz, *Culp's Hill and Cemetery Hill*, 155; Houghton, journal; Barrett, *Reminiscences, Incidents, and Battles of the Old Fourth Michigan Infantry in the War of the Rebellion*, 23.

Unlike many units that had missed the heavy fighting at Gettysburg, the members of the 9th Massachusetts knew that they were fortunate to have been on picket duty and therefore spared the devastation wrecked upon their comrades (Macnamara, *The History of the Ninth Regiment, Massachusetts Volunteer Infantry . . .*, 319, 320).

In a letter written to General Joshua Chamberlain after the war, the commander of the 9th Massachusetts, Colonel Patrick Guiney, said he was ordered to join General Tilton's Brigade, as it was less cut up and therefore more likely to become engaged later in the battle (Patrick Guiney, letter, Joshua Chamberlain Papers, Library of Congress).

48. OR suppl., 5, 194; OR 27, 1, 613.

49. OR 27, 1, 612; "The Sixty-Second Pennsylvania Volunteers Dedicatory Exercises at Gettysburg, September 11, 1889," 12–13; Guiney, letter.

50. Busey and Martin, *Regimental Strengths and Losses*, 61, 248.

51. Dyer, *Compendium*, 303; Tagg, *Generals of Gettysburg*, 89–90.

52. Amos M. Judson, *History of the Eighty-Third Regiment, Pennsylvania Volunteers* (Erie, PA, 1865), 123.

53. Alfred Apted, diary, copy in 16th Michigan folder, GNMP; John Berry, diary, Civil War Times Illustrated Collection, USAMHI.

54. OR 27, 1, 621, 622, 632; Oliver W. Norton, *The Attack and Defense of Little Round Top* (New York, 1913), 285; Robert Ilisevich and Jonathan Helmrieich, *The Civil War Diaries of Seth Waid III* (Meadville, PA, 1993), 103; Ziba B. Graham, "On To Gettysburg," *Michigan MOLLUS*, vol. 1, 473; Marion G. Phillips and Valier P. Parsegian, *Richard and Rhoda—Letters from the Civil War* (Washington, 1981), 30; "Diary of Sgt. H. C. Hosford," copy in 44th New York folder, GNMP.

55. Pullen, *The Twentieth Maine: A Volunteer Regiment in the Civil War* (Philadelphia, 1957), 98; Phillips and Parsegian, *Richard and Rhoda—Letters from the Civil War*, 30; Berry, diary; OR 27, 1, 622; Elisha Coan "Manuscripts," Bowdoin College; Nevins and Styple, *What Death More Glorious*, 68.

56. Theodore Gerrish, "The Twentieth Maine at Gettysburg," *Portland Advertiser*, March 13, 1882; Oliver Norton, letter, copy in 83rd Pennsylvania folder, GNMP.

57. Norton, *Attack and Defense of Little Round Tops*, 264; Norton, letter.

58. Norton, letter.

59. Rufus Jacklin, "Account," copy in 16th Michigan folder, GNMP; Norton, letter; Judson, *History of the Eighty-Third Regiment, Pennsylvania Volunteers*, 127; Kevin E. O'Brien, "Valley of the Shadow of Death," *Gettysburg Magazine* (July 1992), issue 7, 46.

60. Charles H. Salter, letter, copy in 16th Michigan folder, GNMP; Judson, *History of the Eighty-Third Regiment, Pennsylvania Volunteers*, 127; OR 27, 2, 622, 630; Pfanz, *Gettysburg—The Second Day*, 222; *Michigan at Gettysburg*, 108–109.

61. OR 27, 1, 628, 630; Judson, *History of the Eighty-Third Regiment, Pennsylvania Volunteers*, 127; W. W. Colestock, "The 16th Mich. At Little Round Top," *National Tribune*, March 26, 1914; Pfanz, *Gettysburg—The Second Day*, 228; John Michael Gibney, "A Shadow Passing," *Gettysburg Magazine* (January 1992), issue 6, 33.

Several soldiers cast Colonel Welch in a poor light after the battle. Oliver Norton reported seeing Welch and "a large number of his men" nearly a mile to the rear (Norton, *Attack and Defense of Little Round Top*, 218–220), while Captain Benjamin Partridge, who remained in position, reported seeing Welch withdrawing with the colors (Gibney, "A Shadow Passing," 40).

62. Charles Sprague, letter, copy in the 44th New York folder, GNMP; OR 27, 1, 617; Bates, *Pennsylvania Volunteers*, vol. IV, 1255; Nash, *A History of the 44th New York Volunteer Infantry*, 145.

Vincent died a few days later. Soon after his wounding, Vincent asked that his wife join him, but the messages never reached her. Vincent received his commission to the rank of brigadier general on his deathbed.

63. Salter, letter.

64. Nash, *History of the 44th New York Volunteer Infantry*, 145.

65. OR 27, 1, 632; William H. Brown, letter, Brown University Library.

66. OR 27, 1, 623.

67. Gerrish, "The Twentieth Maine at Gettysburg"; OR, 27, 1, 623.

68. OR 27, 1, 623.

69. OR 27, 1, 623; Ellis Spear, *The Civil War Recollections of General Ellis Spear* (Orona, ME, 1997), 33; Pullen, *Twentieth Maine: A Volunteer Regiment in the Civil War*, 117–118.

70. OR 27, 1, 624; Spear, *Civil War Recollections of General Ellis Spear*, 34.

71. OR 27, 1, 624; Joshua Chamberlain to John Bachelder, *Bachelder Papers*, vol. 3, 1885.

72. OR 27, 1, 624.

There is some disagreement on this point. According to Colonel William Oates of the 15th Alabama, his men were in the process of withdrawing when the charge was launched against them (William C. Oates, *The War Between the Union and the Confederacy . . . History of the 15th Alabama Regiment . . .* (Dayton, OH, 1974), 219–220).

73. OR 27, 1, 624.

Captain Spear on the left of the line insisted after the war that he never heard

Chamberlain's orders to charge. Instead, he got his cue when the center of the regiment suddenly began rushing down the slope (Spear, *Civil War Recollections of General Ellis Spear,* 34). In an article in the *National Tribune* ("The Left at Gettysburg by Gen. Ellis Spear," June 12, 1913) Spear related that it was really the enlisted men on the left that started the charge when they were concerned that their wounded in front of the left of the line were exposed. This version is dubious.

74. OR 27, 1, 624–425; Walter G. Morrill to John Bachelder, March 10, 1884, Bachelder Papers, New Hampshire Historical Society.

75. OR 27, 1, 625.

After the war, Chamberlain wrote to John Bachelder that Fisher "emphatically declined [Rice's orders from Sykes that he take Big Round Top] & I remember his saying that his men were armed with some inefficient rifle 'smoothbores' it seems to me he said, & especially that the ground was difficult & unknown to his men. He & his men also were much agitated" (Joshua Chamber-

lain to John Bachelder, January 25, 1884, Bachelder Papers, New Hampshire Historical Society).

76. Bradley M. Gottfried, "Fisher's Brigade at Gettysburg: The Big Round Top Controversy," *Gettysburg Magazine* (July 1998), issue 19, 90–91; Pullen, *Twentieth Maine: A Volunteer Regiment in the Civil War,* 130–131.

77. Thomas Desjardin, *Stand Firm Ye Boys From Maine* (Gettysburg, PA, 1995), 135–136; Elisha Coan, "Round Top: A Shot From the 20th Maine Aimed at Comrade Fisher," *National Tribune,* June 4, 1885.

78. OR 27, 1, 621, 626, 630; Salter, letter; Graham, "On To Gettysburg"; Judson, *History of the Eighty-Third Regiment, Pennsylvania Volunteers,* 137; Ilisevdich and Helmreich, *Civil War Diaries of Seth Waid: Letters from the Civil War,* 104.

79. OR 27, 1, 622, 626; Samuel J. Keene, diary, copy in 20th Maine folder, GNMP; William Livermore, "Diary of William Livermore, Color Guard, 20th Maine" *Lincoln County News,* June, 1883; Apted, diary.

80. Salter, letter.

2ND DIVISION—

Major General George Sykes/
General Romeyn B. Ayres

General Romeyn B. Ayres's Division held the distinction of containing two brigades of U.S. regular troops. Half of these regiments had been in existence since the War of 1812, and all were composed of seasoned regulars. The division was a distinguished one, having served in many of the major eastern theater engagements. Major General George Sykes, who had commanded the division since its inception, was a no nonsense commander who did not put up with much foolishness, even from his commanders. When ordered to make a demonstration against the strong Confederates posted at Fredericksburg on June 6, 1863, Sykes wrote, "I am opposed to any movement across the river with the forces I have . . . it is hardly to be expected that anything reliable would be gained, even supposing it could be obtained from such sources." When he heard this reaction, General Hooker fired off a message to the V Corps commander that read, "you are not to disregard the order to feel the enemy a little." The division had fought with distinction during the Seven Days battles, at Second Bull Run, and at Chancellorsville. Sykes probably began the Gettysburg campaign wondering if he would ever be given a corps. Two of Ayres's brigade commanders had never commanded a brigade prior to the campaign and a third (Colonel Sidney Burbank) was ill.[1]

   Approaching the battlefield at around 6:00 A.M. on July 2, the division formed into line of battle half a mile north of Hanover Road. Ayres assumed command of the division when Sykes was elevated to command the corps. After remaining parallel to the road for about an hour, the division marched back to it, crossed it, and formed a line of battle at a right angle to it. The division now approached the town in this formation. Later that morning the division moved farther to the left and center of the Federal line. The men rested in a massed deployment along Baltimore Pike through the afternoon. Barnes's Division was to their left and Crawford's was behind them. The division followed Barnes's south to support the III Corps at about 4:30 P.M. However, rather than following Barnes's Division on Granite Schoolhouse Lane, Ayres marched his along country roads to Taneytown Road, and finally halted near Little Round Top. Weed's Brigade led the column south, followed by Burbank's; Day's brought up the rear. Weed's Brigade was diverted to climb Little Round Top to help beat off the determined Confederate attack, while the two other brigades continued their march. Burbank's Brigade deployed at the northern base of Little Round Top with its left near Gibbs's Battery and its right extending two hundred yards northward. Day's Brigade deployed behind it.[2]

While the 140th New York of Weed's Brigade was finding immortality on the slopes of Little Round Top, the two regular brigades were ordered northwest to the Wheatfield. Crossing Plum Run, the men took position in woods south of the Wheatfield. While watching the turn of events, Ayres observed troops approaching his right flank. Turning to General Caldwell, whose troops were in the Wheatfield, Ayres asked about their identity. Caldwell replied that they were fresh troops relieving his. When about to give the order to advance and sweep the enemy out of the Wheatfield, Ayres made a horrible discovery, and exclaimed, "Those regiments are being driven back!" When one of his aides tried to reassure him, Ayres blurted out, "A regiment does not shut up like a jack-knife and hide its colors without its retreating." Ayres was correct, as the enemy was wrapping around both flanks of his two brigades, placing them in an untenable position. Parts of four Confederate brigades had overwhelmed Caldwell's men and now were taking on Ayres's men. Ayres ordered an immediate retreat before the two brigades were destroyed. Lieutenant Colonel William Fox noted that the regulars "moved off the field in admirable style, with well-aligned ranks, facing about at times to deliver their fire and check pursuit . . . in this action the regulars sustained severe losses, but gave ample evidence of the fighting qualities, discipline, and steadiness under fire which made them the pattern and admiration of the entire army."[3]

While Weed's Brigade remained on the summit of Little Round Top, the two other shattered brigades took position behind (east) of it. They remained there through July 4, when Day's Brigade was thrown out on a reconnaissance. The division left the battlefield on July 5.[4]

✂

1st Brigade: Brigadier General Romeyn Ayres/
Colonel Hannibal Day[5]

Units: 3rd U.S., 4th U.S., 6th U.S., 12th U.S., 14th U.S.
Strength: 1553
Losses: 382 (46–318-18)—25.6%[6]

Brigadier General Romeyn Ayres was one of several former artillery officers who left that service and entered the infantry to gain faster promotions. A West Pointer, Ayres had commanded a battery at First Bull Run and rose to artillery chief of a VI Corps division. He served with distinction during the Seven Days battles and Antietam. His talents were rewarded when he assumed command of the entire VI Corps artillery at Fredericksburg. He left the artillery on April 21, 1863, to take command of the 1st Brigade. The men were pleased that a seasoned regular was placed in command of them, for they had fought the entire war first under a lieutenant colonel and then under a major of the regulars.[7]

The brigade reached Frederick on June 28. Captain Jonathan Hager of the 14th U.S. found the town "full to overflowing with officers, soldiers, and citizens." The brigade received a new commander when Meade took command of the army, Sykes took over the corps, and Ayres assumed command of the division. This thrust Colonel Hannibal Day of the 6th U.S. Regulars into command of the brigade. Although Day was a West Point graduate and had served in the Mexican War and a variety of other actions, he had been considered too old for field command, so he had spent most of the Civil War in recruitment activities. Now in command of the 6th U.S., he had yet to lead it in battle.[8]

Although reveille sounded at 4:00 A.M. on June 29, the column did not continue its march until sometime between noon and 1:00 P.M. The march of June 30 began at 4:00 A.M., and the brigade (and the remainder of the division) marched twenty-five miles. These marches were long, dreary affairs with few breaks. Reuben Kelly of the 12th U.S. complained that "some of the time the dust was shoe deep and the wether [sic] very hot." The following day, July 1, the men were on the road at 8:00 A.M., crossed the Pennsylvania line at about 11:00 A.M., and reached Hanover by midafternoon. The stop here was a fairly short one, for at 6:00 P.M. the men were ordered back into line and marched to within a few miles of Gettysburg on Hanover Road. Captain Hager was unhappy about the turn of events, for "we were making ourselves comfortable, had brought some provisions and a crock of apple butter, had some clothes washed when lo! The general sounded." The column stopped at about 11:00 P.M. that night. The men were awakened at 3:00 A.M., permitted to have a quick breakfast, and were on the road again at 4:00 A.M. They finally reached the battlefield at 6:00 A.M. on July 2.[9]

The men rested during most of the day, and later in the afternoon, the entire division moved south by the left flank. The column finally halted near the northern base of Little Round Top. There is some confusion about the brigade's deployment during this and subsequent periods of the battle. Richard Robbins of Burbank's Brigade recalled that Day's Brigade was deployed from left to right as 14th U.S.–12th U.S.–6th U.S.–4th U.S.–3rd U.S.

2ND DIVISION �֍ 259

However, in his after-battle report, Captain Levi Bootes reported that his 6th U.S. was on the extreme left of the brigade. Day's Brigade formed behind Burbank's during this time. After a fifteen-minute wait, the two brigades advanced across Plum Run and into Rose Woods in the same arrangement. The trek was short in duration, but deadly, as the men were peppered with sniper fire and many were hit. Captain Thomas Dunn claimed that the brigade formed into three lines in the Rose Woods, with his regiment, the 12th U.S., in the second. The small arms fire, particularly from the left rear, was heavy, so the men were permitted to lie down for safety.[10]

After remaining there for a few minutes, Captain Thomas Dunn (12th U.S.) received orders to "move by the right flank a distance equal to my front." This would take them into the Wheatfield, still behind Burbank's Brigade. As Dunn and presumably the rest of the brigade were carrying out these orders, they could see the Federal troops on their right (probably Sweitzer's Brigade) falling back in some disorder. Sergeant Frederick Conette of the 14th U.S. saw Sweitzer's men "running like flocks of sheep." Conette was a seasoned veteran, so he knew to expect the enemy on his unit's flank. Watching Burbank's Brigade pouring effective volleys into the approaching Confederates (probably Wofford's Brigade), Conette hoped that his unit would advance. However, within moments, Captain Dunn received orders from Ayres to "face by the rear rank and march to the position first occupied [near Little Round Top]." Probably seeing that further resistance was doomed, Day's men gladly obliged, and moved to the rear in "quick time" under a "galling fire." Major Grotius Giddings claimed that his regiment never advanced from its position in the Rose Woods. "After lying in that position about twenty minutes, I received

orders to face the regiment about and fall back, and while in the act of falling back we received a heavy fire of musketry from the rear and right flank, by which we suffered severely."[11]

Sergeant Conette wrote home about the nightmare of retreating through Plum Run Valley, where there was "600 yards of muddly ground, in which you stuck fast at every pace, and the whole line of rebs firing in us." Captain Jonathan Hager of the 14th U.S. watched helplessly as "the men fell fast around me. I was behind, urging the men not to run." Reaching a stone wall in the Valley of Death along Plum Run, Captain Dunn of the 12th U.S. ordered his men to halt, about-face, and fire into the enemy soldiers who were following them. The unit again turned and continued its march to safety, finally stopping on the crest of Little Round Top.[12]

As the men approached Little Round Top, John Page of the 3rd U.S. could see the artillery officers of the Hazlett's battery on the summit, waving their hats "for us to hurry up. We realized that they wished to use canister, so took up the double-quick." Some of the men dove for cover when the artillerymen felt that they could wait no longer, and opened fire on the approaching enemy.[13]

The brigade lay in line of battle at the base of Little Round Top and played no role on July 3. "Shot and spherical case continually crushed through the tops of trees above our heads," recalled Hager. The brigade remained in this position until the morning of July 4, when it was ordered out on a reconnaissance. Advancing about a mile with the 3rd U.S., 4th U.S., and 6th U.S. in the lead, followed by the 12th U.S. and 14th U.S. in support, the troops came under a heavy artillery fire and were ordered to lie down. When the storm subsided the men were ordered onto their feet and back to their original positions. Hager complained that "we had nothing to eat, nothing to drink and nobody to make a speech" on the nation's birthday. The regiments participated in picket duty through the remainder of the day and most of the next. This was anything but a pleasant experience, as "the dead were lying thick on the ground, black, swollen corpses. The air was rank with the horrid perfume," noted Hager. During the night of July 4, he went to sleep "with a piece of tobacco at my nose." He considered it to be the "most disagree-able night I ever spent in or out of the service." The men were relieved when they left Gettysburg sometime between 4:00 and 5:00 P.M. on July 5.[14]

Because Day's Brigade was in support of Burbanks's, its losses were about half of its sister brigade. Richard Robbins of Burbank's Brigade explained that because Day's Brigade "receiv[ed] the order to regain the hill [Little Round Top], they . . . received the order first, and they were not caught so disastrously as the Second Brigade."[15]

2nd Brigade—Colonel Sidney Burbank

Units: 2nd U.S., 7th U.S., 10th U.S., 11th U.S., 17th U.S.
Strength: 954
Losses: 447 (78-342-27)—46.9%[16]

Colonel Sidney Burbank did not assume active command of the veteran 2nd Brigade until April 1863. Prior to this, bouts of illness had caused him to see only limited action during the Civil War. The brigade was only moderately engaged at Chancellorsville. Therefore, the men did not really know their commander's fighting abilities.[17]

As Burbank's Brigade made its way north, it experienced a number of different reactions from the local citizens. Most were thrilled to see the Union troops and were generous with their food and water. J. P. Hackett of the 17th U.S. recalled how "the good people of Pennsylvania had at noon set tables under the trees by the roadside, and we helped ourselves from the abundance of food there awaiting us." He noted that "we could tell by the treatment we received that we were marching through God's country." In some villages, "stalwart men stood unweariedly [sic] pumping water for the thirsty troops, while the women handed more fortunate soldiers broad slices of bread-and butter with rich draughts of pure milk." Flags flew from most houses, and the villagers waved hats and handkerchiefs. "It was an exciting and wonderful scene," George Williams recalled.[18]

Other civilians were not so hospitable. For example, a farmer near Hanover, Pennsylvania, was furious when the brigade marched through his unharvested wheatfield. He could not understand why the columns could not march through his newly cut hayfield, but was told that the artillery were using that route. "I'm a ruined man!" exclaimed the farmer when he next saw the men carry off his fence rails.[19]

The battle began on July 1, while the column trudged toward Hanover, Pennsylvania. It reached this town about midafternoon. Colonel Burbank described it as a "very pleasant day; good roads and the men marched well." The men were pleased to hear the orders to halt and prepare to bivouac. The halt was but momentary, as the men were almost immediately ordered to pack up and continue the march. The column finally halted sometime between 1:00 and 2:00 A.M., and the men were permitted to stack arms and rest. Many simply dropped to the ground and immediately fell asleep. Sleep did not come to many others, for although they were exhausted from their long series of marches, the excitement of the looming battle and the pain emanating from their limbs kept them awake. The ever-present rumble of artillery and wagons moving toward the front also did not help their slumber.[20]

Reveille sounded sometime between 3:00 and 3:30 A.M., and the men began preparing breakfast. Unfortunately, they were ordered to fall in before most of the men could grab a cup of coffee. There was a commotion everywhere around them as the corps prepared to continue its trek toward Gettysburg. "In every direction there were signs of intense activity. Troops were moving up, the wagons had already drawn out of park, and the hum of many voices mingled with the neighing of horses or the bellowing of mules," recalled Williams. The column was finally back on the road by 4:00 A.M., and the march continued until it reached the vicinity of Wolf Hill and formed on the left of Barnes's Division. Skirmishers were thrown out, who quickly engaged their Confederate counterparts.[21]

The brigade was now ordered to take position in the rear. Just as the movement by the right flank began, the division was sent south, near where Baltimore Pike intersects Rock Creek. The men spent the afternoon dozing, smoking, and talking. The sounds of battle grew in intensity during the late afternoon, as the Federal left was assailed. Shortly after 5:00 P.M. a staff officer galloped up to Burbank with orders to "move forward with the utmost dispatch." The men moved out in quick-step, then broke into a double-quick pace. Colonel Burbank soon ordered his men to reduce their speed, lest they be worn out when they entered the fray. He was also concerned that his lines were becoming irregular and confused as the men jogged along. The column passed ambulances and lines of wounded men. A steady stream of Confederate shells flew over their heads, tearing off tree limbs, which fell among the men. The column halted when it reached Little Round Top, where it deployed for battle. The brigade was deployed, from left to right, as 17th U.S.–11th U. S.–10th U.S.–7th U.S.–2nd U.S.[22]

A short time later, Burbank received orders to move his men to the Rose Woods adjacent to the Wheatfield. The brigade double-quicked through the marshy area in the Valley of Death, which Major Arthur Lee of the 2nd U.S. described as being "50 yards wide, ankle-deep and miry." Confederate sharpshooters took their toll as the men rushed across the open area. The brigade then wheeled left at a 45 degree angle and climbed Houck's Ridge, where the men finally entered the southern part of Rose Woods. Robbins (11th U.S.) characterized the fire as "a perfect hail storm of bullets . . . many fell in that short rush." As they entered the woods, the men drove out a horde of enemy sharpshooters. After taking position, the 17th U.S. on the left of the brigade was hit by small arms fire, and Burbank ordered its left-most company refused to face this threat. Before long, the men could see Brooke's Brigade (Caldwell's Division) sweep past in the Wheatfield in front of them, clearing the area of Anderson's Brigade (Hood's Division).[23]

In less than half an hour, the regulars could see Brooke's men quickly retreating in fewer numbers than when they had initially swept past. They could now make out Sweitzer's Brigade (Barnes's Division, V Corps) in the Wheatfield. The men solemnly watched as the 4th Michigan fought to prevent its flag from falling into enemy hands. According to Lieutenant James Pratt of the 11th U.S., it was the only time he ever heard the regulars cheer. Burbank immediately ordered his men forward to occupy a low stone wall on the southern edge of the Wheatfield, near where they had halted. Soon they were ordered into the Wheatfield, wheeling to the left to occupy a position perpendicular to its original one. Knowing that the Rose Woods in front of them must be filled with the enemy, Burbank ordered his men to fire a volley into it. When the fire was not returned, he ordered his men to cease fire.[24]

Suddenly, Confederates could be seen moving around the brigade's right flank, and just as Burbank was about to change his brigade's position to meet this threat, he received orders to withdraw. The Confederates were wrapping around the brigade's right flank and attempting to get into their rear to do some serious damage. Robbins (11th U.S.) recalled Ayres's order as "Face about and wheel to the right at the double quick and form on the general line of battle." In his report, Colonel Burbank wrote that this withdrawal was made "as rapidly and in as good order as the nature of the ground would permit." Some of the men, particularly those in the center, did not see the threat on the right, and therefore complained about the order. Noise was another problem. According to Captain William Clinton of the 10th U.S., "the roar of musketry was so extensive that a great portion of our command did not hear the order to fall back until some minutes after it had been given. The enemy at this time was in front and on both our flanks." During the withdrawal, some companies of the 17th U.S. were squeezed between a rail fence and the rest of the line, and were thrown into disorder, giving the "appearance of confusion, which was impossible to correct," according to Robbins. As a result, the withdrawal was probably less organized than Burbank volunteered in his report.[25]

Seeing the regulars withdrawing, Kershaw's, Wofford's, Anderson's, and Semmes's Brigades threw several volleys into their backs and both flanks. Men fell in heavy numbers, as the brigade rushed back toward Little Round Top to avoid annihilation. Lieutenant Pratt of the 11th U.S. characterized it as an "almost semicircle of fire . . . almost a sheet of fire . . . the slaughter was fearful." The survivors reformed behind the signal station on Little Round Top, where they spent the night.[26]

July 3 was a quiet day until shortly after 1:00 P.M., when the brigade came under the heavy artillery fire preceding the Pickett–Pettigrew–Trimble charge. "The [artillery] pieces showered about us for hours, tops of trees and heavy branches carried off by round shot helped the awful din," recalled Lieutenant Pratt. The next day was quiet. Ira Pettit recorded in his diary, "No firing! Not even national salutes." Burial details plied their ghastly trade during the day, and the men began their trek after Lee's retreating troops during the latter part of the afternoon of July 5.[27]

The battle went badly for the Burbank's Brigade. Although well-trained and well-led, the brigade was placed in an untenable situation when it was thrown into the Wheatfield after Sweitzer's Brigade had already been dispatched by overwhelming numbers. Given the position and numbers of the Confederate troops in the area, Burbank's movement into the Wheatfield was doomed from the start. As a result, the brigade lost almost half its men.

✄

3rd Brigade: Brigadier General Stephen Weed

Units: 140th New York, 146th New York, 91st Pennsylvania, 155th Pennsylvania
Strength: 1491
Losses: 200 (40-142-18)—13.4%[28]

Like many others, Brigadier General Stephen Weed was new to his command, having jumped from captain of the V Corps's artillery to general of infantry on June 6, 1863. He now led General Warren's old brigade, which was a hodgepodge of units. Originally composed of four regiments, two had been mustered out and were replaced by two others in May 1863. Therefore, the brigade's four regiments had yet to fight as a unit.[29]

Singing was very much in evidence as Weed's men trudged northward. Schoolchildren sang the "Star Spangled Banner" and other patriotic songs as the men marched past their school. At various times the citizens, or the soldiers, broke out in song.[30]

The misery of the march was intense. The thousands of feet kicked up massive clouds of dust that blinded the men, parched their throats, and made breathing all but impossible. Because the men were not permitted to remove their shoes when fording streams, blisters formed, which were exacerbated by the long marches with few breaks. The blisters made wearing shoes difficult, so many men removed them and carried them dangling from their fixed bayonets. Other men's shoes completely gave out, and soon they did as well. The regimental surgeons issued passes to these men so the provost guard would not arrest them. The more enterprising soldiers made copies of them so they too could fall out of line without repercussions. So severe was the

march on June 30 that only 30 men answered the 155th Pennsylvania's roll call at its conclusion.[31]

The citizens generally made the hardships more bearable. The men were cheered by the enthusiasm, particularly after their long campaigns in Virginia, where they had been scorned. Crossing the Pennsylvania state line also excited the men. However, anger soon replaced these feelings when the men passed citizens selling food at exorbitant prices. The fact that many of these people were "young athletic farmer boys" who should have been in their ranks made the slight all the more difficult to bear. Farther up the road the citizens were less mercenary, and many freely provided the men with all manner of goods without seeking compensation.[32]

During the march of July 1, some of the men could hear cannon fire in the distance. The column reached Hanover by midafternoon and the men prepared to settle into camp for the night. They did not appreciate seeing a messenger gallop up on a foaming horse and dismount at General Sykes's headquarters. Bugles almost immediately sounded "assembly," and the men were back in line within ten minutes. The 140th New York had just broken ranks after an inspection when the bugler sounded the call to strike tents. Before moving out, the men were read an order from their new army commander, General George Meade. Colonel Patrick O'Rorke also addressed the men. His words are lost now, but one soldier recalled that he told them that "they were to make a forced march of 12 miles to the battlefield, that the hour had now arrived when it was expected that we would annihilate the rebel army, and he expected every man to perform his duty faithfully and honorably. He also called upon the officers to urge their men to the utmost in the performance of their duty." The latter part was added because the men were exhausted even before the march began. Lieutenant Porter Farley, the regiment's adjutant, reported that O'Rorke ended his speech with the words, "I call on the file closers to do their duty, and if there is a man this day base enough to leave his company, let him die in his tracks—shoot him down like a dog."[33]

Citizens lining the roads distributed goods and sang patriotic songs, which helped buoy the men's spirits. Corporal J. Ansel Booth of the 140th New York noted that "the regiment never marched so easily, so cheerily, or sang so lively during the night of their march from Hanover to Gettysburg." The men were, however, totally exhausted when they were finally permitted to rest about 1:00 P.M. They had marched fourteen more miles since leaving Hanover and were now a mere five miles from the battlefield. Most men merely fell to the road surface and were almost asleep before they hit the ground.[34]

After what seemed to be but a few moments, but was really three hours, the men were roused. "Dusky forms arise one after another, and fires are lighted. Make your coffee, and fall in is the word passed along," wrote Captain Henry Curran of the 146th New York. In another letter, Curran accurately summed up the march of the brigade when he stated that "some days we marched from two in the morning until late at night, with nothing but crackers to eat."[35]

The brigade, along with the rest of the corps, finally reached the battlefield at about 7:00 A.M. on July 2 and halted near Wolf Hill to the right of the XII Corps.

The command moved about during the morning, eventually coming to rest where Rock Creek crosses Baltimore Pike. Designated as a unit that would provide aid to Sickles's III Corps, the brigade rested in ranks while awaiting their summons during most of the afternoon. Some of the men, including General Weed and Colonel O'Rorke, joined in singing songs as the unit whiled away the hours. Intense artillery fire could be heard to the brigade's left at about 3:30 P.M., where Longstreet's infantry were about to attack Sickles's Corps. Suddenly a string of orders were issued to the men: "Fall in; Take arms; Shoulder arms; Left face; Forward, double quick." The 1.5-mile march south at a double-quick pace caused extreme misery. Several men fell out of the ranks, as the brigade led Ayres's Division toward the sound of the fighting.[36]

General Weed rode ahead of his brigade to reconnoiter. Just as he left, General Warren rode down from Little Round Top, frantically trying to find troops to counter the Confederates who were now approaching Little Round Top. Colonel Strong Vincent's Brigade occupied the southern part of the hill, but more troops were needed. Spying a column making its way to the west, Warren quickly rode up to it. Bringing up the rear of the brigade, Colonel O'Rorke of the 140th New York, watched as Warren approached. So excited was Warren that he began speaking when he was still some distance away. According to accounts by Adjutant Porter Farley and Captain Joseph Leeper, Warren told O'Rorke that enemy units were advancing up the opposite side of the hill. "Paddy, give me a regiment," he finally exclaimed. O'Rorke replied, "General Weed is ahead and expects me to follow him." Warren impulsively remarked, "Never mind that, bring your regiment up here and I will take the responsibility."

Trusting Warren's instincts, O'Rorke turned his regiment toward Little Round Top, while Warren rode ahead to find General Weed.[37]

The panting men of the 140th New York climbed toward the crest of the hill without stopping. The ascent was made even more difficult because the hill was "covered with sharp flinty rocks—wild blackberry briers, poison ivy and brambles of every kind." Upon reaching the summit, the men immediately came under hostile fire. One private recalled that the "bullets flew around us like hail." There is some disagreement as to whether the men's guns were loaded as they ascended the hill. According to Adjutant Farley, the situation was so critical that the men could not stop to load. Writing to a local paper after the battle, Sergeant James Campbell recalled it slightly differently: "we were delayed a few moments in loading . . . [then were ordered] to the front of a ledge of rocks." There was also no time to get the men into anything that resembled a line of battle, as the Confederates were on the verge of capturing this critical hill. Instead, O'Rorke yelled to his men, "Down this way, boys" as he led them toward the Confederates that were forcing back the right flank of the 16th Michigan of Vincent's Brigade in front of them. "The rebels looked at us for a minute, as we rushed down at them, then they gave us a murderous volley."[38]

The conflict with the 48th Alabama (Law's Brigade) and 4th Texas (Robertson's Brigade) was short and sharp. In actuality, only two of O'Rorke's companies were following right behind him. Many men fell with every step they took toward the enemy. Just as Colonel O'Rorke turned to his men and yelled, "Here they are, men. Commence firing," he was fatally wounded. O'Rorke's men were so enraged that they pumped seventeen bullets into the enemy soldier who shot him. The Confederate charge had brought some of the enemy soldiers so close to the 140th New York that they chose to surrender rather than try their luck at escaping. O'Rorke's remaining companies soon arrived on the right, forming a horseshoe.[39]

While Warren and O'Rorke were conferring, General Weed was meeting with General Sickles at the Trostle farm. Soon one of General Sykes's staff officers galloped up and told the two generals that Weed's Brigade could not be spared after all. Weed rode back to his brigade and turned it back toward Little Round Top. By the time they had arrived, the battle for Little Round Top was all but over. The brigade now was deployed from left to right as 140th New York–91st Pennsylvania–146th New York–155th Pennsylvania.[40]

Weed's men were not the only reinforcements rushing to Little Round Top. Lieutenant Charles Hazlett's battery was also making its way to the hill. However, due to the rocks and steepness of the hill, the guns were not making much headway. Some of Weed's men stopped their ascent, unhitched the horses, and helped pull and push the guns up to the top of the hill. Because the cannon were fired through gaps in their line, several men in the 140th New York suffered permanent hearing loss.[41]

Sniper fire replaced the assaults on Little Round Top, and many were hit, including General Weed. As he lay mortally wounded on the rocks, he beckoned his friend, Lieutenant Hazlett, to his side. Those near could hear him tell Hazlett about debts he owed and about his sister. Before he could finish his statements, a sniper's bullet found Hazlett's brain, killing him instantly. Weed died later that evening.[42]

That night, the men were ordered to build breastworks of stone to help protect them from the deadly snipers in Devil's Den. Except for ongoing sniper fire, July 3 proved to be quiet. The day began unusually because no reveille was sounded. The officers instead roused the men from their slumber. The quiet ended shortly after 1:00 P.M., when the massive artillery barrage preceding Pickett's charge commenced. "The noise was terrible, as their shells burst right in our midst," wrote Captain Henry Hastings of the 146th New York. Casualties were low because the men knelt behind rocks.[43]

With the withdrawal of Lee's army, the men were freed from being prisoners of their breastworks. Many men were sent out to collect muskets and other equipment scattered on the battlefield. July 5 was also quiet. Later in the afternoon the brigade began its trek after Lee.[44]

Except for essentially two companies of the 140th New York, the brigade played a small role in the battle. After repelling the breach in Vincent's line, the brigade occupied the northern side of the hill and could possibility have dissuaded other attacks.

NOTES

1. Pfanz, *Gettysburg—The Second Day,* 295–296; OR 27, 3, 17–18; Tagg, *Generals at Gettysburg,* 81–82.

2. OR 27, 1, 634, 638, 643; Pfanz, *Gettysburg—The Second Day,* 296.

3. OR 27, 1, 634; Powell, *The Fifth Army Corps,* 535; *NYG,* vol. 1, 55.

4. OR 27, 1, 635.

5. Colonel Day's official report was, without a doubt, the most superficial account of any brigade on the field of Gettysburg. Composed of two sentences, it stated that "although not called on myself for a report." In an unusual action, General Ayres added an endorsement to Day's report that stated, "Respectfully forwarded. So much delay has

occurred in getting this paper that I will forward it as a substitute for the report of the brigade commander required by regulations and custom of service from time immemorial." Part of this may have stemmed from the fact that Colonel Day had a desk job up to the Gettysburg Campaign (OR 27, 1, 636–637; Tagg, *The Generals of Gettysburg,* 93–94).

6. Busey and Martin, *Regimental Strengths and Losses,* 62, 248.

7. Tagg, *Generals of Gettysburg,* 91–92; Dyer, *Compendium,* 303.

8. Jonathan B. Hager, "Civil War Memoirs," Alderman Library, University of Virginia; Charles Bowen, diary, copy in the 12th U.S. folder, GNMP; Dyer, *Compendium,* 303; Tagg, *Generals of Gettysburg,* 93–94.

9. Hager, "Civil War Memoirs"; Reuben Kelly, letter, copy in 12th U.S. folder, GNMP.

10. Robbins, "The Regular Troops at Gettysburg"; *Philadelphia Weekly Times,* January 4, 1879; OR 27, 1, 640; B. P. Mimmack, letter, copy in 12th U.S. Folder, GNMP.

11. OR 27, 1, 640–641; 643; Sergeant Frederick Conette, letter, CWTI Collection, USAMHI.

12. Conette, letter; Hager, "Civil War Memoirs"; OR 27,1, 641.

13. William H. Powell, *The Fifth Army Corps . . .* (New York, 1896), 535.

14. OR 27, 1, 637, 639, 641, 644; Hager, "Civil War Memoirs."

The actual time of this movement is disputed. Major Grotius Giddings of the 14th U.S. wrote that it began at 7:30 A.M. His colleague, Captain Julius Adams of the 4th U.S., stated that the time was 10:00 A.M., and Sergeant Charles Bowen recorded in his diary that it was at 11:00 A.M. (OR 27, 1, 639, 641; Bowen, diary).

15. Robbins, "The Regular Troops at Gettysburg."

16. Busey and Martin, *Regimental Strengths and Losses,* 63, 249.

17. Tagg, *Generals of Gettysburg,* 94–95.

18. J. P. Hackett, "The Fifth Corps at Gettysburg," *National Tribune,* July 29, 1915; George F. Williams, *Bullet and Shell* (New York, 1882), 198.

19. Williams, *Bullet and Shell,* 196–197.

20. Robbins, "The Regular Troops at Gettysburg"; Sidney Burbank, journal, Library of Congress; Hackett, "The Fifth Corps at Gettysburg"; Williams, *Bullet and Shell,* 199, 200.

21. Cyrus Bacon, Jr., diary, University of Michigan; Burbank, journal; Williams, *Bullet and Shell,* 203; Robbins, "The Regular Troops at Gettysburg"; OR 27, 1, 644, 646.

22. OR 27, 1, 644–645, 646; James P. Pratt, letter, copy in Brake Collection, USAMHI; Hackett, "The Fifth Corps at Gettysburg"; Robbins, "The Regular Troops at Gettysburg."

23. OR 27, 1, 645, 646; Robbins, "The Regular Troops at Gettysburg."

According to J. P. Hackett, the toll on the officers was becoming so high that they were permitted to remove their shoulder boards, and some even picked up rifles in an effort to blend in with the enlisted men ("The Fifth Corps at Gettysburg").

24. OR 27, 1, 645, 647, 649.

25. OR 27, 1, 645, 647, 649; Pratt, letter; Robbins, "The Regular Troops at Gettysburg."

Lieutenant Pratt of the 11th U.S. wrote home after the battle that his men were exposed to a heavy small arms fire as they entered the wheatfield, but were prevented from returning the fire because units of the II Corps were still in their front. To reduce their losses, the regulars were ordered to lie down until the II Corps passed over them, then rose up and fired a volley against the enemy (Pratt, letter).

26. OR 27, 1, 645; Pratt, letter; W. H. Sanderson, "Sykes's Regulars," *National Tribune,* April 2, 1891.

27. Pratt, letter; Ira S. Pettit, *Diary of a Dead Man* (New York, 1976), 150.

28. Busey and Martin, *Regimental Strengths and Losses,* 64, 249.

29. John T. Porter, *Under the Maltese Cross . . . Campaigns of the 155th Pennsylvania Regiment* (Pittsburgh, PA, 1910), 165; Sifakis, *Who Was Who,* 701; Warner, *Generals in Blue,* 548; Dyer, *Compendium,* 304–305.

30. Porter, *Under the Maltese Cross . . . Campaigns of the 155th Pennsylvania Regiment,* 153.

31. Mary G. Brainard, *Campaigns of the One Hundred and Forth-Sixth Regiment, New York Volunteers* (New York, 1915), 109–110; Porter, *Under the Maltese Cross . . . Campaigns of the 155th Pennsylvania Regiment,* 153, 164.

32. Porter, *Under the Maltese Cross . . . Campaigns of the 155th Pennsylvania Regiment,* 153.

33. Porter, *Under the Maltese Cross . . . Campaigns of the 155th Pennsylvania Regiment* 155–156; True Blue, "From the 140th Interesting Particulars of the Late Fight," *Rochester Evening Express,* July 11, 1863; Porter Farley, "Reminiscences of Porter Farley, 140th New York Infantry," in *Rochester Historical Society* (1944), vol. 22, 217.

34. J. Ansel Booth, "Letter," *Democrat & American,* February 18, 1864; Edward North, *A Memorial to Henry Hastings Curran,* copy in 146th New York folder, GNMP, 107; Porter, *Under the Maltese Cross . . . Campaigns of the 155th Pennsylvania Regiment,* 156.

35. Farley, "Reminiscences of Porter Farley, 140th New York Infantry," 216; North, *Memorial to Henry Curran,* 104, 107.

36. *NYG,* vol. 3, 970; OR 27, 1, 634, 645; Pfanz, *Gettysburg: The Second Day,* 225; Porter, *Under the Maltese Cross . . . Campaigns of the 155th Pennsylvania Regiment,* 165; Joseph M. Leeper, "Gettysburg—The Part Taken in the Battle by the Fifth Corps," *National Tribune,* April 30, 1885; Farley, "Reminiscences of Porter Farley," 217; OR 27, 1, 651; North, *Memorial to Henry Curran,* 108.

37. Farley, "Reminiscences of Porter Farley, 140th New York Infantry," 218; Farley Porter, letter, Brake Collection, USAMHI.

General Sykes was clearly unhappy that Weed moved his brigade away from Little Round Top. When he questioned Weed about his actions, the latter merely replied that he was following Sickles's orders (OR 27, 1, 593).

38. *Rochester Evening Express,* July 11, 1863; Farley, "Reminiscences of Porter Farley, 140th New York Infantry," *Rochester His-*

torical Society, 222; anonymous, letter, Rochester Evening Express, August 20, 1863.

It appears that at least the 148th New York was ordered to load as the men marched south (North, Memorial to Henry Curran, 104).

39. Samuel R. Hazen, "Fighting the Good Fight," National Tribune, September 13, 1894; Farley, "Reminiscences of Porter Farley, 140th New York Infantry," 222; Porter Farley, "Otis's Regiment at Gettysburg and the Wilderness," Army and Navy Journal (April 22, 1899); William Clark, "Memoir," copy in the 140th New York folder, GNMP; Brian A. Bennett, Sons of Old Monroe: A Regimental History of Patrick O'Rorke's 140th New York Volunteers (Dayton, OH, 1992), 216.

40. "Notes on the Taking and Holding of Little Round Top"; Edgar Warren to John Bachelder, November 15, 1877.

41. Charles N. Smith, "Account," New York Times, July 3, 1913; Hazen, "Fighting the Good Fight."

42. "Notes on the Taking and Holding of Little Round Top"; Bennett, Sons of Old Monroe: A Regimental History of Patrick O'Rorke's 140th New York Volunteers, 219.

43. OR 27, 1, 652; Brainard, Campaigns of the One Hundred and Forth-Sixth Regiment, New York Volunteers, 121; Porter, Under the Maltese Cross . . . Campaigns of the 155th Pennsylvania Regiment, 175; North, Memorial of Lt. Colonel Henry Hastings, 104.

44. Farley, "Reminiscences of Porter Farley, 140th New York Infantry," 231; Hazen, "Fighting the Good Fight"; William Crennell, diary, copy 140th New York folder, GNMP.

3RD DIVISION—

Brigadier General Samuel Crawford

The Pennsylvania Reserve Division was one of the storied units in the Army of the Potomac. Originally formed to protect Pennsylvania when so many other units were being shipped to the fronts, the division moved south during the first winter of the war. The division performed splendidly during the Seven Days battles, fighting at Mechanicsville, Gaines's Mill, and White Oak Swamp. The battles of Second Bull Run, Antietam, and Fredericksburg added to its fame. During the latter battle, it was the only division that broke through the Confederate line.[1]

These successes came at a bloody price, however. The division was so badly decimated that it was detached from the army after Fredericksburg and assigned to the XXII Corps, which defended the capital. Here the division was broken apart, and the three brigades guarded different sectors. The men became increasingly agitated when they learned that Lee's army had broken camp in Virginia and was again moving north. According to Colonel M. Hardin of the 41st Pennsylvania, "when they heard that Lee threatened to invade Maryland and probably Pennsylvania, officers and men began to take on the military air, which had been somewhat laid aside after Fredericksburg; and talk of applying to rejoin their comrades of the Army of the Potomac, on their march northward, became prevalent and went so far, in one case at least, as to be put in the form of a written petition." Their request was granted, and the men received orders to "get rid of all surplus baggage and camp equipage, draw extra rations and a full-supply of ammunition," noted Captain John Bard of the 42nd Pennsylvania. The men cheered this order, and before long they were marching northward to join the army, which was concentrating around Frederick, Maryland. The men were also pleased that they were being reassigned to Meade's V Corps. Their excitement was dimmed somewhat when they learned that Meade had assumed command of the army.[2]

The division was under the command of Brigadier General Samuel Crawford. A physician by training, Crawford joined the army's medical corps in the 1850s. Deciding that fighting was more to his liking, he became a major of the infantry prior to the war. Somewhat of a blowhard, he had seen action on a number of battlefields and briefly led a division in combat. He assumed command of the division in May 1863.[3]

The men left the Washington defenses on June 24 and marched rapidly north. The two brigades of the Pennsylvania Reserves were reunited during the afternoon of the following day. The men's excitement dissipated when they heard that the 2nd Brigade was left behind to continue guarding Washington. The two remaining brigades reached the V Corps around Frederick on June 28.[4]

A minor controversy began the next day that continued for much of the march. Because of the long wagon train already on the road, the Pennsylvania Reserves could not break camp and begin the march at daybreak, as ordered. Instead, the march did not begin until 1:00 P.M. Because the division was behind the slow-moving wagon train, its progress was further retarded. As a result, the division did not reach its assigned campground near Liberty, Maryland, until 11:00 P.M. Marching along different roads, the remainder of the V Corps had arrived in camp hours earlier, and those still awake listened with disdain as the reserves trudged past their camps. Colonel M. Hardin (41st Pennsylvania) recalled that "most of us were so hot and tired, we dropped down and went to sleep without even making coffee. A bad beginning for a long march." The following morning the division again experienced frustrating delays, but it made better time in the afternoon. The men were chagrined, however, when it was reported to Meade that their division was unable to march as fast as the other divisions of the corps.[5]

July 1 was one of the most memorable of the men's lives. "The brigade bands and regimental drum corps poured forth their soul-inspiring airs from morning till night, and light was the tread of our feet to their notes," recalled Captain Evan Woodward of the 31st Pennsylvania. The division reached the Pennsylvania state line between 2:00 and 3:00 P.M., and General Crawford gave a speech. "Cheer after cheer rang out from the regiments, which rolled over the hills and through the valleys until lost in the far distance," according to Woodward. Another veteran wrote, "caps flew in air, swords were brandished, and the men shouted and sung National songs."[6]

The division reached Hanover, Pennsylvania, at 5:00 P.M. on July 1 and could see the effects of the cavalry fight waged there the day before. The column moved on, making a sharp left turn toward Gettysburg. The battle had begun, so Sykes pushed his men hard, marching them twenty-five miles. They did not stop until they reached McSherrystown at about 2:00 A.M. on July 2. The men were permitted to rest for two hours before making the final leg of the journey to Gettysburg.[7]

The men were thoroughly exhausted from these long and arduous marches. Private A. P. Morrisson of the 38th Pennsylvania Reserves wrote home that when the column finally halted for the evening, "I was almost too tired to sleep when I did lie down." The final fifteen-mile march to the battlefield began at 6:00 A.M., and the division arrived during the late morning. The division had made an incredible seventy-mile march in about three and a half days.[8]

Upon reaching the battlefield, the division marched along Baltimore Pike to the rear of Cemetery Hill. The thoroughly exhausted men were permitted to rest, and they received their first hot meal since the march had begun. Next, the men were ordered to examine, clean, and load their guns. As the artillery commenced firing, the men realized that an attack was imminent and their anxiety rose. Between 4:00 and 5:00 P.M. they received orders to follow Barnes's Division south to support Sickles's beleaguered troops "should it be necessary for them to fall back." Before moving out, the men were told to leave their knapsacks behind in a pile and to load their guns if they hadn't done so already.[9]

Fisher's Brigade led the column toward Little Round Top. As it scrambled up the rocky hill, the victorious Confederates from McLaws's Division approached, having finally swept all before them from the Wheatfield and Peach Orchard. Realizing the seriousness of the situation, Crawford was ordered to charge the enemy, now traversing Plum Run. He quickly formed McCandless's Brigade into line of battle, along with the 40th Pennsylvania from Fisher's Brigade. Sweeping down, they pushed the Confederates back through the Wheatfield, finally halting at the wall in the middle of the field that had been so hotly contested for several hours before. Crawford actually grabbed his divisional flag, which was snagged in some vegetation, and rode forward with it to lead the charge. Not only did he have the flag, also attached to his leg was the reluctant flag bearer, who refused to give up possession of the treasured flag. The situation was not quite as glorious as Crawford and his men represented after the battle. W. H. Sanderson of Burbank's Brigade (Ayres's Division) saw that the Confederate line approaching Little Round Top was "badly broken . . . it was a crowd without any tangible line."[10]

While McCandless's Brigade was finding immortality in the Valley of Death, Fisher's Brigade was ordered to secure Big Round Top. Confusion reigned as night descended upon the bloody field, and Fisher did not get his troops up to the top until near midnight. They remained there for the rest of the battle. The same was not true of McCandless's Brigade. Ordered to advance into the Wheatfield during the late afternoon of July 3, it caught the 15th Georgia (Benning's Brigade, Hood's Division) off-guard, and after a series of engagements, killed, wounded, and captured a number of its men. The division finally left the battlefield on July 5.[11]

1st Brigade—Colonel William McCandless

Units: 30th Pennsylvania, 31st Pennsylvania, 35th Pennsylvania, 42nd Pennsylvania
Strength: 1248
Losses: 155 (20-132-3)—12.4%[12]

Although Colonel William McCandless had commanded the 1st Brigade for only a few weeks, the men knew him, as he was the colonel of the 31st Pennsylvania. Known for his bravery, he had fought with his unit through all of its major engagements, except Antietam, because he had been wounded at Second Bull Run.[13]

The men could clearly hear the sounds of battle on July 1 as they marched toward Gettysburg. The bands struck up the song, "Home Again" as the brigade entered Pennsylvania, and many men were on the verge of tears. Toward the end of the day, music again was called upon to motivate the men. This time, it was to perk up the exhausted men. Captain Frank Bell of the 42nd Pennsylvania recalled that "our band struck up tune after tune and at times we sang in chorus to keep ourselves awake as we marched steadily on." Bell remembered that this march seemed never-ending; the men were "literally sleeping as they walked and falling at times through sheer exhaustion and drowiness." When the men were finally permitted to halt for the remainder of the night, most simply dropped down and immediately fell asleep, having been awake for about twenty-two hours.[14]

The march continued at daylight on July 2. Many of the men were from the Gettysburg area, and as the column moved along the hot dusty roads, more than a few passed their houses and loved ones standing outside. "With the merest greetings, the boys kept their places in the ranks," noted Captain Henry Minnigh of the 30th Pennsylvania. There were few stops, and those were made to permit the men to refill their canteens. The brigade, with Fisher's, finally rested where Hanover Road intersects Baltimore Pike. Minnigh related that "fatigued by the long and weary marches, we soon were oblivious to all surroundings, wrapped in restful slumber."[15]

The peacefulness was broken shortly after 4:00 P.M., when Minnigh related that "we were hurriedly called into line, and ordered to sling knapsacks, which command to us always meant, 'get ready for quick and devilish work.'" Moving by the left flank (south), the men rapidly followed Fisher's Brigade. Climbing Little Round Top, the men strained to see the events down below in the Valley of Death. The brigade was joined by the 40th Pennsylvania of the Fisher's Brigade, which was detached by one of Crawford's aides and told to "hold this hill at all hazards." According to Colonel S. Jackson, the valley was so choked with smoke that the men could not see much of anything.

Other units who had a better view could see the Federal forces in full retreat. On their heels were enemy soldiers from four Confederate brigades, albeit in a disorganized state. According to Colonel McCandless, "this plain was marshy and difficult to cross; over it however, the enemy passed his infantry in a disordered mass, driving our forces back on my position."[16]

As the Federal troops swarmed back toward Little Round Top in defeat, they heard a "solid, ringing, regular tramp of firm, determined men. Concealed by the smoke and the irregularities of the ground, the sound of the approaching mass was heard before the line appeared in sight. As it drew nearer and nearer, that splendid division, the Pennsylvania Reserves, came suddenly into view."[17]

An officer from Gibbs's battery, which straddled Wheatfield Road just north of Little Round Top, which was in danger of being captured, ran up to the Reserves and yelled, "Dunder and blixen, don't let dem repels took my batteries." Colonel S. Jackson of the 40th Pennsylvania told him to "double-shot his guns, hold his position, and we would see to their safety." Jackson's men hearing this exchange, yelled out, "Stand by your guns, Dutchy, and we will stand by you."[18]

There was not a moment to waste, and Colonel McCandless responded magnificently. He deployed his brigade in two lines. The first line was, from left to right, 30th Pennsylvania–40th Pennsylvania (from Fisher's Brigade)–35th Pennsylvania. The second line was composed of the 42nd Pennsylvania on the left and the 31st Pennsylvania on the right. Waiting until the ground below them was clear of Federal soldiers, the Pennsylvania Reserves fired a volley, then attacked. The charge was vividly described by Woodward after the war:

Immovable and firm stood the Reserves, resting on their arms silently gazing on the magnificent and grand sight, until our broken masses had passed to the right, and the enemy had advanced within fifty paces, when the gallant Crawford, seizing the standard of the First, whose bearer had been shot down, waved it aloft and cried out, "Forward, Reserves." With a simultaneous shriek from every throat, that sounds as if coming from a thousand demons, who had burst their lungs in uttering it, on swept the Reserves.[19]

The Confederate soldiers were probably amazed and demoralized to see the Pennsylvania Reserves charging toward them. They had finally driven the last vestige of Federal troops from the Wheatfield and were about to claim their prize of Little Round Top. Now in front of them loomed a mass of fresh blue-clad soldiers. The Confederate tide probably washed up against the 40th Pennsylvania in the center of the first line. Because the Union troops were armed with smoothbore muskets, deadly at close range, the devastation must have been great. McCandless's men now charged, along with Wheaton's Brigade (VI Corps) on their right. This was more than the Confederates could stand, and they began heading rapidly for the rear. The left flank came under heavy fire during the counterattack, forcing McCandless to move his second line up to connect with the left of his first, thus extending his line. Captain Bell of the 42nd Pennsylvania, on the left of the second line, heard his commanding officer give the order to "by the left flank, march."[20]

Captain Bell called the battle line charging down Little Round Top "the most irregular line that ever made a charge. Many of the men stopping to drop behind a rock or some other cover and fire at the enemy on our left who were busy with their complements." The Federal advance halted at the stone wall midway through the Wheatfield that had been so hotly contested for several hours earlier in the evening. So exuberant was General Crawford at the performance of his men that he rode up to Colonel Jackson of the 40th Pennsylvania and exclaimed, "Colonel Jackson, you have saved the day, your regiment is worth its weight in gold; its weight in gold sir."[21]

The men were choked with thirst, so small groups were permitted to return to Plum Run with their comrades' canteens. Unfortunately, many dead and wounded floated in the stream, making even the thirstiest think twice about drinking the tainted water. The night was spent in the advanced position behind the stone wall. Pickets were thrown out and ammunition distributed. Despite the fact that they were so close to the enemy, most of the men immediately went to sleep. All around them were the thousands who had fallen in the Wheatfield throughout the bloody late afternoon and evening fighting. The situation proved to be too much for some of the veterans to handle. Captain Frank Bell on the picket line saw "the entire left of my line of pickets quit their posts, one after the other without orders and skulked to the rear. An unaccountable panic seemed to seize them and the same men who had so fearlessly faced death in the daylight." The men composed themselves and returned to their posts, proving to Bell that "we are all cowards in the dark."[22]

Confederate sharpshooters were active during the night and all through July 3, forcing the men to keep under cover as much as possible. The fire from Devil's Den to the left became such a nuisance that several companies from the 42nd Pennsylvania were dispatched to pick off the Confederates as they popped up from behind the large rocks to fire. Being in such an advanced position had its rewards—the men were spared the devastation wrought by the cannonade that preceded the Pickett–Pettigrew–Trimble charge.[23]

After the great Confederate charge failed, Sykes sent Crawford orders to clear the enemy from the Rose Woods in front of him. Sykes suspected that the woods were empty, but just in case, Crawford was to send all of McCandless's Brigade, along with the 40th Pennsylvania of Fisher's Brigade, which had not returned to its unit. Captain Henry Minnigh of the 30th Pennsylvania recalled the brigade, "at the word of command, leaping over the wall and deliberately dress[ing] their lines." Almost as soon as the movement through the open Wheatfield began, an enemy battery, probably in the Peach Orchard, opened fire on the reserves. McCandless immediately dispatched his right-most regiment, the 35th Pennsylvania, to capture the battery. Rapidly reaching Stony Hill, they pushed the enemy skirmishers out of their way and made for the battery. Rather than storming it, they dropped down and opened fire on the gunners, causing the cannoneers to slacken their fire.[24]

With this threat removed, the rest of the brigade dashed forward into the Rose Woods. The handful of enemy troops here took to their heels, leaving the woods in the possession of the reserves. McCandless quickly became aware of a large enemy force to his left, and as he put it in his report, "at right angles therewith." This was the 15th Georgia (Benning's Brigade, Hood's Division). "I faced my command by the rear rank, and charged the enemy directly on the left flank, routing him," noted McCandless. Major H. Sloan of the 40th Pennsylvania recalled the order as being more complicated: "By the rear rank right about face, right-turn, march." After making this movement, Woodward (31st Pennsylvania) described the Federal soldiers as "running like hounds, and yelping like devils down through the meadow and up over the steep acclivity on the opposite side, surprising the enemy and taking them on the flank, and doubling them up and driving regiments and brigades pell-mell before them in utter confusion. The gallant efforts of their officers to rally them were useless, we had them fairly on the run, and did not cease following them until we had penetrated far into their lines." The engagement was short, but sharp. On the Confederate side, McLaws's and Hood's Divisions had been given orders to pull back from their exposed position after Pickett's repulse, and were in the process of complying. For some reason, Benning's 15th Georgia was left in position and was assailed by the Pennsylvania Reserves. The Georgians tried to put up a fight, but were overwhelmed, losing their flag and almost two hundred men to capture. The solider who captured the flag later received the Congressional Medal of Honor. General Crawford reported that Robertson's Brigade was nearby, but did not provide assistance to Benning's Brigade, because they "ran, as reported by the prisoners, without firing a shot." The other Confederate brigades were very much in evidence, though, causing McCandless wisely to halt his pursuit.[25]

With the Wheatfield in complete Fed-eral control, the men were ordered to gather the small arms that were scattered about. McCandless estimated that his men collected two thousand to three thousand rifles. Always one to embellish, Crawford stated that the men collected "upward of 7,000 stand of arms." The men also assisted the wounded who lay unattended in high numbers. While engaged in these activities, McCandless's men heard the sounds of the enemy chopping down trees to create formidable defensive positions along Warfield and Seminary Ridges. Around noon on July 4, McCandless was relieved from his advanced position near Devil's Den by the two brigades of regulars (Ayres's Division), and ordered to return to the stonewall within the Wheatfield. The brigade remained there until July 5, when it was ordered to follow Lee's retreating army.[26]

McCandless's Brigade was a classic example of being at the right place at the right time. While its charge on July 2 was heroic and successful, it fought exhausted Confederates who had achieved more than anyone could have expected of them. Similarly, the brigade's vastly successful charge against the 15th Georgia on July 3 was partially the result of poor leadership on the part of the Confederate officers. Nevertheless, these two charges were among the most successful of the battle.

3rd Brigade—Colonel James Fisher

Units: 34th Pennsylvania, 38th Pennsylvania, 39th Pennsylvania, 40th Pennsylvania, 41st Pennsylvania
Strength: 1609
Losses: 55 (6-49-0)—3.4%[27]

Like his counterpart in the 1st Brigade, Colonel James Fisher was present with his regiment (34th Pennsylvania) in all of the brigade's major engagements. Elevated to brigade command in January 1863, he and his brigade did not participate in the Chancellorsville campaign. As a result, unlike McCandless, he did not have prior experience leading a brigade.[28]

Colonel Fisher was excited when he received orders from General Crawford to give his brigade an inspirational speech as they marched into Pennsylvania. According to Colonel S. Jackson of the 40th Pennsylvania, Fisher was "always anxious for an opportunity to make a speech." Jackson recalled that the speech was "excellent and eloquent . . . which seemed to arouse the men very much at the time." Private E. D. Benedict of the 41st Pennsylvania recorded in his diary that the "Colonel halted us at the line and the boys gave three cheers for old Pa and we vowed never to leave the State until we had driven the rebels out, we felt enthused and showed our determination by increasing our speed. There was no nonsense about us." Firing could be heard up ahead and, according to Private Elly Torrance of the 38th Pennsylvania, "every eye brightened & every step quickened as the firing grew more rapid. We were all very tired & anxious to have the Battle over one way or the other so that we might get some rest." The twenty-five-mile-march seemed never-ending and, according to Colonel Jackson, "the long night march before reaching Gettysburg took much of the spasmodic patriotism out of the boys." The column forged on after leaving Hanover, Pennsylvania, at 5:00 P.M. on July 1. "Darkness came on, yet no signs of a halt appeared; on the contrary, the word passed back along the line to 'keep well closed up and press forward,'" recalled Colonel Jackson. "The men became tired, footsore and cross; midnight passed, 1 o'clock passed, but they longed in vain for the order to halt." The men finally got their wish at 3:00 A.M., after marching almost twenty-three hours with few halts.[29]

The men were up at first light and on the march again by about 5 A.M. After a few miles, the column halted and the men fixed a quick breakfast. The brigade continued the march about thirty minutes later, finally reaching the battlefield during the late morning. The men were permitted to rest, clean their guns, and write home. Fisher received orders to lead the division south between 4:00 and 5:00 P.M. to reinforce Sickles's III Corps. "Every heart beat faster & each face became more serious & you could see the poor fellows take their letters up & destroy them & read a hurried chapter from their well worn Bibles, trying to prepare for the very worst," wrote Torrance to his sister.[30]

The column's southward movement was slowed by the increasing stream of wounded men. The brigade finally reached Little Round Top, but the climb up its northern slope was difficult because it was covered with rocks and thick brush. As the brigade advanced to the crest of the hill, the fight for Little Round Top was over.[31]

As Fisher's men filed to the left, General Crawford ordered the 40th Pennsylvania, which was bringing up the rear, detached from the brigade to join Colonel William McCandless's Brigade to attack the onrushing Confederates in the Valley of Death. The regiment formed between two of McCandless's Brigade's regiments in the first line of battle, and successfully drove the enemy back toward the Wheatfield.[32]

The rest of the brigade was rushed to the left to support Weed's and Vincent's (now under Colonel James Rice) Brigades. While Fisher and a number of his veterans made it sound as though the brigade was influential in holding Little Round Top, the truth is that the Confederates had given up their attempts to capture the hill by the time the reserves arrived. In his official report of the battle, Fisher suggested that his troops mounted a charge against the enemy. "I marched my brigade to the left of General Sykes' corps . . . and at once engaged the enemy, although very shortly afterward he retired." He corrected this version in 1878, writing that "my command had not long been in their new position supporting [Vincent's Brigade] until the enemy fell back and left us in peaceful possession of that part of the field." This version was supported by Private E. D. Benedict of the 41st Pennsylvania, who wrote in his diary that "we were first drawn up to go in on [sic] charge on little round top our regt was held as reserve, the others went in." A controversy over this point flared soon after the battle ended, when Professor Reverend M. Jacobs suggested in his book, *Notes on the Rebel Invasion of Pennsylvania and the Battle of Gettysburgh*, that Fisher's Brigade had played the pivotal role in defending Little Round Top. A furious Colonel Rice corrected this assertion in a letter published in the November 28, 1863 issue of the *New York Times*.[33]

Although Fisher's Brigade did not directly engage the enemy, it is possible that its arrival influenced Colonel Oates of the 15th Alabama to call off his attacks on Little Round Top. After the war, Oates wrote that a long line of Federal infantry descended on his right and threatened his rear, necessitating a hasty withdraw. John Bachelder believed that these troops were Fisher's.[34]

Meanwhile, sniper fire from Big Round Top was taking its toll on the officers and men. Realizing that the threat had to be neutralized, a decision was made to move Federal troops up the hill during the evening hours of July 2. Who made this decision is a matter of debate. At least four individuals have claimed the honor: Fisher, Crawford, Rice, and Sykes. Most vocal in his claim was Colonel Fisher, who wrote in his official report that "soon after the close of the fight of the 2d, I discovered in my immediate front a hill called Round Top, from the summit of which the

enemy was doing us great damage. I thought it highly important that we should at once occupy it. I accordingly took two regiments of my brigade . . . and the Twentieth Maine." So obvious was the act of securing Big Round Top, that probably all four men determined that it must be captured.[35]

Fisher wrote after the battle that he left the 38th Pennsylvania and 39th Pennsylvania in the "saddle" between the two hills. "I accordingly took two regiments of my brigade, viz, the Fifth [34th], Lieutenant-Colonel Dare, and the Twelfth [41st], Colonel Hardin, and the Twentieth Maine, commanded by Colonel Chamberlain, and at 10 P.M. ascended the hill, which was occupied by a full brigade of the enemy. We went up steadily in line of battle, taking over 30 prisoners in our ascent."[36]

Colonel Joshua Chamberlain bitterly disagreed with these statements. While he acknowledged that Fisher's Brigade was to take the hill, he stated in his official report that "it was the understanding . . . that Colonel Fisher's Brigade was to advance and seize the western slope of Great Round Top, where the enemy had shortly before been driven." Continuing his narrative, Chamberlain wrote, "but after considerable delay, this intention for some reason was not carried into execution. We were apprehensive that if the enemy were allowed to strengthen himself in that position, he would have a great advantage in renewing the attack on us at daylight or before. Colonel Rice then directed me to make the movement to seize that crest." Elaborating after the war, Chamberlain wrote, "he [Fisher] emphatically declined [Rice's order from Sykes that he take Big Round Top] & I remember his saying that his men were armed with some inefficient rifle 'smooth-bores' it seems to me he said, & especially that the ground was difficult & unknown to his men. He & his men also were much agitated." While three of his regiments carried Springfield or Enfield rifles, Fisher admitted after the war that they were "Harper's Ferry altered muskets" and this is why he asked Chamberlain to take the lead. Fisher contested this account, particularly that he was reluctant to order his men up the hill.[37]

Asking for volunteers, Chamberlain was pleased when all of his exhausted men sprang to their feet. The men started up Big Round Top with their bayonets fixed at about 9:00 P.M. Shots fired in the darkness hit several of the men, but the 20th Maine captured about twenty Confederates. Reaching the top of the hill, Chamberlain deployed his men behind rocks and ordered a skirmish line forward toward the base of the hill. Soon after Chamberlain's men began their ascent, Fisher probably realized that he had erred by not taking the heights himself, and ordered the 34th Pennsylvania and 41st Pennsylvania up the hill. Colonel Hardin of the 41st Pennsylvania recalled after the war that the darkness and rough terrain took their toll on the men's bearings during the ascent, and soon all organization was lost. Confusion reigned. Stopping about a third of the way up, the officers tried to rally their men, but realized that to continue in the darkness was hopeless. A frustrated Colonel Fisher ordered the two regiments back down to the base of the hill, where some semblance of order was restored. The two regiments then ascended the hill again "by the flank" and finally reached its summit.[38]

As Fisher's two regiments approached the heights, Colonel Chamberlain at first thought that they were enemy soldiers, but was relieved to learn their true identity. Unfortunately, the enemy also heard their noise and opened fire. The volley fired in the darkness rattled the Pennsylvanians, and a horrified Chamberlain watched as they "started like antelopes & went down the way they had come up on, & never stopped till they were behind the line on Little Round Top again." Private Benedict (41st Pennsylvania) corroborated Chamberlain's remarks. "Colonel Hardin marched us up to top of Round Top where striking the enemy in the dark and a gun being discharged we fell back off the hill, & in doing so got lost for awhile." Private James Randolph Simpson of the 34th Pennsylvania added in a letter home on July 21, 1863, that we "moved up its rugged ascent and found the top when by a misunderstanding we by order came down it again. On coming down the reb picket fired into me doing no damage . . .on reaching the base of the hill, Col. Fisher halted us and said that we must return and hold it, the hill, at all hazards. This time it was double quick. Many did not reach the top, having played out with continued marches."[39]

As suggested by Private Simpson, Fisher's men did return to the top of Big Round Top and took position near the 20th Maine. Chamberlain was angry at this point and he later wrote, "at some time about midnight, two regiments of Colonel Fisher's Brigade came up the mountain beyond my left, and took position near the summit; but as the enemy did not threaten from that direction, I made no effort to connect with them." The ill-will was evident when Chamberlain wrote that "I had nothing to do with Fisher, nor he with me."[40]

After reaching the summit, the Pennsylvanians threw up a line of breastworks to protect themselves from the Confederates, who continued to fire at them. The sniper fire continued into the next day. The brigade remained there until it left the battlefield on July 5. The real battle began after the war, when Fisher and his men took on the 20th Maine about what really happened on the night of July 2, 1863.[41]

Lieutenant William Grier probably summarized Fisher's Brigade's activities best when he wrote, "the services of the Third Brigade in this battle can be told in a few sentences. On many another hard-fought field the Third Brigade performed greater work and lost many more brave men than it did at Gettysburg, but that was not the fault of the brigade. It was because the opportunity for actual conflict was not presented us."[42]

NOTES

1. Sauers, *Advance the Colors*, vol. 1, 81–83.

2. J. R. Sypher, *History of the Pennsylvania Reserve Corps . . .* (Lancaster, PA, 1865), 448–449; Bates, *Pennsylvania Volunteers*, vol. 1, 821, 852, 885; John P. Bard, "The 'Old Bucktails,' 42d Regt. P.V. at the Battle of Gettysburg," *Philadelphia Weekly Times*, May 19, 1886; Evan M. Woodward, *Our Campaigns— The Second Regiment, Pennsylvania Reserve Volunteers* (Philadelphia, 1865), 204–205; M. D. Hardin, *History of the Twelfth Regiment, Pennsylvania Reserve Volunteer Corps* (New York, 1890), 140; Mark Nesbitt, *35 Days to Gettysburg* (Harrisburg, PA, 1992), 103.

3. Tagg, *Generals of Gettysburg*, 97–98.

4. Nesbitt, *35 Days to Gettysburg*, 113; Hardin, *History of the Twelfth Regiment, Pennsylvania Reserve Volunteer Corps*, 141.

5. OR 27, 1, 595; Nesbitt, *35 Days to Gettysburg*, 135, 139; Hardin, *History of the Twelfth Regiment, Pennsylvania Reserve Volunteer Corps*, 143, 144.

6. Woodward, *Our Campaigns—The Second Regiment, Pennsylvania Reserve Volunteers*, 208; Bates, *Pennsylvania Volunteers*, vol. 1, 552.

7. *PAG*, vol. 1, 277.

8. Nesbitt, *35 Days to Gettysburg*, 145, 149; OR 27, 1, 652; Hardin, *History of the Twelfth Regiment, Pennsylvania Reserve Volun-*

teer Corps, 144; A. P. Morrisson, letter, 38th Pennsylvania File, GNMP Library.

Several different times have been given for the arrival of the Pennsylvania Reserves on the battlefield. Hardin, the historian of the 41st Pennsylvania, gives the time as 12:30 (*History of the Twelfth Regiment, Pennsylvania Reserve Volunteer Corps*, 152); Bates's section on the 41st Pennsylvania (*Pennsylvania Volunteers*, vol. I, 885) lists the time as 10:00 A.M., while the section on the 39th Pennsylvania gives the time as 9:00 A.M. (821). In his after-battle report, General Crawford wrote that the division arrived at noon (OR 27, 1, 652).

9. OR 27, 1, 653; Hardin, *History of the Twelfth Regiment, Pennsylvania Reserve Volunteer Corps*, 144; Elly Torrance, letter, Adam Torrance Papers, Pennsylvania State Archives; Adam Torrance, letter, Adam Torrance Papers, Pennsylvania State Archives; A. P. Morrisson, letter, July 21, 1863, 38th Pennsylvania File, GNMP Library.

10. OR 27, 1, 653; Pfanz, *Gettysburg—The Second Day*, 398; Sanderson, "Sykes's Regulars."

11. OR 27, 1, 625, 654–655, 657.

12. Busey and Martin, *Regimental Strengths and Weaknesses*, 65, 249.

13. Tagg, *Generals of Gettysburg*, 100.

14. Frank Bell, "The Bucktails at Gettysburg," copy in the 42nd Pennsylvania folder, GNMP; Woodward, *Our Campaigns—The Second Regiment, Pennsylvania Reserve Volunteers*, 208.

15. Bell, "The Bucktails at Gettysburg"; H. N. Minnigh, *History of Company K, 1st Penn'a Reserves* (Duncansville, PA, 1891), 23.

16. Minnigh, *History of Company K, 1st Penn'a Reserves*, 24; *PAG*, vol. 1, 278, 279; OR 27, 1, 657.

According to Major Sloan of the 40th Pennsylvania, the men could not ascertain the identity of the soldiers climbing the hill in front of them. Finally realizing that they were the enemy, Colonel Jackson ordered his men to open fire, then ordered his men to fix bayonets and charge (*PAG*, vol. 1, 283).

17. Smith, *History of the 118th Pennsylvania Volunteers, Corn Exchange Regiment*, 252.

18. Minnigh, *History of Company K, 1st Penn'a Reserves*, 26; *PAG*, vol. 1, 278.

According to Captain Minnigh, the German officer sought out the brigade the following day and exclaimed, "The Pennsylvania Reserves saved mine pattery, by ____. I gets you fellers all drunk mit beer."

19. OR 27, 1, 653, 657; Woodward, *Our Campaigns—The Second Regiment, Pennsylvania Reserve Volunteers*, 213.

The official reports are contradictory with regard to the number of volleys fired before the reserves charged. McCandless claimed that his men fired one volley, while Crawford recalled that it was two (OR 27, 1, 653, 657). Since commanding officers reviewed their subordinates' reports before they completed theirs, it appears that Crawford did not agree with McCandless on this issue. Similarly, there were differences of opinion as to who ordered the attack into the Valley of Death. The "honor" was claimed by General Crawford and Colonel Samuel Jackson of the 40th Pennsylvania. The latter claimed to have ordered the charge after seeing the devastation and demoralization caused by his men's initial volley (Edwin A. Glover, *Bucktailed Wildcats: A Regiment of Civil War Volunteers* [New York, 1960], 206). That Crawford carried the flag is confirmed by George Swopes's letters written after the war (copies in 30th Pennsylvania folder, GNMP).

20. OR 27, 1, 657; Glover, *Bucktailed Wildcats: A Regiment of Civil War Volunteers*, 206; Sypher, *History of the Pennsylvania Reserves*, 461.

As might be expected, some of the old veterans embellished the story after the war. For example, Captain John Bard wrote that the enemy had gained the summit of Little Round Top, and that the reserves engaged them in hand-to-hand combat. Both statements were false (Bard, "The 'Old Bucktails'").

21. Bell, "The Bucktails at Gettysburg"; Woodward, *Our Campaigns—The Second Regiment, Pennsylvania Reserve Volunteers*, 213; *PAG*, vol. 1, 279.

22. Woodward, *Our Campaigns—The Second Regiment, Pennsylvania Reserve Volunteers*, 214; Bell, "The Bucktails at Gettysburg."

23. Glover, *Bucktailed Wildcats: A Regiment of Civil War Volunteers*, 210; Minnigh, *History of Company K, 1st Penn'a Reserves*, 26.

24. OR 27, 1, 657; Minnigh, *History of Company K, 1st Penn'a Reserves*, 26.

25. OR 27, 1, 654–655, 657; *PAG*, vol. 1, 283; Woodward, *Our Campaigns—The Second Regiment, Pennsylvania Reserve Volunteers*, 216; Glover, *Bucktailed Wildcats: A Regiment of Civil War Volunteers*, 214–215; Jeffry D. Wert, *Gettysburg—Day Three* (New York, 2001), 284–285.

According to Major William Hartshorne of the 13th Pennsylvania, McCandless arranged his brigade in column of regiments, rather than in a single battle line for this attack. In a letter to John Bachelder, Hartshorne was convinced that had McCandless not deployed his men in this manner, the attack would have failed (William Hartshorne to John Bachelder, July 16, 1866, Bachelder Papers, New Hampshire Historical Society).

26. OR 27, 1, 655, 658; Bates, *History of the Pennsylvania Volunteers*, vol. II, 920; vol. I, 552.

27. Busey and Martin, *Regimental Strengths and Weaknesses*, 66, 250.

28. Tagg, *Generals of Gettysburg*, 101–102.

29. *PAG*, vol. 1, 277, 281; E. D. Benedict, diary, 41st Pennsylvania File, GNMP Library; Torrance, letter.

30. *PAG*, vol. 1, 277, 281.

31. *PAG*, vol. 1, 278; Hardin, *History of the Twelfth Regiment, Pennsylvania Reserve Volunteer Corps*, 153.

32. Pfanz, *Gettysburg—The Second Day*, 396–402; Jeffrey F. Sherry, "The Terrible Impetuosity: The Pennsylvania Reserves at Gettysburg," *Gettysburg Magazine* (January 1997), issue 16, 74–76.

In a letter dated April 8, 1878, Fisher gave a different version of how the 40th Pennsylvania was detached to assist McCandless's Brigade: "the 11th Regt . . .being on the left of my line became somehow mixed up with McCandless [sic] Brigade and participated in a charge made from little Round Top . . .This was owing to one of Crawford's blunder [sic] of which he was prolific" (National Archives, RG 94 War Records, Union Battle Reports, vol. 27, boxes 48–52).

33. Alice Trulock, *In The Hands of Providence: Joshua Chamberlain and the American Civil War* (Chapel Hill, NC, 1992), 444; OR 27, 1, 658; ; J. W. Fisher, letter, National Archives, RG 94 War Records; E. D. Benedict, diary, 41st Pennsylvania file, GNMP Library; *New York Times*, November 28, 1863; Bradley M. Gottfried, "Fisher's Brigade at Gettysburg: The Big Round Top Controversy," *Gettysburg Magazine* (July 1998), issue 19, 88.

34. William C. Oates, "Gettysburg—The Battle on the Right," in *Southern Historical Society Papers* (1878), vol. 6, 176–178; Edwin B. Coddington, *The Gettysburg Campaign: A Study in Command* (New York, 1968), 743–744, n. 48.

35. OR 27, 1, 618, 658; Gottfried, "Fisher's Brigade at Gettysburg: The Big Round Top Controversy," 89.

36. OR 27, 1, 658.

While a number of Confederate soldiers occupied the hill, there was nothing equivalent to a brigade.

37. OR 27, 1, 625, 654; Joshua Chamberlain to John Bachelder, January 25, 1884, Bachelder Papers, New Hampshire Historical Society; Dean S. Thomas, *Ready . . .Aim . . .Fire! Small Arms Ammunition in the Battle of Gettysburg* (Biglersville, PA, 1981), 59–66; Joseph Fisher, "Round Top Again," *National Tribune,* April 16, 1885.

38. Hardin, *History of the Twelfth Regiment, Pennsylvania Reserve Volunteer Corps,* 154–155; Bates, *History of Pennsylvania Volunteers,* I, 154.

39. OR 27, 1, 625; Pullen, *The Twentieth Maine: A Volunteer Regiment in the Civil War,* 130–131; Joshua Chamberlain to John Bachelder, January 25, 1884.

40. Coan, "Round Top"; Joshua Chamberlain to John Bachelder, January 25, 1884; OR 27, 1, 625–626.

41. John O'Connel, "Memoir," Civil War Miscellaneous Collection, USMHI; Hardin, *History of the Twelfth Regiment, Pennsylvania Reserve Volunteer Corps,* 157.

42. *PAG,* vol. 1, 91.

VI CORPS—

MAJOR GENERAL JOHN SEDGWICK

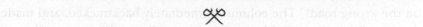

Formed on May 18, 1862, the VI Corps was present during McClellan's Peninsula and Seven Days campaigns, but was only peripherally involved at the battles of Gaines's Mill and Malvern Hill. The corps saw some action during the Second Manassas campaign and again at Crampton's Gap during the Antietam campaign, but played only a supporting role at the battle near Sharpsburg. The corps was lightly engaged at Fredericksburg, and it was not until Chancellorsville that the corps showed its mettle. Under Major General John Sedgwick, the corps crossed the Rappahannock River and successfully stormed Marye's Heights. As the corps moved toward Lee's rear, Sedgwick's men were confronted by a rapidly assembled defense force, which delayed the advance. Hooker had lost his nerve by this time and had halted all offensive maneuvers. The isolated VI Corps was almost cut off and annihilated, but was able to recross the river safety. The corps needed to redeem itself, and the men hoped it would be during the Gettysburg campaign.[1]

"Uncle John" Sedgwick's VI Corps slipped out of its entrenchments on June 14 and began its movement north. After a series of hard marches, the corps crossed the Potomac River on June 27 and camped that night in Maryland. There was no rest for the weary, as the corps continued its march, halting for the night of July 1 near Manchester, Maryland—about thirty-five miles from Gettysburg. Some may have thought the corps would never reach the battlefield in time for the battle, but Sedgwick had other plans. The march began at 10:00 P.M. that night, and continued through much of July 2, without so much as a break to make coffee or sleep. Occasional ten-minute breaks were provided for the men to relieve themselves. One exception was at 1:00 P.M., when, nearing the battlefield, the men were permitted an hour to rest and make coffee after having marched for over fifteen hours. In all, the corps had marched almost a hundred miles in a span of five days. During the final leg, the column marched thirty-five miles in eighteen hours. The march actually began on the wrong foot. Sedgwick initially decided to march to Gettysburg via Taneytown. After the column had traversed two miles, Sedgwick decided to take a more direct route. The men knew something was amiss when an aide shouted, "Make way here, make way, for God's sake; you are all wrong!" Reaching the head of the column, the aide exclaimed, "Halt your men, colonel; you are on the wrong road!" The column immediately backtracked, and made the rest of the trip on Baltimore Pike. According to Lieutenant George Bicknell of the 5th Maine (Bartlett's Brigade, Wright's Division) this caused "much strong language" among the men. The corps' thirty-six regiments stretched over ten miles.[2]

The vanguard reached the Pennsylvania state line by midmorning, where the troops rejoiced. The head of the corps arrived on the battle-field sometime between 4:00 and 4:30 P.M. A newspaper correspondent, Charles Carlton Coffin, was at Meade's headquarters when the situation seemed most desperate. A cloud of dust began materializing on Balti-more Pike. Coffin related what happened next. "There were anxious countenances around the . . . Commander-in-Chief . . . 'It is not cav-alry, but infantry,' said one [aide], 'there is the flag, it is the Sixth Corps.' Faces which a moment before were grave became cheerful."[3]

The column halted near Rock Creek. Coffin related how the men "threw themselves upon the ground, tossed aside their knapsacks, and wiped the sweat from their sun-burnt cheeks." After a short break, the men were ordered to the center of the Union line, where they were permitted to rest for about two hours. At about 6:00 P.M., General Sedgwick received orders to support the left, which was crumbling under heavy attacks by two Confederate divisions. Lieutenant George Bicknell of the 5th Maine noted that the order transformed the weary men. "The men seemed wild with excitement. Drums beat, colors were flying—it was a season of rejoicing. The long weary miles were all for-gotten." The corps was broken apart soon after and its units sent to various parts of the field.[4]

On July 3, the corps had the distinction of having one brigade (Neill's) on the extreme right of the Union line, and another (Grant's) on the extreme left of the army. Although the corps played but a small part in the battle, its arrival helped buoy the other troops and ensured that any breakthrough by Lee's forces would be short-lived.[5]

1ST DIVISION—

Brigadier General Horatio Wright

1st Brigade—Brigadier General Alfred Torbert
Units: 1st New Jersey, 2nd New Jersey, 3rd New Jersey, 15th New Jersey
Strength: 1320
Losses: 11 (0-11-0)—0.8%[6]

2nd Brigade—Brigadier General Joseph Bartlett
Units: 5th Maine, 121st New York, 95th Pennsylvania, 96th Pennsylvania
Strength: 1325
Losses: 5 (1-4-0)—0.4%[7]

3rd Brigade—Brigadier General David Russell
Units: 6th Maine, 49th Pennsylvania, 119th Pennsylvania, 5th Wisconsin
Strength: 1832
Losses: 2 (0-2-0)—0.05%[8]

The men of the 1st Division had many questions about their new commander, Brigadier General Horatio Wright, as they marched north. He had commanded the division since May 23, 1863, so the men did not know much about him. A West Point graduate, Wright had commanded a brigade during the storming of Port Royal South Carolina and a division during the ill-fated battle of Secessionville in June 1862. He then took over the Department of the Ohio. He finally landed at the head of the 1st Division. All agreed that he was a man of great promise, but with little battlefield experience.[9]

The men received a warm reception as they marched northward. "The inhabitants Seem to be pleased to See the army came [sic] to defend them," wrote Sergeant John Hartwell of the 121st New York (Bartlett's Brigade). Bread, milk, meat, and pies were very much in evidence, and they were freely distributed to the men. Lieutenant James Latta of the 119th Pennsylvania (Russell's Brigade) was reminded of a county fair during his stay in Manchester. Citizens streamed in from

miles around just to see the soldiers who had marched north to protect their homes. By the time the column reached the Pennsylvania
state line, the men were too engrossed in their own misery to show
much enthusiasm. However, many were especially pleased with their
reception at Littletown, a small community just south of Gettysburg.
Large pails of cool water were hoisted onto the town's horse blocks,
allowing the men to dip their cups into them as they marched past. To
brighten the men's spirits even more, the flags were unfurled and the
bands struck up lively military airs. On the negative side, the soldiers
could also see the citizens carrying off some of the wounded in their
buggies.[10]

The officers continually told their men to keep the ranks closed
and not to straggle. Some told their men that they would shoot any
man falling out of rank. The men joked about surviving the march,
but were less optimistic about the officers' horses. Frequent songs
broke out and whole companies engaged in singing. These activities
helped the miles go faster and the misery seem less severe. There was
no time to stop and eat so, according to Private Isaac Best of the 121st
New York (Barlett's Brigade), "raw pork and hardtack was our bill of
fare that day." So exhausted were the men that many marched while
almost asleep. As July 2 wore on, the hardships increased. "[Our] eyes
aching from want of sleep, faint from want of nourishment, we
marched along, but without murmur, or complaint," wrote Major F. W.
Morse of the same regiment. "The heat was deadly, dust filled our
throats; but still the march was kept up . . . no time to rest, no time to
east, no time for any thing but suffering." Morse saw that his men's
faces were "haggard and distorted by fatigue, their feet swollen and
their shoes in consequence thrown away . . . but . . . there was a look of
determination in their eyes."[11]

When the column stopped to rest at 1:00 P.M. on July 2, most of the
men merely dropped in their places and went to sleep. The march
continued an hour later, and the column approached the battlefield
within the next two hours. General Torbert was especially proud of his
brigade, as only twenty-five men had fallen out of the ranks during this
arduous trek to the battlefield. The men were permitted to bathe their
tired and blistered feet in Rock Creek. While Torbert's Brigade was
refreshing itself, the sounds of battle could clearly be heard up ahead.
Suddenly, a dusty aide galloped up and inquired about the location of
Sedgwick's headquarters. The men knew what was coming, and within
moments they were on their feet and preparing to enter the fray. As
the column rushed south, "shells were bursting in the air and minnie
balls singing close to our heads," reported Reverend Alanson Haines
of the 14th New Jersey (Torbert's Brigade).[12]

Torbert's and Russell's Brigades took up their reserve positions in the rear of the Federal line, behind, and just north of Little Round Top as the sun was setting. In the meantime, Bartlett's Brigade was detached and sent to the right of Wheaton's (Nevin's) of the 3rd Division, just north of Little Round Top. Wofford's victorious Confederate brigade soon approached. General Bartlett wrote that "before my formation was complete, [Wheaton's Brigade] moved rapidly to the front and right, completely masking my troops, and rendering an advance unnecessary." Barlett and his men could only watch as Wheaton's men dashed down toward the Georgians and routed those still advancing toward the heights. Bartlett's Brigade suffered but two casualties from stray bullets.[13]

The men constructed breastworks during the night of July 2 to protect themselves from another Confederate attack that was anticipated on the morrow. This completed, "we dropped where we stood, and the men instantly fell in a deep dead sleep," recalled Major F. W. Morse of the 121st New York (Bartlett's Brigade).[14]

The division was further broken apart early on July 3, when Torbert's Brigade moved north to fill a gap to the left of the I Corps. Because of the brigade's isolation, General Wright placed it under the command of I Corps commander, General Newton. The men prepared for the Confederate onslaught by piling their cartridges on top of a stone wall and crouching behind it. Additional muskets were loaded and kept within easy reach. The last brigade, Russell's, was ordered to the extreme left of the Federal line. Wright rode along with the brigade and took command of this sector, which included Grant's Vermont Brigade of Howe's 2nd Division, and two batteries of artillery.[15]

Many of Wright's units were exposed to the tremendous cannonade that preceeded the Pickett–Pettigrew–Trimble charge. Major Morse of the 121st New York counted three to six shells bursting per second, and wrote that even the most hardened veteran was amazed at the barrage. "The air grew thicker and fuller and more deafening with the howling and whirling of these infernal missiles," he wrote. As the charge was being repulsed, Wright received orders to send Russell's Brigade north to reinforce the right of the V Corps. The threat was over when it arrived, so the brigade remained in reserve. The following day the brigade moved once again, this time to the left of the V Corps, on the west-facing slope of Big Round Top. This brigade had the distinction of suffering the fewest casualties (two men) during the battle.[16]

July 4 was a quiet day. The men helped tend to the wounded and bury the dead. Many roamed about, replacing their Enfield muskets with Springfields. Some reluctantly made this switch, as they believed that the Enfields shot farther and with greater accuracy.[17]

The division crossed the Valley of Death on July 5, and moved cautiously toward Seminary Ridge. Seeing some enemy to their right, the troops opened fire and dispersed them. This was the last small arms fire on the battlefield. The pursuit of Lee's army began at about 11:00 A.M. with Torbert's New Jersey Brigade leading the column.[18]

Like most of the units in Sedgwick's Corps, Wright's Division played only a supporting role in the battle. It is doubtful that more than a few men even fired their muskets.

2ND DIVISION—

Brigadier General Albion Howe

Grant's Brigade—Colonel Lewis Grant
Units: 2nd Vermont, 3rd Vermont, 4th Vermont, 5th Vermont, 6th Vermont
Strength: 1832
Losses: 1 (0-1-0)—0.05%[19]

Neill's Brigade—Brigadier General Thomas Neill
Units: 7th Maine, 33rd New York, 43rd New York, 49th New York, 77th New York, 61st Pennsylvania
Strength: 1775
Losses: 15 (2-11-2)—0.8%[20]

The officers and men of the VI Corps realized that Brigadier General Albion Howe had friends in high places, for in spite of a minimal combat record, he was given the 2nd Division on November 16, 1862. Howe was a West Point graduate who had seen limited action as a brigade commander during the Seven Days' battles. Not engaged at Second Bull Run or Antietam, Howe had very little combat experience when he assumed command of the division. Howe and the division performed well at Chancellorsville, so the men felt more comfortable with their new commander at the start of the Gettysburg campaign.[21]

Few men in Howe's Division had ever seen the kind of bounty they encountered during the march toward Gettysburg. Lieutenant Colonel Selden Conner of the 7th Maine (Neill's Brigade) told his father that it "would do you good to travel in this country; such farms I never saw before. I have not seen a pauper for three weeks." Despite the long marches north, many of the men did not mind going on picket duty because it meant a license to forage. Being on the extreme right flank of the army, the men marched through towns that had been visited by the Confederates. One such town was Westminster, which they passed through on July 1. "The people welcomed us with demonstrations of joy, which were all the more earnest, as the rebel cavalry had, but two hours before, taken a hasty leave of them." The men were greeted with an outpouring of joy and food. Some towns-people had distilled their own rye whiskey and freely distributed it to the men. As a result, several became intoxicated and fell by the side of the road during the march. [22]

The long march to the battlefield began that evening. Because wagons and other vehicles clogged the road, the initial part of the march was slow. "Marching by rods is like dying in inches, and it gets an impatient man into a hell of a misery. Scolding and swearing is dispensed at an awful rate when a regiment is compelled to halt and wait every few rods, if the road is good and the journey long," complained Private Wilbur Fisk. A thirty-five-mile march in eighteen hours is bad enough, but making it worse was the fact that it was made under a blazing sun on July 2. The men were also burdened with at least fifty pounds of equipment. Water was also a problem, for although the men were able to replenish their canteens occasionally when water was brought by citizens, at all other times the officers refused to let the men stop where natural water was available. Relatively few fell from the ranks during this leg of the march because, according to Private George Stevens of the 77th New York (Neill's Brigade), "few in that corps were willing to be left behind in a fight." Those who could not keep up fell from the ranks and rested for a time, then slowly followed the column toward Gettysburg.[23]

Passing through one town, Colonel Grant ordered his brigade "marched through in an orderly manner, carrying our guns in a uniform position, and keeping our step and places in the ranks as if we were trying to play Fourth of July . . . so that we might show the people how well good Union soldiers behave," Private Fisk of the 2nd Vermont wrote home. The trek through Littletown was fondly remembered, as women and children lugged water containers to the road so the men could fill their canteens. They saw many wounded Federal soldiers being cared for by the citizens.[24]

The division arrived at the battlefield at about 5:00 P.M. After moving to the center of the Union line, the division was split. Grant's Brigade was sent to the left, and Neill's Brigade went off to guard the army's right flank. The latter brigade reported to General Slocum on Powers Hill and was ordered to support Wadsworth's Division on Culp's Hill. General Neill received orders from General Meade at midnight to return to his original position. Grant's Brigade occupied the extreme left flank of the army, to protect it from being turned.[25]

Worried about his right flank during the morning of July 3, General Slocum ordered General Neill to send two regiments to this area.

Neill initially sent the 7th Maine and 43rd New York toward the Taney house, but then decided to send his entire brigade when he realized that Confederate sharpshooters from the 2nd Virginia (Stonewall Brigade, Johnson's Division) were active in this sector. Meanwhile, Grant's Brigade occupied the exact opposite end of the army. Its right flank was rested near the Round Tops; its left, on Taneytown Road. Here the men hastily constructed a breastwork of fence rails and dirt. According to Private Fisk (2nd Vermont), Colonel Grant only smiled when he saw it.[26]

While Grant's Brigade was spared the severe artillery firestorm that preceded the Pickett–Pettigrew–Trimble charge on July 3, the same was not true of Neill's Brigade. "Every size and form of missile known to gunnery crashed, shrieked, whirled, moaned and whistled along the ridge, splintering trees, bounding from rocks, smashing wagons, disabling guns . . . the roar at first was deafening," recalled A. T. Brewster of the 61st Pennsylvania. July 4 was a quiet day for the men. They marched after Lee's army on July 5.[27]

Except for the distinction of guarding both flanks of the army on July 3, Howe's Division played a small role in the battle.

3RD DIVISION—

Brigadier General John Newton/
Brigadier General Frank Wheaton

1st Brigade—Brigadier Alexander Shaler
Units: 65th New York, 67th New York, 122nd New York, 23rd Pennsylvania, 82nd Pennsylvania
Strength: 1770
Losses: 74 (15-56-3)—4.2%[28]

2nd Brigade—Colonel Henry Eustis
Units: 7th Massachusetts, 10th Massachusetts, 37th Massachusetts, 2nd Rhode Island
Strength: 1595
Losses: 69 (3-41-25)—4.3%[29]

Brigadier General John Newton was very familiar to his men. A West Point graduate, he began the war as an engineer and was given a brigade in the fall of 1861. He led his unit at Gaines's Mill and Malvern Hill and received recognition for his actions at both battles. A high point in Newton's career was at the battle of Crampton's Gap, where his brigade helped overwhelm the Confederates. He assumed command of the 3rd Division on October 18, 1862, and led it during the Fredericksburg and Chancellorsville campaigns. As a result of his distinguished career, the men were most comfortable with their leader's abilities.[30]

The division made good progress through the Maryland countryside. Citizens lined the road in abundance, waving small flags and offering food or drink. The men passed through Westminster around noon on June 30, where they saw evidence of a cavalry battle that had been waged only a few hours before. The column continued on to Manchester, where the division bivouacked for the night. July 1 was fairly quiet, so the men cleaned their guns and repaired their clothing after completing the long five-day march. Many thought they would spend another night there and were asleep when the sound of hoofs became louder. A bugle soon sounded "assembly." "Pack up and fall in immediately," yelled the officers. "Blankets were slung, knapsacks packed, belts tightened, and almost sooner than it takes to write it, the Regiment was up the road," wrote Reverend Augustus Woodbury of the 2nd Rhode Island. The men were in good spirits after their almost twenty-four-hour rest.[31]

The march continued long into the night. The officers constantly yelled, "Close up! Close up!" They also offered continual encouragement. "Boys, do your best. We must reach the field; the brave old army needs you," recalled Private Nelson Hutchinson of the 7th Massachusetts (Eustis's Brigade). Night became day and still the officers issued the same orders. Perspiration flowed freely from the men as their heavy loads, coupled with the heat, made marching difficult. A halt was permitted, but before the coffee was even half brewed, the men were ordered back into line. Unfinished coffee is better than none at all, so the men either gulped it down or carefully poured it into their canteens. Many men fell from the ranks in exhaustion, but most of them trudged slowly after the column after resting a while.[32]

Citizens cheered the men as they marched through Littletown. However, the men were unhappy that the troops ahead of them had depleted all the food the citizens of the small town had to distribute. Brewster (10th Massachusetts) told his mother a different story. Many citizens said that they were out of food until some of the men pulled out greenbacks. A veritable banquet of pies and breads suddenly appeared that were sold at exorbitant prices. "Those women sold lots of pies . . . to these tired, hungry, dust begrimed soldiers . . . to save the homes of these worthless wretches from destruction," wrote Brewster. Another short rest was permitted at 2:00 P.M., but the men not allowed to kindle fires, as there was not enough time to make coffee. Earlier, General Newton had been ordered to Gettysburg to take command of the I Corps, leaving General Wheaton in charge of the division. The column finally approached Rock Creek at about 4:00 P.M. Details were quickly sent to fill canteens, but aides arrived almost immediately with orders to move quickly toward the left of the line, where Sickles's III Corps was bearing the brunt of Longstreet's attack. Riding ahead, General Sedgwick surveyed the situation and sent a messenger back with the order, "Tell Colonel Eustis to bring up his brigade as soon as possible!" The men were now ordered to "Fall in; Take arms; right face; forward march," at a double-quick pace. "Forgotten the pain, ignored the stiffness of limb, for help is needed," explained Private

James Bowen of the 37th Massachusetts. The men fixed bayonets as they dashed forward. Upon reaching their assigned position, Eustis's brigade formed the first line and Shaler's behind it. The two brigades bivouacked for the night behind the Round Tops.[33]

While Eustis's Brigade maintained its position during the morning of July 3, Shaler's Brigade was ordered to Culp's Hill at 3:30 A.M., where it came under heavy artillery fire. Before the brigade moved north, General Meade sent word to General Shaler that he was to remain in the center of the line and to report directly to General Newton, now commanding the I Corps. General Newton ordered the brigade about half a mile to the right, where it came under General Geary's (2nd Division XII Corps) orders. The battle for Culp's Hill was raging as the brigade formed in the rear in column of regiments.[34]

Geary skillfully pulled his regiments out of the front line and replaced them with fresh units. Although Geary had been ordered not to use Shaler's Brigade unless absolutely necessary, Confederate pressure on the Union defenders continued to escalate. Shaler's Brigade's time arrived at 9:00 A.M., when the 122nd New York was ordered forward into the entrenchments to relieve the 111th Pennsylvania (Kane's Brigade). Colonel Silas Titus of the 122nd New York recalled Shaler saying to him, "Col., things are a little mixed up there, go in and report to me, I will support you with the balance of the brigade."[35]

Corporal Sanford Truesdell of the 122nd New York recalled the move to occupy the breastworks:

> About fifteen rods in front of our lines, was a breastwork . . . to reach it we had to cross a space of about ten rods, fully exposed to the fire of the enemy, we crawled on our hands and knees, to the top of the bluff, and raising up, ran to our position as fast as our legs could carry us, but O! how the bullets whistled, our companions dropped at every step, but it seemed impossible for one of us to reach there alive.[36]

The regiment lost about forty-four men while in the open. Now safely in the breastworks, the men looked to the left and saw the familiar faces of the 149th New York (Greene's Brigade), which also hailed from Onondaga County. The men now opened fire on the enemy. "Our fire was sharp and effective, while we were in comparative safety," wrote Truesdell. "We had them now in a tight fix, as they could not retreat without exposing themselves, as much as we did, while coming out." Realizing their dilemma, Daniel's Confederate Brigade (Rodes's Division) charged the works again, and again was repulsed. Many Confederates finally decided to surrender rather than risk being shot in the back during their retreat. About twenty minutes after the 122nd

New York arrived in the breastworks, the 23rd Pennsylvania moved up to support them, 150 yards in the rear. The 67th New York was thrown into the fray at about 11:00 A.M., just as the Confederates were pulling back, and succeeded in capturing about twenty of them. Fifteen minutes later, the 65th New York also advanced to the breastworks to support the 23rd Pennsylvania. At 11:30, the 82nd Pennsylvania moved forward and relieved the 122nd New York.[37]

Five companies from the 23nd Pennsylvania were detached at about 12:20 P.M. and moved farther to the right, under heavy enemy fire, to occupy a portion of the breastworks. After silencing the small arms fire, a skirmish line was thrown out, but it encountered exceptionally heavy small arms fire and was compelled to fall back. All of the regiments were pulled back at 3:00 P.M., and the brigade reformed in the rear after holding their positions for several hours.[38]

While Shaler's Brigade was repelling Confederate charges on Culp's Hill, Eustis's was up at dawn. According to Colonel Horatio Rodgers of the 2nd Rhode Island, "wherever the fighting was the thickest there the brigade was sure to be sent, to reinforce the line when hard pressed. But though we had to traverse the bloody, fatal field . . . first to the centre, then back again, then retrace our steps, then to the right, and so on, were not called on to fire a shot." The day was so hot that several men fell out of the ranks because of heat stroke. Although the men did not fire a shot, the 37th Massachusetts suffered twenty-four casualties when it came under the artillery fire preceding the Pickett–Pettigrew–Trimble charge. These losses were three times higher than those of the 10th Massachusetts, which was also moving by the flank. The difference in losses was probably because the 37th Massachusetts was marching "in close order," while the 10th Massachusetts was strung out.[39]

That night, Eustis's men were permitted to make small fires to prepare their coffee, and in the words of Alfred Roe of the 10th Massachusetts, "actually rest, a most gracious privilege." July 4 found the men tending to the wounded and burying the dead. The brigade was ordered to entrench during the early afternoon. Not possessing tools, the men used their bayonets, tin plates, and cups to dig. Some used fence rails and even dead horses as barricades. The division moved out after Lee's army on July 5.[40]

The two sister brigades were both under fire during the second and third days of the battle. However, Shaler's Brigade played a more pivotal role, as it helped repulse several Confederate charges on Culp's Hill, while Eustis's Brigade played only a supporting role, moving from place to place without firing a shot. The 3rd Brigade also played an important role, as described below.

❧

3rd Brigade—Brigadier General Frank Wheaton/
Colonel David Nevin

Units: 62nd New York, 93rd Pennsylvania, 98th Pennsylvania, 102nd Pennsylvania, 139th Pennsylvania
Strength: 1369
Losses: 53 (2-51-0)—3.9%[41]

Brigadier General Frank Wheaton was another officer who did not have extensive combat experience prior to Gettysburg. He began the war as lieutenant colonel of the 2nd Rhode Island Volunteers, and saw action at First Bull Run. Despite seeing almost no action after that, Wheaton was promoted to brigadier general and given command of the 3rd Brigade on December 15, 1862. Although the brigade did well at the battle of Chancellorsville, a question mark still hung over it and its commanding officer.[42]

The order to march with haste to the battlefield arrived during the early evening hours of July 1, and the regiments were on the road by 9:00 P.M. The column trudged toward Gettysburg all night. More than a few men grumbled when the brigade took the wrong road and lost two hours by backtracking. The unit crossed the Pennsylvania state line at daybreak. This was a very special event for the brigade, as most of it was composed of Pennsylvania regiments. "Our bands struck up the 'Star Spangled Banner,' the men fell into close marching order, taking the correct step from the music, and up went three cheers and a 'tiger' that made the air ring," noted Private George Uhler of the 93rd Pennsylvania. Captain William Herbert of the 139th Pennsylvania added that the men waved their caps in the air.[43]

July 2 was hot and the road dusty. Fortunately, citizens lined the road in many

places, providing encouragement, and better still, refreshments to the exhausted troops. Many of the men probably also remembered some of the stirring remarks made by their regimental commanders before the march began.[44]

The brigade led the VI Corps column. Arriving near Rock Creek between 2:00 and 3:00 P.M. that afternoon, the brigade had completed the thirty-four-mile march in 18 hours. As the brigade reached its assigned position, Chaplain S. Lame of the 93rd Pennsylvania recalled the men were "too much exhausted to eat, [and] threw themselves wearily to the ground and lay like logs." Meade assigned John Newton to command the I Corps during the march, so General Wheaton took over the division. This left Colonel David Nevin of the 93rd Pennsylvania in charge of the brigade.[45]

The brigade was ordered to Little Round Top at about 4:30 P.M. According to Captain William Herbert of the 139th Pennsylvania, General Sedgwick was so concerned about the Federal left flank that he rode over to Colonel Nevin and yelled, "Hurry up there; never mind forming your brigade; pitch in by regiments." Upon reaching Little Round Top, the brigade formed behind McCandless's Brigade of Pennsylvania Reserves (Crawford's Division, V Corps). Before long, the men could see Ayres's regular troops approaching. To Private Wesley George of the 139th Pennsylvania, they were "going off the field in such good order that the incoming troops thought . . . [it] was on account of having exhausted their supply of ammunition." This recollection was not universally shared. Another veteran wrote in the *National Tribune* that they "met General Sykes' regulars coming up the hill in very bad order and running for life." What actually occurred was probably somewhere between these two versions, as several victorious Confederate brigades from McLaws's Division had smashed into the regulars and drove them from the field. The enemy was now approaching the prize of Little Round Top. Confederate sharpshooters were active and losses mounted during this period. For example, the 98th Pennsylvania lost ten men.[46]

Colonel Nevins received orders to move to the right of McCandless's Brigade. Leaving the 98th Pennsylvania to support their left flank, the 62nd New York, 93rd Pennsylvania, and 139th Pennsylvania quickly advanced. The men immediately saw Wofford's Brigade (McLaws's Division) approaching and, in the words of Nevins, "delivered two volleys into the ranks of the advancing rebels, and immediately after charged their column, breaking the same and driving them in disorder down the hill." They did not know it, but General Wofford had already received orders to withdraw, and probably was in the process of doing so. Wofford's departure was hastened when Nevin's three regiments charged down the hill, crossed the Valley of Death, and continued on about a hundred yards before halting. Nevin's Brigade also recaptured several lost guns from Walcott's battery during the counterattack.[47]

While Nevin's three regiments charged Wofford's men, the 98th Pennsylvania went into action on the left of McCandless's Brigade. It joined their charge and drove the enemy before it although there was no serious resistance as he Confederate charge was spent. As the men continued through the Valley of Death, Captain Jacob Schmide of the 98th Pennsylvania noted that his regiment "received a livelier

fire from the left (Devil's Den) while crossing the swamp, which, together with the difficulty of crossing through the soft slough [Plum Run valley], had the effect to break our line up somewhat." The line reformed and, in the words of Schmide, "allowed those who become delayed (stuck in the mire) in crossing, to catch up."[48]

Bad blood developed between Nevin's and McCandless's men after the war. It may have begun when McCandless's men either ignored or minimized Nevin's Brigade's role in repelling the enemy onslaught. Wheaton's men reciprocated by suggesting that the reserves were cowards. For example, Captain William Herbert stated in the dedication of the 139th Pennsylvania monument that "the impetuous and fiery New Yorker [Col. Nevins] . . . found General Crawford and his division of the Fifth Corps in his way and unwilling to move. We will never forget how Colonel Nevin relieved his mind in language more vehement than elegant, giving no attention to the rank of the offending general who doubtless overlooked the offense considering the exciting and sulphurous surroundings." Similarly, Captain Schmide (98th Pennsylvania) said during his unit's monument dedication that "this line of our regiment was formed immediately in rear of a line of others . . . we soon found were some of the Pennsylvania Reserves . . . we were ordered to fix bayonets followed immediately by the command 'forward Ninety-eighth, charge,' and forward we did go, advancing through the line of troops mentioned as lying directly in front of us while we formed, they apparently willingly opening their ranks to let us through."[49]

The brigade stayed behind a stone wall on July 3, not far from the base of Little Round Top, "supporting the two regiments of General Crawford's Pennsylvania Reserves," according to Colonel Nevin.

Confederate sharpshooters operating near Devil's Den to their left continually harassed the men. Captain Samuel Schoyer of the 139th Pennsylvania noted that as the men lay behind the wall, the bullets flew overhead "like sheets of hail." The men observed the Confederates making a reconnaissance to their left during the morning, which was quickly driven back, and about 1:00 P.M., they could see and hear the great cannonade that preceded the Pickett–Pettigrew–Trimble charge. The brigade's position precluded it from being exposed to the shelling, however. The brigade remained there until 6:00 P.M. on July 3, when it was ordered to the left to support McCandless's Brigade's strong reconnaissance in force toward the Wheatfield. Two of Nevin's Regiments took an active part in this engagement. The 139th Pennsylvania formed on the right of the McCandless's Brigade and helped recapture a cannon from Bigelow's battery that had been lost the day before near the Trostle farm. The 62nd New York marched to the extreme left of the line, where it participated in driving Benning's Brigade back toward Seminary Ridge. The regiment was without its commanding officer, Colonel F. Collier, who accidentally shot himself in the foot while trying to unjam one of his officers' pistols.[50]

The battle was not yet over for the brigade, for Colonel Nevin received orders at 9:00 A.M. on July 4 to support General Ayres's regulars, who were making a strong reconnaissance toward Seminary Ridge. This completed, the men were either ordered out on picket or helped bury the dead. That evening, General Wheaton returned to assume command of the brigade. It finally left the battlefield on the afternoon of July 5.[51]

While the brigade's losses were modest, it participated in two important engagements. Because it formed on the right of

McCandless's Brigade, the Confederates were confronted by a much more formidable force, which undoubtedly caused them to break off their attack. While of lesser consequence, the actions of two of the regiments during the early evening of July 3 are also noteworthy.

NOTES

1. Dyer, *Compendium*, 308.
2. OR 27, 1, 665, 668; George Bicknell, *History of the Fifth Regiment, Maine Volunteers* (Portland, ME, 1871), 249; James L. Bowen, *History of the Thirty-seventh Regiment, Massachusetts Volunteers in the Civil War* (Holyoke, MA, 1884), 172; Abraham T. Brewer, *History Sixty-first Pennsylvania Volunteers, 1861–1865, Under Authority the Regimental Association* (Pittsburg, PA, 1901), 62; David A. Ward, "Sedgwick's Foot Cavalry: The March of the Sixth Corps to Gettysburg," *Gettysburg Magazine* (January 2000), issue 22, 60.
3. OR 27, 1, 665; Brewer, *History Sixty-first Pennsylvania Volunteers, 1861–1865, Under Authority the Regimental Association*, 63.
4. OR 27, 1, 665; Bicknell, *History of the Fifth Regiment, Maine Volunteers*, 243.
5. OR 27, 1, 665.
6. Busey and Martin, *Regimental Strengths and Losses*, 71, 250.
7. Busey and Martin, *Regimental Strengths and Losses*, 72, 251.
8. Busey and Martin, *Regimental Strengths and Losses*, 72, 251.
9. Dyer, *Compendium*, 308; Tagg, *Generals of Gettysburg*, 106.
10. Bicknell, *History of the Fifth Regiment, Maine Volunteers*, 240; *PAG*, vol. 2, 652–653; Ann H. Britton and Thomas Reed, *To My Beloved Wife and Boy at Home* (Madison, NJ, 1997), 107; Bruce Chadwick, *Brother Against Brother* (New York, 1997), 147.
11. Isaac O. Best, *History of the 121st New York State Infantry* (Chicago, 1921), 86–88; Bicknell, *History of the Fifth Regiment, Maine Volunteers*, 242; F. W. Morse, *Personal Experiences in the War of the Rebellion* (Albany, NY, 1866), 33–34.

12. Chadwick, *Brother Against Brother,* 147; Alanson A. Haines, *History of the Fifteenth Regiment New Jersey Volunteers* (New York, 1883), 668.

13. OR 27, 1, 663, 671; Camille Baquet, *History of the First Brigade, New Jersey Volunteers from 1861–1865* (Trenton, NJ, 1910), 91; Haines, *History of the Fifteenth Regiment New Jersey Volunteers,* 85; Best, *History of the 121st New York State Infantry,* 89.

14. *Maine at Gettysburg,* 366; Morse, *Personal Experiences of the War of the Rebellion,* 35.

15. OR 27, 1, 665; Haines, *History of the Fifteenth Regiment New Jersey Volunteers,* 87; Chadwick, *Brother Against Brother,* 148.

16. Morse, *Personal Experiences of the War of the Rebellion,* 36–37; OR 27, 1, 665, 673.

17. Chadwick, *Brother Against Brother,* 148.

18. OR 27, 1, 666, 670; Bicknell, *History of the Fifth Regiment, Maine Volunteers,* 247; Joseph G. Bilby, *Three Rousing Cheers: A History of the Fifteenth New Jersey* (Hightstown, NJ, 1995), 90; Charles A. Harrison, "Diary of Three Years Service in the United States Army," copy 2nd New Jersey folder, GNMP.

19. Busey and Martin, *Regimental Strengths and Losses,* 73, 251.

20. Busey and Martin, *Regimental Strengths and Losses,* 74, 251.

21. Dyer, *Compendium,* 310; Tagg, *Generals of Gettysburg,* 111.

22. Selden Connor, letter, Brown University Library; Emil Rosenblatt and Ruth Rosenblatt, *Hard Marching Every Day* (Lawrence, KS, 1992), 113–114; George T. Stevens, *Three Years in the Sixth Corps* (Albany, NY, 1866), 239–240.

23. Rosenblatt and Rosenblatt, *Hard Marching Every Day,* 114; Stevens, *Three Years in the Sixth Corps,* 239–240; Brewer, *History Sixty-first Pennsylvania Volunteers, 1861–1865, Under Authority the Regimental Association,* 62.

24. Rosenblatt and Rosenblatt, *Hard Marching Every Day,* 114; Stevens, *Three Years in the Sixth Corps,* 240.

25. OR 27, 1, 675, 679–680.

26. OR 27, 1, 679–680; Rosenblatt and Rosenblatt, *Hard Marching Every Day,* 115.

27. Brewer, *History Sixty-first Pennsylvania Volunteers, 1861–1865, Under Authority the Regimental Association,* 64; OR 27, 1, 679–680.

28. Busey and Martin, *Regimental Strengths and Losses,* 75, 252.

29. Busey and Martin, *Regimental Strengths and Losses,* 75, 252.

30. Tagg, *Generals of Gettysburg,* 112–113; Dyer, *Compendium,* 311.

31. Joseph Newell, *"Ours"—Annals of the Tenth Regiment Massachusetts Volunteers* (Springfield, MA, 1875) 220–221; Bowen, *History of the Thirty-seventh Regiment, Massachusetts Volunteers in the Civil War,* 170–171; Augustus Woodbury, *The Second Rhode Island Regiment* (Providence, RI, 1875), 193; Joseph Taper, diary, copy in the 23rd Pennsylvania folder, GNMP.

32. Nelson V. Hutchinson, *History of the Seventh Massachusetts Volunteer Infantry in the War of the Rebellion* (Taunton, MA, 1890), 153–154.

33. Hutchinson, *History of the Seventh Massachusetts Volunteer Infantry in the War of the Rebellion,* 154–155; Woodbury, *The Second Rhode Island Regiment,* 194–195; Bowen, *History of the Thirty-seventh Regiment, Massachusetts Volunteers in the Civil War,* 173, 174, 176; Charles Brewster, *When This Cruel War is Over* (Amherst, MA, 1992), 241; Mark Nickerson, "Recollections of the Civil War by a High Private in the Front Ranks," copy in the Brake Collection, USAMHI; *PAG,* vol. 1, 187; Alfred S. Roe, *The Tenth Regiment, Massachusetts Volunteer Infantry* (Springfield, MA, 1909), 207; OR 27, 1, 680; *Shaler's Brigade—Survivors of the Sixth Corps: Reunion and Monument Dedications* (Philadelphia, 1888), 43.

34. OR 27, 1, 681–682; *Shaler's Brigade—Survivors of the Sixth Corps: Reunion and Monument Dedications,* 56.

35. Andrew Hug, diary, copy in the 82nd Pennsylvania folder, GNMP; OR 27, 1, 682–683, 829; Pfanz, *Gettysburg—Culp's Hill and Cemetery Hill,* 324.

36. Sandford Truesdell, letter, Special Collections, Joseph Regenstein Library, University of Chicago.

37. OR 27, 1, 682–683; *Shaler's Brigade—Survivors of the Sixth Corps: Reunion and Monument Dedications*, 26–27, 44; Truesdell, letter; John M. Wetherill, "The Eighty-Second Regiment Pennsylvania Volunteers in the Gettysburg Campaign," *The Philadelphia Weekly Press*, February 17, 1886.

38. *PAG*, vol. 1, 188; OR 27, 1, 683; *Shaler's Brigade—Survivors of the Sixth Corps: Reunion and Monument Dedications*, 26–27.

39. Woodbury, *The Second Rhode Island Regiment*, 200; Bowen, *History of the Thirty-seventh Regiment, Massachusetts Volunteers in the Civil War* 190; Newell, *"Ours"—Annals of the Tenth Regiment Massachusetts Volunteers*, 223; Roe, *The Tenth Regiment, Massachusetts Volunteer Infantry*, 208.

40. Roe, *The Tenth Regiment, Massachusetts Volunteer Infantry*, 208; Alonzo Johnson, "War Recollections," copy in 82nd Pennsylvania folder, GNMP; Bowen, *History of the Thirty-seventh Regiment, Massachusetts Volunteers in the Civil War*, 191; Woodbury, *The Second Rhode Island Regiment*, 200.

41. Busey and Martin, *Regimental Strengths and Losses*, 76, 252.

The 102nd New York was detached to guard trains at Manchester, and was therefore not present during the brigade's actions on July 2.

42. Tagg, *Generals of Gettysburg*, 115; Dyer, *Compendium*, 312.

43. George H. Uhler, *Camps and Campaigns of the 93d Regiment, Pennsylvania Volunteers* (n.p., 1898); OR 27, 1, 684, 686; *PAG*, vol. 2, 678.

44. Uhler, *Camps and Campaigns*.

45. Garry Adelman, "The Third Brigade, Third Division, Sixth Corps at Gettysburg," *Gettysburg Magazine* (July 1994), issue 11, 93; OR 27, 1, 684, 686, 688; *PAG*, vol. 1, 506.

46. Penrose G. Mark, *Red: White: and Blue Badge . . . A History of the 93rd Pennsylvania* (Harrisburg, PA, 1911), 217; *PAG*, vol. 2, 678; W. George, "Wheaton's Brigade," *National Tribune*, February 11, 1909; OR 27, 1, 686.

Chaplain Lame recalled that the men were ordered to lie down when they reached their pre-attack position and hold their fire as the enemy advanced. Some of the men fired prematurely into the Confederate ranks. This caused Lame to lament that had this not occurred, the entire Federal line could have sprung up and captured the entire enemy force in front of them (*PAG*, vol. 1, 507).

47. OR 27, 1, 685; Pfanz, *Gettysburg—The Second Day*, 398–399.

48. Adelman, "The Third Brigade, Third Division, Sixth Corps," 95–97; *PAG*, vol. 1, 526.

According to Pfanz (*Gettysburg—The Second Day*, 394), the 98th Pennsylvania became separated from its sister regiments, and following a staff officer, climbed Little Round Top.

Captain Jacob Schmide of the 98th Pennsylvania, who wrote about his regiment moving through McCandless's prone men, admitted that they eventually did rise and charge the enemy. However, he gave the distinct impression that they were merely supporting Nevin's brigade (*PAG*, vol. 1, 525–526).

49. *PAG*, vol. 1, 525–526; vol. 2, 678–679.

Much of the brigade's wrath was directed toward General Crawford. In a letter written after the war, General Wheaton stated, "I quite agree with you that Crawford's innate modesty never prevented his appropriating his full share of all that was done by his own division and by our Newton's division" (Mark, *Red: White: and Blue Badge . . . A History of the 93rd Pennsylvania*, 218).

50. OR 27, 1, 685, 688; *PAG*, vol. 2, 679; William T. Schoyer, *The Road to Cold Harbor* (Pittsburgh, PA, 1986), 20; John Nevin, "93rd Pennsylvania Volunteers," National Archives (RG vol. 27, boxes 48–52); Samuel Harper to John Bachelder, May 7, 1888, in Bachelder Papers, New Hampshire Historical Society.

51. OR 27, 1, 685, 686, 688; *NYG*, vol. 2, 471.

XI CORPS—

Major General Oliver O. Howard/
Major General Carl Schurz

Major General Oliver O. Howard's XI Corps had borne the brunt of the army's disdain since it was crushed at the battle of Chancellorsville. Composed primarily of German-born immigrants, the corps was referred to as "Howard's cowards" and the "flying Dutchmen." Men of other units were fond of taunting the Germans by saying, "I fights mit Sigel . . . and runs mit Schurz!" Negative perceptions of these troops were even held by non-German/Dutch soldiers in the corps. Private Charles Ladley of the 75th Ohio (Ames's Brigade, Barlow's Division) wrote home that the "dutch run and leave us to fight, so we have to fight twice our numbers or run too which we don't like to do at the first fire. Well I hope we shall be able to get out of this soon." Howard fervently hoped that the coming battle would help the XI Corps redeem itself.[1]

There had been few good days on the battlefield for the XI Corps. Formed on September 12, 1862, from Major General Franz Sigel's Corps that had fought in the Shenandoah Valley and had later become part of Pope's Army of Virginia, it spent the Antietam campaign in the defenses of Washington. The corps was not engaged during the battle of Fredericksburg. The battle of Chancellorsville was its first real engagement as a corps, and it was roughly handled during Stonewall Jackson's massive flank attack.[2]

The youngest corps commander in the Army of the Potomac, General Oliver Howard was a West Point graduate who had taught mathematics at the academy after graduation. Beginning the war as colonel of the 3rd Maine, Howard rose to brigade command and led it at First Bull Run. A wound at Fair Oaks caused him to lose his arm, but he was back during the Second Bull Run campaign, where he commanded the Philadelphia Brigade. He took over the 2nd Division of the II Corps during the rout at Antietam when its commander was wounded, and led it at Fredericksburg. He was given command of the XI Corps in April 1863.[3]

General Howard received orders to march from the Middletown Valley in Maryland to Frederick at 2:00 P.M. on June 28. The head of the column arrived at about 8:00 P.M. that night, and the entire corps was in camp by midnight. The next morning the corps continued its march to Emmitsburg, where it bivouacked near St. Joseph College. Around sunset, Howard received a request to meet with General Reynolds. At this meeting General Howard learned that he was assigned to the left wing and was to report directly to Reynolds. The pair spent hours poring over information and discussing what the future might bring. Howard left at about 11:00 P.M.—the last time that he would see his respected colleague. Orders arrived at 8:00 A.M. to march to Gettysburg, and a half hour later his men were in motion. Schurz's and von Steinwehr's Divisions and four batteries made their way northward along Taneytown Road, while Barlow's Division plus a battery followed the I Corps along Emmitsburg Road. A driving rainstorm made the roads slippery, which slowed the march.[4]

Although Schurz's and von Steinwehr's Divisions's route was more circuitous than Barlow's, there were no troops on this road, so the men made faster progress. Upon reaching the Pennsylvania border, the Keystone State regiments beat their drums, dipped their colors, and cheered. A soldier from the 153rd Pennsylvania recalled that "at the state line we were informed that we were crossing into Pennsylvania, our caps went up in the air and gave three cheers for our native State."[5]

The two divisions reached Horner's Mill at 10:30 A.M. and pushed on. A courier arrived as the troops were leaving the town with news of a battle at Gettysburg and orders to make haste in covering the remaining five miles. The day was sultry, but the men rushed forward at a quick-step pace without rests. "The boys thought there was no use marching so fast, for we would be dead before we could get there," wrote one soldier.[6]

With the death of General Reynolds, Howard assumed command of the field, and Brigadier General Carl Schurz of the 3rd Division was placed in charge of the XI Corps. Schurz turned over his division to Brigadier General Alexander Schimmelfennig. The exhausted men of the latter division arrived first, between 12:15 and 12:45 P.M., and were ordered north of Gettysburg to help bolster the I Corps's right flank. Brigadier General Francis Barlow's Division arrived about half an hour later, and was also sent out north of town, forming on Schimmelfennig's right. Brigadier General Adolph von Steinwehr's Division was the last to arrive, and it was placed in reserve on Cemetery Hill.[7]

The townspeople were relieved to see Union troops coming to their rescue. One of them, Professor Henry Jacobs, wrote that the men "kept the pace without breaking ranks; but they flowed through and out into the battlefield beyond, a human tide, at millrace speed."[8]

Schimmelfennig's Division was initially ordered to occupy Oak Hill, but it lost the race to the lead elements of Rodes's Division (Ewell's Corps). Instead, the division deployed several hundred yards north of the town. Barlow's Division also did not occupy its assigned position, which was to extend to the right (east) of Schimmelfennig's right flank. General Barlow instead spied a knoll to the north that he believed would be a better place to meet the enemy and moved his division there. Blocher's Knoll now bears his name. Unfortunately, the position was far in advance of Schimmelfennig's line, which caused both flanks to hang in the air.[9]

With the left of its line at right angles to the right of the I Corps, its right flank exposed, and one division in reserve on Cemetery Hill, the XI Corps prepared to do battle with the Confederates, who were arriving in large numbers from the north. Within a matter of moments, Barlow's Division was defeated on Blocher's Knoll. Then Krzyzanowski's Brigade (Schimmelfennig's Division), moving to Barlow's aid, was crushed. Finally, Coster's Brigade (von Steinwehr's Division) was sent down from Cemetery Hill to halt the Confederate advance from the north, but it, too, was defeated. The retreat became a rout as the troops found chaos in Gettysburg. The Confederates were constantly on their heels, snapping up hundreds of prisoners. The remnants of the XI Corps took refuge on Cemetery Hill, where they were met by General Howard, swinging his sword and yelling, "Rally here, men; rally here! Form a line here! Go no farther, but rally here!" The men essentially remained there for the remainder of the battle.[10]

Howard's men were tested again on the evening of July 2, when two Confederate brigades from Early's Division (Second Corps) attacked Cemetery Hill. Gaps in the line spelled doom to the defenders, and before long, several Confederate units were soon among the guns on the summit of the hill. Marshaling his forces and asking for reinforcements, Howard was able to drive the enemy from the hill and reestablish his defensive line. The remainder of the battle saw the men exchanging shots with the enemy or resting. The corps began its march after Lee's army during the evening of July 5.[11]

1ST DIVISION—

Brigadier General Francis Barlow/
Brigadier General Adelbert Ames

Discouraged by the XI Corps's performance at the battle of Chancellorsville, General Howard brought in Brigadier General Francis Barlow on May 24, 1863, to whip the 1st Division into shape. An attorney by training, Barlow had begun the war as a private, but commanded the 61st New York by the beginning of the Peninsula campaign. Barlow distinguished himself at the battles of Fair Oaks and Malvern Hill. The accolades continued at the battle of Antietam, where he fell gravely wounded. Barlow returned to the army in time to command a XI Corps brigade at Chancellorsville. He was not impressed with his new command, and the men knew it. So began a hostility that continued through June 1863.[12]

Marching behind the I Corps on July 1, Barlow's Division had a much more difficult march to the battlefield than the two other divisions of the XI Corps. After marching through Gettysburg, the division deployed on the right of Schimmelfennig's Division, near the almshouse. Barlow did not like the looks of the position, and after reconnoitering, decided to push his division several hundred yards north to high ground, called Blocher's Knoll, which he considered a fine platform for his artillery. Like General Daniel Sickles the next day, he was also concerned that if he did not seize the high ground, the enemy would, with disastrous results. Some have hypothesized that Barlow ordered the move so he could get on Rodes's Division's left flank as a prelude to destroying it. These plans went awry when Early's Division arrived, and with the help of Doles's Brigade (Rodes's Division), slammed into Barlow's small division. Although the fight was spirited, Barlow's troops could not hold out against the attacks on their front and both flanks. Barlow was severely wounded during this action, and General Adelbert Ames of the 2nd Brigade took over the division.[13]

With their commander severely wounded and the division gravely reduced in numbers, the men retreated into Gettysburg, where hundreds were taken prisoner. Captain Frederick Winkler of the 26th Wisconsin (Schimmelfennig's Division) was unkind to his comrades when he wrote home soon after the battle that "I felt furious when I saw the 1st Division all crowding the sidewalks; think of it, it was a northern village." The survivors took up positions at the base of the northeastern and eastern slopes of Cemetery Hill on the evening of July 1. Many probably wished that their part of the battle was over. It was not. Just after sundown on July 2, the division bore the brunt of Early's Division's desperate attack on Cemetery Hill. Because of several errors by the brigade and divisional commanders, the line was broken and several units were forced up the hill to where the Union cannon were massed. The attack was repelled with assistance from other units and the men returned to their original positions at the base of the hill.[14]

July 3 was uneventful, with the exception of heavy artillery and sniper fire. Losses mounted. The toll among the officers was particularly heavy. Overall, the division marched into battle with about 2500 men and left Gettysburg with under 1200 men, a loss of over 53%.

Colonel Andrew Harris, who took over the 2nd Brigade when Ames replaced the wounded Barlow on July 1, complained to John Bachelder that "Gen. Ames expected more of his weak division than human beings could accomplish. I do not think he made the report of the part taken by his command . . . that the facts warrant." Ames's official report of the battle is surprisingly brief, but what he did write is fairly derogatory to his men, noting that the "First Brigade of this division running through the lines of the regiments . . . of the Second," and "the whole division was falling back with little or no regularity, regimental organizations having become destroyed." Ames's attitude toward his troops was sharply rebuked by General Samuel Carroll, who wrote to Ames on the battlefield, "Damn a man who had no confidence in his troops." [15]

1st Brigade—Colonel Leopold von Gilsa

Units: 41st New York (200 men detached and not present on July 1), 54th New York, 68th New York, 153rd Pennsylvania
Strength: 1136
Losses: 527 (54-311-163)—46%[16]

The road to Gettysburg was a difficult one for the men of the 1st Brigade. Every mile brought them closer to another confrontation with Lee's Army of Northern Virginia. None would ever forget the whipping the corps took when it last met Lee's men at the battle of Chancellorsville. Now, as another battle loomed, something else weighed heavily on them. Division commander Francis Barlow had arrested their no-nonsense leader, Colonel Leopold von Gilsa. Some of the men believed that von Gilsa had run afoul of Barlow when he permitted too many men to break ranks to get water during the march. This was not the case. Von Gilsa decided to remain at Middletown, Maryland, on June 27, 1863, until he received orders from his corps commander, rather than obey his division commander's to rejoin the unit. As the brigade approached Gettysburg, one resident recalled that a "roar of cheers began. It rolled forward, faster than the running of the men . . . its roar of cheering neared and neared, until we saw a group of officers coming at a brisk trot . . . among them rode one man in colonel's uniform who held his head high and smiled." Barlow had restored von Gilsa to his command.[17]

Von Gilsa's Brigade led Barlow's Division's column on the final leg of the march to Gettysburg, and it entered the town at about 1:00 P.M., about half an hour after Schimmelfennig's Division. The 153rd Pennsylvania's band played as townspeople lined the streets. "They stood along the sidewalks with buckets of water, and doing all they could for the men," wrote Private Ruben Ruch of the 153rd Pennsylvania.[18]

The column marched north on Washington Street until it reached the outskirts of Gettysburg. "As soon as we got clear of the town we received another reception, but this was in the shape of solid shot, shells . . . and everything that could be shot out of a cannon," recalled Ruch. The massed column marching out of Gettysburg was a tempting target for some of Rodes's cannoneers on Oak Hill. "The shells were coming pretty thick before we reached the barn [almshouse]." Although the brigade sustained few casualties during this cannonade, it took a psychological toll on the men. Most of the men of the 153rd Pennsylvania ducked as one shell screamed over the column.[19]

Upon leaving town, the brigade crossed open fields and made its way to the almshouse, just northeast of Krzyzanoswki's Brigade's (Schimmelfennig's Division) right flank. Von Gilsa's Brigade formed on the left of the Harrisburg Road and Ames's Brigade was on the right of it. The exhausted men were now permitted to rest while Barlow inspected the ground. During this reprieve the commander of the 153rd Pennsylvania, Major John Frueauff, addressed his men. Explaining that their terms of enlistment had expired on June 22, he said, "If there was a man in [the] ranks who did not wish to go into battle; he should step out, that it was no disgrace; but that the enemy was in our native state, and that the people of Pennsylvania looked to us for relief, and that it was our duty to protect our homes . . . we gave three cheers and not a man stepped out of the ranks."[20]

Barlow decided to occupy Blocher's Knoll and gave orders to that effect to von Gilsa. The men left their knapsacks in a pile by the almshouse, and von Gilsa threw the 54th and 68th New York and two companies of the 153rd Pennsylvania out as skirmishers. He immediately realized that the inexperienced Pennsylvania unit had erred by deploying its color company on the skirmish line. After correcting this problem, von Gilsa probably realized that he needed to assist the regiment's inexperienced skirmishers, so he rode just behind them as they advanced. In addition to providing encouragement, von Gilsa could be heard telling them not to shoot "unless they saw something to shoot at, as ammunition was worth money, and they must not waste it," noted Ruch (153rd Pennsylvania).[21]

The skirmish line took on the sharpshooters of the 5th Alabama (O'Neal's

Brigade, Rodes's Division, Second Corps) and pushed them out of a wheatfield and back toward Rock Creek. About 150 feet to the rear of the skirmish line marched the eight remaining companies of the 153rd Pennsylvania. The day did not bode well for Company D, as its commander, Lieutenant William Beaver, was shot in the chest just as he gave the order to advance. He died later that day.[22]

After his skirmishers had cleared the knoll of Confederates, von Gilsa quickly deployed his brigade in two lines on its summit. In the center of the first line were the two companies of the 153rd Pennsylvania that had formed the skirmish line. The 68th New York was broken up, with one small detachment forming on the left of the 153rd Pennsylvania and stretching toward Carlisle Road. The rest of the regiment formed on the right of the Pennsylvanians. To the right of the 68th New York was the 54th New York, which extended to Rock Creek. The second line was composed of the eight remaining companies of the 153rd Pennsylvania, thinly stretched from the middle of the 68th New York on the left to the center of the 54th New York on the right. The men were ordered to lie down to rest, which also helped them avoid the bullets that continued flying overhead.[23]

The brigade's position was vulnerable, even to the untrained eye. Although the brigade occupied high ground, both flanks floated invitingly in the air. Possibly following prior orders, Barlow decided to keep Ames's Brigade *en echelon*, about one-quarter of a mile to the rear. Just before von Gilsa became engaged, Barlow realized his error and quickly brought up Ames's Brigade, deploying it within supporting distance of von Gilsa's left flank.[24]

With his brigade in position, von Gilsa threw out another line of skirmishers. Dense thickets obscured their view as they moved cautiously toward Rock Creek. By crouching down, the skirmishers could, however, see the enemy's "legs up to their knees," according to Lieutenant J. Clyde Miller of the 153rd Pennsylvania. Seeing many knees, the men realized that a large force was deploying in the open meadow before them. This was Gordon's Brigade (Early's Division, Second Corps), which had just arrived on the battlefield.[25]

The 31st Georgia (Gordon's Brigade) made at least two approaches against the 68th New York, but were driven back both times. A private from the 153rd Pennsylvania accurately assessed the situation when he wrote, "I think it was a feint, their object being to keep us in our position until they got ready."[26]

Lieutenant Clyde Miller of the 153rd Pennsylvania was upset when several of his men on the skirmish line were hit by small arms fire coming from their right and rear. Thinking it was friendly fire, he sent a corporal back to the regiment to stop the firing. The corporal rapidly returned with bad news: the gunfire was from the enemy in their rear. With Doles's Brigade on their left and Gordon's Brigade in front, the Confederate attack was unleashed. Von Gilsa's Brigade initially held its position. General Gordon reported that the "enemy made a most obstinate resistance until the colors on portions of the two lines were separated by a space of less than 50 paces, when his line was broken and driven back." A Georgia private agreed. "We had a hard time moving them. We advanced with our accustomed yell, but they stood firm until we got near them. They then began to retreat in fine order, shooting at us as they retreated. They were harder to drive than we had ever known them before. Men were being mown down in great numbers on both sides."[27]

Both wings of von Gilsa's first line crumbled and retired toward the town.

This left the second line, composed of the inexperienced 153rd Pennsylvania. The regiment's leaders wisely realized that further resistance was useless and ordered a rapid withdrawal. One soldier recalled that the brigade had only been in position about ten minutes before this attack was made. Actually, the attack was probably made at least half an hour later. As the men pulled back, they left Ames's Brigade behind.[28]

The men of the 153rd Pennsylvania could see the results of the battle on Blocher's Knoll as they fell back. Ruch wrote that it "presented a regular swath of blue coats, as far as I could see along the line. They were piled up in every shape, some on their backs, some on their faces, and others turned and twisted in every imaginable shape." Von Gilsa's men insisted that they retreated in an orderly fashion, stopping periodically to fire on Gordon's Brigade. Ruch recalled seeing only one man running to the rear. Another wounded Pennsylvanian called the withdrawal a "stubborn retreat of our regiment."[29]

Several men from Ames's Brigade had different recollections. For example, Private William Warren of the 17th Connecticut recalled that as his regiment approached Blocher's Knoll, "a german regt came running back, hooting and hollowing, right through our lines which broke our regt all up & scattered us . . . the officer was drunk & raised his sword over his head, swinging it carelessly around, cussing & swearing at me to get out of that or he would split my head open."[30]

Von Gilsa tried to rally his broken brigade midway between Blocher's Knoll and the town, "using the German epithets so common to him." Ruch also recalled that "the bullets were whistling about like hail." Seeing Gordon's Brigade continuing its advance, "closing in on them like a gate," von Gilsa realized that further resistance was futile and wisely ordered his men to continue their retreat to Gettysburg. The town was rapidly filling with Union soldiers as von Gilsa's men made their way through it. In a classic understatement, one veteran from the 153rd Pennsylvania recalled that "the retirement through and east of the town was attended with some confusion because our men were not acquainted with the streets. Many of the troops had narrow escapes and some were captured."[31]

The men finally reassembled on the northeastern sector of Cemetery Hill. The 54th and 68th New York deployed behind a low stone wall along Brickyard Lane to the right and rear of Ames's Brigade. The 153rd Pennsylvania, minus two companies on the skirmish line, formed on the right of the New York regiments, behind stone walls, farther up the hill, where they supported Wiedrich's and Cooper's batteries. The brigade's deployment was complete when the 41st New York reached the battlefield at 4:00 A.M. on July 2. Two companies were thrown out as skirmishers and the remaining companies took position behind a stone wall, probably near the Evergreen Cemetery gatehouse.[32]

Von Gilsa was devastated by the sight of the remnant of the brigade. Attempting to relieve the tension, one of his aides told him, "You can now command your brigade easily with the voice, my dear Colonel, this is all that is left."[33]

The night was a sleepless one for most of the men. Although exhausted from their long marches and the day's fight, they were filled with anxiety and concern about missing comrades. Meat and soup were distributed to the hungry men at 2:00 A.M. on July 2, which immediately rejuvenated them. Confederate sharpshooters in upper floors of buildings continually fired upon them for most of the daylight hours that followed. Some were so bothersome that the Union artillery opened fire on the most pesky ones, killing or scattering them.[34]

At about 2:00 P.M., the 41st New York was moved closer to the batteries on the hill and helped support them with the 153rd Pennsylvania. Later, the New Yorkers, along with the 33rd Massachusetts (Smith's Brigade, von Steinwehr Division), were thrown forward about half a mile to Culp's Meadow. Fearing an attack, both regiments were pulled back about a thousand yards to the main line at about 5:00 P.M. The 153rd Pennsylvania also moved at about the same time. All of von Gilsa's Regiments now occupied a low stone wall, facing northeast. The deployment, from left to right, was 54th New York–68th New York–153rd Pennsylvania–41st New York. To the left of the brigade was the 17th Connecticut of the Second Brigade; to their right was the 33rd Massachusetts. According to Harry Pfanz, the position was not a good one, as it was fairly isolated and the Union artillery on the hill could not effectively cover it. A knoll about 120 yards in front gave a decided advantage to the Confederates, who ultimately captured it.[35]

The massed Confederate artillery opened on Cemetery Hill at about 4:00 P.M., and its effect on the infantry was deadly. Private William Simmers and Lieutenant Paul Bachschmidt of the 153rd Pennsylvania wrote after the war that the "enemy's shot and shells which, hitherto had injured us but little, were now doing terrible execution in our ranks. Everywhere men were seen writhing in the agony of death, while the wounded were shrieking for help which no one could render them." Up to this point the men had felt that they could repel any attack on this strong position, bristling with cannon. Private Stephen Wallace of the 153rd

Pennsylvania recorded in his diary on July 2, "our forces have a good position and would rather the Rebs to make an attack. We fired cannon every once in a while in order [to] get them to come out."[36]

The men got their wish between sundown and dark, as three long lines of Confederate infantry emerged from the right of the town. The skirmishers saw the Confederates first. Lieutenant Clyde Miller on the 153rd Pennsylvania's skirmish line recalled that he ordered his men to pull back, but stopped them three times along the way to turn and fire on the enemy.[37]

Although wounded on July 1, Ruch (153rd Pennsylvania) watched the Confederate attack from the upper window of a church that had been converted into a hospital. The attack looked formidable, until the Union batteries opened with canister and grape on the advancing Confederates. "I could see heads, arms, and legs flying amid the dust and smoke . . . it reminded me much of a wagon load of pumpkins drawn up a hill and the end gate coming out, and the pumpkins rolling and bounding down the hill," he wrote.[38]

Miraculously, the Confederate line reached the base of Cemetery Hill. The left of Hays's Louisiana Tiger Brigade and the right of Avery's North Carolina Brigade fell on the undersized and skitterish 54th and 68th New York, and after a brief fight, the two regiments were forced to abandon their positions and scamper up the hill. To the right, von Gilsa brought grief to his own men, when he prevented the 153rd Pennsylvania from firing at the approaching shadowy figures. He believed these troops to be Federal infantry, but they were really from Avery's Brigade. Just returning from the skirmish line, Lieutenant Miller told his commander that he was making a mistake, but von Gilsa stubbornly refused to listen. Finally, Lieutenant William Beidelman of Company F ordered his men to open fire on the enemy. The rest of the regiment opened on the enemy lines as well. It was too little too late, as Miller related that the "first rebel line passed over and up towards the batterys [sic] the second line and our line met, and we were jammed up into the batterys, here a promiscuous fight took place." In another narrative after the war, Miller related that the "fight was on in all its fierceness, muskets being handled as clubs; rocks torn from the wall in front and thrown, fists and bayonets used."[39]

Battery commander Captain R. Bruce Ricketts recalled the events quite differently. "When the charge was made on my position, their conduct on that occasion was cowardly and disgraceful in the extreme. As soon as the charge commenced, they, although they had a stonewall in their front, commenced running in the greatest confusion to the rear, hardly a shot was fired, certainly not a volley, and so panic stricken were they that several ran into the canister fire of my guns and were knocked over."[40]

After the left and center of von Gilsa's Brigade were forced to flee up the hill, the Confederate onslaught reached the left of the 41st New York, and it too took to its heels. However, the right of the regiment, and the 33rd Massachusetts (Smith's Brigade) on its right, held their positions and threw an enfilading fire into the left of the 57th North Carolina (Avery's Brigade), driving it back.[41]

Up at the top of the hill, some of von Gilsa's men took position behind a stone wall and opened fire on the enemy. Looking behind him, Lieutenant Miller of the 153rd Pennsylvania could see troops "coming up and through the archway of the Cemetery." Carroll's Brigade (Hays's Division, II Corps) arrived to help halt the Confederate advance. Captain Ricketts contested von Gilsa's men's claims that they assisted Carroll's Brigade in repelling the Confederate charge at the top of the hill. "I wish to say distinctly, that all the credit due to the infantry in that affair is due to Carroll's Brigade alone. None of the 11th Corps were rallied in time to assist in repulsing the charge." Given the chaos around him and the darkness, it is unlikely that Ricketts could have accurately observed what really occurred that evening. Another officer from the 75th Ohio (Ames's Brigade) wrote that "they (the dutch) commenced running back as usual. My sword was out and if I didn't welt them with it my name ain't O.C.L."[42]

After the enemy charge was finally repelled, von Gilsa's men were ordered back down the hill to reoccupy their old positions at the stone wall. This time, the 153rd Pennsylvania took the place of the 17th Connecticut on the left of the 54th and 68th New York. As the 41st New York reassembled, its commander realized that four companies were missing. They were found the following day in front of the town and were thrown out on the skirmish line.[43]

During July 3, the men again were exposed to sniper fire from the town and the heavy artillery fire that preceded the Pickett–Pettigrew–Trimble charge. Casualties mounted. At about 4:00 A.M. on July 4, skirmishers from the brigade were pushed forward toward Gettysburg. They scooped up almost three hundred prisoners as they cautiously entered the town. The men were permitted to rest in the town's square before returning to their positions on Cemetery Hill.[44]

So ended the battle for von Gilsa's Brigade. Its losses were high—approximately 46% of the men. The greatest losses (60%) were sustained by the 68th New York. Unfortunately, the brigade's performance at Gettysburg did nothing to change the army's perceptions about the "flying dutchmen."[45]

✄

2nd Brigade—Brigadier General Adelbert Ames

Units: 17th Connecticut, 25th Ohio, 75th Ohio (100 men on detached service and not present on July 1), 107th Ohio
Strength: 1337
Losses: 778 (68–366–344)—58%[46]

The men of the 2nd Brigade were anxious as they marched toward Gettysburg. They were led by an officer with only limited experience commanding infantry. To make matters worse, Brigadier General Adelbert Ames had assumed command close to the beginning of the campaign (May 24, 1863). The men did know that he was a West Pointer and had begun the war in command of a battery. Shifting to the infantry in August 1862, he took command of the 20th Maine. He saw limited action with the regiment at Fredericksburg, then volunteered to become an aide on George Meade's staff. When General Howard requested seasoned professionals to assist him in whipping the XI Corps into shape, Ames was promoted and sent to command the 2nd Brigade.[47]

The 2nd Brigade's march to the battlefield began at 7:00 A.M. on July 1, when the men were told to strike their tents and be ready to move in an hour. After marching about five miles without a rest, the men were ordered to "double-quick." One soldier from the 75th Ohio characterized it as a "dog trot. "Exhausting in the heat of mid-day and the thick dust of the road. Some dropped with sunstroke and exhaustion. An ambulance drove along with the column and picked up all it could," noted an anonymous soldier in the 75th Ohio.[48]

The brigade slowed down when it reached Gettysburg. "Townspeople were excited and scared to death, hurrying and scurrying in every direction," wrote a soldier from the 75th Ohio. Private William Warren of the 17th Connecticut recorded in his diary that the "citizens stood in their doorways handing us eatables & water out we went through in such a hurry, we could hardly stop to get anything to eat, we were on business, & we soon had all we wanted."[49]

Marching through town on Washington Street, the brigade moved north on Mummasburg Road behind von Gilsa's Brigade. Crossing fields, the column reached a meadow near Harrisburg Road, where the men were given a well-earned rest. "I dropped on the ground like a dead person, all exhausted and very tired," wrote Warren. They were exposed to artillery fire almost as soon as they left Gettysburg. Private Justus Silliman of the 17th Connecticut wrote that "we were obliged to pass through a raking crossfire from a rebel battery on our right, but most of their shells passed over us as we kept pretty close." Not all of the men from the Nutmeg State were so lucky—two resting by the almshouse were wounded by a bursting shell. Many of the men fired off their guns to ensure that they still worked after the morning's soaking rain. Like its sister brigade (von Gilsa's), Ames's Brigade also massed in double column of companies as it rested near the almshouse. From left to right, the brigade was arranged as 107th Ohio—25th Ohio—17th Connecticut. The 75th Ohio formed a supporting line behind them.[50]

Two bodies of troops were detached from the brigade while resting there. The 25th Ohio was ordered forward to support Lieutenant Bayard Wilkeson's battery. At about the same time, a detachment from the 17th Connecticut was rushed forward to secure a brick house and a small wooden bridge on Harrisburg Road that spanned Rock Creek, northeast of the almshouse. Warren recorded in his diary, "before we had hardly rested a moment in the meadow Lieut Col. Fowler wanted to know what Co's would volunteer to go with him & feel for the enemy . . . he only wanted those Co's that would volunteer." Captain Henry Allen immediately stepped forward, and while saluting said, "Colonel Fowler, Company F is ready." Three other company commanders also volunteered, and this small force, led by Major Allen Brady, was soon cautiously making its way northward.[51]

As the detachment approached Rock Creek, Major Brady sent two of the companies to capture the bridge, while the two others were to advance in line, "loading and firing as rapidly as possible, making at the same time a left wheel, so as to swing our right around the house [Josiah Benner's]." As the men approached the house, guns from Lieutenant Colonel H. P. Jones's Confederate artillery battalion opened on them with "shot, shell, grape, and canister," which stopped the advance in its tracks. Brady now dismounted and led his men the rest of the way on foot. Confederate shells soon found the house, setting it on fire and forcing the men to take whatever cover they could find. They now opened fire on the approaching Confederate infantry. These were the only Union soldiers to fight on the north side of Rock Creek during the battle.[52]

The remainder of the brigade did not have long to savor its rest, because the men were rushed forward at about 3:00 P.M. to support von Gilsa's Brigade. "We staid [sic] in this meadow about an hour, laying flat on the ground to rest, then arose & double quicked it out of the lot, acrost [sic] the road, into another lot. We were about used up," recorded Warren in his diary. In front

of them were skirmishers from the 5th Alabama (O'Neal's Brigade, Rodes's Division, Second Corps).[53]

After Wilkeson's battery pulled back, the 25th Ohio moved up to the left of von Gilsa's Brigade, forming beside a small detachment of the 68th New York. The 107th Ohio formed on the left of the 25th Ohio, facing northwest. Behind these two regiments, under the crest of Blocher's Knoll were the 75th Ohio and the six remaining companies of the 17th Connecticut. It is difficult to conceive of a worse disposition of troops. A gap existed between the left of the 107th Ohio and the right of the 68th New York and to make matters worse, the 107th Ohio and 25th Ohio met at a 45 degree angle, forming a salient.[54]

Because of this formation, the left of the 107th Ohio received an enfilading fire along its left flank from the 21st and 44th Georgia of Doles's Brigade (Rodes's Division). Another of Doles's regiments, the 4th Georgia, fired volleys into the 107th Ohio's front, and the 60th Georgia and 31st Georgia of Gordon's Brigade (Early's Division) ripped the right apart. To its right, the 25th Ohio was receiving a crossfire from the 4th, 60th, 31st, and 13th Georgia of Gordon's Brigade. The lines were so close together that the flag bearers of the 25th Ohio and 31st Georgia actually fought each other with their flagstaffs. One private from Gordon's Brigade later wrote that "we advanced with our accustomed yell, but they stood firm until we got near them. They then began to retreat in fire order, shooting at us as they retreated." [55]

The fighting was desperate and von Gilsa's Brigade began to give way. General Ames ordered the 75th Ohio to "fix bayonets, pass to the front between the 107th and 25th Ohio, and if possible check the advance of the enemy," recalled Colonel

Andrew Harris, commander of the 75th Ohio. "It was a fearful advance and made at a dreadful cost of life. We could go no farther, halted and opened fire. We checked them in our immediate front, but they continued to press on around both flanks." A private from the regiment recalled that the artillery bombardment made the ground shake. "The infantry held their fire until the Johnnies were well within range, then let loose. What a horrible roar of battle! Smoke and fumes thick and acrid. One could scarcely see the comrade beside him." Colonel Harris added that "we could not advance for our strength was exhausted. I expected orders to fall back or assistance to hold on, but neither came . . . without orders, I hesitated to fall back but it was soon evident that we could not stay in our exposed condition."[56]

Over on the right, the 17th Connecticut was having its own problems. Originally lined up in reserve to the right of the 75th Ohio, its six companies were broken as von Gilsa's men fled for safety. Warren recorded in his diary that a "german regt came running back, hooting & hollowing, right through our lines which broke our regt all up & scattered us." The regiment was ordered to advance with the 75th Ohio. Lieutenant Doty recalled that "Colonel Fowler at once rode to the front and gave the command to deploy columns, and swinging his sword, said: 'Now, Seventeenth, do your duty! Forward, double quick! Charge bayonets!' And with a yell, which our boys know how to give, they charged." As the regiment reached the top of the knoll, it engaged in hand-to-hand combat with Gordon's soldiers. Despite pleas from his men, Colonel Fowler refused to dismount from his conspicuous white horse, "fearing he might be deemed cowardly," wrote Albert Peck. Fowler was killed within minutes,

"his head shot off and his brains flew on the Adjutent [sic]," wrote Warren.[57]

No troops could have sustained this type of overwhelming attack. General Gordon later wrote that "under the concentrated fire from front and flank, the marvel is that any escaped." As the 75th Ohio began its retreat, its men realized that it was the last regiment of the brigade to leave the knoll. To reduce further losses, Colonel Harris ordered his men to withdraw in a skirmish line. Upon reaching the town, Harris was ordered to take over the brigade, as Barlow's wounding forced Ames to assume divisional command.[58]

As the men of the six companies of the 17th Connecticut retreated through Gettysburg, the four companies that had been thrown across Rock Creek joined them. This detachment also had had its share of excitement. Ordered to pull back, the four companies quickly learned that Hays's Louisiana Brigade (Early's Division) was between them and the town and appeared very eager to cut them off. However, by taking a circuitous route, the Nutmeggers safely reached the town. The regiment frequently stopped to fire volleys into the ranks of the enemy as it moved through the streets of Gettysburg. Being told to move out of the way for a battery to be deployed, the regiment waited along a sidewalk. Here it was attacked by Confederate infantry and driven back. Major Brady, now commanding the regiment, wrote in his after-battle report that as "we retreated, we loaded, halted, and poured destructive volleys into their ranks, which cleared the main street of them several times, but we found the enemy too many for us. They poured in from every street in overwhelming numbers, which broke our ranks." The 17th Connecticut, and the remainder of the 2nd Brigade, finally reached the safety of Cemetery Hill by early evening.[59]

Not all of the men were interested in stopping and taking position on Cemetery Hill. Private Jacob Smith of the 107th Ohio wrote that "many of the troop, no doubt, thought that it was an utter defeat of our forces, and they made an effort to get as far away from the enemy as possible. It required considerable effort on the part of our officers to get them into line and position again. A strong guard of Cavalry and Infantry was placed just in the rear of Cemetery Hill to stop the fleeing soldiers, and send them back into the ranks again."[60]

In his official report, Major Brady suggested that the 17th Connecticut still retained its desire to confront the enemy. "Major-General Howard . . . asked if he had troops brave enough to advance to a stone wall across a lot toward town, and said he would lead them. We replied, 'Yes, the Seventeenth Connecticut will,' and advanced at once to the place indicated." Lieutenant Albert Peck told a different story after the war. "I can tell you, the loss of the brave Colonel Fowler . . . took the zeal out of our boys for a while, and when we were ordered forward, after reforming on the hill, there was a little hesitation until, I think, General Howard took our colors and moved forward, and our boys followed with a cheer."[61]

After some repositioning during the evening of July 1, the brigade was eventually deployed as follows: the 107th Ohio formed the left of the line, facing Gettysburg to the north. On its right was the 25th Ohio, which occupied an angle in the stone wall, so its left flank faced northwest and the town, and its right faced northeast. On its right was the 17th Connecticut. The 75th Ohio formed the extreme right of the brigade.[62]

The regiments now settled down and counted their losses, which were severe.

Three of the four regiments were led by new commanders—Lieutenant Colonel Douglas Fowler of the 17th Connecticut was killed; Lieutenant Colonel Williams of the 25th Ohio was taken prisoner; and Colonel Seraphim Meyer of the 107th Ohio was "relieved of command by the Genl." Several of the regiments had lost more than 50% of their men.[63]

It was a long night for the men. "We were ordered to be very watchful and vigilant, as our troops were expecting to make an attack on the town that night; I don't think I got any sleep that night," wrote Peck (17th Connecticut).[64]

Smith (107th Ohio) recalled that the morning of July 2nd was "fresh, balmy and pleasant." However, Lieutenant Peck of the 17th Connecticut observed an ominous sight. "As soon as it was light . . . we could see the Johnnies moving along the fences in our front, keeping out of sight as much as possible. It was not long before 'zip' came the bullets from them, and our boys promptly returned their fire, although it was difficult to see them." Thus opened a day-long period of sniping that took its toll on the men. The fire was so effective at one point that the 17th Connecticut was ordered back to the protection of a stone wall. The entire regiment was later sent out on picket duty.[65]

Late in the afternoon, the Confederate batteries to the north opened on Cemetery Hill. The men of the 17th Connecticut could see one of the batteries in a wheatfield, about a mile away. "We hugged the ground pretty close, and some of the shells burst over our heads, but I do not remember that any of our brigade were either killed or wounded, although we were very much exposed," noted Peck.[66]

Just before dark, General Ames became aware of a gap between his brigade and von Gilsa's to the right. He therefore ordered the 17th Connecticut to move to the right of the 75th Ohio. One soldier from the 75th Ohio paid its sister regiment quite a compliment when he wrote after the war, "my company was on the right flank next to the Seventeenth Connecticut. At their place the wall dwindled to a height of about two feet [from the four feet to the left] and was a weak point in event of a charge. That's why the Seventeenth Connecticut, known for their hard fighting, was put there." While this effectively sealed the gap between the two brigades, it created another yawning gap between the 25th Ohio and the 75th Ohio. Colonel Harris attempted to compensate by "thinning the line from the left, moving the regiments farther to the right except the left of the 107th Ohio." While some of the 25th Ohio now occupied the gap, it was not enough. Harris complained after the war that "all of the men could get to the stonewall, used by us as a breastwork, and have all the elbow room he wanted."[67]

Just as the 17th Connecticut reached its new position, the skirmish line erupted in gunfire as two brigades from General Early's Division approached. Attacking Colonel Harris's left and center was General Harry Hays's Louisiana Brigade. Despite his dread, Harris watched the charge with admiration. "They moved forward as steadily, amid this hail of shot shell, and minie ball, as though they were on parade far removed from danger. It was a complete surprise to us . . . we could not have been much more surprised if the moving column had raised up out of the ground amid the waving timothy grass of the meadow." Realizing his brigade's danger, Harris gave encouragement as he rode along the line, telling the men about the "importance of our position, and that we must hold it all hazards."[68]

Despite the hail of lead thrown at them by the artillery on the heights, Hays's men quickly covered the six hundred yards to Cemetery Hill. Changing course a bit to the right, the Lousianians fell on the line between the 107th and 25th Ohio. Unfortunately for the Federals, they found the thinly defended gap between the 25th and 75th Ohio, and drove through it. Hand-to-hand fighting erupted. Sergeant George Clements of the 25th Ohio later recalled that the Confederates "put their big feet on the stone wall and went over like deer, over the heads of the whole . . . regiment, the grade being steep and the wall not more than 20 inches high." The situation was becoming perilous, as Hays's Tigers poured over the wall and attacked the 25th and 107th Ohio from the rear. Captain John Lutz of the 107th Ohio later insisted that his men were ordered to pull back, "fighting step by step to the stone fence in front of Wiedrich's Battery."[69]

The two regiments took position on the top of the hill and prepared to help defend the batteries. The flag bearer of the 107th Ohio, Sergeant Greibel, "stood flaunting them in the faces of the rebels," but was shot in the process; the colors were almost captured. Realizing that his men were about to break for the rear, Captain Peter Young sprung forward at the advancing Confederates and shot the 8th Louisiana's flag bearer, catching the colors before they hit the ground. He paid the price when a bullet pierced his left arm and lung.[70]

The situation was quite different on Harris's right. Here the 75th Ohio and 17th Connecticut occupied a naturally strong position. In their front was a short slope that provided good fields of fire. The left of the 75th Ohio was anchored on a wall that ran up the hill, and in front of them was a clump of trees that could impede the progress of the attackers. The 17th Connecticut's ranks were also swelled by the addition of three hundred men who had been "compelled" by Major Brady to join his depleted regiment. Where these men came from is not known.[71]

The growing darkness prevented the men from getting a good look at the attacking columns. But they could certainly hear them. "They came on us about dark yelling like demons with fixed bayonets," Ladley (75th Ohio) wrote home. Major Brady recorded that "when within 150 paces of us, we poured a destructive fire upon them, which thinned their ranks and checked their advance. We fired several volleys by battalion." Hays's men regrouped and charged again. The fighting was now hand-to-hand, as the 17th Connecticut refused to be pushed back from the wall.[72]

The continued attacks sliced back the two right companies of the 75th Ohio that were positioned next to the 17th Connecticut. More threatening was the fact that the Confederates, who had breached left of the brigade's line, were now in their rear. By this point von Gilsa's regiments on their right had also given way. One soldier from the 75th Ohio derisively wrote, "those Germans could not face the bayonet. How they were slaughtered." While some of the men of these two regiments were forced up the hill, most remained in position by the stone wall.[73]

The fighting at the top of the hill was desperate and at close quarters. One soldier from the 75th Ohio recalled that "it was almost impossible to distinguish who were Union, who were Confederate, to shoot and not kill our own men. Artillerists fought with ramrods, wielding them like ballbats." Help was on the way as Carroll's Brigade (Hays's Division, II Corps), and other units of the XI Corps descended on the area, forcing what was left of Hays's and Avery's commands to withdraw from the heights.[74]

While fighting valiantly to hold their untenable position, the brigade again sustained heavy losses. The sense of loss was especially keen in the 75th Ohio, which had lost its flag to the enemy when their flag bearer was killed. Colonel Harris again led his men down toward the base of the hill after the repulse, "at the stone wall in the rear of and parallel with the one occupied the previous day." The left of the brigade now rested on Baltimore Pike.[75]

When dawn broke on July 3, the men could see the outcome of Early's charge. One veteran could only write, "it was a ghastly battlefield." Sniper fire continued during the morning of July 3. Most of the firing was from the steeples of churches that were being used as hospitals and by snipers in the "brickyard," where Coster's Brigade had fought Hays's and Avery's Brigades on July 1. The men were later exposed to the intense artillery barrage that preceded the Pickett–Pettigrew–Trimble charge.[76]

During this period, the men of the 17th Connecticut became increasingly concerned about the lack of food. Told that they would be drawing three-day rations at the conclusion of the July 1 march to Gettysburg, the men had finished off the contents of their haversacks. Unfortunately, transportation problems hindered their resupply, so the men had not eaten for several days, except for the scraps of food they procured during lulls in the battle.[77]

The brigade was ordered into town on July 4. Leaving their positions at 5:00 A.M., they "charged right through on a run and drove the rebels out and captured about 300 prisoners," wrote Ladley. The charge was not as gallant as Ladley made it sound, as the Confederates had all but vacated the town. Those captured Confederates were, in the words of Andrew Harris, "men who were tired of War and concluded not to go back to 'Dixie.'" During this time, Colonel William Noble of the 17th Connecticut, who had been wounded at Chancellorsville, arrived at Gettysburg and assumed command of the brigade.[78]

Ames's Brigade's reputation was certainly not enhanced by its performance at Gettysburg. Although its losses were close to 60% (the 25th Ohio lost 84%, the second highest in the army), it was driven from Barlow's Knoll on July 1 and several of its units broke during the July 2 charge on Cemetery Hill. In both cases, poor placement of the troops led to their defeat. The men had fought hard, but had little to show for it.[79]

NOTES

1. D. Scott Hartwig, "The 11th Army Corps on July 1, 1863," Gettysburg Magazine (January 1990), issue 2, 55; James S. Pula, For Liberty and Justice—The Life and Times of Wladimir Krzyzanowski (Chicago, 1978), 92; Carol M. Becker and Ritchie Thomas, Hearth and Knapsack: The Ladley Letters (Athens, OH, 1988), 147.

2. Dyer, Compendium, 318.

3. Tagg, Generals of Gettysburg, 121–122.

4. OR 27, 1, 701, 707, 727; Oliver O. Howard, Autobiography of Oliver Otis Howard (New York, 1907), vol. 1, 408; "Gen'l O.O. Howard's Personal Reminiscences in the War of the Rebellion," National Tribune, November 20, 1884.

5. William R. Keifer, History of the One Hundred and Fifty-Third Regiment Pennsylvania Volunteer Infantry (Easton, PA, 1909), 208.

6. Carol Schurz, "The Battle of Gettysburg," McClure's Magazine (July 1907), vol. 29, 273; OR 27, 1, 727; Keifer, History of the One Hundred and Fifty-Third Regiment Pennsylvania Volunteer Infantry, 209; Pula, Liberty and Justice—The Life and Times of Wladimir Krzyzanowski, 96.

7. OR 27, 1, 702, 727.

8. Pfanz, Gettysburg—Culp's Hill and Cemetery Hill, 29.

9. OR 27, 1, 752, 754; Hartwig, "The 11th Army Corps on July 1, 1863," 40.

10. OR 27, 1, 703–705; Edwin Southard, "The 119th N.Y. at Gettysburg," National Tribune, August 19, 1897.

11. OR 27, 1, 705–706.

12. Dyer, Compendium, 318, Tagg, Generals of Gettysburg, 125–126.

13. A. Wilson Greene, "From Chancellorsville to Cemetery Hill—O.O. Howard and Eleventh Corps Leadership," in The First Day at Gettysburg (Kent, OH, 1992), 78. It is unfortunate that Barlow blamed the defeat on the fighting prowess of his men and not on his own poor deployment. In a letter to his mother after the battle, he wrote, "this is the last of my connection with the division . . . I would take a brigade in preference to such a division."

14. Louise W. Hitz, Letters of Frederick C. Winkler (n.p., 1963), 71; OR 27, 1, 713.

15. Andrew Harris to John Bachelder, March 14, 1881, Bachelder Papers, New Hamphire Historical Society; OR 27, 1, 712–713; Pfanz, Gettysburg—Culp's Hill and Cemetery Hill, 274.

16. Busey and Martin, Regimental Strengths and Losses at Gettysburg, 81, 253.

17. Pfanz, Gettysburg—Culp's Hill and Cemetery Hill, 29.

18. OR 27, 1, 715; Keifer, History of the One Hundred and Fifty-Third Regiment Pennsylvania Volunteer Infantry, 209.

19. Keifer, History of the One Hundred and Fifty-Third Regiment Pennsylvania Volunteer Infantry, 209–210.

20. Martin, Gettysburg—July 1, 271; Keifer, History of the One Hundred and Fifty-Third Regiment Pennsylvania Volunteer Infantry, 209–210.

21. Bates, Pennsylvania Volunteers, vol. VII, 775; J. Clyde Miller to John Bachelder, March 2, 1886, Bachelder Papers, New Hampshire Historical Society; Keifer, History of the One Hundred and Fifty-Third Regiment Pennsylvania Volunteer Infantry, 210–211; Pfanz, Gettysburg—The First Day, 231–232.

22. Keifer, *History of the One Hundred and Fifty-Third Regiment Pennsylvania Volunteer Infantry,* 140; J. Clyde Miller to John Bachelder, March 2, 1886.

23. Martin, *Gettysburg—July 1,* 274; Hartwig, "The 11th Army Corps on July 1, 1863," 41; Keifer, *History of the One Hundred and Fifty-Third Regiment Pennsylvania Volunteer Infantry,* 211.

24. Martin, *Gettysburg—July 1,* 276–277.

25. Keifer, *History of the One Hundred and Fifty-Third Regiment Pennsylvania Volunteer Infantry,* 140.

26. Keifer, *History of the One Hundred and Fifty-Third Regiment Pennsylvania Volunteer Infantry,* 211.

27. J. Clyde Miller to John Bachelder, March 2, 1886; OR 27, 2, 492; G. W. Nichols, *A Soldier's Story of His Regiment* (Jessup, GA, 1898), 116.

28. Keifer, *History of the One Hundred and Fifty-Third Regiment Pennsylvania Volunteer Infantry,* 211.

29. Keifer, *History of the One Hundred and Fifty-Third Regiment Pennsylvania Volunteer Infantry,* 178, 214.

30. William Warren, diary, 17th Connecticut folder, GNMP.

31. Keifer, *History of the One Hundred and Fifty-Third Regiment Pennsylvania Volunteer Infantry,* 83, 214–215.

32. Keifer, *History of the One Hundred and Fifty-Third Regiment Pennsylvania Volunteer Infantry,* 86; Pfanz, *Gettysburg—Culp's Hill and Cemetery Hill,* 244–235; David G. Martin, *Carl Bornemann's Regiment* (Hightstown, NJ, 1989), 149–150; OR 27, 1, 713.

33. John T. Butts, ed., *A Gallant Captain of the Civil War* (New York, 1902), 80.

34. William Simmers, *The Volunteers' Manual or Ten Months with the One Hundred and Fifty-Third Pennsylvania Volunteers* (Easton, PA, 1863), 29; Keifer, *History of the One Hundred and Fifty-Third Regiment Pennsylvania Volunteer Infantry,* 85; J. Clyde Miller to John Bachelder, March 2, 1886.

35. OR 27, 1, 714; Martin, *Bornemann's Regiment,* 150; Imhof, *Gettysburg—Day Two,*

228; Pfanz, *Gettysburg—Culp's Hill and Cemetery Hill,* 260.

36. Keifer, *History of the One Hundred and Fifty-Third Regiment Pennsylvania Volunteer Infantry,* 86; Stephen Wallace, diary, Pennsylvania State Archives.

37. J. Clyde Miller to John Bachelder, March 2, 1886.

38. Keifer, *History of the One Hundred and Fifty-Third Regiment Pennsylvania Volunteer Infantry,* 220.

39. Martin, *Bornemann's Regiment,* 152–154; J. Clyde Miller to John Bachelder, March 2, 1886; Keifer, *History of the One Hundred and Fifty-Third Regiment Pennsylvania Volunteer Infantry,* 141–142.

Simmers (*The Volunteers' Manual or Ten Months with the One Hundred and Fifty-Third Pennsylvania Volunteers,* 30) recalled that the fight at the wall at the base of Cemetery Hill took about three-quarters of an hour—his recollection was clearly flawed.

40. R. Bruce Ricketts to John Bachelder, March 2, 1866, Bachelder Papers, New Hampshire Historical Society.

41. Martin, *Bornemann's Regiment,* 156; OR 27, 1, 714; OR 27, 2, 484.

42. OR 27, 1, 714; Keifer, *History of the One Hundred and Fifty-Third Regiment Pennsylvania Volunteer Infantry,* 97; J. Clyde Miller to John Bachelder, March 2, 1886; R. Bruce Ricketts to John Bachelder, March 2, 1866; Becker and Thomas, *Heath and Knapsack: The Ladley Letters,* 147.

43. J. Clyde Miller to John Bachelder, March 2, 1886; Martin, *Bornemann's Regiment,* 159.

44. Keifer, *History of the One Hundred and Fifty-Third Regiment Pennsylvania Volunteer Infantry,* 221; Simmers, *The Volunteers' Manual or Ten Months with the One Hundred and Fifty-Third Pennsylvania Volunteers,* 31; *NYG,* vol. 1, 308.

45. Busey and Martin, *Regimental Strengths and Losses,* 253.

46. Busey and Martin, *Regimental Strengths and Losses,* 82, 253.

47. Dyer, *Compendium,* 319; Tagg, *Generals of Gettysburg,* 129–130.

48. Warren, diary, 17th Connecticut folder, GNMP; Tagg, *Generals of Gettysburg*, 130; anonymous, 75th Ohio folder, GNMP.

49. Warren, diary; anonymous, 75th Ohio.

50. Warren, diary; M. Browne to John Bachelder, April 8, 1864, Bachelder Papers, New Hampshire Historical Society; Edward Marcus, *A New Canaan Private in the Civil War* (New Canaan, CT, 1984), 41; Albert Peck, "Memoir," 17th Connecticut folder, GNMP, 94; Andrew Harris to John Bachelder, March 14, 1881.

51. M. Browne to John Bachelder, April 8, 1864; OR 27, 1, 717; Warren, diary; Hamblen, *Connecticut Yankees at Gettysburg*, 18.

52. OR 27, 1, 717; Hamblen, *Connecticut Yankees at Gettysburg*, 20–21. Josiah successfully extinguished the flames before they consumed the house.

53. Warren, diary; Andrew L. Harris to John Bachelder, September 18, 1882, Bachelder Papers, New Hampshire Historical Society.

54. OR 27, 1, 719; Andrew L. Harris to John Bachelder, September 18, 1882; Martin, *Gettysburg—July 1*, 277, 288–289.

55. Jeremiah William to John Bachelder, June 18, 1880, Bachelder Papers, New Hampshire Historical Society; Nichols, *A Soldier's Story of His Regiment*, 116.

56. Andrew Harris to John Bachelder, March 14, 1881; anonymous, 75th Ohio.

57. Warren, diary; Hamblen, *Connecticut Yankees*, 23–24.

58. John B. Gordon, R*eminiscences of the Civil War* (New York, 1903), 141; Andrew Harris to John Bachelder, March 14, 1881.

59. OR 27, 1, 717–718.

60. Jacob Smith, *Camps and Campaigns of the 107th Regiment Ohio Volunteer Infantry* (n.p., n.d.), 89.

61. OR 27, 1, 718; Albert Peck, "First Day at Gettysburg," 17th Connecticut folder, GNMP, 95–96.

62. Augustus Vignos to John Bachelder, April 17, 1864, Bachelder Papers, New Hampshire Historical Society.; OR 27, 1, 716. This description is speculative—Pfanz wrote, "I have seen no good documentary evidence on the position of the three Ohio regiments" (*Culp's Hill and Cemetery Hill*, 448–449, n. 27).

63. M. Browne to John Bachelder, April 8, 1864; Andrew Harris to John Bachelder, March 14, 1881. According to Harris, Meyer was sick on July 1, but Captain Peter Young of the 107th Ohio reported that the cause was "incapacity and cowardice" (Peter Young to John Bachelder, August 12, 1867, Bachelder Papers, New Hampshire Historical Society).

64. Peck, "First Day at Gettysburg," 96.

65. Smith, *Camps and Campaigns of the 107th Regiment Ohio Volunteer Infantry*, 93; Peck, "Second Day at Gettysburg," 97–98; OR 27, 1, 719.

66. Peck, "Second Day at Gettysburg," 98–99.

67. Anonymous, 75th Ohio; Andrew Harris to John Bachelder, March 14, 1881.

68. Andrew Harris to John Bachelder, March 14, 1881.

69. George S. Clements, "The 25th Ohio at Gettysburg," *National Tribune*, August 6, 1891; Alfred Rider to John Bachelder, August 20, 1885, Bachelder Papers, New Hampshire Historical Society.

70. Peter Young to John Bachelder, August 12, 1867; Smith, *Camps and Campaigns of the 107th Regiment Ohio Volunteer Infantry*, 101; OR 27, 1, 720.

71. Pfanz, *Culp's Hill and Cemetery Hill*, 257–258; OR 27, 1, 718.

72. Becker and Thomas, *Hearth and Knapsack: The Ladley Letters*, 142; OR 27, 1, 718.

73. George Fox to John Bachelder, November 14, 1885, Bachelder Papers, New Hampshire Historical Society; Hamblen, *Connecticut Yankees at Gettysburg*, 60–61; Anonymous, 75th Ohio.

74. Anonymous, 75th Ohio; Edward C. Culp, *The Twenty-Fifth Ohio Veteran Volunteer Infantry in the War for the Union* (Topeka, KS, 1885), 78–79.

75. Anonymous, 75th Ohio; OR 27, 1, 716; William Noble, letter, Leigh Collection, USAMHI.

76. Andrew Harris to John Bachelder, March 14, 1881; Culp, *The Twenty-Fifth Ohio Veteran Volunteer Infantry in the War for the Union*, 79.

77. "17th Conn. Vols," *Gettysburg Compiler*, September 29, 1894.

78. Becker and Thomas, *Hearth and Knapsack: The Ladley Letters*, 142; OR 27, 1, 716; Andrew Harris to John Bachelder, March 14, 1881.

79. Busey and Martin, *Regimental Strengths and Losses*, 253, 262.

2ND DIVISION—

Brigadier General Adolph von Steinwehr

The 2nd Division of the Army of the Potomac had not seen much action, other than during the Shenandoah Valley campaign of 1862. The division was composed of only three regiments at Second Bull Run, but was later expanded with the addition of two brigades. The division finally saw action at Chancellorsville, where it was soundly defeated along with the rest of the XI Corps. The division's commander, Brigadier General Adolph von Steinwehr, was Prussian by birth, and looked every bit the soldier. Although his combat experience was limited, his men respected him.[1]

Bringing up the rear of the corps on July 1, von Steinwehr's Division was ordered to take up a reserve position on Cemetery Hill at about 2:00 P.M. von Steinwehr placed Colonel Charles Coster's 1st Brigade on the northeast end of the hill and Colonel Orland Smith's 2nd Brigade toward the northwest, with orders to support the corps' artillery reserve. As the situation worsened to the north, Coster's Brigade was sent down to help stem the Confederate tide north of town. It was almost destroyed in the subsequent fight against two Confederate brigades in the brickyard.[2]

During July 2, both brigades formed part of the defensive line on Cemetery Hill. Smith's Brigade's position along the Taneytown Road was directly opposite Pender's (Third Corps) and Rodes's Confederate Divisions (Second Corps), and skirmished with them during the three remaining days that the brigade faced the enemy. Coster's Brigade's position to the south was quieter, although at least two of regiments participated in repulsing Early's attack on the evening of July 2.[3]

✂

1st Brigade—Colonel Charles Coster

Units: 134th New York, 154th New York, 27th Pennsylvania, 73rd Pennsylvania
Strength: 1423 (50 men from each regiment were detached from brigade, which did not arrive until 10:00 A.M. on July 2)
Losses: 597 (56-228-313)—41.9%[4]

Morale in the 1st Brigade was low. Its respected commanding officer, Colonel Adolphus Buschbeck, had been wounded at Chancellorsville, and Colonel Charles Coster of the 134th New York served in his place. The two Pennsylvania regiments were composed of German-born immigrants, while non-Germans comprised the two New York regiments. This generated tension, as suggested by Private George Newcomb of the 154th New York. "They are all Dutch in our brigade, except our regiment, and they do not like us very well. We can hardly get any water to use but what some Dutchman has washed his ass in it." Sergeant Horace Smith from the same regiment wrote, "how I would like to give them a volley of musketry from our guns."[5]

The brigade became weaker by two hundred when fifty men from each regiment were detached at Emmitsburg on July 1. Their orders were to march westward to ensure that no Confederate troops could attack the XI Corps's flank during its march toward Gettysburg.[6]

Reaching the Codori house about a mile south of Gettysburg, the remainder of the brigade left Emmitsburg Road and double-quicked across fields to Cemetery Hill. The time of their arrival has been set by participants as 2:00, 3:00, or 4:00 P.M. Three o'clock is probably most accurate.[7]

Soon after arriving on Cemetery Hill, the men were permitted to rest their weary feet and empty their haversacks of what little hardtack and sowbelly remained. They were also ordered to clean their guns and inspect their ammunition to ensure it was still dry after the morning rain. Although none of the soldiers wrote about it, General von Steinwehr stated in his official report that he sent out two regiments on picket duty. "Colonel Coster threw forward one regiment as skirmishers in front of his position, and another one into a large stone church and the surrounding houses in town, in order to prevent the enemy's sharpshooters from annoying our artillery."[8]

Private Charles McKay of the 154th New York recalled that "we stacked arms among the old gravestones and watched with wondering eyes the scene that presented itself in plain view just across the valley." Looking due north, Coster's men could see their XI Corps comrades battling Early's Division, and to the west, the I Corps taking on Heth's and Rodes's Divisions. They did not like what they saw, as Federal units were already approaching their positions in disarray. It did not take long for the men to realize that von Steinwehr's small division was the only reserve unit that could potentially save the two beleaguered Federal corps.[9]

Unbeknownst to von Steinwehr's men, General Carl Schurz, commanding the XI Corps in place of General Oliver Howard, had been clamoring for permission to have one of von Steinwehr's brigades "placed upon the north side of the town, near the railroad depot. My intention was to have that brigade in readiness to charge upon any force the enemy might move around my right." Early's Division had not yet arrived, so a well-positioned brigade from von Steinwehr's Division may have resulted in quite a different outcome.[10]

Coster's Brigade was finally ordered to offer support. Galloping up the hill, General Schurz's adjutant, Captain Frederick Winkler, found that Coster's Brigade had not begun to stir. "I urged haste impetuously and it set in motion at once," he wrote. Although it would arrive too late to take offensive action, Schurz hoped that the brigade would "check the enemy long enough to permit Barlow's Division to enter the town without being seriously molested on its retreat."[11]

As Coster's men double-quicked through the town, they could see the wounded from Schimmelfennig's Division everywhere they looked. "All around was confusion and disaster," recalled McKay. With just a bit of hyperbole, he continued, "it requires the steadiness of veterans of unswerving courage to advance and meet the victorious foe." General Schurz met the brigade and led it through the town.[12]

The 134th New York led the column, followed in turn by the 154th New York, the 27th Pennsylvania, and the 73rd Pennsylvania. As the column reached the railroad depot, the 73rd Pennsylvania was detached to act as the brigade's reserve. The rest of the brigade continued along Stratton Street to Kuhn's brickyard on the edge of town, where the men were exposed to cannon fire for the first time in the battle. Each round exploded a little closer to the column. Private John Wellman of the 154th New York recalled that "I looked for some disorder, but I swear to you today, not one man broke step from the head of the column to the rear."[13]

Upon reaching John Kuhn's brickyard, the column turned right (east), and the orders, "Halt, front, right dress" echoed through the brigade. "Had the regiment been on dress parade it could not have done better," recalled Wellman.[14]

Less than a thousand men of Coster's Brigade now stood between Early's victorious division and the town of Gettysburg. Schurz quickly deployed the brigade behind a rail fence with the brickyard behind it. The 27th Pennsylvania formed on the left, the 154th New York in the center, and the 134th New York on the right. It was not a good position. "The ground in our front was higher than at our position, gently rising until, 40 rods away, it was perhaps 20 feet above us and covered with wheat just ready for the sickle," recalled McKay. This higher ground prevented these troops on the left from firing, except to the right oblique. Colonel Allen of the 154th New York admitted that his regiment should have taken position on this high ground, but the enemy "came down upon us almost before we had got in line."[15]

In front of Coster's men were two brigades of Early's Division. Advancing astride the Harrisburg Road was Hays's Brigade. In front and, to his left, was General Avery's North Carolina Brigade. Gordon's Georgia Brigade, which had almost single-handedly destroyed Barlow's Division, was within supporting distance at the almshouse. Within a startlingly short time, the Confederate line hove into view. "Evidently they deemed themselves sufficiently strong as they advanced upon us in splendid style," related Lieutenant Benjamin Sheldon of the 134th New York. According to McKay, "I shall always remember how the Confederate line of battle looked as it came into full view and started down towards us. It seemed as though they had a battle flag every few rods, which would indicated that their formation was in solid column." The men were told to "reserve our fire until the enemy were close enough to make our volley effective." The wait was a short one, as orders were soon given to fire "and the whole line [was] a blaze of fire." Sergeant

William Howe of the 134th New York noted that the Confederates "fired grape and shell at us and we let them get about sixty yards from us, and then we gave them a volley."[16]

Because a gap had formed between the two New York regiments, Lieutenant Colonel Lorenz Cantador of the 27th Pennsylvania ordered his second battalion to rush to the right to lend assistance. However, because of the din of battle, only fifty of his men heard the order and obeyed it. They followed Lt. Adolphus Vogelbach as he took position between the two New York regiments.[17]

Although outnumbered more than three to one, Coster's men held their ground and fired a smoke-filled volley into the Confederates. McKay recalled that "our fire did good execution when we opened, and their line was stopped in our front." E. Northrup recalled that each man in the 154th New York fired six to nine shots into the enemy's closely packed ranks. The fire halted the 6th and 21st North Carolina in their tracks, but most of the men did not know that the attack column overlapped both of the brigade's flanks. Fearing destruction of his brigade, Coster ordered his men to withdraw. Being close to his left flank, the 27th Pennsylvania heard the order and immediately obeyed it. For some reason, the two New York regiments did not receive the order and continued to battle against overwhelming odds.[18]

The situation became even grimmer with the 27th Pennsylvania gone, especially on the right, where the 134th New York gallantly attempted to hold its position. Colonel Allen of the 154th New York wrote that the enemy line "so far overlapped the 134th on our right that they swung around almost in their rear, and had such an enfilading fire upon them and our whole line, that that regiment was

compelled to give way." Attacked in their front, flank, and rear by the 21st and 57th North Carolina, the regiment lost half of its men in a matter of minutes and was forced to withdraw. Allen quickly issued orders for his regiment to fall back toward the left, where he expected to find more security with the 27th Pennsylvania. He was shocked when he learned that "they had been withdrawn without my knowledge, and that the enemy had outflanked us to a much greater extent on our left than on the right."[19]

The situation was now desperate, as the two New York regiments were all but surrounded and it was every man for himself as the units scattered—all that is, except for Company C of the 154th New York. Seeing that his regiment had halted the enemy advance, Lieutenant Jack Mitchell yelled, "Boys, let's stay right here." He did not know about the danger to his flanks and rear. Those men who had begun their retreat quickly returned to join their comrades at the fence and fired away at the enemy as fast as they could reload their guns. After about five minutes, even Mitchell realized the hopelessness of the situation and called out, "Boys, we must get out of here" and the men ran for the rear. It was too late. Those who had taken flight earlier were also doomed. Lieutenant Alanson Crosby of the 154th New York recalled his retreat. "We entered the road [Harrisburg Pike], and fierce hand to hand conflict ensued" as they ran from Avery's North Carolinians into the arms of Hays's Tigers. Continuing his narrative, Crosby wrote that the "opposing forces were mingled in promiscuous confusion. Four color-bearers in the 154th New York were shot down in rapid succession. The only resource left was to cut through the enemy's ranks. The bayonet was used, but alas, what could a mere handful of men do against thousands that surrounded us on all sides." Private James Quilliam concurred. "We got to the road it was full of Rebels and they were coming up behind us, so there we had to stay, and but few got away." Lieutenant Adolphus Vogelbach with the small detachment of the 27th Pennsylvania that had attempted to plug the gap between the two New York regiments was ordered to surrender. When he refused, he was shot down, and his men subsequently capitulated.[20]

One of the tragedies of this action was the saga of the "Children of the Battlefield." A grave digger preparing to bury a dead Federal soldier noticed that he tightly grasped an ambrotype of three small children in his hand. The soldier carried no identification, and this set off a national search that finally identied the soldier as Sergeant Amos Humiston of the 154th New York.[21]

Although there were some close calls, none of the New York flags were lost in the melee. As Captain Cheney of the 154th New York was running to the rear, he spied what he thought was his regiment's state colors. Picking them up, he made his way to the rear. It was only after he had reached the safety of Cemetery Hill that he learned that he was carrying the colors of the 134th New York. The flag of the 154th New York was also laying on the ground, and it was picked up by a member of the 134th New York and carried to safety. Another flag of the 134th New York was saved when its bearer ripped it from its staff and stuffed it into his tunic before he was captured. Fortunately, his captors never searched him or inquired about the bulge in his shirt.[22]

The losses were horrendous, especially in the 154th New York, which lost all but three officers and fifteen men. As Coster's exhausted survivors trudged up Cemetery Hill, they were again positioned in the cemetery on the east side of Taneytown

Road. Warily waiting for the renewed Confederate attack, which they knew would surely come, the men were formed into line "to make the enemy believe that we had a strong reserve force . . . he was either deceived or from some other cause he did not make any further advance that night," wrote McKay. The New Yorkers slept among the graves in the cemetery that night.[23]

The evening was a bit more exciting for the 73rd Pennsylvania—the regiment left at the train depot and was not involved in the brickyard fight. An officer rode up to the huddled groups and asked if there was a Pennsylvania regiment on the hill. Upon hearing an affirmative answer from the men, he ordered them into town to "ascertain the position of the enemy and how much of the town is occupied." Quickly complying, Companies A, F, and D slowly moved along the streets east of Baltimore Street, while Companies B, C, and K moved along the opposite side. Companies E and H moved up Baltimore Street, and Companies G and I formed the reserve. At a signal from Captain Kelley, the men advanced, but were halted by a volley fired by Confederate troops in the houses and nearby wheatfield. Several men were hit. Realizing that he had acquired the desired information, Captain Kelley quickly pulled his men back to Cemetery Hill.[24]

The night was uneventful. Welcome reinforcements appeared at about 10:00 A.M. on July 2, when the two hundred men detached from the brigade during the march to Gettysburg returned. The detachment from the 154th New York "swelled" its ranks to almost seventy-five men. So small were the two New York regiments that they were consolidated under the command of the 154th New York's commander, Colonel D. B. Allen. Sometime during the day, Company B of the

73rd Pennsylvania punched holes in the roof of the Wagon Hotel and fired at the enemy snipers occupying a nearby tannery. Otherwise, the day was mostly quiet as the brigade occupied the southwestern slope of the hill.[25]

This changed after dark, when Hays's and Avery's Confederate Brigades launched an attack against Cemetery Hill. These were the same brigades that had crushed Coster's Brigade the day before. They drove up the hill and successfully reached the batteries positioned there. General Howard sought immediate assistance. In addition to Carroll's Brigade (Hays's Division, II Corps), Howard called upon other XI Corps units. Among them were the 27th and 73rd Pennsylvania. When the two regiments reached the scene, they engaged in intense hand-to-hand combat. Battery commander Captain Michael Wiedrich wrote that "when the Louisiana Tigers charged my battery, and when we were in a hand-to-hand fight with them, I saw that my position could not be held, and had ordered my battery to limber up and fall back to the Baltimore pike, when the Seventy-third and Twenty-seventh Regiments Pennsylvania Volunteers came to my rescue and repulsed the rebels." The two Pennsylvania regiments had gained a measure of redemption by helping to defeat units from the two brigades that had crushed their brigade the day before. Coster's New York regiments played only a supporting role in this action. Major Lewis Warner of the 154th New York wrote that his regiment "lay for some two hours with shells, canister, round shot and railroad slugs flying around and over in plenteous. But two of the 154th were wounded, which was really miraculous."[26]

A historian of the 27th Pennsylvania related a bizarre story that occurred just before Early's men charged up the hill.

"As the rebels were advancing to the attack, a mounted man in the national uniform, representing himself as a staff officer, rode up and ordered the regiment to fall back some distance to a wall in the rear." While some of the men followed this order, the majority refused. "The pretended officer discovering that his order was not obeyed, leaped the wall and galloped away toward Gettysburg, evidently a rebel in disguise."[27]

Except for some sniper fire during the morning, July 3 was quiet until 1:00 P.M., when Coster's Brigade was exposed to the massive cannon fire that preceded the Pickett–Pettigrew–Trimble charge. As Trimble's and Pettigrew's men left their positions on Seminary Ridge, the 73rd Pennsylvania, and possibly the 27th Pennsylvania, rushed down Taneytown Road to Ziegler's Grove to provide support. They were not needed and returned to Cemetery Hill later that day.[28]

On the morning of July 4 the brigade was one of several from the XI Corps that cautiously entered the town. Deployed as skirmishers, they moved along the streets in the western part of Gettysburg until they reached Chambersburg Street. Here they encountered a small force of Confederate cavalry who stubbornly held its ground. The appearance of Federal cavalry in their rear convinced some of the Confederates to surrender; the rest rapidly vacated the town. The prisoners were left in the care of the 73rd Pennsylvania, which marched them to the town square. The men spent the remainder of the day building breastworks and barricades on several streets.[29]

The brigade lost almost 50% of its men during the battle—most during the short fight in the brickyard. One regiment, the 154th New York, won the distinction of sustaining the greatest losses of *any* Federal regiment during the battle—84%.

Most of these losses were in the form of prisoners (178). The 134th New York's losses were also heavy—about 63%.[30]

The 1st Brigade will always be remembered for its gallant attempt to stem the Confederate tide at the brickyard on July 1. Had the brigade been ordered down from its perch on Cemetery Hill sooner, it could have arrived in time to support Bar-low's Division. The brigade's actions were nevertheless important for, as one veteran wrote, by "checking the advance of the Confederates they permitted the falling back of Northern troops through the town of Gettysburg at a great sacrifice." Another foot soldier probably summed it up best when he wrote, "again the 154th must be sacrificed to bad generalship."[31]

2nd Brigade—Colonel Orland Smith

Units: 33rd Massachusetts, 136th New York, 55th Ohio, 73rd Ohio
Strength: 1639
Losses: 348 (51-278-19)—21.2%[32]

Although the individual units of the 2nd Brigade had fought in several engagements during the 1862 Shenandoah campaign and at Second Bull Run, they did not fight together until the battle of Chancellorsville. The brigade had the distinction of being the only one in the XI Corps to have missed being stampeded during Stonewall Jackson's flank movement. When General Francis Barlow was assigned command of the 1st Division on May 24, Colonel Orland Smith of the 73rd Ohio rose to command the brigade. Like so many others, he had had no prior experience leading a brigade prior to the Gettysburg campaign.[33]

The veterans of Colonel Orland Smith's 2nd Brigade remembered two aspects of their march to Gettysburg: the abundance of the land and the bone-tiring pace. Sergeant John Cate of the 33rd Massachusetts wrote home about the "thousands upon thousands of acres of wheat. It is yellow as it is growing, almost ready to cut. Then there are large corn-fields, then there is any quantity of fruit, the trees are full of green fruit. Cherries are now ripe . . . and people say help yourselves."[34]

The march was a difficult one for the men. "The men marched fully equipped, with haversacks, knapsacks, &c, carrying three days' rations and 60 rounds of ammunition . . . the shoes began to fail, thus leaving many men to march barefooted sometimes over very rough roads . . . every labor and hardship was endured, however, with a cheerfulness which is worthy of commendation," wrote Colonel Smith in his official report. Henry Henney of the 55th Ohio was one of the lucky ones, as he was able to purchase a pair of shoes in Emmitsburg for $2.50. "They are a stubby pair and I think when they are broken in, I can march first-rate in them," he recorded in his diary.[35]

As with so many units, the civilians who lined the roads helped buoy the men's spirits. Private Andrew Boies of the 33rd Massachusetts recalled the young girls saying, "don't the soldiers look pretty," while an old woman was heard to exclaim, "I never seed [sic] such a sight in all the world; so many people . . . they are a mighty smart lot of men, indeed they are."[36]

The brigade broke camp at Emmitsburg about 8:00 A.M. on July 1 and took its place at the rear of von Steinwehr's Division's column. As a result, it was the last brigade of the XI Corps to arrive at Gettysburg. The men were often forced to march in the fields along the sides of the road to keep it open for the artillery. About halfway to Gettysburg, the men learned about the fight there and were ordered to increase their pace.[37]

The men could hear the sounds of battle as the column approached the town. Lieutenant L. A. Smith of the 136th New York recalled how "the distant booming of cannon soon increased the heart beat. The heavy Enfield rifle, accoutrements, knapsack, haversack and canteen were no longer burdensome. Tired limbs, blistered feet and sore muscles no longer absorbed our thoughts or drew upon the will power; the whole man was changed as by magic; quickened and apparently refreshed to a degree not explainable."[38]

Marching north on Taneytown Road, the brigade halted in the rear of Cemetery Hill and formed in line of battle by battalions. The troops next climbed the hill and marched through the cemetery, halting about midway through it. "Our first thoughts were of the seeming desecration, as we trod beneath our feet the grass-grown mounds which marked the resting place of the dead, but other thoughts and scenes soon engrossed our attention," wrote Lieutenant Smith of the 136th New York. These scenes were of the deadly contest between the Confederates and the Federal I and XI Corps to the west and north. The men could see many units retreating and "turning every few rods to fire a volley, facing in every direction." The foot-sore soldiers were given a much-needed rest. Sitting in the cemetery, Henney (55th Ohio) recorded in his diary that it was "one of the pleasantest burial places I ever saw." While waiting here, one out of every twelve men was ordered to collect canteens and fill them with water.[39]

This reprieve did not last long, as the men were again ordered into line and moved to the northern brow of the hill. Their orders were to prepare to repel an expected Confederate attack on the hill and to support the Union troops that were swarming out of town. As the broken units arrived on the hill, Smith received orders to move his brigade to the west to help support the batteries on the hill.[40]

Smith deployed his brigade behind a stone wall along Taneytown Road, about thirty yards in front of the batteries it was to support. Facing west, the 55th Ohio formed the extreme right of the line, with its right extending to the southwest corner of the town and its center where Taneytown and Emmitsburg Roads intersected. The 73rd Ohio and the 136th New York formed the brigade's left flank, connecting with the right of Hays's Division (II Corps) at Ziegler's Grove. The location of the 33rd Massachusetts in this line is not known, but it was probably on the left of the 73rd Ohio. The 136th New York was almost directly under the barrels of the cannon on Cemetery Hill. No sooner had the brigade deployed than it began taking casualties from enemy sharpshooters.[41]

The men could see Confederate troops massing in an orchard in front of them in preparation for an attack on Cemetery Hill. A staff officer rode up to Colonel Underwood of the 33rd Massachusetts and ordered his men not to open fire on the enemy until they were within "short range." Underwood knew this would be a problem because "it was not an easy thing to keep men cool in the fiery impatience that comes in battle, especially when everything seemed to be giving away."[42]

But the enemy's line of battle did not advance. Instead, a strong skirmish line moved steadily toward Smith's Brigade. Smith responded by throwing out his own line of skirmishers, who halted when about 150 yards from the enemy. "The enemy kept up an almost continuous fire upon our skirmishers," wrote Colonel James Wood of the 136th New York. Private Luther Mesnard of the 55th New York complained that the "German regiment to our right did not keep out skirmishers but we threw them out in an open field in our front."[43]

That night the men slept on their arms by the side of the road. "But how we did sleep and rest," Mesnard recalled. At about 10:00 P.M. that night, the 73rd Ohio was pulled into the cemetery, where its men slept on and around the graves. Their reprieve was a short one, as they were moved back into position again at 3:00 A.M. on July 2.[44]

Skirmishing in front of Smith's Brigade began with first light on July 2 and continued through July 3. "This line was exposed not only to the fire of the enemy's front, but to a fire from the flanks and rear by the sharpshooters posted in the houses in the town. Indeed, the main line, though posted behind a stone wall, was constantly subjected to annoyances from the same source," wrote Colonel Smith in his official report. Confederate sharpshooters firing from buildings within the town particularly bothered the regiments on the right of the line. Samuel Hurst of the 73rd Ohio wrote after the war that it "seemed to us unfortunate that the town was given up to the enemy, for it was at once filled with rebel sharp-shooters, and their work of death was begun." The troops were also exposed to artillery fire from Confederate guns on Benner's Hill, and to make matters worse, "some casualties were occasioned by the premature explosion of some of the shells from our own batteries." Because of the heat, details were frequently sent out to fill canteens at a nearby spring. Such excursions

often resulted in some of the men being hit by enemy bullets.[45]

Each regiment rotated its companies on the skirmish line, keeping at least three out at any given time. This duty was extremely hazardous. According to Captain John Hand of the 136th New York, these "skirmishers appeared to be relieved with unnecessary frequency, as the change was never effected during the day without loss of life." Smith of the same regiment agreed, writing that going out on the skirmish line "meant a useless sacrifice of life, as we could see that no preparation had been made for our support." As Smith's company moved slowly forward during the early afternoon of July 2, it pushed back the enemy skirmishers. "We were suddenly confronted by a regiment rising up in our front from what appeared to be an abandoned railroad cut." The resulting volley killed and wounded several of Smith's men and forced the remainder to fall back, Smith recalled. This type of interaction was constantly replayed throughout the two days.[46]

At about 3:00 P.M. on July 2, a company of Confederate infantry took possession of a house (probably the Bliss house) between the two lines and soon men from the 55th Ohio began falling in quick succession. The batteries on the hill tried to open fire on the house, but the barrels of their guns could not be depressed enough. In desperation, Colonel Charles Gambee of the 55th Ohio asked for volunteers to venture out and neutralize the enemy. Captain Frederick Boalt volunteered, as did twenty to twenty-five men of the regiment. Exposed to heavy fire, the men were able to close in on the house and drive out the Confederates. They took possession of the house, but most were later captured.[47]

At about 6:00 P.M. that evening, the Confederates reinforced their skirmish line and pushed back their Federal counterparts. The 55th Ohio responded by sending out several additional companies. Mesnard was one of these men, but they too were forced to return to the protection of their lines as the "Rebs on both flanks and front and quite too close and fired as fast as possible . . . the bullets seemed to come criss cross from every way." Mesnard was wounded in the arm, and made his way to the rear.[48]

The 33rd Massachusetts missed most of these skirmishes because it had been dispatched to support the batteries on the opposite side of Cemetery Hill. Surprisingly, brigade commander Orland Smith did not know of these orders until after the battle ended. In his official report, Smith wrote, "I learned from the report of Colonel Underwood, [his command] was put temporarily under the command of General Ames (Barlow's Division) this, however, being the first intimation to me of such a fact."[49]

The regiment took position in front of the Evergreen Cemetery gate on the east side of Baltimore Pike. Colonel Underwood placed one wing along the road, facing northeast, and another wing perpendicular to it, facing southwest. Both wings were exposed to the cannonade that began at 3:00 P.M. that afternoon. The regiment's historian recalled "splinters of gun carriages, pieces of tombstones, even human legs and arms and palpitating flesh were flying about in every direction." To reduce losses, Underwood frequently changed his men's position from one side of the wall to the other.[50]

Most of the men disdained supporting the batteries. Corporal John Ryder of the 33rd Massachusetts noted that "of all the places in battle excuse me from supporting a battery where one has nothing to take up his mind but to lie waiting to be killed or wounded and no chance to fire

at the enemy unless he should advance to capture the battery. The kind of fighting I prefer is where the officer says, 'Now load and fire at will, and as far as possible make every shot tell.' There's excitement enough to take your mind off of the danger you are in and gives you the feeling you are accomplishing something worthwhile." Lieutenant Smith of the 136th New York on the other side of the hill agreed. "If we could have had something to do, even though it had been to charge the enemy's batteries, it would have been a welcome relief."[51]

Later that afternoon the 33rd Massachusetts was thrown to the right, into Culp's Meadow between Culp's and Cemetery Hills. Here they formed into line of battle with the 41st New York of von Gilsa's Brigade. At about 8:00 P.M. they saw a long line of enemy infantry approaching. These were two brigades of Early's Division launching their attack on Cemetery Hill. Pulled back to the base of Cemetery Hill, the 33rd Massachusetts took its place to the right of von Gilsa's Brigade behind a stone wall and awaited the attack. The men on the skirmish line had an anxious time of it when, during their retreat back to the main lines, they realized that they could be shot by their own men. Ryder recalled that "our colonel was standing on the wall saying, 'These are our skirmishers, don't fire on them.' We jumped the wall and lay down quickly back of it."[52]

After the war, Colonel Underwood recalled the charge of the 57th North Carolina (Avery's Brigade). "The enemy came on gallantly, unchecked by our artillery fire, and my regiment opened a severe musketry fire on them, which caused gaps in their line and made it stagger back a bit. It soon rallied and bravely came within a few feet of our wall, though my men clung unflinchingly to it and steadily poured in their fire. I ordered them to fix bayonets to be ready for the enemy."[53]

The enemy had already breached the wall in several places to the left of the 33rd Massachusetts. Still, the Bay Staters held their ground along with the 41st New York to their left. Bullets from the Confederates who had breached the wall to the left were now hitting Underwood's men from behind. The situation was becoming desperate. "Our colonel just gave the 33d, 'Fix bayonets and remember Massachusetts!' when Stevens' 5th Maine Battery to our right let go all six guns in one volley and swept our front clear of Rebels with canister," recalled Ryder.[54]

After repulsing the attack the regiment buried its dead and then was moved farther to the right, where it formed on the immediate left of Steven's battery. According to Ryder (33rd Massachusetts), the men asked themselves that night, "What will tomorrow bring forth?"[55]

For the remainder of the brigade on the west side of Cemetery Hill, the morrow brought more skirmishing and continued losses. Federal artillery opened fire on some of the structures in Gettysburg that the Confederates were firing from, and in at least one case, caused a barn to catch fire, driving out about fifty enemy soldiers.[56]

At about 1:00 P.M., the cannonade that preceded the Pickett–Pettigrew–Trimble charge opened and continued for almost two hours. The low fence offered little protection, and many of the men were ordered to the rear; the others hugged the ground for safety. Captain Hand of the 136th New York recalled "for two savage hours the air above and about us was filled with hissing, shrieking, howling messengers of death; a roaring, raging, withering hell of missiles, a pandemonium of unearthly sounds." In a letter home, Private James Jones of the same regiment

wrote that the "shells rained in on Cemetery hill tearing up graves, knocking monuments & iron fences killing horses & men & knocking guns endways. There was some noise when those cannons all got to playing."[57]

At first the men thought that the charge would be against their front. But as Pettigrew's Division advanced, it wheeled to its right, making Smith's Brigade little more than spectators. Skirmishing in front of the brigade continued after the charge was repulsed. That evening the skirmishers from the 136th New York thought they could see sheep in the fields to their left. They were not sheep, but dead and wounded Southerners remaining in the fields. Smith of the regiment later wrote that "altogether a night of horror, which the lapse of time has not altogether obliterated from memory." Private George Metcalf of the same regiment agreed. "I see them now when my eyes are shut, and hear the sounds I cannot describe whenever I let my mind dwell upon that night of all nights, as I lay among the dead and dying on the night of July 3rd on the battlefield of Gettysburg."[58]

The 33rd Massachusetts returned on July 4, and with the rest of the brigade, was involved in picket duty. Although Lee was about to pull back to Virginia, the two lines maintained a brisk firing.[59]

Smith's Brigade's losses of 348 (21%) was the lowest of any brigade in the corps, and one of the lowest in the entire army, exclusive of the little-used VI Corps. The small losses are understandable, given the fact that except for the 33rd Massachusetts, the brigade had not come within a hundred yards of the enemy. Most of the losses were sustained on the skirmish line between Cemetery Hill and Seminary Ridge. This makes the losses of the 73rd Ohio (42%) all the more interesting. These high losses were the result of their skirmish line being exposed to a deadly crossfire. The brigade served well during its four days at Gettysburg, and earned the gratitude of its commander. Colonel Smith wrote, "though the situation was at times of the most trying character, never a man faltered, to my knowledge, or complained, but every man seemed inspired by a determination to hold his position, dead or alive." Eminent Gettysburg scholar Harry Pfanz wrote that the brigade's relatively high losses "is a tribute to Union courage and Confederate marksmanship."[60]

NOTES

1. Tagg, *Generals of Gettysburg*, 131–132.
2. OR 27, 1, 721.
3. OR 27, 1, 721–722.
4. Busey and Martin, *Regimental Strengths and Losses*, 83, 254.
5. George Newcomb, letter, Leigh Collection, USAMHI; Mark H. Dunkelman and Michael J. Winey, "The Hardtack Regiment in the Brickyard Fight," *Gettysburg Magazine* (January 1993), issue 8, 17–18.
6. *NYG*, vol. 3, 1050.
7. Charles W. McKay, "Three Years or During the War With the Crescent and Star," *National Tribune Scrap Book* (Washington, n.d.), 130; OR 27, 1, 720; *NYG*, vol. 3, 1055; Daniel B. Allen to John Bachelder, April 5, 1864, Bachelder Papers, New Hampshire Historical Society.
8. Mark H. Dunkelman and Michael J. Winey, *The Hardtack Regiment: An Illustrated History of the 124th Regiment, New York State Infantry Volunteers* (East Brunswick, NJ, 1981), 71; OR 27, 1, 720.
Coster, nor any of his regimental commanders, submitted reports of the battle, and except for the 154th New York, few primary sources are available. As a result, the brigade's activities, particularly the two Pennsylvania regiments', are sketchy.
9. McKay, "Three Years or During the War With the Crescent and Star," 130.

10. OR 27, 1, 728.
11. Hitz, *The Letters of Frederick C. Winkler*, 70; OR 27, 1, 729.
12. McKay, "Three Years or During the War With the Crescent and Star," 131; Wellman, letter; OR 27, 1, 729.
13. Dunkelman and Winey, "The Hardtack Regiment in the Brickyard Fight," 19; Wellman, letter; McKay, "Three Years or During the War With the Crescent and Star," 131.
Colonel Daniel Allen of the 154th New York recalled that there were no other troops in the town when Coster's Brigade entered. The facts do not support this assertion (Daniel B. Allen to John Bachelder, April 5, 1864).
14. Wellman, Letter.
15. *NYG*, vol. 3, 1051; McKay, "Three Years or During the War With the Crescent and Star," 131.
16. Sheldon letter; McKay, "Three Years or During the War With the Crescent and Star," 131; Wellman, letter; Howe letter.
17. Bates, *Pennsylvania Volunteers*, vol. I, 391.
18. McKay, "Three Years or During the War With the Crescent and Star," 131; *NYG*, vol. 3, 1055; George W. Conklin, "The Long March to Stevens Run: The 134th New York Volunteer Infantry at Gettysburg," *Gettysburg Magazine* (July 1999), issue 21, 52.
19. *NYG*, vol. 3, 1051.
20. Wellman, letter; Crosby, letter; Dunkelman and Winey, "The Hardtack Regiment in the Brickyard Fight," 21.
21. Dunkelman and Winey, "The Hardtack Regiment in the Brickyard Fight," 25–26.
22. *NYG*, vol. 3, 1055; Hartwig, "The 11th Army Corps on July 1, 1863," 48–49.
23. *NYG*, vol. 3, 1055; McKay, "Three Years or During the War With the Crescent and Star," 132.
24. *PAG*, vol. 1, 420.
25. Dunkelman and Winey, *The Hardtack Regiment: An Illustrated History of the 124th Regiment, New York State Infantry Volunteers*, 78; *NYG*, vol. 3, 1056; William Kerr, letter, 73rd Pennsylvania folder, GNMP.
26. *Pennsylvania at Gettysburg*, vol. 1, 420–421; Conklin, "The Long March to

Stevens Run: The 134th New York Volunteer Infantry at Gettysburg," 54; Dunkelman and Winey, "The Hardtack Regiment in the Brickyard Fight," 24.

27. Bates, *Pennsylvania Volunteers*, vol. I, 391.

28. *Pennsylvania at Gettysburg*, vol. 1, 421; Bates, *Pennsylvania Volunteers*, vol. I, 391.

29. *Pennsylvania at Gettysburg*, vol. 1, 421; *History of the 134th Regiment, N.Y.S. Vol.* (Schenectady, NY, n.d.), 10; Dunkelman and Winey, *The Hardtack Regiment: An Illustrated History of the 124th Regiment, New York State Infantry Volunteers*, 78.

30. Busey and Martin, *Regimental Strengths and Losses*, 254.

31. *NYG*, vol. 2, 913; Wellman, letter.

32. Busey and Martin, *Regimental Strengths and Losses*, 84, 254.

33. Tagg, *Generals of Gettysburg*, 134–135; Dyer, *Compendium*, 319.

34. John Cate, letter, copy in 33rd Massachusetts folder, GNMP.

35. Henry Henney, diary, USAMHI; John M. Cate, *If I Live To Come Home: The Civil War Letters of Sergeant John March Cate* (Pittsburgh, PA, 1995), 105.

36. Andrew J. Boies, *Record of the Thirty-third Massachusetts Volunteer Infantry, From August 1862 to August 1865* (Fitchburg, MA, 1880), 32.

37. OR 27, 1, 723, 726; L. A. Smith, "Recollections of Gettysburg," in *Michigan MOLLUS* (1898), vol. 2, 299.

Colonel Adin Underwood recalled after the war that his men began to double-quick to the battlefield when they were about two miles away (OR suppl., 5, 216).

38. Smith, "Recollections of Gettysburg," 298.

39. OR 27, 1, 724; Smith, "Recollections of Gettysburg," 299; Adin B. Underwood, *Three Years' Service of the Thirty-Third Massachusetts Infantry Regiment* (Boston, 1881), 118; Henty, diary; George Metcalf, "Reminiscence," USAMHI.

40. Samuel H. Hurst, *Journal of the Seventy-Third Ohio Volunteer Infantry* (Chillicothe, OH, 1866), 66–67.

41. OR 27, 1, 724; Pfanz, *Gettysburg—*

Culp's Hill and Cemetery Hill, 146; Hurst, *Journal of the Seventy-Third Ohio Volunteer Infantry*, 67.

The location of the three regiments along the wall is from Smith's official report. Smith never gave the position of the 33rd Massachusetts, probably because it was detached the following day. Smith gave the positions of the regiments on either flank, and Hurst (*Journal of the Seventy-Third Ohio Volunteer Infantry*, 68) said that the 73rd Ohio was on the left of the 55th Ohio.

42. Underwood, *Three Years' Service of the Thirty-Third Massachusetts Infantry Regiment*, 119.

43. Underwood, *Three Years' Service of the Thirty-Third Massachusetts Infantry Regiment*,119; OR 27, 1, 726; Mesnard, "Reminiscences," 35.

44. OR suppl., 5, 217; Mesnard, "Reminiscences," 35; Hurst, *Journal of the Seventy-Third Ohio Volunteer Infantry*, 68.

45. OR 27, 1, 724; Hurst, *Journal of the Seventy-Third Ohio Volunteer Infantry*, 67; Pfanz, *Gettysburg—Culp's Hill and Cemetery Hill*, 147.

46. OR 27, 1, 726; J. W. Hand, "Gettysburg—A Graphic Account of the Battle by a Eleventh Corps Captain," *National Tribune*, July 24, 1890; Elizabeth S. Kaszubski, "Arzy and Lafayette West Brothers—Together 'Til The End," 136th New York folder, GNMP; Smith, "Recollections of Gettysburg," 301.

47. Hartwell Osborn, *Trials and Triumphs: The Record of the Fifthy-Fifth Ohio Volunteer Infantry* (Chicago, 1904), 99–100; Mesnard, "Reminiscences," 35–36.

48. Mesnard, "Reminiscences," 36–37.

49. OR suppl., 5, 217; OR 27, 1, 724.

50. OR suppl., 5, 217; Underwood, *Three Years' Service of the Thirty-Third Massachusetts Infantry Regiment*,123.

51. John J. Ryder, *Reminiscences Of Three Years' Service In The Civil War By A Cape Cod Boy* (New Bedford, MA, 1928), 34; Smith, "Recollections of Gettysburg," 303.

52. OR suppl., 5, 217–218; Ryder, *Reminiscences Of Three Years' Service In The Civil War By A Cape Cod Boy*, 34–35.

53. OR suppl., 5, 218.

54. Ryder, *Reminiscences Of Three Years' Service In The Civil War By A Cape Cod Boy,* 35; OR suppl., 5, 218–219.

55. OR suppl., 5, 219; Ryder, *Reminiscences Of Three Years' Service In The Civil War By A Cape Cod Boy,* 35.

56. Kaszubski, "Arzy and Lafayette West Brothers—Together 'Til The End."

57. Kaszubski, "Arzy and Lafayette West Brothers—Together 'Til The End;" James Jones, letter, 1863, USAMHI.

58. OR 27, 1, 724; Smith, "Recollections of Gettysburg," 306; Kaszubski, "Arzy and Lafayette West Brothers—Together 'Til The End."

59. OR suppl., 5, 219.

60. Busey and Martin, *Regimental Strengths and Losses,* 254; Osborn, *Trials and Triumphs: The Record of the Fifty-Fifth Ohio Volunteer Infantry,* 100; OR 27, 1, 724; Pfanz, *Gettysburg—Culp's Hill and Cemetery Hill,* 151.

3RD DIVISION—

Major General Carl Schurz/
Brigadier General Alexander Schimmelfennig

General Carl Schurz was unusual, for he entered the army in April 1862 with the rank of brigadier general and in command of a division. Despite the fact that he had had no prior military experience, he had impressed Lincoln and was rewarded when he wanted to join the army. Schurz led his division during the Shenandoah Valley campaign of 1862 and at Second Bull Run, receiving mixed grades for his performance. Caught up in the corps' rout at Chancellorsville, Schurz tried to minimize the negative press coverage that portrayed the XI Corps as ineffective cowards. He marched toward Gettysburg with a firm resolve to clear the corps' name. With the death of General Reynolds and the elevation of General Howard, Schurz took over the corps, General Alexander Schimmelfennig took over the 3rd Division, and Colonel George von Amsberg of the 45th New York assumed command of the 1st Brigade.[1]

The division marched through a driving rain during the early morning of July 1. However, the sun broke through the clouds as the column passed Horner's Mill at 10:30 A.M. Howard ordered the division to occupy Oak Hill after it marched through Gettysburg. Unfortunately, Rodes's Division (Second Corps) reached the hill first, forcing Schurz to link up with the I Corps instead. To accomplish this order, von Amsberg's Brigade moved toward the left and formed perpendicularly to Robinson's Division of the I Corps. Seeing these movements, Rodes's batteries on Oak Hill concentrated such an immense fire on the troops that they were not able to connect with Robinson's men, resulting in a yawning four hundred-yard gap beween them. This gap never became much of an issue because of the uncoordinated nature of Rodes's initial attacks on the I Corps. Krzyzanowski's 2nd Brigade moved due north and rested in reserve. However, when Barlow's Division, which had ventured too far north, was about to be overwhelmed, Krzyzanowski's Brigade was rushed to its aid.[2]

Holding the extreme left of the line, the 45th New York assisted in repelling O'Neal's Brigade's (Rodes's Division) charge against Baxter's Brigade (Robinson's Division, I Corps) on Oak Ridge. The rest of von Amsberg's Brigade took position to its right and merely skirmished with the enemy. However, the heavy artillery fire from Oak Hill racked up many casualties. Krzyzanowski's Brigade, moving to the aid of Barlow's Division, ran into two Confederate brigades and was forced to retreat with heavy losses. The 157th New York of von Amsberg's Brigade was now ordered to stem the Confederate tide and was almost destroyed in the process. Hundreds of men from the division fell captive during the retreat to Cemetery Hill. Most made it to the safety of Cemetery Hill, and some, like General Schimmelfennig, hid from the enemy in houses or farmyards.[3]

Schimmelfennig's Division occupied the western side of Cemetery Hill on July 2 and 3. Both of its brigades had opportunities for glory on the evening of July 2, when two regiments from the Krzyzanowski's Brigade participated in the repulse of Early's attack on the east side of Cemetery Hill, and von Amsberg's Brigade was ordered to Culp's Hill to help repulse General Johnson's night attack. During most of the time on Cemetery Hill, the men dodged bullets from Confederate snipers who fired from houses and other structures. Except for continued sniper fire, July 4 was relatively quiet. The division moved with the remainder of the XI Corps after Lee's army at about 6:00 P.M. on July 5.[4]

1st Brigade—Brigadier General Alexander Schimmelfennig/ Colonel George von Amsberg

Units: 82nd Illinois, 45th New York, 157th New York, 61st Ohio (104th did not arrive until 8:00 A.M. on July 2), 74th Pennsylvania
Strength: 1683
Losses: 807 (58-296-453)—48%[5]

A no-nonsense commander, Brigadier General Alexander Schimmelfennig had had extensive military experience before he immigrated to the United States. Although he had been in the country for less than a decade, Schimmelfennig immediately rose to command the 74th Pennsylvania. Schimmelfennig was a strict disciplinarian who believed in constant drilling and unfailing discipline. The brigade, to which the 74th Pennsylvania was assigned, participated in the Shenandoah Valley campaign, but Schimmelfennig was not present because of illness. He returned and commanded the brigade at Second Bull Run, where it lost heavily trying to extract Stonewall Jackson's men from their position along the railroad. The brigade missed Antietam and Fredericksburg because it was helping man the Washington defenses. It rejoined the Army of the Potomac in time for the battle of Chancellorsville, where it was forced out of its position and fled with the rest of the XI Corps. The men wanted redemption, and all hoped that the Gettysburg campaign would provide it.[6]

The 45th New York had the distinction of leading Schurz's Division during its march to and through Gettysburg, and was therefore the first regiment of the XI Corps to reach the battlefield. Although the unit's historians placed its arrival north of the town at 11:30 A.M., it was probably thirty to forty-five minutes later. The regiment headed toward the right of the I Corps, and eventually formed the left-most unit of the XI Corps's line of battle.[7]

Because of the strenuous march, only four companies of the 45th New York initially arrived on Mummasburg Road; the remainder were some distance in the rear. Captain Francis Irsch assumed command of these companies with orders to form a skirmish line with its left on the road and its right extending as far as it could to the east. Irsch's objective was McLean's red barn on Oak Hill. He was more reassured when told that the regiment's other companies would join him on the picket line when they arrived.[8]

As Irsch deployed his right wing in a wheatfield or ryefield about three-quarters of a mile from the town, his men came under fire from Page's battery near McLean's barn and a second battery on a hill to their right (probably Reese's battery). The fire was ineffective and caused few casualties. As Irsch moved his men toward McLean's farm buildings, they came under fire from a battalion of the 5th Alabama (O'Neal's Brigade), who were deployed as sharpshooters. The Alabamians's line stretched along a lane at the foot of Oak Hill to an apple orchard near the Hagy farm near Mummasburg Road. Pushing forward, Irsch's men sustained heavy losses from the small arms

and artillery fire. Undeterred, they continued northward, pushing the enemy skirmishers before them for about four hundred yards. They finally took refuge behind some fences running northwestward from the Hagy farm's apple orchard. The New Yorkers were at an advantage, for many were equipped with long-range Remington rifles. When the remainder of the regiment arrived, the entire unit moved forward to the next fence line.[9]

Irsch was joined around this time by a section of Captain Hubert Dilger's battery. The two remaining sections were left behind on Cemetery Hill. The battery had already received a rousing welcome from the 157th New York of the brigade, when it galloped past them in Gettysburg. After sizing up the situation, Dilger brought up his remaining four guns and deployed them for action. Dilger's initial fire was exceptionally accurate, causing Page's battery to limber up and move to a safer position.[10]

Irsch's men were also relieved when they looked behind them to see the 61st Ohio and 74th Pennsylvania of their brigade approaching at a double-quick pace up Mummasburg Road. Both extended the skirmish line to the right of Irsch's companies. The 45th New York faced northwest, the 61st Ohio faced north-northwest, and the 74th Pennsylvania faced north-northeast, with its right touching Carlisle Road. The three regiments therefore extended over a half-mile front. They were almost immediately exposed to an "incessant fire . . . pouring grape, canister, solid shot, and shell on our position." After a sharp exchange, the 61st Ohio was able to drive back the enemy skirmishers in the open fields in front of them. When the two remaining regiments of the brigade arrived at about 1:30 A.M., they were deployed about a quarter-mile to the rear. The 157th New York formed behind the 45th New York on the left of the line and the 82nd Illinois was behind the right of the 61st Ohio and the left of the 74th Pennsylvania. Dilger's battery was just in front of the 82nd Illinois, which continued to engage the enemy. Because of its position behind the Dilger's guns, the 82nd Illinois was pounded by the Confederate artillery.[11]

Seeing O'Neal's Alabama Brigade making for the gap to his left, between his regiment and Baxter's Brigade (Robinson's Division), Captain Irsch directed his four companies of the 45th New York to concentrate their fire on this attack column. When he realized that the small arms fire was not halting O'Neal's attack, Irsch asked Dilger to open on it with canister. So massive was the response that Irsch ordered his men to lie down, lest they too be hit by this storm of lead. No troops could have survived this pounding, and O'Neal's troops began to waver. As the left of O'Neal's uncertain and "half resolute" line passed the 45th New York's position, Irsch's four companies opened fire on the Alabamians's flank and rear from a distance of fifty to one hundred yards. The remainder of the regiment, which had performed a left oblique, fired into its left front and flank. Some of Baxter's regiments also engaged O'Neal's front. "The enemy's line halted, gradually disappeared on the same spot where they stood, and the remainder, finding they could not retrace their steps, surrendered," wrote Lieutenant Colonel Adolphus Doebke. Many of O'Neal's men retreated to the McLean farm, closely followed by Irsch's four companies of the 45th New York, who drove forward as far as McLean's red barn, capturing many enemy soldiers in the process.[12]

The New Yorkers did not have time to savor their success because another large body of Confederates emerged from Oak Hill to attack Robinson's line. This was Iverson's Brigade, making its ill-fated attack that left 65% of its men killed, wounded, or captured. While the historian of the 45th New York believed that his regiment was instrumental in repelling the charge, it probably played only a minor role.[13]

The situation became more complex when Doles's Brigade (Rodes's Division) and Early's Division (II Corps) advanced on their right. General Schimmelfenning ordered the 157th New York to the right to bolster Kryzanowski's Brigade, which had taken position on the east side of Carlisle Road. Advancing from the southwest, the 157th New York fell on the flank of the 44th Georgia, which formed Doles's right flank. The New Yorkers opened fire when a mere thirty or forty yards from the startled Georgians. The timing was unfortunate, for Kryzanowski's Brigade had just been driven from its position, permitting Doles to concentrate his regiments' attention on the New Yorkers. The 44th Georgia responded to this new threat by wheeling to the right and returning the fire. Both units stood face to face, firing into each other's ranks. The stalemate was broken when the 4th Georgia rushed into position on the 44th Georgia's left. While fighting it out with the two Confederate regiments in front and right flank, the New Yorkers did not see that the 21st Georgia was concealed along a farm lane on their left flank. Private Henry Thomas of Doles's Brigade wrote that "the Federals had advanced to within a short distance of them [21st Georgia], when at the command of their colonel, they sprang to their knees and poured such a volley into the enemy that they were not only checked but stampeded." Still another of Doles's Regiments, the 12th Georgia, rushed to take position on the left of the 21st Georgia. Major W. Peebles of the 44th Georgia wrote in his report that "the

Twenty-first Georgia now came up to our right, and we captured, killed, or wounded nearly every man that came upon our right flank. We soon had nothing in our front."[14]

Hit in front, both flanks, and rear, the men of the 157th New York fell in droves. Their commander, Colonel Philip Brown, recalled that "the men were falling rapidly and the enemy's line was taking the form of a giant semi-circle . . . concentrating the fire of their whole brigade upon my rapidly diminishing numbers." Without orders to withdraw, Brown attempted to hold his position, but it was suicide. He later learned that one of Schimmelfennig's aides carried orders for his withdrawal, but he had returned the way he had come when his horse was killed rather than risk the firestorm that raged up ahead. Brown bitterly wrote that the aide "hallooed to me to retreat" before running to the rear. A general retreat was ordered, but now the men had to rush through a hail of artillery fire coming from Rodes's batteries on Oak Hill. Roughly 75% of the regiment was listed as killed, wounded, or captured—only five other regiments in the entire Army of the Potomac sustained greater losses during the battle. Even some Confederates felt sorry for the regiment's plight. Sidney Richardson of the 21st Georgia wrote home soon after the battle that "one time I felt sad, one Yankee regiment charge [sic] us, we fired a volley into them and then charged them as quick as we could, they turned to run and we continued the charge untill [sic] they got away." After the war, some of the men's traumas were reduced when they learned that their regiment had advanced farther than any other XI Corps unit.[15]

Back on the left flank, the 45th New York, 61st Ohio, and 74th Pennsylvania remained under intense artillery fire for most of the afternoon. The commander of the 45th New York, Lieutenant Colonel Doebke, reported that the "most raging fire and the most horrible scenes . . . one after another, were killed, and some shattered to pieces, not a single man flinched, but all were cheering, and fulfilled their duties nobly." Colonel Adolph von Hartung of the 74th Pennsylvania was severely wounded during this period. The men received orders to pull back at about 4:00 P.M. The brigade, with the 82nd Illinois bringing up the rear, stopped near the college. The 45th New York's historical committee noted after the war that the withdrawal was anything but harried. "We were marching leisurely to the College." Looking over to Seminary Ridge, the men could see the I Corps's line broken and its men streaming toward the town. The bugle sounded after about fifteen or twenty minutes, and the men were ordered to double-quick toward the town. The same writer recalled that most of the men ignored the orders and instead pulled back more slowly.[16]

The brigade was fired upon by Confederate troops (probably Perrin's Brigade) approaching from the right when it reached the Eagle Hotel. Losses mounted as the brigade continued its trek toward the safety of Cemetery Hill. Gettysburg was filled with men from the various shattered units, which precluded an orderly march through the town. The regiments stopped periodically, turned, and fired volleys into the enemy to keep them at a more respectable distance. Several men entered houses, where they had a better shot at the harassing Confederates. All through the afternoon the Confederates demanded the men's surrender. These demands were usually answered with determined volleys. As the 45th New York approached the public square in the center of town, it encountered a sea of disorganized and demoralized troops. Attempting to avoid the confusion, Lieutenant Colonel Doebke led his regiment down a side street. It ran into enemy soldiers who opened fire. Not knowing their strength, Doebke quickly ordered his men into a nearby alley, which led into a spacious yard. There was no exit, and when the men turned around, they saw Confederates barricading the entrance with the bodies of dead Union soldiers. Only about a hundred men escaped—the remainder of the 45th New York was ordered to destroy their arms and ammunition and surrender.[17]

The remnant of the brigade finally took position behind a stone fence on the northwest corner of Cemetery Hill. It had all but been destroyed during the few hours it occupied the fields north of town. Now less than five hundred men took defensive positions on Cemetery Hill. The 45th New York could muster but one hundred men, or one-third of its original strength. The other regiments also fared poorly. Four officers and eighteen men were all that was left of the 74th Pennsylvania; the 157th New York mustered about forty. Krzyzanowski's Brigade formed behind von Amsberg's on the northwest side of the hill.[18]

The brigade spent much of the second day skirmishing with the enemy occupying the town. Sometime between 6:00 P.M. and 7:00 P.M. that evening, four of von Amsberg's regiments (61st Ohio, 157th New York, 82nd Illinois, and 45th New York), mustering a mere 475 men, were rushed to Culp's Hill to support General George Greene's Brigade (Geary's Division, XII Corps), which was about to be overwhelmed by vastly superior numbers of Confederates. As a result of this movement, the brigade missed Early's Division attack on Cemetery Hill. The first two regiments were led to their positions by a I Corps staff officer; the 82nd Illinois and

45th New York were led by one of Schurz's staff officers. Unfamiliar with the terrain, the latter staff officer got lost, causing the two regiments to wander about before reaching their assigned positions.[19]

The activities of von Amsberg's Brigade on Culp's Hill are sketchy. According to Harry Pfanz, the ill-fated 157th New York took position on Greene's right. During Steuart's Brigade's (Johnson's Division) night attack, the regiment's flag bearer was wounded and the flag lost to the 37th Virginia. The 82nd Illinois was apparently effective in helping to halt the further advance of Steuart's Brigade. After the repulse, an unknown officer intending to pay a compliment to the commander of the 82nd Illinois said, "If you had been here yesterday instead of that d__d 11th Corps, we would not have been driven back." After receiving a sharp rebuke, the unknown officer vanished without uttering another word.[20]

The brigade remained there during the night, and on the morning of July 3 some of the units may have participated in a charge on the rifle pits that had been captured by Steuart's Brigade the evening before. The brigade returned to its old positions on Cemetery Hill later that morning. During the afternoon, General Schurz called for volunteers to dislodge Confederate snipers who were taking their toll on the Union artillerymen on the Cemetery Hill. Ten men from the 45th New York were selected, who helped oust the bothersome sharpshooters. This ended von Amsberg's Brigade's role in the battle. The brigade remained on Cemetery Hill until 6:00 P.M. on July 5, when it began its march toward Emmitsburg.[21]

Like so many other units of the XI Corps, the brigade's effectiveness was ultimately related to its position and leadership. Although the 45th New York effectively helped blunt O'Neal's attack on

Oak Ridge, the 157th New York was almost destroyed in its ill-fated charge on Doles's Brigade. The rest of the brigade occupied an untenable open position north of town that was hammered by Confederate artillery during the afternoon of July 1. The brigade's other actions were of minor significance.

2nd Brigade—Colonel Wladimir Krzyzanowski

Units: 58th New York (8 companies on detached duty until late afternoon of July 1), 119th New York, 82nd Ohio, 75th Pennsylvania (50 men on detached duty), 26th Wisconsin
Strength: 1420
Losses: 669 (75-388-206)—47%[22]

A Polish immigrant, Wladimir Krzyzanowski jumped at the chance to serve his new country. He helped organize the 58th New York and became its first colonel during the fall of 1861. Krzyzanowski saw his first action at Cross Keys, where his regiment was soundly defeated. He rose to brigade command during the Second Bull Run campaign and appeared to handle his men well. Then came the fiasco at Chancellorsville, where the brigade lost heavily. The men were ready to redeem themselves at Gettysburg.[23]

Krzyzanowski's Brigade marched behind Schimmelfennig's during the final miles to the battlefield. Crossing the Pennsylvania state line at 10:00 A.M. on July 1, the 75th Pennsylvania responded by "ruffling their drums, dipping their colors, and cheering as they stepped upon her soil." Hundreds of people gathered along the roadside to dispense food, water, and encouragement. "God bless you, boys!" was commonly heard along the route. The men could hear gunfire in the distance about an hour after crossing into Pennsylvania. Captain Frederick Winkler of the 26th Wisconsin noted that it was "the same kind of firing that we have heard very often on our marches of late, and we attributed it to a cavalry fight." The officers soon received orders to double-quick toward Gettysburg. The march was slowed by the heavy rains, which made the roads muddy.[24]

The firing increased as the brigade approached Gettysburg and so did the pace of the march. The brigade finally reached Gettysburg at about 1:00 P.M. and immediately moved northward. The town was in chaos. Captain Alfred Lee found "the rush of artillery galloping to the front, the eager movement of infantry, the hurry-scurry of cavalry, the scamper of the terror-stricken inhabitants, the clatter of amulances [sic] and other vehicles, all accentuated by the clatter of musketry and the thunder of cannon, constituted about as wild a scene of excitement as the tumult of war ever presents." Sergeant Charles Wickesberg of the 26th Wisconsin noted that "we were wet as cats, hungry as wolves, our thirst was satisfied by the good citizens when we ran in full gallop through their town." The men knew that they would soon be engaged. "Everyone's blood flows quicker, every pulse beats louder, every nerve is more sensitive, and every one feels that he is living faster than he was half an hour since," wrote a soldier in the same regiment.[25]

Leaving Gettysburg on Carlisle Road, the brigade took position in the open fields and orchards between Mummasburg and Carlisle Roads, northeast of the college. The brigade was deployed in double column of companies, from left to right, as 82nd Ohio–75th Pennsylvania–119th New York–26th Wisconsin. One company from the 119th was thrown forward as skirmishers to prevent the enemy from taking a large barn on the right.[26]

The men were now given a well-earned rest in an apple orchard. Theodore Dodge, the 119th New York's adjutant, wrote that "we then had a few minutes to ourselves. The men were allowed to rest in line, and each one sat or lay down in the most comfortable position just where he was, some reclining at full length and closing their eyes, some merely squatting down to discuss a hard tack and the situation, while the first sergeants called the roll." Captain Alfred Lee of the 82nd Ohio added that "the men quietly responded to their names amid the boom of cannon and the screech of exploding shells." The sight of massed columns of blue-clad soldiers well within range to the east was probably too irresistible for the Confederate cannoneers on Oak Hill and they opened fire on the brigade. While the losses were slight, probably under twenty, the bombardment took its toll in other ways. No matter how ineffective, massed cannon fire was psychologically difficult for infantry—more so than even effective small arms fire. To make matters worse, the men could look to their left and see their I Corps comrades wavering under the Confederate hammer blows. They also reflected on the fiasco at Chancellorsville. The men therefore entered the battle somewhat demoralized.[27]

Sometime around 2:00 P.M., the order to "fall in" rang through the brigade. The men knew what was in store for them because the skirmish fire in their front had been increasing in intensity. As the brigade moved forward, it encountered a series of fences. Some were torn down; the stouter ones were climbed over. The brigade remained deployed in column, probably to facilitate rapid movement.[28]

Shortly before this time, General Barlow had pushed his division farther north, so Schurz ordered Krzyzanowski to advance and support Barlow's left flank. As the brigade moved forward, "the enemy's batteries swept the plain completely from two or three different directions, and their shells plunged through our solid squares, making terrible havoc. Gaps made in the living mass by the cannon-shot were closed again as quickly and quietly almost as though nothing particular had happened," recalled Captain Lee. The brigade halted after advancing about four hundred yards and deployed in line of battle. The left of the 82nd Ohio on the left flank of the brigade touched Carlisle Road; the right stretched over open fields and ended close to woods on the right of the 26th Wisconsin. Several officers experienced dread during this advance when they realized that both of the brigade's flanks were "in the air." A similar situation had occurred a few months before, when Stonewall Jackson crushed the XI Corps at the battle of Chancellorsville. According to Captain Lee, Krzyzanowski's "face grew pale and distressed, when he realized his brigade's precarious position."[29]

Krzyzanowski's men had been unable to see the Confederate infantry in front of them up to this point. When their skirmishers came running back to their lines, they knew it was merely a matter of minutes before they would be engaged. Captain Dodge of the 119th New York recalled what occurred next. "A moment or two of breathless anxiety and impatience, and the irregular line of butternut and gray hove gradually in sight—their officers all mounted, waving their swords and cheering on their men." Prior to this, it had been difficult for the men not to fire their rifles. This evoked a "volley of oaths from the delinquents' supervisors, and not a few by a sound rap over the head . . . by a testy file closer." With the enemy in sight the officers finally gave the order to "fire." "This in no way checked the enemy's advance, but it drew their fire; and they continued slowly to push on, keeping it up in a desultory manner as they drew near," wrote Dodge. General Krzyzanowski nervously rode back and forth behind his lines, shouting both encouragement and orders to his men.[30]

The men were up against the 21st Georgia, which had been on the right of Doles's line as it faced Barlow's Division. Seeing Krzyanowski's Brigade advancing, it obliqued to the right to face this new threat. After battling the Union troops for a few minutes, the regiment's commander realized that his unit was no match for the enemy force in front of him, so he pulled back to Blocher's farm lane and ordered his men to lie down. Major August Ledig of the 75th Pennsylvania gleefully reported in his official report that "we charged upon them and drove them back."[31]

This would be the last positive comment that any member of the brigade would write, for Doles wheeled the 44th and 4th Georgia to the right to face Krzyzanowski's men. "Their movements were firm and steady, as usual, and their banners, bearing the blue Southern cross, flaunted impudently [sic] and seemed to challenge combat. On they came, one line after the other, in splendid array," recalled Captain Lee of the 82nd Ohio. [32]

The two lines now stood less than seventy-five yards apart in a wheatfield. So close were the lines that the "names of battles printed on the Confederate flags might have been read, had there been time to read them," recalled Captain Lee. The gunfire was having an effect on both sides. Dodge noted that "every five or six seconds some poor fellow would throw up his arms

with an 'ugh!' and drop." Lee added that "bullets hummed about our ears like infuriated bees." After about ten minutes, at least a quarter of the men were down. Because the regiment was deployed more diagonally than parallel, the companies on the far left were closer to the enemy and experienced heavier casualties.[33]

While Doles's regiments took on Krzyzanowski's left and center, the 31st and 60th Georgia from Gordon's Brigade turned their attention from Barlow's fleeing men to Krzyzanowski's right flank and rear. Smashing into the 26th Wisconsin, the Georgians left the field littered with men from the Badger State. A total of twenty-six men were killed and 129 wounded within a matter of minutes. Few troops could have sustained this attack, and the regiment began stampeding to the rear. This movement exposed the right flank of the 119th New York, which in turn was forced to flee. Captain Dodge admitted after the war that there was "no disguising the fact that we were fairly driven off the field." The flag bearer of the 119th New York was killed during the latter part of their stand, and the standard was left behind on the ground.[34]

As Gordon's Georgians rolled up Krzyzanowski's right flank, Doles's Georgians continued to pressure the brigade's left. Caught between these two forces, Krzyzanowski's two remaining regiments, the 82nd Ohio and 75th Pennsylvania, were forced to withdraw as well. The latter regiment lost 111 men in fifteen minutes, including its commander, Colonel Francis Mahler. After the battle, the men from the 75th Pennsylvania tried to claim that they were the last unit to leave their position. The veterans of the 82nd Ohio took issue with this assertion, and vehemently stated that *they* were the last to leave. Taking the middle ground, one old soldier accurately suggested that Gordon's flanking movement rolled up the brigade so fast that no regiment was able to hold its ground for any length of time. One of the casualties was General Krzyzanowski, who fell heavily to the ground after his horse was killed.[35]

Retreating about two hundred yards to the south, some of the men stopped to rest briefly in an orchard before continuing their retreat. A number of casualties were sustained as the men ran across the open fields, exposed to both artillery and small arms fire. Several units tried to turn and face the enemy. One officer later wrote that it was "useless, of course, to try to resist the long rebel forces that were approaching, but we could delay them and thus ensure a safe retreat to the rest of the troops." The futility of these attempts was soon obvious, and the men either fled or were ordered to enter Gettysburg. Here they found the streets clogged with demoralized troops. Many aimlessly wandered about. Winkler (26th Wisconsin) admitted that the "retreat [was] less orderly than it should have been." In the same letter, Winkler wrote that prior to the retreat through the town, "everywhere there were manifestations of day; handkerchiefs were waving everywhere, and the ladies stood in the streets offering refreshments to the solders as they passed. It seemed so awful to march back through those same streets whipped and beaten. It was the most humiliating step I ever took."[36]

Krzyzanowski's Brigade was the last of the XI Corps to enter Gettysburg. A band of men from the 119th New York halted at the foot of Washington Street and fired volleys, temporarily halting the Confederate advance. The retreat then continued through the town, where many men were captured. Those who successfully reached the safety of Cemetery Hill were led to the brigade's position in a cornfield just to the west of the Evergreen gatehouse, behind von Amsberg's Brigade on the west side of Emmitsburg Road. Upon their arrival they encountered the eight remaining companies of the 58th New York which had been on detached duty. The brigade was deployed in two lines. The first was composed of the 75th Pennsylvania on the left and the 82nd Ohio on its right. The second line was probably composed, from left to right, of the 26th Wisconsin–58th New York–119th New York. The full magnitude of the brigades' losses was finally tallied here.[37]

A patrol composed of men from the 75th Pennsylvania and the 58th New York entered Gettysburg that night to see if they could recover any of their wounded comrades. Enemy pickets fired into them, killing and wounding several of the men. Realizing that the town was still filled with enemy troops, the patrol was pulled back to the safety of Cemetery Hill.[38]

On July 2, the brigade came under continuous sniper fire from Confederate soldiers in houses and steeples. Later, the brigade was exposed to a heavy cannon fire from A. P. Hill's artillery on Seminary Ridge. One veteran wrote that a "perfect storm of cannon projectiles was hurled against the position . . . the exploding fragments dealing death and wounds throughout the ranks of every regiment." The tension was broken by the strains of a Confederate band playing a variety of waltzes and polkas. Early's Division's two-brigade attack on Cemetery Hill was launched as darkness descended. Driving up the east side of the hill, the Confederates successfully captured the crest of the hill. Krzyzanowski quickly ordered the men of the 119th New York and 58th New York to their feet, had them fix bayonets, and personally led them toward the scene of the action. It was dark, so the Confederates could only be located by the flashes from their muskets. The 119th New York led Krzyzanoswski's three hundred-man relief column, and the 58th New York brought up the rear. The distance between the two units must have been fairly great because only the 119th New York participated in the repulse. Several other units joined in the counterattack against the Louisiana Tigers, and the enemy was finally driven from the hill. Historian Harry Pfanz believed that the Union counterattack to reclaim Wiedrich's battery was made in two columns (actually masses, because of the confused conditions). Not content to help drive the Confederates from the hill, the 119th New York followed them to the base, where the men flopped down to rest. Losses to the regiment were low—only four men.[39]

Professor Michael Jacobs recorded in his diary that night that the returning Confederates "expressed their most earnest indignation at the foreigners—the Dutchmen—for having shot down so many of their men. This led us to believe that the Eleventh Corps . . . had done their duty and had nobly redeemed their character."[40]

The brigade continued exchanging shots with the Confederate snipers in the town during the morning of July 3. At about 6:00 A.M., a company of skirmishers was ordered to take possession of houses to the left of Baltimore Pike, where the Confederate snipers were particularly troublesome. The brigade's only fresh regiment, the 58th New York, was shifted to the right of Baltimore Pike to help support Wiedrich's battery should the Confederates make another attempt to capture Cemetery Hill. At about 1:00 P.M., the brigade was exposed to the cannonade that preceded the Pickett–Pettigrew–Trimble charge, and several men were hit. Krzyzanowski moved about offering encouragement to the men, while they dis-

tracted themselves by cleaning their guns, sewing their clothes, and shining their buttons. This ended Krzyzanowski's Brigade's participation in the battle. The unit finally left the battlefield on July 5.[41]

Krzyzanowski's Brigade was placed in an untenable position when ordered to aid Barlow's Division on July 1. With both flanks "in the air," the brigade formed an inviting target for Doles's and Gordon's Confederate Brigades. No troops could have held their positions in this situation. The brigade was crushed, sustaining a loss of 53%, and the 119th New York lost almost 60%.[42]

NOTES

1. Tagg, *Generals of Gettysburg*, 136–137.
2. OR 27, 1, 727–728; Martin, *Gettysburg—July 1*, 260.
3. OR 27, 1, 734, 740; George L. Warren, "The Eleventh Corps—The First Day at Gettysburg," *National Tribune*, July 21, 1887.
4. OR 27, 1, 730, 731, 735, 743.
5. Busey and Martin, *Regimental Strengths and Losses*, 85, 254.
6. Tagg, *Generals of Gettysburg*, 138–139.
7. *NYG*, vol. 1, 378; OR 27, 1, 734; Hartwig, "The 11th Army Corps on July 1, 1863," 35.
8. *NYG*, vol. 1, 378.
9. *NYG*, vol. 1, 378.
10. OR 27, 1, 734; Arthur Lee to John Bachelder, February 16, 1888, Bachelder Papers, New Hampshire Historical Society; John Applegate, *Reminiscences and Letters of George Arrowsmith of New Jersey* (Red Bank, NJ, 1893), 211–212.
11. Bates, *Pennsylvania Volunteers*, vol. I, 896; OR 27, 1, 734, 738–739; Martin, *Gettysburg—July 1*, 650 (n. 11); Jonathan Boynton, "Memoir," Civil War Miscellaneous Collection, USAMI.

A number of reporting errors were made by officers and men of two of the regiments. The commander of the 61st Ohio claimed in his report that his regiment had the privilege of leading the 3rd Division. This claim appears false, as the 45th New York led the column. The account of the 74th Pennsylvania in Bates states that the regiment was on the extreme left of the brigade with its left extending toward the I Corps. This assertion is also incorrect.

12. *NYG*, vol. 1, 379; OR 27, 1, 734.

The 45th New York claimed to have captured three hundred prisoners. This is grossly overstated as, all told, O'Neal's Brigade lost under two hundred prisoners (Busey and Martin, *Regimental Strengths and Losses*, 288).

13. *NYG*, vol. 1, 379; Martin, *Gettysburg— July 1*, 264.

14. Martin, *Gettysburg—July 1*, 260, 301– 302; Applegate, *Reminiscences and Letters of George Arrowsmith of New Jersey*, 214–215; OR 27, 2, 584–585; Henry W. Thomas, *History of the Doles'-Cook Brigade* (Atlanta, GA, 1906), 475–476.

With the 45th New York, 61st Ohio, and 74th Pennsylvania on the picket line, and the 82nd Illinois supporting the artillery, only the 157th New York was available to Schurz.

15. Applegate, *Reminiscences and Letters of George Arrowsmith of New Jersey*, 217; Martin, *Gettysburg—July 1*, 302; Sidney J. Richardson, letter, Georgia Department of Archives and Records; *NYG*, vol. 1, 21.

16. OR 1, 1, 734–735; Illinois Adjutant General's Report, vol. 5, copy in GNMP Library; *NYG*, vol. 1, 379–380.

17. *NYG*, vol. 1, 25, 380; OR 27, 1, 735.

18. OR 27, 1, 730, 735; Pfanz, *Culp's Hill and Cemetery Hill*, 241; Bates, *Pennsylvania Volunteers*, vol. I, 896 Applegate, *Reminiscences and Letters of George Arrowsmith of New Jersey*, 222.

19. OR 27, 1, 731; *NYG*, vol. 1, 63.

The 74th Pennsylvania was so badly battered that it was left behind to "reinforce" the right flank of the 1st Division.

20. Pfanz, *Culp's Hill and Cemetery Hill*, 213–214.

21. Illinois Adjutant-General's Report, vol. 5; *NYG*, vol. 1, 63, 381; *NYG*, vol. 1, 381; OR 27, 1, 736.

22. Busey and Martin, *Regimental Strengths and Losses*, 86, 255; OR 27, 1, 739–740.

23. Tagg, *Generals of Gettysburg*, 140–141.

24. Alfred Lee, "Reminiscences of the Gettysburg Battle," *Lippincott's Magazine of Popular Literature and Science* (July 1883), vol. 6, 54–55; *Address of General Robinson, Dedication of the 82nd Ohio Memorial* (Columbus, OH, 1887), 73; Hitz, *Letters of Frederick Winkler*, 69; Pula, *For Liberty and Justice— The Life and Times of Wladimir Krzyzanowski*, 95.

25. Pula, *For Liberty and Justice—The Life and Times of Wladimir Krzyzanowski*, 96; *Address of General Robinson, Dedication of the 82nd Ohio Memorial*, 73; Lee, "Reminiscences of the Gettysburg Battle," 55; Hinz, *Letters of Frederick Letters*, 69; James S. Pula, *The Sigel Regiment: A History of the Twenty-Sixth Wisconsin Volunteer Infantry, 1862–1865* (Campbell, CA, 1998), 161.

26. OR 27, 1, 742, 745, 746; Arthur Lee to John Bachelder, February 16, 1888.

Some erroneously wrote that the brigade left Gettysburg on Mummasburg Road.

27. Theodore A. Dodge, "Left Wounded on the Field," *Putnam's Monthly Magazine* (1869), vol. 4, 319; Lee, "Reminiscences of the Gettysburg Battle," 55.

The barn was probably part of the almshouse complex.

28. Hartwig, "The 11th Army Corps on July 1," 45.

29. Dodge, "Left Wounded on the Field," 319; Lee, "Reminiscences of the Gettysburg Battle," 56.

30. Dodge, "Left Wounded on the Field," 320–321; Pula, *For Liberty and Justice—The Life and Times of Wladimir Krzyzanowski*, 100.

31. OR 27, 2, 585; OR 27, 1, 745.

32. Lee, "Reminiscences of the Gettysburg Battle"; Pula, *For Liberty and Justice— The Life and Times of Wladimir Krzyzanowski*, 56; OR 27, 2, 585.

33. Dodge, "Left Wounded on the Field," 321; Lee, "Reminiscences of the Gettysburg Battle," 56; David Thomson to John Bachelder, February 28, 1888, Bachelder Papers, New Hampshire Historical Society.

34. OR 27, 1, 746; Martin, *Gettysburg—July 1*, 298; Dodge, "Left Wounded on the Field," 321; Ralph Whitehead, "The 119th New York Volunteers and Their Participation in the Gettysburg Campaign, June 12–July 4, 1983," 119th New York folder, GNMP, 9–10; Kevin E. O'Brien, "Bullets Came as Thick as Hail," *Gettysburg Magazine* (January 2001), issue 24, 66.

35. OR 27, 1, 745; David Thomson to John Bachelder, February 28, 1888; Arthur Lee to John Bachelder, February 16, 1888; Pula, *For Liberty and Justice—The Life and Times of Wladimir Krzyzanowski*, 102–103.

36. OR 27, 1, 740, 742, 744; Hitz, *Letters of Frederick Winkler*, 71; Pfanz, *Gettysburg—Culp's Hill and Cemetery Hill*, 241.

37. Pula, *For Liberty and Justice—The Life and Times of Wladimir Krzyzanowski*, 103; OR 27, 1, 740, 742, 744, 745; Hitz, *Letters of Frederick Winkler*, 70–71.

38. OR 27, 1, 740

39. OR 27, 1, 743; *NYG*, vol. 1, 431; Pula, *The Sigel Regiment: A History of the Twenty-Sixth Wisconsin Volunteer Infantry, 1862–1865* 176; Whitehead, "The 119th New York Volunteers and Their Participation in the Gettysburg Campaign, June 12–July 4, 1983," 10; Pfanz, *Gettysburg—Culp's Hill and Cemetery Hill*, 268, 272.

40. Michael M. Jacobs, *Notes on the Rebel Invasion of Maryland and Pennsylvania and the Battle of Gettysburg* (Philadelphia, 1864), 38.

41. Pula, *For Liberty and Justice—The Life and Times of Wladimir Krzyzanowski*, 113; *NYG*, vol. 1, 431.

42. Busey and Martin, *Regimental Strengths and Losses*, 255.

The percentage does not include the 58th New York, most of which arrived too late to participate in the fight on July 1.

Like so many unit historians who wrote about Gettysburg, the 75th Pennsylvania's tried to paint a positive picture of his regiment's actions. Two of his statements are illustrative of this approach. "Of the wild disorderly retreat the Eleventh Corps has maliciously been accused, the Seventy-Fifth Regiment at least was not guilty." Writing about the unit's losses of 55%, the historian erroneously concluded that "no other regiment in the Eleventh Corps met with a similar loss" (*PAG*, vol. 1, 434).

XII CORPS—

MAJOR GENERAL HENRY SLOCUM/
BRIGADIER GENERAL ALPHEUS WILLIAMS

The XII Corps was formed on September 12, 1862, and placed under the command of Major General Joseph Mansfield. The first major test of the corps occurred less than a week later, when Mansfield led it into the battle of Antietam. The corps entered the fray after General Joseph Hooker's I Corps had been soundly defeated. Mansfield's corps met the same fate, and the old general was mortally wounded. General Howard Slocum assumed command of the corps on October 20, 1862, but it did not see any action at Fredericksburg. The corps participated in the flanking action against Lee's army at the battle of Chancellorsville, and lost over 20% in the ensuing fight.[1]

Although only thirty-six years old, Major General Howard Slocum was the senior-ranking officer in the army. Considered overly cautious at times, he was a stickler for details and order, but was a competent fighter as long as the orders he received were clear and precise.[2]

The XII Corps crossed the Potomac River at Edwards Ferry on June 26 and made good progress marching along the dusty roads after Lee's army. This was not true on June 29, however. Beginning their march before 3:00 A.M., the men were forced to wait four hours while a long wagon train passed. Resuming the march at about 10:30 that morning, the column finally made better time. The corps marched through Frederick, Maryland, that day and crossed into Pennsylvania on the morning of June 30.[3]

After spending the night about a mile beyond Littlestown, the corps reformed at 7:00 A.M. on July 1. The column, led by Geary's 2nd Division, retraced its steps about a mile to Baltimore Pike, which took the men the final ten miles to Gettysburg. Upon taking command of the field after Reynolds's death, General O. O. Howard sent urgent pleas for assistance to the III Corps and XII Corps. While General Sickles of the former corps immediately complied, Slocum did not, instead allowing his men to cook their noontime meal and nap at Two Taverns, a mere five miles from Gettysburg. According to modern historian Larry Tagg, Slocum may have put too much faith in Meade's original plan of falling back to defensive positions along Pipe Creek, and hence did not want to get entangled in a fight that was contrary to his commander's wishes. Slocum also had a nickname that applied well to his cautious nature—"Slow Come."[4]

After a halt of about three hours, the column continued its march, arriving about one mile from Gettysburg at 4:00 P.M. on July 1. Because the XI Corps had already fallen back, Slocum's corps could not form on its right, north of town, as planned. Instead, the corps continued marching east toward Wolf Hill. Later, Geary's Division was detached and sent south to the Round Tops. Changes in command occurred during the night. Because Slocum outranked Howard, he took command of the army (and later, when Meade arrived, he oversaw this sector). General Alpheus Williams replaced him as commander of the XII Corps, General Thomas Ruger of the 3rd Brigade assumed command of the 1st Division, and Colonel Silas Colgrove of the 27th Indiana took command of his brigade.[5]

At about 8:00 A.M. on July 2, Williams received orders to reunite the corps on the slopes of Culp's Hill. Geary's Division formed on the left of Wadsworth's Division, and Ruger's Division continued the line to the right. The men spent most of the day entrenching. At about 6:00 P.M. Williams ordered Ruger's men to march south to assist in repulsing Longstreet's attack on the left of the Federal line. Because of the addition of Lockwood's green brigade, and presumably Ruger's inexperience, Williams elected to accompany the 1st Division during its march south. Williams was astounded when he later learned that Slocum had personally ordered two brigades of Geary's Division to follow. Thinking they were following Ruger's Division, Geary's men took the wrong road and headed toward Littlestown instead. While five of the six XII Corps brigades were out of the breastworks, the remaining brigade, General George Greene's, was attacked by Johnson's Division (II Corps). While most of the attacks were beaten off, the Confederates succeeded in capturing a portion of the XII Corps's breastworks.[6]

The XII Corps returned, and its orders for July 3 were to retake the lost breastworks. The Confederates attacked first, and they continued fighting all morning. The Confederate troops fell in heaps, but still they charged the Federal lines. Private James Baum of the 46th Pennsylvania wrote after the war that to "those soldiers of the southern army, who stood without qualling [sic] before that terrible storm of iron hail and leaden bullets, the greatest praise should be given. They were heroes in deed and fact." The corps remained in its breastworks until July 5, when it began its movement after Lee's army.[7]

1ST DIVISION—

Brigadier General Alpheus Williams/
Brigadier General Thomas Ruger

Brigadier General Alpheus Williams led a division longer than any other in the Army of the Potomac. After he took command on March 13, 1862, his division saw action in the Shenandoah Valley campaign of 1862 and the Second Bull Run campaign. Both were significant defeats for the North. When Pope's Army of Virginia was disbanded, the XII Corps was formed. Williams led his division into the Antietam campaign, where it was soundly defeated. After missing the battle of Fredericksburg, Williams's Division was heavily engaged repulsing numerous Confederate attacks during the battle of Chancellorsville. The men felt good about Williams's fighting abilities as they made their way north during the Gettysburg campaign.[8]

During their trek toward Pennsylvania, General Alpheus Williams's men made good time marching along the dusty roads. Citizens along the route often distributed food and water. Many children wore red, white, and blue outfits. General Williams was not impressed with the Pennsylvania Dutch citizens his troops passed. Noting their large and imposing barns, he called them "a people of barns, not brains." The men were ordered to unload and inspect their guns on June 30 to ensure that they were in good working order. The ammunition was also closely inspected. This completed, the men reloaded their guns. After a stream of artillery passed, the line reformed and orders of "forward, double-quick" rang through the column. After trotting along for about two miles in this manner, the column passed through Littlestown. Here they could see the entire population outside, waving handkerchiefs, some smiling, others crying. Many held baskets filled with cakes, cold meats, and bread, or pails of water.[9]

After double-quicking another mile, the men were permitted to rest for the night in a large field. The 1st Division led the corps on July 1, when the march continued at daybreak. The division reached Two

Taverns at about 11:00 A.M., and rested there for several hours. The pace was fast when the march resumed that afternoon. Because no breaks were permitted, many men could not keep up and fell by the side of the road. When the order to halt was finally given, "in a minute every man was flat on the ground resting while perspiration ran from our bodies in streams," wrote Sergeant Lorenzo Coy of the 123rd New York.[10]

Before reaching Rock Creek, about a mile from Gettysburg, Williams's Division halted and marched about three-quarters of a mile to the right, along a farm lane. Here it formed in line of battle and advanced toward Wolf Hill. Describing this period of the battle, General Ruger wrote that the "appearance of the division in this position at the time it occurred was apparently a timely diversion in favor of our forces, as the farther advance of the enemy ceased." This was probably not bravado, as Confederate General William Smith may have seen these troops approaching, and this caused at least two brigades of Early's Division to be kept northeast of town.[11]

Since the XI Corps had been defeated, there was no need for Williams's Division to come to its aid north of town. According to Williams, "as the Rebels had already driven back our troops in front of Gettysburg and occupied the town, we were in danger of being cut off from our line towards the main road." Instead, the division was pulled back about three-quarters of a mile, at sunset. Here the men remained for the night, without food. At daylight on July 2, the division's pickets exchanged fire with the enemy and sustained some casualties. The men were relieved when the V Corps arrived soon after and took position on the right of the division. During this period, Williams was ordered to take command of the corps, General Thomas Ruger took over the division, and Colonel Silas Colgrove of the 27th Indiana assumed command of his brigade. Ruger received orders at 9:00 A.M. to move the division about 1.5 miles south on Baltimore Pike to form on the right of Geary's Division on Culp's Hill. Under the watchful eye of General Williams, Ruger deployed his men in two lines, with McDougall's Brigade on the left and Colgrove's Brigade on the right. Upon taking up these positions, the men were immediately put to work constructing breastworks. Lockwood's Independent Brigade, which arrived during the morning, formed southeast of Colgrove's Brigade, but did not construct breastworks.[12]

At about 6:00 P.M., the division was ordered south to support the left wing of the army, now under attack by General Longstreet's Divisions. In his report, Williams noted that the division "occupied the woods on the left of Lockwood, and pushed forward in two lines, the enemy retiring with but little resistance." Ruger reported, "having approached the point of heavy fire of musketry, which had become feeble, I formed the division in line of masses preparatory to moving forward." While Lockwood's men did not fire a shot, their presence may have acted as a deterrent to any further Confederate advance. Williams ordered the division back to its original position on Culp's Hill after dark. Colgrove's Brigade probably led the column back toward Culp's Hill, followed by McDougall's; Lockwood's brought up the rear.[13]

Concerned that the enemy may have occupied some of his breastworks, Ruger threw several companies forward in the darkness. This was a wise move because Stueurt's Brigade (Johnson's Division) had captured the breastworks earlier that evening. Although seventeen of Ruger's men were captured, the division's losses could have been much higher. After considering his options, Ruger decided not to attack. He included his reasoning in his official report. "I deemed it unwise to attack the enemy, owing to the darkness, difficult character of the ground, and want of knowledge of the force of the enemy, and immediately placed the division in line along the crest of a slight ridge . . . the position best adapted to prevent the enemy from advancing toward the turnpike if he should attempt it." There being nothing left for the division to do, Ruger ordered it to settle in for the night.[14]

The Confederate attack on the Federal line began at 4:30 A.M. on July 3, when Confederate cannon on Ruger's right and left opened fire on his position. The attacks continued all morning. According to Ruger, the Confederates had two things against them: the ground was covered by large rocks, making rapid movement difficult, and depositions of the Federal brigades permitted them to send an enfilading fire into the ranks of the attackers. The Confederates finally pulled back, allowing Ruger's Division to regain its lost breastworks. The division remained there through the early afternoon of July 5, when it began its march after Lee's army.[15]

1st Brigade—Colonel Archibald McDougall

Units: 5th Connecticut, 20th Connecticut, 3rd Maryland, 123rd New York, 145th New York, 46th Pennsylvania
Strength: 1835
Losses: 80 (12-60-8)—4.4%[16]

Although on paper the 1st Brigade was a veteran unit that had fought on many bat-

tlefields, it had been reorganized in May 1863 from what had been the 1st and 2nd Brigades. Hence, it was essentially a new brigade with little experience fighting as a unit. Colonel Archibald McDougall of the 123rd New York commanded the brigade during the Gettysburg campaign because its regular commander, Brigadier General

Joseph Knipe, had been sent to Pennsylvania to assume command of a militia brigade. Thus, the 1st Brigade marched toward Gettysburg with six veteran regiments that had not fought together as a unit, and were under the command of a colonel who had seen action in only one battle.[17]

Marching behind Ruger's 3rd Brigade, Colonel McDougall's men took in all of the sights during their march to Gettysburg. Many men were disappointed that the rapid pace through the town of Littlestown, Pennsylvania, did not permit them to partake of the goods offered by its citizens. Some were nevertheless able to grab a handful of food as they double-quicked down Baltimore Pike. While marching toward Gettysburg on July 1, "we heard the deep booming of cannon and soon an orderly came dashing along our column and we learned that the 2nd [1st] and 11th Corps were then engaged with Jackson's old Corps under General Ewall [sic]. On learning this we halted and rested about three hours and then 'fell in and forward,'" recalled Sergeant L. R. McCoy of the 123rd New York. When about a mile or so from Gettysburg, the brigade was ordered to march about a half mile to the right of the road, where it formed into line of battle behind Colgrove's Brigade. Nothing materialized, so the men pulled back, and were permitted to rest on their arms for the remainder of the night. This was not true of the 5th Connecticut, which was detached as skirmishers to support a battery.[18]

The men were awakened at 4:00 A.M. on July 2 and immediately ordered to form into line of battle without breakfast. With a line of skirmishers preceding them, the brigade retraced the route it took the night before, when it had approached the battlefield. They had not gone far when they were ordered to halt and grab a quick breakfast of hardtack and coffee, then they rested for an additional three hours. The brigade welcomed back the 3rd Maryland during the morning, which had been detached to guard the division's ordnance wagons. At 9:00 A.M., General Ruger received orders to move the division to Culp's Hill, and he immediately complied. Cutting across fields, the men reached Baltimore Pike, then marched south to Culp's Hill, where they formed on the right of Geary's Division. The brigade's left met Kane's Brigade's right. From this point, the right of the line ran along the crest of the rocky, wooded lower hill, with its right flank extending almost to Rock Creek. Here it connected at an angle with Colgrove's Brigade. McDougall's Brigade was deployed in two lines. The first line was on the crest of the hill; the second was behind a stone wall, about seventy-five yards in the rear. Colonel McDougall considered it to be a very strong position, made more so by the construction of breastworks, so that it "was able to resist almost any assault that could have been made in front." Colonel E. Livingston Price of the 145th New York reported that his regiment formed on the second line with the 3rd Maryland on the left and the 5th Connecticut on the right. Historian Harry Pfanz agreed, believing the regiments on the first line were deployed, from left to right, as 123rd New York–20th Connecticut–46th Pennsylvania. Colonel James Rogers of the 123rd New York confirmed that his regiment was on the first line.[19]

The men set to work building breastworks with a vengeance. Henry Morhous of the 123rd New York explained why: "the boys, remembering Chancellorsville, were determined to have good works this time, and went to work with a will." The men first felled large trees, stripped off the branches, and piled up the trunks until they were breast-high. These were kept in place by notching smaller trees and sticking them upright into the ground. A space of about three inches was left between the two top upper timbers, through which the men could push their gun barrels. A ditch ensured that no man's head extended above the top log, and a shelf was built to allow shorter men to fire through the space. Earth thrown against the logs on the opposite side of the breastwork prevented the enemy shells from splintering the timbers. Finally, many of the limbs cut from the tree trunks were sharpened and used to form an abatis. Enemy skirmishers hindered the construction of the works.[20]

The men were proud of their engineering accomplishments and hoped they would now be permitted to rest after their long hours of exertion. This was not the case, for at about 6:00 P.M. the entire division was ordered south to help repel Longstreet's attack against the Union left flank. The two-mile march took the brigade across fields, then up onto Cemetery Ridge and south to the Wheatfield, where it formed behind units of the V Corps. Along the way the men came under sporadic artillery fire. Private Abner Smith of the 20th Connecticut wrote home that the "rebs had a battery playing onto us all the way from where we started till we got where it was thought we should be needed . . . one in our regiment was knocked down by a cannonball . . . but did not hurt him very much." The march southward left a vivid impression on Sergeant L. R. Coy of the 123rd New York, who wrote home, "never shall I forget that time. Eight thousand men in steady line with guns at the 'right shoulder shift' all on the run while fugitives from the 3rd Corps were continually breaking through our lines and shot and shell fell thick and fast around us." The welcome order,

"Halt, Front, Rest," was heard, and Coy and his comrades "fell to the ground tired out and exhausted." Their reprieve did not last long. "We commenced forming a line of battle by way of relieving and re-enforcing our exhausted and wearied troops, which had been maintaining the fight on this part of the line," wrote McDougall in his report. If the men were looking forward to engaging the enemy, they were disappointed. "We expected warm work here but just as we came in sight the enemy gave way and we were ordered back to the right," wrote Coy.[21]

Upon approaching their original breastworks on Culp's Hill at about 10:00 P.M., an officer rode up to Colonel McDougall with word that they were occupied by the enemy. McDougall threw a company from the 123rd New York and one from the 5th Connecticut cautiously forward in the darkness as skirmishers. Their orders, according to Colonel W. Packer of the 5th Connecticut, were "not to fire upon or otherwise alarm the enemy, but merely to ascertain and report their strength and position." Lieutenant Marcus Beadle with a portion of the 123rd New York's Company I was soon challenged in the darkness. Upon identifying himself, Beadle heard the words, "Come on, it's all right." As he advanced, he learned that he had been conversing with Confederate soldiers, who quickly captured him. As he was hustled to the rear he yelled out, "Fall back men." Firing broke out, but no other men from his company were captured. The same was not true of the 5th Connecticut, which lost five men to the enemy. Because the main body of the 123rd New York was lower on the slope than the 145th New York behind it, when the Confederates fired, the shots went over the 123rd New York's heads and into the 145th New York. Several men were wounded, "causing some confusion," as their commander put it. Others painted quite a different picture, saying that the regiment panicked in the darkness and fired into the 123rd New York in front of it, killing at least one soldier. Still frightened, many of the men fled to the rear, leaving their colors behind.[22]

The men were now permitted to rest on their arms in a cornfield between Baltimore Pike and McAllister Woods near Rock Creek. Coy wrote home that the brigade was deployed in the following order from left to right: 3rd Maryland–145th New York–20th Connecticut–5th Connecticut–46th Pennsylvania. Coy did not list the position of the 123rd New York, but it appears to have occupied a slightly advanced position.[23]

That night, several men were sent to Spangler's Springs to fill canteens. Despite the darkness, they knew that they were not alone, as Confederate soldiers were also filling their canteens. Not a word was muttered, as each side quickly completed their task and left the area.[24]

During the morning of July 3 McDougall ordered the 20th Connecticut forward to reconnoiter and attempt to retake the breastworks. After the war, its colonel, William Wooster, explained why his regiment was selected for this important mission. "The 20th C.V. had stood a hard fight at Chancellorsville. The 123rd N.Y., had not been so well tried & I understood at the time this was reason [sic] why I received the advance. The 5 Conn. & 46 Pa., two tried regts. were not both in numbers equal to the work."[25]

Wooster received orders to be ready to advance as early as 3:00 A.M. on July 3. Enemy artillery opened fire at about 4:30 A.M., and Wooster ordered his men forward soon after. His orders were to advance to "prevent the enemy [from] getting around the right of General Geary's forces in the entrenchments on our left, and holding the enemy back so

that our artillery could have free play upon his columns without destroying our own troops." Even with the 20th Connecticut in its advanced position, a gap of two hundred to three hundred yards existed between the Nutmeggers and Geary's troops. For five hours, a bitter struggle ensued between the 20th Connecticut and the 10th Virginia of Steuart's Brigade. Rocks and trees protected Wooster's men during this struggle. Every one of the Confederate attacks was halted. In addition to dealing directly with the enemy infantry, Wooster sent back information about the enemy's movements so that the batteries could adjust their range and improve their effectiveness. John Storrs vividly recalled this part of the battle. "The sharp and almost continuous reports of the twelve pounders, the screaming, shrieking shell that went crashing through the tree tops; the deadened thud of the exploding shell; the whizzing sound of the pieces as they flew in different directions; the yells of the rebels when they gained a momentary advantage; the cheers of the men when the surging tide of battle turned in our favor."[26]

Sometime during the morning, the 20th Connecticut was able to advance to a stone wall which afforded them some protection. A short time later they were evicted by a Confederate counterattack. So began a seesaw battle over a wall that lasted for several hours. Wooster's men also had to contend with errant Federal artillery shells. McDougall wrote that the 20th Connecticut "encountered great difficulty, while resisting the enemy, in protecting himself against the fire of our own artillery . . . his [Wooster's] greatest embarrassment was, the farther he pushed the enemy the more directly he was placed under the fire of our own guns." Wooster lost several men to this friendly fire.[27]

The remainder of the brigade was also

exposed to Union artillery fire and several men were killed and wounded. These events led to some hostility between McDougall and the commander of the 145th New York, E. Livingston Price. The latter described the incident in his official report: "deeming it advisable and proper to report the facts [about the friendly fire] to my commanding officer, I dispatched . . . to inform the colonel commanding the brigade that several of my men had been wounded by the fire of our own artillery." According to Price, the aide returned with a message, "Tell Colonel Price 'not to fret.'" Colonel James Selfridge of the 46th Pennsylvania purportedly went to see McDougall and, drawing his revolver, said that he would shoot the battery commander if additional shells fell on his troops. When three additional men were hit, an enraged Price and an equally angry Selfridge decided to take matters into their own hands and rode over to the offending battery, where they met General Slocum. The regiment was subsequently pulled back out of cannon range. McDougall took issue with this version of the story, writing that upon questioning Price's aide, he was told that none of the troops had been injured.[28]

While the 20th Connecticut skirmished with Steuart's troops, the remainder of McDougall's Brigade also attempted to advance. However, between the small arms and artillery fire, they found it easier to lie flat on the ground. "The sharpshooters were very active, and any of the least rise on our part was a leaden answer. Once I lifted my cap. I did not repeat it, as a bullet was sent after it," wrote Baum (46th Pennsylvania).[29]

Wooster reported that the 20th Connecticut finally drove the Confederates out of their breastworks at about 10:30 A.M. Almost out of ammunition, the regiment was pulled back and replaced by the 123rd New York. After replenishing their ammunition, the Nutmeggers returned to the breastworks, along with the remainder of the brigade. In his official report, Colonel James Rogers of the 123rd New York wrote that the "regiment lay in this position as a reserve . . . when the enemy having been driven from the breastworks, it moved forward and occupied them." The story was embellished somewhat after the battle, when Lieutenant L. R. Coy wrote home on July 6, 1863, "we charged over the wall only to see the rebels spring over the breastworks and by the time we reached them they were on a wild run through the woods beyond." Morhous recalled that "as soon as the Regiment came in sight of the works they had left the day before they gave a cheer and a rush, and gained them without a loss of life, the Rebels being driven over the works with great slaughter." What really seems to have occurred is that neither the 20th Connecticut nor the 123rd New York drove the Confederates out of the works. After long hours of fighting, and nothing to show for it, General Steuart finally pulled his men back. This was confirmed by McDougall's report, which stated that at "about 2 P.M. this regiment [20th Connecticut] was relieved by the One Hundred and twenty-third New York Volunteers, which soon reported to me that, not finding any enemy, they had entered and then held the breastworks." Colonel Wooster was incensed that some veterans of the 123rd New York claimed to have driven the enemy out of the breastworks, so he wrote a letter to John Bachelder. "When the 123 N.Y. came to relieve the 20th C.V. there was no occasion for a gun to be discharged at anything, nor was there a <u>living moving rebel within our lines at which a charge could be directed</u> [underlining is Wooster's]." The 123rd

New York probably saw the Confederates retreating, but did not fire a shot.[30]

The men were subjected to sniper fire after the brigade had settled back into its captured works. The 5th Connecticut was detached and ordered to the foot of McAllister's Hill to support a battery and watch for enemy troops on the army's right flank. A signal gun was heard at 1:00 P.M. and the ground shook as almost 150 Confederate artillery pieces opened fire on the Union line. Colonel McDougall explained that "the artillery of the enemy, covering us with an enfilading fire, shells and solid shot passing through and crushing the tops of trees over our heads and falling within and on both sides of our works. The command bore this dangerous fire with commendable coolness." Lieutenant Charles Warner of the 145th New York wrote home, "I could not distinguish the different reports, but it was one continual roar. I tell you it was perfectly horrible."[31]

Sometime between 4:00 and 5:00 P.M. that afternoon, the brigade, minus the 5th Connecticut, was pulled out of their breastworks a second time in two days and marched to the rear to assist in the repulse of the Pickett–Pettigrew–Trimble charge. Several regiments from Colgrove's Brigade took their places as they vacated their breastworks. Marching along Baltimore Pike, McDougall's Brigade was met by one of Meade's staff officers near the Leister house and led to its position behind the II Corps. The men waited here for about three-quarters of an hour and then were abruptly ordered back to their original positions as the attack had been repulsed and they were no longer needed. Because Colgrove's Brigade was still in their fortifications, McDougall's troops were ordered to occupy a position behind them, which exposed them to sniper fire. Colgrove's Brigade was pulled out during the early evening, and McDougall's men

eagerly took their places behind the protective breastworks. The detached 5th Connecticut was also busy during this period. About 5:00 P.M. it marched two miles down Hanover Road, and with the 13th New Jersey, supported General David Gregg's cavalry division.[32]

About 7:00 A.M. on July 4, the 5th Connecticut, 123rd New York and 46th Pennsylvania were placed under the command of Colonel Colgrove of the 3rd Brigade, and ordered to the northeast, to conduct a reconnaissance of the enemy's positions. With a detachment of cavalry in the lead and a cannon sandwiched between the regiments, the reconnaissance force moved slowly forward, eventually passing through the town and beyond it. No enemy soldiers were seen, so the men returned to their breastworks by 10:00 A.M., after the eight-mile trek. The remainder of the day was spent collecting weapons and equipment, and burying the dead. The scenes were horrible. Coy (123rd New York) wrote that "in one spot not 12 feet square I saw 8 dead but I cannot describe what I saw it was too horrid— truly thought as I passed over the field none but Demons can delight in way."[33]

The brigade pulled out of its breastworks for good at 10:30 A.M. on July 5 and joined the rest of the XII Corps in the march back to Littlestown. It arrived there at about dark.[34]

Compared with other units of the XII Corps, McDougall's Brigade's losses were fairly light. As one might expect, the highest losses were in 20th Connecticut, which skirmished with the enemy during most of the morning of July 3. Yet, they lost only twenty-eight, or 9%, of their men. The brigade did little actual fighting during the battle and had the advantage of the protection afforded by a well-built fortification for most of it. Nevertheless, the brigade probably deserved the following accolades heaped upon the 145th New York by its commanding officer, Colonel Edward Price:

> I cannot omit speaking of the nobleness with which my command endured the privations, hardships, and trials of these fifteen days. It marched over 150 miles, engaged the enemy for two or three days at Gettysburg, built breastworks and abatis, was deprived continually of both rest and sleep, performed forced marches of nearly 30 miles per day through mud and rain, sometimes with inadequate rations, and many of my men without shoes or sufficient clothing. . . . not a man faltered; that not a single case of disobedience of orders occurred.[35]

2nd Brigade—Brigadier General Henry Lockwood

Units: 1st Maryland Eastern Shore (Did not arrive until the morning of July 3), 1st Maryland Potomac Home Guard, 150th New York
Strength: 1818
Losses: 174 (35-121-18)—9.6%[36]

Henry Lockwood's Brigade marched toward Gettysburg with a mixture of awe and discomfort. This was a new brigade—two of the regiments were linked just a few days before the march began, and the third did not join the brigade until the morning of July 3. While the brigade was composed of only three regiments, it outnumbered most of the others in the Army of the Potomac because each regiment was large. For example, the 1st Maryland Potomac Home Guard had over seven hundred men in its ranks. The regiment had been raised to protect railroads and other important sites in Maryland, so it had not seen much action. The 150th New York (the Dutchess Regiment) had been mustered into service in 1862, but had not seen any action. Neither regiment had seen service with the Army of the Potomac. It was not until June 27 that the green 150th New York finally saw the fabled Army of the Potomac. "What a spectacle for a recruit to look upon," wrote one of the men. Although they were now part of the army, they certainly did not look the part. "With our full ranks, bright colors and clean uniforms, we were readily distinguished from the veteran regiments." Because these men were new, they had trouble keeping up with the veteran units.[37]

Although the brigade was to be part of the XII Corps's 1st Division, Williams decided to consider it an "Independent Brigade." Otherwise Lockwood, who outranked Ruger, could claim the right to command the 1st Division after Williams took command of the corps. Williams explained that he had nothing against Lockwood, but he was "a stranger to the division. . . . I did not like while a battle was pending, to give him command of the division." Therefore, Williams "directed him to take his orders directly from me, as an unassigned brigade during the pending operations."[38]

The men camped outside Bruceville, Maryland, on the evening of June 30 and reached Littlestown on the evening of July 1. The men could hear the sounds of battle that day, causing their anxiety levels to rise. Roused early on July 2, they continued their march to the battlefield, arriving there sometime between 8:00 and 9:00 A.M. Prior to this final march, the two regimental commanders felt a need to calm and motivate their men, but they did so in a very different manner. Colonel William Maulsby of the 1st Maryland Potomac Home Guard told his men of the perils that awaited them and "in patriotic words encouraged them to bravely do their duty." Colonel John Ketcham of the 150th New York took a different approach. "It was not his custom to harangue us with loud-sounding phrases," wrote one of his men. Instead, he walked along the line, providing encouragement and imparting advice.[39]

Arriving at the battlefield on July 2, the brigade finally joined the rest of the XII Corps and was soon exposed to cannon fire. The Confederate shells flew uncomfortably close to their heads, with many exploding in a nearby field. "We turned our heads one side, with eyes upward, trying to see them as they passed, much as a flock of turkeys will do to catch sight of a hawk," wrote Major Henry Gildersleeve of the 150th New York. The novelty soon wore off, but not the concern for their safety.[40]

The brigade formed the right flank of the division, and it moved at least twice during the day. At 5:00 P.M., Lockwood received orders to move his men south immediately, and then west, to assist Sickles's hard-pressed III Corps. During the rapid march along Granite Schoolhouse Lane, which they made in column of four abreast, the men were exposed to artillery fire. They soon passed a stream of wounded men. The first wounded soldier they encountered had blood on his hand and arm. "We looked from one to another with serious faces which expressed what we all felt but no one put into words . . . jesting ceased; a strange silence fell upon the marching column . . . strange that a little wound in a man's arm should affect us so," wrote Private Charles Benton of the 150th New York. As they approached the scene

of the fighting, the men could hear the victorious Rebel yell, and the stream of wounded men increased. The officers were especially concerned about how the men would react to these sights—"whether it unnerved them, or stiffened their sinews, and 'summoned up the blood.'" One of the shells hit a nearby wagon, sending provisions flying in all directions. The hungry men could not resist breaking ranks to scoop up hardtack.[41]

The march finally halted around the Trostle house. The Confederates massing in their front were from Barksdale's Brigade (probably the 21st Mississippi), which had crushed the Union position at the Peach Orchard and were now moving forward to breach the Federal line. General Williams wrote that he knew the situation was critical because, "though we passed large masses of our disorganized men, we saw not one line or body of our troops in position. The enemy seemed to have a clear field in that part of our lines." Lockwood immediately ordered his two regiments (the 1st Maryland Eastern Shore had not yet arrived) to face right and form line of battle on the left of Willard's Brigade (Hays's Division, II Corps). The 1st Maryland Potomac Home Guard was in the front line and the less experienced 150th New York was in the second. The men were ordered to fix bayonets and charge at the double-quick. A soldier in Colgrove's Brigade wrote after the war that the "brilliant charge of Lockwood's Brigade was well executed; and their first work under fire was worthy of veterans."[42]

What occurred next is contested. The officers and men of the brigade wrote that they directly engaged the enemy. Both Lockwood's and Maulsby's official reports use almost identical terms to explain the role played by the 1st Maryland Potomac Home Guard—"driving the enemy before them/us and entirely cleared the field." After the war, Lockwood recalled that the brigade "rushed with many cheers into the thickest of the fight, over ground strewn with dead and wounded." Benton (150th New York) agreed: "in the field before us, just skirting the woods, was a long line of men in gray, firing continuously. Our own line paused a line in forming, then a cloud of blue smoke, pierced with a thousand jets of flame, sprang from their front, and before the echoes of the volley had died away they dashed forward with a cheer." The enemy then "gave way completely and ran scattering through the wood before this impetuous charge of fresh men."[43]

However, corps commander Alpheus Williams noted that "fortunately, he [1st Maryland] met little resistance, for the Rebs. ran and left the captured guns, which were thus recaptured without firing a gun." Colonel Ketcham of the 150th New York and others agreed, suggesting that Barksdale's troops were already retreating when the brigade arrived. Gildersleeve, also of the 150th New York, recalled that the men "were not called upon to fire a gun." This view is also confirmed by the historian of the 150th New York, who wrote that the "enemy had fallen back upon the first approach of reinforcements and were now concealed from view." Although the brigade did not "drive" the Mississippians from the field, its approach could have been instrumental in discouraging the disordered and exhausted Confederates from continuing the attack. In his report, General Williams wrote that the brigade was to "deploy his line and occupy the woods, which he did in gallant style, pushing a considerable distance to the front." He clarified his rhetoric the following year when he wrote to John Bachelder that "the enemy fell back with but little opposition, indeed

they must have been retiring as I came upon the ground. They had probably seen the reinforcements of the 6th and 12th Corps advancing."[44]

Not contested is that Companies B and G of the 150th New York were ordered to help pull off three artillery pieces of Bigelow's battery that had been briefly captured by the enemy. "The credit of recapturing [the cannons] belongs to that brigade," wrote General Williams after the battle. The men tended to the wounded now that the enemy was finally repulsed. The regiment remained there until about 9:00 P.M., when it was ordered back to the right of the army.[45]

Where the brigade initially halted is not known. At 2:00 A.M. on July 3, "after a short march," they halted and deployed on either side of Rugg's and Kinzie's batteries on Baltimore Pike. The 1st Maryland Potomac Home Guard formed on the left, not far from the Spangler house, and the 150th New York formed on the right, near the Lightner house. Here they observed the batteries open fire at about 4:30 A.M.[46]

At about 6:00 A.M., Lockwood received orders to send a regiment to engage the enemy troops in the woods to the right. Probably recalling the 1st Maryland Potomac Home Guard's success the evening before, he sent orders to Colonel Maulsby to advance and engage the enemy. In front of him was the 2nd Virginia (Walker's Brigade), crouched behind a low stone wall. The seven hundred-man regiment advanced rapidly in bright blue uniforms under heavy small arms fire. Members of the 150th New York watched their advance. One soldier wrote that "it was a fine display . . . they were all out of sight at once, and we waited in dread suspense, but not long. A thousand rifles opened from the contending forces." Maulsby halted his line when it was within thirty-five feet of the wall. The lines were dressed, bayonets were fixed, and orders to charge were about to be given when General Lockwood ordered the men to break off the attack and fall back. "Information reached me that another regiment was taking him on his [Maulsby's] right, and that our fire would damage that movement," Lockwood explained in his report. A frustrated Maulsby wrote that "at this moment numbers of the enemy were distinctly seen fleeing from behind the stone wall to the rear." The historian of the regiment believed that the real reason for the order may have been "to save it from the murderous fire to which it was exposed." Lockwood seems to support this supposition in his official report. "Having already lost in killed and wounded some 80 men, and our ammunition being short, I withdrew the regiment, and returned to the turnpike."[47]

Soon after the 1st Maryland Potomac Home Guard returned to Baltimore Pike, the 150th New York was ordered to move by the flank to the left. "'Forward, 150th!' was given, we advanced at the double-quick with a rush and a cheer, " recalled one of the men. Their destination was General Greene's embattled position at the height of Culp's Hill. Upon their arrival at about 7:40 A.M., the men could see "a long line of hastily built breastworks filled with soldiers who were pouring an incessant fire into the valley below." The regiment replaced the 78th New York and moved into their rifle pits. According to Benton, "the ground descended sharply in our front here, and the enemy's line was not more than fifteen or twenty rods distant. The smoke had settled so thickly in the timber that we could not distinguish them clearly, and the spurts of smoke from their guns furnished the principal indication which showed our men

where to aim." Benton was surprised by the men's calmness. "I was struck by the cool and mater-of-fact way in which our men were loading and firing, while the dead lay at frequent intervals, and not infrequently some of our number fell . . . what magic art had suddenly transformed these timid youths into hardened veterans?" Fighting behind a strong breastwork at the top of a steep hill can do wonders for any new troops.[48]

The 150th New York remained in the rifle pits for about two and a half hours, until the 102nd New York relieved it. The men returned to the breastworks an hour later to relieve the 102nd New York. Each man shot off about 150 rounds of ammunition into the woods in front of him during his stay in the rifle pits. Rarely did the men see the enemy, but the green troops still kept up a steady fire. "The woods in our front were branched low and full of undergrowth. Very seldom was there a living target to be seen, but our shots went down into that valley continuously," wrote one of the men. Colonel Ketcham reported that "it is evident the shots did good execution." White flags could been seen several times along the enemy positions. "Presently a straggling line of Confederates came running up the hill, and, springing over the breastworks, gave themselves up as prisoners," wrote Benton.[49]

The brigade's numbers increased by a third when the five hundred-man 1st Maryland Eastern Shore finally arrived at 8:00 A.M. It was immediately formed into line of battle and sent to support Greene's Brigade. The men stopped briefly to drop their knapsacks and blankets, before advancing. Musketry fire broke out as they approached the breastworks. This confused the green troops, for while they had been in the service for two years, they had had no prior combat experience. Slaveholder Colonel James Wallace explained what happened next to his regiment. "Owing to some misunderstanding as to the point of the works designated to be supported, four companies . . . passed to the left, and five . . . moved directly to the front." As the latter five companies reached the brow of the hill, they saw what the men in the breastworks below them could not: a Confederate charge. Halting, they opened fire on the advancing Confederates. This caused considerable consternation among the 111th Pennsylvania (Kane's Brigade) and the 149th New York (Greene's Brigade). "The officer in command of the men in the breastworks, supposing we were firing into his command, requested that the fire should cease," wrote Wallace. However, the men of the 1st Maryland Eastern Shore beleived that their volley, along with that of other regiments, apparently broke the Confederate attack.[50]

The five companies of the 1st Maryland Eastern Shore continued forward to relieve the 149th New York (Greene's Brigade) behind the breastworks, while the four remaining companies that had veered to the left, probably joined the 150th New York behind their breastworks. The two wings of the regiment remained in their positions for several hours. Wallace reported that the "conduct of my men was very satisfactory." Others strenuously disagreed with this conclusion, as Wallace's men began drifting to the rear, despite the pleas and actions taken by their officers. It appears that the 149th New York was called back to help stem the tide. The gap in the line was partially filled when the right wing of the 150th New York shifted to its right, and the 107th New York (Colgrove's Brigade) was ordered to advance from Baltimore Pike.[51]

After its aborted advance, the 1st Maryland Potomac Home Guard was sent forward again at 9:00 A.M., following the 1st

Maryland Eastern Shore to the front. Upon arriving in the breastworks, it relieved the 29th Pennsylvania and fought well for the next three hours. Its activities there were controversial, however. Concerned about the condition of his inexperienced men—they had returned late the night before, were exhausted, and were without rations—Colonel Maulsby sought permission to pull his men out of the front line for a rest, as the attacks seemed to have ceased. Lockwood readily gave his consent, but wisely told Maulsby to also check with Greene. Finding an officer "representing himself to be an aide to General Greene," Maulsby made his case, and the officer consented, with the understanding that the two regiments on either side would be asked to spread their lines to cover the gap. Thinking this was a reasonable request, Maulsby made the necessary arrangements and pulled his men out of the breastworks. No sooner had his men settled in the rear than General Williams ordered them back to the breastworks.[52]

Later that day, Lockwood's men were pulled out of the breastworks, and along with McDougall's Brigade, marched rapidly to the center of the Union line, which was trying to stop the Pickett–Pettigrew–Trimble charge. They had almost reached the Leister house when an aide arrived to tell them that the attack had been repulsed, and their services were no longer needed. The weary men returned to Cemetery Hill to await further orders.[53]

Little is known about the brigade's activities on July 4 and 5. At least the 150th New York, and possibly the others, were ordered to occupy rifle pits to the right of the position they occupied the day before at about 7:00 A.M. The men remained there about two hours before being relieved. They probably assisted in burying the dead and collecting equipment the remainder of the day. The return march to Littlestown began on July 5.[54]

The 10% losses (174 men) sustained by the brigade exceeded those of McDougall's Brigade, probably because of the two charges the unit made against the enemy. The greatest losses (104 men, or 15%) were sustained by the 1st Maryland Potomac Home Guard, which charged Barksdale's Brigade on July 2, and Steuart's Brigade on July 3. Overall, the brigade did fairly well for an inexperienced unit. The behavior of Colonel Maulsby in withdrawing the 1st Maryland Potomac Home Guard during its

first advance on Culp's Hill is suspect, as is the 1st Maryland Eastern Shore's behavior when it occupied the breastworks the same day. The brigade received no special recognition, but caused a controversy. Part of the reason was that it was new to the army and there was insufficient time to integrate it into the division. Indeed, General Ruger's divisional report does not even mention the brigade. The brigade passed out of existence on July 16, when the two Maryland regiments were detached and the 150th New York became part of the Ruger's Brigade of the 1st Division.[55]

3rd Brigade—General Thomas Ruger/Colonel Silas Colgrove

Units: 27th Indiana, 2nd Massachusetts, 13th New Jersey, 107th New York, 3rd Wisconsin
Strength: 1598
Losses: 279 (49-225-5)—17.5%[56]

The 3rd Brigade was a cohesive unit that was formed from veteran regiments in September 1862. The individual regiments had seen action in the Shenandoah Valley in 1862 and during the Second Bull Run campaign as part of Pope's Army of Virginia. The new 3rd Brigade fought well at Antietam and Chancellorsville. Its leadership was also stable, as Brigadier General Thomas Ruger had commanded it since February 1863. A West Point graduate, Ruger had left the service prior to the war, but at its outbreak raised the 3rd Wisconsin and became its commander. The brigade was a tough fighting unit that was itching for a chance to get at Lee's troops.[57]

The men were pleased by their reception as they marched through Maryland and Pennsylvania. A soldier from the 13th New Jersey wrote home that "everywhere the troops were warmly welcomed. Every

body turned out to see us; from miles on either side of the turnpike. They came in carriages & wagons, bringing with them smiling faces warm hearts & their offerings of bread pies milk cake etc. The citizens refused to take anything from Union soldiers but freely gave all they had."[58]

The rugged 27th Indiana led the march as the brigade neared the battlefield on July 1, halting about two miles away. The five-minute break was all too short. The men were then ordered onto a small road on the right. After about half a mile, the troops turned to face Wolf Hill, thought to be occupied by Confederate cavalry. General Ruger deployed his brigade and moved it forward, led by skirmishers from all of the regiments except the 107th New York. The 27th Indiana apparently led the advance, followed by the 2nd Massachusetts, 3rd Wisconsin, and 13th New Jersey. The 107th New York was left behind on the road. Because the enemy occupied the town and endangered the division, the skirmishers were halted as they climbed the hill and were ordered back to their regiments. Returning to the farm lane, the brigade retraced its steps. The men were permitted to lie on their arms for the night about half a mile northeast of Baltimore Pike. The brigade's formation is not known during this period, except that the 2nd Massachusetts formed a reserve behind the main body.[59]

During the early morning hours of July 2, the 27th Indiana retraced its steps toward Hanover Road and Benner Hill. After advancing about half a mile, the regiment's skirmish line engaged in a sharp contest with the enemy's from the Stonewall Brigade. This lasted for about an hour, during which time the Hoosiers took position near a stone dwelling that housed Confederate snipers. Colonel Silas Colgrove of the 27th Indiana assumed command of the brigade during this period as General Thomas Ruger took over Williams's 1st Division. Lieutenant Colonel John Fesler, now in command of the 27th Indiana, received orders at 8:00 A.M. to return to the brigade, which was still in the bivouac area.[60]

The brigade marched half a mile on Baltimore Pike before turning right onto a small lane, on which it marched another half mile before taking position in a rocky woods. The brigade thus became the right-most unit of the entire army. Because of a swale, the brigade was actually divided into two parts. The 107th New York faced Rock Creek on the left, at a 45 degree angle to McDougall's Brigade and just north of Spangler's Spring. Massed about seventy-five paces behind it in double columns was the 13th New Jersey. To the southeast, on the other side of the swale, were the three remaining regiments in McAllister's Woods. According to Colgrove, the 2nd Massachusetts formed on the left, facing northeast; the 3rd Wisconsin formed on the center, facing east; and the 27th Indiana was on the right, fac-

ing south, adjacent to Rock Creek. This caused Colgrove to refer to the brigade's position as forming "three sides of an irregular square." Because of the width and depth of Rock Creek, Colgrove was confident that no Confederate attack could be made from that direction. To protect the other parts of his line, Colgrove ordered his men to use stone walls where available, or to build breastworks of fence rails, timber, and stone. Fesler (27th Indiana) was generally pleased with his position, which he said was behind a "cliff of rocks." This did not, however, extend all the way to his left, so the two exposed companies were ordered to build some stone breastworks.[61]

As events worsened along Sickles's front on the left of the Federal line, Colgrove received orders between 6:00 and 7:00 P.M. to join the remainder of Ruger's Division in its trek down Baltimore Pike. The men were exposed to artillery fire during this march, but few casualties resulted. During the march south, the men passed an old woman. Many of the men were unsettled by the Rebel yell, which sounded "more devilish than anything which *could* come from human throats." The old crone called out reassuringly, "Never mind, boys, they're nothing but MEN!" For some reason, these words helped to calm them. It was already dark when the brigade reached its assigned position near the Wheatfield. Skirmishers were thrown out, while the rest of the brigade waited anxiously in the rear. After spending about forty-five minutes there, Colgrove received orders to return to his original position just south of Culp's Hill.[62]

Colgrove halted his brigade upon arriving within three hundred yards from his former position. General Ruger ordered him to throw a company of skirmishers forward from the lead regiment, the 2nd Massachusetts, to make sure that it was safe to continue venturing forward in the darkness to reoccupy its old position. The men soon returned with the welcome news that no enemy troops were detected in McAllister's Woods. Colgrove then sent these skirmishers across the swale to the left side of their former position. They returned with twenty-three prisoners and the unwelcome news that Confederate troops occupied it. Colgrove heaped praise on this company (F): "They advanced into the wood, where it was impossible to tell friend from foe, and before they scarcely knew it were in the midst of a brigade of the enemy, from whom they captured 23 prisoners . . . with a loss of only 2 captured on their side."[63]

Another company of the 2nd Massachusetts, apparently followed by the remainder of the regiment, continued across the swale. They heard members of the 23rd Virginia (Steuart's Brigade, Johnson's Division) talking, before cautiously retracing their steps. The 107th New York also ventured forward across the swale, and when its commander ascertained that his breastworks were occupied by the enemy, pulled his regiment back as well. After resting in the woods in double column for a while, the regiment was ordered northward to support McDougall's Brigade.[64]

Many of Colgrove's soldiers were unhappy with the situation. "It was exasperating to see them benefiting by our labors, but we were somewhat consoled by the capture of twenty Confederates," wrote Captain Julian Hinkley of the 3rd Wisconsin. Some of the soldiers overheard a conversation near Baltimore Pike involving several officers, including Williams, Colgrove, and probably Ruger. One or two wanted to retake the lost breastworks immediately as they believed that relatively few troops occupied them and they were probably not expecting an attack. To delay would result in the arrival of additional

enemy troops and the construction of more formidable breastworks. Others felt that it was just too risky. Finally, the men heard Williams's clear voice saying, "We will hold the position we now have until morning. Then, from these hills back of us, we will shell hell out of them."[65]

The troops remained there all night. Realizing that the enemy could enfilade his line, Colgrove ordered the 3rd Wisconsin to vacate its position between the 2nd Massachusetts and 27th Indiana, and to move north to a position adjacent and perpendicular to its original one. Between 5:00 and 6:00 A.M. on July 3, Colgrove ordered the 27th Indiana to shift to the left to occupy the breastworks that had been built by the 3rd Wisconsin the day before, which faced Rock Creek. The 13th New Jersey occupied its old breastworks on the right of the line. The line south of the swale was now composed of the 3rd Wisconsin on the left, and the 2nd Massachusetts, 27th Indiana, and the 13th New Jersey on the right. The latter regiment faced Rock Creek, with its two left companies refused to face the swale.[66]

As the battle opened against Geary's Division, farther up Culp's Hill, Colgrove's Brigade was exposed to deadly sniper fire. Sergeant Edwin Bryant of the 3rd Wisconsin noted that the "enemy before us were well sheltered by the huge boulders that lie like hundreds of sleeping elephants along the slopes of Culp's Hill just above Spangles [sic] Spring." Colgrove quickly responded by sending sharpshooters from the 3rd Wisconsin and 2nd Massachusetts to a small belt of trees in front of the brigade's position, where they fired away at the enemy for two hours. This firing was not restricted to the sharpshooters, as all of Colgrove's men opened fire on the unseen enemy. About this time, the men could hear a noticeable reduction in the battle's intensity on Geary's front and, looking to their left, they could see McDougall's Brigade move en masse into their old position in the breastworks.[67]

The detached 107th New York was also having its share of excitement. After daybreak, it moved to Baltimore Pike to support Best's battery. During their stay there, the men could see the 1st Maryland Eastern Shore (Lockwood's Brigade) charging the enemy in the woods to their left. Seeing that the attack had failed after about twenty minutes, they were subsequently ordered to form line of battle and advance to hold the 1st Maryland's position as long as possible. The men were permitted to lie down when they reached the position, so only one soldier was wounded. The greater danger was from their own batteries, whose shells occasionally burst prematurely overhead. The men remained in this position all morning and well into the afternoon.[68]

As the sun rose, so too did the men's spirits. "We felt entire confidence that no force that the Southerners could bring against us could by direct assault break our line at any point," wrote Hinkley (3rd Wisconsin). Although Colgrove's men had not been tested, they clearly heard the cheers of their comrades, suggesting that every Confederate charge was repulsed.[69]

The brigade's passive role ended when Lieutenant W. M. Snow of Ruger's staff galloped up to Colonel Colgrove with fresh orders. Slocum believed that the attacks on the XII Corps appeared to be weakening, and he reported that "the enemy were becoming shaky or showed signs of falling back." Not going through Williams, Slocum apparently ordered Ruger to attack the works at 10:00 A.M. His order was to "try the enemy with two regiments on the right of the line of breastworks to the left of the swale, and, if practical, to force him out." Ruger, who had

been watching the enemy position for several hours, rode over to Slocum and convinced him that "any attack would fail and result in serious loss." He instead convinced Slocum to allow him to first send skirmishers across the swale to ascertain the enemy's strength. If weak, then he would launch a full attack.[70]

The nature of Ruger's subsequent orders to Colgrove is disputed. According to General Ruger, Colgrove was to "advance skirmishers against the enemy at that point [the swale], and, if not found in too great force, to advance two regiments, and dislodge him from the breastworks." If these were the orders, then Snow had garbled them or Colgrove heard them incorrectly, for the latter went off thinking "the general directs that you advance your line immediately." After the war, Snow insisted that he was not at fault. "Realizing the importance of correct delivery of such an order, I returned to General Ruger, after first starting, and requested him to repeat his instructions, which he did." Snow characterized Colgrove as an "enthusiastic fighter . . . he enjoyed the reputation of being an officer who would much rather fight than eat." Given his certainty, Snow wrote that "I could never quite understand why General Colgrove should have advanced two regiments under the order delivered by me, when he, being on the spot, must have known that it was 'Murder.'" Coming to the defense of his commanding officer, the historian of the 27th Indiana wrote that when Colgrove heard the orders, he pulled his nose and repeated, almost talking to himself, "It cannot be done, it cannot be done." He then added, "If it can be done, the Second Massachusetts and the Twenty-seventh Indiana can do it." General Ruger expressed the opinion after the war that Colgrove had not exceeded his orders, but that miscommunication resulted in tragedy.[71]

Colgrove now gave orders to the 27th Indiana and 2nd Massachusetts to rise and immediately charge the enemy's works behind the swale. He should have understood the futility of the charge before he ordered the men forward. He wrote in his official report that the "enemy was entirely sheltered by the breastworks and ledges of rock. It was impossible to send forward skirmishers. The enemy's advantages were such that a line of skirmishers would be cut down before they could fairly gain the open ground that intervened. The only possible chance I had to advance was to carry his position by storming it." If skirmishers could not survive the passage through the open swale, Colgrove should have realized that dense masses of men would have even greater difficulty. Behind the breastworks was Smith's Brigade (Early's Division). Added to this firepower were some units of Steuart's Brigade (Johnson's Division, II Corps), which were positioned to send an enfilading fire into the ranks of Colgrove's two regiments. Colgrove's attacking force was therefore outnumbered by almost two to one.[72]

Lieutenant Colonel Charles Mudge of the 2nd Massachusetts was incredulous when he received Colgrove's orders. After quietly listening, he asked the orderly, "Are you sure that is the order?" Upon receiving an affirmative answer, Mudge said, "Well, it is murder: but it's the order." Walking over to his men, Mudge gave the order, "Up, men, over the works! Forward, double quick." One veteran recalled that Mudge's demeanor was cheerful as always. These were the last words that anyone recalled Mudge utter.[73]

The men of the 27th Indiana on the right of the 2nd Massachusetts heard Colgrove give the orders in his characteristic "shrill, piercing tones—Twenty-seventh, charge! Charge those works in your front." Fesler (27th Indiana) knew it was

not as easy as that, for his regiment was almost at right angles to the direction it must charge, as it was facing Rock Creek. He therefore ordered his men to "about face" and make a "half wheel in battalion formation." At the same time, the 13th New Jersey, on the right, was to move by the left flank to clear a space. The latter regiment apparently did not move fast enough, for the two regiments collided, creating great confusion.[74]

Both regiments jumped over their breastworks and were off with a shout. Ruger was incredulous. He had ordered a skirmish line to advance against the Confederate position, not two full regiments. Springing forward, he attempted to halt the attack, but it was too late. He probably saw the 2nd Massachusetts first, as the 27th Indiana's charge was delayed by its complex turning movement.[75]

For the first hundred yards, the 27th Indiana ran down a gentle slope thickly covered with oak and hickory saplings. The pace quickened when the regiment hit the edge of the swale. Now the men could see the Confederate position behind a stone wall on the opposite side of the open, boggy meadow, a mere hundred yards away. Their advance would be all the more difficult because Colgrove ordered it to oblique to the right. After advancing several yards into the swale, a well-directed Confederate volley staggered the regiment and scores of men fell. "To those who had the whole view it almost appeared that a crevasse had opened in the earth and swallowed the regiment, bodily," wrote Edmund Brown of the 27th Indiana. The survivors merely closed ranks and continued on. With each foot, the Confederate fire seemed to become hotter, and men continued to fall. The survivors recalled that the air was "alive with singing, hissing and zipping bullets." Still they advanced, seeing the distance between them and the wall diminishing. "We were invincible. We must not and could not fail. A supreme, concerted dash, which we were capable of making, would land us inside the enemy's entrenchments," recalled Brown.[76]

The urge to stop and fire into the enemy position was overwhelming. Most were able to resist this urge until the line reached the middle of the field. Here the men halted and fired a volley. This was a deadly mistake. Their motion halted, the survivors made targets that the Confederate marksmen dreamed about. After sustaining additional losses, Colgrove realized that "scarcely a man could live to gain the position of the enemy," so he ordered them to fall back to avoid total annihilation. The veterans, of course, recalled that the withdrawal was slow and orderly. "Once faced to the rear, our line moved rapidly, but without undue haste or disorder, back to the breastworks we had crossed in our advance."[77]

The 2nd Massachusetts was having its own problems on the left. Its men had stopped to fire into the Confederate skirmishers just after entering the meadow, and it took heavy losses as it charged forward. Lieutenant Colonel Mudge fell in the middle of the field. The regiment forged on despite the staggering losses. The fire was too intense to continue, so the survivors veered to the left, miraculously reaching the woods on the opposite side of the swale. Looking around, the men could see that they were all alone. According to Chaplain Alonzo Quint of the 2nd Massachusetts, "the regiment on its right [27th Indiana], its single help, had melted back. The troops in support were motionless. From behind every tree and rock, the enemy poured an overwhelming fire." To their left the men could see a thin line of Confederate troops moving around their right flank. Realizing

their vulnerability, the unit's new commander, Major Charles Morse, ordered his men to return to the Union lines. Before doing so, Morse sent a messenger to the commander of the regiment on his left, which he believed to be a "Home Guard Maryland Regiment," to "call his men to *attention* and make an appearance, at least, of advancing, which would perhaps give an opportunity to fall back with small loss." The 1st Maryland Eastern Shore commander replied that he could not comply without orders from his commanding officer. Realizing that he could not retrace his steps without further loss, Morse had his men veer toward Baltimore Pike, and the regiment arrived about two hundred yards west of its original position. Morse proudly remarked that the retreat of his regiment "was made with the same precision that would have accompanied an ordinary drill movement."[78]

Five flag bearers carried the 2nd Massachusetts's banner during the charge, and never once did it touch the ground. A roll call made immediately after the charge revealed that about 44% of the men had been killed or wounded crossing the field in the futile charge. General Williams remarked that "few if any regts. in the service that could have stood the almost instantaneous loss of half its force and maintained, as the 2nd Mass. did, almost perfectly the order and regularity of a battalion drill."[79]

The brigade's other regiments watched the charge in awe. They could see the long lines move into the swale, but awe changed to grief when "the "gleam of thousands of gun-barrels were seen among the rocks in their front," which blew apart the two regiments. Confederate regiments on the opposite side of Rock Creek also fired into the flank of the 27th Indiana. Sergeant A. Sheridan Jones of the 3rd Wisconsin recalled that the

Massachusetts men in front of him were "being cut down in our front like grass before a prairie fire . . . it was an awful moment." The troops tried to provide support by firing at the Southerners. However, as the 2nd Massachusetts veered to the left, it moved in front of the 3rd Wisconsin, forcing its men to hold their fire.[80]

No sooner had the remnants of the two regiments reached the safety of their own breastworks than they were ordered to help repel the ill-conceived counterattack of Smith's Confederate Brigade. The repulse was sharply administered by frontal fire from the 3rd Wisconsin, 27th Indiana, and 13th New Jersey, and enfilading fire of the 2nd Massachusetts. Colgrove proudly recalled that "at the first fire they [Smith's Brigade] were completely checked, and at the second they broke in confusion and fled, leaving their dead and wounded on the field."[81]

After the charge and countercharge, the troops returned to their prior dispositions. Sniper fire was a constant irritation through the remainder of the day. It was especially bad for the men of the 13th New Jersey, who were fired upon from a stone house in front of them across Rock Creek and from a meadow on their flank. Artillery fire momentarily quieted these enemy soldiers from the 2nd Virginia (Walker's Brigade, Johnson's Division), but they soon returned to fire into the Union lines. This was repeated several times during the late morning and early afternoon hours. The other regiments suffered as well because their low breastworks provided little protection against the Southern marksmen. The men took special effort to avoid exposing any part of their anatomy, lest a bullet fly in their general direction. When this fire slackened around midday, Colgrove sent the 3rd Wisconsin forward, which found the

breastworks abandoned. It remained there for the remainder of the day.[82]

The men were startled by the massive artillery barrage that preceded the Pickett–Pettigrew–Trimble charge in the afternoon. "The limbs were crashing and falling from the trees above us. Huge shells were striking the great rocks about us, either exploding or breaking. . . .others, with spent force, went whirling overhead, with a screeching sound, terrible in itself," noted Brown (27th Indiana).[83]

The 13th New Jersey was detached at about 6:00 P.M. and moved to the right, where it remained for about ninety minutes. At about the same time, the 107th New York relieved the 46th Pennsylvania in their breastworks. At about 7:30 P.M., both regiments joined the 5th Connecticut (McDougall's Brigade) and marched down Hanover Road to support cavalry. They arrived after dark—too late to provide assistance.[84]

Little is known about the brigade's activities on July 4. It appears that it was ordered to make a reconnaissance. Backtracking, the brigade reached Baltimore Pike, then marched to Hanover Road. The men passed through Gettysburg and reached Baltimore Pike again. No healthy enemy soldiers were encountered during this five- or six-mile circuit, only their dead and wounded. The brigade left Gettysburg on July 5. As the 2nd Massachusetts passed, Slocum and his staff bared their heads in silent tribute to the men's efforts and losses.[85]

Had it not been for the ill-fated charge of the 2nd Massachusetts and 27th Indiana, the activities of Colgrove's Brigade would have merited but a footnote. The brigade's losses of 18% are deceptive. Three of the regiments lost a total of thirty-four men (under 4%), mostly from sniper fire. The two regiments involved in the charge lost almost 38% of their men.[86]

NOTES

1. Dyer, *Compendium*, 320; Tagg, *Generals of Gettysburg*, 143–144.

2. Tagg, *Generals of Gettysburg*, 143–144.

3. Alpheus Williams, *From the Cannon's Mouth* (Detroit, MI, 1959), 223–224; Henry C. Morhous, *Reminiscences of the 123rd Regiment, New York State Volunteers* (Greenwich, NY, 1879), 46.

4. OR 27, 1, 758; Pfanz, *Gettysburg—Culp's Hill and Cemetery Hill*, 92–93; Tagg, *Generals of Gettysburg*, 144.

General Williams and Edmund Brown of the 27th Indiana recalled that the orderlies arrived while the troops were at Two Taverns (OR 27, 1, 773; Edmund R. Brown, *History of the Twenty-Seventh Indiana Volunteer Infantry* [Monticello, NY, 1899], 366).

5. Coddington, *The Gettysburg Campaign*, 310–313; L. R. Coy, letter, copy in 123rd New York folder, GNMP; Warren W. Packer, diary, copy in USAMHI; OR 27, 1, 758–759, 771, 773, 778; *PAG*, vol. 1, 308.

Some officers reported that the halt around Two Taverns lasted only about an hour, from 11 A.M. to noon, but these assertions are incorrect (OR 27, 1, 790).

6. OR 27, 1, 759, 773–774; Williams, *From the Cannon's Mouth*, 228, 229.

7. OR 27, 1, 761; James H. Baum, "A Boy Soldier Tell the Story of Gettysburg," *The East Liverpool Morning Tribune*, July 9, 1910.

8. Tagg, *Generals of Gettysburg*, 146–147.

9. Baum, "A Boy Soldier Tell the Story of Gettysburg"; Robert Cruikshank, "Memoirs," Bancroft Library, Salem, NY; Williams, *From the Cannon's Mouth*, 224; Morhous, *Reminiscences of the 123rd Regiment, New York State Volunteers*, 46; OR 27, 1, 771.

10. Coy, letter; Williams, *From the Cannon's Mouth*, 224.

11. OR 27, 1, 773, 777; Pfanz, *Gettysburg—Culp's Hill and Cemetery Hill*, 77

12. OR 27, 1, 773, 777–778; Williams, *From the Cannon's Mouth*, 225–226.

13. OR 27, 1, 774, 783, 779, 804; Pfanz, *Gettysburg—Culp's Hill and Cemetery Hill*, 230.

14. OR 27, 1, 780.

15. OR, 27, 1, 781.

16. Busey and Martin, *Regimental Strengths and Losses*, 91, 255.

17. Dyer, *Compendium*, 320; Tagg, *Generals of Gettysburg*, 149–150.

18. Morhous, *Reminiscences of the 123rd Regiment, New York State Volunteers*, 46–47; OR 27, 1, 782, 788; Coy, letter.

19. OR 27, 1, 778, 783, 796, 800; Coy, letter; Edwin E. Marvin, *The Fifth Regiment, Connecticut Volunteers: A History Compiled from Diaries and Official Reports* (Hartford, CT, 1899), 275; Hamblen, *Connecticut at Gettysburg*, 70–71; John Storrs, *The Twentieth Connecticut* (Ansonia, CT, 1886), 92; Pfanz, *Gettysburg—Culp's Hill and Cemetery Hill*, 428–429 (n. 44).

McDougall recalled that he moved his men at 11:00 A.M., but his memory seems flawed.

20. Morhous, *Reminiscences of the 123rd Regiment, New York State Volunteers*, 47; Cruikshank, "Memoirs"; Packer, diary; Marvin, *The Fifth Regiment, Connecticut Volunteers: A History Compiled from Diaries and Official Reports*, 275.

Charles Warner of the 145th New York noted that the brigade was deployed in two lines—the first was behind a stone wall, and the second was behind the breastworks the men constructed (Charles Warner, letter, copy in 145th New York folder, GNMP).

21. Hamblen, *Connecticut Yankees at Gettysburg*, 72–73; Coy, letter; OR 27, 1, 783.

22. OR 27, 1, 783–784, 800; Morhous, *Reminiscences of the 123rd Regiment, New York State Volunteers*, 48–49; Cruikshank, "Memoirs."

Morhous erroneously suggested that his own 123rd New York fired into the ranks of the 74th Pennsylvania, which broke for the rear.

23. Coy, letter; Morhous, *Reminiscences of the 123rd Regiment, New York State Volunteers*, 48.

24. Cruikshank, "Memoirs"; *PAG*, vol. 1, 308; Pfanz, *Gettysburg—Culp's Hill and Cemetery Hill*, 377–378.

25. William Wooster to John Bachelder, December 19, 1886, Bachelder Papers, New Hampshire Historical Society.

26. William Wooster to John Bachelder, December 11, 1886; OR 27, 1, 784, 793; Hamblen, *Connecticut Yankees at Gettysburg,* 79–81; Storrs, *The Twentieth Connecticut,* 92–93.

27. Storrs, *The Twentieth Connecticut,* 92–93; OR 27, 1, 784.

28. OR 27, 1, 785, 801; Cruikshank, "Memoirs."

29. Baum, "A Boy Soldier Tell the Story of Gettysburg."

30. OR 27, 1, 784, 794, 797; Morhous, *Reminiscences of the 123rd Regiment, New York State Volunteers,* 50; Coy, letter; Pfanz, *Gettysburg—Culp's Hill and Cemetery Hill,* 351; William Wooster to John Bachelder, December 11, 1886, and December 19, 1886.

McDougall's recollection of time is incorrect—it was closer to noon.

31. OR 27, 1, 785, 789; Hamblen, *Connecticut Yankees at Gettysburg,* 84; Packer, diary; Warner, letter.

32. OR 27, 1, 785, 790; Harlan Rugg, diary, copy in USAMHI.

The official reports of both the 123rd and 145th New York indicate that no sooner had the men reached this position than they were turned around and marched back to their original positions on Culp's Hill (OR 27, 1, 797, 801).

33. OR 27, 1, 786, 791, 794, 795; Morhous, *Reminiscences of the 123rd Regiment, New York State Volunteers,* 52; Coy, letter.

34. OR 27, 1, 786, 796.

35. Busey and Martin, *Regimental Strengths and Losses,* 255; OR 27, 1, 802.

One of the heroes of the battle was Private George Warner. Despite losing both arms to an artillery shell, he returned home to support and raise a family. He was given the honor of unveiling the regiment's monument on July 3, 1885. A drape attached to a rope covered the monument. The other end of the rope was tied to Warner's body, and when he walked a few steps, the drape fell, revealing the statue (*Gettysburg Complier,* July 7, 1885; Hamblen, *Connecticut Yankees at Gettysburg,* 140–141).

36. Busey and Martin, *Regimental Strengths and Losses,* 92, 256.

37. Pfanz, *Gettysburg—The Second Day,* 62–3; *NYG,* vol. 3, 1032–1033; OR 27, 1, 804.

38. Alpheus Williams to John Bachelder, December 1863 and April 21, 1864, Bachelder Papers, New Hampshire Historical Society.

39. *NYG,* vol. 3, 1032.

40. OR 27, 1, 773; *NYG,* vol. 3, 1033.

41. Charles E. Benton, *As Seen From the Ranks* (New York, 1902), 24–25; *NYG,* vol. 3, 1042; Stephen G. Cook and Charles E. Benton, eds., *The "Dutchess County Regiment"in the Civil War* (Danbury, CT, 1907), 316.

42. Alpheus Williams to John Bachelder, December 1863; OR 27, 1, 804, 805–806, 810; Edwin C. Bryant, *History of the Third Regiment Wisconsin Veteran Volunteer Infantry* (Madison, WI, 1891), 188–189.

43. OR 27, 1, 804, 805–806, 810; *Report of the State of Maryland Gettysburg Monument Commission* (Baltimore, MD, 1891), 56; Benton, *As Seen From the Ranks,* 27–28.

44. Williams, *From the Cannon's Mouth,* 228; OR, 27, 1, 774, 809; *NYG,* vol. 3, 1033; Cook and Benton, *The "Dutchess County Regiment" in the Civil War,* 31; Alpheus Williams to John Bachelder, December 1863.

Colonel Maulsby took issue with Gildersleeve's statement that the brigade had not fired a gun, writing that "we were not called on to fire minies on this occasion, but to use bayonets." He did admit that "the bayonets were not bloodied . . . because they did not stand long enough to give the bayonets a chance to show what metal they were made of" (*NYG,* vol. 3, 1043).

45. OR 27, 1, 809–810; Alpheus Williams to John Bachelder, April 21, 1864; David Topps, "The Dutchess County Regiment," *Gettysburg Magazine* (January 1995), issue 12, 50.

46. Cook and Bartlett, *The "Dutchess County Regiment" in the Civil War,* 32–33; Pfanz, *Gettysburg—Culp's Hill and Cemetery Hill,* 286–287; Alpheus Williams to John Bachelder, November 10, 1865.

47. OR 27, 1, 804–805, 806; Cook and Bartlett, *The "Dutchess County Regiment" in the Civil War,* 33; *Report of the State of Maryland Gettysburg Monument Commission,* 57–58.

48. Cook and Bartlett, *The "Dutchess County Regiment" in the Civil War*, 34–35; Benton, *As Seen From the Ranks*, 34–35; Pfanz, *Gettysburg—Culp's Hill and Cemetery Hill*, 307.

49. Cook and Bartlett, *The "Dutchess County Regiment" in the Civil War*, 34–35; OR 27, 1, 810; Pfanz, *Culp's Hill and Cemetery Hill*, 307; Topps, "The Dutchess County Regiment," 54; Benton, *As Seen From the Ranks*, 36.

50. OR 27, 1, 808–809; Pfanz, *Gettysburg—Culp's Hill and Cemetery Hill*, 307–308.

51. OR 27, 1, 808–809, 820; John H. Shane, "Getting into the Fight at Gettysburg," *National Tribune*, November 27, 1924; George K. Collins, *Memories of the 149th Regiment, New York Volunteer Infantry* (Syracuse, NY, 1891), 143; Pfanz, *Gettysburg—Culp's Hill and Cemetery Hill*, 308.

52. OR 27, 1, 807–808; Pfanz, *Gettysburg—Culp's Hill and Cemetery Hill*, 308–309.

53. *Report of the State of Maryland Gettysburg Monument Commission*, 58; OR 27, 1, 805, 806.

54. OR 27, 1, 810; *Report of the State of Maryland Gettysburg Monument Commission*, 59; Topps, "The Dutchess County Regiment," 55.

55. Busey and Martin, *Regimental Strengths and Losses*, 256; OR 27, 1, 777–782; Topps, "The Dutchess County Regiment," 58.

According to a letter from General Williams to John Bachelder, the two Maryland regiments "objected to leaving their state and the brigade was broken up" when the units reached Harper's Ferry (Alpheus Williams to John Bachelder, April 21, 1864).

56. Busey and Martin, *Regimental Strengths and Losses*, 93, 256

57. Dyer, *Compendium*, 321; Tagg, *Generals of Gettysburg*, 152–153.

58. S. Duncan, letter, copy in 13th New Jersey folder, GNMNP.

59. OR 27, 1, 811, 816, 819; Julian W. Hinkley, *A Narrative of Service With the Third Wisconsin Infantry* (Madison, WI, 1912), 82–83; Brown, *History of the Twenty-Seventh Indiana Volunteer Infantry*, 367; Charles F. Morse, *History of the Second Massachusetts Regiment of Infantry* (Albany, NY, 1882), 7.

60. OR 27, 1, 811–812, 815; Brown, *History of the Twenty-Seventh Indiana Volunteer Infantry*, 368–369; Pfanz, *Gettysburg—Culp's Hill and Cemetery Hill*, 153.

61. OR 27, 1, 812, 818, 819; Brown, *History of the Twenty-Seventh Indiana Volunteer Infantry*, 370; Hinkley, *A Narrative of Service With the Third Wisconsin Infantry*, 83–84.

According to Colgrove's report, Ruger ordered him to change his troop dispositions. The 3rd Wisconsin took the 107th New York's position on the left of the swale, the 13th New Jersey moved into the 3rd Wisconsin's old position on the right, and the less experienced 107th New York was moved to a supporting position behind the three regiments on the right. None of the regimental reports mention this change, making the accuracy of Colgrove's report questionable.

62. OR 27, 1, 779, 812–813, 818, 819; Morse, *History of the Second Massachusetts Regiment of Infantry*, 8–9.

63. OR 27, 1, 813.

64. OR 27, 1, 817, 820; "Account of the part taken by the 'Second Mass. Inf.' In the battle of 'Gettysburg,' July 1 , 2, and 3, 1863, Bachelder Papers, New Hampshire Historical Society.

65. Hinkley, *A Narrative of Service With the Third Wisconsin Infantry*, 85; Brown, *History of the Twenty-Seventh Indiana*, 373–374.

66. OR 27, 1, 815, 824; Brown, *History of the Twenty-Seventh Indiana Volunteer Infantry*, 377; Bryant, *History of the Third Regiment Wisconsin Veteran Volunteer Infantry*, 191; Toombes, *New Jersey Troops in the Gettysburg Campaign*, 79–80.

67. OR 27, 1, 813, 818; Bryant, *History of the Third Regiment Wisconsin Veteran Volunteer Infantry*, 192.

68. OR 27, 1, 820.

69. Hinkley, *A Narrative of Service With the Third Wisconsin Infantry*, 86; Bryant, *History of the Third Regiment Wisconsin Veteran Volunteer Infantry*, 192–193.

70. Thomas Ruger to John Bachelder, August 12, 1869, Bachelder Papers, New Hampshire Historical Society.

71. Thomas Ruger, letter, copy in 2nd Massachusetts folder, GNMP; OR 27, 1, 781;

813; W. M. Snow, letter, copy in 2nd Massachusetts folder, GNMP; Brown, *History of the Twenty-Seventh Indiana Volunteer Infantry*, 379; Thomas Ruger to John Bachelder, August 12, 1869.

72. OR 27, 1, 813.

73. Alonzo H. Quint, *The Record of the Second Massachusetts, 1861–1865* (Boston, 1867), 180; Morse, *History of the Second Massachusetts Regiment of Infantry*, 13; Everett W. Pattison, "Some Reminiscences of Army Life," in *Massachusetts MOLLUS*, 262–263.

74. Brown, *History of the Twenty-Seventh Indiana Volunteer Infantry*, 380.

75. Thomas Ruger to John Bachelder, August 12, 1869.

76. Brown, *History of the Twenty-Seventh Indiana Volunteer Infantry*, 381–382, 396–398.

77. OR 27, 1, 814; Brown, *History of the Twenty-Seventh Indiana Volunteer Infantry*, 383–384; Pfanz, *Gettysburg—Culp's Hill and Cemetery Hill*, 348.

78. Quint, *Record of the Second Massachusetts*, 181; Morse, *History of the Second Massachusetts Regiment of Infantry*, 14–16.

The 2nd Massachusetts remained at the wall for about ten minutes ("Account of the part taken by the 'Second Mass. Inf.' In the battle of 'Gettysburg' ").

79. Pattison, "Some Reminiscences of Army Life," 16–17; Alpheus Williams to John Bachelder, April 7, 1864.

80. A. Sheridan Jones, "Battle of Gettysburg," *National Tribune*, December 29, 1892; Bryant, *History of the Third Regiment Wisconsin Veteran Volunteer Infantry*, 194–195.

81. OR 27, 1, 814; Bryant, *History of the Third Regiment Wisconsin Veteran Volunteer Infantry*, 195–196.

82. OR 27, 1, 814, 824; Toombes, *New Jersey Troops in the Gettysburg Campaign*, 80–81; John Grimes to John Bachelder, April 2, 1864, Bachelder Papers, New Hampshire Historical Society; Brown, *History of the Twenty-Seventh Indiana Volunteer Infantry*, 386–387.

83. Toombs, *New Jersey Troops in the Gettysburg Campaign*, 81; Brown, *History of the Twenty-Seventh Indiana Volunteer Infantry*, 390–391.

84. OR 27, 1, 818, 821; John Grimes to John Bachelder, April 2, 1864.

85. Brown, *History of the Twenty-Seventh Indiana Volunteer Infantry*, 393–394; W.W. Clayton, *History of Steuben County, New York . . .* (Philadelphia, 1878), 399; Hinkley, *A Narrative of Service With the Third Wisconsin Infantry*, 89; *NYG*, vol. 2, 771.

86. Busey and Martin, *Regimental Strengths and Losses*, 256.

2ND DIVISION—

Brigadier General John Geary

The 2nd Division was commanded by six-foot, six-inch John Geary. Because he was a large target, he had been wounded nine times prior to Gettysburg. Although he was not a West Point graduate, Geary did serve in the Mexican War, where he commanded a militia regiment. When the war broke out, Geary formed the 28th Pennsylvania and led it with distinction. Promoted to brigadier general in the spring of 1862, he participated in the Shenandoah Valley and Second Bull Run campaigns. He was elevated to division command and performed well at Chancellorsville. The "White Star" Division was a veteran unit under effective leadership as it marched northward.[1]

After breaking camp at Knoxville, Maryland, at 6:30 A.M. on June 28, the 2nd Division reached Frederick at 2:00 P.M. The march continued at 4:00 A.M. on June 29, and the column made good progress until it reached the XI Corps camp at 6:00 A.M. The men were forced to wait four hours while Howard's men cleared the road. Following Williams's 1st Division, Geary's men trudged through Taneytown, and reached Littlestown during the afternoon of June 30. Here they found the streets lined with well-wishers. After camping outside the town, the division backtracked to Baltimore Pike and headed for Gettysburg. Arriving at Two Taverns on July 1, the men were permitted to rest and eat their midday meal. The men received orders to form into column to complete the march to Gettysburg at about 4:00 P.M. and they made swift progress. One veteran wrote that an observer on Cemetery Hill at about 5:00 P.M. on July 1 would have seen approaching "amid clouds of curling dust, a column of Union troops carrying aloft the stars and stripes . . . the day was hot, sultry and cloudless . . . as the column drew nearer to the crest of the hill, it filed off to the left through open fields . . . with Geary's 2nd Division in the lead, whose headquarters flag of dark blue with its inspiring big white star emblazoned in the center, was at the head."[2]

As he arrived in the vicinity of Gettysburg, Geary happened upon General Winfield Hancock, who told him that "the right could maintain itself, and the immediate need of a division on the left was imperative." Kane's Brigade and two cannon were detached about two miles from Gettysburg and left by the side of the road while the rest of the division marched to the base of Little Round Top. By 5:00 P.M. they formed the left flank of the army.[3]

Geary's troops were relieved by Birney's Division (III Corps) at about 5:00 A.M. on July 2 and marched back toward Culp's Hill. Here they rejoined Williams's Division, which had spent the night northeast of Gettysburg. Geary was ordered to place his command on the heights of Culp's Hill with its left connecting at right angles with Wadsworth's Division (I Corps), and its right connecting with Williams's Division. Greene's Brigade was placed on the left, Kane's (Cobham's) on the right, and Candy's behind and in support of Greene's. The men spent most of the day constructing breastworks. Sergeant Lawrence Wilson of the 7th Ohio (Candy's Brigade) later wrote that Geary's actions in ordering the construction of the breastworks "rendered the defenses of Culp's Hill comparatively safe and harmless to the Union troops who fought in them."[4]

Geary received orders from General Slocum at about 7:00 P.M. to leave Greene's Brigade in the entrenchments and follow Williams's (Ruger's) Division to assist the Federal left. Unfortunately, the 1st Division had a half hour head start on Geary, and by the time the column moved out, their comrades were out of sight. To make matters worse, Slocum's staff officer had not thought to tell Geary the route he was to take or his destination. Geary could see some men in the distance. He thought they were Williams's, and ordered his men to follow. When he reached the position where the Baltimore Pike crosses Rock Creek, Geary received orders to stop and hold his position until further notice. General Slocum called it an "unfortunate and unaccountable mistake." Geary later wrote that he "received no specific instructions as to the object of the move, the direction to be taken, or the point to be reached, beyond the order to move by the right flank and to follow the First Division." While Geary was losing his way, Greene's Brigade, which was left behind to hold the crest of Culp's Hill, was savagely attacked by General Johnson's Division (II Corps). After a series of attacks, Steuart's Brigade managed to capture part of the Union entrenchments to the right of Greene's line.[5]

The division was ordered back to its former position at 9:00 P.M. that night. It was met by small arms fire as it approached. Rather than taking on the unseen enemy, Geary wisely decided to wait until morning to throw the Confederates out of his works.[6]

On July 3, the brunt of Johnson's attack on Culp's Hill fell on Geary's Division. Through a skillful approach of relieving units on a regular basis to rest and resupply themselves with ammunition, Geary was able to maintain an exceptionally high firepower against the Confederate attacks. Every attack was blunted and heavy casualties were inflicted upon the attackers. Geary estimated that his division fired an incredible 277,000 rounds of ammunition during the battle. The division remained here until July 5, when it followed Lee's army south.[7]

1st Brigade—Colonel Charles Candy

Units: 5th Ohio, 7th Ohio, 29th Ohio, 66th Ohio, 28th Pennsylvania, 147th Pennsylvania
Strength: 1798
Losses: 139 (18-119-2)—7.7%[8]

Colonel Charles Candy had led the 1st Brigade off and on since September 12, 1862. His most recent stint was since March 1863. Candy was an enlisted man in the regular army, but was promoted to the rank of captain when the war began, and then assumed command of the 66th Ohio in December 1861. The brigade fought in the Shenandoah Valley campaign of 1862, Second Bull Run, Antietam, and Chancellorsville. The Confederates roughly handled the men at the latter battle, so they were ready for redemption when the Gettysburg campaign began.[9]

The brigade's strenuous march to Gettysburg was fairly uneventful. During the march through Taneytown, Maryland, the column was met by "loyal citizens and ladies who could sympathize with us in our tired and worn out condition," recalled Private Henry Tallman of the 66th Ohio. As the brigade passed over the Pennsylvania state line on June 30, its two native regiments understood the significance. At the dedication of the 28th Pennsylvania monument, one of the veterans told his comrades, "with what glad hearts you pressed your feet on Pennsylvania soil, and the huzzas that were sent up as each command entered the State, and how light the step that gave outward signs of your eagerness to meet Lee's forces." The column reached Littlestown, where the veterans fondly remembered how the citizens "received us very kindly, giving us plenty to eat, and supplied us with good clear cold water to quench our thirst." Skirmishing between the opposing cavalry could be seen up ahead, and the brigade was ordered into the woods to the right of the road while the rest of the division continued its march. Here Colonel Candy was to throw out skirmishers and form his brigade "in column by two battalion front." The cavalry action soon broke off, and Candy's men were permitted to camp for the night. Tallman noted "here we remained all night—enjoying our situation very much, because we were with our own friends and out of Rebeldom [sic]."[10]

The brigade rejoined the division the following day and the march continued to Gettysburg. The men reached Two Taverns at about 11:00 A.M. on June 1, where they were permitted to prepare their midday meal and rest. Some soldiers from the 29th Ohio even had time for a swim. Off in the distance, the men could clearly hear the sounds of battle. As the division continued its march at about 2:00 P.M., Candy's Brigade proudly led the XII Corps's column. Sergeant William Tallman remembered that the weather was oppressive. "The sun was hot. The breezes that fanned our brows was hot, and the men panted like dogs on the chase and sweat [sic] and sweltered through cloudy dust." The column began passing knots of civilians fleeing from the battlefield. The men could not resist yelling out, "Oh come back; we are going to have lots of fun," and similar sentiments. The merriment ended when a steady stream of wounded passed the column.[11]

After reaching the vicinity of Gettysburg, the brigade moved with the rest of Geary's Division southward on Baltimore Pike, and halted just northeast of the Round Tops during the early evening. Around dark, Candy was ordered to send two regiments out on picket duty. The 5th Ohio and 147th Pennsylvania were selected and trotted toward the valley between Little Round Top and Emmitsburg Road in the fading light. To their left the men could see the large rocks of Devil's Den and to their right was Cemetery Ridge. Finding a stone fence, they hunkered down and waited. The skirmishers had a peaceful time of it, as the Confederates had not yet extended their line this far south. The men were nevertheless filled with anxiety, as they had little information about the day's events and they did not know the exact location of the enemy. They felt alone and vulnerable on the army's left flank. Most dreaded what tomorrow might bring.[12]

Sometime between 5:30 and 6:00 A.M. on July 2, the brigade marched to Culp's Hill with the remainder of Geary's Division. Greene's Brigade was formed on the left of the line, and initially, Candy's

Brigade was ordered to connect with its right flank. These orders were never carried out, as the brigade was ordered to form a line (with a double column on the center) behind Greene's Brigade and Kane's Brigade took its place on the right of the division. The 28th Pennsylvania was ordered down to the base of the hill to support Greene's skirmishers almost as soon as the brigade took its new position. There the Pennsylvanians helped engage the skirmishers from Nicholls's and Jones's Brigades (Johnson's Division), losing about three men during the day. The remainder of the brigade stacked arms and constructed breastworks. Captain Joseph Moore grumbled after the war that "as usual . . . the pioneer corps was not at hand, and bayonets, tin pans, tin cups, etc., were improvised as implements in the construction of earthworks."[13]

Sergeant Sherman Norris of the 7th Ohio could not have been more pleased with his position, which he considered "simply impregnable." He described it as a "stone wall [that] had been thrown up along the crest of Culp's Hill high enough to protect our bodies when kneeling, on top of which, leaving space through which to put our guns, a log was placed to protect our heads."[14]

Although there was some skirmishing in their front, Candy's men were relatively safe. About 4:00 P.M., they could hear the sounds of battle coming from the south, as Longstreet unleashed his attack on the III Corps. Sometime between 6:00 and 7:00 P.M., the brigade received orders to march south with Kane's Brigade in support of the Union left flank. Leading the column, the brigade was forced to cross an open area that was exposed to Southern artillery fire. Some of the men were hit as they quickly traversed it. Halting on the east bank of Rock Creek and McAllister's Mill, Candy deployed his brigade with its left on the creek and its right near a bridge. Pickets were thrown out to watch for the enemy, and the rest of the men slept and talked while Geary decided his next move. The two brigades remained there until about midnight, when they were ordered back to their original positions on Culp's Hill.[15]

The march back to Culp's Hill was extremely difficult, as related by Captain Joseph Moore of the 147th Pennsylvania:

> The task of such a movement, in utter darkness, amid heavily-timbered ridges and ravines on Culp's Hill, was one of extreme danger and uncertainty . . . it seemed to be a night of bewilderment to all . . . It was a night of slow, tiresome, round-about maneuvering, through fields, over fences, now on the pike; then a whispered halt! A rest for some minutes; the men asleep! Wake up! . . . Then, again, began the slow, silent movement forward, over rough, stony, stumpy ground, through bushes and briars, over stones, ditches . . . until near daybreak, when the regiment was faced in line of battle for the third and last day's fight.

The men had at least one consolation. Since the column had "about-faced," they were no longer in the lead.[16]

After "wandering through brush, briars, and boulders" in a confused manner, the brigade finally reclaimed its position in the rear of Greene's Brigade at about 1:30 A.M. on July 3. It now lay just behind Spangler's Lane, with its right in the orchard north of the Spangler house. The men assumed their positions very quietly, as the enemy was close by. They were permitted to grab what little rest they could. All realized that the rising sun would bring a hot contest for the hill. The exact disposition of the brigade is not known, but it is probable that the deployment was, from left to right, 147th Pennsylva-

nia–7th Ohio–5th Ohio. The remaining three regiments, the 29th and 66th Ohio and 28th Pennsylvania, were to the right of the line, but their actual positions are unknown. These initial positions are immaterial, however, for they were soon to relieve units on the front lines.[17]

Colonel Candy recalled that the Confederate artillery opened on the Federal lines at 3:45 A.M. on July 3. Knapp's battery lay directly behind the 29th Ohio, and when it opened fire, "The blaze of the guns would almost reach us, and the concussion would lift us up bodily," noted J. Lynn. Realizing that an attack was imminent, Candy ordered the 7th Ohio right toward Baltimore Pike, followed by the 147th Pennsylvania and 5th Ohio. They formed to the right of the brigade, facing Kane's (Cobham's) former breastworks, deployed from left to right as 5th Ohio–147th Pennsylvania–7th Ohio behind a low stone wall. In front of them was an open field, later named "Pardee Field" in honor of the commander of the 147th Pennsylvania. The remainder of the brigade (29th and 66th Ohio and 28th Pennsylvania) remained behind Greene's men in a "hollow." This protected area became the spot where regiments pulled out of the front lines came to rest and replenish their ammunition.[18]

The men did not have long to wait for the Confederate attack to begin. Although they were mere spectators during the opening phases of the engagement, they were soon thrown forward to relieve some of Greene's and Kane's regiments. For example, soon after daylight, the 7th Ohio was ordered to move by the left flank back up the hill, then double-quick forward to relieve the 60th New York (Greene's Brigade) in the trenches. Sergeant Lawrence Wilson found that the breastworks were built "so that a trench dug on the inside made them breast high; then a space was left of say six inches to fire through, and then a 'head log' placed on top." The regiment remained there until about 8:00 A.M., when the 60th New York returned to relieve it. The 7th Ohio then returned to the hollow and rested until 9:30 A.M., when it was ordered to relieve another regiment. It remained there for about twelve hours. While in this position the men participated in repelling the Stonewall Brigade's last charge. They could see the Virginians forming down in the valley before moving rapidly up the slope. Norris recalled that "the enemy formed his line of battle at the foot of the hill and came up across the intervening space of woods and rock in splendid order." Colonel Creighton ordered his men to hold their fire until he gave the orders. As the Virginians closed in on the summit of the slope, Creighton ordered firing by rank, beginning with the first, then the second. The Confederate line melted away before these concentrated volleys. Taking cover behind rocks and trees, the Virginians returned the fire. In some cases, the two lines were less than fifteen yards apart. Realizing that they could not take the heights, the Southerners retreated as best they could to the base of the hill.[19]

Some of the Confederates realized that surrender was their only option, and soon makeshift white flags could be seen fluttering along the line. Major B. Watkins Leigh of Johnson's staff saw these flags and became enraged. Spurring his horse up the hill, he "was seen to come forward and endeavor to stop the surrender, when he was fired upon by my men and instantly killed," recalled Colonel Creighton. A total of seventy-eight men (including seven officers) from Walker's Stonewall Brigade surrendered to the 7th Ohio.[20]

The 29th Ohio was ordered to relieve the 137th New York (Greene's Brigade) in the breastworks at 5:45 A.M. The 29th Ohio's commander, Captain Wilbur

Stevens, was struck by a spent ball, causing "severe pain and giddiness." He therefore temporarily passed command of the unit to Captain Edward Hayes. Somewhat cautious because he had not commanded a regiment before, Hayes decided to make a personal reconnaissance, as he did not know the exact position of the 137th New York. After reaching the desired location and conversing with the New York regiment's commander, Hayes bounded back to his own troops. Hayes later reported that "the regiment moved over the ridge at a run without firing a shot until fairly in the trenches, when it opened a heavy fire upon the enemy, under cover of which Colonel Ireland [of the 137th New York] was able to withdraw his regiment with but small loss."[21]

The regiment remained there for about two hours and ten minutes when the 28th Pennsylvania of its own brigade relieved it. After the men had rested and replenished their ammunition, Hayes received word from Colonel Candy to prepare to help repel an attack on the position held by the 147th Pennsylvania and 5th Ohio on its right. The men were not needed, but Captain Charles Horton, Greene's Brigade's adjutant general, came running up to Hayes with a desperate request for assistance. One of the regiments in the front line was being hard pressed and was almost out of ammunition. This posed a dilemma for the new regimental commander. "Ordinarily, I should not have felt justified in moving without an order from the commander of our own brigade, but the men in front were falling back by twos and threes, and there did not seem to be any time to lose." He made up his mind when he received word from Lieutenant Hitt of Candy's staff that he would be ordered forward in the near future. "The regiment responded to the order in the most splendid manner, cheering as they charged,"

Hayes recalled. It was now just before 10:00 A.M., and the regiment remained heavily engaged until about 11:00 A.M., when the enemy withdrew from its front.[22]

The Confederate charges against the upper slopes of Culp's Hill are hard to imagine. One soldier from the 28th Pennsylvania did a fairly good job of describing it after the war:

> Down the opposite slope they came in beautiful alignment, their officers gallantly leading—now up the hillside in our front, in solid column, as if by sheer force of weight to bear us down. There was no retreat for the poor fellows in the front ranks who, with blanched faces, came up to be mowed down in companies. At twenty paces, ten, five, and even less intervening space, our minnie balls were planked [sic] into their unprotected bodies . . . The faces of the men in the front ranks exhibited that fear and dread that is akin to insanity, and yet without any hope of success, they were driven to the slaughter.[23]

The 28th Pennsylvania was subsequently relieved by a New York regiment and moved to the rear, where the men cleaned their guns and replenished their ammunition. Despite being actively engaged, the regiment lost only twenty-five men during the morning.[24]

While the 7th and 29th Ohio, and 28th Pennsylvania were relieving Greene's Brigade, the 66th Ohio was ordered toward the summit of the hill, where it crossed the breastworks and formed perpendicular to and facing Greene's line. This allowed them to pour an enfilading fire into the charging Confederates from Walker's Stonewall Brigade. The advanced position also exposed the Buckeyes to enemy fire. An officer from a different command was incredulous when he overheard the order, and said, "I am expecting an attack every moment; if you go out

there with your regt. they will simply swallow you." The regiment's commander, Lieutenant Colonel Eugene Powell, reported that "we poured a murderous fire on the enemy's flank. After a short time, I found that the enemy had posted sharpshooters at the foot of the hill, behind a fence, who were annoying us very much. I ordered my regiment to take up a sheltered position behind trees and stones, and direct their fire on the sharpshooters, whom we soon dislodged." Powell beamed after the war—"I am confident that this diversion of but a single regiment assisted very materially in recovering our works." The regiment was pulled back at about noon and moved east to relieve the 150th New York (Lockwood's Brigade). It remained here until 9:00 P.M., when it was pulled back for a well-deserved rest.[25]

Over to the right of Kane's Brigade, the 147th Pennsylvania and 5th Ohio were experiencing stressful times. Colonel Warren Packer of the 5th Ohio ordered Company F to occupy a stone wall just to the left of his position, "to fret the enemy as much as possible, for the purpose of drawing him from his entrenchments." The ploy was successful, for a line of Confederates now appeared in front of the men. Caught between the skirmishers and the 5th Ohio's regimental line, the enemy "received volley after volley, until they were forced to retire." A second attempt was made with the same result. Packer believed these repulses caused the Confederates, probably from Steuart's Brigade, to abandon their breastworks.[26]

Soon after arriving, the exhausted men of the 147th Pennsylvania were ordered to "keep firing continually and without intermission through these trees in our front." When the men protested that they could not see any enemy, their officers merely shrugged and replied that they were merely obeying orders. At about 10:25 A.M., the Pennsylvanians, who were holding the right of the 2nd Division's line, could see the 3rd North Carolina (Steuart's Brigade) slowly advancing up the hill. "They boldly advanced to within about 100 yards without discovering my regiment. I then ordered the regiment to fire, and broke their line. They reformed as a body and advanced. Their advance was checked by the heavy fire they received, when they broke and ran," wrote Lieutenant Colonel Ario Pardee. Captain George Thomas, a member of the 1st Maryland battalion (Steuart's Brigade) trying to dislodge the 147th Pennsylvania, recalled that a "burst of flame and shot and shell" swept his men to their destruction. Colonel Candy indicated that the Pennsylvanians caused "considerable casualties and havoc among [the enemy.]" Pardee explained that he would have ordered a counterattack, but being on the right of the line, he did not feel that he had the support needed to be successful. Because the regiment was not relieved during the entire morning, boxes of ammunition were frequently carried to the stone wall and distributed to the men.[27]

The attacks on the Federal works ended by 11:00 A.M. The men did not have long to savor the reprieve, because the artillery barrage preceding the Pickett–Pettigrew–Trimble charge caught them by surprise. "The scene now became terrific and indescribable. Projectiles of all sorts rained mercilessly above us, among us and all around us, as if the infernal regions had broken loose . . . they can whistling, shrieking, moaning, whirling, fluttering, bouncing, bursting and crashing with fearful force and rapidity," wrote one of the men.[28]

The movement of Candy's troops continued throughout the day and night. For example, the 28th Pennsylvania relieved the 7th Ohio at about 3:00 P.M. and was exposed to sniper fire until 9:00 P.M., when a half-hearted charge was made

against the works. The Pennsylvanians were pulled out of the breastworks shortly after, and received rations. The regiment moved forward again at midnight, this time to relieve the 60th and 78th New York of Greene's Brigade. The 147th Pennsylvania on the right was finally pulled out of line and moved up toward the highest point of Culp's Hill, where it deployed just to the right of Wadsworth's Division (I Corps). Not permitted to sleep for three nights, the men were exhausted. The 7th Ohio was also active during the night, relieving another regiment behind the breastworks at 1:00 A.M. on July 4. About the same time, the 29th Ohio relieved the 137th New York.[29]

After the battle, both Candy and Colonel William Creighton claimed that the 7th Ohio captured the 14th Virginia battle flag. This was impossible, as the 14th belonged to Armistead's Brigade of Pickett's Division. It was actually the flag of the 4th Virginia, which was all but annihilated on the morning of July 3. The 7th Ohio almost lost its own flag when an enterprising Confederate sergeant crept up and tried to knock it over the breastworks. His efforts woke the 7th Ohio's flag sergeant, who shot and killed the offender. This roused the rest of the men, who thought they were under attack, so they opened fire.[30]

The men were ordered out to bury the dead and collect equipment on July 4. The quiet also gave them a chance to take stock of the situation. They were stunned not only by the massive losses of the enemy, but also by their own light casualties. The Confederates had launched what amounted to a suicide attack on the Federal works. The dead lay in heaps in front of Geary's Division's line. The historian of the 29th Ohio was left pondering another issue. "Still the mystery exists how any rebels escaped, as each soldier of the

Union army had, in the seven hours' fight, fired two hundred and fifty rounds of ammunition, sufficient to have annihilated the entire Southern army." Others felt sorry for the common Confederate foot soldier. One soldier from the 28th Pennsylvania merely wrote,"brave men, they deserved better success for their undaunted courage."[31]

On July 5, the brigade began its march back toward Littlestown. Given the destruction it inflicted on Johnson's Division, the brigade's losses of 139 (8%) were exceptionally low. Like the rest of Geary's Division, the brigade fought behind breastworks, which reduced its losses. Most losses occurred when the regiments approached or left the breastworks. The men had performed well, particularly on July 3. Yet, many groused, with some validity, that they did not receive the credit they deserved.[32]

2nd Brigade—Brigadier General Thomas Kane/Colonel G. A. Cobham

Units: 29th Pennsylvania, 109th Pennsylvania, 111th Pennsylvania
Strength: 700
Losses: 98 (23-66-9)—14.0%[33]

No fewer than eleven regiments had been part of the 2nd Brigade. By the Gettysburg campaign, only three remained—the other eight having been assigned elsewhere. Because of the men's distinctive headgear, the unit was called the "Bucktail Brigade." The regiments had much in common, so it was a cohesive veteran unit. Unfortunately, commanding officer General Thomas Kane was recuperating from a bout of pneumonia, so the brigade was commanded by Colonel G. Cobham of the 111th Pennsylvania.[34]

The brigade reached Littlestown on June 30 with the rest of the division and camped just beyond the town that night. The march continued at 7:00 A.M. on July 1, and a halt was permitted at Two Taverns for a midday rest and repast. Just as the column was about to move out at 2:00 P.M., a messenger from Slocum's headquarters ordered Geary to leave one brigade and a section of artillery behind to cover the right flank of the army. Geary selected Cobham's. No record of the men's reactions to this order exists. However, they could hear the sounds of battle coming from Gettysburg, and since they were defending their own state, they were probably unhappy to be left behind. Yet the brigade had suffered so many severe losses in past battles that it is likely that some men did not regret missing the opportunity of tangling with Lee's legions once again.[35]

While the two remaining brigades of Geary's Division made their way to Little Round Top, the 2nd Brigade remained all night by the side of Baltimore Pike, two miles from Gettysburg. The men did not sleep well that night, as they were ordered to "sleep on their arms" and to expect an attack at any time. The men welcomed back General Kane at 6:00 A.M. on July 2. Because of the danger posed by Stuart's cavalry, Kane was forced to make his way in civilian clothes. An added complication was that Kane's condition did not permit him to ride a horse, so he arrived in an ambulance. According to Cobham's report, he turned the brigade over to Kane and returned to his 111th Pennsylvania. "But in a few minutes General Kane sent me an order by one of his aides to resume the command of the brigade. I reported to the general, when he repeated the order to me . . . [he] being too much prostrated to continue it." Kane's report says nothing about relinquishing his command to Cobham. Adding to the confusion are the reports of the regimental commanders. Colonel William Rickards of the 29th Pennsylvania reported receiving orders from Kane, while Lieutenant Colonel Thomas Walker of the 111th Pennsylvania said he had received his orders from Cobham.[36]

The brigade was ordered to rejoin the division on the morning of July 2. As Candy's and Greene's Brigades marched northward from the Round Tops, Cobham's Brigade moved west, and the two contingents met at Culp's Hill. As the men approached Powers Hill, they spied Generals Meade and Geary sitting on their horses by the side of the road. Meade asked Geary about the identity of some of the troops. After being told they were from the 29th Pennsylvania, Meade pondered a bit, and then said, "It is a very small one but order them up. We will want every man today." Geary placed Cobham's Brigade to the right of Greene's, "at an angle of about 45 degrees forward, conforming its line to the crest of the ridge." Candy's Brigade formed on their right. The 109th Pennsylvania was on the left of the brigade, with the 111th Pennsylvania on its right along the top of the lower hill. The 29th Pennsylvania deployed behind a stone wall about a hundred yards to the rear. Its right flank connected with the 3rd Maryland of Candy's Brigade. The men were then set to work throwing up breastworks. Both Kane and Cobham remarked that the position was "excellent." Cobham added that the position was "admirably located to command the approaches by Rock Creek." McDougall was on Cobham's right.[37]

The crushing attack on the Union left

by two divisions of Longstreet's Corps caused Meade to pull most of the XII Corps out of their entrenchments to support Sickles's III Corps. Geary received his orders at about 7:00 P.M., and ordered Kane's Brigade to follow Candy's down Baltimore Pike. The movement got off to a bad start when Candy's Brigade began the movement without Kane's, because the latter was slow in gathering its equipment. An impatient Geary rode up to the 29th Pennsylvania and ordered it to "Follow me." The regiment's commanding officer, Colonel William Rickards, took issue with Geary's direct orders to his men, and immediately protested that all such orders should go through him. Realizing that Rickards was right, Geary apologized, and both led the brigade down the road. The column was exposed to enemy artillery fire at one point, but sustained few casualties. After marching about a mile, Geary halted his column and took stock of the situation. He was clearly on the wrong road and was perplexed about what to do next. The left of his division rested on Rock Creek and his right was on the turnpike. At about 9:00 P.M. the line was ordered to "about face," and now Kane's Brigade led the division's march back to Culp's Hill.[38]

The men let out a "hurrah" as they approached their former breastworks to hearten Greene's men, who had been trying to hold off Johnson's Division's attacks. The sounds of encouragement were also clearly heard by the men of Steuart's Brigade, who had captured part of the XII Corps's breastworks. A volley erupted from a distance of about twenty-five paces, killing four men from the 29th Pennsylvania and wounding another ten. Colonel Rickards had a nagging suspicion that Greene's men had fired the volley. After pulling his men back to safety, Rickards rode back to the breastworks and "called to those behind it, telling them who I was, and was answered by a heavy discharge of musketry." Finally realizing that the enemy did indeed occupy their breastworks, the brigade retraced its steps to Baltimore Pike, and filed back into the woods via a small lane near the Spangler house. The 111th Pennsylvania now led the column. Skirmishers were thrown forward to feel for the enemy. A detail from the 29th Pennsylvania moved slowly forward in the darkness under the command of Captain George Johnson. Without knowing it, they had entered the enemy lines, and Johnson and five of his men were quickly captured by the enemy. Likewise, two companies forming the left of the 111th Pennsylvania ventured too close to the enemy and received a volley at close range. Lieutenant Colonel Thomas Walker ordered his eight remaining companies to turn and face the Confederates. Colonel Cobham was not so sure that the Confederates occupied the 111th Pennsylvania's former breastworks, so he ordered the regiment to reclaim them. It was only through strenuous efforts that Walker convinced Cobham to countermand the order which, if executed, surely would have resulted in a blood bath.[39]

Moving forward to the right and rear of Greene's Brigade in the area between the two hills forming Culp's Hill that was called the "saddle," the brigade relieved the 84th New York (Cutler's Brigade, Wadsworth's Division) and 6th Wisconsin (Iron Brigade, Wadsworth's Division). Facing southeast, the brigade was positioned at right angles to its original breastworks. The 111th Pennsylvania was on the left, the 29th Pennsylvania was on its right, and the 109th Pennsylvania formed the brigade's right flank. Half of the 29th Pennsylvania was placed behind a stone fence. The 111th Pennsylvania was pulled back later that night to occupy a reserve

position. This was a dangerous maneuver, as the enemy troops were close by. According to Walker, "I was endeavoring to move my regiment, a man at a time, with the utmost caution, when our watchful enemy detected a move, and, supposing we were about to retire, opened fire upon us. My men returned the fire, silencing theirs, and then moved to the position assigned to them, awaiting daylight for the work to begin."[40]

About 3:00 A.M. on July 3, movement was observed on Cobham's front. While the Federal officers speculated about its nature, Steuart's Confederate Brigade opened fire. A spirited firefight occurred until the Southern troops pulled back to safety. The brigade was then pulled back about fifty paces, behind a ledge of rocks that offered good protection. The Confederate troops returned at about 3:30 A.M., and firing again broke out. "The enemy advanced with a yell. We opened fire briskly, quickly compelling them to take the shelter of the rocks and of our own trenches that were in their possession," wrote one soldier. The men were ordered to fire into the wooded ravine in front of them for most of the morning. The regiments were pulled out of line and replaced by others, so they could rest, clean their guns, and replenish their ammunition. For example, the 111th Pennsylvania replaced the 29th Pennsylvania behind the ledge. The regiment remained in reserve for about forty-five minutes, then was ordered back to regain its original position in the breastworks. It was withdrawn again at 11:00 A.M. and replaced by the 1st Maryland Potomac Home Guard (Lockwood's Brigade). The periods when the men entered or left the protective cover were hazardous, and several were killed and wounded.[41]

Because of the deeply sloping ground in front of Company A of the 109th Pennsylvania, the men could not get off good shots at the enemy. One veteran recalled that "we were obliged to run out in advance of the rest behind a large tree, and await an opportunity, which constantly offered, to shoot rebels. This tree was in constant use by our company . . . when one had discharged his piece and run back, another ran forward to occupy his place."[42]

A major Confederate attack was launched at 10:30 A.M., when Steuart's Brigade rushed up the hill. To Kane and his men, the attack formation was "closed in mass." In actuality, three lines of infantry moved swiftly forward. The Federal troops initially held their fire, which emboldened the Confederates. As the range closed, the men were ordered to open fire. The opening volleys were not effective. "Noticing by the falling leaves that our men were firing too high the colonel gave the command to shoot at their knees, the effect of which was noticeable at once," recalled one of the men. Colonel Rickards of the 29th Pennsylvania proudly reported that "our men stood to their ground well, firing with great rapidity and execution. When within 70 paces, their column began to waver, and soon after broke and ran from reach of our fire, leaving a large number of their dead and wounded on the field."[43]

After the war, General Kane recalled the steady approach of the 1st Maryland and 3rd North Carolina of Steuart's Brigade. The enemy soldiers carried their rifles at right shoulder shift, constantly redressing their lines as men fell. Just as the Confederate line began to waver under the heavy volleys from the Union soldiers, its officers ordered a double-quick pace, then a run, as they approached. Many Confederates realized that they could go no farther, but others forged on, only to be destroyed as they

approached the Union position. A dog suddenly broke from the Confederate ranks and bounded forward. The dog apparently found his master lying on the ground and, while licking his hand, was killed by a Federal volley. After the battle, Kane ordered his men to bury the dog, as he was "the only Christian minded being on either side."[44]

The Confederate attacks all but ceased with the repulse of this charge. The 109th Pennsylvania was withdrawn and replaced by a regiment from Shaler's Brigade (Newton's Division, VI Corps). At about 2:30 P.M., the regiment was ordered to reoccupy its original breastworks, now abandoned by the enemy. The 29th Pennsylvania, which had been withdrawn at 11:00 A.M., was also ordered forward at about 3:00 P.M.[45]

The men spent the remainder of the afternoon dodging sniper bullets. Curiously, none of the officers or men reported the tremendous cannonade that preceded the Pickett–Pettigrew–Trimble charge. The Confederates launched one final assault on the Union line at 9:00 P.M. It too was repulsed. This caused alarm among the officers, so they ordered their men to sleep on their arms and be vigilant for another attack.[46]

During the morning of July 4, Colonel Rickards of the 29th Pennsylvania threw out a company as skirmishers to ascertain the position of the enemy. Moving slowly down the slope, the men were both surprised and relieved to find that the enemy had withdrawn and no longer posed a threat. When word reached the brigade, many men sprang forward to have a better look around them. "Before advancing many paces we came upon numberless forms clad in grey, either stark and stiff or else still weltering in their blood," wrote Dr. August Zeitter. The sights and smells were enough to send many of the men back up the hill. Most of the men had fired as many as 160 rounds at the enemy, and they could easily see the deadly results of their work. The brigade spent the remainder of the day collecting equipment, tending to the wounded, and burying the dead. It began the march back toward Littlestown on July 5.[47]

Kane's small band of less than seven hundred men acquitted itself well in the battle. Its commander simply wrote that they "justified their reputation as marksmen." Lieutenant Colonel Thomas Walker reported, "I am proud to say they fought feeling they were Pennsylvanians in Pennsylvania."[48]

3rd Brigade—Brigadier General George Greene

Units: 60th New York, 78th New York, 102nd New York, 137th New York, 149th New York
Strength: 1424
Losses: 303(67-212-24)—21.3%[49]

None of the New Yorkers who trudged toward Gettysburg as part of the 3rd Brigade could have ever imagined what lasting fame awaited their unit. This was a veteran fighting unit that at one time contained five other regiments from other states. It was now an all-New York brigade. At its head rode General George Greene, who had commanded the brigade since September 18, 1862. At sixty-two, he was easily one of the oldest officers in either army. This was a brigade to be reckoned with, given its stability and battlefield experience.[50]

The late afternoon of June 30 found the brigade approaching the small community of Littlestown, Pennsylvania. Corporal James Hyde of the 137th New York recorded in his diary that the "citizens did not know anything about our coming until they saw us. They cut their bread into slices and spread it with butter to give to the soldiers . . . water stood in pails in front of every house and a young lady ready to hand you a drink . . . this was a real union place." Since Greene's Brigade

brought up the rear of the XII Corps, Hyde and his comrades grumbled when they realized that "the eatibles [sic] were nearly all gone when we got there." The men spent the night about a mile north of town, where they received much-needed clothing.[51]

Halting halfway between Gettysburg and Littlestown on July 1, the men were permitted to rest and eat whatever food was available. For some, it was merely a cup a coffee. While resting there, perhaps about 1:00 P.M., many men could plainly hear the sounds of battle coming from Gettysburg. The march continued at about 4:00 P.M. that afternoon. As the brigade approached the town, it passed artillery, infantry, and stragglers by the side of the road. A few men slipped from the ranks, realizing that a fight was in the offing. They also passed a stream of women and children making their way to safety. "In the faces of many were evidences of weeping, and in all a look of horror and despair," wrote George Carr of the 149th New York. Sergeant Sam Lusk of the 137th New York added that this "scine [sic] looked heart renching [sic] & I can tell you it kindled a war spirit in us so that it seemed impossible for the whole rebble [sic] force to whip our Brigade." Continuing their march at the double-quick, the men finally approached Gettysburg, then were directed southward to Little Round Top. The men were told to load their muskets and dispose of all unnecessary equipment. They were pleased to learn that they would spend the night there. Most of the men slept only fitfully. "The night was cool, but the slumbers of the men were not peaceful, although they had undergone great fatigue," wrote Carr.[52]

The men were roused at daybreak and with the rest of Geary's Division, marched to the right, eventually halting on Culp's Hill at about 6:00 A.M.. Greene's Brigade took position at the top of the upper slope, with its left flank connected to the I Corps and its right attached at right angles to Kane's (Cobham's) Brigade at the saddle between the higher and lower hills. The regiments were arranged, along the four hundred-yard front, from left to right, as 60th New York–102nd New York–78th New York–149th New York–137th New York.[53]

The men were immediately ordered to build breastworks. They had done this once before, at Chancellorsville, and were not overly enthusiastic about the enterprise. A story circulated after the war that Geary did not wish to entrench, but "Pap" Greene insisted. According to one version, Geary called a conference of his brigade commanders to address the issue and immediately announced his position, saying, "It unfitted men for fighting without them." Greene purportedly said that he was more interested in saving lives, and ordered his men to construct the breastworks. Whether true or not, the men energetically set to work, using any and all materials available to them, including, rocks, tree stumps, cords of wood, soil, and anything else that could be moved and could potentially stop a bullet. Captain Jesse Jones of the 60th New York recalled that the more experienced men

went about their tasks in a methodical manner. "Right and left the men felled the trees, and blocked them up into a close log fence. Piles of cordwood which lay near by were quickly appropriated. The sticks, set slanting on end against the outer face of the logs, made excellent battening." Greene could be seen everywhere along the line, encouraging the men and providing advice. In some places, large rocks and stone ledges precluded the need for construction. The breastworks were completed by noon, and the men were given a well-deserved rest. They also took the opportunity to visit with their comrades in other regiments.[54]

A skirmish line composed of about 180 officers and men was thrown down the northern slope of Culp's Hill at about 8:00 A.M. Moving cautiously toward Rock Creek, it relieved two companies of the 7th Indiana. The men remained there throughout the day, supported by the 28th Pennsylvania of Candy's Brigade. Occasional firing broke out between the opposing pickets. About 4:00 P.M., Geary brought up two batteries to the main Union line to respond to the Confederate artillery that had opened fire. In a letter to his father after the battle, Steuben Coon of the 60th New York wrote that the "shells burst over and all around us, but only a few were hurt—for it is a fact that unless troops are massed together, shells or shot do very little damage except to scare raw recruits. They do make an unearthly noise." When a number of artillerymen fell victim to sniper's bullets, men from the 60th and 78th New York sprang forward to help carry ammunition and work the guns. This artillery fire and the twenty-five snipers sent forward to pick off the Confederate artillerymen forced the enemy battery to retire.[55]

About 7:00 P.M., Lieutenant Colonel John Redington, commanding the skirmish line, could see a thick line of Confederate infantry moving slowly toward him. Realizing that the long-delayed attack was in the offing, he ordered his men back across Rock Creek. Pulling every man he could into line, he opened a brisk fire on the Confederates, forcing the opposing skirmishers to take cover in the grass. Surveying the situation, Redington decided to pull back to a position about a hundred yards from the creek. Redington judged that his men could pour a concentrated fire into the Confederate infantry as they crossed the stream. He also requested support from the 28th Pennsylvania (Candy's Brigade). The response was both rapid and unwelcome. The Pennsylvanians had been ordered back to the entrenchments and could not provide assistance. This left Redington with no choice but to pull his men slowly back to their own entrenchments. The Confederates were advancing so rapidly that Redington's men were able to turn and capture twelve prisoners in the growing darkness. When within fifty yards of the breastworks, Redington yelled for his men to sprint the rest of the way, culminating in a rapid leap over the breastworks. The men encountered the 78th New York as they were retreating, which had been ordered forward to relieve the 28th Pennsylvania. However, seeing the powerful Confederate attack force, composed of three separate lines, the New Yorkers wisely returned to their breastworks, but not before firing at least one volley. "The flashes from their rifles glowed with an angry light," noted Captain John Peck of the 78th New York.[56]

Redington was unaware of the momentous decisions being made on the hill behind him. First Williams's (Ruger's) Division and then Candy's and Kane's Brigades of Geary's Division were pulled from their breastworks to help support

the Union left flank. This was the reason why the 28th Pennsylvania was pulled back from its position. Before he left, Geary told Greene to extend his line to the right to occupy the now abandoned breastworks of the remainder of the division. No sooner had Geary's two brigades left, than Confederate General Edward Johnson launched his division's attack.[57]

The movement by the right flank began immediately. Coon, whose 60th New York held the left of the brigade, wrote that "now a singular thing took place . . . the commander of our brigade came riding up and ordered every regiment except the 60th to fall into line. He told our Colonel that the other regiments were needed in another place and that he must put the men in a single rank and far enough apart so to cover the ground before occupied by the whole brigade. So away they all went, the last thing the General said, was that we must hold the position!" The remainder of the brigade moved to the right so that the 102nd New York occupied the 149th New York's position, the 149th New York occupied the 137th New York's, and the 137th New York moved into part of Kane's now abandoned breastworks. Gunfire now erupted along Rock Creek, and before long the men could see their own skirmishers speedily approaching. The final leap of Redington's skirmishers over the breastworks brought welcome relief for the rest of the brigade, for it meant that they could open fire on the enemy now climbing the hill. Word passed along the line that Greene's orders were to "hold the works under all circumstances."[58]

George Carr recalled that moments felt like years. "The pale faces, staring eyeballs, and nervous hands grasping loaded muskets, told how terrible were those moments of suspense." Coon noted that "not a shot was fired at them until they got within about 15 rods. Then the order was given (Fire!) and we did fire, and kept firing. If ever men loaded and fired more rapidly than the 60th did on that occasion, I never saw them do it. The rebels yelled like wild indians and charged upon us on a double quick. They acted bravely, they came as close as they could but very few got within 2 rods of us, those that did never went away again." Carr added that after each man fired, "he involuntarily drew back and sought safety behind the works as if alarmed at the sound of his own musket and the murderous work he had done." This wasted movement stopped after the men fired a few shots. Despite firing as rapidly as they could, the enemy still advanced. Sergeant Lusk (137th New York) wrote home that the enemy infantry "charged and pouring a perfect shower of lead with their hideous yells tried to drive us back. But we stood firm, not flinching, and give them what they say was the most murderous fire that they ever came in contact with."[59]

The attack finally faltered and the enemy soldiers retreated toward the base of the hill. While the men were relieved by their success, they were plainly worried about what laid ahead. They were up against a substantial enemy force, yet were expected to occupy a large front that forced the line to be spread thinly. In most places, one man occupied a yard of breastworks—too diluted to be effective. The Rebel yells were now replaced with pleas for help from the Confederate wounded. Many of Greene's soldiers leaped over the breastworks to provide assistance. Suddenly, the men could hear the Confederates moving forward again to attack the works. "Our men sprang to their places. This time they came with a rush—they had been reinforced, and thought to drive us out certain. Again death met them in the face," wrote Coon to his father.[60]

It was dark now, and the men hoped the Confederates would not launch additional attacks. They could hear the sounds of another advance, and the destruction was repeated. Again, the Confederates were forced to retreat. Because no other troops were available to relieve Greene's men, ammunition was brought to the breastworks between attacks. At least once, the ammunition was not forthcoming, and the men were ordered to fix bayonets. The Confederates made a total of four attacks that evening. All were met with defeat, with one exception.[61]

A dangerous situation developed when the left flank of Steuart's Brigade overlapped the right of Greene's line. To bolster the line, the 71st Pennsylvania of Webb's Philadelphia Brigade (Gibbon's Division, II Corps) was sent to the right of the 137th New York. Moving forward in the darkness and probably making too much noise, the Philadelphians were fired upon by the enemy, probably by the 10th Virginia (Steuart's Brigade). The regiment's colonel, R. Penn Smith, ordered his men to return to their position on Cemetery Ridge. When one of Greene's flabbergasted aides asked Smith what he was doing, he responded that he had orders to return to his brigade. This was clearly not the case. In response to the renewed pressure (he was outnumbered about five to one), Colonel David Ireland of the 137th New York ordered his rightmost company (Company A) to pull back and form at right angles to the rest of the regiment. Receiving fire from three sides, the company was forced to pull back again. Perhaps most disconcerting were the volleys fired by the 10th Virginia, who occupied a stone wall behind them. The 137th New York was forced to fall back so that its left rested in its original breastworks; its right ran parallel to Kane's works, but two hundred feet behind them.

Seeing the 137th New York's problems, Lieutenant Colonel Charles Randall of the 149th New York attempted to change the front of his three right companies. The order was misunderstood by the company commanders, who thought they were to withdraw. The movement to the rear was well under way when Randall realized the mistake and ordered the men back to their breastworks. Being exposed at the time, the regiment sustained a number of casualties. Some of Steuart's men surged forward and claimed Kane's breastworks to the right of the 137th New York.[62]

Greene now turned to General Wadsworth for help. Wadsworth commanded a I Corps division that was positioned on Greene's left on Culp's Hill. Wadsworth responded by sending the 6th Wisconsin, 84th New York, and 147th New York. General Howard also assisted by sending the 82nd Illinois, 45th New York, and 61st Ohio. These regiments provided valuable service to Greene's men, permitting them to leave their breastworks to clean their guns and replenish their ammunition during the night. In a few cases they engaged the enemy, helping to discourage further attacks that night.[63]

Most of the firing died down after 9:00 P.M. Concerned that the enemy occupied the dark wood in front of him, Colonel Abel Godard of the 60th New York made a difficult decision. "I ordered an advance of a portion of my regiment, who eagerly leaped the works and surrounded about 50 of the enemy . . . and took at the time two flags." At the opposite end of the line, Captain Gregg of the 137th New York ordered a squad of men to make a bayonet charge against a group of Confederates who were harassing them. Gregg fell leading this ill-advised charge.[64]

By 10:00 P.M. the men realized that the battle was over for the night. The rest of the night was very dark and tensions were high. Peering out of their breastworks, the men could make out large numbers of dead and wounded Confederates lying within fifty feet of them. At least twice, once at 1:00 P.M., and again an hour later, volleys rang out in the night. These were isolated incidents, however, and quiet returned to the battlefield. The fight for Culp's Hill on the evening of July 2 was magnificent. Greene's five regiments held out against three Confederate brigades. Jones's Brigade had taken on the 60th New York; Nicholls's Brigade had fought the 78th New York and 102nd New York; and Steuart's Brigade fought the 149th and 137th New York. Despite these uneven odds, only a portion of the breastworks on the right was lost.[65]

Few doubted that the attacks would be renewed the following day. Greene prepared for them by ordering the 78th New York, which had been supporting the picket line, and subsequently the 102nd New York to advance and occupy the breastworks in the center of the line between the 60th and 102nd New York. To its right, Colonel Randall of the 149th New York walked along his lines, sharing his whiskey with his officers. He told them that it would probably be the last drink they would take together, and he hoped it would "sustain them in doing their duty and to meet the consequences." As soon as the last drop was expended, some of the men yelled out that they could again see the Confederates advancing. The time was sometime between 3:30 and 4:00 A.M. The firing became intense along many parts of the line. The three left regiments faced four brigades: Jones's, Nicholls's, O'Neal's, and Daniel's Brigades; the two right regiments faced parts of Nicholls's, Walker's, and Steuart's Brigades.[66]

Although Wadsworth's men had returned to their former positions, the remainder of XII Corps had returned to provide aid to Greene's men. As a result, Greene was able to pull his men out of line periodically for brief periods to clean their rifles, replenish their ammunition, and rest. For example, at about 7:40 A.M., the 150th New York (Lockwood's Brigade) replaced the 78th New York. The latter returned at 9:00 A.M., and the 150th New York slid to the right and replaced the 102nd New York. The 102nd New York returned about twenty minutes later to replace the 150th, and the two regiments again exchanged positions about an hour later. The men had scarcely settled down near Greene's headquarters when they were ordered forward to close the gap in the line formed when the 1st Maryland Eastern Shore abandoned its works. The 102nd New York remained there until 2:00 P.M., when the 60th New York relieved it. Likewise, the 137th New York, now on the right of Greene's line, was relieved by the 29th Ohio (Candy's Brigade) at 5:45 A.M. It returned at 7:00 A.M., and was again relieved at 9:30 A.M.[67]

The 1st Maryland Eastern Shore Regiment caused other hardships for Greene's Brigade. The regiment had originally been sent in to relieve the 149th New York. Approaching to within four or five rods, the green Maryland troops fired in the direction of the New Yorkers, then ran away. We will never know whether the Marylanders were firing at the enemy or at their own men. When the Maryland regiment returned to relieve the 149th New York, the latter regiment formed behind them for a few moments to ensure that they would not "gig out" a second time. Many New Yorkers insisted that the Maryland troops did just that after they left.[68]

The regiments stayed in a protected hollow when relieved. Getting to the hollow was usually more dangerous than remaining in the breastworks. Carr recalled that the men first fired their guns "while the men of another regiment mid deafening cheers leaped over them into their vacant places. Under cover of the fire from the relief, the men made a lively retreat back to the hollow." The act of cleaning the guns was critical during this stage of the battle. The guns, Carr recalled, "were so foul that a ball could not be driven home without difficulty, and the barrels so hot as to be painful to the touch." Lacking cleaning materials, the men often tore off pieces of their shirts.[69]

During midmorning, Colonel Randall (149th New York) ordered his men not to fire unless they had a target. Almost immediately, a private rose and deliberately fired. Angered by this action, Randall stormed over and demanded to know why he had fired. The soldier merely pointed, and Randall could see the Confederates (probably the Stonewall Brigade) advancing in line of battle. Randall screamed, "Give them h_____l boys, give it to them right and left." The Confederate line soon disintegrated, as those still standing retreated backward—all except for one large sergeant, who rushed the works in an effort to capture the 149th New York's flag, which was resting on the breastworks. He reached the breastworks, only to be cut down by a dozen bullets.[70]

The 149th New York's flag was hit by over eighty bullets and its staff by at least seven. The staff broke at one point and was spliced by William Lilly, the flag sergeant. "Coolly, under fire [he], mended the broken member with splints from a cracker box and straps from his knapsacks," noted Captain George Collins. Lilly was wounded while accomplishing this much-needed act.[71]

Firing continued throughout the morning, until after 11:00 A.M., when the men could see the enemy pulling back. White flags appeared, as knots of Confederates chose to surrender rather than risk the move down the hill under a hail of bullets. Cheers erupted from the Union lines when the men realized that their lines had held.[72]

The men now had a chance to look around. They could see large numbers of the enemy literally lying in heaps in front of them. Corporal James Hyde of the 137th New York could stand anywhere and count at least fifty to sixty dead bodies. He also observed how the trees suffered. "The limbs were cut from the trees, and the trees were pushed up as much as if each had been a target for many months. On some trees there was not a piece of bark left as large as your hand . . . the only wonder is that there was a live rebel left." The men could barely recognize their comrades. "Their clothes ragged and dirty, their faces black from smoke, sweat and burnt powder, their lips cracked and bleeding from salt-petre in the cartridges bitten by them," wrote Carr. The men's clothes were also covered with dirt and blood. They spent considerable time caring for the dead and wounded. During the initial phases of the battle, their dead comrades were tenderly pulled out of the way, but as the battle raged, they were either unceremoniously tossed aside, or more likely stepped or sat on as the men repelled attack after attack. The flesh of the dead began to putrefy in the hot July sun, making the men all the more miserable. While most of the wounded in the trenches had head or upper body wounds as a result of the protection of the breastworks, ricocheting bullets often caused wounds to other parts of the body as well. The most dangerous times were not in the trenches, however, but when the men were leaving or entering them. Each company lost at least one man during these times.[73]

While tending to the killed and wounded, an occasional sniper bullet made them aware that a still-dangerous enemy lurked nearby. Several of the regiments were also moved around. For example, the 102nd New York was sent to Wadsworth's Division to the left, and remained in a reserve position until the army pulled out. At about 1:00 P.M. on July 1 the air was filled with projectiles of every sort, as the cannonade preceding the Pickett–Pettigrew–Trimble charge was unleashed. Carr recalled that each man had to make a decision: protect himself against the artillery shells or from the sniper fire that continued through the afternoon. Burying of the dead took place in earnest on July 4, and the men finally were ordered from the battlefield at noon on July 5.[74]

General Greene's exploits have not always received the recognition they deserve. Even George Meade failed to mention the brigade in his official report. Yet, historian Harry Pfanz wrote that while "others had fought well and had done their full duty, Greene's Brigade more than any other had foiled the Confederate attacks and had held the line." The reasons for Greene's success are summarized in his official report of the battle. "The regiments in the intrenchments were relieved from thirty to ninety minutes by others with fresh ammunition and clean arms, going forward at a double-quick and with a cheer, the regiments relieved falling back through their files when they arrived in the trenches, so that the fire was kept up constantly and efficiently over our whole line, and the men were comparatively fresh and their arms in good order, the regiments relieved going to work with alacrity to clean their arms as soon as in rear." Greene's men counted almost 400 dead Confederates in their front and 150 more across the creek. Another 130 were captured. The number wounded was at least double that of the killed, for a loss of over 1500. The losses to Greene's Brigade were minor in comparison—about 300. Almost half of the losses were sustained by the 137th New York, which occupied the embattled right flank. The actions of the brigade were the envy of most of the army. Indeed, General Slocum wrote in his report, "Greene handled his command with great skill, and . . . his men fought with gallantry never surpassed by any troops under my command."[75]

NOTES

1. Tagg, *Generals of Gettysburg*, 155–156.

2. *PAG*, vol. 2, 713; OR 27, 1, 824–825.

3. OR 27, 1, 825, 848.

4. OR 27, 1, 825; Lawrence Wilson, "Charge Up Culp's Hill," *Washington Post*, July 9, 1899.

5. OR 27, 1, 759, 826–827; Tagg, *Generals of Gettysburg*, 156.

6. OR 27, 1, 827–828.

7. Charles Horton to John Bachelder, January 23, 1867, Bachelder Papers, New Hampshire Historical Society; OR 27, 1, 833.

8. Busey and Martin, *Regimental Strengths and Losses*, 94, 256.

9. Dyer, *Compendium*, 321; Tagg, *Generals of Gettysburg*, 157–158.

10. *PAG*, vol. 1, 202; OR 27, 1, 835–836; William H. Tallman, "The War of the Rebellion or the Slaveholders War," USAMHI; Nathanial Parmeter, diary, Ohio Historical Center.

11. John Hamilton Se Cheverell, *Journal History of the Twenty-Ninth Ohio Veteran Volunteers* (Cleveland, OH, 1883), 69–70; OR 27, 1, 825; Henry J. Knapp, "Gettysburg By a Soldier in the Ranks," *Jefferson Gazette*, February 12, 1912; William H. Tallman, "The War of the Rebellion or the Slaveholders War," USAMHI.

Sergeant William Tallman recalled that the column continued its march later, between 3:00 and 4:00 P.M.

12. OR 27, 1, 836, 839; *PAG*, vol. 1, 202; vol. 2, 714–715; Bates, *Pennsylvania Volun-*

teers, vol. VII, 552; Lawrence Wilson, "Candy's Brigade at Little Round Top: The First Union Troops to Occupy Little Round Top," *National Tribune*, June 26, 1902.

Both regiments were under the command of Colonel J. H. Patrick of the 5th Ohio.

13. Kevin E. O'Brien, "A Perfect Roar of Musketry: Candy's Brigade in the Fight for Culp's Hill," *Gettysburg Magazine* (July 1993), issue 9, 84; OR 27, 1, 836, 845; *PAG*, vol 2, 715; Se Cheverell, *Journal History of the Twenty-Ninth Ohio Veteran Volunteers*, 70.

14. S. R. Norris, "Ohio at Gettysburg," *National Tribune*, June 9, 1887.

15. OR 27, 1, 836, 840; *PAG*, vol. 1, 203–204; Se Cheverell, *Journal History of the Twenty-Ninth Ohio Veteran Volunteers*, 70.

There is a great deal of confusion regarding when the brigade began its trek back to Culp's Hill. According to Geary, it was 9:00 P.M., Colonel William Creighton of the 7th Ohio believed it was 11:30 P.M., Candy recalled it was midnight, Captain John Flynn of the 28th Pennsylvania thought it was 12:30 A.M. on July 3, and Captain Wilbur Stevens of the 29th Ohio recalled it was 2:00 A.M. on July 3 (OR 27, 1, 827, 836, 840, 841, 845).

16. *PAG*, vol. 2, 717.

17. J. R. Lynn, "At Gettysburg—What the 29th Ohio Did During the Three Days' Fighting," *National Tribune*, October 7, 1897; O'Brien, "A Perfect Roar of Musketry: Candy's Brigade in the Fight for Culp's Hill," 87; Bates, *Pennsylvania Volunteers*, vol. VII, 552; OR 27, 1, 836–837; Pfanz, *Gettysburg—Culp's Hill and Cemetery Hill*, 228–229.

18. OR 27, 1, 836–837, 839; O'Brien, "A Perfect Roar of Musketry: Candy's Brigade in the Fight For Culp's Hill," 87.

19. OR 27, 1, 841; Wilson, "Charge Up Culp's Hill"; Norris, "Ohio at Gettysburg"; Pfanz, *Gettysburg—Culp's Hill and Cemetery Hill*, 323.

20. OR 27, 1, 841; George L. Wood, *The Seventh Regiment: A Record* (New York, 1865), 158–159; Bertholf, "The Twelfth Corps at Gettysburg," *National Tribune*, May 22, 1893.

21. OR 27, 1, 843.

22. OR 27, 1, 843.

23. *Re-union of the 28th & 147th Regiments, Pennsylvania Volunteers* (Philadelphia, 1872), 6.

24. OR 27, 1, 845; *PAG*, vol. 1, 204–205.

25. OR 27, 1, 837, 844; Eugene Powell to John Bachelder, May 15, 1878 and March 23, 1886, Bachelder Papers, New Hampshire Historical Society; John Mitchell to John Bachelder, August 15, 1887, Bachelder Papers, New Hampshire Historical Society.

26. OR 27, 1, 839.

There is some confusion about the position of these two regiments. Joseph Moore of the 147th Pennsylvania clearly recalled that "to our right one of the Ohio regiments of the brigade was posted." Candy wrote in his report that the 5th Ohio was on the right of his line, but he may have been referring to the time that they had just returned to Culp's Hill. On the other hand, the stone wall that Colonel Patrick referred to would have put the 147th Pennsylvania on the right of the line, and Pfanz believed that this was indeed the alignment (*PAG*, vol. 2, 718; OR 27,1, 836; Pfanz, *Gettysburg—Culp's Hill and Cemetery Hill*, 311).

27. OR 27, 1, 836, 846; *PAG*, vol. 2, 717–718; George Thomas, "The Confederate Monument at Gettysburg," in *Southern Historical Society Papers* (1886), vol. 14, 444–446.

O'Brien believes that the charge was later than 8:00 A.M. Pardee recalled in his official report ("A Perfect Roar of Musketry: Candy's Brigade in the Fight for Culp's Hill," 93).

28. *PAG*, vol. 2, 719.

29. *PAG*, vol. 1, 205, vol. 2, 720; Wood, *The Seventh Regiment: A Record*, 158; OR 27, 1, 841.

30. OR 27, 1, 837, 841; Wilson, "Charge Up Culp's Hill"; O'Brien, "A Perfect Roar of Musketry: Candy's Brigade in the Fight for Culp's Hill," 94.

31. Lawrence Wilson, *Itinerary of the Seventh Ohio Volunteer Infantry, 1861-1864, With Roster, Portraits, and Biographies* (New York, 1907), 254; Se Cheverell, *Journal History of the Twenty-Ninth Ohio Veteran Volunteers*, 72; *PAG*, vol. 1, 204–205.

Candy reported that few men were buried until July 5, when the brigade's pioneer corps arrived with appropriate tools (OR 27, 1, 837).

32. Busey and Martin, *Regimental Strengths and Losses*, 256; *PAG*, vol. 1, 204; vol. 2, 722.

33. Busey and Martin, *Regimental Strengths and Losses*, 95, 256.

34. Dyer, *Compendium*, 321; Tagg, *Generals of Gettysburg*, 159–160.

35. OR 27, 1, 825, 848; Bates, *Pennsylvania Volunteers*, vol. I, 489.

36. *PAG*, vol. 1, 569; "Notes of a Conversation with Brig. Gen. Thomas L. Kane 2d Brigade, 2d Division, 12th Corps," Bachelder Papers, New Hampshire Historical Society; OR, 27, 1, 846, 848–849, 851, 854.

37. OR 27, 1, 825–826, 847, 849, 854; David Mouart, "Three Years in the 29th Pennsylvania Volunteers," Historical Society of Pennsylvania; *PAG*, vol. 1, 569–570, 598; Pfanz, *Gettysburg—Culp's Hill and Cemetery Hill*, 112; William Alexander to John Bachelder, September 2, 1887, Bachelder Papers, New Hampshire Historical Society.

38. OR 27, 1, 849, 853, 854; Mouart, "Three Years in the 29th Pennsylvania Volunteers"; Pfanz, *Gettysburg—Culp's Hill and Cemetery Hill*, 227.

39. *PAG*, vol. 1, 220; Mouart, "Three Years in the 29th Pennsylvania Volunteers"; OR 27, 1, 854; William Rickards to John Bachelder, April 12, 1864, Bachelder Papers, New Hampshire Historical Society.

40. *PAG*, vol. 1, 220, 570–571; OR 27, 1, 849, 855.

41. OR 27, 1, 847, 849, 852, 855; Bates, *Pennsylvania Volunteers*, vol. I, 490.

42. Bates, *Pennsylvania Volunteers*, vol. VI, 957.

43. OR 27, 1, 847, 849, 852; *PAG*, vol. 1, 220.

44. Thomas Kane to Peter Rothermel, March 21, 1874, Pennsylvania State Archives.

45. OR 27, 1, 852, 853.

46. Bates, *Pennsylvania Volunteers*, vol. I, 490.

47. Bates, *Pennsylvania Volunteers*, vol. I, 490; vol. VI, 958; *PAG*, vol. 1, 597; OR 27, 1, 850, 852.

48. OR 27, 1, 847, 855.

49. Busey and Martin, *Regimental Strengths and Losses*, 96, 257.

50. Dyer, *Compendium*, 321; Warner, *Generals in Blue*, 186.

51. James S. Hyde, diary, 137th New York folder, GNMP; Richard Eddy, *History of the Sixthieth Regiment of New York State Volunteers* (Philadelphia, 1864), 259.

52. George K. Carr, *Memoirs of the 149th N.Y. Infantry* (Syracuse, NY, 1891), 134–136; Charles Horton to John Bachelder, January 23, 1867; Sam Lusk, letter, 137th folder, GNMP; OR 27, 1, 855–856.

53. OR 27, 1, 856, 860, 863, 864; *NYG*, vol. 1, 450; Pfanz, *Gettysburg—Culp's Hill and Cemetery Hill*, 211.

54. Carr, *Memoirs of the 149th N.Y. Infantry*, 137; *NYG*, vol. 3, 1013; Jesse H. Jones, "The Breastworks at Culp's Hill," in *Battles and Leaders of the Civil War*, vol. 3, 316; Spence Jansen, diary, 137th New York Folder, GNMP; OR 27, 1, 856, 860.

55. OR 27, 1, 856, 862; *NYG*, vol. 1; 450, vol. 2, 629; Steuben Coon, letter, copy in 60th New York folder, GNMP.

56. OR 27, 1, 862, 863, 866; *NYG*, vol. 2, 629.

57. OR 27, 1, 826–827.

58. OR 27, 1, 861, 862; *NYG*, vol. 3, 1013; Coon, letter.

59. Carr, *Memoirs of the 149th N.Y. Infantry*, 138–139; Lusk, letter.

60. Coon, letter.

61. OR 27, 1, 861.

62. George S. Greene, "The Breastworks at Culp's Hill," in *Battles and Leaders of the Civil War*, vol. 3, 317; OR 27, 1, 826–827, 856, 857, 866; Jay Jorgensen, "Holding the Right: The 137th New York Regiment at Gettysburg," *Gettysburg Magazine*, (July 1996), issue 15, 65; Henry Rudy, "Memoir," DeWitt Historical Society of Tompkins County, copy in 137th folder, GNMP); Carr, *Memoirs of the 149th N.Y. Infantry*, 139.

63. OR 27, 1, 857.

64. OR 27, 1, 861, 865, 867, 868.

65. OR 27, 1, 861, 865; Hyde, diary; *NYG*, vol. 1, 451; Pfanz, *Gettysburg—Culp's Hill and Cemetery Hill*, 217.

66. Carr, *Memoirs of the 149th N.Y. Infantry*, 140; OR 27, 1, 861, 863, 865; Eddy, *History of the Sixtieth Regiment of New York State Volunteers*, 261.

67. OR 27, 1, 863, 865, 867.

68. Carr, *Memoirs of the 149th N.Y. Infantry*, 143; Pfanz, *Gettysburg—Culp's Hill and Cemetery Hill*, 457 (n. 61).

69. James Hyde, diary; Carr, *Memoirs of the 149th N.Y. Infantry*, 140–141.

70. Carr, *Memoirs of the 149th N.Y. Infantry*, 141.

71. OR 27, 1, 868; *NYG*, vol. 3, 1019.

72. Rudy, diary.

73. Carr, *Memoirs of the 149 N.Y. Infantry*, 143–144; Hyde, diary; Lusk, letter.

74. OR 27, 1, 861, 865; Carr, *Memoirs of the 149th N.Y. Infantry*, 146; Rudy, diary; Jansen, diary; Ira Jeffers, letter, copy in the 137th New York folder, GNMP; Hyde, diary.

75. OR 27, 1, 759, 857–858; Pfanz, *Gettysburg—Culp's Hill and Cemetery Hill*, 352, 381; Alpheus Williams to John Bachelder, December 1863; Busey and Martin, *Regimental Strengths and Losses*, 257.

CONFEDERATE BRIGADES

FIRST CORPS—

Lieutenant General James Longstreet

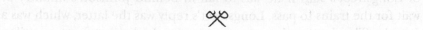

With the death of Stonewall Jackson, General James Longstreet became Robert E. Lee's closest confidant. A poor student at West Point, he found glory in the Mexican War while carrying the flag at Chapultapec. He served as paymaster at a series of outposts, and intended to enter the Confederate army in the same capacity. His experience was too valuable for this duty, however, and he was assigned a brigade at First Manassas. Promoted to the rank of major general on October 7, 1861, and given a division, he fought in the Peninsula and the Seven Days battles. Given one of the two newly formed wings of the army, Longstreet performed well in subsequent battles. With the army's reorganization following the battle of Chancellorsville, Longstreet retained three veteran divisions. Two of them, McLaws's and Hood's, were among the finest fighting units in the army. Not enthralled with Lee's plan to invade the North a second time, Longstreet agitated for a defensively-offensive campaign. This put him at odds with Lee and helped spell doom for the Confederates at Gettysburg.[1]

Longstreet's Corps broke camp at Fredericksburg and marched toward Culpeper Courthouse on June 3. After spending almost two weeks around the latter town, the three divisions left for the Blue Ridge Mountain gaps on June 15. Here the corps helped General Jeb Stuart's cavalry, which was tangling with persistent Union troopers. The corps continued northward in the Shenandoah Valley on June 23, and Pickett's Division crossed the Potomac River on June 25. The two other divisions crossed into Maryland the following day. The officers found a large supply of whiskey in Williamsport, and the general officers decided to give each man a gill. According to division commander Lafayette McLaws, "I never heard of any one refusing it." The men were therefore in "good humor" despite their wet condition.[2]

The corps entered Pennsylvania and reached Chambersburg on June 27, going into camp about a mile beyond it. Leaving Pickett's

Division behind, the two other divisions continued their march toward Gettysburg on June 30. July 1 found the two divisions by the side of Chambersburg Road at 8:00 A.M., while Johnson's Division (Second Corps) marched past. Knowing that the Second Corps's train was behind Johnson's Division, General McLaws asked Major John Fairfax of Longstreet's staff if he was to fall in behind Johnson's infantry or wait for the trains to pass. Longstreet's reply was the latter, which was a mistake. The slow-moving wagon train stretched about fourteen miles, and seriously delayed the arrival of the two divisions that most believed were the best in Lee's army.[3]

Longstreet's Corps did not finally take to the road until 4:00 P.M. on July 1. Within an hour, the men could hear the sounds of battle up ahead. They responded with cheers and instinctively increased their pace. The weary solders were finally permitted to bivouac after midnight. The final leg of the march to Gettysburg began around 3:00 A.M. the following day, and the column reached Seminary Ridge a few hours later.

General Longstreet was unhappy with Lee's battle plan. He believed that Lee originally contemplated a defensive campaign, where the First Corps would hold off the Army of the Potomac, while the two other corps would destroy it. Lee abandoned the concept of a defensive campaign, and Longstreet's frustrations boiled over when his commanding officer began giving direct orders to General Lafayette McLaws, one of his division commanders. After a short confrontation, Lee prevailed, but according to McLaws, Longstreet "appeared as if he was irritated and annoyed." The plan was to move into position on the Confederate right without being seen, then wheel to the left and find Meade's flank.[4]

Although Lee wanted to continue the battle on the morning of July 2, Longstreet convinced him to wait until Law's Brigade arrived from picket duty near New Guilford. While waiting for orders to move his division to its assigned position, McLaws could see the enemy arriving, "hour after hour, on to the battleground." Orders to move out finally arrived at about 1:00 P.M., and McLaws's Division led the column. Marching along Herr Ridge, McLaws realized that his men could be plainly seen by Federal troops on Little Round Top as they ascended a hill near Black Horse Tavern. McLaws immediately halted the column and conferred with Longstreet, who decided to order a countermarch. McLaws returned to his command in a foul mood, "saying things I would not like to teach my grandson . . . to repeat," reported one of the foot soldiers. Retracing their steps, the two divisions followed Willoughby Run to their jumping off points on Seminary and Warfield Ridges. The ordeal lasted over two hours, so the units were not in position until just after 3:00 P.M. Hood's Division formed on McLaws's right on the southern portion of Seminary Ridge and Warfield Ridge.[5]

The attacks began between 4:00 and 4:30 P.M., when Law's Brigade (Hood's Division) stepped off. Hood's three other brigades attacked in succession. McLaws's Division continued the attacks on Hood's left, beginning at about 5:00 P.M. Ultimately, the corps captured Devil's Den/Houck's Ridge, the Wheatfield, the Peach Orchard, and the southern end of Cemetery Ridge. However, rapidly fading light, the exhausted condition of the men, and the appearance of fresh enemy infantry ultimately spelled doom to Longstreet's attempts to crush the Federal left. The men remained in their positions that night.

Pickett's Division arrived by midafternoon of July 2. After much discussion and disagreement, Longstreet was assigned the task of crushing the Union center on July 3. In addition to Pickett's fresh division, Longstreet was given Heth's entire division (now under General James Pettigrew) and two brigades of Pender's Division (now under General Isaac Trimble). Captain James Hutter of the 11th Virginia (Kemper's Brigade) recalled that General Lee and Longstreet conversed in an apple orchard near his regiment on Seminary Ridge. The men could see that their corps commander was against the charge. Longstreet apparently told Lee that "his command would do what anybody of men on earth dared to do but no troops could dislodge the enemy from their strong position." General Pickett disagreed, as did Lee, and the South's fate was sealed.[6]

The repulse of "Pickett's Charge" did not end the battle for Longstreet's men. Later that afternoon, a charge by units of the Federal V Corps resulted in the capture of a large chunk of the 15th Georgia (Benning's Brigade, Hood's Division). Farther to the south, General Elon Farnsworth launched an ill-fated cavalry charge against Hood's right flank that was easily beaten off.

After the war, a number of old soldiers and historians concluded that Longstreet's sulking caused the attacks on July 2 to be delayed and uncoordinated and, ultimately, to fail. Although Longstreet vigorously defended his actions and attacked others after the war, many modern historians continue to believe that his behavior contributed to the Southern defeat.[7]

MCLAWS'S DIVISION—

Major General Lafayette McLaws

Major General Lafayette McLaws had much in common with his corps commander, James Longstreet. Both were large, stout men who sported heavy beards, were poor students at West Point, and excelled on battle-fields where a rugged defense was required. Although he began the war at the head of a regiment, McLaws was quickly promoted and assumed command of a division during the siege of Yorktown. Promotion to the rank of major general occurred on May 23, 1862.[8]

McLaws's Division was one of the finest in the army. Composed of brigades from Georgia, Mississippi, and South Carolina, it was a stable fighting force that had won accolades on many battlefields. The division's high point was at the battle of Fredericksburg, where it occupied rifle pits at the base of Marye's Hill and beat back charge after Federal charge. It also had the potential for glory at the battle of Chancellorsville, where it helped blunt the Federal drive against Lee's rear. McLaws was reluctant to seize the offensive, but if he had, he could have potentially destroyed a Federal army corps. McLaws had also received criticism during the Sharpsburg campaign for not pushing his troops hard enough as they came to the aid of Lee's beleaguered army.[9]

McLaws's Division marched with Longstreet's column from its camps around Fredericksburg to the Gettysburg battlefield, arriving near Marsh Creek after midnight on July 2. The march continued later that morning, when McLaws approached Herr Ridge. General Lee summoned McLaws and told him, "General, I wish you to place your division across this road [Millerstown Road] . . . and I wish you to get there if possible without being seen by the enemy," while pointing to a map at the same time. When asked if he could do it, McLaws told Lee that he saw no reason why he couldn't, but requested permission to reconnoiter. Lee rejected this request, telling McLaws that Captain Samuel Johnston of his staff was about to venture forward. McLaws immediately asked permission to accompany him. General Longstreet, who had been pacing back and forth a short distance away, entered the conversation at this point and blurted out, "No, sir, I do not wish you to leave your division." Then approaching the map, he contradicted Lee's placement of the division. Lee immediately replied, "No, General, I wish it placed just perpendicular to that." McLaws's second request to accompany Johnston was rejected, and instead, the bulky commander sent an aide in his place.[10]

After completing the circuitous march to his position in the late afternoon, McLaws positioned his division on the southern end of Seminary Ridge, with Kershaw's Brigade on the right and Barksdale's on the left. Semmes's Brigade was behind Kershaw's and Wofford's was behind Barksdale's. The men were almost immediately exposed to Federal artillery fire. Told that no enemy troops were in front of him, McLaws was shocked to actually see the enemy "massed in my front, and extended to my right and left as far as I could see." Matters only got worse when Longstreet insisted that McLaws post a battery along his front. McLaws protested that it would draw Federal cannon fire, but Longstreet was not to be denied, and soon shells were falling among the infantry.[11]

Kershaw's Brigade did not attack until shortly after 5:00 P.M., and Barksdale, Semmes, and Wofford followed in succession, but with gaps of time in between. As a result, the attacks were disjointed. McLaws's men captured the Peach Orchard, and with Anderson's Brigade (Hood's Division), took the Wheatfield. Although several of McLaws's units approached Cemetery Ridge and Little Round Top, they were not successful in forcing the enemy off these strategic points. One Federal soldier watching this approach wrote that the "rebel line was badly broken . . . it was a crowd without any tangible line." McLaws's men were not engaged on July 3. Shortly after the Pickett–Pettigrew–Trimble charge, McLaws received orders from Longstreet to pull his men back to Seminary Ridge. McLaws was clearly unhappy with these orders—his men had fought hard to capture these advanced positions. Longstreet permitted no discussion, so McLaws reluctantly withdrew his troops.[12]

Kershaw's Brigade—Brigadier General Joseph Kershaw

Units: 2nd South Carolina, 3rd Carolina, 7th South Carolina, 8th South Carolina, 15th South Carolina, 3rd South Carolina Battalion
Strength: 2183
Losses: 649 (179-419-51)—29.7%[13]

Brigadier General Joseph Kershaw's Brigade was one of the most stable in the army. General Milledge Bonham initially commanded it during the summer and fall of 1861, but when he resigned in January 1862, the unit passed to Joseph Kershaw of the 2nd South Carolina. The brigade had seen action on many battlefields. During Seven Days campaign, the brigade had opened the fight at Savage Station, and a few days later, charged up Malvern Hill in what amounted to a suicide mission. The brigade helped captured Maryland Heights overlooking Harper's Ferry during the Maryland campaign, thus sealing the town's fate, and it performed admirably at the battle of Sharpsburg. The brigade's finest hour was at the battle of Fredericksburg, where it took position behind a stone wall, and, with Cobb's (later Semmes's) Brigade, beat back charge after charge.[14]

General Joseph Kershaw was considered by many to be among Lee's finest brigadiers. An influential South Carolina attorney before the war, Kershaw had fought in the Mexican War and was a member of the South Carolina legislature that voted to secede from the Union. Orphaned at the age of seven, he gained his station through hard work and effective performance. His bravery was unquestioned. At Fredericksburg his insistence on remaining on his horse earned the accolades of both friend and foe.[15]

Kershaw's men were proud to be part of Lee's invading army. A veteran unit, it had fought in all of the campaigns of the Army of Northern Virginia. Corporal Tally Simpson of the 3rd South Carolina wrote home, "our army is strong and in fine spirits, and has the most implicit confidence in Genl Lee." He was less enthusiastic about the quantity of food available, writing that "I ate my day's ration at one mouthful—not one meal, but one mouthful. What do you think of that?" Another soldier wrote that "we had to live on one pound of flour to the man for four days. I had to eat wheat. I would take it and Boil it in a cup and salt it and then eat it and it was good at least it [was] good to a hungry man." This soldier

also pointed out another shortcoming: "I am Bare Footed—havent [sic] got a Shoe to my name." Poor food and deteriorating shoes made the long marches especially difficult.[16]

Being so far from home, the men paid close attention to the women. An unidentified member of the 2nd South Carolina wrote home that Pennsylvania "has [some] of the finest land in it in the world and some of the ugliest women that I ever saw. They are mostly Dutch." Simpson (3rd South Carolina) agreed. "I saw a great many young ladies, but none very pretty. In fact I have not seen a really pretty girl since I have been in Penn." He wrote home that "the women are what you would call the flat-headed dutch, while gals are ugly, broad-mouthed specimens of humanity." But he did find them "always neat and clean and very industrious." Lieutenant Colonel Franklin Gaillard of the 2nd South Carolina observed that many of the women and girls wore U.S. flags on their smocks, and many "held their noses and made faces" at the Southern soldiers.[17]

Since many of the men were from rural parts of South Carolina, they were keenly interested in the countryside. Simpson wrote that the "country is very thickly settled . . . each farmer, whether rich or poor, has a fine barn or granary as large [as] . . . the hotels in Pendleton [S.C.]." He also found, "it strange to see no negros [sic]." A soldier from the 2nd South Carolina wrote, "they have the finest houses you ever saw. All made of Brick and there is a house every half mile."[18]

Simpson found the citizens they passed to be "frightened almost to death. They won't take our money, but for fear that our boys will kill them, they give away what they can spare." The soldiers, Simpson wrote, "harbor a terrific spirit of revenge and steal and pillage in the most sinful manner." Soldiers, like Simpson, with an upper-class upbringing, could not bring themselves to plunder, but were powerless to stop it.[19]

The men reached Chambersburg on June 27 and remained in the vicinity though June 30, when the march continued to Fayetteville. Any hopes of quickly reaching the battlefield on July 1 were quickly dashed, as Anderson's and Johnson's Divisions were ahead of them, as were the Second Corps's wagon trains. The men were ordered to cook three days' rations while waiting. The column reformed in the road at 4:00 P.M., and marched to within two miles of Gettysburg, halting at about midnight. The men could hear the distant sound of cannon fire during parts of the march, and Captain Pulliam of the 2nd South Carolina exclaimed, "Boys, that sounds familiar," as the column hurried on. The 2nd South Carolina came to rest for the night near a large house filled with the wounded of Hill's Third Corps.[20]

Kershaw was told that night that he was to lead McLaws's column, which was to leave at about 4:00 A.M. on July 2. The time came and went, and it was not until sunrise that the column got under way. Kershaw was ordered to halt at the road leading to Black Horse Tavern. The men rested there until noon to begin the infamous march to the right, where Longstreet attempted to shield his two divisions from the view of the enemy on Little Round Top. The men watched as Longstreet and McLaws rode forward to reconnoiter, then returned, "both manifesting considerable irritation," according to Kershaw. A soldier in the 3rd South Carolina described McLaws's language as being very "raw," noting that their division commander was "saying things I would not like my grandson to repeat."[21]

After completing the circuitous march, Kershaw deployed his brigade behind a stone wall on Seminary Ridge shortly after 3:00 P.M. The South Carolinians could see General Longstreet and his staff up in front of them, observing the Federal position with their binoculars. The men marveled that their commander never flinched despite the intense artillery fire that this group attracted. Upon returning, Longstreet gave orders directly to Kershaw. He recalled that they were to "advance my brigade and attack the enemy at that point [Peach Orchard], turn his flank, and extend along the crossroad, with my left resting toward the Emmitsburg Road." After the attack commenced, Kershaw was to "sweep down the enemy's line in a direction perpendicular to our then line of battle." This action would hit the supposedly vulnerable Federal left flank. A battery arrived and took position along Millerstown Road, parallel to Kershaw's line of attack. With his men in position, Kershaw had a chance to scrutinize the enemy's position. He did not like what he saw. "An advanced line occupied the Peach Orchard, heavily supported by artillery . . . the intervening ground was occupied by open fields, interspersed and divided by stone walls. The position here seemed almost impregnable." Even if he were successful in capturing the Peach Orchard, his right and rear would be exposed to a deadly fire from other parts of the Federal line. Kershaw communicated these concerns to General McLaws, who responded that Hood's Division would clean out the Federals on his right, and Barksdale's Brigade would hit the line on his left. Behind him was Semmes's Georgia Brigade, ready to give support when needed.[22]

At 4:00 P.M. Kershaw was told to commence the attack when he heard the signal from Cabell's Battalion. This would take the form of three individual guns firing sequentially. To ensure that all of his regiments stepped off at the same time, Kershaw conveyed this order to each commanding officer. They would all be expected to commence their attack without receiving orders from their commanding officer. The brigade was deployed from left to right as 8th South Carolina–3rd South Carolina Battalion–2nd South Carolina–3rd South Carolina–7th South Carolina. The 15th South Carolina was deployed farther to the right, where it supported Cabell's artillery.[23]

The men could hear the sounds of battle on their right and knew that Hood's men were engaging the enemy. Suddenly, at about 5:00 P.M., three cannon shots rang out, and Kershaw's men leaped to their feet and began their charge. Kershaw proudly wrote after the war that his men moved forward "with great steadiness and precision, followed by Semmes with equal promptness." Because of the numerous obstructions, Kershaw and his officers advanced on foot. During the initial phases of the attack, at least until the men reached Emmitsburg Road, General Longstreet accompanied Kershaw. As Longstreet wished him well and began his journey back to Seminary Ridge, Kershaw was stunned to hear Barksdale's drummers beating assembly. He had expected the Mississippians to advance at the same time on his left, but now he knew that his left would be "squarely presented to the heavy force of infantry and artillery at and in rear of Peach Orchard."[24]

This caused Kershaw to change his plans. He had originally intended to hit Stony Hill in front of him, then wheel around and hit the Peach Orchard in the flank. Now knowing that there would be nothing to distract the Federal artillerymen from raking his lines, Kershaw decided to send the left side of his line, composed of the 8th South Carolina, 3rd South Carolina Battalion, and 2nd South Carolina, against the Federal batteries in the Peach Orchard. The right side of his brigade continued its march toward Stony Hill. Kershaw noted that prior to making this change, the regiments advanced "majestically across the field . . . with the steadiness of troops on parade." The line was raked with a severe artillery fire which, in the words of Kershaw, "rendered it difficult to retain the line in good order." Lieutenant Alex McNeill of the 2nd South Carolina called this "the most terrible fire to which they ever were exposed."[25]

Private John Coxe of the 2nd South Carolina would never forget the "deathly surging sounds of those little black balls as they flew by us, through us, between our legs, and over us!" Private William Shumate of the same regiment graphically described what it was like to charge across an open field in the face of massed Federal cannon fire:

> Kershaw's Brigade moved . . . in perfect order and with the precision of a brigade drill, while upon my right and left comrades were stricken down by grape and canister which went crashing through our ranks. It did seem to me that none could escape. My face was fanned time and again by the deadly missiles. We had arrived within one hundred yards of the battery and had not fired a shot. The artillerists were limbering up their pieces to retire.[26]

To the right of the 2nd South Carolina, the 3rd South Carolina and 7th South Carolina passed on either side of the Rose farm buildings, causing the two regiments to overlap. Seeing this development, Kershaw ordered the 7th South Carolina to move to the right to correct the alignment. This order caused many casualties in the 2nd South Carolina, which had been steadily advancing against the Federal artillery in the Peach Orchard. The men knew that it would take but a few more minutes to reach their objective. However, an unknown officer from the 2nd South Carolina, seeing a sister regiment move to the right, ordered his men to conform to this movement. Writing slightly tongue in cheek, Private W. Johnson of the regiment wrote, "guess they thought we had had enough sight-seeing from the front, and now we were to have a side view." According to Private Shumate, the men were stunned when they heard the order, but "true to our sense of duty we immediately obeyed the command." The Federal gunners were also stunned, but it was for a different reason. In the process of abandoning their positions, they stopped, loaded their guns, and poured a destructive fire into the ranks of the almost helpless South Carolinians. Lieutenant Colonel Gaillard wrote that "we were in ten minutes or less, terribly butchered . . . I saw half a dozen at a time knocked up and flung to the ground like trifles . . . there were familiar forms and faces with parts of their heads shot away, legs shattered, arms torn off, etc."[27]

The survivors of the 2nd South Carolina found a depression and quickly sought shelter there from the murderous hail of canister. However, a Federal cannon was positioned to fire into it, killing and wounding many more South Carolinians. The losses became less severe when the men lay down, and some enterprising souls fired at the artillerymen to silence the deadly gun.[28]

While the left regiments were being slaughtered, the right wing had driven back the Union line and reached Stony Hill between the Peach Orchard and Wheatfield, where they opened fire on the Federal batteries in the Peach Orchard. Looking to his left, Kershaw was relieved to see Barksdale's men appearing, and with his own 8th South Carolina and 3rd South Carolina Battalion, moving to engage the enemy in the Peach Orchard. The results were better than expected. While the Mississippians hit Graham's Brigade (Humphreys's Division, III Corps) head on from the west, the two South Carolina units hit them from the south, causing the line to crumble. Kershaw's anger with General Barksdale was evident in his official report: "this brigade [Barksdale's] then moved so far to the left as no longer to afford me any assistance."[29]

Kershaw's angst was compounded when his right wing was assailed by Zook's Brigade and the Irish Brigade (Caldwell's Division, II Corps) as it took position on Stony Hill. Kershaw's two regiments, numbering eight hundred men, were up against almost double their number. So sudden was this attack that the South Carolinians were not able to take up sound defensive positions. While Zook's Brigade engaged the two regiments in their front, part of the Irish Brigade hit the 7th South Carolina on its right flank. A resourceful Kershaw immediately undertook three activities to bolster his precarious position: he ordered his right flank refused; he ordered his 15th South Carolina, which was over to the right supporting Cabell's artillery battalion, to move quickly to the aid of his beleaguered line; and he loped back to find General Semmes to request immediate assistance. Semmes had been wounded just before Kershaw reached him, but was lucid enough to order his successor, Major William Gist, to move the brigade forward to the South Carolinians's assistance by plugging the gap between the latter and Anderson's Brigade. During this action the 3rd South Carolina's flag was attracting a hot fire. Four color guards had already been shot down, causing the men near the flag to yell, "Lower the colors, down the flag." The color bearer, in an act of defiance against his own comrades, waved the flag even more forcefully and yelled out "this flag never goes down until I am down." The flag did not go down on this day. [30]

As the 7th South Carolina exchanged volleys with the Irish Brigade at a distance of less than two hundred yards, one of Semmes's regiments, probably the 50th Georgia, advanced at a double-quick pace and opened fire on the enemy. A gap of about a hundred yards still existed between the right of the 7th South Carolina and the left of the 50th Georgia, which the veterans of the Irish Brigade were quick to exploit. According to Kershaw, the two sides exchanged fire from less than thirty paces, and the right of the 7th South Carolina was refused even more, until, in the words of Kershaw, "the two wings of the regiment were nearly doubled on each other." The 15th South Carolina arrived shortly thereafter, and found that parts of Semmes's Brigade prevented it from linking up with the rest of its brigade. For some reason, Kershaw did not bring it around the rear of Semmes's Brigade to plug the gap in the line. Instead, it fought separately from its sister units. Kershaw admitted after the war that the "position of the 15th Regiment [was] wholly unknown to me." [31]

Over on Kershaw's left, the combined charge of Barksdale's Brigade, the 8th South Carolina, and at least part of the 3rd South Carolina Battalion had forced the Federal batteries from their positions in the Peach Orchard. This relieved the 2nd South Carolina from the deadly enemy artillery fire it was receiving and which had caused the regiment to lose over 40% of its men—the highest losses in the brigade. Seeing that the 2nd South Carolina was now able to rise, Kershaw quickly ordered it to the rescue of his beleaguered right flank. Almost immedi-

ately after giving this order, the pressure on the 7th South Carolina was so great that it finally broke, and Kershaw ordered its commanding officer, Colonel D. Wyatt Aiken, to reform it at a stone wall, two hundred yards to his right, in the rear of the Rose farm. Aiken described the movement as being made with "considerable confusion, though no demoralization." Parts of the 50th Georgia were also forced back, leaving only the 3rd South Carolina on Stony Hill, which was now under a furious attack on its front and right flank by Zook's Brigade and the Irish Brigade. Like the 7th South Carolina before it, its right flank was refused to face the enemy on two fronts. To complicate matters even further, some soldiers from the 50th Georgia had become mingled with the 3rd South Carolina, reducing the officers' ability to direct their men competently. General Kershaw later wrote that "amid rocks and trees, within a few feet of each other, these brave men, Confederates and Federals, maintained a desperate conflict." Realizing that the 3rd South Carolina was in danger of being cut off and captured en masse, Kershaw reluctantly ordered it back to the Rose farm as well. [32]

A dejected Kershaw followed his defeated men back to the buildings. With Semmes's Brigade also defeated and Barksdale's moving north, the situation looked grim. As Kershaw emerged from the woods, he was overjoyed to see General William Wofford leading his Georgia brigade into battle on the left. Private John Coxe of the 2nd South Carolina described it as "an almost perfect Confederate line of battle just entering the woods, hotly engaging and driving the Federal infantry." Wofford rode up to the 2nd South Carolina and asked its men to join him. Thus, while the 7th and 3rd South Carolinians assumed defensive positions at the Rose farm against the still advancing

Federal troops, Wofford, with Kershaw's left wing, composed of the 8th South Carolina, 3rd South Carolina battalion, and 2nd South Carolina, hit Stony Hill, which was occupied by Zook's Brigade. The 15th South Carolina, and some of Semmes's regiments, also attacked the Irish Brigade at this time. Before long, the exhausted Federal soldiers from both brigades were streaming to the rear.[33]

As the two Federal brigades pulled out, Sweitzer's Brigade was ill advisedly returned to the Wheatfield to stem the Confederate drive. It was a major blunder, resulting in the near destruction of the brigade, as it was hit by Anderson's Brigade, the 3rd South Carolina Battlion, 8th South Carolina, 2nd South Carolina, 15th South Carolina, and assorted regiments from Semmes's Brigade. Coxe (2nd South Carolina) noted that as the men rushed forward to engage the Federal troops, a "tremendous Rebel yell went up from our powder-choked throats." Kershaw's men continued fighting hard here, capturing two Federal flags in the process. The commander of the 4th Michigan fought valiantly to prevent his flag's capture. A newspaper account written shortly after the battle accurately described what occurred. "A Federal officer attempted to use his sword, which one of the men wrenched from his grasp and thrust his bayonet into him." Colonel Harrison Jeffords lost both his flag and his life in the process. Still another Federal brigade, Burbank's, ventured into the Wheatfield, and it too was attacked by Kershaw's, Semmes's, Anderson's, and Wofford's Brigades, and forced to retire. With the defeat of Sweitzer's and Burbank's Brigades, the now exhausted Confederate units continued their advance toward Little Round Top.[34]

Darkness was now descending on the battlefield, and the men were ordered to break off the assault. Few men from Kershaw's Brigade described the attack of the Pennsylvania Reserves (V Corps) and Wheaton's Brigade (Shaler's Division, VI Corps). As Johnson (2nd South Carolina) approached Little Round Top, he saw "several lines of battle posted on the hillside so that they could shoot over the heads of the men in front. We got close up and kept the men who were attempting to fire some guns which were posted there thinned out so that they could not do much. But the lines of battle fired into us and many of our troops fell . . . the men began to fall back . . . we retreated in good order, loading and firing on the Yanks. We reached the edge of a woods and here we made a stand." Colonel Gaillard of the same regiment recalled that the bullets "literally came down upon us as thick as hailstones."[35]

Kershaw assembled his brigade and Semmes's behind a stone wall at the Rose farm. Here the men built fires and rummaged through the Federal haversacks for food. Later that night, the brigade moved to the left to the Peach Orchard, which the unit's left wing had helped clear earlier in the evening. About noon on July 3, Kershaw was ordered to reoccupy the position near the Rose farm. Later that afternoon, Longstreet ordered Kershaw to the right, to connect with the right of Hood's Division, parts of which were under attack by Farnsworth's Brigade of cavalry.[36]

One of the finest brigades in the Army of Northern Virginia, Kershaw's Brigade met with mixed success at Gettysburg. When the brigade cooperated with others, the results were usually positive, as it helped clear the Wheatfield and Peach Orchard of Federal troops. However, such was not the case on the right of the line, where, possibly because of the early wounding of Semmes, there was little cooperation. It was a very confused evening for Kershaw, as he admitted in his official report that his brigade was so scat-tered that he lost touch with much of it. For example, he did not know the location of the 15th South Carolina.[37]

Barksdale's Brigade—Brigadier General William Barksdale

Units: 13th Mississippi, 17th Mississippi, 18th Mississippi, 21st Mississippi
Strength: 1620
Losses: 804 (156-470-178)—49.6%[38]

Barksdale's Brigade had forged a distinguished record on every battlefield. The individual regiments initially tasted battle at First Manassas, but were not brigaded together. That occurred when they were shifted to Brigadier General Nathan Evans's Brigade soon after the battle. The brigade next took on Colonel Edward Baker's expeditionary force at the battle of Ball's Bluff in early October 1861, exacting a dreadful toll on the Federal troops. The Mississippians received a new brigade commander the following month. Brigadier General Richard Griffith led the brigade during the Peninsula campaign, but was mortally wounded at the battle of Savage Station.[39]

William Barksdale of the 13th Mississippi assumed command of the brigade after Savage Station and led it to Gettysburg. A strong fire-eater, Barksdale was an attorney by training and subsequently served as a quartermaster in the Mexican War. He was a congressman when the war broke out, but quickly resigned to join the Confederate army. His first battle as brigade commander was at Malvern Hill, where he grabbed a flag and led his men up the hill. His fiery nature and love of battle were exhibited in many subsequent engagements. During the Maryland campaign, Barksdale's men were influential in capturing Harper's Ferry and then at the battle of Sharpsburg helped crush a Federal division. These were but preludes to even more glory. Barksdale's men patrolled the streets of Fredericksburg prior to the great battle there in December 1862. They tenaciously restricted the Federal troops from crossing the Rappahannock River, and when they finally did cross, Barksdale's men engaged them in street fighting. The Mississippians's star rose even higher at the battle of Chancellorsville, where they alone stood on Marye's Heights and held off a Federal corps for several hours.[40]

The brigade crossed the Potomac River on June 26. The men noted that the water was very cold and two feet deep. The brigade, along with the rest of the division, made swift progress through Maryland and crossed the Pennsylvania state line the next day. Private Robert Moore of the 17th Mississippi recorded in his diary that "we find but few sympathizers & and are not disappointed." The same day, General Lee's orders about respecting private property were read to the men. Nevertheless, Moore recorded that the "souldiers [sic] are committing some depredation on private property."[41]

The men were not above playing tricks on others, including their commanding officer. Private John Henley of the 17th Mississippi recalled that when the men saw General Barksdale approaching, they began looking up into a tree, pretending to see someone in its upper branches. "I reckon you will come down out of that tree, now, the General has come," they yelled out. Curious, Barksdale halted below the tree and intently gazed upward. "Of course there was no one up the tree, so we had a good laugh," reported Henley. Barksdale did not think it funny, and angrily announced that it was "insubordination." The men played a similar prank on a farmer, causing him to rush over to his apple trees.[42]

The men received rations of flour and "some pretty good beef" at about noon on July 1. Many used the flour to make shortening bread. Before it was completely cooked, however, the Long Roll beat, and the men rolled up their blankets, collected their other scant belongings, and took their place in line. However, General Edward Johnson's Division appeared on the road, causing a delay in the march. Private William Abernathy of the 17th Mississippi uncharitably wrote after the war that Johnson's Division "came piling into the road from some place they ought not to have been, and we lay there waiting for them to pass."[43]

After Johnson's men had passed, a wagon train appeared. According to Abernathy, the major who led it "had less sense and more obstinacy than any army mule in Longstreet's Corps." When the wagon train finally passed, Barksdale's men jumped to their feet and the march to Gettysburg continued. According to Private Moore, the march finally got under way at about 4:00 P.M., and continued until about midnight, when the column reached Marsh Creek.[44]

The men were roused at about 4:00 A.M. on July 2, and the final leg of the march to Gettysburg began soon after. Henley (17th Mississippi) recalled that the brigade reached the vicinity of Gettysburg at about 9:00 A.M. The column halted near Lee's headquarters, where Chambersburg Pike intersected Seminary Ridge. The men rested there until approximately 11:30

A.M., when they received orders to march to the right. None of the participants described the circuitous march to the Confederate right flank on Warfield and Seminary Ridges, but Major George Gerald of the 18th Mississippi recalled the men turning to the right off Chambersburg Pike "into the woods and after moving through the timber for some distance halted and the order was given to 'strip for the fight.'"[45]

When the two-division column about-faced to retrace its steps, Barksdale's Brigade now formed the rear of the division. As a result, it formed the left flank of the division when it finally reached its final position on Seminary Ridge. To its left was Wilcox's Brigade (Anderson's Division, Third Corps) and to its right was Kershaw's Brigade. The brigade was deployed from left to right as 18th Mississippi–13th Mississippi–17th Mississippi–21st Mississippi. The men could see open fields, fences, and scattered farmhouses in front of them. According to General Longstreet, Barksdale's orders were to capture the elevated ground at the Peach Orchard "that General Lee desired me to take and hold for artillery."[46]

The men watched as Moody's and Gilbert's batteries plied their trade in front of them. Unfortunately, many of the Federal rounds hit both the batteries and Barksdale's infantry. A veteran of many battles, Private William Hill of the 13th Mississippi recorded in his diary that the cannonading was the "most terrific that I ever heard." George Leftwich of the 17th Mississippi noted that the projectiles "tore the limbs off of the trees and plowed gaps through his men." Those units occupying unprotected positions were especially hard hit. "They killed so many of our artillerymen that some of the infantrymen had to go and help them handle the guns," recalled Henley (17th Mississippi).

The men remained under this artillery fire for at least ninety minutes. Despite the psychological difficulty of being under an artillery barrage, Barksdale's men held up well. In fact, they were ready for a fight. "Never was a body of soldiers fuller of the spirit of fight, and the confidence of victory," wrote John McNeily of the 21st Mississippi. The men chatted with each other and filled their canteens; some broke off branches of cherry trees to get the fruit.[47]

Speaking at a reunion of veterans in 1878, division commander Lafayette McLaws noted that "Barksdale had been exceedingly impatient for the order to advance, and his enthusiasm was shared in by his command." Barksdale was probably both anxious to get at the enemy and also to vacate his present position in Pitzer's Woods, which was being raked by artillery fire. Two or three times Barksdale approached McLaws, pleading, "General, let me go; General let me charge." But McLaws had not yet received orders to this effect and told his "fiery impetuous Mississippian" to be patient. When Longstreet appeared, Barksdale could not restrain himself and rode up to his corps commander, saluted and blurted out, "I wish you would let me go in, General; I would take that battery in five minutes." Longstreet's reply was as patient as McLaws's—"Wait a little—we are all going in presently."[48]

Barksdale was at least now given his orders. Assembling his regimental officers, he pointed to the high ground along Emmitsburg Road and said, "The line before you must be broken—to do so let every officer and man animate his comrades by his personal presence in the front line." The officers below the rank of general were told that they would make the charge on foot because of the "difficulty of replacing the horses killed," noted Major George Gerald.[49]

The time had finally arrived. Captain G. B. Lamar noted that "when I carried him the order to advance his [Barksdale's] face was radiant with joy!" Just before 6:00 P.M., the men could see General Barksdale riding along the rear of their line, which was the signal for the regimental commanders to prepare for action. The men stripped off their scant belongings and threw them in a pile by regiment, with one man left to guard them. The command of "Attention" could soon be heard ringing through the ranks. McNeily likened the command to an electric shock, for it "brought every man of his regiment up standing." By this time Barksdale had reached the end of the line, turned, and rode in front of his line, stopping in front of his old regiment, the 13th Mississippi. The men could see that "stamped on his face, and in his bearing, as he rode by, was a determination 'to do or die.'" As Barksdale halted and faced the enemy, Colonel Benjamin Humphreys of the 21st Mississippi yelled for his men to "move forward and swing to the left." Major Gerald of the 18th Mississippi recalled that the order was "dress to the colors and forward to the foe!" Private Joseph Lloyd of the 13th Mississippi noted that his colonel gave the following string of orders: "Attention! Fix bayonets! Forward march. Double quick march. Charge bayonets."[50]

The men had not gone far when they heard the command, "Double-quick, charge!" and the line of battle responded accordingly. McNeily noted that the brigade, "yelling at the top of their voices, without firing a shot, . . . sped swiftly across the field and literally rushed the goal." Henley (17th Mississippi) recalled that "we went in perfect line. They would knock great gaps in our line. Then we would fill up the gaps and move on." Leftwich of the same regiment agreed. "When a solid shot tore a gap in your ranks it was instantly closed up, and the Brigade came on in almost perfect line."[51]

As the line moved rapidly forward, some of the men of the 21st Mississippi on the right flank could see that Kershaw's Brigade had obliqued toward the right, leaving their own right flank exposed. Those on the opposite flank could not see any support on their left either, as Wilcox's Brigade had not yet stepped off. As a result, Barksdale's men moved swiftly forward unsupported. The 21st Mississippi on the right of the line smashed into the Peach Orchard salient occupied by Graham's Brigade (Birney's Division, III Corps), while the 18th Mississippi on the left of the line approached the Sherfy buildings, filled with Pennsylvanians. In between, the 13th Mississippi and 17th Mississippi took on the rest of Graham's Brigade.[52]

The 21st Mississippi on the right crossed Emmitsburg Road and continued on without pausing. It soon ran into the 68th Pennsylvania of Graham's Brigade and the 2nd New Hampshire of Burling's Brigade (Humphreys's Division, III Corps). The Federal troops held their ground, forcing the 21st Mississippi to stop at a fence, probably the one bordering Wheatfield Road, until the 17th Mississippi arrived on its left. Before long the Federal troops began to back out. McNeily recalled that the Federal troops "fought back bravely, retiring slowly until the firing was at close quarters, when the retreat became a rout in which our men took [a] heavy toll for the losses inflicted on them." Many of the Federal troops tried to hide behind boulders, but were quickly captured. General Joseph Graham supervised the defense along this part of the line, and several Confederate soldiers observed his actions. "General Graham with becoming courage rode out of the orchard behind

his men. His horse was wounded and pitched the General over his head, leaving him in a dazed state of mind," recorded McNeily. The 21st Mississippi quickly snatched him up along with hundreds of other prisoners, and sent them rapidly to the rear. Several cannon were also captured at this point in the battle.[53]

Over on the opposite end of the brigade, the 18th Mississippi rapidly approached the Sherfy buildings, where it encountered units of the 57th Pennsylvania. After driving these troops back, the men could see that many Federal troops had taken refuge in the farm buildings and were throwing a deadly fire into their ranks. According to Major George Gerald, "[I] called to the colonel and the lieutenant colonel that the barn was occupied by the enemy and must be taken; they failed to respond promptly and I called to the men that the barn must be captured and to follow me and I would open the door." So heavy was the Federal fire that Gerald and his men could only see dense smoke filling the barn. "They followed me with a rush . . . and within less than two minutes we had killed, wounded or captured every man in the barn," Gerald recounted.[54]

In the center of the brigade, the 13th Mississippi and part of the 17th Mississippi ran into the 114th Pennsylvania and parts of the 57th Pennsylvania. Lloyd (13th Mississippi) recalled that "scarcely a minute and we are at the barn and scaling the fences at the lane and right across and in among the enemy and literally running over them." The 17th Mississippi to the right hit the 114th Pennsylvania in the front and flank. Henley wrote that the Federal "regiment began to run, and we commenced firing on them, and they ran in crowds. You could not shoot without hitting two or three of them." He recalled that as the Mississippians continued forward, they ran into other Pennsylvania units, probably remnants of the 114th and 57th Pennsylvania and the intact 105th Pennsylvania "posted behind an embankment, and they killed lots of our boys." Most of the 17th Mississippi, with the 21st Mississippi to their right, crossed Emmitsburg Road where they took on the flank of the 68th Pennsylvania and 2nd New Hampshire, driving them back. Federal reinforcements in the form of the 73rd New York from Brewster's Brigade (Humphreys's Division, III Corps) were also swept away. A wounded Captain Frank Moran of the latter regiment recalled how the 13th Mississippi charged past him, "firing and shrieking like Indians."[55]

These troops were quickly dispatched, and the 13th, 17th, and 18th Mississippi swung northward along the Emmitsburg Road, where they caught Carr's and Brewster's Brigades on the flank and sent them reeling as well. Barksdale actively encouraged his men, shouting to them, "Forward men, forward," which Major Gerald recalled was the only command he uttered.[56]

As the three regiments swung to the north, Colonel Humphreys's of the 21st Mississippi could see several batteries in front of him taking a toll on Kershaw's Brigade on his right. He realized that they could also send an enfilading fire against Barksdale's men, so he drove his men toward the guns, causing Clark's battery to limber up to leave. However, the volleys from the Mississippians, combined with the Confederate artillery fire, killed and wounded a number of horses, forcing the battery to leave a caisson behind. Thompson's battery on the right of Clark's suffered a similar fate. Some of the cannons, like Bigelow's, were pulled back with prolonges, or long ropes while they continued firing. Up ahead, Bigelow's battery took a new position near the Trostle barn.

Whitelaw Reid, the former minister to England, was present on the battlefield as a correspondent for the *Cincinnati Gazette* and happened to see the desperate fight between the battery and the 21st Mississippi. "Reserving his fire a little, then with depressed guns opening with double charges of grape and canister, he smites and shatters, but cannot break the advancing line . . . he falls back on spherical case, and pours this in at the shortest range. On, still onward, comes the artillery-defying line, and still he holds his position. They are within six paces of the guns—he fires again. Once more, and he blows devoted soldiers from his very muzzles . . . They spring upon his carriages and shoot down his forces." John Bigelow wrote that the "enemy crowded to the very muzzles . . . but were blown away by the canister . . . the air was dark with smoke . . . the enemy were yelling like demons, yet my men kept up a rapid fire, with their guns each time loaded to the muzzle." In the end, the 21st Mississippi captured four of Bigelow's guns.[57]

After dispatching Bigelow's battery, Watson's battery galloped up and deployed for action, again preventing Humphreys from reuniting with the rest of the brigade. The 21st Mississippi overwhelmed this battery in short order as well. In fact the regiment was moving so rapidly that it captured the battery before it even had a chance to fire a shot. After the war, Humphreys recalled this moment:

> From the position I occupied then, no enemy could be seen or heard in my front. Nor a gun was being fired at me. The federal army was cut in twain. Eight hundred yards, to my right a confused mass was retreating, driven by McLaws, and Hood. I attempted to turn the guns just captured on them but no rammers or friction wires could be found. Eight hundred yards to my left, the enemy's line was kept busy by Barksdale.[58]

Before long, Humphreys could see both groups giving way. The situation quickly changed when the 39th New York (Willard's Brigade, Hays's Division, II Corps) drove forward on the Mississippians' left. A short time later, a dense mass of blue-clad figures suddenly materialized in front of him, which proved to be Lockwood's Brigade (Ruger's Division, XII Corps). Humphreys quickly ordered his men to retreat. They reluctantly left the five guns from Watson's battery, and in their haste, could not pull any of Bigelow's guns off the field either. They did spike one of the Napoleons though.[59]

While Humphreys's 21st Mississippi was crossing Plum Run, driving a wedge in the Union line, the rest of the brigade continued northward. While seemingly achieving great success, its future was becoming increasingly precarious. Barksdale's three remaining regiments were badly disorganized. Major Gerald of the 18th Mississippi vividly recalled that during this part of the battle "Our entire line of battle . . . were badly scattered and in great confusion." Still the three regiments moved on under the orders of "forward with bayonets." The colonels of the 17th Mississippi and 18th Mississippi pleaded with Barksdale to halt to reform his line, but he would hear nothing of it. "No—Crowd them—we have them on the run," was his reply. The men approached Plum Run. No Federal troops were in view and it appeared that they had successfully breached the Federal center, possibly forcing the enemy to vacate Cemetery Ridge. A volley suddenly rang out from the other side of the run. Barksdale's slim and disordered lines were now up against a fresh Federal brigade, Willard's (Hays's Division, II Corps).[60]

Barksdale was mortally wounded around this time. He was hit several times in his leg and foot, and sustained a large wound to his left breast, which was thought to have been caused by a cannon projectile. One of his men later noted that Barksdale "had a very thirst for battlefield glory, to lead his brigade in the charge." According to one of the men, Barksdale's last words were to "tell his family that he loved them, and that he died at his post." Colonel Thomas Griffin of the 18th Mississippi now took command of the brigade, but he was wounded in a matter of minutes.[61]

After exchanging volleys with Willard's Brigade for several minutes, the remaining officers realized that they were without support and that their lines were sadly depleted. The sun was setting, and the men soon heard the orders to retire. Falling back to Emmitsburg Road, the regiments reunited with the 21st Mississippi and bivouacked near the Peach Orchard. While some of the men fell into a deep sleep, others, like Major George Gerald, resisted, as he was afraid that the full moon could encourage a night attack, similar to the one made at Chancellorsville a few months before.[62]

Colonel Humphreys took command of the brigade during the morning of July 3, and was ordered to "drive the enemy pickets as far as they will go." General Lee rode by that morning and asked about the identity of the troops. Major George Gerald responded that "it is what is left of Barksdale's Brigade." Lee ordered the unit back toward Seminary Ridge to "prevent the artillery from being harassed by federal infantry." While there, the brigade was ordered to take cover down when the great bombardment preceding the Pickett–Pettigrew–Trimble charge began. After losing over half its men during July 2, the brigade lost but six on July 3, mostly through "premature explosion from both sides during the bombardment."[63]

Many of the men jumped to their feet to watch Pickett's men attack the Union center. "The enemy concentrated their fire on the charging line, endeavoring to demoralize it, and at one time I saw a concentrated fire cut out nearly all of the men in the line for thirty or forty yards like grass before a reaper, but the line closed up and moved on towards the heights without ever losing the step," recalled Major George Gerald. The brigade spent July 4 resting, and began the retreat at 2:00 A.M. on July 5.[64]

Barksdale's Brigade's actions were among the most spectacular of the battle. It almost single-handedly defeated two Federal brigades (Graham's and Brew-

ster's), causing each to sustain heavy losses, and materially helped defeat a third (Carr's). It also temporarily captured at least nine cannon. The cost was heavy, as the Mississippians lost about half of their men in an attack that was eventually blunted. Private Moore probably best summed up the men's feelings when he recorded in his diary during the evening of July 2, "our loss was heavy . . . Every man acted the hero. Miss. has lost many of her best & bravest sons. How thankful should all be to God who have escaped. Oh! The horrors of war." Moore would not be so lucky in his next battle—he would die at the battle of Chickamauga.[65]

Semmes's Brigade—Brigadier General Paul Semmes

Units: 10th Georgia, 50th Georgia, 51st Georgia, 53rd Georgia
Strength: 1334
Losses: 432 (80-261-91)—32.4%[66]

Although the 10th Georgia had been with the Army of Northern Virginia since September 1861, the three other regiments were not mustered into service until the late winter–early spring of 1862, and spent their initial months on the South Carolina–Georgia coast. They were transferred to the Army of Northern Virginia in June–July 1862 and were finally combined into Semmes's Brigade in November 1863. Thus, while all four regiments had seen combat, they did not enter a battle as a unit until the Fredericksburg campaign.[67]

Their commander, Brigadier General Paul Semmes, was a banker and plantation owner prior to the war. Entering the war as colonel of the 2nd Georgia, he was in command of General Lafayette

McLaws's old brigade by the spring of 1862. He fought at Savage Station and Malvern Hill, and helped capture Harper's Ferry during the Maryland campaign. After the battle of Sharpsburg, the brigade was reorganized to contain only Georgia regiments. Semmes's Brigade served in a reserve capacity at Fredericksburg, but showed its mettle at the battle of Chancellorsville, where it helped blunt the advance of a Federal V Corps division and later helped halt an entire Federal corps. After their successes at Chancellorsville, the men were ready for more action as the army moved north.[68]

The brigade crossed the Potomac with "much jollity and merriment," recalled Judge L. Cochran of the 10th Georgia. It marched rapidly through Maryland and then into Pennsylvania. The townspeople of Greencastle, Pennsylvania, lined the streets to watch the Confederates pass "with as much apparent curiosity as if we had been orangoutangs [sic] or baboons," wrote one of the soldiers of the 10th Georgia. "We were clad in garments very much damaged by hard usage," noted the soldier. When a private overheard a smirk about the soldiers' clothes, he merely smiled and said, "We don't put on our best clothes when we go out to kill hogs."[69]

The men spent the next day and a half in Chambersburg, where, as one soldier put it, the men spent time "testing the qualities of Pennsylvania poultry." Despite Lee's orders to the contrary, many of the men "seemed to consider the private impressment of supplies an imperative duty incumbent upon us in retaliation for the marauding of the Yankees in our country," wrote one of the men. William Stillwell of the 53rd Georgia wrote home that the "peple [sic] hear [sic] are mostly Duch [sic] it hurts them very bad to see the rebble [sic] occupying thare [sic] country we don't disturb eny [sic] thing but what we need [sic] to eat . . . the peple [sic] looked very sour and crest faling [sic] though they hope we will git [sic] whiped [sic] at the capital [Harrisburg]." The men were also issued whiskey along the way, and cherries were to be had in abundance.[70]

Marching second in line behind Kershaw's Brigade, Semmes's men arrived near Herr Ridge on the morning of July 2. Here they participated in the circuitous march to their position on the southern part of Seminary Ridge. "We kept marching to and fro, backward and forward, until about three o'clock P.M.," wrote Private Stocker of the 10th Georgia. The brigade finally took position about fifty to seventy-five yards in the rear of Kershaw's Brigade, which it was to support. According to modern historian John Imhof, the brigade was arrayed, from left to right, as

50th Georgia–10th Georgia–51st Georgia–53rd Georgia. Cochran (10th Georgia) recalled surveying the ground in front of the brigade. "In our front was an open field, some six or eight hundred yards across. Beyond this, and on our left were hills and mountains, bristling with Federal bayonets and cannon." The regimental officers encouraged the men while waiting for orders to advance. Sergeant William Pendleton of the 50th Georgia noted that Lieutenant Colonel Francis Kearse "addressed each company, telling the men to fight and win." Any enthusiasm that was generated by the short speech was probably dissipated when the men were ordered to fall in before the canteen carriers had returned. The men would thus go into the fight without water.[71]

The Federal artillery took its toll as the line of battle advanced across the open plain. Pendleton noted that "we moved forward over a hill into an open field where we were under fire. We came to a road [Emmitsburg Road] with high fences on both sides; the firing was getting hotter. I wondered if I would ever get across the fences. We were going toward a Peach Orchard, but were ordered to right oblique. The firing was very heavy and dangerous." Cochran (10th Georgia) recalled how the "men sprang quickly into line, and the brigade moved slowly forward into the open field, and then 'hell broke loose' from every hill in our front, and on our left burst such a roar of artillery and such a storm of shot and shell as we had never faced before; it was Malvern Hill all over again, but on a grander scale." Another soldier from the regiment agreed. "Charge after charge of grape shot, canister shot, shells, etc., came whizzing through the air in a continuous stream of destruction . . . the greatest wonder with us was how any of us survived."

Many didn't, including Lieutenant Colonel Kearse.[72]

The line of battle halted to the right of the Rose farm buildings. Up ahead and to their left, they could see Kershaw's South Carolinians engaged with the enemy. As the sounds of the conflict escalated, the men knew that it was just a matter of time before they would be called forward. Some of the soldiers on the left of the line may have seen General Kershaw striding quickly toward General Semmes with a plea for assistance. General Semmes was mortally wounded at this time.

As the brigade swept forward to try to close the gap between Kershaw's and Anderson's Brigade, the 50th Georgia on the left of the line advanced faster than the others and took position to the right of Kershaw's 7th South Carolina. A gap still existed between the two brigades, however. Major Peter McGlashan of the 50th Georgia noted, "a dense and large mass of infantry suddenly arose, poured in a destructive fire of musketry and charged." The 50th Georgia threw a volley into the Irish Brigade (Caldwell's Division, II Corps), causing it to halt momentarily. Over to the right, the rest of the brigade ran through an open meadow and into the concentrated firepower of Brooke's Brigade, which had just taken position behind trees and boulders at the edge of Rose Woods. "We then advanced about 60 yards and stopped behind some rocks, which however, did not afford much protection because they only projected from 12 to 18 inches above the surface. . . . .many fell along this line," recalled a soldier in the 10th Georgia. The line buckled, and then fell back.[73]

Over on the left, the relentless pressure in the gap caused Kershaw's right-most regiment, the 7th South Carolina, to pull back. The pressure was also too great for

some of the 50th Georgia of Semmes's Brigade, and they too fell back. Some of the remaining members of the 50th Georgia became mingled with the 3rd South Carolina on Stony Hill, weakening the overall command structure.

Caldwell's Division, which had valiantly held its ground in the Wheatfield, was in a tough position. With Wofford's Brigade now bearing down on its right flank, Kershaw's and Semmes's on its front, and Anderson's Brigade on its left, it was finally forced to retreat through the Wheatfield. As Semmes's Brigade followed, some of the men stopped at Rose Run for a quick drink, even though swirls of blood were evident in the water. Continuing on, the brigade, together with Anderson's, Kershaw's, and Wofford's Brigades, smashed into Sweitzer's Brigade (Barnes's Division, V Corps) and then Burbank's (Ayres Divison, V Corps). In a fit of excitement, Pendleton (50th Georgia) yelled to his men, "Let's show we can fight in Pennsylvania as well as in Virginia."[74]

Moving forward, the brigade approached Little Round Top. But night was falling, and soon the men received orders to fall back. That night, few men could sleep because of the groans of the wounded all around them. The next day, the men cared for the wounded and helped bury the dead. Later in the day, the brigade was moved to the right to relieve Anderson's Brigade. The men returned to their original position during the morning of July 4 and remained there until after nightfall, when they joined the retreat to Virginia.[75]

Semmes's Brigade played a small role during the battle. After its commanding officer was killed, the brigade battled Brooks's Brigade, and ultimately assisted in the destruction of Sweitzer's Brigade in the Wheatfield.

✄

Wofford's Brigade—Brigadier General William Wofford

Units: 3rd Georgia Sharpshooters Battalion, 16th Georgia, 18th Georgia, 24th Georgia, Cobb's Legion, Phillips's Legion
Strength: 1627
Losses: 370 (48-184-138)—22.7%[76]

Although most of the units were initially brigaded together under Brigadier General Howell Cobb, the 18th Georgia was part of Hood's Texas Brigade during the Peninsula campaign and subsequent Seven Days battles and did not join the brigade until November 1862.[77]

The brigade first tasted battle at Yorktown, where it helped defend the town from McClellan's forces. It was subsequently involved in battles at Seven Pines, Savage Station, Malvern Hill, and Sharpsburg. General Howell Cobb left the army in October 1862, and command of the brigade passed to his brother, Brigadier General Thomas Cobb. The subsequent battle of Fredericksburg was Cobb's and his brigade's finest hour. Stationed behind a stone wall, they beat back a series of Federal charges. Cobb was mortally wounded during the fight, and Colonel William T. Wofford of the 18th Georgia was promoted to the rank of brigadier general to date from January 1863 and given the brigade.[78]

A lawyer and planter prior to the war, Wofford also served in the Georgia legislature and, as a Democrat, voted against secession. Because of his prominence and limited experience in the Mexican War, Wofford assumed command of the 18th Georgia and fought with Hood's Texans for most of 1862. When Hood was elevated to division command, Wofford was temporarily given command of the Texas Brigade, which he fought with at the battle of Antietam. Ambitious by nature, he assumed command of Cobb's Brigade before the battle of Chancellorsville and showed skilled and tenacity. Like all of McLaws's other brigade commanders, Wofford had been tested on the battlefield.[79]

The Georgians enjoyed the bounty of food around them as they marched through Maryland and southern Pennsylvania. Lieutenant Marcus Green of Phillips's Legion recorded in his diary on June 28, "I got plenty of good brandy and chickens, butter, load of bread, cherry last night." Corporal Tally Simpson of the 3rd South Carolina (Kershaw's Brigade) was not at all pleased that Wofford's men were living it up, and wrote to his family, "last night Wofford's Brig of this div stole so much that they could not carry what rations they drew from the commissary."[80]

As could be expected, the Northern citizens were less than enthusiastic about their Southern "guests." Surgeon William Shine of the Phillip's Legion noted that the Chambersburg residents "all look very sour at us as we passed through. A great many sharp things were said to them by the troops who seemed to be in a fine humor." The men could not resist teasing the citizens by asking the distances to Philadelphia, Baltimore, and Washington, D.C.[81]

After spending a few days at Chambersburg, the brigade was ordered to take the road to Gettysburg with the rest of McLaws's Division on July 1. Because two other divisions preceded them, as did the Second Corps's wagon trains, the brigade did not move out until about 4:00 P.M. Earlier that day, at about 10:00 A.M., the men cold see General Lee and his staff ride by them toward Cashtown. "He was looking in perfect health, & seemed happy as the troops cheered him, he rode by hat in hand," noted Surgeon Robert Myers of the 16th Georgia. The march continued until about midnight, when the column reached the vicinity of Marsh Creek. Surgeon Myers felt the fatigue, admitting in his diary that he, "marched or rather dragged along with Capt Conyers." The next morning the men waited until almost noon when they were finally ordered to the right on their circuitous march to form the right flank of Lee's army.[82]

The trek to their positions in Pitzer's Woods on Seminary Ridge finally ended when they halted in the rear of Barksdale's Brigade. None of the officers in Wofford's Brigade filed an official report of their actions at Gettysburg, so the disposition of the units is not known. Two modern historians differed in their perspectives. John Imhof had the brigade arranged from left to right as Cobb's Legion–Phillip's Legion–24th Georgia–18th Georgia–16th Georgia. A recent Wofford biographer believed that the brigade was disposed in its "typical" manner, from left to right, as Phillip's Legion–Cobb's Legion–16th George–24th Georgia–18th Georgia. The 3rd Georgia Sharpshooters was deployed as skirmishers.[83]

The men watched intently as first Kershaw's Brigade attacked the Federal positions along Emmitsburg Road, followed by Barksdale's Brigade. The Mississippians of the latter brigade were achieving greater success with the Federals at the Peach Orchard than Kershaw's men in the Wheatfield/Stony Hill sector. After being in reserve, Wofford was finally ordered forward. Almost immediately, a hundred-yard gap formed within the 24th Georgia as it moved through the row of Confederate artillery. Seeing the problem, Wofford rode over to the regiment and waved his hat as he urged them on. The men responded by double-quicking. Watching

Wofford's heroics, Confederate battery commander Captain W. W. Parker yelled, "Hurrah for you of the bald-head." His cannoneers took up the cry and cheered the men as they rushed past. Enemy artillery opened fire on the brigade as it broke into the open ground. One shell took out most of one company, leaving only eight men uninjured. Another shell landed in the ranks of the 16th Georgia, killing eight and wounding twenty-one. However, the gunners were much more concerned about the immediate threats posed by Kershaw's and Barksdale's Brigades, and therefore the losses in the rest of the brigade were light. General Longstreet apparently rode part of the way with the brigade, and told the men to "cheer less and fight more."[84]

As the victorious Mississippians of Barksdale's Brigade swung left (north) to take on Humphreys's Division on Cemetery Ridge, Wofford ordered his men to continue moving straight ahead, which caused their line of battle to stretch across Wheatfield Road and move parallel with it. The left of the brigade skirted the Peach Orchard, while the right of the four hundred-yard line moved toward Stony Hill and the Wheatfield. Surgeon William Shine of the Phillips's Legion noted that "our Men charged the Enemy with a terrific Yell, peculiar to the Southerners on all such occasions." The right side of the 18th Georgia on the brigade's right wing approached the exposed flank of Zook's Brigade, forcing it to the rear. Sergeant Gilbert Frederick of the 57th New York recalled that Wofford's Brigade was "marching steadily with colors flying as though on dress parade, and guns at right-shoulder-shift." Zook's withdrawal caused a chain reaction, which ultimately forced Caldwell's entire division from the Wheatfield. This was a critical time, as Kershaw's Brigade had been roughly handled by Zook's Brigade and the Irish Brigade. John Coxe, a member of the 2nd South Carolina, recalled how Wofford rode over to his regiment with a request that the South Carolinians form on his right as the charge continued:

Wofford took off his hat and, waving it at us, turned back and charged along his line to the left. And here was seen how the right sort of officer can inspire his men to accomplish next to superhuman results. Always Wofford rode right along with his men during a fight, continually furnishing examples and cheering them with such words as, "Charge them, boys." Those who saw it said they never saw such a fine military display as Wofford's line of battle as it advanced from the pike. He went right for those Federal cannons that were firing at us. Nor did it take him long to reach those batteries and smash them even before the gunners had time to turn their guns upon him. Rushing over the artillery, he kept right on and tackled the Yankee infantry in the woods beyond. And his assault was so sudden and quickly executed that the Federal lines of infantry were smashed and gave way at every point in Wofford's way . . . it became a regular rout.[85]

While Wofford's Brigade did not actually engage Caldwell's Division on Stony Hill and the Wheatfield, or Birney's Division in the Peach Orchard, it played a major role in the Federal defeats. According to historian Harry Pfanz, Wofford's Brigade "was a fresh, disciplined body of men that intimidated the battered and disorganized Federals . . . its appearance gave new life and hope to Kershaw's and Semmes's men on it right." A member of the 118th Pennsylvania of Tilton's Brigade, which was forced to fall back under the irresistible advance of the Georgians, described them as "moving obliquely, loading and firing with deliber-

ation as they advanced, begrimed and dirty-looking fellows, in all sorts of garb, some without hats, others without coats, none apparently in the real dress of uniform of a soldier."[86]

With Tilton's Brigade and Caldwell's Divisions extracted from their positions, the Georgians continued their advance. Although they probably did not directly engage Sweitzer's Brigade when the latter reentered in the Wheatfield, Wofford's Brigade probably acted as one arm of a pincer, which forced the ill-fated Federal brigade to retreat with heavy losses. Wofford's Brigade also engaged the right flank of Burbank's Brigade (Ayres's Division, V Corps), when it attempted to relieve Sweitzer's Brigade.[87]

Wofford's men quickly took on Walcott's battery, just south of the J. Weikert farm. According to a Federal soldier, "General Wofford's Confederate Brigade leaped over the wall, driving back the Regulars, and demanding the battery to surrender. No one seemed to know where they came from, because they sprang over the wall and came up to the guns so quick." All six cannon fell into Wofford's hands.[88]

The grandest prize loomed before them: Little Round Top. As the brigade made its way forward, its men continually overtook the fleeing Federal soldiers, resulting in hand-to-hand combat. "The men would club their guns and use the stocks, killing more than one of the enemy by this novel mode of fighting," reported a newspaper account. As Wofford approached the hill, he could see that it bristled with the men of the newly arrived Federal VI Corps. Upon reaching the hill, the men "met a terrible volley," probably fired by Wheaton's Brigade, which looked ready to charge. General Longstreet was also closely watching the hill and could see that his worn-out men were no match for the fresh muskets of the VI Corps, so he ordered them to break off the attack and return to safety.[90]

A bitter Colonel Goode Bryan of the 16th Georgia wrote after the war, "no troops went so far as my 16th Georgia . . . there were no enemy either in front or on our right to cause us to fall back . . . I was ordered to fall back by a courier from Gen Longstreet . . . seeing Longstreet some distance to my rear I went to him, and requested him not to order us back . . . his reply was I order you to fall back." Bryan went to his grave believing that his men could have won the battle had they been permitted to continue their advance. "If Gen L[ongstreet] had not ordered us to fall back we could have won the day," he wrote.[91]

General Wofford was also angry about the order to withdraw. Following his men through the Trostle Woods with pistol in hand, he spied his division commander, General McLaws, and angrily told him that he should not have been ordered to withdraw. He demanded to know who had ordered it. McLaws replied that he assumed that the order came from Longstreet, and he had to obey it. Always mindful of his reputation, Wofford was especially concerned that his withdrawal might be misconstrued, but he was assured that this would not be the case.[92]

The brigade fell back toward the Wheatfield that night, and the 3rd Georgia Sharpshooters was thrown out on the skirmish line. Wofford ordered the sharpshooters into Trostle Woods the following morning, where they engaged the Federal skirmish line. The fire became so strong at one point that Wofford anticipated an attack and advanced his entire brigade, forming it to the right of the sharpshooters. Generals Lee and Longstreet rode up to him in the morning to ask him if he thought a renewal of the attack could be successful. "I told him that the afternoon

before, I nearly reached the crest. He asked if I could go there now. I replied, 'no General, I think not.'" Lee quickly asked why, and Wofford answered, "General, the enemy have had all night to intrench and reinforce. I had been pursuing a broken enemy and the situation was now very different."[93]

The brigade assumed the role of spectator when Pickett's Division launched its ill-fated charge against the Federal line. The brigade remained in its advanced position until sometime between 4:30 and 5:00 P.M, when it returned to its original position on Seminary Ridge, and was severely shelled by Federal artillery. The following day, the men helped tend the wounded and bury the dead. The retreat began about midnight.[94]

Wofford's charge through the Wheatfield was one of the great actions of the battle. Flanking Zook's Brigade, the Georgians helped to crush Caldwell's Division and force it from the Wheatfield. Little remaining light, growing Federal reinforcements, and hesitant Southern commanders denied Wofford's men the opportunity to try to take Little Round Top. If they had, they probably would have failed.

NOTES

1. Larry Tagg, *Generals of Gettysburg* (Mason City, IA, 1998), 204; Ezra J. Warner, *Generals in Gray* (Baton Rouge, LA, 1959), 192.

2. OR 27, 2, 357–358; Lafayette McLaws, "Gettysburg," *Southern Historical Society Papers* (1879), vol. 7, 64–66; Edwin B. Coddington, *The Gettysburg Campaign* (New York, 1968), 114.

3. OR 27, 2, 358; McLaws, "Gettysburg," 66–67.

4. Richard Rollins, "The Ruling Ideas of the Pennsylvania Campaign: James Longstreet's 1873 Letter to Lafayette McLaws,"

Gettysburg Magazine (July 1997), issue 17, 7; McLaws, "Gettysburg," 68.

5. McLaws, "Gettysburg," 69; William M. Abernathy, *Our Mess: Southern Gallantry and Privations* (McKinney, TX, 1977), 31.

In a letter to his wife after the battle, McLaws placed much of the blame for the defeat of his division on Longstreet. "Longstreet is to blame for not reconnoitering the ground . . . during the engagement he was very excited, giving contrary orders to everyone and was exceedingly overbearing" (Lafayette McLaws to wife, July 7, 1863, McLaws Papers, UNC).

6. J. R. Hutter, letter, Daniel Papers, University of Virginia.

7. Robert K. Krick, "If Longstreet . . . Says So, It Is Most Likely Not True," in Gary W. Gallagher (ed.), *The Second Day at Gettysburg* (Kent, OH, 1993), 57–86.

8. Tagg, *Generals of Gettysburg,* 210; Warner, *Generals in Gray,* 204.

9. Douglas S. Freeman, *Lee's Lieutenants* (New York, 1943), vol. 2, xxxiv; Tagg, *Generals of Gettysburg,* 210–211.

10. Jay Jorgensen, "Wofford Sweeps the Wheatfield," *Gettysburg Magazine* (January 2000), issue 22, 32–33; McLaws, "Gettysburg," 68.

11. McLaws, "Gettysburg," 70, 72, 73.

12. McLaws, "Gettysburg," 87–88; W. H. Sanderson, "Sykes's Regulars," *National Tribune,* April 2, 1891.

13. John W. Busey and David G. Martin. *Regimental Strengths and Losses at Gettysburg* (Hightstown, NJ, 1994), 138, 281.

14. Clement A. Evans, *Confederate Military History.* 12 vols. (Atlanta, GA, 1899), vol. 5, 26, 66, 72–73, 147, 154; Tagg, *Generals of Gettysburg,* 214.

15. Tagg, *Generals of Gettysburg,* 214.

16. Guy R. Everson and Edward W. Simpson, Jr., *Far, Far From Home* (New York, 1994), 249; unidentified, letter, Mike Musick Collection, USAMHI.

17. Unidentified, letter; Everson and Simpson, *Far, Far From Home,* 252, 263; Mac Wycoff, *A History of the Second South Carolina Infantry, 1861–1861* (Fredericksburg, VA, 1994), 177.

18. Everson and Simpson, *Far, Far From Home,* 250, 252; unidentified, letter.

19. Everson and Simpson, *Far, Far From Home,* 250–251.

20. OR 27, 2, 366; Mac Wycoff, *A History of the Third South Carolina Infantry, 1861–1861* (Fredericksburg, VA, 1995), 117; John Coxe, "The Battle of Gettysburg," *Confederate Veteran* (1913), vol. 21, 433.

21. J. B. Kershaw, "Kershaw's Brigade at Gettysburg," in *Battles and Leaders of the Civil War,* vol. 3, 118.

22. OR 27, 2, 367; W.T. Shumate, "With Kershaw at Gettysburg," *Philadelphia Weekly Times,* May 6, 1882; Kershaw, "Kershaw's Brigade at Gettysburg," vol. 3, 332.

23. Joseph Kershaw to John Bachelder, April 3, 1876, Bachelder Papers, New Hampshire Historical Society; Kershaw, "Kershaw's Brigade at Gettysburg," vol. 3, 334; David Aiken, letter, copy in 7th South Carolina file, GNMP.

24. Kershaw, "Kershaw's Brigade at Gettysburg," vol. 3, 334–335.

25. OR 27, 2, 368; Kershaw, "Kershaw's Brigade at Gettysburg," vol. 3, 335; Alex McNeill, letter, 2nd South Carolina folder, GNMP.

26. Coxe, "The Battle of Gettysburg," 434; Shumate, "With Kershaw at Gettysburg."

27. Joseph Kershaw to John Bachelder, March 20, 1876; Wycoff, *A History of the Third South Carolina Infantry, 1861–1861,* 121–122; W. A. Johnson, "The Battle of Gettysburg," copy in the 2nd South Carolina folder, GNMP; Shumate, "With Kershaw at Gettysburg"; Gerald J. Smith, *One of the Most Daring of Men* (Murfreesboro, TN, 1997), 83.

The utter dismay caused by this order did not fade with time. John Coxe wrote, "to think of it makes my blood curdle even though nearly fifty years afterwards—the insane order was given by 'right flank'" (Coxe, "The Battle of Gettysburg," 434).

28. Johnson, "The Battle of Gettysburg."

29. OR 27, 2, 368.

Unfortunately, no first-person accounts are available from the two South Carolina units.

30. OR 27, 2, 368; John Hard, "Memoirs," copy in 7th South Carolina folder,

GNMP; August Dickert, *History of Kershaw's Brigade* (Newberry, SC, 1899), 241.

31. OR 27, 2, 368; Kershaw, "Kershaw's Brigade at Gettysburg," vol. 3, 336, 337.

32. OR 27, 2, 369; Kershaw, "Kershaw's Brigade at Gettysburg," vol. 3, 336–337; D. Wyatt Aiken, "The Gettysburg Reunion," *Charleston News and Courier,* June 21, 1882.

According to W. Johnson of the 2nd South Carolina, his regiment fired into the flank of Zook's Brigade, causing numerous casualties (Johnson, "The Battle of Gettysburg").

33. OR 27, 2, 369–370; Kershaw, "Kershaw's Brigade at Gettysburg," vol. 3, 337; Coxe, "The Battle of Gettysburg," 435.

34. OR 27, 2, 369; Cox, "The Battle of Gettysburg," 435; Wofford Flag Report, National Archives, Microfilm M 474 Roll 71.

35. OR 27, 2, 369; Johnson, "The Battle of Gettysburg"; Coxe, "The Battle of Gettysburg," 435; Gaillard, letter.

36. Coxe, "The Battle of Gettysburg," 435; OR 27, 2, 369.

37. OR 27, 2, 369.

38. Busey and Martin, *Regimental Strengths and Losses and at Gettysburg,* 139, 282.

39. Stewart Sifakis, *Compendium of the Confederate Armies: Mississippi* (New York, 1995), 94, 101, 103; Evans, *Confederate Military History,* vol. 7, 25–26.

40. Evans, *Confederate Military History,* vol. 7, 117, 119, 120, 178; Tagg, *Generals of Gettysburg,* 218–219; Ernest B. Furguson, *Chancellorsville, 1863* (New York, 1993), 261.

41. Robert A. Moore, *A Life for the Confederacy* (Jackson, TN,: McCowat-Mercer Press, 1959), 152; J. S. Henley, "On the Way to Gettysburg," copy in 17th Mississippi Folder, GNMP.

42. Henley, "On the Way to Gettysburg."

43. Abernathy, *Our Mess: Southern Gallantry and Privations,* 29–30.

44. Abernathy, *Our Mess: Southern Gallantry and Privations,* 30; Moore, *A Life for the Confederacy,*153; J. S. McNeily, "Barksdale's Mississippi Brigade at Gettysburg," *Publications of the Mississippi Historical Society* (1914), vol. 14, 233.

45. J. W. Duke, "Mississippians at Gettysburg," *Confederate Veteran* (1906), vol. 14,

216; Henley, "On the Way to Gettysburg"; McNeily, *Barksdale's Mississippi Brigade at Gettysburg,* 234; Judge G. B. Gerald, "The Battle of Gettysburg," *Waco Daily-Times,* July 3, 1913.

46. McNeily, *Barksdale's Mississippi Brigade at Gettysburg,* 235.

47. Henley, "On the Way to Gettysburg"; William H. Hill, diary, Mississississippi Department of Archives and History; George J. Leftwich, "The Carreer [sic] of a Veteran," *The Aberdeen Examiner,* August 22, 1913; McNeily, *Barksdale's Mississippi Brigade at Gettysburg,* 235–236.

48. McNeily, *Barksdale's Mississippi Brigade at Gettysburg,* 241; McLaws, "Gettysburg," 70, 73; William M. Owen, *In Camp and Battle with the Washington Artillery* (Boston, 1885), 245.

49. Claiborne Papers, Southern Historical Collection, University of North Carolina; Gerald, "The Battle of Gettysburg."

50. McLaws, "Gettysburg," 74; McNeily, *Barksdale's Mississippi Brigade at Gettysburg,* 236, 238, 241; Gerald, "The Battle of Gettysburg."

51. McNeily, *Barksdale's Mississippi Brigade at Gettysburg,* 236; Leftwich, "The Carreer [sic] of a Veteran."

52. McNeily, *Barksdale's Mississippi Brigade at Gettysburg,* 235.

53. McNeily, *Barksdale's Mississippi Brigade at Gettysburg,* 236–237; Harry W. Pfanz, *Gettysburg—The Second Day* (Chapel Hill, NC, 1987), 326.

54. Gerald, "The Battle of Gettysburg."

55. McNeily, *Barksdale's Mississippi Brigade at Gettysburg,* 238; Henley, "On the Way to Gettysburg"; Francis E. Moran, "About Gettysburg," *National Tribune,* November 6, 1890.

56. Gerald, "The Battle of Gettysburg."

57. Pfanz, *Gettysburg—The Second Day,* 338–339; McNeily, *Barksdale's Mississippi Brigade at Gettysburg,* 248; John Bigelow to John Bachelder, n.d., Bachelder Papers, New Hampshire Historical Society.

58. McNeily, *Barksdale's Mississippi Brigade at Gettysburg,* 249.

59. Benjamin Humphreys to John Bachelder, May 1, 1876, Bachelder Papers,

New Hampshire Historical Society; Pfanz, *Gettysburg—The Second Day,* 405–406.

60. Gerald, "The Battle of Gettysburg"; McNeily, *Barksdale's Mississippi Brigade at Gettysburg,* 243; Abernathy, *Our Mess: Southern Gallantry and Privations,* 33–34.

61. Jack D. Welsh, *Medical Histories of Confederate Generals* (Kent, OH, 1995), 13–14; McNeily, *Barksdale's Mississippi Brigade at Gettysburg,* 236; Hill, diary.

62. Gerald, "The Battle of Gettysburg."

Major Gerald believed that he was the ranking officer and took command of the brigade during the evening of July 2, and that command shifted to Colonel Humphreys the next morning.

63. Benjamin Humphreys to John Bachelder, May 1, 1876; Gerald, "The Battle of Gettysburg."

64. Gerald, "The Battle of Gettysburg."

65. Moore, *A Life for the Confederacy,* 153–154.

66. Busey and Martin, *Regimental Strengths and Losses at Gettysburg,* 140, 282.

67. Stewart Sifakis, *Compendium of the Confederate Armies: South Carolina and Georgia* (New York, 1995), 205, 264, 265, 267.

68. Evans, *Confederate Military History,* vol. 6, 435–436; Tagg, *Generals of Gettsyburg,* 216–217.

69. "Some Incidents on the March to Gettysburg," copy in the 10th Georgia Folder, GNMP.

70. "Some Incidents on the March to Gettysburg"; William Stillwell, letter, copy in 53rd Georgia folder, GNMP; Constance Pendleton, *Confederate Memoirs* (Bryn Athyn, PA, 1958), 34.

71. "Stocker Recollections," Robert Woodruff Library, Emory University; John D. Imhof, *Gettysburg—Day Two, A Study in Maps* (Baltimore, MD, 1999), 99; Hon. L. L. Cochran, "The Tenth Georgia Regiment at Gettysburg," *Atlanta Journal,* February 23, 1901; Aiken, "The Gettysburg Reunion; Pendleton," *Confederate Memoirs,* 35.

72. Keith Bohannon, "Wounded and Captured at Gettysburg," *Military Images* (May–June, 1988), 14; Pendleton, *Confederate Memoirs,* 35; "Some Incidents on the

March to Gettysburg"; Cochran, "The Tenth Georgia Regiment at Gettysburg"; Lafayette Mclaws, "McLaws Division and the Pennsylvania Reserves," *Philadelphia Weekly Press,* October 20, 1886.

73. "Some Incidents on the March to Gettysburg."

Some of the most famous photographs of Confederate dead are those of Semmes's men in the meadow near the Rose farm buildings. Originally labeled "McPherson" woods, the correct location was ascertained by William Frassanito (*Gettysburg—A Journey in Time* [New York, 1975], 198–201).

74. Pendleton, *Confederate Memoirs,* 35.

75. *Atlanta Journal,* August 31, 1901; Pendleton, *Confederate Memoirs,* 36; OR 27, 2, 403.

76. Busey and Martin, *Regimental Strengths and Losses at Gettysburg,* 141, 282.

77. Sifakis, *Compendium of the Confederate Armies: South Carolina and Georgia,* 215, 219, 229.

78. Evans, *Confederate Military History,* vol. 6, 159–160; Sifarkis, *Who Was Who in the Civil War,* 130, 727.

79. Warner, *Generals in Gray,* 343–344.

80. Everson and Simpson, *Far, Far From Home,* 251.

81. William F. Shine, diary, J. B. Clifton Collection, North Carolina Department of Archives and History.

82. Robert P. Myers, diary, Museum of the Confederacy.

83. Imhof, *Gettysburg, Day Two,* 139; Smith, "One of the Most Daring of Men," 81.

84. "Wofford's Georgia Brigade," *Richmond Daily Enquirer,* August 5, 1863; Jorgensen, "Wofford Clears the Wheatfield," 37; Smith, "One of the Most Daring of Men," 85; McLaws, "Gettysburg," 73; Royal W. Figg, *Where Men Only Dare to Go!: Or the Story of a Boy Company by an Ex-Boy* (Richmond, 1885), 140; Goode Bryan, letter, Southern Historical Collection, University of North Carolina.

85. Shine, diary; Gilbert Frederick, *The Story of a Regiment—The Fifty-seventh New York* (Chicago, 1895), 170–171; Coxe, "The Battle of Gettysburg," 435.

86. Pfanz, *Gettysburg—The Second Day,* 328; Smith, *History of the 118th Pennsylvania Volunteers, Corn Exchange Regiment* (Philadelphia, 1990), 244.

87. "Wofford's Georgia Brigade"; Imhof, *Gettysburg: Day Two,* 184, 191

88. John L. Parker and Robert G. Carter, *Henry Wilson's Regiment—History of the 22nd Massachusetts Infantry . . .* (Boston, 1887), 313.

89. "Wofford's Georgia Brigade"; John L. Smith, *History of the 118th Pennsylvania Volunteers, Corn Exchange Regiment* (Philadelphia, 1909), 244; Wofford Flag Report, National Archieves, Microfilm M 474 Roll 71.

90. "Wofford's Georgia Brigade."

91. Bryan, letter.

92. Smith, *One of the Most Daring of Men,* 90–91; Lafayette McLaws, "Federal Disaster on the Left," *Philadelphia Weekly Press,* August 4, 1886.

93. "Wofford's Georgia Brigade"; Myers, diary; Smith, *One of the Most Daring of Men,* 93.

94. Abner Doubleday, *Chancellorsville and Gettysburg* (New York, 1885), 188; "Wofford's Georgia Brigade"; Myers diary; Smith, *One of the Most Daring of Men,* 93.

HOOD'S DIVISION—

Major General John Hood/
Brigadier General Evander Law

Major General John Hood was arguably the finest division commander in the Army of Northern Virginia. An undistinguished West Point graduate, he served on the Texas frontier under Robert E. Lee. Because his native state of Kentucky did not secede, Hood offered his services to the State of Texas and was given the rank of lieutenant of cavalry. By March 1862, he commanded the Texas Brigade. The brigade soon developed a reputation that was nonparalleled in the army, and equaled that of the Iron Brigade in the Army of the Potomac.[1]

Given command of a division after the Peninsula campaign, Hood and his men nearly destroyed Major General John Pope's army at the battle of Second Manassas. Hood continued to lead the division effectively at the battle of Sharpsburg, where his men slugged it out with the enemy at Miller's Cornfield. The battle of Fredericksburg was relatively quiet for Hood's command, and it missed the battle of Chancellorsville because the division was sent to southwest Virginia with General Longstreet. Therefore, Hood's men were ready for a fight since they had not really engaged the enemy for over eight months.[2]

After crossing the Potomac River at Williamsport on June 26, Hood's men made good time marching through Maryland. Reaching Chambersburg, Pennsylvania, on the afternoon of June 27, the division continued an additional mile, camping in a "grove of magnificent timber." The division remained there until June 30, when Hood's march resumed at 8:00 A.M. The march was a short one, consuming only six miles. The march on July 1 was delayed by the arrival of Johnson's Division of the Second Corps and by army trains. Beginning again at about 4:00 P.M., the division marched until midnight, and finally reached Seminary Ridge at about 9:00 A.M. on July 2.[3]

The division was composed of only three brigades at the time, as Law's Brigade had been detached to guard Lee's flank at New Guilford.

The march to the division's pre-attack position occurred after Law returned during the early afternoon. Following McLaws's Division, the march ground to a halt when the officers realized that the column could be seen from Little Round Top as it ascended a hill near Black Horse Tavern. The men were ordered to backtrack, and reached its jumping off point on Warfield Ridge just before 4:00 P.M. The brigades were arranged in two lines. The first line was composed of Robertson's Brigade on the left and Law's on the right. Anderson's formed behind Robertson's and Benning's behind Law's.[4]

Sitting astride his horse in front of his old Texas Brigade, Hood gave a short speech, then rose in his stirrups and in a commanding voice yelled, "Fix bayonets, my brave Texans; forward and take those heights!" Law's and Robertson's Brigades immediately advanced. Hood was hit by a shell fragment soon after, and General Law took over the division. According to modern historian Harry Pfanz, Law exercised poor leadership of the division. He neglected to appoint one of the regimental commanders to take over his brigade until later in the day, and he did not appear to have provided much guidance to the other brigades. As a result, the division's attacks were uncoordinated. Both Law's and Robertson's Brigades split apart and their regiments fought individually. Benning's Brigade, which was to follow Law's up Little Round Top, instead drove straight forward and wound up slugging it out with the Federal troops holding Devil's Den/Houck's Ridge. While Hood's Division ultimately captured these areas and helped take the Wheatfield, it was unsuccessful in securing the most important prize, Little Round Top. The problems continued on July 3, when during the confused withdrawal back to Warfield Ridge, Benning's 15th Georgia was left behind and subsequently almost destroyed by a Federal attack.[5]

Law's Brigade—Brigadier General Evander Law

Units: 4th Alabama, 15th Alabama, 44th Alabama, 47th Alabama, 48th Alabama
Strength: 1933
Losses: 500 (99-253-148)—25.9%[6]

Although Brigadier General Evander Law commanded an all-Alabama brigade, its history as a fighting unit was fairly short. Prior to being brigaded together, the five regiments had been assigned to no less than three brigades. The 4th Alabama saw heavy fighting at the first battle of Manassas as part of Brigadier General Barnard Bee's Brigade and the 15th Alabama was a member of Brigadier General Isaac Trimble's Brigade that saw considerable action in the Shenandoah Valley campaign. By the battle of Fredericksburg, only the 4th and 44th Alabama had joined Law's Brigade, and it was not until January 1863 that all five regiments were assigned to the brigade. As a result, the brigade had never fought as a unit prior to Gettysburg.[7]

A graduate of The Citadel, Evander Law had established his own military high school in Alabama prior to the war. He recruited a company from the school and soon rose to lieutenant colonel of the 4th Alabama. Wounded at the first battle of Manassas, he assumed command of the regiment when he returned during the fall of that year. When Brigadier General William Whiting assumed command of a division, Law took over his brigade. Law led the brigade at Seven Pines, Gaines's Mill, Malvern Hill, Second Manassas, and Sharpsburg, and was finally promoted to the rank of brigadier general on October 3, 1862. His brigade was only lightly engaged at Fredericksburg and was not present at Chancellorsville. By the Gettysburg campaign, he was acknowledged to be an effective brigade commander.[8]

The brigade had the distinction of being one of the last Confederate brigades to reach the battlefield. Left at New Guilford, Pennsylvania on June 30, the brigade made a "rapid and fatiguing marching of about 24 miles," according to Lieutenant Colonel Lawrence Scruggs of the 4th Alabama. This was the first segment of the march that the men could complain about, as most of the prior ones were not exhausting. After crossing the Potomac, each man had been issued a half gill of whiskey. Most added it to the contents of their canteens to make the treat go farther. As the brigade marched through Greencastle on June 27, the fife and drum corps of the 48th Alabama played the "Bonnie Blue Flag." The brigade stopped there to replenish its supplies. Some of the soldiers walked up to citizens and snatched off their hats, offer-

ing their old ones in return. When the column broke ranks, the men foraged and returned with a wealth of edibles. Captain Henry Figures reported that "some of the army treated the citizens very badly, stole their chickens, milk, butter etc." Figures was particularly repulsed by the waste. "There were a great many sheep killed that were not used."[9]

The brigade continued its march and reached Chambersburg on June 27. As it made its way through the town, some of the women yelled out in derision, "This ain't the way to Harrisburg, now you are skedadling [sic], thought you was going to Washington." The brigade rested nearby with the rest of the division. On the morning of June 30, the brigade was ordered to New Guilford to perform "outpost duty," which amounted to guarding Lee's flank. It was from this small town that the men began what Private W. C. Ward called "the most fatiguing march of the war." Asleep on July 1, "we were awakened by the unwelcome voice of a courier asking to be directed to the Colonel commanding," recalled Captain R. Coles of the 4th Alabama. The messenger was from General Longstreet, ordering the brigade to Gettysburg without delay. According to Coles, the men were on the march at 2:00 A.M.; Longstreet thought it was by 3:00 A.M. Either way, by daybreak the men were ascending the passes through South Mountain and, without a halt, descended toward Cashtown. The men's spirits were buoyed by the large number of Federal prisoners passing to the rear and by the news that the Southern arms had been victorious during the first day's battle. The march continued, and many men began complaining about the lack of rest stops, and more vocally about their empty canteens. General Longstreet wrote long after the battle that Law's twenty-eight-mile march in eleven hours was "the best marching done in either army to reach the field of Gettysburg." It certainly helped that no obstructions blocked their way to the battlefield. As the men approached Gettysburg, Colonel William Oates of the 15th Alabama recalled seeing Generals Lee and Longstreet intently studying the Federal positions while on a nearby hill. The men were finally permitted to rest. Private Ward and others carried their comrades' canteens to a ditch still containing the long-past spring rains. The water was hot and greenish in color, but the men were parched, and they greedily filled their canteens with the vile liquid. The rest was all too short, for the men were ordered up to participate in Longstreet's long circuitous loop to reach its position on Warfield Ridge.[10]

After reaching their assigned position on the extreme right of the Confederate line at about 3:30 P.M., General Law sent out six men to locate the Federal left flank. While waiting for their return, he deployed the brigade in line of battle from left to right as 4th Alabama–47th Alabama–15th Alabama–44th Alabama–48th Alabama. The brigade would have the distinction of being the "brigade of direction" and would lead the assault on the Federal left. The cannonade preceding Hood's charge began shortly after the men had taken position. A total of five companies from the 48th and 47th Alabama were thrown out as skirmishers. Shortly after 4:00 P.M. the brigade prepared to advance. Most of the men probably had the same reaction as Private Ward of the 4th Alabama: "O God, just for a half hour's rest!" Almost immediately after coming to attention, the men heard the commands, "Shoulder arms," then "Right shoulder; shift arms!" followed by "Forward; Guide center; March!" The Rebel yell now erupted from every throat. The Federal artillery opened fire on the line,

but it did not dissuade the impetuous Alabamians. Private Rufus Franks, who had just returned from Alabama with a new uniform, screamed to his comrades in the 4th Alabama, "Come on, boys; come on! The Fifth Texas will get there before the Fourth! Come on boys; come on!" He would soon be lying dead on the field. Because the line was rushing forward so impetuously, it soon became ragged, causing Adjutant Leigh Terrell to yell for them to emulate the disciplined, orderly advance of the nearby 5th Texas.[11]

General Law rode up to Colonel Oates of the 15th Alabama and told him that he was on the extreme right of the line and ordered him to "hug the base of Great Round Top and go up the valley between the two mountains, until I found the left of the Union line, to turn it and do all the damage I could." Oates also recalled being told that the 47th Alabama on his left was to keep in close contact with him, and if the two regiments became separated from the rest of the brigade, he was to oversee the actions of both. Looking to his right, Oates was not happy to see the 44th and 48th Alabama gone. As Colonel William Perry of the 44th Alabama advanced on Oates's right, he received orders from General Law to move north, behind the rest of the brigade. Law told him that "he expected my regiment to take a battery [Smith's]which had been playing on our line from the moment the advance began." After the 44th had pulled out of line, Law also sent orders for the 48th Alabama to silence the pesky battery. These regiments actually formed on the left of the 4th and 5th Texas (Robertson's Brigade), and helped seal a gap that has formed in the latter brigade. The movement placed the 15th Alabama on the extreme right of the brigade.[12]

As the brigade dashed forward, it was hit by a volley from the 2nd U.S. Sharpshooters (Ward's Brigade, Birney's Division), which was deployed in its path, west of the Slyder farm. A few soldiers in the 15th Alabama fell. The losses to the 47th Alabama were apparently greater, as their colonel wrote, "then the slaughter commenced in earnest[;] we were in good range of the sharpshooters, but we could get no crack at them," owing to their concealed position behind the fence. The 15th Alabama and 47th Alabama continued on, only to be hit by a second volley. Not knowing the size of the force in front of him, Oates ordered his men to wheel to the right to take on the unknown enemy. Colonel James Jackson of the 47th Alabama proudly wrote his wife that "we got in about a hundred yards of the first line when the men gave a shout & charged it at double quick. The Yanks waited until we came in forty or fifty paces & gave way and fled." The 4th Alabama in the center of the line also dashed against the sharpshooters and assisted in dislodging them. Oates admitted that because his force had four times more men than the sharpshooters, he had little difficulty extracting them from their positions. The sharpshooters took position again behind a stone wall at the foot of Big Round Top, and again were dislodged, this time scrambling up Big Round Top.[13]

Full of fight, Oates chose to ignore Law's orders and sent his men up the steep, rocky slope of Big Round Top, after the retreating sharpshooters. The 47th Alabama also surged up the hill. The sharpshooters periodically stopped to fire at their pursuers, but invariably fired over their heads. About halfway up the hill, the sharpshooters split—one group moved north, and joined Company B of the 20th Maine; the other moved around the south side of the hill. Oates rested his exhausted men when they reached the top of the hill. Many fainted because of the heat,

their exhausted state after their thirteen-hour march to the battlefield, and lack of water. A water detail of twenty-two men that had been sent to fill the canteens had not returned before the attack began. Colonel Jackson of the 47th Alabama noted only half of his men made it up to the top of the hill. The others had either been killed or wounded, or more likely were felled by exhaustion.[14]

After about five minutes on the hill, Captain Leigh Terrell of General Law's staff rode up and demanded to know why Oates was not attacking Little Round Top as ordered. Oates explained that he wanted to remain on this hill for "within half an hour I could convert it into a Gibraltar that I could hold against ten times the number of men that I had . . . it should be held and occupied by artillery as soon as possible, as it . . . would command the entire field." An exasperated Terrell listened impatiently, then said he had no authority to change orders. He informed Oates that Hood was wounded, that Law was in charge of the division, and the Colonel James Sheffield of the 48th Alabama was now in command of the brigade. Before riding off, Terrill repeated Oates's orders: "Lose no time, but press forward and drive the enemy as far as possible." Realizing the futility of further protest, Oates ordered his regiment down the hill to attack Little Round Top.[15]

While the 15th and 47th Alabama were engaging the 2nd U.S. Sharpshooters and climbing up Big Round Top, the 4th Alabama, in the middle of the line, had driven straight ahead until it reached the base of Little Round Top. Here it found itself on the right of the 5th Texas of Robertson's Brigade. Colonel L. Scruggs fell from sheer exhaustion. In fact, he was one of three of the five regimental commanders who fell from exhaustion that afternoon. Colonel William Perry of the

44th Alabama complained after the war that the officers were ordered to dismount prior to the charge, and this led to the high incidence of fainting among the higher-ranking officers.[16]

After briefly resting to reform its lines, the 4th Alabama scrambled up Little Round Top. Dodging rocks and Federal bullets, the men approached the enemy line, only to be forced back. A wounded Private William Ward lay on the side of the hill, listening to the sounds of battle: "Minie balls were falling through the leaves like hail in a thunderstorm." They tried it again with the same result. A third charge was ordered, and it too failed. Ordered down toward the base of the hill, the exhausted men rested. Soon one of General Longstreet's aides rode up to the regiment and asked to speak with the commanding officer. Thinking it was Captain Coles, the aide yelled, "Get your men into line, sir, and charge that position." After being told his error, he merely turned his horse and rode away. Coles lamented that his 4th Alabama had never lost more men as prisoners—25% of its men, with nothing to show for its efforts. Colonel Scruggs wrote in his official report, "owing to the exhausted condition of the men and the roughness of the mountainside, we found it impossible to carry this position."[17]

What had been the extreme right of the brigade, the 44th and 48th Alabama, was ordered during the charge to move to the left to take on Smith's battery in the Devil's Den sector. To accomplish this, the two regiments actually passed behind the 4th and 5th Texas and formed on their left. How the battery was to be captured was left up to the regimental commanders. As the 44th Alabama approached Devil's Den, Colonel Perry did not like what he saw—"a valley destitute of trees and filled with immense bowlders [sic]

between them." Although he believed he saw two regiments defending the guns, probably only the 4th Maine (Ward's Brigade, Birney's Division) was present at this point. Realizing that his regiment was too far to the east, Perry ordered a left wheel, bringing his left wing opposite the battery, while his right extended toward Little Round Top. Perry ordered this movement when his regiment was not more than two hundred yards from the Federal line. The obstructions prevented most of the Maine troops from seeing Perry's movements.[18]

The enemy troops lay hidden in the rocks of Devil's Den and opened fire as Perry's men cleared the woods. "A few scattered shots in the beginning gave warning in time for my men to fall flat, and thus largely to escape the effect of the main volley," wrote Perry after the war. Before the enemy soldiers had time to reload their guns, Colonel Perry ordered his men to attack with the simple word, "Forward!" "The response was a bound, a yell, and a rush, and in less than a minute the right wing of the regiment was pouring into the Den," recalled Perry. In an untenable situation, the 4th Maine pulled back. Unbeknownst to the Alabamians, the 1st Texas (Robertson's Brigade) and the 15th and 20th Georgia (Benning's Brigade) were also charging Smith's guns from the triangular field to the left. The fight between these regiments and the 4th Maine, 99th Pennsylvania, and 124th New York was short and sharp, but ultimately three cannon were captured. Subsequent Federal counterattacks failed to retake the guns. Two regiments from Benning's Brigade, the 2nd and 17th Georgia, arrived and plugged the gap that had formed between the 44th and 48th Alabama. While Smith's battery had been neutralized, the sector was still pounded by Hazlett's battery atop Little Round Top.[19]

The 48th Alabama took position just southeast of the 44th Alabama, and acted independent of it. Part of its line occupied what is now called the "Slaughter Pen." Colonel Sheffield led his men forward until they were within about "20 paces" of the 4th Maine. Both sides opened fire at about the same time. The fire was too hot on the left of Sheffield's line, forcing it to fall back. The rest of the regiment initially held its position, but it too withdrew before long. Another attack on the pesky 4th Maine failed, and so did a third. At this point a messenger sought out Sheffield with the news that with Law's ascension to division command, he was in charge of the brigade. With the arrival of Benning's Brigade the enemy were finally driven from Devil's Den.[20]

Although the accounts are sketchy, it appears that the 48th Alabama continued forward toward Little Round Top, where it formed on the left of the 4th Texas. The 4th and 5th Texas and 4th Alabama had pushed their way up the hill twice before, and were preparing for yet another charge when the 48th Alabama arrived. Adjutant Henry Figures wrote home after the battle that the "enemy were upon the top of the mountain[;] the steepest place I ever saw in my life." The 48th Alabama's position on the left of the line permitted the Confederates to overlap Colonel Strong Vincent's Brigade on Little Round Top. As the 4th Texas and 48th Alabama scaled the heights, they could see the flag of the 16th Michigan moving back toward the summit. Victory was theirs—they had but to exploit it. Suddenly a mass of blue soldiers appeared at the crest of the hill. The 140th New York had arrived. The men fired at the newly arrived enemy force and its commanding officer, Colonel Patrick O'Rorke, fell dead. Feeling the fatigue from their exertions and realizing the futility of the situation, the

Confederates fell back toward the base of the hill.[21]

Just prior to this point, the 47th Alabama on the right of Law's line was scrambling down the side of Big Round Top. Lieutenant Colonel Michael Bulger's plan was to conceal his men behind boulders, fire at the enemy, and advance under cover of the rocks, until the regiment was close enough to charge the enemy. The plan soon unraveled when the regiment came face to face with the left flank of the 83rd Pennsylvania and right and center of the 20th Maine. This occurred as the 4th Alabama was into its third and last attack on Little Round Top, on the 47th Alabama's left, and may have been why Bulger did not wait until the 15th Alabama arrived to launch its initial attacks. As the men advanced to take the southwest slope of Little Round Top, an aide from General Law rode up to Bulger with a one-word order—"Charge." An exasperated Bulger retorted, "Tell Law I am charging to the best of my ability. Put the 15th Alabama on my right and we will drive them when we come to them." The fighting between the 20th Maine and 47th Alabama was bitter and hand-to-hand. Colonel Chamberlain reported that Bulger's men "burst upon us in great fury." Bulger was wounded, and when the 4th Alabama fell back, the 47th Alabama's left flank was exposed to a withering flank fire.[22]

As the 47th Alabama engaged the enemy, Oates's 15th Alabama streamed down the north side of the hill. Suddenly, Oates saw something that most officers only dream about—a large number of unprotected Federal ordnance wagons to his right. Just as he had deployed Company A to capture them, he received a brisk fire from the 20th Maine, so Oates ordered his men to quick-step to form on the right of the 47th Alabama. Unfortunately for Oates and his men, Colonel Joshua Chamberlain had extended his line to the left (to the right of Oates) and refused two companies to face this new threat. Moving forward, the 15th Alabama was hit with a hot volley when only forty or fifty paces from the Federal line. The sudden fire caused the Alabamians to halt and close ranks. They now opened fire, causing heavy losses to Chamberlain's left. After a second volley, the two left companies on the Federal left began to waver and Oates ordered a charge. The Alabamians now faced a fire that was "so destructive that my line wavered like a man trying to walk against a strong wind." The line of battle finally halted, and started backward. Private William Jordan of the 15th Alabama complained that "they [the enemy] could see every movement we made, they would shoot down, we would have to elevate our guns."[23]

Lieutenant Colonel Bulger of the 47th Alabama was wounded at this time. The unit's next in command, Major James Campbell, could not hold the regiment in its position, and it finally gave way. The fact that the left flank of the 47th Alabama hung in the air and was hit by an enfilading fire from the 44th New York and a frontal fire from the 83rd Pennsylvania was a growing problem. According to Colonel James Jackson, the 47th Alabama charged the Federal works four times and four times it was driven back. Jackson believed that the assigned task was just too great for men who had been marching most of the night without water. "[They] were completely exhausted before they began this charge & they fainted on the field by the hundreds." After the last repulse, Major Campbell pulled the regiment back about three hundred yards, where the men threw up stone breastworks.[24]

As the 47th Alabama was being driven back, Colonel Oates ordered four of his left companies to change position from front to left to enfilate the 20th Maine's

right flank, giving the remnants of the 47th Alabama time to withdraw. They received an enfilading fire from the 83rd Pennsylvania at this point. Realizing how exposed his men were, Oates passed through his the line to the front with his sword drawn, yelling, "Forward, men, to the ledge!" According to Oates, his men drove the Maine men back five times, and five times the enemy countercharged to regain their positions. Twice the battle was so close that bayonets were used.[25]

Realizing that he was getting nowhere, Oates sent an aide to the 4th Alabama for help. The aide quickly returned with sobering news: enemy troops were swarming along the 15th Alabama's left flank. Oates summarized the situation after the war: "The Fifteenth Alabama had infantry in front of them, to the right of them, dismounted cavalry to the left, and infantry in the rear of them." Looking at his dead and dying men littering the forest floor all around him, Oates decided to launch one more charge. Within seconds, he changed his mind and instead decided to withdraw. "When the signal was given we ran like a herd of wild cattle," wrote Oates. He never acknowledged that the 20th Maine's bayonet charge helped hasten his retreat and added to his losses. As his men retreated, Company B of the 20th Maine and a detachment of the 2nd U.S. Sharpshooters, occupying an advanced position, fired into Oates's rear and then pounced on the fleeing Alabamians, capturing many more.[26]

Most of the remnants of Oates's 15th Alabama sought safety by yet again climbing Big Round Top. So exhausted was Colonel Oates that he fainted before reaching the top and was carried the rest of the way by two of his stout men. He went to his grave with heartfelt gratitude toward them, believing that capture was a fate worse than death.[27]

The brigade was withdrawn a short distance on the morning of July 3. Still on the extreme right of the army, the men threw up stone breastworks near the base of Big Round Top and grimly waited for the enemy to attack. The brigade was deployed, from left to right, as 44th Alabama–48th Alabama–4th Alabama–47th Alabama–15th Alabama. Late in the afternoon, after the Pickett–Pettigrew–Trimble attack had failed, two regiments of Farnsworth's Federal cavalry brigade broke through the Confederate picket line. One of Law's aides found help in the form of the 4th Alabama. Captain Coles reported that "everyone without the semblance of order, with rear in front and only keeping with each other, companies all commingled, the most fleet-footed leading, ran through the woods in the direction of the firing." Rushing through a woods and emerging on the other side, the men saw the 1st Vermont bearing down on them. "Cavalry boys, cavalry! This is no fight, only a frolic, give it to 'em," yelled Lieutenant Vaughan. Because the horsemen were only thirty or forty paces away, most of the bullets found their mark. Each man loaded as fast as he could, but the cavalrymen veered away from them to the north.[28]

Colonel Oates's 15th Alabama was ordered to rush toward Reilly's battery to help prevent its capture. Soon an enemy detachment was riding down on the regiment's skirmishers at the southern end of the Plum Run Valley. According to Oates,

General Farnsworth rode up to the soldiers and demanded their capture. The soldiers opened fire, felling the general from his horse. They claimed that rather than being taken prisoner, he pointed his pistol at himself and fired.[29]

The brigade spent the remainder of the day and all of July 4 awaiting another Federal attack, which never came. The brigade joined the army's retreat on the early morning hours of July 5.[30]

Despite their exhaustion after their long march to the battlefield, Law's Brigade performed remarkably well. It fought essentially without any coordination after Law ascended to division command, and it was some time before Colonel Sheffield learned that he was in command of the brigade. As a result, the brigade fought in three clusters. The 15th and 47th Alabama fought near the southern end of Little Round Top; the 4th Alabama took on the east-facing slope of the hill; and the 44th and 48th Alabama attacked the Devil's Den/Houck's Ridge sector. Two of the regiments (15th and 48th Alabama) came close to capturing Little Round Top, and the 44th Alabama and 48th Alabama were instrumental in driving the Federal infantry from Devil's Den and assisting in capturing several pieces of Smith's battery. On July 3, the 4th Alabama and 15th Alabama were skillfully maneuvered to cut off, and ultimately defeat, General Farnsworth's ill-fated expedition against Lee's right flank.

Robertson's Brigade—Brigadier General Jerome Robertson

Units: 3rd Arkansas, 1st Texas, 4th Texas, 5th Texas
Strength: 1734
Losses: 603 (152-313-138)—34.8%[31]

The fabled Texas Brigade was reorganized after the Maryland campaign of 1862 with the removal of Georgia and South Carolina units and the addition of the 3rd

Arkansas. The Texas nucleus remained and so did the brigade's fighting abilities, which were the best in Lee's army. The brigade, under General John Hood, crushed the Federal line at Eltham's Landing on the Virginia peninsula and won further distinction at the battle of Gaines's Mill, where it helped to finally breach the Federal line. The brigade helped spearhead the attack on General John Pope's forces at Second Manassas. Although equally aggressive at the battle of Antietam, the brigade sustained heavy losses in the cornfield without anything to show for it. The brigade was not involved in the fight at Fredericksburg and was with Longstreet near Suffolk, so it missed the Chancellorsville campaign. The men were ready for a fight after so many months of inactivity.[32]

Brigadier General Jerome Robertson had an unusual past. After losing his father at an early age, Robertson worked for a physician and ultimately went to medical school. His education was cut short by the War for Texas Independence. At the age of twenty, Robertson raised a company of Kentuckians and took them south to serve under Sam Houston. Robertson remained in Texas after the war, where he married and began a medical practice. An acclaimed Indian fighter, Robertson was elected to the Texas legislature and voted in favor of secession. He subsequently raised a company of volunteers and brought them to Richmond, where they became part of the 5th Texas. Elevated to colonel of the regiment in early June 1862, he fought in most of the regiment's subsequent battles. Robertson finally assumed command of the brigade in the fall of 1862. Nicknamed "Aunt Polly," because he cared so much about his men's welfare, Robertson had proven himself to be a no-nonsense fighter who had won the respect of his Texans.[33]

Many of the men grumbled when ordered to ford the armpit-deep Potomac River on June 26 while fully clothed and holding their guns and accoutrements over their heads. The grumbling stopped when the men were issued captured whiskey. The more temperate gave their share to their comrades, causing more than a few to become intoxicated. While most of the officers chose to look the other way, Colonel Van Manning of the 3rd Arkansas "ordered the sober ones to dunk the drunken ones in the creek to bring a reaction," recalled Captain Miles Smith of the 4th Texas. Tongue in cheek, Smith wrote that the "Texas Brigade was in four states in one day. The State of Virginia, the State of Maryland, the State of Pennsylvania, and a state of drunkenness." The sober soldiers enjoyed the beauty of the countryside. Private John West commented that the barns were "more substantially and carefully built and fitted out than any house I have ever seen in the country in Texas."[34]

The brigade reached Chambersburg on June 27. To Colonel Robert Powell of the 5th Texas, it was a "city of banners . . . a Union flag surrounded every house . . . every lady held a flag in her hand, varying in size from a postage stamp to a table cloth." The women were less than congenial, as they "congregated on the sidewalks and did jeer and ridicule the Johnny Rebs, who received in return compliments equally gracious," recalled Smith. Some of their scorn turned to horror when they realized who they were dealing with. At least one remarked, "They are the ones that have killed so many of our soldiers." One woman smugly remarked, "Thank God, you will never come back alive." This was answered by, "No, as we intend to go to Cincinnati by way of New York."[35]

Marching another mile north of the town, the men halted and went into bivouac with the rest of the division. The soldiers were most unhappy when they realized that their commissary wagons had not yet arrived. They finally arrived after dark, but the men were dismayed to find that they contained slender rations of rancid bacon and musty flour. This caused the men to reason that the "Federal soldiers that had marched through Virginia had taken, with the strong hand, whatever they wanted . . . not even offering to pay in greenbacks," recalled Corporal Joseph Polley of the 4th Texas. Lee had issued strong orders against depredations on private property, but the men did not consider it a violation if they paid for the goods with Confederate script or if it was voluntarily offered. "No violence used, no threats of any kind made by any Confederate soldier, and none of the citizens complained of having been intimidated and robbed," claimed Polley.[36]

Polley awoke to a wondrous sight on June 28. "Every square foot of an acre of ground not occupied by a sleeping or standing soldier, was covered with choice food for the hungry. Chickens, turkeys, ducks, and geese . . . scattered around in bewildering confusion and gratifying profusion . . . loaves of bread and chunks of corned beef, hams, and sides of bacon . . . bowls of yellow butter, demijohns of buttermilk, and other eatables too numerous to mention."[37]

The march resumed on June 30, and the brigade reached Fayetteville. It was to continue early the next day, but was delayed because Johnson's Division and the Second Corps's wagon train filled the road, so the men waited. The men were ordered to form into column when the last wagon passed. A frustrated Corporal Polley recalled that the men marched only about a hundred yards before being ordered to stop. No one wanted to sit down, because they expected the march

to be resumed momentarily. "Nothing is so wearing on infantry as such halting process," he wrote after the war. The subsequent march over the mountains in the dark was a tiring one. Colonel Powell of the 5th Texas noted that there was not nearly as much "hilarity" on this march, as the men understood that they would soon be in battle. The brigade was finally permitted to rest outside Cashtown at 2:00 A.M. on July 2. The men were awakened less than two hours later, as the officers conducted an inspection of every soldier's arms and equipment. The final leg of the march to Gettysburg was exceedingly slow—only about six miles in four hours. The brigade finally reached the battlefield at about 9:00 A.M. During the last portion of its march, the brigade passed "the bloody shirts"—men who had been wounded the day before and were attempting to return to Virginia.[38]

After completing a circuitous march to Warfield Ridge, General Robertson aligned his regiments, from left to right, as 3rd Arkansas–1st Texas–4th Texas–5th Texas. Many of the men were apprehensive when they looked across the wide swath of ground. "Hitherto, the Texans had fought on ground over which they could move rapidly in line, and where the enemy was accessible—where the terror caused by their dashing rush and swift oncoming counted large. Here at Gettysburg the foe lay concealed behind stone fences at the base of the ridge and mountains, or flat on the ground on a crest of ridge or mountain," noted Corporal Polley.[39]

Reilly's battery opened fire from its position in the front of the brigade. The enemy guns replied, "knocking out a man here and there," according to Private A. C. Sims of the 1st Texas. John Wilkerson of the 3rd Arkansas could look down the line "and see our men knocked out constantly . . . I don't know how long we were held there under fire, but the time seemed endless," he recalled. Private John West noted that the "infernal machines came tearing and whirring through the ranks with a most demoralizing tendency." The losses were heaviest in the 4th Texas, which lost fifteen men to a single shell. Captain Decimus Barziza of that regiment found that these cannonades were exceedingly difficult for the men because "one has time to reflect upon the danger, and the utter helplessness of his present condition. The men are all flat on the ground, keeping their places in ranks, and as a shell is heard, generally try to sink themselves into the earth." At the height of the shelling, a private stood up and, moving to the front of the 5th Texas, offered a prayer. Seeing the effect of this cannon fire, General Robertson moved the men to a safer location and ordered them to lie down. Colonel Manning (3rd Arkansas) calmed his men by walking among them, quietly saying, "Steady men, steady."[40]

General Hood ordered them to charge the enemy and take the heights at about 5:00 P.M. Colonel Phillip Work of the 1st Texas pointed to his regiment's flag and yelled, "Follow the Lone Star Flag to the top of the mountain!" Almost immediately, commands to "Forward-Guide Right-March!" were heard, and off they went. The Federal artillery fire now increased, causing the line to move faster. As the brigade advanced, Robertson ordered it to throw down a rail fence in its front. Riding forward, he yelled, "We're going in there, men. There's a rail fence down there on the road. Grab it by the bottom rail and heave." With this obstruction out of the way, the men swept across Emmitsburg Road. As the line rushed forward, it encountered a skirmish line composed of the tough 2nd U.S. Sharpshooters (Ward's Brigade, Birney's Division), who took their toll on the attackers. Pri-

vate Mark Smither of the 5th Texas wrote home after the battle that "our men tumbl[ed] out of ranks at each step, knocked over by the Enemy's sharpshooters who lined the side of the mountain."[41]

The brigade almost immediately ran into problems. After the war, Robertson complained that Law started his charge prematurely, "a full mile from the enemy's line of battle." Because Law's Brigade had a head start and was moving so fast, Robertson's men had to go from quickstep to a trot to keep up with the Alabamians. Another problem was Hood's orders to Robertson, which were to "keep my right well closed on Brigadier-General Law's left, and to let my left rest on the Emmitsburg Pike." As his line of battle rushed forward, Robertson realized that Emmitsburg Road "[bore] sharply to the left . . . while Law on my right bore to the right." Robertson knew that his brigade was too small to cover the desired space. Colonel Manning's 3rd Arkansas stubbornly held his regiment's left on Emmitsburg Road, while the 5th Texas linked up with Law's Brigade on the right. The 4th Texas aligned with the latter regiment, but the next regiment in line, the 1st Texas, aligned with the right of the 3rd Arkansas. This caused a yawning gap to form in the middle of the brigade. Despite the fact that Robertson explained in his report that the "separation of my regiments . . . was remedied as promptly as the numerous stone and rail fences . . . would allow," in reality, the two wings fought independently for the remainder of the day. Robertson admitted this later in his report, indicating that he tried to send the left wing to the assistance of the right, but when he realized that it was too heavily engaged, he tried to move the 4th and 5th Texas to the left. However, that too was impossible, as these two regiments had already encountered the enemy. He did not mention that the gap was partially filled by the arrival of the 44th and 48th Alabama (Law's Brigade). Realizing that he could not supervise both diverging wings, Robertson sent a message to Law, asking him to look after the 4th and 5th Texas, while he stayed with the left wing. Equally concerning to Robertson was the fact that McLaws's Division had not advanced on his left.[42]

The left wing probably engaged the enemy first, just south of the Wheatfield. With the 3rd Arkansas on the left, in the Rose Woods, and the 1st Texas on the right, the two regiments swept forward. According to Colonel Phillip Work, Company I of the 4th Texas became separated from its regiment during the charge and joined the 1st Texas. The fact that both flanks hung in the air did not seem to bother either regimental commander at this time. Up ahead were regiments from Ward's Brigade (Birney's Division, III Corps). With a yell, the two regiments charged the Federal line, which opened fire. A volley suddenly tore into the 3rd Arkansas's vulnerable left flank. The 17th Maine of de Trobriand's Brigade (Birney's Division) had just sprinted to a stone wall on the edge of the Wheatfield to cut down the 3rd Arkansas's left flank. Colonel Manning ran to the left and ordered the three companies there to change position to face this new threat. But the din of battle was so great that none heard his command, so Manning had to physically push the men into position. Up against the 86th New York, 20th Indiana, and 99th Pennsylvania of Ward's Brigade in his front, and the 17th Maine on its left flank, Manning wisely broke off the attack and pulled his men back to safety. He stretched out his regiment to about double its original length, hoping that he would find the vulnerable flank of the enemy, and charged again, but the results

were the same. The 3rd Arkansas's repulses are easy to understand, given that its 479 men were up against about 1300 of the enemy.[43]

Coming up on the right of the 3rd Arkansas, the 1st Texas was exposed to a devastating artillery fire from Smith's battery on Houck's Ridge. According to Private A. C. Sims of the 1st Texas, "we loaded and fired, the front rank on their knees and the rear standing." They found a measure of safety when they reached a stone wall at the base of the triangular field. Fortunately for the Texans, Smith's cannon could not depress their barrels enough to fire into them as they crouched behind the wall. The Texans opened fire on Smith's gunners and silenced the battery. The men now jumped over the wall and dashed toward the guns. All was confusion. First the men heard orders to retreat, which the regiment began to do. Then the order was quickly countermanded. "No one seemed to know whence it came, nor from whom," recalled Private James Bradfield. "It cost us dearly, for as we lay in close range of their now double lines, the enemy poured a hail of bullets on us, and in a few minutes a number of our men were killed or wounded." The 124th New York closely watched these events while stationed atop Houck's Ridge. According to Captain Charles Weygant of the regiment, the Texans advanced to within fifty yards of the battery, when the Federal troops opened fire. The "crash of riflery [sic] perceptibly thinned their ranks and brought them to a stand . . . it seemed to paralyze their whole line." The Texans soon recovered, and continued forward.[44]

Upon the command of its officers, the 124th New York let out a cheer and charged into the 1st Texas, driving it back about two hundred yards to a rail fence. Here the Texans rallied and held their ground, inflicting terrible losses on the New Yorkers. Help was on the way, as Benning's veteran brigade moved up behind the Texans and opened fire on the New Yorkers, forcing them back to their original position on Houck's Ridge. Not knowing that the 1st Texas was in front of them, the 20th Georgia opened fire. The 1st Texas's flag bearer quickly moved to an open area and waved his flag until the firing stopped.[45]

Colonel Work (1st Texas) was initially relieved when the 15th Georgia arrived to support his regiment. This relief quickly changed to frustration, as the Georgians barreled forward and "commingled" with his troops. Despite the efforts of both commanding officers, the regiments could not be separated and fought most of the day together. With the threat from the 124th New York dissipated, both regiments stormed toward Smith's battery on Houck's Ridge. Private James Bradfield insisted that no orders to charge were given. "Without awaiting orders, every man became his own commander and sprang forward toward the top of the hill at full speed." The charge was successful, and several of Smith's guns were captured. During this melee, the two commingled regiments were joined by the 20th Georgia and the 44th Alabama (Law's Brigade), who took on the 124th New York, 4th Maine, and 99th Pennsylvania, often in hand-to-hand combat.[46]

Over to the left, Colonel Manning's 3rd Arkansas was still not making any progress. General Robertson now ordered Colonel Work to leave two companies on Houck's Ridge and move the rest of his regiment to the left to support the 3rd Arkansas. Manning was also relieved to see the 11th and 59th Georgia of Anderson's Brigade form on his endangered left flank. Just at that moment, a shell exploded almost in Manning's face, knocking him senseless.

Despite these reinforcements, the Federal troops in this sector were just too strong to be displaced, and every attack failed. The persistence of these attacks caused the 3rd Arkansas to lose more men than any other regiment in the brigade, save one. Eventually, the growing pressure on the Federal line was so great that Ward's Brigade and the 17th Maine were finally forced to fall back.[47]

The first-person accounts of the 1st Texas survivors are confusing after this point. There is, however, ample evidence from the 15th Georgia that two regiments continued to advance to the Wheatfield, where they slugged it out with the newly arrived 5th New Hampshire of Cross's Brigade (Caldwell's Division, II Corps), but were forced back. The two regiments were later pushed farther back by the arrival of Brooke's Brigade of the same division. Worried about his ability to withdraw his regiment, Colonel Work ordered the color bearer and several men to maintain their position, while the rest of the regiment was ordered to the rear. It did not work out like Work had intended, as the men refused to leave their beloved flag. These men continued to fire away at the newly arrived Federal reinforcements. Soon after, the 1st Texas and the 3rd Arkansas were ordered to Devil's Den on the right, where they opened fire on the Federal troops on Little Round Top. One soldier from the 3rd Arkansas merrily sang, "Now let the wide world wag as it will, I'll be gay and happy still!" as he methodically loaded his gun and fired it at the Federal troops on the hill. The men replenished their supplies of ammunition by rifling through the pouches of fallen soldiers.[48]

While the left of the line was engaged with several regiments from Ward's and de Trobriand's Brigades, the right of the line, consisting of the 4th and 5th Texas, drove toward Little Round Top. To the right of the 5th Texas was the 4th Alabama of Law's Brigade. About a quarter mile from Little Round Top they encountered skirmishers from the 2nd U.S. Sharpshooters, who occupied thick undergrowth. So tenacious were the skirmishers that the Texans had to stop and reform their ranks before charging. Although the skirmish line was finally pushed back, it bought valuable time for the Federals. All the while, artillery played upon the ranks of the Texans, causing many casualties. Advancing another two hundred yards, Major John Bane of the 4th Texas believed that he had finally encountered the Union line. These troops were probably from the 2nd U.S. Sharpshooters making another stand, along with skirmishers from Vincent's Brigade. The men leaped a low stone fence and rushed the sharpshooters, forcing them to retreat.[49]

The three regiments were now alone at the base of Little Round Top. Near the summit, the men could see the 16th Michigan, 44th New York, and 83rd Pennsylvania (Vincent's Brigade) taking cover behind rocks. The two Texas regiments were aligned directly in front of the first two regiments. Moving slowly up the hill, the officers found it increasingly difficult to keep anything that resembled an orderly line of battle. The hill was just too steep and studded with numerous large rocks and other obstructions. "The huge rocks form[ed] defiles through which not more than 3 or 4 men could pass abreast, thus breaking up our alignment and rendering its reformation impossible," wrote Lieutenant Colonel K. Bryan of the 5th Texas in his official report. So steep were some areas that West (4th Texas) thought that "a mountain goat would have reveled" in them. Still, the men moved on. Halting his men, Bryan ordered them to open fire on the enemy. The Federal troops

returned the fire, which Bryan likened to "being showered like hail upon us."[50]

Private J. Mark Smither of the 5th Texas wrote home after the battle that "nothing daunted . . . our boys . . . until they had arrived within 25 steps of the works on finding that the plan of scaling the heights was impossible, for we could hardly have gone over them if there had been no Yankees there." Private William Fletcher noted that "we stopped advancing, without orders as far as I was concerned, as I had heard none." Smither related how his comrades "immediately took shelter, Indian fashion, behind rocks and trees and commenced popping away at the Yankees whenever they showed their heads . . . the Yankees . . . pouring volley after volley down on us with frightful effect." The men were in an impossible situation. They could not advance, and to raise their heads invited having them shot off by the Federal troops above them. Jonathan Stevens of the same regiment honestly recalled after the war that "for the first time in the history of the war, our men began to waver. We [were] suffering terribly."[51]

Realizing that they were not making progress, but taking additional casualties with each moment they remained on the side of the hill, the officers pulled their men back to the woods at its base. According to Major J. C. Rogers, who took command of the 5th Texas after its colonel and lieutenant colonel had been wounded, he pulled his men back only when the withdrawal of the other regiments left his flanks unguarded.[52]

Another charge was ordered, but it too met with defeat. Three regiments charging a steep hill against a similar size force, protected by cover, is folly. Yet the Texans and Alabamians never gave up. The veterans of Robertson's Brigade realized an impossible situation when they saw it, and began streaming back down the slope, despite their officers' orders to "halt." While resting in the woods, the 48th Alabama arrived and formed on the left of the 4th Texas. Another charge was ordered. This time, four Confederate regiments stormed Vincent's three well-positioned ones. The 5th Texas stormed up the hill, getting farther than it had on its first two attempts. A courier for General Law scrambled up the hill and told Major Rogers, "General Law presents his compliments and says hold the place at all hazards." Rogers roared back, "Compliments, hell! Who wants compliments in such a damned place as this? Go back and ask General Law if he expects me to hold the world in check with the Fifth Texas Regiment." Rogers apparently obeyed the order, for Private Val Giles saw him mount a log and "begin a Fourth of July speech. He was a little ahead of time, for that was about six thirty on the evening of July 2nd." All was chaos. "Every fellow was his own general. Private soldiers gave commands as loud as the officers. Nobody paid attention to either," recalled Giles. Actually, the din of battle was so loud that few could hear beyond a few feet.[53]

Polley explained the hellish conditions on the hill:

> Their fire [Federal artillery] and that of our own batteries, and the constant roar and rattle of thousands of muskets, made the earth tremble beneath our feet, while the fierce, angry shriek, the strident swirl of grape and canister as they tore hurtling through the air and broke like a wave from the ocean of death upon that devoted spot, the hissing bullets, and their "spat" as they struck rock, tree or human flesh—all this, with the shouts and imprecations, the leaping to and fro and from boulder to boulder of powder-begrimed men, seemingly gone wild with rage and excitement, created a scene of such indescribable, awe-inspiring confusion.[54]

This attack should have ended like the others, except for the fact that the 48th Alabama appeared to have flanked Vincent's right-most regiment, the 16th Michigan, while the 4th Texas hit its front. Before long, the Michiganders were streaming to the rear. It looked like the Texans and Alabamians would finally take the hill. Colonel Strong Vincent rushed over to rally his men, but was mortally wounded as he shouted encouragement while standing on a large rock.[55]

Help was on the way. Before the Confederates could exploit the breach in the Federal line, the 140th New York (Weed's Brigade, Ayres's Division, V Corps) arrived and smashed into the Texans and Alabamians. The fight was now at close quarters, but the Confederates were at a disadvantage and forced to fall back yet again. The officers could see that further attacks were futile, as their men were exhausted, their ranks were decimated, the Federal position was all but impregnable, and enemy reinforcements were now arriving.[56]

A bitter Smither told his mother, "now it was to be expected that our men having tried it and seeing the impossibility of taking the place would have refused to have gone in again, but no they tried it a second and third time and formed to go in a 4th time when night came on forced us to abandon the fight." Another private from the regiment, Rufus Felder, wrote home that "it seemed like madness in Lee to have attempted to storm such a position. He came very near loosing [sic] his whole army by it." The 5th Texas had the dubious honor of having sustained the brigade's greatest losses—52%.[57]

Nightfall ended the bloodletting. Fletcher recalled orders to prepare to charge the hill once again. "The order shook me, and my feelings were indescribable; in fact, I had a bad case of cowardly horror." Common sense prevailed and the attack was never launched. One of the casualties was General Robertson, who was wounded above his knee and unable to walk.[58]

At about 2:00 A.M. on July 3, the 1st Texas and 3rd Arkansas moved to the right, where they rejoined the two Texas regiments. The exhausted men threw themselves down in front of Little Round Top and caught whatever sleep they could, given the continual moans and groans of the wounded. Fearing an attack by the enemy, the men were awakened to erect breastworks. By dawn, Major John Bane of the 4th Texas could report that they stood two feet high. The brigade remained in this position through July 3. The only event of any importance was the skirmishing in their front. Several men were killed or wounded during the sharpshooting that occurred during the day. Several were also wounded during the grand cannonade that preceded Pickett's charge, when, according to Fletcher, "the guns were not elevated enough and were doing fine work on our position. The bursting and flying pieces of shell and rock put us in a panic condition."[59]

At about 3:00 P.M., Colonel Work was ordered to move his 1st Texas south to help repel an anticipated cavalry charge. As the column approached the Bushman house, the men were ordered to tear down part of a fence that obstructed their passage. Proceeding another two hundred yards or so, the regiment took position behind a stone wall on the edge of the Bushman Woods. Here the men deployed in one line. Given the large area to cover and the losses the day before, Sims called it a "skirmish line." Captain George Hillyer from the 9th Georgia (Anderson's Brigade) noted that the 1st Texas did not have "men enough to have more than about one to every five or six steps." Sev-

eral units were thrown out to the left and right to protect the flanks. On the left, some of the men took down a "staked and ridered" fence and rebuilt it, attaching it to the stone wall. Reilly's battery also joined the regiment, deploying about 250 yards in the Texans's rear. Hardly had the men completed building the breastwork than the 1st West Virginia of Farnsworth's cavalry brigade charged. One unknown Texan recorded in his diary that the charge began about 4:30 P.M.[60]

Thomas McCarthy vividly described the Federal cavalry charge:

We formed behind a Bunch of Timber in our front between it and us, being an open field for Two Hundred yards[.] The ground trembled as they came, they rode down our skirmishers & charged us, and in a few seconds were on us, our Boys arose and pitched in to them. They went through us cutting right & left[.] The firing for a few minutes was front, rear & towards the flanks[.] In a few minutes, great numbers of riderless horses were galloping around & and others with riders on were trying to surrender, a fusilade of shot 7 shell from Rileys [sic] Battery passed a couple of feet above our heads.[61]

Private W. T. White of the 1st Texas noted that "they formed line of battle in plain view of us and charged. We held our fire until they were within fifty or sixty yards of us, when, taking deliberate aim, we fired on them, bringing down many men and horses. Instead of continuing the assault, which probably would have resulted in our capture, they retreated to their original starting point, reformed, and recharged, with the same result as before." Many of the cavalrymen continued their charge. "All of the boys had fired off their pieces, and Yankees would not give them time to load, so the boys were using the butts of their guns." Private James

Hendrick agreed, stating that some of the Federal cavalrymen came "up [with]in ten steps of the regiment. Some of the regiment knocked them off of their horses with rocks. We killed a great many of them and captured over one-hundred prisoners. They could not break our lines."[62]

The reprieve was short-lived, for within a few minutes, the 18th Pennsylvania galloped toward the Texans's position. The result was the same, and many horses trotted away with empty saddles. Private White noted, "having repulsed the second charge, we felt that we could almost whip all the cavalry the enemy had, and from that time on, for about two hours, they continued making demonstrations against us."[63]

During the evening of July 3, the brigade was ordered to move by the right

flank to its original jump off position on Warfield Ridge. Here the men remained through July 4, finally retreating from Gettysburg late that night.[64]

One of the toughest brigades in either army, Robertson's Brigade was not effectively utilized on July 2. The problems began almost immediately, when the brigade broke into two separate and independent wings, fighting separately throughout the remainder of the day. Although outnumbered, the left wing fought well and eventually captured three cannon from Smith's battery. The right also did as well as could be expected, given that it was assigned the impossible task of storming Little Round Top. That the two Texas regiments almost captured the heights is a testament to their fighting abilities.[65]

Benning's Brigade—Brigadier General Henry Benning

Units: 2nd Georgia, 15th Georgia, 17th Georgia, 20th Georgia
Strength: 1420
Losses: 519 (95-275-149)—36.5%[66]

Unlike so many other brigades in the Army of Northern Virginia, Benning's had been fairly stable since its inception. First commanded by Brigadier General Robert Toombs, the brigade was initially was composed of the 2nd, 15th, and 17th Georgia. The 20th Georgia was originally been part of General Jubal Early's Brigade, but was transferred to Toombs's in June 1862. The brigade fought on the peninsula, in the Seven Days battles, and at Second Manassas. However, it was at Sharpsburg that the brigade achieved lasting fame. Stationed near Burnside's Bridge, the brigade held off an entire Federal corps for several hours, thus saving Lee's army from certain defeat.[67]

Upset about being passed over for promotion, General Toombs resigned his commission on March 4, 1863. The brigade's senior regimental commander, Colonel Henry Benning of the 17th Georgia, was promoted the following month and given command of the brigade. This was not the first time that Benning had commanded the brigade. With Toombs away on business, Benning first commanded the brigade at Second Manassas. He panicked in this role, but General Longstreet helped him regain his composure. Because Toombs was wounded at Sharpsburg, Benning commanded the brigade again at Fredericksburg, where it was not heavily engaged. "Old Rock" Benning had been a Georgia Supreme Court Justice prior to the war, and although he was considered for a post in Jefferson Davis's cabinet, he instead opted for field command. His brigade was a cohesive unit that had shown its mettle on several battlefields.[68]

Crossing the Potomac was a presage of the hardships Benning's men were to face in the future. Sergeant Thomas Ware of the 15th Georgia complained that the men were not permitted to strip before crossing the river, but admitted, "it was still raining & we were very wet any way." The column marched rapidly into Pennsylvania. At Greencastle, the men experienced the local citizens who, "looked mad & sullen at our appearance . . . several Federal flags were seen the girls had them on their bonnets." Upon reaching Chambersburg, the brigade was given a much-needed rest. Ware observed that the "stores all closed & a great many people out to see us & looked frightened & mad." He was surprised to see so many young men not in the army. The farms were also a constant source of interest. "People very thickly settled & live in fine houses . . . [but] seem to think more of their gardens and barns than any thing else, as they had the largest & finest barns I ever saw."[69]

According to Ware, there was little respect for personal property. "We marched through fields of wheat & corn tearing down fences & not respecting scarcely any thing. The soldiers hardly respecting any thing, robbing bee gums & poultry yards." While camped near Chambersburg on June 28, Ware noted that over half of his regiment were out foraging. "The soldiers are taking everything. Camps full of chickens, butter & milk." He did admit that the men paid for at least some of the goods, as they could get "almost any thing at your own price." Despite the fact that few knew the exact location of the enemy, surveillance was light. Ware noted that "we kept one sentinel on watch all night in case of a surprise."[70]

The men knew something was up when they were ordered to prepare three days'

rations on June 29. Next, orders arrived for the brigade to tear up railroad tracks and destroy a railroad bridge. The cavalry had already burned the latter once, but it had been immediately rebuilt, only to be destroyed again by Hood's men. The men left Chambersburg on June 30 and camped at Fayetteville, where, in the words of Ware, "we made fences fly." The men were awakened the next day, and, according to Ware, "soon the drum beat & all in lines." There was a delay in beginning the march, so the men made the most of it by having "our usual fun in guying the teamsters, cavalry and stragglers as they passed us," recalled Private William Fluker of the 15th Georgia. He noted that after the wagons cleared the road, General Longstreet rode up to General Benning and said, "General, put your brigade in motion." Soon the men could hear the command of "Attention men, fall in; right face, forward march." So it was that Benning's Brigade led Hood's Division on the difficult final leg of the march to Gettysburg. According to Private John Bowden of the 2nd Georgia, "the march was awful, and the soldiers were exhausted. Under the intense heat of double-quick time some fainted and fell by the way." The march seemed to be endless. In growing desperation, some of the men yelled out, "Rest, rest!" but their pleas were ignored. Some of the men half-slept while they marched and in many instances bumped into the soldier in front of them. In the words of Fluker, the offender was "cussed for tramping on his heels."[71]

The brigade marched until midnight, when the men were permitted to rest for a few hours. "As soon as we stopped every man dropped to the ground where he stood and was soon asleep," recalled Fluker. The three-hour rest seemed like but a few minutes to the exhausted men, and none were happy when they were ordered to continue the march at 3:00 A.M. on July 2. The column marched another three miles to reach the battlefield. Turning right, the men marched another three hundred yards to a cloverfield, where they were permitted to rest until 1:00 P.M.[72]

After making the circuitous march to its pre-attack position, the Benning's Brigade formed behind Law's on Warfield Ridge. Colonel Wesley Hodges of the 17th Georgia noted with pride that "notwithstanding the excessive heat of the day, and the circuitous route to reach said position, officers and men bore up cheerfully under the annoyances." Shortly after taking his position, Benning was informed by General Hood that the division would attack the Federal troops in front of them, and that his brigade "would follow Law's Brigade at the distance of about 400 yards." Benning arranged his brigade from left to right as 15th Georgia–20th Georgia–17th Georgia–2nd Georgia.[73]

The men watched as Law's men in front of them, and Robertson's to their left stepped off to attack the Federal left flank. The sounds of battle escalated as the 1st Texas and 3rd Arkansas (Robertson's Brigade) and the 44th and 48th Alabama (Law's Brigade) attacked Ward's Brigade (Birney's Division, III Corps) on Houck's Ridge. The men could see Generals Hood and Longstreet "riding coolly up and down in front of us, seeming to examine every man," recalled Private Fluker. Earlier, the men had been ordered to leave everything behind but their canteens, cartridge boxes, and haversacks. Fifty additional cartridges were issued to each man. The enemy soldiers stubbornly held their ground against Law's and Robertson's onslaught, and before long Benning received orders to move forward in support. With the order, "Forward, guide center, march!" the advance began.[74]

Benning could see troops up ahead, and he ordered his men to support them. He wrote in his report, "in truth, it was Robertson's, Law's being farther to the right. This I did not discover until late in the fight, a wood on the right concealing from me most of Law's Brigade." This was yet another mistake that spelled doom to the Confederates on July 2. Many have speculated that if Benning had moved to the right and supported Law's assault on Little Round Top, the heights might have been captured.[75]

The brigade was exposed to heavy shelling from Federal batteries almost as soon as it stepped off. "As soon as we came in sight a furious blast of cannon broke from the tops of the hills and mountains around and the terrific cry and scream of shells began," wrote a soldier from the 17th Georgia. Although the Confederate batteries opened on their counterparts, the Federal artillery did not take the bait, instead continuing to pour their destructive fire on the advancing infantry. "Down the plunging shot came, bursting before and around and everywhere tearing up the ground in a terrific rain of death." The brigade halted after advancing about four hundred yards. The shells continued to scream overhead, but few men bolted from the ranks. The line was again ordered forward after a few minutes in this position. The minié balls now came in "showers," and, according to an anonymous soldier in the 17th Georgia, "the ranks began to melt away, but springing forward, with a shout, the undismayed line steadily rushed on."[76]

The 15th Georgia on the left of the brigade apparently outdistanced its sister regiments because it faced fewer obstructions. Benning halted the regiment when it was within 150 yards of the first enemy line until the rest of the brigade could catch up. The regiment's commander,

Colonel Dudley DuBose, could see the 1st Texas behind a stone wall up ahead and, in front of it the 124th New York. Fluker noted that "the blue lines of infantry instantly changed to one of white smoke," and eventually the Texans were forced back toward the Georgians. DuBose brought up his regiment after watching several charges. The commander of the 1st Texas, Colonel P. A. Work, was not at all happy to see the Georgians approach, because he felt they were needed farther to the left, which was under heavy attack. The two regiments became commingled and could not be separated despite the best efforts of both regimental commanders, and therefore fought together for the rest of the day. The two commanders turned their attention to the enemy, and ordered their men to open fire on the 124th New York up ahead. Seeing that the rest of the brigade was heavily engaged with the enemy, Colonel DuBose ordered his men to jump over the stone wall and drive the enemy away from his front. The Texans followed suit. "We raised a deafening yell and went over the rock fence and up the hill shouting and yelling like demons," wrote Fluker. The two regiments' attack was irresistible, driving the 124th New York back to Ward's main line.[77]

To the right of the 15th Georgia, the men of the 20th Georgia the man could see Smith's battery near Devil's Den and, to their left, the 1st Texas and 15th Georgia preparing to charge the ridge. Colonel James Waddell ordered his men to oblique to the left so that they directly faced the battery, then ordered them to charge with the two regiments on its left. Colonel Waddell estimated that it took fifteen minutes to scale Houck's Ridge, where it helped capture Smith's three cannon. To secure the guns for good, the men had to repel the charge of the 99th

Pennsylvania, 4th Maine, and perhaps part of the 124th New York (Ward's Brigade). So intense was the fighting in this sector that Colonel Waddell counted eighty-seven holes in his battle flag. Thirty-eight were made by minié balls, and the remainder by shell fragments.[78]

The right of the brigade, composed of the 17th and 2nd Georgia, moved to the right and entered Plum Run Gorge. Here they encountered the 44th and 48th Alabama, which were slugging it out with the 4th Maine. Two pieces from Smith's battery were firing into the gorge, making it a hellish place. Lieutenant Colonel William Shepard of the 2nd Georgia reported that "the entire regiment moved forward in splendid order until it came to a deep gorge, where the nature of the ground was such that it was impossible to preserve an alignment, but not withstanding the rocks, undergrowth, and the deadly fire of the enemy . . . [we] moved forward with dauntless courage, driving the enemy." According to Sergeant William Houghton of the 2nd Georgia, "above us then, quite twenty feet, on the edge of the rock stood a line of blue coated United States regulars firing straight down at our line which had become broken in passing over and around the huge boulders which barred our way." They were really up against the large 40th New York of de Trobriand's Brigade (Birney's Division), which had been rushed to the scene to help stem the Confederate advance. The two Georgia requirements were pushed back into the rocky area called "Devil's Den," where they repelled charge after charge by the New Yorkers. Private Theodore Fogle of the 2nd Georgia proudly wrote after the battle, "our brigade charged over a ravine filled with large rocks . . . we drove back the enemy and captured three guns. The enemy in turn charged us three (some say six) times but were gloriously repulsed."[79]

The progress of Benning's right flank was enhanced when the rest of the line finally captured Houck's Ridge. The men knew it because, according to Captain John Martin of the 17th Georgia, "the music of the unmistakable Confederate yell announced to us the joyous tidings that our men were on top [of Houck's Ridge] and were charging, and soon those firing upon us were routed from the mountain top." Benning's orders to his men were simple ones: "Give them hell, boys—give them hell."[80]

In his report, Benning discussed the difficulties that his brigade faced in dealing with the enemy. "The ground was difficult—rocks in many places presenting, by their precipitous sides, insurmountable obstacles, while the fire of the enemy was very heavy and very deadly. The progress was, therefore, not very rapid, but it was regular and uninterrupted." Although Ward's Brigade gallantly held its position, Benning's Brigade's sheer numbers and aggressiveness finally forced the Federals off Houck's Ridge.[81]

The 15th Georgia on the left of the line also continued forward and gobbled up over 150 prisoners. Looking up, Private Fluker never saw the sun bigger or redder, but worse, it seemed to just hang in the sky, seemingly unwilling to cause a halt to the death and destruction. Colonel DuBose suddenly noted a strong Federal force in his front, moving toward the gap between his left and Anderson's Brigade. This was the 5th New Hampshire, which, along with the rest of Cross's Brigade (Caldwell's Division, II Corps), had been sent into the Wheatfield to clear it of Confederates. "We stood ready, taking shelter behind rocks and trees," recalled Fluker. "They raised a hip, hurrah, and charged on our forces, and it seemed as if they were determined to run

over us." Afraid that his regiment would be cut off and surrounded, DuBose pulled his men back to the stone wall it had occupied at the beginning of his charge. Seeing Anderson's Brigade about to charge, DuBose attached his men to the right of the 59th Georgia and joined in. While meeting with initial success, the attack finally failed and Anderson's men fell back. This left DuBose with little choice but to do the same. He halted his men behind one of the stone walls of the triangular field.[82]

In the meantime, Brooke's Brigade (Caldwell's Division) arrived. The 15th Georgia opened fire on these troops, but did not attack them. Colonel DuBose received a message from the commander of the 59th Georgia (Anderson's Brigade) on his left that another attack was planned and it would meet with greater success if the 15th Georgia participated. DuBose readily agreed and the 15th Georgia advanced once again. With the growing pressure, Colonel John Brooke decided that it was time to pull his Federal brigade back to safety. DuBose now swung his regiment around to form at right angles to Anderson's Brigade and fired into Brooke's men, further hastening their withdrawal. The men did not have much time to rest, as DuBose received a report that the enemy was again moving toward his left flank. "I changed my line back about 200 yards, and fronted differently," he wrote in his report. "I had not gotten through this movement before I discovered that the enemy were moving forward rapidly, and were within 200 yards of the left of my line. I halted, faced about, and commenced fighting them, and, after a few well-directed volleys, succeeded in checking their advance." These troops appeared to be from Burbank's Brigade (Ayres's Division, V Corps). Moving his men back to the safety of a stone wall, DuBose ordered them to rest.[83]

While the 15th Georgia was hammering it out with brigades from Caldwell's and Ayres's Divisions, the rest of Benning's Brigade had full control of Houck's Ridge. From this position Benning scanned Little Round Top. He did not like what he saw, considering it all but impregnable. In the absence of orders (Hood was wounded and Law, his replacement, was all but invisible), Benning decided to hold the ridge. This he considered to be a difficult task, as the artillery on Little Round Top was making it uncomfortable for his men and the snipers were bringing down many others. Benning ordered his men behind rocks and trees; they opened a deadly fire on the enemy on the hill, killing and wounding many of them. Private John Bowden noted that "the enemy had concealed themselves, and we considered it impossible to drive them back with anything like an orderly advance. So here we came to a halt, and Indian fashioned, each man selected a rock" from behind which he could fire at the enemy.[84]

Not all of the men halted on the ridge. Lieutenant Colonel William Harris of the 2nd Georgia led his men across Plum Run and toward Little Round Top. "He crossed the creek, but few if any of his men crossed with him, they seeing that it was impossible to climb the mountain up which he was endeavoring to charge under the terrific fire of the enemy. At this point, still about twenty yards in advance of his command, he fell, pierced by the enemy bullets," recalled Private Bowden of the same regiment. As night descended, Benning's men awaited a final charge by the enemy. General Benning was heard to tell his men, "Hold your fire until they come right up. Then pour a vol-

ley into them, and if they don't stop, run your bayonets into their bellies."[85]

That night, Benning rearranged his line, established pickets, and removed the wounded. Of the three activities, Benning considered the latter to be the most difficult, "owing to some fault or mistake in the surgeon having charge of the brigade ambulances, but two of them made their appearance, so that the labor to the litter-bearers became very heavy." The enemy was also busy that night throwing up breastworks. These sounds were easily heard, and portended problems in the future. The enemy skirmish line pushed Colonel DuBose's skirmishers on the left of the line so persistently that two additional companies were sent out, resulting in a heavy skirmish.[86]

Words escaped Fluker (15th Georgia) when he tried to relate what the battlefield looked like at the end of July 2. "The slaughter in our front was simply beyond description. The ground in front of us was covered in places with dead men. Where a line would stand for a few moments it was marked as distinctly by a line of dead as it ever was by the living. I saw them in one place as they fell, three deep piled on each other." Fluker thought that the slaughter in the Wheatfield occurred because "the breeze on the hill took the smoke out of the way and every man could see his mark at each fire." The lack of cover also explained the high losses.[87]

The men rested for most of July 3 on the left flank of Hood's Division. General Benning received disquieting news at about 5:00 P.M.—McLaw's units on his left had moved several hours before, leaving his flank vulnerable to attack. "I immediately ordered the strongest picket force I could spare to the abandoned post of General McLaws's line," Benning noted in his report. Not long afterward, Benning received orders from General Law to move to the crest of a hill. His initial relief turned to concern when he realized he didn't know which hill Law was referring to. Asking the courier, he was told that Law "waved his hand thus (making a wave of his hand)." Thinking it was Rose's Woods to the left formerly occupied by McLaws's men, Benning ordered his left regiment, the 15th Georgia, to move in that direction. After the 15th Georgia had departed, another messenger arrived with more specific orders from Law—move back to Warfield Ridge. Benning immediately ordered his three remaining regiments to march to the rear. His heart must have sunk when he heard small arms fire coming from the direction of the 15th Georgia.[88]

Colonel DuBose didn't know it, but he was marching toward Colonel William McCandless's Brigade of Pennsylvania Reserves (V Corps), which was advancing into the Wheatfield. DuBose was apparently not told that McLaws's men had moved, for he was dismayed to see no Confederate troops on his left when he took his assigned position. He was also concerned about the yawning quarter-mile gap to his right. DuBose threw out skirmishers to patrol the gap and almost immediately saw McCandless's men advancing. "The enemy came up rapidly in heavy force, turning my left entirely, and also advancing in front and moving upon my right in the space between my right and the left of the position where I had left the balance of our brigade," wrote DuBose in his report. Seeing the desperateness of the situation, DuBose immediately ordered his line back about seventy-five yards and, at the same time, changed front to face the enemy. Deploying his men behind rocks and trees, DuBose steeled his men against the attack. "I had a desperate fight, the enemy

moving upon my right and left flanks and front. I fought them until they had gotten within 20 to 40 yards of my men," wrote DuBose. Seeing that no assistance was on the way, DuBose quickly ordered a retreat, and the men eventually reformed about 350 yards in the rear behind a stone wall. McCandless's men could smell blood and quickly followed. After a brief firefight, DuBose realized that his small regiment was about to be overwhelmed, so he again ordered it to the rear. He rallied the regiment again, and again it was overwhelmed.[89]

The remnants of the regiment finally rejoined the rest of the brigade during the next withdrawal. DuBose reported that "my loss was immense." Of the 330 men who had entered the battle, only seventy were killed, wounded, or missing during the series of engagements on July 2. However, the regiment lost over a hundred on July 3, as well as its flag. As a result, his regiment lost more than any other in Benning's Brigade—almost 50%. Benning's poor handling of his brigade caused the unnecessary losses. Why he allowed a single regiment to move to the left to occupy an isolated position has never been explained. He did report that "I did not go to his assistance because, when I heard the fire, it seemed to be (and was, indeed) so far on my left that I thought some of General McLaws's men had been sent forward to check an advance of the enemy, and that it came from a collision between them and the enemy." The excuse was lame—just a few paragraphs before, Benning admitted knowing that McLaws had withdrawn from its former positions.[90]

The brigade faced Emmitsburg Road on Warfield Ridge on July 4. Here they erected breastworks to help repel the Federal advance, which never came. The retreat began at midnight.[91]

While Benning's Brigade performed reasonably well during the battle, it suffered from poor leadership. It was to have followed Law's Brigade into battle, but, in the confusion, Benning went to Robertson's aid. Many have wondered what would have happened if it had attacked Little Round Top. However, in the absence of orders, Benning was content to hunker down on the Houck's Ridge. Similarly, Benning's handling of the 15th Georgia on July 3 bordered on extreme incompetence, causing the loss of many effective soldiers.[92]

Anderson's Brigade—Brigadier General George Anderson

Units: 7th Georgia, 8th Georgia, 9th Georgia, 11th Georgia, 59th Georgia
Strength: 1874
Losses: 722 (152-468-102)—38.5%[93]

General George Anderson's Brigade was a unit itching for a fight. It was a veteran brigade, whose roots extended back to the first battle of Manassas, where the 7th and 8th Georgia were part of Bartow's Brigade. Brigadier General Samuel Jones assumed command of the brigade after the battle and the 9th and 11th Georgia were added. After a short stint under D. R. Jones, the brigade was assigned to Colonel George Anderson. The brigade fought at Yorktown and Williamsburg. The 59th Georgia arrived in June 1862, in time for the Seven Days battles. The brigade charged up the Malvern Hill, but had better luck when it helped take on General John Pope's army at the battle of Second Manassas. It played only a minor role at the battle of Sharpsburg, and in October 1862 the brigade was transferred to General John Hood's fighting division. The brigade saw little action at the battle of Fredericksburg and was with Longstreet in southwest Virginia during the Chancellorsville campaign. Therefore, it had been almost a year since the brigade had been in heavy combat.[94]

"Tige" (short for "tiger") Anderson served in the war with Mexico and later commanded a company in the regular army. He was a wealthy landowner at the outbreak of the war, initially the colonel of the 11th Georgia, Anderson took over the brigade just prior to the Seven Days battles. A tough fighter, he was well liked by his men.[95]

Anderson's men were in good spirits as they marched into Chambersburg, Pennsylvania, during the Gettysburg campaign. The men noted that the townspeople were wary of them, so they tried to reassure them. "Why they won't hurt you. All their muskets and equipment are marked U.S.," yelled one of the men in the 8th Georgia. Lieutenant J. Reid of the same regiment recalled that as the brigade marched through Chambersburg "with streaming banners and lively martial airs, the streets were crowded with women. Each one had a small United States flag on her bosom, and somehow held them so that you couldn't hardly see anything else." Hillyer (9th Georgia) noted that private property rights were "universally accepted" because of Lee's orders. This was probably stretching the truth, as many men actively "appropriated" needed materials. Those caught were often punished. One private stealing a chicken was ordered to carry a heavy pole across his shoulders for two miles.[96]

The men were issued extra ammunition and rations on July 1 and told that they would move out that day. Anderson finally received the order to "proceed as rapidly as possible to Gettysburg" at 2:00 P.M. One of the men recalled that Anderson gave the order of "Attention" so loudly, that it could be heard half a mile away. While an exaggeration, the order was immediately obeyed, as was the following one, "Forward, March!" So began the twenty-four-mile march to reach the battlefield. Trains and other troops slowed the march, so it was not until shortly before daybreak that the brigade reached Marsh Creek, where the men were finally permitted to rest.[97]

As the sun rose, the men stirred and ate their rations. Several spoke with their counterparts from A. P. Hill's Corps and learned about the first day's battle. Lieutenant John Reid of the 8th Georgia noted that "this raised the ardor of our men to white heat." Some of the men were heard to say, "These Yanks say that we whip them in Virginia because we are at home and they are away from home; today we shall whip them at home." Sometime during the morning, the men could see General Lee conferring with other officers. One private remarked, "Boys, there are ten thousand men sitting on that one horse."[98]

None of the men spent much time writing about the circuitous march to Warfield Ridge. Major M. Bass of the 59th Georgia simply wrote to his wife that "after maneurving [sic] all day until 3 P.M., we finally got fully into the fight." The brigade was aligned to the extreme left of Hood's Division, in the rear of Biesecker's Woods, in support of Robertson's Brigade. Other supporting brigades were near—Benning's Brigade was on its right, and Semmes's Brigade (McLaws's Division) was on its left. The brigade was deployed from left to right as 9th Georgia–8th Georgia–11th Georgia–59th Georgia. The 7th Georgia was not there

because it had been detached and moved to the right to watch for Federal cavalry. Federal cannon fire commenced almost immediately. According to Reid, "we were lying down behind a skirt of small forest trees. The shells were striking among us, and I had made my men get before the fence to avoid splinters."[99]

The brigade was not in position long when Law's Brigade on the extreme right of the division launched its attack shortly after 4:00 P.M. Because of the *en echelon* nature of the attack, a span of time elapsed before Law's and then Robertson's Brigades were launched. Hood went down with a wound and Law assumed command of the division. A courier arrived from Robertson soon after with word that he was being sorely pressed and requested that Anderson advance to support his left flank. Anderson immediately ordered his men forward, and according to a private in the 8th Georgia, "the line rose from the grass upon which they were resting and boldly marched to the field." The men gave a rousing Rebel yell. Anderson did not know the exact location of Robertson's Brigade (General Robertson's messenger merely pointed in the general direction), but reasoned that he would find it if he marched toward the firing on his right. As the line of battle broke from the protection of Biesecker's Woods it attracted the attention of the Federal artillery near the Wheatfield. "Had our advance been slow they would have swept all of us away. We understood that too well to loiter, and so we dashed on through small wheat fields and over stone fences, filling up every gap made by a hit, and maintaining a line which would have delighted Ney himself," wrote Reid (8th Georgia). The brigade did not experience much relief until it had finally traversed the three hundred-yard open space and reached Rose's Woods.[100]

Anderson did not know it, but he was moving rapidly toward the right flank of Ward's Brigade, de Trobriand's Brigade to its right, and the 8th New Jersey and 115th Pennsylvania of Burling's Brigade in Rose's Woods. After crossing Rose Run, the men continued their charge. The ground was irregular, populated with large rocks and trees that destroyed the regiments' formations. The Federal troops opened fire on Anderson's men. "Our line did not waver under the galling musketry, but came on almost at a run, firing vigorously. I have never read in military history of any soldiers who could deliver such deadly volleys as ours when charging," Reid related proudly.[101]

The 59th Georgia on the right of the line linked up with the 3rd Arkansas (Robertson's Brigade) and together they swept forward against Ward's Brigade's right flank, composed of the 86th New York, 20th Indiana, and 99th Pennsylvania. As the 59th Georgia rushed forward, its left flank was hit by deadly fire from the 17th Maine (de Trobriand's Brigade). The opposite flank of the brigade was having no more success. The 5th Michigan and 110th Pennsylvania extended beyond the left flank of the 9th Georgia and, as a result, Hillyer found that "bullets were coming from our front; enfilading from our left; and also diagonally from our rear." Large rocks provided a measure of protection, causing Hillyer to write home, "if it had not been for the shelter of the rocks and trees behind which we fought, not one of us would have escaped." Reid also saw the menace on the left. "At about seventy yards their muskets were leveled, and they gleamed in the sun . . . a scythe of fire leaped forth, and the air all around me turned to hissing lead." Anderson ordered the three companies of the 8th Georgia to face this threat. After yelling out, "Attention three left companies,"

Hillyer realized that his men could not hear him over the din of the battle. "I ran to the left of the line," he wrote, "and touching the men on the back, made the movement mainly by signs."[102]

The right side of the 9th Georgia and the left side of the 8th Georgia met with more success, as it found a gap between the 8th New Jersey and 115th Pennsylvania, forcing both Federal regiments to retreat back through the Wheatfield. The 17th Maine, farther to their right, held firm, however. Although it was forced from its stone wall at least once, the Federal regiment rallied and drove back Anderson's men. Its efforts were assisted by Winslow's battery in the Wheatfield, which continued to throw a deadly fire against Anderson's men. Major M. Bass of the 59th Georgia recalled that the "musket balls fell in a shower like hail around us. I could hear bones crash like glass in a hailstorm. The ground was covered with the dead and dying, Federals and Confederates lying in piles together." The 17th Maine held its ground, despite being assailed on its front by the 8th and 11th Georgia, as the 9th Georgia poured deadly oblique volleys into it. This tenacious stand, together with the continued oblique fire from the 5th Michigan and 110th Pennsylvania on the right of Federal line, caused Anderson's Brigade to pull back to reform after the fighting had raged for about an hour.[103]

Knowing that he could not renew the fight until he extended his line to the left, Anderson went in search of help. He found it in the form of the 15th South Carolina (Kershaw's Brigade, McLaws's Division), which formed on the left of the 9th Georgia. Anderson now ordered a second attack on the Federal position in the Wheatfield, Rose's Woods and Stony Hill. Anderson was hit by a minié ball in the thigh about this time and knocked out of action for the remainder of the battle. Lieutenant Colonel William Luffman of the 11th Georgia took his place. This attack, would be in conjunction with Kershaw's to the northwest, against parts of three Federal brigades—de Trobrand's, Sweitzer's, and Tilton's. Anderson's men again smashed into the Federal defensive line. Sweitzer's and Tilton's Brigades pulled back, leaving de Trobriand's men to go it alone. The pressure was just too great, and even the tough 17th Maine was finally pushed back from its position behind a stone wall. Anderson's men joyfully occupied their hard-won prize. Any attempt to advance farther into the Wheatfield was discouraged by Winslow's deadly guns, now supported by the 115th Pennsylvania (Burling's Brigade, Humphreys's Division, III Corps).[104]

The men's rest behind the stone wall was cut short by the appearance of Cross's Brigade (Caldwell's Division, II Corps), which was thrown into action to push the Confederates out of the Wheatfield and off Stony Hill. The 148th Pennsylvania, 61st New York, and 81st Pennsylvania steadily advanced against the right of Anderson's Brigade, composed of the 11th Georgia and 59th Georgia. The two regiments hopped down behind the wall, and with their guns poised on the stones, the men opened a deadly fire on the attackers. The defenders should have successfully held their positions, but seven companies of the 148th Pennsylvania were detached and sent around the 59th Georgia's right flank, forcing it from the wall. Like a row of dominos, the entire brigade fell back, one regiment at a time, leaving Cross's Brigade in sole possession of the stone wall.[105]

While Cross's Brigade was content to halt its attack at the stone wall, Brooke's Brigade from the same division soon arrived and continued the advance, pushing Anderson's men completely out of

Rose's Wood. This must have been maddening for the Georgians, as they had fought for several hours, only to be pushed back to their starting point. Together with Semmes's Brigade on their left, Anderson's men exchanged fire with Brooke's soldiers, but were unable to drive them from the woods. Events were occurring in other parts of the Wheatfield, however, that would have a profound effect on Anderson's men. Wofford's Brigade (McLaws's Division) hit Caldwell's Division's right flank, destabilizing the entire line. With the brigades to the left tumbling backward in succession, it was just a matter of time before Brooke ordered his men back through the Wheatfield.[106]

Anderson's men probably couldn't believe their eyes when they realized that Rose's Woods were vacant. Before they could savor the moment, another Federal line of battle approached. Captain Hillyer (9th Georgia) on the left of the line ordered his men to hold their fire as Sweitzer's Brigade approached. After having fought in the Wheatfield earlier, this Federal brigade was thrown back into the Wheatfield to help stem the Confederate tide. A Federal flag bearer marched six feet in front of the line. The soldier suddenly fell back into the line and the Georgians knew what was coming next. "With the precision of a dress parade, that magnificent line of Federals lowered their pieces and the volley came." Most of Hillyer's men had taken cover behind the bank of Rose Run, so the bullets passed harmlessly overhead. Hillyer now screamed for his men to open fire and swore that every shot hit its mark, for as the smoke cleared, "there was not one of the enemy left standing in our front." He admitted that many of the enemy had taken flight, but in front of them "there was a long blue line on the ground so close together than anyone could have walked over them as far as their front extended, without touching the earth." Anderson's men now sprinted forward with Semmes's, Kershaw's, and Wofford's Brigades and threw the remnants of Sweitzer's Brigade out of the Wheatfield. It is a wonder that any of Sweitzer's men survived this attack.[107]

While Sweitzer's men were fleeing from the Wheatfield, Burbank's Brigade (Ayres's Division, V Corps) approached. None of Anderson's men mention their encounter with the U.S. Regulars, as by this time the battle had become very confused as one enemy unit fed into the battle seemed to merge into the next. Continuing forward, Anderson's men collided with the enemy, and with the assistance of Semmes's and part of Kershaw's Brigades, pushed it and Day's Brigades out of the Wheatfield as well.

Little Round Top loomed before them. Struggling forward with their lines in disarray, Anderson's men could see Semmes's, Kershaw's, and Wofford's Brigades to their left in similar confusion. As the men reached the foot of the heights, they could see masses of Federal troops crowning its crest. All but the most foolish knew that there was no way that the relatively few men remaining, exhausted from hours of fighting in the blazing sun, would be able to take these important heights. Captain Hillyer (9th Georgia) claimed that his men began climbing the hill, when "our little attacking column hesitated. They were all veterans in the highest sense. I heard no order to retreat and gave none, but everybody, officers and men, seemed to realize that we could not carry the position . . . by common consent we fell back." The proud Hillyer took pains to explain that the withdrawal was executed at a leisurely pace. The night was spent caring for the wounded, and when possible, sleeping.[108]

The 7th Georgia, which had missed the battle on July 2 because it was watching for a cavalry attack on Hood's right flank, returned to the brigade on the morning of July 3. The regiment's commander, Colonel William White, was now the ranking officer and took command of the brigade. No sooner had his men broke ranks than one of General Law's aides galloped up with orders to send a regiment to the right to help ward off what appeared to be a pending cavalry attack. White sent the 9th Georgia off with an aide. Possibly because White had just returned, he did not know that the regiment had lost over half of its men the day before. Another aide soon arrived with a request for two more regiments, and White complied again, this time sending his own 7th Georgia along with the 8th Georgia. About an hour later, Semmes's Brigade relieved White's two remaining regiments, permitting him to march them to the scene of the brewing action. General Law actually personally escorted these two regiments to the right.[109]

The 9th Georgia took position along Emmitsburg Road near the Kern house, with the 1st Texas off to their left. When it arrived later, the 7th Georgia formed across Emmitsburg Road on the right of the 9th Georgia, and the 8th formed on its right. The men could see General Hugh Kilpatrick's cavalry division's skirmish line in front of them. The men of Farnworth's Brigade were so active that Law was forced to stretch his already thin line, and the 9th Georgia was moved several times. When the 11th and 59th Georgia arrived, they were deployed on the extreme right of his line with orders to attack the cavalry in front of them. These regiments took on Merritt's Brigade (Kilpatrick's Division), driving them from their front.[110]

Later in the day, some units of Farnsworth's cavalry brigade broke through the skirmish line on the far right flank and made for Riley's and Bachman's batteries. Captain Hillyer set his men in motion on the half-mile quick-time march to the northeast to help protect the batteries. According to Hillyer, his men made good time and passed through the batteries. As the men emerged from behind some bushes, they came in full sight of the Federal cavalry. "When they saw our battle flag they seemed to hesitate," recalled Hillyer, "as they did not expect to find any infantry at that point. . . .I gave the command to fire, and . . . the enemy's column seemed to partly go down, and what remained scattered right and left." Many of the men scattered into Law's old brigade, which killed and wounded many more.[111]

The regiments remained in their respective positions after the repulse, expecting the attack to be renewed. The attack never came and the brigade remained there during the night. It moved back to its original position near Biesecker's Woods on the morning of July 4, where the men constructed breastworks in anticipation of a Federal attack. The attack never materialized, and the brigade began its retreat during the early morning hours of July 5.[112]

Anderson's Brigade probably had the distinction of fighting more enemy brigades than any other unit in either army. It engaged at least ten brigades to some degree (de Trobriand's, Sweitzer's, Tilton's, Cross's, Brookes's, Burbank's, Day's, McCandless's, Merritt's, and Farnsworth's), and defeated, or helped to defeat seven of them (de Trobriand, Sweitzer's Tilton's, Burbank's, Day's, Merritt's, and Farnsworth's). The brigade's actions in the Wheatfield were tenacious, and it is doubtful that any troops in either army could have done better. The 39% losses sustained by the brigade is deceptively low because it includes the 6% losses

of the 7th Georgia, which was detached and did not participate in the Wheatfield fight. If this unit is removed from the calculations, the brigade lost, 47%—far more than any other brigade in Hood's Division.

NOTES

1. Warner, *Generals in Gray,* 142–143.

2. Tagg, *Generals of Gettysburg,* 224; Warner, *Generals in Gray,* 143.

3. John C. West, *A Texan in Search of a Fight* (Waco, TX, 1901), 81; Joseph B. Polley, *Hood's Texas Brigade* (New York, 1910), 146–147; Captain D. U. Barziza, diary, Cobb and Hunter Family Papers, Southern Historical Collection, University of North Carolina.

4. Calvin L. Collier, *"They'll Do to Tie to!"—The Story of the Third Regiment Arkansas* (Little Rock, AR, 1988), 136–137.

5. F. B. Chilton, *Unveiling and Dedication of Monument to Hood's Texas Brigade* (Houston, 1911), 350; Pfanz, *Gettysburg—The Second Day,* 173; Tagg, *Generals of Gettysburg,* 226, 228–229.

Another Texan recalled that Hood ordered the men to, "Forward—Steady—Forward" (West, *A Texan in Search of a Fight,* 94).

6. Busey and Martin, *Regimental Strengths and Losses,* 132, 280.

7. Stewart Sifakis, *Compendium of the Confederate Armies: Alabama* (New York, 1992), 59, 76, 114, 117, 119.

8. Warner, *Generals in Gray,* 174–175; Tagg, *Generals of Gettysburg,* 227.

9. OR 27, 2, 391; W. C. Ward, "Incidents and Personal Experiences on the Battlefield at Gettysburg," *Confederate Veteran* (1900), vol. 8, 345; Henry L. Figures, letter, copy in Brake Collection, USAMHI.

10. Figures, letter; Ward, "Incidents and Personal Experiences on the Battlefield at Gettysburg," 346; R. T. Coles, "History of the Fourth Regular Alabama Volunteer Infantry," Alabama Department of Archives and History, chap. 12, 6–7; James Longstreet, *From Manassas to Appomattox* (Phila-

delphia, 1903), 365; William C. Oates, *The War Between the Union and Confederacy and Its Lost Opportunities* (New York, 1905), 206.

Private Ward told a slightly different story. Before turning in, the men were told that they would be roused at 2:00 A.M. on July 2 to begin the march. True to their word, the officers had the men on the road at the appointed time. Colonel Oates agreed, stating that at dark he received orders to be ready to march at any moment. Later he was told that the brigade would move out at 3:00 A.M., but it was not until just before 4:00 A.M. that the column actually moved out (Ward, "Incidents and Personal Experiences on the Battlefield at Gettysburg," 346; Oates, *The War Between the Union and Confederacy and its Lost Opportunities*, 206).

11. Evander M. Law, "The Struggle for Little Round Top," in *Battles and Leaders of the Civil War*, vol. 3, 321; Gary J. Laine and Morris M. Penny, *Law's Alabama Brigade in the War Between the Union and the Confederacy* (Shippensburg, PA, 1996), 80; Oates, *The War Between the Union and Confederacy and its Lost Opportunities*, 207; Ward, "Incidents and Personal Experiences on the Battlefield at Gettysburg," 347.

12. Oates, *The War Between the Union and Confederacy and its Lost Opportunities*, 210; William Oates letter, William Clements Library, University of Michigan; OR 27, 2, 392, 393.

Lieutenant Colonel Michael Bulger never suggested that he was aware of these orders. Bulger commanded the regiment until he was wounded because Colonel J. W. Jackson was somewhere in the rear. In the regiment's official report of the battle, Major James Campbell wrote that "there was some confusion in these companies, owing to the fact that in the charge the lieutenant-colonel expected the colonel to give all necessary commands, and the colonel remained so far behind that his presence on the field was but a trammel to the lieutenant-colonel." Yet in a letter to his wife on July 7, Colonel Jackson suggests that he was in the thick of the battle. Colonel Jackson subse-

quently resigned from the army (OR 27, 2, 395; J. W. Jackson, letter, copy in 47th Alabama folder, GNMP; "General M.J. Bulger, A Hero," *New Orleans Picayune*, September 18, 1898).

13. Oates, *The War Between the Union and Confederacy and its Lost Opportunities*, 210; J. W. Jackson, letter; Coles, "History of the Fourth Alabama," 8; John J. Pullen, "Effects of Marksmanship—A Lesson From Gettysburg," *Gettysburg Magazine* (January 1990), issue 2, 56–58.

William Oates believed that the 2nd U.S. Sharpshooters should have the tallest monument on the field, as it caused the two Alabama regiments to change their course and delay their attack on Little Round Top, which ultimately led to their defeat (Charles A. Stevens, *Berdan's Sharpshooters in the Army of the Potomac* [St. Paul, MN, 1892], 326–328).

14. Oates, *The War Between the Union and Confederacy and its Lost Opportunities*, 210–212; Jackson, letter.

In his report, Oates justified disobeying his orders by stating that the "regiment on my left was crowding me on the left, and running into my regiment, which had already created considerable confusion . . . If I had obeyed the order, I should have come in contact with the regiment on my left, and also have exposed my right flank to an enfilading fire from the enemy" (OR 27, 2, 392).

15. Oates, *The War Between the Union and Confederacy and its Lost Opportunites*, 212–213; Oates, letter; William C. Oates, "Gettysburg—The Battle on the Right," in *Southern Historical Society Papers* (1878), vol. 6, 174–176.

16. William F. Perry, "The Devil's Den," in *Confederate Veteran* (1901), vol. 9, 161.

17. OR 27, 2, 391; Ward, "Incidents and Personal Experiences on the Battlefield at Gettysburg," 347–348; Cole, "History of the Fourth Alabama," 9–10, 19.

18. OR 27, 2, 393–394; Perry, "The Devil's Den," 161; Laine and Penny, *Law's Brigade in the War Between the Union and Confederacy*, 90.

According to modern historian Gary Bruner, Law shifted the two regiments when he realized that they were too far to the right (Gary P. Bruner, "Up Over Big Round Top: The Forgotten 47th Alabama," *Gettysburg Magazine* [January 2000], 12).

19. Perry, "The Devil's Den," 161–162; OR 27, 2, 394; Kathleen G. Harrison, "Our Principal Loss Was in this Place," *Gettysburg Magazine* (July 1989), issue 1, 62; Imhof, *Gettysburg—Day Two*, 102.

20. OR 27, 2, 395–396.

Colonel Sheffield was not told that he was to assume command of the brigade until the second day's battle was all but over (OR 27, 2, 396).

21. Figures, letter.

22. Laine and Penny, *Law's Brigade in the War Between the Union and the Confederacy*, 100–101; "General M.J. Bulger, A Hero"; J. Jackson, letter, *Montgomery Daily Mail*, July 26, 1863; Oates, "Gettysburg—The Battle on the Right," 176.

According to Lieutenant Holman Melcher, the 20th Maine was just taking position when the 47th Alabama burst upon them (Holman S. Melcher, "The 20th Maine at Gettysburg," in *Battles and Leaders of the Civil War*, vol. 3, 315).

23. Oates, *The War Between the Union and Confederacy and its Lost Opportunities*, 217–218; William C. Jordan, *Incidents During the Civil War* (Montgomery, AL, 1909), 43; Oates, letter.

24. Jackson, letter.

Despite a severe chest wound, Lieutenant Colonel Bulger refused to surrender his sword to an officer of lower rank. Colonel James Rice of the 44th New York was sent for, and the old lieutenant colonel willingly tendered his sword to him. Oates believed that had Bulger not been wounded, his regiment would have held their ground and Little Round Top would have been captured (Oates, *The War Between the Union and Confederacy and its Lost Opportunities*, 217; Oates, letter).

25. OR 27, 2, 623; Oates, *The War Between the Union and Confederacy and its Lost Opportunities*, 218–219; Oates, letter.

26. Oates, *The War Between the Union and Confederacy and its Lost Opportunities*, 219–220; Oates, letter.

27. Oates, *The War Between the Union and Confederacy and its Lost Opportunities*, 222.

28. H. C. Parsons, "Farnsworth's Charge and Death," in *Battles and Leaders of the Civil War*, vol. 3, 394; William Oates to John Bachelder, September 16, 1888, Bachelder Papers, New Hampshire Historical Society; OR 27, 2, 391–392; Coles, "History of the Fourth Alabama," 21–23.

29. Oates, *The War Between the Union and Confederacy and its Lost Opportunities*, 236–237; "Gen. E. M. Law at Gettysburg," in *Confederate Veteran* (1922), vol. 30, 49–50; William Oates to John Bachelder, September 16, 1888.

30. Oates, *The War Between the Union and Confederacy and its Lost Opportunities*, 239.

31. Busey and Martin, *Regimental Strengths and Losses*, 133, 280.

32. Sears, *To the Gates of Richmond*, 241–242; Sears, *Landscape Turned Red*, 200–201; Tagg, *Generals of Gettysburg*, 232.

33. Tagg, *Generals of Gettysburg*, 231–232; Warner, *Generals in Gray*, 261.

34. Gregory Coco, *Recollections of a Texas Colonel at Gettysburg* (Gettysburg, PA, 1990), 7; Polley, *Hood's Texas Brigade*, 146–147; Miles V. Smith, "Reminiscences of the Civil War," Civil War Miscellaneous Collection, USAMHI, 34–35, West, *Texan in Search of a Fight*, 81.

35. R. M. Powell, "With Hood at Gettysburg," *Philadelphia Weekly Times*, December 13, 1884; Smith, "Reminiscences of the Civil War," 35; Barziza, diary; J. Mark Smither, letter, 5th Texas folder, GNMP; West, *Texan in Search of a Fight*, 82.

36. Polley, *Hood's Texas Brigade*, 147.

37. Polley, *Hood's Texas Brigade*, 148.

38. Smither, letter; Polley, *Hood's Texas Brigade*, 154; Barziza, diary; Coco, *"Recollections of a Texas Colonel at Gettysburg* (Gettysburg, 1990); Collier, *They'll Do to Tie to!* 135; A. C. Sims, "Recollections of A. C. Sims at the Battle of Gettysburg," copy in Brake Collection, USAMHI.

39. Polley, *Hood's Texas Brigade*, 154.

40. Sims, "Recollections of A. C. Sims at the Battle of Gettysburg"; John A. Wilkerson, "Experiences of 'Seven Pines' At Gettysburg," copy in the 3rd Arkansas folder, GNMP; Decimus Barziza, *The Adventures of a Prisoner of War* (Austin, TX, 1964), 44; Polley, *Hood's Texas Brigade,* 167; Collier, *They'll Do to Tie to!* 138.

41. Chilton, *Unveiling and Dedication of Monument to Hood's Texas Brigade,* 350; Collier, *They'll Do to Tie to!* 139; W. A. Fletcher, *Rebel Private, Front and Rear* (Austin, TX, 1954), 59; Smithers, letter.

According to Private A. Sims, it was General Hood who ordered the men to lie down. Sims also recalled that Hood was the officer that led the small detail of men to knock down the fence (Sims, "Recollections of A. C. Sims at the Battle of Gettysburg").

42. OR 27, 2, 404, 405, 407; Jerome Robertson to John Bachelder, May 11, 1882, Bachelder Papers, New Hampshire Historical Society.

Many years after the war, Colonel Phillip Work of the 1st Texas insisted that he had no contact with Robertson before, during, or after his initial charge (P. A. Work, letter, copy in 1st Texas folder, GNMP).

After the charge began, the 48th and 44th Alabama moved from the extreme right of Law's Brigade and partially plugged this gap.

43. Collier, *They'll Do to Tie to!* 140–141; OR 27, 2, 407; Busey and Martin, *Regimental Strengths and Losses,* 245, 246, 280.

44. James E. Smith, *A Famous Battery and Its Campaigns* (Washington, 1892), 111–112; Garry E. Adelman and Timothy H. Smith, *Devil's Den—A History and Guide* (Gettysburg, PA, 1997), 31; *New York Monuments Commission for the Battlefields of Gettysburg and Chattanooga—Final Report on the Battlefield of Gettysburg* (Albany, NY, 1900), vol. 2, 869; Polley, *Hood's Texas Brigade,* 169.

45. Sims, "Recollections of A. C. Sims at the Battle of Gettysburg"; Harrison, "Our Principal Loss Was in this Place," 62.

46. OR 27, 2, 407, 408–409; Daniel M. Laney, "Wasted Gallantry: Hood's Texas

Brigade at Gettysburg," *Gettysburg Magazine* (January 1997), issue 16, 41–42; Sims, "Recollections of A. C. Sims at the Battle of Gettysburg"; Polley, *Hood's Texas Brigade,* 169; Maine Gettysburg Commission, *Maine at Gettysburg: Report of the Main Commissioners Prepared by the Executive Committee* (Portland, ME, 1898), 182.

Over forty years after the battle, Colonel Work still fumed that the 20th Georgia had claimed credit for capturing the battery. Work also insisted that Robertson was wounded early in the attack and did not give orders the remainder of the day. While Robertson does not discuss it in his official report, he was wounded, but later than when Work recalled (Work letter; OR 27, 2, 404–407; Collier, *They'll Do to Tie to!* 144).

47. OR 27, 2, 405, 406; Collier, *They'll do to tie to!* 142; Busey and Martin, *Regimental Strengths and Losses,* 280.

48. Collier, *They'll Do to Tie to!* 143; OR 27, 2, 409, 422.

49. OR 27, 2, 411, 412.

50. OR 27, 2, 411, 413; Imhof, *Gettysburg—Day Two,* 78, 80; West, *A Texan in Search of a Fight,* 94.

51. Smither, letter; Fletcher, *Rebel Private Front and Rear,* 79; Stevens, *Reminiscences of the Civil War,* 114.

52. OR 27, 2, 413.

53. "Gettysburg Trip—The Lone Star Flag Over Devil's Den," copy in Brake Collection, USAMHI; Fletcher, *Rebel Private,* 80; Valerius C. Giles, *Rags and Hope: The Recollections of Val C. Giles . . .* (New York, 1961), 180; Stevens, *Reminiscences,* 114–115.

Giles recalled that the Major Rogers's "speech" occurred before Law's aide arrived. However, it appears more likely that it occurred after.

54. Polley, *Hood's Texas Brigade,* 170.

55. OR 27, 1, 617, 628; Oliver W. Norton, *Attack and Defense of Little Round Top, Gettysburg, July 2, 1863* (New York, 1913), 243; Zack Landrum, letter, copy in Brake Collection, USAMHI.

56. Norton, *Attack and Defense of Little Round Top, Gettysburg, July 2, 1863,* 260.

57. Smither, letter; Rufus K. Felder, letter, copy in 5th Texas folder, GNMP; Busey and Martin, *Regimental Strengths and Losses*, 280.

58. Fletcher, *Rebel Private*, 82; Tagg, *Generals at Gettysburg*, 233.

59. OR 27, 2, 406, 411; Collier, *They'll Do to Tie to!* 143; Fletcher, *Rebel Private Front and Rear*, 82.

60. Thomas McCarthy, "The Battle of Gettysburg July 1st, 2nd, & 3d 1863," copy in Brake Collection, USAMHI; Sims, "Recollections of A. C. Sims at the Battle of Gettysburg"; George Hillyer, "Battle of Gettysburg Address," Walton Tribune, copy in the 9th Georgia folder, GNMP; Todd, "Recollections of Gettysburg," 240; unknown diary, Brake Collection, USAMHI; Paul M. Shevchuk, "The 1st Texas Infantry and the Repulse of Farnsworth's Charge," *Gettysburg Magazine* (January 1990), Issue 2, 85.

Several of the above authors (e.g., Sims and Todd) believed that the cavalrymen were intoxicated. However, modern historian Paul Shevchuk believed that, given the rigorous ride to the battlefield, it is unlikely that the men had an opportunity to drink. He believed that it was more likely that the men were simply exhausted from their exertions (Shevchuk, "The 1st Texas Infantry and the Repulse of Farnsworth's Charge," 88–89).

61. McCarthy, "The Battle of Gettysburg." Unfortunately, no official reports from the 1st Texas about its actions against Farnsworth's cavalry exist. Colonel Work wrote in a 1908 letter, "it is simply incredible and not a fact, that I failed to report on the conduct of the brigade on the 3rd." The letter contained Work's strong assertions that the report included in the official records was not his (Work, letter).

62. W.T. White, "First Texas Regiment at Gettysburg," in *Confederate Veteran* (1922), vol. 30, 185; H.W. Berryman, "Company I, 1st Texas at Gettysburg," in *New York Times*, July 3, 1913; James H. Hendrick, "Letter," copy in 1st Texas folder, GNMP.

63. Shevchuk, "The 1st Texas Infantry and the Repulse of Farnsworth's Charge," 87–88; White, "First Texas Regiment at Get-tysburg," 185; Jeffrey D. Wert, *Gettysburg—Day Three* (New York, 2001), 277.

64. OR 27, 2, 411, 413.

65. Some writers acknowledge that the 16th Michigan fell back because of incorrect orders, not because of the pressure of the 4th Texas and 48th Alabama.

66. Busey and Martin, *Regimental Strengths and Losses*, 134, 281.

67. Sifakis, *Compendium of the Confederate Armies: South Carolina and Georgia*, 181, 214, 216–217, 222.

68. Tagg, *Generals of Gettysburg*, 234–235; Warner, *Generals in Gray*, 25–26, 306.

69. Thomas Lewis Ware, papers, Southern Historical Collection, University of North Carolina, 124, 125,126.

70. Ware, papers, 125, 126.

71. Ware, papers, 127, 128; William J. Fluker, "An Account of the Battle of Little Round Top Hill at Gettysburg," copy in 15th Georgia folder, GNMP; John Malachi Bowden, "Recollections," Theodore Fogle Collection, Emory University Library.

72. OR 27, 2, 420, 424; Ware Papers, 128; Fluker, "Account of the Battle of Little Round Top Hill at Gettysburg."

73. OR 27, 2, 420, 421, 424, 425.

74. Fluker, "Account of the Battle of Little Round Top Hill at Gettysburg."

75. OR 27, 2, 414–415

76. OR 27, 2, 415; "A Letter From the Army," *The Savannah Republican*, July 22, 1863.

Because some of the soldiers referred to Houck's Ridge as "the heights" or "peak," it is often confused with Little Round Top. Thus, in his report, Benning wrote, "when my line reached the foot of the peak, I found there a part of the First Texas, struggling to make the ascent." In reality, the 1st Texas was battling the 124th New York in the triangular field, near Devil's Den (OR 27, 2, 415).

77. OR 27, 2, 409, 421; Fluker, "Account of the Battle of Little Round Top Hill at Gettysburg."

78. OR 27, 2, 426–427; J. W. Lokey, "Wounded at Gettysburg," in *Confederate Veteran* (1914), vol. 22, 400.

Although none of the Georgians mentioned it, Private A. C. Sims of the 1st Texas complained that in the confusion, the 20th Georgia fired into them (Sims, "Recollections of A. C. Sims at the Battle of Gettysburg").

79. OR 27, 2, 420, 424–425; William R. Houghton, *Two Boys in the Civil War and After* (Montgomery, AL, 1912), 220; Bowden, "Recollections."

John Bowden recalled that the smoke was so dense that some of the men, believing themselves to be in the front ranks, fired into their comrades in front of them until stopped.

80. John H. Martin, "Accurate Historical Records," in *Confederate Veteran* (1904), vol. 12, 114; "Gettysburg Trip—The Lone Star Flag Over Devil's Den," copy in Brake Collection, USAMHI.

81. OR 27, 2, 415.

82. OR 27, 2, 422; Fluker, "Account of the Battle of Little Round Top Hill at Gettysburg"; Pfanz, *Gettysburg—The Second Day*, 273–274.

83. OR 27, 2, 422.

84. OR 27, 2, 415; John Bowden, "Recollections."

85. John Bowden, "Recollections"; Sims, "Recollections of A. C. Sims at the Battle of Gettysburg."

86. OR 27, 2, 416, 423.

87. Fluker, "Account of the Battle of Little Round Top Hill at Gettysburg."

88. OR 27, 2, 416–417.

General Law never a filed a report after the battle, but did write to Colonel John Bachelder after the war, indicating that much of the gap to the left of Benning's Brigade was caused by the movement of Anderson's Brigade. The latter brigade was moved south to help repel an anticipated charge by Federal cavalry. Law also believed that Benning misunderstood his orders when he moved the 15th Georgia to the north (Evander Law to John Bachelder, June 13, 1876, in Bachelder Papers, New Hampshire Historical Society).

89. OR 27, 2, 423–424.

90. Busey and Martin, *Regimental Strengths and Losses*, 281; OR 27, 2, 417.

91. OR 27, 2, 417.

92. Modern historian Garry Adelman believes that the errant movement of Benning's Brigade was actually a positive development because it helped plug the gap between the two wings of Robertson's Brigade which had moved in different directions. Adelman also had a different perception of Benning's leadership during the battle, considering it to have been very effective. Few of Benning's regimental commanders, however, mentioned him in their reports of the battle, suggesting that they were fighting it out alone without much supervision (Garry E. Adelman, "Benning's Georgia Brigade at Gettysburg," *Gettysburg Magazine* [January 1998], issue, 18, 61, 66).

93. Busey and Martin, *Regimental Strengths and Losses*, 135, 280.

94. Sifakis, *Compendium of the Confederate Armies: South Carolina and Georgia*, 196–197, 200, 202–203, 206–207, 272–273; Evans, *Confederate Military History*, vol. 6, 391.

95. Warner, *Generals in Gray*, 6–7; Tagg, *Generals of Gettysburg*, 229–230.

96. Travis Hudson, "Soldier Boys in Gray, A History of the 59th Georgia Infantry Regiment," *Atlanta Historical Society Journal* (Spring 1979); 52; J. C. Reid, diary, Alabama State Archives, 65; George Hillyer, "Battle of Gettysburg Address," *Walton Tribune*, copy in the 9th Georgia folder, GNMP.

97. Hillyer, "Battle of Gettysburg Address," 2.

98. Reid, diary, 67; Hillyer, "Battle of Gettysburg Address," 3.

99. M. J. Bass, letter, copy in the 59th Georgia folder, GNMP; OR 27, 2, 396; Reid, diary.

Although the 7th Georgia's position is not known, modern historian Harry Pfanz believed that it was in a position where it could guard both Emmitsburg Road and the countryside around it. It probably did not see any cavalry during July 2 (Pfanz, *Gettysburg—The Second Day*, 160).

100. Hudson, "Soldier Boys in Gray, A History of the 59th Georgia Infantry Regiment," 55–56; George Anderson to John

Bachelder, March 15, 1876, Bachelder Papers, New Hampshire Historical Society; Reid, diary.

101. Reid, diary.

102. Imhof, *Gettysburg—Day Two*, 70; Hillyer, "Battle of Gettysburg Address," 6; "Letter From Captain Hillyer," *Southern Banner*, July 29, 1863; Reid, diary.

103. Reid, diary; Bass, letter; Jay Jorgenson, "Anderson Attacks the Wheatfield," *Gettysburg Magazine* (January 1996), issue 14, 68–69.

Major B. H. Gee of the 59th Georgia explained that his men were not successful because they were exhausted from double-quicking over 400 yards "under a severe shelling and a scorching sun" (OR 27, 2, 403).

Captain George Hillyer of the 9th Georgia gave the distinct impression that his men never pulled back, but instead held their positions along Rose Run (Hillyer, "Battle of Gettysburg Address," 7).

104. George Anderson to John Bachelder, December 4, 1894, Bachelder Papers, New Hampshire Historical Society; Pfanz, *Gettysburg—The Second Day*, 257, 263.

105. Pfanz, *Gettysburg—The Second Day*, 273–274.

106. Pfanz, *Gettysburg—The Second Day*, 285–287.

107. Pfanz, *Gettysburg—The Second Day*, 294–295; Hillyer, "Battle of Gettysburg Address," 8.

108. Hillyer, "Battle of Gettysburg Address," 9; E. Rich account, copy in 59th Georgia folder, GNMP; Bass, letter.

Some Confederates claimed to have captured Little Round Top. For example, Captain Benton Miller of the 59th Georgia stated to the Christian Commission at Pont Lookout, where he was a prisoner of war, "[We] got possession of Little Round Top and beyond it" (Andrew B. Cross, *The War, Battle of Gettysburg and the Christian Commission*, copy in the 59th Georgia folder, GNMP).

109. OR 27, 2, 397; Evander Law to John Bachelder, June 13, 1876 and April 22, 1886.

110. Evander Law to John Bachelder, June 13, 1876; OR 27, 2, 402.

111. Eric J. Wittenberg, "Merritt's Regulars on South Cavalry Field: Oh, What Could Have Been," *Gettysburg Magazine* (January 1997), 120–121; Hillyer, "Battle of Gettysburg Address," 13–14.

In his official report, Captain Hillyer claimed that he was already moving the regiment on his own, when the orders arrived (OR 27, 2, 400).

112. Hillyer, "Battle of Gettysburg Address," 14–15; OR 27, 2, 398.

PICKETT'S DIVISION—

Major General George Pickett

Major General George Pickett was one of the most well known divisional commanders in Lee's army. Sporting long curls and considered somewhat of a clown, Pickett was a West Pointer who had the distinction of graduating dead last in his class. He served with distinction during the Mexican War, and in one instance carried the flag up the parapet at Chapultapec. He also made headlines when he took on the British in what is now Washington State in a territorial dispute. Initially receiving a colonel's commission at the outbreak of the Civil War, he was placed in charge of the defenses along the lower Rappahannock River. He was promoted in February 1862 and took command of Brigadier General Philip St. George Cocke's Virginia Brigade after the latter committed suicide. Pickett fought well at Williamsburg, Seven Pines, and Gaines's Mill. Wounded at the latter battle, he returned to the army after the Maryland campaign and was promoted to the rank of major general and given a reorganized division composed of four Virginia brigades and one of South Carolina troops.[1]

Pickett's new division was only marginally engaged at the battle of Fredericksburg and was not present at the battle of Chancellorsville. As a result, the division had never fought as a unit prior to the Gettysburg campaign. To make matters worse, the division was only at three-fifths strength, as Corse's and Jenkins's brigades had been left behind to guard the approaches to Richmond. Even without these brigades, the men were happy to be moving northward. Pickett was justifiably proud of his division, for its morale was high and its ranks full. Most of the men were actually quite young. Colonel David Johnston of the 7th Virginia estimated that the average age of the troops did not exceed nineteen years old.[2]

The division crossed the Potomac River on June 25. While the river was fairly shallow and easily fordable, it posed some difficulties, as related by Captain John James of the 11th Virginia. "The crossing was anything but pleasant, as the bottom was full of rock and a great crowd of men shoving and jostling you about the whole time you were in the river." Sergeant Catlett Conway of the 7th Virginia recalled that the men quickly recovered from their ordeal and burst out singing, "Maryland, My Maryland," as they marched away from the river.[3]

The division reached Chambersburg, Pennsylvania, during the evening of June 27. It was left behind when Longstreet's two other divisions continued their march toward Gettysburg on June 30. Pickett's march to the battlefield finally commenced at 2:00 A.M. on the morning of July 2, when Imboden's cavalry brigade arrived to take over for the Virginians's. While in Chambersburg, the men took advantage of the region's "hospitality" and also spent time tearing up the tracks of the Cumberland Valley Railroad. The rails were first heated, then twisted around trees. Later in the war these twisted rails were called "Sherman's bowties." Although July 2 was exceedingly hot and the road was dusty, the men made good time, arriving within two miles of Gettysburg by midafternoon that day, after a twenty-five-mile march. When the division was about five miles from the battlefield, Pickett rode ahead to confer with Longstreet. At the same time, Pickett sent his adjutant, Major Walter Harrison, to inform General Lee that his division was approaching, and although tired from the long march, would be ready to fight after a two-hour rest. Because of Longstreet's initial successes during the late afternoon of July 2, Lee decided it was best to let the division rest and prepare for action the following day.[4]

This information did not filter down to the men, so many could not understand why they were not moved to the front, particularly since the sounds of battle were so loud. Lieutenant John Dooley of the 1st Virginia believed that Pickett protested the orders to move to the front because of the "jaded" condition of the men from their twenty-five-mile march that day. However, Colonel Joseph Mayo of the 3rd Virginia knew that Pickett had sent Harrison to find General Lee and inform him "of our arrival and readiness for action."[5]

Lee's plan for July 3 was fairly straightforward: send twelve brigades forward to breach the Federal center, 1300 yards away. The Federal line on Cemetery Ridge had been successfully breached the day before by 1400 Georgians of Wright's Brigade (Anderson's Division, Third Corps). Now the Confederates would return, but this time with almost ten times that number. While Longstreet doubted that any troops could successfully storm the heights, Pickett was more optimistic.[6]

Reveille sounded at 3:00 A.M. on July 3. After a quick breakfast, the men were back on Chambersburg Pike. Taking back roads, the division marched from Chambersburg Pike to Seminary Ridge, on the right. Because the division formed for battle in its marching order, Kemper's Brigade, which led the column, formed on the right and Garnett's on the left. Heth's Division (now under General Johnston) was on Garnett's left. Not knowing whether he should form in front of Heth's Division or behind his two sister brigades, Armistead asked for assistance and was told to form behind the latter.[7]

The cannonade that preceded the charge was fairly destructive to Pickett's men, particularly Kemper's Brigade on the right, where the men were most exposed. After the massive cannonade ended, Pickett received permission to launch the charge. The men stepped off Seminary Ridge as if on parade. The line moved at "route step," or 110 paces per minute. About halfway to Cemetery Ridge, the Federal artillery, and then the infantry, opened fire on the line. One Federal soldier marveled, "I can see no end to the right nor left to the line that is coming . . . men are being mowed down with every step. And men are stepping into their places. There is no dismay, no discouragement, no wavering." As Pickett's men broke through Major James Dearing's now silent artillery, the youthful officer yelled, "For God's sake wait till I get some ammunition and I will drive every Yankee from the heights." Unfortunately, none was to be found and this contributed to Pickett's defeat. The division sustained frightful losses during the charge and the survivors' subsequent retreat back to Seminary Ridge.[8]

A crestfallen Pickett returned to Seminary Ridge, where he was approached by Lee, who told him to "place your division in rear of this hill, and be ready to repel the advance of the enemy should they follow up their advantage." With head lowered, Pickett sadly replied, "General Lee, I have no division now, Armistead is down, Garnett is down, and Kemper is mortally wounded." Lee's fatherly response was, "Come, General Pickett, this has been my fight and upon my shoulders rests the blame. The men and officers of your command have written the name of Virginia as high today as it has ever been written before."[9]

Kemper's Brigade—Brigadier General James Kemper

Units: 1st Virginia, 3rd Virginia, 7th Virginia, 11th Virginia, 24th Virginia
Strength: 1634
Losses: 703 (171-367-165)—43.0%[10]

Brigadier General James Kemper's Brigade was one of the oldest and most distinguished in Lee's army. All but one regiment (3rd Virginia) were present at the battle of First Manassas in Longstreet's and Early's Brigades. By the siege of Yorktown,

the nucleus of the future brigade had formed, with the placement of the 1st, 7th, and 11th Virginia in A. P. Hill's Brigade. With the elevation of Hill to divisional command, James Kemper was promoted to brigadier general and given the brigade on June 3, 1862.[11]

Kemper was an attorney by training. He volunteered for service during the Mexican War, but did not see any action. He entered politics and served in the Virginia legislature. Soon after the war began, Kemper became the colonel of the 7th Virginia and saw action at First Manassas, Yorktown, Williamsburg, and Seven Pines. After his promotion, he led his brigade with distinction at the battle of Glendale and then assumed temporary command of three brigades in what would become part of Pickett's Division. He participated in crushing Pope's flank during the battle of Second Manassas. Back in command of his brigade, Kemper and his men battled units of the Federal IX Corps at Sharpsburg, but were roughly handled, causing Lee's flank to be dangerously exposed. The brigade was in reserve at Fredericksburg and participated in the Suffolk campaign, therefore missing the Chancellorsville campaign.[12]

The spirits of Kemper's Virginians were exceptionally high as they marched northward. In a letter home, Captain Thomas Pollock noted that the army was in much better condition than it had been during the prior September when it had first invaded the North. The men enjoyed watching the reactions of the local citizens. "It is almost amusing to witness the curious stare with which we are regarded as our sunburnt, motley dressed regiments—but moving in closed ranks with the cadence step to the tune of Dixie and with Enfield muskets glistening and the red battle flag inscribed all over with the names of our victories—pass through." Pollock related that the citizens' reactions ranged from sadness to anger. Many of the latter told them that they would never make it back home again. How right they were.[13]

After spending most of the war in warravaged Virginia, the men were astounded to see the bounty all around them. "It is a beautiful country overflowing with wealth and fatness. Every inch of ground seems to be producing something," wrote Pollock.[14]

In spite of all this temptation, the men did a fairly good job of restraining themselves because of Robert E. Lee's general orders against pillaging. The men's faith in their leader was exceptionally strong. Pollock summed up this feeling, writing that "they would go into any battle with as much assurance of victory as if it was already won—simply because they have an almost fanatical confidence in him." Harold Walthall of the 1st Virginia recalled that while "we were pretty tough soldiers . . . I didn't hear of any aggravated vandalism, but can't vouch for the fate of any pig or rooster who wouldn't get out of the way." The men were generous in their attempts to pay for their purchases with Confederate script, but few farmers accepted their offers.[15]

Not all of the men were happy about this northward excursion. Johnston (7th Virginia) was one of them. "We had uniformly insisted upon defensive warfare on our own soil . . . we steadfastly contended against the claim of the enemy to invade our own land, and logically we should be bound by the same reasoning." Still, Johnston admitted that the men's morale was exceptionally high, as they knew that the army could "beat its old antagonist anywhere he chose to meet it."[16]

During the march from Chambersburg to the edge of Gettysburg on July 2, the men choked on the dense dust that hung heavily in the air. Sergeant Catlett Conway of the 7th Virginia recalled that "water was scarce and we suffered much." The men could hear the boom of cannons in the distance, and soon officers were yelling orders to "close up, men, quick-step; we are needed at the front." Men threw away their belongings in an effort to keep up. They sighed with relief when the column finally halted outside of Gettysburg at about midafternoon on July 2. The men immediately scattered. Some hunted for water, others ate, and still others rested and talked with their comrades.[17]

The division was back on the road sometime between 2:00 and 3:00 A.M. on July 3. This time, Kemper's Brigade was in the lead. The column halted behind Seminary Ridge and remained there until about 10:00 A.M., when Pickett moved his division to the right and took a position about two hundred yards behind the Confederate batteries. The brigade was arranged from left to right as 3rd Virginia–7th Virginia–1st Virginia–11th Virginia–24th Virginia. Johnston noted that the men were "cheerful and seemed to realize their weighty responsibilities and the importance . . . of success . . . that probably in their hands rested." The men passed General Lee during their short trek, and Dooley (1st Virginia) recalled that his face "does not look as bright as tho' he were certain of success."[18]

Because the brow of Seminary Ridge protected the men on the center and right of the brigade, they could not see the enemy's position without venturing forward. This was not the case with the left of the line, where the men of the 3rd and 7th Virginia were exposed. Almost immediately, fifteen men from each regiment were thrown out as skirmishers. The sun grew hotter as the day progressed, and the men sought the cool shade provided by nearby trees. Those men in an apple orchard relieved some of the stress by throwing green apples at each other. This not withstanding, the officers detected a distinct change in the men, "from being unusually merry and hilarious they on a sudden had become as still and thoughtful as Quakers at a love feast," related Colonel Joseph Mayo of the 3rd Virginia. Johnston (7th Virginia) observed that the men were "grave and thoughtful, but showed no signs of fear." In observing the Union position, the officers and men knew that the chances for success were not good.[19]

Several distinguished visitors made their appearance while the men rested. Generals Lee, Longstreet, and Pickett could be seen conferring. General Kemper later told Colonel Mayo that the 3rd Virginia had been given the "post of honor" during the charge.[20]

As the hour of 1:00 P.M. approached, the men were told that a cannonade would soon begin and that when they heard the two signal guns they were to "lie down with our faces to the ground," recollected Johnston. Dooley recalled that after the cannonade ended, they were to "charge straight ahead over the open field and *sweep from our path* any thing in the shape of a Yankee that attempts to oppose our progress." The order caused anxiety, even in the most seasoned veteran. The guns opened fired soon after, and the sound was deafening. The Union batteries responded, but the shells did not merely hit their Confederate counterparts, they hit Kemper's men as well. Johnston recalled,

The very atmosphere seemed broken by the rush and crash of projectiles, solid shot, shrieking, bursting shells. The sun, but a moment before so brilliant, was now almost darkened by smoke and mist enveloping and shadowing the earth, and through which came hissing and shrieking, fiery fuses and messengers of death, sweeping, plunging, cutting, ploughing through our ranks, carrying mutilation, destruction, pain, suffering and death in every direction . . . at almost every moment of time, guns, swords, haversacks, human flesh and bones, flying and dangling in the air, or bouncing above the earth, which now trembled beneath us as if shaken by an earthquake.[21]

The men prayed. They prayed like never before. They prayed for the ordeal to end. They prayed that they might live through it. Recalling his orders to lie flat, Walthall (1st Virginia) wanted to disobey them and crawl *into* the ground. In looking to his left, Johnston saw one shell kill or wound eight men. Some, like Major John Dearing, were oblivious to the danger. He grabbed a flag and waved it as he rode along his artillery battalion. Captain John Smith of the 11th Virginia felt some alarm when General Longstreet rode along between the artillery and infantry. "He was as quiet as an old farmer riding over his plantation on a Sunday morning, and looked neither to the right or left."[22]

After what must have seemed like an eternity, the cannonading slackened, then stopped. The toll exacted by the cannonade was high. One soldier estimated that no less than three hundred of Pickett's men were killed or wounded. General Cadmus Wilcox, whose brigade lay nearby, estimated that Kemper's Brigade lost about two hundred men, and a modern historian estimated the losses to be about 15% of the men, or almost 250. The unprotected men of 3rd and 7th Virginia on the left of the line sustained the highest casualties.[23]

Soon after the cannonade ended, Pickett sent Captain Robert Bright of his staff to Kemper with his orders. "You and your staff and field officers to go in dismounted; dress on Garnett and take the red barn [Codori] for your objective point." Kemper recalled this interaction slightly differently after the war, noting that the young staff officer said, "Gen. Pickett orders you to advance your brigade immediately." Kemper added that it was "the only order I received during the battle." He recalled after the war that he was shocked when he saw Garnett's and Armistead's Brigades already in line and ready to advance. They had apparently been given their instructions and

were in the process of stepping off. Kemper immediately ordered his men to fall in, and Pickett rode by, yelling, "Up men, and to your posts! Don't forget today that you are from old Virginia!" before riding away. Johnston recalled that the words had an electrical effect on the men.[24]

Dooley (1st Virginia) honestly wrote after the war, "I tell you, there is no romance in making one of these charges . . . when you rise to your feet . . . I tell you the enthusiasm of ardent breasts in many cases *ain't there.*" Not all of the men took their places in the ranks. According to Dooley, these men fell into four categories: the dead, the wounded, those suffering from heat stroke, and the cowards. He was quick to point out that "but of these last there are but few." Some of the men who did join the line of battle quickly fainted— some from the heat, others from the dread of what awaited them. Captain James Hutter looked down on these prone men and appealed to them "in the name of Virginia to go if possible." When Hutter leaned over one of his men, Captain John Smith brusquely told him, "Col. [Captain] Hutter, when he says he is sick, he is sick."[25]

The flag bearers advanced four paces to the front, and the long lines stood motionless. The men could easily see their commander, George Pickett, astride his coal-black horse, riding from the left of the division to the center, wheeling toward the enemy and advancing about a hundred yards. Conway (7th Virginia) recalled that Pickett, "look[ed] back at his men as they [stood] in long straight lines, steady as rocks and their bayonets flashing in the sunlight. He lift[ed] his hat and rides slowly forward, while orders to 'forward march! Guide right!' [rang] out in the clear, quick command of Kemper." Captain John Smith of the 11th Virginia recalled that the orders were, "forward, quick time, march" and the men rapidly advanced. The men cried out to their wounded comrades, "Goodbye, boys! Goodbye!" As the line of battle passed the artillery, Dearing's gunners raised their hats and cheered. One of Kemper's bands was playing "in the same manner that it would, had the division been passing in review," noted Sergeant James Walker of Armistead's Brigade.[26]

Because the plain in front of them was fairly flat and the Union position somewhat elevated, the men could easily see their objective. Walthall wrote after the war that "it was the first time I had such a clear view of a fight." Despite the long distance the men would need to traverse in the open, most were cautiously optimistic of success. Captain John Smith of the 11th Virginia wrote soon after the battle that "we fully expected to take them."[27]

The beginning of the charge went fairly smoothly. The officers gave a continuous stream of orders to their men. "Onward—steady—dress to the right—give way to the left—steady, not too fast—don't press upon the center—keep well in line." The enemy's skirmishers, who were about four hundred yards in front of Cemetery Ridge, were tenacious and held their ground until the line of battle bore down on them. Captain John Smith admired their behavior, writing that they "retreated in perfect order, firing as they fell back." The Federal artillery had opened fire when the brigade was about halfway into the plain. Projectiles flew from batteries on Cemetery Ridge in front of them, from Hazlett's battery on Little Round Top, and from massed artillery near the Peach Orchard. Dooley (1st Virginia) called them "black monsters." At first few casualties were sustained, but the deadly missiles soon found their mark, tearing large holes in the line. Rank closers quickly filled these, but not without making the line "unsteady."[28]

While most of the brigade encountered no serious obstructions until they reached Emmitsburg Pike, the Roger's house posed a serious problem to the 11th Virginia. Ordered to move around it with his right wing, Captain James Hutter found the maneuver exceptionally difficult to perform, particularly under the heavy artillery fire.[29]

Additional men fell with each cannon blast, often spattering their comrades with blood. The men were ordered to "oblique to the left" as Pickett's Division attempted to connect with Pettigrew's Division on the left. This caused some initial confusion, because the 24th Virginia apparently made the move first, which crowded the 11th Virginia, which in turn crowded the 1st Virginia to its left. An angry Colonel Lewis Williams of the latter regiment rode up to Captain Hutter, now commanding the 11th Virginia, and yelled, "Col. Hutter can you do nothing with you men they are crowding me out of line." An utterly frustrated Hutter immediately retorted, "If you will go and attend to that damned little squad of yours (his regiment was very small . . .) and let my regiment alone we will get along better."[30]

As the men approached Emmitsburg Road they again encountered the Federal skirmishers who had taken position on the other side. Colonel Mayo (3rd Virginia) also saw a number of other things, like "a small body of men, compact and solid as a wedge, moving swiftly to the left oblique," which proved to be Armistead's Brigade. He also noted a "disorderly crowd of men breaking to the rear" that neither Pickett, nor his staff, could stem. A magnificently mounted officer was seen galloping along the crest of Cemetery Ridge and as the men raised their muskets, Mayo and others yelled out, "Don't shoot him! Don't shoot him!" Mayo finally saw General Kemper rise in his saddle, and pointing with his sword, yell, "There are the guns, boys, go for them."[31]

Private Ralph Sturtevant of the 13th Vermont watched the destruction of Kemper's men as they approached the Federal defensive line on Cemetery Ridge.

> Up rose the Green Mountain Boys, 3,000 strong as if by magic . . . [they] took deliberate aim and with a simultaneous flash and roar fired into the compact ranks of the desperate foe and again and again in quick succession until a dozen or more volleys had been discharged with deadly effect. We saw at every volley the grey uniforms fall quick and fast and the front line hesitated, moved slowly and melted away, could not advance against such a furious and steady storm of bullets in their faces and the raking fire of McGilvery's batteries against their flank . . . and with an awful menacing yell dashed forward with the evident purpose of carrying the crest of Cemetery Ridge at our right and rear.[32]

The troops on the right, the 11th and 24th Virginia, had a more serious threat than their comrades, for as they passed the Codori house, a dense mass of Federal soldiers suddenly materialized on their right flank. These soldiers were from the large 13th and 16th Vermont (Stannard's Vermont Brigade), who had left their position on Cemetery Ridge to take on Pickett's right flank. A Confederate sergeant on the right of Garnett's Brigade asked Captain Henry Owen about the identity of a large mass of troops on the right of Kemper's Brigade. Owen replied, "Yankees march straight ahead and say nothing." When Major Edmund Berkeley told Kemper about this threat, he initially discounted it, saying that they were their own troops. Berkeley could not resist saying to Kemper, "You will soon see your mistake." Watching it, Owen commented that it was "the grandest sight I have ever

seen." What he witnessed was a mass of Vermonters, eight hundred or a thousand yards away, running toward them. Their uniforms looked black and their muskets gleamed in the bright sunlight. Owen instinctively knew that these troops were desperately trying to stem the tide before it hit the stone wall on Cemetery Ridge.[33]

The 24th Virginia immediately fired a volley into the inexperienced Vermont troops, throwing them into disarray. Regaining their composure, the enemy opened a devastating fire on the Virginians. The immediate inclination was to crowd to the left to avoid this musket fire. Colonel Terry turned his 24th Virginia and part of the 11th Virginia at right angles to the rest of the line to face the enemy, both to stave off their counterattack and to keep them from getting into their rear. Colonel Mayo of the 3rd Virginia also learned of the threat on the right and he later related that "I hastily gathered a small band together and faced them to meet the new danger." The battle became a "wild kaleidoscopic whirl" for Mayo at this point. "Seeing the men as they fired, throw down their guns and pick up others from the ground, I followed suit, shooting into a flock of blue coats that were pouring down from the right, I noticed how close their flags were together." The Vermont troops returned the fire and Sturtevant (13th Vermont) saw "the gray uniforms fall quick and fast and the front line hesitated, moved slowly and melted away." The oblique to the left caused even more of Kemper's flank to be exposed to the Vermont troops, who took full advantage of it. Colonel Wheeler Veazey of the 16th Vermont recalled that the "ground over which we passed after striking their flank was literally covered with dead and wounded men."[34]

The line of battle was fearfully thinned by now, but still the men continued on toward the Federal main line on Cemetery Ridge. In front of them were Hall's and Harrow's Brigades (Gibbon's Division). Looking at the relatively few men left in the ranks, Walthall wondered "what we would do when the impact occurred. It looked to me like we would be swallowed whole if we got in that maelstrom." Many of Kemper's men halted at a "slashing" just in front of the Union position and opened a murderous fire on the enemy. After firing a few volleys, many men jumped up, and with a Rebel yell, ran toward their goal of the stone wall. Sergeant Conway (7th Virginia) recalled reaching the wall which sheltered the enemy, and then the "blue coats rose and poured a murderous volley right into their faces [Conway had been wounded by this time]. A moment the line halted and staggered as so many men went down, but steadying themselves, the whole line bent forward, gave the southern yell, charged and went over the stone wall and in turn poured into the blue line a terrific fire which compelled them to give way." Over to the right, Captain John Smith of the 11th Virginia recalled that the pace was at "top speed and as we neared the works I could see a good line of battle, thick and substantial, firing upon us." As Smith's men continued forward, he spied "first, a few, and then more and more, and presently, to my surprise and disgust, the whole [enemy] line break away in flight." This was apparently the 59th New York (Hall's Brigade). According to Smith, his men now held the Federal works, which he called a "hasty trench and embankment, and not a stone wall." Looking around, Smith was concerned about the small numbers that had reached the wall and that "our regiment was a mass or ball, all mixed together, without company organization." Realizing that they needed help, Smith quickly dispatched one of his

men, and then a second, back to Seminary Ridge for reinforcements.[35]

The fighting was hand-to-hand at this point. "Men fired into each other's faces; there were bayonet thrusts, cutting with sabres, hand-to-hand contests, oaths, curses, yells and hurrahs . . . the Second Corps fell back behind the guns to allow the use of grape and double cannister [sic], and as it tore through the rebel ranks at only a few paces distant, the dead and wounded were piled in ghastly heaps; still on they came up to the very muzzles of their guns; they were blown away from the cannon's mouth, but yet they did not waiver," related Johnston (7th Virginia).[36]

Up on the ridge, just in front of them were Cowan's and Rorty's batteries—still full of fight. Using double canister, they blew gaping holes in Kemper's line. One of Rorty's guns was loaded with triple canister, causing it to topple over after it fired. Kemper's men reached the guns and engaged in hand-to-hand combat with the rammer-wielding cannoneers. A Confederate officer leading a small group of men charged up the hill and yelled out, "Take the gun!" as he approached Cowan's battery. Cowan ordered the gun fired when the band was only ten yards away and 220 pieces of lead blew away this small, but gallant band of men. So impressed was Cowan with this enemy officer's bravery that he had him buried with honors near the graves of his own cannoneers.[37]

Dooley, shot through both thighs, lay about thirty yards from the Federal position. Although racked with pain, he desperately wanted to know the fate of the charge that had prostrated him. "There . . . a new shout, and cheer after cheer rends the air. Are those fresh troops advancing to our support? No! no! That huzza never broke from southern lips . . . Virginia's bravest, noblest sons have perished here today and perished all in vain."

Captain Smith estimated that he and his small band of men waited about twenty minutes for reinforcements, and when he realized that the enemy was massing for a counterattack, he ordered his men back to the safety of Seminary Ridge. Corporal Charles Loehr of the 1st Virginia gathered as many of his regiment as he could find, as he had been ordered to move "by the right flank." Only twelve men answered the call, and most were immediately felled by enemy small arms fire. It was time for the brigade to retreat, but this would be no easy task, so the officers ordered their men to "scatter as they retired."[38]

Upon reaching Seminary Ridge, the survivors learned that most of the brigade's officers and men had been killed, wounded, or captured. Among the wounded, and temporarily captured, was James Kemper, who was shot within a hundred yards of the Federal position. His men recaptured him almost immediately. The brigade lost several stands of colors, including those of the 7th Virginia, which

was carried by nine men. When the last one fell, a soldier from the 82nd New York (Harrow's Brigade, Gibbon's Division, II Corps) grabbed it.[39]

Seeing General Lee, the flag bearer of the 24th Virginia waved his colors and said, "General, let us go it again!" Before Lee could respond, a stretcher carrying General Kemper passed by. Lee expressed his hope that Kemper was not badly hurt, to which he responded, "They tell me it is mortal." Lee then asked if there was anything he could do for him, and Kemper painfully replied, "Yes, General Lee; do full justice to this division for its work to-day." Lee bowed his head and said, "I will."[40]

Kemper's Brigade had the misfortune of being assigned the unsupported right flank of Pickett's charge. As a result, it was racked by concentrated artillery fire from its front and right and then hit by Stannard's Brigade's savage flank attack. Losses were heavy, but the men did as well as could be expected.

Armistead's Brigade—Brigadier General Louis Armistead

Units: 9th Virginia, 14th Virginia, 38th Virginia, 53rd Virginia, 57th Virginia
Strength: 1950
Losses: 1223 (187-447-587)—62.7%[41]

Brigadier General Louis Armistead commanded his brigade longer than any other brigadier in Pickett's Division. Thrown out of West Point for disciplinary reasons, Armistead entered the regular army and saw considerable service during the Mexican War. He entered the War Between the States as colonel of the 56th Virginia, which he commanded in western Virginia and northern North Carolina. Promoted to the rank of brigadier general on April

1, 1862, he was given a brigade and sent north to join General Joseph Johnston's army near Richmond. The brigade's first action was at the battle of Seven Pines, where most of the regiments retreated, leaving Armistead and thirty men to take on a Federal brigade. Chosen to spearhead the drive up Malvern Hill, Armistead's Brigade sustained heavy losses. Good judgment prevailed when Armistead refused to launch a night attack at the second battle of Manassas. The brigade saw action at the battle of Sharpsburg, but was not engaged during the Fredericksburg campaign and was absent during the Chancellorsville campaign. Therefore, crusty and opinionated Louis Armistead and his men were ready for a fight at the start of the Gettysburg campaign.[42]

The march from Richmond to Gettysburg was a harsh one for Armistead's men. The land's bounty and the citizens' hostile reactions helped to mitigate their weariness. Private Joseph Payne of the 38th Virginia observed the great crops of wheat and corn and wrote home that the "people is [sic] very kind to us but I think it is thru [sic] fere [sic] for I don't think they have eny [sic] love for us." Private James Booker of the same regiment agreed, adding that "most of our Virginia boys treat them verry [sic] kind though there is some [of] our . . . troops has treated the people badly [sic]. I am sorry thay [sic] do so." Booker was surprised that the citizens refused to take payment for the food, but was intuitive enough to know that they were not doing this through good will.[43]

Surgeon Charles Lippitt of the 57th Virginia was pleased to hear an old farmer say that "he could not blame our army for taking horses &c for he had heard the yankees boast of what they have taken from the southern people." Sergeant John Beaton of the 9th Virginia added that the "people say we treated them a great deal better than they expected." According to orders, the soldiers were to offer payment for anything they took from citizens. Lippitt and some of the men caught some chickens on the road, "but were made to offer to pay for them."[44]

Not surprisingly, many of the soldiers felt ambivalent toward the Northern citizens. Beaton wrote home that "it was truly heart rendering to see a country so beautiful and under such a high state of cultivation suffering so much from the march of an invading army." Private William Ross of the 14th Virginia agreed. "We are now in the very midst of Yankeedom . . . I can't

help feel sorry for the citizens . . . when I see how frightened they are . . . but when I think again of the waste the Yankees have made in my native state, I can't have much sympathy for them." Beaton also observed that "one more invasion and the army will not respect Genl Lee's orders as it did before but will retaliate in kind, a house for a house will be their motto."[45]

July 1 found the brigade in Chambersburg with the two other brigades of Pickett's Division engaged in tearing up railroad tracks, heating them, and twisting them around trees. In addition to these exertions, the men were "visiting Pensilvanians [sic] and finding cherries a plenty." The men were issued three days' rations that night. Leading the division, Armistead's Brigade was on the road toward Gettysburg by 3:00 A.M. on July 2. Marching through South Mountain, the men were fired on by "bushwhackers." After a long twenty-three-mile march brought them within three miles of Gettysburg, the men were permitted a midafternoon rest. The march was not an easy one, as the roads were choked with wagons, artillery, and wounded soldiers marching to the rear. The weary men were overjoyed when told they would rest for the night. Lieutenant John Lewis of the 9th Virginia recalled that "we of Pickett's division were tired and hungry, and paid attention to the part of hunger at once. After eating and resting a short time we were ready to hear the news of the day."[46]

The men were up at 3:00 A.M. on July 3 and each was issued 20 additional cartridges. If the men didn't know that they would soon be thrown into battle before, they did now. The brigade brought up the rear during the last leg of the march to the battlefield. Private Thomas Oakes of the 14th Virginia complained that they stopped "in a large open field with not a shade tree nearer than a body of woods and there we were not allowed to go." The sun was blazing hot and the men suffered in the open. The men stayed there less than an hour, when at noon they were moved to the left to take their positions behind Seminary Ridge. They were ordered to lie down, particularly when the artillery opened fire. The brigade was deployed from left to right as 38th Virginia–57th Virginia–53rd Virginia–9th Virginia–14th Virginia.[47]

The men were in high spirits because of the results of the first two days of the battle. They knew they would soon be engaged and felt supremely confident in their ability to make a difference in the outcome of the battle. Sergeant James Walker of the 9th Virginia admitted that "the men did not seem to dread this battle as many others they had been in." They were Virginians, in a crack division, under the command of Robert E. Lee, so everything would work out in the end. This euphoria may have dissipated somewhat when Armistead told some of them that if the artillery barrage did not successfully dislodge the enemy, Pickett's infantry would be forced to charge the Federal position.[48]

The great cannonade began shortly after 1:00 P.M., and soon both sides were firing with abandon. "The smoke soon darkened the sun, and the scene produced was similar to a gigantic thunder-storm, the screeching of shot and shell producing the sound of the whistling blast of winds," noted Lewis (9th Virginia). "Death was in every foot of space, and safety was only in flight, but not one of the men did that." J. F. Crocker of the same regiment added that "nothing can be seen but the flashing light leaping from the cannon's mouth amidst the surrounding smoke." Private Erasmus Williams of the 14th Virginia was chastised by a lieutenant for pulling out a pocketknife and digging a crude breast-work prior to the cannonade. The officer who called him a coward was "swept away by a shot or shell, and his blood sprinkled all over me," related Williams. As the cannonading continued, the Federal shells began to overshoot the Confederate position. Unlike the more exposed men of Kemper's Brigade, Armistead's lost relatively few during the cannonade.[49]

As the cannonade faltered, then ceased, General Armistead ordered his men into line. The adjutant of the 9th Virginia, John Crocker, recalled that the "men with alacrity and cheerfulness fell into line." Whether because of his own exuberance, or because he felt his men needed it, Armistead could be seen providing encouragement to his men as he walked down the line. Some of his men recalled Armistead saying, "Men, remember what you are fighting for. Remember your homes, your firesides, your wives, mothers, sisters and your sweethearts." When he reached the flag bearer of the 53rd Virginia, the center regiment, he stopped and said in a voice loud enough for most of the men to hear, "Sergeant, I want you and your men to plant your colors on those works. Do you think you can do it?" The sergeant immediately replied, "Yes, sir, if God is willing!" Armistead then told his men to "follow their colors and to remember the brave words of their color bearer," according to Colonel Rawley Martin. Before he walked away, Armistead pulled out a small flask and offered it to the sergeant. The other members of the color guard were disappointed when Armistead put the precious flask away without offering them a drink.[50]

The men were ordered to strip off their knapsacks, blankets, cooking utensils, and anything else that might serve as an impediment during their charge as they quietly took their positions. Armistead then took a position about twenty paces in front of the 53rd Virginia's color bearer and watched as Kemper's and Garnett's brigades stepped off in front of him. Lewis (9th Virginia) thought that "his place was in the rear, properly." But Armistead's blood was up, and he would personally guide his brigade into the greatest fight of its existence. "His men saw him. They saw his example. They caught his fire and determination, and then and there they resolved to follow that heroic leader until the enemy's bullets stopped them. It was his example, his coolness, his courage that led that brigade over that field of blood," Lewis wrote after the war.[51]

It was deathly quiet. Armistead finally gave the order, "Right shoulder, shift arms. Forward march." Sergeant William Walker (9th Virginia) recalled that "not a sound was heard; not a shot was fired from any part of the field. The command 'forward' was given, and in five minutes they had left the woods which had concealed them during the artillery fight." Being one of the three brigades serving in a supporting role (Scales's and Lane's of Trimble's Division were the other two), the brigade was ordered forward after the first line had made considerable progress across the plain between the two ridges.[52]

The brigade first ventured forward in relative peace at a quick time pace. Captain James Poindexter of the 38th Virginia noted that "before us, one hundred and fifty yards away, moving on like waves of the sea, marched Garnett and Kemper, their battle flags flashing in the sun light . . . marching in perfect order, with disciplined thread, [we] followed where they led." Somewhat disconcerting was a band playing somewhere to the right, where Kemper's noncombatants were located. Before long, the "heavy guns on Round-Top were trained upon us, and the howling shells burst around us or crashed through our ranks," recalled Poindexter.[53]

"The shells flew far over us at first, but this lasted but a moment. They soon obtained the range, and then Death commenced his work of destruction," recalled James Walker (9th Virginia), who suggested that the artillery fire began when the troops were about halfway to Cemetery Ridge. Lieutenant John Crocker noted that "as the killed and wounded dropped out, our lines closed and dressed up, as if nothing had happened, and went on with steady march." Lewis agreed, stating that "the crash of shell and solid shot, as they came howling and whistling through our lines, seemed to make no impression on the men. There was not a waver, but all was as steady as if on parade." It was not unusual for eight, ten, or even fourteen men to fall with the explosion of a single shell. The grass even caught fire in some places. Sergeant William Robertson of the 14th Virginia noted that "now and then a man's hand or arm or leg would fly like feathers before the wind."[54]

According to Colonel Martin (53rd Virginia), General Kemper rode up when the brigade had reached the halfway mark and told Armistead, "General, hurry up, my men can stand no more." Armistead merely replied, "I'll do it!" and issued orders to "double quick," which soon changed to a run. Armistead took off his hat and placed it on the tip of his sword, which he held aloft. Whitehead recalled that Armistead "kept fifteen or twenty steps in front of his brigade all the way, was cheering all the time and calling his men to follow." The sword's blade cut through the hat several times, causing Armistead to readjust it.[55]

The two fences along Emmitsburg Road posed a strong obstacle to the men, as they had to break ranks to scale both of them before reforming on the opposite side. The Federal infantry waited until the

Confederates reached the road before opening fire. One soldier wrote that "a new storm of missiles—canister, shrapnel, and rifle shot belched forth from the Federal position, and even more men fell." According to Lewis, men were "falling in heaps." One veteran described the ordeal at Emmitsburg Road as a matter of timing and luck. The men had to "climb up to the top of the fence, tumble over it, and fall flat into the bed of the road. All the while the bullets continued to bury themselves into the bodies of the victims and the sturdy chestnut rails." After a few moments' rest, the men rose and repeated the process by climbing the fence on the opposite side of the road. Losses mounted, and as Armistead's rapidly dwindling brigade moved toward Cemetery Ridge, it left behind "scores of dead and wounded comrades in the dust of the road." Up to this point, Armistead's men had been denied doing what they so desperately wanted—fire on the enemy. With his men falling by the second, Armistead ran behind his troops and finally gave the order to fire. Federal soldiers fell in droves. The enemy fire only increased, "as no tongue can describe."[56]

This momentary pause by Emmitsburg Pike gave Armistead time to survey the field. He was delighted to see that Garnett's Brigade had captured the stone wall to his left. Realizing that he must exploit this breach, he ordered his men to oblique in that direction. This caused his men to run parallel to the line held by the 69th Pennsylvania of the Philadelphia Brigade. The Irishmen of this regiment were only too happy to open fire again with a vengeance. Armistead's men continued to fall by the score, but they were not to be denied, joining Garnett's men at the wall.[57]

Although they had planted their flags by the wall, Armistead's men were still in trouble. Near the top of the ridge in front of them stood the 72nd Pennsylvania (Webb's Brigade, Gibbon's Division, II Corps), which was firing into their ranks. Armistead turned to Colonel Martin and yelled through the din, "Martin, we can't stay here; we must go over that wall." Martin agreed and immediately gave the order, "Forward with the colors." At the same time, Armistead yelled his immortal words, "Follow me boys; give 'em the cold steel, boys!" as he leaped over the wall. At least 100 men, and perhaps as many as 300, followed him. Colonel Martin went down with a shattered thigh within a few steps of clearing the wall.[58]

Armistead was gravely wounded as he touched one of Cushing's now abandoned cannon and fell by one of its wheels. The 72nd Pennsylvania now charged down the hill as other Federal troops also descended on the area. Captain Benjamin Farinhold of the 53rd Virginia noted that "pandemonium reigned complete, and for a time no quarter was asked nor given, and many on each side lost their lives." Farinhold related how the combatants were so close together that their clothes and flesh were burned with every musket discharge. Lewis (9th Virginia) noted that "death lurks in every foot of space. Men fall in heaps, still fighting, bleeding, dying." There were but a handful of men now with virtually no officers in view. "We see ourselves being surrounded. The fire is already on both flanks and front," recalled Lewis. He finally ordered his men to "look out for themselves, and my duties ceased as an officer from that time." Every man now had to make a decision: continue fighting, attempt to flee, or surrender. Lewis believed that it was his duty to remain at the wall, and he questioned whether he would die or be captured. "I chose the latter, and found myself a prisoner of war."[59]

As the prisoners were led away, they could not help but be dismayed by the devastation around them. "Here at the stone wall they lie in solid heaps along its foot; and here within the Federal lines they are as autumnal leaves," wrote Crocker (9th Virginia). The charge was deadly for the brigade. In addition to losing Armistead and most of the officers, the brigade lost over 1200 men, or about 63% of its strength. All of the regiments' colors were also lost.[60]

Of Pickett's three brigades, Armistead's role in the charge is probably best known, probably because it advanced farther than its two sister brigades and because of Armistead's flamboyant utterances during the charge. No troops in Lee's army could have gone farther or acquitted themselves more gallantly.

Garnett's Brigade—Brigadier General Richard Garnett

Units: 8th Virginia, 18th Virginia, 19th Virginia, 28th Virginia, 56th Virginia
Strength: 1459
Losses: 948 (231-393-324)—65.0%[61]

Brigadier General Richard Richard Garnett's Brigade had a long and distinguished history with the army. All but the 56th Virginia were recruited in May 1861 and served at the first battle of Manassas in Brigadier General Philip St. George Cocke's Brigade. When the latter committed suicide after Christmas of that year, the brigade was assigned to Brigadier General George Pickett, who commanded it at Williamsburg, Seven Pines, and Gaines's Mill. When Pickett was wounded at the latter battle, Colonel Eppa Hunton of the 8th Virginia took over the brigade. The 56th Virginia, which had seen some action in Tennessee, was added to the brigade prior to the Seven Days battles.[62]

Colonel Hunton temporarily led the brigade at the second battle of Manassas. Because Pickett was slow in mending, Brigadier General Richard Garnett was assigned temporary command of the brigade prior to the Maryland campaign. His was a checkered past. A West Point graduate, Garnett showed his mettle as an Indian fighter. Entering the Confederate army as a major of artillery, he shifted to the infantry in November 1861, when he was promoted to the rank of brigadier general and given command of the Stonewall Brigade. Problems with Stonewall Jackson began almost immediately, when during the Romney campaign he allowed his exhausted men to rest, and then at the battle of Kernstown he ordered a withdrawal when his men were out of ammunition and in danger of being flanked. Jackson finally arrested him. A full trial never materialized, and Lee put Garnett in temporary command of Pickett's Brigade during the Maryland campaign. Garnett performed well, and when Pickett was given a division, the disgraced general was given permanent command of the brigade.[63]

Because the brigade had not seen action since the battle of Sharpsburg, Garnett was ready for a fight. These plans were complicated by medical problems. Because he had been severely kicked by his aide's horse, Richard Garnett rode in an ambulance to the front. To make matters worse, an infection set in just prior to the battle, furthering his misery. Colonel Hunton (8th Virginia) assumed command of the brigade during Garnett's incapacity. A veteran of First Bull Run and many subsequent battles, Hunton was not enthusiastic about the invasion of Pennsylvania. Seeing General Lee, he rode up to him and expressed his concerns. The fatherly Lee replied that "the movement was a necessity; that our provisions and supplies of every kind were very nearly exhausted in Virginia, and that we had to go to Pennsylvania for supplies." Lee's conviction that the army would be successful, swayed Hunton. "I threw away my doubts and [I] became as enthusiastic as he was."[64]

Most of men were proud of the army and agreed with Lee's assessment. Still, they were a ragtag bunch. Private Henry Owen of the 18th Virginia admitted that "slouched hat, the faded threadbare jacket and patched pantaloons" were the order of the day. Many were without shoes and blankets. Most of the men in the ranks were quite young, but it was not easily discernible because of their tanned faces and unkempt beards.[65]

The men usually obeyed Lee's orders against pillaging. Private Randolph Shotwell of the 8th Virginia noted that "many of the citizens express surprise at the civil treatment they are receiving from our men. It is much more than they expected, and far more than their due." The soldiers did get their due, however. Colonel William Stuart of the 56th Virginia admitted that "there was an abnormal amount of chickens and fresh meat being cooked around the campfires at night." One soldier from the 18th Virginia wrote home that a "great many of our Soldiers are pilladging [sic] & destroying every thing they can lay their hands on." He also commented on the "great many long faces" of citizens as the troops passed through the small towns on their journey to Gettysburg. One soldier recalled that these loyal Northerners were not shy

about telling the troops that "we [would] soon be driven from Pa by McClellan Hooker & others."[66]

The men were amazed by the land's bounty. "The whole State seems to be one large field of wheat," wrote a soldier in the 18th Virginia. "There is no danger of starving out these wretches." The army lived off the land, supposedly paying for confiscated items with Confederate script. However, Private Edmund Irby of the 18th Virginia felt that the men fared worse in Pennsylvania than they did in Virginia "because we had no greenbacks with which to buy anything." During the brigade's stay in Chambersburg, the men helped destroy the railroads and shops in the area. Many of the men of the 8th Virginia who had witnessed the destruction of their homes and properties, yelled out, "Boys, remember Haymarket" as they destroyed the railroad equipment.[67]

The march to Gettysburg began during the predawn hours of July 2. This came as no surprise to the men, as they had been issued three days' rations the night before. After a quick breakfast, the brigade was on the road to Gettysburg. The column reached Cashtown at about 4:00 P.M. and continued until it stopped by Marsh Creek, about three miles west of Gettysburg. Shotwell (8th Virginia) bragged that his division "had fewer 'stragglers' than ever before, and while all the men realized that they were to have bloody work, none despaired of ultimate triumph." The men could easily hear the sounds of battle to the left as they bivouacked.[68]

Reveille sounded at about 3:00 A.M. on July 3, and the men were soon marching toward the battlefield, which they reached at about 8:00 A.M. Lieutenant William Wood of the 19th Virginia recalled that "the usual jests and hilarity were indulged in . . . and no gloomy foreboding hovered over our ranks." Upon reaching the battle-field, the men were permitted to rest until noon, when they were moved to the right, behind Dearing's artillery battalion. They were ordered to lie down and wait for the order to advance. Some of the men cautiously peered over the lip of Seminary Ridge to survey the Union line. "My heart almost failed me," wrote Private Sam Paulett. "This is going to be a heller! Prepare for the worst!" he told his comrades.[69]

The day became intolerably hot. The men could see their field officers conducting frequent conversations, and Wood overheard Major Dearing say, "That hill must fall," referring to Cemetery Ridge. The brigade was lying in line of battle, from left to right, as 56th Virginia–28th Virginia–19th Virginia–18th Virginia–8th Virginia.[70]

The great cannonade began at about 1:00 P.M. "The sound startles us, though we have been expecting it," recalled Shotwell. Fortunately for Garnett's men, most were protected by the brow of the hill, but casualties mounted. As the cannonade continued, however, many of the shells sailed over the infantry's heads.[71]

The men were both incredulous and excited when they observed General Garnett arrive to lead the brigade. Mounted on a coal-black horse and wearing a beautiful new uniform, Garnett was every inch a soldier. A number of officers rode up to confer with Garnett soon after he arrived. One of the first was General Cadmus Wilcox, who told him that this would be the most difficult assault he would make in the war. "I lost several hundred men there yesterday in fifteen minutes without making an impression." Pickett also discussed the charge with him, saying, "Get across the field as soon as you can, for I believe you are going to catch hell." The men could also see General Longstreet riding slowly by them, looking straight

ahead. He caught the attraction of enemy snipers and cannoneers and minié balls and shells whirled around him. More than once he had to control his horse. The men lying prone in the grass finally yelled, "Go to the rear . . . we'll fight without you leading us . . . you'll get your old fool head knocked off."[72]

Few officers rode in the charge that day, apparently because Lee discouraged it. Those with physical disabilities were permitted to ride. This clearly referred to Garnett and to Colonel Hunton, who had a fistula. Colonel William Stuart of the 56th Virginia begged Garnett not to make the charge, but he would not hear of it. The men were on their feet when the order, "Attention! Attention!" rippled down the line. Knowing the tall odds against them, many of the men cried out to their comrades, "Good-by, boys! Good-by!" Not everyone jumped to their feet when the order was given. Some had sunstroke and were foaming at the mouth. Others pretended to be stricken.[73]

The men could see Pickett coolly riding along the lines. Private Shotwell (8th Virginia) thought Pickett "rather *dandyish* in his ruffles and curls." Pickett stopped to confer one last time with Garnett. The latter asked him if he had any further orders and Pickett replied that he had none. Riding on, Pickett reached the front of the division, and those close enough could hear him yell, "Column, forward! Guide center." Stuart had ordered his men to fix their bayonets before the charge began. He also assigned certain men the task of being file closers with orders to shoot anyone who lagged behind.[74]

As the men passed through Dearing's artillery, the gunners raised their hats in tribute to the infantry. Colonel Stuart yelled to his men, "See that wall there," pointing to Cemetery Ridge, "It's full of

Yankees. I want you to help take it." As the men moved forward they could see Kemper's men to the right and slightly behind them. From the rush of trampling feet behind them, they knew that Armistead's men had begun their movement as well. The order was now, "Quick-time," and for at least half the distance to the enemy's position, the men were not exposed to enemy fire. The officers issued a stream of orders to their men. "Steady, boys," "Don't fire," "Close up," were the most frequent.[75] Shotwell (8th Virginia) could not hide his awe of the attack, when he wrote,

Colonels on horseback ride slowly over the brow of the ridge; followed by a glittering forest of bright bayonets. The whole column is now within sight, coming down the slope with steady step and superb alignment. The rustle of thousands of feet amid the stubble stirs a cloud of dust . . . The flags flutter and snap—the sunlight flashes from the officer's swords—low words of command are heard—and thus in perfect order, this gallant array of men marches straight down into the valley of Death![76]

When the line of battle was well into the plain, the Federal batteries in front of them and those on Little Round Top to their right opened fire. "Shot, shell, spherical case, shrapnel and cannister [sic] — thousands of deadly missiles racing through the air to thin our ranks!" recalled Shotwell. "Whole regiments stoop like men running in a violent storm." The results were dreadful. Major Charles Peyton of the 19th Virginia saw as many as ten of his men go down after a single shell hit the line. And always, the command of "close up!" was heard. Major Nathaniel Wilson of the 28th Virginia screamed to his men, "Now boys, put your trust in God and follow me." Wilson was mortally wounded within a matter of seconds.[77]

At least three breast-high fences stood between Seminary Ridge and the enemy's position. The line briefly halted to reform after the men climbed each one. The historian of the Philadelphia Brigade, which was directly in front of Garnett's men, noted that "none who saw this magnificent charge . . . could refrain from admiring its grandeur." However, as Pickett's men approached the fences along Emmitsburg Road, he noted that "their formation was irregular, and near the front and centre were crowded together the regimental colors of the entire division." The artillery fire was so severe that Private William Jesse of the 28th Virginia was incredulous that any of his comrades survived the climb over the first set of fences, which were about midway between the two ridges. Along the way, the brigade dispatched the Federal skirmish line, which was "swept away before the division like trash before the broom," remarked Captain H. T. Owen. As the line reached the last set of fences on either side of Emmitsburg Road, Garnett could be heard encouraging his men, saying, "Steady, men! Close up! A little faster; not too fast! Save your strength!" Matters were complicated when Kemper's men were hit by a flank attack by Stannard's Vermont Regiments (Doubleday's Division, I Corps) and crowded the right side of Garnett's line. Parts of three companies of the 8th Virginia on the right were refused to meet this new threat.[78]

Garnett's men did not see the Philadelphia Brigade lying concealed behind a low stone wall at the base of Cemetery Ridge. As Garnett's men climbed over the fences along Emmitsburg Road, they could see "polished musket barrels . . . glitter for an instant. Then burst forth a puff, a blinding withering, wasting blaze, a long sheet of lightning, as if from the summit of the hill had suddenly sprung a vomiting volcano of deadly gases," recalled Private Shotwell. Many Confederates fell during this monstrous initial volley. They could not know that each soldier in the Philadelphia brigade had two to six loaded guns laying near him that were fired in quick succession. Shotwell could not understand how any of his comrades survived this unrelenting hail of bullets from the 69th and 71st Pennsylvania.[79]

Still Garnett's men continued on, and soon they were permitted to give their Rebel yell and fire at the enemy. Private Robert Damron recalled that the yell was "awe inspiring and the earth fairly trembled." Men dropped at every step. Lieutenant George Finley of the 56th Virginia wrote that "men were falling all around us and cannon and muskets were raining death upon us. The 56th was being torn to pieces, but the men never faltered or wavered." As the men approached, they could see the 71st Pennsylvania holding the Bloody Angle begin to break for the rear. Garnett's men surged forward to capture their prized stone wall. The fighting was now hand to hand, and the remaining Federal soldiers were overwhelmed and either ran for safety or surrendered. Finley recalled after the war that many men from the 71st Pennsylvania approached, shouting, "Don't shoot! We surrender. Where shall we go?" Not being able to spare any men, the Confederates merely pointed toward Seminary Ridge, and the Union soldiers began the long trek to imprisonment. Because of the complex obliqueing movements, the brigade was densely packed over a small area, with some ranks as much as thirty deep.[80]

Two guns from Cushing's battery were double loaded with canister and were fired as Garnett's men approached, clearing a fifty-foot-wide swath in the Confederate line. Finley distinctly felt the "flame of the explosion." They were overwhelmed

as Garnett's men experienced the ecstasy of victory. The men now looked back for their support, and they were relieved to see Armistead's men approaching. It appears that all of Garnett's regiments planted their flags on the stone wall—all that is, except the 8th Virginia, on the right flank, which was facing the tough and immovable 69th Pennsylvania of the Philadelphia Brigade. General Garnett, still mounted, looked over the situation, ready to give fresh orders to his men. Lieutenant Finley would never forget what happened next.

> At that instant, suddenly a terrific fire burst upon us from our front, and looking around I saw close to us, just on the crest of the ridge, a fresh line of Federals attempting to drive us from the stone fence, but after exchanging a few rounds with us they fell back behind the crest, leaving us still in possession of the stone wall. Under this fire, as I immediately learned, Gen. Garnett had fallen dead.[81]

This was quite a blow to Garnett's survivors. After the war, some of Garnett's veterans stated that Garnett fell from an artillery projectile. However, the evidence supports Finley and other survivors who believed that it was the muskets of the 72nd Pennsylvania of the Philadelphia Brigade that brought down Garnett. One of Garnett's couriers, Private R. H. Irvine, estimated that Garnett fell approximately fifteen to twenty paces from the stone wall, hit by a single bullet, which entered just above and behind his left ear. Death was instantaneous. Seeing the mass of the 72nd Pennsylvania near the top of the ridge, Garnett's survivors decided to wait until Armistead's reinforcements arrived. Lying behind the stone wall, they fired at the unprotected Fire Zouaves.[82]

Armistead, swinging his hat on his sword, now approached. Jumping over the stone wall, he led his troops up the ridge. Some of Garnett's troops followed. Most appear to have remained at the wall, continuing to fire at the Federal troops on the ridge. Armistead was struck down, and the men could see fresh Federal troops massing for a counterattack. Those who did not retreat took on the overwhelming numbers of Federal troops in hand-to-hand combat. "Men fired into each other's faces; there were bayonet thrusts, cutting with sabers, hand-to-hand contests, oaths, curses, yells, and hurrahs," wrote Lieutenant John Lee of the 28th Virginia. The men soon realized that further defense was futile. Shotwell wrote that "to retreat was nearly as dangerous as to advance, and scores of men threw themselves behind some piles of stone in front of the works, and held up their hands in token of surrender." Finley (56th Virginia) recalled that "the bullets seemed to come from front and both flanks, and I saw we could not hold the fence any longer." While weighing his odds of getting back to Seminary Ridge alive, the Federal line approached, and Finley told his men to cease fire and surrender. He dejectedly wrote that the "sharp, quick huzza of the Federals told of our defeat and their triumph."[83]

The retreat back to Seminary Ridge was a difficult one, as the Federal infantry and artillery continued to take their toll. As the men reached the ridge they encountered General Pickett. Some were concerned that their failure had disgraced the army. However, when Pickett sobbed, "My brave men! My brave men!" they knew that they were anything but cowards. The men were rallied, and it was now that they saw the immensity of their losses. Resting there the following day, the survivors began the march for home during the night of July 4–5. As the men trudged away, many felt like William

Jones, who wrote, "I never want to get back to Pennsylvania."[84]

Garnett's Brigade lost a higher percentage of men than either of its two sister brigades in Pickett's Division. It had the distinction of piercing the Federal line near the Bloody Angle, and may have been more successful in capturing the ridge if it had continued its charge, rather than waiting for Armistead's men to arrive. However, in the end, there were too few men in gray and an overwhelming number of Federal troops.

NOTES

1. Warner, *Generals in Gray*, 239; Tagg, *Generals of Gettysburg*, 237–238.

2. Kathy G. Harrison and John W. Busey, *Nothing But Glory* (Gettysburg, PA, 1993), 1–2, 8; Tagg, *Generals of Gettysburg*, 237–238; David E. Johnston, *The Story of A Confederate Boy in the Civil War* (Portland, OR, 1914), 202

3. Coddington, *The Gettysburg Campaign*, 114; Harrison and Busey, *Nothing But Glory*, 2; Thomas D. Houston, "Storming Cemetery Hill," *Philadelphia Weekly Times*, October 21, 1882; Catlett Conway, "The Battle of Gettysburg," *Atlanta Journal*, December 7, 1901.

4. David E. Johnston, *Four Years a Soldier* (Princeton, WV, 1887), 243–244; Walter Harrison, *Pickett's Men: A Fragment of War History* (New York, 1870), 88.

5. Joseph T. Durkin, *John Dooley, Confederate Soldier, His War Journal* (Washington, DC, 1945), 101; Joseph Mayo, "Pickett's Charge at Gettysburg," *Richmond Times-Dispatch*, May 6, 1906.

There is some confusion over the actual time of arrival. Johnston put the time at 2:00 P.M.; Colonel Joseph Mayo of the 3rd Virginia recalled it was 3:00 P.M. ("Pickett's Charge at Gettysburg"), and John Dooley believed that it was between 5:00 and 6:00 P.M. The actual time was probably between 2:00 and 3:00 P.M.

6. Henry J. Greenberg, "Pickett's Charge: The Reason Why," *Gettysburg Maga-*

zine (July 1991), issue 5, 105–106; J. R. Hutter, letter, Daniel Papers, University of Virginia.

Major James Hutter recalled that after this exchange with Longstreet and Pickett, Lee said, "Ask the men if they can dislodge them." At least two companies of the 11th Virginia were moved to the crest of the ridge, and Hutter heard his men say, "Boys, many a one of us will bite the dust here today but we will say to Gen. Lee if he wants us them driven out we will do it." There is no other indication that this incident occurred, and Harrison and Busey (*Nothing But Glory*, 16–17) discounted it.

7. Harrison and Busey, *Nothing But Glory*, 12–15; Harrison, *Pickett's Men*, 91–92.

8. Harrison and Busey, *Nothing But Glory*, 42; "Terrific Fight of Third Day," *The Scranton Truth*, July 3, 1913; Eppa Hunton, letter, University of Virginia.

Pickett's location during the charge has been questioned. According to his aide, Captain Robert Bright, Pickett followed about twenty yards behind the advance for the first 750 yards. While many believed that Pickett watched the rest of the fight from the Codori house, Harrison and Busey were noncommittal (Robert A. Bright, "Pickett's Charge, The Story of It Told by a Member of His Staff," in *Southern Historical Society Papers* [1903], vol. 31, 230–231; Harrison and Busey, *Nothing But Glory*, 128–134.)

9. Bright, "Pickett's Charge, The Story of It Told by a Member of His Staff," 234.

10. Busey and Martin, *Regimental Strengths and Losses*, 144, 283.

11. Sifakis, *Compendium of the Confederate Armies: Virginia*, 155–156, 163–164, 176, 183–184, 204; Sears, *To the Gates of Richmond*, 364, 375; Warner, *Generals in Gray*, 169.

12. Tagg, *Generals of Gettysburg*, 241.

13. Thomas Pollock, letter, Southern Historical Collection, University of North Carolina.

14. Pollock, letter.

15. Pollock, letter; Harold M. Walthall "Memoirs," copy in 1st Virginia file, GNMP.

16. Johnston, *Story of a Confederate Boy*, 194.

17. Johnston, *Story of a Confederate Boy*, 197–198.

18. Houston, "Storming Cemetery Hill"; Mayo, "Pickett's Charge at Gettysburg"; Johnston, *Four Years a Soldier*, 245; Durkin, *John Dooley, Confederate Soldier*, 101.

19. Mayo, "Pickett's Charge at Gettysburg"; Charles T. Lohr, *War History of the Old First Virginia Infantry Regiment, Army of Northern Virginia* (Richmond, VA, 1884), 36; Durkin, *John Dooley, Confederate Soldier*, 102; Johnston, *The Story of a Confederate Boy*, 204.

20. Houston, "Storming Cemetery Hill."

21. Johnston, *Four Years a Soldier*, 249, 253; Durkin, *John Dooley Confederate Soldier*, 103.

22. Johnston, *Four Years a Soldier*, 254; Walthall, "Memoirs"; Johnston, *Story of a Confederate Boy*, 207; Rawley W. Martin and John H. Smith, "Battle of Gettysburg and Charge of Pickett's Division," *Southern Historical Society Papers* (1904), vol. 32, 190.

23. Johnston, *Four Years a Soldier*, 255; C. M. Wilcox, letter, in *Southern Historical Society Papers* (1877), vol. 4, 116; Ralph W. Gunn, *Twenty-fourth Virginia* (Lynchburg, VA, 1987), 45.

24. R. A. Bright, " Pickett's Charge at Gettysburg," in *Confederate Veteran* (1930), vol. 37, 264–265; Kemper, letter; Johnston, *Story of a Confederate Boy*, 207–208.

Colonel Lewis Williams of the 1st Virginia protested this order, and Bright agreed to make an excuse for him. According to Harrison and Busey, Williams was wounded in the shoulder during the advance, but was killed when he fell off his horse and onto his own sword (Bright, "Pickett's Charge at Gettysburg"; "Harrison and Busey, *Nothing But Glory*, 181).

25. Durkin, *John Dooley, Confederate Soldier*, 104–105; Hutter, letter.

26. John Smith, "Account," *Southern Historical Society Paper* (1904), vol. 32, 190; Conway, "The Battle of Gettysburg"; James Walker, "The Charge of Pickett's Division by a Participant," Virginia State Library.

27. Martin and Smith, "Battle of Gettysburg and Charge of Pickett's Division," 190; Johnston, *Story of a Confederate Boy*, 208; Walthall, "Memoirs."

According to General Kemper, the charge got off on the wrong foot, when he saw Garnett's Brigade prematurely stepping off. As a result, Kemper's Brigade lagged behind Garnett's during the charge.

28. Durkin, *John Dooley Confederate Soldier*, 105–106; Martin and Smith, "Battle of Gettysburg and Charge of Pickett's Division," 191.

The modern historian of the 7th Virginia estimated that the brigade was first exposed to cannon fire after about four minutes into the march. (Davis F. Riggs, *Seventh Virginia Infantry* [Lynchburg, VA, 1882]), 25.

29. Hutter, letter.

30. Hutter, letter.

While this crowding may have occurred later in during the oblique movements to the left, Hutter does not mention that this was in response to this attack.

31. Mayo, "Pickett's Charge at Gettysburg."

32. Ralph O. Sturtevant, *Pictorial History of the Thirteenth Vermont Volunteers in the War of 1861–1865* (Burlington, VT, 1910), 303.

33. Henry T. Owen, letter, copy in GNMP; Richard Rollins, *Pickett's Charge— Eyewitness Accounts* (Redondo Beach, CA, 1994), 174–175; Edmund Berkeley, letter, University of Virginia.

34. Charles T. Loehr, "The Famous Pickett Charge," *Richmond Times-Dispatch*, October 16, 1904; Gunn, *Twenty-Fourth Virginia*, 46; Joseph Mayo, "Report," Duke University; Mayo, "Pickett's Charge at Gettysburg"; Sturtevant, *Pictorial History of the Thirteenth Regiment*, 301; Harrison and Busey, *Nothing But Glory*, 68; Wheelock Veazey letter, copy in 16th Vermont folder, GNMP.

35. Walthall, "Memoirs"; Durkin, *John Dooley, Confederate Soldier*, 106; Conway, "The Battle of Gettysburg"; Martin and Smith, "Battle of Gettysburg and Charge of Pickett's Division," 191–192.

36. Johnston, *Story of a Confederate Boy*, 210.

37. Andrew Cowan, "When Cowan's Battery Withstood Pickett's Charge," *New York Herald*, July 2, 1911; Harrison and Busey, *Nothing But Glory*, 102, 116.

38. Durkin, *John Dooley, Confederate Soldier*, 107; Smith, "Account," 193; Charles T. Loehr, "Casualties in the Old First at Gettys-

burg," in *Southern Historical Society Papers* (1890), vol. 17, 408.

39. Johnston, *Story of a Confederate Boy*, 211, 215; Colonel W. Fry, "Report," Duke University; Edward Cook Barnes, letter, University of Virginia.

40. Gunn, *Twenty-fourth Virginia*, 47; Bright, "Pickett's Charge at Gettysburg," 265–266.

Kemper recovered from his wounds, but never again returned to active duty. He was elected governor of Virginia after the war (Warner, *Generals in Gray*, 169–170).

41. Busey and Martin, *Regimental Strengths and Losses at Gettysburg*, 145, 283

42. Warner, *Generals in Gray*, 11–12; Tagg, *Generals of Gettysburg*, 243–244.

43. Gregory, *Thirty-eighth Virginia Infantry* (Lynchburg, VA, 1988), 37.

44. Charles Lippitt, diary, Southern Historical Collection, University of North Carolina; John Beaton, letter, copy in 9th Virginia file, GNMP.

45. Beaton, letter; Edward R. Crews, *Fourteenth Virginia Infantry* (Lynchburg, VA, 1995), 36.

46. B. L. Farinholt, "Battle of Gettysburg—Johnson's Island," in *Confederate Veteran* (1897), vol. 5, 468; Levin C. Gayle, diary, copy in 9th Virginia folder, GNMP; George K. Griggs, diary, Museum of the Confederacy; James H. Walker, "The Charge of Pickett's Division," in *Blue and Gray* (1893), vol. 1, 221; John H. Lewis, "Memoirs," copy in Brake Collection, USAMHI.

47. Charles Lippitt, diary; Thomas H. Oakes, "The Battle of Gettysburg," copy in 14th Virginia file, GNMP; Walker, "The Charge of Pickett's Division," 222; Gregory, *Thirty-eighth Virginia*, 38.

48. James H. Walker, "A Survivor of Pickett's Division," in *Blue and Gray* (1893), vol. 2, 27; Walker, "The Charge of Pickett's Division," 222.

49. Lewis, "Memoirs"; J. F. Crocker, "Gettysburg—Pickett's Charge and Other War Addresses," 40–41, copy in 9th Virginia file, GNMP; Erasmus Williams, "Account," Daniel's Papers, University of Virginia; Gregory, *Thirty-eighth Virginia*, 39.

50. Crocker, "Gettysburg—Pickett's Charge," 41; Rawley W. Martin, "Armistead at the Battle of Gettysburg," in *Southern Historical Society Papers* (1914), vol. 39, 186; James T. Carter, "Flag of the Fifty-Third Virginia Regiment," in *Confederate Veteran* (1902), vol. 10, 263.

51. Gregory, *Thirty-eighth Virginia*, 39; Martin,, "Armistead at the Battle of Gettysburg," 186; Lewis, "Memoirs."

52. Harrison and Busey, *Nothing But Glory*, 56; Walker, "The Charge of Pickett's Division," 222.

53. Walker, "The Charge of Pickett's Division," 222; James E. Poindexter, "General Armistead's Portrait Presented," in *Southern Historical Society Papers* (1909), vol. 37, 146. There is some disagreement on this point. While most veterans recollected that the fire began when they were about halfway across the plain, John Lewis of the 9th Virginia estimated that it began when they were only two hundred yards into the charge.

54. Walker, "The Charge of Pickett's Division," 222; J. F. Crocker, "Gettysburg—Pickett's Charge and Other War Addresses," copy in 9th Virginia folder, GNMP, 42; Lewis, "Memoirs"; Harrison and Busey, *Nothing But Glory*, 54; William B. Robertson, "Account," Daniel's Papers, University of Virginia.

55. Martin, "Armistead at the Battle of Gettysburg," 186. Another version of the conversation had Kemper saying to Armistead, "I am going to charge those heights and carry them and I want you to support me." To this request, Armistead immediately responded, "I'll do it! Look at my line. It never looked better on dress parade" (Maude C. Clement, *History of Pittsylvania County, Virginia*, [Lynchburg, VA, 1929], 249).

56. Lewis, "Memoirs"; Crocker, *Gettysburg—Pickett's Charge*, 43; Gregory, *Thirty-eighth Virginia*, 40; Clement, *History of Pittsylvania County*, 249.

57. Bradley M. Gottfried, *Stopping Pickett—The History of the Philadelphia Brigade* (Shippensburg, PA, 1999), 173–174.

58. "Col. And Dr. R. W. Martin, of Virginia," in *Confederate Veteran* (1897), vol. 5, 70; J. Irving Sale, "Gettysburg"; *Philadelphia Weekly Press*, July 4, 1887; Poindexter, "General Armistead's Portrait Presented," 149.

59. Farinholt, "Battle of Gettysburg—Johnson's Island," 468; D. B. Easley, letter, copy at USAMHI; Lewis, "Memoirs."

60. Crocker, *Gettysburg—Pickett's Charge*, 46; Busey and Martin, *Regimental Strengths and Losses*, 283.

61. Busey and Martin, *Regimental Strengths and Losses at Gettysburg*, 146, 283.

62. Sifarkis, *Compendium of the Confederate Armies: Virginia*, 177–178, 193, 194–195, 212–213, 250; Warner, *Generals in Gray*, 57;

63. Warner, *Generals in Gray*, 99; Tagg, *Generals of Gettysburg*, 246–247.

64. Eppa Hunton, *Atutobiography of Eppa Hunton* (Richmond, VA, 1933), 86–87.

65. James I. Robertson, *Eighteenth Virginia* (Lynchburg, VA, 1984), 20; Hunton, *Atutobiography of Eppa Hunton*, 87.

66. Randolph A. Shotwell, *The Shotwell Papers* (Raleigh, NC, 1929–1931), vol. 1, 496; Richard Irby, *Historical Sketch of the Nottoway Grays* (Richmond, VA, 1878), 27; William A. Young, *Fifty-sixth Virginia* (Lynchburg, VA, 1990), 78; Anonymous, letter, copy in the 18th Virginia file, GNMP.

67. Anonymous, letter, copy in the 18th Virginia file; Irby, *Historical Sketch of the Nottoway Grays*, 27; Norborne Berkeley, "Account, " copy in the 8th Virginia file, GNMP.

68. Young, *Fifty-sixth Virginia*, 79; Shotwell, *The Shotwell Papers*, vol. 1, 500; vol. 2, 4.

69. Robertson, *Eighteenth Virginia*, 21; William N. Wood, *Reminiscences of Big I* (Charlottesville, VA, 1909), 43; George Findley, "Bloody Angle," *Buffalo Evening News*, May 29, 1894; Randolph A. Shotwell, "Virginia and North Carolina in the Battle of Gettysburg," in *Our Living and Our Dead* (1876), vol. 4, 88.

70. Wood, *Reminiscences of Big I*, 44; Young, *Fifty-sixth Virginia*, 81.

71. Shotwell, "Virginia and North Carolina in the Battle of Gettysburg," 89–90; William P. Jesse, "Account," copy in 28th Virginia file, GNMP.

72. Berkeley, "Memoirs"; Young, *Fifty-sixth Virginia*, 81.

73. John E. Divine, *Eighth Virginia Infantry* (Lynchburg, VA, 1983), 21; Hunton, *Autobiography of Eppa Hunton*, 91; Wood, *Reminiscences of Big I*, 45.

74. Shotwell, "Virginia and North Carolina in the Battle of Gettysburg," 90; Ida L. Johnson, "Over the Stone Wall at Gettysburg," in *Confederate Veteran* (1923), vol. 31, 249; Young, *Fifty-sixth Virginia*, 82.

75. Young, *Fifty-sixth Virginia*, 82; Wood, *Reminiscences of Big I*, 46.

76. Shotwell, "Virginia and North Carolina in the Battle of Gettysburg," 91.

77. Shotwell, "Virginia and North Carolina in the Battle of Gettysburg," 91–92; OR 27, 2, 386; Frank E. Fields, *Twenty-eighth Virginia Infantry* (Lynchburg, VA, 1985), 26.

78. Charles H. Banes, *History of the Philadelphia Brigade . . .* (Philadelphia, 1876), 190; Jesse, "Memoir"; Jacob Hoke, *The Great Invasion* (New York, 1959), 385–386; R. H. Irvine, "Brig. Gen. Richard B. Garnett," in *Confederate Veteran* (1915), vol. 23, 391; Divine, *Eighth Virginia*, 22.

79. Shotwell, "Virginia and North Carolina in the Battle of Gettysburg," 93; Gott-fried, *Stopping Pickett—The History of the Philadelphia Brigade*, 170, 172.

80. Young, *Fifty-Sixth Virginia*, 84–85; Finley, "Bloody Angle."

81. Young, *Fifty-Sixth Virginia*, 85; Finley, "Bloody Angle."

82. Irvine, "Brig. Gen. Richard B. Garnett," 391; Winfield Peters, "The Lost Sword of General Richard B. Garnett, Who Fell at Gettysburg," *The Baltimore Sun*, November 4, 1905; Stephen Davis, "The Death and Burial of General Richard Brooke Garnett," *Gettysburg Magazine* (July 1991), issue 5, 113; Harrison and Busey, *Nothing But Glory*, 85.

Garnett's body was never found and was probably buried in a long trench with the other men of his brigade. A Union soldier apparently ripped off the star and wreath from his collar, making his rank unclear to the men who were burying the dead the next day (Irvine, "Brig. Gen. Richard B. Garnett," 391).

83. Shotwell, "Virginia and North Carolina in the Battle of Gettysburg," 94; Finley, "Bloody Angle."

84. Wood, *Reminiscences of Big I*, 47; William H. Jones, letter, Duke University.

SECOND CORPS—

Lieutenant General Richard Ewell

After Stonewall Jackson was mortally wounded at Chancellorsville, the Army of the Northern Virginia was subdivided into three corps. The Second Corps was given to Major General Richard Ewell, who had recently returned to the army after losing a leg at Second Manassas. A West Point graduate, Ewell had spent most of his career in the Southwest. Upon entering the Confederate service, he was given the rank of lieutenant colonel in April 1861, colonel a month later, and brigadier general in June. He commanded an infantry brigade at the first battle of Manassas, and was a close ally of Stonewall Jackson during the Valley campaign, where he commanded a division. After serving in the Seven Days battles, Ewell led his division to Second Manassas, where he was seriously wounded.[1]

The campaign started well for Ewell, when he defeated General Robert Milroy's command at the second battle of Winchester on June 14–15, 1863. The corps began crossing the Potomac on the evening of June 15, and on June 21, Ewell received choice orders from Lee: enter Pennsylvania and capture Harrisburg.[2]

While Rodes's and Johnson's Divisions marched toward Greencastle, Pennsylvania, and then on to Carlisle, Early's Division approached Gettysburg. The three divisions scrounged the countryside for supplies along the way. Early continued on to York, which he captured on June 28. One of his brigades, under Brigadier General John Gordon, marched on Wrightsville to capture the 1.5-mile long bridge over the Susquehanna River. Early was to cross the river, capture Lancaster, and then march on Harrisburg from the rear, while the remainder of the corps approached from the opposite direction. Militia thwarted the plan when they fired the bridge before fleeing for safety. It really didn't matter, as Ewell received orders on June 29 to return to the western side of the South Mountain and rejoin Lee's army.[3]

On the night before the battle, Ewell's three divisions were still dispersed: Rodes's was at Heidlersburg, Early's was three miles away on the road leading to Berlin, and Johnson's was between Greenville and Scotland. The next day, July 1, Rodes's Division was ordered to march toward Cashtown, Early, was to move via Hunterstown, and Johnson's was to continue to Fayetteville. Learning that A. P. Hill's Third Corps was approaching Gettysburg, Ewell turned the head of Rodes's column toward that crossroads town, marching it down the Middletown Road, and ordered Early to hurry down Heidlersburg Road. As a result, Rodes's Division approached the battlefield first from the north, Early's came next, from the northwest, and Johnson's arrived that evening from the west, along Chambersburg Pike.[4]

Two of Ewell's three divisions were engaged on July 1. Rodes's Division opened the corps' fight by attacking the Federal I Corps's right flank, and after some initial set-backs, caused the line to crumble. The same occurred to the east, where Early's Division barreled into the XI Corps in the open fields north of town, driving it back through Gettysburg to Cemetery Hill. Concerned about the fatigue of his two divisions, and warned of fresh enemy troops arriving on his left, Ewell elected to wait until Johnson's Division arrived to storm the heights. Deciding that Culp's Hill might provide a better route to Cemetery Hill, Ewell ordered Johnson to take the hill. Assuming that Johnson was following his orders, Ewell rested. He did not know that Johnson sent a scouting party up the hill to ascertain whether the enemy occupied it. Johnson got his answer when his scouts were fired upon in the growing darkness. He subsequently decided to rest his men and wait for first light before attacking. Unfortunately for the Confederates, few Federal troops held the hill at this time.[5]

When Ewell learned that Johnson had not taken the hill the night before, he ordered an immediate attack. It was too late, as the XII Corps had arrived and the V Corps was close by. The attack was halted. After much reflection, Lee ordered Ewell to attack the right of the Union line with all three of his divisions on July 2 while Longstreet took on the left. Both actions were to be launched at 4:00 P.M. While Ewell's artillery opened fire at the appointed time, the infantry attack was not launched until after 7:00 P.M., when two brigades of Early's Division stormed Cemetery Hill and Johnson's Division attacked Culp's Hill. Both attacks met with only limited success, sustaining heavy losses in the process. Rodes's Division was also to attack Cemetery Hill, but it was late in taking position and its advance was aborted.[6]

Johnson's Division, with assistance from some brigades from Rodes's and Early's Divisions, stormed Culp's Hill again and again, beginning at about 4:30 A.M. on July 3. The attacks finally ended at about 11:00 A.M., when Ewell finally realized that his men could not take the heavily fortified heights. The losses were dreadful. Pulling back to Seminary Ridge, the corps spent July 4 waiting for an attack that never came. It began the long march back to Virginia during the night of July 4–5.[7]

EARLY'S DIVISION—

Major General Jubal Early

Crusty Major General Jubal Early commanded the crack division since the battle of Antietam. Two of the brigades bore special merit. Hays's Brigade was composed of rowdy Lousianians who loved to fight, and Gordon's Brigade was led by a charismatic commander who whipped his troops into an effective fighting unit. Formerly Ewell's old division, it had seen extensive action in the Shenandoah Valley as part of Stonewall Jackson's forces, during the Seven Days battles, and again at Second Manassas. When Ewell went down with his leg wound at the latter battle, Brigadier General Alexander Lawton assumed command of the division prior to the Maryland campaign. Lawton was wounded at the battle of Sharpsburg and Early continued the fight. Early effectively led the division at the battle of Fredericksburg when it helped seal a breach in Stonewall Jackson's line. Promoted in April 1863, Early was given permanent command of the division. During the subsequent Chancellorsville campaign, Early was ordered to hold the heights over Fredericksburg against overwhelming odds. Ultimately forced to retreat, he was able to organize a counterattack and help defeat the Federal VI Corps. Although not well-liked, Early had gained a well-earned reputation for being an outstanding division commander.[8]

General Early boasted after the war that his men were the first Confederate troops to enter and "capture" Gettysburg. Hearing that there were enemy troops in the town, Early moved his division in that direction, arriving there on June 26. According to Early's official report, "the object of this movement was for Gordon to amuse and skirmish with the enemy while I should get on his flank and rear, so as to capture his whole force." As Early approached the town, he found General John Gordon's Brigade just entering it and quickly learned that the Federal force was simply a regiment of Pennsylvania militia (26th Pennsylvania Militia), which had no intention of standing in the way of Early's veterans. Fleeing across the fields, they left behind about 175 men as prisoners, who were quickly paroled. Early wanted supplies, but was disappointed to find few in the town. Gordon's Brigade was now sent toward York, while the remainder of Early's Division marched toward Dover. Gordon's men entered York on the morning of June 28. Early was more successful here, receiving about 1500 pairs of shoes, hats, socks, rations, and about $28,600 in cash.⁹

Early's next goal was to capture the Columbia Bridge over the Susquehanna River. After crossing, the division was to cut the Pennsylvania Central Railroad, secure supplies from Lancaster, and then attack Harrisburg in the rear, while Ewell's other divisions attacked from other directions. Early's plans were dashed when Pennsylvania militia torched the bridge before Gordon's Brigade could secure it. The division reassembled at York, and on the evening of June 29, Early received orders to pull back to the western side of South Mountain. Leaving York on the morning of June 30, Early began the twenty-two-mile march toward Hunterstown. That night, Ewell informed him that the road to Hunterstown was "very circuitous and rough," and so on the morning of July 1, Early struck out for Heidlersburg, about three miles from his camp. Early's van arrived on the battlefield at about 3:00 that afternoon—just in time to see Doles's Brigade (Rodes's Division) about to be attacked in front and flank by Barlow's Division (XI Corps).¹⁰

Early quickly deployed his division by placing Hoke's (Avery's) Brigade on the left, Gordon's on the right, and Hays's in the center, astride Harrisburg Road. General William Smith's Brigade formed the reserve. Wasting little time, he sent Gordon's men forward, to be followed by the remainder of the division. The Confederates made short work of Barlow's Division on Blocher's Knoll. While Doles's Brigade attacked Barlow's left flank, Gordon hit his front, causing the Union line to collapse. It now boiled down to a foot race, and hundreds of XI Corps soldiers were captured. Upon approaching the town, Coster's reserve brigade (von Steinwehr's Division, XI Corps) was sent down from Cemetery Hill to halt the Confederate onslaught. Hays's and Hoke's (Avery's) Brigades made short work of defeating this lone Federal brigade, which joined in the race for the safety of Cemetery Hill.¹¹

The division's last important action occurred on the evening of July 2, when Hays's and Hoke's (Avery's) Brigades successfully captured the crest of Cemetery Hill. Unsupported by Gordon's Brigade and by Rodes's Division, the remnants of the two brigades were forced to vacate the hill. Early was criticized for not supporting the two brigades, but he felt that "the attempt would be attended with a useless sacrifice of life." Except for Smith's Brigade's detachment and subsequent action at the eastern base of Culp's Hill, where it halted an attack by two Federal regiments, the division was inactive on July 3. After spending July 4 on Seminary Ridge, the division began its retreat during the early morning hours of July 5.[12]

Gordon's Brigade—Brigadier General John Gordon

Units: 13th Georgia, 26th Georgia, 31st Georgia, 38th Georgia, 60th Georgia, 61th Georgia
Strength: 1813 (26th Georgia detached to protect artillery and participated in only part of July 1 fight).
Losses: 537 (112-297-128)—30%[13]

Although about eleven months separated the mustering in of the brigade's first regiment (13th Georgia) and its last (61st Georgia), all six regiments initially served in Georgia. The 13th and 26th Georgia were sent north in June and saw some service in Stonewall Jackson's Valley campaign, and all were organized into Brigadier General Alexander Lawton's Brigade by the start of the Seven Days campaign. The brigade fought well at the battles of Gaines's Mill and Second Manassas. When General Lawton was given Ewell's Division, the brigade was led by Colonel Marcellus Douglass at the battle of Sharpsburg, where the men helped blunt the attack of the Federal I Corps. The brigade sustained exceptionally heavy losses, including the death of Colonel Douglass. Colonel E. N. Atkinson of the 26th Georgia assumed command of the brigade after the battle and led it during the Fredericksburg campaign. The brigade helped seal a breach in Stonewall Jackson's line, and when the enemy was reinforced and charged again, the brigade counterattacked, but advanced too far.

With its flanks exposed, the brigade sustained heavy losses, including the mortal wounding of Colonel Atkinson.[14]

The brigade's new commander was Brigadier General John Gordon. An attorney by training, he was active politically before the war. He entered the Confederate army as a captain in the 6th Alabama and was present at the first battle of Manassas. By April 1862, he was in command of the regiment. During the Peninsula campaign he temporarily commanded Robert Rodes's Brigade and saw action at Gaines's Mill and Malvern Hill, where he gained a reputation for being an aggressive fighter. He fought well at South Mountain and was wounded five times at the Sunken Road at the battle of Sharpsburg. When he returned to the army at the end of March 1862, he was given Lawton's old brigade. He performed well at the battle of Chancellorsville, and he and his men were ready for their next encounter with the Union army.[15]

General John Gordon's Brigade's pre-Gettysburg exploits were almost as exciting as its later escapades on the battlefield. Ordered to capture the city of York, Gordon was surprised to see a knot of men approaching as he was about to enter the town. They proved to be the mayor and other influential citizens, who negotiated the town's surrender. Gordon immediately ordered the removal of the large Federal flag flying over the main street.

After securing supplies and cash, Gordon was ordered to march on Wrightsville, where he was to capture the Columbia Bridge. This would allow Early's Division to cross the Susquehanna River in its quest to capture Harrisburg. Gordon learned that the militia defending the bridge were strongly entrenched in front of it. At first Gordon hoped that he could cut off the enemy, but after realizing that this was impossible, he ordered a battery to open fire on the enemy. "By a few well-aimed shots and the advance of my lines, caused this force to retreat precipitately, with the loss of about 20 prisoners," he noted in his report.[16]

As Gordon's men stepped onto the bridge, they realized that the fleeing militia had set it on fire. Requesting buckets from the citizens of Wrightsville, Gordon was told that none were to be had. Before long, the flames consumed not only the bridge, but they also leaped to the town itself, causing several buildings to burn. The citizens miraculously produced a wealth of buckets, which were quickly grabbed by Gordon's men. A bucket brigade formed and the flames were soon extinguished, but not before the bridge was destroyed. Gordon's men were later enraged when they learned that the Northern press said that *they* had set the town on fire. The Georgians turned the table later that day, burning fourteen railroad bridges around York.[17]

Upon reaching the battlefield at about 3:00 P.M. on July 1, Gordon was ordered to form his brigade on the right of the division along a sunken farm lane. One of his regiments, the 26th Georgia, was detached at this point to support the division's artillery. The brigade's remaining regiments were deployed from left to right as 38th Georgia–61st Georgia–13th Georgia–31st Georgia–60th Georgia. Gordon wrote in his official report that his men "were much fatigued from long marches, and I therefore caused them to move forward slowly until within about 300 yards of the enemy's line, when the advance was as rapid as the nature of the ground and a proper regard for the preservation of my line would permit."[18]

Gordon's timely arrival helped thwart an attack on Doles's Brigade to his right by Barlow's Division (XI Corps), which had occupied Blocher's Knoll. In front of Gordon's Brigade was two- or three-foot-deep Rock Creek with steep four-foot banks. As Gordon's men splashed across they encountered von Gilsa's Brigade. Sergeant Francis Hudgins of the 38th Georgia recalled after the war that Gordon "gave his ringing order to 'forward at right shoulder shift arms.'" Gordon later bragged, "moving forward under heavy fire over rail and plank fences, and crossing a creek whose banks were so abrupt as to prevent a passage excepting at certain points, this brigade rushed upon the enemy with a resolution and spirit, in my opinion, rarely excelled."[19]

Colonel Leopold von Gilsa's Brigade held its positions along the eastern portion of Blocher's Knoll despite what must have looked like an irresistible charge. Gordon's men were equally impressed. Hudgins recalled the "grand sight, to see the Federal infantry on the bank of the stream, waiting motionless our approach." Barlow ordered his men to open fire when Gordon's men were about seventy-five yards away. Private G. Nichols of the 61st Georgia recalled that "we met the enemy at Rock Creek. We attacked them immediately, but we had a hard time moving them. We advanced with our accustomed yell, but they stood firm until we got near them." The two lines now stood less than fifty paces apart, each firing volleys into the other. One of them had to break, and it turned out to be von Gilsa's line, which fled to the rear. Nichols recalled that the Federal troops "then began to retreat in fine order, shooting at us they retreated. They were harder to drive than we had ever known them before. Men were being mowed down in great numbers on both sides." While running for his life, Private Ruben Ruch of the 153rd Pennsylvania happened to look back and saw "a regular swath of blue coats as far as I could see along the line. They were piled up in every shape."[20]

With von Gilsa's Brigade gone, Ames's Brigade alone occupied the west side of the hill. Hit on its front and left flank by Doles's Brigade, and receiving an enfilading fire on their right flank from Gordon's regiments, it was only a matter of minutes before this Federal unit also withdrew. After the war, General Gordon marveled that any troops escaped from the hell on Blocher's Knoll.[21]

Colonel Krzyzanowski's Brigade (Schimmelfennig's Division) now approached from the southwest. It was to form on Ames's left flank, but the latter was defeated before it could do so. Several of Doles's regiments, including the 12th, 44th, and 4th Georgia, and to their left, Gordon's 31st and 60th Georgia, wheeled to face this new threat. Gordon's regiments overlapped Krzyzanowski's right flank, held by the 26th Wisconsin. Hit on the flank and front, the Federal regiment crumbled. One of the many fictions of the battle occurred when Colonel William Jacobs of the 26th Wisconsin wrote that the "regiment was furiously attacked by vastly superior numbers, but held its own until ordered by you [Krzyzanowski] to retreat, when a retreat in good order was effected." In actuality, the retreat was anything but orderly.[22]

Gordon's men now hit the next regiment in line, the 119th New York, and sent it flying to the rear as well. Within a very short time, Krzyzanowski's entire brigade was completely broken by Gordon's and Dole's Georgians' determined attacks. In his report, Gordon described the attack in but one sentence: "An effort was here made by the enemy to change his front and check our advance, but the effort failed, and this line, too, was driven back in the greatest confusion, and with immense loss in killed, wounded, and prisoners."[23]

Early now ordered Gordon to continue his advance to the almshouse, where some of the shattered Federal units were attempting to make a stand. Private Nichols recalled that the Federal "officers were cheering their men and behaving like heroes and commanders of the 'first water.'" After driving these demoralized Union troops from the almshouse, Gordon rested his men and reformed their disorganized ranks. They were merely spectators to the destruction of Coster's Brigade (von Steinwehr's Division, XI Corps) by Hays's and Hoke's (Avery's) Brigades.[24]

As Gordon's men surveyed the fields behind them, they could see the landscape dotted with hundreds of blue-clad men. Lieutenant Joseph Hilton of the 26th Georgia wrote home after the battle, "it makes me feel sick when I think of the piles of dead men I saw upon that field." In his official report, Gordon added, "I had no means of ascertaining the number of the enemy's wounded by the fire of this brigade, but if these were in the usual proportion to his killed, nearly 300 of whom were buried on the ground where my brigade fought, his loss in killed and wounded must have exceeded the number of men I carried into action." Gordon was also credited with capturing an additional 1800 men. He could not resist referring to the fact that because one of his regiments had been detached, he carried only 1200 men into battle.[25]

General Gordon left a lasting impression on his men on July 1. Riding a magnificent coal-black stallion, which could be seen "close upon the heels of the battle line, his head right in among the slanting barrels and bayonets . . . his rider [Gordon] standing in his stirrups, bareheaded, hat in hand, arms extended, and, in a voice like a trumpet, exhorting his men. It was superb; absolutely thrilling," wrote Confederate artilleryman Robert Stiles. When asked where his dead were, Gordon replied, "I haven't got any, sir; the Almighty has covered my men with His shield and buckler." One of Gordon's men called him the "prettiest thing you ever did see on a field of fight. It'ud put fight into a whipped chicken just to look at him."[26]

Hilton (26th Georgia) accurately summed up July 1, when he wrote home on July 18, 1863, that "the first days [sic] fight was a Glorious and [a] complete victory, the enemy was badly cut up and routed all along the line, they fled in confusion through the town for the heights where their reserve was stationed, . . . the almost impregnable position which they fled to was all that saved their army from capture."[27]

Although a gallant and talented officer, General Gordon made several incorrect assertions after the war. One was that he personally aided General Barlow after the young Federal officer was wounded trying to rally his troops. It is doubtful that the two ever met that day. A second erroneous assertion was that he wanted to continue his advance through the town and take Cemetery Hill during the afternoon of July 1. In his memoirs, Gordon recalled,

The whole of that portion of the Union army in my front was in inextricable confusion and in flight. . . . Large bodies of the Union troops were throwing down their arms and surrendering, because in disorganized and confused masses they

were wholly powerless either to check the movement or return the fire. As far down the lines as my eye could reach the Union troops were in retreat. . . . In less than half an hour my troops would have swept up and over those hills, the possession of which was of such momentous consequence.[28]

Exaggerating what occurred next, Gordon wrote, "it is not surprising, with a full realization of the consequences of a halt, that I should have refused at first to obey the order. Not until the third or fourth order of the most peremptory character reached me did I obey. I think I should have risked the consequences of disobedience." Nowhere else is there any reference to Gordon's unwillingness to halt his exhausted men.[29]

Unlike Hays's and Hoke's (Avery's) Brigades, which entered the town, General Early had other plans for Gordon's men. Repeated messages from General Billy Smith suggesting that a large Federal force was approaching their left flank and rear from York Road could no longer be ignored by Early. He wrote in his official report, "though I believed this an unfounded report, as it proved to be, yet I thought it best to send General Gordon with his brigade out on that road, to take command of both brigades, and to stop all further alarms from that direction." Gordon quickly ascertained that the report was indeed false, but it broke Early's momentum. That night, and through the following day, Gordon's Brigade remained with Smith's astride York Road.[30]

During the afternoon of July 2, Gordon received orders to move his brigade to the railroad on the eastern part of town. Here it formed behind Hays's and Hoke's (Avery's) Brigades, which were to form the first line of attack on Cemetery Hill. The two brigades launched their attack at about 8:00 P.M. that night. Rodes's Division was to attack the hill from the west, while Early attacked from the northeast.[31]

Early's two brigades gallantly advanced against a storm of Federal lead, but they received no support, and the survivors were forced to flee to safety after briefly capturing Cemetery Hill. In his official report, Early explained that he did not launch Gordon's Brigade because Rodes's Division did not attack as planned. To do so would "have been a useless sacrifice." Instead, the brigade "was retained as a support for the other brigades to fall back upon."[32]

Hays's and Hoke's (Avery's) Brigades were withdrawn to the town during the early morning hours of July 3, leaving only Gordon's Brigade in front of Cemetery Hill. It remained there throughout the day. Curiously, Gordon chose not to report on any of these activities in his official report, writing instead, "the movements during the succeeding days of the battle (July 2 and 3), I do not consider of sufficient importance to mention."[33]

Gordon joined the rest of the division on Chambersburg Pike at 2:00 A.M. on July 4, where it prepared to repel a Federal attack. None came, and the brigade pulled out on the early morning hours of July 5. Forming the rear guard on July 5, the 26th Georgia was detached to hold the Federal pursuit in check outside of Fairfield, "until the wagon and division trains could be moved forward," noted General Gordon. He reported that "a spirited skirmish succeeded in driving back the enemy's advance guard and in withdrawing this regiment through the woods, with the loss of 8 or 10 killed and wounded."[34]

Gordon performed flawlessly on July 1, earning richly deserved accolades. The brigade's role during the remaining parts of the battle was minor in comparison. Given the fact that it was outnumbered during most of the fighting on July 1, and caused over a thousand Federal casualties, it is amazing that it lost only slightly more than half of the losses of the Federal troops it engaged, or about 30% of its effectives.[35]

Hoke's (Avery's) Brigade—Colonel Isaac Avery

Units: 6th North Carolina, 21st North Carolina, 57th North Carolina
Strength: 1244
Losses: 412 (92-213-107)—33%[36]

Two of Brigadier General Robert Hoke's regiments were at the battle of First Manassas—the 6th North Carolina was a member of Bee's Brigade and the 21st North Carolina was in Bonham's. The 57th North Carolina was not mustered into service until a year later. In between, the two original regiments saw action in different theaters. As part of Whiting's Brigade, the 6th North Carolina fought in the Peninsula campaign, while the 21st North Car-

olina was assigned to Crittenden's Brigade and then Trimble's, and saw extensive action during Stonewall Jackson's Valley campaign. Both regiments fought in the Seven Days battles. The 57th North Carolina was added to Trimble's Brigade in November 1862, and all were combined under Brigadier General Robert Hoke when he assumed temporary command of the brigade in January 1863.[37]

Starting the war as a lieutenant of the 1st North Carolina, Robert Hoke rose to the rank of colonel and commanded the 21st North Carolina. He took over command of Trimble's Brigade at the battle of Fredericksburg and effectively led it in an irresistible counterattack. His reward was a brigadier general's commission and permanent command of Trimble's Brigade. After he was severely wounded at the battle of Chancellorsville, Colonel Issac Avery of the 6th North Carolina assumed command prior to the Gettysburg campaign.[38]

The brigade was missing still another key element as it marched north. One of its regiments, the 54th North Carolina, was left behind in Virginia to transport prisoners captured at the second battle of Winchester. As a result, the brigade marched to Gettysburg with but three veteran regiments.[39]

Major John W. Daniel of Early's staff galloped up to the column on July 1 with the news that General A. P. Hill was being hard pressed at Gettysburg and the division must double-quick to the battlefield. Avery's men threw off their blankets and other encumbrances, knowing that the rear guard would pick up their valued possessions and throw them in the wagons. The men had already been warned of an impending battle, for earlier in the day they were ordered to inspect their arms and cartridge boxes. Artillery flying up the road caused the column to scatter several times during the march.[40]

Upon reaching the outskirts of Gettysburg, Hoke's Brigade formed the left of the division, on the left (east) of Harrisburg Road. The 57th North Carolina formed the extreme left of the line, followed by the 21st and then the 6th North Carolina on the right. Hays's Louisianians formed on their right. Jones's artillery battalion was directly in their front. Just ahead, the men could see Gordon's Brigade preparing to advance on the Federal troops on Blocher's Knoll.[41]

The men were now permitted a ten-minute reprieve. Some used the time to scan the area around them. "From our position we could see the Confederate and Federal lines arrayed one against the other in open ground, no breastworks, no fortifications, but they stood apart in battle array and were in plain view for two miles," wrote Colonel Hamilton Jones of the 57th North Carolina. The men exchanged fire with several companies of the 17th Connecticut, which had been thrown across Rock Creek during this period. When finally ordered to advance, the men were pleased to be able to finally push the pesky Nutmeggers out of their way. Although the brigade advanced to support Gordon's Brigade as it drove Barlow's Division off Blocher's Knoll, Avery's men were not involved in the actual fighting.[42]

Unlike the other units of Early's Division, Avery's men did not approach Rock Creek until they were southeast of the almshouse because of the curving nature of the stream. Up ahead, they could see Coster's Brigade (von Steinwehr's Division, XI Corps) take position behind "a strong fence, portions of which were made of stone." Colonel Archibald Godwin of the 57th North Carolina reported that "our advance was made with great deliberation until we approached a sluggish stream, or slough, about 200 yards in front of the enemy's lines, when the batteries opened upon us with grape and canister, seconded by a very destructive fire from the infantry." Avery immediately yelled for his men to double-quick across the stream to close with the enemy. The brigade must have made a lasting impression upon the Union defenders, for one wrote after the war, "it seemed as though they had a battle flag every few rods, which would indicate the formation was in solid column." Avery's men approached to within thirty or forty yards of Coster's line when the Union defenders began to waver. The 57th North Carolina hit the flank and front of the 134th New York, holding Coster's right flank, and drove it back. Coster also withdrew his left regiment, the 27th Pennsylvania, before it had time to engage in hand-to-hand combat with the 6th North Carolina. Nevertheless, Coster's center regiment, the 154th New York, held its ground behind a stout fence. Godwin reported that the "enemy stubbornly [held] their position until we had climbed over into their midst." The fight was short, but sharp, and after capturing the fence line, Avery ordered his men to capture the fleeing Federal troops. Bartlett Yancy Malone summed up the engagement in a succinct sentence: "Our Bregaid [sic] and General Hases [Hays'] charged the enemy and soon got them routed and run them threw [sic] the town and then we stopt [sic]." Two cannon from Heckman's Battery were also captured by the 6th North Carolina during this charge.[43]

After entering Gettysburg, Avery was ordered to break off the pursuit and move to the railroad in the eastern part of town. Batteries on Cemetery Hill soon opened fire with little effect on Avery's men, who were protected in the railroad cut. Remaining in the protective railroad cut, the brigade moved about four hundred yards by the left flank. The men were now ordered out of the cut, but the Union cannon again found the brigade's range, so Avery ordered his men to get into a depression, protected by a hill. Here they remained through the night with the ominous sounds of picks and shovels ringing in their ears, as the enemy fortified Cemetery Hill. Their anxiety levels increased because of the continual rumble of guns and the tramp of infantry, as enemy reinforcements streamed in all through the night.[44]

Except for the skirmishers thrown forward toward the enemy position, the brigade rested for most of the day. Captain John McPherson recalled that "the Sharp-shooters kept up a brisk fire all day,

so that a man could not show himself along the line without being shot at." The order to fall into line for the attack on Cemetery Hill arrived at about 8:00 that night. After lying in the hot July sun all day, constantly pestered by enemy sharpshooters, the men "hailed with delight the order to again meet the veteran foe, regardless of his advantage in numbers and position," recalled Major James Beall of the 21st North Carolina. The sun was now low in the sky.[45]

Avery gave the order, "Forward, Guide Right!" and the movement began. Hays's Brigade was on their right. Colonel Hamilton Jones of the 57th North Carolina recalled that as a bugle sounded the order to move out, "the line advanced in beautiful order, and as it pointed to the south-west there was a glint all along the line of bayonets that was very striking and marked how beautifully they were aligned." The brigade retained the same alignment as the day before—the 57th North Carolina on the left, 6th North Carolina on the right, and 21st North Carolina in the center.[46]

Gettysburg scholar Harry Pfanz noted that none of the veterans described the route they took to attack the heights, but he hypothesized that Avery's Brigade probably moved astride the fence line that is today marked by East Confederate Avenue. Passing through an orchard, the unit probably advanced through Culp's Meadow. Here Colonel Avery stopped the brigade to dress its lines. Realizing that a gap loomed between his brigade and Hays's, Avery wheeled his North Carolinians to the right, which put his left regiment, the 57th North Carolina, perilously close to Stevens's battery on their left flank. Lieutenant Colonel Archibald Godwin described the movement as one in "which none but the steadiest veterans could have executed under such circumstances."[47]

A wounded Private Ruben Ruch of the 153rd Pennsylvania watched the charge from the upper floor of a church and saw that "between the Rebel and Union positions was a ridge about six or eight feet high. The Johnnies started stooped over, scattered like a drove of sheep, till they got to this ridge. Then every man took his place, and giving the Rebel yell . . . they closed up like water, and advanced on a double-quick."[48]

Their objective was the guns atop the hill, and many men vowed that they would not stop until they were captured. Captain Neill Ray of the 6th North Carolina noted that as the brigade approached Cemetery Hill, "his sharp-shooters emptied their rifles at us and fell back to their main line at once, and every gun was brought to bear on us." One of the Federal officers on the skirmish line concurred, noting that after emptying their rifles at the advancing Confederate troops, his men made their way back to the main Union line of defense at the base of Cemetery Hill. The men turned several times and fired on Avery's advancing men.[49]

The Union artillery opened on the attacking columns almost as soon as they left the town. Private Ruch of the 153rd Pennsylvania wrote that he "could see heads, arms, and legs flying amid the dust and smoke . . . it reminded me much of a wagon load of pumpkins drawn up a hill and the end gate coming out, and the pumpkins rolling and bounding down the hill." No less than four batteries poured a frontal and enfilading fire on the Confederate line. Lieutenant Charles Brockway of Rickett's battery wrote that "we threw in their midst shrapnel and solid shot; but when they charged, we used single and finally double rounds of canister."[50]

Avery's men weathered this storm without hesitation and reached the wall that sheltered von Gilsa's Brigade. The 6th

North Carolina and the left flank of Hays's Brigade squarely hit the 54th New York and 68th New York, which had been defeated on Blocher's Knoll the day before. After a brief hand-to-hand encounter, they drove the New Yorkers up the hill. About seventy-five men from the 6th North Carolina, and a handful from Hays's 9th Louisiana, followed them up toward the batteries at the top of the hill. To the left, the 21st North Carolina reached the line of rifle pits, when the Federal brigade commander, Colonel Leopold von Gilsa, mistook the North Carolinians for his own skirmishers and ordered his men to hold their fire. Leaping over the rifle pits with a cheer "like an unbroken wave, our maddened column rushed on, facing a continual stream of fire," described Major James Beall of the 21st North Carolina. The two lines now met. An officer from the 153rd Pennsylvania recalled that the "fight was on in all its fierceness, muskets being handled as clubs; rocks torn from the wall in front and thrown, fists and bayonets used." Twice the North Carolinians charged the wall, but were unsuccessful each time in driving away the defenders. A few probably did cross the line and made their way individually to the summit.[51]

Because of an "indentation" in the hill, the left flank of the 57th North Carolina was forced to "swing round almost half a turn" before it struck the Federal line composed of the 41st New York and 33rd Massachusetts, well protected by the stone wall. Colonel Adin Underwood of the latter regiment recalled the 57th North Carolina's charge. "The enemy came on gallantly, unchecked by our artillery fire, and my regiment opened a severe musketry fire on them, which caused gaps in their line and made it stagger back a bit. It soon rallied and bravely came within a few feet of our wall, though my men clung unflinchingly to it and steadily poured in their fire. I ordered them to fix bayonets to be ready for the enemy." Facing sheets of flames from the two enemy regiments and canister from Stevens's battery to their left, these North Carolinians never made it to the wall.[52]

Beall (21st North Carolina) could never forget this phase of the engagement. "The hour was one of horror. Amid the incessant roar of cannon, the din of musketry, and the glare of bursting shells making the darkness intermittent—adding awfulness to the scene—the hoarse shouts of friend and foe, the piteous cries of wounded and dying."[53]

The handful of men, no more than a hundred from the 6th North Carolina and 9th Louisiana who had successfully breached the wall, hustled up the hill to capture the Union artillery. By now it was dark and the combatants could only be seen by the flashes from their muskets as they fired into the artillerymen. With a final rush they threw themselves upon the left section of Captain R. Bruce Ricketts's battery. The fighting was hand-to-hand, as the gunners refused to abandon their guns. At least one gun was captured and another was spiked during this bloody confrontation.[54]

Knowing that they were on the verge of a great victory, but realizing that too few Confederates were present to hold the hill, Major Samuel Tate of the 6th North Carolina sent back for immediate assistance before moving his men a few paces to the protection of a stone wall. They anxiously waited there for reinforcements. In the darkness and dense smoke "we could not see what the enemy was doing, but we could hear him attempting to rally his men, and more than once he rallied close up to us," recalled Captain Neill Ray of the 6th North Carolina. "Soon they came over the hill in pursuit,

when we again opened fire on them, and cleared the hill a second time," wrote Tate in his report. These troops were probably from the 153rd Pennsylvania and other units from von Gilsa's Brigade, which had been forced back from their original positions at the base of the hill.[55]

Although Major Tate didn't know it, Colonel Samuel Carroll's Federal Brigade (Hays's Division, II Corps) had rushed to the area and charged through Rickett's guns. As he did so, he received small arms fire from his left—probably from Tate's gallant men behind the stone wall. Concerned about growing resistance in his front and rear, Tate finally gave the order to vacate the hill. He boasted in his report that "under cover of the darkness, I ordered the men to break and to risk the fire. We did so, and lost not a man in getting out." All told, Tate and his men probably occupied the top of the hill for fifteen to twenty minutes.[56]

Anger simmered in Tate and his men that exploded when they reached the Confederate lines around the town. "I demanded to know why we had not been supported, and was coolly told that it was not known that we were in the works," he wrote in his report. Tate and his men had every right to be outraged, for within supporting distance was Gordon's Brigade. Early, however, chose not to commit fresh troops to the fray, because he realized that Rodes's Division had not moved forward against Cemetery Hill, as planned. Early reasoned that "the attempt would be attended with a useless sacrifice of life." Instead, it was Avery's and Hays's men who were sacrificed.[57]

The losses were tallied as the brigade's survivors reassembled in the southeastern part of the town, to the right of Gordon's Brigade. In addition to the loss of about three hundred men, the brigade also lost its acting commander, Isaac Avery, who was mortally wounded midway between the brigade's jump off point in front of the town and the Union position. Avery had intended to lead the charge on foot, but at the last moment decided to remain mounted on his conspicuous white horse. Both Avery and his horse were hit at the same time, and both fell together, the animal pinning his rider to the ground. In the fading light, Avery took out a scrap of paper and pencil and wrote his last words: "Major, tell my father I died with my face to the enemy." Avery died the next day. Colonel Hamilton Jones of the 57th North Carolina believed that Avery's death seriously impeded the attack, "as it was not known to some parts of the line for some time that he had fallen."[58]

After a restless night, Early ordered the brigade moved to the railroad outside town, and later that day, to the northern part town to form on the left of Hays's Brigade. Except for firing along their skirmish line, the battle was over for Avery's Brigade. Remaining on the southern edge of town, it could hear the Pickett–Pettigrew–Trimble charge, but did not partici-

pate. Malone (6th North Carolina) summed it up when he wrote, "the 3 morning we went back in town and laid in a line of battel [sic] all day in the Streets And thar [sic] was a great deel [sic] of fiting [sic] don [sic] that day but our divishion [sic] was not cauld [sic] on." The brigade marched by the right flank to the west of Gettysburg at 2:00 A.M. on July 4, where the army was massing. Here the men formed into line of battle to the left of Hays's Brigade, and remained there until 2:00 A.M. on July 5, when the retreat began.[59]

The brigade mounted two successful charges against strong Union positions during the battle. The second one against Cemetery Hill was especially tragic, for the opportunity was wasted when no reinforcements came to their aid. The brigade's losses of 33% were the highest of any brigade in Early's Division. Colonel Archibald Godwin, who commanded the brigade after Avery's fall, proudly proclaimed in his report, "no body of men of equal number could have accomplished greater results against such overwhelming odds."[60]

Hays's Brigade—Brigadier General Harry Hays

Units: 5th Louisiana, 6th Louisiana, 7th Louisiana, 8th Louisiana, 9th Louisiana
Strength: 1295
Losses: 334 (51-187-86)—25.8%[61]

While all five regiments were mustered into service between May and July 1861, only three, the 6th, 7th, and 8th Louisiana, were present at the first battle of Manassas, where each served in a different brigade. These regiments, and 9th Louisiana, were joined after the battle to form the 1st Louisiana Brigade, which saw considerable service during Stonewall Jackson's Valley

campaign under Brigadier General Richard Taylor. Because Taylor was ill, Colonel Isaac Seymour commanded the brigade at the start of the Seven Days campaign. The brigade's first battle at Gaines's Mill was not auspicious, as Seymour became confused in Boatswain's Swamp, and when one of one of the brigade's most popular officers was killed, the men turned back after sustaining heavy losses.[62]

The 5th Louisiana was added in July 1862 and its commander, Colonel Henry Forno, assumed command of the brigade. His tenure was short, as he was wounded during the savage fighting during the battle of Second Manassas. Harry Hays of the 7th Louisiana was promoted to the rank of brigadier general and given permanent command of the brigade prior to the Maryland campaign. An attorney and local politician, Hays had seen service in the Mexican War. At the outbreak of the war he assumed command of the 7th Louisiana, where he became known as a hard drinker and an even harder fighter. Badly wounded after an attack on a larger Federal force at the battle of Port Republic, Hays returned to the army in September 1862. Hays lost over 60% of his men in the savage fighting that occurred in the cornfield during the battle of Sharpsburg. The brigade was lightly engaged at Fredericksburg. That winter, Hays got into a fight with his division commander, Major General Jubal Early, because of the brigade's "thievery." The brigade redeemed itself at Salem Church during the battle of Chancellorsville, when it slammed into to Federal line, sending it reeling. By the start of the Gettysburg campaign the brigade had firmly established its reputation of being out of control, yet among the finest fighting forces in the army.[63]

The campaign started well for Hays's Brigade when it helped capture the Federal works at the second battle of Winchester, thus guaranteeing the Federal garrison's demise. The brigade continued northward and crossed into Pennsylvania to the sounds of "Dixie." Lining the road were scores of citizens warily watching the threadbare and haggard invaders. One Louisianian could not help but tell the crowd that they had "eat up [sic] the last mule we had and had come over to get some beef & bacon." Others joked about "going back into the Union at last." The townspeople generously shared food with the invaders, "only asking that their barns

and dwellings be spared," noted Lieutenant Charles Batchelor of the 2nd Louisiana. The Tigers had already gained quite a reputation from friend and foe alike for their unruliness and fighting prowess. Although the men had generally behaved themselves during the invasion, the entire brigade did go on a four-day drinking binge. They also found stores of whiskey during their first visit to Gettysburg on June 26. When it was time to move out the following day, Captain William Seymour of the 6th Louisiana recalled that "the men having had too much free access to liquor . . . caused me much trouble to make them keep up with the column."[64]

The brigade broke camp at 9:00 A.M. on July 1 and marched on Heidlersburg Road toward Gettysburg. The men could smell a fight, and were not too happy to be stuck in the rear of the column during the twelve-mile march. As the column drew closer, the Tigers could hear the sound of cannon, and the pace subsequently quickened. Arriving on the battlefield at about 3:00 P.M., the men were greeted by a solid shot from one of the enemy batteries. "It struck the pike or dirt road about 50 yards in our front and ricocheted turning to the right," recalled Captain R. J. Hancock of the 9th Louisiana. They could see that Hoke's (Avery's) Brigade was deployed to the left of the road, and Gordon's Brigade to the right of it. A space astride the road was left for the Tigers. The 5th Louisiana formed to the right of the road, next to Gordon's men, followed by the 6th Louisiana and part of the 9th Louisiana. The left wing of the 9th Louisiana, the 7th Louisiana, and the 8th Louisiana formed on the left of the road. As they took position, the men could see Rodes's men on their right, "driving the Yankees before him like sheep. It was the prettiest sight I ever saw," commented Lieutenant R. Stark

Jackson of the 8th Louisiana. Gordon's Brigade moved forward in a matter of moments. The men could see the thick masses of Federal troops on Blocher's Knoll and few thought that the Georgians would be successful. One of the brigade's staff officers, Captain Seymour, recalled that "in a few minutes the firing ceased, & the smoke lifting from the field, revealed to our sight the defeated Federals in disorderly flight, hotly pursued by the gallant Georgians."[65]

Early ordered Hays's and Avery's Brigades to sweep down toward the town of Gettysburg at approximately 4:00 P.M. The brigade engaged several companies from the 17th Connecticut that had been thrown across Rock Creek. After pushing this small force out of their path, the Tigers continued toward the town. Because of the brigade's rapid movement, they cut off some Federal units making for the rear. Taking some literary license, Captain Seymour wrote that the brigade took "whole regiments belonging to the 11th Corps." He described how one "Dutch Colonel" at the head of 250 men approached him to surrender, "evidently wishing to get from under fire as soon as possible." So happy were they to be out of the fight that Seymour was able to send them to the rear under the guard of a single Confederate soldier.[66]

"We crossed about 20 fences & 1 creek [Rock Creek] and at last came right slap up on the '11th corps' & a battery," wrote Lieutenant Jackson (8th Louisiana). This was Coster's Brigade (2nd Division, XI Corps) and Heckman's battery, which had been rushed forward to stem the Confederate tide. Because trees and Gordon's Brigade obstructed their path, Hays's Brigade lagged behind Avery's. As a result, Hays's left flank was behind Avery's right when it reached Coster's Brigade. Although most of the fighting was done by

Avery's Brigade to their left, Hays's men played a major role in flanking Coster's Brigade and getting into its rear, thus forcing it into a more desperate situation. Sweeping forward through canister and small arms fire, they shoved Coster's left flank back. "We ran them thro town & caught more prisoners than we had men in the brigade. We also captured 2 pieces of the battery," wrote Jackson.[67]

Continuing their advance, Hays's men came under a "galling fire" from batteries on Cemetery Hill. As the Tigers approached the railroad on the edge of town, General Hays quickly became aware of a "heavy column of the enemy's troops" on his right flank. In reality, they were merely scattered Federal units attempting to make a last stand at the edge of the town. Wheeling the 5th, 6th, and right wing of his 9th Louisiana around, Hays ordered them to open fire. "With this line, after several well-directed volleys, I succeeded in breaking this column on my right, dispersing its men in full flight through the streets of the city," he recalled. A chagrined Hays soon realized that this movement gave the Federal cannoneers enough of a reprieve to limber up their guns and get them to safety before the Tigers could charge them.[68]

Hays now ordered his men into Gettysburg, where they scooped up hundreds of prisoners. This posed a dilemma for Hays, as he refused to weaken his brigade by sending detachments to the rear with hundreds of prisoners. Instead, he simply told the captives to march northward, where they were collected by Rodes's troops. Hays insisted that he captured more men than he had in his command. So far, his losses were exceptionally low—seven killed, forty-one wounded, and fifteen missing.[69]

After all the Union troops were either captured or driven out of the town, Hays assembled his men along Middle Street. Many grumbled when they realized that they would not be ordered to take Cemetery Hill that night. No one was more upset than General Hays, who persistently pushed Ewell to order the assault. Ewell laughingly asked Hays if his Tigers ever got a bellyful of fighting. His anger growing, Hays replied that his only concern was to prevent the unnecessary slaughter of his men. Never did the men miss Stonewall Jackson more. "All night long the Federals were heard chopping away and working like beavers, and when day dawned, the ridge was found to be crowned with strongly built fortifications, and bristling with a most formidable array of cannon," wrote Captain Seymour in his journal. The men's slumber was broken at 2:00 A.M., when Early ordered Hays to take his men out on a reconnaissance into the no-man's-land between the town and Cemetery Hill. Hays finally halted his men in an open field at the base of Cemetery Hill, southeast of the town. Here the brigade remained throughout the remainder of the night and through the next day, "prominently exposed to the fire of the enemy's skirmishers and sharpshooters," noted Seymour. Any man standing upright faced almost certain death.[70]

That afternoon, Hays received orders from Early to hold his brigade in readiness for a possible assault on Cemetery Hill. At about 4 P.M., the men observed a tremendous artillery duel between the two opposing armies. Captain Seymour recorded in his journal that the "roar of the guns was continuous and deafening; the shot and shell could be seen tearing through the hostile batteries, dismounting guns, killing and wounding men and horses, while ever and anon, an ammunition chest would explode, sending a bright column of smoke far up towards the heavens." The Federal gunners found

the range of the Confederate batteries, and pounded them until they withdrew.[71]

Hays finally received orders to advance with Avery's Brigade shortly before 8:00 P.M., and immediately issued orders to this effect. Captain R. J. Hancock of the 9th Louisiana wrote that "Gen'l Harry Hays, who was no man to deceive his men nor any one, rode along the line about dusk and told his men that Gen'l Early had said we must go Cemetery Hill and silence those guns and Gordon would reinforce us and hold them." Lieutenant Jackson (8th Louisiana) received the orders to advance with dread. "I felt as if my doom was sealed, and it was with great reluctance that I started my skirmishers forward." Captain Seymour recalled it differently. "The quiet, solimn [sic] mien of our men showed plainly that they fully appreciated the desperate character of the undertaking; but on every face was most legibly written the firm determination to do or die."[72]

Although Hays did not describe the brigade's formation, Harry Pfanz deduced that it formed a single line, in the following order from left to right: 8th Louisiana–7th Louisiana–9th Louisiana–6th Louisiana–5th Louisiana. Pfanz also believed that the brigade's right flank followed the eastern side of Brickyard Lane for about 250 yards, and when it approached the Federal line, it wheeled to the right. The brigade's left flank was probably where the school sits today.[73]

Driving up the hill they had been resting behind, the men reached the top, only to be met by cannon and small arms fire. "But we [were] too quick for them, and [were] down in the valley in a trice, while the Yankee missiles [were] hissing, screaming & hurtling over our heads, doing but little damage," recalled Seymour. Directly in front of them was Ames's Brigade (1st Division, XI Corps), protected by a stone wall. These troops opened fire on the Tigers, and at the same time, Federal artillery fired canister into their ranks.[74]

Colonel Andrew Harris, now commanding Ames's Brigade, marveled at the advance. "When they came into full view in Culp's meadow our artillery . . . [we] opened on them with all the guns that could be brought to bear. But on, still on, they came, moving steadily to the assault, soon the infantry opened fire, but they never faltered. They moved forward as steadily, amid this hail of shot shell and minnie ball, as though they were on parade far removed from danger."[75]

Hays believed that the growing darkness, coupled with the dense smoke, reduced his losses at the time, as "our exact locality could not be discovered by the enemy's gunners, and we thus escaped what in the full light of day could have been nothing else than horrible slaughter." Captain R. J. Hancock of the 9th Louisiana agreed. "The enemys [sic] cannon lighted up the heavens but most of the charges they shot over us but even at that we suffered terribly."[76]

Although Hays did not know it at the time, good fortune grinned at him a second time. Just before the charge, the 17th Connecticut was moved to the right side of the Federal line, creating a gap in the defenses that was only partially closed by the 25th Ohio. Dispersing the first line, Hays's men came upon the second, and drove the Ohioans back from this one as well. A soldier from the 75th Ohio wrote home that Hays's men "came on us about dark yelling like demons with fixed bayonets. We opened on them when they were about 500 yards off but still they came their officers in advance. We lay behind a stone wall and received them with our bayonets." Those Federal soldiers who did not run were captured. Sergeant George

Clements of the 25th Ohio later recalled that the Confederates "put their big feet on the stone wall and went over like deer, over the heads of the whole . . . regiment, the grade being steep and the wall not more than 20 inches high." A third line of rifle pits behind fallen timbers was also taken in short order. Lieutenant Jackson wrote home that Hays's men had arrived "at a stone fence behind which mr. Yank had posted himself and he did not want to leave. But with bayonets & clubbed guns we drove them back." It was now so dark that Jackson was concerned about shooting his own men. Nothing stood between the artillery on the summit of the hill and Hays's men.[77]

Hays triumphantly wrote in his official account of the battle that "arriving at the summit, by a simultaneous rush from my whole line, I captured several pieces of artillery, four stands of colors, and a number of prisoners. At that time every piece of artillery which had been firing upon us was silenced." Although Hays did not mention it, hand-to-hand combat erupted around the guns of Wiedrich's battery. One of Hays's men threw himself at the muzzle of one of the guns, exclaiming, "I take command of this gun." A German artilleryman yelled, "Du sollst sie haben!" and pulled the lanyard, blowing away the Confederate soldier. The Federal infantry and artillerymen fought with bayonets, clubbed muskets, pistols, rammers, and rocks. Particularly intense was the fight over several flags. The Confederates lost, and the 8th Louisiana's flag was captured.[78]

An eerie quiet now settled over the battlefield. In the darkness, however, Hays could discern the sound of troops massing in the darkness and soon detected a dim line of battle moving slowly toward him. Thinking it could be reinforcements, he ordered his men to hold their fire. After three volleys were fired against his men at a distance of less than a hundred yards, Hays finally realized that the unknown troops were not friendly, and when they were less than twenty feet from his line, he ordered his men to return the fire. Captain Seymour recalled that the "Yankee line melted away in the darkness." Another line appeared in their front, while others approached from their flanks.[79]

Realizing that help was not forthcoming and his command was in danger of being surrounded, Hays reluctantly ordered his men to relinquish their hold on the summit and fall back to the stone wall at the foot of the hill. This accomplished, Hays ordered his men to fall back another seventy-five yards to a fence, where he awaited the enemy. Rushing back, Hays found Gordon's Brigade, "occupying the precise position in the field occupied by me when I received the order to charge the enemy on Cemetery Hill, and not advancing." Realizing that Early had no intention of assisting, Hays returned to his command and ordered his men to move by the right flank around the hill between Cemetery Hill and the town to avoid detection by the enemy. The men reached the town at about 10:00 P.M. and rested here for the remainder of the night. Major John Daniel of Early's staff rode along the streets of Gettysburg after the charge and observed Hays's and Avery's men lying on the sidewalks, many bleeding from their wounds. "All was in confusion, distress," he recalled. Yet, he admired the men greatly, for "it is manhood indeed which faces danger & does not shrink."[80]

The men in the ranks were too angry to consider their gallantry. One captured Federal soldier in the town that night recalled how the men bitterly talked about how they had breached the enemy line,

only to see others not take advantage of it. "A madder set of men I never saw. They cursed their officers in a way and manner that showed experience in the business . . . it was simply fearful . . . they said their officers didn't care how many were killed, and especially old Hays, who was receiving his share of the curses." A civilian who happened by later recalled that "there seemed now to be an entire absence of that elation and boastfulness which they manifested when they entered the town on the evening of the first of July."[81]

The capture of Cemetery Hill was one of the greatest feats in the annuals of the Army of Northern Virginia. It was also one of the more tragic, for it was unsupported, and many died in vain. Captain Seymour accurately explained the problem when he wrote, "the Army was fought by Divisions instead of by Corps, which was a great and most unfortunate mistake."[82]

At daybreak, Early ordered Hays back to the position he had occupied on Middle Street on July 1. The brigade remained there through July 3, skirmishing with the enemy, resulting in the loss of at least sixty-two additional men. The brigade pulled back to Seminary Ridge during the early morning hours of July 4, and it began its retreat at 2:00 A.M. on July 5.[83]

In summing up his brigade's feats, Hays wrote, "in all the operations in the neighborhood of Gettysburg, I am happy to state that both officers and men, while animated with a spirit of daring that disdained to concede any obstacle to their progress insurmountable, were yet amenable to all the orders of their leaders, and accepted readily any position assigned them." The brigade performed admirably on both July 1 and 2. Clearly, ineptitude at the higher command levels prevented it from realizing even greater glory.[84]

✖

Smith's Brigade—Brigadier General William Smith

Units: 31st Virginia, 49th Virginia, 52nd Virginia
Strength: 806
Losses: 213 (46-115-52)—26%[85]

Some might say that William Smith's Virginia Brigade had two strikes against it during the Gettysburg campaign. Having left two of its five regiments back in Virginia, it mustered barely eight hundred men. The three remaining regiments had had a long history of service, having been mustered into the Confederate army between June and August 1861. While the 49th Virginia was engaged at the first battle of Manassas as a part of Cocke's Brigade, the two other regiments were in northwestern Virginia at the time. By the start of the Second Bull Run campaign, the regiments were under the command of Brigadier General Jubal Early, and fought under him at Sharpsburg and Fredericksburg. Colonel William Smith of the 49th Virginia was promoted to the rank of brigadier general and took over the brigade when Early was given a division.[86]

The second strike against the brigade was that Smith commanded it. An attorney and ex-governor of Virginia, "Extra Billy" Smith became colonel of the 49th Virginia at the start of the war and led it at the first battle of Manassas. Unable to give up politics, he won a seat in the First Confederate Congress and attempted to balance his two responsibilities. This undoubtedly bothered his commander, Jubal Early, who barely tolerated him and trusted him even less. He gave up his seat and was wounded at Seven Pines and again at Sharpsburg. He also led his regi-

ment during the Seven Days campaign and at Second Bull Run.[87]

Early had already exchanged harsh words with Smith after the latter had stopped his brigade in York, Pennsylvania, to make a speech to the citizens. That night, most of Smith's men went on a drinking binge with captured whiskey, and many were drunk the following morning.[88]

John Cleek of the 52nd Virginia wrote home that the "people all treated us very kindly and the most of them seemed anxious for the war to end. Though I think that their kindness was more through fear than any thing else." The brigade had the dubious honor of bringing up the rear of the division on June 30, and as a result, ate more than its share of dust. This, coupled with the fact that many men sported new shoes that tore at their feet, made this leg of the march a miserable one.[89]

The march toward Gettysburg continued on July 1, and the sounds of battle could be heard when the brigade was within a few miles of the town. Early deployed his division when it was about a mile and a half out of town. Gordon's Brigade was deployed to the right of the road, Hays's Brigade straddled it, and Hoke's (Avery's) Brigade formed on the left of the road. Early directed Smith to position his brigade behind Hoke's (Avery's), thus assigning it a reserve role, a fitting place for a small brigade with suspect leadership. As Gordon's Brigade, and then Hays's and Avery's, were ordered forward, Smith's remained behind to support the artillery. His orders were to advance when the artillery was called forward.[90]

The brigade advanced twice toward Gettysburg. At the conclusion of the second movement, the brigade formed on York Road, to the east of the town. This put the brigade on the extreme left flank of the army, and in a position to detect any enemy movement from that direction. By about 5:00 P.M., Early's other brigades had driven the XI Corps back toward the town. Fearing for the safety of his left flank due to the rapid retreat of the Federal forces, Early sent a message to Smith to rejoin the rest of the division to provide support.[91]

Instead of seeing the brigade march toward a point north of Gettysburg, however, Early saw an aide galloping in his direction. Smith's aide told Early that "a report having been brought to General Smith that a large force of the enemy was advancing on the York road on our then rear, he [Smith] thought proper to detain his brigade to watch that road." Not satisfied with this explanation, Early repeated his order for Smith to quit York Road and rejoin the rest of the division. This brought another aide from Smith, who told Early that the "enemy was advancing a large force of infantry, artillery, and cavalry on the York road, menacing our left flank and rear."[92]

Exasperated by reports that he felt fairly certain were false, Early sent General John Gordon and his brigade to the area to "take command of both brigades, and to stop all further alarms from that direction." This action took Gordon's Brigade out of the fight and ensured that Early's Division would not storm Cemetery Hill that evening. After the war, Early defended the action of sending his most able brigadier general and his brigade to the left. "I had no faith in the report myself, but knowing the effect such a report must have on the men in Gettysburg and to the right and left of it, as if true, it would bring the enemy in their rear, I immediately ordered one of my staff officers to go and

tell Gordon to take his brigade . . . and stop that 'stampeding.'"[93]

In reality, there were no Federal troops approaching on the road—the closest were at least 1.5 miles away on Wolf Hill. Some of Smith's own troops were frustrated by their commander's actions on July 1. Lieutenant Cyrus Coiner of the 52nd Virginia wrote that "Gen. Smith from some cause I do not know what, unless he mistook a fence with a growth of small trees for a line of troops, was so impressed with the idea the enemy was advancing on him that he called his son and sent him to Gen. Early with the report that the enemy was advancing and that he needed reinforcements at once."[94]

Smith was not the only officer in the brigade having problems that day. While on York Road, the 49th Virginia was thrown out as skirmishers. One soldier wrote disparagingly, "the major had not sense enough or was scared too badly to deploy the Regiment and it was a general jumble up and we advanced like a set of rabbits." The guns on Cemetery Hill opened on the regiment, causing the soldier to write, "it was a terribly disagreeable place to be, not half deployed and worse commanded."[95]

Smith's and Gordon's Brigades remained there through noon of July 2, when cavalry pickets galloped up to inform Smith that enemy cavalry were approaching on York Road. While the two brigades prepared to meet this new threat, the 49th Virginia was again ordered forward as skirmishers. Once, again, it was a false alarm.[96]

The "noncombatant" role played by the brigade ended at 3:00 A.M. on July 3, when Smith was awakened and told to prepare his men to move to the extreme left of Johnson's Division. The division had attacked the Federal lines on the evening of July 2 and Steuart's Brigade held a portion of the Federal breastworks. Another attack was planned that morning.[97]

Leaving the 31st Virginia behind to guard against the phantom Federal troops on York Road, Smith led the 49th and 52nd Virginia toward their assigned position. Federal artillery opened on the column, causing a number of casualties and serving notice that the men were in for some combat before the sun set that night. As they approached Johnson's position, they were ordered to march by the left flank, about another half mile.[98]

The two regiments halted behind a stone wall at right angles to Johnson's line, which bordered the two hundred-yard long by one hundred-yard wide Spangler's Meadow. To their right was the Stonewall Brigade. No Confederate troops were on their left. Between 10:30 and 11:00 A.M., two Federal regiments, the 2nd Massachusetts and the 27th Indiana (Colgrove's Brigade, Williams's Division, XII Corps), with "deafening cheers, . . . sprang forward" toward the wall occupied by Smith's two regiments. They were met by sheets of flames from Smith's men. Halfway through the meadow, the 27th Indiana was forced to stop and then withdraw. The 2nd Massachusetts continued its advance, obliquing to the left, where the men took refuge.[99]

Waving his hat over his snow-white hair, Smith "goaded" his men to counterattack. The 49th Virginia jumped over the wall, followed by the 52nd Virginia. As they crossed the meadow of death already littered with blue-clad figures, they were hit with small arms fire from the 27th Indiana, 3rd Wisconsin, and 13th New Jersey in front of them, and the 2nd Massachusetts to their right and rear. Just as the Federals had proved a few minutes before, nothing could survive a charge through the open meadow, and Smith's troops were slaughtered. The survivors were

forced to return to the protection of the stone wall on the edge of the field. In a matter of minutes, the 49th Virginia lost 100 of its 250 men; the 52nd Virginia lost 54 men. Fortunately, the arrival of the 31st Virginia helped steady the survivors.[100]

Major R. W. Hunter of Johnson's staff recalled the events prior to the charge. "At the supreme moment was heard the voices of Smith and his men . . . taking the highest position he could find, reckless of shot and shell, with bare head and sword in hand, pointing to the enemy, he harangued each regiment as it double quicked past into the area of blood & fire." Not everyone was so inspired by Smith's behavior. Lieutenant Coiner recalled, "Gen. Smith took us into battle with out orders and had us badly cut up and we accomplished nothing."[101]

As the three regiments settled down behind the wall, they came under increasingly intense hostile fire. Some believed that the artillery fire was the heaviest they had ever experienced. They were also receiving enfilading small arms fire. Private Newton Bosworth of the 31st Virginia bragged that "our regiment acted as though they were on drill. Everyone seemed to be perfectly cool."[102]

After sustaining a growing number of casualties, Smith pulled his brigade back across Rock Creek to the rear at around noon, where the men rested. In the afternoon, Smith ordered his men to recross the creek and form behind the Stonewall Brigade, to the right of their former position. According to Colonel John Hoffman of the 31st Virginia, the brigade moved farther to the rear and the right after dark. The men were awakened after midnight on July 4, and at 1:00 A.M., marched to Seminary Ridge to the west of town. Here they rested in an orchard near Gettysburg College on the left of Gordon's Brigade and the right of Hays's. Remaining here during the day, they received orders at 9:00 P.M. to prepare to leave Gettysburg. The movement began at about 2:00 A.M. on July 5.[103]

So ended the strange experiences of "Extra Billy" Smith's Virginians. Had it not been for the ill-fated countercharge on July 3, their losses would have been minimal. Some have posited that Smith's messages about phantom troops on York Road helped lose the battle. Captain R. J. Hancock of the 9th Louisiana (Hays's Brigade) probably summed it up accurately when he wrote after the war, "Gen'l Smith's heart and soul were with the South as much so as any man but he was too old for rough campaigning." General Billy Smith apparently agreed. Feeling all of his sixty-six years, he decided to call it quits, tendering his resignation on July 10. Deciding that he could serve the Confederacy in another way, he was again elected governor of Virginia during the fall 1863 elections. Jefferson Davis recognized Smith by promoting him to the rank of major general on August 13, 1863.[104]

NOTES

1. Tagg, *Generals of Gettysburg*, 251–252; Warner, *Generals in Gray*, 84–85.

2. OR 27, 2, 440–443.

3. OR 27, 2, 443–444.

4. OR 27, 2, 444.

5. OR 27, 2, 444–446; Donald C. Pfanz, *Richard S. Ewell—A Soldier's Life* (Chapel Hill, NC, 1998) 302–312; Tagg, *Generals at Gettysburg*, 270–271.

6. OR 27, 2, 446–447.

7. OR 27, 2, 447–448.

8. Tagg, *Generals of Gettysburg*, 256–257; Warner, *Generals in Gray*, 79.

9. OR 27, 2, 443, 465–466.

10. OR 27, 2, 443–444, 466–468; Jubal A. Early, *Autobiographical Sketch and Narrative of the War Between the States* (Philadelphia, 1912), 266–268.

11. OR 27, 2, 468–469.

12. OR 27, 2, 470–471.

13. Busey and Martin, *Regimental Strengths and Losses*, 158, 286.

14. Sifakis, *Compendium of the Confederate Armies: South Carolina and Georgia*, 210, 232, 241, 38, 60, 61; William C. Davis, *The Confederate General*, 6 vols. (Harrisburg, PA, 1991), vol. IV, 27; Sears, *Landscape Turned Red*, 186; OR 21, 554.

15. Davis, *The Confederate General*, vol. III, 8–9.

16. OR 27, 2, 491–492.

17. OR 27, 2, 466–467, 492; John B. Gordon, *Reminiscences of the Civil War* (New York, 1903), 147–148.

18. OR 27, 2, 492; Alton J. Murray, *South Georgia Rebels: The True Wartime Experiences of the 26th Regiment, Georgia Volunteer Infantry . . .* (St. Marys, GA, 1976), 134–135.

19. OR 27, 2, 492; F. L. Hudgins, Gettysburg Campaign," copy in the 38th Georgia Folder, GNMP; Michael W. Hofe, *That There Be No Stain Upon My Stones* (Gettysburg, PA, 1995), 33–34; Charles Stuart, "Recollections," copy in the 26th Georgia file, GNMP.

20. OR 27, 2, 492; Hudgins, Gettysburg Campaign," copy in 38th Georgia Folder, GNMP; G. W. Nichols, *A Soldier's Story of His Regiment . . .* (Jesup, GA, 1898), 116; William R. Kiefer, *History of the One Hundred and Fifty-Third Pennsylvania Volunteer Infantry* (Easton, PA, 1909), 213.

21. Gordon, *Reminiscences of the Civil War*, 151.

22. OR 27, 2, 492; OR 27, 1, 746.

23. OR 27, 2, 492.

24. Nichols, *A Soldier's Story of His Regiment . . .* ,116.

25. Joseph Hilton, letter, copy in the 26th Georgia Folder, GNMP; OR 27, 2, 493.

26. Robert Stiles, *Four Years Under Marse Robert*, 210–212.

27. Hilton, letter.

28. Gordon, *Reminiscences of the Civil War*, 153–154.

29. Gordon, *Reminiscences of the Civil War*, 154; Harry W. Pfanz, "'Old Jack' Is Not Here," in *The Gettysburg Nobody Knows*, ed. Gabor S. Boritt, (Oxford, 1997), 63.

30. OR 27, 2, 270.

31. Early, *Autobiographical Sketch and Narrative of the War Between the States*, 272–273.

32. Early, *Autobiographical Sketch and Narrative of the War Between the States*, 274.

33. Early, *Autobiographical Sketch and Narrative of the War Between the States*, 275; OR 27, 2, 493.

34. OR 27, 2, 493.

35. Busey and Martin, *Regimental Strengths and Losses*, 253, 255, 286.

36. Busey and Martin, *Regimental Strengths and Losses*, 159, 287.

37. Sifakis, *Compendium of the Confederate Armies: North Carolina* (New York, 1992), 91, 114, 157; Davis, *The Confederate General*, vol. III, 114.

38. Davis, *The Confederate General*, vol. III, 114.

39. OR 27, 2, 484; Walter Clark, ed., *Histories of Several Regiments and Battalions from North Carolina in the Great War, 1861-'65*, 5 vols. (Raleigh, NC, 1901), vol. 3, 270. Hereafter cited as *N.C. Regiments*.

40. *N.C. Regiments*, vol. 1, 311; vol. 3, 413.

41. Clark, *N.C. Regiments*, vol. 3, 413.

42. Clark, *N.C. Regiments*, vol. 3, 413; David G. Martin, *Gettysburg—July 1* (Conshohocken, PA, 1996), 283, 310–311.

43. OR 27, 2, 484; *NYG*, vol. 3, 1055; *National Tribune Scrap Book: Stories of the Camp, March, Battle, Hospital and Prison Told by Comrades* (Washington, DC, 1909), 131.

44. OR 27, 2, 484; Clark, *N.C. Regiments*, vol. 3, 414; Samuel Eaton, diary, Southern Historical Collection, University of North Carolina.

45. John McPherson, "The Death of Colonel Isaac Avery," copy in 6th North Carolina folder, GNMP; Clark, *N.C. Regiments*, vol. 2, 136.

46. Clark, *N.C. Regiments*, vol. 3, 415.

47. OR 27, 2, 484; Harry W. Pfanz, *Gettysburg—Culp's Hill and Cemetery* (Chapel Hill, NC, 1993), 251–252.

48. Kiefer, *History of the One Hundred and Fifty-Third Pennsylvania*, 219–220.

49. Clark, *N.C. Regiments*, vol. 1, 313; J. Clyde Miller to John Bachelder, March 2, 1884, Bachelder Papers, New Hampshire Historical Society.

50. Kiefer, *History of the One Hundred and Fifty-Third Pennsylvania*, 152; Pete Tomasak, "An Encounter with Battery Hell," *Gettysburg Magazine* (January 1995), 36–37.

51. J. Clyde Miller to John Bachelder, March 2, 1886; Clark, *N.C. Regiments*, vol. 2, 136–137; Kiefer, *History of the One Hundred and Fifty-Third Pennsylvania*, 141–142; David G. Martin, *Carl Bornemann's Regiment: The Forty-First New York Infantry in the Civil War* (Hightstown, NJ, 1987), 156; OR 27, 1, 714; OR 27, 2, 484; Clark, *N.C. Regiments*, vol. 2, 136–137.

In a departure from the Gettysburg norms, the historian of the 21st North Carolina may have actually downplayed the regiment's success, as both Pfanz and the Union defenders wrote that some of these Tar Heels did cross the wall and climbed the heights (Pfanz, *Gettysburg—Culp's Hill and Cemetery Hill*, 262; J. Clyde Miller to John Bachelder, March 2, 1886).

52. Clark, *N.C. Regiments*, vol. 3, 415; OR suppl., 5, 218.

53. Clark, *N.C. Regiments*, vol. 2, 137.

54. Pfanz, *Gettysburg—the Second Day*, 268–270; Clark, *N.C. Regiments*, vol. 1, 313–314.

After the battle, emotions continued to rage and petty rivalries were not uncommon. For example, Major Tate of the 6th North Carolina wrote bitterly to Governor Vance of North Carolina soon after the battle about the capture of the Federal batteries on Cemetery Hill. "This battery will be credited to Early's Division—see if it don't." Sure enough, Early stated in his report, "Two pieces of artillery (Napoleons) were also captured outside of the town, the capture being claimed by both brigades; but it is unnecessary to decide which reached these pieces first, as the capture was unquestionably due to the joint valor of both brigades" (OR 27, 2, 469, 486)

55. Clark, *N.C. Regiments*, vol. 1, 313–314; OR 27, 2, 486.

56. OR 27, 2, 486; Thomas E. Causby, "Storming the Stone Fence at Gettysburg," *Southern Historical Society Papers* (1901), vol. 29, 340; "A Southern Keepsake," *Gettysburg*

Compiler, December 13, 1909; Clark, N.C. Regiments, vol. 3, 416.

57. OR 27, 2, 470, 486.

58. Early, Autobiographical Sketch and Narrative of the War Between the States, 275; McPherson "The Death of Colonel Isaac Avery," copy in the 6th North Carolina folder, GNMP; Robert W. Iobst and Louis H. Manarin. The Bloody Sixth: The Sixth North Carolina Regiment, Confederate States of America (Durham, NC, 1965), 138–139; Causby, "Storming the Stone Fence at Gettysburg," 340; Clark, N.C. Regiments, vol. 3, 416.

59. Clark, N.C. Regiments, vol. 1, 317; vol. 3, 416; Bartlett Malone, Whipt 'Em Everytime: The Diary of Bartlett Yancey Malone (Jackson, TN, 1960), 86; OR 27, 2, 485; Samuel Eaton diary, copy at GNMP.

60. Busey and Martin, Regimental Strengths and Losses, 287; OR 27, 2, 485.

61. Busey and Martin, Regimental Strengths and Losses, 160, 287.

62. John Hennessy, The First Battle of Manassas (Lynchburg, VA, 1989); Sifakis, Compendium of the Confederate Armies: Louisiana (New York, 1995), 76, 78, 80–81, 83, 85–86; Sears, To the Gates of Richmond, 229.

63. Davis, The Confederate General, vol. III, 78–80.

64. Terry L. Jones, Lee's Tigers (Baton Rouge, LA, 1987), 163–166; Charles Batchelor, letter, LSU Library.

65. OR 27, 2, 479; Charles Moore, diary, copy in the Brake Collection, USAMHI; Captain R. J. Hancock, letter, John Daniel Papers, University of Virginia; OR 27, 2, 479; R. Stark Jackson, letter, LSU Library; R. Stark Jackson, "Going Back Into the Union at Last," Civil War Times Illustrated (January–February 1991), 56; William Seymour, journal, William L. Clements Library, University of Michigan.

66. Seymour, journal.

Hays stated in his official report that the order came at 2:00 P.M. (OR 27, 2, 479).

67. Jackson, letter; Martin, Gettysburg—July 1, 311.

Avery's and Hays' Brigades captured over three hundred of Coster's men during this short engagement north of town. Both brigades claimed to have captured these two guns (Busey and Martin, Regimental Strengths and Losses, 254).

68. OR 27, 2, 479.

69. OR 27, 2, 479–480.

70. OR 27, 2, 280; Jones, Lee's Tigers, 168–169; Seymour, journal.

71. OR 27, 2, 280; Seymour, journal.

72. Hancock, letter; Jackson, letter; Seymour, journal.

73. Pfanz, Gettysburg—Culp's Hill and Cemetery Hill, 237, 250–251.

74. Seymour, journal.

75. Andrew L. Harris to John Bachelder, March 14, 1881, Bachelder Papers, New Hampshire Historical Society.

76. OR 27, 2, 280; Hancock, letter.

77. Andrew L. Harris to John Bachelder, March 14, 1881; OR 27, 2, 280; Jackson, letter; Carol M. Becker and Ritchie Thomas, Heath and Knapsack: The Ladley Letters, 1857–1880 (Athens, OH, 1988), 142; George S. Clements, "The 25th Ohio at Gettysburg," National Tribune, August 6, 1891.

78. OR 27, 2, 280; Jackson, letter; William Simmers, The Volunteer's Manual . . . (Easton, PA, 1863), 30; Jones, Lee's Tigers, 173.

79. OR 27, 2, 280–281; Seymour journal.

80. OR 27, 2, 281; J. W. Daniel, "Memoir of the Battle of Gettysburg," Virginia Historical Society.

81. Jones, Lee's Tigers, 175; Austin C. Stearns, Three Years with Company K (Cranbury, NJ, 1976), 190–192; Earl Schenck Miers and Richard A. Brown, eds., Gettysburg (New Brunswick, NJ, 1948), 182–184.

82. Seymour, journal.

83. OR 27, 2, 281.

84. OR 27, 2, 282.

85. Busey and Martin, Regimental Strengths and Losses, 161, 287.

86. Sifakis, Compendium of the Confederate Armies: Virginia, 218, 239, 244; OR 27, 2, 488.

87. Davis, The Confederate General, vol. V, 187.

88. Driver, Fifty-Second Virginia Infantry (Lynchburg, VA, 1986), 39.

89. John Cleek, Sr., letter, Duke University Rare Book, Manuscript, and Special Col-

lections Library; Laura V. Hale and Stanley S. Phillips, *History of the Forty-Ninth Virginia Infantry, CSA: "Extra Billy Smith's Boys* (Lanham, MD, 1981), 76.

90. OR 27, 2, 468; Early, *Autobiographical Sketch and Narrative of the War Between the States,* 268.

91. OR 27, 2, 468; John M. Ashcroft, *Thirty-First Virginia Infantry* (Lynchburg, VA, 1988), 53; Early, *Autobiographical Sketch and Narrative of the War Between the States,* 269.

92. Early, *Autobiographical Sketch and Narrative of the War Between the States,* 269–270.

93. Early, *Autobiographical Sketch and Narrative of the War Between the States,* 270; Jubal Early, "Leading Confederates in the Battle of Gettysburg," *Southern Historical Society Papers* (1877), vol. 4, 255–256.

94. Martin, *Gettysburg—July 1, 1863,* 510; Driver, *Fifty-Second Virginia Infantry,* 40.

95. Hale and Philips, *History of the Forty-Ninth Virginia Infantry, CSA: "Extra Billy Smith's Boys,* 77–78.

96. Hale and Philips, *History of the Forty-Ninth Virginia Infantry, CSA: "Extra Billy Smith's Boys,* 78.

97. Driver, *Fifty-Second Virginia Infantry,* 40.

98. Hale and Philips, *History of the Forty-Ninth Virginia Infantry, CSA: "Extra Billy Smith's Boys,* 79; Driver, *Fifty-Second Virginia Infantry,* 40–41.

99. Ashcroft, *Thirty-First Virginia Infantry,* 54.

100. Driver, *Fifty-Second Virginia Infantry,* 40–42.

101. Driver, *Fifty-Second Virginia Infantry,* 41–42.

102. Ashcroft, *Thirty-First Virginia Infantry,* 54–55.

103. Ashcroft, *Thirty-First Virginia Infantry,* 55; OR 27, 2, 490; Driver, *Fifty-Second Virginia Infantry,* 42; Hale and Philips, *History of the Forty-Ninth Virginia Infantry, CSA: "Extra Billy Smith's Boys,* 83–84.

104. OR 27, 2, 488; Captain R. J. Hancock, letter, John Daniel Papers, University of Virginia; Davis, *The Confederate General,* vol. 5, 188–189.

RODES'S DIVISION—

Major General Robert E. Rodes

Major General Robert Rodes's Division had had a distinguished record up to the Gettysburg campaign. Originally under Major General Daniel H. Hill, it fought well at the battles of Williamsburg, Seven Pines, Mechanicsville, Gaines's Mill, and Malvern Hill during McClellan's drive toward Richmond. The division held the center of Lee's line along the Sunken Road at the battle of Sharpsburg and fought well there. Rodes assumed temporary command of the division during the Chancellorsville campaign and formed the front line of Stonewall Jackson's successful flank attack.

Robert Rodes was a Virginia Military Institute graduate who held a series of railroad positions prior to the war. He raised a company of the 5th Alabama and was made captain of it. He took command of the regiment in May, and although he did not see action at First Manassas, Rodes was promoted to the rank of brigadier general in October. Severely wounded at Seven Pines, Rodes rejoined the army prior to the Maryland campaign, where his brigade tenaciously held the South Mountain passes. Permanent command of the division and promotion to major general came in May 1863.[1]

Rodes's command was the first infantry division to enter Northern territory when it crossed the Potomac River on June 15. It continued to Hagerstown, where it remained until June 22, when it was ordered to resume its march. The route was through Greencastle and Chambersburg, Pennsylvania, and the command reached Carlisle on June 27. Daniels's, Iverson's, and Ramseur's Brigades occupied the U.S. barracks there, while Doles's Brigade bivouacked on the Dickinson College campus. O'Neal's Brigade performed picket duty outside town.[2]

The men greatly anticipated June 30—the day they were to march on Harrisburg. Fate intervened, however, and the division instead was ordered to march on Cashtown. It reached Heidlersburg after the twenty-two-mile march and camped for the night. The march was a very difficult one, so the officers ordered the 4th Georgia's (Doles's Brigade) band to play. "The music had a most exhilarating effect, and off the men marched, inspired by the presence of the generals and the strains of the 'Tom, March On' by the band. I never saw anything so magical in its effect," wrote Private Charles Grace of Doles's Brigade.[3]

The division continued its march early the next morning. Upon reaching Middletown, Ewell ordered General Rodes to turn his column toward Gettysburg. Sounds of the battle between Heth's Division and the Federal I Corps could be heard when the division was within four miles of the town, and the men were ordered to double-quick to the battlefield. Upon scanning the area north and west of Gettysburg, Rodes was delighted to learn that he was on the enemy's flank, and with some fast movements and good luck, he could roll up the Union line. He quickly ordered one brigade deployed. Devin's Federal cavalry brigade detected Rodes's presence and deployed to meet this new threat from the north. This forced Rodes to stop his advance and deploy two more of his brigades as they arrived. General George Doles's Georgia Brigade occupied the left, Rodes's old Alabama Brigade, now under Colonel Edward O'Neal, formed in the center, and General Alfred Iverson's North Carolinians formed on the right. The two remaining brigades, both Tar Heels under General Junius Daniel and General Stephen Ramseur, took a reserve position behind the others.[4]

The division now advanced about a mile and performed a complicated right wheel maneuver, crossing a creek and marching through wheatfields, and finally arriving on Oak Hill at about 1:00 P.M. Here the men could clearly see the battle raging about half a mile in front of them. Rodes immediately deployed Carter's artillery battalion on the hill to open fire on the Union troops. He was especially pleased to see that no enemy troops faced his, making the Union rout all the more certain. Modern historian Larry Tagg believed that Rodes erred by not remaining on Carlisle Road, for such a route would have put him in the Federal I Corps's rear.[5]

Rodes must have been greatly disappointed when he saw large bodies of Union troops streaming out of Gettysburg and heading toward his left flank. This was von Amsberg's Brigade (Schimmelfennig's Division, XI Corps), which had just arrived after a long march. Rodes also observed that the Union line battling Heth's Division was being extended toward his position. Facing the center of his line was Robinson's Division (I Corps).

In his official report, Rodes wrote that "being thus threatened from two directions, I determined to attack with my center and right, holding at bay still another force, then emerging from the town." Rodes retained his three-brigade deployment, but ordered Daniel's Brigade to extend the line to the right, so that it could either support Iverson or attack on its right. This left Ramseur's Brigade in reserve. Rodes's initial deployment has been severely criticized, as he launched his attack with his least experienced brigade commanders.[6]

"I caused Iverson's Brigade to advance, and at the same moment gave in person to O'Neal the order to attack, indicating to him precisely the point to which he was to direct the left of the four regiments then under his orders. . . . Daniel was at the same moment instructed to advance to support Iverson, if necessary; if not, to attack on his right as soon as possible," wrote Rodes in his official report. If these were the orders, then his commanders did not obey them, for O'Neal launched his brigade's attack first, and as he was being repulsed, Iverson sent his men forward. Iverson's men were subsequently slaughtered. Rodes reorganized his troops, and at about 3:00 P.M., launched a coordinated attack on the Federal position on Oak Ridge, sending the enemy streaming toward the rear. Daniel's Brigade's attack on Stone's Brigade (Wadsworth's Division, I Corps) on McPherson's Ridge was also successful at the time.[7]

During the pursuit of the fleeing Federal troops, Rodes estimated that his men captured about 2500 men—"so many as to embarrass [his division's] movements materially," he noted. The division spent the night, and most of July 2, in and around Gettysburg. That night, the division made arrangements to attack Cemetery Hill from the west in conjunction with Early's Division. Rodes, however, underestimated the time it would take to get his troops into position, and by the time they were ready, Early's Division was already repulsed. Curiously, Rodes placed the attack column under the command of brigade commander General Stephen Ramseur. According to Tagg, Rodes may have been sick during this period.[8]

After midnight on July 3, Rodes received orders to send "all the troops I could spare without destroying my ability to hold my position" to General Johnson, who was planning on renewing his attacks on Culp's Hill. Rodes responded by sending O'Neal's and Daniel's Brigades, which took position behind Johnson's Division. The two brigades attacked the XII Corps repeatedly later that morning without success. The other brigades rested along Long Lane and were merely spectators to the devastation of Pettigrew's Division as it attacked the Federal line on Cemetery Ridge during the afternoon.[9]

Daniel's Brigade—Brigadier General Junius Daniel

Units: 32nd North Carolina, 43rd North Carolina, 45th North Carolina, 53rd North Carolina, 2nd North Carolina Battalion
Strength: 2052
Losses: 926 (227-583-116)—45%[10]

The regiments comprising Brigadier General Junius Daniel's Brigade were mustered into service between March and April 1862, and except for two regiments initially serving in Holmes's Division during the Seven Days campaign, the brigade spent most of its time guarding the James River near Drewry's Bluff and then in North Carolina. With the pending invasion of the North, this large unit of over two thousand fighting men was called up and added to Lee's army in May 1862. The men were excited to leave the tedium behind.[11]

A West Point graduate, Junius Daniel left the U.S. army and became a planter. He entered the Confederate as colonel of the 14th North Carolina. During the winter of 1861–1862, he assumed command of three regiments and a cavalry battalion. Promotion to brigadier general came in September 1862. Although he had had limited battlefield experience, he had impressed his superiors.[12]

During Rodes's short stay in Carlisle, the 32nd North Carolina was honored by receiving the first new battle flag that was to symbolize the Confederacy for the remainder of the war and long after. According to Private Henry London, the flag was sent to Lee, who passed it on to Ewell, who bestowed it on Rodes, who finally gave it to "his most favored Brigadier, General Daniel, and he ordered

it to be presented to the Thirty-second Regiment." It seems odd that this honor was given to an untested regiment. The unit would earn its honor before the battle was over.[13]

The stay in Carlisle was a pleasant one. "We were treated very good by the ladies. They thought we would do as their soldiers do, burn every place we passed through, but when we told them the strict orders of General Lee they were rejoiced," noted Louis Leon of the 43rd North Carolina. Cutting down the Stars and Stripes flying over the barracks and replacing it with a Confederate flag was one of the Southerners' first acts. Many of the troops were stationed in the barracks there, causing Lieutenant William Beavans of Daniel's staff to confide in his diary, "sleeping in the Barracks drinking ice water and Whiskey."[14]

The brigade, along with the remainder of the division, left the friendly confines of Carlisle on June 30, and marched toward Heidlersburg. The long march continued on July 1, when the men were ordered back into line at about 6:00 A.M. on July 1. The morning, although dusty, was uneventful. Beavans noted that "we marched, without thinking any danger was at hand, very soon we heard canonading [sic] ahead." All but the ordnance wagons were ordered to the rear, and the men became uneasy. Leon (43rd North Carolina) related that "a deep feeling of anxiety pervaded the minds of the troops."[15]

Rodes deployed his units as they reached the vicinity of Gettysburg. Being in the rear of the column, Daniel's Brigade was ordered to protect the division's right flank by deploying about two hundred yards behind and to the right of Iverson's Brigade. The brigade was deployed, from left to right, as 2nd North Carolina Battalion–45th North Carolina–43rd North Carolina–53rd North Carolina–32nd North Carolina. The men were ordered to lie down when their artillery opened fire on the Federal troops on McPherson's Ridge. A Federal shell fell among the prone men of the 2nd North Carolina Battalion within a matter of minutes, killing and wounding nine. After remaining there for about half an hour, Daniel was told that Iverson's Brigade was about to advance, and that he should also move forward in support. Because the information was incomplete, Daniel believed that Iverson's movement immediately went awry, as "he changed his line of direction considerably to the left, thus unmasking such of my regiments as were in his rear." This threw Daniel in a quandary. He believed that his orders were to drive south to strike the Federal I Corps, and at the same time, support Iverson's right flank. With Iverson moving to the southeast, Daniel decided to split his brigade into two wings. After ordering the 43rd North Carolina and 53rd North Carolina to swing to the left to support Iverson's Brigade, he rode back to the 2nd North Carolina Battalion and the 45th North Carolina and ordered them to continue moving southward. The 32nd North Carolina was apparently kept in reserve between the two wings at the time.[16]

If these were Daniel's orders, they too were miscommunicated. While the 53rd North Carolina moved by the left flank in support of Iverson, the 43rd North Carolina never budged from the vicinity of the Forney house along Mummasburg Road. The regiment's commanding officer, Lieutenant Colonel W. G. Lewis, believed that his orders were to take a position between

the 2nd North Carolina Battalion (which was moving due south to take on Stone's Brigade) and the 53rd North Carolina (which was moving to the aid of Iverson's Brigade), and "support either on the right or left, as necessity demanded." The regiment finally advanced to try to support both units. It came under a "severe fire in front and on flank," and was ordered to fall back to the cover of Oak Hill.[17]

While the 43rd North Carolina dallied around the Forney house, the 53rd North Carolina made its way toward Iverson's right flank, all the while torn by small arms and cannon fire. As the regiment approached Oak Ridge, it encountered the 3rd Alabama (O'Neal's Brigade), which was also to the right of Iverson. It first formed on the Alabama unit's left, but then moved around to its right. Although Iverson's charge had been repulsed, the two regiments continued their advance toward Oak Ridge and Cutler's Brigade (Wadsworth's Division, I Corps) on its south slope. This movement apparently caused Cutler to pull his men back to a more protected position in Sheads's Woods. As the two regiments continued forward, they were hit by a crossfire from Cutler's troops in the front and Stone's Brigade on their right. Colonel William Owens, commander of the 53rd North Carolina, halted his men when the Alabamians on his left suddenly stopped and fell back. Without support on the right or left, Owens also ordered his men to fall back about fifty yards to reconnect with the 3rd Alabama. The men had not settled down long, when the 3rd Alabama again moved, this time to form on the right flank of Ramseur's Brigade, as he did not receive orders from General Daniel.[18]

As these events unfolded, the 2nd North Carolina Battalion and the 45th North Carolina were moving southward to protect the division's right flank. In front of them was Colonel Roy Stone's Brigade (Rowley's Division, I Corps) along Chambersburg Pike. Watching them approach, Stone noted that "their line [was] being formed not parallel but obliquely to ours." About halfway to the Federal line, the men were ordered to lie down so the batteries in their rear could soften up the enemy's position. Continuing on again, the men reached a position about two hundred yards north of Chambersburg Pike, where the two regiments halted to fire into skirmishers who had taken refuge behind a stout fence. As Daniel's men scaled the fence, the 143rd and 149th Pennsylvania, lying on the south lip of Chamberburg Pike, opened fire, killing and wounding large numbers of Tar Heels. At least three Federal batteries opened fire at the same time. Lieutenant James Stewart of Battery B, 4th U.S. Artillery, later wrote that "it was more than they [Daniel's men] could stand. They broke to the rear where they halted, faced about and advanced again, but meeting with such a storm of lead and iron, they broke and ran over the rising ground entirely out of sight." Other Federal officers recalled how the North Carolinians's ranks wavered, and many fell back. Those that reached the unfinished railroad cut were swept aside by the canister fired into it by a Federal battery. Many men jumped into the railroad cut to avoid the deadly artillery fire. However, a battery opened an enfilading fire from their left, "sweeping the cut with terrible effect," recollected Lieutenant Colonel Wharton Green of the 2nd North Carolina Battalion.[19]

The 149th Pennsylvania now charged across Chambersburg Pike, forcing the two Confederate regiments to retreat about a quarter of mile, where they were rallied by General Daniel. "In his stento-

rian tones audible in command a quarter of a mile or more away, he ordered the men to halt and reform on him. This they did without regard to company or regimental formation almost to a man," recalled Green. Realizing that he could not drive the enemy from Chambersburg Pike with these two small units, Daniel ordered his three other regiments forward in support. The 43rd and 53rd North Carolina formed on the left, and at right angles to the 2nd North Carolina Battalion, while the 32nd North Carolina formed on the right of the 45th North Carolina. Just to the right of the 32nd North Carolina were units from Davis's (Heth's Division, III Corps) broken brigade. Daniel later wrote that he "sent an officer with a request that they would act in conjunction with me in my . . . advance, and with which request they had for some cause failed to comply." Given the rough handling of Davis's Brigade in the unfinished railroad cut, it is not surprising that they were not interested in reentering the fray.[20]

Daniel now ordered his three units to move in the direction of Chamberburg Pike and Stone's Brigade. Upon reaching the fence again, the line of battle received a terrific volley from the 149th Pennsylvania that had taken refuge in the unfinished railroad cut, a mere twenty-two paces from the fence. Captain Francis Jones of the Federal regiment watched from the railroad cut as "three lines of the enemy [Daniel's Brigade] came into view and close enough for our fire to cut all three ranks down at one firing." Not to be denied, Daniel's men forged on. A well-placed Confederate battery forced the Pennsylvanians to flee from the deep trench. Because the sides were so steep, many had trouble scaling the wall and were captured by Daniel's men. While Colonel S. H. Boyd of the 45th North

Carolina saw no reason to pursue the Pennsylvanians toward Chamberburg Pike, Lieutenant Colonel H. L. Andrews of the 2nd North Carolina Battalion ordered his unit forward. Approaching Chambersburg Pike, they were met by a withering fire from the 143rd Pennsylvania, forcing them to seek shelter in the unfinished railroad cut. Two more times they charged, and both times they were repulsed.[21]

Daniel's men in the railroad cut now opened an unmerciful fire against Stone's Brigade. Realizing that his losses were mounting, the new commander of Stone's Brigade, Colonel Langhorne Wistar, knew that he must either order a charge to drive Daniel's men out of the railroad cut or retreat. He decided on the former, turning around the 149th Pennsylvania, which had just returned from its first charge, to attack again. Daniel's men immediately opened fire, causing the field between the railroad cut and Chambersburg Pike to be littered with Federal dead and wounded. The lucky ones made it back to their original position.[22]

Over on the right, Daniel ordered Colonel E. C. Brabble to make a charge toward McPherson's barn with his 32nd North Carolina. As they moved swiftly forward, Brabble's men did not see several companies from the 150th Pennsylvania crouching behind a fence north of Chambersburg Pike. When within fifty yards, the Federal troops opened fire, cutting down many of Brabble's men. While staggered, they did not retreat until hit by a second volley, which forced them back to the protection of the railroad cut.[23]

A stalemate existed until about 3:00 P.M., when Brockenbrough's Brigade (Heth's Division, III Corps) attacked Stone's Brigade from the west. Watching the Virginians approach, Daniel ordered

his brigade to renew its attack. The pressure was too great, and Stone's men began their retreat toward Seminary Ridge. The victorious Tar Heels took hundreds of prisoners during this period of the battle, and the 45th North Carolina was able to recapture the flag of the 20th North Carolina of Iverson's Brigade. Around this time, the 43rd and 53rd North Carolina, along with Iverson's 12th North Carolina on their left, drove against Paul's (Robinson's Division) and Cutler's (Wadsworth's Division) Brigades on Oak Ridge in conjunction with Rameur's and O'Neal's attacks from the north. Together, they crushed the final stand of the Federal I Corps's right flank. Although none of the reports or memoirs from Daniel's men referred to the sharp engagement on Seminary Ridge, historian David Martin believed that the brigade attacked from the north side of Chambersburg Pike. Stewart's battery may have kept the 32nd, 45th, and 2nd North Carolina Battalion at bay, but it had more difficulty with the 43rd and 53rd North Carolina, which attacked farther north and ultimately flanked the battery, forcing its retreat.[24]

With the Federal troops in full retreat toward Gettysburg, Daniel reformed his men and moved them to the cover afforded by the unfinished railroad cut on Seminary Ridge. Lack of water was a problem. Private James Green of the 53rd North Carolina described the situation. "It was a very hot day & our men sufered [sic] very much for Water for they were marched in quick time for severel [sic] miles before they got to the Battle field & did not have the chance of getting [sic] Water in there [sic] Canteens so they don [sic] without from 10 in the Morning till 5 P m." The brigade spent the night there. The men slept soundly despite not having their blankets, instead using captured ones that were scattered about the fields in profusion.[25]

The brigade moved southwest the next morning to occupy the area around the seminary, and remained there for the remainder of the day. Rodes placed O'Neal's Brigade under Daniel's command at this time—an indication of the high esteem the division commander held for his subordinate. The Federal artillery opened fire on Daniel's position at about 4:00 P.M. Green described this cannonade as "the heaviest Commandeing [sic] I ever heard by half." General Daniel wrote in his official report that his men, "owing much to their exposed situation, they suffered much." The losses in the 45th North Carolina amounted to one killed and ten to twelve wounded.[26]

Just after sunset, Daniel received orders to form his men in the open fields between Seminary Ridge and the town to support an attack that was to be made on Cemetery Hill by Doles's, Iverson's, and Ramseur's Brigades. After marching about three-quarters of a mile behind Ramseur's Brigade, Daniel received word that the assault on the heights was canceled. Soon after, Federal sharpshooters opened fire on the brigade, but losses were few as the men were told to get down. The brigade remained in this position until 10:00 P.M., when it was ordered into Gettysburg, and occupied a stretch of Middle Street.[27]

The weary men did not get much sleep that night, for about two hours later (1:30 A.M. on July 3), they received orders to again fall in and move to the left. They reached their assigned positions after several miles of marching. Daniel reported to General Edward Johnson at 4:00 A.M., and was informed that his brigade would support Jones's Brigade in its assault on

Culp's Hill. Daniel was also relieved of direct responsibility of O'Neal's Brigade. The Federal artillery opened fire during its march to its position behind Jones's Brigade, causing several casualties in the 32nd North Carolina. Colonel Brabble bitterly wrote after the battle that his regiment lost "many men and doing little injury to the enemy."[28]

A feeling of dread filled General Daniel as daybreak approached. "The hill in front of this position was, in my opinion, so strong that it could not have been carried by any force," he wrote in his report. After waiting several hours, Daniel received orders to file to the left, where his brigade was to storm the heights in conjunction with Steuart's Brigade. The men were exposed during this movement, and Federal shells rained down on them, killing and wounding as many as a hundred. Sergeant Albert Marsh of the 53rd North Carolina wrote after the war that "being in open ground for about a half mile, it is a wonder that our loss was not greater."[29]

Both Generals Daniel and Steuart protested the order to charge the hill, but their pleas fell on deaf ears. Daniel dejectedly returned to his command, now facing the lower hill. To his left was Steuart's Brigade; the Stonewall Brigade was on his right. The brigade was formed into two lines. The 43rd North Carolina formed the left of the first line, with its left flank at right angles with the 3rd North Carolina of Steuart's Brigade. To the right of the 43rd North Carolina was the 45th North Carolina, and then the 2nd North Carolina Battalion. In the second line, the 32nd North Carolina formed behind the 43rd North Carolina, and the 53rd North Carolina was behind the 45th North Carolina. Against them were Candy's and Kane's Brigades

(Geary's Division, XII Corps), occupying strong breastworks.[30]

Steuart's Brigade was repulsed even before the 43rd North Carolina on its right had a chance to advance. As the North Carolinians launched their attack, they were exposed to a severe fire, causing heavy losses, particularly among its left companies. Lieutenant Colonel W. Lewis finally ordered the regiment back to the protection of some abandoned breast-works. He could not understand why the two units on his right did not advance. Captain Van Brown of the 2nd North Carolina Battalion on the right of the front line wrote in his report that the unit did not attack, but instead "was employed during the day chiefly as skirmishers."[31]

Despite Lewis's assertions, the 45th North Carolina did its share of fighting. Captain J. A. Hopkins described what he saw as his men moved up the heights to take their positions. "The enemy was on a height, and well fortified. The line of for-tification was not parallel with our line of battle, lacking perhaps 15 or 20 degrees, and about half the length of our line in front, and a short [distance] to the right and in rear of this line was another, leaving an open space between the two." The Federal troops quickly sprinted from the first line of defenses to the second soon after Daniel's men arrived. "At that time almost every man of the regiment [45th North Carolina] was firing into them as they passed the opening, cer-tainly killing a number. At times it seemed as if whole masses of them would fall," wrote Captain Hopkins. Daniel called it a "most destructive fire with the whole of the Forty-Fifth Regiment for five minutes upon a crowd of the enemy who were dis-organized and fleeing in great confu-sion." Not able to advance, Daniel's men remained in their positions and poured a destructive fire into Federal units attempt-

ing to relieve the troops in the front lines. When their ammunition was depleted, the 43rd North Carolina was pulled back and the 32nd North Carolina took its place.[32]

The 53rd North Carolina apparently relieved the 45th North Carolina and charged the heights several times. Green wrote that "we could not rout them from there [sic] strong hold, for they had an advantage of hight [sic] & Breastworks of us." Private Louis Leon of the same regi-ment wrote that his regiment "stayed all day—no here, I may say, we melted away." Leon would never forget this day, when "our poor boys fall by our sides—almost as fast as the leaves that fell as cannon and musket balls hit them."[33]

At about noon, Daniel finally received orders to pull back to the base of the hill. The brigade remained there until almost midnight, when Daniel followed General Smith's Brigade back to Gettysburg, again with O'Neal's Brigade in tow. He reported to General Rodes, but it could not have been a happy reunion. July 4 found the command in defensive positions along Seminary Ridge. The retreat back to Vir-ginia began sometime between midnight and 1:00 A.M. on July 5.[34]

It appears that Daniel's Brigade acquit-ted itself well in its first battle with the army. It stubbornly battled Stone's men on July 1, and apparently was instru-mental in helping to knock the Federal I Corps's right flank off Seminary Ridge. Despite the horrendous odds against it, the brigade apparently did as well as any other in the ill-fated attempt to take Culp's Hill. It lost more men (969) than any other Confederate brigade, with the exception of Pettigrew's, Armistead's, Davis's, and Garnett's. The brigade remained with Lee's army and ultimately surrendered at Appomattox Courthouse.[35]

✀

Doles's Brigade—Brigadier General George Doles

Units: 4th Georgia, 12th Georgia, 21st Georgia, 44th Georgia
Strength: 1323
Losses: 219 (46-106-67)—17%[36]

Although General George Doles's Brigade contained four veteran regiments, only two, the 4th and 44th Georgia, had served together for any length of time. During the Seven Days battles, the four regiments served in four different brigades. By the battle of Cedar Mountain, the 4th and 44th Georgia were brigaded together in Early's Brigade and were shifted to Ripley's Brigade at the onset of the Maryland campaign. This arrangement continued up to the Chancellorsville campaign, when the two remaining regiments were added to the brigade, now commanded by Brigadier General George Doles.[37]

Although he had little formal education prior to the war, Doles was elected colonel of the 4th Georgia in May 1861. Doles led his regiment at the battle of Malvern Hill and again at Sharpsburg, where Brigadier General Roswell Ripley was wounded and he assumed command of the brigade. Doles was assigned permanent command of the brigade in November 1862 and was promoted to the rank of brigadier general. After playing a supporting role at Fredericksburg, Doles led his newly reformed brigade on the flank attack at Chancellorsville, where he and his command drew praise. The brigade was a confident unit, ready to face the enemy again when the Gettysburg campaign began.[38]

The men found the march from Carlisle on June 30 to be especially wearying. Their spirits rose when they saw their commanders at the head of their brigade and the 4th Georgia's band was ordered to play "Tom, March On." "I never saw anything so magical in its effect," noted C. D. Grace after the war. The men were on the road early the next day, and could soon hear the ominous booming of cannon in the distance. This brought orders to double-quick.[39]

Feeling threatened by Federal forces in his front and left as his division approached Gettysburg, Rodes decided to attack the former and hold the latter in check until Early's Division arrived along Harrisburg Road. The difficult job of holding the growing horde of Union troops from the XI Corps on his left at bay was assigned to Doles's veteran Georgia brigade. It was a gamble, as it appeared that the Union troops were interested in turning Rodes's left flank. But Rodes expected Early's men momentarily, who "would strike this portion of the enemy's force on the flank before it could overpower Doles."[40]

Obliquing to the left (east), Doles deployed his men aside Newville Road, just north of where Carlisle Road branches at the Smithy farm. Most of the brigade deployed to the right of the road, facing the town, from left to right, as 12th Georgia–4th Georgia–44th Georgia–21st Georgia. The 12th Georgia extended the line beyond Newville Road to the east. In front of the brigade were the 61st Ohio and 74th Pennsylvania (von Amsberg's Brigade, Schimmelfennig's Division) and Dilger's and Wheeler's batteries, supported by the 82nd Illinois. A large gap extended between Doles's right flank and O'Neal's left flank, which was partially protected by skirmishers from O'Neal's 5th Alabama. Doles also deployed his sharpshooters as skirmishers, extending from York Pike almost to the base of Oak Hill—a distance of about half a mile.[41]

At about 3:30 P.M., skirmishers from Barlow's Division (XI Corps) arrived on Blocher's Knoll, near Doles's left flank, forcing their Confederate counterparts backward. Concerned about being flanked, Doles quickly responded. "The enemy moved his force from our front, made a strong demonstration on our left, driving our skirmishers from the hill . . . the command was then moved by the left flank, to meet any attack the enemy might attempt on our left and rear," Doles reported after the battle. Reconnoitering the Union line, Doles could see solid masses of enemy troops taking position on the hill, along with batteries. Directly in front was Ames's Brigade and von Gilsa's was to the left. The Federal batteries on the knoll opened on Doles's Brigade, "and they soon made it very unpleasant for us," wrote Private Henry Thomas of the 4th Georgia.[42]

It was clear that the Union troops had more on their minds than holding the hill—they were making preparations to attack Doles's flank. General Jubal Early wrote after the war, "Doles's Brigade was getting in a critical situation." Fortunately for Doles, Early's first brigade, Gordon's, arrived just at this point. Immediately deploying his Georgians, Gordon ordered them to advance slowly toward Barlow's position on the knoll. Not to be outdone, Doles ordered his men to attack Ames's front and flank. General Rodes briefly summarized Doles's Brigade's activities during the remainder of the afternoon, when he wrote that "Doles, thus relieved, without waiting for orders, and though greatly outnumbered, boldly attacked the heavy masses of the enemy in his front. After a short but desperate contest, in which his brigade acted with unsurpassed gallantry, he succeeded in driving them

before him." Rodes's description is too short, for Doles's men took on not one group of Union troops, but three, in separate actions.[43]

The first action occurred when the center of Doles's line, composed of the 4th Georgia on the left and the 44th Georgia on its right, advanced against the left side of Ames's line. Thomas recalled that "our brigade charged with that soul-stirring rebel yell, which once heard on the field of battle can never be forgotten." The Union artillery on the knoll had been taking its toll on Doles's men, causing one to remark that they "advanced through a field midst grape shot and cannister [sic.]" The officers of the 4th and 44th Georgia disputed what occurred next. Major W. Peebles of the 44th Georgia wrote that "we charged the line in our front, and immediately put it to flight." However, Major W. Willis, who took over the 4th Georgia after Colonel D. R. E. Winn had been mortally wounded, wrote that the "enemy was a little stubborn, but soon gave way, with considerable loss." Either way, Ames's regiments were soon fleeing to the rear.[44]

The situation was quite different on the right of the line, where Colonel John Mercer of the 21st Georgia spied a strong Federal force approaching to aid Barlow's beleaguered division. Wheeling his regiment to the right, he advanced across a wheatfield to meet Krzyzanowski's Brigade (Schimmelfennig's Division, XI Corps). Seeing the Georgians approach, Krzyzanoswki halted his men in the wheatfield and awaited their attack. Captain Theodore Dodge of the 119th New York recalled that within a matter of moments "the irregular line of butternut and gray hove gradually in sight—their officers all mounted, waving their swords and cheering on their men." The Federal line opened fire, but, according to Dodge, "this in no way checked the enemy's advance, but it drew their fire; and they continued slowly to push on, keeping it up in a desultory manner as they drew near."[45]

Colonel Mercer soon learned that four regiments against one are poor odds, and pulled his men back about forty yards to Blocher's farm lane, where he ordered his men to lie down. This Southern reversal permitted an officer of the XI Corps a rare opportunity to write, "we charged upon them and drove them back." Help was on the way. Having dispatched Ames's Brigade, the 4th and 44th Georgia were ordered to wheel to the right to face Krzyzanowski's new threat. The 12th Georgia was also moved from the left of the line to the right to face these Federal units. Captain Alfred Lee of the 82nd Ohio watched with a sinking heart. "Their movements were firm and steady, as usual, and their banners, bearing the blue Southern cross, flaunted impudently [sic] and seemed to challenge combat. On they came, one line after the other, in splendid array."[46]

While Doles's regiments took on Krzyzanowski's left and center, two regiments from Gordon's Brigade turned their attention to the Federal brigade's right flank and rear. In some places the two opposing lines stood less than seventy-five feet apart—so close that "names of battles printed on the Confederate flags might have been read, had there been time to read them," noted one Federal soldier. Men dropped by the score on both sides. After about ten minutes, the Federal troops could stand no more and were ordered to the rear.[47]

Prior to these events, General Doles was involved in a serious incident that could have cost him his life. His powerful sorrel horse took the bit between his teeth and galloped straight for the Federal lines, with Doles pulling frantically on the reins. When within about fifty yards of the enemy line Doles either fell or jumped off his horse, and scrambled for safety. The horse continued on, until reaching within ten or fifteen feet of the Federal line, when he wheeled and rushed back the way he had come. Neither rider or horse was injured in this escapade.[48]

Having defeated two Federal brigades, Doles's men began their advance toward Gettysburg. Suddenly, a Federal force appeared out of nowhere on their right flank and rear. This was the 157th New York (von Amsberg's Brigade, Schimmelfennig's Division, XI Corps), which was dispatched to assist Barlow and Krzyzanowski in their desperate fight. Unfortunately, these Federal troops were now fleeing toward Gettysburg, leaving this single regiment to face Doles's entire brigade, already flushed with victory.[49]

The 157th New York fell on the 44th Georgia's flank and opened fire when it was a mere thirty or forty yards away. They were probably able to advance so closely without detection because the Georgians were too busy setting their sights on the town. "As soon as it was discovered that we were flanked, we made a wheel to the right, faced the new foe, and began to fire upon him. Thus checked in his movement, he faced us, and opened a severe fire upon us," wrote Major Peebles of the 44th Georgia. The 4th Georgia also wheeled to face the enemy. While the New Yorkers could see these movements in their front, they did not see the men of the 21st Georgia lying along Blocher's farm lane on their left. This was the regiment that had been driven to this location by Krzyzanowski's Brigade about twenty minutes earlier. When the 157th New York had advanced to within a short distance of them, "at the command of their colonel, they sprang to their knees and poured such a volley into the enemy that they were not only checked but stampeded," noted Thomas. The 12th Georgia arrived and took position on the 21st Georgia's right. The New York regiment was now enveloped by a wide semicircle of Georgia troops. The result was its almost total destruction. As Major Peebles wrote, "we captured, killed, or wounded nearly every man that came upon our right flank. We soon had nothing in our front." Corporal Sidney Richardson of the 21st Georgia expressed sympathy for the New Yorkers—"I was glad when the yankees turned to run back, but one time I felt sad, one Yankee regiment charge [sic] us, but we all fell down behind a fence, and received the charge just before they got to us, we fired a volley into them and then charged them as quick as we could, they turned to run and we continured [sic] the charge untill [sic] they got away. I think they fight harder in their own Country, then they do in Virginia."[50]

In a remarkably short time, Doles's Brigade had participated in the defeat of two Federal brigades and the almost total destruction of a regiment of a third. In his report of the battle, Rodes wrote, "in this affair, Doles handled his men with a skill and effect truly admirable, exhibiting marked coolness and courage." The lion's share of the fighting had been done by the 4th and 44th Georgia. One soldier from the 21st Georgia wrote home, "it is the first fight we every [sic] was in that we was not put in the heardest [sic] part of the battle."[51]

After reforming his ranks, Doles ordered his men forward toward the town. To Grace, the afternoon's action "was a fearful slaughter, the golden wheatfields, a few minutes before in beauty, now gone, and the ground covered with the dead and wounded in blue." The brigade made determined efforts to cut off the retreating Federal units, including Paul's Brigade (Robinson's Division, I Corps). These attempts were unsuccessful, for as General Doles explained, "we did not succeed, as he retired faster than we advanced." Major Peebles (44th Georgia) added that "had not our men been so nearly exhausted, we should doubtless have captured the greater portion of the artillery and men; but only a few who could not flee so rapidly as the main body fell into our hands." The brigade continued firing into the ranks of the retreating men, causing additional casualties.[52]

As the brigade reached the northwestern edge of the town, Doles ordered it to enter by the left flank. Thomas recalled that "we continued the pursuit through town, and had a sharp engagement in the streets, killing, wounding, and capturing a good many men, with small loss to ourselves." Reaching West Middle Street, Doles was ordered to halt for the night. Iverson's Brigade formed on the right.[53]

The brigade remained there through July 2, when at 8:00 P.M., it was ordered to march by the right flank through town, forming in the fields just to the southwest. Here the men formed a line of battle with the rest of Rodes's Division in what was to be a charge on the strongly held Federal position on Cemetery Hill. Doles's Brigade formed on the left of the line, with Iverson's Brigade on its right, followed by Ramseur's Brigade. O'Neal's Brigade formed behind Doles's. The three brigades marched to within a hundred yards of the Federal line, where the brigade commanders halted their troops and conferred. Fearing the Union defenses were too strong to attack, Rodes called off the attack, ordering his three brigades withdrawn to Long Lane, about 300 yards in the rear. As a result, they did not participate in the attack on Cemetery Hill that was to be coordinated with Early's Division.[54]

Thomas accurately described the brigade's subsequent activities when he wrote, "we were not actually engaged again, though continually under an annoying fire." July 3 was spent on Long Lane, with its left touching the outskirts of Gettysburg and its right connecting with Iverson's Brigade. The brigade pulled back to a position near the seminary during the early morning hours of July 4, arriving there at sunrise. The troops were immediately ordered to construct breastworks.[55]

In an appendix to his official report, Doles reported that Confederate batteries fired upon his men on both July 1 and July 3. He was particularly infuriated when, on the latter day, "we waved our flag, and sent them word that they were firing on us. They did not cease firing. I lost several men wounded by the fire of this bat-tery . . . I have made every effort to find out the batteries, and have failed so far."[56]

In its battles with parts of three Federal brigades on July 1, Doles's men caused over 800 casualties—an incredible figure, given the brigade's strength was just over 1300. Their own losses were just as unbelievable—only 219 (17%)—the lowest of any brigade in Rodes's Division.[57]

The brigade's activities are best summarized by P. E. Pryor, who wrote after the battle, "they had the advantage in position the 2nd & 3rd day; the first wee [sic] whiped [sic] them badly . . . the first day wee drove them two miles like chaff. They did not stand atall [sic] untwill [sic] dark, then they worked all knight [sic] and fortified a small mountain that wee [sic] would have sacrifised [sic] too much to have taken it."[58]

Iverson's Brigade—Brigadier General Alfred Iverson

Units: 5th North Carolina, 12th North Carolina, 20th North Carolina, 23rd North Carolina
Strength: 1384
Losses: 903 (182-399-322)—65%[59]

Five regiments were linked together to form Brigadier General Samuel Garland's Brigade by the Seven Days battles. Prior to this campaign, only the 5th and 23rd North Carolina were in his brigade at the battle of Seven Pines. The brigade was credited with boldness in its attack on the Federal position at Gaines's Mill. It remained near Richmond during July and August 1862, missing the Second Manassas campaign. Rejoining Lee's army in time for the Maryland campaign, Garland's Brigade held Fox's Gap in South Mountain. General Garland was killed there and his men routed. Colonel Dun-can McRae of the 5th North Carolina took over the brigade for the rest of the campaign. Promoted to the rank of brigadier general, Alfred Iverson of the 20th North Carolina took command of the brigade after the campaign. The brigade did not see action at Fredericksburg, but fought well at the battle of Chancellorsville.[60]

The men had a burning dislike of their brigade commander. Their disdain had boiled over during the previous winter, when, after being elevated to brigade command, Iverson sought to install a friend as his replacement in command of his old regiment. The men would have none of it, and fired off petitions to Richmond. Iverson was probably still smarting from his defeat in this matter. He probably could not understand his men's feelings because his own career had always advanced because of political influence.[61]

The several days of rest at Carlisle, Pennsylvania, refreshed the men. They secured Federal Government whiskey and all was well until they got into a tussle with Doles's Brigade's Georgians, who also had too much to drink. During the march toward Gettysburg, the "black-hearts" (cherries) could be found in abundance along the sides of the roads, but because of Lee's strict orders against pilfering, the men were discouraged from helping themselves. Fortunately, the limbs of the cherry trees "obstructed the advance of the regiment and had to be incontinently topped off with the camp hatchet. As these offending limbs were invariably heavily ladened the fruit there on had to be eaten or else good victuals had to be thrown anyway which every body knew was a sin," noted Charles Bicknall.[62]

The brigade led Rodes's column toward Gettysburg, during the last phase of the march on July 1. The sounds of battle could be clearly heard when the men were about four miles from town. "Many a canteen filled with proceeds of the Yankee treat at Carlisle was now emptied without compunction. The best of soldierery [sic] never harden beyond the point that the approach of the battle had its sobering effect," wrote Bicknall. Arriving on Oak Hill, Rodes ordered Iverson to deploy his brigade and move forward. As the ridge widened, O'Neal's and Doles's Brigades were thrown out on Iverson's left.[63]

As the men arrived on Oak Hill, they could see A. P. Hill's Divisions engaged with units from the Federal I Corps to the southwest. They could also see hostile flags behind stone walls and waves of men in gray surging against them, only to break and recoil. Looking due south and to the east, they could see streams of the enemy moving northward as well. Seldom had the men been treated to such a panoramic view.[64]

Rodes halted the line and ordered Iverson's Brigade to support Carter's artillery battalion, which was softening up the enemy's position. Thinking that the enemy was about to attack his position, Rodes organized three of his brigades for an attack on the Federal I Corps's right flank, and informed Iverson that he was to advance with O'Neal. He was also told that he could call upon Daniel's Brigade for support, if needed. Iverson had just sent notification to Daniel that he was about to advance, and ordered another staff officer to the left to find out when Colonel O'Neal was going to launch his attack. To his surprise, he learned that O'Neal's men were already advancing. Without the coordinated attack that Rodes had ordered, O'Neal's Alabamians were decisively repulsed. Now, all of Baxter's Brigade (Robinson's Division, I Corps) on Oak Ridge could change direction from the north to the west, to face Iverson's North Carolinians.[65]

None of this was known by Iverson's men, who were being formed at the base of Oak Hill. Marching across Mummasburg Road, the brigade was arranged from left to right as 5th North Carolina–20th North Carolina–23rd North Carolina–12th North Carolina. Whether Rodes gave Iverson specific directions about the route of this charge is not known. Modern historian David Martin believes that Iverson was to sweep southeast along Mummasburg Road. However, the line veered to the right, and instead aimed toward the southeast corner of open, clover-planted Forney's field, where a gap existed between Cutler's (Wadsworth's Division) and Baxter's (Robinson's Division) Brigades. As a result, Iverson's left flank hung dangerously in the air as the brigade marched obliquely toward Baxter. Iverson's four hundred-yard line of battle probably stepped off sometime between 2:00 and 2:30 P.M.[66]

Several soldiers on both sides commented on the splendor of the attack. Private John Vautier of the 88th Pennsylvania recalled that "Iverson's men, with arms at a right shoulder, came on in splendid array, keeping step with an almost perfect line." Except for a rail fence that was oriented roughly parallel, and seven hundred yards south of the Mummasburg Road, the men's march was unobstructed.[67]

Iverson did not accompany the charge, and therefore could not provide needed leadership and direction. The son of Major Charles Blacknall of the 23rd North Carolina, Oscar Blacknall recounted a rumor that Iverson "not only remained in the rear but that a big chestnut log intervened between him and the battle and that more than once he reminded his staff that for more than one at a time to look over was an unnecessary exposure of person." Captain V. C. Turner and Sergeant H. C. Wall of the same regiment wrote that "Iverson's part in the heroic struggle of his brigade seems to have begun and ended with the order to move forward and 'Give them hell.'" Distinguished modern historian, Harry Pfanz, was much less critical of Iverson's performance, however. Compounding the problem was the fact that most of the officers' ranks had been depleted at the battle of Chancellorsville and had not been filled. The worst situation was in the 5th North Carolina, which carried no officers above the rank of captain into the battle. As fate would have it, this regiment was placed on the vulnerable left flank during the attack, without the leadership the men needed.[68]

Soon after Iverson's men got under way, the 90th Pennsylvania, 83rd New York, and 88th Pennsylvania quickly shifted from facing O'Neal's men to the north, to a position behind the stone wall facing Forney's open field, facing west. No fewer than nine Federal regiments from Baxter's and Cutler's Brigades watched in anticipation as Iverson's men marched across Forney's field. The lead elements of Paul's Brigade were also arriving at the time. Tragically, Iverson's men never knew what they were up against until it was too late. Lieutenant Walter Montgomery of the 12th North Carolina wrote that the "troops bounded forward not knowing certainly where the enemy was, for his whole line, with every flag, was concealed . . . not one of them was to be seen." The Union soldiers were constantly reminded by their officers to hold their fire and stay concealed. Iverson's men's march across Forney's field was not unscathed during this period, as Union artillery found their range, and men fell here and there.[69]

Reaching a small gully in the center of the field, Iverson's men continued on, "as orderly as if on brigade drill, while behind the stone wall the Union soldiers, with rifles cocked and fingers on the triggers, waited and bided their time, feeling confident," wrote Vautier (88th Pennsylvania). And well they should have, for not only was Iverson not present to direct his men, he had not thought to send skirmishers forward, who probably would have unmasked the Federal position.[70]

When the North Carolinians were within fifty yards of the Federal position, Baxter's men were ordered to rise and open fire. "A sheet of fire and smoke belched from the wall, flashing full in the faces of the Confederates," recollected Vautier. "Hundreds of the Confederates fell at the first volley, plainly marking their line with the ghastly row of dead and wounded men, whose blood trailed the course of their line with a crimson stain clearly discernable for several days after the battle, until the rain washed the gory record away." Oscar Blacknall wrote, "a solid wall of blue rose behind the one of stone and poured in a plunging, crushing fire. The range was point blank and largely enfilading." This was not war, it was murder, as hundreds fell at the first volley, particularly the men from the 5th, 20th, and 23rd North Carolina on that part of the line closest to Baxter's men.[71]

A young artilleryman, Private Henry Berkeley, saw the effect of this initial volley the following day:

> There were . . . seventy-nine North Carolinians laying dead in a straight line. I stood on their right and looked down their line. It was perfectly dressed. Three had fallen to the front, the rest had fallen backward; yet the feet of all these dead men were in a perfectly straight line. . . . They had evidently been killed by one volley of musketry and they had fallen in their tracks without a single struggle. . . . I turned from this sight with a sickened heart and tried to eat my breakfast, but had to return it to my haversack untouched.[72]

Although shocked by the sudden chaos around them, most of Iverson's survivors stopped and returned the Federal fire. However, as one Federal soldier recalled, "the men were falling like leaves in a storm . . . but no troops could long withstand that pelting fire." Lieutenant George Grant of the 88th Pennsylvania recalled how his men were able to rest their rifles on boulders and "fire coolly and with unerring aim." There were not many options available to Iverson's men. To retreat would force them to recross the open field behind them. Instead, most took refuge in a nearby shallow gully, from where they returned the fire. Captain V. C. Turner of the 23rd North Carolina wrote, "unable to advance, unwilling to retreat, the brigade lay down in the hollow or depression in the field and fought as best it could." Many from Baxter's Brigade fell, still flushed with victory.[73]

While the gully offered some protection, the men were still vulnerable, as the Federal troops "emptied their ammunition boxes in a point blank, plunging fire upon the prostrate line," noted Oscar Blacknall. To rise meant certain death, as Colonel Daniel Christie of the 23rd North Carolina learned when he tried to lead a charge from the gully. All the regiment's officers, save one, were killed or wounded, further hampering a cohesive response to the threat. Glancing behind them, the men forlornly looked for any movement that would suggest that help was at hand. There was none, and many of the men now realized that their only option was surrender. According to Captain Lewis Hicks of the 20th North Carolina, this realization occurred after the men lay stranded for about ten minutes, and "in the absence of white flags the wounded men hoisted their boots and hats on their bayonets to show their desperation."[74]

Other men were not so sure they wanted to surrender. Captain Hicks vividly described these tortured moments. "The smoke was so dense you could not perceive an object ten feet from you. . . . while we felt and heard the tread of the enemy, our minds were in a tumult, whether to lie still or to yield or to die fighting." When the Union troops ventured forward to scoop up the prisoners, they became outraged when they were fired upon instead. Their reaction was often to try to kill those around them who had betrayed this unspoken rule of war.[75]

Scores of prisoners were scooped up and taken to the rear. Around this time, Ramseur's Brigade, along with the 3rd Alabama (O'Neal's Brigade), arrived, and let loose volleys that killed and wounded not only Baxter's men, but also some of Iverson's. The colors of the 5th, 23rd, and 20th North Carolina were also captured by the Federal troops. The latter's was desecrated soon after. Colonel Charles Wheelock of the 97th New York taunted the Confederates by standing atop the stone wall and waving the 20th North Carolina's flag. General Baxter rode up and ordered the flag sent to the rear for safekeeping, Wheelock refused. Instead, he drew his sword and ran it through the flag, tearing it from its staff. He then waved it tauntingly at the enemy, while his aide waved the staff. Within moments a sharpshooter deposited a bullet into the aide's brain, thus discouraging Wheelock from further antics. The odyssey was not over yet, however, for during the retreat, a Confederate soldier came up to a Union soldier carrying the flag and demanded it. A pulling match ensured, and because of Wheelock's saber slash, the flag separated in two nearly equal parts, each taken by a combatant. By chance, the two old soldiers met at the fiftieth anniversary of the battle and reunited the two pieces. A similar happy ending was not true of the 23rd North Carolina's flag, which its captors tore it up that afternoon rather than allow it to be recaptured.[76]

Watching from the safety of Oak Hill, Iverson was beside himself. "When I saw white handkerchiefs raised, and my line of battle still lying down in position, I characterized the surrender as disgraceful; but when I found afterward that 500 of my men were left lying dead and wounded on a line as straight as a dress parade, I exonerated . . . the survivors." Captain V. C. Turner of the 23rd North Carolina recalled that the blood "ran like a branch. And that too, on the hot, parched ground."[77]

Hardest hit were the regiments on the left flank, closest to Baxter's Brigade. The 12th North Carolina, on the right flank, escaped the bloodbath with fewer casualties because it was farther from Baxter's line and was protected by a slight rise in the ground. Seeing what was happening to the other regiments, Lieutenant Colonel Davis ordered his men to move at once by the right flank to a protected position. Davis wisely realized that his 175 men were no match for the thousands of Federal infantry in his front. Instead, he bided his time, finally charging forward with Daniel's Brigade on his right, as the Federal right flank was crumbling. The regiment ultimately reached the unfinished railroad cut, and captured scores of prisoners.[78]

Captain Don Halsey of Iverson's staff collected the remnants of the three other regiments. An officer wrote that "there was so much consternation, so much confusion," that the three regiments ceased to be much of a fighting force for the reminder of the battle. The remnant of the brigade was attached to Ramseur's Brigade and operated with it during the remainder of the battle. The brigade formed along Middle Street that evening, with Doles's Brigade on its left and Ramseur's on its right. The three brigades advanced on the evening of July 2 to participate in the storming of Cemetery Hill. Iverson wrote that his brigade "advanced with him [Ramseur], got under the fire of the enemy's skirmishers and artillery without returning the fire, and perceiving, as I believe every one did, that we were advancing to certain destruction, when other parts of the line fell back, I also gave the order to retreat, and formed in the road [Long Lane], in which we maintained a position during that night and the whole of July 3." Lying on Long Lane, flanked by Doles's and Ramseur's Brigades, the men merely watched the Pickett–Pettigrew–Trimble charge. At 3:00 A.M. on July 4, the brigade was pulled back to Seminary Ridge, where it took defensive positions. It left the battlefield at 2:00 A.M. on July 5 to help escort the wagon train along Fairfield Road.[79]

Captain Turner of the 23rd North Carolina probably summed up best what occurred to Iverson's men during that fateful July 1 afternoon: "unwarned, unled as a brigade, went forward Iverson's deserted band to its doom. Deep and long must the desolate homes and orphan children of North Carolina rue the rashness of that hour." General Rodes wrote in his report that Iverson's men "fought and died like heroes. His dead lay in a distinctly marked line of battle." Rejoining the 20th North Carolina in Virginia after recuperating from a wound that prevented him from participating in the Gettysburg Campaign, Private E. Faison Hicks was not able to find his company. He finally stumbled upon its lone survivor, who dejectedly told him, "Hicks, I'll be d____n if we ain't whipped. [80]

Whipped was an understatement. Iverson's Brigade lost 65% of its men, tying with Garnett's Brigade for the brigade with the heaviest losses at Gettysburg. The greatest loss was sustained by the 23rd North Carolina, which lost over 89% of its men. Only one other regiment, the 8th Virginia of Garnett's Brigade, lost more men.[81]

The men refused to serve under Iverson after the battle. Ordered to take command of Nichols's Louisiana Brigade (Johnson's Division, Second Corps) on July 19, 1863, Iverson was transferred to Georgia in October of that year. One veteran wrote after the war that Iverson "was relieved at once & sent back to await trial." But politics reared its head again and Iverson was "forwarded to Richmond, got off scot free & had a brigade of reserves given to him in Georgia."[82]

Ramseur's Brigade—Brigadier General Stephen Ramseur

Units: 2nd North Carolina, 4th North Carolina, 14th North Carolina, 30th North Carolina
Strength: 1024
Losses: 275 (39-149-87)—27%[83]

Mustered into Confederate service between June and September 1861, all but the 4th North Carolina spent their early months in Norfolk or North Carolina. By June 1862, all four regiments were under the command of Brigadier General George B. Anderson. The brigade performed well at the battles of Gaines's Mill and Malvern Hill, but lost almost nine hundred men in the process. After missing the Second Manassas campaign, the brigade helped seal the breach in the Confederate line near Fox's Gap during the Maryland campaign. Three days later, the brigade fought savagely along the Sunken Road, where

Anderson was wounded. Although the wound was thought to be minor, Anderson died in October 1862.[84]

Colonel Stephen Ramseur of the 49th North Carolina was given the brigade on November 1 and promoted to the rank of brigadier general. An 1860 West Point graduate, Ramseur resigned his commission at the outbreak of the war and assumed command of a battery. He rose in the ranks and then switched to the infantry in April 1862. Meritorious service during the Seven Days battles won him the brigade and a general's star, despite the fact that he missed the Second Manassas and Maryland campaigns because of a severe wound. He was unable to return in time for the Fredericksburg campaign, so Colonel Bryan Grimes of the 4th North Carolina commanded the brigade. The brigade saw little action there, and Ramseur returned to assume command of his new brigade in January 1863. At Chancellorsville, Ramseur effectively threw his brigade into a growing gap in the line, and was later highly commended by his superiors. By the start of the Gettysburg campaign, Ramseur was feeling comfortable with his new brigade and his ability to command it.[85]

Although the smallest in the division, Ramseur's Brigade was given the honor of crossing the Potomac River before the other commands. This and other actions caused the men in the other brigades to sneer, "Be bound if there is any advantage given, Ramseur's Brigade will get it." Captain James Harris of the 30th North Carolina marveled at the number of towns so close to each other, and the number of children in them, causing him to remark, "I am glad I have them to fight this generation for I should be afraid to risk it the next." Arriving at Carlisle, Pennsylvania, on June 27, the men were quartered in the U.S. barracks. The men found whiskey and ice during their stay there, and mint juleps were the order of the day. Colonel Risden Bennett of the 14th North Carolina recalled that the men enjoyed their stay, "flirting with the dutch girls" and procuring supplies.[86]

The peace and serenity ended on June 30, when the troops were assembled and marched out of town. During the twenty-two-mile march to Heidlersburg, the troops encountered a number of Southern sympathizers who "treated us very nicely." During the final fourteen-mile march the next day, July 1, the brigade occupied the unusual position of rear guard, where it guarded the wagons. When about six miles from Gettysburg, the men began hearing the booming of the cannon. The pace quickened, sometimes to a double-quick. Various times are given for the brigade's arrival on Oak Hill.

The commander of the 2nd North Carolina reported 1:00 P.M., the 14th North Carolina's commander reported 2:00 P.M., and the 4th North Carolina's commander stated it was 4:00 P.M. The actual time was probably about 3:00 P.M.[87]

Ramseur's men were given a much-deserved rest when they arrived on Oak Hill. The reprieve was a short one, for one of Rodes's messengers galloped up with orders to enter the fray about fifteen minutes later. Prior to Ramseur's arrival, O'Neal's Brigade had been repulsed in its charge against the extreme right flank of the I Corps, and Iverson's Brigade was in the process of being destroyed. Rodes ordered Ramseur to split his brigade, ordering the 2nd North Carolina and 4th North Carolina to O'Neal's support and the 14th and 30th North Carolina to aid Iverson. Seeing that the action was probably going to be hotter in Iverson's sector, Ramseur personally led the 14th and 30th North Carolina forward mounted on a steel-gray horse. The men thought Ramseur looked magnificent.[88]

As Ramseur rushed his two regiments to Iverson's aid, he encountered Colonel Cullen Battle of the 3rd Alabama (O'Neal's Brigade). Probably concerned about the hot work that lay ahead of his small force, Ramseur could not resist asking the seemingly idle 3rd Alabama to join him. The request was "cheerfully" accepted, and the three regiments maneuvered into position. Around this time, Captain James Crowder, who commanded the 3rd Alabama's sharpshooters, strode up to Ramseur. Having watched Iverson's bloody repulse, Crowder saw that the way Ramseur was deploying the three regiments would lead to the same fate. Instead, he suggested that Ramseur move his troops to the left, where they could take on the I Corps's flank. This was the position that O'Neal was to hit, but the attack was made too far to the west, so it did not encounter the vulnerable Union flank. Ramseur agreed, and moved his troops down Mummasburg Road until they approached the Federal position, then cut across the fields in O'Neal's front. Wheeling to the left, Ramseur's men took their final positions. Adjutant Frederick Phillips of the 30th North Carolina proudly proclaimed that "Ramseur could handle troops under fire with more ease than any officer I ever knew."[89]

Ramseur's three regiments were now formed on O'Neal's left flank, perpendicular to the stone wall that had caused Iverson's men such grief. To their left they could see Doles's Brigade taking on the Federal XI Corps. Sitting astride his horse, Ramseur closely watched as his men marched past him to form line of battle. Many were still winded from their strenuous march. Pointing, Ramseur told them, "Boys, do you see that stone wall over yonder? Well, I want you to drive the Yankees from behind it, and then you can rest."[90]

Ramseur's two other regiments, the 2nd and 4th North Carolina, which were supposed to be sent to aid O'Neal's, were recalled by Rodes and ordered to defend Oak Hill against a possible attack. Realizing that the Union troops were not going to attack the hill, and instead seeing an enemy regiment marching to reinforce the sector that Ramseur and his other regiments were going to attack, Rodes released these two regiments and sent them back to their brigade.[91]

The 14th North Carolina formed the brigade's left flank, with the 30th North Carolina on its right. The two remaining regiments formed somewhat behind and to the right of their comrades. Colonel Bennett of the 14th North Carolina suggested that the entire brigade be shifted farther to the left to take advantage of the Federal flank dangling invitingly in the

air. Ramseur was, however, anxious to launch the charge and could not wait the additional time it would take to complete this maneuver.[92]

Captain James Harris of the 30th North Carolina recalled that Ramseur's line began its advance when within six hundred yards of the Federal line, but it was not visible until within three hundred yards. The advance was diagonal to the stone fence so that the left of the line was closest to the Federal line.[93]

Charging across the field, the troops came to a board fence. So many men mounted it at the same time that it collapsed, throwing some as far as ten feet. While Ramseur's men pressed forward, they were joined by O'Neal's Brigade and the 12th North Carolina (Iverson's Brigade). Against this formidable and coordinated force was Paul's Brigade (Robinson's Division, I Corps). Upon reaching Mummasburg Road, Ramseur's troops momentarily halted and fired volleys into the enemy. This allowed the 2nd and 4th North Carolina to come up on the right. Since the 14th North Carolina overlapped the Union right flank, Ramseur's men were able to get into the enemy's rear and throw volleys the enemy's front, flank, and rear. Other Confederate troops added their weight to the attack. General Ramseur's horse was killed within a few yards of the stone fence that protected the Union troops. No troops could long withstand this fire, and soon Paul's men were withdrawing toward the unfinished railroad cut to the south.[94]

Describing the charge in his official report, Rodes wrote that Ramseur's Brigade was "ordered forward, and was hurled by its commander with the skill and gallantry for which he is always conspicuous, and with irresistible force, upon the enemy just where he had repulsed O'Neal and checked Iverson's advance."[95]

Although winded from their charge, Ramseur's men stormed after the fleeing enemy troops. William Smith of the 14th North Carolina recalled that the enemy withdrawal was not panic-stricken, "but in one heroic stand after another till we drove them back a mile and a half to the town of Gettysburg." After a short time, the men could see Daniel's Brigade coming up on their right, boxing in the Federal troops. Hundreds of prisoners were scooped up. Many Federal soldiers saw that the only hope of reaching safety was along the unfinished railroad cut. Ramseur's troops began yelling, "Bring us a battery! Bring us a battery!" and in response, the general turned to an aide and snapped, "D___it, tell them to send me a battery! I have sent for one a half dozen times." One soon arrived and began throwing shells at the retreating enemy troops. Concentrated in the cut, the enemy's losses were horrendous. Colonel Bennett of the 14th North Carolina recalled that one could "almost hear their bones crunch under the shot and shell."[96]

Several of Ramseur's men remarked after the battle that they could have captured far more prisoners had they not been so exhausted by their march to the battlefield. Several claimed to have been the first troops to enter Gettysburg, where they captured many more Federal soldiers. Lieutenant F. Harney of the 14th North Carolina captured the flag of the 150th Pennsylvania during the chaos. The brigade, which was disorganized as it entered the town, became even more so while rounding up prisoners. This, coupled with the heat and the men's exhaustion, caused most of them to welcome the orders to halt and reform their ranks along Middle Street.[97]

Even before the battle ended, many men rued the decision not to storm Cemetery Hill when it was most vulnera-ble. Colonel Bryan Grimes of the 4th North Carolina recalled after the war,

The enemy were routed and retreating in great confusion. General Ramseur, with my regiment in advance, was rushing up and following the enemy, and, without the slightest doubt in my mind, could have captured these guns and occupied the hill, but a officer of rank rode up and advised that we await re-enforcements, which was done, and we were drawn back to the main street of Gettysburg, and there remained, without firing a shot the whole of the evening—several hours of daylight.[98]

A controversial event occurred that evening, when Ramseur rode over to Seminary Ridge to ask artillery chief William Pendleton not to shell Cemetery Hill, for fear that some of his own troops would be hit.[99]

The men rested quietly that night, although it appears that many may have visited private homes. Lieutenant William Calder of the 2nd North Carolina wrote home that the "town afforded us any quantity of butter and preserves of all kinds on which we supped most sumptuously." Calder noted that this was the first anniversary of the bloody battle of Malvern Hill, where so many young Confederate soldiers had been needlessly slaughtered. How different the present day had been, he thought.[100]

The morning of July 2 dawned bright and promised to be another hot one. Quiet reigned all through the morning, except for an occasional shot from a picket or sniper. At about 4:00 P.M., the men could see Longstreet's attack launched against the Union left flank. Without orders to advance, the men thought they would be spared from additional fighting. As the sun set, the men received orders to reform, and they marched about five hundred yards to the right, stopping in a large wheatfield. Seeing this movement, the Federal artillery on Cemetery Hill opened fire, but most of the shells flew harmlessly over the men's heads. It was here that the men were told that they would finally be given an opportunity to storm Cemetery Hill.[101]

Ramseur had been informed that the other brigades of the division "would be governed by my movements." As Ramseur watched his men pass him, he remarked, "Boys, I want you to take off your canteens and haversacks and leave them in a pile right here. We've got to take those breastworks up yonder, and we don't want any noise. Take nothing but your cartridge-boxes and guns. The Yankees have got a strong picket-line and if they shoot don't return the fire, but keep advancing until you've driven them back into the works. 'North Carolina to the rescue!' will be the watch-word."[102]

The men were exceptionally nervous. They knew that the enemy had had over twenty-four hours to reinforce the hill, and the continual sounds of axes and shovels told the men that the enemy had made the most of this reprieve. Private Hufham of the 30th North Carolina recalled that he could feel his "heart rise in my throat, for I didn't like the idea of getting my life snatched out there in the dark."[103]

As the brigade moved silently forward, many men were as worried about Daniel's Brigade in their rear as much as the enemy in their front. Yesterday's battle had been the first for Daniel's men, and as Captain James Harris of the 30th North Carolina wrote home, "you know how much men become excited under fire in the day, much less in the night." Phillips of the same regiment recalled that the "rattle of musketry and the flash of artillery was terrible." When within two hundred yards of the Union position, Ramseur ordered his men to lie down. Colonel R. Tyler Bennett recalled it was "so near were we that you could almost hear the movements of the enemy's men as they moved about with as little noise as possible."[104]

Ramseur had an opportunity to scrutinize the Federal position during this time. He did not like what he saw. "Batteries were discovered in position to pour upon our lines direct, cross, and enfilade fires. Two lines of infantry behind stone walls and breastworks were supporting these batteries." After conferring with General Doles, Ramseur decided to send this information to Rodes and await further orders. The orders were soon in coming—"retire quietly to a deep road some 300 yards in rear, and be in readiness to attack at daylight." The men were immensely relieved when ordered to withdraw. "It was well for us that we did for in the confusion of the darkness we would have lost nearly every man and gained nothing," wrote Calder to his mother.[105]

This decision has been questioned ever since that night. Unbeknownst to Ramseur, two of Early's Brigades had captured the summit of Cemetery Hill and held it for several minutes. During this time they waited forlornly for the support expected from Rodes's Division—support that never materialized. According to his report, Rodes already knew that Early's attack had been repulsed by the time his division approached the hill. No one will ever know whether the attack could have been successful if the troops had pressed on.[106]

When the sun rose on July 3, the men could see the vulnerability of their position along Long Lane, between Iverson's Brigade on their left and Perrin's on their right, as they were closer to the Union line than to their own. "So the only thing to be done, and which was done with amazing rapidity, was for the men to bury themselves in this farm road, using as implements of excavation, pocket knives, bayonets, tin cups and everything else at command," wrote Phillips (30th North Carolina). A fence in front of the 14th North Carolina was hastily pulled down and the rails piled up to form a barricade. These efforts paid off, as Federal snipers soon opened on the Confederate line. Enemy bullets quickly hit those foolish enough to stand, like Colonel Bennett of the 14th North Carolina.[107]

That afternoon, the men witnessed the tremendous cannonade that preceded the Pickett–Pettigrew–Trimble charge. Unfortunately, several Confederate shells fell among Ramseur's men, killing or wounding seven. Ramseur reported that this was the result of "careless use [of the guns] or imperfect ammunition." They later witnessed the great charge. That night, Ramseur's men, and the rest of Rodes's Division, were pulled back to Seminary Ridge. The retreat back to Virginia commenced during the early morning hours of July 5.[108]

After a brilliant first day, Ramseur's Brigade was essentially relegated to bystander status during the two remaining days of the battle. Questionable decisions by Ramseur on the evening of July 1 and July 2 unfortunately clouded his brigade's magnificent performance, when it was instrumental in rolling up the Federal I Corps's right flank during the afternoon of July 1.

O'Neal's Brigade—Colonel Edward O'Neal

Units: 3rd Alabama, 5th Alabama, 6th Alabama, 12th Alabama, 26th Alabama
Strength: 1688
Losses: 696 (90-422-184)—41%[109]

The 5th and 6th Alabama had the distinction of being present at the first battle of Manassas (in Ewell's Brigade), although they were not engaged. By the beginning of the Peninsula campaign, these two regiments, plus the 12th Alabama, were in Rodes's Brigade, the 3rd Alabama was in Mahone's Brigade, and the 26th Alabama was in Rains's Brigade. Rodes's Brigade distinguished itself at the battle of Seven Pines, but suffered exceptionally high casualties. By the beginning of the Seven Days battles, all five regiments were together in Rodes's Brigade. Because Rodes was wounded at Seven Pines, Colonel John Gordon of the 6th Alabama commanded the brigade with distinction at Gaines's Mill and Malvern Hill. Rodes returned to the brigade during the Mary-land campaign and it fought tenaciously at Turner's Gap in the South Mountain and then a few days later along the Sunken Road at the battle of Sharpsburg. The next battle for the brigade was Chancellorsville, where Rodes commanded D. H. Hill's Division and Colonel Edward O'Neal commanded the Alabama brigade. The brigade did well under the watchful eye of its permanent commander.[110]

With the elevation of Rodes to permanent division command, O'Neal was given the brigade. O'Neal didn't know it, but Robert E. Lee carried his brigadier general's commission, dated June 6, 1863, in his pocket as he rode to Gettysburg. Although many of his superiors, including General Rodes did not want him, well-connected friends lobbied to get O'Neal Rodes's old brigade and hopefully, his general's star.[111]

Several of O'Neal's men commented about the "good times" they had during the march. "We had plenty to eat and drink, and if an old soldier is ever happy it is when grub is plentiful and not fighting," wrote Private James Thompson of the 12th Alabama. The men marveled at the bounty around them. Thompson commented on the "finest fields of wheat just ready for the harvest . . . but the advent of the terrible Rebels had caused the reapers to stop." The scarcity of fresh fruit, except for cherries, disappointed him, however. The march north was made at a somewhat leisurely pace, and occasionally an officer could be seen asleep on his horse by the side of the road.[112]

A few of the men had relatives in Carlisle, which posed a dilemma when they stopped at this small city, as some were tempted to shuck army life and remain behind with their families. Most couldn't make up their minds, so they rejoined the column as it left the city. The nineteen-mile June 30 march was especially hard on the men, as periods of rain made the road muddy and slippery.[113]

The march toward Gettysburg began again at about 6:30 A.M. on July 1. After marching about seven miles, the men could hear the sound of cannon fire. "This sullen sound was soon followed by others more distinctly . . . the deadly vollies [sic] of infantry could be distinctly heard," recalled Thompson. They halted and formed into line of battle when about two miles north of the town. The brigade occupied a position between Iverson's Brigade on its right and Doles's Brigade on its left. Realizing the importance of Oak Hill, Rodes ordered his division to perform a right wheel movement. This 1.5-mile movement was particularly difficult for the 5th Alabama, the left regiment of the brigade, as it was forced to move more rapidly than the other units because it was farthest from the pivot point. Colonel J. Hall wrote in his official report that the men often moved at a run

through very rough ground. "In places the regiment moved through full-grown wheat, in others over plowed ground, through orchards, gardens, over wood and stone fences, which with the rapidity of the movement, fatigued the men, causing many of them to faint from their exhaustion." Corporal Samuel Pickens (5th Alabama) commented in his diary that "I was perfectly exhausted & never suffered so from heat & fatigue in my life. A good many fell out of ranks being completely broken down & some fainted."[114]

The men were grateful when this movement ended and they could rest. Some still had enough life in them to watch the artillery duel between their batteries stationed about 150 yards in front of them and an enemy battery (probably Dilger's) over to their left. Artillery rounds soon found their way to the resting Alabamians, killing and wounding a number of them and forcing Rodes to pull the brigade back under cover.[115]

Rodes planned to unleash a three-brigade attack against Robinson's Division, which formed the right flank of the I Corps. While O'Neal's Brigade attacked down the east slope of Oak Hill, Iverson's North Carolinians were to attack on its right, followed *en echelon,* by Daniel's Brigade. O'Neal's Brigade was deployed from left to right as 5th Alabama–6th Alabama–26th Alabama–12th Alabama–3rd Alabama. Worried about the gap between Doles's Brigade on the left and the remainder of the division, Rodes detached the 5th Alabama and ordered a battalion of its sharpshooters under Eugene Blackford to move to the left. Rodes was not confident about O'Neal's ability to implement his orders, so to ensure coordination with the other attacking units, he ordered the 3rd Alabama on the right to connect with the left of Daniel's Brigade. Rodes reported that "for reasons explained to Colonel O'Neal, the Third having been permitted by Colonel O'Neal to move with Daniel's Brigade." O'Neal professed that he did not know this, writing in his report that the "Third Alabama . . . was ordered by General Rodes to connect with the brigade of General Daniel . . . General Rodes said he would command in person, so I only moved forward with the Twelfth, Twenty-sixth, and Sixth Alabama Regiments. Why my brigade was thus deprived of two regiments, I have never been informed." A more experienced brigade commander would have probably taken charge of the 3rd Alabama as well. Thus, O'Neal moved forward with only a thousand of his 1700 men.[116]

Confident of a decisive victory, Rodes ordered his three brigades forward at about 2:15 P.M. At the same time, Rodes precisely told O'Neal the point he was to attack. According to Rodes, "the Alabama brigade went into action in some confusion, and with only three of its regiments . . . the three . . . regiments moved forward with alacrity (but not in accordance with my orders as to direction) and in confusion into the action." For some reason, O'Neal's three regiments began their attack before Iverson's, and therefore advanced alone. Seeing their advance, General Henry Baxter of Robinson's Division shifted the 88th Pennsylvania, 12th Massachusetts, and 90th Pennsylvania of his brigade to the north to face the Alabamians as they approached Mummasburg Road.[117]

Three attacking regiments against an equal number of strongly posted defenders does not bode well for success. A soldier from the 88th Pennsylvania vividly recalled the charge. "Their line of battle, covered by a cloud of busy skirmishers, came driving through the woods from the right of the Mummasburg Road. Waiting until they were in easy range, the order

was given, 'Commence firing.' With the sharp crack of the muskets a fleecy cloud of smoke rolled down the front of the brigade [Baxter's] and the Minie balls zipped and buzzed with a merry chorus toward the Southern line, which halted, and after a brief contest, retired to the shelter of the woods." Few Confederate soldiers left descriptions of this attack. Captain Robert Park recalled that many of the troops lay down. All the while "balls were falling thick and fast around us, and whizzing past and often striking someone near." Corporal Pickens (5th Alabama) reported that "we attacked them in a strong position. After a desperate fight of about fifteen minutes, we were compelled to fall back, as the regiments on our left gave way, being flanked by a large force." This force was the 45th New York (von Amberg's Brigade, Schimmelfennig's Division, XI Corps), which poured an enfilating fire into the 6th Alabama, while the 90th Pennsylvania threw volleys into their front. Compounding the problem, Dilger's battery poured canister into O'Neal's left flank. Unable to resist this musket fire from two sides, the regiment was forced to fall back, causing a chain reaction with the other regiments on its right. Captain Francis Irsch of the 45th New York recalled that as a result of his regiment's fire, the Alabamians "began to break and run up the slope of Oak Hill." The sympathetic historian of the 88th Pennsylvania recalled that O'Neal's men had many difficulties to overcome. "Marching over the hill, through the brush, over fences and rocks, and being in the advance, he came in collision with Baxter before Iverson was up."[118]

Rodes closely watched O'Neal's advance and, when he saw that "we were making no impression upon the enemy," rode forward to find Colonel Hall of the 5th Alabama to order him forward to form on the left of the 6th Alabama. When he arrived, Rodes was surprised to see that "Colonel O'Neal, instead of personally superintending the movements of his brigade, had chosen to remain with his reserve regiment. The result was that the whole brigade . . . was repulsed quickly, and with loss." O'Neal's rather lame explanation was that just as the attack was ordered, he realized that he and his staff did not have horses and were therefore forced to remain behind.[119]

As the 5th Alabama rushed forward, its commander could see the enemy line composed of "two heavy lines of infantry in front and a line of sharpshooters, supported by infantry and artillery, on my left flank." After the regiment passed the McLean farmhouse, Colonel Hall responded by sending his right companies forward toward Mummasburg Road, while refusing his left flank at right angles to handle the threat on his left. Major Albert Van de Graaff reported that his unit came within fifty yards of the Federal line. However, learning that the regiments on his right were pulling back, Hall did the same, bitterly remarking in his report that "my command was under a front and enfilading fire, with no support, and suffering a very severe loss."[120]

The addition of the fourth regiment to the attacking line made little difference to the outcome. One of the reasons for the defeat was that O'Neal had not extended his line far enough to the east. If he had, he would have taken on Baxter's regiments from the front and flank, quite possibly with different results. Rodes apparently had this in mind when he ordered the attack, but O'Neal blundered. The brigade sustained heavy casualties in this ill-fated charge, and many men were captured. Lieutenant Colonel John Goodgame of the 12th Alabama stated that forty of his men were lost in this fash-

ion, explaining in his report that "every man could have escaped being captured had they done their duty. In all, the attack lasted but 15 minutes."[121]

The shattered regiments formed about three hundred yards in the rear. Most of the men simply lay down to rest and to avoid the heavy small arms fire being directed at them. Pickens (5th Alabama), who had been detached from his regiment, now returned and remarked in his diary that "I never saw troops so scattered & in such confusion . . .the Brig. was rallied by Col. O'Neal & Genl Rodes." The men were assembled after about half an hour, and ordered to attack the Federal line again, this time in concert with Ramseur's Brigade. Rodes commented in his report that "O'Neal's shattered troops, which had assembled without order on the hill, rushed forward, still without order, but with all their usual courage, into the charge." The results were quite different, as Baxter's replacement, Paul's Brigade, was unable to hold the exposed position for very long in the face of overwhelming numbers of Confederate troops.[122]

Just to the south, Daniel's Brigade was prepared to support Iverson's, with O'Neal's 3rd Alabama on its right. Because changes in Daniel's Brigade position would take the 3rd Alabama farther south and away from the rest of O'Neal's Brigade, Colonel Cullen Battle asked General Daniel for orders. "He had no orders for me, and [said] that I must act on my own responsibility," reported Battle. Seeing Rameur's Brigade arriving, Battle rode up to its commander "and offered him my regiment. The offer was accepted, and my command acted under this gallant officer in a charge which drove the enemy from one of his strongholds." In his report, Ramseur told a slightly different version of the story, saying that *he* asked Battle to join his command. Ramseur reported that

Battle "rendered brilliant and invaluable service . . . he came in at the right place, at the right time, and in the right way." Captain William May of the 3rd Alabama recalled that the enemy "became demoralized and disorganized, doubling up and making poor resistance." Seeing the remainder of O'Neal's Brigade moving toward Gettyburg, Battle bid farewell to Ramseur and rejoined his fellow Alabamians with his regiment.[123]

Driving southward, the brigade approached the unfinished railroad cut, where it again encountered units from Paul's Brigade and captured many enemy soldiers. Members of the 3rd Alabama claimed that they were the first Confederate troops to enter the town. Perhaps to cover his ineptitude, O'Neal inaccurately reported that his brigade was "in the act of charging the hill [Cemetery Hill], when I was recalled, and ordered to form my brigade beyond the railroad." The men rested on northern edge of Gettysburg. They remained there through July 2, with Daniel's Brigade on their right. They were exposed to severe shelling from the guns on the heights from time to time, but sustained few casualties because of the protection provided by the embankment.[124]

While the remainder of the brigade engaged units of the I Corps on July 1, Major Blackford's sharpshooters of the 5th Alabama were dispersed along a broad front. Before them were dismounted cavalry from Devin's Brigade (Buford's Division). Moving southward, Blackford's men drove the cavalrymen before them. When about half a mile from Gettysburg, they came up against Devin's main body, and were attacked twice, beating off both of them. The XI Corps began arriving after about an hour of skirmishing. Except for Doles's Brigade, Blackford's sharpshooters was the only unit in the sector, and its line was stretched exceptionally thinly. The right company of Blackford's line skirmished with von Amsberg's Brigade, and, according to Blackford, "annoyed these very much, holding their position steadily until our infantry came up." Blackford's center company faced a double line of sharpshooters, which they charged, forcing them back toward the town. The left company faced Barlow's Division, which was intent on claiming Blocher's Knoll. Advancing in three lines, the Federal troops were met by Blackford's sharpshooters, who fired at them from behind trees. As they slowly fell back, the Alabamians were relieved to see Gordon's Brigade (Early's Division, Second Corps) arriving to take on the Federal infantry. A bugle call assembled the troops in the center of the line, and the small unit marched south along Carlisle Road to the town. It was not until after dark that the Blackford's men reunited with the rest of the brigade.[125]

After nightfall on July 2, O'Neal received orders to advance in preparation for an assault on Cemetery Hill. After moving a short distance, the column halted in a wheatfield and were ordered to lie down. Rodes, however, decided not to risk an attack on the highly fortified heights that night. At about 2:00 A.M., Rodes ordered General Daniel to take his brigade and O'Neal's to the left to support Johnson's planned attack on Culp's Hill. Rodes's frustration had probably reached the point where he felt O'Neal needed to be directed at all times. Since the movement in the dark was a difficult endeavor, Rodes decided to entrust both brigades to Daniel. The 5th Alabama was left behind, where it was attached to Doles's Brigade to help bolster its position.[126]

The brigade arrived in position at the base of Culp's Hill at about sunrise and took position behind Nicholls's Brigade. O'Neal was informed that he would receive orders directly from General Johnson. While waiting, the men came under severe artillery and small arms fire. They were almost relieved when at 8:00 A.M. they were told that they would charge the enemy works in front of them. An officer from Nicholls's Brigade was not pleased to see O'Neal's Brigade arriving. The Alabamians approached with a yell, he said, which served "no other purpose but to intensify a galling fire in our front." Soldiers fell by the score. "The troops coming to our relief were much more exposed to the enemy's fire than ourselves, as we were so close to their line that they would fire over us . . . we regretted that we were being relieved." O'Neal reported that the "brigade moved forward in fine style, under a terrific fire of grape and small-arms, and gained a hill near the enemy's works, which it held for three hours, exposed to a murderous fire." The key word here is "near," as there is no evidence that O'Neal's men were successful in forcing the Federal infantry from their strong breastworks. Captain May (3rd Alabama) called this action a "hopeless undertaking" that accomplished little except to lose many men. He recalled reaching a position in advance of the others, and looking back "at our poor fellows and see[ing] them shot down one after another." An enlisted man wrote home soon after the battle that "I thought I had been in hot places before—I thought I had heard Minnie balls; but that day [July 3] capped the climax. All day long it was one continuous roar."[127]

For three long hours, the men clung to the side of Culp's Hill. Some were so exhausted that they fell asleep, despite the din and danger around them. They finally received orders to retire at about 11:00 A.M., and the survivors sprinted down the hill, where they remained until midnight, mostly under artillery and small arms fire. The brigade now marched to a position north of the town, where it rejoined the remainder of the division.[128]

While most of the brigade's units were being sacrificed on Culp's Hill, the members of the 5th Alabama were dodging shells and minié balls along Long Lane with Dole's Brigade. There was no shade and the sun shone brightly. To make matters worse, some of the Confederate shells fell among Doles's men beside them. In this position, they watched the repulse of Trimble 's and Pettigrew's Divisions on July 3. Blackford's sharpshooters were a bit more active during this period. Before daybreak on July 3, they took position in houses at the base of Cemetery Hill and opened fire on the Union gunners. Blackford proudly wrote in his report that the "the Northern papers confess that their gunners could not stand to their guns, and that the officers were picked off by rebel sharpshooters. One battery near us, after firing several shots at us, was removed out of our sight."[129]

July 4 found the division on Seminary Ridge, not far from were it had fought on July 1. "There were a good many of the enemy's dead & dead horses lying back of our position which produced a most disagreeable smell," wrote Pickens. The men entrenched while there. The retreat toward Hagerstown began at about 1:00 A.M. on July 5. This march was particularly disagreeable because the heavy rains had made the road exceptionally slippery.[130]

Robert Rodes's old brigade did not fare well at Gettysburg. If handled properly by O'Neal, Robinson's Division could have been swept off of Oak Hill before 3:00 P.M. Instead, the brigade suffered a bloody repulse. Its hasty demise had a direct influence on the disaster that befell Iverson's Brigade a few minutes later. An eminent historian wrote that "even misdirected and under-strength as it was, the Alabama brigade's attack would have served to ease Iverson's plight had it been pressed with ordinary tenacity." The situation was not much better on July 3, when the brigade had virtually no chance of taking the Federal breastworks crowning the summit of Culp's Hill. O'Neal was punished for his ineptitude by losing his brigade, and his commission to the rank of brigadier general was revoked. He left the army before the end of the year, a bitter man.[131]

O'Neal's men experienced even more frustration before the campaign ended. Enemy cavalry captured the brigade's supply train, taking among other things $11,235 in a money chest that was earmarked for paying and feeding them.[132]

NOTES

1. Davis, *The Confederate General*, vol. V, 107.

2. OR 27, 2, 550–552.

3. OR 27, 2, 551–552; C. D. Grace, "Rodes's Division at Gettysburg," in *Confederate Veteran* (1897), vol. 5, 614.

4. OR 27, 2, 552; Grace, "Rodes's Division at Gettysburg," 614.

5. OR 27, 2, 552; Grace, "Rodes's Division at Gettysburg," 614; Tagg, *Generals at Gettysburg*, 285.

6. OR 27, 2, 552–553.

7. OR 27, 2, 553.

8. OR 27, 2, 555–556; Tagg, *Generals at Gettysburg*, 286.

9. OR 27, 2, 556–557.

10. Busey and Martin, *Regimental Strengths and Losses*, 164, 288.

11. Sifakis, *Compendium of the Confederate Armies: North Carolina*, 130, 141–142, 144; Davis, *The Confederate General*, vol. II, 46–47.

12. Davis, *The Confederate General*, vol. II, 46–47.

13. Clark, *N. C. Regiments*, vol. 2, 525–526; A. T. Marsh, "North Carolina Troops at Gettysburg," in *Confederate Veteran* (1908), vol. 16, 516.

14. Louis Leon, *Diary of a Tar Heel* (Charlotte, NC, 1913); 33; diary of William Beavans, copy in USAMHI, Clark, *N.C. Regiments*, vol. 4, 255.

15. Leon, *Diary of a Tar Heel*, 34; William Beavans diary; "43rd North Carolina in the War," copy in 43rd North Carolina folder, GNMP.

16. OR 27, 2, 566, 574; Clark, *N.C. Regiments*, vol. 4, 255.

17. OR 27, 2, 573.

18. OR 27, 2, 576; Martin, *Gettysburg, July 1*, 239–240. Martin suggested that the 53rd North Carolina was sent to the aid of the beleaguered Iverson. However, there is no confirmation of this in Rodes's report, and Daniel wrote in his report that his left was to maintain contact with Iverson's right. A strange interpretation of the 53rd North Carolina's movement was given by the regiment's historian, who wrote that the unit was "dropped out of line" and forced to remain exposed to enemy fire because there was not enough room for all of the regiments on the field (Clark, *N.C. Regiments*, vol. 3, 256).

19. OR 27, 1, 330; OR 27, 2, 566; James Stewart, "Battery B, Fourth United States Artillery at Gettysburg," in *Ohio MOLLUS*, vol. 4, 185; OR 27, 1, 332.

20. Scott Hartwig, "The Defense of McPherson's Ridge," *Gettysburg Magazine* (July 1989), issue 1, 20; Clark, *N.C. Regiments*, vol. 4, 255–256.

21. Hartwig, "The Defense of McPherson's Ridge," 21; "Chronicles of Francis Bacon Jones," copy in Brake Collection, USAMHI.

22. Martin, *Gettysburg, July 1*, 145–146.

23. OR 27, 2, 567; Hartwig, "The Defense of McPherson's Ridge," 21.

24. OR 27, 2, 575, 577, 578; Martin, *Gettysburg, July 1*, 389, 432–433.

25. Manly W. Wellman, *Rebel Boast* (New York, 1956), 125–126, 238; James E. Green, diary, copy at USAMHI.

26. OR 27, 2, 567, 568, 572, 573, 575; Marsh, "North Carolina Troops at Gettysburg," 517; Green, diary.

27. OR 27, 2, 568, 575.

28. OR 27, 2, 568, 572.

29. OR 27, 2, 568; "Thirty-Second Reg't Troops at the late Battles of Gettysburg," copy in 32nd North Carolina folder, GNMP; Marsh, "North Carolina Troops at Gettysburg," 517.

30. McKim, "Steuart's Brigade at the Battle of Gettysburg," 297; Pfanz, *Gettysburg—Culp's Hill and Cemetery Hill*, 311.

31. OR 27, 2, 573–574, 578

32. OR 27, 2, 568, 575.

33. Green, diary; Leon, *Diary of a Tar Heel*, 36.

34. OR 27, 2, 569, 570.

There are a number of different recollections of the time Daniel's men were pulled off the hill. Daniel infers it was around noon (OR 27, 2, 569), Lieutenant Colonel Lewis of the 43rd North Carolina reported that it was at 2:00 P.M. (OR 27, 2, 574), and Colonel Brabble of the 32nd North Carolina stated that it was at 5:00 P.M. (OR 27, 2, 572).

35. Busey and Martin, *Regimental Strengths and Losses*, 283, 288, 290.

36. Busey and Martin, *Regimental Strengths and Losses*, 167, 289.

37. Sifakis, *Compendium of the Confederate Armies: South Carolina and Georgia*, 188–189, 208–209, 224–225, 256–257.

38. Davis, *The Confederate General*, vol. II, 72–73.

39. Grace, "Rodes's Division at Gettysburg," 614.

40. OR 27, 2, 552–523.

41. OR 27, 2, 584; Hartwig, "The Defense of McPherson's Ridge," 37–38; Grace, "Rodes's Division at Gettysburg," 614.

42. OR 27, 2, 581–582; Henry W. Thomas, *History of the Doles-Cook Brigade, Army of Northern Virginia* (Atlanta, GA, 1903), 73.

43. Early, *Autobiographical Sketch and Narrative of the War Between the States*, 267; OR 27, 2, 554.

44. Thomas, *History of the Doles-Cook Brigade, Army of Northern Virginia*, 7–8; R. W. Tanner, "Reminiscences of the War Between the States," GNMP Library; OR 27, 2, 584, 586.

45. OR 27, 2, 584–585; Theodore A. Dodge, "Left Wounded on the Field," *Putnam's Monthly Magazine* (1869), vol. 4, 320–321.

46. OR 27, 2, 585; OR 27, 1, 745; Alfred E. Lee, "Reminiscences of the Gettysburg Battle," *Lippincott's Magazine of Popular Literature and Science* (July 1883), 56.

47. Lee, "Reminiscences of the Gettysburg Battle," 56; Dodge, "Left Wounded on the Field," 321.

48. Grace, "Rodes's Division at Gettysburg," 614.

49. Martin, *Gettysburg—July 1*, 301–302.

50. John Applegate, *Reminiscences and Letters of George Arrowsmith of New Jersey* (Red Bank, NJ, 1893), 214–215; OR 27, 2, 584–585; Thomas, *History of the Doles-Cook Brigade, Army of Northern Virginia*, 475–476; Sidney Jackson Richardson, letter, Georgia Department of Archives and Records, copy in 21st Georgia folder, GNMP.

According to one Confederate soldier, because Doles was without a horse and all of the field-officers were to the left of the brigade, no one knew who gave the order to "by the right flank." The order was nevertheless obeyed (Grace, "Rodes's Division at Gettysburg," 615).

51. OR 27, 2, 554; Richardson, letter.

52. Grace, "Rodes's Division at Gettysburg," 614; Martin, *Gettysburg—July 1*, 390–391; S. G. Pryor, *A Post of Honor: The Pryor Letters* (Fort Valley, GA, 1989), 374; OR 27, 2, 582, 585.

53. OR 27, 2, 582, 585; Thomas, *History of the Doles-Cook Brigade, Army of Northern Virginia*, 8–10; Pfanz, *Gettysburg—Culp's Hill and Cemetery Hill*, 278.

54. OR 27, 2, 582; Pfanz, *Gettysburg—Culp's Hill and Cemetery Hill*, 280–281.

55. Thomas, *History of the Doles-Cook Brigade, Army of Northern Virginia*, 476; OR 27, 2, 582. "Report of Colonel Edward Willis, Twelfth Georgia Infantry, Doles' Brigade," in *Southern Historical Society Papers* (1889), vol. 17, 185; Pryor, *A Post of Honor: The Pryor Letters*, 375.

56. OR 27, 2, 583.

57. Busey and Martin, *Regimental Strengths and Losses*, 253, 254, 255, 289.

58. Pryor, *A Post of Honor: The Pryor Letters*, 378.

59. Busey and Martin, *Regimental Strengths and Losses*, 165, 288.

60. Sifakis, *Compendium of the Confederate Armies: North Carolina*, 89, 99–100, 112, 117–118; Davis, *The Confederate General*, vol. II, 165–166; vol. III, 142–143.

61. OR 27, 2, 551; Robert K. Krick, "Three Confederate Disasters on Oak Hill," in Gary Gallagher, ed., *The First Day at Gettysburg* (Kent, OH, 1992), 131.

62. Clark, *N.C. Regiments*, vol. 2, 233; Charles Blacknall, "Memoir," Brake Collection, USAMHI.

63. Blacknall, "Memoir"; OR 27, 2, 552.

64. Blacknall, "Memoir."

65. OR 27, 2, 553, 579.

66. Martin, *Gettysburg—July 1*, 226.

67. John Vautier, "At Gettysburg," *Philadelphia Weekly Press*, November 10, 1886; Thomas L. Elmore, "Attack and Counterattack," *Gettysburg Magazine* (July 1991), issue 5, 128.

68. Blacknall, "Memoir"; Clark, *N.C. Regiments*, vol. 2, 239; Krick, "Three Confederate Disasters on Oak Hill," 131–132; Harry Pfanz *Gettysburg—The First Day* (Chapel Hill, NC), 177–178.

69. Clark, *N.C. Regiments*, vol. 1, 635; George W. Grant, "The First Army Corps at Gettysburg," in *Minnesota MOLLUS*, vol. 5, 49.

70. Vautier, "At Gettysburg."

71. Vautier, "At Gettysburg"; John D. Vautier, *History of the Eighty-Eighth Pennsylvania in the War for the Union* (Philadelphia, 1884), 135; Blacknall, "Memoir."

72. Henry R. Berkeley, *Four Years in the Confederate Artillery* (Richmond, VA, 1991), 50.

73. Vautier, "At Gettysburg"; Grant, "The First Army Corps at Gettysburg," 50; Blacknall, "Memoir"; Clark, *N.C. Regiments*, vol. 2, 236.

74. Blacknall, "Memoir"; Hicks, "Memoirs."

75. Hicks, "Memoirs."

76. Grant, "The First Army Corps at Gettysburg," 51; Samuel Boone, "Personal Experiences," USAMHI.

77. OR 27, 2, 579; Clark, *N.C. Regiments*, vol. 2, 238.

78. Clark, *N.C. Regiments*, vol. 1, 637–638; OR 27, 2, 579. Iverson intimated that he played a role in the activities of the 12th North Carolina, but there is little evidence to support his claim.

79. Don P. Halsey, Jr., *A Sketch of the Life of Capt. Don P. Halsey of the Confederate States Army* (Richmond, VA, 1904), 10–12; Clark, *N.C. Regiments*, vol. 1, 636.

80. Clark, *N.C. Regiments*, vol. 2, 235, 239; OR 27, 2, 554; E. Faison Hicks, "My War Reminiscences," USAMHI.

81. Busey and Martin, *Regimental Strengths and Losses*, 283, 288.

82. Krick, "Three Confederate Disasters on Oak Ridge;" 136; OR 27, 3, 1025.

83. Busey and Martin, *Regimental Strengths and Losses*, 168, 289.

84. Sifakis, *Compendium of the Confederate Armies: North Carolina*, 83–84, 87–88, 103–104; Davis, *The Confederate General*, vol. I, 19.

85. Davis, *The Confederate General*, vol. V, 74–75; OR 21, 541.

86. Michael W. Taylor, "Ramseur's Brigade in the Gettysburg Campaign . . . ," *Gettysburg Magazine* (July 1997), issue 17, 29, 31; J. D., Hufham, Jr. "Gettysburg," *The Wake Forest Student* (1897), vol. 16, 452; Colonel Risden T. Bennett, "Memoir," 14th North Carolina folder, GNMP.

87. Bennett, "Memoir"; Taylor, "Ramseur's Brigade in the Gettysburg Campaign . . . ," 31; OR 27, 2, 589, 590.

88. OR 27, 2, 587.

89. OR 27, 2, 587; Bennett, "Memoir"; John J. McClendon, "Memoir," copy in 14th North Carolina folder, GNMP; Frederick Phillips, letter, N.C. State Archive, copy in 30th North Carolina folder, GNMP.

90. Phllips, letter; Hufham, "Gettysburg," 454.

While the Bachelder maps show Ramseur's position to be to the right of O'Neal's Brigade, historian Michael Taylor convincingly showed that the unit actually formed on the opposite side of the Alabamians (Taylor, "Ramseur's Brigade in the Gettysburg Campaign . . . ," 31–34).

91. OR 27, 2, 589.

This was probably the 16th Maine of Paul's Brigade.

92. Taylor, "Ramseur's Brigade in the Gettysburg Campaign. . . ." 30; R. T. Bennett, letter, copy in 14th North Carolina folder, GNMP.

93. Taylor, "Ramseur's Brigade in the Gettysburg Campaign . . . ," 31.

94. Clark, *N.C. Regiments*, vol. 1, 719; Hufham, "Gettysburg," 454–455; Phillips, letter; T. M. Gorman, in *Pierce's Memorandum Account Book Designed for Farmers, Mechanics, and All People*, typescript in 2nd North Carolina folder, GNMP; Phillips, letter.

95. OR 27, 2, 554.

96. W. A. Smith, *The Anson Guards, Company C, Fourteenth Regiment, North Carolina Volunteers, 1861–1865* (Charlotte, NC, 1914), 207; Hufham, "Gettysburg," 455–456; Clark, *N.C. Regiments*, vol. 1, 719.

In his memoirs, Colonel Bennett of the 14th North Carolina described how some of the Federal troops who had already surrendered and were seeking refuge in the railroad cut were unintentionally killed by the gunfire from Daniel's Brigade.

97. Taylor, "Ramseur's Brigade in the Gettysburg Campaign . . . ," 34; McClendon, "Memoir"; William Calder, letter, copy in Brake Collection, USAMHI; Bennett, "Memoir"; Clark, *N.C. Regiments*, vol. 1, 719.

Rodes claimed that Doles's Brigade entered the "heart" of the town (OR 27, 2, 555).

98. William Calder, letter, copy in Brake Collection, USAMHI; Taylor, "Ramseur's Brigade in the Gettysburg Campaign . . . ," 34; Bryan Grimes, *Extracts of Letters of Major-General Bryan Grimes* (Wilmington, NC, 1986), 130–131.

99. Gary W. Gallagher, *Stephen Dodson Ramseur—Lee's Gallant General* (Chapel Hill, NC, 1985), 73–74.

100. Calder, letter.

101. T. M. Gorman, *Pierce's Memorandum Account*; Taylor, "Ramseur's Brigade in the Gettysburg Campaign . . . ," 34–35.

102. OR 27, 2, 587; Hufham, "Gettysburg," 453.

103. Hufham, "Gettysburg," 453.

104. Taylor, "Ramseur's Brigade in the Gettysburg Campaign . . . ," 35; OR 27, 2, 588; Phillips, letter; Bennett, letter.

105. OR 27, 2, 588; Calder, letter.

106. OR 27, 2, 556.

107. Phillips, letter; McClendon, "Memoir"; Clark, *N.C. Regiments*, vol. 1, 720.

108. McClendon, "Memoir"; Taylor, "Ramseur's Brigade in the Gettysburg Campaign . . . ," 37; OR 27, 2, 588.

109. Busey and Martin, *Regimental Strengths and Losses*, 166, 288.

110. Sifakis, *Compendium of the Confederate Armies: Alabama*, 56, 62–63, 64–65, 72, 93–94; Davis, *The Confederate General*, vol. III, 9; vol. V, 107.

111. Krick, "Three Confederate Disasters on Oak Hill," 122; Tagg, *Generals at Gettysburg*, 299.

112. *Mobile Evening News*, July 24, 1863; J. M. Thompson, *Reminiscences of the Autauga Rifles Read Before the Historical Association, December 19, 1879*, copy in the 12th Alabama folder, GNMP.

113. Thompson, *Autauga Rifles*; Samuel Pickens, diary, 5th Alabama folder, GNMP.

114. Thompson, *Autauga Rifles*; Pickens, diary; OR 27, 2, 596.

115. OR 27, 2, 553.

Curiously, no one from O'Neal's Brigade mentioned this retrograde movement.

116. Krick, "Three Confederate Disasters On Oak Hill," 120, 125; OR 27, 2, 553, 592; Martin, *Gettysburg—July 1*, 221.

Thomas Elmore supported the idea that the reason the 3rd Alabama did not advance was because there was insufficent space for them to deploy prior to the advance (Elmore, "Attack and Counterattack," 128).

117. OR 27, 2, 553; Vautier, "At Gettysburg."

118. Vautier, "At Gettysburg"; Robert E. Park, "War Diary of Captain Robert Emory Park, Twelfth Alabama Regiment, January 28, 1863 —January 27, 1864," *Southern Historical Society Papers* (1898), vol. 26, 13; OR 27, 2, 601; *New York at Gettysburg*, vol. 1, 378–379; Vautier, *History of the Eighty-Eighth Penna. Volunteers*, 134.

119. OR 27, 2, 553–554.

120. A. S. Van de Graaff, letter, 5th Alabama Battalion folder, GNMP; OR 27, 2, 595.

121. Krick, "Three Confederate Disasters on Oak Hill," 128; OR 27, 2, 602.

122. de Graaff, letter; Pickens, diary; OR 27, 2, 554.

123. OR 27, 2, 587, 595; W. H. May, "First Confederates to Enter Gettysburg," *Confederate Veteran* (1897), vol. 5, 620.

124. May, "First Confederates to Enter Gettysburg," 620; OR 27, 2, 593, 596.

A soldier from Doles's Brigade told a slightly different story after the war, explaining how O'Neal rode up to Doles and asked him to take command of the division and "drive the Federals from cemetery ridge." O'Neal purportedly said that the Federals were demoralized and their position could be easily taken. Doles, however, refused to do anything without orders (Grace, "Rodes's Division at Gettysburg," 614).

125. OR 27, 2, 597–598.

126. OR 27, 2, 556, 568, 593, 596; Pickens, diary.

127. Pfanz, *Culp's Hill and Cemetery Hill,* 289; OR 27, 2, 518, 568, 593; 601; May, *Reminiscences,* 281; *Mobile Evening News,* July 24, 1863.

128. *Mobile Evening News,* July 24, 1863; OR 27, 2, 593, 601.

129. Pickens, diary; OR 27, 2, 598.

130. Pickens, diary; OR 27, 2, 593; 601, 602.

131. Krick, "Three Confederate Disasters on Oak Hill," 131; Davis, *The Confederate General,* vol. 4, 204–205.

132. Krick, "Three Confederate Disasters on Oak Hill," 138.

JOHNSON'S DIVISION—

Major General Edward Johnson

Major General Edward Johnson commanded one of the most distinguished units in the army—Stonewall Jackson's old division. A cavalcade of individuals led the division after Jackson. Brigadier General Charles Winder led it during the Seven Days campaign, but when he was killed at the battle of Cedar Mountain, Brigadier General William Taliaferro took over. Taliaferro was wounded during the battle of Second Manassas. Brigadier General John R. Jones led the division at the battle of Sharpsburg, and when he was wounded, Brigadier General William Starke assumed command. He was killed, so the bloody day ended with Colonel Andrew Grisby in command of the division. General Taliaferro was back in command during the Fredericksburg campaign, but he requested a transfer from the army when he failed to win promotion. Brigadier General Raleigh Colston became the next of a seemingly endless line of division commanders. Colston performed so poorly at Chancellorsville that Lee removed him with "uncharacteristic speed and finality."[1]

Major General Edward Johnson became the division's next commander. A West Point graduate, Johnson had seen action against the Seminole Indians and then again during the Mexican War. Initially entering Confederate service as a lieutenant colonel, Johnson took over the 12th Georgia and fought effectively in the mountains of western Virginia in 1861. In command of a brigade during Stonewall Jackson's Valley campaign, Johnson went down with a severe foot wound at the battle of McDowell. Although he had had limited experience in commanding a brigade, in April 1863, Johnson was assigned Jackson's old division.[2]

The Gettysburg campaign started well for Johnson and his new command. Although his division was not heavily engaged during the second battle of Winchester, it swung around the rear of General John Milroy's Division. Milroy's troops unexpectedly ran into Johnson's trap during the retreat, and after several charges, thousands surrendered.

Johnson's Division crossed the Potomac River and moved to Sharps-burg on June 15. On subsequent days, the column passed Hagerstown and Chambersburg, and finally reached the outskirts of Carlisle. The division, along with Rodes's Division, remained there until June 29, when it was ordered to rejoin Lee's concentrating army.[3]

Johnson ordered his division to countermarch to Greenville, where it camped on the night of June 30. On July 1, the division struck Chambersburg Pike and headed east toward Gettysburg. They encoun-tered two divisions from Longstreet's Corps near Fayetteville, leisurely camped along both sides of the road. Pressing on in the heat, the men could hear the sounds of battle just prior to reaching Cashtown. The march was a difficult one because of the slow pace and frequent halts caused by the wagon train in front of them. The division reached the battlefield at about 7:30 P.M., after a long twenty-five-mile march. Filing into the field on the left of Chambersburg Pike, they skirted the town to the north, and eventually stopped at the railroad depot. All around them during this march were the grisly results of the army's first day's fight with the I Corps and, farther on, the fight with the XI Corps. After resting in Gettysburg for at least an hour, the division continued its march along the railroad, finally stopping northeast of town, where the men rested for the night. In line of battle, the brigades were aligned from right to left as Nicholls's–Jones's–Steuart's–Walker's. Unbeknownst to most of them, a drama was being played out. Ewell ordered the division to secure Culp's Hill that night, but not liking the foreboding look of the steep hill, Johnson first sent scouts up to deter-mine if it was occupied by Federal soldiers. Only one Federal regiment was nearby, the 7th Indiana (Cutler's Brigade, Wadsworth's Division, I Corps), and, as fate would have it, the two forces made contact. As a result, Johnson decided to wait until morning to take the hill. By that time the hill was fully occupied, and Johnson was ordered to wait.[4]

At about 4:00 P.M. on July 2, Johnson ordered Major Joseph Lati-more to deploy his artillery on Benner's Hill and open fire on the enemy's position. This brought a swift and violent reaction from the Union batteries, and within an hour, the Confederate guns were silenced. Receiving orders from Ewell to advance, Johnson sent three of his brigades toward Rock Creek, but retained Walker's to guard against a flank movement. Johnson was not optimistic about his divi-sion's chances of success, calling the Union position on Culp's Hill "a rugged and rocky mountain, heavily timbered and difficult of ascent; a natural fortification, rendered more formidable by deep intrench-ments and thick abatis."[5]

As the men stumbled forward in the growing darkness, they were met by the concentrated volleys of the Union troops behind the entrenchments. Johnson thought that he was outnumbered, but all he was facing was General George Greene's Brigade (Geary's Division, XII Corps), and later, some regiments from the I Corps. The remainder of the XII Corps had been called south to help repel Longstreet's attack against the Union left flank. Greene had thinned his brigade to cover as much of the abandoned breastworks as possible. Several charges were made, but all were repulsed. Part of Steuart's Brigade was, however, successful in taking possession of part of the Union breastworks. The hostilities ended about 10:00 P.M. that evening.[6]

The battle for Culp's Hill reopened sometime between 3:30 and 4:00 A.M. on July 3. While the battle raged for seven hours, and included numerous attacks on the Federal breastworks, none were successful and the losses were fearful. The dead and wounded literally lay in heaps in several places. Johnson lost almost a third of his men on the well-fortified hill. Ted Barclay of the Stonewall Brigade wrote home to his sister that "our regiment [4th Virginia] has only 66 men left and the whole division suffered proportionally through the folly of our hard fighting Johnson. He has none of the qualities of a general but expects to do everything by fighting. Three or four times did he throw our gallant band against powerful breastworks and Yankees without number each time mowing them down."[7]

Steuart's Brigade—Brigadier General George Steuart

Units: 1st Maryland Battalion, 1st North Carolina, 3rd North Carolina, 10th Virginia, 23rd Virginia, 37th Virginia
Strength: 2121
Losses: 769 (149-385-235)—36%[8]

Brigadier General George Steuart's Brigade was an anomaly. In an army where brigades composed of regiments from the same state were the rule, Steuart's Brigade had regiments from three. The six units were all veteran, having fought in three different brigades during the campaigns of 1862. By the Chancellorsville campaign, the North Carolina and Virginia regiments were in Brigadier General Raleigh Colston's Brigade. During this campaign, Colston also commanded the division.[9]

A delicate situation arose after Chancellorsville when General Lee removed Colston from the army for his ineptitude. Because Colston hailed from Virginia, an uneasy rivalry existed between the North Carolina and Virginia troops. To ameliorate the situation, Lee decided to add the 1st Maryland Battalion to the brigade and appoint Marylander General George Steuart as its commander.[10]

A West Point graduate, George Steuart had limited military service prior to the war. He took command of the 1st Maryland prior to the first battle of Manassas. He did well there and was promoted to the rank of colonel. Promoted to the rank of brigadier general, Steuart was given command of a brigade in Stonewall Jackson's Valley command and was severely wounded at the battle of Cross Keys. When he finally returned to the army in May, he was given command of Colston's Brigade.[11]

June 30 found the brigade, along with the rest of the division, marching through a number of small Pennsylvania towns on its way to Gettysburg. Sergeant John Stone of the 1st Maryland Battalion noted that "at each place the inhabitants seemed most astonished at seeing so many soldiers, some expressed the belief that nearly the entire world had turned out to pay them a visit." The Maryland troops believed that they were on the road leading to Baltimore, and one soldier recalled that "a tremendous shout arose from our Battalion at the thought of such a destination." Others thought that the army was retreating and clearly expressed their disdain while the local citizens rejoiced. After camping for the night at Greenville, the brigade began to march again at about 7:00 A.M. on July 1. Passing through South Mountain and Cashtown on Chambersburg Pike, they could faintly hear the sounds of battle in front of them. "The hurried to and fro of couriers and staff officers proved to us that a battle was imminent," wrote S. Z. Ammen of the 1st Maryland battalion. As they continued their march, orders came to "Close up, men; close up; Hill's corps is in," and, amid shouts and cheers, the pace quickened. The men were itching for a fight. They would get their wish and never forget the resulting horrors.[12]

After passing lines of wounded men and field hospitals, the brigade finally reached the battlefield at about 7:30 P.M. on July 1. Leaving Chambersburg Pike west of Gettysburg, the brigade cut across fields north of town. After a short rest and a march along the railroad, the men could hear orders to "on the right by file into line." Turning to their right, the thor-

oughly exhausted men threw themselves down for a much-needed rest after the twenty-eight-mile march. Looking out in the darkness, the men could see the outline of Culp's Hill looming in front of them. Several suspected that the hill would be their destination when the sun rose, and a few would have liked to secure it that night—at least, that's how they recalled it after the war.[13]

As the sun rose on July 2, the men could hear the Union troops hard at work fortifying Culp's Hill. Many shook their heads, not understanding why they were just standing by while the enemy was entrenching. A spirited attack now could drive the enemy off the hill. They did not know that Lee was waiting for Longstreet to get into position before launching the attack. The defenses became more impregnable with every passing minute. The brigade was deployed at this time from left to right as 23rd Virginia–37th Virginia–10th Virginia–1st Maryland Battalion–3rd North Carolina. Six companies of the 1st North Carolina formed the reserve on the right side of the line. Its four other companies were on picket duty on the east side of Rock Creek. Skirmishers were thrown out, but the remainder of the brigade waited, growing more anxious with each passing moment.[14]

At about 4:00 P.M. the men observed an artillery duel between the two armies. The better-positioned Union artillery soon had the upper hand, driving the Confederate guns from Benner's Hill. Although Steuart's Brigade did not sustain any casualties because of the protection afforded by the woods and undulating land, they did have some anxious moments. "Perhaps nothing in battle is so trying to an infantryman's nerves and patience as the preliminary artillery fire that precedes it," wrote Major William Goldborough of the 1st Maryland.[15]

Seeing mounted officers galloping down the line from right to left, the men knew it was their turn to enter the fray. "As they pass[ed] the men [sprang] to their feet, and quickly form[ed] their ranks. We [knew] what it [meant], and [took] our places unordered," wrote Ammen (1st Maryland). No one knew that Johnson's Division was up against one Federal brigade on Culp's Hill—the rest had been moved south. Their commanding officer, Lieutenant Colonel James Herbert, yelled, "Forward—guide center." The brigade moved through woods and cornfields and over fences at a fast clip. The men encountered enemy skirmishers as they approached Rock Creek, driving them across it. Because the hill was southeast of his position, Steuart ordered his left wing to perform a right half-wheel, or move in a clockwise fashion, with the 3rd North Carolina maintaining its connection with Nicholls's Brigade. As a result of this movement and because of the greater natural obstructions on the left, the right wing crossed the creek before the left. There was not enough time for the men to select their crossing points. Instead, they splashed across when they arrived, often in waist-high water. The steep banks did not make the crossing any easier.[16]

Once across the creek, the men let out a Rebel yell and dashed up the wooded slope. Little did they know that the two brigades on their right (Nicholls's and Jones's) were already meeting with defeat. At this point, Steuart's right wing, composed of the 3rd North Carolina and 1st Maryland Battalion, was considerably ahead of the left regiments—so much so that a gap existed between them and the remainder of the brigade. The two units drove forward, despite having no support on their left flank, but with their right still connected with Nicholls's Brigade. After they had easily driven the enemy skirmish-ers before them, an eerie quiet settled in. Some wondered whether the enemy had fled the hill. Suddenly, "the heavens [were] lighted up by the flash of thousands of muskets and the deadly minnies [tore] and [rent] our ranks fearfully. Our column reeled and staggered like a drunken man," wrote Major William Goldsborough. They had been hit by a deadly crossfire from the 137th and 149th New York of Greene's Brigade. Captain George Thomas of the 1st Maryland described the horrors of the charge. "The fire thicken[ed] and the shrieking shells fill[ed] all the air with horrid sound, but still the line move[d] on over the huge projecting rocks, men falling at every step." It was dark now and the men stumbled over the rocks and other obstructions. Their way was lit, however, by the incessant discharges from the Union muskets on top of Culp's Hill. All around them was the "buzzing and hissing" of minié balls and the screams of their comrades, as many bullets found their mark. Lieutenant Colonel James Herbert of the 1st Maryland went down with three wounds and was succeeded by Major Goldsborough.[17]

The men were ordered to lie down to avoid taking further casualties when about thirty yards from the enemy's breastworks. Some believed that this order was a mistake, because over eighty casualties were sustained while the men lay exposed in front of the Union position. To make matters worse, the battalion's return fire was ineffective since the men were firing from below the breastworks. The men could barely hear their officers' orders above the din, and those they did hear were often contradictory—"Cease fire," "Give it to them boys," "Move here," were among the more commonly heard commands. The former command was often given because of the mistaken belief that they were firing into their own men.[18]

While the brigade's right wing was pinned down, Johnson ordered Steuart to bring up his left—something a brigade commander should have known to do without being told by his superior officer. But Steuart was new to his command and Johnson was probably watching him closely. Because of the right-half wheel maneuver, Steuart's left regiment, the 23rd Virginia, arrived first. The unit contained only about fifty men at the time, as the remainder had been left behind as skirmishers and as the brigade guard. The handful of men could see that the breastworks in front of them were weakly defended, so they swept up the hill and scattered some enemy soldiers from the works that had once been held by Kane's now-departed brigade. The Virginians scrambled into the breastworks. With no enemy to their left, but Greene's main line to their right, Lieutenant Colonel Simeon Walton alertly ordered his men to file to the right to roll up the Federal flank. The drive eventually reached the 137th New York, which had been refused to ward off an attack from that sector. When the 10th and 37th Virginia arrived, they drove forward in support of the 23rd Virginia.[19]

"We gained the enemy's breastworks and poured our fire up their line to our right, thus relieving our men of the other Regts. of the Brigade to our right from the murderous fire they were receiving—pinned down as they were," wrote Lieutenant Charles Raine of the 23rd Virginia after the war. Relieved of the crossfire it had been receiving for about forty-five minutes, the 1st Maryland was ordered to spring up and continue its attack in conjunction with its sister regiments on its left.[20]

Steuart ordered the 1st North Carolina forward to support the right wing in its quest to capture the Federal breastworks. Led by Lieutenant Randolph McKim, who used the musketry flashes to orient him,

the regiment moved up the hill. Seeing a force in front of them and bullets flying over his head, McKim assumed that they were enemy troops, so he screamed, "Fire on them, boys; fire on them!" Major William Parsley from the 3rd North Carolina angrily rushed up to McKim with a plea to stop the firing, as they were shooting his own men. Although reinforced, the North Carolinians were not able to breach the strong Federal line in front of them.[21]

This was a pivotal time for Steuart. He had captured a portion of the Federal breastworks at the "saddle" area between the upper and lower slopes of Culp's Hill, and was pouring a destructive fire on Greene's right flank. Some of the officers became agitated when they believed that their men were firing on their own troops. Orders to cease fire soon echoed along the heights, permitting Greene's men to regroup. Raines (23rd Virginia) recalled that "when we gained the earthworks we discovered by the flashes of the guns (it was dark) that these troops (the enemy) were firing in the direction we had come from. The Col. was puzzled and ordered his men to cease firing and asked for a volunteer to ascertain and report what troops these were." Raines crept went forward and found enemy soldiers in front of him. On the right side of Steuart's line, a conference between Lieutenant Colonel Walton of the 23rd Virginia and Major Goldsborough of the left wing of the 1st Maryland led to a concerted attack on the Federal breastworks, finally driving the 137th New York out of them.[22]

At about the same time, the 10th Virginia was ordered forward to a stone wall, which was supposed to be in the enemy's rear. Here they poured a destructive fire into Greene's right flank, driving part of it backward in confusion in the darkness. The Virginians soon came under attack from Federal troops in its rear (probably the 6th Wisconsin from the Iron Brigade and the 84th New York of Cutler's Brigade), forcing its commander to order his men to turn and beat back this new threat. It was clear that additional Federal troops were descending on the area, and with the growing confusion caused by the darkness, Steuart ordered his men back to the captured breastworks, ending the action, between 10:00 and 11:00 P.M.[23]

Little did Steuart know that his men were but a few hundred yards from the vital Baltimore Pike, which was loaded with supplies and artillery. Although many subsequent "armchair historians" speculated the "what if's" of the situation, in reality, the road was filled with returning infantry from Ruger's Division (XII Corps). Nevertheless, like Hays's and Hokes's (Avery's) Brigades (Early's Division) on Cemetery Hill, Steuart's men had captured a portion of the Federal heights. The difference was that Steuart's troops were able to hold them through the night.[24]

Except for the North Carolina regiments, which were still in front of the occupied Federal line, the remainder of the brigade took pride in the fact that it had captured the enemy's breastworks. Sargent Thomas Betterton of the 37th Virginia had even captured the 157th New York's flag. Their joy turned to anxiety, as they could hear the sounds of thousands of men approaching in the night, and too much artillery being wheeled into position. Several clashes occurred during the night as the Federal infantry probed the Confederate position. One occurred when the 111th Pennsylvania (Kane's Brigade's, Geary's Division, XII Corps) attempted to return to its breastworks, only to be peppered by a volley from Steuart's men. A similar fate occurred to McDougall's Brigade (Ruger's Division, XII Corps) and to the 2nd Massachusetts

(Colgrove's Brigade), when they ran into the 23rd Virginia. The Federal troops were in all cases turned back and forced to wait until daylight for the issue to be settled. As bad as July 2 seemed, July 3 would be much worse, and none of Steuart's survivors would ever forget it. In a letter written soon after the battle, Stone (1st Maryland) simply wrote, "the worst was to come."[25]

The guns opened fire at about 3:30 A.M. on July 3. Because most of the brigade occupied the breastworks, the men could simply hunker down, and few casualties resulted. The 1st Maryland and 3rd North Carolina took turns occupying the safety of the captured breastworks on the right of the line; the rest took refuge behind large boulders. Some men from the 3rd North Carolina had but one or two cartridges remaining, forcing them to scrounge from the dead and wounded who lay in abundance all around them. Except for the four companies still on picket duty on the other side of Rock Creek, the 1st North Carolina was moved from the right to the left of the brigade.[26]

The firing along the line was incessant. Leaves and bark were swept from the trees, and the ground literally trembled from the concentrated cannon fire. One soldier from the 1st Maryland vividly recalled the hell on Culp's Hill. "The whole hillside seemed enveloped in a blaze. Minnie balls pattered upon the breastworks . . . like hail upon a housetop. Solid shot went crashing through the woods, adding the danger from falling limbs of trees to that from erratic fragments of exploding shells. The whole hill was covered with the smoke and smell of powder. No enemy could be seen." Rifles often became clogged because of the sustained firing, which occurred hour after hour without cessation. Unlike Geary's Division in front of them, there were no reinforcements to spell the men while they rested and cleaned their guns. A scarcity of ammunition continued to plague the men. At one point, Lieutenant Randolph McKim of the 1st Maryland took a few men back to the wagons beyond Rock Creek and returned carrying the cartridges in blankets suspended on a rail.[27]

At about 10:00 A.M. on July 3, Steuart received orders to launch an attack from his position at the top of the lower slope. Surveying his front, Steuart realized that any attack was futile. He lodged a complaint with General Johnson, but knew that he had no choice but to obey his orders. Major William Goldsborough, commander of the 1st Maryland, is said to have protested the order to charge the Federal works. "Sir, I consider it murder; I take my men in under protest." Several other officers also lodged protests, but all ultimately followed their fatal orders. Using the 3rd North Carolina as a pivot, Steuart swung the remainder of the brigade in a clockwise manner, to face northwest. In all, he had about nine hundred men to make the attack. This maneuver accomplished, the men spied a strong line of Federal troops in line of battle, composed of the 5th Ohio and 147th Pennsylvania (Candy's Brigade, Geary's Division, XII Corps) in front of them, across Pardee's Field. Kane's Brigade (Geary's Division) was to their right. Steuart formed his brigade at right angles to the captured breastworks, from left to right, as 1st North Carolina–23rd Virginia–37th Virginia–1st Maryland–3rd North Carolina. The 10th Virginia was ordered down to protect the brigade's left flank by forming perpendicular to the 1st North Carolina. In front of them was the 20th Connecticut of McDougall's Brigade. Moving forward as a strong skirmish line, they pushed the enemy's skirmishers back.[28]

Advancing across Pardee's field, the center and left side of Steuart's line was staggered by sheets of bullets as it approached the middle of the field. The men could not resist halting and firing at the enemy. Realizing that they could not remain exposed, and not wishing to go forward, the men began drifting to the rear. Steuart despaired that the left "did not maintain its position in line of battle." Lieutenant Colonel Walton of the 23rd Virginia merely wrote that "here we were exposed to a terrible fire and had to retire." Many of the men decided to surrender rather than attempt to recross the deadly field of fire.[29]

Steuart had positioned himself to the right of the line, behind his own 1st Maryland. "Attention! Forward, double-quick! March!" he yelled, and the line moved forward. The battalion was joined by the handful of men remaining from the 3rd North Carolina. Most realized that this might be their last moment on earth, and a solemn mood descended on the battalion. Some prayed that they would do their duty and not embarrass themselves during the approaching charge. As they emerged from the woods and entered Pardee field, cannon fire blew holes in the line and scores of men fell by the second. A member of the 147th Pennsylvania (Candy's Brigade, Geary's Division) noted, "down the opposite slope they came in beautiful alignment, their officers gallantly leading, —now up the hillside in our front, in solid column, as if by sheer force of weight to bear us down. There was no retreat for the poor fellows in the front ranks who, with blanched faces, came up to be mowed down by companies." To their left the Marylanders could see the prone men of the Virginia regiments refusing to obey the curses and pleading of their officers to advance. "Never shall I forget the expressions of contempt on the faces of the men of the left companies of the Second [First] Maryland as they cast a side glance upon their comrades who had proved recreant in this supreme moment," wrote Goldsborough.[30]

Kane's and Candy's Brigades (Geary's Division, XII Corps) held their fire until Steuart's men were within a hundred yards of their position. The devastation was almost indescribable, as small arms fire now added to the destruction and the men were mowed down by fire from the front and both flanks. A veteran from the 147th Pennsylvania recalled that his men "poured a deliberate and most deadly fire into their ranks. This was done with cool and well-aimed precision, such as old veterans alone could do, and the destruction of the rebel column was almost complete." All was confusion, as no one seemed to be in charge. Many of the officers, including Major Goldsborough, had fallen early in the charge. Private Thomas Webb wrote home that the "men fell on my right and left and in front of me and I thought sure my time had come." The men finally received orders to retire.[31]

Oliver Taylor of the 37th Virginia recalled how the Marylanders lay in heaps. Sergeant George Pile of the same regiment noted that the murderous fire almost wiped out the Maryland battalion and left only him and one other man from his company unhurt. Most of the men now made their way back to their former position, but others continued the charge, only to be struck down as they approached the breastworks. A dog appeared before the Federal line, apparently looking for his dead or dying master. He too was riddled by bullets. After the battle, General Kane ordered him to be buried "as the only Christian minded being on either side."[32]

Tears streamed down Steuart's face when he saw how few of his men had sur-vived the ill-fated charge. "My poor boys! My poor boys!" was all that he could say. In his report, Steuart wrote that the "enemy's position was impregnable, attacked by our small force, and any further effort to storm it would have been futile, and attended with great disaster, if not total annihilation." Only about a dozen men were left of the 3rd North Carolina when it fell back after its second charge. The return of a detached company and some lost men subsequently raised its numbers to seventy-seven.[33]

Reforming behind some rocks and a stone fence, the men expected to repel a counterattack. None came, however, and Steuart was ordered to pull his men back to the base of Culp's Hill about an hour later. The brigade remained there for the remainder of the day, during which time half of it was deployed as skirmishers. They quickly drove back Federal skirmishers who were attempting to ascertain the position and strength of the Confederates. Ammen (1st Maryland) vividly remembered his feelings at the time. "At the foot of the hill, along whose crest lie so many of our dead, we sleep—poor, worn out, powder stained soldiers, our guns grasped that we may be ready to rise at a moment's notice." At about the midnight, the brigade recrossed Rock Creek, marched to the rear of Gettysburg, and took defensive positions along Seminary Ridge, where the men threw up their own breastworks.[34]

The men were thoroughly exhausted. They had been on the firing line for over seventeen hours with little food or sleep, and had fought two pitched engagements. They could be proud of their achievements of breaching the Federal defenses on Culp's Hill, albeit with a little help from the Union commanders. The brigade's losses of just over a third, while high, could have been much higher, had some of the units fought as tenaciously as the 1st Maryland, which lost almost 50%. The figures are deceiving, however, as Reverend Randolph McKim noted: "very few men in that battle in our brigade but were touched by shot or shell, even if they escaped without being wounded." McKim

himself was hit four times, but none caused injury. Colonel John Futch of the 3rd North Carolina ended a letter about his brother's death on Culp's Hill with the sentence, "I believe he is happy and no doubt is better off than any of us . . . we are living the worst life men ever <u>have</u>."[35]

Nicholls's Brigade—Colonel Jesse Williams

Units: 1st Louisiana, 2nd Louisiana, 10th Louisiana, 14th Louisiana, 15th Louisiana
Strength: 1104
Losses: 393 (66-287-36)—35%[36]

Although the five regiments hailed from the same state, and all but the 15th Louisiana were formed between April and June 1861, they served in four separate brigades between the latter part of 1861 and July 1862. The five regiments were finally regimented together in July 1862 to form the 2nd Louisiana Brigade under the command of Brigadier General William E. Starke. The brigade performed well at the battle of Groveton. The following day, the brigade was ordered to fix bayonets and launch a counterattack against a Federal force that had broken through a portion of the Confederate line. The subsequent counterattack was successful, and the Louisianians captured two cannon in the process. Starke was killed leading a charge at the battle of Sharpsburg and was replaced by Brigadier General Francis Nicholls. Previously wounded, Nicholls did not return to take command until January 1863, so Colonel Edmund Pendleton of the 15th Louisiana took command during the Fredericksburg campaign.[37]

General Nicholls commanded the brigade at Chancellorsville, where he lost a foot to go along with the arm he had lost earlier in the war. Therefore, the Gettys-

burg campaign began with the Louisiana Tigers marching north under the temporary command of Colonel Jesse Williams. The brigade took full advantage of its reputation as "blood-thirsty killers" during the march. The citizens along the route were only too happy to tend to their every need, and seldom did a man go hungry. "Never did soldiers appear more buoyant and cheerful than Lee's army and never did men fare more sumpously [sic] than they up to the battle," wrote Lieutenant Charles Batchelor of the 2nd Louisiana. Batchelor recalled that the Pennsylvanians gave "with cheerfulness only asking that their barns and dwellings be spared." The Louisianian estimated that all of the men who were afflicted with "sore mouth," caused by a deficiency of meat and vegetables in the diet, were cured during the invasion. The men were so courteous to the citizens that even their own officers were surprised, causing one to remark that the men behaved better in enemy territory than in their own. Morale was exceptionally high. Colonel David Zable of the 14th Louisiana wrote after the war that "we believe[d] we could surmount every obstacle; that there was no foe we could not defeat; such was our faith in our Commander and in our powers to do."[38]

The brigade trudged toward Gettysburg at the head of Johnson's column on

July 1, arriving between 6:00 and 7:00 P.M. They had heard gunfire during their march, which had quickened their pulses. Had it not been for the wagon train in front of them, they would have made better time. At one point, some of the men sneered when they passed McLaws's and Hood's Divisions (I Corps) sprawled along the sides of Chambersburg Pike. Moving through Gettysburg, the brigade halted at the railroad depot while the rest of the division came up. The men continued the march easterly along the railroad, stopping after a three-quarter-mile march. Here they formed line of battle and moved south another six hundred yards, where the men were permitted to rest on their arms. About five hundred yards in front of them was Hanover Road and Culp's Hill loomed a mile in the distance.[39]

Many of the men had an uneasy feeling as they rested their weary feet. They knew that their comrades had driven the enemy out of this part of the battlefield and into the hills to the south of the town. But with daylight still available, they could not understand why they were not ordered forward to complete the destruction of the Union army. "The troops realized there was something wanting somewhere, there was an evident feeling of dissatisfaction among our men, we were not doing Stonewall Jackson's way," recalled Colonel Zable.[40]

The following morning, the troops displayed renewed enthusiasm when they were ordered toward Culp's Hill. After marching a few hundred yards in line of battle, the men were again halted and permitted to rest. They again were perplexed, particularly when their returning skirmishers reported that Culp's Hill was unoccupied. The quiet was broken by the sounds of axes and trees falling. With each passing minute, the Federal breast-

works on Culp's Hill became stronger. The men knew all this and more, and grimly considered the chances that they would survive this battle.[41]

The relative quiet was broken at about 3:00 P.M., when the XII Corps's artillery on Culp's Hill opened on Johnson's Division. Nicholls's Brigade suffered as much, if not more, in their exposed position, as any of Johnson's men. The Louisianians could merely take whatever cover they could find and wait. According to one soldier, "perhaps nothing in battle is so trying to an infantryman's nerves and patience as the preliminary artillery fire." Finally, at about 7:00 P.M., they received orders to exchange positions with Jones's Brigade, placing them second from the right in Johnson's line of battle. About three-quarters of a mile in front of them loomed their target—Culp's Hill.[42]

According to Imhof, the brigade was deployed from left to right: 15th Louisiana–14th Louisiana–10th Louisiana–and Louisiana–1st Louisiana. After splashing across Rock Creek, Colonel Williams briefly reformed the brigade's disordered ranks, then ordered the charge. The men had taken but a few steps when Lieutenant Colonel Michael Nolan of the 1st Louisiana was fatally wounded. The growing darkness and obstructions made the charge difficult. Colonel Zable (14th Louisiana) recalled that "with a yell our men rushed forward as best they could up the steep hill side over rocks and through the timber up to the enemy's line of works."[43]

Straining his eyes, Lieutenant George Collins of the 149th New York (Greene's Brigade, Geary's Division, XII Corps) could not see the Louisianians's initial approach. Suddenly, the Federal skirmish line "came running back followed by a Confederate line of battle, yelping and howling in its particular manner." With night falling and the dense smoke, the Federal troops were guided more from hearing the Confederates than seeing them.[44]

It appears that Williams's men ran from tree to tree and from boulder to boulder to try to avoid the minié balls zipping down on them from the crest. The incline was steep, making the ascent all the more difficult. In front of them were the 78th and 102nd New York, forming General Greene's Brigade's left and center. Within a hundred yards of the Federal position the fire from Greene's units was so severe that the men halted, dropped to the ground, and returned the fire—all, that is, except for the 1st Louisiana on the right of the line. Continuing its advance, the regiment briefly drove part of Greene's men from their defenses. However, since Jones's Brigade on the right and its sister regiments on the left had failed to move up, the 1st Louisiana was forced to abandon its gains and fall back. The firing continued until after 10:00 P.M., when peace finally returned to the battlefield. Williams's men remained so close to Greene's line that they had to talk in whispers that night.[45]

Sometime during the charge, the 14th Louisiana's flag bearer was cut off and captured. However, shortly before he was taken, he was able to tear the precious flag from the staff, carefully fold it, and stuff it into his tunic. The enemy never knew the prisoner had the flag and both returned to the regiment when prisoners were exchanged a few months later.[46]

According to Colonel Zable, the brigade opened fire again on Greene's Brigade at about 4:00 A.M. on July 3, as part of a ruse. Realizing that they were outnumbered and vulnerable to an attack, "our best plan to mask our weakness would be to open fire on the enemy before daylight in the morning so as to cause them to believe that we were about

to make another effort to capture the works." The fire was quickly returned. Zable recalled that it was "the most terrific and deafening we ever experienced," and soon the entire area was enveloped by smoke. The firing was so intense that the officers could only give orders by yelling directly into the ears of their men.[47]

Some of Williams's men were incredulous that any of them survived the firestorm. "Had the enemy fired with greater deliberation they would have annihialated [sic] the Brigade . . . our foe were evidently demoralized, shooting wild into the tree tops so that the leaves and limbs were falling so thick and fast that it seemed it was raining," recalled Zable.[48]

It appears that Williams's men did not attack the Federal breastworks on July 3, instead they merely held their ground and fired at the enemy. After several hours of suspenseful waiting for the Federal troops to launch their counterattack, Williams's men were pleased when they looked back and saw O'Neal's Brigade (Rodes's Division, II Corps) advancing to relieve them. This reaction soon turned to horror as the Federal fire found their mark. "The troops coming to our relief were much more exposed to the enemy's fire than ourselves, as we were so close to their line that they would fire over us . . . we regretted that we were being relieved," wrote Colonel Zable. Realizing that Culp's Hill could not be taken, the men were ordered to race down the hill, across the field of fire, to safety. Many men met their fate. The brigade reformed at the base of the hill, about three hundred yards from their farthest advance. The men remained there until 3:00 A.M. on July 4, when they were ordered west of town to take defensive positions on Seminary Ridge.[49]

Although Williams's Brigade made only one series of charges on Culp's Hill on July 2, its losses (estimated to be 35%)

ranked with those of Steuart's Brigade, which charged the Federal works on both July 2 and 3. Only one regiment's losses were recorded (10th Louisiana's) and it was 49%. As they trudged home, many soldiers probably contemplated what might have been if they had charged the hill earlier in the battle.[50]

Walker's Brigade—Brigadier General James Walker

Units: 2nd Virginia, 4th Virginia, 5th Virginia, 27th Virginia, 33rd Virginia
Strength: 1323
Losses: 338 (65-173-100)—26%[51]

Walker's men had every right to march with heads held high. The only brigade to have a name other than its commander's, this was the Stonewall Brigade. It was the brigade led by Stonewall Jackson, the one that helped turn the tide at First Manassas. That was almost two years ago, and only a dim memory for most of the men. A somewhat disappointed Sir Arthur Fremantle wrote that "in appearance the men differed little from other Confederate soldiers, except, perhaps, that the brigade contains more elderly men and fewer boys."[52]

A series of officers commanded the brigade after Jackson. Brigadier General Richard Garnett led the unit during the early phases of the Valley campaign, but was removed from command by Stonewall Jackson for perceived misconduct at the battle of Kernstown. Garnett was replaced by Brigadier General Charles Winder, who led the brigade conspicuously through the rest of the Valley campaign and during the Seven Days battles. When Winder was killed at the battle of Cedar Mountain, Colonel W. Baylor assumed command, but he subsequently lost his life at the second battle of Manassas. Colonel Andrew Grigsby commanded the brigade at the battle of Sharpsburg, but when he took over the division, two others assumed command during the battle. Brigadier General Elisha Paxton assumed command of the brigade in November 1862 and led it at Fredericksburg. He entered the battle of Chancellorsville with premonitions of death which proved to be accurate.[53]

The brigade's new commander, Brigadier General James Walker, had been expelled from the Virginia Military Institute by Stonewall Jackson, but finished his education at the University of Virginia. An attorney by training, he progressed through the ranks of the Confederate army because of his fighting abilities. He participated in every campaign from the Valley campaign to Chancellorsville in command of the 13th Virginia. A stream of influential supporters finally gained his promotion to the rank of brigadier general in May 1863, and with it came the Stonewall Brigade.[54]

The men looked in wonder at the large barns and fat livestock they passed. The citizens were generous, but the men questioned their sincerity. Private John Garibaldi of the 27th Virginia wrote home that the "people of Pennsylvania treated us very kindly but I think it was only from their teeth out. When we went to their houses they gave us plenty of everything they had."[55]

After their long, round-a-bout march to the battlefield, the men climbed South Mountain on Chambersburg Pike. Near the top, they could barely discern the sounds of battle emanating in the distance. On the descent, they were heartened when they passed other units resting by the side of the road. "We [began] to pass the encampments of Anderson's Division, Hill's corps, and as we [saw] the men leisurely cooking and eating, as if nothing of importance [was] occurring, we [began] to feel more assured that all [was] right," wrote Private Charles Rollins of the 27th Virginia. During this, the last phase of the march to Gettysburg, the men were chagrined to be at the rear of Johnson's column. They could not see what was happening in front of them and they consumed their share of dust.[56]

The brigade finally reached the battlefield during the early evening of July 1. Leaving Chambersburg Pike, it followed the rest of Johnson's Division, swinging to the left to approach Gettysburg from the north. The column made its way along the York and Gettysburg Railroad for about two miles, then filed to the right, where the men formed into line of battle. The men wondered whether they would advance against the enemy in the growing darkness. That is what their old commander would have done. Their answer soon arrived when they were ordered to rest in line of battle. That night, they could hear the tramp of feet and sound of axes, as the enemy reinforced the hills south of town and strengthened them against an attack. The brigade's position was on the extreme left of Johnson's line, near Hanover Road and Culp's farm. Except for throwing out some pickets, Walker took no offensive action that night.[57]

Federal skirmishers from the 27th Indiana (Colgrove's Brigade, Ruger's Division, XII Corps) appeared in the brigade's front at dawn on July 2, resulting in a long-range dual for most of the day. Rollins (27th Virginia) recalled that the skirmishers from his brigade used the "lie down" method. Lying on their backs to reload, the men rolled onto their stom-

achs to fire, then repeat the process. They occasionally jumped to their feet and advanced with a yell before resorting to the "lie down" method again. Johnson ordered his division forward in preparation for the attack on Culp's Hill at about 6:00 P.M. and halted them south of Hanover Road. Walker's vulnerable left flank came under fire from enemy sharpshooters posted in a nearby wheatfield and woods. Deployed behind them on Brinkerhoff's Ridge was the 9th Massachusetts (Sweitzer's Brigade, Barnes's Division, V Corps) and three cavalry regiments from McIntosh's Brigade. As losses mounted, Walker ordered Colonel John Nadenbousch to about-face his 2nd Virginia and move north to drive the pesky enemy away, "which he did at a single dash, his men advancing with great spirit," reported Walker after the battle. Nadenbousch's men had taken on the 10th New York cavalry and forced it to retire.[58]

Johnson had planned for Jones's Brigade to lead the attack on Culp's Hill, followed by Nicholls's and Steuart's. Johnson wrote later that "General Walker was directed to follow, but reported to me that the enemy were advancing upon him from their right, he was ordered to repulse them and follow on as soon as possible." Johnson was undoubtedly referring to the actions of the 2nd Virginia. Walker did not follow Johnson's other brigades after driving the skirmishers away. He explained in his report that "our flank and rear would have been entirely uncovered and unprotected in the event of my moving with the rest of the division, and as our movement must have been made in full view of the enemy, I deemed it prudent to hold my position after dark, which I did." The 2nd Virginia returned at about 8:00 P.M., and the entire brigade later advanced toward Rock Creek to support Steuart's Brigade, which had successfully captured a portion of the Federal breastworks. Colonel Funk of the 5th Virginia recalled that this movement was not made until 2:00 A.M. on July 3. It is tempting to speculate what might have been had Walker's Brigade participated in the charge up Culp's Hill on July 2, as the area in its front was devoid of Federal troops at this time because most the XII Corps had departed to other parts of the field.[59]

The battle reopened at about 3:30 A.M. on July 3 as the now-returned Federal XII Corps desperately tried to regain its trenches lost to Steuart's Brigade the night before. Realizing he needed support, Steuart requested Walker's aid, and the Stonewall Brigade came up behind him. The 2nd Virginia was sent to the left flank of Steuart's Brigade, where it formed at right angles to the 1st North Carolina, where it helped repulse a Federal charge. One company was sent across Rock Creek "for the purpose of attracting the fire of the enemy in front and turning his right flank, " wrote Nadenbousch in his report. The remainder of the 2nd Virginia opened on the enemy when they were only twenty-five yards away. Still the enemy advanced. Nadenbousch detached two more companies to run to the bend in the creek and fire into enemy's rear and left flank. Nadenbousch recalled that "with this concentrated fire, he was soon forced to retire in confusion." Although the identity of these Union troops is not definitively known, historian Harry Pfanz believed that they were the large and inexperienced 1st Maryland-Potomac Home Guard (Lockwood's Brigade, Ruger's Division), which had been ordered to turn the Confederate left flank.[60]

"Extra Billy" Smith's Brigade arrived at 7:00 A.M. and relieved the 2nd Virginia. Seeking to protect his brigade's left flank, Walker sent the regiment across the creek, where it joined the four companies of the 1st North Carolina that were skirmishing with Colgrove's Brigade (Ruger's Division) on the creek's west bank. Federal skirmishers soon appeared on the 2nd Virginia's left flank. Although they did not know it at the time, General Thomas Neill had brought his brigade (Howe's Division, VI Corps) up to support the XII Corps, to prevent the enemy "from turning us." Colonel Nadenbousch reported that "I advanced some distance on the left, driving the enemy's skirmishers from and taking possession of the heights at this point, where I remained during the day, skirmishing with and inflicting some injury on the enemy . . . and keeping the left flank clear." Despite the mismatch, Neill never pushed the weak force out of the way to advance on Johnson's rear.[61]

While the 2nd Virginia was taking on Colgrove's and Neill's Brigades, the remainder of Walker's Brigade had formed behind Steuart's Brigade. It remained there for about five hours, exchanging fire with units from Kane's and Candy's Brigades (Geary's Division). Losses, particularly on the right of the line, were heavy. This appears to have been the position of the 4th Virginia. Funk (5th Virginia) suggested that his regiment began the fight in reserve, and after about an hour, he was ordered to move to his right and relieve the 4th Virginia, which had expended its ammunition. The unit remained here for over two hours, until it too ran out of ammunition.[62]

The brigade was relieved by Daniel's Brigade (Rodes's Division, II Corps) sometime between 8:30 and 9:00 A.M. and moved to the rear, where the men were permitted to clean their guns, replenish their ammunition, and rest. Walker apparently pulled his men back without permission. Rollins (27th Virginia) recalled that after about an hour, Johnson approached the brigade and asked its identity. When so informed, he angrily asked, "Where is your commander? What in the ___ are you doing here?" Directed to Walker, the two had an animated conversation, which ended when Johnson ordered the brigade to march about four hundred yards to the extreme right of the division to relieve Nicholls's and O'Neal's Brigades. Here the brigade was ordered to attack the steep heights at about 10:30 A.M. in conjunction with Steuart's and Daniel's Brigades to their left. The disposition of the brigade is again not known, except that the 5th Virginia probably occupied the extreme right.[63]

With the 2nd Virginia still over to the east, Walker had less than a thousand men. Against them were at least four Federal regiments—60th and 149th New York of Greene's Brigade, and the 7th and 66th Ohio of Candy's. The latter regiment was actually positioned perpendicular to the others at the northern end of the line, so it could pour an enfilading fire into the right flank of the Stonewall Brigade. The Federal troops held their fire as Walker's men advanced. There seemed to be an endless quantity of Confederates being thrown against the hill, and the officers wanted to make sure that their men had enough ammunition to kill and maim them all. The gray line moved unsteadily up the steep and rocky hill, when the world suddenly exploded, as the Federal officers yelled for their men to open fire. It was a particularly deadly fire, and the Federal troops recalled that the Confederate line simply melted away. Some of the men dropped down and hid behind anything that might stop a bullet. After a while, some of the men continued to inch forward, protecting themselves by moving from rock to rock to tree. Some got to within fifteen yards of the breastworks, and one sergeant actually reached the

works and grabbed the flag of the 149th New York before being cut down by a hail of bullets. Lieutenant Collins later recalled that he was "a large noble-looking man, and no one who afterwards saw him lying with his head and arm against the works, could help admiring his manly appearance and evident courage."[64]

After about forty-five minutes, the left side of the brigade could no longer withstand the murderous fire and began falling back. The 4th Virginia, which was probably being held in reserve, was now sent forward to support the 33rd Virginia. Closely watching his men's progress, Walker realized that the renewed attack "was done with equally bad success as our former efforts, and the fire became so destructive that I suffered the brigade to fall back to a more secure position, as it was a useless sacrifice of life to keep them longer under so galling a fire." The order brought a sense of relief to the men, and many bounded down the hill with a silent prayer for safety. Others were not relieved, because they realized that they had advanced too far, and therefore any attempt to escape would result in certain death. Almost seventy men from the 4th Virginia surrendered, and the 14th Connecticut captured the regiment's flag. Most of the Federal troops were magnanimous in victory. As one Confederate soldier approached the works with hands held high in the air, he was told, "Gim-me your hand, Johnny Reb; you've given us the bulliest fight of the war."[65]

Major B. Watkins Leigh, Johnson's assistant adjutant general, was so incensed when he saw the white flags that he spurred his horse up the hill. Before he could utter a word of protest, a volley ripped through the forest and Leigh and his horse went down. Federal soldiers who ventured down to see him after the engagement rifled his pockets and desecrated his body for souvenirs. They described him as "a man of small stature with a smart and intelligent look." Struck with admiration for Leigh, General Greene ordered that he be buried along with the Federal troops—the other Confederate troops were left to rot in the hot sun.[66]

About an hour later, Walker again moved his command partly up the hill. This was not done to launch an attack, but to discourage a counterattack by the Federal troops on the hill. Walker received orders at about midnight to pull back with the rest of the division to Seminary Ridge. Here the men rested all of July 4, waiting and hoping for a Federal attack. The men left Gettysburg at about 11:00 P.M. that

night, marching in the direction of Fairfield. For Private Benjamin Coffman of the 33rd Virginia, "the worst of all was we did not get to bury our dead." Private Barclay (4th Virginia) poignantly wrote home that "I feel rather lonesome sometimes with the few of us who are left, but don't cry."[67]

Because of Walker's insistence on remaining on Johnson's left flank and not assaulting Culp's Hill on July 2, the Stonewall Brigade lost a lower percentage of men (25%) than any other brigade in Johnson's Division. As a result, he squandered an opportunity to damage the Federal right flank. If Stonewall Jackson was looking down, he could not have been pleased by the brigade's leadership.

Jones's Brigade—Brigadier General John M. Jones

Units: 21st Virginia, 25th Virginia, 42nd Virginia, 44th Virginia, 48th Virginia, 50th Virginia
Strength: 1467
Losses: 453 (78-293-82)—30%[68]

The Virginia regiments comprising Brigadier General John Jones's Brigade were all mustered into service between April and September 1861 and were scattered into two separate brigades. During the Seven Days campaign, the 21st, 42nd, and 48th Virginia were in John R. Jones's Brigade, while the 25th and 44th Virginia were in Arnold Elzey's Brigade. The regiments were combined under Jones's command prior to the Chancellorsville campaign. After more than a year of incompetence, Jones was removed from command and replaced by Brigadier General John M. Jones.[69]

John M. Jones was a West Point graduate who began the war as a major of artillery. He served several months as a

staff officer and was promoted to the rank of brigadier general and given John R. Jones's Brigade. Although he had had an alcohol problem, Jones threw himself into shaping up the brigade for the Gettysburg campaign.[70]

Leaving camp near Scotland, Pennsylvania, at 7:00 A.M. on July 1, Jones's Brigade was the second brigade in Johnson's column. Lieutenant Thomas Boatwright of the 44th Virginia marveled at the bounty of the countryside. He was, however, saddened by his comrades' behavior, for "though we was not allowed to interfere with private property," looting of unoccupied houses was fairly common. "I was made sorry at times," he wrote.[71]

After a brief reprise at Gettysburg's railroad depot on the evening of July 1, the brigade moved along the railroad to the east of the town. It halted in a ravine just northeast of Cemetery Hill, where the men were permitted to lie on their arms for the night. The brigade occupied the extreme right of Johnson's Division. Not all of the troops were so lucky to be able to rest—four companies of the 25th Virginia were thrown out as pickets. The brigade was arranged from left to right as 21st Virginia–48th Virginia–50th Virginia–42nd Virginia–25th Virginia. The 44th Virginia's position is unclear.[72]

Except for the sounds of Federal troops constructing breastworks on the hills in front of them, all was quiet through the night and into the following day. During this time, Jones ordered the 25th Virginia's picket line to move forward to observe the enemy's movements. Sometime around 3:00 P.M., Jones received orders to advance to support Latimer's artillery battalion on Benner's Hill. While the brigade halted about three hundred yards behind and to the left of the hill, the 50th Virginia was ordered to continue its advance and directly support the artillery. The regiment ultimately formed just to the left of the guns on the south slope of Benner's Hill. Although Latimer's guns were ultimately driven away by superior Federal firepower, the 50th Virginia lost only one man killed and two wounded. The remainder of the brigade did not suffer many losses either, as it was protected by Benner's Hill.[73]

While making these movements, Jones recalled seeing a Federal force making a demonstration on his right and responded by sending the remainder of the 25th Virginia to the scene. The regiment's commander, Colonel John Higginbotham, took issue with this recollection, stating that the remainder of his regiment was ordered to the skirmish line.[74]

At about 4:00 P.M., Johnson rode up to Jones and ordered him to move his brigade to the position recently vacated by Nicholls's Louisianians. This placed Jones's Brigade back on Johnson's right flank northeast of town. The rest of the

order probably sent a shiver up Jones's spine. After completing the movement, he was to move forward behind his skirmish line and take Culp's Hill. Johnson tried to reassure him by explaining that Nicholls's and Steuart's Brigades would join the attack on his left. As the brigade moved forward, it was probably arranged from left to right as 21st Virginia–48th Virginia–42nd Virginia–50th Virginia. The position of the 44th Virginia is again not known.[75]

Advancing steadily, the 25th Virginia on the skirmish line scattered the enemy's counterparts, who were especially numerous on the regiment's left flank. The men soon came under artillery fire, but continued to drive forward until they reached the banks of Rock Creek. Their move was hastened by a strong desire to get out of the range of the Union artillery on the heights while crossing the open fields. Lieutenant Colonel L. Salyer of the 50th Virginia wrote that "our whole line moved forward in handsome order." Incredibly, they sustained no casualties during this movement. This ended when they encountered Federal troops behind large rocks. Although the 25th Virginia was able to extract them, "just here my casualties were the heaviest," wrote Colonel Higginbotham.[76]

Jones's main line quickly reached the creek. Captain Jesse Richardson of the 42nd Virginia recalled that his regiment now "advanced up the mountain some 75 yards, when it opened fire upon the enemy. It continued loading and firing, and pressing forward up the hill."[77]

Because Jones's Brigade occupied the extreme right of Johnson's Division, his troops had to scale the steepest part of Culp's Hill. General Jones noted that the hill was "steep, heavily timbered, rocky, and difficult of ascent." Captain T. Buckner of the 44th Virginia recalled that the "works in front of our lines were of a formidable character, and in some places they could scarcely be surmounted without scaling-ladders." These characteristics, combined with the growing darkness and the Union small arms fire directed against it, caused the line to fall into disarray. "All was confusion and disorder," wrote Buckner. The confusion was greatest on Jones's left, where there was a "mixing up of the files and the derangement of the general line." Jones rushed over to help correct the situation, but a Federal bullet tore into his thigh, forcing him to relinquish command to Colonel John C. Higginbotham of the 25th Virginia, who was almost immediately wounded. Lieutenant Colonel R. Dungan of the 48th Virginia now took over the brigade.[78]

Recalling the advance, Steuben Coon of the 60th New York (Greene's Brigade, Geary's Division, XII Corps) noted that "not a shot was fired at them until they got within about 15 rods. Then the order was given and we did fire and kept firing. If ever men loaded and fired more rapidly . . . I never saw them do it. The rebels yelled like wild indians and charged upon us on a double quick. They acted bravely, they came as close as they could but very few got within 2 rods of us, those that did never went away again. We gave them a welcome with leaden bullets that sent many a brave rebel, for they are brave, to his last account."[79]

Realizing that he could not reorganize the brigade while still on the hill, Dungan ordered the men to fall back to its base. The entire brigade did not retire, however, for the 44th Virginia apparently retreated about 150 yards down the hill and took position behind a rocky ledge. Because Dungan pulled his men off the hill to regroup, Nichols's (Williams's) Brigade on their left was hit by the fire of the 102nd and 78th New York in front of them and the oblique fire from the 60th New York on their right (which had faced Jones's men).[80]

Satisfied that the brigade was now ready to take on Greene's troops, Dungan again sent the brigade back up the hill, probably to the dismay of more than a few of the men. Moving unsteadily forward, the line halted when it was about three hundred yards from the enemy's breastworks. Dungan now ordered a charge. Some of the troops advanced to within twenty-five feet of the breastworks before being forced to turn back. Lieutenant Colonel Salyer recalled that "we tried again and again to drive the enemy from their position, but at length we were compelled to fall back, worn down and exhausted, but not till every round of cartridge had been discharged. At one time we were within a few feet of their works, but the fire was so heavy we could not stand it." Coon agreed. "Soon we heard the rebels coming again . . . this time they came with a rush—they had been reinforced, and thought to drive us out certain . . .they charged again, and again retreated." Dungan now pulled what was left of the brigade back about two hundred yards, and the firing ended at about 10:00 P.M.[81]

While it appears that the brigade maintained a steady fire against the Union position, it did not actually charge the works on July 3. About 4:00 A.M., General Junius Daniel's Brigade moved up to support the brigade. Both came under severe artillery fire during this time. "The bums [bombs] fell that thick that I did not know which way to go. They throwed the dirt all over me a time or too [sic] but did not hurt me, but [I] thought of the other world rite [sic] smart," wrote Private Abisha Gum of the 25th Virginia. Dungan received orders to pull back at about 10:00 P.M. on July 3. Moving with the rest of the division, the brigade took position on Seminary Ridge and prepared to resist a counteroffensive. Colonel Bradley Johnson arrived on July 4, and took command of the brigade.[82]

The horrors of the battle remained with most of Jones's survivors until they died. Private Benjamin Jones of the 44th Virginia recalled years after the battle that "the roar of artillery and rattle of musketry was awfully severe. The mountain trembled under our feet like an aspen leaf, as the great number of artillery belched forth death in our ranks." Because of their position on the steepest part of the line, it is doubtful that any troops could have successfully stormed the heavily defended breastworks during the evening of July 2.[83]

NOTES

1. Davis, *The Confederate General*, vol. II, 13; vol. VI 15.

2. Davis, *The Confederate General*, vol. III, 186–187.

3. OR 27, 2, 441, 442, 503–504.

4. OR 27, 2, 503–504; William W. Goldsborough, "With Lee at Gettysburg," *Philadelphia Record*, July 8, 1900; *The Telegram*, n.d., copy in 2nd Maryland Battalion folder, GNMP; Company F, First North Carolina Infantry at the Battle of Gettysburg," Brake Collection, USAMHI; Pfanz, *Gettysburg—Culp's Hill and Cemetery Hill*, 85–86.

5. OR 27, 2, 504.

6. OR 27, 2, 504; OR 27, 1, 579, 773–774.

7. Ted Barclay, *Ted Barclay, Liberty Hall Volunteers* . . . (Natural Bridge Station, VA, 1992), 28.

8. Busey and Martin, *Regimental Strengths and Losses*, 152, 285.

9. OR 21, 561–562; OR 25, 1, 809

10. Warner, *Generals in Gray*, 59; Pfanz, *Gettysburg—Culp's Hill and Cemetery Hill*, 5–6; Freeman, *Lee's Lieutenants*, vol. 2, 702–703.

11. Davis, *The Confederate General*, vol. VI, 2–3.

12. John Stone, "Memoir," copy in 1st Maryland Battalion folder, GNMP; S. Z. Ammen, *The Telegram*, n.d.; George Thomas, "The Confederate Monument at Gettysburg," *Southern Historical Society Papers* (1886), vol. 14, 444.

13. OR suppl., vol. 5, 394–395; *The Telegram*.

14. OR suppl., vol. 5, 393, 394–395; Clark, *N.C. Regiments*, vol. 1, 148; Pfanz, *Gettysburg—Culp's Hill and Cemetery Hill*, 330.

15. OR 27, 2, 509; William W. Goldsborough, *The Maryland Line* (Port Washington, NY, 1972), 146; Washington Hand, "Memoirs," University of Virginia.

16. OR 27, 2, 509; *The Telegram*.

17. *The Telegram*; OR 27, 2, 509–510; OR suppl., vol. 5, 394–395; Hand, "Memoirs"; Clark, *N.C. Regiments*, vol. 1, 195; Thomas L. Elmore, "Courage Against the Trenches," *Gettysburg Magazine* (July 1992), issue 7, 86; Thomas, "The Confederate Monument at Gettysburg," 445;" Goldsborough, "With Lee at Gettysburg."

18. *The Telegram*, n.d.; William Zollinger, Lamar Hollyday, and D. R. Howard, "General George H. Steuart's Brigade at the Battle of Gettysburg," *Southern Historical Society Papers* (1876), vol. 2, 106.

19. OR 27, 2, 510; OR suppl., vol. 5, 399.

20. Lamar Holliday, "The Second Maryland Again," *The Telegram*, May 19, 1903; Charles Raine, "Memoir," Fredericksburg-Spotsylvania Military Park.

21. Thomas Boone, "History of Company F, First North Carolina Infantry," *The Index*, March 8, 1895; Randolph McKim, "Steuart's Brigade at the Battle of Gettysburg," *Southern Historical Society Papers* (1878), vol. 5, 293.

22. OR 27, 2, 510; Raines, "Memoirs."

23. OR suppl., vol. 5, 397; Samuel Firebaugh, diary, Southern Historical Collection, UNC; Rufus R. Dawes, *Service with the Sixth Wisconsin Volunteers* (Marietta, OH, 1890), 181–182; C. V. Tevis, *The History of the Fighting Fourteenth* . . . (Brooklyn, NY, 1911), 91–92.

This force was probably from the I Corps that had been rushed to support Greene.

Terrence V. Murphy, *Tenth Virginia Infantry* (Lynchburg, VA, 1989), 78, believes it was the 84th New York.

24. Thomas Rankin, *Thirty-Seventh Virginia Infantry* (Lynchburg, VA, 1987), 69.

25. OR 27, 2, 506; OR suppl., vol. 5, 401; Pfanz, *Gettysburg—Culp's Hill and Cemetery Hill*, 288; Pennsylvania Battlefield Commission, *Pennsylvania at Gettysburg . . .* 2 vols. (Harrisburg, PA, 1904), vol. 1, 598; OR 27, 1, 783, 789, 791; 817; Stone, letter.

26. OR 27, 2, 511; Clark, *N.C. Regiments*, vol. 1, 195.

27. Stone, letter; *The Telegram*; Hand, "Memoirs."

28. OR 27, 2, 511; Pfanz, *Gettysburg—Culp's Hill and Cemetery Hill*, 313, 315, 320; McKim, "Steuart's Brigade at the Battle of Gettysburg," 298; *The Telegram*; Thomas, "The Confederate Monument at Gettysburg," 445–446.

29. OR 27, 2, 511; OR suppl., vol. 5, 397, 399; Thomas Rankin, *Twenty-Third Virginia* (Lynchburg, VA, 1985), 68.

30. *The Telegram*; Winfield Peters, "A Maryland Warrior and Hero," in *Southern Historical Society Papers* (1901), vol. 29, 248; *The 28th and 147th Pennsylvania Reunion*, 6; Goldsborough, *The Maryland Line*, 109.

31. Thomas Webb, letter, copy in 1st Maryland folder, GNMP; *Pennsylvania at Gettysburg*, vol. 2, 718.

32. Oliver Taylor, *The War Story of a Confederate Soldier Boy*, copy in the 37th Virginia folder, GNMP; Rothermel Papers, Pennsylvania State Archives.

33. Goldsborough, *The Maryland Line*, 109; OR 27, 2, 511, OR suppl., vol. 5, 395. Although John Cowan (*N.C. Regiments*, vol. 1, 196), claimed that the regiment had three hundred men when it began the battle, Busey and Martin (*Regimental Strengthens and Losses*, 285) believed that it was much higher—548. While both agree that losses were about 220, the differences in initial strength estimates would mean that the regiment lost either 74% or 40%.

One company and part of another from the 3rd North Carolina were on detached duty at the time.

34. OR 27, 2, 511; Firebaugh, diary; *The Telegram*.

35. Randolph McKim, *The Second Maryland Infantry—An Oration Delivered . . . May 9, 1909* (n.p., 1909), 11; Randolph McKim, *A Soldier's Recollections* (New York, 1911), 185; John Futch, letter, Brake Collection, USAMHI.

36. Busey and Martin, *Regimental Strengths and Losses*, 153, 285.

37. Sifarkis, *Compendium of the Confederate Armies: Louisiana*, 64–65; 68–69, 88, 96–97, 98–99; Davis, *The Confederate General*, vol. IV, 197, 200; vol. V, 199.

38. Jones, *Lee's Tigers*, 163–164; Charles Bachelor, letter, copy in the 2nd Louisiana folder, GNMP); David Zable, "Memoir," Tulane University.

39. OR 27, 2, 518; Zable, "Memoir"; Pfanz, *Gettysburg—Culp's Hill and Cemetery Hill*, 80–81.

40. Zable, "Memoir."

41. Zable, "Memoir"; W. G. Lloyd, "Second Louisiana at Gettysburg," *Confederate Veteran* (1898), vol. 6, 417.

42. Pfanz, *Gettysburg—Culp's Hill and Cemetery Hill*, 180; OR 27, 2, 518.

43. Jones, *Lee's Tigers*, 170; Zable, "Memoir"; Imhof, *Gettysburg: Day Two*, 255.

44. George K. Collins, *Memoirs of the 149th Regiment New York Volunteer Infantry* (Syracuse, NY, 1891), 138–139.

45. Thomas W. Brooks and Michael D. Jones, *Lee's Foreign Legion: A History of the 10th Louisian Infantry* (Gravenhurst, ONT, 1995), 47; OR 27, 2, 518; Pfanz, *Gettysburg—Culp's Hill and Cemetery Hill*, 217; Zable, "Memoir"; Watha Rawlings, *War Stories, Being the Thrilling Experiences and Adventures of Captain Watha Rawlings During the War of 1861–1865* (McCauley, TX, 1909), 3.

46. W. P. Snakesberg, "Memoir," copy in Brake Coll., USAMHI.

47. Zable, "Memoir."

48. Zable, "Memoir."

49. OR 27, 2, 518.

50. Busey and Martin, *Regimental Strengths and Losses*, 285.

51. Busey and Martin, *Regimental Strengths and Losses*, 154, 285.

52. Lowell Reidenbaugh, *Twenty-Seventh Virginia* (Lynchburg, VA, 1993), 87; Walter Lord, *Three Months in the Southern States* (New York, 1954), 252.

53. Davis, *The Confederate General*, vol. IV, 213, vol. VI, 147.

54. Davis, *The Confederate General*, vol. VI, 86.

55. John Garibaldi, letter, Brake Collection, USAMHI.

56. C. A. Rollins, "Jackson's Foot Cavalry Reach the Gettysburg Battlefield," *Lexington Gazette and Citizen*, August 16, 1888; George Buswell, diary, copy in 33rd Virginia folder, GNMP.

57. OR 27, 2, 518, 526.

58. OR 27, 2, 518, 521; Pfanz, *Gettysburg—Culp's Hill and Cemetery Hill*, 153–154; Charles Rollins, "Playing Cavalry," *Lexington Gazette and Citizen*, September 27, 1888.

59. OR 27, 2, 504, 518–519, 521, 526.

60. OR 27, 2, 521–522; Pfanz, *Gettysburg—Culp's Hill and Cemetery Hill*, 292–293.

61. OR 27, 2, 522; OR 27, 1, 680.

62. OR 27, 2, 526.

63. OR 27, 2, 519, C. A. Rollins, "A Private's Story," *Lexington Gazette and Citizen*, July 26, 1888.

64. Pfanz, *Gettysburg—Culp's Hill and Cemetery Hill*, 322–323; Collins, *Memoirs of the 149th Regiment New York Volunteer Infantry*, 141.

65. OR 27, 2, 519, 523; William G. Bean, *The Liberty Hall Volunteers* (Charlottesville, VA, 1964), 150; James I. Robertson, *The Fourth Virginia Infantry* (Lynchburg, VA, 1982), 27–28; Pfanz, *Gettysburg—Culp's Hill and Cemetery Hill*, 325–326.

66. Collins, *Memoirs of the 149th Regiment New York Volunteer Infantry*, 148.

67. OR 27, 2, 519; B. H. Coffman, letter, Civil War Miscellaneous Collection, USAMHI; Barclay, *Ted Barclay, Liberty Hall Volunteers . . .*, 92.

68. Busey and Martin, *Regimental Strengths and Losses*, 155, 286.

69. Sifakis, *Compendium of the Confederate Armies: Virginia*, 197, 206, 229–230, 232–233, 237–238; Davis, *The Confederate General*, vol. III, 206–207.

70. Davis, *The Confederate General*, vol. III, 203, 205.

71. Thomas F. Boatright, "Letter," Southern Historical Collection., University of North Carolina.

72. OR 27, 2, 531, 536, 537.

73. OR 27, 2, 531–532, 539; John D. Chapla, *The Forty-Second Virginia Infantry* (Lynchburg, VA, 1983), 37.

74. OR 27, 2, 531–532, 536

75. OR 27, 2, 504, 532, 533, 537.

76. OR 27, 2, 536, 538, 539.

77. OR 27, 2, 532, 538, 539.

While Jones's men did not come under artillery fire from Culp's Hill while they were ascending it, Jones reported that his line received fire from cannon on Cemetery Hill, but sustained few casualties from it (OR 27, 2, 532).

78. OR 27, 2, 532, 537.

79. Steuben H. Coon, letter, copy in 60th New York folder, GNMP.

80. OR 27, 2, 518, 538.

81. OR 27, 2, 553, 539; Coon, letter.

82. OR 27, 2, 533, 534; Richard L. Armstrong, *Twenty-fifth Virginia Infantry and Ninth Virginia Infantry* (Lynchburg, VA, 1990), 64.

83. Benjamin Jones, "Memoirs," CWTI Collection, USAMHI.

THIRD CORPS—

Lieutenant General A. P. Hill

With the death of Stonewall Jackson, Lee created three corps to replace the two-corps system he had used before. None of the three corps was affected as much as A. P. Hill's. Not only was he promoted and assigned command of the new Third Corps, two of his brigadiers, Henry Heth and Dorsey Pender, were elevated to division command. Fate would have Lee's least experienced corps lead the advance toward Gettysburg, with perhaps his least experienced division commander in the lead.[1]

Major General Ambrose Hill was a West Point graduate who hailed from an influential Virginia family. By the outbreak of the war, Hill had already resigned his commission and became colonel of the 13th Virginia. Promoted to brigadier general in February 1862, he led his brigade into action at Williamburg a little more than two months later. Later that month, Hill was promoted again, this time to major general, and was given command of a division styled the "Light Division." Hill led it with distinction. He opened the Seven Days campaign with an unauthorized attack at Mechanicsville, and also sustained exceptionally heavy losses at Gaines's Mill and Frayser's Farm. He performed solidly at the battles of Cedar Mountain and Second Manassas. Hill literally saved Lee's army at Sharpsburg, when his division appeared on the field late in the day. Lapses in judgment caused unnecessarily high casualties at Chancellorsville. Although slightly wounded with Stonewall Jackson, Hill was promoted yet again, about a year after his last one, and given the newly formed corps.[2]

Left behind to watch Hooker's Army of the Potomac along the Rappahannock, General A. P. Hill waited until the enemy had begun its pursuit of the rest of Lee's army before moving northward with his powerful corps. General Richard Anderson's Division began its movement on June 14 and Henry Heth's Division followed the next day. Hill's last division, under Dorsey Pender, remained behind to make sure the Federal army did not turn around and drive for Richmond.

Finding this not to be the case, Pender put his division on the road north as well. The march was uneventful, and the evening of June 27 found the Third Corps encamped at Fayetteville, Pennsylvania.[3]

When Lee finally realized that the enemy had crossed the Potomac and was rapidly heading toward Pennsylvania, he gave orders to concentrate his army near Cashtown or Gettysburg. Hill received orders to this effect during the night of June 28–29. He must have been disappointed, because his former orders were to march toward York, cross the Susquehanna, and menace Harrisburg's communications with Philadelphia. He was also to cooperate with General Ewell, as needed. Hill accordingly directed Heth's Division to take the lead, followed by Pender's. Anderson's Division was ordered to break camp and follow the next morning.[4]

After a reconnaissance by Pettigrew's Brigade (Heth's Division) on June 30 found enemy forces near Gettysburg, Hill ordered Anderson to begin his march sooner and informed Ewell of his intention "to advance the next morning and discover what was in my front." Despite Lee's orders not to engage the enemy until the entire army had assembled, Hill moved two powerful divisions along Chambersburg Pike during the early hours of July 1. Thinking he was going to encounter militia that could be swept aside, he instead was confronted by John Buford's cavalry, which held Henry Heth's Division at bay on the hills west of Gettysburg long enough for Wadsworth's Division (I Corps) to arrive. Heth's initial piecemeal attack at about 10:30 A.M. was defeated with heavy losses. The subsequent attacks, beginning at 3:00 P.M. that afternoon, proved more successful. Heth's two brigades swept three Federal brigades off McPherson Ridge, and then General Dorsey Pender's Division was brought up to finish the job. With the Federal troops now pushed off Seminary Ridge and retreating toward the town of Gettysburg, Hill decided to halt his men, rather than pursue and destroy the enemy. He wrote in his official report that "under the impression that the enemy were entirely routed, my own two divisions exhausted by some six hours' hard fighting, prudence led me to be content with what had been gained, and not push forward troops exhausted and necessarily disordered, probably to encounter fresh troops of the enemy."[5]

On July 2, Anderson's Division was part of the *en echelon* attack against the Federal left and center. Anderson performed poorly, as he did not properly coordinate his brigades' attacks against the Federal line. While some brigades met with limited success, none supported the others, and ultimately, the entire division was defeated. Just as the *en echelon* attack reached Pender's Division, its commander was wounded. In the absence of direct orders, General James Lane, now commanding the division, decided not to commit his troops to the fray. That night, two of Pender's brigades were moved up to support Rodes's attack on Cemetery Hill, which was never launched.[6]

One and a half divisions from Hill's Corps were tapped to participate in the massive charge on July 3. Heth's thoroughly worn out division, now under James Pettigrew, formed to the left of Pickett's Division; behind it were two brigades from Pender's Division, now under Major General Isaac Trimble. Hill probably erred when he assigned command of these two brigades to Trimble just before the attack—too late for their new leader to examine their positions and make needed adjustments. Two brigades from Anderson's Division (Wilcox's and Lang's) were to attack, but they were merely to protect Pickett's right flank. Although most of Hill's units attacked valiantly, they were ultimately repulsed with heavy losses. The corps remained on Seminary Ridge during July 4, and began the retreat back to Virginia that night.[7]

A. P. Hill's performance at Gettysburg is an enigma. Recently elevated to command a corps after the death of Stonewall Jackson, Hill performed poorly. After giving each of his division commanders general orders, he appeared to adopt a "hands off" approach, and as a result, there was poor coordination, limited success, and much higher losses than there should have been.

ANDERSON'S DIVISION—

Major General Richard H. Anderson

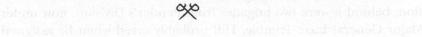

With the exception of Lafayette McLaws, Major General Richard Anderson commanded a division longer than any other officer in Lee's army. He briefly commanded Longstreet's Division during the Peninsula campaign and was promoted to the rank of major general on July 14, 1862, and given command of Huger's Division, which consisted of three brigades. By the Gettysburg campaign, one of the original three had been removed and three additional added for a total of five.

A South Carolinian by birth, Anderson graduated from West Point and then fought in the Mexican, Mormon, and Comanche Wars. Like his commander, A. P. Hill, Anderson resigned prior to the bombardment of Ft. Sumter, and he was present at its fall. He remained in South Carolina and commanded its forces. Ordered to join the army in Virginia, Anderson was assigned a brigade of South Carolina regiments and led them at the battles of Williamsburg, Seven Pines, Gaines's Mill, and Frayer's Farm. After so distinguishing himself on these fields it was just a matter of time before he received his division.[8]

Anderson's Division broke camp around Fredericksburg on the afternoon of June 14 and marched for Culpeper Courthouse. After marching through the Shenandoah Valley, the division crossed the Potomac on July 24 and reached Hagerstown the next day. The weary men reached Fayetteville, Pennsylvania, on June 27 and were permitted to camp just outside it until July 1. Now refreshed, the men formed into column early that morning, and headed for Cashtown, which they reached that afternoon. The sounds of cannon fire could be plainly heard coming from the direction of Gettysburg at about 10:00 A.M., but rather than pushing on, the division was ordered to halt for about ninety minutes at Cashtown. It remained there until 1:00 P.M., when the march to Gettysburg continued. A steady stream of wounded soldiers soon began to pass them. The men paid the wounded little heed, for according to Englishman James Fremantle, the hardened veterans had seen many of them before. Arriving in the vicinity of Gettysburg sometime between 4:00 and 5:00 P.M., Anderson's Division was ordered to form line of battle in Pender's Division's former position on Herr Ridge. Anderson threw out Wilcox's Brigade to the right to detect enemy movement from that direction. The division did not stir for the remainder of the day, causing more than a few men to openly question why they did not push on to enter the fray, which could be clearly heard up ahead.[9]

Anderson had his division in motion again early on July 2. After a mile and a half march, the column reached Seminary Ridge, where Anderson deployed his men on the right of Pender's. The division formed the right flank of the army at the time. The division's brigades were deployed from left to right as Mahone's–Posey's–Wright's–Perry's–Wilcox's. The men felt more comfortable when McLaws's Division formed on their right several hours later. When the *en echelon* attack reached Anderson's three right brigades during the early evening, they advanced on Cemetery Ridge. The actual time is subject to debate, varying from 5:00 to 7:00 P.M. It was probably between 6:00 and 6:30 P.M.[10]

Anderson described the attack of his three right brigades in his report:

> Never did troops go into action with greater spirit or more determined courage. The ground afforded them but little shelter, and for nearly three-quarters of a mile they were compelled to face a storm of shot and shell and bullets; but there was no hesitation nor faltering. They drove the enemy from his first line, and possessed themselves of the ridge and of much of the artillery which it had been crowned.[11]

Parts of Anderson's report were exaggerated. While all three brigades drove the Federal troops from their front, Wilcox's and Perry's Brigades never reached the crest of Cemetery Ridge, as they were forced to pull back because of inadequate support. Wright's Brigade in the center of the division briefly reached the crest of Cemetery Ridge, but it too was forced back because no reinforcements helped it hold the ridge.

Wilcox's and Perry's Brigades were again ordered to attack Cemetery Ridge on the afternoon of July 3, this time in conjunction with Pickett's Division on their left. The attack was not launched until after Pickett's Division was repulsed, however, and some have questioned its significance. It appears to have distracted the Federal troops, thereby allowing some of Pickett's men to reach Seminary Ridge safely. Private Randolph Shotwell of Kemper's Brigade wrote that "this demonstration was mainly useful in allowing time for the fragments of the two attacking divisions, with many of their slightly wounded to get out of range of the Federal sharpshooters." Noted historian George Stewart agreed with this assessment and added that the charge also convinced Meade that Lee had additional troops hidden in the forest along Seminary Ridge. As a result, the Federal commander decided to abort his planned counterattack.[12]

Anderson had also intended to throw Wright's and Posey's Brigades against Cemetery Ridge that afternoon. He noted in his report "at what I supposed to be the proper time, I was about to move forward . . . the brigades, when Lieutenant-General Longstreet directed me to stop the movement, adding that it was useless, and would only involve additional losses."[13]

Anderson's effectiveness and behavior during the battle have been questioned. Most serious was the charge that Anderson did not exercise control and leadership over his division on July 2. While three of his brigades were on or close to Cemetery Ridge, and their commanders were pleading for reinforcements, Anderson permitted Posey's Brigade to be marginally engaged, and Mahone's not at all. One of General Cadmus Wilcox's aides purportedly found Anderson and his staff lying on the ground near a ravine behind Seminary Ridge, as though nothing of importance was occurring.[14]

Wilcox's Brigade—Brigadier General Cadmus Wilcox

Units: 8th Alabama, 9th Alabama, 10th Alabama, 11th Alabama, 14th Alabama
Strength: 1726
Losses: 778 (78-443-257)—45.1%[15]

Brigadier General Cadmus Wilcox's Brigade was perhaps the most stable in the army, as its commander and its regiments had all served together since the Peninsula campaign. As a result, it had been forged into an effective fighting force. Wilcox was only a recent West Point graduate when he was sent south to fight in the Mexican War, where he won honors for his gallantry. He began the war as colonel of the 9th Alabama. On the field at the first battle of Manassas, Wilcox was disappointed with his small role. He was promoted to the rank of brigadier general and given a brigade in October 1861. His new brigade performed meritoriously at Williamsburg and again at Seven Pines. So aggressive was Wilcox during the Seven Days battles that his brigade lost about half of its men. He commanded a small division at the Second Manassas campaign, but was back with his brigade at Sharpsburg, Fredericksburg, and Chancellorsville. The latter campaign was perhaps Wilcox's greatest as a brigade commander, as he skillfully thrust his units between a Federal infantry corps and Lee's rear at Salem Church.

With the Gettysburg campaign in full swing, Wilcox's men could hear the sounds of battle up ahead as they approached Cashtown, Pennsylvania, on July 1. Many Alabamians believed that Lee's army would be eminently successful during this invasion. One soldier from the 10th Alabama related that the "opinion prevailed among subordinate and privates that it was only the Pennsylvania militia that had marched out of Harrisburg to give us battle." The men were pleased to be given a rest when they reached Herr Ridge during the afternoon of July 1. However, when valuable minutes passed, many of the men posed the question, "Why are we not put in?" According to Colonel Hilary Herbert of the 8th Alabama, the answer was usually, "If we were needed 'Marse Bob' would have us there."[16]

After the rest, the division formed into line of battle on Herr Ridge. Wilcox's Brigade was detached, and marched about a mile south, stopping near the Black Horse Tavern, where it formed at a right angle with the rest of the division. Wilcox's men spent the night on picket duty there, watching for a Federal flank attack. Their only companion was Ross's battery. Little did they know that Humphreys's Division (III Corps) almost stumbled into them during the night as it approached the battlefield.[17]

The brigade returned to the division at 7:00 A.M. the next day and marched with it east along Chambersburg Pike. Turning south, the brigade trudged behind its sister brigades, which had already taken their positions on Seminary Ridge. Anderson rode with Wilcox as the brigade moved by the right flank toward Pitzer's Woods and pointed out where he wanted the brigade positioned. The brigade now formed the right flank of the army. Wilcox had an uneasy feeling as he examined the woods with his field glasses. Were they occupied by the enemy, and if so, by how many? He ordered the 10th and 11th Alabama to move cautiously forward and feel for the enemy. So concerned was Wilcox about this possible threat, that he decided to retain the remainder of his regiments in the rear, lest they be overwhelmed by a strong enemy force.[18]

Because the 11th Alabama was advancing southward in an unobstructed wheatfield, it made faster progress than the 10th Alabama on its right, which was moving through rock-strewn Spangler's Woods. Reaching its assigned position, the 11th Alabama wheeled to the left, which had the effect of facing front at right angles to its original line of march. This also presented its right flank to the woods that would soon be occupied by the 10th Alabama. A heavy volley of musketry from the right and rear broke the stillness, and several men on the right flank of the 11th Alabama fell. So unexpected was this fire that the regiment was thrown into confusion. The officers felt that the only sensible thing to do was to pull the unit back to the safety of its supporting line. As the men rushed back toward the rest of the brigade, the soldiers of the 8th Alabama were told to lie down to permit their comrades to pass through their ranks. The Alabamians did not know it, but hiding behind rocks and trees in Pitzer's Woods were the veterans of the 3rd Maine and Berdan's 1st U.S. Sharpshooters (Ward's Brigade, Birney's Division, III Corps). The 10th Alabama double-quicked forward, and when close enough, let loose several volleys into the Federal troops which had ventured into the open field. The enemy troops scurried back to the woods. During this time, the 8th Alabama also moved forward and now occupied the 10th Alabama's former position. After a fifteen- to twenty-minute firefight with the Federal troops in the woods, Colonel William Forney ordered his 10th Alabama to charge. The order was successfully carried out, and the last remnants of Federal troops on Seminary Ridge were driven out. The 11th Alabama's Fleming Thompson proudly wrote home that "[we] advanced on them and made them move in double quick from there [sic] stronghold . . . I tell you we made the ground look blue with yanks." J. J. Renfroe told the folks back home that Wilcox rode up to the 10th Alabama's commander and exuded, "Col. Forney, from my heart I thank you and to your gallant regiment I pull off my hat," as he bowed to the men.[19]

The brigade continued to occupy not only the extreme right of the division, but also the army, until Longstreet's men arrived a few hours later. It appears that the brigade was deployed from left to right as 9th Alabama–14th Alabama–11th Alabama–8th Alabama–10th Alabama. At about 2:00 P.M., the men could see a long column of troops pass behind them— McLaws's and Hood's Divisions of Longstreet's Corps had finally arrived. Because Wilcox's Brigade had formed the right-most unit of the army up to this time between Pitzer's and Spangler's Woods, its two right regiments (8th and 10th Alabama) were refused to the right, so they faced south, while the other regiments faced east. It does not appear that Wilcox changed the position of these two regiments when Barksdale's Brigade (McLaws's Division) took position on the right and rear of his brigade. As a result, these two regiments faced friends, not foe.[20]

While there was scattered musket and artillery fire during the late morning and early afternoon, it was mostly quiet. The men rested and chatted with their comrades. Private George Clark of the 11th Alabama recalled that "the sun was fiercely hot and there was no shade or other protection for the men. Here they sweated, sweltered and swore." Wilcox took the opportunity to brief his officers of the attack plans as he understood them. The brigade's first action was to move by the left flank, to give Barksdale's Brigade on the right space to get into line, prior to their attack.[21]

Wilcox received his orders to prepare to attack at about 6:00 P.M. First, he moved farther south. "This was done as rapidly as the nature of the ground with its opposing obstacles (stone and plank fences) would admit. Having gained 400 or 500 yards to the left by this flank movement, my command faced by the right flank and advanced," wrote Wilcox in his official report. After analyzing the voluminous writings of Colonel Hilary Herbert, modern historian Harry Pfanz believed that the 8th Alabama, which had been facing south, marched by the left flank, but this took him into the no-man's-land between Seminary and Cemetery Ridges. As the regiment approached the Staub house, approximately three hundred yards from Pitzer's Woods, it was fired on by Federal troops. Herbert wrote that "we were greeted . . . with a shower of musket balls and grape shot from a line of Infantry, about 200 yards off, and a battery of Artillery on their right." This caused Herbert to deploy his regiment in line of battle. Continuing his narrative, Herbert noted that "the regts. in our rear were obliged to make a detour to our left and then came 'forward into line,' which this occupied considerable time." During this time, Herbert's line, particularly his right-most companies, came under heavy fire.[22]

While Herbert's 8th Alabama was forming, it appears that the remaining regiments of the brigade marched by the left flank, and therefore closed the gap with Perry's Brigade on their left. The 10th Alabama, which had formed the right flank, did not follow the 8th Alabama's lead, but instead rushed over to form on the right of the 11th Alabama. This left a two hundred-yard gap between the 8th Alabama and the rest of the brigade.[23]

With the brigade in line of battle, Wilcox issued orders to charge. Cheers filled the air, as the men felt supremely confident that they would drive the enemy as they had earlier in the day. More than a few, however, probably felt some dread, for in front of them was an open plain, and farther on, masses of Federal troops. Lieutenant Edmund Patterson of the 9th Alabama felt more like praying than cheering. Uttering a silent prayer, he asked God to help him do his duty to his country. The men of the 8th Alabama were especially satisfied to receive the order, for it permitted them to escape the intense pounding they were taking from the federal artillery.[24]

Driving forward, the brigade, minus the 8th Alabama (see below), swept toward Emmitsburg Road, quickly dissipating the Federal skirmish line in front of it. Seeley's battery also galloped off, leaving two guns behind because so many horses were disabled or killed. The Alabamians now climbed the fences on either side of Emmitsburg Road and continued on. They were soon hit by artillery fire along their front and both flanks.[25]

Carr's Brigade (Humphrey's Division, III Corps) was up ahead in two lines of battle. After climbing the fence, Wilcox's men exchanged volleys with the enemy along Emmitsburg Road for several minutes. Carr's men could not sustain the pressure, particularly with Barksdale's Brigade on their left flank, and began pulling back. Four cannon from Turnbull's Battery fell into Wilcox's hands. So far, Wilcox's men had driven the infantry before them, and captured six cannon. Total victory seemed within their grasp. So quickly was the brigade moving forward that there was no time to stop and reform their disordered ranks. Some units, such as the 10th and 11th Alabama, had become terribly jumbled up during the charge. Clark (11th Alabama) noted with dismay that the units were "in marked confusion, mixed up indiscriminately, offi-

cers apart from their men, men apart from their officers, but all pushing forward notwithstanding."[26]

The 8th Alabama was rushing forward a few hundred yards to the south, essentially on its own. It finally encountered Barksdale's regiments on its right, and the units from the two brigades swept forward. While the men could see some Federal troops up ahead, most had already been routed. Making a half-wheel to the left, the 8th Alabama changed position to attack the Federal troops there and to make contact with the remainder of the brigade. Up ahead was a Federal battery, which was wheeled about and opened fire. According to Colonel Herbert, a "storm of grape shot whizzed around our heads." He ordered a charge, and "we swept like a hurricane over cannon and caissons." To Colonel Herbert, this was the supreme moment for his men during the entire war. "Victory was with our army and we ourselves were the victors," he wrote after the war.[27]

None of Wilcox's men probably realized it, but two fresh Federal regiments (19th Massachusetts and 42nd New York) took position behind Carr's withdrawing brigade. After firing a few volleys, these two regiments also withdrew. Wilcox could see two Federal batteries firing at his brigade from Cemetery Ridge. He quickly sent the 9th and 14th Alabama charging against the battery on the left (probably Thomas's), and the 10th and 11th Alabama against the one on the right (probably Rorty's). A mass of blue-clad infantry suddenly appeared in their front. Wilcox described the appearance of the 1st Minnesota (Harrow's Brigade, Gibbon's Division, II Corps) in his report, writing that "still another line of infantry descended upon the slope in our front at a double-quick, to the support of their fleeing comrades and for the defense of their batteries."[28]

Looking around him, Wilcox and his men were dismayed to see no other Confederate troops in the area. Wilcox quickly dispatched his adjutant general, Captain Walter Winn, to General Anderson with a plea for support. He was unsuccessful in getting aid, despite the fact that Posey and Mahone's Brigades were only modestly engaged.[29]

Sergeant John Plummer of the 1st Minnesota was surprised "to see some of the rebs, not fifty yards from us, standing out openly and loading and firing as deliberately as though they were in no danger whatever . . . Ah! There is no mistake but what some of those rebs are just as brave as it is possible for human beings to be. I expected they would turn and run when they see us coming so determinedly."[30]

Wilcox's Brigade and the 1st Minnesota both advanced and collided near Plum Run. Wilcox recalled that the 1st Minnesota charged his men three times, and three times they were stopped. All the while, Federal artillery poured shells into the Alabamians. The fight lasted about fifteen minutes. Other Federal units arrived from Harrow's (Gibbon's Division, II Corps) and Willard's (Hays's Division, II Corps) Brigades. The 111th New York of the latter brigade attacked Wilcox's right flank, driving it back. Now with pressure on his front and on both flanks, and with no support forthcoming, Wilcox realized his brigade's dilemma, and reluctantly ordered his men back to the safety of Seminary Ridge. "With a second supporting line, the heights could have been carried," Wilcox lamented.[31]

The retreat across the open plain was no easy task, as the Federal infantry and cannon continued to fire into the backs of the retreating Alabamians. The survivors regrouped at their old positions on Seminary Ridge and bivouacked for the night. The men were saddened, not only by their lost comrades and lost opportunities, but also by the thoughts of the Federal cannon they had captured but were forced to leave behind.[32]

The brigade rested during the morning of July 3. As the men laid about they could see Colonel Porter Alexander rearrange his batteries near Emmitsburg Road. Some of the men could see Wilcox stride rapidly to the summit of the ridge and closely examine the Federal position on Cemetery Ridge with his field glasses. The men were ordered to move up directly behind the artillery soon after he returned. This order unnerved some of the men. One remarked that "Old Billy Fixin (the Brigadier's nickname), was not satisfied with having lost half of his brigade the day before, but was determined to sacrifice the 'whole caboodle' today."[33]

The Confederate artillery opened fire soon after 1:00 P.M., and the Federal guns quickly replied in kind. Clark (11th Alabama) remembered that the cannonade was beyond description. "The earth seemed to rise up under the concussion, the air was filled with missiles, and the noise of all was so furious and overwhelming as well as continuous that one had to scream to his neighbor beside him to be heard." The smoke was so dense that the men could not see the cannoneers, despite being less than fifty yards away. According to Colonel Herbert, it was only when "a breath of air blew aside the smoke to let in the yellow sunlight or the lurid glow of burning powder lighted up the scene" that the cannoneers could be seen. Renfroe (10th Alabama) added that "bombs were exploding in every direction, and nature trembled under the terrors of the hour." Despite the noise, the brigade suffered few casualties.[34]

More than a few men cringed at the sight of Pickett's Division stepping off to their left. The Federal artillery opened fire, and the men could see gaping holes appear in Kemper's Brigade's lines. Kemper's men then obliqued to the left and marched out of sight of Wilcox's men. A courier galloped up to Wilcox, then a second, and then a third, all with the same order: to move forward with Perry's (Lang's) Brigade to support Pickett's right flank. One of Pickett's aides, Captain Robert Bright, related how Wilcox "was standing with both hands raised waving and saying to me, 'I know, I know.' I said, 'But, General, I must deliver my message.'" Despite the fact that Pickett's men had already been defeated, Wilcox had no choice but to order his men forward. Colonel Hilary Herbert of the 8th Alabama admitted that "every private saw at once the madness of the attempt." They could also see Lang's men advance on their left.[35]

Artilleryman Edward Alexander wrote after the war, "just then, Wilcox's Brigade passed by us, moving to Pickett's support. There was no longer anything to support, and with the keenest pity at the useless waste of life, I saw them advance. The men, as they passed us, looked bewildered, as if they wondered what they were expected to do, or why they were there."[36]

As the 1000 men advanced over the same ground they had traversed the afternoon before, the regiments were arranged from left to right as 14th Alabama–8th Alabama–11th Alabama–10th Alabama–9th Alabama. Since he was to cover Pickett's right flank, Wilcox ordered his men to oblique slightly to the left to cover the same ground as the Virginians. McGilvery's artillery battalion opened fire as Wilcox's men came into view. "All of the enemy's terrible artillery that could bear on them was concentrated upon them from both flanks and directly in front, and more than on the evening previous," noted Wilcox. It might have

been easier for Wilcox if he had seen a reason to advance, but he admitted in his report that "not a man of the division that I was ordered to support could I see." Colonel Herbert recounted that the Federal artillery had no one but Wilcox's and Perry's (Lang's) Brigades to concentrate upon. "Shells bursting in the ranks made great gaps in the regt. These at the command of 'guide centre' were closed up as if on drill & we continued forward."[37]

To make matters worse, Wilcox could see Stannard's Brigade (Doubleday's Division, I Corps) moving toward Lang's vulnerable left flank. Because the Federal troops were exposed, Wilcox was confident that the Confederate artillery would quickly disperse them. Riding rapidly back to the batteries along Seminary Ridge, Wilcox was horrified to learn that they were out of ammunition. "Not getting any artillery to fire upon the enemy's infantry that were on my left flank, and seeing none of the troops that I was ordered to support, and knowing that my small force could do nothing save to make a useless sacrifice of themselves, I ordered them back," he wrote. Despite the fact that they had only come under artillery fire as he reached Plum Run before turning back, Wilcox's Brigade lost over two hundred men during their aborted charge.[38]

After resting on July 4, the brigade joined the rest of the army in its retreat back to Virginia. The brigade had done well under the steady hand of its commander. On July 2 it came very close to capturing a section of Cemetery Ridge, and would have been more successful had reinforcements been forthcoming. Despite the great odds against it, the brigade advanced valiantly against Cemetery Ridge on July 3. Fortunately for the men, Wilcox had the good sense to abort the mission and return to Seminary Ridge.

✂

Mahone's Brigade—Brigadier General William Mahone

Units: 6th Virginia, 12th Virginia, 16th Virginia, 41st Virginia, 61st Virginia
Strength: 1542
Losses: 102 (12-51-39)—6.7%[39]

Brigadier General William Mahone's men knew no other brigade commander during the war. A Virginia Military Institute graduate, Mahone spent his prewar years in the railroad industry. When the war broke out, he received a lieutenant colonel's commission and within a month became the colonel of the 6th Virginia. During the autumn and winter of the first year of the war, Mahone was given a brigade of Virginia regiments and served in the Norfolk Department. He next moved his brigade to Drewry's Bluff, where it helped repel a Federal naval squadron attempting to approach Richmond. Transferred to the army, the brigade participated in the battle of Seven Pines. The brigade performed poorly at Glendale, but redeemed itself at Malvern Hill, when it drove to within seventy-five yards of the enemy. Mahone was wounded at Second Manassas, and as a result, the brigade was attached to Pryor's Brigade during the Maryland campaign. During the Chancellorsville campaign, Mahone helped take on the Federal VI Corps at Salem Church. While the brigade had been engaged in many battles, there were lingering questions about its mettle.[40]

"Little Billy" Mahone's men experienced a mixture of emotions as they marched through Maryland. Certain towns, like Funkstown and Hagerstown, had Southern leanings, and Confederate flags hung from many houses. Other towns, like Boonsboro and Frederick,

were more pro-Union and the inhabitants showed it with their grim expressions. During the much needed rest at Chambersburg, the men roamed around the countryside in search of food. Despite Lee's orders not to steal from civilians, the men often returned with their arms loaded with food and other goods. When queried about how they got them, the answer was invariably, "I bought them." However, Sergeant James Whitehorne of the 12th Virginia knew better, as his men had not been paid in weeks.[41]

Morale was high, but many had nagging feelings about enemy soldiers, or more precisely, the lack of them anywhere in the vicinity. They could not believe that they were being permitted to march into Pennsylvania unmolested. This did not stop them from admiring the lush farms and the well-built barns that were usually larger than the houses. According to Private Westwood Todd of the 12th Virginia, "the people whom we saw looked glum and even sorrowful. Some were badly frightened." Todd, however, related that the civilians had little to worry about.[42]

The march to Gettysburg continued on July 1 after a few days' reprieve at Fayetteville. Crossing South Mountain, the brigade, with the rest of the division, reached Cashtown around noon and rested before continuing its march. The men could hear the sounds of battle up ahead, and before long, a steady stream of wounded men and prisoners walked and limped past them. The brigade bivouacked near Seminary Ridge that night. On July 2, the men were marched to the right, to take their positions near the McMillan house, where they formed the left flank of Anderson's Division. A line of skirmishers was thrown out, which battled their counterparts near the Bliss farm.[43]

Most of the men spent a quiet day in the shade of McMillan's Woods through the early evening of July 2. Beginning at 6:00 P.M., the three right brigades of Anderson's Division (Wilcox's, Lang's, and Wright's) launched their *en echelon* attacks on Cemetery Ridge and met with initial success. Realizing that he could not capture and hold the ridge, General Ambrose Wright sent his aide-de-camp to find General Anderson and get help from Posey's and Mahone's Brigades. Anderson told Wright to continue his attack, as he would quickly provide assistance. Posey's Brigade, to Mahone's immediate right, launched its attack and captured the Bliss farm, and some of his units were driving for Emmitsburg Road. He too needed assistance, and asked Mahone for help. In his official report, Posey wrote, "I . . . requested Brigadier-General Mahone, who was on my left, in the rear of another division, to send me a regiment to support my left. He being at this time ordered to the right, could not comply."[44]

It appears that Mahone used Anderson's order to move to Wright's aid as an excuse for not sending a regiment to support Posey. Yet Mahone never moved any of his troops to support Wright either. Thus, while the rest of Anderson's Division was engaged in desperate combat, Mahone's men were merely spectators. These actions helped substantiate a growing feeling in the army that Mahone "was a little too careful in looking after his men—a suspicion that he sometimes kept them out of the fighting." While some historians believed that Mahone's Brigade was to act as the divisional reserve, it is clear that it was arrayed in a manner to continue the *en echelon* attack of Anderson's Division. Some have speculated that because Mahone did not move forward,

the attack wave never reached Pender's Division, which could have continued the assault on Cemetery Ridge.[45]

Mahone's men expected to be committed at any time. Private Todd (12th Virginia) related that "we were lying on our arms, expecting every minute to take a hand. It was a day of painful suspense." While in McMillan's Woods, the brigade supported some of William Pegram's batteries and was exposed to severe artillery fire during the day. Private William Moseley of the 6th Virginia recorded in his diary that the "fire was terrible—one continual roar—air filled with bursting shells and shrapnel and other infernal machines to kill." George Barnard of the 12th Virginia believed that this artillery fire was the heaviest the brigade had experienced up to this time in the war, and added that the "ordeal of being subjected for hours to this fire from an unseen foe, without any prospect of suppressing or returning it was trying; but the casualties were not numerous."[46]

The brigade apparently spent most of July 2 resting and building breastworks. Although it did apparently advance toward Cemetery Ridge later that night, it did not go far before turning around and retracing its steps, much to the relief of the men, who dreaded night charges.[47]

The men were thankful to have built breastworks when the great cannonade of July 3 commenced. "Our little breastwork was hit 23 times and pieces of shell fell all around us nearly covering us with dirt," recorded Private Moseley in his diary. Later the men could soon see the three Confederate divisions advancing toward Cemetery Ridge. Incredibly, Lee and A. P. Hill did not choose to use Mahone's Brigade in the Pickett–Pettigrew–Trimble charge, despite the fact that it had lost but a handful of men thus far. Some have suggested that Lee's staff did not know the exact condition of the brigades committed to the charge. Others have suggested that Mahone's recalcitrant behavior on July 2 may have played a role. Either way, this fresh brigade was not deployed in the charge until the remnants returned, when it was finally thrown forward to help cover the retreat of the broken units.[48]

As a result of Mahone's actions and Anderson's and Hill's mismanagement, the brigade lost only 102 men during the battle, or 7% of its strength. This was the lowest of any brigade in Lee's army at Gettysburg. Charges were never filed against Mahone, and the following year he was promoted to the rank of major general and became one of Lee's most capable and aggressive division commanders. No one could have predicted this turn of events, given Mahone's performance at Gettysburg.[49]

Perry's Brigade—Colonel David Lang

Units: 2nd Florida, 5th Florida, 8th Florida
Strength: 742
Losses: 455 (80-228-147)—61.3%[50]

Perry's Brigade had a number of distinctions as it marched toward Gettysburg. It was the smallest brigade in Lee's army, partly because it was composed of only three regiments. These three regiments were the only ones in Lee's army that hailed from Florida. Finally, the brigade's commander, General Edward Perry, was recuperating from a bout with typhoid fever and was not with the army. Colonel David Lang of the 8th Florida now led the brigade.[51]

The three regiments had seen variable service with the Army of Northern Virginia. The 2nd Florida had been mustered into service in July 1861 and the brigade's last regiment (8th Florida) formed a year later. Although not brigaded, the 2nd Florida participated in the battle of Williamsburg. It later joined Garland's Brigade, and at Seven Pines captured a Federal battery, with losses approaching 45%. The regiment was also engaged at Gaines's Mill and Frayser's Farm. The two other Florida regiments arrived in Virginia and participated in the Second

Manassas campaign. The three were placed in Pryor's Brigade prior to the Maryland campaign, but were later pulled away to form a separate brigade under General Perry.[52]

As the brigade crossed the waist-deep Potomac River, the men began singing "Maryland, My Maryland." The pace of the march slowed to only twelve to fifteen miles a day when the men marched through Maryland. They appreciated the slower pace and the abundant food in the region. Toward the end of a long rest period in Chambersburg, Captain C. Seton Fleming of the 2nd Florida wrote home that the men were "'resting on our oars' here for three days, living on the fat of the land." Fleming was amazed that the price of food was actually lower than it was in Florida, prior to the war. He did express some concern over the fact that many men were stealing chickens and other commodities, despite Lee's strict orders to the contrary. Yet, he quickly rationalized that these men's families had suffered at the hands of the enemy, and their theft was therefore justified. Fleming was not impressed with the people who populated southern Pennsylvania, whom he called, "low Dutch." Writing to his brother, he said that "I have scarcely seen a refined and highly intelligent person since I have been in the State."[53]

During the march toward Gettysburg on July 1, the brigade was designated as the division's rear guard and traveled with the wagon train. However, as the battle raged, Anderson was ordered to bring up his division, and one of his first actions was to recall Lang's Brigade. As a result of being in the rear of the division, the men choked on clouds of dust kicked up by the troops ahead of them. Anderson halted the division about two miles from town, where the men could clearly hear the sounds of battle up ahead. They anxiously waited to join the fray. The orders never materialized, however, and the brigade, with the remainder of the division, bivouacked on Herr Ridge.[54]

The next morning, July 2, the brigade marched to Seminary Ridge, where it turned to the right and occupied a position south of the McMillan farm buildings. Wilcox's Brigade was on its right and Wright's was on its left. Firing soon erupted to their right, where Wilcox's Brigade was taking position. Anderson immediately alerted Lang to move to Wilcox's assistance, but before they had gone very far, he received word that his brigade was not needed. The men spent the remainder of the day resting behind a low stone wall, which they strengthened with rails and dirt. Many chafed at the delay in launching the attack, probably knowing that every minute brought more enemy troops to the area and permitted them to build stronger defenses. Some men played cards to while away the hours, but tore them up and threw them away when they received orders to prepare to engage the enemy.[55]

Lang reported that he received orders from Anderson at about 5:00 P.M. He was told that Longstreet's men were successfully driving the enemy, and that Wilcox's

Brigade would advance when the last of Longstreet's men had been launched. "I was ordered to throw forward a strong line of skirmishers, and advance with General Wilcox, holding all the ground the enemy yielded," he noted in his report. Because of Lang's inexperience, it appears that Anderson put him under Wilcox's wing.[56]

Colonel Lang anxiously watched as Wilcox's men began their advance. Lieutenant J. B. Johnson of the 5th Florida also observed this movement. "There [went] Wilcox's Brigade, and soon all to the right [was] hidden by dense smoke, and the rebel yell [could] be heard above the rattle of musketry." Almost immediately, Johnson heard the orders: "Attention, forward, charge," and the men began their attack. Lang's regiments were deployed from left to right: 2nd Florida–8th Florida–5th Florida.[57]

Both Lang and Johnson recalled how their double-quicking line was pounded by Federal artillery as it marched steadily toward Cemetery Ridge. Lang wrote that his brigade was met at the first hill "with a murderous fire of grape, canister, and musketry." Johnson described how the "enemy's guns [were] making great gaps in our lines, and the air seem[ed] filled with musket balls, our men [were] falling on all sides."[58]

Continuing forward, Lang's three small regiments slammed into the left flank of Carr's Brigade (Humphreys's Division), positioned along Emmitsburg Road composed of the 1st and 11th Massachusetts and the 26th Pennsylania. The left and center of Wilcox's Brigade also hit Carr's Brigade almost at the same time. Unable to sustain such an intense attack on its front and flank, Carr's men broke for the rear. Modern historian Harry Pfanz credited Lang's attack with rolling up Carr's Brigade. Many of Carr's men halted beyond their artillery and attempted to regroup, but Lang's men soon reappeared and poured volleys into the Federal troops, causing them to continue their retreat toward Cemetery Ridge. Lang wrote that the "men opened a galling fire upon them, thickly strewing the ground with their killed and wounded. This threw them into confusion, when we charged them, with a yell, and they broke and fled in confusion into the woods and breastworks beyond, leaving four or five cannon in my front."[59]

Flushed with victory, Lang ordered his men forward. As they reached the foot of Cemetery Ridge, Lang could see how winded and scattered his regiments had become. He therefore ordered a halt "for the purpose of reforming, and allowing the men to catch breath before the final assault on upon the heights," he reported. According to Sergeant William Pigman of the 8th Florida, they had driven the enemy "like chaff." He noted that "after driving them at least 1 mile & just as we were ready to make a grand charge on their last line of entrenchments, the order came to fall back." Almost immediately after the men halted, a series of events conspired to completely change the situation. An aide arrived with information that a heavy force was advancing against Wilcox's Brigade on the right. Almost immediately, several volleys erupted from the woods about fifty yards in front of the brigade, which felled many Floridians. This was apparently was from the four hundred-man 19th Maine (Harrow's Brigade, Gibbon's Division, II Corps). They returned the fire. Lang characterized it as being "gallantly met and handsomely replied to by my men." Another aide arrived with more ominous news: Wilcox's men had now pulled back and the enemy was attempting to get behind his right flank. Deciding to investigate

himself, Lang found that the "enemy had passed me more than 100 yards, and were attempting to surround me."[60]

Johnson (5th Florida) also watched the buildup of Federal troops in this sector. "As we [stood] panting for breath, we [saw] the artillery coming around the foot of the Ridge with the horses at full speed, and long lines of infantry after them. Reinforcements [were] coming to the enemy. We look[ed] back but there [was] no support in sight. The battle [was] won, but the battle [would] be lost."[61]

With the possibility of being surrounded, and no aid forthcoming, Lang had no choice but to pull his brigade back. He halted his command at Emmitsburg Road, hoping to rally his men and put up stiff resistance. He soon realized, however, that the area did not provide a good defensive position, and he reluctantly ordered his men back to is starting point on Seminary Ridge. The retreat was almost as difficult as the advance, as the Federal troops "poured a perfect torrent of grape cannister [sic] and shell after us with terrible effect," noted Lieutenant James Wentworth of the 5th Florida. The men were somewhat surprised that the enemy had fought so well. According to D. E. Maxwell of the 8th Florida, "the fighting was the most desperate of the War (the enemy fighting much harder on their own soil, and having the best position imaginable)." The small brigade lost about three hundred men, or more than 40%, during this charge. Among the missing was the prized flag of the 8th Florida, which had fallen to the ground after several of its flag bearers were hit. No one knew it was missing until the men had reached the safety of Seminary Ridge. Sergeant Raymond Reid of the 2nd Florida summarized the men's feelings when he wrote home, "worn out weary and sad we prepared to rest for the night."[62]

During the early morning hours of July 3, Lang received orders from Anderson to "connect my right with General Wilcox's left, and conform my movements during the day to those of his brigade." The orders also contained a strange statement for a division commander to make—that Lang "would receive no further orders." At about 7:00 A.M., Lang saw Wilcox's men moving forward toward Emmitsburg Road to support the batteries taking position there. True to his orders, Lang ordered his men forward to connect with Wilcox's left. The men set about crafting breastworks. "The men went to work in good earnest and in a little while had quite a formidable breastwork built of stone, rails and dirt which was dug with bayonets," noted Reid (2nd Florida)."[63]

The men were not ready for the great cannonade that occurred shortly after 1:00 P.M. "The roar of our cannon and the bursting shells from the enemy's was something indescribable and terrific," wrote Johnson (5th Florida). He characterized the sound as "one continuous and awful roar." Reid wrote home that "the earth trembled beneath us. We could not raise our heads."[64]

After about an hour and a half, Pickett's Division could be seen stepping off smartly into the valley of death between Cemetery and Seminary Ridges. About fifteen to twenty minutes later, General Wilcox's men were on their feet and seemed ready to move forward. Lang reported that "in accordance with previous orders to conform to his movments [Wilcox's] I moved forward also." Johnson recalled how at the order of "attention," "we [sprang] to our feet, forward and we [were] marching to meet the enemy." It is hard to imagine that after the severe losses that the brigade took the day before the men were in any mood to risk losing more in a futile charge across the

valley. It appears that the brigade was aligned as it was the day before.[65]

Being on the left and closest to Kemper's Brigade, Lang's men received the same pounding that the Virginians had sustained several minutes before. He sent back a request for aid from the artillery in his rear, but they had run out of long-range ammunition. Pigman (8th Florida) admitted that "knowing what we had to encounter, it [the order to charge] was not obeyed with the same alacrity as was the case yesterday." Wentworth (5th Florida) truly captured the horrors of the charge, when he wrote in his diary that the Floridians charged "amid a terrible shower of shell grape cannister [sic] and bullets. It was the hottest work I ever saw. My men falling all around me with brains blown out, arms off and wounded in every direction." Reid (2nd Florida) wrote home that "as we raised the Yell they poured a deadly fire of grape and canister upon us. On we rushed. Our men fell fast and thick. At last we were flanked."[66]

The flanking column was the 16th Vermont of Stannard's Brigade (Doubleday's Division, I Corps). After assisting in repulsing Kemper's Brigade, the Green Mountain men were incredulous to see yet another line of battle bearing down on them along their left and rear. Changing direction and charging forward, they approached Lang's left flank as it entered the woods surrounding Plum Run, south of the Codori farm, while McGilvery's artillery battalion on Cemetery Ridge continued to pour a withering frontal fire into the Floridians. Some of the men halted and returned the fire, while others continued their march toward Cemetery Ridge. With their own huzzah, the Federal troops charged into the 2nd Florida's left flank. Colonel Wheeler Veazey of the 16th Vermont explained that upon his order "the men cheered and rushed forward at a run without firing a shot and quickly struck the rebel flank and followed it until the while line had disappeared. The movement was so sudden and rapid that the enemy could not change front to oppose us." Colonel Lang reported that the "noise of artillery and small-arms was so deafening that it was impossible to make the voice heard above the din, and the men were by this time so badly scattered in the bushes and among the rocks that it was impossible to make any movement to meet or check the enemy's advance." As a result, the Federal troops scooped up scores of prisoners. Lang acknowledged that despite the fact that he immediately ordered a retreat, "it was not in time to save a large number of the Second Florida Infantry, together with their colors, from being cut off and captured by the flanking force on the left." The men did not go easily, firing from

behind rocks and trees until they were overwhelmed.[67]

The brigade lost hundreds of men and the flags of the 2nd and 8th Florida. The survivors of this once proud brigade now numbered less than 175. The officers rallied the men in their former positions on Seminary Ridge, where they remained through the night and the next day. The brigade began its retreat during the early morning hours of July 5.

Isaac Barineau of the 8th Florida best summed up the brigade's actions at Gettysburg when he wrote to his sister, "I never saw such fighting as was done on thursday [sic] and friday [sic] the yanks had a spendid [sic] position and we charged them twice and run them both times but we couldn't hold it we didn't get reinforced in time." Captain Fleming (2nd Florida) added, "no troops could have fought better than our Floridians."[68]

Posey's Brigade—Brigadier General Carnot Posey

Units: 12th Mississippi, 16th Mississippi, 19th Mississippi, 48th Mississippi
Strength: 1322
Losses: 112 (15-80-17)—8.5%[69]

Like so many other brigades that fought at Gettysburg, Posey's four regiments were recruited at about the same time (mid-1861), but were initially organized into four different brigades. While the 2nd Mississippi Battalion (which later became the 48th Mississippi) and the 12th and 19th Mississippi were sent directly to Johnston's army and participated in the Peninsula campaign and the battle of Seven Pines, the 16th Mississippi became part of Trimble's Brigade and fought in the Shenandoah Valley. All but the 16th Mississippi were placed in Featherston's

Brigade just prior to the Seven Days battles, and they saw action at Gaines's Mill and Glendale. The 16th Mississippi was added to the brigade prior to the Second Manassas campaign and saw action there and at Sharpsburg, where Colonel Carnot Posey of the 16th Mississippi temporarily commanded the brigade.[70]

With the transfer of General Winfield Featherston to Mississippi, Colonel Posey was promoted to the rank of brigadier general and assumed command of the brigade on January 19, 1863. An attorney by training, Posey was a lieutenant in the Mexican War. It did not hurt that he served under Jefferson Davis. Entering the Confederate service as a captain in the 16th Mississippi, Posey rose to command the regiment in June 1861. He saw continuous combat until elevated to brigade command. Chancellorsville was Posey's first battle as a brigadier general, where the brigade played only a supporting role. Therefore, Posey marched with his men toward Gettysburg with limited experience commanding a brigade in battle.[71]

As Lee's army began its march northward, Private Frank Foote from the 48th Mississippi noted that "we were braced by a consciousness of superior valor and contempt for our foe which in the end proved our ruin." An early reminder of the horrors of battle occurred when the men marched through the recent Chancellorsville battlefield. The men were hardened, though, and when they came upon a fleshless skull lying along the road, the men took turns kicking it. One officer even carried it aloft on his sword for a while. A disgusted soldier finally retrieved the skull and buried it.[72]

The men approached the Pennsylvania state line with much anticipation. But first they had to find it, since it was not clearly marked. The men relied on the citizens' guidance, and when the men were sure they had reached the invisible line, they let out an "old-fashioned, prolonged yell [that] attested the fact and vented our joy," recalled Foote. The special event was marked that night with a whiskey ration served to all the men. According to Foote, it was "about as foul as the average Northern estimate of Jeff Davis and his cause."[73]

The inhabitants of Chambersburg, Pennsylvania were found to "like us even less than did the Marylanders. Many can't speak English," wrote Private Frank Riley of the 16th Mississippi. The men were chagrined when the women made fun of their ragged appearance. The mood lightened, however, when one of the men yelled out, "We always put on our dirty clothes when we go hog killing." Riley went so far as to call the women "insolent and ugly."[74]

The men readily partook of the local bounty. Cherries were plentiful, and the commissary officers often returned with many other luxuries. The men were not above playing tricks on the inhabitants of Pennsylvania. In one case, the men "captured" a young civilian and "inducted" him into the Confederate army before releasing him. Another instance found the men removing some milk and cream from crocks in small enough quantities that the farmer would not miss them. Some acts of pillage apparently occurred during the march, and guards were posted around the camps to keep the soldiers from wandering, but, as Riley noted, "soldiers are hard to restrain."[75]

The march on July 1 began early. Many of the men believed that they were heading toward Harrisburg, but a sense of anticipation rose when they learned that they were marching on the road leading toward Baltimore. Cannon fire could be heard up ahead at about 10:00 A.M., and soon after, the men saw General Lee riding toward the firing. The column began encountering knots of prisoners and wounded heading to the rear. The men were next ordered to "load at will." According to Private David Holt of the 16th Mississippi, "the effect was magical. Every man tightening up and was on the alert. No need then for orders to keep the ranks closed up, for every man had had become a good soldier by instinct."[76]

It was therefore a surprise when the men received orders to halt, file to the right of the road, and stack arms. Foote (48th Mississippi) later considered this to be a fatal error, as the division's five brigades could have made a thirty-minute march to "the very ridge for which the next two days both sides struggled so hard to possess." Instead, the men prepared to bivouac for the night near Herr Ridge.[77]

On the morning of July 2, after several movements, Posey's Brigade finally reached its position between McMillan and Spangler's Woods on Seminary Ridge. To its left was Mahone's Brigade; to the right was Wright's. The morning was quiet. Captain John Lewis of the 16th Mississippi recalled that the men were ordered to "make such protection as would shelter them . . . fences were pulled down and the rails piled up and a little dirt thrown up." Skirmishers were sent out to relieve those from Scales's Brigade at about 1:00 P.M. Advancing to a fence line, they knocked off several boards so they could better see the enemy in front of them. As the sun rose, the temperatures soared. Private James Kirkpatrick noted, "day very hot & we are much exposed."[78]

Later that afternoon, General Posey received orders to "advance after Brigadier General Wright, who was posted on my right." Posey's orders were straightforward: as the wave of the *en echelon* attack reached the center of Anderson's Division, Posey was to launch his attack against Cemetery Ridge. The situation became more complicated at 4:00 P.M., when Anderson's aide-de-camp, Captain Samuel Shannon, arrived with fresh orders to, "advance but two of my regiments, and deploy them closely as skirmishers." Posey already had a thin line of skirmishers between the two armies at this point, but now ordered the 19th and 48th Mississippi out onto the skirmish line toward the Bliss farm buildings. Colonel Nate Harris of the 19th Mississippi recalled his orders differently, writing in his official report that he was to "advance the right wing of my regiment until I encountered the enemy's skirmishers, and drive them back."[79]

After dressing their lines on Seminary Ridge, the officers of the 19th Mississippi ordered their men to double-quick the 250 or so yards to the rail fence that sheltered their skirmishers. Colonel Harris could see that the enemy occupied an orchard in front of his men. About ready to push forward, Harris was informed by one of his company commanders that he if did so, "without my right being supported, there was imminent danger, from the nature of the ground, of my being flanked easily." Harris was content to wait at the fence line until the 48th Mississippi arrived on his right.[80]

Seeing growing activity around the Bliss farm buildings, primarily from the 1st Delaware and several companies of the 12th New Jersey (Smyth's Brigade, Hay's Division, II Corps), Posey ordered the 16th Mississippi forward to form on Colonel Harris's left. While the 19th and 48th Mississippi apparently waited at the fence line, the 16th Mississippi swept forward and drove the enemy out of an orchard and captured the farm buildings. The men found the barn to be an effective position for sniping at the Union line on Cemetery Ridge, "and soon every window, door, and crevice showed the protruding muzzles of long range rifles ready to do their deadly work," wrote Charles Page of the 14th Connecticut. In an ill-fated move, a company from the 106th Pennsylvania (Webb's Brigade, Gibbon's Division, II Corps) advanced against the barn, but was driven back with a loss of thirteen men. The sniper fire was so deadly that II Corps division commander, Alexander Hays, ordered four companies of the 12th New Jersey to recapture the buildings. Not seeing this attack until it was too late, seven officers and eighty-five enlisted Confederates, including a number from the 16th Mississippi and possibly some from the 19th Mississippi, were captured, and the buildings again fell into enemy hands.[81]

When he received word that the enemy was threatening both flanks of the 16th Mississippi, Posey sent his last regiment, the 12th Mississippi, forward in relief. At the same time, he sent an aide to General Mahone on his left, with a request for a regiment to support him. Posey wrote in his report that, "he [Mahone] being at this time ordered to the right, could not comply."[82]

With Posey's men arranged from left to right as 12th Mississippi–16th Mississippi–19th Mississippi–48th Mississippi, the brigade rushed forward and recaptured the Bliss buildings. Not content to take the buildings, the 19th Mississippi and at least part of the 48th Mississippi continued to advance at least "400 paces" beyond the farm buildings. Here they opened fire on the gunners on Cemetery Ridge, killing and wounding a number of them and driving the rest from their guns. The artillerymen returned to their guns, and again were driven away. This happened three times, finally forcing the gunners to move their cannon to more protected locations. Riley (16th Mississippi) noted that his regiment "advanced nearly to the batteries on the ridge." The reason why the men did not try to take the batteries was illuminated by Kirkpatrick of the same regiment, who wrote that the "enemy by being reinforced, would force us back to the orchard, our starting point."[83]

Foote told a slightly different story. As Wright's men swept by during their magnificent charge against Cemetery Ridge at about 6:30 P.M., they yelled to the prone men of the 48th Mississippi on their left, "Get up and fight!" and "Come forward Mississippians!" According to Foote, "the effect was felt and the entire regiment left its place in the flank and went into action against the earnest efforts of Colonel Jayne to stop them." If anything, Foote was certainly dramatic, recalling his unit's attack on Cemetery Ridge in conjunction with Wright's Brigade's:

> Wild with enthusiasm and ardor, on we pressed, while every instant the enemy thundered their shot and shell in our midst. Shells amongst us, shells over us and shells around us tore our bleeding ranks with ghastly gaps. . . . The ground roared and rumbled like a great storm, and the shower of minnie balls was pitiless and merciless. We pressed on, knowing that the front was safer now than to turn our backs, and with a mighty yell, we threw ourselves upon the batteries and passed them, still reeking hot. An attempt was made to reform the line, but before it could be done a heavy column of infantry in blue came up at double quick; we were too detached to cope successfully with them, and in a moment we were hurled, bleeding a crippled, from our hard-won trophies. Wright's men, with whom we still were, began to fall back, and then came the dreadful part of the whole matter—a falling back across the wide, open fields, with an exultant enemy thundering at our heels with every contrivance of death.[84]

In reality, the 48th Mississippi probably advanced only as far as Emmitsburg Road. General Wright wrote in his official report, "I had observed that Posey's Brigade, on my left, had not advanced . . . on my left we were entirely unprotected, the brigade [Posey's] ordered to support having failed to advance." Wright's men continued on and captured several cannon from Brown's battery before throwing themselves against Cemetery Ridge. As a result, the brigade was beaten to a bloody pulp. The 48th Georgia on the left of Wright's line sustained casualties of close to 60%. Contrasted with the 48th Mississippi's 15% casualties, the truth is revealed. It is true, however, that these losses exceeded those of the three other regiments of Posey's Brigade, and therefore the 48th Mississippi probably advanced farther than its sister regiments, but not as far as Wright's. Foote wrote that the regiment "rallied behind the other regiments of the brigade, who look on our struggle without participating. They had no orders to attack."[85]

Posey decided to ride forward to see how his four regiments were faring as the sun was setting. After a quick inspection, Posey sent an aide back to General Anderson for instructions. The aide came back within a short time with orders to return to Seminary Ridge.[86]

So ended Posey's actions on July 2. David Holt of the 16th Mississippi summarized them: "we wasted the second day of July in a fool preparation to repel a fancied attack when we were the attacking party." Some modern historians have tried to make a case that the tenacious defense of Bliss farm buildings by Smyth's Federal Brigade prevented Posey's Brigade from participating in the *en echelon* attack on Cemetery Ridge, and this contributed to Lee's overall defeat at Gettysburg. While Posey believed that his orders were not to make the charge, it is possible that a full-fledged attack in conjunction with Wright could have materially changed the battle's outcome. Whatever the cause, Wright's men were never supported and the attack failed.[87]

Except for the skirmishing around the Bliss farm buildings, July 3 was spent quietly on Seminary Ridge. The men had retaken the buildings the evening before, and now with the sun rising they again opened fire on the Federal position. The 12th New Jersey was sent out again at

about 7:30 A.M., and it again recaptured the buildings. However, heavy pressure from the Mississippians pushed the Union troops back to the safety of Cemetery Ridge. Hays countered with the 14th Connecticut, which succeeded in capturing the buildings. Their success was short-lived, as heavy cannonading, coupled with fire from Posey's skirmishers, forced the Nutmeggers to abandon the buildings, but not before burning them to the ground.[88]

Although the brigade had sustained relatively few casualties on July 2, Lee did not include it in Longstreet's grand charge, instead opting for Wilcox's and Perry's (Lang's) bloodied brigades. Kirkpatrick (16th Mississippi) watched the charge, but was not impressed by the intensity of the North Carolinians in his sector. "The distance they had to traverse was nearly a mile, there was no intermediate sheltered point to rally at and the sun's heat was intolerable, is the only excuse that can be plead in their behalf." Riley of the same regiment suggested that Posey's Brigade was to support the charge. "Around 3 [P.M.] again in echelon, we moved out of our breastworks until Gen. Longstreet stopped us, for, he said, since the assault had failed, further attack would be useless."[89]

The men spent July 4 waiting for a Federal attack that never came. Captain Lewis (16th Mississippi) indicated that the men felt that the "cowards would not charge our shattered lines. They knew that the lion was hurt but not killed." The march from the battlefield began that night. Except for the afternoon of July 2 and the morning of July 3, the brigade was not actively engaged in the battle. Its actions around the Bliss farm were insignificant in relation to other sectors of the battlefield.[90]

Wright's Brigade—Brigadier General Ambrose Wright

Units: 3rd Georgia, 22nd Georgia, 48th Georgia, 2nd Georgia Battalion
Strength: 1413
Losses: 696 (184-343-169)—49.3%[91]

The 3rd and 22nd Georgia and the 2nd Georgia Battalion were organized between May and August 1861 and their initial assignments included Norfolk, North Carolina, Georgia, and Florida. By March 1862, all four units were with Johnston's army in Virginia. The Seven Days battles found the four units in three different brigades—two of them, the 3rd and 22nd Georgia, were in Wright's Brigade. The 48th Georgia joined Wright's Brigade prior to the Second Manassas campaign, and the 2nd Georgia Battalion was transferred in November 1862. The brigade was finally intact by the Fredericksburg campaign, so by the start of the Gettysburg campaign it was a seasoned unit that had fought on several battlefields.[92]

Born and raised in Georgia, Ambrose Wright was an attorney and politician who enthusiastically supported secession. He enlisted as a private in the 3rd Georgia and was elected the regiment's colonel within a few weeks. He performed well in his early engagements, and was promoted to brigadier general on June 3, 1862, and given a brigade in time for the Seven Days campaign. Severely wounded at Sharpsburg, Wright returned to the army in time for the Chancellorsville campaign, where he was again wounded, this time only slightly. Although not particularly liked by his men, he had shown himself to be a good fighter.[93]

Wright's Brigade made the final leg of the journey to Gettysburg without its com-mander. Suffering from "severe indisposition," Wright was precluded from riding, and finally sought shelter at a house along Chambersburg Pike at about 2:00 P.M. on July 1. While Wright rested, his brigade continued its march toward Gettysburg. Earlier that day, at about 10:00 A.M., Wright clearly heard the report of cannon fire from the direction of Gettysburg. Wright's Brigade followed Mahone's during this march. The Wright-less Brigade went into bivouac that night, about two miles from Gettysburg. Feeling better, Wright rejoined his command at about 7:00 A.M. on July 2. Shortly thereafter, Anderson personally led Wright's men by the right flank to a point on the right (south) of Chambersburg Pike, where they relieved Davis's Brigade of Heth's Division on Seminary Ridge. By 11:00 A.M., the brigade was in position with Lang's (Perry's) Brigade on its right and Posey's on its left.[94]

At about noon, Wright was informed by Anderson that "an attack upon the enemy's lines would soon be made by the whole division, commencing on our right by Wilcox's Brigade, and that each brigade of the division would begin the attack as soon as the brigade on its immediate right commenced the movement." Wright was also told that he would begin his advance simultaneously with Lang's on his right, and that "Posey's Brigade, on my left, would move forward upon my advance."[95]

The day was a quiet one for the men, except for one company of the 3rd Georgia, which was sent out on skirmish duty. These men battled Union skirmishers and dodged cannon shells throughout the morning and afternoon. Because of the intensity of skirmishing in his front, Wright ordered the 2nd Georgia to reinforce the line at about 3:00 P.M. This force was large enough to drive back the enemy skirmishers who were crouching behind a fence line directly south of the Bliss house and about three hundred yards west of the Emmitsburg Road. This action continued for about an hour.[96]

At about 4:00 P.M. the men could hear the opening of the battle on their right, as Hood's Division began its attack. The wave of battle moved slowly but steadily northward, until it reached Anderson's Division. Wilcox's Brigade opened Anderson's attack against Humphreys's Division, followed in quick succession by Perry's (Lang's). Sometime between 6:15 and 6:30 P.M., Wright began his attack on Cemetery Ridge.[97]

Wright's line of battle was arranged from left to right as 48th Georgia–3rd Georgia–22nd Georgia. According to Wright's official report, the 2nd Georgia Battalion on the skirmish line behind a fence between Cemetery and Seminary Ridges was to form on the left of the 48th Georgia as it swept by. If these were the orders, the battalion's second in command, Captain James Moffett, never received them. Moffett's official report states: "in the absence of orders, or any definite instructions in the event of an advance of our forces, the skirmishers did not assemble, but went forward with the line as it moved past them. In this way the battalion was scattered along the whole line of the brigade, and some of the men went into action with General Perry's Florida Brigade, it pressing upon our right. This being the case, the battalion did not perform a separate and united part in the charge upon the enemy's position."[98]

The brigade must have presented a magnificent sight as it marched toward the Federal position. Corporal John Buckley of the 69th Pennsylvania (Webb's Brigade, Gibbon's Division, II Corps) later recalled that Wright's men were "the best clothed soldiers that we had ever come across on their side." When the brigade reached the fence line occupied by their skirmishers midway between the two ridges, it briefly halted to rest and redress its lines. This completed, the brigade continued into a hail of artillery fire that Wright considered "the most furious fire of arty. I had ever seen." Losses were light up to this point, however, because of the undulations in the ground. In Wright's path were the 15th Massachusetts and 82nd New York (Harrow's Brigade, Gibbon's Division, II Corps) along the Emmitsburg Road. Prior to the attack, these worried Federal soldiers had hastily thrown up flimsy breastworks of fence rails. Many were subsequently knocked down by the Southern artillery shells that were raining down on them. Neither side could see the other because of the tall grass that stood between them. It was probably just as well, for the Federal soldiers might have been tempted to run if they saw Wright's magnificent charge. Their new brigade commander, General William Harrow, had made it very clear earlier that he expected nothing less than success. He even went so far as to draw his pistol and tell his men that if he found anyone skulking, he would "blow him to hell in an instant." The men now grimly listened for the approaching enemy.[99]

Upon their approach, the Confederates let out a "demoniac yell." This was quickly answered by a effective volley from the veteran troops behind the barricade. Private Roland Bowen of the 15th Massachusetts recalled that "with a shout we sprang up on our knees and resting our muskets over the rails, we gave them one of the most destructive volleys I ever witnessed . . . they hesitated, then reeled, they staggered and wavered slightly, yet there was no panic." Wright's soldiers were undeterred by the large number of men that fell, and pressed on.[100]

Attacked in their front and left flank, the 82nd New York crumbled first. This further exposed the 15th Massachusetts on its right, and despite their efforts to hold their position, they too were overwhelmed. Just as Colonel J. H. Ward gave the order to retire, he was mortally wounded. The 82nd New York's commander also went down with a serious wound during this engagement. It became a footrace, as the men from the two Federal regiments tried to get away. The number of prisoners mounted by the second, as many Federal soldiers were hauled down by their pursuers. One soldier called it a "stampede." In describing the fight between his brigade and the two Federal regiments, Captain M. R. Hall of the 48th Georgia reported that the "enemy made but a short stand before our fire before they commenced retreating; at first in order, but we pushed them so rapidly that they broke and fled in great confusion, a large number of them running into our lines for safety. We pursed them some distance beyond their first line of batteries."[101]

The Georgians now turned their attention to Brown's six-rifled cannon, which had been personally positioned by General Gibbon that morning. So intent were the men on capturing these guns that when Private Bowen of the 15th Massachusetts tried to surrender, he was ignored, as the Southerners "spoke not a word to me but passed over and on, every rebs' eye seemed to be fixed on our artillery wich [sic] they were after." Lieutenant Brown warily watched Wright's advance, but the enemy approached so quickly that only four of his guns could be turned in their direction. These guns opened with spherical case shells filled with seventy leaden or iron balls set to explode in four seconds. As Wright's men advanced, John Rhodes remembered that "our fuses were cut at 3, 2, and one second, and then canister at point blank range, and finally, double charges were used."[102]

Brown's guns tore gaping holes in Wright's line, but still they advanced. Rhodes noted that "as artillery fire cut down their men, they would waver for a second, only to close up and continue their advance, with their battle flags flying in the breeze, and the barrels of their muskets reflecting the sun's dazzling rays." Losses mounted, but on they came. A Southern private who participated in the attack later recalled that "shells around us tore our bleeding ranks with ghastly gaps . . . we pressed on, knowing that the front was safer now than to turn our backs, and with a mighty yell, we threw ourselves upon the batteries and passed them, still reeking hot."[103]

Despite inflicting terrible losses on the Georgians, Brown's battery was in serious trouble. Heavy volleys from both Wright's men in its front, and Posey's to its right were decimating the gunners and horses. Not able to wait any longer, Brown gave the order to "limber to the rear." However, Sergeant Albert Straight elected to load and fire his piece one last time. Although it took but a few seconds, two of his horses went down and Straight was forced to leave the cannon behind. A second piece was also left behind, while the other four galloped to safety toward a stone wall on Cemetery Hill. Deployed behind the wall were the battle-hardened veterans of the 69th Pennsylvania (Webb's Brigade, Gibbon's Division, II Corps), who were ordered to open fire on Wright's men once the cannon cleared their front. One cannonner recalled that the Pennsylvanians sent a "vivid flame sending messengers of death to the foe."[104]

Wright's men surged over Brown's two abandoned, but still red-hot guns. Some tried to turn the guns around to fire on the troops on Cemetery Ridge. These efforts were soon halted by a withering fire that erupted from Cushing's and Arnold's batteries on Cemetery Ridge. The area around the guns became a no-man's-land, as any attempt to go near them resulted in certain injury or death.[105]

Watching the charge, Lieutenant Frank Haskell of Gibbon's staff marveled that "the whole slope in our front is full of them; and in various formations, in line, in columns, and in masses which are neither, with yells and thick volleys, they are rushing toward our crest." General Gibbon wrote that Wright's men advanced with "impetuosity."[106]

The closer Wright's men came to Cemetery Ridge, the more concerned he became about his vulnerable right and left flanks. Both were hanging in the air for different reasons. On his right, Perry's (Lang's) Brigade's charge had lost steam at the base of Cemetery Ridge, so its commander decided to rest and reform his men. Realizing that the Federal troops were massing in his front, and seeing that Wilcox's Brigade on his right had fallen back, brigade commander Colonel David Lang also decided to withdraw. Posey's Mississippi Brigade on Wright's left was nowhere to be seen, so he dispatched his aide-de-camp to General Anderson with a plea for help. Anderson ordered Wright to press on, as Posey had been ordered forward, but he said he would reiterate the order.[107]

Some soldiers of Posey's Brigade may have joined in Wright's charge. Private Foote noted that as the men of the 48th Mississippi lay under arms in the Bliss farmyard, they watched Wright's men charging past on their right. The Georgians cried out, "Get up and fight" and "Come forward with us Mississippians." Despite the efforts of their commanding officers to stop them, at least some of the soldiers of the 48th Mississippi rose and joined the attack on Wright's left flank.[108]

As Wright's men approached Cemetery Ridge, they faced the 69th Pennsylvania, and the 7th Michigan and 59th New York (Hall's Brigade, Gibbon's Division), behind a low stone wall. Behind the copse of trees were the three remaining regiments of the Philadelphia Brigade. The unit's commander, General Alexander Webb, now ordered these regiments forward to help counter Wright's attack. While the 71st Pennsylvania deployed to the right of the grove of trees, and the 72nd Pennsylvania deployed to the left of it, the 106th Pennsylvania approached the top of the ridge.[109]

Wright's men surged over a third abandoned cannon, this one within fifty yards of the stone wall. A Confederate officer mounting the cannon to spur on his men so infuriated Captain Michael Duffy of the 69th Pennsylvania that he ordered his men to "knock that d___d officer off the gun." Both Captain Duffy and the Southern officer fell soon after. Private Anthony McDermott of the 69th Pennsylvania observed that "still came on the mad Georgians until they reach point-blank range of our rifles. We met their charge with such a destroying fire that they were forced back in confusion. They rall[ied] again and [made] a second effort and again [were] their lines broken and thinned as we pour[ed] volley upon volley into their disordered ranks, until they finally retire[d] a dispirited mob." Company I of the 48th Georgia came within twenty yards of the stone fence, but could go no farther.[110]

Just as the 48th Georgia was recoiling in confusion, the 106th Pennsylvania appeared at the crest of the ridge and poured several volleys into the advancing Confederates from a distance of about sixty yards. Seeing the enemy line waver, Colonel William Curry of the 106th Pennsylvania ordered his men to fix bayonets and charge. The sight of a regiment of cheering Northerners jumping over a stone fence, and attacking their flank, while another was sending a hail of bullets into their ranks from behind a stone wall in their front, was too much for the men of the 48th Georgia. Their numbers had already been decimated during the charge—seven times their flag fell to the ground only to be picked up by another soldier. The last time it fell, no one picked it up, and it was captured. The men knew it was time to turn around and begin the long retreat back to Seminary Ridge.[111]

Over on the right side of Wright's line, the 7th Michigan and 59th New York were also pouring a rapid and destructive fire into the oncoming 3rd and 22nd Georgia. The 20th Massachusetts backed up the two Federal regiments, and behind it, the remaining guns of Brown's battery were unlimbered and ready for action. Approximately thirty to forty yards from the Union line was an area that offered Wright's men some protection. Here they stopped briefly to send a "galling fire" into the Union ranks. Weir's battery was overwhelmed and a battle flag was posted on one of the guns. The Union troops then poured a deadly fire into the Southerners around the cannon, piercing the color guard with at least a dozen bullets. Still Wright's men came on, approaching to within twenty yards of the Union line. According to Colonel Norman Hall's report, Wright's men could not overcome the destructive fire being thrown at it, so they began to retreat. Some men chose to crawl forward to the Union line to surrender rather than attempt to retreat with their backs exposed to the destructive

enemy fire. Colonel Edward Walker of the 3rd Georgia disagreed, stating that "the regiment during this advance was hotly engaged with infantry . . . which, though far superior in numbers, were steadily driven back."[112]

A gap in the line to the left of the 59th New York, which formed when Caldwell's Division moved south, had caused grave concern to Colonel Hall. Now the 22nd Georgia and part of the 3rd Georgia were aiming for it. Incredibly, a number of Georgians reached the stone wall, crossed it, and began climbing toward the crest of the ridge. They were suddenly attacked by the 13th Vermont of Stannard's Brigade, which was rushed from Cemetery Hill. Seeing their approach, the 22nd Georgia fired a volley into them, but it was poorly aimed and ineffectual. Instead of returning the fire, the Vermont soldiers sprang forward with fixed bayonets. So sudden was this counterattack that a number of Wright's men threw themselves to the ground and surrendered. The 13th Vermont passed over them in their haste to recapture Weir's guns. Other units were also converging on the gap and Weir's captured guns, including units from Brewster's Brigade (Humphreys Division), Harrow's Brigade (Gibbon's Division), and Stone's Brigade (Doubleday's Division). Colonel Walker of the 3rd Georgia stated that, "having no reserve, and fearing a flank movement, I was forced to fall back."[113]

Wright realized that his position was precarious. "We were now in a critical condition. The enemy's converging line was rapidly closing upon our rear; a few moments more, and we would be completely surrounded; still, no support could be seen coming to our assistance, and with painful hearts we abandoned our captured guns, faced about, and prepared to cut our way through the closing lines in our rear." The losses during the retreat across the open fields were exceptionally heavy, as the men were exposed to artillery and small arms fire the entire way. The 106th Pennsylvania, on Wright's left, also continued its charge down Cemetery Ridge and, with the 71st Pennsylvania, recaptured Brown's three abandoned cannon and twenty of Wright's men.[114]

About halfway to Seminary Ridge, Colonel Walker was able to rally the remnants of his 3rd Georgia near the fence line that had been held by the 2nd Georgia Battalion earlier that day. The unit then marched back to its position on Seminary Ridge. As the exhausted men stumbled back to their original positions on Seminary Ridge, their thoughts were merely on resting from their ordeal, not on tallying their losses. That grim task would come later. All but one of Wright's regimental/battalion commanders had been killed, and about half the brigade was killed, wounded, or captured. Wright bitterly complained in his official report about the lack of support he had received from Posey's and Perry's Brigades. "I have not the slightest doubt but that I should have been able to have maintained my position on the heights, and secured the captured artillery, if there had been a protecting force on my left, or if the brigade on my right had not been forced to retire," he wrote after the battle. Colonel Walker of the 3rd Georgia concurred. "Had the whole line advanced and [had we] been properly supported, there would have been no trouble about holding our position, as the enemy seemed panic-stricken, and were fleeing before us in every direction, and in my opinion, could not have been rallied at their second line." In a newspaper article written soon after the battle, Wright pinned the blame for his defeat on his sister brigades, writing, "we were about to be sacrificed to the bad management and cowardly conduct of others."[115]

The night was spent caring for the wounded. Wright wrote, "I need not tell you that sleep was not thought of by us that night." The men spent most of the following day resting on their arms. Later, the brigade was moved forward five hundred to six hundred yards into the no-man's-land between the two ridges to cover the retreat of Pickett's shattered division. This done, Lee ordered the brigade back to Seminary Ridge, where it formed several hundred yards behind Wilcox's Brigade "to support the latter in case the enemy should advance upon it, and which was now threatened." The attack never materialized, so the brigade trudged back to its original position after nightfall.[116]

A controversy emerged about whether Wright's right wing actually reached the summit of Cemetery Ridge. Wright's official report strongly suggests that it did. "We were now within less than 100 yards of the crest of the heights, which were lined with artillery, supported by a strong body of infantry, under protection of a stone fence. My men, by a well-directed fire, soon drove the cannoneers from their guns, and, leaping over the fence, charged up to the top of the crest . . .we were now complete masters of the field, having gained the key, as it were, of the enemy's whole line." The inaccuracies in the terrain Wright described in his report caused many to discount his assertions. However, General Gibbon's report tended to support Wright's claim. "The enemy came on with such impetuosity that the head of his column came quite through a vacancy in our line to the left of my division, opened by detaching troops to other points." Distinguished modern historian Harry Pfanz believed that Wright's men did indeed reach the summit of Cemetery

Ridge before being driven back by converging Union troops. As such, Wright's single brigade, wholly unsupported, actually did what nine brigades could not do the following day: pierce the Union line and take the summit of Cemetery Ridge. Wright's pride in his men was evident after the battle when he wrote home, "although I know their character well; knew they were capable of doing what any other troops dare do, I must confess that I was surprised at the vigor of their attack and the tenacity with which they held their ground under such adverse circumstances."[117]

NOTES

1. Freeman, *Lee's Lieutenants*, vol. 2, 698–699.
2. Davis, *The Confederate General*, vol. III, 96–97.
3. Freeman, *Lee's Lieutenants*, vol. 3, 74–75; Douglas C. Haines, "A. P. Hill's Advance to Gettysburg," *Gettysburg Magazine* (July 1991), issue 5, 4–6.
4. OR 27, 2, 606–607.
5. OR 27, 2, 607.
6. OR 27, 2, 607–608.
7. William K. McDaid, *Four Years of Arduous Service*, Ph.D. Dissertation, Michigan State University (1987), 216–217; OR 27, 1, 608–609.
8. Davis, *The Confederate General*, vol. I, 28–29.
9. OR 27 2, 607, 613, 622; Lord, *The Fremantle Diary*, 202–203; Wilcox, letter, 114.
10. OR 27, 2, 608, 613–14, 622–623.
The official reports of Wright, one of his unit commanders, and the commander of the 7th Michigan recalled that the charge began at 5:00 P.M. Colonel David Lang, who commanded Perry's Brigade, reported that it was 6:00 P.M., as did one of Wright's commanders, and the official report and historian of the 82nd New York. In their official reports, General Wilcox and General Alexander Webb reported the time to be

about 6:30 P.M. This was also supported by the historian of the 69th Pennsylvania. Tucker split the difference between Perry's and Wilcox's estimates, and put the time at 6:15 P.M. Tucker also indicated that Wright's attack began approximately half an hour later, at 6:45 P.M., but there is little evidence that so much time elapsed between these two advances (OR 27, 1, 426, 427, 448; OR 27, 2, 617, 623, 627, 628, 629, 630, 631; *New York at Gettysburg*, vol. 2, 664; Glenn Tucker, *High Tide at Gettysburg: The Campaign in Pennsylvania* [Indianapolis, IN, 1968], 283, 286; Anthony W. McDermott and John E. Reilly, *History of the 69th Regiment, Pennsylvania Veteran Reserves* [Philadelphia, 1889], 28).
11. OR 27, 2, 614.
12. Shotwell, "Virginia and North Carolina in the Battle of Gettysburg," 94; George R. Stewart, *Pickett's Charge—A Microhistory of the Final Attack at Gettysburg, July 3, 1863* (Boston, 1959), 252; OR 27, 2, 614–615.
13. OR 27, 2, 615.
14. Douglas S. Freeman, *R.E. Lee*, 4 vols. (New York, 1935), vol. 3, 555.
15. Busey and Martin, *Regimental Strengths and Losses*, 186, 293.
16. J. J. Renfroe, *South Western Baptist*, August 13, 1863; Maurice S. Fortin, "Colonel Hilary A. Herbert's History of the Eighth Alabama Volunteer Regiment, CSA," in *The Alabama Historical Quarterly* (1977), vol. 39, 114.
17. OR 27, 2, 613, 616–617; Pfanz, *Gettysburg—July 2*, 98.
18. OR 27, 2, 617.
19. OR 27, 2, 617; Hilary A. Herbert to John Bachelder, July 9, 1884, Bachelder Papers, New Hampshire Historical Society; Fortin, "Colonel Hilary A. Herbert's History of the Eighth Alabama Volunteer Regiment, CSA," 114–115; George Clark, *A Glance Backward or Some Events in the Past History of My Life* (Houston, 1914), 36; Fleming W. Thompson, letter, copy in Brake Collection, USAMHI; Renfroe, *South Western Baptist*.
20. OR 27, 2, 617; Pfanz, *Gettysburg—July 2*, 355.
21. Clark, *A Glance Backward or Some Events in the Past History of My Life*, 36.

22. OR 27, 2, 618; Pfanz, *Gettysburg—July 2*, 362–363; Hilary A. Herbert, "A Short History of the 8th Alabama Regiment," McLaws Papers, Southern Historical Collection, University of North Carolina.

23. Pfanz, *Gettysburg—July 2*, 362–363.

24. John Barrett, ed., *Yankee Rebel: The Civil War Journal of Edmund DeWitt Patterson* (Chapel Hill, NC, 1966), 116; Herbert, "A Short History of the 8th Alabama Regiment."

25. OR 27, 2, 618.

26. Clark, *A Glance Backward or Some Events in the Past History of My Life*, 37; Bailey G. McClellan, *Civil War History of Company D, 10th Alabama Regiment* (Anniston Station, AL, 1901), 2.

27. Fortin, "Colonel Hilary A. Herbert's History of the Eighth Alabama Volunteer Regiment, CSA," 116–117; OR 27, 2, 618.

Harry Pfanz believed that these guns were from Turnbull's Battery (Pfanz, *Gettysburg—July 2*, 373).

28. Wilcox, letter; OR 27, 2, 618; Pfanz, *Gettysburg—July 2*, 379–380..

Pfanz was uncertain about the identity of the battery on the left, but he was fairly certain that the one on the right was Battery C, 4th Artillery, under Lieutenant Evan Thomas (Pfanz, *Gettysburg—July 2*, 374).

29. OR 27, 2, 618.

30. Plummer, letter.

31. OR 27, 2, 618; OR 27, 1, 475, 476; Clark, *A Glance Backward or Some Events in the Past History of My Life*, 38.

According to Imhof (*Gettysburg—Day Two*, 197), the 1st Minnesota collided with the 11th Alabama.

32. OR 27, 2, 618.

33. Wilcox, letter, 116; Clark, *A Glance Backward or Some Events in the Past History of My Life*, 38–39; Thompson, letter.

34. Clark, *A Glance Backward or Some Events in the Past History of My Life*, 39; Herbert, "A Short History of the 8th Alabama Regiment"; Renfroe, *South Western Baptist*, August 13, 1863; OR 27, 2, 620.

35. OR 27, 2, 620; Thompson, letter; Bright, "Pickett's Charge, The Story of it Told by a Member of His Staff," 232; Herbert, "A Short History of the 8th Alabama Regiment."

36. E. Porter Alexander, "The Great Charge and Artillery Fighting at Gettysburg," in *Battles and Leaders of the Civil War,* vol. 3, 366.

37. OR 27, 2, 620.

38. OR 27, 2, 620.

Wilcox erroneously wrote after the war that his brigade had advanced to within a hundred yards of the Federal position before turning back, as he could then see that Pickett's men had been repulsed (Wilcox, letter, 117).

39. Busey and Martin, *Regimental Strengths and Losses*, 187, 294.

40. Davis, *The Confederate General*, vol. IV, 143.

41. J. E. Whitehorne, *Diary of J. E. Whitehorne* (Louisville, KY, 1995), 22–24.

42. Whitehorne, *Diary of J. E. Whitehorne*, 22–24; Westwood Todd, "Reminiscences," 12th Virginia folder, GNMP.

43. Bradley M. Gottfried, "Mahone's Brigade: Insubordination or Miscommunication," *Gettysburg Magazine* (January 1998), issue 18, 69–70; William D. Henderson, *Twelfth Virginia Infantry* (Lynchburg, VA, 1984), 56.

44. OR 27, 2, 623–624, 633–634.

45. Gottfried, "Mahone's Brigade: Insubordination or Miscommunication," 73–74; William W. Hassler, "'Fighting Dick' Anderson," in *Civil War Times Illustrated* (1974), vol. 12, 10, 40.

46. Todd, "Reminiscences"; William Moseley, "Confederate Diary," copy in 6th Virginia folder, GNMP; George Bernard Papers, copy in 12th Virginia folder, GNMP.

47. William H. Stewart, *A Pair of Blankets: War-Time History in Letters to the Young People of the South* (Wilmington, NC, 1990), 97.

48. Moseley, "Confederate Diary"; Coddington, *The Gettysburg Campaign*, 460–462; Gottfried, "Mahone's Brigade: Insubordination or Miscommunication," 75–76.

49. Gottfried, "Mahone's Brigade: Insubordination or Miscommunication," 76.

50. Busey and Martin, *Regimental Strengths and Losses*, 188, 294.

51. Francis P. Fleming, *Memoir of Capt. C. Seton Fleming of the Second Florida Infantry CSA* (Jacksonville, FL, 1884), 194.

52. Stewart Sifakis, *Compendium of the Confederate Armies: Florida and Arkansas* (New York, 1992),16–17, 21, 24; Davis, *The Confederate General*, vol. V, 20–21.

53. J. B. Johnson, "A Limited Review of What One Man Saw of the Battle of Gettysburg," copy in 5th Florida folder, GNMP; Francis P. Fleming, "Francis P. Fleming in the War for Southern Independence," *The Florida Historical Quarterly* (1949), vol. 27, 145–146.

54. OR 27, 2, 631.

According to Lang's report, the brigade was ordered to move to the right about one mile. We know that Anderson issued these orders to Wilcox, but there is no evidence that Lang's Brigade also received them, despite the commander's assertion.

55. OR 27, 2, 631; Raymond J. Reid, letter, Raymond Reid Papers, St. Augustine Historical Society; Johnson, "A Limited Review of What One Man Saw of the Battle of Gettysburg."

56. OR 27, 2, 631.

57. OR 27, 2, 631; Johnson, "A Limited Review of What One Man Saw of the Battle of Gettysburg"; Pfanz, *Gettysburg—Day Two*, 364.

58. OR 27, 2, 631; Johnson, "A Limited Review of What One Man Saw of the Battle of Gettysburg."

59. OR 27, 2, 631; Pfanz, *Gettysburg—July 2*, 374.

60. OR 27, 2, 631–632; David Lang, "Letter To General Edward Perry," in *Southern Historical Society Papers* (1899), vol. 27, 195; William Pigman, diary, Pigman Papers, Georgia Historical Society; Thomas L. Elmore, "The Florida Brigade at Gettysburg," *Gettysburg Magazine* (July 1996), 50; Pfanz, *Gettysburg—July 2*, 414.

Harry Pfanz believed that the troops in front of the Floridians were from the 19th Maine and those on the right may have belonged to Willard's Brigade (Hays's Division), possibly the 111th New York.

According to Colonel Francis Heath of the 19th Maine, his regiment briefly withdrew from Lang's front after the initial sharp encounter. Receiving erroneous information that his right flank was being turned, Heath pulled his men back, but soon realizing the error, marched his men back to face Lang's Brigade. This may have been construed by Colonel Lang as at least part of the reinforcements (John D. Smith, *The History of the Nineteenth Regiment of Maine Volunteer Infantry, 1862–1865* [Minneapolis, MN, 1909], 68–69).

61. Johnson, "A Limited Review of What One Man Saw of the Battle of Gettysburg."

62. OR 27, 2, 632; "James Wentworth Wrote Diary of Civil War Days," *Perry News*, n.d., copy in 5th Florida file, GNMP; D. E. Maxwell, "Letters from a Florida Confederate," *Florida Historical Quarterly* (1958), vol. 36, 365; Fleming, *Memoir of Capt. C. Seton Fleming of the Second Florida Infantry, CSA*, 84; Reid, letter; Elmore, "The Florida Brigade at Gettysburg," 51.

63. OR 27, 2, 632; Reid, letter; *Perry News*.

This order probably emanated from the fact that Longstreet had overall command of the attacking units.

64. Johnson, "A Limited Review of What One Man Saw of the Battle of Gettysburg"; Reid, letter.

65. OR 27, 2, 632; Johnson, "A Limited Review of What One Man Saw of the Battle of Gettysburg."

Lang reported that he began his charge after Pickett had been repulsed. This is probably not correct, although he may have observed a stream of wounded men making their way back to Seminary Ridge.

66. *Perry News*, n.d.; Pigman, diary; Reid, letter; Hess, *Pickett's Charge*, 298–299.

67. OR 27, 1, 350; Wheeler Veazey, letter, copy in 16th Vermont folder, GNMP; OR 27, 2, 632–633.

According to Wheeler Veazey, as his 16th Vermont approached the Floridians, they were "crouching behind the low bushes and rocks which afforded some shelter from our artillery and infantry fire in front" (Veazey, letter).

68. Isaac S. Barineau, letter, Civil War Misc. Collection, USAMHI; Fleming, *Memoir*

*of Capt. C. Seton Fleming of the Second Florida Infantry, CSA.,*148.

69. Busey and Martin, *Regimental Strengths and Losses at Gettysburg,* 189, 294.

70. Sifakis, *Compendium of the Confederate Armies: Mississippi,* 92–93, 99, 104–105, 138–139; Davis, *The Confederate General,* vol. II, 119.

71. Davis, *The Confederate General,* vol. V, 51

72. Frank Foote, "Marching in Clover," *Philadelphia Weekly Times,* October 8, 1881.

73. Foote, "Marching in Clover."

74. Franklin L. Riley, *Grandfather's Journal . . .* (Dayton, OH, 1988), 147–148.

75. Foote, "Marching in Clover."

76. Riley, *Grandfather's Journal . . .* , 148; James J. Kirkpatrick, diary, University of Texas at Austin;

David Holt, *A Mississippi Rebel in the Army of Northern Virginia . . .* , (Baton Rouge, LA, 1995), 194.

77. Foote, "Marching in Clover."

78. Elwood Christ, *The Struggle for the Bliss Farm at Gettysburg . . .* (Baltimore, MD, 1993), 21; John S. Lewis, "The Battle of Gettysburg," in *The Woodville Republication;* Foote, "Marching in Clover"; Kirkpatrick, diary.

79. OR 27, 2, 633, 634.

80. OR 27, 2, 634; Christ, *The Struggle for the Bliss Farm at Gettysburg . . .* , 27–28.

81. Charles D. Page, *History of the Fourteenth Regiment, Connecticut Volunteer Infantry* (Meriden, CT, 1906), 144; R. C. Ward, *History of the One Hundred and Sixth Regiment, Pennsylvania, Pennsylvania Volunteers* (Philadelphia, 1883), 160; Terrence J. Winschel, "Posey's Brigade at Gettysburg, Part II," *Gettysburg Magazine* (July 1991), issue 5, 96; Christ, *The Struggle for the Bliss Farm at Gettysburg . . .* , 38–39.

82. OR 27, 2, 633.

83. OR 27, 2, 634; Christ, *The Struggle for the Bliss Farm at Gettysburg . . .* , 38; Riley, *Grandfather's Journal . . .* , 148; Kirkpatrick, diary.

In his report, Posey said his men advanced "200–300 yards" beyond the farm buildings (OR 27, 2, 633).

84. Foote, "Marching in Clover."

85. OR 27, 2, 623–624; Bradley M. Gottfried, "Wright's Charge at Gettysburg: Piercing the Union Line or Inflated Glory?" *Gettysburg Magazine* (July 1997), issue 17, 76; Busey and Martin, *Regimental Strengths and Losses,* 294; Foote, "Marching in Clover."

86. OR 27, 2, 633–634.

87. Holt, *A Mississippi Rebel in the Army of Northern Virginia . . .* ,195; Christ, *The Struggle for the Bliss Farm at Gettysburg . . .* , 46; Gottfried, "Mahone's Brigade: Insubordination or Miscommunication," 74

88. Winschel, "Posey's Brigade at Gettysburg, Part II," 99–100.

89. Kirkpatrick, diary; Riley, *Grandfather's Journal . . .* ,149.

90. Riley, *Grandfather's Journal . . .* ,149–150; John Lewis, "Article," *The Woodville Republican,* July 19, 1924.

91. Busey and Martin, *Regimental Strengths and Losses,* 190, 294.

92. Sifakis, *Compendium of the Confederate Armies: South Carolina and Georgia,* 185, 225–226, 261, 179.

93. Davis, *The Confederate General,* vol. VI, 161.

94. *Daily Constitution* (Augusta, Georgia), July 23, 1863; OR 27 2, 613, 622, 630.

95. OR 27, 2, 622.

96. OR 27, 2, 627–628, 630.

97. OR 27, 2, 617, 623, 627, 628, 629, 630, 631.

98. OR 27, 2, 623, 630.

99. OR 27, 1, 423; *Augusta Daily Constitutionalist,* July 23, 1863; OR 27, 2, 627–629; Foote, "Marching in Clover"; John H. Rhodes, *History of Battery B, First Regiment, Rhode Island Artillery* (Providence, RI, 1914), 202; Andrew E. Ford, *Story of the Fifteenth Regiment, Massachusetts Volunteer Infantry in the Civil War* (Clinton, MA, 1898), 267; Pfanz, *Gettysburg—The Second Day,* 385–386; Gregory Coco, *From Ball's Bluff to Gettysburg . . .* (Gettysburg, PA, 1994), 196–201.

100. Ford, *Story of the Fifteenth Regiment, Massachusetts Volunteer Infantry in the Civil War,* 267; Coco, *From Ball's Bluff to Gettysburg . . .* , 196–201.

101. OR 27, 1, 419–420, 425–426; OR 27, 2, 628, 629; Ford, *Story of the Fifteenth Regi-*

ment, *Massachusetts Volunteer Infantry in the Civil War*, 268–269; Coco, *From Ball's Bluff to Gettysburg* . . . , 201–202; Wiley Sword, "Defending the Codori House and Cemetery Ridge: Two Swords with Harrow's Brigade in the Gettysburg Campaign, *Gettysburg Magazine* (July 1995) issue 13, 46–47; *New York at Gettysburg*, vol. 2, 664; William Paul, "Severe Experiences at Gettysburg," in *Confederate Veteran* (1912), vol. 19, 85.

102. Rhodes, *History of Battery B, First Regiment, Rhode Island Artillery*, 200–202.

103. Rhodes, *History of Battery B, First Regiment, Rhode Island Artillery*, 201.

104. Rhodes, *History of Battery B, First Regiment, Rhode Island Artillery*, 202–203.

105. Frederick Fuger, "Battle of Gettysburg, Recollections of the Battle," Webb Papers, Yale University Library, 20–21.

106. OR 27, 1, 417; Frank A. Haskell, *The Battle of Gettysburg* (New York, 1910), 373.

107. OR 27, 2, 631–632; Lang, "Letter to General Edward A. Perry," 192–205.

108. Foote, "Marching in Clover"; Pfanz, *Gettysburg—The Second Day*, 383–384.

Given the number of losses sustained by the 48th Mississippi and the fact that none of their officers reported this movement, it is doubtful that more than a handful of companies participated in the charge.

109. *Pennsylvania at Gettysburg*, vol. 1, 415, 550–551; Ward, *History of the One Hundred and Sixth Regiment, Pennsylvania, Pennsylvania Volunteers*, 191; McDermott and Reilly, *History of the 69th Regiment, Pennsylvania Veteran Reserves*, 28; OR 27, 1, 434; Gary Lash, "The Philadelphia Brigade at Gettysburg," *Gettysburg Magazine* (July 1992), issue 7, 100.

110. McDermott and Reilly, *History of the 69th Regiment, Pennsylvania Veteran Reserves*, 28; Ward, *History of the One Hundred and Sixth Regiment, Pennsylvania, Pennsylvania Volunteers*, 191–192; Paul, "Severe Experiences at Gettysburg," 85.

111. Foote, "Marching in Clover"; Paul, "Severe Experiences at Gettysburg," 85; Ward, *History of the One Hundred and Sixth Regiment, Pennsylvania, Pennsylvania Volunteers*, 191–192; McDermott and Reilly, *History of the 69th Regiment, Pennsylvania Veteran Reserves*, 28; *Pennsylvania at Gettysburg*, vol. 1, 550–551; OR 27, 1, 434. Anthony McDermott to John Bachelder, 2 July 1886, Bachelder Papers, New Hampshire Historical Society; OR 27, 2, 626.

112. OR 27, 1, 436, 447–448; OR 27, 2, 628.

113. Pfanz, *Gettysburg—The Second Day*, 421; Sturtevant, *Pictorial History of the Thirteenth Vermont Volunteers in the War of 1861–1865*, 267–269; George H. Scott, "Vermont at Gettysburg," in *Proceedings of the Vermont Historical Society* (1930), vol. 1, 65; OR 27, 1, 349, 351–352; OR 27, 2, 623–625, 628.

114. OR 27, 2, 624, 628; OR 27, 1, 427, 432, 434; Ward, *History of the One Hundred and Sixth Regiment, Pennsylvania, Pennsylvania Volunteers*, 192–193.

115. OR 27, 2, 623–624, 628; *Augusta Daily Constitutionalist*, July 23, 1863.

116. *Augusta Daily Constitutionalist*, July 23, 1863; OR 27, 2, 624–625.

117. OR 27, 2, 623; OR 27 1, 417; Pfanz, *Gettysburg—The Second Day*, 417; *Augusta Daily Constitutionalist*, July 23, 1863.

Wright reported driving the enemy's infantry into a "rocky gorge on the eastern slope of the heights." No such terrain exists on this part of the field.

HETH'S DIVISION—

Major General Harry Heth/
Brigadier General James Pettigrew

It was certainly a bad omen when General A. P. Hill permitted Major General Harry Heth's Division to lead the Confederate advance on Gettysburg. Historian David Martin questioned why A. P. Hill made this decision, as he considered it a "makeshift" division under a new commander. Graduating at the bottom of his West Point class, Henry Heth saw action in the Mexican War and then spent time with the 19th U.S. Infantry "chasing buffalo, Indians, and Mormons." He entered Confederate service as a major and rose quickly to lieutenant colonel and then colonel, and commanded the 45th Virginia. Promotion to brigadier general occurred on January 6, 1862, and Heth was sent to the mountains of western Virginia, where his command was soundly defeated. After service in Kentucky, Heth was transferred to the Army of Northern Virginia and given command of what had been Field's Brigade just prior to Chancellorsville. Heth was slightly wounded at the battle, and when the army was restructured, he received a division composed of two brigades from A. P. Hill's Light Division, an inexperienced one newly arrived from North Carolina and a recently reformed brigade.[1]

The division first made contact with the Federal forces around Gettysburg on June 30, when Heth sent General James Pettigrew's Brigade toward the town to see if it could procure needed supplies. Running into pickets from General John Buford's cavalry division at about 10:30 A.M., and hearing drums beating on the opposite side of the town Pettigrew thought it best to return to Cashtown, in accordance with Heth's orders, which were not to fight any organized troops.[2]

While Pettigrew was giving his report to Heth, A. P. Hill rode up. After listening to what had transpired, Hill remarked that the "only force at Gettysburg is cavalry, probably a detachment of observation. I am just from General Lee, and the information he has from his scouts corroborates that I have received from mine—that is, the enemy are still at Middleburg, and have not yet struck their tents." Heth quickly said to Hill, "If there is no objection, I will take my division tomorrow and go to Gettysburg and get those shoes!" Hill replied, "None in the world." Pettigrew listened in disgust. It was clear that Hill and Heth did not yet trust their new brigade commander.[3]

Breaking camp promptly at 5:00 A.M. on July 1, Heth ordered his entire division to march on Gettysburg. Because he had no cavalry, Major William Pegram's artillery battalion was ordered to lead the march, and the infantry followed. Modern historian David Martin considered this to be "dangerous." Archer's Brigade led the infantry column, followed in turn by Davis's, Brockenbrough's, and finally Pettigrew's. Whether through ignorance or sheer confidence, Heth pushed his men blindly forward, admitting in his official report that he was "ignorant [of] what force was at or near Gettysburg." Martin also questioned why Heth ordered Archer's and Davis's Brigades to lead the division, as both units were badly depleted and, in the case of the latter brigade, led by an untried officer.[4]

Approaching Gettysburg at 9:00 A.M., Heth did not see any Federal troops, so he deployed Pegram's artillery and ordered them to open fire to "see if he could get a response." None was received, and the infantry arrived about half an hour later. Deploying Archer to the right of Chambersburg Pike and Davis to the left, Heth ordered them forward. "The object being to feel the enemy; to make a forced reconnaissance, and determine in which force the enemy were . . . whether or not he was massing his forces on Gettysburg," he noted. Heth admitted that he knew that there were "infantry, cavalry and artillery in and about the town." Therefore, it is hard to understand why he did not bring up his two other brigades to provide support.[5]

Archer's Brigade crossed Willoughby Run and ran into the fabled Federal Iron Brigade (Wadsworth's Division, I Corps); it suffered significant losses, including the capture of General James Archer. Events were not much better on the left of the road, where Davis's Brigade met with initial success against Cutler's Brigade (Wadsworth's Division, I Corps), only to be trapped in an unfinished railroad cut. Hundreds of men were captured. Heth had blundered by leaving half of his division too far in the rear to provide support. Further attacks on McPherson Ridge were halted, as Lee reiterated his orders that the enemy not be engaged until the army was assembled. Watching Ewell's troops appear to the north and engage the enemy, Heth sought out General Lee, saying, "Rodes is very heavily engaged, had I not better attack?" General Lee replied: "No; I am not prepared to bring on a general engagement today—Longstreet is not up." Returning to his division, Heth believed that the enemy was moving troops from his front to face Rodes. This information finally convinced Lee to permit Heth to renew his attack.[6]

Advancing with Brockenbrough's and Pettigrew's fresh brigades, the Federal troops were finally pushed off McPherson Ridge, but not before the latter brigade sustained horrendous losses. At this point, Dorsey Pender's Division moved up and, passing through Heth's exhausted ranks, pursued the enemy troops toward Seminary Ridge. Heth was not able to relish this victory, as he was shot in the head. He survived, only because a clerk had added several layers of paper to make his new hat fit better. As a result, the ball never entered Heth's skull, but did give him a concussion that knocked him out of the battle. Command of the division devolved upon General Pettigrew.[7]

The division rested on July 2. The following day was a fateful one for the division, as it was included in the Pickett–Pettigrew–Trimble charge. Major Charles Venable of Lee's staff admitted after the war that "it was a mistake to reckon Heth's Division in planning the assault, for it suffered more on the first day than was reported and had not recuperated." Lee realized his mistake when he rode along his lines just before the attack and saw Heth's depleted ranks. The sight "made General Lee shed tears and say, 'they should not be here.'" It was too late, as the men stepped off. The division was positioned, from left to right, as Brockenbrough–Davis–Pettigrew–Archer. Two brigades from Pender's Division (now under Trimble) formed behind Pettigrew and to his right was Pickett's Division.[8]

Aligned opposite Heth's Division was General Alexander Hays's Division. He vividly described the attack in his official report:

> Their march was as steady as if impelled by machinery, unbroken by our artillery, which played upon them a storm of missiles. When within 100 yards of our line of infantry, the fire of our men could no longer be restrained. Four lines rose from behind our stone wall, and before the smoke of our first volley had cleared away, the enemy, in dismay, and consternation, were seeking safety in flight.[9]

The remnant of the division remained on Seminary Ridge during July 4, waiting to repel a Federal counterattack that never materialized. The trip south began during the evening of July 4–5.

Pettigrew's Brigade—Brigadier General James Pettigrew

Units: 11th North Carolina, 26th North Carolina, 47th North Carolina, 52nd North Carolina

Strength: 2581

Losses: 1450 (386-915-149)—56.2%[10]

Pettigrew's Brigade had the distinction of being the largest in the army. Composed of four large regiments, only the 26th North Carolina had been near a battlefield, and that was over a year before, during the Seven Days campaign. Since that time, the brigade had been assigned to "surveillance and containment" duty in southeastern Virginia and eastern North Carolina. This changed in early June, when Pettigrew's Brigade was assigned to Heth's new division of the Army of Northern Virginia. Despite its lack of combat experience, the brigade's morale was high and the men were looking forward to engaging the enemy.[11]

Brigadier General James Pettigrew was a highly educated and cultured North Carolinian born into a wealthy family. He studied law, and at the outbreak of the war, was commanding a militia unit. He became colonel of the 22nd North Carolina and was appointed brigadier general on February 26, 1862. He led his mixed brigade at the battle of Seven Pines, where he was badly wounded and captured. After being exchanged, he took command of a brigade that he would ultimately lead at Gettysburg. The unit remained in North Carolina and saw some action at New Berne. Pettigrew was ordered to join Lee's army just before the beginning of the Gettysburg campaign.[12]

As the brigade crossed the Potomac River into Maryland, the men asked the musicians to play "Maryland, My Maryland." The musicians were reluctant to honor this request, but General Pettigrew heard about the situation and ordered the band to strike up the tune. The men were pleased by the large number of women who waved small Confederate flags by the side of the roads. The men's demeanor changed when they crossed into Pennsylvania. The bands were prohibited from playing as the brigade marched through the towns. The men tried to obey Lee's strict orders against taking food and other

commodities from private citizens. "It was impossible for the officers to keep the men from 'flanking' to some extent, but upon the whole there was less depredating than might have been expected," recalled Julius Lineback of the 26th North Carolina.[13]

Leading Heth's Division, the brigade arrived at Cashtown on June 30. Pettigrew's men did not have long to rest, for the North Carolinians were ordered toward Gettysburg on a reconnaissance and to secure supplies. Pettigrew took the 11th, 26th, and 47th North Carolina with him; the 52nd North Carolina was left behind near Cashtown. Taking the road at about 6:30 A.M., the three regiments moved off smartly, reaching the vicinity of Seminary Ridge sometime between 9:30 and 10:00 A.M. Seeing Buford's cavalry approach at about 10:30 A.M., Pettigrew wisely decided to march back toward Cashtown. According to Heth, Pettigrew told him that "some of his men reported the beat of drums (including infantry) on the further side of the town; that if he entered the town his men when searching for shoes would have become scattered, and if there was a large force there, it might have proved disastrous to his command."[14]

Pettigrew did not march his three regiments back to Cashtown that night, instead deploying the 26th North Carolina as pickets near Marsh Creek, with his two other regiments within supporting distance. That night, two women were prevented from reaching their homes, which were beyond the brigade's picket line. They were taken to the Lieutenant Colonel John Lane, who commanded the line. Telling them that "the Confederate soldier did not make war upon women and children," he extended the picket line to encompass their homes.[15]

Because they had led the division on June 30, the brigade rotated to the rear during the march on July 1. The brigade merely held its advanced position, and when the column passed it, fell into line at the rear. When some cavalry ambushed the lead regiment (the 47th North Carolina), the brigade was forced to halt and deploy. The march resumed after the enemy fled. About two and a half miles from Gettysburg, the brigade was ordered to deploy on the left of Chambersburg Pike. Before the men had a chance to settle down, they were ordered to march by the right flank to the right of the road. "Then, as each regiment of the brigade marching to the right, uncovered the regiment in its front, its commander gave the order 'By the left flank, March,' and thus in a few moments, and by the quickest tactical movement the brigade was in line of battle," recalled Lieutenant George Underwood of the 26th North Carolina. The men took position behind Major William Pegram's artillery battalion. Remaining there about half an hour, the brigade was exposed to Federal artillery fire, which killed and wounded about a dozen. "There [was] some little excitement, but it soon disappear[ed] as Colonel [Henry] Burgwyn riding along the line in his grandest style, command[ed] in his clear, firm voice, 'Steady boys, steady,'" noted one of the men. Gunfire erupted in front of them, as the Iron Brigade overwhelmed Archer's Brigade. Ordered to advance about half a mile, the brigade halted at the edge of a strip of woods on Herr Ridge. At this point, the brigade was aligned from left to right as 26th North Carolina–11th North Carolina–47th North Carolina–52nd North Carolina. They did not form a straight line of battle, though. Instead, each regiment was arranged *en echelon* on the 26th North Carolina, which was closest to the enemy; the 11th North Carolina was formed a short distance behind it and to

its right; the 47th and 52nd North Carolina was behind and to its right. On the brigade's left was Colonel John Brockenbrough's Brigade of Virginians.[16]

Major John Jones noted that "a wheatfield about a fourth of a mile wide; then came a branch [Willoughby Run], with thick underbrush and briars skirting the banks. Beyond this was again an open field" in front of them. Throwing out a line of skirmishers, the brigade rested. Squads of men were sent to Marsh Creek to refill their comrades' canteens during this time. While waiting there, some of the men were hit by sniper fire from an old house to the right. Colonel Henry Burgwyn ordered one of his men to take them out, and peace soon returned. This minor episode helped to distract Burgwyn, who, according to Lieutenant Colonel John Lane, "became quite impatient to engage the enemy, saying we were losing precious time."[17]

Two Federal brigades lay in front of Pettigrew's Brigade in dispositions that were anything but adequate. In front of the 26th North Carolina was the 24th Michigan, and the 19th Indiana blocked the path of the 11th North Carolina. The 19th Indiana's left flank hung in the air, because Biddle's Brigade (Rowley's Division; I Corps) had not formed next to it, but instead deployed 300 yards to its left and rear. As a result, the left flank of Biddle's Brigade, held by the 121st Pennsylvania, also hung in the air. Pettigrew's two right regiments, the 47th and the 52nd North Carolina, extended beyond the Iron Brigade, and overlapped Biddle's Brigade as well. There were also gaps between the Federal regiments.[18]

A sense of relief flooded over Pettigrew's men when they were finally ordered to advance at about 2:00 P.M. Colonel Burgwyn of the 26th North Carolina gave the command, "Attention," followed by "Forward March," and the regiment was off. Captain John Thorp of the 47th North Carolina recalled that "the morale of the men was splendid, and when it [sic] advanced to its first grand charge it was with the feelings of conquerors." The enemy opened fire as Pettigrew's men approached Willoughby Run. Most of these shots were too high and caused little damage to the large regiment of almost nine hundred men. Lieutenant Colonel John Lane proudly recalled after the war that "all kept the step and made as pretty and perfect line a regiment ever made, every man endeavoring to keep dressed on the colors." Colonel Henry Morrow of the 24th Michigan noted that the North Carolinians "advanced in two lines of battle . . . they came on with rapid strides, yelling like demons." As the brigade moved down the ravine, men began to fall more regularly. Those soldiers on the left of the regiment began crowding toward the center, as Reynold's battery on McPherson Ridge opened an accurate enfilading fire. The briers and undergrowth also made the descent difficult and wrecked havoc on the finely dressed lines. The men quickly splashed across Willoughby Run and then immediately halted to redress their lines. They now began their final rush toward McPherson Ridge. The enemy's small arms fire was becoming deadly. Underwood found it as "thick as hail stones in a storm." The officers were everywhere, cheering on their green troops. A colonel riding behind his troops on a mule had his hat knocked off by a musket ball. Catching it with one hand, he continued pressing his men onward, yelling to them, "Give 'em _____, boys."[19]

After breaking the first line of the 24th Michigan, the 26th North Carolina met its second line and the fighting became desperate. Some survivors recalled that the adversaries stood about twenty paces apart, pouring volleys into each other. Over on the 26th North Carolina's right, the 11th North Carolina was advancing against the 19th Indiana, which formed the left flank of the Iron Brigade. Waiting until the distance closed, the Hoosiers finally poured volleys into the North Carolinians. The Tar Heels stopped, redressed their lines, and continued forward. Finding the exposed left flank of the 19th Indiana, the North Carolinians attacked the beleaguered unit along its front and flank. The left companies crumbled, and were forced toward the center, but they too were rolled up. The Hoosiers had no choice but to drift toward Seminary Ridge, with the triumphant 11th North Carolina behind them. Lieutenant William Taylor wrote to his mother that "we drove the enemy like sheep . . . we just mowed them down."[20]

The situation was more desperate to the left of the 11th North Carolina, where the 26th North Carolina and 24th Michigan were embraced in a deadly struggle. Ten flag bearers had held the 26th North Carolina's flag aloft, and all were now dead or wounded. One of Pettigrew's staff officers now took up the fallen banner, but was almost immediately stricken. Another captain took the colors, and he too fell. Seeing the flag lying on the ground, Colonel Burgwyn picked it up and yelled, "Dress on the colors!" Just then, a private ran up to Burgwyn and asked for the honor of carrying the flag. As Burgwyn handed it to him, he was struck by a minié ball with such force that it spun him around. The beloved "boy colonel" died before the sun set. The private who was given the flag was soon shot in the head, and the fourteenth flag bearer, Lieutenant Colonel John Lane, hoisted the flag and carried it forward. He too was severely wounded, yielding the flag to a fifteenth flag bearer.[21]

Despite horrendous losses, the 26th North Carolina was not to be denied. "We raised a cheer [and] the Yankee line gave way; we charged to the top of the hill where we found another line, which we charged," wrote Captain Thomas Cureton. The victorious men of the 26th North Carolina probably did not realize that the 24th Michigan's line was also broken by the flanking action of the 11th North Carolina, which had already disposed of the 19th Indiana.[22]

Over on the right of the brigade, the 47th and 52nd North Carolina were also advancing. "It is a grand spectacle," reported Lieutenant J. Rogers of the 47th North Carolina. "In the line of the Forty-seventh there are over 650 muskets, the men marching steadily to meet the foe . . . artillery which at every step rakes through our lines, cutting great gaps, which are quickly filled up by our boys." Crossing Willoughby Run, the two regiments ran into the 121st Pennsylvania and 80th New York (Biddle's Brigade). Buford's troops on the right of the 52nd North Carolina briefly caused the North Carolinians to form a square against them. After dispersing them, the unit continued its advance. They also reluctantly burned the Harman (McClean) house that harbored enemy sharpshooters. Lieutenant Colonel Alexander Biddle of the 121st Pennsylvania wrote in his official report that "I saw the line of the enemy slowly approaching up the hill, extending far beyond our left flank, for which we had no defense." Captain Frank Sterling of the same regiment noted that the 52nd North Carolina's advance was "a beautiful sight . . . to see the rebels advancing from the woods in line of battle with their flags flying as they marched steadily on until they were within the range." Farther to the right, Private Edwin Gearhart of the 142nd Pennsylvania watched as the 47th North Carolina "kept steadily advancing until we could see their officers stepping in front swinging their swords. Suddenly a cloud of smoke arose from their line and almost instantly the balls began to whistle about us and the men next to my right fell." Biddle now yelled for his men to open fire on Pettigrew's slowly advancing men.[23]

John Thorp of the 47th North Carolina recalled that the men's guns became so hot that they had trouble ramming home charges, so they pounded the ramrods on rocks and the ground. The 52nd North Carolina finally found the left flank of the 121st Pennsylvania, and savagely attacked on two fronts, forcing the Pennsylvanians back. Like what had occurred with the Iron Brigade, this rolled up the 80th New York. As the 47th North Carolina moved through the breast-high wheat, a new line of enemy soldiers suddenly materialized. "Though taken by surprise the roar of our guns sounded along our whole line. We had caught the drop on them. Redoubling our yells and a rush, and the work is done. The earth just seemed to open and take in that line which five minutes ago was so perfect," wrote Thorp. He was referring to the ill-fated counterattack of the 142nd Pennsylvania, which was quickly defeated, with its survivors sent fleeing toward Seminary Ridge.[24]

With the two Federal brigades in full retreat, Pender's Division moved up and pursued them to Seminary Ridge. Except for the 52nd North Carolina, which was thrown to the right to watch Buford's cavalry, this ended Pettigrew's first day's fight. The losses were horrendous—about 1100 of the 2500 men the brigade carried into battle. The regimental losses formed a gradient, the 26th North Carolina on the left of the line suffering the greatest losses (588) and the 52nd North Carolina on the right, the least (147). A South Carolinian from Perrin's Brigade provided an interesting analysis of Pettigrew's performance, when he wrote that "they had fought well, but, like most new soldiers, had been content to stand and fire, instead of charging."[25]

Perhaps because the officers were concerned that the men might become demoralized when the euphoria of victory wore off and they realized the severity of their losses, the bands were ordered to play. At least one surgeon objected because the musicians were assisting the wounded. He was overruled, and the bands struck up some tunes to cheer the soldiers.[26]

During the night of July 1 and most of July 2, the men rested in the woods near Willoughby Run. Captain Thomas Cureton of the 26th North Carolina noted that during July 2 "every effort was made by General Pettigrew and all the officers of the brigade to recruit [into] our ranks all the men that were not too severely wounded to bear arms, many sent from the hospital to their companies. The cooks were given muskets, etc.; in fact everything was done to get as many fighting men in ranks as possible." Pettigrew's Brigade received orders to move with the rest of the division to Seminary Ridge, where it spent the evening of July 2 and the morning of July 3 quietly waiting for events to unfold.[27]

The men were disappointed when they heard that the chaplains of Pickett's Division were holding religious services prior to the charge. Their own chaplains had their hands full caring for the wounded and could not tend to the souls of the fit.[28]

After the conclusion of the memorable artillery barrage, General Pettigrew, now commanding the division because of Heth's concussion, rode up to his replacement, Colonel James Marshall. Captain Cureton noted that Pettigrew wore the "bright look he always wore in the hour of danger, and said, 'Now, Colonel, for the honor of the good old North State, forward.'" Marshall repeated the command, and the line marched smartly into the open fields between the two ridges. Cureton related what happened next:

We marched past the valley down the hill, into the valley between the lines (with the Confederate yells); as we marched forward, our artillery would occasionally fire a shot over our heads, as if to let us know we had friends in the rear. The enemy's artillery did not open on us till we got within half a mile of the works . . . [I] looked to the right and left and as far as the eye could see on either side saw that splendid sight of perfect line of battle.[29]

Lieutenant Rogers (47th North Carolina) did not like the looks of the terrain. "Passing our batteries the field . . . was entirely open except here and there an old homestead, and one or two roads with a number of strong rail and post fences, some of them high and difficult to pass over." With Archer's Brigade on the right and Davis's on the left, Pettigrew's Brigade slowly advanced. The arrangement of the regiments was, from left to right, 11th North Carolina–26th North Carolina–47th North Carolina–52nd North Carolina. Behind a stone wall on Cemetery Hill in front of them was the 14th Connecticut and 1st Delaware of Smyth's Brigade (Hays's Division, II Corps) as well as Arnold's battery. There was apparently some momentary confusion as Pickett's Division made its oblique movement to the left to bring it in contact with Pettigrew's Division. Captain Albert Haynes of the 11th North Carolina reported that the line of battle halted twice. "When we dressed the line I did not see one falter . . . it required more courage to dress a line under fire than to continue the charge."[30]

The enemy soldiers could distinctly hear the brigade's officers issuing orders to "close up, guide center, give way to the right or left." As the Tar Heels reached Emmitsburg Pike, the Federal infantry opened a devastating fire. According to one soldier in the 1st Delaware, "they not only crossed the Emmettsburg [sic] Pike but they dressed their line as if on parade after crossing it." Modern historian Earl Hess estimated that perhaps 700 North Carolinians crossed the road.[31]

According to Captain Cureton of the 26th North Carolina, "the enemy's artillery opened on us with grape canister, etc., but our lines crossed the lane [Emmitsburg Pike] in splendid order. When about 200 yards from their works, the musketry opened on us, but nothing daunted our brave men, [who] pressed quickly forward."[32]

Captain Haynes added that the "storm of lead which now met us is beyond description. Grape and canister intermingled with minies and buckshot. The smoke was dense, and at times I could scarcely distinguish my own men." The losses mounted with each step as the line of battle approached the Union position. Major John Jones, now commanding the 26th North Carolina, wrote in his official report that "we were met with a perfect hail-storm of lead from their small arms. The brigade dashed on, and many had reached the wall, when we received a deadly volley from the left." The veterans of the 1st Delaware contested this claim. Their historian wrote that "from the moment we poured the first volley into them they ceased to exist as a compact military organization. They never got fairly formed after they crossed Emmitsburg Pike." While the losses were staggering, the men stopped and sent volleys into the ranks of the 1st Delaware and 14th Connecticut, killing and wounding scores

of the enemy. There was not much of Heth's Division left. Brockenbrough's Brigade and some of Davis's were forced back to Seminary Ridge. Most of Archer's troops on the right that reached the wall were either killed or wounded. Now Pettigrew's Brigade was facing Federal troops on its left flank and front.[33]

The commander of the 14th Connecticut, Theodore Ellis, noted that the initial Federal volleys were so destructive that only "detached portions of the [Confederate] line were rallied, and for a short time maintained their ground, but being rapidly mown down by our terribly destructive fire, they commenced falling back." The situation was becoming desperate. Trimble's two supporting brigades had not yet arrived, and additional Federal troops were massing in front of the men. "With our thinned ranks and in such a position, it would have been a folly to stand, and against such odds," wrote Major Jones. "We therefore fell back to our original position in rear of the batteries." Lieutenant Gaston Broughton of the 26th North Carolina estimated that a handful of his regiment remained at the stone wall for ten to fifteen minutes before falling back. As he made his way back, Captain Cureton came across General Pettigrew, whose horse had been killed and who was now wearily walking back to Seminary Ridge.[34]

Honor precluded some of the men from retreating, however. Lieutenant Colonel John Graves of the 47th North Carolina and about 150 men halted about forty yards from the stone wall. Knowing he could go no farther, he ordered the men to remain there until Trimble's two brigades arrived to provide relief. All of these men were ultimately captured, wounded, or killed.[35]

Soon after the remnants of his command had returned to Seminary Ridge,

General Pettigrew turned to Major Jones, who was now commanding the brigade because of the death of Marshall, and purportedly said with tears in his eyes, "My noble brigade had gained the enemy's works, and would have held them had not _____'s Brigade (names the brigade), on the left, given way. Oh! had they have known the consequences that hung upon their action at that moment, they would have passed on." Pettigrew was undoubtedly referring to Brockenbrough's Brigade on the left of the line.[36]

At least two of Pettigrew's battle flags were lost during the charge on July 3. The men of the 12th New Jersey were awed by the gallantry of the 26th North Carolina's flag bearer, and held their fire until he reached the stone wall in front of them. Then they cried out, "Come over on this side of the Lord!" Realizing his impossible situation, the color bearer surrendered. The 52nd North Carolina's flag was apparently left laying on the ground and was picked up by members of the 14th Connecticut.[37]

Pettigrew's Brigade remained on Seminary Ridge, with the remainder of the division, on July 3 and 4, and began the retreat late that night. The horrors did not end with the retreat, however, as the brigade lost additional men, including General Pettigrew, during the rear guard action at Falling Waters on July 14.[38]

The losses to this once large brigade were high—close to 60%. The greatest loss was sustained by the 26th North Carolina, which carried close to nine hundred men into the battle and marched away with only sixty-seven privates and three officers. Its loss of 83% was fourth highest among Lee's regiments. The 11th North Carolina lost almost 60%. The 47th and 52nd North Carolina, which were on the right of the line during both charges lost only about a third of their men. While the ranks of the 11th and 26th North Carolina were restocked with men after the battle, they were never the same. The survivors could not recover from the shock of losing so many comrades in such a short period of time, and the officer corps never attained its prior high standards. The historians of the 11th North Carolina explained that "owing to the number of officers captured in the Gettysburg battles and not exchanged, many of the vacancies could not be filled, and this defective organization continued to mar the efficiency of the regiment to the end of the war."[39]

Davis's Brigade—Brigadier General Joseph Davis

Units: 2nd Mississippi, 11th Mississippi, 42nd Mississippi, 55th North Carolina
Strength: 2305 (1508 on July 1 as 11th Mississippi not present)
Losses: 1030 (289-677-66+)—44.7%[40]

Two of Brigadier General Joseph Davis's regiments had had significant battlefield experience prior to the Gettysburg campaign, and the two others had none. The 2nd and 11th Mississippi served in Bee's Brigade at First Manassas and saw heavy fighting. After the battle, they were transferred to Whiting's Brigade and fought in the Peninsula campaign and at Seven Pines. Part of Law's Brigade, the two regiments saw heavy action at Gaines's Mill and Malvern Hill, Second Manassas, and Sharpsburg. They were transferred to the Department of North Carolina and Southern Virginia in December 1862, so they missed the Fredericksburg campaign.

Here they were brigaded with the 42nd Mississippi and the 55th North Carolina under the command of Brigadier General Joseph Davis. The latter two regiments had been mustered into service the previous May and had spent most the intervening period in North Carolina.[41]

A nephew of President Jefferson Davis, Joseph Davis was a Mississippi attorney who entered the war as a lieutenant colonel of the 10th Mississippi. Promoted to colonel, he joined his uncle's staff in Richmond in August 1861. The family ties helped, for Davis was promoted to brigadier general on October 8, 1862. This was not the first time that Davis had been put forward for promotion—the Senate had rejected the first one. Toward the end of that year he assumed command of the Mississippi and North Carolina regiments that he would lead at Gettysburg. The brigade was summoned to join Lee's army in May 1863. Its leader had absolutely no prior military experience. According to historian Robert Krick, Joseph Davis's promotion to the rank of brigadier general was "unadulterated" nepotism. Davis had not a shred of combat experience, and to make matters worse, the brigade was bereft of experienced field officers. Only one of the nine could boast a military education or prior experience, and that was in the navy.[42]

Davis's men were keen observers during the trek north into Pennsylvania. Private Samuel Hankins of the 2nd Mississippi recalled how most of the houses along the route were abandoned, as their owners had fled to the mountains for safety. "Some in their haste to depart had not even closed their doors, leaving everything exposed." Hankins proudly recalled that "nothing was molested by our men." By this he meant that the houses were not burned, but he did admit that the men helped themselves to food and the army

"exchanged" their tired mules for the fat horses found in this region.[43]

As the brigade trudged toward Gettysburg on July 1, one of its most experienced regiments, the 11th Mississippi, had been left behind to guard the division's trains. As fate would have it, Davis's Brigade was second in line during the march toward Gettysburg, and as a result, was involved in the opening stages of the battle. The 42nd Mississippi had already skirmished with units from Buford's Federal cavalry division at Fairfield on June 30.[44]

As the column approached Marsh Creek, it came under artillery fire from Calef's battery, and by 8:00 A.M., one Mississippian had been killed and three more wounded. Continuing on, the men encountered Buford's dismounted cavalry, armed with new six-shot Spencer repeating rifles. The Mississippians had never been exposed to this type of weapon before, and it apparently caused considerable confusion, particularly among the less experienced troops. The Mississippians pressed on, however, and eventually pushed their way to Herr Ridge.[45]

Up to this point, the 2nd Mississippi had been on detached duty in Cashtown, but now joined its comrades on Herr Ridge. Davis halted his brigade along the eastern slope of the ridge at about 9:00 A.M. on July 1 and formed his men into line of battle. The experienced 2nd Mississippi was placed in the center of the line to the left of Chambersburg Pike, flanked on either side by an inexperienced regiment. The 55th North Carolina formed the left flank and the 42nd Mississippi formed with its right flank resting on Chambersburg Pike. Hankins (2nd Mississippi) recalled that the regiment's commander, Colonel John Stone, "came down the line, stopping in front of each company and giving instructions. On reaching ours he remarked: 'Men clean out your guns, load, and be ready. We are going to have it!"' The men were in high spirits, as they had been told that only militia were behind the cavalry.[46]

As the men advanced again they could see open fields of grass and grain between them and the town. The enemy skirmishers scattered as the brigade approached McPherson Ridge. During this movement, the 2nd and 42nd Mississippi moved due east, while the 55th North Carolina made a circuitous route to the left (north) that broke its connection with the two other regiments. At about 10:30 A.M., a wall of blue-clad Federal infantry from Cutler's Brigade (Wadsworth's Division, I Corps) suddenly materialized and fired a volley into the North Carolinians. Two members of the color guard fell, and Colonel John Connelly ordered his men to halt and return the volley. Their volley was better aimed than the one they had received, and scores of Federal troops from the 56th Pennsylvania fell. The North Carolinians also fired into the 76th New York, which was on the right of the 56th Pennsylvania. These volleys were the first ever fired by the 55th North Carolina, and no veteran unit could have delivered them any better.[47]

While the 55th North Carolina was aligned on the right flank of these two Federal regiments, the 2nd Mississippi was advancing straight against them. Because of the tall wheat, the Mississippians were not seen by the Federal troops. Colonel Stone ordered the regiment to halt and fire a volley into the enemy. Then a second. Then a third. The commander of the 76th New York initially thought the troops might be "friendly" and ordered his men to hold their fire, despite the fact that his men were falling by the second. Finally realizing his error, he ordered his men to return the fire.[48]

Seeing that his left flank overlapped the Federal right, Colonel Connelly

ordered his 55th North Carolina on the left of the line to wheel to the right with bayonets fixed. The regiment's flag bearer went down during this movement, and Connelly seized the flag before it hit the ground. Rushing forward with it, he was hit in the arm and hip. When Major Alfred Belo of the regiment stooped down to ask Connelly if he was badly wounded, the colonel said, "Yes, but do not pay any attention to me; take the colors and keep in front of the Mississippians." Lieutenant Colonel Maurice Smith took command, but was soon mortally wounded, and Belo stepped forward to lead the regiment. Around the same time, Colonel John Stone of the 2nd Mississippi dismounted and was hurrying forward with the right of his regiment. Coming to a high fence, he climbed it with his men. He later recalled that he was "shot off the fense [sic] as I was climbing over." After the war, Stone admitted to his old brigade commander that "in battle I rarely knew anything that occurred beyond the immediate vicinity of my own command."[49]

One Union soldier described the fighting as "at very short range and very destructive." Despite the fact that the 76th New York refused its right flank to try to deal with the 55th Carolina, Cutler's two regiments could not resist the vice-like pressure for long, and were ordered to fall back within half an hour of its arrival. Over four hundred men from these two Union regiments were left lying on the field or hustled to the rear as prisoners. Seeing the Federal troops in retreat, Davis's men let out a wild yell and dashed forward.[50]

On the right side of the line, the men of the 42nd Mississippi saw a tempting sight—Hall's unsupported Federal battery along Chambersburg Pike. Opening fire on the horses and gunners, the men sprang forward to claim their prize. "We poured such a deadly fire into them that they left their gun and ran for life," wrote one veteran of the 2nd Mississippi. Captain Leander Woollard of the 42nd Mississippi recalled that "just as we were charging them we came to the top of a hill in a wheat field & beheld a *regiment* of the blue bellies immediately in front & not over 100 yards from me & just as they leveled their guns . . . I gave the command to 'lay down,' and a shower of balls passed over our heads—wounding a few of my men." This was the 147th New York from Cutler's Brigade, which had sprinted up and taken position near the battery. Fortunately for the Mississippians, the wheat saved many a life that morning. The stress was too much for several of the green soldiers, who tried to break for the rear. Seeing this, Captain Woollard stationed himself behind his company with his sword drawn, telling them that he would run it through any man who attempted to run. "Not a man showed a willingness to go back but rather an anxiety to go ahead," he recalled.[51]

The Union soldiers held their ground, despite the gradual advance of the 42nd Mississippi. Having disposed of the 56th Pennsylvania and 76th New York, the two other regiments of Davis's Brigade turned their attention to the 147th New York. The beleaguered Federal regiment had been told to retreat with the others, but its commander was wounded before he could give the order. Captain J. V. Pierce of the 147th New York noted that the 55th North Carolina, "press[ed] far to our right and rear, and came over to the south side of the rail fence. The colors drooped to the front. An officer in front of the centre corrected the alignment as if passing in review. It was the finest exhibition of discipline and drill I ever saw, before or since, on the battlefield."[52]

The 147th New York finally received its orders to retreat, and the men sprinted for the rear. By this time, Hall's battery had limbered up and galloped to safety, but not without the loss of one gun. According to Private William Murphy of the 2nd Mississippi, "we poured such a deadly fire into them that they left their gun and ran for [their] life." There is also evidence that the gun may have been lost when some Confederate soldiers bayoneted its team of horses.[53]

Davis's men had gained a great victory after only forty-five minutes of fighting. They had decisively defeated an equal number of Federal regiments and were now rushing after the fleeing Union soldiers. A wheel to their right would put them on the flank of the Iron Brigade and total victory. Davis suddenly saw a movement of Federal troops on the other side of Chambersburg Pike, "and soon after [they] opened a heavy fire on our right flank and rear." These troops were from three Federal regiments, the 6th Wisconsin (Iron Brigade) and the 84th and 95th New York (Cutler's Brigade) that had been rushed to face Davis's threat. Opening fire while on the south side of Chambersburg Pike, Lieutenant Colonel Rufus Dawes of the 6th Wisconsin observed that "the rebel line swayed and bent, and suddenly stopped firing." Seeing this threat, the men broke off their chase of Cutler's men. Major Belo of the 55th North Carolina ran over to Major Blair, now commanding the 2nd Mississippi, and suggested that the regiment quickly charge the enemy, for "the side charging first would hold the field."[54]

This was an extremely critical time for Davis's Brigade. Its commander had lost control of his regiments as they had swept after the fleeing Union soldiers. Two of the three regiments had lost their commanders, and Davis had not thought to halt his troops to reform their ranks. Now three fresh Federal regiments were bearing down on them. Seeing the enemy charging across Chamberburg Pike, Davis's men peppered them with withering volleys. Hundreds fell, but still they advanced. Some of Davis's men jumped into the unfinished railroad cut, thinking it would provide a safe haven from the Federal bullets. One sergeant wrote that "our men thought [it] would prove a good breastwork, but it was too steep and in changing front the men were all tangled up and confused."[55]

Captain Woollard of the 42nd Mississippi vividly recalled what happened after they saw the fresh Union troops. "An order [came] down the line from whom I cannot tell, to lay down in a cut for a rail road near by. Well we obeyed—& in obeying sacrificed our freedom . . . for the cut was too deep to fire over except at the extreme left and the 2nd Mississippi & 55th N.C. having passed over my company were too thick to either fight or escape." Major John Blair, now in command of the 2nd Mississippi, wrote that "all the men were jumbled together without regard to regiment or company."[56]

Davis's men continued firing into the three Federal regiments, who were now approaching their position. According to Lieutenant Lloyd Harris of the Iron Brigade Guard, the "fire was the worst I ever experienced." The enemy fell by the score, but still they charged toward the railroad cut. Realizing the danger his men were in, Davis sprang into action. "In this critical condition, I gave the order to retire, which was done in good order, leaving some officers and men in the railroad cut who were captured," he wrote in his report. Like so many accounts of the battle, Davis's was flawed. While the thoughts of the men in the railroad cut were obviously on escape, the Federal troops had other ideas, as they quickly lined the banks of the railroad cut, and a detachment from the 6th Wisconsin flanked it

on the Confederate left. Colonel Dawes (6th Wisconsin) recalled seeing "hundreds of rebels . . . four feet deep" in the railroad cut. Many Union soldiers jumped into the cut to engage the trapped Confederates in hand-to-hand combat. "I tried to make my way out & escape but the press was very great and just as I was trying to squeeze through, a *big* Wisconsin man thrust his bayonett [sic] at me and said 'Give me that Sword & Stop your men from shooting here or we will kill the last damned one of you,'" wrote a chagrined Captain Woollard.[57]

The fight for the 2nd Mississippi's colors was especially brutal. Murphy, the color bearer, recalled after the war,

> My color guards were all killed and wounded in less than five minutes, and also my colors were shot more than one dozen times, and the flag staff was hit and splintered two or three times. Just at that time a squad of soldiers made a rush for my colors and our men did their duty. They were all killed or wounded, but still rushed for the colors with one of the most deadly struggles that was ever witnessed during any battle of the war. They still kept rushing for my flag and there were over a dozen shot down like sheep in their madly [sic] rush for the colors. The first soldier was shot down just as he made for the flag . . . and at the same time a lieutenant made a desperate struggle for the flag, and was shot through his right shoulder. Over a dozen men fell killed or wounded, and then a large man made a rush for me and the flag. As I tore the flag from the staff he took hold of me and the color.

The "large man" was Corporal Frank Waller of the 6th Wisconsin, who later received the Congressional Medal of Honor for his deed.[58]

Most of the 55th North Carolina apparently did not enter the railroad cut, instead opting to line up just north of it.

Their orders were to cover the retreat of the remainder of the brigade. Some, like Major Belo, jumped down into it. When the Federal troops approached from the south, an officer yelled, "Kill that officer, and that will end it," and threw his sword at Belo, missing him, but hitting a soldier behind him. Belo ordered one of his men to shoot the officer, who was soon lying at the bottom of the railroad cut.[59]

Colonel Dawes approached Major Blair of the 2nd Mississippi and demanded his surrender. "The officer replied not a word, but promptly handed me his sword, and his men, who still held them, threw down their muskets," recalled Dawes. He later marveled at his men's "coolness, self possession and discipline" that prevented them from firing into Davis's trapped troops in the railroad cut.[60]

There are differences of opinion about the number of troops captured in the railroad cut. According to Colonel Dawes of the 6th Wisconsin, 7 officers and 227 men were captured. Murphy (2nd Mississippi) argued that the number was closer to 87. Dawes's figure is probably closer to the truth.[61]

The indignity of capture continued as the men were hustled through Gettysburg. "Some of the citizens, a few miserable cravens who were too cowardly to engage in honest warfare against us, jeered and laughed at us from their doors, tops of houses & other places of safety—miserable creatures," wrote Captain Woollard.[62]

The first day's battle had not yet ended for Davis's Brigade. At about 2:30 P.M., the brigade was formed on the left of Heth's Division. General Daniel complained in his official report that "some troops of General A. P. Hill's corps who where lying down in line of battle, and to whom I had sent an officer with a request that they would act in conjunction with me in my previous advance, and with which request

they had for some cause failed to comply." This was confirmed by Major Thomas Chamberlin of the 150th Pennsylvania, who wrote to Colonel John Bachelder, "I do not question your statement that Davis' Brigade did not come forward until the close of the fight near the McPherson's place." However, not all of the men were passive. Seeing two stands of colors of the 149th Pennsylvania (Stone's Brigade) behind some fence rails, a group of men from the 42nd Mississippi decided to capture them. Sergeant Frank Price recalled that "[I] . . . rose upon my feet, waved my hat, and made directly for the flags." After a tug of war, Price successfully captured one of the flags. Later, the remnants of the 42nd Mississippi helped capture a number of men from the 149th Pennsylvania who were trying to retreat toward Cemetery Ridge. Continuing, the brigade finally reached the outskirts of Gettysburg. "The men, being much exhausted by the heat and severity of the engagement were here rested," wrote Davis. At about sunset, the brigade moved about one mile to the rear.[63]

It was here that the full extent of the brigade's losses was ascertained. Only two of the brigade's nine field officers were unhurt and remained with the troops. All of the regiments were thoroughly decimated, but none more than the 2nd Mississippi, which could count but sixty men present that night. This figure included men with minor wounds. Although the brigade's overall losses were not tallied that day, some have estimated it to be about two-thirds of the number that had entered the battle.[64]

July 2 was a quiet day for the brigade, as it rested and collected rifles and other accoutrements. That night the men moved up to Seminary Ridge and halted in McMillan's Woods. Archer's Brigade formed on its right and Brockenbrough's on its left. The evening also brought the welcome addition of the 11th Mississippi, which swelled Davis's ranks by almost six hundred men. So desperate was Davis for reinforcements that he actually rode down Chambersburg Pike for several miles to find the regiment, which was marching swiftly toward Gettysburg. The 11th Mississippi responded with cheers, "in acknowledgment of our approval of the conduct of himself & the balance [sic] of the brigade," noted Lieutenant William Peel in his diary.[65]

At about 9:00 A.M. on July 3, the men were ordered into line and marched about a quarter mile to the left, where they formed behind Pegram's artillery battalion. They did not know it at the time, but they were to be involved in the Pickett–Pettigrew–Trimble charge on Cemetery Ridge. The brigade deployed from left to right as 11th Mississippi–2nd Mississippi–42nd Mississippi–55th North Carolina. The grand cannonade that preceded the charge opened at about 1:00 P.M. and soon drew return fire from the Union batteries positioned on Cemetery Hill and Cemetery Ridge. Some of the shells sailed over Pegram's guns and exploded among Davis's men, killing two and wounding twenty-one. According to Davis, his orders were that "when the artillery in our front ceased firing, the division would attack the enemy's batteries, keeping dressed to the right, and moving in line with Major-General Pickett's Division, which was on our right, and march obliquely to the left."[66]

The artillery ceased firing at about 3:00 P.M., and almost immediately, Archer's and Pettigrew's Brigades moved smartly forward. For some reason, Davis's Brigade, the third from the right, did not follow. Horror-stricken, General Pettigrew, now in command of the division, sent an aide back to the thick woods to get Davis moving. However, Davis's men almost immediately broke from the woods and, with an "impetuous rush," soon overtook the two brigades. They marched forward as if on parade. The enemy did not open fire until the division was about three-quarters of a mile from Cemetery Ridge. At first, the shells flew harmlessly over the line, causing Peel to write that it was "a storm of screaming, howling shells, across the field, that burst & tore the timber behind us in frightful manner." Before long, the artillery found the advancing line of battle, and "we were met by a heavy fire of grape, canister, and shell, which told sadly upon our ranks," wrote General Davis. Some of the shells took out four or five men. To Peel, the sound of the artillery became louder than an ongoing thunderclap. "Shells, screaming & bursting around us, scattered their fragments & projectiles in very direction," he wrote. All that the officers could yell was, "Steady boys" or "Don't break yourself down by running." Davis noted that "under this destructive fire, which commanded our front and left with fatal effect, the troops displayed great coolness, were well in hand, and moved steadily forward, regularly closing up the gaps made in their ranks."[67]

Davis's Brigade presented an imposing sight to the men of Smyth's Brigade (Hays's Division, II Corps), who were manning the Federal line directly in front of them. "Looking up we saw them advancing out of the woods across the field coming in three lines of battle, their bayonetts [sic] fixed, lines dressed as if on parade," wrote Captain George Bowen of the 12th New Jersey. Private Chauncey Harris of the 108th New York added that "I never saw troops march out with more military precision. Their lines were unbroken and they looked in the distance like statues. On they came, steady, firm, moving like so many automatons."[68]

A number of fences were encountered along the way, which had to be climbed. In each case, the regiments halted to reform after scaling them before marching on. Looking around them, the men could see that the artillery was taking a ghastly toll. As they crossed Emmitsburg Road, Smyth's Brigade opened fire. Peel (11th Mississippi) estimated that the enemy infantry opened fire when they were within two hundred yards of Cemetery Ridge. According to General Davis, "we suffered severely; but this did not for a moment check the advance." Captain Bowen (12th New Jersey) wrote that "we open[ed] fire, pouring in the most deadly kind of fire, they fell like wheat before the garner." Most of the enemy were armed with buck and ball ammunition that had a deadly effect at short distances.[69]

Brockenbrough's small brigade of Virginians on their left had given way under the devastating artillery fire from over thirty cannon on Cemetery Hill and from the 8th Ohio, which had ventured out to pour an oblique fire into them. This exposed Davis's left to the brunt of this gunfire. Still, the line surged on. The outline of the Bryan farm could be seen through the smoke just ahead. A number of officers from the 11th Mississippi went down, and no one seemed to know who was in command of the regiment. Captain John Moore stood with his back to Cemetery Ridge, trying to reorganize the shattered ranks of Company A. "John, for heaven's sake give the command to charge," yelled Lieutenant A. J. Baker of the same company. "No," replied Moore, "I cannot take the responsibility." Realizing that to delay meant the destruction of his company, Baker took it upon himself to scream, "Charge." Baker fell when within ten feet of the stone wall, and was ultimately captured. The same fate befell most of the 11th Mississippi.

Company G entered the attack with forty-five men, but only five returned unhurt.[70]

Because of the orientation of Cemetery Ridge, the right side of the brigade was the first to make contact with the Federal infantry behind the stone wall. "Here we were subjected to a most galling fire of musketry and artillery, that so reduced the already thinned ranks that any further effort to carry the position was hopeless, and there was nothing left but to retire to the position originally held, which was done in more or less confusion," wrote Davis. The 55th North Carolina, on the right of the brigade, came within nine yards of the stone wall before being turned away.[71]

Private William Love remarked after the battle that "this mere skeleton of the Davis Brigade went as far as human strength and endurance could go." At least some of the men did get as far as the Bryan farm buildings. One was Lieutenant Peel, who soon after had to make a decision about retreating into the teeth of death or surrendering. He chose the latter. Three of the four officers commanding regiments were killed during the charge, and the fourth, Colonel Green of the 11th Mississippi, was wounded.[72]

The brigade, or what was left of it, returned to the position it had occupied earlier in the morning and remained there for about thirty hours. During this time, the men prepared breastworks in the event the enemy decided to attack. A soldier from Posey's Mississippi Brigade, who knew General Davis before the war, spied him after the charge and asked him where his brigade was. "He pointed his sword up to the skies, but did not say a word, and stood there for a moment knocking pebbles out of the path with the point of his sword. He could not talk . . . he walked on." The brigade began its retreat toward Virginia during the early morning hours of July 5.[73]

The battle was not kind to Davis's Brigade. After initial success, the brigade was caught in the unfinished railroad cut and sustained heavy losses. That should have been the end of the battle for the brigade, but it was included in the ill-fated Pickett–Pettigrew–Trimble charge. It fought as well as could be expected, given its inexperienced leadership on July 1 and its impossible task on July 3.[74]

Brockenbrough's Brigade—Colonel John Brockenbrough

Units: 40th Virginia, 47th Virginia, 55th Virginia, 22nd Virginia Battalion
Strength: 971
Losses: 186 (35-130-21)—19.2%[75]

One of the smallest brigades in Lee's army, Brockenbrough's Brigade had already seen heavy combat in most of the army's campaigns since the Seven Days battles, when they all fought in Field's Brigade. As part of A. P. Hill's Light Division, the brigade sustained heavy losses at the battles of Mechanicsville, Gaines's Mill, and Glendale. During the latter battle it had the distinction of capturing Brigadier General George McCall. The men also fought in the Second Manassas campaign, where Brigadier General Charles Field went down with a severe wound. Temporarily replaced by Colonel John Brockenbrough of the 40th Virginia, the brigade helped save Lee's army at Sharpsburg along with the rest of A. P. Hill's Division. Brockenbrough remained in charge of the brigade during the Fredericksburg campaign, where it launched several counterattacks on the enemy. Although Colonel Brockenbrough had led the brigade at Sharpsburg and Fredericksburg, it was never officially assigned to him, and it went to Brigadier General Henry Heth prior to the Chancellorsville campaign. It fought hard there, with some of its units sustaining losses of almost 50%. As a result, the brigade was worn out and not in good fighting trim when the Gettysburg campaign began. With Heth's elevation to division command, Brockenbrough was again assigned "temporary" command of the brigade.[76]

During the march north, Brockenbrough's troops were not among the most well-behaved. Private Tom Luttrell of the 40th Virginia wrote, "inhabitants alarmed. Bad behavior in our troops, plundering &c." June 29 found Heth's Division at Cashtown. That evening, Brockenbrough ordered Colonel W. Christian to take his 55th Virginia out on picket duty along the Chambersburg Pike toward Gettysburg. Brockenbrough apparently went to great trouble telling his subordinate "not to mistake friends from foes, that we probably might meet some of Ewells [sic] command or Stuarts [sic] and a great deal more than was not very clear to me," wrote Christian after the war. Not understanding all of this order, Christian rode back to Brockenbrough for additional information. "Col. B. told me he knew no more than I did, that it was an exact copy of an order he had gotten from Gen. Heth." Undeterred, Christian sought out Heth, who told him that he had received the order from General Hill. The sun was beginning to set, so Christian turned his horse and rode back to his waiting regiment. After marching them along the pike for about a mile and a half, he halted his men at Marsh Creek for the night.[77]

After a breakfast of "confiscated chickens," Christian spied "a considerable body of our troops advancing from Cashtown." This turned out to be most of General Pettigrew's Brigade, conducting a reconnaissance toward Gettysburg. Pettigrew apparently asked Christian to "attend him with my Regiment." Informing Pettigrew that his men had spent a sleepless night along the road, and he had no orders to move farther to Gettysburg, the general admitted that "he had no right to command my presence." Pettigrew explained that while his men were "splendidly drilled and equipped," they were inexperienced, and he would like nothing better than to have a veteran unit accompany them on their journey. Christian agreed, and they all set off toward Gettysburg. Bumping into Federal cavalry, Pettigrew sent a courier to Christian to "call me back, and said that he had found out all he came for."[78]

Brockenbrough's Brigade was third in line, behind Archer's and Davis's, during Heth's advance toward Gettysburg on July 1. Firing could be heard up ahead at about 10:00 A.M., but Brockenbrough's men did not expect a fight. The brigade halted while Archer's and Davis's men ventured forward. Gunfire suddenly erupted around Willoughby Run, and the men were ordered to file to the right of the road. Their officers yelled, "Left face, load." It wasn't long before they saw Archer's men fleeing from the woods with the victorious Iron Brigade close behind. Brockenbrough's men raised their guns to fire into the advancing Federals, but were prevented from doing so because of the "flying Tennesseans." Realizing that it was too late to help Archer's men, Brockenbrough ordered his brigade back to Herr Ridge.[79]

With Pettigrew's Brigade on his right, Brockenbrough was again ordered forward at about 2:00 P.M. The brigade was deployed from left to right as 55th Virginia–47th Virginia–40th Virginia–22nd Virginia Battalion. Brockenbrough's men approached Willoughby Run and the Federal line on the ridge behind it. The brigade obliqued to the right before crossing the stream, undoubtedly to link up with Pettigrew's Brigade that was advancing on its right. The right of Brockenbrough's line was positioned to take on the 2nd and 7th Wisconsin (Iron Brigade, Wadsworth's Division, I Corps), numbering about 550 men, while the left would take on the 150th Pennsylvania (Stone's Brigade, Rowley's Division, I Corps), numbering about 400. After dispersing the four companies of Federal skirmishers, Brockenbrough's small brigade moved against the well-placed Federal troops on the ridge, whose numbers roughly approximated their own.[80]

The 150th Pennsylvania, facing the left of Brockenbrough's Brigade, watched these movements from behind a stout fence. Major Thomas Chamberlin of the regiment recalled that his regiment's opening fire "failed to scatter or confuse him." Brockenbrough's men now returned the fire, which Chamberlin likened to a hailstorm. "Back and forth, for a few minutes, swept the tempest of bullets. . . . Suddenly, as if elsewhere something decisive, for which they had been waiting, had occurred, our antagonists ceased firing, fell back a short distance, and obliquing to their right were soon hidden from view by the woods," noted Chamberlin.[81]

The outcome of this initial assault could have actually turned out differently. Several companies of the 150th Pennsylvania had been sent to Chambersburg Pike to help repel Daniel's Brigade's charge from the north. If Brockenbrough had attacked immediately, he would have faced but a handful of companies. Instead, his men advanced very slowly, giving time for the 150th Pennsylvania to reform and open fire. Their concentrated volleys encouraged the Virginians to beat a hasty retreat. Major Chamberlin noted that "for some unexplained reason the strong force approaching from the west . . . moderated its movements, as if awaiting developments on other portions of the field, and by the time it came within musket reach of our regiment was firmly established in its position."[82]

The brigade apparently made two unsuccessful attacks on the Federal line. Neither appears to have been "spirited." Those units in front of the 7th Wisconsin of the Iron Brigade lay down and opened a galling fire against them. At about 3:00 P.M., Scales's Brigade (Pender's Division) moved into position behind Brockenbrough's men. By this time, Pettigrew's men had finally flanked the Iron Brigade, forcing its retreat. The Wisconsinites withdrew, firing as they left their positions. This left the 150th Pennsylvania isolated. Attacked on three sides, it was overwhelmed and joined the retreat toward Seminary Ridge. As Brockenbrough's men approached the McPherson barn, they came upon fifty dead Pennsylvanians in a straight line, marking the regiment's former position on the ridge. While resting around the barn, the men saw several Union soldiers running toward them with the flag of the 149th Pennsylvania. Jumping to their feet, they opened fire, and Private James Lumpkin of the 55th Virginia captured the flag.[83]

This essentially ended Brockenbrough's Brigade's first day's fight. "Used up" by their exertions against the Federal line on McPherson Ridge, they were relieved by Scales's Brigade who pursued the enemy to Seminary Ridge. Scales wrote with some disdain in his official report that when he came upon Brocken-

brough's men, they had halted and were lying down. "The officers on this part of the line informed me that they were without ammunition, and would not advance farther." Brockenbrough ordered his men to follow Scales toward the town, scooping up scores of prisoners in the process. The brigade's losses were modest—just under 150. That night, and most of July 2, the brigade occupied Seminary Ridge with the rest of the division.[84]

During the evening of July 2, the brigade was ordered to the right, halting near the McMillan house, where it formed the left of Heth's Division. The next morning, the men learned that they would participate in the attack on the strongly held Union position on Cemetery Ridge. To make matters worse, they would have the dubious honor of forming the extreme left of the attack column.

As the time for the charge approached, Brockenbrough was told to begin his advance when Davis's Brigade, on his right, began its movement. To assure that there was adequate supervision of the men, Brockenbrough decided to break the brigade into two parts. On the left would be the 47th and 55th Virginia under the command of Colonel Robert Mayo of the former regiment. Brockenbrough retained direct command of the 40th Virginia and 22nd Virginia Battalion, which formed on the right, next to Davis's men. This added an unnecessary complication. As Davis's men stepped off at about 3:00 P.M., Brockenbrough followed the lead, and the 40th Virginia and 22nd Virginia Battalion grimly moved forward. For some reason, the word never reached the left side of the line. Colonel Christian (55th Virginia), watching the right side of the brigade moving forward, could not understand why his regiment had not received orders to advance. Noticing that Brockenbrough's Brigade had not advanced, one of Pettigrew's aides offered to gallop over and get them moving. Pettigrew told him not to bother, as "it might follow, and if it failed to do so it would not matter." According to the staff officer, the brigade had been "so badly handled that it was in a chronic state of demoralization and was not to be relied upon; it was virtually of no value in a fight."[85]

Colonel Christian rode over to confer with Lieutenant Colonel Lyle of the 47th Virginia, and the two realized that Colonel Mayo was nowhere to be found. Recalling Brockenbrough's direct orders "not to move till Col. Mayo said so," the two officers were in a quandary. Realizing that they could wait no longer, they ordered their men to dash forward to try to catch up with the right side of the brigade. They finally caught up with the remainder of the brigade.[86]

Some writers believed that despite the official returns, Brockenbrough's Brigade numbered less than five hundred men at this time. These veterans still moved grimly forward. Suddenly, screaming artillery shells from over thirty guns on Cemetery Hill began landing uncomfortably close to the men. Being on the left of the line, Brockenbrough's Brigade provided a perfect target. The shells began finding their mark. Major T. W. Osborn, commanding these batteries, wrote in his report that the "havoc produced upon their ranks was truly surprising." One of his battery commanders, Captain Frederick Edgell, wrote that his oblique fire against Brockenbrough's Brigade had a "destructive effect." Reaching a swale just past the burned-out Bliss barn, about five hundred yards from the Federal line on Cemetery Ridge, the men halted to reform their lines. It was here that many of the men realized that to continue was suicide, and either remained there or began their retreat toward Seminary Ridge. More and more men began

making for the rear as the shells again played on their ranks. The remaining men continued on, in what looked more like a skirmish line at this point.[87]

Without warning, a volley erupted from their left. Looking over, they saw the 8th Ohio (Carroll's Brigade, Hays's Division) on their flank. This was the final straw, and Lieutenant W. F. Dunaway of Brockenbrough's staff noted that "out of this corner the men without waiting for orders turned and fled." The movement had a domino effect, as the volleys hit the new left flank and it too crumbled. Soon the entire brigade was making its way back to safety. The artillery on Cemetery Hill and the infantry on the flank now turned their attention on Davis's Brigade, with devastating results. As Brockenbrough's men retreated, several remarked bitterly, "If Old Jack [Stonewall Jackson] had been here, it wouldn't have been like this."[88]

Although Colonel Mayo did not participate in the charge, he did provide a report on the battle. Exaggerating, he stated that the brigade did not number more than two hundred, and that "we succeeded, however, in holding the enemy in check until everything on our right had given way. Our brigade was the last to leave field." After the war, Colonel Christian repeated this outrageous claim. "We remained out in that field till all of the troops on our right had fallen back . . . and did not retire until AFTER the retreat had become general."[89]

Almost as soon as the battle was over, comrades from other units attacked Brockenbrough's Brigade's poor performance during the charge. Most of these attacks were made by North Carolinians, who were upset that Pickett's Virginians had gotten most of the glory from the charge. Therefore, these detractors went after Brockenbrough's Virginians. This can be clearly seen in William McLaurin's

(Lane's Brigade) account. "Brockenbrough's, Va. Brigade did not come up to its usual standard, and the shafts of detraction were hurled at all its comrades under Pettigrew, on that account." Captain L. Young of Pettigrew's Brigade wrote that Brockenbrough's men never really got into the charge at all; "it advanced to the protection of some rifle pits in front of Seminary Ridge, . . . it took no part in the charge." He also bluntly stated that Brockenbrough's men were "the only troops on the ground which really behaved badly." Others suggested that the brigade fled almost immediately when the Federal artillery opened fire on it. Another member of Pettigrew's Brigade described an alleged incident where one of Brockenbrough's wounded soldiers wandered over to the North Carolinians for assistance because there were "none wounded but himself and none killed in his company."[90]

Brockenbrough's men were quick to refute these claims, but they tended to stick through the years. Modern historian George Stewart supported the Virginians when he wrote, "actually the brigade did better than the statements of its worst detractors suggest," as they did advance as a unit to beyond the Bliss farm. One Union soldier observed that "no human flesh could have stood in front of the terrible cannon fire . . . on the point occupied by Brockenbrough's Brigade." Flank attacks are difficult to withstand, no matter how high the morale. One needs only to recall the flank attack on July 1 that forced Biddle's Brigade to retreat from McPherson Ridge. The same occurred nearby, when the storied Iron Brigade was flanked and forced back to Seminary Ridge. Some have also blamed General Pettigrew for putting his two weakest brigades in the attack column's most vulnerable position.[91]

The brigade began its retreat during the early morning hours of July 5. The unit's problems continued during the retreat. Federal cavalry caught up with Heth's Division near Falling Waters on July 14. The cavalrymen made several ill-fated attacks on Brockenbrough's Brigade, all of which were repelled. For some reason, still not understood, Colonel Brockenbrough ordered his brigade to attack the enemy while he and the rest of the division marched away toward the safety of the Potomac River. Outnumbered and unsupported, the small brigade was overwhelmed and all of its flags and many of the men were captured. After the fiasco, the 40th Virginia numbered fewer than a hundred men. So small was the brigade that it was consolidated with Archer's.[92]

Brockenbrough was relieved of his command in late July 1863, and he resumed command of the 40th Virginia. His lieutenant colonel, Henry Walker, was promoted to the rank of brigadier general, and assumed command of the consolidated brigade. Outraged, Brockenbrough resigned his commission in January 1864.[93]

Archer's Brigade—Brigadier General James Archer

Units: 13th Alabama, 5th Alabama Battalion, 1st Tennessee, 7th Tennessee, 14th Tennessee
Strength: 1198

Losses: 684 (69-219-396)—57.1%[94]

Brigadier General James Archer's Brigade could trace its roots to Brigadier General

Samuel Anderson's Brigade from the summer of 1861. Composed of the 1st, 7th, and 14th Tennessee, the brigade first tasted combat under Robert E. Lee in the mountains of western Virginia. It fought well at the Battle of Cheat's Mountain and later participated in the Romney campaign in January 1862. The brigade transferred to Johnston's army in late February and fought with Hood's Brigade at Eltham's Landing during the Peninsula campaign. General Anderson resigned his commission a short time later because of ill health, and was replaced by Brigadier General Robert Hatton, who had been colonel of the 7th Virginia. Entering into thick, tangled woods during the battle of Seven Pines, the brigade blundered into a full division of fresh Federal troops and was forced to beat a hasty retreat, but not before Hatton was killed instantly. Additional units were added to the brigade, including the 5th Alabama, and a new commander also arrived. An attorney by trade, James Archer had served as a captain in the Mexican War. He remained in the army in that capacity and became colonel of the 5th Texas at the outbreak of the war. Although he had seen limited service in the war, Archer was promoted to the rank of brigadier general on June 3, 1862, and given Hatton's Brigade.[95]

The brigade saw action in A. P. Hill's Division at Mechanicsville and Gaines's Mill, where it launched bloody charges against strong Federal positions. More casualties were sustained at Frayer's farm, where its counterattack helped stabilize the Confederate line. The brigade lost over five hundred men in one week of fighting. Another counterattack helped win the day at the battle of Cedar Mountain and later, the brigade beat back several Federal attacks during the battle of Second Manassas. It continued to provide gallant service during the Maryland cam-

paign. Archer's finest hour may have been at Fredericksburg, where the brigade plugged a dangerous hole in the Confederate line caused by Lane's Brigade's untimely retreat. Chancellorsville brought new commendations, as the brigade charged the high ground at Hazel Grove, allowing the Confederate artillery to mass there. By the start of the Gettysburg campaign, the brigade could boast that it had never been defeated on any battlefield.[96]

As Archer's men trudged through the Pennsylvania countryside, they were impressed by the farms they passed. Although the houses all looked about the same, Sergeant Robert Mockbee of the 14th Tennessee noted that "we were struck too, with the good barns, sometimes better than the dwellings of the owners, and a big bell on top of each barn. The clover and wheat fields looked very enticing to us who were from the cotton fields." Although the soldiers had received strict orders against pillaging, they "seemed to consider chickens and fruits of all kinds to be exempt from this general order," wrote Lieutenant William Fulton of the 5th Alabama.[97]

Archer threw out pickets, who moved toward Gettysburg on June 30, when the division was camped outside Cashtown. In the distance, the men could see Federal cavalry riding to the top of a distant hill; after quickly looking around, they rode off in the direction from which they had come. The next morning, the pickets were called back to the main body when the brigade received orders to continue the march along Chambersburg Pike.[98]

The brigade led the division's march toward Gettysburg on July 1. The men did not expect a fight, instead thinking that this day would be no different from all of the others they had experienced since entering Northern territory. The day before, General Pettigrew had conducted a reconnaissance toward Gettysburg and did not like what he saw. Returning to the division, he sought out General Archer. According to Lieutenant L. Young of Pettigrew's staff, his commanding officer had gone to great lengths explaining the topography and the potential dangers that were ahead. "General Archer listened but believed him not, marched on unprepared," wrote Young after the war. Archer, like most of the men of Heth's Division, did not believe that the Army of the Potomac was anywhere near.[99]

As the column continued marching on Chambersburg Pike, Colonel Birkett Fry of the 13th Alabama rode back to the color bearer and ordered him to unsheath the colors. Up ahead, Private E. Boland saw a squad of Federal cavalry in the fields to the right of the road. Three companies from the 13th Alabama and the 5th Alabama Battalion were thrown forward as skirmishers on the same side of the road. As the men deployed, they loaded their rifles. Moving forward, they quickly scattered Buford's skirmishers. The first casualty in Archer's Brigade was actually a mascot—a dog that had joined the 13th Alabama.[100]

As Archer's skirmishers continued driving Buford's counterparts back toward Herr Ridge, the men approached a house, from which issued "a fierce dog [that] raised an objection" to their presence. The homeowner emerged, and after inquiring about the presence of Archer's men on his property, asked them to "Tell Lee to hold on just a little until I get my cow out of the pasture." A large yellow dog, whether the same one or not, "did not like so much company; so he thought he would intercept our progress by biting a lot of us, and so put in to put [sic] his thoughts into effect, when he was shot by several, and of course layed him out," recalled Private W. Bird of the 13th Alabama. The dog's owner rushed out upon hearing the shots, and yelled that "the Rebels were terrible fellows; and she did not fail to tell us so."[101]

After driving the Federal pickets about three miles, Archer could see dismounted cavalry (Gamble's Brigade) drawn up across the pike. Suddenly, a battery from Major William Pegram's artillery battalion galloped up, deployed in front of the brigade, and opened fire on the dismounted cavalry. After firing several shots, Archer ordered his column to the right of the road, marching in "fours," where the brigade formed line of battle. Bird called it the "pretiest [sic] line of battle I think I ever saw." The brigade was deployed, from left to right as 7th Tennessee–14th Tennessee–1st Tennessee–13th Alabama.[102]

Federal artillery shells fell among the men as the line of battle moved forward, so they were ordered to double-quick across the fields. Lieutenant John Calef, commanding Company A, 2nd U.S. Artillery, closely watched Archer's advance, writing that "their battle-flags looked redder and bloodier in the strong July sun than I had ever seen them before." Calef ordered his gunners to aim at the Confederate banners, throwing the lines "into some confusion." As the brigade advanced, it forced Pegram's guns to fall silent, lest they hit their own men. After progressing about a mile, Pegram's guns were able to reopen on the enemy. "As soon as we were below the range of our guns, they fired a volley at the Federal battery, and I thought it the sweetest music I had ever heard as the balls went whizzing just above our heads," wrote Private W. Moon of the 13th Alabama. The second volley knocked over one of the Federal guns. "This raised a terrible Rebel yell all along the line," recalled Moon.[103]

The brigade again encountered Buford's men, and opened fire. Private

John McCall recalled that the "engagement soon became very warm." The
enemy made a stubborn resistance, but
were finally forced across Willoughby
Run. Because of the terrain, the 13th
Alabama and 1st Tennessee advanced
faster than the 7th and 14th Tennessee on
the left. As a result, General Archer
ordered his advanced regiments to halt.
Private Moon recalled that the men
"halted to reform, reload, catch our
breath, and cool off a little." Up ahead
was Willoughby Run. Private Bird recalled
that the stream was clear with "pebbles in
bottom nearly knee deep." By this time,
the 7th and 14th Tennessee had reached
the west bank of the stream. Lieutenant
Colonel Samuel Shepard of the 7th Tennessee was concerned about the terrain,
which he described as having "a fence and
undergrowth, which was some disadvantage to our line in crossing, but the
brigade rushed across with a cheer."[104]

Up ahead, on the other side of the
stream, was a steep incline. No one in
Archer's Brigade knew what was ahead. So
far, the troops had faced only dismounted
Federal cavalry, who were driven back.
While the brigade halted, Heth rode up
to Archer and ordered him forward to
ascertain the "strength and line of battle
of the enemy." Captain J. Turney of the
1st Tennessee recalled that Archer told
Heth that his "brigade was light to risk so
far in advance of the enemy." Undeterred,
Heth ordered the brigade forward.
Because of the terrain, the brigade did
not cross the stream all at once in a solid
mass. Instead, gaps formed between several of the regiments.[105]

Once across the stream, the left of the
line moved rapidly up the hill and ran
right into the advancing Iron Brigade,
perhaps the finest fighting unit in the
Army of the Potomac. "We were not 40 or
50 yards from the enemy's line when we
opened fire. Our men fired with great
coolness and deliberation, and with terrible effect," recorded Shepard in his official report. He was up against the 2nd Wisconsin, the first regiment to arrive. The
smoke was so dense that the Tennesseans
in the center and left of the brigade could
not see the ememy in front of them. But
they could tell they were there, for bullets
zipped into them regularly. The Federal
fire suddenly ceased, and Captain Turney
in the center of the line "dropped on my
knees, and, looking beneath the hanging
smoke, saw the feet and legs of the enemy
moving to our left." Rushing over to General Archer, Turney communicated this
information, but received the rebuke. "I
guess not, Captain, since Gen. Joe Davis is
to occupy that timber to our left." This
was the first glimpse Captain Turney had
of the rapidly deploying Iron Brigade.[106]

To Turney's right, the the 13th Alabama
was ordered to climb to the crest of the
ridge and hit the 2nd Wisconsin in the
flank. Wheeling to the left, the Alabamians
stopped "about seventy-five yards from the
bluecoats, into whom we were pouring volley after volley as fast as we could," recalled
Private Moon. Many of the men "were
rather enjoying the fray." Suddenly, the
men were ordered to fall back.[107]

The order astounded the men, but they
did not know that the situation on the
right wing of the regiment was growing
grim. As the right wing climbed the ridge
on the east side of Willoughby Run, it ran
directly into the rapidly approaching 19th
Indiana. Private W. Bird of the 13th
Alabama related what occurred next,
when "all of a sudden a heavy line of battle
rose up out of the wheat, and poured a
volly [sic] into our ranks, it wavered and
they charged us, and we fell back to the
ravine again, and before we could rally, it
seemed to me there were 20,000 Yanks
down in among us hollowing surrender."

Being on the extreme right of the brigade had its dangers, especially now, because the 24th Michigan on the left of the 19th Indiana found no enemy in front of it, and was able to wrap around the Alabamians's right flank and rear. Private E. Boland of the 13th Alabama recalled that "we discovered that we had tackled a hard proposition . . . we had Yankees on the front, Yankees on the flanks, and seen Yankees behind us." With the two Federal regiments on their right flank and rear, and the 7th Wisconsin attacking their front, the 13th Alabama and 1st Tennessee were in a desperate situation. "After a short, furious fight, surrounded by infantry and cavalry, nothing was left for us to do but lay down in the field and allow the enemy to come on or surrender, which we did," wrote a chagrined Boland. Lieutenant James Simpson felt that many men fell into Northern hands because "most of the brigade refused to fall back."[108]

To the left of the 13th Alabama, the 1st Tennessee continued to engage the 7th Wisconsin in front of them. Looking over, Private Moon of the 13th Alabama saw that the men were "hotly engaged at close quarters, the Yanks charging in column, the Tennesseans lying on their backs to load and whirling over to fire." Before long, the pressure on their right flank from the 19th Indiana and 24th Michigan forced the Tennessee regiment to fall back as well. Many realized that flight was foolhardy, as Colonel Robinson of the 7th Wisconsin wrote, "the enemy . . . what was left of them able to walk . . . threw down their guns, ducked between our files, and passed to the rear."[109]

While this fiasco was occurring on the brigade's right flank, the left, composed of the 7th and 14th Tennessee, was hit by the 2nd Wisconsin's vicious bayonet charges. The Badgers had so unexpectedly encountered the enemy that the men had not had time to load their muskets. Archer's men calmly opened fire on the enemy when they were but forty or fifty yards away, and in a short time, almost half of the men of the 2nd Wisconsin were lying dead and wounded on the forest floor. Not to be deterred by these heavy losses, the survivors slowly pushed Archer's men back across Willoughby Run. According to Major Mark Finnicum of the 2nd Wisconsin, "the Rebels sullenly fell back, firing on our advancing line, killing and wounding many of our men." Archer's men finally knew that they were not up against cavalry or militia, as one exclaimed, "There are those damned black-hatted fellows again. Taint no militia. It's the Army of the Potomac."[110]

As the men of the 2nd Wisconsin approached a fence, they saw a knot of Confederates in the thick undergrowth, who were quickly overcome and captured. Among the prisoners was General James Archer, who was so exhausted from his morning exertions that he could not retreat any farther. Captain William Harries of the 2nd Wisconsin recalled that Archer "wore a splendid gray uniform and while I was looking him over, the lieutenant of my company stepped up to him and said, 'I'll relieve you of that sword.'" Archer at first refused, saying "courtesy permitted him to retain his sidearms." Archer was the first general that Lee lost as a prisoner.[111]

Remarkably, none of the regiments' flags were captured. The 13th Alabama came closest, but its flag bearer, Private W. A. Castleberry, ripped the flag from its staff and stuffed it into his tunic. Despite curses from Federal troops, Castleberry was able to flee to safety.[112]

The survivors fell back a safe distance, and opened fire upon any Federal soldier foolish enough to expose himself. A bitter Lieutenant Colonel Shepard (7th

Tennessee) wrote after the battle, "being completely overpowered by numbers, and our support not being near enough to give us any assistance, we fell back across the field, and reformed just in rear of the brigade [Pettigrew's] that had started in as our support." Shepard estimated that about seventy-five men had been captured by the Iron Brigade. The number was probably closer to 240, with overall losses totaling about 374.[113]

Colonel Birkett Fry of the 13th Alabama assumed command of the brigade, which spent the next several hours resting in the woods near Herr Ridge. At about 2:30 P.M., the brigade was ordered to its feet and formed into line of battle as General Heth prepared his next attack on McPherson Ridge, this time with Brockenbrough's and Pettigrew's Brigades. Archer's depleted brigade formed on the latter's right and warily advanced. Although they did not see any Federal troops in front of them, enemy cavalry materialized on their right flank. Colonel Fry immediately halted his command and wheeled the men to face this new threat. Neither side advanced upon the other, as the two combatants merely watched each other during the remainder of the day.[114]

That night, and all the following day, the men rested on the right of Heth's Division, with their right on a farm lane. During the evening of July 2, the men received orders to march to Seminary Ridge, stopping on the left flank of Wright's Brigade (Anderson's Division). The brigade was formed from left to right as 5th Alabama Battalion–7th Tennessee–14th Tennessee–13th Alabama–1st Tennessee. Pickett's fresh division arrived during the morning of July 3 and deployed to the right of Archer's Brigade.[115]

Sometime after noon, Colonel Fry observed Generals Lee, Longstreet, and A. P. Hill ride up to a spot between the

right of Archer's Brigade and the left of Garnett's (Pickett's Division). Dismounting, they sat on a log and intently studied a map. After completing their discussion, they remounted and rode off. Staff officers and couriers soon galloped about, and General Pettigrew approached Fry to inform him that Heth's Division would charge the Federal position after a cannonade had softened up the enemy line. "They will of course return the fire with all the guns they have; we must shelter the men as best we can, and make them lie down," Pettigrew told Fry.[116]

Fry was told to ride over to General Pickett at the conclusion of this conversation "and have an understanding as to the *dress* in the advance." Fry recalled that Pickett was in "excellent spirits," and was optimistic that the Southern troops would drive the enemy off the heights after they had been "demoralized by our artillery." General Richard Garnett joined the two men, and the three agreed that the Virginians would dress on Fry's command. This concluded the discussion, and Fry rode back to brief General Pettigrew. An initial gap of several hundred yards yawned between the right of Archer's Brigade and the left of Pickett's Division, but a left oblique maneuver by the latter would close the gap during the advance.[117]

The great cannonade preceding the charge began at about 1:00 P.M. The Federal batteries responded. "For two hours the old hills trembled as if affrighted. The limbs and trunks of trees were tron [sic] to pieces and sent crashing to the earth to add to the havoc among the gallant boys who waited anxiously an order to charge," wrote Captain J. Turney of the 1st Tennessee. A number of Archer's men were killed and wounded during the bombardment, including Colonel Fry, who was hit by a shell fragment in his shoulder. The wound was not serious enough to prevent him from personally leading his men in the charge. All was suddenly quiet, and then the men heard the order to advance. "After lying inactive under that deadly storm of hissing and exploding shells, it seemed a relief to go forward to the desperate assault," noted Fry.[118]

Recalling the event after the war, Colonel Fry wrote, "at a signal from Pettigrew I called my command to attention. The men sprang up with cheerful alacrity, and the long line advanced." Fry recalled that his line was "stormed at with shot and shell," but moved steadily on. However, modern historian George Stewart did not believe that many guns were focusing on Archer's men, instead aiming against Brockenbrough's Brigade on the left of the line and Pickett's Division on the right.[119]

The brigade, along with the other units, cut an imposing image, one that would never be forgotten by the men on either side. "We charged in unbroken line, across the fields, through ravines, over fences—on we went, bent on victory or death," wrote Captain Jacob Turney (1st Tennessee). When his commanding officer fell wounded, Turney was told to take command of the regiment and ordered to "proceed with the charge, but don't stop to fire a gun."[120]

Up ahead, the 14th Connecticut (Smyth's Brigade, Hays's Division, II Corps) silently watched as Archer's Brigade approached. Its historian wrote that "it was, indeed, a scene of unsurpassed grandeur and majesty . . . their gay war flags fluttering in the gentle summer breeze, while their sabers and bayonets flashed and glistened in the midday sun. Step by step they came, the music and rhythm of their tread resounding upon the rock-ribbed earth." Major Theodore Ellis characterized the march as "magnificent."[121]

As the advance continued, many of the men could hear General Garnett issuing indecipherable commands to his brigade. "Seeing my look or gesture inquiring he called out 'I am dressing on you.' A few seconds after he fell dead," wrote Colonel Fry. The brigade's losses were probably light up to this point. McCall recalled that "the enemy held their fire until we were in fine range, then opened on us a most galling fire of musketry and artillery, but this did not for a moment check the advance." Colonel Fry went down with yet another wound. So confident was he of victory, that he yelled to his men who tried to carry him to safety, "Go on; it will not last five minutes longer!" As they approached Emmitsburg Road, the men saw stout fences on both sides of it. Some of the men rushed forward to knock down the closest with their rifle butts. This effort met with little success, so the men were forced to climb it. "How like hail upon a roof sounded the patter of the enemy's bullets upon that fence," wrote Captain Turney. Private James Moore of the 7th Tennessee recalled that the climb over the fence was "not a leaping over; it was rather an insensible tumbling to the ground, in the nervous hope of escaping the thickening missiles that buried themselves in falling victims." Many an Alabamian and Tennessean were hit when they were halfway over the fence. Those who survived these volleys dropped down along the sunken road to catch their breath and regain their composure. Then it was up again and over the next fence. Despite the withering fire, Archer's men calmly redressed their ranks before their final rush against the Federal line. Looking back, Moore estimated that he saw about half of his regiment remaining along the road. As few as 250 may have continued toward the Federal works.[122]

The smoke was so dense that the men could not see much around them, and the roll of musketry was incessant. There were far fewer men, as Archer's line was "thinned now and weakened." But the Federal line behind a low stone wall (probably the 14th Connecticut and 1st Delaware) was now a mere two hundred yards away across an open field. The right of the brigade attacked the Bloody Angle. Lieutenant Colonel Shepard of the 7th Tennessee, now commanding the remnants of the brigade, indicated that his men finally reached the first defensive line, which was composed of "rough stones." "The enemy abandoned this, but just in rear was massed a heavy force. By the time we had reached this work, our lines all along, as far as I could see, had become very much weakened; indeed, the line both right and left, as far as I could observe, seemed to melt away until there was but little of it left. Those who remained at the works saw that it was a hopeless case, and fell back."[123]

While Shepard's remarks about the left of the line were accurate, he probably did not see the successes of the right of his line, where the 1st Tennessee drove to the wall of Bloody Angle. Captain Turney recalled that "in wonderful order, at double-quick time, we continued the charge; and not until we were within about fifteen steps of the stone wall did I give the command to fire. The volley confused the enemy. I then ordered a charge with bayonets [sic], and on moved our gallant boys. Another instant, and we were engaged in a desperate hand-to-hand conflict for possession of the fragile wall of masonry that held out as the sole barrier between the combatants. Each man seemed to pick his foe." Before long, several companies of the 71st Pennsylvania (Webb's Brigade, Gibbon's Division, II Corps) were fleeing to the rear.[124]

Being on the extreme right of the line, the fifty or so members of the 1st Tennessee mingled with Garnett's and Armistead's men as they breached the Bloody

Angle and moved up the ridge. They captured prisoners and sent them to the rear. Seeing Pickett's men being repulsed on his right, Turney ordered his men to the left, to pour a enfilading fire into the enemy troops still holding the wall. Men from other regiments now stormed forward in victory. Up ahead, the men could see troops from Webb's Philadelphia Brigade forming at the top of the ridge, so Turney ordered his men back to the stone wall. According to Turney, his men repelled the first counterattack, then ordered his own men to attack, but this also met with failure. It was just a matter of time before the 1st Tennessee was overwhelmed. "To the left of the First Tennessee our lines had entirely given way, thus enabling the enemy to concentrate their fire . . . directly on my command," recalled Turney. Realizing that any attempt to retreat to the safety of Seminary Ridge was suicidal, many men laid down their rifles.[125]

The situation along the center and left of the brigade was more desperate. Here the men charged against Arnold's battery and at least the left flank of the 14th Connecticut (Smyth's Brigade, Hays's Division, II Corps), who were behind a low stone wall in a single line. Major Theodore Ellis of the 14th Connecticut waited until Archer's men were within two hundred yards of the stone wall, and then ordered his men to open fire. "The enemy's first line was broken and hurled back upon the second, throwing that also into confusion. Detached portions of the line were rallied, and for a short time maintained their ground, but being rapidly mown down by our terribly destructive fire, they commenced falling back." The color bearer of the 14th Tennessee made it to the wall, propped his flag up against it, and, while looking calmly into the faces of his enemy, was shot dead.[126]

After the battle, perhaps in response to the criticism of Pickett's men, the survivors steadfastly maintained that they had remained at the stone wall as long as any other command. The brigade lost four of its five regimental colors during the intense fighting there. Only the 7th Tennessee's flag was saved, and this occurred when Captain A. Norris ripped it from its staff and hid it in his coat.[127]

The dazed survivors were reformed in their original position on Seminary Ridge and ordered to prepare for an enemy counterattack. The attack never materialized, and on the night of July 4–5, the brigade began its long trek home. The campaign of horrors did not end with the retreat, for on July 5, ninety-seven men were scooped up by Federal cavalry who had descended upon the wagon train carrying the wounded back to Virginia.[128]

Like Davis's Brigade, Archer's was decimated on the first and third days of the battle, losing about the same number of men (about 375) each day. As a result, the brigade lost almost two-thirds of its men during the battle. Better leadership would have made a difference on July 1, but little could have helped it on July 3. Because of the heavy casualties, including the loss of General Archer, the brigade was consolidated with Brockenbrough's and assigned to newly promoted General Henry Walker after the battle.[129]

NOTES

1. Davis, *The Confederate General*, vol. III, 89.

2. Martin, *Gettysburg—July 1*, 60–61; Harry Heth, *The Memoirs of Harry Heth* (Westport, CT, 1974), 173; OR 27, 2, 637; Harry Heth, "Letter From Major General Heth of A.P. Hill's Corps, A.N.V.," *Southern Historical Society Papers* (1877), vol. 4, 157.

3. Heth, "Letter From Major General Heth of A.P. Hill's Corps, A.N.V.," 157; Heth,

The Memoirs of Harry Heth, 73; Clark, *N.C. Regiments*, vol. 5, 116.

4. OR 27, 2, 637; Martin, *Gettysburg—July 1*, 60–61.

5. OR 27, 2, 637; Heth, *The Memoirs of Harry Heth*,173.

6. Heth, "Letter From Major General Heth of A.P. Hill's Corps, A.N.V."; Heth, *The Memoirs of Harry Heth*, 175.

7. Heth, *The Memoirs of Harry Heth*,174.

8. Stewart, *Pickett's Charge*, 38, 42; William A. Love, "Mississippi at Gettysburg," in James L. McLean and Judy W. McLean, eds., *Gettysburg Sources* (Baltimore, MD, 1987), vol. 1, 145; OR 27, 2, 650.

9. OR 27, 1, 454.

10. Busey and Martin, *Regimental Strengths and Losses*, 174, 290.

11. Archie K. Davis, *The Boy Colonel: The Life and Times of Henry King Burgwyn, Jr.* (Chapel Hill, NC, 1985), 314–315; Clark, *N.C. Regiments*, vol. 3, 235.

12. Davis, *The Confederate General*, vol. V, 24–25.

13. Julius Lineback Papers, Southern Historical Collection, University of North Carolina.

14. Clark, *N.C. Regiments*, vol. 2, 342–343; Michael Jacobs, *Notes on the Rebel Invasion of Maryland and Pennsylvania . . .* (Philadelphia, 1864), 21; Heth, *The Memoirs of Harry Heth*,173; Martin, *Gettysburg—July 1*, 25–27.

15. Clark, *N.C. Regiments*, vol. 2, 342; Jacobs, *Notes on the Rebel Invasion of Maryland and Pennsylvania . . .*,22.

16. OR 27, 2, 607, 642–643; Clark, *N.C. Regiments*, vol. 2, 343–344; vol. 3, 103–104; George Underwood, *History of the Twenty-Sixth Regiment of the North Carolina Troops in the Great War, 1861-'65* (Goldsboro, NC, 1901), 46.

17. OR 27, 2, 643; John Lane, "Address at Gettysburg," John Lane Papers, Southern Historical Collection, University of North Carolina.

18. Hartwig, "The Defense of McPherson's Ridge," 17, 23–24.

19. Underwood, *History of the Twenty-Sixth Regiment of the North Carolina Troops in the Great War, 1861-'65*, 49; Clark, *N.C.*

Regiments., vol. 2, 351; vol. 3, 89; Lane, "Address at Gettysburg"; OR 27, 1, 268; R. Lee Hadden, "The Deadly Embrace," *Gettysburg Magazine* (July 1991), issue 5, 28; Orson B. Curtis, *History of the Twenty-Fourth Michigan of the Iron Brigade* (Detroit, MI, 1891), 160.

20. OR 27, 2, 643; OR suppl., vol. 5, 417; William T. Venner, *Hoosiers' Honor: The Iron Brigade's 19th Indiana Regiment* (Shippensburg, PA, 1998), 173–174; William Taylor, letter, copy in 11th North Carolina folder, GNMP.

21. Underwood, *History of the Twenty-Sixth Regiment of the North Carolina Troops in the Great War, 1861-'65*, 50–51; Lane, "Address at Gettysburg"; OR suppl., vol. 5, 424; Davis, *The Boy Colonel: The Life and Times of Henry King Burgwyn, Jr.*, 332–333; Fred A. Olds, "A Brave Carolinian Who Fell at Gettysburg," in *Southern Historical Society Papers* (1908), vol. 36, 245–247; Clark, *N.C. Regiments*, vol. 5, 119.

22. OR suppl., 5, 424–425.

23. OR 27, 1, 323; Captain Benjamin Little, "Account," copy in the 52nd North Carolina folder, GNMP; Clark, *N.C. Regiments*, vol. 3, 89–90, 236–237; vol. 3, 105–106; Captain Frank Sterling, letter, copy in 121st Pennsylvania folder, GNMP; Edwin R. Gearhart, "Account," copy in 142nd Pennsylvania folder, GNMP; Hartwig, "The Defense of McPherson's Ridge," 23.

24. Clark, *N.C. Regiments*, vol. 3, 89.

In defending themselves against Buford's cavalry, Lieutenant J. Rogers of the 47th North Carolina observed that Colonel Marshall refused three companies of his 52nd North Carolina to meet this threat. He did not mention the formation of a square (Clark, *N.C. Regiments*, vol. 3, 106).

25. Clark, *N.C. Regiments*, vol. 2, 361; J.F.J. Caldwell, *The History of a Brigade of South Carolinians* (Marietta, GA, 1951), 97.

26. Julius Lineback, "Papers"; Underwood, *History of the Twenty-Sixth Regiment of the North Carolina Troops in the Great War, 1861-'65*, 60.

27. OR 27, 2, 263; OR suppl., 5, 427.

28. OR suppl., 5, 428.

29. OR suppl., 5, 429.

30. Clark, *N.C. Regiments*, vol. 3, 107; Michael W. Taylor, "North Carolina in the Pickett-Pettigrew-Trimble Charge," *Gettysburg Magazine* (January 1993), issue 8, 69; OR 27, 2, 644; OR suppl., 5, 409.

31. *Report of Joint Committee to Mark the Positions Occupied by the 1st and 2 nd Delaware at the Battle of Gettysburg* (Dover, DE, 1887), 14, 15; Hess, *Pickett's Charge*, 203.

32. OR suppl., 5, 429.

33. OR 27, 2, 644; OR suppl., 5, 410; "Report of Joint Committee," 14.

34. OR 27, 2, 644; OR suppl., 5, 430–431; OR 27, 1, 467.

35. OR suppl., 5, 421.

36. OR suppl., 5, 412.

37. Stewart, *Pickett's Charge—A Microhistory of the Final Attack at Gettysburg*, 226; Page, *History of the Fourteenth Regiment, Connecticut Volunteer Infantry*, 161.

38. Clark, *N.C. Regiments*, vol. 1, 591; vol. 3, 240–241.

39. Underwood, *History of the Twenty-Sixth Regiment of the North Carolina Troops in the Great War, 1861-'65*, 64; Busey and Martin, *Regimental Strengths and Losses*, 290, 298; and Clark, *N.C. Regiments*, vol. 1, 590–591.

40. Busey and Martin, *Regimental Strengths and Losses*, 175, 290.

The "64+" that the authors list as missing seems too low, given the engagement at the unfinished railroad cut on July 1 and the attack on Cemetery Ridge on July 3.

41. Sifakis, *Compendium of the Confederate Armies: Mississippi*, 71–72, 90–91, 133; Sifakis, *Compendium of the Confederate Armies: North Carolina*, 155.

42. Davis, *The Confederate General*, II, 51; Krick, "Failures of Brigade Leadership," 99–102.

43. Samuel W. Hankins, *Simple Story of a Soldier* (Nashville, TN, n.d.), 43.

44. OR 27, 1, 926.

45. Perry A. Synder, ed. "Gallantry at Gettysburg," copy in GNMP, 4–5; Love, "Mississippi at Gettysburg," 127.

46. OR 27, 2, 649; Martin, *Gettysburg—July 1*, 86; Krick, "Failures of Brigade Leadership," 99–102; Hankins, *Simple Story*, 43.

While Davis reported that his attack began at 10:30 A.M., historian David Martin believed that it was an hour earlier (OR 27, 2, 649; Martin, *Gettysburg—July 1*, 86).

47. "The Battle of Gettysburg," *The Galveston Daily News*, June 21, 1896.

48. James L. McLean, *Cutler's Brigade at Gettysburg* (Baltimore, MD, 1994), 66–68.

49. Clark, *N.C. Regiments*, vol. 3, 297; A. H. Belo, "The Battle of Gettysburg," in *Confederate Veteran* (1900), vol. 8, 165; John Stone to John Bachelder, n.d. and March 27, 1890, Bachelder Papers, New Hampshire Historical Society.

50. *New York at Gettysburg*, vol. 3, 1001; McLean, *Cutler's Brigade at Gettysburg*, 77.

51. W. B. Murphy, letter, copy in 2nd Mississippi file, GNMP; Leander G. Woollard, "Journal of Events and Incidents as They Came to the Observation of the 'Senatobia Invincibles,'" Memphis State University Library.

52. *New York at Gettysburg*, vol. 3, 992.

53. Terrence J. Winschel, "Heavy Was Their Loss, Part 1," *Gettysburg Magazine* (January 1990), issue 2, 11; Murphy, letter.

54. OR 27, 2, 649; Dawes, *Service with the Sixth Wisconsin Volunteers*, 167; Belo, "The Battle of Gettysburg," 165.

55. Winschel, "Heavy Was Their Loss, Part 1," 11; Louis H. Manarin, *North Carolina Troops, 1861–1865: A Roster*, 13 vols. (Raleigh, NC., 1966), vol. 13, 377–378.

Colonel Dawes of the 6th Wisconsin wrote after the war that his regiment lost 40 killed and 160 wounded during the charge.

56. Woollard, diary; *New York Gettysburg*, vol. 3, 1006.

57. Lloyd G. Harris, "With the Iron Brigade Guard at Gettysburg," *Gettysburg Magazine* (July 1989), issue 1, 32; Woollard, diary.

58. Murphy, letter; "Capture of the Colors of the 2nd Mississippi Regiment. Notes of a Conversation With Veterans on the Field at Gettysburg," Bachelder Papers, New Hampshire Historical Society.

59. Clark, *N.C. Regiments*, vol. 3, 298; Belo, "The Battle of Gettysburg," 165.

60. Dawes, *Service with the Sixth Wisconsin Volunteers*, 169.

61. OR 27, 1, 275–276; OR 27, 2, 649; Murphy, letter.

62. Woollard, diary.

63. Winschel, "Heavy Was Their Loss, Part 1," 13–14; OR 27, 2, 567; Frank Price to John Bachelder, January 27, 1878, Bachelder Papers, New Hampshire Historical Society; Thomas Chamberlin to John Bachelder, June 8, 1889, Bachelder Papers, New Hampshire Historical Society; OR 27, 2, 649–650.

64. OR 27, 2, 649, Love, "Mississippi at Gettysburg," 129.

65. Clark, *N.C. Regiments*, vol. III, 299; OR 27, 2, 650; Baxter McFarland, "The Eleventh Mississippi at Gettysburg, in *Mississippi Historical Society* (1918), vol. 2, 550; Terrence J. Winschel, "The Gettysburg Diary of Lieutenant William Peel," *Gettysburg Magazine* (July 1993), issue 9, 103.

66. OR 27, 2, 650–651.

67. OR 27, 2, 651; Clark, *N.C. Regiments*, vol. 5, 125; Love, "Mississippi at Gettysburg," 142; Winschel, "The Gettysburg Diary of Lieutenant William Peel," 105.

William Peel of the 11th Mississippi, who left a detailed account of the battle, did not mention anything about the brigade getting off late or rushing to catch up.

68. George A. Bowen, *"Diary of Captain George D. Bowen, 12th New Jersey Volunteers,"* *The Valley Forge Journal* (June 1984), vol. 2, 133; George H. Washburn, *A Complete Military History and Record of the 108th Regiment N.Y. Volunteers . . .* (Rochester, NY, 1894), 52.

69. OR 27, 2, 651; Bowen, *"Diary of Captain George D. Bowen, 12th New Jersey Volunteers,"* 133; Winschel, "The Gettysburg Diary of Lieutenant William Peel," 105.

70. Love, "Mississippi at Gettysburg," 142, 144; Maud Morrow, *The University Greys: Company A, Eleventh Mississippi Regiment, Army of Northern Virginia* (Richmond, VA, 1940), 45; Andrew J. Baker, "Tribute to Captain Magruder and Wife," *Confederate Veteran* (1898), vol. 6, 507.

71. OR 27, 2, 651; Clark, *N.C. Regiments*, vol. 3, 301; Baxter McFarland, "Losses of the Eleventh Mississippi Regiment at

Gettysburg," *Confederate Veteran* (1923), vol. 31, 258.

72. Love, "Mississippi at Gettysburg," 145; Winschel," The Gettysburg Diary of Lieutenant William Peel," 105; Terrence J. Winschel, "Heavy was Their Loss, Part II," *Gettysburg Magazine* (July 1990), issue 3, 83.

These figures are at odds with those in Busey and Martin's *Regimental Strengths and Losses* (290), who estimated that the 2nd Mississippi lost only 232 men in the battle. However, they apparently did not include the number of men captured on July 1 (over 200). If these are added to their figures, the number who marched away from Gettysburg would be less than 50. Similarly, they estimate that the 11th Mississippi only lost 53% of their men.

73. Hankins, *Simple Story of a Soldier,* 45; Thomas D. Cockrell and Michael B. Ballard, *A Mississippi Rebel in the Army of Northern Virginia* (Baton Rouge, LA, 1995), 198.

74. Winschel, "Heavy was Their Loss," Part II, 85.

75. Busey and Martin, *Regimental Strengths and Losses,* 176, 291.

76. Sifakis, *Compendium of the Confederate Armies: Virginia,* 199, 227–228, 236; Davis, *The Confederate General,* vol. II, 124; vol. III, 89; Robert K. Krick, *Fortieth Virginia Infantry* (Lynchburg, VA, 1985), 29; Stewart Sifakis, *Who Was Who in the Civil War* (New York, 1987), 75; Stewart, *Pickett's Charge: A Microhistory of the Final Attack at Gettysburg,* 38–39.

77. Krick, *Fortieth Virginia Infantry,* 25; W. S. Christian "55th Virginia Infantry (Brockenbrough) Account of Col. W. S. Christian" copy in 55th Virginia folder, GNMP.

78. Christian, "55th Virginia Infantry ... "

79. Jaquelin M. Meredith, "The First Day at Gettysburg, "*Southern Historical Society Papers* (1896), vol. 24, 184; Homer D. Musselman, *Forty-seventh Virginia Infantry* (Lynchburg, VA, 1989), 49; Richard O'Sullivan, *Fifty-Fifth Virginia Infantry* (Lynchburg, VA, 1989), 53.

80. Musselman, *Forty-seventh Virginia Infantry,* 50; Martin, *Gettysburg—July 1,* 368; OR 27, 1, 274.

81. *Pennsylvania at Gettysburg,* vol. 2, 756.

82. *Pennsylvania at Gettysburg,* vol. 2, 756

83. Harry W. Pfanz, "The Regiment Saved, the Colors Lost," copy in the 149th Pennsylvania folder, GNMP; Musselman, *Forty-seventh Virginia Infantry,* 50; O'Sullivan, *Fifty-fifth Virginia Infantry,* 54.

84. Musselman, *Forty-seventh Virginia Infantry,* 50; OR 27, 2, 670.

85. Krick, *Fortieth Virginia Infantry,* 27; Clark, *N.C. Regiments,* vol. 5, 125.

86. Christian, "55th Virginia Infantry ..." Several recent regimental histories (O'Sullivan, *Fifty-fifth Virginia Infantry,* 55; Musselman, *Forty-seventh Virginia Infantry,* 51) state that Brockenbrough's right wing also got off late as "Davis missed his cue." The origin of this idea is unknown.

87. OR 27, 1, 893; O'Sullivan, *Fifty-fifth Virginia Infantry,* 55; Musselman, *Forty-seventh Virginia Infantry,* 53; OR suppl., 5, 415.

88. W. F. Dunaway, *Reminiscences of a Rebel* (New York, 1913), 92; Musselman, *Forty-seventh Virginia Infantry,* 53; O'Sullivan, *Fifty-Fith Virginia Infantry,* 55; OR 27, 2, 651.

89. OR suppl., 5, 415.

90. Clark, *N.C. Regiments,* vol. 2, 44; vol. 5, 125, 130; OR suppl., 5, 410.

91. Stewart, *Pickett's Charge—Microhistory of the Final Attack at Gettysburg,* 189–190.

92. Krick, *Fortieth Virginia Infantry,* 31–34.

93. Sifakis, *Who Was Who in the Civil War,* 75; Davis, *The Confederate General,* vol. 6, 85.

94. Busey and Martin, *Regimental Strengths and Losses,* 177, 291.

95. Sifakis, *Compendium of the Confederate Armies: Tennessee* (New York, 1992), 88, 102, 113; Davis, *The Confederate General,* vol. I, 35, 37; vol. III, 73.

96. Davis, *The Confederate General,* vol. I, 37–38.

97. R. T. Mockbee, *Historical Sketch of the 14th Tennessee,* Eleanor Brockenbrough Library, Museum of the Confederacy, Richmond, 39; W. F. Fulton, *War Reminiscences of William Frierson Fulton II, 5th Alabama Battalion ...* (Gaithersville, MD, 1986), 75.

98. A. H. Moore, "Heth's Division at Gettysburg," *Southern Bivouac* (1885), vol. 3, 384; Marc Storch and Beth Storch, "What a Deadly Trap We Were In," *Gettysburg Magazine* (January 1992), issue 6, 16.

99. Clark, *N.C. Regiments*, vol. 5, 117; Hadden, "The Deadly Embrace," 25.

100. E. T. Boland, "Beginning of the Battle of Gettysburg," in *Confederate Veteran* (1906), vol. 14, 308; Fulton, *War Reminiscences . . .* , 79–80.

101. Fulton, *War Reminiscences . . .* , 79; W. H. Bird, *Stories of the Civil War, Company C, 13th Regiment of Alabama Volunteers* (Columbiana, AL, n.d.), 6–7.

102. Bird, *Stories of the Civil War, Company C, 13th Regiment of Alabama Volunteers Stories*, 7; OR 27, 2, 646; Storch and Storch, "What a Deadly Trap,"18.

103. Moon, "Beginning the Battle at Gettysburg," 449; Boland, "Beginning of the Battle of Gettysburg," 308; J. Calef, "Gettysburg Notes: The Opening Gun," *Journal of the Military Service Institute of the U.S.* (1907), vol. 40, 48.

104. John T. McCall, "What the Tennesseans Did at Gettysburg;" *The Louisville Journal*, 1902; Martin, *Gettysburg—July 1*, 84; Bird, *Stories of the Civil War, Company C, 13th Regiment of Alabama Volunteers*, 7; Moon, "Beginning the Battle at Gettysburg," 449.

Colonel Birkett Fry of the 13th Alabama insisted that the resistance of the Union cavalry was "inconsiderable" (Birkett Fry to John Bachelder, February 10, 1878, Bachelder Papers, New Hampshire Historical Society).

105. J. B. Turney, "The First Tennessee at Gettysburg," *Confederate Veteran* (1900), vol. 8, 535; Storch and Storch, "What a Deadly Trap We Were In," 22.

106. OR 27, 2, 646; Turney, "The First Tennessee at Gettysburg," 535.

107. Moon, "Beginning the Battle at Gettysburg," 449.

108. Alan D. Gaff, "Here Was Made Our Last and Hopeless Stand," *Gettysburg Magazine* (January 1990), issue 2, 29; Boland, "Beginning of the Battle of Gettysburg," 308; Bird, *Stories of the Civil War, Company C, 13th Regiment of Alabama Volunteers*, 7; Lt. James Simpson, letter, Southern Historical Collection, University of North Carolina.

109. Moon, "Beginning the Battle at Gettysburg," 449; OR 27, 1, 279.

110. "'The Iron Brigade'—7th Wis. Infantry at Gettysburg, Pa.—Report of Lt. Col. John Callis," Bachelder Papers, New Hampshire Historical Society; Cornelius Wheeler, "Reminiscences of the Battle of Gettysburg," in *Wisconsin MOLLUS*, vol. 2, 210; Marc Storch and Beth Storch, "Unpublished Gettysburg Reports by the 2nd and 7th Wisconsin Infantry Regimental Officers," *Gettysburg Magazine* (July 1997), issue 17, 21; Doubleday, *Chancellorsville and Gettysburg*, 132.

111. William H. Harries, "The Iron Brigade in the First Day's Battle at Gettysburg," in *Minnesota MOLLUS*, vol. 4, 340.

Archer was interred at Fort Delaware and then at Johnson's Island Prison. Exchanged in August 1864, he returned to duty at Petersburg, but died of exhaustion on October 24, 1864.

112. W. A. Castleberry, "Thirteenth Alabama—Archer's Brigade," in *Confederate Veteran* (1911), vol. 19, 338.

113. OR 27, 2, 646; Storch and Storch, "What a Deadly Trap We Were In," 26–27.

The position of the 5th Alabama Battalion is unclear. Although on the skirmish line, its casualties were light, causing Harry Pfanz to believe they were deployed in front of two of Cutler's regiments, who were to the right of the Iron Brigade (Pfanz, *Gettysburg—The First Day*, 106).

114. Fulton, *War Reminiscences*, 79; OR 27, 2, 646.

115. OR 27, 2, 647.

116. B. D. Fry, "Pettigrew's Charge at Gettysburg," *Southern Historical Society Papers* (1879), vol. 7, 92.

117. Birkett Fry to John Bachelder, December 27, 1877, Bachelder Papers, New Hampshire Historical Society; Fry, "Pettigrew's Charge at Gettysburg," 92; Stewart, *Pickett's Charge—A Microhistory of the Final Charge at Gettysburg*, 188.

118. Turney, "The First Tennessee at Gettysburg," 535; Birkett Fry to John Bachelder, December 27, 1877.

119. Fry, "Pettigrew's Charge at Gettysburg," 92; Stewart, *Pickett's Charge—A Microhistory of the Final Charge at Gettysburg*, 188.

120. Turney, "The First Tennessee at Gettysburg," 535.

121. Page, *History of the Fourteenth Regiment, Connecticut Volunteer Infantry*, 151; OR 27, 1, 467.

122. McCall, "What the Tennesseans Did at Gettysburg"; Birkett Fry to John Bachelder, December 27, 1877; Fry, "Pettigrew's Charge at Gettysburg," 93; Moore, "Heth's Division at Gettysburg," 391; Stewart, *Pickett's Charge—Microhistory of the Final Attack at Gettysburg*, 203; Hess, *Pickett's Charge*, 203.

123. Turney, "The First Tennessee at Gettysburg," 535; OR 27, 2, 647.

124. Turney, "The First Tennessee at Gettysburg," 535.

125. Turney, "The First Tennessee at Gettysburg, " 536.

126. Henry S. Stevens, letter, N.C. Department of Archives and History; OR 27, 1, 467; Hess, *Pickett's Charge*, 205.

127. OR 27, 2, 647.

128. OR 27, 2, 647–648; McCall, "What the Tennesseans Did at Gettysburg"; Storch and Storch, "What a Deadly Trap We Were In," 27; Moore, "Heth's Division at Gettysburg," 393.

129. Storch and Storch, "What a Deadly Trap We Were In," 26; Krick, *Fortieth Virginia Infantry*, 34.

PENDER'S DIVISION—

Brigadier General Dorsey Pender/
Brigadier General James Lane/
Major General Isaac Trimble

✂

With the death of Stonewall Jackson and the reorganization of the army, Brigadier General Dorsey Pender was given a newly formed division. It was really A. P. Hill's Light Division minus Archer's and Brockenbrough's Brigades, and therefore a veteran division that had fought on many battlefields.

A West Point graduate, Pender spent his prewar days on the frontier. He entered Confederate service as a captain of artillery and two months later was elected colonel of the 3rd North Carolina. His gallantry under fire in his first engagement (Seven Pines) was observed by President Jefferson Davis, who promoted him to brigadier general. Given a brigade in A. P. Hill's Light Division, Pender fought with distinction at Mechanicsville, Gaines's Mill, Frayser's Farm, Second Manassas, Sharpsburg, Fredericksburg and Chancellorsville. Although not well liked by his men because he was a strong disciplinarian, Pender was promoted and given command of the division just prior to the start of the Gettysburg campaign.[1]

Pender's Division followed Heth's toward Gettysburg on the morning of July 1. Ordered to support Heth's Division, Pender brought his men up for the afternoon assault on McPherson Ridge. After Pettigrew's and Brockenbrough's Brigades had successfully driven the Federal troops off the ridge, Pender ordered his division forward to continue the pursuit to Seminary Ridge. Only Scales's and Perrin's Brigades were involved in the assault—the former was repulsed with heavy losses, but the latter found the enemy's left flank and forced it to abandon Seminary Ridge. Lane's Brigade did not participate in the charge, as its commander formed a square, reminiscent of Napoleon's era, to fend off a cavalry charge he thought was in the offing. The fourth brigade, Thomas's, was off to the northwest, supporting artillery.[2]

The division subsequently took position on Seminary Ridge, just south of Gettysburg, and spent a quiet day on July 2. About sunset, Pender was struck by a two-inch-square piece of artillery shell as he rode along the lines. As he was carried to the rear, he assigned command of the division to General Lane. Lane's orders were vague: "advance, if I saw a good opportunity for doing so." Some believe that Pender's wounding at this critical juncture was one cause of the Confederate defeat at Gettysburg.[3]

Major H. A. Whiting of Rodes's staff arrived with information that the division was going to make an assault on Cemetery Hill at dark, and requested Lane's help in protecting his right flank. Lane probably thought it strange that he was directly receiving the request, rather than it first going through A. P. Hill. He decided to send an aide to Hill for orders, but, realizing that he could not wait, he honored Rodes's request by moving Thomas's and Perrin's Brigades to the right of Rodes's Division. Hill subsequently confirmed what Lane had already decided to do. The attack was aborted, but the two brigades remained on Rodes's right. After the attack on Cemetery Hill failed, both Ewell and Early attempted to shift the blame to Lane. Ewell wrote in his official report that "the want of co-operation on the right made it more difficult for Rodes' division to attack . . . I have every reason to believe . . . that the enemy lines would have been carried." These criticisms appear unfounded.[4]

On the morning of July 3, Lane learned that his brigade and Scales's (now under Colonel William Lowrance) would form a supporting line behind Heth's (Pettigrew's) Division during the charge planned for that afternoon. However, not long before the men stepped off, Lee placed General Isaac Trimble in charge of the two brigades. Whether this action, so close to the start of the charge, was because Lee did not trust Lane, or was to placate Trimble, who had been a volunteer aide to Ewell but was becoming a nuisance, is unknown.

Lieutenant Octavius Wiggins of the 37th North Carolina recalled that Trimble "rode down the line and halted at different regiments and made us little speeches—saying he was a stranger to us and had been sent to command us . . . and would lead us upon Cemetery Hill at 3 o'clock." General Trimble recalled what he said somewhat differently. Wishing to inspire confidence in this new command, he ordered that "no guns should be fired until the enemy's line was broken, and that I should advance with them to the farthest point."[5]

Advancing smartly, the two brigades finally neared Emmitsburg Road. Here, according to General Trimble, they encountered several of Pettigrew's men who had halted in a ditch on the west side of Emmitsburg Road and would go no farther. Someone yelled, "Three cheers for the old North State," and the men of Lane's and Scales's

Brigades responded with "a hearty shout." Hearing this, Trimble turned to his aide, and said, "Charley, I believe those fine fellows are going into the enemy's line." Trimble was seriously wounded soon after, and the two brigades were repulsed with heavy losses. Trimble recalled a bitter conversation he had with an aide, who came up to him while he was lying on the ground. "General, the men are falling back, shall I rally them?" asked the aide. "No! let them get out of this, its all over," replied Trimble, who was later captured.[6]

Trimble believed the grand charge failed because "it was a mistake to charge batteries & lines over so great a distance, every yard exposed to a hot fire—Had we marched at night to ¼ mile of the works it is I think certain we could have carried them."[7]

McGowan's Brigade—Colonel Abner Perrin

Units: 1st South Carolina (Provisional Army), 1st South Carolina (Rifles), 12th South Carolina, 13th South Carolina, 14th South Carolina
Strength: 1882 (1516 as the Rifles were guarding the wagons on July 1)
Losses: 593 (128-451-16)—31.5%[8]

The distinguished brigade of South Carolinians had its roots at Ft. Sumter, where the 1st South Carolina (Provisional) was present. The regiment's commander, Colonel Maxcy Gregg, was chagrined when only half of his regiment consented to accompany him to Virginia. Promoted to brigadier general, Gregg received a brigade composed of the 12th, 13th, and 14th South Carolina. After spending the winter in South Carolina, Gregg returned to Virginia, where the 1st Provisional and 1st Rifles were added. The brigade performed brilliantly at the battle of Gaines's Mill. Further accolades resulted when the brigade anchored the Confederate left at the battle of Second Manassas and beat off attack after attack. The brigade performed well at Sharpsburg, where it helped rescue

Lee's army. General Gregg was killed at Fredericksburg and replaced by Colonel Samuel McGowan of the 14th South Carolina. McGowan was wounded at Chancellorsville, and Colonel Abner Perrin of the 14th South Carolina replaced him at the start of the Gettysburg campaign.[9]

As the brigade moved north, the men could not believe the bounty of the land around them. They saw the fattest cattle, orchards brimming with fruit, and lush fields of grain. It was a far cry from what they had been experiencing in Virginia. The men treated private property with respect, as related by Lieutenant James Caldwell of the 1st South Carolina. "It is true that numbers of men flanked patrols and slipped through to capture what they needed to eat, but it is equally true that only such articles of food were captured as were of solid importance, that nothing was wantonly destroyed, that no man or woman was insulted." Caldwell observed that the citizens were "amazed at our moderation." While provisions around the countryside were abundant, and the farmers were more than willing to sell them, few of the soldiers had Confederate currency, much less greenbacks. As a result, the men relied on the "charity" of the citizens, and, as one soldier put it, the "lightness of our fingers." The men did not need to rely much on the latter, as the citizens were so frightened about the safety of their families and homes that they cheerfully gave away food and other supplies. In some ways, the officers were considered just as generous, as they provided whiskey rations on June 26 and again on June 30. The men were especially interested to know when they crossed into Pennsylvania. The problem was that no signs marked this important landmark, so they guessed, and when they were fairly certain, "there was great rejoicing," recalled Caldwell.[10]

Colonel Perrin's orders for July 1 were to have his men ready for the day's march by 8:00 A.M. The regiments moved out at the head of Pender's column, except for the 1st South Carolina (Orr's Rifles), which was left behind to guard the wagon train. After marching three to four miles, the men could hear the sounds of battle from the direction of Gettysburg. "Couriers began to pass to the rear, and orders given to hurry up—canteens to be filled with water," recalled Corporal Thomas Littlejohn of the 12th South Carolina. Surgeon Spencer Welch of the 13th South Carolina knew that a battle was brewing, simply by looking at the expressions on the faces of his veterans. It was a look of "intense seriousness and solemnity." Another sign was the growing number of women and children rushing past them to the rear. "I remember a woman leading a cow with some little children following crying," observed Littlejoin.[11]

Halting along the road during midmorning, the men rested for about an hour. Up ahead, Archer's and Davis's Brigades of Heth's Division were making initial contact with the rapidly arriving infantry of the Federal I Corps. The men were then ordered up again, and after marching about two miles, filed to the right of the road. Pender's orders to his inexperienced acting brigade commander were precise during the battle. This time it was to "form line of battle, leaving sufficient room between my left and the Gettysburg Road [Chambersburg Pike] for General Scales' brigade, and to throw out skirmishers to cover my right flank," reported Perrin. The brigade was arranged, from left to right as 14th South Carolina–1st South Carolina–12th South Carolina–13th South Carolina.[12]

Perrin soon received another order. He was to follow and support Heth's Division as it renewed its attack on McPherson Ridge. Pender made sure that Perrin knew how to advance, for he also added that he would do so by "preserving my alignment with General Scales, on my left." By ordering Perrin to follow the movements of his more experienced brigade commander, Pender was confident that everything would go smoothly. After advancing across open fields for about a mile, the brigade was halted. Perrin was probably relieved when he saw Lane's Brigade forming on his right to face Buford's Division of cavalry.[13]

Ordered forward another half mile at about 3:00 P.M., the brigade was exposed to artillery fire. Littlejohn (12th South Carolina) observed that "they began throwing grapeshot at us by the bushel it seems. They shot too high for us as the shot went over our heads. Had they been a little lower, I don't see how any of us could have escaped."[14]

The brigade stopped just behind Brockenbrough's and Pettigrew's Brigades (Heth's Division), who were engaging the enemy. With the increasing heat, the perspiration poured out of the men while they rested. Captain Washington Shooter of the 12th South Carolina wrote that after advancing, the "fire and smoke and dust and noise and confusion and disorder of battle had begun." Welch (13th South Carolina) marveled that Heth's advance "was really a magnificent sight." Welch was equally impressed with his own division's appearance, which stretched "nearly a mile in length." The men remained there in the role of observers until about 4:00 P.M., when Perrin finally received orders to "advance, and to pass General Heth's division should I come up to it at a halt, and to engage the enemy as circumstances might warrant." Perrin's Brigade would take the lead only if Heth's Division halted because it was repulsed or exhausted. It turned out to be the latter, as Perrin's men passed through Pettigrew's Brigade, which was decimated and worn out after throwing several Federal brigades off McPherson Ridge.[15]

Perrin's men came under enemy artillery fire as they advanced in line of battle. Using the protection of Willoughby Run to reform his men, Perrin gave orders to his regimental commanders. According to Sergeant B. Brown of the 1st South Carolina, Colonel Perrin addressed the men, saying, "Men, the order is to advance; you will go to the crest of the hill. If Heth does not need you, lie down and protect yourselves as well as you can; if he needs you, go to his assistance at once. Do not fire your guns; give them the bayonet; if they run, then see if they can outrun the bullet." Colonel Joseph Brown of the 14th South Carolina recalled another part of the order—the men were not to stop for any reason until they had driven the enemy off Seminary Ridge.[16]

Rushing forward, they passed by Pettigrew's exhausted men, who yelled out, "Go in, South Carolina! Go in, South Carolina!" recollected Brown. "Our line

passed over Hill's [Heth's] and drove the enemy rapidly before us without firing a gun . . . we could see the Yankees running in wild disorder and everything went merry as a marriage bell until we ascended a hill where we saw their batteries and their last line of entrenchment-a stone wall," wrote Captain Shooter. Up against Perrin's men were the remnants of Biddle's (Rowley's) Brigade of primarily Pennsylvania troops.[17]

Perrin noted that as the men ascended McPherson Ridge and set foot upon the open ground leading to Seminary Ridge, "we were met by a furious storm of musketry and shells from the enemy's batteries to the left of the road near Gettysburg." Caldwell (1st South Carolina) recalled that "the artillery of the enemy now opened upon us with fatal accuracy. They had a perfectly clear, unobstructed fire upon us. Still we advanced, with regular steps and a well-dressed line. Shell and canister continued to rain upon us." Great gaps soon appeared in the brigade's line.[18]

Perrin could not see what happened to the enemy infantry. "Some lines of infantry had shown themselves across the field, but disappeared as we got within range of them," he noted in his report. Pressing forward, the men came to a fence, about two hundred yards from the seminary. The world suddenly exploded, as Perrin explained that the "brigade received the most destructive fire of musketry I have ever been exposed to." Perrin now knew that the enemy had taken position on Seminary Ridge. Ordering his men forward, still without firing, they were hit by another volley. "Here the Fourteenth Regiment was staggered for a moment by the severity and destructiveness of the enemy's musketry. It looks to us as though this regiment was completely destroyed," Perrin noted. Daniel Tompkins of the 14th South Carolina could hear the Federal officers "distinctly encouraging their men to hold their fire, until the command to fire was given. They obeyed their command implicitly, and rose to their feet and took as deliberate aim as if they were on dress parade." His company lost thirty-four of their original thirty-nine that it carried into battle.[19]

When it looked as though the brigade was wavering, Perrin rode up to the front line to lead his men personally. Seeing their gallant leader so exposed, the men continued their advance. Some threw away their knapsacks and blankets so they could keep up, despite the withering fire that claimed more men with each step. Lieutenant Colonel Joseph Brown of the 14th South Carolina, succinctly explained his emotions during this period when he wrote, "to stop was destruction. To retreat was disaster. To go forward was 'orders.'" While Brown never forgot the destructiveness of the Federal artillery fire, he was quick to affirm the deadliness of the small arms fire as well. "Not a foot of ground presented a place of safety. The Union troops fired low, and their balls swept close to the ground," he wrote after the war.[20]

Perrin now faced a dilemma. On his left, Scales's Brigade had halted and taken position behind a fence, about two hundred yards from the seminary. There was no sign of Lane's Brigade on his right. Perrin's fighting blood probably did not permit him to weigh his opinions for any length of time. His orders were to take the ridge, and he was not going to allow a lack of support stop him, despite the fire he was receiving from three directions. During his quick observation of the Federal position, Perrin probably saw a gap in the Federal line between the left of Biddle's Brigade and the right of Gamble's cavalry brigade (Buford's Division). "I now directed the First Regiment . . . to oblique to the right, to avoid a breastwork of rails

behind which I discovered the enemy was posted, and then to change front to the left, and attack in flank," wrote Perrin. It was a masterful plan and the movement was made without hesitation. "Struggling and panting, but cheering and closing up, they [1st and 14th South Carolina] went, through the shell, through the Minie balls, heeding neither the dead who sank down by their sides, nor the fire from the front which killed them, until they threw themselves desperately on the line of Federals and swept them from the field," recalled Caldwell. It was now the supreme moment for the South Carolinians, and they took advantage of it, firing into the flank of the 121st Pennsylvania. The Pennsylvanians were soon fleeing to the rear, and like dominos, the rest of the Federal line collapsed. The only act that would have made the victory more complete would have been to capture some of the Federal artillery. However, the guns quickly galloped for safety before Perrin's men could overwhelm them, but not before many cannoneers and horses went down in a storm of bullets. Perrin later lamented to the governor of South Carolina, "if we had any support at all we could have taken every piece of artillery they had and thousands of prisoners." They did capture four Federal colors, including the I Corps's flag.[21]

While the 1st South Carolina was driving toward the gap in the Federal line, Perrin ordered the 12th and 13th South Carolina on the right of his line to oblique to the right. This put them up against Gamble's dismounted cavalrymen, who were behind a stout stone wall. "They rushed up to the crest of the hill and the stone fence, driving everything before them, the Twelfth gaining the stone fence, and pouring an enfilading fire upon the enemy's right flank. The Thirteenth now coming up, made it an easy task to drive the enemy down the opposite slope and across the open field west of Gettysburg," reported Perrin. He did not report the heavy losses sustained by these regiments, however. Surgeon Welch wrote that "as the enemy were concealed, they killed a great many of our men before we could get at them." Wheeling to the left, the South Carolinians poured a devastating fire into the flank of Biddle's Brigade, causing it to withdraw as well.[22]

Perrin's Brigade had achieved the same feat that Pettigrew's had on McPherson Ridge—it found the Federal left flank, enfiladed the line, and forced the enemy to flee for safety. Like Pettigrew's Brigade, losses were heavy, but probably not as severe, because they had not stopped to return the fire, but dashed forward instead. It was a classic charge made by veteran troops. The greatest losses were sustained by the 14th South Carolina on the left of the line, which was raked by the severe artillery fire. Not willing to stop and savor their victory, the 1st and 14th South Carolina, followed the retreating Union troops to Gettysburg, capturing scores along the way. Because of their rapid movement, these were among the first Confederate units to enter Gettysburg. The 1st South Carolina marched directly up Chambersburg Pike; the 14th South Carolina, swung to the left and entered North Boundary Street, and eventually reached Main Street.[23]

Watching the charge, General Pender became anxious when he saw the brigade disappear from view. Thinking it was repulsed and the remainder had been captured, he rode forward to ascertain the fate of the brigade. Learning of its success, he ordered the 12th and 13th South Carolina to occupy a position between the town and the seminary, and then rode through Gettysburg to compliment the officers of the 1st and 14th South Carolina, who later passed these words on to their men. The lead elements of Rodes's Division soon entered the town, allowing the two regiments to rejoin the brigade. Skirmishers were thrown out, and the brigade rested through the remainder of the day. Perrin bitterly wrote in his report that "now it was that the first piece of artillery fired by the enemy from Cemetery Hill . . . was opened upon command, and it was the same artillery which we had driven from our left near Gettysburg. I saw it move off from my left, and file into position over the hill."[24]

The men did not understand why they were not ordered to scale Cemetery Hill. "If 'Old Stonewall' had been alive and there, it is no doubt [what] would have been done. Hill was a good division commander, but he is not a superior corps commander. He lacks the mind and sagacity of Jackson," wrote Dr. Welch. Upon arriving at their new position, the men stacked arms, and many returned to the site of their charge to provide assistance to their fallen comrades. The brigade moved to the right, and according to Colonel John Bachelder's maps, occupied a position behind Lane's Brigade, with its left flank touching Hagerstown Road. Night did not bring peace and quiet. "All night it was tramp, tramp, tramp. The rumble of artillery moving to positions, wagons with supplies of all kinds needed by soldiers, coming up," complained Littlejohn.[25]

The men spent most of July 2 resting and dodging artillery shells thrown by the batteries on Cemetery Hill. Skirmishing was particularly sharp between Seminary and Cemetery Ridges. Perrin received orders at about 6:00 P.M. to throw out a line of skirmishers to drive away a heavy mass of the enemy who had taken control of a road in front of the brigade. The 1st South Carolina moved forward to support the skirmishers. The attack was a success, and the position was held until 10:00 P.M., when Perrin received orders to advance his brigade to the right of Ramseur's brigade (Rodes's Division, Second Corps) along Long Lane. Littlejohn (12th South Carolina) recalled that the men pulled down a fence lining the road and used it "as a kind of breastwork." The plan was for the brigade to support Ewell's attack on Cemetery Hill. Rodes's attack was aborted before it really began and the South Carolinians remained in this position for the remainder of the battle.[26]

July 3 brought continued skirmishing. According to Colonel Perrin, it was "the heaviest skirmishing I have ever witnessed . . . the enemy made desperate efforts to recapture the position." Because of their proximity to Cemetery Hill, the skirmishers had to dodge both infantry minié balls and artillery shells. At one point in the morning, the Federals threw out such a heavy force of skirmishers that Perrin's men were swept back toward the main line. In response, he sent out the 14th South Carolina, who drove back this

enemy force from von Steinwehr's division (XI Corps). The rest of the troops were exposed to the heavy cannon fire that preceded the Pickett–Pettigrew–Trimble charge as they lay along Long Lane. Littlejohn believed that some of the enemy's guns were aimed directly at his regiment. When the artillery fire ceased, the men looked behind them to see their comrades massing for the attack. The South Carolinians had a great view of the charge as Pettigrew's men swept past them in their futile assault on Cemetery Ridge. The brigade remained there through July 4, when it joined the retreat toward Virginia during the early morning hours of July 5.[27]

Colonel Abner Perrin and his brigade performed as well as any during the battle. Finding the gap in the Federal line on July 1, it was able to single-handedly knock the enemy off Seminary Ridge. Unlike Scales's Brigade, which had also sustained heavy losses on July 1, the brigade was spared the bloodletting of the Pickett–Pettigrew–Trimble charge.

Lane's Brigade—Brigadier General James Lane

Units: 7th North Carolina, 18th North Carolina, 28th North Carolina, 33rd North Carolina, 37th North Carolina
Strength: 1734
Losses: 792 (178-376-238)—45.7%[28]

Brigadier General Jim Lane's Brigade was composed of a collection of veteran regiments that had fought together since March 1862. The brigade's initial commander was Brigadier General Lawrence Branch, who first led the brigade into action during the New Berne campaign. General Ambrose Burnside's small army

shoved the brigade aside and captured the town. The brigade was transferred to Piedmont, Virginia, but was never called upon to join Stonewall Jackson's small army. The brigade was next sent to Hanover Courthouse, where it was thoroughly thrashed by a large Federal force in a battle that preceded the Seven Days campaign. The brigade was transferred to A. P. Hill's Light Division and fought well at Gaines's Mill and Frayser's Farm. It was an important factor in the Confederate victory at Cedar Mountain, and saw action at Second Manassas and Sharpsburg, where Branch was killed.[29]

Branch was succeeded by Colonel James Lane of the 28th North Carolina. A graduate of the Virginia Military Academy, he returned after a few years and became a faculty member. Elected major of the 1st North Carolina, Lane saw action at Big Bethel—one of the earliest battles of the war. Because he was small in stature, his men referred to him as first the "little major" and then the "little general." Lane was promoted on November 1, 1862, and given formal command of the brigade. The brigade had some difficulties at the battle of Fredericksburg because of a gap in the line, causing it to be forced back. The brigade partially redeemed itself at Chancellorsville, where it played a large role in Jackson's flank attack. Unfortunately, the brigade had mistakenly fired on Stonewall Jackson that night, mortally wounding him. As the brigade marched to Gettysburg it sought redemption.[30]

Lane's veteran North Carolinians were surprised by the reaction of the Northern citizens to Lee's men. Captain John Turner of the 7th North Carolina wrote that the "North American Indian could not have been more surprised or frightened when Columbus landed than these people. They agreed to any proposition—grant any request—take Confederate money, give provisions." Others, like Lieutenant Iowa Royster, believed that guilt feelings played a role. "They know how their soldiers have behaved in Virginia and they fear that ours will retaliate." Many farmers provided food to the men without asking for payment, probably because they hoped their property would be spared. Most prized were the farm animals, who were confiscated as soon as they were found.[31]

The brigade, along with the remainder of Pender's Division, reached Cashtown on June 30. Pender's march to Gettysburg began at about 8:00 A.M., or about three hours after Heth's Division had departed. The sounds of battle could be heard when the brigade was about four miles from Gettysburg, and the pace increased. After marching an additional mile, the brigade was ordered to the left of Chambersburg Pike in the following order, from left to right: 33rd North Carolina–18th North Carolina–28th North Carolina–37th North Carolina–7th North Carolina, with the latter's right flank resting on the road. After advancing in line of battle for almost a mile, Lane received orders to move to the right of the road, to form the extreme right of the division. While the men rested, Lane ordered the 7th North Carolina to deploy as a strong line of skirmishers at right angles to the rest of the brigade to counter Buford's cavalry in this sector. At about 3:00 P.M., the brigade advanced toward McPherson Ridge and formed behind Heth's Division. The 7th North Carolina made this movement by marching by the left flank. Passing through Archer's defeated brigade, Lane's men now formed the right flank of the army. The 7th North Carolina was detached to engage the Federal cavalry, about half a mile away, which, according to Lane, "were annoying us with an enfilade fire."[32]

Rushing forward at quick time toward Seminary Ridge at about 4:00 P.M., the brigade came under small arms fire from the dismounted cavalry "and a few infantry . . . when the men gave a yell, and rushed forward at a double-quick, the whole of the enemy force beating a hasty retreat to Cemetery Hill." At least that's what Lane wrote in his report. What really occurred appears to be quite different.

Coming up against units of Gamble's Brigade (Buford's Division), Lane formed his men into a hollow square. Some hypothesized that these cavalry, armed with Sharps repeating rifles, caused Lane to think that there were more of the enemy behind a stone wall than were really present. When the cavalry feigned an attack, Lane responded by employing the obsolete maneuver. However, as modern historian William McDaid explained, cavalry attacks against infantry were almost always repelled without resorting to squares, and Lane had actually done so at the battle of Cedar Mountain. All this maneuver achieved was to make his men more vulnerable to the cavalrymen's carbines. After realizing that the cavalry were not going to charge, Lane formed his men back into line of battle. This maneuver caused the brigade to be a "no show" during Pender's attack on the Federal infantry on Seminary Ridge. Instead, Perrin's and Scales's Brigades were forced to make frontal charges on the strong positions with disastrous losses. Lane's Brigade had extended far beyond the Federal infantry's left flank, and could have easily gotten into the enemy's rear, forcing them off of Seminary Ridge with many fewer Confederate losses. An angry Colonel Abner Perrin wrote after the battle, "Lane's Brigade never came up at all until the Yankees were clear out of reach."[33]

Finally advancing into a peach orchard near the McMillan house on Seminary Ridge, Lane was ordered to halt for the day, "unless there was another general forward movement." Seeing the chances of this to be slim, Lane allowed his men to rest behind a stone wall. The brigade remained there through the night and most of July 2. That afternoon, Pender ordered Lane to help secure the portion of Emmitsburg Road in front of his posi-

tion. This would not be an easy task. Colonel Clark Avery of the 33rd North Carolina was ordered to provide seventy-five men and two officers to carry out the mission. Riding up to Lieutenant Wilson Lucas, one of the two officers selected, Pender asked, "Can you take that road in front?" Surveying the situation, Lucas honestly replied that he was not sure. That was not the response that Pender was seeking and angrily replied, "If you can't take it say so and I will get some one who can." That "touched me up," recalled Lucas, and he quickly responded, "We can take it if any other 75 men in the Army of Northern Virginia can." Pender eyed the young officer and responded, "That is the way I love to hear you talk," and ordered the men to hold their fire as long as possible, but reiterated that the road must be taken. Rushing forward, the enemy held their ground until Lucas's men were within twenty yards of them, when most turned and fled back toward Cemetery Ridge or surrendered. Some, however, first fired into Lucas's men, killing and wounding a number of them.[34]

Later that afternoon, the 18th and 33rd North Carolina were ordered to the left to support Lieutenant Colonel Garnett's artillery battalion near the seminary, where they were exposed to heavy Federal artillery fire. During the early evening, Pender was wounded, Lane assumed command of the division, and Colonel C. M. Avery of the 33rd North Carolina took over the brigade. That night the brigade was held in readiness to support Rodes's Division's attack on Cemetery Hill.[35]

At noon on July 3, Lane was ordered to move his brigade, and Scales's, to the right, where they formed behind Pettigrew's Brigade (Heth's Division, III Corps). Almost immediately after taking position, Lane received word that he was to return to his brigade, as General Isaac

Trimble would assume command of the two brigades during the charge. Lane's brigade was aligned from left to right as 33rd North Carolina–18th North Carolina–28th North Carolina–37th North Carolina–7th North Carolina.[36]

By 1:00 P.M., the men had reached their positions behind Davis's and Marshall's (Pettigrew's) Brigades, and the officers informed them of their mission. They were specifically told to keep cool, preserve their alignment, press steadily to the front, and gain the enemy's works. The men could not be happy about what they saw in front of them—clear fields with an occasional fence. This was certainly not like Virginia, where open fields were not as abundant. Just as the brigade emerged from the woods, at the conclusion of the bombardment, an unknown staff officer galloped up and cautioned the men "not to fire into, nor pass the front line unless it wavered and he added with an apparent feeling of pride, 'the men in front never waver,'" noted Major James Harris of the 7th North Carolina. Major J. Weston of the 33rd North Carolina noted that "I never saw, even in drill, a more beautiful line than my brigade kept as it advanced under that murderous fire." Lane added in his report that "my command never moved forward more handsomely." They could see Davis's men already engaged to their left-front. The tremendous frontal and flanking fire caused Davis's men to begin falling back. Unfortunately, Trimble's supporting line was about 150 yards to the rear—too far away to provide assistance—so he ordered the men to double-quick. Because of the enfilading fire, some of Davis's men crowded Lane's advancing brigade and could only be driven away at the point of the bayonet. Pettigrew and Archer in front of Lane's men had gone farther, and were nearing the wall that sheltered the enemy. When Lane's men were about 150 yards from Emmitsburg Road, the two brigades in front of them were suddenly pounded in their front and flank. General Trimble wrote after the war that "they seemed to sink into the earth under the tempest of fire poured into them." Lieutenant Colonel W. Morris of the 37th North Carolina noted that " they laid down, some in the road, some on the crest of the hill near the stone fence and beckoned to us to come on."[37]

A serious miscommunication occurred on the right of the brigade as it neared Emmitsburg Road. The 7th North Carolina and the companies of the 37th North Carolina to the right of the color guard heard General Trimble order an oblique to the right. The remainder of the brigade heard Lane order an oblique to the left to take the place of Davis's now departed brigade, on Pettigrew's Brigade's left. As a result, a gap formed in the brigade, inviting fire from the flank and front. It also caused the right of the brigade to crowd Scales's men. The men now opened fire, as General Lane put it, "with telling effect, repeatedly driving the cannoneers from their pieces, completely silencing the guns in our immediate front, and breaking the line of infantry which was formed on the crest of the hill." Lieutenant Colonel Turner of the 7th North Carolina insisted that he saw Federal troops running away from the stone wall as his men approached the road. "I called the attention of the men to this fact, and the whole line rushed forward with increased vigor." Pulling down the fence on the west side of Emmitsburg road, the men rapidly crossed to the other side. Here, the fence was much stronger, and the men could not pull it down. Looking up, Turner saw enemy reinforcements approaching the stone wall and Pettigrew's and Archer's men falling back. The situation did not look good.[38]

Because they were a supporting line, the brigade's losses up to this point were relatively light. However, the amount of shot and shell thrown at the men increased dramatically as they approached the fence along Emmitsburg Road. Lieutenant Colonel Turner led his 7th North Carolina over the fence, but was wounded about ten yards beyond it, and his men pulled back to the safety of the roadway. Captain Harris of the same regiment noted that Turner ordered his men to fall back because Lane's left regiments did not seem to be advancing. Another officer from the regiment, Lieutenant Thomas Mulloy, recalled that only half of the regiment climbed the fence. The rest remained along the road. He noted that not more than a dozen men made their way to the stone wall, only to be killed, wounded, or captured. All of the color guard were shot down, and the flag fell to the ground; it was later captured by the enemy. Major Weston of the 33rd North Carolina claimed that many of his men advanced to within a few feet of the wall, and some on his right actually jumped over it. Before long, Weston's men were hit by small arms fire from their left.[39]

Captain John Thorp of Pettigrew's 47th North Carolina recalled seeing General Lane on horseback "quite near the stone wall, riding just behind and up to his men, in the attitude of urging them forward with his hand; a moment later a large spurt of blood leaped from the horse as he rode up, and rider and horse went down in the smoke and uproar." Dismounting, Lane ordered his left regiment, the 33rd North Carolina, to turn to the left and face the enemy attacking from that direction. The regiment's commander, Colonel Charles Avery, screamed, "My God! General, do you intend rushing your men into such a place unsupported when the troops on the right are falling

back." A glance told Lane that Avery was right, and he ordered a withdrawal. Lieutenant Thomas Norwood of the 37th North Carolina was rushing toward the wall, when he was told to break off the attack because the remainder of the brigade was retreating. Most of the men knew it was futile to continue the struggle and they began making their way back to Seminary Ridge. Some of the enemy jumped over the works at this point and captured additional Tar Heels. The men's exhaustion caused many to capitulate with little resistance.[40]

General Lane wrote after the war that Trimble told him, "If the troops I had the honor to command today couldn't take that position, all hell can't take it." Trimble denied ever using profane language, but did admit that he "used some emphatic expression of commendation." The retreat back to Seminary Ridge was almost as hazardous as the advance. "Our loss in this retreat was immense, as we were raked by a cross fire for a mile and a half by the guns of the enemy, without any protection whatever to shield us," wrote one private. On July 4, Lane's Brigade returned to its original position near the McMillan house and rested. That night, they began their long march home.[41]

The performance of General Lane and his brigade was mixed. Lane performed poorly on July 1, when he missed an opportunity to almost single-handedly roll up the Federal left flank on Seminary Ridge. Instead, he formed obsolete hollow squares against a cavalry attack that never materialized. As a result, hundreds of men in Perrin's and Scales's Brigades were needlessly sacrificed. The brigade did much better on July 3, when it mounted its attack on Cemetery Ridge. However, no troops could have successfully captured and held the enemy position.

✄

Scales's Brigade—Brigadier General Alfred Scales

Units: 13th North Carolina, 16th North Carolina, 22nd North Carolina, 34th North Carolina, 38th North Carolina
Strength: 1351
Losses: 704 (175-358-171)—52.1%[42]

Although the regiments entered the war in four different brigades, by June 1862, all but the 13th North Carolina were in Brigadier General Dorsey Pender's Brigade. The 13th North Carolina was in Garland's Brigade. Pender's Brigade saw heavy fighting at Gaines's Mill, Frayser's Farm, Second Manassas, and Antietam. After the death of General Samuel Garland during the Maryland campaign, the 13th North Carolina petitioned to be transferred to Pender's Brigade and its request was honored on October 17. The now complete brigade helped beat off a determined Federal charge at the battle of Fredericksburg.[43]

When General Pender received command of the division, Colonel Scales of the 13th North Carolina took over the brigade. An attorney and U.S. congressman, Scales actually joined the army as a private, but was quickly elected captain of a company in what was to become the 13th North Carolina. He was elected colonel of the regiment on October 3, 1861. The rigors of the Peninsula and Seven Days campaigns took their toll on Scales, causing him to collapse from exhaustion. He did not return to the army until mid-November, having missed the Second Manassas and Maryland campaigns. He left the army again in February 1863 to marry a woman half his age, then returned in time for the battle of Chancellorsville. With the reorganization of the army, General Pender was given a divi-

sion, and Scales was promoted to the rank of brigadier general in mid-June 1863 and given permanent command of the brigade. As a result, the Gettysburg campaign was his first experience as a brigade commander.[44]

Scales's men had a number of memorable experiences during the march through Maryland and Pennsylvania. After one particularly long march, Private A. J. Dula of the 22nd North Carolina fell asleep almost immediately, while several of his comrades decided to forage. Dula's slumber was soon broken by the sounds of chickens, geese, and ducks brought into camp. Not wanting to miss these delicacies, Dula jumped up and helped prepare the grand feast. While most of the citizens were respectful, some openly vented their emotions. Once when the 13th North Carolina struck up, "Maryland My Maryland," an old woman yelled at the men, "Oh, yes! Oh, yes! It's 'Maryland My Maryland,' but when you come back it will be 'fire in the mountains; run, boys, run'!"[45]

Upon reaching the vicinity of Gettysburg on July 1, General Scales deployed his men to the right of Chambersburg Pike with his left flank resting on it. The brigade was arranged from left to right as 38th North Carolina–13th North Carolina–34th North Carolina–22nd North Carolina–16th North Carolina. Scales noted that his left flank was fifty to sixty "steps" from Chambersburg Pike. After Lane's Brigade moved to the opposite end of the line, Scales's Brigade became the left-most unit of Pender's Division. A few minutes later, Scales was ordered to advance, and a quarter-mile march put the brigade behind Pegram's batteries on Herr Ridge. The men were able to rest for about half an hour before being ordered forward again. This time, the men were exposed to a fairly heavy artillery fire and several were hit with shell fragments. Seeing the struggle between Stone's Federal Brigade (Rowley's Division, I Corps) and Daniel's Brigade (Rodes's Division, Second Corps), Scales ordered his men to hasten their pace. He indicated in his report that his men "pressed on with a shout to their assistance."[46]

Quick-stepping through a meadow, they came up behind Brockenbrough's Brigade (Heth's Division, Third Corps), whose men were lying down in line of battle in front of the Federal line on McPherson Ridge. The Tar Heels watched as Brockenbrough's Virginians rose and advanced in quick time. After a few minutes, Scales also ordered his men forward to remain within supporting distance. A quarter-mile march brought them up to Brockenbrough's men again, who were lying down on McPherson Ridge. Scales was told that Brockenbrough's men "were without ammunition, and would not advance further." With some disdain, Scales later wrote that "I ordered my men to march over them, they did so." The brigade now made for the seminary buildings on the ridge in front of him. Referring to Bachelder's map, historian David Martin believed that the movement of Perrin's Brigade forced Scales to the left, and as a result, the left-most regiment, the 38th North Carolina, was pushed across Chambersburg Pike. However, General Scales wrote after the war that "this road [Chambersburg Pike] was from thirty to fifty yds. From my left until we reached the point where we were checked [west of Seminary Ridge]."[47]

The remnants of three I Corps's brigades were safely behind barricades on Seminary Ridge by this time. Although decimated in numbers, they were still full

of fight. In addition, Scales was marching into the teeth of the I Corps's massed artillery, whose axles were almost touching in some places. The North Carolinians stopped and poured volleys into the Federal line, and the latter responded with a tremendous artillery barrage. One observer believed that it was the most desperate fight ever waged between infantry and artillery. General Scales described what happened from his vantage point:

> Here the brigade encountered a most terrific fire of grape and shell on our flank, and grape and musketry in our front. Every discharge made sad havoc in our line, but still we pressed on at a double-quick until we reached . . . a distance of about 75 yards from the ridge we had just crossed, and about the same distance from the college [Seminary], in our front . . . Our line had been broken up, and now only a squad here and there marked the place where regiments had rested.[48]

Colonel Charles Wainwright, commander of the I Corps's artillery, wrote in his diary, "never have I seen such a charge. Not a man seemed to falter. Lee may well be proud of his infantry; I wish ours was equal to it." Colonel William Robinson of the Iron Brigade's 7th Wisconsin also observed Scales's men steady approach. He wrote in his official report, "it was with some difficulty I restrained the men from firing until the enemy got as near as I wanted them. When they were within easy range, the order was given, and their ranks went down like grass before the scythe from the united fire of our regiments and the battery. There were very few, if any, of that brigade [that] escaped death or wounds."[49]

The survivors lay down to avoid the deadly artillery fire when they were about seventy-five yards from the ridge. They could do no more. An artilleryman from Stevens's battery noted that "the whole line of battle from right to left was one continuous blaze of fire . . . completely filled with the thick blue smoke of infantry, making it difficult to distinguish friend from foe, while the artillery . . . belched forth a tremendous fire of shot and shell, moving their deadly missiles in rapid succession into the ranks of the enemy." The battery expended fifty-seven rounds of deadly canister in a short time. Marveling at the sight of the charge, Captain Robert Beecham of the 2nd Wisconsin observed that the "charging Confederates were brave men—in fact, no braver ever faced a more certain death!"[50]

Every field officer except one was killed or wounded, including Scales. Every unit experienced heavy losses. According to Adjutant Nathaniel Smith, his 13th North Carolina lost 150 men of the 180 that entered the battle. A careful analysis by Busey and Martin found that the regiment's battlefield losses were somewhat less, totalling "only" 77%, the sixth highest for any Confederate regiment at Gettysburg. One casualty was the surgeon of the 16th North Carolina, who, in his excitement, rode forward with the line of battle. The historian of the regiment later wrote that "our surgeon was shot in the head, and ought to have been killed for being there and for not attending to his duty."[51]

The battered remains of the brigade rallied in the rear, before advancing to a fence, about two hundred yards from Seminary Ridge. They opened fire on the Union position, but were asked to advance no farther. Command of the brigade devolved upon Colonel William Lowrance of the 34th North Carolina. Surveying their condition, he found the men to be in a "depressed, dilapidated, and almost unorganized condition." After nightfall, the brigade was ordered to the left. Lowrance ordered a picket line to be posted at 1:00 A.M. on July 2, and told "the few who were still in ranks [sic] to stack arms for the night."[52]

As morning dawned on July 2, the brigade was detached from the division and ordered to move to the right to support Pegram's batteries on Seminary Ridge. This movement caused the brigade to form the extreme right flank of the army. Lowrance was not happy with this order, as he considered it "hazardous in the extreme, taking into consideration our weakness and the importance of the position." Throwing out a line of skirmishers, Lowrance ordered the rest of his command to rest and wait. Lowrance was clearly relieved when the head of Anderson's Division (Third Corps) arrived, and he was ordered to return to his division, forming on the right of Lane's Brigade. The brigade remained here through the morning of July 3. The men could not understand why it was so quiet. "Our men becoming impatient would call out and say, 'If we had Jackson we would move and do something,'" recalled a soldier from the 16th North Carolina. The men hunkered down during the artillery duel that began at 1:00 P.M. that day, and there were few casualties. Lowrance referred to it as "a most galling fire," and further stated that "I am proud to say the men endured with the coolness and determined spirit of veterans, for such they are."[53]

Hearing about the grand charge that General Longstreet was to oversee, the men were incredulous to learn that they would form the supporting line behind Heth's Division, now under General Pettigrew. One of General Pickett's staff officers, Captain Robert Bright, overheard Lieutenant Colonel George Gordon of the 34th North Carolina, say, "Pickett, my men are not going up to-day." Pickett told him he must take the men back into battle, but

Gordon simply shook his head, saying that "for the last day or two they have lost heavily under infantry fire and are very sore, and they will not go up to-day." The grand cannonade abruptly ended this discussion.[54]

Lee rode by to inspect the attack formation and observed the condition of Scales's Brigade. According to one observer, Lee, "noticing many of Scales' men with their heads and hands bandaged, . . . said to General Trimble: 'Many of these poor boys should go to the rear, they are not able for duty.' Passing his eyes searchingly along the weakened ranks of Scales' brigade he turned to General Trimble and touchingly added, 'I miss in this brigade the faces of many dear friends.'" Within the next hour, Lee would lose many more of them.[55]

The firing stopped, and Lowrance's men could see Archer's Brigade of Heth's Division advancing in front of them against the strongly held Federal position on Cemetery Ridge. "Then we were ordered forward over a wide, hot, and already crimson plain," Lowrance recorded in his official report. The brigade was deployed from left to right as 16th North Carolina–22nd North Carolina–34th North Carolina–13th North Carolina–38th North Carolina. The men of the 14th Connecticut (Smyth's Brigade, Hays's Division, II Corps) watched as the brigade broke out of the woods. The historian of the regiment counted four lines of battle approaching, two each from Archer's and Scales's Brigades. The brigade's movement, which included Gordon's 34th North Carolina, was ignored by the enemy until it reached about halfway to Cemetery Ridge, when the Federal artillery opened on it. Lowrance referred to the Union position as "on an eminence in our front, strongly fortified and supported by infantry." The command came

to a fence running diagonally across the field, which, according to Adjutant Henry Moore of the 38th North Carolina, "deranged our line very much." Lowrance described another complication when his command had marched about two-thirds of the distance to the enemy line—"troops from the front came tearing through our ranks, which caused many of our men to break, but with the remaining few we went forward." The enemy fire was becoming more severe. Moore wrote after the battle that "our men were falling in every direction but we managed to struggle on with a tolerably good line as we had rearranged it the best we could."[56]

Moore further noted that "about 150 yards from the enemy a part of our line struck another fence, which confused us considerably. The fire from the enemy's artillery and infantry was now terrible, and we were reduced to a mere skirmish line. We reached another fence, which was on the other side of the road [Emmitsburg]. Here we halted and endeavored to reform our line with the men who had become mixed up from different commands."[57]

Lowrance observed that because his line was marching in a "rather oblique line," the regiments on the right side of the brigade approached the enemy position first. While the artillery in their front line had been silenced, other cannon were still issuing deadly shells. "Here many were shot down, being exposed to a heavy fire of grape and musketry." It appears that the hostile fire was greater along the flanks than from the front.[58]

The 16th North Carolina on Lowrance's right flank advanced rapidly against Arnold's battery and Smyth's infantry brigade. One of the cannoneers wrote after the war that "one of the guns . . . was double-shotted with canister . . . and [the Confederate troops] had almost reached the wall just in front of us . . . [after firing] the gap made in that North Carolina regiment was simply terrible." The historian of the 14th Connecticut wrote that "Major Ellis gave the order to the regiment to fire left oblique to dislodge some Confederates who had come uncomfortably near the front of an adjoining battery [Arnold's]." There were few other Federal accounts of Scales's Brigade's activities, probably because from their point of view, they blended into Archer's attack.[59]

The situation was chaotic. After the first day's fiasco, few officers remained to make the charge and most of these were now out of action. To make matters worse, Trimble was down and Lowrance could not be everywhere. The men were confused. Trimble recalled that "Scales' brigade . . . passed over Pettigrew's line, reached the fence and began firing— (contrary to the orders I had given at the start). Amid the roar of the battle it was impossible to make them hear orders to advance. Scales' men stood at the fence for some *ten* minutes discharging their muskets—and then slowly fell back." This was not true of all of Scales's troops. At the fence, Adjutant Moore (38th North Carolina) ran over to Captain Abel Cloud of the 16th North Carolina and asked him what they should do. His reply was, "We will hold on here until we get help." Although Moore saw some fresh troops approaching, they soon disappeared. With the fire in front of them slackening, Moore ordered his men over the last fence bordering Emmitsburg Road and onto the enemy position. As they ran forward, a group of enemy soldiers emerged from their breastworks and gobbled up Moore and those who had followed him. Acting brigade adjutant Lieutenant D. McIntyre claimed after the war that a large number of the men

did reach the wall, writing, "I suppose we held the works some fifteen minutes or more." This was probably an exaggeration, as very few even approached the wall.[60]

The men felt forsaken as all of the other Confederate troops, except Lane's and theirs, had now retreated back to the safety of Seminary Ridge. Many wondered what to do. According to Colonel Lowrance, "the men answered for themselves, and, without orders, the brigade retreated, leaving many on the field unable to get off, and some, I fear, unwilling to undertake the hazardous retreat." Although wounded, General Trimble recalled that "Scales brigade faced right about and marched off the field after heavy loss, in as good order as they advanced, and in no disorder whatever."[61]

The stragglers were collected and the brigade was reformed at its original position on Seminary Ridge. Adjutant Moore thought frequently about the doomed charge for the rest of his life. He attributed the defeat to an interesting object. "Had there been no fence in the way in the third day's fight at Gettysburg . . . [we] would have driven the Federals from their line." The men immediately began throwing up breastworks on Seminary Ridge. As a wounded General Trimble rode by, he said to them, "That's right boys, stand your ground and we will serve the Yanks as they have served us." The attack never came, however. Remaining there through July 4, the brigade joined the retreat back home later that evening.[62]

Scales's men were not to taste the fruits of victory at Gettysburg. The charges on both July 1 and July 3 were futile and resulted in many casualties—over 50% of the brigade. Some could argue that the charges should never have been made, as no troops could have been successful in these situations.

✕

Thomas's Brigade—Brigadier General Edward Thomas

Units: 14th Georgia, 35th Georgia, 45th Georgia, 49th Georgia
Strength: 1326
Losses: 264 (34-127-103)—19.9%[63]

Most of the regiments of Thomas's Brigade entered the war as part of Brigadier General Joseph Anderson's Brigade. The brigade initially served in North Carolina, but was transferred to Virginia in early May 1862, and was positioned near the Rappahannock River to watch Major General Irwin McDowell's Federal Corps. Withdrawn to join the main Confederate army, the brigade saw action as part of A. P. Hill's Division at the battles of Mechanicsville, Gaines's Mill, and Frayser's Farm. The brigade's activities during these battles were less successful than Hill's other brigades, and it lost fewer than half the men as the others.[64]

Anderson resigned his commission on July 19, 1862, and Colonel Edward Thomas of the 35th Georgia was given command of the brigade. Thomas quickly showed that he was a hard-hitting fighter, and he and his brigade performed well at the battles of Cedar Mountain and Second Manassas. The brigade was stationed behind the unfinished railroad in the latter battle and helped beat back several determined attacks. The battle of Sharpsburg may have been a disappointment to some of the men, as the brigade was left behind at Harper's Ferry to parole the prisoners and therefore missed the battle. Thomas was promoted to brigadier general on November 1, 1862, and his men fought with distinction at Fredericksburg and Chancellorsville.[65]

The marches to Gettysburg were long and arduous. Private George Hall of the 14th Georgia recorded in his diary that "my feet was [sic] so sore I could hardly put them to the ground." The men marveled at the countryside. "This is the finest country I ever saw and if . . . our army had never come here they [the inhabitants] would not know that any war was going on at all, every thing is as cheap as in time of peace and there looks like there is enough wheat here to suply [sic] the world."[66]

On the morning of July 1, the 35th Georgia was left behind to the guard the wagon train. The men knew that a battle was imminent and assumed that they would miss it. Orders suddenly arrived to rejoin the brigade, and the men trotted for about three miles to reach the brigade.[67]

Marching at the rear of the division, Thomas's Brigade could hear the report of artillery and soon were double-quicking forward. They halted as they approached Gettysburg from the west and deployed on the north side of Chambersburg Pike, now on the left of the division. The brigade swept forward in line of battle for about a mile with its sister brigades. A soldier in the 14th Georgia reported that "the enemys [sic] Batterys [sic] throw shell all around us and our Batterys [sic] just in front of us keep up a continual roar." As the division advanced again in the afternoon to support Heth's attack on McPherson Ridge, General A. P. Hill held Thomas's Brigade back to support Pegram's artillery. Assistant Adjutant-General Major Joseph Engelhard reported that the brigade was "retained by Lieutenant-General Hill to meet a threatened advance from the left." This was a strange use of a strong brigade, given the fact that the Federal troops in this sector were making no suggestion of taking offensive action. This was but another example of Hill's mismanagement of his troops during the battle. One soldier reported that the brigade "had nothing to do save dodging shells and witnessing the first day's engagement." The brigade remained there until sunset, when Pender ordered it to take position on the right of the division, where it again pulled artillery support duty.[68]

The brigade remained quietly in its position until the evening of July 2. Lieutenant David Champion of the 14th Georgia recalled that "we lay in line of battle but were not engaged." Hall of the same regiment spoke of the enemy artillery fire throughout the day—"we lie down in line of Battle to keep the enemys [sic] Batterys [sic] from having such affect on us. Cannon balls, bombs, grape and canisters fall thick and fast among us killing and wounding several of our regt." The same was not true for the brigade's skirmishers, which were involved in a seesaw battle for control of the Bliss farm. It was on the skirmish line that the brigade suffered most of its casualties. Captain Charles Conn of the 45th Georgia wrote home that "the skirmishing was the *heaviest* I have ever heard of, being almost equal to a pitch [sic] battle all the time . . . I think twas [sic] the *hottest* place I have yet been in." According to Hall, his regiment maintained three companies on the skirmish line at all times, which were periodically replaced by others during the course of the day.[69]

During the evening of July 2, the brigade was ordered forward to support Rodes's attack on Cemetery Hill. The attack was called off and the brigade subsequently formed along Long Lane, with its right resting a short distance from an orchard near the Bliss farm. Its left was at an obtuse angle to Perrin's Brigade, leaving an interval of "100 paces" between the two units. Hall complained that the "battle continue[d] near 10 oclock at night, we [got] no rest nor sleep this night."[70]

The artillery duel between the armies on July 3 left an indelible impression on the men. Lt. David Champion wrote that the "horrors of the artillery duel are indescribable . . . the shells came hissing and shrieking past us, sometimes bursting over us and the earth seemed as though it were in the throes of a great earthquake . . . amid the deafening noise of bursting shells, the only other sounds which pierced our ears were neighing of wounded horses and the cries of dying men." Hall added that "the air was so hot that a great number of our men fainted."[71]

Because Thomas's Brigade occupied the right of Long Lane, they had an unobstructed view of the Pickett–Pettigrew–Trimble charge, particularly the destructive fire thrown against Brockenbrough's Brigade by the artillery on Cemetery Hill and by the 8th Ohio, which flanked it. With better leadership, it is conceivable that Thomas's fresh brigade could have been thrown forward to thwart the destructive actions of the Ohio regiment. The historian of the 35th Georgia claimed that Thomas ordered his brigade forward to participate in the charge and part of it did. Likewise, Lieutenant Chapman noted that the company of the 14th Georgia next to his, also joined the charge. James McElvany's diary contains the statement, "General Heaths [sic] Division with Thomas Brigade charged the enemys [sic] battery at 5 o'clock." However, Thomas makes no mention of his brigade's participation in the charge, and if some of the units did advance, they played virtually no role in the outcome of the offensive. The most outrageous claim was made in a letter written soon after the battle in which Major James Carter of the 45th Georgia claimed that his unit charged half a mile to within a hundred yards of the batteries before turning back. The brigade remained here through the night of July 3, when it was pulled back to a wood lot north of Gettysburg. The brigade began its retreat on the night of July 4–5.[72]

Only one other brigade in Lee's army (Mahone's) lost as few men in the battle as Thomas's. It played but minor roles on July 1 and July 3. In between, the unit was involved in heavy skirmishing between Cemetery and Seminary Ridges. Why this fresh, veteran brigade did not play more of a role in the battle is open to question.

NOTES

1. Davis, *The Confederate General*, vol. V, 10–11.

2. OR 27, 2, 656–657.

3. Tagg, *Generals of Gettysburg*, 327; OR 27, 2, 665.

4. OR 27, 2, 447, 666.

5. James S. Harris, *Historical Sketches: Seventh Regiment, North Carolina Troops* (Ann Arbor, MI, 1972), 35–36; Clark, *N.C. Regiments.*, vol. 2, 661; James Lane, letter, Southern Historical Collection, University of North Carolina.

6. Lane, letter; Isaac Trimble to John Bachelder, February 8, 1883, Bachelder Papers, New Hampshire Historical Society; Isaac Trimble, "The Campaign and Battle of Gettysburg," in *Confederate Veteran* (1917), vol. 25, 213.

7. Isaac Trimble, "The Civil War Diary of Isaac Ridgeway Trimble," *Maryland Historical Magazine* (1922), vol. 17, 12.

8. Busey and Martin, *Regimental Strengths and Losses*, 180, 292.

9. Sifakis, *Compendium of the Confederate Armies: South Carolina and Georgia*, 53–54, 56, 85, 86; Davis, *The Confederate General*, vol. III, 41–43; vol. IV, 122–123.

10. Sifakis, *Who Was Who In the Civil War*, 416; Caldwell, *The History of a Brigade of South Carolinians*, 93–94.

11. OR 27, 2, 661; Thomas M. Littlejohn, "Recollections of a Confederate Soldier," copy in 12th South Carolina file, GNMP; U. R. Brooks, *Stories of the Confederacy*, in *Confederate Veteran* (Columbia, SC, 1912), 37.

12. OR 27, 2, 661.

13. OR 27, 2, 661.

14. Littlejohn, "Recollections."

15. Caldwell, *A Brigade of South Carolinians*, 97; Captain Shooter, letter, *Drumbeat*, newsletter of the Charleston Civil War Round Table (June 1989), copy in 12th South Carolina file, GNMP; Brooks, *Stories of the Confederacy*, 37; OR 27, 2, 661.

16. OR 27, 2, 661; B. F. Brown, "Some Recollections of Gettysburg," in *Confederate Veteran* (1923), vol. 31, 53; Varina D. Brown, *A Colonel at Gettysburg and Spotsylvania* (Columbia, SC, 1931), 77.

17. Brown, "Some Recollections of Gettysburg," 53; Shooter, letter.

18. OR 27, 2, 661; Caldwell, *A Brigade of South Carolinians*, 96; Shooter, letter.

19. OR 27, 2, 661–662; Daniel A. Thompkins, *Company K, Fourteenth South Carolina Volunteers* (Charlotte, NC, 1897), 19–20.

20. Caldwell, *A Brigade of South Carolinians*, 97–98; Brown, *A Colonel at Gettysburg and Spotsyvania*, 80, 84.

21. OR 27, 2, 662; Brown, *A Colonel at Gettysburg and Spotsylvania*, 79; Caldwell, *A Brigade of South Carolinians*, 98; Abner Perrin, "A Little More Light on Gettysburg," in *Mississippi Valley Historical Review* (1938), vol. 24, 522; J. Michael Miller, "Perrin's Brigade on July 1, 1863," *Gettysburg Magazine* (July 1995), issue 13, 31.

22. OR 27, 2, 662; Brooks, *Stories of the Confederacy*, 37; Shooter, letter.

23. Brown, *Colonel at Gettysburg and Spotsylvania*, 82–83, 85; Caldwell, *A Brigade of South Carolinians*, 97.

24. Brown, *Colonel at Gettysburg and Spotsylvania*, 82–83; OR 27, 2, 663.

25. Brooks, *Stories of the Confederacy*, 38.

26. OR 27, 2, 663, 666; Caldwell, *A Brigade of South Carolinians*, 100; Littlejohn, "Recollections."

27. OR 27, 2, 663–664; Littlejohn, "Recollections."

28. Busey and Martin, *Regimental Strengths and Losses*, 181, 292.

29. Sifakis, *Compendium of the Confederate Armies: North Carolina*, 93–94, 110, 124–125; Davis, *The Confederate General*, vol. I, 118–119.

30. Davis, *The Confederate General*, vol. IV, 17.

31. McDaid, *Four Years of Arduous Service*, 204.

32. OR 27, 2, 665.

33. OR 27, 2, 665; Harris, *Historical Sketches: Seventh Regiment, North Carolina Troops*, 34; McDaid, *Four Years of Arduous Service*, 207–209.

34. W. H. Lucas, letter, North Carolina Department of Archives and History.

Lane reported that the 38th North Carolina was the regiment involved in this action, but Lucas served in the 33rd North Carolina.

35. OR 27, 2, 665–666; McDaid, *Four Years of Arduous Service*, 215.

36. OR 27, 2, 666; William Morris, letter, Southern Historical Collection, University of North Carolina.

37. Lane, letter; Harris, *Historical Sketches: Seventh Regiment, North Carolina Troops*, 36; Clark, *N.C. Regiments*, vol. 2, 565; OR 27, 2, 666; W. G. Morris, letter, Southern Historical Collection, University of North Carolina.

38. Lane, letter; Morris, letter; OR 27, 2, 666; John Turner, letter, Southern Historical Collection, University of North Carolina.

39. OR 27, 2, 666; Turner, letter; Harris, *Historical Sketches: Seventh Regiment, North Carolina Troops*, 37; OR suppl., 5, 451; McDaid, *Four Years of Arduous Service*, 219; Clark, *N.C. Regiments*, vol. 2, 74.

40. Clark, *N.C. Regiments*, vol. 3, 91; Lane, letter; OR suppl., 5, 453, 459.

41. Clark, *N.C. Regiments*, vol. 2, 564; McDaid, *Four Years of Arduous Service*, 221.

42. Busey and Martin, *Regimental Strengths and Losses*, 182, 292.

43. Sifakis, *Compendium of the Confederate Armies: North Carolina*, 102, 107, 116, 133–134; Davis, *The Confederate General*, vol. V, 10–11.

44. Warner, *Generals in Gray*, 268–269; Evans, *Confederate Military History—North Carolina*, 349; Davis, *The Confederate General*, vol. V, 128–129.

45. A. J. Dula, "Civil War Incidents," Duke University; Clark, *N.C. Regiments*, vol. 1, 698.

46. OR 27, 2, 669; Mills, *History of the 16th North Carolina Regiment*; Alfred M. Scales to John Bachelder, February 22, 1890, Bachelder Papers, New Hampshire Historical Society.

47. Mills, *History of the 16th North Carolina*, 36; OR 27, 2, 670; Alfred M. Scales to John Bachelder, February 22, 1890; Martin, *Gettysburg—July 1*, 401.

48. Nathaniel Smith letter, Southern Historical Collection, University of North Carolina; Silas Felton, "The Iron Brigade Battery at Gettysburg," *Gettysburg Magazine* (July 1994), issue 11, 60; OR 27, 2, 670.

Scales apparently did not undertake a reconnaissance prior to the charge, and this was criticized by David Martin who believed that if he had, he would have called on the Confederate artillery to neutralize the guns. Whether such an observation would have allowed him to halt his charge, is however, open to question.

49. Charles Wainwright, *A Diary of Battle* (New York, 1962), 236; OR 27, 1, 280.

50. Clark, *N.C. Regiments*, vol. 1, 698; *Maine at Gettysburg*, 85; Brown, *Colonel at Gettysburg and Spotsylvania*, 211.

51. Smith, letter; Clark, *N.C. Regiments*, vol. 1, 698; Busey and Martin, *Regimental Strengths and Losses*, 292, 298; Mills, *History of 16th North Carolina*, 36.

According to Smith, Scales asked a regiment from Brockenborough's Brigade to assist on his left flank. No evidence exists of this request.

52. OR 27, 2, 658, 662, 671.

53. OR 27, 2, 671; Mills, *History of 16th Carolina*, 37.

The position became less vulnerable a short time later, when the lead elements of Anderson's Division (III Corps) arrived and took position to the right of Scales's Brigade.

54. Bright, "Pickett's Charge, The Story of It Told by a Member of his Staff," 229; Burwell T. Cotton, *The Cry is War, War, War:*

The Civil War Correspondence of Lts. Burwell Thomas Cotton and George Job Huntley . . . (Dayton, 1994), 24.

55. William Swallow, "The Third Day at Gettysburg," in *Southern Bivouac* (1886), vol. 4, 565.

56. OR 27, 2, 671–672; Page, *History of the Fourteenth Regiment, Connecticut Volunteer Infantry,* 151; Henry Moore, letter, Southern Historical Collection, University of North Carolina.

57. Moore, letter.

58. OR 27, 2, 672.

59. Thomas A. Aldrich, *History of Battery A, First Regiment Rhode Island Light Artillery, in the War to Preserve the Union* (Providence, RI, 1904), 216; Page, *History of the Fourteenth Regiment, Connecticut Volunteer Infantry,*153.

Aldrich stated that the 26th North Carolina of Pettigrew's Brigade was the target of the cannon fire. However, a careful analysis by Bruce Trinque showed that the regiment in question was the 16th North Carolina (Trinque, "Arnold's Battery and the 26th North Carolina," 67).

60. OR suppl., 5, 469; D. M. McIntyre, letter, Southern Historical Collection, University of North Carolina; Isaac Trimble to John Bachelder, February 8, 1883.

61. OR 27, 2, 672; Elijah Withers, "Letter," Southern Historical Collection, University of North Carolina; Isaac Trimble to John Bachelder, February 8, 1886.

62. OR 27, 2, 672; Moore, letter; Isaac

Trimble to John Bachelder, February 8, 1886.

63. Busey and Martin, *Regimental Strengths and Losses,*183, 293.

64. Sifakis, *Compendium of the Confederate Armies: South Carolina and Georgia,* 212–213, 244–245, 258; Davis, *The Confederate General,* vol. I, 27.

65. Davis, *The Confederate General,* vol. VI, 45.

66. Diary of George Washington Hall, Library of Congress.

67. Folsom, *Heroes and Martyrs of Georgia* . . . (Baltimore, MD, 1995), 140.

68. OR 27, 2, 656; Hall, diary; James M. Folsom, *Heroes and Martyrs of Georgia,* 140; C. A. Conn, "Letters From Charles A. Conn," *Georgia Historical Quarterly* (1962), vol. 46, 188.

69. OR 27, 2, 666, 667–668; "Reminiscences as told by David Champion," copy in 14th Georgia file, GNMP; Hall, diary; Conn, "Letters From Charles A. Conn," 189.

70. OR 27, 2, 666; Hall, diary.

71. "Reminiscences as told by David Champion"; Hall, diary.

72. OR 27, 2, 669; Folsom, *Heroes and Martyrs of Georgia . . . ,* 140; "Reminiscences as told by David Champion"; "The Diary and Letters of James Thomas McElvany," *Virginia Country,* March/April, copy in 35th Georgia folder, GNMP; Major James Carter, letter, Middle Georgia Archives, Washington Library, Macon, Georgia.

BIBLIOGRAPHY OF UNION AND CONFEDERATE BRIGADES

"A Letter From the Army." *The Savannah Republican*, July 22, 1863.

"A Southern Keepsake." *Gettysburg Compiler*, December 13, 1909.

Abbott, Henry. *Fallen Leaves—The Civil War Letters of Major Henry Abbott*. Kent, OH: Kent State University Press, 1991.

Abernathy, Willliam M. *Our Mess: Southern Gallantry and Privations*. McKinney, TX: McKintex Press, 1977.

Acken, J. Gregory. *Inside the Army of the Potomac*. Mechanicsburg, PA: Stackpole Books, 1998.

Adams, A. J. "The Fight at the Peach Orchard." *National Tribune*, April 23, 1885.

Adams, Silas. "The Nineteenth Maine at Gettysburg." *Maine MOLLUS*, vol. 4, 249–263.

Address of General Robinson, Dedication of the 82nd Ohio Memorial at Gettysburg. Columbus, OH: Nitschke Bros., 1887.

Adelman, Garry E. "The Third Brigade, Third Division, Sixth Corps at Gettysburg." *Gettysburg Magazine* (July 1994), issue 11, 91–101.

Adelman, Garry E. "Benning's Georgia Brigade at Gettysburg." *Gettysburg Magazine*, (January 1998), issue 18, 57–66.

Adelman Garry E., and Timothy H. Smith, *Devil's Den—A History and Guide*. Gettysburg: Thomas Publications, 1997.

Aiken, D. Wyatt. "The Gettysburg Reunion." *Charleston News and Courier*, June 21, 1882.

Aldrich, Thomas A. *The History of Battery A, First Regiment Rhode Island Light Artillery, in the War to Preserve the Union, 1861–1865*. Providence, RI: Snow & Farnham Printers, 1904.

Alexander, E. Porter. "The Great Charge and Artillery Fighting at Gettysburg." In *Battles and Leaders of the Civil War*, vol. 3, 357–368.

Applegate, John. *Reminiscences and Letters of George Arrowsmith of New Jersey*. Red Bank, NJ: John H. Cook, 1893.

Armstrong, Richard L. *Twenty-fifth Virginia Infantry and Ninth Virginia Infantry*. Lynchburg, VA: H. E. Howard, Inc., 1990.

Ashcroft, John M. *Thirty-first Virginia Infantry*. Lynchburg, VA: H. E. Howard, Inc., 1988.

"At Gettysburg. How A Proposed Night Attack by the Enemy was Foiled." *National Tribune*, February 11, 1886.

Ayars, Peter B. "The 99th Pennsylvania." *National Tribune*, February 4, 1886.

Bachelder, John B. "The Third Day's Battle." *Philadelphia Weekly Times*, December 15, 1877.

Baker, Andrew J. "Tribute to Captain Magruder and Wife." *Confederate Veteran Magazine* (1898), vol. 6, 507.

Banes, Charles H. *History of the Philadelphia Brigade: Sixty-ninth, Seventy-first, Seventy-second, and One Hundred and sixth Pennsylvania Volunteers*. Philadelphia: J. B. Lippincott, 1876.

Banes, Charles H. *History of the Philadelphia Brigade . . .* Philadelphia: J. B. Lippincott, 1876.

Baquet, Camille. *History of the First Brigade, New Jersey Volunteers, From 1861 to 1865*. Trenton, NJ: MacCrellish & Quigley, State Printers, 1910.

Bararella, Michael. *Lincoln's Foreign Legion*. Shippensburg, PA: White Mane Publishing, 1996.

Barclay, Ted. *Ted Barclay, Liberty Hall Volunteers: Letters From the Stonewall Brigade (1861–1864)*. Natural Bridge Station, VA: Rockbridge Pub. Co., 1992.

Bard, John P. "The 'Old Bucktails,' 42d Regt. P.V. at the Battle of Gettysburg." *Philadelphia Weekly Times,* May 19, 1886.

Bardeen, Charles W. *A Little Fifer's War Diary.* Syracuse: C. W. Bardeen, Publisher, 1910.

Barziza, Decimus et Ultimus, *The Adventures of a Prisoner of War, 1863–1864.* Austin: University of Texas Press, 1964.

Barrett, John G., ed. *Yankee Rebel: The Civil War Journal of Edmund DeWitt Patterson.* Chapel Hill: University of North Carolina Press, 1966.

Barrett, O. S. *Reminiscences, Incidents, and Battles of the Old Fourth Michigan Infantry in the War of the Rebellion, 1861–1864.* Detroit: W. S. Ostler, 1888.

Bartlett, Asa W. *History of the Twelfth Regiment, New Hampshire Volunteers in the War of the Rebellion.* Concord, NH: Ira C. Evans, Printer, 1897.

Bassler, J. H. "The Color Episode of the One Hundred and Forty-ninth Regiment, Pennsylvania Volunteers." *Southern Historical Society Papers,* vol. 37, 272–300.

Bates, Samuel P. *History of Pennsylvania Volunteers, 1861–5.* Wilmington, NC: Broadfoot Publishing Co., 1993.

Baum, James H. "A Boy Soldier Tell the Story of Gettysburg." *The East Liverpool Morning Tribune,* July 9, 1910.

Bayles, Jonah. "On Cemetery Hill." *National Tribune,* September 1, 1910.

Bean, William G. *The Liberty Hall Volunteers.* Charlottesville: University of Virginia Press, 1964.

Beaudot, William J., and Lance J. Herdegen. *An Irishman in the Iron Brigade, The Civil War Memoirs of James P. Sullivan* . . . New York : Fordham University Press, 1993.

Becker, Carol M., and Ritchie Thomas, eds. *Hearth and Knapsack: The Ladley Letters, 1857–1880.* Athens: Ohio University Press, 1988.

Belo, A. H. "The Battle of Gettysburg." In *Confederate Veteran* (1900), vol. 8, 165–168.

Benedict, George G. *Vermont at Gettysburg, A Sketch Of The Part Taken By The Vermont Troops, In The Battle Of Gettysburgh.* Burlington, VT: Free Press Association, 1870.

Benedict, George G. *A Short History of the Fourteenth Regiment, Vermont Volunteers.* Bennington, VT: Co. F, 14th Vermont Regiment, 1887.

Benedict, George G. *Army Life In Virginia: Letters from the Twelfth Vermont Regiment and Personal Experiences of Volunteer Service in the War for the Union, 1862–63.* Burlington. VT: The Free Press Association, 1882.

Benedict, George G. *Vermont in the Civil War, A History of the Part taken by the Vermont Soldiers and Sailors in the War for the Union, 1861–5.* Burlington, VT: Free Press Association, 1886–1888.

Bennett, Brian A. *Sons of Old Monroe: A Regimental History of Patrick O'Rorke's 140th New York Volunteer.* Dayton, OH: Morningside House, Inc., 1992.

Bennett, Edward. "The Battle as Seen by a Member of the 44th N.Y." *National Tribune,* May 6, 1886.

Benton, Charles E. *As Seen From the Ranks.* New York: G.P. Putnam's Sons, 1902.

Berkeley, Henry R. *Four Years in the Confederate Artillery.* Richmond: Virginia Historical Society, 1991.

Berryman, H. W. "Company I, 1st Texas at Gettysburg." *New York Times,* July 3, 1913.

Bertholf, D. "The Twelfth Corps." *National Tribune,* May 11, 1893.

Best, Isaac O. *History of the 121st New York State Infantry.* Chicago: J. H. Smith, 1921.

Beyer, W. F., and O. F. Keydel. *Deeds of Valor.* Stamford, CT: Longmeadow Press, 1994.

Bicknell, George. *History of the Fifth Regiment, Maine Volunteers* . . . Portland, ME: H. L. Davis, 1871.

Bilby, Joseph G. *Three Rousing Cheers: A History of the Fifteenth New Jersey from Flemington to Appomattox.* Hightstown, NJ: Longstreet House, 1993.

Bilby, Joseph G. *Remember Fontenoy! The 69th New York Irish Brigade in the Civil War.* Hightstown, NJ: Longstreet House, 1995.

Bingham, Daniel. "From the 64th New York." *The Cattaraugus Freeman,* July 30, 1863.

Bird, W. H. *Stories of the Civil War, Company C, 13th Regiment of Alabama Volunteers.* Columbiana, AL: Advocate Printing, n.d.

Blake, Henry N. *Three Years in the Army of the Potomac.* Boston: Lee and Shepard, 1865.

Bloodgood, John D. *Personal Reminiscences of the War.* New York: Hunt and Eaton, 1893.

Blue, True. "From the 140th Interesting Particulars of the Late Fight." *Rochester Evening Express,* July 11, 1863.

Bohannon, Keith. "Wounded and Captured at Gettysburg." In *Military Images* (May–June 1988), 14.

Boies, Andrew J. *Record of the Thirty-third Massachusetts Volunteer Infantry, From August 1862 to August 1865.* Fitchburg, MA: Sentinel Printing Company, 1880.

Boland, E. T. "Beginning of the Battle of Gettysburg." *Confederate Veteran Magazine* (1906), vol. 14, 308–309.

Boone, Thomas. "History of Company F, First North Carolina Infantry." *The Index,* March 8, 1895.

Bowen, Edward R. "Collis' Zouaves—The 114th Pennsylvania Infantry at Gettysburg." *Philadelphia Weekly Times,* June 22, 1887.

Bowen, George A. "The Diary of Captain George A. Bowen, 12th New Jersey Volunteers." *The Valley Forge Journal* (June 1984), vol. 2.

Bowen, James L. *History of the Thirty-Seventh Regiment, Mass., Volunteers, in the Civil War of 1861–1865 . . .* Holyoke, MA: C. W. Bryan & Company, 1884.

Bradley, Thomas W., and Peter B. Ayars. "At Gettysburg." *National Tribune,* February 4, 1886.

Brainard, Mary G. *Campaigns of the One Hundred and Forty-Sixth Regiment, New York State Volunteers . . .* New York: G. P. Putnam's Sons, 1915.

Brewer, Abraham T. *History Sixty-first Pennsylvania Volunteers, 1861–1865, Under Authority the Regimental Association.* Pittsburgh, PA: Art Engraving & Printing Company, 1911.

Brewster, Charles. *When This Cruel War is Over: The Civil War Letters of Charles Harvey Brewster.* Amherst: University of Massachusetts Press, 1992.

Bright, R. A. "Pickett's Charge at Gettysburg." *Confederate Veteran Magazine* (1930), vol. 37, 263–266.

Bright, Robert A. "Pickett's Charge, The Story of It Told by a Member of his Staff." In *Southern Historical Society Papers* (1903), vol. 31, 228–236.

Britton Ann H., and Thomas Reed. *To My Beloved Wife and Boy at Home.* Madison, NJ: Fairleigh Dickinson University Press, 1997.

Brooks, Thomas W., and Michael D. Jones. *Lee's Foreign Legion: A History of the 10th Louisiana Infantry.* Gravenhurst, ONT: Watts Printing, 1995.

Brooks, U. R. *Stories of the Confederacy.* Columbia, SC: The State Company, 1912.

Brown, B. F. "Some Recollections of Gettysburg." In *Confederate Veteran* (1923), vol. 31, 53.

Brown, Edmund R. *History of the Twenty-Seventh Indiana Volunteer Infantry.* Monticello: n.p., 1899.

Brown, Henri L. *History of the 3d Regiment, Excelsior Brigade, 72d New York Volunteer Infantry, 1861–1865.* Jamestown, NY: Journal Print. Co., 1902.

Brown, Varina D. *A Colonel at Gettysburg and Spotsylvania.* Columbia, SC: The State Company, 1931.

Bruce, George A. *The Twentieth Regiment of Massachusetts Volunteer Infantry.* Cambridge, MA: Houghton-Mifflin & Company, 1906.

Bruner, Gary P. "Up Over Big Round Top: The Forgotten 47th Alabama." *Gettysburg Magazine* (January 2000), issue 22, 6–22.

Bryant, Edwin C. *History of the Third Regiment of Wisconsin Veteran Volunteer Infantry.* Madison, WI: Democrat Printing Company, 1891.

Busey, John W., and David G. Martin. *Regimental Strengths and Losses at Gettysburg.* Hightstown, NJ : Longstreet House, 1994.

Butts, John T., ed., *A Gallant Captain of the Civil War: From the Record of the Extraordinary Adventures of Friederich Otto Baron von Fritsch.* New York: F. Tennyson Neely, 1902.

Caines, H. H. "A Gettysburg Diary." *National Tribune,* December 23, 1909.

Caldwell, J. F. J. *The History of a Brigade of South Carolinians.* Marietta, GA: Continental Book Company, 1951.

Calef, J. "Gettysburg Notes: The Opening Gun." *Journal of the Military Service Institute of the U.S.* (1907), vol. 40, 40–58.

Campbell, Eric. "Remember Harper's Ferry": The Degradation, Humiliation and Redemption of Col. George L. Willards's Brigade. *Gettysburg Magazine* (July 1992), issue 7, 51–76.

Campbell, Eric. "Caldwell Clears the Wheatfield." *Gettysburg Magazine* (July 1990), issue 3, 27–50.

Carr, George K. *Memoirs of the 149th N.Y. Infantry.* Syracuse, NY: Author, 1891.

Carter, James T. "Flag of the Fifty-Third VA. Regiment." In *Confederate Veteran* (1902), vol. 10, 263.

Castleberry, W. A. "Thirteenth Alabama— Archer's Brigade." In *Confederate Veteran* (1911) vol. 19, 338.

Cate, John M. *If I Live to Come Home: The Civil War Letters of Sergeant John March Cate.* Pittsburgh, PA: Dorrance Publishers, 1995.

Causby, Thomas E. "Storming the Stone Fence at Gettysburg." In *Southern Historical Society Papers* (1901), vol. 29, 339–341.

Chapla, John D. *The Forty-Second Virginia Infantry.* Lynchburg, VA: H. E. Howard, Inc., 1983.

Chadwick, Bruce. *Brother Against Brother.* New York: Carol Publishing Group, 1997.

Chamberlin, Thomas. *History of the One Hundred and Fiftieth Regiment Pennsylvania Volunteers, Second Regiment, Bucktail Brigade.* Philadelphia: J. B. Lippincott Co., 1895.

Child, William A. *A History of the Fifth Regiment, New Hampshire Volunteers in the American Civil War.* Bristol, NH: R. W. Musgrove, Printer, 1893.

Chilton, F. B. *Unveiling and Dedication of Monument to Hood's Texas Brigade.* Houston: F. B. Chilton, 1911.

Christ, Elwood. *The Struggle For the Bliss Farm at Gettysburg, July 2nd and 3rd, 1863: "Over a Wide, Hot, Crimson Plain.* Baltimore: Butternut and Blue, 1993.

Clark, Almond E. "A Yankee at Gettysburg— The Stand Made by the Remnant of the 27th Connecticut." *National Tribune,* October 10, 1918.

Clark, George. *A Glance Backward or Some Events in the Past History of My Life.* Houston: n.p., 1914.

Clark, Walter, ed. *Histories of the Several Regiments and Battalions from North Carolina in the Great War, 1861-'65.* 5 vols. Raleigh: E. M. Uzzell, Printer, 1901.

Clay, James. "About the Death of General Garnett." *Confederate Veteran* (1905), vol. 14, 81.

Clayton, W. W. *History of Steuben County, New York . . .* Philadelphia: Lewis, Peck & Co., 1879.

Clements, George S. "The 25th Ohio at Gettysburg." *National Tribune,* August 6, 1891.

Clement, Maude C. *History of Pittsylvania County, VA.* Lynchburg, VA: n.p., 1929.

Coan, Elisha. "Round Top: A Shot From the 20th Maine Aimed at Comrade Fisher." *National Tribune,* June 4, 1885.

Cochran, Hon. L. L. "The Tenth Georgia Regiment at Gettysburg." *Atlanta Journal,* February 23, 1901.

Cockrell, Thomas D., and Michael B. Ballard, *A Mississippi Rebel in the Army of Northern Virginia.* Baton Rouge: Louisiana State University Press, 1995.

Coco, Gregory A. *Recollections of a Texas Colonel at Gettysburg.* Gettysburg, PA: Thomas Publications, 1990.

Coco, Gregory A., ed. *From Ball's Bluff to Gettysburg . . . And Beyond: The Civil War Letters of Private Roland E. Bowen, 15th Massachusetts Infantry 1861–1864.* Gettysburg: Thomas Publications, 1994.

Coddington, Edwin B. *The Gettysburg Campaign: A Study in Command.* New York: Charles Scribner's and Sons, 1968.

Coey, James. "Sketches and Echoes—Cutler's Brigade." *National Tribune,* July 15, 1915.

Cole, Jacob H. *Under Five Commanders.* Patterson, NJ: News Printing Company, 1906.

Colestock, W. W. "The 16th Mich. At Little Round Top." *National Tribune,* March 26, 1914.

Collins, George K. *Memories of the 149th Regiment, New York Volunteer Infantry.* Syracuse, NY: Author, 1891.

"Col. and Dr. R. W. Martin of Virginia." In *Confederate Veteran* (1897), vol. 5. 70.

Collier, Calvin L. *"They'll do to tie to!"—The Story of the Third Regiment Arkansas Infantry, C.S.A.* Little Rock, AR: Civil War Roundtable Associates, 1988.

Collins, George K. *Memories of the 149th Regiment, New York Volunteer Infantry.* Syracuse: Author, 1891.

Conklin, George W. "The Long March to Stevens Run: The 134th New York Volunteer Infantry at Gettysburg." *Gettysburg Magazine* (July 1999), issue 21, 45–56.

Conn, C. A. "Letters From Charles A. Conn." *Georgia Historical Quarterly* (1962), vol. 46, 169–195.

Conway, Catlett. "The Battle of Gettysburg." *Atlanta Journal,* December 7, 1901.

Cook, Benjamin F. *History of the Twelfth Massachusetts Volunteers (Webster Regiment).* Boston: Twelfth Regiment Association, 1882.

Cook, John "Personal Reminisces of Gettysburg." *Kansas MOLLUS,* 321–341.

Cook, Stephen G., and Charles E. Benton, eds. *The "Dutchess County Regiment" in the Civil War.* Danbury, CT: Danbury Medical Printing Company, 1907.

Cotton, Burwell, T. *The Cry is War, War, War: The Civil War Correspondence of Lts. Burwell Thomas Cotton and George Job Huntley . . .* Dayton, OH: Morningside House, 1994.

Cowan, Andrew. "When Cowan's Battery Withstood Pickett's Charge." *New York Herald,* July 2, 1911.

Cowtan, Charles W. *Services of the Tenth New York Volunteers (National Zouaves) in the War of the Rebellion.* New York: C. H. Ludwig, 1882.

Coxe, John. "The Battle of Gettysburg." In *Confederate Veteran* (1913), vol. 21, 433–436.

Craft, David. *One Hundred and Forty-First Regiment Pennsylvania Volunteers.* Towanda, PA: Reporter-Journal Printing Company, 1885.

Crews, Edward R. *Fourteenth Virginia Infantry.* Lynchburg. VA: H. E. Howard, 1995.

Curtis, Orson B. *History of the Twenty-fourth Michigan of the Iron Brigade.* Detroit, MI: Winn and Hammond, 1891.

Dalton, Cyndi. *Sixteenth Maine Regiment; The Blanket Brigade: The Soldier's Story of the 16th Maine Infantry in the War Between the States.* Union, ME: Union Pub. Co., 1995.

Davis, Archie K. *The Boy Colonel: The Life and Times of Henry King Burgwyn, Jr.* Chapel Hill: University of North Carolina Press, 1985.

Davis, Charles E. *Three Years in the Army: The Story of the Thirteenth Massachusetts Volunteers from July 16, 1861 to August 1, 1864.* Boston: Estes & Lownat, 1864.

Davis, Stephen. "The Death and Burials of General Richard Brooke Garnett." In *Gettysburg Magazine* (July 1991), issue 5, 107–116.

Davis, William C. *The Confederate General.* 6 vols. Harrisburg, PA: National Historical Society, 1991.

Dawes, Rufus R. *Service with the Sixth Wisconsin Volunteers.* Marietta, OH: E. R. Alderman & Sons, 1890.

Dawes, Rufus R. "Align on the Colors," *Milwaukee Sunday Telegraph,* April 27, 1890.

Dedication of the Monument to the Fourth New York Company, First Regiment, U.S. Sharpshooters. n.p.: n.d., 1889.

de Trobriand, P. Regis. *Four Years With the Army of the Potomac.* Boston: Ticknor and Company, 1889.

Desjardin, Thomas. *Stand Firm Ye Boys From Maine.* Gettysburg: Thomas Publications, 1995.

Dickelman, J. L. "Gen. Carroll's Gibraulter Brigade at Gettysburg." *National Tribune,* December 10, 1908.

Dickert, August. *History of Kershaw's Brigade.* Newberry, SC: Elbert H. Hull Company, 1899.

Dickson, Christopher C. "Col. Francis Voltaire Randall and the 13th Vermont Infantry." *Gettysburg Magazine* (July 1997), issue 17, 83–102.

Dickson, D. J. "At Culp's Hill—Gallant Fighting by the First Corps." *National Tribune,* March 15, 1915.

Divine, John E. *Eighth Virginia Infantry.* Lynchburg: H. E. Howard, Inc., 1983.

Dodge, Theodore A. "Left Wounded on the Field." *Putnam's Monthly Magazine* (1869), vol. 4, 17–326.

Doubleday, Abner. *Chancellorsville and Gettysburg.* New York: Charles Scribner's Sons, 1885.

Downey, James W. *A Lethal Tour of Duty: A History of the 142nd Pennsylvania Volunteer Infantry, 1862–1865.* M.A. Thesis, Indiana University of Pennsylvania, 1995.

Driver, Robert J. *Fifty-second Virginia Infantry.* Lynchburg, VA: H. E. Howard, Inc., 1986.

Duke, J. W. "Mississippians at Gettysburg," In *Confederate Veteran* (1906), vol. 14, 216.

Dunaway, W. F. *Reminiscences of a Rebel.* New York: Neale, 1913.

Dunkelman, Mark H., and Michael J. Winey. *The Hardtack Regiment: An Illustrated History of the 154th Regiment, New York State Infantry Volunteers.* East Brunswick, NJ: Fairleigh Dickinson University Press, 1981.

Dunkelman, Mark H., and Michael J. Winey. "The Hardtack Regiment in the Brickyard Fight." *Gettysburg Magazine* (January 1993), issue 8, 17–30.

Dunn, Craig L. *Iron Men, Iron Will.* Indianapolis: Guild Press, 1995.

Durkin, Joseph T. *John Dooley, Confederate Soldier, His War Journal.* Washington: Georgetown University Press, 1945.

Dyer, Frederick H. *A Compendium of the War of the Rebellion.* New York: Thomas Yoseloff, 1959.

Early, Jubal A. "Leading Confederates in the Battle of Gettysburg." In *Southern Historical Society Papers* (1877), vol. 4, 241–281.

Early, Jubal A. *Autobiographical Sketch and Narrative of the War Between the States.* Philadelphia: J. B. Lippincott Company, 1912.

Eddy, Richard. *History of the Sixthieth Regiment of New York State Volunteers.* Philadelphia: Author, 1864.

Ellis, Franklin, ed. *History of Cattaraugus County, New York.* Philadelphia: L. H. Everts, 1879.

Elmore, Thomas L. "Attack and Counterattack." *Gettysburg Magazine* (July 1991), issue 5, 128.

Elmore, Thomas L. "Courage Against the Trenches." *Gettysburg Magazine* (July 1992), issue 7, 83–96.

Elmore, Thomas L. "The Florida Brigade at Gettysburg." *Gettysburg Magazine.* (1996), issue 15, 45–59.

Evans, Clement A., ed. *Confederate Military History.* 12 vols. Atlanta, GA: Confederate Publishing Company, 1889.

Everson Guy R., and Edward W. Simpson, Jr. *Far, Far From Home.* New York: Oxford University Press, 1994.

Fairfield, George. "The Capture of the Railroad Cut." *National Tribune,* September 1, 1910.

Farinholt, B. L. "Battle of Gettysburg—Johnson's Island." In *Confederate Veteran* (1897), vol. 5, 467–470.

Farley, Porter. "Otis's Regiment at Gettysburg and the Wilderness." *Army and Navy Journal,* April 22, 1899.

Farley, Porter. "Reminiscences of Porter Farley, 140th New York Infantry." *Rochester Historical Society* (1944), vol. 22, 199–252.

Faust, Patricia, ed. *Historical Times Illustrated Encyclopedia of the Civil War.* New York: Harper Perennial, 1986.

Favill, J. *Diary of a Young Officer.* Chicago: R. R. Donnelly & Sons, 1909.

Felton, Silas. "The Iron Brigade Battery at Gettysburg." *Gettysburg Magazine* (July 1994), issue 11, 56–70.

Fields, Frank E. *Twenty-eighth Virginia Infantry.* Lynchburg: H. E. Howard, Inc., 1985.

Figg, Royall W. *Where Men Only Dare to Go!: Or the Story of a Boy Company by an Ex-Boy.* Richmond: Whittet and Shepperson, 1885.

Finley, George W. "The Bloody Angle." *Buffalo Evening News,* May 29, 1894.

Fisher, Joseph. "Round Top Again." *National Tribune,* April 16, 1885.

Fleming, Francis P. *Memoir of Capt. C. Seton Fleming of the Second Florida Infantry, CSA.* Jacksonville, FL: Times Union Publishing House, 1884.

Fleming, Francis P. "Francis P. Fleming in the War for Southern Independence." *The Florida Historical Quarterly* (1949), vol. 27, 143–155.

Fletcher, W. A. *Rebel Private, Front and Rear.* Austin: University of Texas Press, 1954.

Flynn, Frank. *The Fighting Ninth For Fifty Years and the Semi-centennial Celebration.* Ann Arbor, MI : University Microfilms, 1972.

Floyd, Frederick C. *History of the Fortieth (Mozart) Regiment, New York Volunteers . . .* Boston : F. H. Gilson Company, 1909.

Folsom, James M. *Heroes and Martyrs of Georgia . . .* Baltimore, MD: Butternut and Blue, 1995.

Foote, Frank. "Marching in Clover." *Philadelphia Weekly Times,* October 8, 1881.

Ford, Andrew E. *The Story of the Fifteenth Regiment, Massachusetts Volunteer Infantry in the Civil War.* Clinton, MA: Press of W. J. Coulter, 1898.

Fortin, Maurice S., ed. "Colonel Hilary A. Herbert's History of the Eighth Alabama Volunteer Regiment, CSA." *The Alabama Historical Quarterly* (1977), vol. 39, 5–321.

Frassanito, William. *Gettysburg—A Journey in Time.* New York: Scribners, 1975.

Frederick, Gilbert. *The Story of a Regiment— The Fifty-seventh New York Volunteer Infantry in the War of the Rebellion.* Chicago: C. H. Morgan Company, 1895.

Freeman, Douglas S. *R. E. Lee.* 4 vols. New York: Scribners, 1935.

Freeman, Douglas S. *Lee's Lieutenants.* 3 vols. New York: Charles Scribner's Sons, 1949–1951.

Fry, B. D. "Pettigrew's Charge at Gettysburg." *Southern Historical Society Papers* (1879), vol. 7, 91–93.

Fuhrman, Robert. "The 57th Pennsylvania Volunteer Infantry at Gettysburg." *Gettysburg Magazine* (July 1997), issue 17, 62–69.

Fuller, Charles A. *Personal Recollections of the War of 1861 . . . In the 61st New York Volunteer Infantry.* Sherburne, NY: News Job Printing House, 1906.

Fulton, W. F. *The War Reminiscences of William Frierson Fulton II, 5th Alabama Battalion, Archer's Brigade . . .* Gaithersville, MD: Butternut Press, 1986.

Gaff, Alan D. "Here Was Made Our Last and Hopeless Stand." *Gettysburg Magazine* (January 1990), issue 2, 25–32.

Gaff, Alan D. "The Kid." *Civil War Times Illustrated* (1998), vol. 37, number 4, 38–41.

Gallagher, Gary W. *Stephen Dodson Ramseur— Lee's Gallant General.* Chapel Hill: University of North Carolina Press, 1985.

Galway, Thomas F. *The Valiant Hours: Narrative of "Captain Brevet," An Irish-American in the Army of the Potomac.* Harrisburg, PA: Stackpole, 1961.

Gambone, A. M. *Hancock at Gettysburg . . . and Beyond.* Baltimore, MD: Butternut and Blue, 1997.

Gates, Theodore B. *The "Ulster Guard" (20th N.Y. State Militia) and the War of the Rebellion . . .* New York: B. H. Tyrrel, Printer, 1879.

Gerald, Judge G. B. "The Battle of Gettysburg." *Waco Daily-Times Herald,* July 3, 1913.

"Gen. E. M. Law at Gettysburg." In *Confederate Veteran* (1922), vol. 30, 49–50.

"General M.J. Bulger, A Hero." *New Orleans Picayune,* September 18, 1898.

"Gen'l O.O. Howard's Personal Reminiscences of the War of the Rebellion." *National Tribune,* November 20, 1884.

George, W. "Wheaton's Brigade." *National Tribune,* February 11, 1909.

Gerrish, Theordore. "The Twentieth Maine at Gettysburg." *Portland Advertiser,* March 13, 1882.

Gibney, John Michael. "A Shadow Passing." *Gettysburg Magazine* (January 1992), issue 6, 33–42.

Giles, Valerius C. *Rags and Hope: The Recollections of Val C. Giles . . .* New York: Coward-McCann, 1961.

Glover, Edwin A. *Bucktailed Wildcats: A Regiment of Civil War Volunteers.* New York: T. Yoseloff, 1960.

Goldsborough, William W. "With Lee at Gettysburg." In *Philadelphia Record,* July 8, 1900.

Goldsborough, William W. *The Maryland Line.* Port Washington, NY: Kennikat Press, 1972.

Gordon, John B. *Reminiscences of the Civil War.* New York: Charles Scribner's Sons, 1903.

Gottfried, Bradley M. Wright's Charge at Gettysburg: Piercing the Union Line or Inflated Glory?" *Gettysburg Magazine* (July 1997), issue 17, 70–82.

Gottfried, Bradley M. "Fisher's Brigade at Gettysburg: The Big Round Top Controversy." *Gettysburg Magazine* (July 1998), issue 19, 84–93.

Gottfried, Bradley M. "Mahone's Brigade: Insubordination or Miscommunication?" *Gettysburg Magazine* (January 1998), issue 18, 67–76.

Gottfried, Bradley M. *Stopping Pickett—The History of the Philadelphia Brigade.* Shippensburg, PA: White Mane Publishing Company, 1999.

Gottfried, Bradley M. "To Fail Twice: Brockenbrough's Brigade at Gettysburg." *Gettysburg Magazine* (July 2000), issue 23, 66–75.

Gottfried, Bradley M. "'Friendly Fire' at Gettysburg," *Gettysburg Magazine* (July 2002), issue 27, 78–84.

Gottfried, Bradley M. *Roads to Gettysburg,* Shippensburg, PA: White Mane Publishing Company, 2002.

Grace, C. D. "Rodes's Division at Gettysburg." In *Confederate Veteran* (1897), vol. 5, 614–615.

Graham, Ziba B. "On To Gettysburg." *Michigan MOLLUS,* vol. 1, 1–16.

Grant, George W. "The First Army Corps on the First Day at Gettysburg." *Minnesota MOLLUS,* vol. 5, 43–58.

Greenberg, Henry J. "Pickett's Charge: The Reason Why." *Gettysburg Magazine,* (July 1991), issue 5, 105–106.

Greene, George S. "The Breastworks at Culp's Hill." *Battles and Leaders of the Civil War,* vol. 3, 317.

Greene, A. Wilson. "From Chancellorsville to Cemetery Hill—O.O. Howard and Eleventh Corps Leadership." *The First Day at Gettysburg.* Kent, OH: Kent State University Press, 1992.

Gregory, G. Howard. *Thirty-eighth Virginia Infantry.* Lynchburg, VA: H. E. Howard, 1988.

Grimes, Bryan. *Extracts of Letters of Major-General Bryan Grimes.* Wilmington, NC: Broadfoot Publishing Company, 1986.

Gunn, Ralph W. *Twenty-fourth Virginia Infantry.* Lynchburg, VA: H. E. Howard, Inc., 1987.

Hackett, J. P. "The Fifth Corps at Gettysburg." *National Tribune,* July 29, 1915.

Hadden, R. Lee. "The Deadly Embrace." *Gettysburg Magazine* (July 1991), issue 5, 43–58.

Hagerty, Edward J. *Collis' Zouaves: The 114th Pennsylvania Volunteers in the Civil War.* Baton Rouge: Louisiana State University Press, 1997.

Haines, Alanson A. *History of the Fifteenth Regiment New Jersey Volunteers.* New York: Jenkins & Thomas, Printers, 1883.

Haines, William P. *History of the Men of Co. F, With Description of the Marches and Battles of the 12th New Jersey Volunteers.* Woodbury, NJ: Gloucester County Historical Society, 1983.

Hale, Laura V., and Stanley S. Phillips. *History of the Forty-Ninth Virginia Infantry, C.S.A.: "Extra Billy Smith's Boys."* Lanham, MD: S. S. Phillips, 1981.

Haley, John W. *The Rebel Yell & the Yankee Hurrah: The Civil War Journal of a Maine Volunteer.* Camden, ME: Down East Books, 1985.

Halsey, Don P., Jr., *A Sketch of the Life of Capt. Don P. Halsey of the Confederate States Army.* Richmond, VA: Wm Ellis Jones, 1904.

Haines, Douglas C. "A. P. Hill's Advance to Gettysburg." *Gettysburg Magazine* (July 1991), issue 5, 4–12.

Hall, Isaac. *History of the Ninety-Seventh Regiment New York Volunteers ("Conkling Rifles") in the War for the Union.* Utica, NY: L. C. Childs and Son, 1890.

Hamblen, Charles P. *Connecticut Yankees at Gettysburg.* Kent, OH: Kent State University Press, 1993.

Hancock, Almira R. *Reminiscences of Winfield Scott Hancock.* New York: Charles L. Webster & Company, 1887.

Hand, J. W. "Gettysburg—A Graphic Account of the Battle by a Eleventh Corps Captain." *National Tribune,* July 24, 1890.

Hanford, J. Harvey. "The Experiences of a Private of the 124th N.Y. in the Battle." *National Tribune,* September 24, 1885.

Hankins, Samuel W. *Simple Story of a Soldier.* Nashville: Confederate Veteran, n.d.

Hardin, M. D. *History of the Twelfth Regiment, Pennsylvania Reserve Volunteer Corps.* New York: Author, 1890.

Harries, William H. "The Iron Brigade in the First Day's Battle at Gettysburg." *Minnesota MOLLUS,* vol. 4, 335–350.

Harris, James S. *Historical Sketches: Seventh Regiment, North Carolina Troops.* Ann Arbor, MI: University Microfilms, 1972.

Harris, Lloyd G. "With the Iron Brigade Guard at Gettysburg." *Gettysburg Magazine* (July 1989), issue 1, 29–34.

Harrison, Kathleen R. "Our Principal Loss Was in this Place." *Gettysburg Magazine* (July 1989), issue 1, 45–69.

Harrison, Kathy G., and John W. Busey. *Nothing But Glory.* Gettysburg, PA: Thomas Publications, 1993.

Harrison, Walter. *Pickett's Men: A Fragment of War History.* New York: D. Van Nostrand, 1870.

Hartwig, Scott. "The Defense of McPherson's Ridge." *Gettysburg Magazine* (July 1989), issue 1, 15–24.

Hartwig, D. Scott. "The 11th Army Corps on July 1, 1863." *Gettysburg Magazine* (January 1990), issue 2, 33–50.

Haskell, Frank A. *The Battle of Gettysburg.* New York: P. F. Collier and Sons, 1910.

Hassler, Warren W. *Crisis at the Crossroads: The First Day at Gettysburg.* Tuskaloosa: University of Alabama Press, 1970.

Hassler, William W. "'Fighting Dick' Anderson." In *Civil War Times Illustrated* (1974), vol. 12, 4–10, 40–41.

Haynes, Martin A. *History of the Second New Hampshire Regiment: Its Camps, Marches, and Battles.* Manchester, NH: Charles F. Livingston, Printer, 1865.

Haynes, Martin A. *A History of the Second Regiment, New Hampshire Volunteer Infantry in the War of the Rebellion.* Lakeport. NH: n.p., 1896.

Hays, Gilbert A. *Under the Red Patch—The Story of the Sixty-Third Regiment, Pennsylvania Volunteers, 1861–1864.* Pittsburgh, PA: Sixty-Third Pennsylvania Volunteers Regimental Association, 1908.

Hazen, Samuel R. Fighting the Good Fight." *National Tribune,* September 13, 1894.

Henderson, William D. *Twelfth Virginia Infantry.* Lynchburg, VA: H. E. Howard, Inc., 1984.

Hennessy, John. *The First Battle of Manassas: An End to Innocence July 18–21, 1861.* Lynchburg, VA., H. E. Howard, Inc. 1989.

Hennessy, John. *Return to Bull Run: The Campaign and Battle of Second Manassas.* New York: Simon & Schuster, 1993.

Herdegen, Lance J. "The Lieutenant Who Arrested a General." *Gettysburg Magazine* (January 1991), issue 4, 25–32.

Herdegen Lance J., and William J. K. Beaudot. *In the Bloody Railroad Cut.* Dayton, OH: Morningside House, 1990.

Hess, Earl J. *Pickett's Charge—The Last Attack at Gettysburg.* Chapel Hill, NC: University of North Carolina Press, 2001.

Heth, Harry. *The Memoirs of Harry Heth.* Westport, CT: Greenwood Press, 1974.

Heth, Harry. "Letter from Major General Heth, of A.P. Hill's Corps, A.N.V. *Southern Historical Society Papers* (1877), vol. 4, 151–160.

Hicks, Lewis. "Memoirs." In *State Journal,* April 27, 1917.

Hinkley, Julian W. *A Narrative of Service With the Third Wisconsin Infantry.* Madison: Wisconsin History Commission, 1912.

History of the 121st Regiment Pennsylvania Volunteers, by the Survivors' Association: An Account From the Ranks. Philadelphia: Catholic Standard & Times, 1906.

History of the 134th Regiment, N.Y.S. Volunteers. Schenectady: J. J. Marlett, n.d..

History of the Fifty-seventh Regiment, Pennsylvania Veteran Volunteer Infantry, First Brigade, First Division, Third Corps, and Second Brigade, Third Division, Second Corps, Army of the Potomac. Kearny, NJ: Belle Grove, 1995.

Hitz, Louise W., ed. *The Letters of Frederick C. Winkler.* Privately printed, 1963.

Hofe, Michael W. *That There Be No Stain Upon My Stones: Lieutenant Colonel William L. Mcleod, 38th Georgia Regiment, 1842–1863.* Gettysburg, PA: Thomas Publications, 1995.

Hofmann, J. William. *Remarks on the Battle of Gettysburg: Operations On The Right Of The First Corps, Army Of The Potomac: First Day Of The Fight.* Philadelphia: A.W. Auner, Printer, 1880.

Hofmann, J. William. "Gettysburg Again." *National Tribune,* June 5, 1884.

Hofmann, J. William. "56th Pennsylvania Volunteers in the Gettysburg Campaign." *Philadelphia Weekly Times,* January 13, 1886.

Hoke, Jacob. *The Great Invasion.* New York: Thomas Yoseloff, 1959.

Holcombe, R. I. *History of the First Regiment Minnesota Volunteer Infantry, 1861-1864.* Gaithersburg, MD: VanSickle, 1987.

Holliday, Lamar. "The Second Maryland Again." *The Telegram,* May 19, 1903.

Holt, David. *A Mississippi Rebel in the Army of Northern Virginia: The Civil War Memoirs of Private David Holt.* Baton Rouge: Louisiana State University Press, 1995.

Houghton, Edwin B. *Campaigns of the Seventeenth Maine.* Portland, ME: Short and Loring, 1866.

Houghton, William R. *Two Boys in the Civil War and After.* Montgomery, AL: Paragon Press, 1912.

Houston, Thomas D. "Storming Cemetery Hill." *Philadelphia Weekly Times,* October 21, 1882.

Howard, Oliver O. *Autobiography of Oliver Otis Howard.* 2 vols. New York: Baker and Taylor Company, 1907.

Hudson, Travis. "Soldier Boys in Gray: A History of the 59th Georgia Infantry Regiment." *Atlanta Historical Society Journal,* (Spring 1979).

Hufham, J. D., Jr. "Gettysburg." *The Wake Forest Student* (1897), vol. 16, 452–454.

Hunton, Eppa. *Autobiography of Eppa Hunton.* Richmond, VA: William Byrd Press, 1933.

Hurst, Samuel H. *Journal of the Seventy-Third Ohio Volunteer Infantry.* Chillicothe, OH: n.p., 1866.

Hussey, George A. *History of the Ninth Regiment N.Y.S.M. (Eighty-third N.Y. Volunteers).* New York: J. S. Ogilvie, 1889.

Hutchinson, Gustavus. *A Narrative of the Formation and Services of the Eleventh Massachusetts Volunteers.* Boston: n.p., 1893.

Hutchinson, Nelson V. *History of the Seventh Massachusetts Volunteer Infantry in the War of the Rebellion* . . . Taunton, MA: Published by Authority of the Regimental Association, 1890.

Ilisevich, Robert, and Jonathan Helmrieich. *The Civil War Diaries of Seth Waid III.* Meadville, PA: Crawford County Historical Society, 1993.

Iobst, Robert W., and Louis H. Manarin. *The Bloody Sixth: The Sixth North Carolina Regiment, Confederate States of America.* Durham, NC: Christian Printing Company, 1965.

Imhof, John D. *Gettysburg, Day Two, A Study in Maps.* Baltimore, MD: Butternut and Blue, 1999.

Imholte, John Q. *The First Volunteers: History of the First Minnesota Volunteer Regiment, 1861-1865.* Minneapolis, MN: Ross & Haines, 1963.

Irby, Richard. *Historical Sketch of the Nottoway Grays* . . . Richmond, VA: J. W. Ferguson and Son, 1878.

Irvine, R. H. "Brig. Gen. Richard B. Garnett." In *Confederate Veteran* (1915), vol. 23, 391.

Jackson J. Letter. *Montgomery Daily Mail,* July 26, 1863.

Jackson, R. Stark. "Going Back Into the Union at Last." In *Civil War Times Illustrated* (January–February 1991), 12, 55–56.

Jacobs, Michael. *Notes on the Rebel Invasion of Maryland and Pennsylvania* . . . Philadelphia: J. B. Lippincott and Company, 1864.

"James Wentworth Wrote Diary of Civil War Days." *Perry News,* n.d.,

Johnston, David E. *Four Years a Soldier.* Princeton, WV: n.p., 1887.

Johnston, David E. *The Story of A Confederate Boy in the Civil War.* Portland, OR: Glass and Prudhomme Company, 1914.

Johnson, Ida L. "Over the Stone Wall at Gettysburg." In *Confederate Veteran* (1923), vol. 31, 248–249.

Johnston, John W. *The True Story of John Burns.* Philadelphia: William, Brown & Earle, 1916.

Jones, A. Sheridan. "Battle of Gettysburg." *National Tribune*, December 29, 1892.

Jones, Jesse H. "The Breastworks at Culp's Hill." *Battles and Leaders of the Civil War*, vol. 3, 316.

Jones, Paul. *The Irish Brigade*. Washington: R. B. Luce, 1969.

Jones, Terry L. *Lee's Tigers*. Baton Rouge: Louisiana State University Press, 1987.

Jordan, William C. *Incidents During the Civil War*. Montgomery, AL: The Paragon Press, 1909.

Jorgenson, Jay. "Anderson Attacks the Wheatfield," In *Gettysburg Magazine* (January 1996), issue 14, 64–76.

Jorgensen, Jay. "Holding the Right: The 137th New York Regiment at Gettysburg." *Gettysburg Magazine* (July 1996), issue 15, 60–67.

Jorgensen, Jay. "Wofford Sweeps the Wheatfield." *Gettysburg Magazine* (January 2000), issue 22, 28–41.

Judson, Amos M. *History of the Eighty-Third Regiment, Pennsylvania Volunteers*. Erie, PA: B. F. H. Lynn, 1865.

Keifer, William R. *History of the One Hundred and Fifty-Third Regiment Pennsylvania Volunteer Infantry*. Easton, PA: Press of the Chemical Publishing Company, 1909.

Keppler, Thomas. *History of the Three Months and Three Years' Service from April 16, 1861, to June, 1864, of the Fourth Regiment Ohio Volunteer Infantry in the War for the Union*. Cleveland, OH: Leader Printing Company, 1886.

Kershaw, J. B. "Kershaw's Brigade at Gettysburg." In *Battles and Leaders of the Civil War*, vol. 3, 331–338.

Kiefer, William R. *History of the One Hundred and Fifty-third Regiment Pennsylvania Volunteer Infantry*. Easton, PA: Press of the Chemical Publishing Company, 1909.

Kimball, George. "Iverson's Brigade." *National Tribune*, October 1, 1885.

Kimball, W. S. "The 13th Massachusetts at Gettysburg." *National Tribune*, May 14, 1885.

Knapp, Henry J. "Gettysburg by a Soldier in the Ranks." *Jefferson Gazette*, February 12, 1912.

Krick, Robert. K. *Fortieth Virginia Infantry*. Lynchburg, VA: H. E. Howard Company, 1985.

Krick, Robert K. "Failures of Brigade Leadership," In Gary W. Gallagher, ed., *The First Day at Gettysburg*. Kent, OH: Kent State University Press, 1992.

Krick, Robert K. "If Longstreet . . . Says So, It Is Most Likely Not True . . . " In Gary W. Gallagher, ed., *The Second Day at Gettysburg*. Kent, OH: Kent State University Press, 1993.

Krick, Robert K. "Three Confederate Disasters on Oak Ridge." In Gary Gallagher, ed., *The First Day at Gettysburg*. Canton, OH: Kent State University Press, 1992.

Krumwiede, John F. "A July Afternoon on McPherson's Ridge." *Gettysburg Magazine* (July 1999), issue 21, 21–44.

Ladd, David L. and Audrey J. *Bachelder Papers*. Dayton, OH: Morningside Press, 1994.

Lader, Paul J. "The 7th New Jersey in the Gettysburg Campaign." *Gettysburg Magazine* (January 1997), issue 16, 46–67.

Laine, Gary J., and Morris M. Penny. *Law's Brigade in the War Between the Union and the Confederacy*. Shippensburg, PA: White Mane Publishing Company, 1996.

Laney, Daniel M. "Wasted Gallantry: Hood's Texas Brigade at Gettysburg." *Gettysburg Magazine* (January 1997), issue 16, 27–45.

Lang, David. "Letter To General Edward Perry, 19 July 1863." *Southern Historical Society Papers* (1899), vol. 27, 195–196.

Lash, Gary. "The Philadelphia Brigade at Gettysburg." *The Gettysburg Magazine* (July 1992), issue 7, 97–113.

Law, Evander M. "The Struggle for Little Round Top." In *Battles and Leaders of the Civil War*, vol. 3, 318–330.

Lash, Gary G. "Brig. Gen. Henry Baxter's Brigade at Gettysburg, July 1." *Gettysburg Magazine* (January 1994), issue 10, 6–27.

Lash, Gary G. "The March of the 124th New York to Gettysburg." *Gettysburg Magazine* (July 1993), issue 9, 5–16.

Lash, Gary G. "'A Pathetic Story'—The 141st Pennsylvania (Graham's Brigade) at Gettysburg." *Gettysburg Magazine* (January 1996), issue 14, 77–101.

Lee, Alfred E. "Reminiscences of the Gettysburg Battle." *Lippincott's Magazine of Popular Literature and Science* (July 1883), 54–55.

Leeper, Joseph M. "Gettysburg—The Part of the Taken in the Battle by the Fifth Corps." *National Tribune,* April 30, 1885.

Leftwich, George J. "The Carreer [sic] of a Veteran." *The Aberdeen Examiner,* August 22, 1913.

"Letter From Captain Hillyer." *Southern Banner,* July 29, 1863.

Leon, Louis. *Diary of a Tar Heel.* Charlotte, NC: Stone Publishing Company, 1913.

Livermore, William. "Diary of William Livermore, Color Guard, 20th Maine." *Lincoln County News,* June 1883.

Lloyd, W. G. "Second Louisiana at Gettysburg." In *Confederate Veteran* (1898), vol. 6, 417.

Lochren, William. "The First Minnesota at Gettysburg." *Minnesota MOLLUS,* vol. 3, 41–56.

Locke, William H. *Story of the Regiment.* New York: James Miller, 1872.

Loehr, Charles T. *War History of the Old First Virginia Infantry Regiment, Army of Northern Virginia.* Richmond, VA: William Ellis Jones, Printer, 1884.

Loehr, Charles T. "Casualties in the Old First at Gettysburg." *Southern Historical Society Papers* (1890), vol. 17, 408.

Loehr, Charles T. "The Famous Pickett Charge." *Richmond Times-Dispatch,* October 16, 1904.

Lokey, J. W. "Wounded at Gettysburg," In *Confederate Veteran* (1914), vol. 22, 400.

Longacre, Edward. *To Gettysburg and Beyond: The Twelfth New Jersey Volunteer Infantry, II Corps, Army of the Potomac, 1862-1865.* Hightstown, NJ: Longstreet House, 1988.

Longstreet, James. *From Manassas to Appomattox.* Philadelphia: J. B. Lippincott, 1903.

Lord, Walter L., ed. *The Fremantle Diary.* New York: Little, Brown and Company, 1954.

Loring, William E. "Gettysburg." *National Tribune,* July 9, 1885.

Love, William A. "Mississippi at Gettysburg." In *Mississippi Historical Society* (1906), vol. 9, 25–51.

Lynn, J. R. "At Gettysburg—What the 29th Ohio Did During the Three Days' Fighting." *National Tribune,* October 7, 1897.

McCall, John T. "What the Tennesseans Did at Gettysburg." *The Louisville Journal,* 1902.

McClellan, Bailey G. *Civil War History of Company D, 10th Alabama Regiment.* Anniston Station, AL: n.p., 1901.

McDaid, William K. *Four Years of Arduous Service.* Ph.D. Dissertation, Michigan State U., 1987.

McDermott, Anthony W., and John E. Reilly, *A Brief History of the 69th Regiment, Pennsylvania Veteran Reserves.* Philadelphia: D. J. Gallagher & Company, 1889.

McFarland, Baxter. "Losses of the Eleventh Mississippi Regiment at Gettysburg." In *Confederate Veteran* (1923), vol. 31, 258–260.

McFarland, Baxter. "The Eleventh Mississippi at Gettysburg." In *Mississippi Historical Society* (1918), vol. 2, 549–568.

McKay, Charles W. "Three Years or During the War With the Crescent and Star." *National Tribune Scrap Book,* Washington, D.C., n.d.

McKim, Randolph. *The Second Maryland Infantry—An Oration Delivered . . . May 7, 1909.* n.p: n.p., 1909.

McKim, Randolph. *A Soldier's Recollections.* New York: Longmans Green, 1911.

McKim, Randolph. "Steuart's Brigade at the Battle of Gettysburg." In *Southern Historical Society Papers* (1878), vol. 5, 291–300.

McLaws, Lafayette. "Gettysburg." In *Southern Historical Society Papers* (1879), vol. 7, 64–90.

McLaws, Lafayette. "Federal Disaster on the Left." *Philadelphia Weekly Press,* August 4, 1886.

McLean, James L. *Cutler's Brigade at Gettysburg.* Baltimore, MD: Butternut and Blue, 1994.

McNeily, J. S. "Barksdale's Mississippi Brigade at Gettysburg." In *Publications of the Mississippi Historical Society* (1914), vol. 14, 231–265.

Macnamara, Daniel G. *The History of the Ninth Regiment, Massachusetts Volunteer Infantry,*

Second Brigade, First Division, Fifth Army Corps, Army of the Potomac, June, 1861–June, 1864. Boston: E. B. Stillings, 1899.

Mahood, Wayne. *Written in Blood.* Shippensburg, PA: White Mane Publishing Company, 1997.

Maine Gettysburg Commission. *Maine at Gettysburg; Report of the Maine Commissioners Prepared by the Executive Committee.* Portland, ME: The Lakeside Press, 1898.

Malone, Bartlett Y. *Whipt 'Em Everytime; The Diary Of Bartlett Yancey Malone.* Jackson, TN: McCowat-Mercer Press, 1960.

Manarin, Louis H. *North Carolina Troops, 1861–1865: A Roster.* 13 vols. Raleigh, NC: State Department of Archives and History, 1966.

Marbaker, Thomas B. *History of the Eleventh New Jersey Volunteers.* Hightstown, NJ: Longstreet House, 1990.

Marcus, Edward. *A New Canaan Private in the Civil War: Letters of Justus M. Sullivan, 17th Connecticut Volunteers.* New Canaan, CT: New Canaan Historical Society, 1984.

Mark, Penrose G. *Red: White: and Blue Badge . . . A History of the 93rd Regiment.* Harrisburg, PA: The Aughinbaugh Press, 1911.

Marsh, A. T. "North Carolina Troops at Gettysburg." In *Confederate Veteran* (1908), vol. 16, 516–517.

Martin, David G. *Carl Bornemann's Regiment: The Forty-first New York Infantry (DeKalb Regt.) in the Civil War.* Hightstown, NJ: Longstreet House, 1987.

Martin, David G. *Gettysburg—July 1.* Conshohocken, PA: Combined Books, 1996.

Martin, James M. *History of the Fifty-Seventh Regiment, Pennsylvania Veteran Volunteer Infantry.* Meadville, PA: McCoy and Calvin, 1904.

Martin, John H. "Accurate Historical Records," In *Confederate Veteran* (1904), vol. 12, 114.

Martin, Rawley W. "Armistead at the Battle of Gettysburg." In *Southern Historical Society Papers* (1914), vol. 39, 186–187.

Martin, Rawley W., and John H. Smith, "Battle of Gettysburg and Charge of Pickett's

Division." In *Southern Historical Society Papers* (1904), vol. 32, 183–195.

Marvin, Edwin E. *The Fifth Regiment, Connecticut Volunteers: A History Compiled from Diaries and Official Reports.* Hartford, CT: Wiley, Waterman & Eaton, 1899.

Matthews, Richard E. *The 149th Pennsylvania Volunteer Infantry Unit in the Civil War.* Jefferson, NC: McFarland & Company, 1994.

Mattocks, Charles. *Unspoiled Heart, The Journal of Charles Mattocks of the 17th Maine.* Knoxville, TN: University of Tennessee Press, 1994.

Maxwell, D. E. "Letters from a Florida Confederate," *Florida Historical Quarterly* (1958), vol. 36, 365.

May, W. H. "First Confederates to Enter Gettysburg," In *Confederate Veteran* (1897), vol. 5, 620.

Mayo, Joseph. "Pickett's Charge at Gettysburg." *Richmond Times-Dispatch*, May 6, 1906.

Meinhard, Robert W. "The First Minnesota at Gettysburg." *Gettyburg Magazine* (July 1991), issue 5, 79–88.

Melcher, Holman S. "The 20th Maine at Gettysburg." In *Battles and Leaders of the Civil War*, vol. 3, 314–315.

Meredith, Jaquelin M. "The First Day at Gettysburg." In *Southern Historical Society Papers* (1896), vol. 24, 184.

Michigan at Gettysburg, July 1st, 2d and 3rd, 1863 . . . Detroit, MI: Winn and Hammond, 1889.

Miers, Earl Schenck, and Richard A. Brown, eds. *Gettysburg.* New Brunswick, NJ: Rutgers University Press, 1948.

Miller, J. Michael. "Perrin's Brigade on July 1, 1863." *Gettysburg Magazine* (July 1995), Issue 13, 22–32.

Miller, William H. "They All Helped to Do It." *National Tribune,* October, 15, 1885.

Mills, George H. *History of the 16th North Carolina Regiment (originally 6th N.C. Regiment) in the Civil War.* Hamilton, NY: Edmonston Pub., 1992.

Minnigh, H. N. *History of Company K, 1st (Inft.) Penn'a Reserves.* Duncansville, PA: Home Print Publisher, 1891.

Moon, W. H. "Beginning the Battle at Gettysburg." In *Confederate Veteran* (1925), vol. 33, 449–450.

Moore, James H. "Heth's Division at Gettysburg." In *Southern Bivouac* (1885), vol. 3, 383–395.

Moran, Francis E. "About Gettysburg." In *National Tribune*, November 12, 1891.

Moran, Frank E. "A New View of Gettysburg." *Philadelphia Weekly Times*, April 22, 1882.

Moran, Frank E. "A Fire Zouave—Memoirs of a Member of the Excelsior Brigade." *National Tribune*, November 6, 1890.

Morhous, Henry C. *Reminiscences of the 123rd Regiment, New York State Volunteers.* Greenwich, NY: People's Journal Book and Job Office, 1879.

Morrow, Maud. *The University Greys: Company A, Eleventh Mississippi Regiment, Army of Northern Virginia, 1861–1865.* Richmond, VA: Garrett and Massie, Inc., 1940.

Morse, Charles F. *History of the Second Massachusetts Regiment of Infantry.* Boston: George H. Ellis, 1882.

Morse, F. W. *Personal Experiences in the War of the Rebellion, From December, 1862, to July, 1865.* Albany, NY: Munsell Printer, 1866.

Muffly, Joseph W., ed. *The Story of Our Regiment: A History of the 148th Pennsylvania Volunteers.* Des Moines, IA: Kenyon Printing and Manufacturing Company, 1904.

Mulholland, St. Clair A. *The Story of the 116th Pennsylvania Infantry.* Philadelphia: F. McManus Jr. & Company Printers, 1899.

Murphy Terrence V. *Tenth Virginia Infantry.* Lynchburg, VA: H. E. Howard, 1989.

Murphy, T. L. *Kelly's Heroes: The Irish Brigade at Gettysburg.* Gettysburg, PA: Farnsworth House Military Impressions, 1997.

Murray, Alton J. *South Georgia Rebels: The True Wartime Experiences Of The 26th Regiment, Georgia Volunteer Infantry, Lawton-Gordon-Evans Brigade, Confederate States Army, 1861–1865.* St. Marys, GA: Author, 1976.

Murray, R. L. *Redemption of the Harper's Ferry Cowards: The Story of the 111th and 126th New York State Volunteer Regiments at Gettysburg.* Wolcott, NY: n.p., 1994.

Musselman, Homer D. *Forty-seventh Virginia Infantry.* Lynchburg, VA: H. E. Howard, Company, 1991.

New York Monuments Commission for the Battlefields of Gettysburg and Chattanooga—Final Report on the Battlefield of Gettysburg. 3 vols. Albany, NY: J. B. Lyon Company, Printers, 1900.

Nichols, G. W. *A Soldier's Story Of His Regiment (61st Georgia): And Incidentally Of The Lawton-Gordon-Evans Brigade, Army Northern Virginia.* Jesup, GA: n.p., 1898.

Nash, Eugene A. *A History of the 44th New York Volunteer Infantry.* Chicago: R. R. Donnelley & Sons Company, 1911.

National Tribune Scrap Book; Stories of the Camp, March, Battle, Hospital and Prison Told by Comrades. Washington, DC: The National Tribune, 1909.

Nelson, Alanson H. *The Battles of Chancellorsville and Gettysburg.* Minneapolis: Author, 1899.

Nesbitt, Mark. *35 Days to Gettysburg.* Harrisburg, PA: Stackpole Books, 1992.

Nevins James H., and William B. Styple. *What Death More Glorious.* Kearney, NJ: Belle Grove Publishing Company, 1997.

Newell, Joseph. *"Ours" Annals of the Tenth Regiment Massachusetts Volunteers.* Springfield: C. A. Nichols & Co., 1875.

Nichols, G. W. *A Soldier's Story of His Regiment (61st Georgia).* Jessup, GA: n.p., 1898.

19th Inf Regt.Reunions of the Nineteenth Maine Regiment Association. Augusta, ME: Sprague, Owen & Nash, 1878.

Nolan, Allen T. *The Iron Brigade.* New York: Macmillan Company, 1961.

Norris, S. R. "Ohio at Gettysburg." *National Tribune,* June 9, 1887.

Norton, Oliver, W. *Attack and Defense of Little Round Top, Gettysburg, July 2, 1863.* New York: Neale Publishing Company, 1913.

Oates, William C. "Gettysburg—The Battle on the Right." In *Southern Historical Society Papers* (1878), vol. 6, 72–182.

Oates, William C. *The War Between the Union and Confederacy and its Lost Opportunites.* New York: Neale Publishing Co., 1905.

O'Brien, Kevin E. "Valley of the Shadow of Death." *Gettysburg Magazine* (July 1992) issue 7, 41–50.

O'Brien, Kevin E. "A Perfect Roar of Musketry: Candy's Brigade in the Fight for Culp's Hill." *Gettysburg Magazine* (July 1993), issue 9, 81–97.

O'Brien, Kevin E. "To Unflinchingly Face Danger and Death: Carr's Brigade Defends Emmitsburg Road." *Gettysburg Magazine* (January 1995), issue 12, 7–23.

O'Brien, Kevin E. "'Give Them Another Volley, Boys': Biddle's Brigade Defends the Union Left on July 1, 1863." *Gettysburg Magazine* (July 1998), issue 19, 37–52.

O'Brien, Kevin E. "'Hold Them with the Bayonet': de Trobriand's Brigade Defends the Wheatfield." *Gettysburg Magazine* (July 1999), issue 21, 74–87.

O'Brien, Kevin E. "'Bullets Came as Thick as Hail': Krzyzanoswki's Brigade Defends the Union Right on July 1, 1863. *Gettysburg Magazine* (January 2001), issue 24, 56–75.

O'Flaherty, Patrick. *History of the 69th Regiment in the Irish Brigade, 1861–1865.* New York: n.p., 1986.

Olds, Fred A. "A Brave Carolinian Who Fell at Gettysburg." In *Southern Historical Society Papers* (1908), vol. 36, 245–247.

Osborn, Hartwell. *Trials and Triumphs: The Record of the Fifty-fifth Ohio Volunteer Infantry.* Chicago: A. C. McClurg, 1904.

Osborn, S. A. "The Battle of Gettysburg as I Remember It. " *Shenango Valley News* (Greenville, PA), April 2, 1915.

Osborne, Seward R. *Holding the Left at Gettysburg: The 20th New York State Militia on July 1, 1863.* Hightstown, NJ: Longstreet House, 1990.

O'Sullivan, Richard. *Fifty-Fifth Virginia Infantry.* Lynchburg, VA: H. E. Howard Company, 1989.

Owen, William M. *In Camp and Battle with the Washington Artillery of New Orleans.* Boston: Ticknor and Company, 1885.

Page, Charles D. *History of the Fourteenth Regiment, Connecticut Volunteer Infantry.* Meriden, CT: The Horton Printing Co., 1906.

Palmer, Edwin F. *The Second Brigade or Camp Life.* Montpelier, VT: Printed by E. P. Walton, 1864.

Park, Robert E. "War Diary of Captain Robert Emory Park, Twelfth Alabama Regiment, January 28, 1863–January 27, 1864." In *Southern Historical Society Papers* (1898), vol. 26, 1–31.

Parker, Francis J. *The Story of the Thirty-Second Massachusetts Infantry.* Boston: C.W. Calkins & Company, 1880.

Parker, John L. *Henry Wilson's Regiment: History of the Twenty-second Regiment, Massachusetts Infantry.* Boston: Press of Rand Avery Company, 1887.

Parker John L., and Robert G. Carter, *Henry Wilson's Regiment—History of the 22nd Massachusetts Infantry . . .* Boston: Press of Rand Avery Company, 1887.

Parkhurst, B. E. "At Gettysburg—Heroism of the 147th New York." *National Tribune,* January 1, 1888.

Parsons, H. C. "Farnsworth's Charge and Death." In *Battles and Leaders of the Civil War,* vol. 3, 393–396.

Pattison, Everett W. "Some Reminiscences of Army Life." *Massachusetts MOLLUS,* 262–263.

Paul, William. "Severe Experiences at Gettysburg." In *Confederate Veteran* (1912), vol. 19, 85.

Peck, Henry T. *Historical sketch of the 118th Regiment Pennsylvania Volunteers.* n.p., n.p., 1884.

Pendleton, Constance. *Confederate Memoirs.* Bryn Athyn, PA: n.p., 1958.

Pennsylvania Battlefield Commission. *Pennsylvania at Gettysburg. Ceremonies at the Dedication of the Monuments . . .* Harrisburg, PA: Stanley Ray, State Printer, 1904.

Perrin, Abner. "A Little More Light on Gettysburg." *Mississippi Valley Historical Review* (1938), vol. 24, 519–525.

Perry, William F. "The Devil's Den." In *Confederate Veteran* (1901), vol. 9, 161–163.

Peters, Winfield. "A Maryland Warrior and Hero." In *Southern Historical Society Papers* (1901), vol. 29, 248.

Peters, Winfield. "The Lost Sword of General Richard B. Garnett, Who Fell at Gettysburg." *The Baltimore Sun,* November 4, 1905.

Pettit, Ira S. *Diary of a Dead Man.* New York: Eastern Acorn Press, 1976.

Pfanz, Donald C. *Richard S. Ewell—A Soldier's Life.* Chapel Hill: University of North Carolina Press, 1998.

Pfanz, Harry W. *Gettysburg—The Second Day.* Chapel Hill: University of North Carolina Press, 1987.

Pfanz, Harry W. *Gettysburg-Culp's Hill and Cemetery Hill.* Chapel Hill: University of North Carolina Press, 1993.

Pfanz, Harry W. "'Old Jack' is Not Here." In Gabor S. Boritt, ed., *The Gettysburg Nobody Knows.* Oxford: Oxford University Press, 1997.

Pfanz, Harry W. *Gettysburg—The First Day.* Chapel Hill, NC: University of North Carolina Press, 2001.

Phillips Marion G., and Valerie P. Parsegian, *Richard and Rhoda—Letters From the Civil War.* Washington: Legation Press, 1981.

Pierce, J. V. "Gettysburg—Last Words as to What Regiment Opened the Battle." *National Tribune,* April 3, 1884.

Plummer, John W. Letter. *The Star Atlas (Minneapolis),* August 26, 1863.

Poindexter, James E. "General Armistead's Portrait Presented." In *Southern Historical Society Papers* (1909), vol. 37, 146.

Polley, Joseph B. *Hood's Texas Brigade.* New York: Neale Publishing Company, 1910.

Poriss, Gerry H., and Ralph G. Porris. *While My Country is in Danger: The Life and Letters of Lieutenant Colonel Richard S. Thompson.* Hamilton, NY: Edmonston Pub., 1994.

Porter, John T. *Under the Maltese Cross . . . Campaigns of the 155th Pennsylvania Regiment.* Pittsburg, PA: 155th Regimental Association, 1910.

Potter, T. S. "The Battle of Gettysburg." *National Tribune,* August 5, 1882.

Powell, R. M. "With Hood at Gettysburg." *Philadelphia Weekly Times,* December 13, 1884.

Powell, William H. *The Fifth Army Corps . . .* New York: G. P. Putnam's Sons, 1896.

Powelson, Benjamin F. *History of Company K of the 140th Regiment Pennsylvania Volunteers, 1862–1865.* Ann Arbor, MI: University Microfilms, 1970.

Priest, John Michael. *Into the Fight—Pickett's Charge at Gettysburg.* Shippensburg,

PA: White Mane Publishing Company, 1998.

Pryor, S. G. *A Post of Honor: The Pryor Letters . . .* Fort Valley, GA: Garret Publications, 1989.

Pula, James S. *For Liberty and Justice—The Life and Times of Wladimir Krzyzanowski.* Chicago: Polish American Congress Charitable Foundation, 1978.

Pula, James S. *The Sigel Regiment: A History of the Twenty-sixth Wisconsin Volunteer Infantry, 1862–1865.* Campbell, CA: Savas, 1998.

Pullen, John J. "Effects of Marksmanship—A Lesson From Gettysburg." *Gettysburg Magazine* (January 1990), issue 2, 55–60.

Pullen, John J. *The Twentieth Maine: A Volunteer Regiment in the Civil War.* Philadelphia: Lippincott, 1957.

Purcell, Hugh D. "The Nineteenth Massachusetts Regiment at Gettysburg." *Essex Institute Historical Collections* (October 1963), 277–288.

Purman, J. J. "General Zook at Gettysburg." *National Tribune,* March 25, 1909.

Quint, Alonzo H. *The Record of the Second Massachusetts Infantry, 1861–1865.* Boston: James P. Walker, 1867.

Rankin, Thomas. *Twenty-Third Virginia.* Lynchburg, VA: H. E. Howard, Inc., 1985.

Rankin, Thomas. *Thirty-Seventh Virginia Infantry.* Lynchburg, VA: H. E. Howard, Inc., 1987.

Rauscher, Frank. *Music on the March: 1861-'65 with the Army of the Potomac, 114th Regiment P.V., Collis' Zouaves.* Philadelphia: Fell, 1892.

Rawlings, Watha. *War Stories, Being the Thrilling Experiences and Adventures of Captain Watha Rawlings During the War of 1861–1865.* McCauley, TX: n.p., 1909.

Reidenbaugh, Lowell. *Twenty-Seventh Virginia Infantry.* Lynchburg, VA: H. E. Howard, Inc., 1993.

Renfroe, J. J. *South Western Baptist,* August 13, 1863.

"Report of Colonel Edward Willis, Twelfth Georgia Infantry, Doles' Brigade." In *Southern Historical Society Papers* (1889), vol. 17, 184–185.

Report of the Joint Committee to Mark the Positions Occupied by the 1st and 2nd Delaware at the Battle of Gettysburg. Dover, DE: n.p., 1887.

Report of the State of Maryland Gettysburg Monument Commission. Baltimore, MD: William K. Boyle and Son, 1891.

Re-union of the 28th & 147th Regiments, Pennsylvania Volunteers, Philadelphia, Nov. 24th, 1871. Philadelphia: Pawson & Nicholson, 1872.

Rhodes, John H. *The History of Battery B, First Regiment, Rhode Island Artillery.* Providence: RI: Snow and Farnham, Printers, 1914.

Rice, Edmund. "Repelling Lee's Last Blow at Gettysburg." *Battles and Leaders of the Civil War,* vol. 3, 387–390.

Riley, Franklin L. *Grandfather's Journal . . .* Dayton, OH: Morningside, 1988.

Riggs, David F. *Seventh Virginia Infantry.* Lynchburg, VA: H. E. Howard, Inc., 1982.

Robertson, James, I. *The Fourth Virginia Infantry.* Lynchburg, VA: H. E. Howard, Inc., 1982.

Robertson, James I. *Eighteenth Virginia Infantry.* Lynchburg, VA: H. E. Howard, Inc., 1984.

Robbins, Richard. "The Regular Troops at Gettysburg." *Philadelphia Weekly Times,* January 4, 1879.

Roe, Alfred S. *The Tenth Regiment, Massachusetts Volunteer Infantry, 1861–1864 . . .* Springfield, MA: Tenth Regiment Veteran Association, 1909.

Rollins, C. A. "Jackson's Foot Cavalry Reach the Gettysburg Battlefield." *The Lexington Gazette and Citizen,* August 16, 1888.

Rollins, C. A. "Playing Cavalry." *The Lexington Gazette and Citizen,* September 27, 1888.

Rollins, C. A. "A Private's Story." *The Lexington Gazette and Citizen,* July 26, 1888.

Rollins, Richard. "The Ruling Ideas of the Pennsylvania Campaign: James Longstreet's 1873 Letter to Lafayette McLaws." *Gettysburg Magazine* (July 1997), issue 17, 7–16.

Rollins, Richard, ed. *Pickett's Charge—Eyewitness Accounts.* Redondo Beach, CA: Rank and File Publications, 1994.

Rosenblatt, Emil and Ruth. *Hard Marching Every Day.* Lawrence: University Press of Kansas, 1992.

Ryder, John J. *Reminiscences of Three Years' Service In The Civil War By A Cape Cod Boy.* New Bedford, MA: Reynolds Printing, 1928.

"St. Louisans Among Gettysburg Heroes." *St. Louis Globe-Democrat,* March 9, 1913.

Sale, J. Irving. "Gettysburg." *Philadelphia Press,* July 4, 1887.

Sanderson, W. H. "Sykes's Regulars." *National Tribune,* April 2, 1891.

Sauers, Richard A. *Advance the Colors!* Volume 1. Harrisburg, PA: Capitol Preservation Committee, 1987.

Sauers, Richard A. "The 53rd Pennsylvania Volunteer Infantry in the Gettysburg Campaign." *Gettysburg Magazine* (July 1994), issue 11, 80–90.

Sauers, Richard A. "The Sixteenth Maine Volunteer Infantry at Gettysburg." *Gettysburg Magazine* (July 1995), issue 13, 33–42.

Sauers, Richard A. *Fighting Them Over—How the Veterans Remembered Gettysburg in the Pages of the National Tribune.* Baltimore, MD: Butternut and Blue, 1998.

Sawyer, Franklin. *A Military History of the 8th Regiment, Ohio Volunteers Infantry: Its Battles, Marches, and Army Movements.* Cleveland, OH: Leader Printing Company, 1881.

Schoyer, William T. *The Road to Cold Harbor.* Pittsburgh, PA: Closson Press, 1986.

Schurz, Carl. "The Battle of Gettysburg." *McClure's Magazine* (July 1907), vol. 29, 272–285.

Scott, George H. "Vermont at Gettysburg." In *Proceedings of the Vermont Historical Society* (1930), vol. 1, 51–74.

Searles, J. N. "The First Minnesota Volunteer Infantry." *Minnesota MOLLUS,* vol. 2, 80–113.

Sears, Stephen. *Landscape Turned Red: The Battle of Antietam.* New York: Ticknor & Fields, 1983.

Sears, Stephen. *To the Gates of Richmond: The Peninsula Campaign.* New York: Ticknor & Fields, 1992.

Sears, Stephen. *Chancellorsville.* New York: Houghton-Mifflin Company, 1996.

Se Cheverell, John Hamilton. *Journal History of the Twenty-Ninth Ohio Veteran Volunteers, 1861–1865.* Cleveland, OH: n.p., 1883.

"17th Conn. Vols." *Gettysburg Complier,* September 29, 1894.

Seville, William P. *History of the First Regiment, Delaware Volunteers, From the Commencement of the "Three Months' Service" to the Final Muster-Out at the Close of the Rebellion.* Baltimore, MD: Gateway Press, 1986.

Shaler's Brigade—Survivors of the Sixth Corps: Reunion and Monument Dedications, at Gettysburg, June 12th, 13th and 14th, 1888 . . . Philadelphia: Published by Order the Brigade Association, 1888.

Shane, John H. "Getting into the Fight at Gettysburg." *National Tribune,* November 27, 1924.

Shevchuk, Paul M. "The 1st Texas Infantry and the Repulse of Farnsworth's Charge." *Gettysburg Magazine* (January 1990), issue 2, 81–90.

Sheldon, Winthrop D. *The "Twenty-Seventh," A Regimental History.* New Haven, CT: Morris & Benham, 1866.

Sherry, Jeffrey F. "The Terrible Impetuosity: The Pennsylvania Reserves at Gettysburg." *Gettysburg Magazine* (July 1997), issue 16, 68–80.

Shotwell, Randolph A. "Virginia and North Carolina in the Battle of Gettysburg." In *Our Living and Our Dead* (1876), vol. 4, 80–97.

Shotwell, Randolph. *The Shotwell Papers.* 2 vols. Raleigh: North Carolina Historical Commission, 1929–1931.

Shumate, W. T. "With Kershaw at Gettysburg." *Philadelphia Weekly Times.* May 6, 1882

Sifakis, Stewart. *Who Was Who in the Civil War.* New York: Facts on File, 1987.

Sifakis, Stewart. *Compendium of the Confederate Armies.* 10 vols. New York: Facts on File, 1992–1995.

Simmers, William. *The Volunteer's Manual: Or, Ten Months With The 153d Penna. Volunteers . . .* Easton, PA: D. H. Neiman, Printer, 1863.

Simons, Ezra D. *A Regimental History: The One Hundred and Twenty-fifth New York State Volunteers.* New York: E. D. Simons, 1888.

Small, A. R. *The Sixteenth Maine Regiment in the War of the Rebellion 1861–1865.* Portland, ME: Thurston & Co., 1886.

Small, Harold A. *The Road to Richmond—The Civil War Memoirs of Major Abner R. Small of the 16th Maine.* Berkley: University of California Press, 1959.

Smith, A. P. *The Seventh-Sixth Regiment, New York Volunteers.* Cortland, NY: Truair, Smith and Miles, Printers 1867.

Smith, Donald L. *The Twenty-Fourth Michigan of the Iron Brigade.* Harrisburg, PA: The Stackpole Company, 1962.

Smith, Gerald J. *One of the Most Daring of Men.* Murfreesboro, TN: Southern Heritage Press, 1997.

Smith, James E. *A Famous Battery and Its Campaigns, 1861–1864.* Washington: W. H. Lowdermilk and Co., 1892.

Smith, Jacob. *Camps and Campaigns of the 107th Regiment Ohio Volunteer Infantry.* n.p., n.d.

Smith, John. "Account." In *Southern Historical Society Papers* (1904), vol. 32, 193.

Smith, John D. *The History of the Nineteenth Regiment of Maine Volunteer Infantry, 1862–1865.* Minneapolis, MN: Great Western Printing Company, 1909.

Smith, John L. *History of the 118th Pennsylvania Volunteers, Corn Exchange Regiment.* Philadelphia: J. L. Smith, Publisher, 1909.

Smith, L. A. "Recollections of Gettysburg." *Michigan MOLLUS,* vol. 2, 295–308.

Smith, R. Penn. "The Battle of Gettysburg— The Part Taken by the Philadelphia Brigade in the Battle." *Gettysburg Compiler,* June 7, 1887.

Smith, Robert G. *A Brief Account of the Services Rendered by the Second Regiment Delaware Volunteers in the War of the Rebellion.* Wilmington, DE: Historical Society of Delaware, 1909.

Smith, W. A. *The Anson Guards, Company C, Fourteenth Regiment, North Carolina Volunteers, 1861–1865.* Charlotte, NC: Stone Publishing Company, 1914.

Southard, Edwin. "The 119th N.Y. at Gettysburg." *National Tribune,* August 19, 1897.

Spear, Ellis. *The Civil War Recollections of General Ellis Spear.* Orono, ME: University of Maine Press, 1997.

Stackpole, Edward J. *Drama on the Rappahannock: The Fredericksburg Campaign.* Harrisburg, PA: Stackpole Publishing Company, 1957.

Stearns, Austin C. *Three Years with Company K.* Cranbury. NJ: Fairleigh Dickinson University Press, 1976.

Stevens, Charles A. *Berdan's Sharpshooters in the Army of the Potomac.* St. Paul, MN: Price-McGill Company, 1892.

Stevens, Jno. W. *Reminiscences of the Civil War.* Hillsboro, TX: Hillsboro Mirror Print, 1902.

Stewart, George R. *Pickett's Charge—A Microhistory of the Final Attack at Gettysburg, July 3, 1863.* Boston: Houghton Mifflin, 1959.

Stevens, George T. *Three Years in the Sixth Corps* . . . Albany: S. R. Gray, 1866.

Stevens, H. S. *Souvenir of the Excursion to the Battlefield by the Society of the 14th Connecticut Regiment.* Washington: Gibson Brothers, 1893.

Stewart, James. "Battery B, Fourth United States Artillery at Gettysburg." *Ohio MOLLUS*, vol. 4, 179–193.

Stewart, Robert L. *History of the One Hundred and Fortieth Regiment, Pennsylvania Volunteers.* n.p.: Regimental Association, 1912.

Stewart, William H. *A Pair of Blankets: War-Time History in Letters to the Young People of the South.* Wilmington, NC: Broadfoot, 1990.

Stiles, Robert. *Four Years Under Marse Robert.* New York: Neale Publishing Company, 1903.

Storch, Marc and Beth. "What a Deadly Trap We Were In." *Gettysburg Magazine* (January 1992), issue 6, 13–28.

Storch, Marc and Beth. "Unpublished Gettysburg Reports by the 2nd and 7th Wisconsin Infantry Regimental Officers." *Gettysburg Magazine* (July 1997), Issue 17, 20–25.

Storrs, John. *The Twentieth Connecticut.* Ansonia, CT: Press of the Naugatuck Valley Sentinel, 1886.

Sturtevant, Ralph O. *Pictorial History of the Thirteenth Vermont Volunteers in the War of 1861–1865.* Burlington, VT: Regimental Association, 1910.

Styple, William B. *Our Noble Blood.* Kearny, NJ: Belle Grove Publishing Co., 1997.

Sullivan, James P. "The Iron Brigade at Gettysburg." *Milwaukee Sunday Telegraph,* December 20, 1984.

Sullivan, James P. "Gettysburg: A Member of the 6th Wis. Takes Issue with Carleton." *National Tribune,* May 14, 1885.

Sullivan, James P. "The Sixth Wis. At Gettysburg." *Milwaukee Sunday Telegraph,* June 21, 1885.

Supplement to the Official Records of the Union and Confederate Armies. Wilmington, NC : Broadfoot Publishing Company, 1994.

Survivors of the Seventy-second Regiment of Pennsylvania Volunteers, Plaintiffs. Vs. Gettysburg Battlefield Memorial Association . . . in Supreme Court of Pennsylvania, Middle District, May Term, 1891.

Swallow, William. "The Third Day at Gettysburg." In *Southern Bivouac* (1886), vol. 4, 562–572.

Swanberg, W. A. *Sickles The Incredible.* New York: Charles Scribner's Sons, 1956.

Sweetland, A. F. "Repulsing the 'Tigers' at the Cemetery." *National Tribune,* October 21, 1909.

Sweetland, A. F. "Sketches and Echoes—First Day at Gettysburg." *National Tribune,* November 2, 1916.

Sword, Wiley. "Defending the Codori House and Cemetery Ridge: Two Swords with Harrow's Brigade in the Gettysburg Campaign." *Gettysburg Magazine* (July 1995), Issue 13, 43–49.

Sword, Wiley. *Sharpshooter: Hiram Berdan, His Famous Sharpshooters and Their Sharps Rifle.* Lincoln, RI : Andrew Mowbray Inc., 1988.

Sypher, J. R. *History of the Pennsylvania Reserve Corps* . . . Lancaster, PA: Published by E. Barr & Co., 1865.

Tagg, Larry. *The Generals of Gettysburg.* Mason City, IA: Savas Publishing Company, 1998.

Taylor, Michael W. "North Carolina in the Pickett-Pettigrew-Trimble Charge at Gettysburg." *Gettysburg Magazine* (January 1993), issue 8, 67–94.

Taylor, Michael W. "Ramseur's Brigade in the Gettysburg Campaign: A Newly Discovered Account by Captain James I. Harris, Col. I, 30th Regt. N.C.T." *Gettysburg Magazine* (July 1997), issue 17, 26–40.

"Terrific Fight of Third Day." *The Scranton Truth,* July 3, 1913.

Tevis, C. V. *The History of the Fighting Fourteenth . . .* Brooklyn, NY: Brooklyn Eagle Press, 1911.

"The Battle of Gettysburg." *The Galveston Daily News,* June 21, 1896.

"The Left at Gettysburg by Gen. Ellis Spear." *National Tribune,* June 12, 1913.

Thomas, Dean S. *Ready . . . Aim . . . Fire! Small Arms Ammunition in the Battle of Gettysburg.* Biglersville, PA: Thomas Publishing, 1981.

Thomas, George. "The Confederate Monument at Gettysburg." In *Southern Historical Society Papers* (1886), vol. 14, 439–446.

Thomas, Henry W. *History of the Doles-Cook Brigade, Army of Northern Virginia.* Atlanta, GA: Franklin Publishing Co., 1903.

Thomas, Howard. *Boys in Blue From the Adirondack Foothills.* Prospect, NY: Prospect Books, 1960.

Todd, George T. "Recollections of Gettysburg." In *Confederate Veteran* (1900), vol. 8, 240.

Thompkins, Daniel A. *Company K, Fourteenth South Carolina Volunteers.* Charlotte, NC: Observer Printing and Publishing Company, 1897.

Thomson, Orville. *Narrative Of The Service Of The Seventh Indiana Infantry In The War For The Union.* Baltimore, MD: Butternut and Blue, 1993.

Toombes, Samuel. *New Jersey in the Gettysburg Campaign.* Orange, NJ: Evening Mail Publishing House, 1888.

Topps, David. "The Dutchess County Regiment." *Gettysburg Magazine* (January 1995), issue 12, 42–60.

Tremain, Henry E. *Two Days of War: A Gettysburg Narrative and Other Experiences.* New York: Bonnell, Silver and Bowers, 1905.

Trimble, Isaac. "The Campaign and Battle of Gettysburg." In *Confederate Veteran Magazine* (1917), vol. 25, 209–213.

Trimble, Isaac. "The Civil War Diary of Isaac Ridgeway Trimble." *Maryland Historical Magazine* (1922), vol. 17, 1–29.

Trimble, Tony L. "Paper Collars: Stannard's Brigade at Gettysburg." *Gettysburg Magazine* (January 1990), issue 2, 75–80.

Trinque, Bruce. "Arnold's Battery and the 26th North Carolina." *Gettysburg Magazine* (January 1995), Issue 12, 61–67.

Truitt, Paul, "The 7th Indiana Fighters." *National Tribune,* November 11, 1925.

Trulock, Alice. *In The Hands of Providence: Joshua Chamberlain and the American Civil War.* Chapel Hill: University of North Carolina Press, 1992.

Tucker, A. W. "Orange Blossoms—Services of the 124th New York at Gettysburg." *National Tribune,* January 21, 1886.

Tucker, Glenn. *High Tide at Gettysburg: The Campaign in Pennsylvania.* Indianapolis, IN: Bobbs-Merrill Company, 1968.

Turney, J. B. "The First Tennessee at Gettysburg." In *Confederate Veteran* (1900), vol. 8, 535–537.

Uhler, George H. *Camps and Campaigns of the 93d Regiment, Penna. Vols.* n.p.: n.p., 1898.

Underwood, Adin B.. *Three Years' Service of the Thirty-Third Massachusetts Infantry Regiment.* Boston: A. Williams, 1881.

Underwood, George. *History of the Twenty-Sixth Regiment of the North Carolina Troops in the Great War, 1861–'65.* Goldsboro, NC: Nash Brothers, Book and Job Printers, 1901.

U.S. War Department. *The War of the Rebellion: A Compilation of the Official Records of the Union and Confederate Armies.* 128 vols. Washington, DC: U.S. Government Printing Office, 1880–1901.

Vanderslice, John M. *Gettysburg Then and Now.* New York: G.W. Dillingham Company, 1899.

VanSantvood, Cornelius. *The One Hundred and Twentieth N.Y.S. Volunteers, A Narrative of its Services in the War for the Union.* Rondout, NY: Regimental Association & Kingston Freeman Press, 1894.

Vautier, John D. *History of the Eighty-Eighth Pennsylvania Volunteers in the War for the*

Union, 1861–1865. Philadelphia: J. B. Lippincott Company, 1984.

Vautier, John. "At Gettysburg." *Philadelphia Weekly Press,* November 10, 1886.

Venner, William T. *Hoosiers' Honor: The Iron Brigade's 19th Indiana Regiment.* Shippensburg, PA : Burd Street Press, 1998.

Verrill, George W. "The Seventeenth Maine at Gettysburg and in the Wilderness." *Maine MOLLUS,* vol. 1, 259–282.

Wainwright, Charles. *A Diary of Battle.* New York: Harcourt, Brace & World, 1962.

Waitt, Ernest L. *History of the Nineteenth Regiment Massachusetts Volunteer Infantry.* Salem, MA: Salem Press Company, 1906.

Walker, James H. "The Charge of Pickett's Division." In *Blue and Gray* (1893), vol. 1, 221–223.

Walker, James H. "A Survivor of Pickett's Division. " In *Blue and Gray* (1893), vol. 2, 27.

Walters, Sara G. *Inscription at Gettysburg: In Memoriam to Captain David Acheson, Company C, 140th Pennsylvania Volunteers.* Gettysburg, PA: Thomas Publications, 1990.

Ward, David A. "Sedgwick's Foot Cavalry: The March of the Sixth Corps to Gettysburg." *Gettysburg Magazine* (January 2000), issue 22, 42–65.

Ward, Joseph R. C. *History of the One Hundred and Sixth Regiment, Pennsylvania Volunteers.* Philadelphia: Grant, Faires & Rodger, 1883.

Ward, W. C. "Incidents and Personal Experiences on the Battlefield at Gettysburg." In *Confederate Veteran* (1900), vol. 8, 345–349.

Warner, Ezra J. *Generals in Blue.* Baton Rouge: Louisiana State University Press, 1964.

Warner, Ezra J. *Generals in Gray.* Baton Rouge: Louisiana State University Press, 1959.

Warren, George L. "The Eleventh Corps—The First Day at Gettysburg." *National Tribune,* July 21, 1887.

Warren, Horatio N. *Two Reunions of the 142nd Regiment, Pennsylvania Volunteers.* Buffalo: The Courier Company, 1890.

Warren, Horatio N. *The Declaration of Independence and War History. Bull Run to Appomattox,.* Buffalo: The Courier Company, 1894.

Washburn, George H. *A Complete Military History and Record of the 108th Regiment N. Y. Vols. From 1862 to 1894 . . .* Rochester, NY: Press of E. R. Andrews, 1894.

Wehrum, Charles. "The Adjutant of the 12th Massachusetts Replies to the Captain of the 97th N.Y." *National Tribune,* December 10, 1885.

Wellman John F. Letter. *Ellicottville Post,* September 5, 1888.

Wellman, Manly W. *Rebel Boast.* New York: Henry Holt and Co., 1956.

Welsh, Jack D. *Medical Histories of Confederate Generals.* Kent, OH: Kent State University Press, 1995.

Wert, Jeffry D. *Gettysburg—Day Three.* New York: Simon & Schuster, 2001.

West, John C. *A Texan in Search of a Fight.* Waco, TX: Press of J. S. Hill and Company, 1901.

West, Oscar W. "On Little Round Top—The Fifth Corps Fight at Gettysburg—Particularly the 32nd Mass's Part." *National Tribune,* November 22, 1906.

Westbrook, C. D. "The 120th N.Y.'s Firm Stand on the Second Day at Gettysburg," *National Tribune,* September 20, 1900.

Wetherill, John M. "The Eighty-Second Regiment Pennsylvania Volunteers in the Gettysburg Campaign." *The Philadelphia Weekly Press,* February 17, 1886.

Weygant, Charles H. *History of the One Hundred and Twenty-Fourth Regiment, N.Y.S.V.* Newburgh, NY: Journal Printing House, 1877.

Wheeler, Cornelius. "Reminiscences of the Battle of Gettysburg." *Wisconsin MOLLUS,* vol. 2, 205–220.

White, W. T. "First Texas Regiment at Gettysburg." In *Confederate Veteran* (1922), vol. 30, 185, 197.

Whitehorne, J. E. *Diary of J. E. Whitehorne.* Louisville, KY: F. L. Elmore, Jr., 1995.

Wilcox, C. M. Letter. In *Southern Historical Society Papers* (1877), vol. 4, 111–117.

Williams, Alpheus. *From the Cannon's Mouth.* Detroit, MI: Wayne State University Press, 1959.

Williams, George F. *Bullet and Shell* . . . New York: Fords, Howard and Hulbert, 1882.

Williams, John C. *Life In Camp: A History of the Nine Months' Service of the Fourteenth Vermont Regiment.* Claremont, NH: Author, 1864.

Willson, Arabella M. *Disaster, Struggle, Triumph: The Adventures of 1000 "Boys in Blue," from August, 1862, to June,1865.* Albany: Argus Company Printers, 1870.

Wilson, Lawrence. "Charge Up Culp's Hill." *Washington Post,* July 9, 1899.

Wilson, Lawrence. "Candy's Brigade at Little Round Top: The First Union Troops to Occupy Little Round Top." *National Tribune,* June 26, 1902.

Wilson, Lawrence. *Itinerary of the Seventh Ohio Volunteer Infantry, 1861-1864, With Roster, Portraits, and Biographies.* New York: Neale Publishing Company, 1907.

Winschel, Terrence J. "Heavy Was Their Loss: Joe Davis's Brigade at Gettysburg, Part 1." *Gettysburg Magazine* (January 1990), Issue 2, 5–14.

Winschel, Terrence J. "Heavy was Their Loss: Joe Davis' Brigade at Gettysburg, Part II." *Gettysburg Magazine* (July 1990), issue 3, 77–86.

Winschel, Terrence J. "Posey's Brigade at Gettysburg. Part II." *Gettysburg Magazine* (July 1991), issue 5, 89–102.

Winschel, Terrence J. "The Gettysburg Diary of Lieutenant William Peel." *Gettysburg Magazine* (July 1993), issue 9, 98–108.

Winthrop, D. Sheldon. *The Twenty-Seventh: A Regimental History.* New Haven, CT: Morris & Benham, 1866.

"With Reference to the 95th." *Rockland County Messenger,* June 1, 1893.

Wittenberg, Eric J. "Merritt's Regulars on South Cavalry Field: Oh, What Could Have Been." *Gettysburg Magazine* (January 1998), issue 16, 120–121.

"Wofford's Georgia Brigade." *Richmond Daily Enquirer,* August 5, 1863.

Wood, George L. *The Seventh Regiment: A Record.* New York: J. Miller, Company, 1865.

Wood, William N. *Reminiscences of Big I.* Charlottesville, VA: Michie Company, 1909.

Woodbury, Augustus. *The Second Rhode Island Regiment: A Narrative of Military Operations* . . . Providence, RI: Valpey, Angell, and Company, 1875.

Woodward, Evan M. *Our Campaigns—The Second Regiment, Pennsylvania Reserve Volunteers.* Philadelphia: J. E. Potter, 1865.

Wyatt Aiken, D. "The Gettysburg Reunion. What is Necessary and Proper for the South to Do." *Charleston News and Courier,* June 21, 1882.

Wychoff, Mac. *A History of the Second South Carolina Infantry, 1861–1865.* Fredericksburg, VA: Sargent Kirkland's Museum and Historical Society, 1994.

Wyckoff, Mac, *A History of the Third South Carolina Infantry, 1861–1865.* Fredericksburg, VA: Sergeant Kirkland's Museum and Historical Society, 1995.

Young, Jesse B. *What a Boy Saw in the Army: A Story of Sight-Seeing and Adventure in the War for the Union.* New York: Hunt & Easton, 1894.

Young, William A. *Fifty-sixth Virginia Infantry.* Lynchburg: H. E. Howard, Inc., 1990.

Zollinger, William, Lamar Hollyday, and D. R. Howard. "General George H. Steuart's Brigade at the Battle of Gettysburg. In *Southern Historical Society Papers* (1876), vol. 2 (1876), 105–107.

INDEX